The APSAC
Handbook on
CHILD
MALTREATMENT

SECOND EDITION

The APSAC Handbook on CHILD MALTREATMENT

SECOND EDITION

Editors

John E. B. Myers
Lucy Berliner
John Briere
C. Terry Hendrix
Carole Jenny
Theresa A. Reid

 APSAC *American Professional Society on the Abuse of Children*

 Sage Publications
International Educational and Professional Publisher
Thousand Oaks ■ London ■ New Delhi

For information:

Sage Publications, Inc.
2455 Teller Road
Thousand Oaks, California 91320
E-mail: order@sagepub.com

Sage Publications Ltd.
6 Bonhill Street
London EC2A 4PU
United Kingdom

Sage Publications India Pvt. Ltd.
M-32 Market
Greater Kailash I
New Delhi 110 048 India

Printed in the United States of America

Library of Congress Cataloging-in-Publication Data

The APSAC handbook on child maltreatment /
    edited by John E.B. Myers [et al.].– 2nd ed.
        p. cm.
    Includes bibliographical references and index.
    ISBN 0-7619-1991-0 – ISBN 0-7619-1992-9 (pbk.)
    1. Child abuse–Handbooks, manuals, etc. 2. Child abuse–Prevention–
Handbooks, manuals, etc. I. Myers, John E. B. II. American Professional
Society on the Abuse of Children.
    HV6626.5 .A83 2001
    362.7′6–dc21   2001004082

        03 04 05 10 9 8 7 6 5 4 3

Acquiring Editor: Nancy Hale
Editorial Assistant: Vonessa Vondera
Copy Editor: Gillian Dickens
Production Editor: Claudia A. Hoffman
Typesetter: Marion Warren
Indexer: Molly Hall
Cover Designer: Jane M. Quaney

This book is dedicated to Kenneth V. Lanning.
Ken, you are one of the pioneers.
You led the way. You opened our eyes.
You taught us. You were always one step ahead.
You're the coolest FBI agent we know.
You've done more than we can count to protect kids.

Thanks.

Contents

Preface

The *APSAC Handbook on Child Maltreatment,* Second Edition, is divided into five parts: (1) overview of child maltreatment, (2) psychosocial treatment, (3) medical aspects, (4) legal issues, and (5) prevention and service delivery. Part One provides in-depth analysis of the most common forms of child maltreatment. Thus, Part One describes neglect, physical abuse, sexual abuse, and psychological maltreatment. Part One also discusses Munchausen Syndrome by Proxy, the relationship between substance abuse and child abuse, and child abuse in the context of domestic violence. Part Two offers theoretically driven models for psychosocial treatment of child, adolescent, and adult survivors of child abuse. Part Two also addresses treatment of sexual offenders. Part Three describes medical aspects of physical abuse and sexual abuse. Additionally, Part Three analyzes medical neglect and fatal child abuse. Part Four examines legal issues, beginning with an overview of the legal system. Part Four describes police investigation, interviewing children, and expert testimony. Part Four ends with discussion of risk management for professionals working in child protection. Part Five addresses prevention of child abuse, reporting maltreatment, cultural competence of professionals, utilization of mental health services, and community organization to end child maltreatment.

J.E.B.M.

November 2001

Introduction

DAVID FINKELHOR

The year 2002 marks what many regard as the 40th anniversary of modern professional concern about child maltreatment. This anniversary sees a field that is well into a new and more mature phase that reflects both its history and some new challenges. The following considers briefly this history and current challenges.

Child Abuse as a Social Movement

Modern concern about child abuse is not the product of some epidemic increase in the scope or nature of the problem. It is rather the result of a broad social movement and a historic moral transformation. The social movement around child protection has been gathering momentum for almost a century and was rooted in two profound social changes. One was the rise of a new, large class of professional workers who specialized in dealing with children and families. These included specialized workers in health care, such as pediatricians and school nurses; in education, such as school counselors and special education teachers; in family law and child advocacy; and in mental health and social service, such as child psychologists and family therapists.

The other social change behind the child abuse movement was the emancipation of women from the domestic sphere and their widespread entry into the workforce and the professions. In a variety of ways, these two changes catalyzed a moral transformation in our view of children and a social and political initiative to intervene on their behalf.

These changes lifted the veil of privacy around many aspects of family life, revealing the hidden existence of violence and abuse. This happened in part because newly independent women with increased access to divorce could afford to acknowledge and disclose some of the seamier realities of family life. The new professionals, for their part, were in positions to confirm these realities and welcomed such opportunities to justify their expertise. Professional receptivity to child welfare concerns was further increased as women moved in larger numbers into the higher-status and influential professions such as medicine, law, and government, bringing with them their interest in children.

Child Abuse as a Moral Transformation

The moral transformation brought about by these changes can be summarized in two propositions. The first arose from a growing consensus that children should be socialized primarily through love, not discipline, and that harsh methods of child rearing, including the hitting and humiliating of children, are detrimental to their development. The second proposition was that parental authority is not absolute; parents are not in all cases the best judges of their children's own welfare, nor are they entitled to unrestricted authority over them. The growing acceptance of these propositions created the basis for the concept of child maltreatment—the misuse of parental power—and the notion that professionals and public authorities have the right to intervene in families on behalf of children.

The modern "discovery" of child abuse is sometimes attributed to C. Henry Kempe, the University of Colorado pediatrician, and his colleagues, with the publication of their 1962 paper on the "battered child syndrome" (Kempe, Silverman, Steele, Droegemueller, & Silver, 1962). But, in fact, concern about child abuse in the United States has a much longer history, dating back to before the turn of the twentieth century (Gordon, 1988). What the Kempe work signaled, though, was that influential medical professionals had joined the ranks of those advocating for child protection and were prepared to lead a new social movement to greatly expand governmental activity in this area (Pfohl, 1977). The physicians had little problem mobilizing other child-oriented professionals, who readily saw this coalition

as a chance to improve conditions for children, promote the new values, and in the process create new opportunities for their own authority and expertise (Nelson, 1983). The coalition was very successful in the early 1970s in establishing the current child protection system with its mandatory reporting laws, its codified definitions of child maltreatment, and its corps of state-funded child protection workers.

The cause of child protection benefited from a second mobilization in the late 1970s, as the growing women's movement gave political momentum to the problem of sexual abuse. In consciousness-raising groups, women around the country discovered the common experience of having suffered childhood rapes and sexual abuse that they had never discussed (Brownmiller, 1975). They began to speak publicly and to write about these experiences and eventually prevailed on young professionals to seek such cases. The result was a flood of new knowledge, publicity, and governmental action around the problem of sexual abuse.

Unfortunately, to describe the concern about child abuse as the product of a moral transformation and a social movement, rather than a scientific discovery, can appear to some as a discounting of the problem itself. But nothing could be further from the truth. Humanity's advance cannot be separated from the social and historical conditions that have allowed social problems to become recognized. And many serious social problems have languished without attention for want of a social movement to highlight them. Thus, it is important to recognize the social movement behind the problem to understand how the problem is formulated and what its future may be (Spector & Kitsuse, 1977).

An Epidemic of Child Abuse?

One of the early tasks of social movements is often to provide evidence to substantiate the seriousness of their concern, and, in the case of child abuse, this has not been hard. A variety of studies (cited in later chapters) suggest that the various forms of child abuse touch the lives of an important fraction of all children in the United States (Garbarino, 1989; Russell, 1986; Straus, Gelles, & Steinmetz, 1980), a scope that has surprised both the public and professionals. Other studies clearly implicate child abuse in the etiology of a broad spectrum of social and psychological problems, ranging from crime and spouse abuse to alcoholism and depression.

Until recently, cases being reported to child welfare authorities continued to grow in number at the rate of more than 10% per year. This escalation in reporting generated much discussion about whether the frequency of child abuse has actually increased in the current era. Most observers believe that the large annual increases in reported cases were principally a result of new public and professional sensitivity to the problem (Sedlak, 1991). Reinforcing this view, retrospective studies of adults showed large quantities of abuse suffered by earlier generations at a time when little was being disclosed (Finkelhor, Hotaling, Lewis, & Smith, 1990). Those taking an even longer historical perspective note that many of the most severe forms of popularly approved chastisement—including whippings with sticks, switches, and belts, as well as washing children's mouths with soap and other substances—have lost their popular endorsement, which probably signals a long-term decline in the routine mistreatment of children (DeMause, 1998). But, at the same time, the rise of contemporary social problems may contribute to the exacerbation of certain forms of abuse and neglect previously unknown or less common. For example, the drug abuse epidemic is certainly responsible for a new problem with cocaine-addicted babies (Bays, 1990). The increase in isolated and poor households headed by a single parent has probably worsened the problem of neglected and latchkey children. And the creation of video technology and the advent of the Internet have created a new market and dissemination mechanism for child pornography (Lanning & Burgess, 1989). Because our ability to monitor undisclosed maltreatment is very limited, we may never be able to say whether the true incidence has been increasing.

Child Abuse: The Second Stage

Whether or not the underlying problem is changing, the nature of our professional response is. All social movements and social problems go through stages of development, and child abuse is no exception. In recent years, child abuse has been moving out of the stage in which advocates had to struggle for public attention and acceptance and has entered a second, more mature, stage (Spector & Kitsuse, 1977). This stage is characterized not only by increasing institutionalization and professional acceptance but also by the recognition of the need for greater accountability.

One harbinger of the new stage was a change in epidemiology. After two decades of rapid growth, child maltreatment reports began to level off in the mid-1990s, and in 1998, they evidenced their first real decline. Sexual abuse reports, for their part, had started to decline as early as 1992 and, by 1998, were down 31% nationwide (Jones & Finkelhor, 2001). As with the increases in previous decades, it is still unclear whether the declines mark true improvements in the treatment of children. But they clearly signal that professionals are no longer dealing with constantly mushrooming caseloads and rapidly expanding responsibilities.

Recent trends can create resource issues for the field. One important problem continuing into the second stage is the ongoing need to exact more political and financial commitment from governmental authorities, a task commensurate with the size and seriousness of the problem and the public's articulated concern. For example, child welfare has not received the kind of support that has gone into some other social problem areas such as health care, crime control, and education. This penury of public funding is the result of two factors: the relatively recent arrival of the child abuse problem on the social agenda and the fact that its arrival has coincided with a period when political philosophies opposed to state intervention are ascendant. Child abuse also suffers along with other social problems that appear more likely to affect certain stigmatized segments of the population. Although new funding does not seem imminent, opinion surveys clearly indicate that, despite cynicism about government, the public is strongly in favor of increased governmental action on behalf of abused children (Schulman, Ronca, & Bucuvalas, Inc., 1988). Hence, the changing epidemiology poses new opportunities and new challenges in trying to persuade policymakers to provide adequate funding for child maltreatment prevention and intervention.

Another ongoing challenge for the field of child abuse has been coping with its very interdisciplinary character. What has been an asset in establishing a robust political coalition supportive of the problem has also allowed conflicting disciplinary priorities and styles (e.g., prosecution vs. therapy) and an uncertain forum for the development of professional dialogue. As the field moves into a more mature phase, it is replacing former ad hoc structures for this dialogue with more permanent ones.

The American Professional Society on Abuse of Children (APSAC) is one of these new structures. Founded in 1987, APSAC has brought together the diverse disciplines concerned with child abuse to create a context in which conflicts can be negotiated and standards established while providing a unified voice that speaks for professionals working in the field.

New Research Agenda

The second stage also has brought a transformation in the nature of child abuse research. Much of the early research in the field was dedicated to drawing attention to the problem. Thus, prevalence studies tried to establish its scope, impact studies tried to establish its seriousness and connection to other social and psychological problems, and studies of professionals tried to highlight the misconceptions that needed to be corrected.

As the field enters a more mature phase, the research agenda has shifted. Of much greater interest now is the evaluation of programs and professional practice to find out what works (if anything) and what does not. As it has become more successful, the field has been able to be more self-critical and ask hard questions. Thus, recent studies have begun to scrutinize intervention programs (e.g., Daro, Jones, & McCurdy, 1993), treatment methods for abusers and victims (e.g., Finkelhor & Berliner, 1995; Marques, Day, Nelson, & West, 1994), and the practices of child protective agencies and investigators (e.g., Kendall-Tackett, 1992). Some of the cherished programs of the field, such as home visitation, are being subjected to welcome scrutiny (Gomby, Culross, & Behrman, 1999). Although these studies may result in some discouraging and possibly embarrassing findings, they also hold the promise of truly improving the work.

The Rise of an Organized Opposition

In this second stage of its development, the child abuse movement is faced with responding to an increasingly well-organized political opposition. During its first stage, child protection had unusually little organized opposition, drawing very broad support from across the political spectrum.

In recent years, however, opposition has coalesced and gained visibility on a number of fronts. An increasing number of parents who believe they have suffered wrongful investigations and accusations are bringing suits and lobbying for restrictions on state child welfare authorities (Hechler, 1988). Moreover, efforts to teach children skills for avoiding abuse and sexual victimization have aroused opposition from some academic critics (Berrick & Gilbert, 1991) as well as from conservative and religious groups concerned about undermining parental authority and the teaching of sex education in the schools. The prosecution of child molesters has resulted in more, better-organized, and specialized defense attorneys, armed with a systematic critique of investigative practices, therapeutic techniques, and research evidence, not to mention their own cadre of expert witnesses (Hechler, 1988). Meanwhile, the growing state child welfare bureaucracies, with their large budgets and diffuse mandates, have become easy targets for the axes of state legislators and budget managers.

The rise of this opposition has been termed the *child abuse backlash*. It has complicated the work of some practitioners not used to operating in an adversarial environment, has been the source of anguish for those who have been personally targeted, and, in some cases, has compromised the ability to advocate on behalf of abused children. Nevertheless, the opposition has had salutary effects by way of curbing excesses of zeal, introducing discussion about efficiency and equity, and focusing attention on the interests of groups (e.g., parents under investigation) that were previously overlooked. At the beginning of the new century, the field appears to have weathered the backlash and retained a substantial degree of public and policy support.

A perhaps even more serious long-term threat to the field of child abuse than a backlash is the problem of public saturation. Social problems tend to follow an "issue attention" cycle, such that after an issue has been in the spotlight for a certain period, the media, the public, and politicians tend to lose interest (Downs, 1972). Child abuse has resisted the problem of saturation, in part by the discovery of "new" aspects of the problem that have reinvigorated public interest. For example, the spotlight on sexual abuse in the late 1970s spurred new interest after a decade of focus on physical abuse.

Although the fascination with the topic of sexual abuse shows few signs of flagging, the attention cycle will inevitably wane at some time in the future. In the meantime, still other issues may arise to sustain public interest. One concerns children who are the victims of emotional maltreatment. Another deals with Internet victimization. Another targets children victimized by peers and schoolmates. Although these "fad cycles" in social problems are in many ways regrettable and do little to produce rational social policy, they are to some extent an unavoidable feature of maintaining support for child abuse as a social problem.

The APSAC Handbook

The APSAC Handbook on Child Maltreatment has proven a welcome compendium of advances in the field. The interdisciplinary richness of the subject is very much on display, as demonstrated by the relevant juxtaposition of sections on medicine, law, and psychotherapy. Furthermore, a newfound capacity for self-evaluation and self-criticism and a growing foundation in research and evaluation are evident. On the basis of a synthesis of the sort available in the following chapters, a field can create a picture of where it has come from and where it has yet to go. It is clear that the domain of child abuse has taken on one of the larger moral and humanitarian challenges in our society today. This volume testifies to the enormous fund of professional expertise, scientific objectivity, social activism, and human compassion that has been unleashed in response to that challenge.

References

Bays, J. (1990). Substance abuse and child abuse: Impact of addiction on the child. *Pediatric Clinics of North America, 37*(4), 881-903.

Berrick, J. D., & Gilbert, N. (1991). *With the best of intentions*. New York: Guilford.

Brownmiller, S. (1975). *Against our will: Men, women and rape*. New York: Simon & Schuster.

Daro, D., Jones, E., & McCurdy, K. (1993). *Preventing child abuse: An evaluation of services to high-risk families*. Philadelphia: William Penn Foundation.

DeMause, L. (1998). The history of child abuse. *Journal of Psychohistory, 25*(3), 216-236.

Downs, A. (1972). Up and down with ecology: The "issue-attention cycle." *Public Interest, 28,* 38-50.

Finkelhor, D., & Berliner, L. (1995). Research on the treatment of sexually abused children: A review and recommendations. *Journal of the American Academy of Child and Adolescent Psychiatry, 34*(11), 1408-1423.

Finkelhor, D., Hotaling, G., Lewis, I. A., & Smith, C. (1990). Sexual abuse in a national survey of adult men and women: Prevalence, characteristics, and risk factors. *Child Abuse & Neglect, 14,* 19-28.

Garbarino, J. (1989). The incidence and prevalence of child maltreatment. In L. Ohlin & M. Tonry (Eds.), *Family violence* (pp. 219-261). Chicago: University of Chicago Press.

Gomby, D. S., Culross, P. L., & Behrman, R. E. (1999). Home visiting: Recent program evaluations: Analysis and recommendations. *Future of Children, 9*(1), 4-26.

Gordon, L. (1988). *Family violence and social control*. New York: Viking.

Hechler, D. (1988). *The battle and the backlash: The child sexual war*. Lexington, MA: D. C. Heath.

Jones, L., & Finkelhor, D. (2001). *The decline in sexual abuse cases: Exploring the causes* (Juvenile Justice Bulletin). Washington, DC: Office of Juvenile Justice and Delinquency Prevention.

Kempe, C. H., Silverman, F. N., Steele, B. F., Droegemueller, W., & Silver, H. K. (1962). The battered child syndrome. *Journal of the American Medical Association, 181,* 17-24.

Kendall-Tackett, K. (1992). Professionals' standards of "normal" behavior with anatomical dolls and factors that influence these standards. *Child Abuse & Neglect, 16*(5), 727-733.

Lanning, K. V., & Burgess, A. W. (1989). Child pornography and sex rings. In D. Zillman & J. Bryant (Eds.), *Pornography: Research advances and policy considerations* (pp. 235-255). Hillsdale, NJ: Lawrence Erlbaum.

Marques, J. K., Day, D. M., Nelson, C., & West, M. A. (1994). Effects of cognitive and behavioral treatment on sex offender recidivism: Preliminary results of a longitudinal study. *Criminal Justice and Behavior, 21,* 28-54.

Nelson, B. J. (1983). *Making an issue of child abuse: Political agenda setting for social problems.* Chicago: University of Chicago Press.

Pfohl, S. J. (1977). The discovery of child abuse. *Social Problems, 24,* 310-323.

Russell, D. E. H. (1986). *The secret trauma: Incest in the lives of girls and women.* New York: Basic Books.

Schulman, Ronca, & Bucuvalas, Inc. (1988). *Public attitudes and actions regarding child abuse and its prevention: 1988.* Chicago: National Committee for Prevention of Child Abuse.

Sedlak, A. J. (1991). *National incidence and prevalence of child abuse and neglect: 1988—Revised report.* Rockville, MD: Westat.

Spector, M., & Kitsuse, J. L. (1977). *Constructing social problems.* Menlo Park, CA: Cummings.

Straus, M. A., Gelles, J., & Steinmetz, S. K. (1980). *Behind closed doors.* Beverly Hills, CA: Sage.

PART ONE

Aspects of Child Maltreatment

Part One offers in-depth and up-to-date analysis of child maltreatment. In Chapter 1, Martha Farrell Erickson and Byron Egeland reprise and expand their excellent analysis of neglect from the first edition of the *APSAC Handbook*. Neglect is notoriously difficult to define, but Erickson and Egeland are up to the task, and they begin their chapter with a useful definitional framework for understanding neglect. From there, they discuss the impact of neglect on children's development. Erickson and Egeland end their chapter with thoughtful analysis of the origins of neglect.

David Kolko uses Chapter 2 to good advantage to provide an exhaustive and valuable analysis of physical abuse. Chapter 2 updates Dr. Kolko's chapter from the first edition. He begins with definitions, moves to prevalence and incidence, and then thoroughly reviews the literature on etiology. This done, Kolko turn his attention to the medical and psychological consequences of physical abuse. He concludes the chapter with discussion of intervention and treatment.

Chapter 3 focuses on sexual abuse of children, and one would be hard pressed to find two more authoritative authors than Lucy Berliner and Diana Elliott. Berliner and Elliott discuss the rate of sexual abuse and the characteristics of the abuse experience. The authors direct particular attention to how children disclose sexual abuse. Next, Berliner and Elliott review the voluminous literature on the short- and long-term effects of sexual abuse. Berliner and Elliott end with discussion of psychological treatment for child and adult survivors of sexual abuse. This excellent chapter updates and expands the authors' contribution to the first edition.

Psychological maltreatment lies at the core of child abuse. In Chapter 4, Stuart Hart, Marla Brassard, Nelson Binggeli, and Howard Davidson unravel the complexities of this form of maltreatment and exhaustively update the chapter from the first edition. Psychological maltreatment does not lend itself to simple definitions. Yet, definitions are important, and the authors devote ample attention to defining psychological maltreatment in a way that is helpful to practitioners in the trenches of child protection. The authors make a convincing case for the harm inflicted by psychological maltreatment. They review the literature on assessment and conclude their valuable contribution with discussion of intervention and treatment issues.

Chapter 5 is new in the second edition of the *Handbook*. Susan Kelley provides a very useful analysis of the role of substance abuse in child maltreatment. Dr. Kelley begins by discussing substance abuse as a risk factor for child abuse and neglect. From there, she analyzes the impact of substance abuse on kinship care. Kelley concludes with discussion of the implications of substance abuse for practice, research, and policy.

Chapter 6 is also new in the second edition. Sandra Graham-Bermann discusses child abuse in the context of domestic violence. When the first edition of the *Handbook* appeared in 1996, experts understood that there was a relationship between domestic violence and child abuse, but little was known at that time. Much has been learned during the past six years, and Dr. Graham-Bermann brings us up to speed. She begins with definitions of child abuse in the context of domestic violence. From there she addresses the prevalence and incidence of overlapping domestic violence and child abuse. She reviews the literature on the effects on children of witnessing domestic violence. Finally, Graham-Bermann describes interventions to help battered women and their children.

Munchausen Syndrome by Proxy is an uncommon, baffling, and dangerous form of child abuse. In Chapter 7, which is new to the second edition, Teresa Parnell delves into this disturbing form of maltreatment. Dr. Parnell traces the history of this form of abuse, beginning with Sir Roy Meadow's classic article in 1977. From there, Parnell discusses the definition of Munchausen Syndrome, and provides useful information on reaching a diagnosis. She concludes Chapter 7 with discussion of treatment for the perpetrator of Munchausen Syndrome by Proxy.

J.E.B.M.

1

Child Neglect

MARTHA FARRELL ERICKSON

BYRON EGELAND

Although the bruises and scars of physical abuse are more readily apparent, the quiet assault of child neglect often does at least as much damage to its young victims. Typically defined as an act of omission rather than commission, neglect may or may not be intentional. It is sometimes apparent (as in the unkempt appearance of the child who comes to school without a bath or adequate clothing) and sometimes nearly invisible until it is too late. Neglect is often fatal, due to inadequate physical protection, nutrition, or health care. Sometimes, as in the case of "failure to thrive," it is fatal because of a lack of human contact and love. In some cases, neglect slowly and persistently eats away at children's spirits until they have little will to connect with others or explore the world.

In this chapter, we present a brief overview of what is known about child neglect. First, within the context of a historical look at society's increasing awareness of neglect, we discuss definitions of neglect and its various subtypes. Second, we review research findings on the impact of neglect on children's health and development, including data from our own longitudinal study of the consequences of emotional neglect. Then we discuss what is known about the underlying causes and correlates of neglect, with an emphasis on those factors that may be amenable to change through preventive intervention. Finally, we briefly discuss what this information suggests for future research and practice.

Developing Awareness of Neglect

Although children have been abused and neglected for centuries, the recognition of maltreatment as a social problem is relatively recent. Forty years ago, Kempe's landmark paper on the "battered child" (Kempe, Silverman, Steele, Droegemueller, & Silver, 1962) spurred a dramatic increase in public awareness of the impact of overt, intentional physical abuse. Widespread recognition of neglect, however, lagged far behind, even though neglect is more prevalent than abuse (McDonald & Associates, 1999) and has been shown to have consequences that are just as serious (e.g., Egeland, 1997; Erickson, Egeland, & Pianta, 1989). Some experts have contended that neglect (emotional neglect, in particular) is the central feature of all maltreatment. For example, Newberger wrote as early as 1973 that "the essential element in child abuse is not the intention to destroy a child but rather the inability of a parent to nurture [his or her] offspring" (p. 15). Nevertheless, neglect continued to receive far less attention than abuse, both publicly and professionally, even into the mid-1980s (Wolock & Horowitz, 1984). A perusal of current popular publications suggests that even now public attention still is aimed primarily at sensational cases of severe physical assault and injury. Neglect may or may not be intentional. It is sometimes apparent (as in the unkempt appearance of the child who comes to school without a bath or adequate clothing) and sometimes nearly invisible until it is too late.

> *Neglect may or may not be intentional. It is sometimes apparent (as in the unkempt appearance of the child who comes to school without a bath or adequate clothing) and sometimes nearly invisible until it is too late.*

Furthermore, the attention given to neglect (and also to abuse) for many years focused only on observable physical effects. Neglect often leaves obvious physical signs, as in the case of gross malnourishment or accidents stemming from a caregiver's failure to protect the child from injury. But many types of neglect, including emotional neglect, typically leave no physical marks. These less obvious forms of neglect nevertheless can have a devastating impact on the child's development (Egeland, 1997; Egeland & Erickson, 1987; Erickson & Egeland, 1995).

It was only in the late 1980s that public awareness began to expand to include recognition of the often profound psychological consequences that stem from even the most subtle neglect. Some experts contended that psychological consequences were the unifying factor in all types of maltreatment (e.g., see Brassard, Germain, & Hart, 1987). Subsequent research by Crittenden and her associates presented a strong case for the impact of psychological maltreatment, regardless of the presence or severity of physical injury (Claussen & Crittenden, 1991). Whether or not the child sustained physical injury, at the core of maltreatment was lasting damage to the child's sense of self and the resultant impairment of social, emotional, and cognitive functioning.

Definitions and Subtypes of Neglect

Neglect means many things to many people (Black & Dubowitz, 1999; Zuravin, 1999). Definitions may vary depending on whether one takes a legal, medical, psychological, social service, or lay perspective (see Chapter 14, this volume, for a discussion of neglect from the medical perspective). Out of necessity, legal definitions tend to be the most elaborate and at least aspire to some level of precision (Flannery, 1979; Giovannoni, 1989; Wald, 1976). But even within the legal arena, there is great variability among definitions of neglect. Some of that variability is due to the fact that maltreatment statutes fall into three different categories, each with a different purpose and therefore a somewhat different interpretation of what constitutes neglect. The three categories include reporting laws that define who should make reports of maltreatment and under what conditions, dependency statutes that define which children may be made wards of the court, and criminal statutes that define a criminal act for purposes of prosecution. Even within any given category of legislation, definitions often include a mixture of precision (i.e., spelling out various kinds and degrees of neglect) and vagueness (i.e., broad, ambiguous phrases, such as "interfering with the child's welfare") (Giovannoni, 1989).

Other perspectives beyond the legal system may take an even broader, more inclusive view of neglect. For example, some groups of professionals advocate intervention in neglect cases that would not necessarily meet the criteria of the law. In an early study of perceptions of neglect, Boehm (1962) surveyed a large sample of community leaders from various professions, asking them to respond to vignettes describing various kinds of neglect. Teachers, nurses, social workers, and clergy were more likely to judge the cases as requiring intervention than were lawyers.

An even broader view of neglect was put forth in *Today's Children: Creating a Future for a Generation in Crisis* (1992) by David Hamburg, president of the Carnegie Corporation Foundation. Calling attention to the plight of today's children, Hamburg indicted U.S. society for "collective neglect" in failing to provide adequate health care, child care, preschool education, and policies that support families in caring for their children.

A general definition of neglect was embedded in the Child Abuse Prevention and Treatment Act of 1974 (P.L. 93-247), which defined abuse and neglect as

> the physical or *mental injury,* sexual abuse or exploitation, *negligent treatment,* or maltreatment of a child under the age of 18, or the age specified by the child protection law of the state in question, by a person who is responsible for the child's welfare under circumstances which indicate that the child's health or welfare is harmed or threatened thereby as determined in accordance with regulations prescribed by the Secretary. (emphasis added)

It is common for states to define abuse and neglect together rather than provide separate legal definitions for each. It is a moot issue in most courts whether the child was injured through an act of commission (abuse) or omission (neglect).

Beyond such overarching definitions of maltreatment, specific interpretations of what "neglect" encompasses vary along several dimensions. One controversy has centered on whether actions can be defined as neglectful regardless of their apparent impact on the child. Must there be clear, immediate evidence of harm or "mental injury," or is an apparent "threat" to the child's well-being sufficient? For example, Brassard et al. (1987) cite one definition of mental injury as referring to *substantial, observable impairment* in the child's ability to perform and behave within a normal range with due regard to his or her cultural background.

Others would argue that actions could be neglectful regardless of their immediate observable impact on the child's functioning. Certainly our own research on the long-term consequences of various patterns of maltreatment, discussed later in this chapter, suggests that the impact of neglect may become apparent later in the child's development, even if it is not immediately obvious. Thus, a definition that demands immediate, observable effects would overlook many cases of neglect. At the groundbreaking 1983 International Conference on Psychological Abuse, the interdisciplinary group of participants proposed a definition of psychological maltreatment that included both immediate and ultimate (i.e., manifest at a later point) damage to the child's behavioral, cognitive, affective, or physical functioning (Brassard et al., 1987). This raises the question of whether we know enough about the impact of neglect to say with some confidence that a given act would be expected ultimately to do damage to the child. Many working in this field would argue strongly that we do know enough.

Another definitional issue regarding neglect that is of particular salience within the legal arena has to do with the intentionality of the act. Dubowitz and his colleagues have argued for a definition based on the unmet needs of the child, regardless of parental intentions (Dubowitz, 1999; Dubowitz, Black, Starr, & Zuravin, 1993). Although intentionality can be a critical variable in determining legal culpability, the end result for the child may be the same whether the parent is willfully neglectful (e.g., out of hostility) or neglectful due to factors such as ignorance, depression, or overwhelming stress and inadequate support. From either an intervention or prevention perspective, identifying the factors that underlie the neglect is important to eliminate or ameliorate those factors and ensure that children receive the care and protection they need and deserve.

In considering neglect, parental motives cannot be dichotomized simply as intentional or unintentional. Motives also need to be considered within the context of the parents' culture and beliefs. Garbarino (1991) cites the example of Hispanic parents who sometimes avoid using car seats for their infants because they believe the infants will feel abandoned if they cannot be held in their parents' arms. Nevertheless, the law requires that infants be restrained in protective car seats, and parents who refuse to comply are neglecting their duty to protect their children from potential harm. In a recent chapter on cultural competence and child neglect, Korbin and Spilsbury (1999) make a compelling case that respecting culture and protecting children are compatible goals. When professionals who serve children and families become culturally competent, the result is neither acceptance of all behavior as culturally appropriate nor a single global standard of parenting to which all societies must adhere (see Chapter 23, this volume).

As health care providers, mental health professionals, and lawmakers have grown in their understanding of neglect, definitions have been refined and elaborated. Several subtypes of neglect have been identified, including the following:

Physical neglect. This is the most widely recognized and commonly identified form of neglect. It includes failure to protect from harm or danger and provide for the child's basic physical needs, including adequate shelter, food, or clothing.

Emotional neglect. In many cases, this type of neglect is more difficult to document or substantiate because of the absence of clear physical evidence and the fact that it goes on quietly in the privacy of the home, often beginning when children are too young to speak out or even know that they are not receiving appropriate care (see Chapter 4, this volume). In its extreme form, however, emotional neglect can lead to nonorganic failure to thrive. This produces stunted growth and physical illness or anomalies and is often fatal.

In discussing definitions of emotional neglect, Brassard et al. (1987) cited the American Humane Association, which describes emotional neglect as "passive or passive/aggressive inattention to the child's emotional needs, nurturing, or emotional well-being" (p. 267). In our own research, we have used the term *psychologically unavailable* to describe parents who overlook their infants' cues and signals, particularly the children's cries and pleas for warmth and comfort. As discussed later in this chapter, we have found this sub-

tle form of neglect to have serious long-term consequences for young victims. The antithesis of emotional neglect is emotional availability, thoughtfully discussed by Biringen and Robinson (1991). These authors reconceptualized availability as a relational construct, taking into account both parent and child behavior, and proposed a multidimensional approach to describing emotional availability that includes parental sensitivity, child responsiveness, parental nonintrusiveness, and child involvement of the parent. In their representation of availability as a continuous variable, emotional neglect would be at the extreme end of that continuum.

Definitions of neglect, however, are in part a function of time and place. What we today call emotional neglect would not have been recognized as such not so many years ago. In fact, in the 1920s, experts advised parents against sentimental handling of babies and urged them to let their babies cry so that they would learn that their parents were in charge (Newson & Newson, 1974). (As we discuss later, that notion has not disappeared completely.)

What we today call emotional neglect would not have been recognized as such not so many years ago.

Definitions of emotional neglect also may vary somewhat depending on cultural context. For example, Korbin (1980) pointed out that in some cultures, our Western practice of making young children sleep alone in their rooms at night would be viewed as emotional neglect. This illustrates that although there is agreement that emotional neglect involves inattention to the child's needs, there is not universal agreement on exactly what those needs are.

Medical neglect. This refers to caregivers' failure to provide prescribed medical treatment for their children, including required immunizations, prescribed medication, recommended surgery, or other intervention in cases of serious disease or injury. This type of neglect has raised some of the most controversial legal issues in the field of child protection, particularly in regard to cases in which the parents' religious beliefs conflict with the recommendations of the medical community (see Chapter 14, this volume). No doubt the courts will continue to grapple with the painful issues raised when children's apparent need for medical intervention clashes with parents' freedom of religion and choice.

Mental health neglect. Similar to medical neglect, this refers to caregivers' refusal to comply with recommended corrective or therapeutic procedures in cases in which a child is found to have a serious emotional or behavioral disorder. Although Hart (1987) proposed standards and procedures for legal and social service intervention in regard to this subtype of neglect, it is not addressed widely as a form of maltreatment.

Educational neglect. In the legal arena, educational neglect refers to caregivers' failure to comply with state requirements for school attendance. Among educators and mental health professionals, it also may be used more broadly to encompass the parents' lack of cooperation or involvement in their children's schooling or the parents' resistance to follow through with special programs or interventions recommended by the schools. However, given the scope of parental rights and choices in regard to their children's education, such broad definitions are not likely to be incorporated into legal definitions of neglect.

The Impact of Child Neglect

Although abuse still garners more public attention, neglect is the most common type of reported maltreatment. Based on a 50-state survey of child protective services (CPS) agencies in the United States, an estimated 2.3 million children were reported as victims of child abuse and neglect in 1997. Of those, approximately 54% were reported for neglect, as compared with 24% for physical abuse, 12% for sexual abuse, 6% for emotional maltreatment (some of whom experienced emotional neglect), and 13% for other forms of maltreatment (McDonald & Associates, 1999). Approximately 55% of reported neglect cases received postinvestigative services. It is likely that the actual incidence of neglect is much higher than reporting statistics indicate. Because neglect (particularly emotional neglect) often leaves no visible scars, it is likely to go undetected.

Furthermore, many victims of neglect are infants who are too young to speak out about the treatment they experience. Because neglect is often chronic rather than episodic, these children also may grow up thinking this is the way life is, not realizing that their experience constitutes maltreatment.

Long-Term Developmental Consequences of Neglect

The 1970s saw a burgeoning interest in studies of the consequences of maltreatment. Early studies, which focused primarily on children who were physically abused, usually presented clinical evidence or descriptive statistics without using control groups. These studies pointed to a disproportionate number of children who performed below average on standardized intelligence tests (e.g., Martin, Beezley, Conway, & Kempe, 1974; Morse, Sahler, & Friedman, 1970; Sandgrund, Gaines, & Green, 1974) and who exhibited varied social and emotional problems, including hostility, aggression, and passive, withdrawn behavior (e.g., Galdston, 1971; Kempe & Kempe, 1978; Martin & Beezley, 1977). In one of the first studies specifically to include neglected children among maltreated subjects, Steele (1977) found learning problems, low self-esteem, and, in subsequent years, a high incidence of juvenile delinquency.

The 1980s saw reports from several studies comparing maltreated children with control groups of nonmaltreated children. Some studies also made comparisons between children who were abused and those who were neglected. For example, Reidy (1977) found that both abused and neglected children behaved more aggressively in school than nonmaltreated children, but abused children exhibited more aggression during fantasy and free play than the neglected children.

Hoffman-Plotkin and Twentyman (1984) reported that abused children were more aggressive than either neglected or nonmaltreated children, but the neglected children interacted less with peers than either abused or nonmaltreated children. Similarly, Crittenden (1985b; Crittenden & Ainsworth, 1989) found that abused children were described as having difficult temperaments, became angry under stress, and exhibited mild developmental delays. Neglected children, on the other hand, were passive, tended toward helplessness under stress, and showed significant developmental delays. In a review of studies from 1975 to 1992, Katz (1992) found that both abused and neglected children had language delays or disorders, but the problems of neglected children were more severe. And a longitudinal study of the school behavior and achievement of neglected children documented a notable decline in performance when children entered junior high (Kendall-Tackett & Eckenrode, 1996).

These findings on the apparent differences in developmental consequences of abuse and neglect point to the importance of separating types of maltreatment when studying their consequences. Otherwise, combining abused and neglected children for group data may obscure the ways in which they differ from nonmaltreated children. On the other hand, many children experience more than one type of maltreatment; groups will overlap, and the line between subtypes usually is blurred. Thus, it is important to keep this in perspective when considering differences between neglect and abuse and recognize that such research is not always the hard science we would hope it to be. Also, it may be important to consider the consequences of multiple types of maltreatment. (Our own Minnesota Parent-Child Project, discussed later, has attempted to address these questions.)

Emotional neglect. As difficult as it is to draw a clear line between abused and neglected children, it is even more difficult to distinguish between children who are physically neglected and those who are emotionally neglected. Most, if not all, children who are physically neglected are also emotionally neglected at least to some extent. However, the converse is not always true. We have seen a number of cases of children who were emotionally but not physically neglected (e.g., Egeland & Erickson, 1987). They were fed adequately, well clothed, and received proper health care, but their caregivers did not respond to their emotional needs.

As mentioned earlier, the most extreme consequences of emotional neglect are labeled as the *nonorganic failure to thrive syndrome,* which involves failure to grow—or sometimes even to survive—despite adequate nourishment (Gardner, 1972; MacCarthy, 1979; Patton & Gardner, 1962). Even after diagnosis and intervention, the psychological consequences of emotional neglect per-

sist. In a clinical follow-up of infants who had been diagnosed as failure to thrive, MacCarthy (1979) reported notable attention-seeking behavior and superficial displays of affection after these children were placed out of the home. Later in their childhood, these children were described as spiteful and selfish, and they reportedly engaged in stealing. Likewise, Polansky, Chalmers, Buttenwieser, and Williams (1981) chronicled the defiant, hostile behavior of young adolescents who, in infancy, had been diagnosed as failure to thrive. Hufton and Oates (1977) also found that failure-to-thrive children presented varied academic and behavior problems in the early elementary grades.

Even in cases much less profound than failure to thrive, the long-term consequences of emotional neglect are remarkable. As reported in detail in earlier papers (Egeland & Erickson, 1987; Egeland, Sroufe, & Erickson, 1983; Erickson et al., 1989), our own research on children with psychologically unavailable parents provides powerful testimony to the impact of this form of neglect. We examined the development of these same children through adolescence and again compared them with nonmaltreated children within our same high-risk sample (Egeland, 1997). Both our earlier findings and the more recent preliminary analyses of our follow-up data are summarized in a subsequent section of this chapter.

Some Methodological Considerations in Studying the Effects of Neglect

It is not easy to examine the impact of neglect and sort it from the many variables that influence a child's development. It often has been noted that many maltreated children live in poverty or in families characterized by other kinds of problems. Therefore, it can be difficult to ascertain to what extent a child's subsequent problems are due to the maltreatment itself or to other aspects of the environment. For example, in a frequently cited study, Elmer (1977) found few differences between abused and nonabused children within a poverty sample, leading her to conclude that the impact of poverty and other environmental factors associated with it may override the effects of abuse. It has been noted elsewhere, however (e.g., Aber & Cicchetti, 1984; Erickson et al., 1989), that the nonabused children in Elmer's sample were matched to the abused children not only for poverty but also for hospitalization experience. Specifically, the nonabused comparison groups included (a) children who were hospitalized for accidental injury and (b) children who were not victims of trauma but were matched for history of hospitalization (i.e., for things such as acute illness). This may have blurred the lines between abused and "nonabused" children in this study. Given the relation of neglect to accidental injury and illness, it is plausible that a number of these children in the so-called nonabused group actually had experienced neglect. (As described below, our own longitudinal research does provide strong evidence that maltreatment has consequences above and beyond the effects of poverty.)

Although it is relatively easy to control for poverty and other sociodemographic variables, it is more challenging to separate the effects of maltreatment from other aspects of the home environment and family functioning. For example, other researchers have pointed to the general dysfunction among families in which intrafamilial sexual abuse has occurred, and some contend that general dysfunction, rather than the sexual abuse per se, accounts for children's poor psychological outcomes (e.g., Giaretto, 1976; Herman & Hirschman, 1981; Rosenfeld, 1977). Likewise, child neglect is often embedded in a larger pattern of dysfunction and, in many cases, environmental chaos, making it difficult or impossible to separate the impact of neglect from other environmental influences. Although this is problematic from a research perspective, such distinctions may be less meaningful from a prevention or treatment perspective; intervention efforts most likely will need to address the entire matrix of home and family variables that support or impede children's development.

Another critical methodological issue involves taking into account the age and developmental stage of the children being studied. Early studies of maltreatment described consequences with little regard for age, often combining children of widely varying ages. Yet, given how rapidly and dramatically children's behavior changes over time, consequences of maltreatment will probably be manifest in different ways at different periods of development. Neglect may be operationalized differently, depending on the age and developmental needs of the child (Biringen & Robinson, 1991; Erickson & Egeland, 1987). More recently, cross-sectional studies have looked at children within a narrower age range, and longitudinal studies have followed children through different stages of development, assessing child behavior within the framework of salient issues at each stage.

Many of the developmentally sensitive studies have focused on infancy and early childhood. For example, in one of the early studies in that wave of research, Gaensbauer, Mrazek, and Harmon (1980) examined the development of affective communication between infants and their caregivers, comparing maltreated and nonmaltreated infants. They observed developmental and affective delays among one group of children who were hypothesized to have experienced extreme neglect. Other children who performed normally on developmental tasks but presented depressed affect were believed to have received adequate care in early infancy, followed by separation from their caregivers or emotional neglect due to maternal depression.

Much of the more recent research on maltreated infants has been guided by attachment theory (Bowlby, 1969, 1973, 1980) and facilitated by the Strange Situation Procedure for assessing the quality of parent-infant attachment (Ainsworth, Blehar, Waters, & Wall, 1978). This assessment procedure, used most often when the child is 1 or 2 years of age, has been demonstrated to be a valid and reliable measure of the infant's adaptation within the context of the infant-caregiver relationship, and it is predictive of the child's subsequent behavior in a variety of situations (e.g., see Bretherton & Waters, 1985). Infants who have secure relationships with their primary caregivers are more competent at later ages than children whose attachment was classified as anxious-resistant or anxious-avoidant in the Strange Situation. Anxiously attached children are more likely to exhibit problems in cognitive and emotional functioning (e.g., Erickson, Sroufe, & Egeland, 1985; Sroufe, 2000; Warren, Huston, Egeland, & Sroufe, 1997).

Several studies have found maltreated children, including those who are neglected, to have a high incidence of anxious attachment. This is not surprising because primary determinants of the quality of attachment are the parent's responsiveness and sensitivity to the baby's cues and signals—the antithesis of maltreatment (Egeland & Farber, 1984; van Ijzendoorn, 1995). In the Harvard Maltreatment Project, maltreated infants were more likely than nonmaltreated infants to be insecurely attached (Schneider-Rosen, Braunwald, Carlson, & Cicchetti, 1985). Lamb, Gaensbauer, Malkin, and Schultz (1985) also reported that children who were maltreated by their primary caregivers were more likely to have insecure relationships with their biological mothers and, to a lesser extent, with their foster mothers. Crittenden (1985b) also reported a high incidence of anxious attachment among abused and neglected children.

Illustrative of the importance of taking development into account when looking at the consequences of maltreatment, Crittenden (1985a, 1992) found interesting differences between abused and neglected children at 2 years of age. Abused children appeared angry during their first year of life but inhibited that anger with their mothers at 2 years of age. Neglected children did not show such a change in strategy, and Crittenden contends that the abused children's inhibition reflects the 2-year-olds' new ability to form expectancies about their parents' behavior.

The Minnesota Parent-Child Project. One of the first major studies to address systematically the methodological considerations discussed earlier was the Minnesota Mother-Child Project. This is a prospective, longitudinal study designed to follow the development of a sample of 267 children born to first-time mothers identified as being at risk for parenting problems due to poverty, youth, low education, lack of support, and unstable life circumstances. Recruited through obstetric clinics during the second trimester of pregnancy, these women, their children, and their life circumstances have been assessed regularly, using multiple methods and measures, through early adulthood (see Egeland, 1997; Erickson et al., 1989; Pianta, Egeland, & Erickson, 1989).

Although the Minnesota Parent-Child Project has examined the entire qualitative range of caregiving, a major focus has been on the antecedents of abuse and neglect, as well as the long-term consequences of maltreatment on children's development. At different points in time, we identified three groups of children who were maltreated, based on observations and other data collected since birth. For example, in the period of 0 to 54 months, we identified physically abused, neglected, and children whose mothers were psychologically unavailable, that is, emotionally neglectful.

(Note that there was overlap in the groups, with some children experiencing physical abuse in addition to other types of maltreatment.)

Of particular interest for this chapter are the neglected children and those with psychologically unavailable caregivers. Mothers in the "neglectful" group did not provide appropriate health care, physical care, or protection for their children—either through incompetence or irresponsibility. Although these mothers sometimes expressed concern and interest in their children's welfare, their care for their children was inconsistent and inadequate. Mothers in the psychologically unavailable group appeared detached and unresponsive to their children's bids for care and attention. When they did interact with their children, it was in a mechanical and perfunctory manner, with no apparent joy or satisfaction in the relationship.

As reported in detail in previous publications, we compared each of these maltreatment groups with a group of nonmaltreated children from within the same high-risk sample (Egeland & Sroufe, 1981; Egeland et al., 1983; Erickson et al., 1989), using as outcomes a wide range of measures administered over time and across multiple situations. Children in all maltreatment groups functioned poorly in a variety of situations from infancy through the preschool period. For those who were maltreated in infancy, there was a high incidence of anxious attachment compared with the control group.

At almost 2 years of age, neglected children lacked enthusiasm, were easily frustrated, displayed considerable anger, and were noncompliant.

Among neglected children, two thirds were anxiously attached at 1 year of age. At almost 2 years of age, when videotaped in a problem-solving task with their mothers, neglected children lacked enthusiasm, were easily frustrated, displayed considerable anger, and were noncompliant. When videotaped with their mothers in a series of teaching tasks, neglected children showed little enthusiasm or persistence and were angry, noncompliant, and often avoidant and unaffectionate toward their mothers, even though they were highly dependent on them for help. Also at 42 months, in an independent problem-solving task, these children showed poor impulse control, rigidity, a lack of creativity, and more unhappiness than all other groups. Later, at 54 months of age, when observed in a preschool or child care setting, neglected children demonstrated poor impulse control, extreme dependence on their teachers, and general adjustment problems in the classroom.

In many ways, our study shows the consequences of *emotional neglect* (or what we call psychologically unavailable parenting) to be even more profound than physical neglect and the other types of maltreatment. Nearly all of the children in this group were anxiously attached, with the majority of those classified as anxious-avoidant. In each of the assessments at 24 and 42 months, they displayed anger, noncompliance, lack of persistence, and little positive affect. Probably the most dramatic finding for these children was their steep decline in performance on the Bayley Scales of Infant Development between 9 and 24 months. In the preschool classroom, at approximately 54 months of age, these children presented varied and serious behavior problems. They continued to be noncompliant and negativistic, impulsive, and highly dependent on teachers, and they sometimes displayed nervous signs, self-abusive behavior, and other behaviors considered to be indicators of psychopathology (Egeland et al., 1983). Although the maltreatment they experienced was the most subtle of all groups, the consequences for the children were the most striking.

For children who were maltreated during the preschool period, the physically neglected presented the most problems. In kindergarten, they were inattentive and uninvolved in learning, anxious, aggressive, and unpopular with peers. Their performance on standardized tests of intellectual functioning and academic achievement were the lowest of all the maltreatment groups. Children who experienced emotional neglect (psychologically unavailable parents) at this stage of life also presented significant problems in the classroom. However, the impact was not as dramatic as for the children who experienced that kind of maltreatment during the first 2 years of life.

Follow-up assessments of emotionally neglected children. Assessments done when the children in this sample were in elementary school included information gathered from the classroom teachers in Grades 1, 2, 3, and 6. Teachers completed the Child Behavior Checklist on each child (Achenbach & Edelbrock, 1980), and, before they knew who the target child was, they also rank-ordered all the students in their classroom on dimensions of peer acceptance and emotional health. Children also were administered the Peabody Individual Achievement Test (Dunn & Markwardt, 1970) in each of the four grades.

Analyses indicate that children who experienced psychologically unavailable parenting in the first 2 years of life continued to have problems throughout the elementary school years. When compared with nonmaltreated children from the same high-risk sample, these emotionally neglected children were ranked low by their teachers on both peer acceptance and overall emotional health. On the Child Behavior Checklist, they were rated at all grade levels as being more socially withdrawn, unpopular with peers, and, in general, exhibiting more problems of the internalizing type. In the early grades, they also were rated as more aggressive and less attentive. On the Peabody Individual Achievement Test, these children performed significantly lower at every grade level than the nonmaltreated children in the sample. When these emotionally neglected children were compared with children who had been physically abused in the early years of life, there were no variables on which the physically abused children did significantly worse than the emotionally neglected children, although the emotionally neglected children were more withdrawn and inattentive than the physically abused children (Erickson & Egeland, 1996). The physically and emotionally neglected children were high on the internalizing and externalizing scores of the Child Behavior Checklist–Teacher's Report Form (CBC-T) compared with the control groups. In addition, both neglect groups were ranked low on peer acceptance and emotional health compared with the control group. The physically neglected children were low academically and had difficulty organizing themselves to cope with the everyday demands of school. Only one neglected child from a total of 19 was not receiving some level of special education services in kindergarten through Grade 3. The physically neglected children missed more than 60 days of school between kindergarten and the third grade compared with 41 days for the control children, and for all maltreated children, the teachers indicated that maltreating parents seldom had knowledge or interest in their children's school life.

According to Erik Erikson (1963) and others, the salient development issue of middle childhood is initiative. Using items from teacher ratings on the Devereux Elementary School Rating Scale (e.g., works independently, persistent, well organized, able to follow directions, stays on task until completed), we constructed an initiative scale and found that all maltreated children, particularly the physically neglected, were lower on this scale compared with the control group (Egeland, Hyson, Yates, & Roisman, 1999).

In summary, the impact of neglect on children's development was at least as damaging as other more overt types of abuse. Physical neglect, particularly during the preschool and primary grades, seriously impaired the children's school behavior. And emotional neglect, especially during the first 2 years of life, had a particularly striking and long-lasting impact on children's adaptation within the family, with peers and teachers, and in regard to learning and problem solving. The effects of neglect are above and beyond the negative impact of poverty and its correlates on children's development.

A further follow-up in adolescence of children who were maltreated in the early years indicated that maltreated children in general were experiencing a variety of problems. The problems that seemed to be more severe in the physical neglect group involved low achievement scores on an individually administered achievement test and high teacher ratings on the delinquency scale of the Child Behavior Checklist, heavy alcohol use, expulsion from school, and dropout. Compared with the control group and other maltreatment groups, the adolescents whose parents were psychologically unavailable at an early age displayed a number of behavior problems. They were high on the social problem, delinquency, and aggression scales of the CBC-T, and significantly more attempted suicide compared with the other maltreatment groups and the controls. At age 17½, we gave the K-SADS (Kiddie–Schedule for Affective Disorders and Schizophrenia), a diagnostic interview for mental illness based on the *DSM-III-R* (American Psychiatric Association, 1987). The majority of maltreated children (90%) received at least one diagnosis. The highest rate was in the psychologically unavailable group in which all but one of the children received at least one diagnosis of psychiatric disorder and 73% were comorbid for two disorders or more. Fifty-four percent of the physically neglected children were comorbid compared with 30% for the control group. In summary, maltreatment in the early years had devastating consequences for the children's overall functioning in adolescence. According to teacher ratings, both the physically and emotionally neglected children had a variety of behavior problems at age 16. In addition, the physically neglected had high rates of academic failure and school dropout, and the emotionally neglected displayed high rates of psychopathology (Egeland, 1997).

Antecedents of Neglect

A critical research question that has important implications for prevention involves the identification of variables that predict which children are likely to be neglected. The more we know about the antecedents of neglect, the more precise our attempts will be to identify and support families most at risk. Unfortunately, little in the research points to specific antecedents of neglect as opposed to physical abuse or other types of maltreatment. However, several studies provide useful information about antecedents and concomitants of maltreatment in general. Historically, many studies followed a psychiatric model, whereby abuse was seen as a result of the parent's emotional illness, with little attention paid to child characteristics or to environmental conditions in which the family functioned. In the past two decades, however, literature reflects a shift toward more interactive processes that take into account the multiple variables that influence quality of care. For example, in 1980, Belsky proposed an ecological model of maltreatment that included four levels of analysis: (a) ontogeny (the individual characteristics associated with being a perpetrator of maltreatment), (b) the microsystem (family factors), (c) the exosystem (community factors), and (d) the macrosystem (cultural values and beliefs that serve to perpetuate maltreatment). (See Belsky, 1993, for a more recent elaboration of these ideas.) Similarly, Cicchetti and Lynch (1993) elaborated a transactional model suggesting that maltreatment occurs when *potentiating factors* (i.e., factors that increase the likelihood of maltreatment) outweigh *compensatory factors* (i.e., those that decrease the risk for maltreatment). Factors were categorized further into (a) enduring vulnerability factors, (b) transient challengers, (c) enduring protective factors, and (d) transient buffers.

Acknowledging that no single factor is sufficient to explain maltreatment, studies have begun to shed light on how these multiple variables interact to render parents more or less able to sustain adequate, appropriate care for their children. Variables of interest can be grouped broadly into parental characteristics and attitudes, child characteristics, and environmental factors. The findings that have accumulated over the past decade can be summarized briefly as follows.

One set of variables that has distinguished between maltreating and non-maltreating parents has to do with social-cognitive and affective processes that are tied to the parents' perceptions of their children and the parent-child relationship. Specifically, maltreating parents often are characterized by a *lack of understanding* the emotional complexity of human relationships, especially the parent-child relationship. They have difficulty seeing things from the child's perspective or understanding behavior in terms of the child's developmental level and the context or situation.

Maltreating parents tend to think in global, all-or-nothing terms rather than see the shades of gray that more realistically capture human behavior (Brunnquell, Crichton, & Egeland, 1981; Newberger & Cook, 1983; Sameroff & Feil, 1984). Aber and Zigler (1981) pointed to the importance of the parents' own developmental level as a determinant of how they think and behave in regard to their children. Parental development reflects the parents' own history of care, their struggles with issues of dependency and autonomy, and their level of cognitive functioning. Parents with unresolved issues of trust, dependency, and autonomy are more likely to have difficulty understanding and meeting the demands of their children and may seek to meet their own needs through the parent-child relationship (Pianta et al., 1989). Maltreating parents also have been found to have a high incidence of depression (Lahey, Conger, Atkenson, & Treiber, 1984) and lack impulse control, particularly when stressed (Altemeier, O'Connor, Vietze, Sandler, & Sherrod, 1982; Wolfe, 1985).

Some researchers have focused on child behavior as a contributing factor to child maltreatment. Bell (1968) was one of the first to call attention to the child's influence on the parent in his important paper on the bidirectionality of influence in the par-

ent-child relationship. Research in the 1970s focused on infant irritability and fussiness as contributing factors (Gil, 1970; Parke & Collmer, 1975; Thomas & Chess, 1977). However, retrospective designs and reliance on temperament measures that may have reflected parental perception more than actual child behavior made it difficult to interpret findings from such studies (Vaughn, Deinard, & Egeland, 1980). Others have cited the relationship between maltreatment and such child features as disabilities, prematurity, and facial features (Belsky, 1980; McCabe, 1984). Biringen and Robinson (1991) summarize studies that provide some limited evidence of the child's contribution to parental availability or unavailability.

Although few would dispute that some children are more difficult to care for than others, there is strong evidence from observational studies that child characteristics alone do not account for maltreatment. Research taking a transactional view of parent-child relationships demonstrated the power of parental sensitivity and responsiveness in overcoming the child's difficulty (Brachfield, Goldberg, & Sloman, 1980; Sameroff & Chandler, 1975). To muster the emotional resources to counter the challenges posed by a difficult child, parents may need extra support, education, and encouragement.

Data from the Third National Incidence Study indicate that, of all subtypes of maltreatment, physical neglect is most clearly associated with poverty.

Finally, research on the etiology of maltreatment points to several environmental characteristics that are contributing factors. Again, these findings are not specific to neglect but appear to be robust in regard to maltreatment in general. Major environmental factors include violence in the marital relationship, parental unemployment, and the availability of a helpful, supportive social network, perhaps especially among single parents who lack intimate emotional support (Dubowitz, 1999). Data from the Third National Incidence Study indicate that, of all subtypes of maltreatment, physical neglect is most clearly associated with poverty (Sedlak & Broadhurst, 1996).

In our own data from the Minnesota Parent-Child Project, we examined the antecedents of specific subtypes of maltreatment, including physical abuse, neglect, and emotional neglect (psychologically unavailable parenting). This work was described in detail in Pianta et al. (1989). Specifically, we found lack of social support and insularity to characterize families in all maltreatment groups. Maltreating families also experienced more stressful life events than nonmaltreating families within the same high-risk sample. The home environments of maltreating families differed from nonmaltreating homes in terms of provision of play materials and parental involvement and responsivity to the child. The homes of neglectful and sexually abusive families also were observed to be more disorganized than the homes of nonmaltreating families. Maltreating mothers also presented more mood disturbances. Psychologically unavailable mothers were more tense, depressed, angry, and confused than nonmaltreating mothers. Neglectful mothers also were more tense, and they functioned at a lower level intellectually than mothers who provided adequate care. Overall, the maltreating parents differed markedly from nonmaltreating parents on many variables, but the differences by specific type of maltreatment were small.

Another variable of particular interest in our study was the care the mother had received in her own childhood. Among mothers who were abused or neglected when they were children, 40% maltreated their children in the early years of their children's lives, and an additional 30% provided borderline care. Among mothers who were neglected children, seven out of nine maltreated their own children, and most of these were cases of neglect (Pianta et al., 1989).

Perhaps the most important question of all is, What characterizes parents who rise above their own history of abuse and provide good care for their children? As described elsewhere (Egeland, 1988; Egeland & Susman-Stillman, 1996), four major factors distinguished between mothers who broke the cycle of maltreatment and those who did not: (a) the presence of a loving, supportive adult during their childhood, someone who gave them a different view of themselves and others; (b) a supportive partner at the time they became parents; (c) therapeutic intervention that enabled mothers to

come to some resolution of their early issues and achieve greater emotional stability and maturity, and (d) the fourth variable had to do with mothers' integration of the maltreating experiences into a coherent view of self. Specifically, mothers who repeated the cycle of maltreatment had significantly higher scores on a measure of disassociation compared with mothers who broke the cycle of maltreatment.

Summary and Discussion: Implications for Practice and Future Research

Based on the research summarized here, it is clear that neglect is a major societal problem. According to CPS, more than 1.5 million children were reported for this form of maltreatment in 1997 (McDonald & Associates, 1999). And those were only the children who showed up in child protection reports. Considering how easily neglect can be overlooked, it seems impossible to estimate the actual scope of the problem.

We also can say with reasonable certainty that neglect has a serious impact on children's behavior across time and varied situations. Neglected children, if they survive physically, often fail to develop the confidence, concentration, and social skills that would enable them to succeed in school and in relationships. The behavior they bring to the classroom sets them up for a continuing cycle of failure and disappointment unless something happens to make a difference.

Even the most subtle kinds of emotional neglect have a dramatic effect on children's development, especially during the early years of life. As we have discussed in detail elsewhere, attachment theory provides a useful framework for understanding the impact of neglect. This theory proposes that the infant's relationships with primary caregivers are the prototypes for subsequent relationships. Within those early relationships, children develop expectancies about how others will respond and about how effective they will be in soliciting the responses they need and want. Children then behave in accordance with those expectancies, and that, in a way, helps to perpetuate the kind of relationship experiences they have had.

For example, the child whose mother fails to respond to his or her signals will eventually shut down, no longer seeking or accepting contact with her (as did the anxious-avoidant children in our sample of emotionally neglected children). Then, when the child enters the new social world of school, those old expectancies and behaviors continue to play out in regard to learning, peer relations, and response to teachers.

Emotionally neglected children expect not to get what they need from others, and so they do not even try to solicit care and warmth. They expect not to be effective and successful in tasks, and so they do not try to succeed. Or perhaps, these children's dependence needs are so overwhelming that they are barely able to concern themselves with being motivated and task oriented. As we have discussed elsewhere (e.g., Egeland & Erickson, 1999; Erickson & Pianta, 1989), teachers and peers are often put off by these children's behavior, thus perpetuating their previous relationship experience and reinforcing their negative expectations of others and self.

Even the most subtle kinds of emotional neglect have a dramatic effect on children's development, especially during the early years of life.

It is ironic that the impact of emotional neglect is most profound when it is least likely to be detected—when the child is too young to speak out to others. (It is not surprising that early neglect has such a strong influence, because an infant's whole world revolves around his or her primary caregivers.) It is also ironic that, unless the child shows clear physical signs of neglect (e.g., failure to thrive), intervention is not likely to be mandated in cases of emotional neglect. (At least that has been our experience; we have not seen data to that effect.)

An interesting and useful direction for research would be to see how professionals are able to secure intervention or supportive services for emotionally neglectful families and to what extent they can get the system to respond to these families who may not meet the criteria for intervention by CPS. Again, it has been our experience that it is easy to fall into a catch-22 situation: Neglectful families who may not qualify for man-

dated intervention also may be the most difficult to engage in voluntary service. Either their lives are extremely disorganized (as is often the case with the physically neglectful) or the parents are distancing and perhaps depressed (as is often the case with the emotionally neglectful). The same factors that make it difficult for parents to connect emotionally with their children probably also make it difficult for them to connect with service providers or other potential sources of support. If they feel that they are being judged as failures in parenting, it will not be any easier for parents to connect with service providers.

Although the effectiveness of intervention with neglecting families has not been studied adequately, limited evidence suggests that interventions are successful with no more than 50% of families. The most effective interventions are comprehensive and relatively long term (Gaudin, 1993; Holden & Nabors, 1999).

Research does point to some of the early indicators of parents who are likely to be physically or emotionally neglectful, and models of family support and early intervention offer promise as prevention strategies (Wolfe, 1993). In particular, maltreatment is likely to occur among parents who lack an understanding of their children's behavior and the parent-child relationship, experience a great deal of stress, are socially isolated or unsupported, and have a history of inadequate care themselves.

It is important to use knowledge of the antecedents of maltreatment to find ways to identify families at risk and address those underlying factors in an effort to prevent neglect. Health care providers, especially in obstetric, perinatal, and pediatric settings, may be in the best position to identify potentially neglectful families. Because neglect is particularly damaging in infancy, it is important to work with families as early in the infant's life as possible—or, preferably, even before the baby is born. In our own preventive intervention program, Project STEEP (Egeland & Erickson, 1990; Erickson & Egeland, 1999; Erickson, Korfmacher, & Egeland, 1992), we have found expectant parents to be open to supportive, therapeutic services prior to the birth of their first child. Because they are not parents yet, they do not feel that their child rearing is being judged. And, as they anticipate the new experiences of childbirth and parenting, they are relatively open to the idea of sharing that adventure with their STEEP home visitor and other parents who will be giving birth at about the same time.

In our opinion, one of the major directions for both practice and research in the area of child neglect is the implementation and careful evaluation of programs designed to prevent neglect. Neglect takes many forms and reflects a variety of underlying problems. It is likely that different strategies will be needed for different families facing different issues. One analysis of 34 prevention studies pointed to individualization as a key to success (Wekerle & Wolfe, 1993). Approaches will vary, depending on factors such as the age and gender of the child, the stage of family development, race, ethnicity, and age and education of the parents. Although it is impossible to design a program to suit each unique family situation, programs should be flexible enough to meet families where they are, identifying and building on individual and family strengths. Programs must be designed, targeted, and evaluated within a clearly articulated theory on the development of maltreated children and the factors that lead to and perpetuate maltreatment. We believe that attachment theory provides a good place to begin.

The challenge for research then will be to assess to what extent, for whom, and under what conditions a program is effective in preventing neglect and other types of maltreatment. As we discover what really helps to build strong families, we prevent harm not only to the children in those families but also to the children of subsequent generations.

References

Aber, J. L., & Cicchetti, D. (1984). The social-emotional development of maltreated children: An empirical and theoretical analysis. In H. Fitzgerald, B. Lester, & M. Yogman (Eds.), *Theory and research in behavioral pediatrics* (Vol. 2, pp. 147-205). New York: Plenum.

Aber, J. L., & Zigler, D. (1981). Developmental considerations in the definition of child maltreatment. In R. Rizley & D. Cicchetti (Eds.), *New directions in child development: Developmental perspectives in child maltreatment* (pp. 1-29). San Francisco: Jossey-Bass.

Achenbach, T., & Edelbrock, C. (1980). *Child Behavior Checklist—Teacher's Report Form.* Burlington: University of Vermont.

Ainsworth, M. D. S., Blehar, M., Waters, E., & Wall, S. (1978). *Patterns of attachment.* Hillsdale, NJ: Lawrence Erlbaum.

Altemeier, W., O'Connor, S., Vietze, P., Sandler, H., & Sherrod, K. (1982). Antecedents of child abuse. *Journal of Pediatrics, 100,* 823-829.

American Psychiatric Association. (1987). *Diagnostic and statistical manual of mental disorders* (3rd ed., rev.). Washington, DC: Author.

Bell, R. (1968). A reinterpretation of the direction of effects in studies of socialization. *Psychological Review, 75,* 81-95.

Belsky, J. (1980). Child maltreatment: An ecological integration. *American Psychologist, 35,* 320-335.

Belsky, J. (1993). Etiology of child maltreatment: A developmental-ecological analysis. *Psychological Bulletin, 114*(3), 413-434.

Biringen, Z., & Robinson, J. (1991). Emotional availability in mother-child interactions: A reconceptualization for research. *American Journal of Orthopsychiatry, 61*(2), 258-271.

Black, M. M., & Dubowitz, H. (1999). Child neglect: Research recommendations and future directions. In H. Dubowitz (Ed.), *Neglected children: Research, practice, and policy* (pp. 261-277). Thousand Oaks, CA: Sage.

Boehm, B. (1962). An assessment of family adequacy in protective cases. *Child Welfare, 41,* 10-16.

Bowlby, J. (1969). *Attachment and loss: Vol. 1. Attachment.* New York: Basic Books.

Bowlby, J. (1973). *Attachment and loss: Vol. 2. Separation.* New York: Basic Books.

Bowlby, J. (1980). *Attachment and loss: Vol. 3. Loss, sadness, and depression.* New York: Basic Books.

Brachfield, S., Goldberg, S., & Sloman, J. (1980). Parent-infant interaction in free play at 8 and 12 months: Effects of prematurity and immaturity. *Infant Behavior in Development, 3,* 289-305.

Brassard, M., Germain, R., & Hart, S. (1987). *Psychological maltreatment of children and youth.* Elmsford, NY: Pergamon.

Bretherton, I., & Waters, E. (Eds.). (1985). Growing points of attachment theory and research. *Monographs of the Society for Research in Child Development, 50*(1-2, Serial No. 209).

Brunnquell, D., Crichton, L., & Egeland, B. (1981). Maternal personality and attitude in disturbances of child rearing. *American Journal of Orthopsychiatry, 51,* 680-691.

Cicchetti, D., & Lynch, M. (1993). Toward an ecological transactional model of community violence and child maltreatment. *Psychiatry, 56,* 96-118.

Claussen, A. H., & Crittenden, P. M. (1991). Physical and psychological maltreatment: Relations among the types of maltreatment. *Child Abuse & Neglect, 15*(1/2), 5-18.

Crittenden, P. M. (1985a). Maltreated infants: Vulnerability and resilience. *Journal of Child Psychology and Psychiatry, 26*(1), 85-96.

Crittenden, P. M. (1985b). Social networks, quality of child-rearing, and child development. *Child Development, 56,* 1299-1313.

Crittenden, P. M. (1992). Children's strategies for coping with adverse home environments: An interpretation using attachment theory. *Child Abuse & Neglect, 16*(3), 329-343.

Crittenden, P. M., & Ainsworth, M. D. S. (1989). Child maltreatment and attachment theory. In D. Cicchetti, & V. Carlson (Eds.), *Child maltreatment: Theory and research on the causes and consequences of child abuse and neglect* (pp. 432-463). New York: Cambridge University Press.

Dubowitz, H. (Ed.). (1999). *Neglected children: Research, practice and policy.* Thousand Oaks, CA: Sage.

Dubowitz, H., Black, M., Starr, R. H., & Zuravin, S. (1993). A conceptual definition of child neglect. *Criminal Justice and Behavior, 20*(1), 8-26.

Dunn, L. M., & Markwardt, F. C. (1970). *Peabody Individual Achievement Test.* Circle Pines, MN: American Guidance Service.

Egeland, B. (1988). Breaking the cycle of abuse: Implications for prediction and intervention. In K. D. Browne, C. Davies, & P. Stratton (Eds.), *Early prediction and prevention of child abuse* (pp. 87-99). New York: John Wiley.

Egeland, B. (1997). Mediators of the effects of child maltreatment on developmental adaptation in adolescence. In D. Cicchetti & S. L. Toth (Eds.), *Rochester symposium on developmental pscyhopathology: Vol. VIII. The effects of trauma on the developmental process* (pp. 403-434). Rochester, NY: University of Rochester Press.

Egeland, B., & Erickson, M. F. (1987). Psychologically unavailable caregiving. In M. Brassard, B. Germain, & S. Hart (Eds.), *Psychological maltreatment of children and youth* (pp. 110-120). Elmsford, NY: Pergamon.

Egeland, B., & Erickson, M. F. (1990). Rising above the past: Strategies for helping new mothers break the cycle of abuse and neglect. *Zero to Three, 11*(2), 29-35.

Egeland, B., & Erickson, M. F. (1999). Findings from the Parent-Child Project and implications for early intervention. *Zero to Three, 20*(2), 3-10.

Egeland, B., & Farber, E. A. (1984). Infant-mother attachment: Factors related to its development and changes over time. *Child Development, 55,* 753-771.

Egeland, B., Hyson, D., Yates, T., & Roisman, G. (1999, December). *A longitudinal study of the developmental consequences of maltreatment.* Paper presented at Overcoming Adversity: Child Maltreatment, School Success and Transition to the Workforce, University of California, Davis.

Egeland, B., & Sroufe, L. A. (1981). Developmental sequelae of maltreatment in infancy. In B. Rizley & D. Cicchetti (Eds.), *New directions for child development: Developmental perspectives in child maltreatment* (pp. 77-92). San Francisco: Jossey-Bass.

Egeland, B., Sroufe, L. A., & Erickson, M. F. (1983). Developmental consequences of different patterns of maltreatment. *Child Abuse & Neglect, 7*(4), 456-469.

Egeland, B., & Susman-Stillman, A. (1996). Disassociation as a mediator of child abuse across generations. *Child Abuse & Neglect, 20*(11), 1123-1132.

Elmer, E. (1977). A follow-up study of traumatized children. *Pediatrics, 59*(2), 273-314.

Erickson, M. F., & Egeland, B. (1987). A developmental view of the psychological consequences of maltreatment. *School Psychology Review, 16*(2), 156-168.

Erickson, M. F., & Egeland, B. (1995). Consequences of neglect: Insights from longitudinal research. In E. Wattenberg (Ed.), *Children in the Shadows conference proceedings* (pp. 113-126). Minneapolis: University of Minnesota.

Erickson, M. F., & Egeland, B. (1996). Child neglect. In J. Briere, L. Berliner, J. Bulkley, C. Jenny, & T. Reid (Eds.), *APSAC handbook on child maltreatment* (pp. 4-20). Thousand Oaks, CA: Sage.

Erickson, M. F., & Egeland, B. (1999). The STEEP program: Linking theory and research to practice. *Zero to Three, 20*(2), 11-16.

Erickson, M. F., Egeland, B., & Pianta, R. C. (1989). The effects of maltreatment on the development of young children. In D. Cicchetti & V. Carlson (Eds.), *Child maltreatment: Theory and research on the causes and consequences of child abuse and neglect* (pp. 647-684). New York: Cambridge University Press.

Erickson, M. F., Korfmacher, J., & Egeland, B. (1992). Attachments past and present: Implications for therapeutic intervention with mother-infant dyad. *Development and Psychopathology, 4,* 495-507.

Erickson, M. F., & Pianta, R. C. (1989). New lunchbox, old feelings: What kids bring to school. *Early Education and Development, 1*(1), 29-35.

Erickson, M. F., Sroufe, L. A., & Egeland, B. (1985). The relationship between quality of attachment and behavior problems in preschool in a high-risk sample. In I. Bretherton & E. Waters (Eds.), *Child development monographs* (pp. 147-166). Chicago: University of Chicago Press.

Erikson, E. (1963). *Childhood and society* (2nd ed.). New York: Norton.

Flannery, E. J. (1979). Synopsis: Standards relating to abuse and neglect. In R. Bourne & E. H. Newberger (Eds.), *Critical perspectives on child abuse* (pp. 89-95). Lexington, MA: D. C. Heath.

Gaensbauer, T. J., Mrazek, D., & Harmon, R. J. (1980). Affective behavior patterns in abused and/or neglected infants. In N. Frude (Ed.), *The understanding and prevention of child abuse: Psychological approaches* (pp. 120-135). London: Concord.

Galdston, R. (1971). Violence begins at home. *Journal of the American Academy of Child Psychiatry, 10,* 336-350.

Garbarino, J. (1991). Not all bad developmental outcomes are the result of child abuse. *Development and Psychopathology, 3,* 45-50.

Gardner, L. I. (1972). Deprivation dwarfism. *Scientific American, 22*(7), 76-82.

Gaudin, J. M. (1993). Effective intervention with neglectful families. *Criminal Justice and Behavior, 20*(1), 66-89.

Giaretto, H. (1976). Humanistic treatment of father-daughter incest. In R. Helfer & H. Kempe (Eds.), *Child abuse and neglect* (pp. 143-162). Cambridge, MA: Ballinger.

Gil, D. G. (1970). *Violence against children: Physical abuse in the United States.* Cambridge, MA: Harvard University Press.

Giovannoni, J. (1989). Definitional issues in child maltreatment. In D. Cicchetti & V. Carlson (Eds.), *Child maltreatment: Theory and research on the causes and consequences of child abuse and neglect* (pp. 3-37). New York: Cambridge University Press.

Hamburg, D. (1992). *Today's children: Creating a future for a generation in crisis.* New York: Times Books.

Hart, S. (1987). Mental health neglect: Proposed definition, standards, and procedures for legal and social services intervention. In M. Brassard, B. Germain, & S. Hart (Eds.), *Psychological maltreatment of children and youth* (pp. 268-270). Elmsford, NY: Pergamon.

Herman, J., & Hirschman, L. (1981). Families at risk for father-daughter incest. *American Journal of Psychiatry, 138,* 967-970.

Hoffman-Plotkin, D., & Twentyman, C. T. (1984). A multimodal assessment of behavioral and cognitive deficits in abused and neglected preschoolers. *Child Development, 35,* 794-802.

Holden, E. W., & Nabors, L. (1999). The prevention of child neglect. In H. Dubowitz (Ed.), *Neglected children: Research, practice, and policy* (pp. 174-190). Thousand Oaks, CA: Sage.

Hufton, I. W., & Oates, R. K. (1977). Non-organic failure to thrive: A long-term follow-up. *Pediatrics, 59,* 73-77.

Katz, K. (1992). Communication problems in maltreated children: A tutorial. *Journal of Childhood Communication Disorders, 14*(2), 147-163.

Kempe, C. H., Silverman, F. N., Steele, B. F., Droegemueller, W., & Silver, H. K. (1962). The battered-child syndrome. *Journal of the American Medical Association, 181*(17), 17-24.

Kempe, R., & Kempe, C. H. (1978). *Child abuse.* London: Lontana/Open Books.

Kendall-Tackett, K. A., & Eckenrode, J. (1996). The effects of neglect on academic achievement and disciplinary problems: A developmental perspective. *Child Abuse & Neglect, 20*(3), 161-169.

Korbin, J. E. (1980). The cultural context of child abuse and neglect. *Child Abuse & Neglect, 4,* 3-13.

Korbin, J. E., & Spilsbury, J. C. (1999). Cultural competence and child neglect. In H. Dubowitz (Ed.), *Neglected children: Research, practice and policy* (pp. 69-88). Thousand Oaks, CA: Sage.

Lahey, B., Conger, R., Atkenson, B., & Treiber, F. (1984). Parenting behavior and emotional status of physically abusive mothers. *Journal of Consulting and Clinical Psychology, 52,* 1062-1071.

Lamb, M. F., Gaensbauer, T. J., Malkin, C. M., & Schultz, L. A. (1985). The effects of child maltreatment on security of infant-adult attachment. *Infant Behavior and Development, 8,* 34-45.

MacCarthy, D. (1979). Recognition of signs of emotional deprivation: A form of child abuse. *Child Abuse & Neglect, 3,* 423-428.

Martin, H. P., & Beezley, P. (1977). Behavioral observations of abused children. *Developmental Medicine in Child Neurology, 19,* 373-387.

Martin, H. P., Beezley, P., Conway, E. F., & Kempe, C. H. (1974). The development of abused children. In I. Schulman (Ed.), *Advances in pediatrics* (Vol. 21, pp. 25-73). Chicago: Year Book.

McCabe, V. (1984). Abstract perceptual information for age level: A risk factor for maltreatment? *Child Development, 55,* 267-276.

McDonald, W. R., & Associates. (1999). *Child maltreatment 1997: Reports from the states to the national child abuse and neglect data system* (DHHS Pub. No. ACF10055951849). Washington, DC: Government Printing Office.

Morse, W., Sahler, O. J., & Friedman, S. B. (1970). A three-year follow-up study of abused and neglected children. *American Journal of Diseases of Children, 120,* 439-446.

Newberger, C. M., & Cook, S. J. (1983). Parental awareness and child abuse: A cognitive developmental analysis of urban and rural samples. *American Journal of Orthopsychiatry, 53,* 512-524.

Newberger, E. H. (1973). The myth of the battered child syndrome. *Current Medical Dialog, 40,* 327-330.

Newson, J., & Newson, E. (1974). Cultural aspects of childrearing in the English-speaking world. In M. P. M. Richard (Ed.), *The integration of a child into a social world* (pp. 53-82). Cambridge, UK: Cambridge University Press.

Parke, R. D., & Collmer, C. W. (1975). Child abuse: An interdisciplinary analysis. In F. D. Horowitz (Ed.), *Review of child development research* (pp. 509-590). Chicago: University of Chicago Press.

Patton, R. G., & Gardner, L. I. (1962). Influence of family environment of growth: The syndrome of "maternal deprivation." *Pediatrics, 30,* 957-962.

Pianta, R., Egeland, B., & Erickson, M. F. (1989). The antecedents of maltreatment: Results of the Mother-Child Interaction Research Project. In D. Cicchetti & V. Carlson (Eds.), *Child maltreatment: Theory and research on the causes and consequences of child abuse and neglect* (pp. 203-253). Cambridge, UK: Cambridge University Press.

Polansky, N. A., Chalmers, M. A., Buttenwieser, E., & Williams, D. P. (1981). *Damaged parents: An anatomy of child neglect.* Chicago: University of Chicago Press.

Reidy, T. J. (1977). Aggressive characteristics of abused and neglected children. *Journal of Clinical Psychology, 33,* 1140-1145.

Rosenfeld, A. (1977). Sexual misuse and the family. *Victimology: An International Journal, 2,* 226-235.

Sameroff, A. J., & Chandler, M. J. (1975). Reproductive risk and the continuum of caretaking casualty. In F. D. Horowitz (Ed.), *Review of child development research* (pp. 187-244). Chicago: University of Chicago Press.

Sameroff, A. J., & Feil, L. A. (1984). Parental concepts of development. In I. Sigel (Ed.), *Parental belief systems: The psychological consequences for children* (pp. 83-105). Hillsdale, NJ: Lawrence Erlbaum.

Sandgrund, A., Gaines, R., & Green, A. H. (1974). Child abuse and mental retardation: A problem of cause and effect. *American Journal of Mental Deficiency, 79,* 327-330.

Schneider-Rosen, K., Braunwald, K. G., Carlson, V., & Cicchetti, D. (1985). Current perspectives in attachment theory: Illustration from the study of maltreated infants. *Monographs of the Society for Research in Child Development, 50*(1-2, Serial No. 209), 194-210.

Sedlak, A. J., & Broadhurst, D. D. (1996). *Executive summary of the third national incidence study of child abuse and neglect* (DHHS Pub. No. ACF-105-94-1840). Washington, DC: Government Printing Office.

Sroufe, L. A. (2000). Early relationships and the development of children. *Infant Mental Health Journal, 21,* 67-74.

Steele, B. F. (1977, February). *Psychological dimensions of child abuse.* Paper presented to the American Association for the Advancement of Science, Denver, CO.

Thomas, A., & Chess, S. (1977). *Temperament and development.* New York: Bruner-Mazel.

van Ijzendoorn, M. H. (1995). Adult attachment representations, parental responsiveness, and infant attachment: A meta-analysis on the predictive validity of the Adult Attachment Interview. *Psychological Bulletin, 117,* 387-403.

Vaughn, B., Deinard, A., & Egeland, B. (1980). Measuring temperament in pediatric practice. *Journal of Pediatrics, 96,* 510-514.

Wald, M. S. (1976). State intervention on behalf of "neglected" children: Standards for removal of children from their homes, monitoring the status of children in foster care, and termination of parental rights. *Standard Law Review, 28,* 629-706.

Warren, S. L., Huston, L., Egeland, B., & Sroufe, L. A. (1997). Child and adolescent anxiety disorders and early attachment. *Journal of the American Academy of Child and Adolescent Psychiatry, 36,* 637-644.

Wekerle, C., & Wolfe, D. A. (1993). Prevention of child physical abuse and neglect: Promising new directions. *Clinical Psychology Review, 13*(6), 501-540.

Wolfe, D. A. (1985). Child-abusive parents: An empirical review and analysis. *Psychological Bulletin, 97,* 462-482.

Wolfe, D. A. (1993). Prevention of child neglect: Emerging issues. *Criminal Justice and Behavior, 20*(1), 90-111.

Wolock, I., & Horowitz, B. (1984). Child maltreatment as a social problem: The neglect of neglect. *American Journal of Orthopsychiatry, 54,* 530-543.

Zuravin, S. J. (1999). Child neglect: A review of definitions and measurement research. In H. Dubowitz (Ed.), *Neglected children: Research, practice and policy* (pp. 24-46). Thousand Oaks, CA: Sage.

2

Child Physical Abuse

DAVID J. KOLKO

Introduction and Significance of the Problem

Since the first edition of this book was published in 1996, child physical abuse has continued to represent a significant concern of the child practitioners in the United States. On the basis of reports from the states to the National Center on Child Abuse and Neglect, physical abuse accounted for 24% of all reports, which is second only to reports of neglect (52%) (U.S. Department of Health and Human Services, 2000). Using the harm standard for definition purposes, one national estimate reported that the total number of children who experienced physical abuse increased from 1986 to 1993 by 42%, and the incidence rate rose from 4.3 to 5.7 children per 1,000, a 33% rate increase (Sedlak & Broadhurst, 1996). As these figures suggest, the physical abuse of children still remains all too common.

Besides a change in prevalence, more recent information has highlighted the significant financial costs of child maltreatment. As summarized by Courtney (1999), one estimate of the costs of providing various services to maltreated children and their families in 1993 was approximately $11.4 billion. During the 1980s, estimates of lost earnings associated with a group of maltreated children with serious injuries (about 24,000 in 1985) ranged from $658 million to $1.3 billion per year (Daro, 1988). The costs of child abuse and neglect services attributed to a particular definition of "incompetent parenting" was estimated at $8.4 billion (Westman, 1994). Overall expenditures for child welfare services in 1996 were estimated at $14.4 billion (Geen, Boots, & Tumlan, 1999).

Evolving empirical evidence confirms various adverse consequences of abuse (e.g., developmental, psychological, medical), risk or contributing factors to the origins of abusive behavior (e.g., child, parent, family), and intervention outcomes (e.g., individual, family systems). For a more complete and in-depth review of the extensive literature that has developed on this topic, the reader is referred to several excellent sources (Azar & Wolfe, 1998; English, 1998; Kaplan, Pelcovitz, & Labruna, 1999; Wolfe, 1999).

It is important to remind the reader that what constitutes child physical abuse is still debated to this day, especially given the broad array of behaviors subsumed by this category. Furthermore, the abusive acts described in the reports and studies to be summarized in this chapter differ considerably in several parameters, not the least of which are their topography, frequency, severity, and temporal stability. In light of the breadth of this topic and the many forms and definitions of abuse, this review incorporates recent research and programmatic descriptions based on both substantiated cases of physical abuse and the more general forms of child physical maltreatment. Cases involving child sexual abuse are reviewed when comparison studies are discussed. The topics to be covered are based on empirical studies of prevalence and incidence, risk factors, developmental effects, treatment outcome, and follow-up status. A summary of the implications of this research for practice and research, as well as topics for further exploration, is provided.

Body of Knowledge, Definitions, and Prevalence/Incidence

Definitions

The nature and specificity of the definition used to identify cases of physical abuse are among the more salient influences on recent estimates of prevalence and incidence rates. Unlike more traditional categories of health or mental health diagnoses, the determination of child abuse reflects a social judgment process that seeks to integrate several social-demographic details (e.g., risk factors, safety issues) with the child's physical/medical status (e.g., severity of injury) (see Emery & Laumann-Billings, 1998). Certainly, whether a given incident under consideration represents physical abuse or just simply an extreme form of parent-to-child discipline (e.g., beating vs. spanking/slapping) is not easy to determine; thus, there are blurred distinctions between abusive and subabusive or nonabusive behavior. Reporting rates also may fluctuate as a function of the interpretation of individual state definitions, as well as other case characteristics (e.g., prior history of agency involvement), caseworker characteristics (e.g., caseload, history of experience, training), and/or social service system factors (e.g., degree of supervision/monitoring, population size), among other variables. Thus, the task of determining when a specific parental behavior or set of behaviors represents child physical abuse and deserves to be reported is complex and multidetermined, yielding different rates of substantiation across states in the United States (see American Humane Association, 2000; for discussion of the child abuse reporting laws, see Chapter 22, this volume).

Different definitions have been used to examine the nature and extent of child physical abuse. The definition of child physical abuse used in the Third National Incidence Study of Child Abuse and Neglect (NIS-3) (Sedlak & Broadhurst, 1996) defined physical abuse as present when a child younger than 18 years of age has experienced an injury (harm standard) or risk of an injury (endangerment standard) as a result of having been hit with a hand or other object or having been kicked, shaken, thrown, burned, stabbed, or choked by a parent or parent-surrogate. In contrast, the definitions used in the National Child Abuse and Neglect Data System study understandably varied by state, but, interestingly, the item used to capture this information for physical abuse was described by the phrase "number of victims of physical acts that caused or could have caused physical injury" (U.S. Department of Health and Human Services, 2000, Appendix B, p. 8).

Prevalence/Incidence

Several methods have been used to document the prevalence of child physical abuse, such as compiling reports to child protective services (CPS) and national prevalence studies, with each method yielding unique information. The U.S. Department of Health and Human Services aggregates annual data from CPS in each state to determine the prevalence of different forms of child maltreatment. The most recent document (for 1998) indicates that reports of suspected abuse were made to CPS agencies on more than 2.8 million children (U.S. Department of Health and Human Services, 2000). Of those reported, 22.7% suffered physical abuse; for comparison purposes, 53.5% suffered neglect, 11.5% suffered sexual abuse, and 6.0% were emotionally maltreated. Rates of physical abuse did not vary significantly by age or sex. Nearly two thirds of all maltreatment fatalities were associated with physical abuse. One limitation of this database is that it includes only reported cases and may underestimate the actual number of children who have been abused.

The NIS-3 (Sedlak & Broadhurst, 1996) is a congressionally mandated study that followed two studies published in 1981 and 1988. NIS-3 included children investigated by CPS and those not reported to CPS but seen by community professionals. According to study results, 1,553,800 children in the United States were abused or neglected in 1993. The estimated number of physically abused children was 381,700. These data were based on a very stringent definition of abuse or neglect in that demonstrable harm must occur. When a less stringent criterion was included (i.e., children who were not yet harmed by maltreatment if a non-CPS sentinel considered them to be endangered or if maltreatment was substantiated or indicated by CPS), the estimated number of maltreated children was 2,815,600, and the number of children physically abused was 614,000. This study estimates that 42 children per 1,000 children in the population were harmed or endangered by abuse or neglect in 1993. Using just the harm standard for definition purposes, this study reported an incidence rate of 5.7 children per 1,000 (Sedlak & Broadhurst, 1996).

National prevalence studies based on violence surveys capture a sample of the general population and may detect abuse that was never reported to an official agency. Finkelhor and Dziuba-Leatherman (1994) conducted a study consisting of telephone interviews with a nationally representative sample of 2,000 youths, ages 10 to 16 years, and their caregivers. Twenty-two percent of youth reported experiencing a completed nonfamily assault, and 7.5% reported a family assault in their lifetime; 7.5% of youth reported experiencing violence to their genitals at some point in their lifetime. The Second National Family Violence Survey of 1985 (Gelles & Straus, 1987) also included telephone interviews with a national probability sample of 6,002 households who were administered the Conflicts Tactics Scales (CTS). Approximately 700,000 children were subjected to very severe violent behavior; 6.9 million children were assaulted by parents (i.e., kicking, biting, punching, choking, beating, and using weapons) at a rate of 110 incidents per 1,000 children during a 1-year period (Straus & Smith, 1990).

Altogether, child physical abuse affects hundreds of thousands of children annually, with physical trauma ranging from the mild (e.g., bruising) to the very severe (e.g., broken bones, skull fractures), including fatalities. However, the impact extends well beyond physical and emotional injury to the individual child and family and includes consequences for society in general. Such information is only now being examined and understood (see Chadwick, 1999).

It is necessary to note how varied are the data sources, definitions, and actual assessment items reported in these studies. Indeed, there have been updates in existing assessment or identification tools, such as the revised CTS (Parent-Child Conflict Tactics Scales; Straus, Hamby, Finkelhor, Moore, & Runyan, 1998), which may yield new information with which comparisons may be difficult. Such developments are necessary to enhance both the reliability and validity of reports documenting the prevalence of child physical abuse.

Etiology and Risk: Predisposing Characteristics

Conceptualization and Models of Child Physical Abuse

The articulation of models of child physical abuse provides a framework for understanding individual findings across studies, describing processes or factors associated with the development of abusive interactions, and identifying worthy intervention targets and programs (see National Academy of Sciences, 1993). Numerous theories that explain the origins and maintenance of the physical abuse of children have been described (e.g., Ammerman, 1990b; Azar & Siegel, 1990; MacKinnon, Lamb, Belsky, & Baum, 1990). Such theories differ on important model parameters that are often only minimally articulated (e.g., definitions, assumptions of origins of abuse, complexity and level of analysis, individual vs. contextual emphasis, child vs. family focus).

Most contemporary models of child physical abuse emphasize the interplay among individual (e.g., psychological state), family-interactional (e.g., use of hostile and aggressive behaviors), and social-system variables (e.g., availability of resources and presence of stress). For example, one model emphasizing both parental cognition and its relationship to other family characteristics is the stress and coping model outlined by Hillson and Kupier (1994). This model posits that parental appraisals that interpret a stressor as a threat yield secondary appraisals that elicit internal sources, which, in turn, stimulate coping dispositions that are influenced by the availability of external supports. The use of alternative parental coping responses described in the model may yield contrasting outcomes, such as facilitative caregiver behavior (e.g., active planning, seeking social support), child neglect (e.g., behavioral or mental disengagement), or child abuse (e.g., venting of emotion). Finally, the model indicates that these appraisals are influenced by child (e.g., child deviance), parent (e.g., parenting behavior), and ecological (e.g., unemployment) factors.

Most contemporary models of child physical abuse emphasize the interplay among individual, family-interactional, and social-system variables.

A related approach proposed by Milner (2000) has articulated a social information-processing model that consists of three cognitive stages and a cognitive-behavioral stage. The cognitive stages include perceptions of social behavior, interpretations and evaluations that give meaning to social behavior, and information integration and response selection activities. The cognitive-behavioral stage involves response implementation and monitoring processes. Cognitive activities at one or more of the first three stages are seen as mediating events at

the response implementation and monitoring stage, whereas stressful circumstances may lead to heightened problems in these areas among abusive parents.

A recent elaboration of a cognitive-behavioral model emphasizes the influence of parents' cognitive and behavioral repertoires on their children's abilities to negotiate developmental tasks (Azar & Gehl, 1999). This model identifies key parental skills or behaviors worthy of evaluation, such as developmentally sensitive expectations, adaptive attributions, adequate child-rearing and problem-solving skills, and constructive self-management (coping and social) skills. The model also considers how the child's personal competencies and clinical status, among other contextual obstacles to effective parenting, may influence parental behavior.

Wolfe's (1987, 1999) transitional model emphasizes the role of psychological processes in relation to other factors associated with child abuse, which are conceptualized in three stages. Each stage postulates a set of either destabilizing or compensatory factors that determine the negative or positive outcomes found in the parent-child relationship. Accordingly, these respective factors in Stage 1 (reduced tolerance for stress and disinhibition of aggression) include poor child-rearing preparation and stressful life events, as well as socioeconomic stability and social supports. In Stage 2 (poor management of acute crises and provocation), these respective factors include multiple sources of anger or aggression and the belief that the child's behavior is threatening or harmful, as well as improvements in the child's behavior and good coping resources. Finally, in Stage 3 (chronic patterns of anger and abuse), these respective factors include parental reinforcement for using strict control techniques and increased child problem behavior, as well as parental dissatisfaction with physical punishment and the availability of community resources. This model is one of the few to describe the development of abusive behavior within the family context in terms of the nature and course of interactions that influence the parent-child relationship over time.

Ecologically based or transactional models also incorporate dysfunctional caregiver-family-environment interactions in understanding the precipitants and correlates of child physical abuse (e.g., Belsky, 1993; Lynch & Cicchetti, 1998). Rather than positing the importance of a specific set of precursors to abuse, this model is concerned with identifying the various interactions among characteristics related to family functioning, such as children's coping efforts, parental caregiving and discipline, and other family system characteristics. Belsky's (1993) developmental-ecological model emphasizes the developmental (i.e., child and parent characteristics), immediate interactional (i.e., parenting, parent-child interactional processes), and broader contextual (i.e., community, cultural, and evolutionary) characteristics associated with child maltreatment. Thus, within this interactional perspective, child physical abuse seems to represent the interplay among child, parent, and family factors and is unlikely to be accounted for by some unique individual or family characteristic.

In one of the rare empirical evaluations of a conceptual model of parenting, Greenwald, Bank, Reid, and Knutson (1997) tested a discipline-mediated model with a sample of adolescents and their parents. It was hypothesized that harsh discipline would result from inadequate discipline tactics and skills. The findings revealed that parental discipline did mediate the relationship between stress and punitive parental practices. Parental irritability was not found to be a significant predictor, but child coercion contributed to parental discipline but not to punitive parenting practices. The relationship between stress and punitive parenting was completely mediated by parental discipline. In addition to evaluating ineffective parenting behaviors, the authors encourage careful assessment of the parent's perceptions of and affective reactions to parent-child interactions in understanding abusive interactions.

Support for the role of variables in different domains in the origins of abusive behavior has been found in other empirical studies. Christman, Wodarski, and Smokowski (1996) examined the empirical evidence found for seven abuse risk factors. Consistent evidence was found for a parental history of abuse, depression, single parenthood, low socioeconomic status, isolation, low maternal age, and substance abuse.

In general, the literature reviewed in this section suggests that physically abusive behavior represents an exaggerated aggressive or hostile response that occurs within a continuum of parenting practices and that abusive behavior must be interpreted in its family-social context. To enhance the clinical merit and empirical testing of these models,

both the processes responsible for coercive interpersonal interactions and the specific interrelationships proposed among the various processes by each model would be important to articulate. The next section examines variables believed to serve as risks for or contributors to abusive behavior based on studies comparing abusive and nonabusive individuals on various characteristics (see Black, Heyman, & Smith-Slep, 2001). One caveat worth mentioning is that a group difference on such characteristics does not necessarily convey that these variables indeed increased the child's risk for abuse. Nonetheless, information aggregated across studies may promote models examining the emergence of abuse, model evaluation, and the design of intervention strategies based on these models. To this end, some of the more salient factors are discussed next.

Child Characteristics

Age. Some data suggest that the severity of children's injuries is associated with being of younger age (Lung & Daro, 1996). Indeed, child fatalities are much more common among very young children (U.S. Department of Health and Human Services, 2000; for a discussion of fatal child abuse, see Chapters 13 and 15, this volume).

Health/medical status. There is little new information regarding the contribution of children's early health and medical problems to their heightened risk for being physically abused. Although early studies suggested certain medical, intellectual, or developmental aberrations (e.g., birth complications, physical disability, low IQ) (Belsky & Vondra, 1989), these characteristics have not significantly increased a child's risk above and beyond parent characteristics (Ammerman, 1990a, 1990b, 1991). Nonetheless, disabilities in one study were found to be twice as prevalent among a maltreated than nonmaltreated hospital sample and were especially related to a history of physical abuse (Sullivan & Knutson, 1998). Of course, whether this correlational finding reflects on disabilities as a precursor or consequence of abuse cannot be determined.

Temperament/behavior. A child's difficult temperament or behavioral deviance is also recognized as a potential risk factor for child physical abuse (Belsky & Vondra, 1989), in part, based on early empirical studies of their contribution to abusive incidents (Herrenkohl, Herrenkohl, & Egolf, 1983; Youngblade & Belsky, 1990). One recent study found that children with oppositional defiant disorder had much higher rates of early child maltreatment than those with other externalizing or internalizing disorders (Ford et al., 1999). Still, there is minimal evidence to support this characteristic as a significant risk factor (Ammerman, 1991; Pianta, Egeland, & Erickson, 1989).

Certainly there are cases in which serious medical problems place considerable personal and financial burdens on the parent(s) and family, especially by reducing parent-child attachments and altering family routines. Likewise, behavioral deviance may disrupt parenting practices and effective parent-child interactions (Webster-Stratton, 1990), so such child characteristics, along with a prosocial behavioral repertoire, warrant further examination in risk factor and assessment studies. What is less clear is how children's early developmental problems affect parental effectiveness, parent-child attachment, and family relationships. Potentially, such children may impose excessive child-rearing responsibilities on parents, which may increase parental expectations and irritability, inconsistent care, or punitive discipline.

Parent Characteristics

Reviews of perpetrator characteristics have examined this literature carefully (see Black et al., 2001). Certain characteristics are discussed here because of their importance to the maintenance and treatment of abusive interaction patterns. Many of these parent characteristics reflect heightened levels of distress, psychological dysfunction (e.g., depression, physical symptoms), or inappropriate parenting strategies. Some evidence highlights the potential role of specific psychiatric disorders.

Childhood history of abuse. The early experience of harsh punishment or abusive experiences and even repeated spanking during childhood is regarded as a potential vehicle for the transmission of abusive behavior (Straus, 1994; Straus, Gelles, & Steinmetz, 1980). Early physical punishment has been related to the use of physical violence with children (Gelles & Straus, 1987; Pianta et al.,

1989; Simons, Whitbeck, Conger, & Chyi-In, 1991; Whipple & Webster-Stratton, 1991). Recent studies show that a history of abuse by one's own mother differentiates abusive from nonabusive mothers (Coohey & Braun, 1997), and that violence experienced during childhood is a significant contributor to heightened child physical abuse risk (Merrill, Hervig, & Milner, 1996). Adults who experience or witness abuse during childhood are exposed to aversive models and may learn to use aggressive methods of disciplining children (Dolz, Cerezo, & Milner, 1997); indeed, the overall relative exposure to spanking may increase a child's risk for abuse (Whipple & Richey, 1997).

These findings notwithstanding, the percentage of abused children who appear to become abusive parents is estimated to be about 30% (Kaufman & Zigler, 1987). Indeed, most abused children do not become abusive parents (Widom, 1989). Nor does early abuse always distinguish abusers from comparison parents (e.g., Salzinger, Feldman, Hammer, & Rosario, 1991) or high- from low-risk parents (Cadzow, Armstrong, & Fraser, 1999). Early physical punishment may increase the risk of later maltreatment (Straus & Smith, 1990) or becoming the target (vs. source) of aggression (Cappell & Heiner, 1990).

The likelihood of child physical abuse may be associated with other psychological or contextual factors associated with general aggressivity, such as gender, maternal depression, high IQ, poverty, poor parenting practices, social support/competence, and stress, among other factors (Cappell & Heiner, 1990; Mash & Johnston, 1990; Simons et al., 1991; Webster-Stratton, 1985, 1990; Whipple & Webster-Stratton, 1991; Widom, 1989).

Other background/demographic characteristics. As reviewed by Milner (1998), some evidence suggests that the likelihood of child physical abuse is higher among parents who are younger, single, and nonbiological. Lower educational level has been found to distinguish parents classified as being at high (vs. low) risk for physical abuse (Cadzow et al., 1999).

Cognitive style. Early and recent evidence provides some support for the presence of various cognitive problems associated with child physical abuse. For example, abusive parents have been reported to perceive their children in a more negative light than nonabusive parents (Azar & Siegel, 1990), which may reflect limited acceptance of their children (see Mash & Johnston, 1990). Abusive parents have reported higher levels of behavioral dysfunction among their children than those of comparison parents, even though home observations failed to reveal group differences (Whipple & Webster-Stratton, 1991). Abusive parents have attributed responsibility for failure to their children but responsibility for success to themselves (Bugental, Mantyla, & Lewis, 1989).

Controlling for IQ, high-risk mothers gave evidence for neuropsychological problems in terms of limited conceptual ability, cognitive flexibility, and problem-solving skill (Nayak & Milner, 1998). Interestingly, when IQ, depression, and anxiety were controlled, no such differences were found. Other problems among high-risk mothers include perceiving children's conventional and personal transgressions as more wrong, expecting less compliance from one's children, and appraising one's own disciplinary responses as less appropriate (Caselles & Milner, 2000). When faced with a noncompliant child, high-risk mothers perceived this situation as more threatening and uncontrollable, rated the child's behaviors as more stressful, and reported more stable, global, and intentional attributions (Dopke & Milner, 2000).

The use of harsh parenting may also relate to parental beliefs in the appropriateness of strict physical discipline and having high expectations of children's behavior (Simons et al., 1991). Relative to comparison parents, abusive parents have been more accepting of physical punishment and have displayed high and potentially unrealistic expectations of their children's behavior (Azar, Robinson, Hekimian, & Twentyman, 1984).

Possible reasons for excessive parental negativity toward children's misbehavior include parental distortions regarding the children's responsibility for certain actions, parental unhappiness and psychiatric disturbances, and reduced tolerance for child problems, but the impact of these conditions among abusive parents awaits further inquiry (Azar, 1997). Certainly, emerging evidence supports a negative cognitive-attributional style, or an attributional bias, that may dispose abusive parents to viewing children in a negative light, making it important to better understand parents' attributions and perceptions (Bugental & Cortez, 1988).

Behavioral functioning. Abusive parents have been noted to exhibit inconsistent child-rearing practices (Susman, Trickett, Ianotti, Hollenbeck, & Zahn-Walker, 1985) that often reflect the presence of critical, hostile, or aggressive management styles (Trickett & Kuczynski, 1986; Whipple & Webster-Stratton, 1991). Some abusive parents exhibit limited attention, positive affect or experiences, and social behavior (Kavanagh, Youngblade, Reid, & Fagot, 1988; Salzinger, Samit, Krieger, Kaplan, & Kaplan, 1986; Schindler & Arkowitz, 1986); poor problem-solving strategies (Azar et al., 1984; Hansen, Pallotta, Tishelman, Conaway, & MacMillan, 1988); and less attention-directing verbal and physical strategies (Alessandri, 1992), with the Alessandri (1992) study showing less mutual interaction in both free-play and problem-solving situations. In some cases, abusive parents have actually responded aversively to child prosocial behavior (Reid, Kavenaugh, & Baldwin, 1987). A strength of many of these studies is their inclusion of structured behavioral observations.

In extensions of this initial work, high-risk mothers likewise have used more power assertion techniques (physical and verbal force) in response to simulated child interactions (Caselles & Milner, 2000). In a related observational study of mother-child interactions, high-risk mothers made fewer neutral approaches to their children, made more indiscriminate responses to their children's prosocial behavior, and displayed more negative behaviors toward their children, although no differences were found in the number of positive responses they made (Dolz et al., 1997). Only the first two differences remained when controlling for educational differences.

Coping skills. Deficits in parental coping skills have been identified in diverse areas (e.g., child management, anger control, financial), making it important to incorporate multidimensional measures to evaluate these broad domains of parental functioning. Based on independent ratings, abusive mothers have shown patterns of coping characterized by greater use of emotion-focused coping (e.g., emotional reactance) and less use of effective problem-solving strategies (e.g., avoidance) than mothers of conduct problem children (Cantos, Neale, &

O'Leary, 1997). Abusive mothers also rated their coping efforts as less effective. Similarly, high-risk parents reported higher levels of negative affect following exposure to a noncompliant child (Dopke & Milner, 2000).

Personality and psychiatric disturbances. Specific characteristics of parental personality may increase the likelihood of parental aggressivity. Hostile personality has been found to be significantly related to the use of harsh parenting (Simons et al., 1991), whereas parental explosiveness, as well as irritability and the use of threats, has been associated with child aggressivity or explosiveness (Caspi & Elder, 1988; Patterson, DeBaryshe, & Ramsey, 1989). Although these characteristics may increase the probability of harsh parenting and child aggressivity, further studies are needed to determine whether hostile or explosive personality is a precursor to or consequence of harsh parenting.

Psychiatric disturbances such as depression (Whipple & Webster-Stratton, 1991) and substance abuse (Kelleher, Chaffin, Hollenberg, & Fischer, 1994; Murphy et al., 1991; Whipple & Webster-Stratton, 1991) have been associated with child physical abuse, although some evidence shows no differences in depression or self-worth between mothers with versus without a history of child physical abuse (Kinard, 1996). Depression and substance abuse may render parents less able or willing to maintain a high level of involvement with a child and more likely to exhibit irritability or anger in response to child misbehavior. Substance abuse may increase the risk of court noncompliance and, along with alcohol abuse in particular, may increase a child's removal from the home (Famularo, Fenton, & Kinscherff, 1992; Murphy et al., 1991). Likewise, maternal drug use has been associated with child maltreatment and child removal (Kelley, 1992). The two disorders have also been found to increase a child's risk for physical abuse (Chaffin, Kelleher, & Hollenberg, 1996). Evidence based on structured interviews has shown that current mood disorder, alcohol abuse, and personality disorder were more common in maltreating than control parents (Famularo et al., 1992). Interestingly, the onset of maltreatment was found to be earlier for children whose mothers did versus did not meet criteria for posttraumatic stress disorder (PTSD) (Famularo, Fenton, Kinscherff,

Ayoub, & Barnum, 1994). Psychiatric disorders are infrequently evaluated in this literature, however, so it is difficult to determine the representativeness of these selected findings and the significance of certain disorders (e.g., PTSD), relative to other forms of distress. For in-depth discussion of substance abuse and child maltreatment, see Chapter 5 (this volume).

Depression and substance abuse may render parents less able or willing to maintain a high level of involvement with a child and more likely to exhibit irritability or anger in response to child misbehavior.

Biological factors. Few biological variables have been examined in relation to child physical abuse, but one characteristic, hyperarousal to stressful child-related stimuli, has been documented among physical child abusers, especially on skin conductance measures (e.g., Friedrich, Taylor, & Clarke, 1985; Wolfe, Fairbanks, Kelly, & Bradlyn, 1983). Greater autonomic activity has also been found in response to non-child-related stimuli perceived as stressful (Casanova, Domanic, McCanne, & Milner, 1991), which may contribute to parents' impulsive behavior and problem-solving difficulties (see McCanne & Milner, 1991). Because there is little new evidence on this topic, additional studies are needed to more fully document the impact of biological responding on child-directed aggressivity and whether parental reactivity is associated with cognitive or behavioral response patterns related to abusive behavior.

Family System Characteristics

Coercive parent-child interactions. Family influences on abusive behavior reflect a broad range of functional and structural characteristics. For example, observational studies have shown that abusive parents and their victimized children exhibit aggressive or coercive behavior toward one another (see Azar, Barnes, & Twentyman, 1988; Fantuzzo, 1990). Parents' aversive behaviors are often negatively reinforced during coercive interchanges because they terminate children's deviant behavior. Other factors contributing to coercive interactions include the use of ineffective child management techniques, such as the limited use of positive affect and general discussion (Bousha & Twentyman, 1984; Kavanagh et al., 1988; Oldershaw, Walters, & Hall, 1986). Indeed, limited positive interactions actually may be more characteristic of abusive families than excessive negativity (Caliso & Milner, 1992).

Overall, social-interactional studies identify patterns characterized by excessive family coercion and limited positive exchanges, with some evidence for aversive child behaviors (Azar, 1989; Conaway & Hansen, 1989). These findings stress the potential significance of aversive confrontations with family members as antecedents to child physical abuse. It should be pointed out that gender effects sometimes qualify these overall patterns. For example, Whipple and Webster-Stratton (1991) found that increased harsh physical punishment was observed for fathers but not mothers in abusive families, but only mothers were more verbally critical.

Poor family relationships. Physically punitive family environments may support psychologically abusive or coercive communications that contribute to the level of psychopathology shown by child victims (Claussen & Crittenden, 1991). This family context of hostility may interact with other child and parent variables that maintain abusive behavior (Wolfe, 1987), such as heightened conflict and decreased cohesion (Azar et al., 1988) or partner abuse (Fantuzzo et al., 1991; Salzinger et al., 1991). Physical abuse potential has also been related to characteristics of the family environment, such as limited family cohesion, expressiveness, marital satisfaction, and heightened family conflict (Mollerstrom, Patchner, & Milner, 1992). Some recent evidence also shows that physically abusive fathers received fewer emotional and instrumental supports from friends, in-laws, and other family members than comparison fathers and were only minimally connected to members of their social networks (Coohey, 2000), although no such difference was found when evaluating the social support of abusive mothers (Kinard, 1996). Although hostile, conflictual, or distant relationships may contribute to abusive behavior, more empirical evidence examining these relationships is needed.

A rare home-observational study by Howes, Cicchetti, Toth, and Rogosch (2000) comparing different maltreatment subgroups (child sexual abuse, child physical abuse, neglect) with low-income comparison families examined family interaction patterns in an effort to understand their unique affective, organizational, and relationship characteristics. The findings revealed no group differences between the child physical abuse group and the other groups on several measures of family climate and structure (e.g., anger regulation, positive affect, chaos, organization, reaching common goals, adaptive relational style). In fact, the sexual abuse group appeared to show dysfunction on several of these measures relative to the other groups, which was not due to family size or overlap with other forms of family violence. Studies of this nature provide novel information regarding the structure and functioning of the family systems of abusive families.

Other family context/social-system variables. Diverse stress-eliciting factors or family socioeconomic disadvantage (e.g., limited income, unemployment, family size, youthful parenthood, single parenthood) contribute to the expression of violent behavior (Belsky & Vondra, 1989). Poverty alone has emerged as a significant predictor of abuse status (Whipple & Webster-Stratton, 1991). Relatedly, indices of financial deprivation, especially male unemployment rate, have been found to be associated with physical abuse more so than for neglect or sexual abuse (Gillham et al., 1998).

Abusive families have experienced numerous child and parent stressors (Holden, Willis, & Foltz, 1989) and social disadvantage (Pianta et al., 1989). The experience of serious parental stressors in some families (e.g., low parental social support, marital discord) may further restrict parents' abilities to support their children's efforts to cope with adversity (see Erickson, Egeland, & Pianta, 1989; Pianta et al., 1989; Webster-Stratton, 1985; Whipple & Webster-Stratton, 1991). Exposure to domestic violence has also emerged as a parental correlate of child physical abuse (Appel & Holden, 1998), more so in some studies than the level of general stress (Coohey & Braun, 1997). Exposure to domestic violence is also a significant correlate of high-risk status (Cadzow et al., 1999). Overall, the experience of few positive family and extrafamilial relationships and heightened conflicts with others is believed to compromise parents' overall effectiveness. For detailed discussion of the relationship between domestic violence and child abuse, see Chapter 6 (this volume).

Summary. Although many of the aforementioned characteristics have been noted in abusive parents, whether they are necessary antecedents or correlates of abuse individually cannot be clearly determined. This is perhaps one of the reasons why it is difficult to identify abusers using individual self-report measures (see Milner, 1998). In addition, recent studies have examined parents classified as being at high risk for abuse rather than parents who have actually engaged in and been reported for recent abusive behavior, which may not reflect comparable groups. At present, the psychological characteristics of abusive parents do not conform consistently to any specific traits or diagnostic profile beyond concerns related to their parenting role and stressful family circumstances (Wolfe, 1999). Abusive adults tend to experience symptoms of affective, somatic, and behavioral distress believed to impair their parenting functions, which may contribute to unrealistic expectations of their children's conduct and capabilities.

The broad characteristics attributed to abusive families underscore the multidimensional nature of aggressive interactions and strongly argue against unitary conceptualizations of etiology (see Black et al., 2001). Greater consideration of the bases of parenting and parent-child relationships, as well as the environmental conditions that precipitate extreme responses along a continuum of parenting experiences, will further our understanding of abusive behavior. In addition, the field needs longitudinal studies that examine risk factors for the emergence of child physical abuse, as was reported in a follow-up study of 644 families over a 17-year period (Brown, Cohen, Johnson, & Salzinger, 1998). The findings indicated that three factors uniquely place a child at risk for physical abuse (low maternal involvement, early separation from mother, perinatal problems). Two other variables, maternal sociopathology and young maternal age, were associated with risk for physical abuse, sexual abuse, and neglect. Such findings underscore the complex etiology of physical abuse and the importance of longitudinal studies that evaluate predictors in multiple domains.

Sequelae and Consequences of Child Physical Abuse

Medical/Health and Psychobiological Problems

Physically abused children experience injuries and pain of varying severity and intensity (see Chapter 13, this volume). In many instances, information is missing as to the nature of these injuries and their implications for children's everyday functioning and health. Although few controlled studies have been reported, medical problems in victims of child physical abuse have included greater neonatal problems and failure to thrive (Famularo et al., 1992) and more early developmental delays, neurological soft signs, serious physical injuries, skin markings, and scars (Kolko, Moser, & Weldy, 1990). The latter study also found that sexual abuse, but not physical abuse, was related to heightened sexuality and physical signs of genital manipulation.

Neurobiological consequences of abuse have been reported in recent years (Perry, 1997), implicating compromised brain and central nervous system development. Among the few studies reported in this domain, impairments have been found in neurological functioning (Lewis, Lovely, Yeager, & Femina, 1989) and in physiological functioning, as reflected by decreased serotonin and increased dopamine and testosterone (Lewis, 1992). A mixed sample of physically and sexually abused children with PTSD has also been found to exhibit greater concentrations of urinary dopamine and norepinephrine than either anxious or control cases, as well as greater concentrations of urinary free cortisol than controls (DeBellis, Baum, Birmaher, Keshavan, Eccard, Boring, Jenkins, & Ryan, 1999). Relative to nonabused peers, physically and sexually abused children and adolescent psychiatric patients had an increased probability of left-sided frontotemporal abnormalities and a higher prevalence of left (vs. right) hemisphere deficits on neuropsychological tests, among other brain abnormalities (Teicher et al., 1997). Similar findings in terms of smaller intracranial and cerebral volumes among maltreated PTSD children and adolescents (vs. controls) have been reported (DeBellis, Baum, et al., 1999).

It is important to note that the recent NIS-3 study found that 20% to 35% of maltreated children (nearly 50,000 children) had suffered from a serious injury defined as "long-term impairment of physical, mental, or emotional capacities or requiring professional treatment aimed at preventing such long-term impairment" (Sedlak & Broadhurst, 1996, p. 13). Examples of such injuries included loss of consciousness, broken bones, and third-degree burns, among other problems. Large numbers of children become severely disabled due to child physical abuse.

Intellectual/Academic Problems

Exposure to severe child physical abuse may produce cognitive or intellectual deficits or other related problems in academic achievement. Certain early studies showed reduced task initiation and motivation (Aber & Allen, 1987; Allen & Tarnowski, 1989) and limited intellectual functioning among maltreated youngsters (Alessandri, 1991; Erickson et al., 1989) and schoolchildren (Salzinger, Kaplan, Pelcovitz, Samit, & Krieger, 1984), whereas other studies have failed to find differences in these areas (Augoustinos, 1987; Azar et al., 1988; Fantuzzo, 1990; Slade, Steward, Morrison, & Abramowitz, 1984). Language deficits also have been found in both receptive and expressive areas, including more limited syntactic expression, functional communication, and self-related language (Coster, Gersten, Beeghly, & Cicchetti, 1989; McFayden & Kitson, 1996).

Problems with academic performance include low scores on both mathematics and reading tests and both school discipline referrals and suspensions (Eckenrode, Laird, & Doris, 1993). Overall, maltreated children were 2.5 times more likely to repeat a grade. These effects were not attributable to socioeconomic status (SES), gender, or age. As suggested by the authors, the academic careers of maltreated children may be marked by considerable discontinuity due to frequent moves, school transfers, and tardiness. In contrast, no relation between child physical abuse and school grades or receptive language was found in a large community study (Flisher et al., 1997).

The varied outcomes in this area may be attributable to several background factors, such as the failure to distinguish among types (severity) of maltreatment or to use objective measures (Augoustinos, 1987). Cognitive functioning may be closely related to the quality of the caretaking environment, as shown in one study that found that young victims of physical abuse had more receptive language problems than nonabused children but did not differ from children residing in low SES families (Vondra, Barnett, & Cicchetti, 1990). Given that the degree of enrichment in the home environment influences a child's cognitive abilities (Aber, Allen, Carlson, & Cicchetti, 1989), the impact of family environmental variables may be considerable. The impact of physical injuries on children's cognitive abilities and their level of academic achievement merits further evaluation.

Cognitive/Perceptual and Attributional Problems

Certain perceptions or attributions related to an experience of physical violence have been reported among children with a history of child physical abuse. Relative to controls, abused children have reported a greater willingness to use physical punishment (Carlson, 1986, 1991), were more likely to assimilate aggressive stimuli (Rieder & Cicchetti, 1989), and have been found to more often attribute hostile intent to their peers' behavior (Dodge & Pettit, 1990).

A more recent study found that abuse-specific attributions and general attributional style were predictive of the level of psychopathology experienced by child physical abuse victims, beyond the variance accounted for by the severity of the parent-to-child violence experienced by the child (Brown & Kolko, 1999). In particular, the findings showed that self-oriented (e.g., self-blame) attributions were associated with internalizing symptoms; other-oriented attributions (e.g., perceiving the world as dangerous) showed a trend toward an association with externalizing symptoms. Such findings suggest that specific attributions may be related to specific types of symptoms.

More generally, abused children have given evidence of having deficiencies in various social-cognitive skills. These limitations include exhibiting greater problems with perspective taking (e.g., Howes & Espinosa, 1985), generating fewer alternative solutions to hypothetical social problems and perseverating on negative solutions (Dodge & Pettit, 1990; Haskett, 1990), and showing difficulties in understanding appropriate affective responses to interpersonal situations (Rogosch, Cicchetti, & Abre, 1995). At the same time, young children with a history of physical harm have been characterized by heightened attributions of hostile intent (Dodge & Pettit, 1990).

Maltreated children also have shown limited self-esteem on self-report (Allen & Tarnowski, 1989; Kinard, 1982; Oates, Forrest, & Peacock, 1985) and parent-report measures (Kaufman & Cicchetti, 1989) relative to controls, with some exceptions (Stovall & Craig, 1990). Although these findings suggest that victims of child physical abuse view themselves more negatively than their nonabused peers, it is not clear whether these differences reflect problems with self-esteem following physical abuse or the presence of broad aspects of personal and family dysfunction. Also, the long-term impact of lowered self-esteem among victims of physical abuse merits investigation.

Although these few studies provide some understanding of the cognitive deficits or distortions evinced by abused children, there is a need to more carefully examine the cognitive repertoires of physically victimized children. Potential cognitive problems include their belief in the appropriateness of violent behavior as a coping skill and their difficulties identifying nonaggressive solutions to interpersonal problems. It would be instructive to learn, for example, whether victims of child physical abuse show negative attributional biases comparable to those of aggressive children (Dodge & Pettit, 1990) or the types of cognitive distortions commonly seen in depressed children (Kendall, Stark, & Adam, 1990). If so, then specific methods designed to enhance children's use of prosocial, verbal mediation skills would be likely to affect these cognitive processes.

Aggression/Behavioral Dysfunction

One of the most extensively documented clinical consequences in child physical abuse victims is heightened aggression and related externalizing behaviors (see National Academy of Sciences, 1993), including poor anger modulation (Beeghly & Cicchetti, 1994; Shields, Cicchetti, & Ryan, 1994). Group differences have been reflected on adult ratings (Cummings, Hennessy, Rabideau, & Cicchetti, 1994; Dodge, Pettit, & Bates, 1997; Feldman et al., 1995; Hotaling, Straus, & Lincoln, 1990; Manly, Cicchetti, & Barnett, 1994; Okun, Parker, & Levendosky, 1994), self-ratings (Pelcovitz, Kaplan,

Goldenberg, & Mandel, 1994; Wolfe, Werkele, Reitzel-Jaffe, & Lefebvre, 1998), and observations in both the home (Bousha & Twentyman, 1984) and play or social settings (Alessandri, 1991; Howes & Espinosa, 1985; Kaufman & Cicchetti, 1989; Klimes-Dougan & Kistner, 1990; Rieder & Cicchetti, 1989). Many of these studies are notable due to the use of objective measures and comparison groups. As suggested by Dodge and colleagues (1997), the experience of child physical abuse provides instruction in the use of aggressive behavior and conveys its appropriateness as a problem-solving skill.

One of the most extensively documented clinical consequences in child physical abuse victims is heightened aggression and related externalizing behaviors, including poor anger modulation.

Other externalizing behavior problems have been documented, such as increased rule violations, oppositionalism, and delinquency (Trickett & Kuczynski, 1986; Walker, Downey, & Bergman, 1989); property offenses and criminal arrests (Gelles & Straus, 1990; Hotaling et al., 1990); and drinking, drug use, and cigarette smoking (Gelles & Straus, 1990; Hotaling et al., 1990; Kaplan, Pelcovitz, Salzinger, Mandel, & Weiner, 1998), highlighting involvement in serious antisocial acts (Lewis et al., 1989).

The level of externalizing dysfunction may be related to the experience of witnessing family violence and other adverse family environment factors, such as negative life events (Wolfe, 1999). Both heightened family conflict that includes verbal and physical aggression (vs. verbal only) and shelter residence (vs. home) have been found to be significantly related to the clinical severity of children's conduct and emotional problems and diminished social functioning (Fantuzzo et al., 1991).

Internalizing Problems

Consistent with reports describing the primary role of changes in affective regulation following trauma (Shields & Cicchetti, 1998), studies have documented the presence of negative affect in younger (Schneider-Rosen & Cicchetti, 1984) and older abused children (Kinard, 1980, 1982). Standardized measures have yielded higher levels of depression and hopelessness among abused versus nonabused psychiatric patients (Allen & Tarnowski, 1989; Kazdin, Moser, Colbus, & Bell, 1985), but no such differences were found on items reflecting affective symptoms (Kazdin et al., 1985) or parent reports (Kolko, Moser, & Weldy, 1988), perhaps because parents may be less aware of their children's internalizing symptoms. Higher levels of internalizing symptoms have been found among abused preschoolers (Fantuzzo, delGaudio, Atkins, Meyers, & Noone, 1998) and adolescents (Pelcovitz et al., 1994). The abused children's limited affective expressiveness has been attributed to underlying deficits in cognitive-perceptual (information-processing) skills as reflected in specialized assessment tasks (Barahal, Waterman, & Martin, 1981; Camras, Grow, & Ribordy, 1983).

There is some evidence for an association between child physical abuse and suicidality, such as increased involvement in suicidal behavior (Riggs, Alario, & McHorney, 1990), although no such association was found in a large community-based probability sample (Flisher et al., 1997) and a smaller comparison study (Kaplan, Pelcovitz, Salzinger, Mandel, & Weiner, 1997). The latter studies are noteworthy for their inclusion of standardized diagnostic interviews with children and adolescents used to evaluate multiple diagnoses and their use of analyses controlling for potential confounders (e.g., family background).

Psychiatric Disturbances and Posttraumatic Stress Disorder

In recent years, studies have examined the nature and extent of psychiatric disturbances in victims of child physical abuse. One of the primary clinical consequences associated with a history of trauma is PTSD, whose symptom picture and severity (e.g., recurrent memories, abuse-repetitive behaviors, attributional changes, trauma-specific fears) have been described for some time (Famularo, Kinscherff, & Fenton, 1990; Terr, 1991). In terms of the prevalence of PTSD in victims of child physical abuse, 36% of maltreated children and youth met criteria for PTSD (Famularo et al., 1994),

and 33% of a subset of those with PTSD were later found to retain the full diagnosis at 2-year follow-up (Famularo, Fenton, Augustyn, & Zuckerman, 1996).

In terms of controlled studies, one clinical study did not find higher proportions of abused and nonabused adolescents diagnosed with PTSD (Pelcovitz et al., 1994), whereas a study based on a large national telephone sample found that reports of parental physical violence were associated with heightened PTSD-related symptoms (Boney-McCoy & Finklehor, 1995). Interestingly, in the latter study, parental violence also was associated with a threefold increase in experiencing trouble with a teacher for girls, but no such association was found for boys. The study is noteworthy due to its effort to control for several background covariates.

One of the larger studies examining diagnostic correlates of child physical abuse was conducted using a community-based probability sample of children and adolescents (Flisher et al., 1997). A history of physical abuse was reported in 26% of the sample. Child physical abuse was associated with several diagnoses: major depression, conduct disorder, oppositional defiant disorder, agoraphobia, overanxious disorder, and generalized anxiety disorder. The findings were not due to the impact of several background covariates, such as family income, family psychiatric history, and perinatal problems.

Higher rates of depression and conduct disorder have been found in abused adolescents (Pelcovitz et al., 1994). A history of maltreatment also has been associated with borderline personality disorder (Famularo, Kinscherff, & Fenton, 1991), attention deficit hyperactivity disorder, and oppositional disorder (Famularo et al., 1992). This latter study is noteworthy for its finding that maltreated cases differed from controls in certain disorders depending on whether children (e.g., greater psychotic symptoms, personality/adjustment disorders) or parents (conduct/mood disorders) were interviewed. Physical abuse has been found to contribute to the prediction of current diagnoses of several disorders (unipolar depression, disruptive disorders, cigarette smoking), as well as other lifetime disorders and problems (e.g., conduct disorder, drug abuse), when added to other identified risk factors (Kaplan et al., 1998). Finally, traumatic victimization (e.g., assault, mugging, sexual molestation) has also been found to contribute to the prediction of oppositional defiant disorder but not attention deficit/ hyperactivity disorder in outpatient child psychiatry clinic referrals (Ford, et al., 1999).

Numerous psychiatric disorders and related forms of dysfunction have been found in victims of child physical abuse based on the use of standardized diagnostic interviews and multivariate analyses. Although the use of matched comparisons and controls for background variables is a more recent advance, the reasons for such diverse psychopathology in this population and whether such clinical problems precede or follow an abusive experience cannot be determined given the cross-sectional nature of most studies.

Social/Interpersonal Competence and Relationship Problems

Disturbances in the formation of stable attachments are of developmental import due to their association with childhood adjustment, such as the child's individuation, personal sense of competence, and ability to regulate affect (Cicchetti, Toth, & Maughan, 2000). Studies examining the quality of the parent-child relationship have shown insecure attachments as reflected by increased avoidance and resistance (Cicchetti & Barnett, 1991; Crittenden, 1992) and separation problems (Lynch & Cicchetti, 1991) among maltreated youngsters, with some longitudinal evidence showing that maltreatment is associated with having an insecure-disorganized/disoriented (Type D) attachment (Barnett, Ganiban, & Cicchetti, 1999). In terms of peer relations, abused children also have been found to exhibit less friendly or positive peer interactions (Howes & Espinosa, 1985; Kaufman & Cicchetti, 1989), engage in less parallel or group play (Alessandri, 1991), and initiate and receive fewer positive peer interactions. Abused children were less well liked by peers (Haskett & Kistner, 1991). Likewise, older child victims have been described as showing limited social competence (Feldman et al., 1989), having problems making friends (Gelles & Straus, 1990), and being socially withdrawn, and they have been rated as more disliked and unpopular than controls (Dodge, Pettit, & Bates, 1994).

In recent studies, peer and classroom teacher reports have acknowledged greater difficulties in the peer relationships of young maltreated children; in particular, they were characterized by lower social competence and greater peer rejection than nonmaltreated children (Rogosch et al., 1995). Similar problems in terms of less observed interactive peer play, self-control, and interpersonal skill in social situations, as well as lower peer sociometric ratings, have been identified using multiple measures in a sample of maltreated (vs. nonmaltreated) Head Start youngsters (Fantuzzo et al., 1998). Another multi-informant study with older children found that abused (vs. control) children were rated by peers as less cooperative, were rated by both parents and teachers as more disturbed, and described their social networks as more insular, atypical, and negative (Salzinger, Feldman, Hammer, & Rosario, 1993). A novel observational study of young adolescents examined the interactions of abused children with their best friends. Relative to the interactions involving nonabused children, the interactions involving abused children displayed less overall intimacy, were more conflictual, and were characterized by more negative affect (Parker & Herrera, 1996). In adolescents, a history of physical abuse has been associated with greater social competence deficits than controls (Pelcovitz et al., 1994) and heightened coercion in dating relationships (Wolfe et al., 1998). These studies are noteworthy for their use of matched comparison cases.

Long-Term Follow-Up Outcomes

Prospective longitudinal studies. The experience of child physical abuse may result in long-term physical and psychosocial adjustment problems (see Herrenkohl, 1990), which have been demonstrated in several long-term outcome studies. Problems of this nature are suggested in a 20-year follow-up of 19 abused children that described considerable variability in their overall adult adjustment, with certain problems noted in terms of financial, social, emotional, marital, and behavioral functioning (Martin & Elmer, 1992). This uncontrolled report provides interesting clinical information but precludes any definitive conclusions regarding the impact of abuse in childhood due to the absence of a nonabused comparison group.

Early controlled longitudinal studies of maltreated samples have documented various clinical concerns, including developmental and externalizing behavior problems, excessive anger, and observed compliance and negative emotions, but not social skills, in both younger and older abused children (Egeland & Sroufe, 1981; Erickson et al., 1989). Hostile parental behavior experienced in childhood also has been associated with reduced social and school competence and increased angry-rejecting behaviors in children at follow-up (Herrenkohl, Herrenkohl, Egolf, & Wu, 1991). This study found that a supportive parent figure, high intellectual functioning, and higher SES helped to compensate for an early adverse parenting experience. Subsequent evidence from this sample showed that victims of child physical abuse were at risk for engaging in violent and criminal behaviors in adolescence (Herrenkohl, Egolf, & Herrenkohl, 1997) and for sexual risk taking (Herrenkohl, Herrenkohl, Egolf, & Russo, 1998).

Widom (1989) found that children with a history of physical abuse were at 2 times greater risk for being arrested of a violent crime and were at higher risk for chronic involvement in criminal activities, relative to controls from the same neighborhood. When followed into adulthood, childhood victims of abuse or neglect from this sample were also more likely than controls to have a juvenile or adult arrest for any nontraffic offense and for a violent crime (Maxfield & Widom, 1996), and in adulthood, they were more likely to have lifetime symptoms of antisocial personality disorder (Luntz & Widom, 1994), engage in prostitution (Widom & Kuhns, 1996), have a lower IQ and reading ability (Perez & Widom, 1994), and show greater alcohol use in women but not men (Widom, Ireland, & Glynn, 1995). Other studies have shown that child physical abuse is a risk factor for aggression (Dodge et al., 1997) and delinquency (Smith & Thornberry, 1995; Zingraff, Leiter, Myers, & Johnsen, 1993).

A 17-year longitudinal study of community cases found that abused (vs. nonabused) cases demonstrated significant impairments in clinical functioning in adolescence and early adulthood, including more depressive and anxiety symptoms, emotional-behavioral problems, suicidal ideation, and suicidal attempts (Silverman, Reinherz, & Giaconia, 1996). Several gender differences in personal functioning also emerged. Related evidence for increased risk for repeated suicide attempts in adolescence and adult depressive disorder has been reported in another 17-year longitudinal study of abused and nonabused children (Brown et al., 1999).

Retrospective cross-sectional studies. A number of recent studies have examined health and clinical problems in adults who retrospectively reported histories of being abused as children. These studies document in the abused samples heightened health problems, including poor current health status (Lesserman et al., 1997), increased hospital admissions and surgical procedures in adulthood (Salmon & Calderbank, 1996), and chronic pain (Goldberg, Pachas, & Keith, 1999).

In terms of clinical problems, controlled studies of adults who report histories of child physical abuse have found higher levels of dissociative symptoms and amnesia for abuse memories (Chu, Frey, Ganzel, & Matthews, 1999), major depression and mania (Levitan et al., 1998), lifetime suicidality (Bryant & Range, 1997), the absence of contraception (Mason, Zimmerman, & Evans, 1998), and, among females, alcohol problems (Langeland & Hartgers, 1998).

Other studies have documented the relationship between adult reports of childhood abuse and their own use of physical violence as adults. In one study, the conflict tactics used by university student respondents were found to be highly related to the reported tactics of their parents and the experience of being maltreated by parents in their early years (Browne & Hamilton, 1998). Another study reported that parent-child violence experienced during childhood accounted for the most variance in explaining child abuse risk in male and female Navy recruit trainees (Merrill et al., 1996).

Summary

Additional empirical evidence has accumulated to suggest that child physical abuse has various short-term and several long-term adverse consequences in terms of heightened clinical and health problems. Although physical abuse may increase a child's risk for dysfunction, this relationship is not always a straightforward one. For example, several problems in the social information-processing skills of young children were found to mediate the relationship between their experience of early physical harm and subsequent aggression (Dodge & Pettit, 1990; Dodge et al., 1997). In more recent studies, the relationship between child physical abuse and adult self-concept was mediated by the negative effect on parent-child relationships (Lopez & Heffer, 1998), and the relationship between child physical abuse and current psychiatric illness was mediated by the presence of child sexual abuse (Mulder, Beautrais, Joyce, & Fergusson, 1998).

Other studies have reported moderators of the long-term impact of abuse, including maltreatment characteristics and individual, family, and environmental factors (Malinosky-Rummell & Hansen, 1993). Sexually abused women, especially those with a history of child physical abuse, had a higher risk of developing complex PTSD (Roth, Newman, Pelcovitz, van der Kolk, & Mandel, 1997). Furthermore, relationships to parental violence may vary depending on the specific parental figure being examined. Among women, lower self-esteem was related to father-to-daughter but not mother-to-daughter verbal aggression and violence (Downs & Miller, 1998). Research should continue to explore moderator and mediator relationships.

Intervention and Treatment

Treatment Considerations

Comprehensive clinical formulation. Numerous treatment prerequisites, approaches, and issues have been described to guide the practitioner, only some of which will be reviewed in this section (see Azar & Wolfe, 1998; Cohen, Berliner, & Mannarino, 2000; Wolfe, 1999). Given the varied types of maladjustment documented among abused children and their parents or families, an initial prerequisite involves the careful assessment of family strengths in addition to the family's various clinical problems. Suggested domains in a comprehensive clinical evaluation include the nature and extent of child and family dysfunction, the child's adjustment problems and family functioning, and potential resources or compensatory skills (Azar & Wolfe, 1998). The evaluation should facilitate identification of the types of therapeutic problems that need to be targeted at the child, parent, family, and social-system levels. The clinical targets commonly reported in prior clinical reports (e.g., deviant child behavior, heightened parental anger, or family conflict) are important to change because they may place the child at heightened risk for reabuse, interfere with successful social adjustment, or increase personal distress.

Recent work by Carlson (2000) has provided a conceptual framework for understanding the effects and persistence of traumatic experiences. These authors provide useful details of the factors that influence children's reactions to trauma, which may bear implications for the overall nature and selection of treatment strategies. Cohen and colleagues (2000) offer specific treatment recommendations for work with traumatized children that are worth examination.

Treatment Approaches, Targets, and Parameters

Although, as noted earlier, several models outline explanations of the origins and maintenance of abusive behavior, fewer descriptions of important therapeutic principles and procedures have been articulated for this population than is the case for child sexual abuse (Cohen, Cohen, & Brook, 1993). Azar and Wolfe (1998) review several significant treatment prerequisites, such as client motivation, the impact of reporting requirements, the child's role in treatment, and the role of therapist values.

To ensure selection of the appropriate treatment, we must consider other parameters of service delivery (e.g., goals and targets, content, format, setting, participants, providers). There is increasing recognition of the need to conduct parent-directed treatments to eliminate abusive behavior in conjunction with the evaluation, education or treatment, and follow-up of abused children to promote their social-psychological development (Graziano & Mills, 1992). Relatedly, there is more attention to ensuring that the goals of intervention both promote a prosocial repertoire and minimize the psychological sequelae of abusive behavior. Also important is the coordination of services and professional roles.

The treatment approaches themselves are heterogeneous, in accord with the need to serve a diverse client population. Several approaches emphasizing different clients, targets, content or methods, or modalities have been reported. For example, Wolfe (1999) provides a brief listing of common treatment approaches in the area of child physical abuse separated by client (e.g., parent/family vs. child centered) and then by target (e.g., child management, anger management). As shown in that review and others (e.g., Azar & Wolfe, 1998), few outcome studies in this area have been reported. Briefly reviewed in the following sections are selected examples of various intervention studies and both their outcomes and treatment implications.

Child-focused treatment outcome studies. Few studies have evaluated services directed toward children (Azar & Wolfe, 1998; Kolko, 1998a, 1998b; Stevenson, 1999). In some studies, child intervention has been reported as one component of a parent's or family's overall treatment (e.g., Brunk, Henggeler, & Whelan, 1987; Wolfe, Edwards, Manion, & Koverola, 1988). In one abuse-specific, cognitive-behavioral treatment program, children and parents have participated extensively, and progress has been evaluated (Kolko, 1996a, 1996c). This study is discussed later.

Day/residential treatment. One of the earlier approaches to child treatment reflects the use of day and residential treatment programs, primarily for maltreated preschoolers, which offers access to different developmentally appropriate and therapeutic activities (e.g., recreation, learning, play) and modalities (e.g., child play groups, family counseling) with trained staff who work closely with each group (Culp, Heide, & Richardson, 1987; Sankey, Elmer, Halechko, & Schulberg, 1985). These clinical reports noted improvements in several developmental skill areas. One program consisting of a therapeutic preschool and home visitation found improved intellectual functioning and receptive language at discharge 1 year later (Oates & Bross, 1995).

Day or residential treatment programs that combine skills training and experiential methods may be most useful in targeting the diverse social-psychological problems of the more seriously dysfunctional child victim and family.

A controlled study examined the efficacy of intensive, group-based treatment programming (mean duration = 8.9 months) aimed at encouraging supportive peer relationships and identification of personal feelings, along with play, speech, and physical therapy (Culp, Little, Letts, & Lawrence, 1991). The program incorporated other family services (e.g., family and individual therapy, support group counseling, parent education, crisis line). Relative to a control group, treated children saw themselves as having higher cognitive competence, peer acceptance, and maternal acceptance and received higher developmental quotients on standardized measures. Teacher ratings supported these improvements. Still, most children scored below the "normal" range in most areas. Unfortunately, the incorporation of multiple therapeutic components precludes evaluation of the specific contribution of the child's day treatment to these outcomes. Day or residential treatment programs that combine skills training and experiential methods may be most useful in targeting the diverse social-psychological problems of the more seriously dysfunctional child victim and family.

Peer social initiation. A second approach reflects the application of specific behavioral and social learning procedures directed toward improving the peer relations and social adjustment of young child victims by arranging play buddy sessions in which withdrawn maltreated children are exposed to social initiation techniques demonstrated by trained peer confederates (Fantuzzo, Stovall, Schachtel, Goins, & Hall, 1987). Systematic studies of these individual sessions have shown that this intervention (resilient peer treatment or RPT) is more effective than adult initiations in improving children's social adjustment and peer initiations (Davis & Fantuzzo, 1989; Fantuzzo, Jurecic, Stovall, Hightower, & Goins, 1988). In particular, RPT has been effective with withdrawn children but not with aggressive children, who actually exhibited higher levels of deviant behavior following intervention (Davis & Fantuzzo, 1989; Fantuzzo et al., 1987; Fantuzzo et al., 1988).

Maintenance effects 2 months following RPT also have been documented (Fantuzzo et al., 1996). This research identifies important differences between intervention procedures and documents short-term follow-up improvements. Further evidence is needed to document the long-term benefits of treatment and its impact on abuse recidivism.

Group therapy. Unlike other forms of maltreatment, it does not appear that controlled group therapy studies have been reported with child physical abuse victims (see Berliner & Saunders, 1996). One recent application described a multiple-module cognitive-behavioral group conducted over a

16-week period with six physically abused children, four of whom completed the group (Swenson & Kolko, 2000). The program emphasized content in three primary domains (trauma-specific work, anger management, social skills training). Outcome assessment based on child reports revealed improvements for some but not all group participants (anger reactions, posttraumatic symptoms), with parent reports indicating some increase in emotional and behavioral problems at posttreatment. Certainly, further evaluation of the feasibility and efficacy of this type of structured group program is warranted. Other group applications for this population are currently under investigation (Silovsky, Valle, & Chaffin, 1999). Certainly, there are potential advantages to group work, especially the ability to draw on shared group experiences and problems, although it is not always easy to find suitable group members at a given time. Other approaches have been applied, including attachment theory (Berlin, 1997) and functional assessment and treatment techniques (Luiselli, 1996).

Parent-Focused Treatment Outcome Studies

Behavioral parent training. Emphasizing the social-interactional model, one of the most common intervention strategies entails parent training in positive and nonviolent child management practices (Egan, 1983; Golub, Espinosa, Damon, & Card, 1987; Szykula & Fleischman, 1985). Parents receiving such training have been trained to monitor behavior, provide judicious reinforcement, apply time-out and response cost in lieu of physical punishment, and set up home-based behavioral programs, among other skills. These brief, early interventions have been demonstrated to improve skills acquisition (e.g., more prosocial interaction, conflict resolution), which, to some extent, has been maintained at follow-up.

Expanded parent training. An extension of the parent training approach examined the addition of individualized parent training in diverse management procedures and parent-child simulation training to standard, informational groups with at-risk families (Wolfe et al., 1988). The combined program was associated with improvements in both parent (e.g., child abuse potential, parental depression) and child (e.g., behavior prob-

lems) targets, but there was little improvement in family interaction. Other beneficial outcomes include reduced out-of-home placement for children from homes rated as low (but not high) in family difficulty (Szykula & Fleischman, 1985).

Cognitive-behavioral treatment for parents. Interventions for parents have broadened beyond the focus on child management by targeting parents' cognitive-behavioral repertoires to deal with a variety of clinical problems. Thus, treatment has been directed toward altering parental dysfunction related to distorted beliefs or attributions, limited problem-solving skills, and heightened anger reactivity, each of which may contribute to parental aggression (Azar & Wolfe, 1998; Kolko, 1998b). For example, programs have helped parents to become aware of their negative self-statements and to generate prosocial alternatives to these statements while providing realistic developmental information (e.g., Barth, Blythe, Schinke, Stevens, & Schilling, 1983). Training has also been directed toward using coping self-statements and relaxation (Egan, 1983) or learning anger management, communication, and problem-solving skills (Acton & During, 1992; Nuris, Lovell, & Edgar, 1988). The addition of cognitive restructuring and problem solving to other stress management methods has been associated with reduced child assault, anger arousal and higher empathy in parents, and fewer complaints concerning child behavior problems (Acton & During, 1992; Whiteman, Fanshel, & Grundy, 1987). The clinical merit of these programs notwithstanding, a few of these studies were uncontrolled reports, and none of the studies reported follow-up or abuse recidivism data.

Parent education and support. Another approach, parental education and support, has been used with at-risk parents and their young children (Whipple & Wilson, 1996). This program incorporated several procedures in a community-based center (e.g., respite, support groups, training in discipline and developmental expectations, parent and child sessions). Clinical improvements were noted in some outcomes (parental depression and stress) but not others (social support, child misbehavior). Controlled studies are needed to document the efficacy of this intervention approach with abusive families.

The short-term effects of a related program (Systematic Training for Effective Parenting, or STEP) were examined relative to a control group. STEP parents were found to show a significant increase in positive perceptions of their children and had less child abuse potential (Fennell & Fishel, 1998).

Family-Focused Treatment

Family casework. Among the various interventions directed toward families, some have emphasized the application of specific treatment procedures/content or protocols. One comparative treatment study administered a family casework condition consisting of the development and discussion of individualized family treatment plans and training in behavioral parenting techniques (Nicol et al., 1988). Relative to clinic play sessions in which behavioral contingencies were used with the child, family casework resulted in greater change in coercive, but not prosocial, behavior.

Abuse-focused family treatment. Kolko (1996a, 1996c) described an abuse-focused family treatment condition that consisted of specific procedures in three phases: engagement (e.g., assessment of the family's structural roles and interactions, reframing to enhance cooperation, discussion of negative effects of physical force, agreement to a no-violence contract), skill building (e.g., problem solving and communication skills training), and application/termination (e.g., establishing problem-solving family routines). A second condition consisted of parallel individual child and parent abuse-specific, cognitive-behavioral treatment (CBT). Sessions in these two conditions were conducted in both the clinic and the home. An initial report examining the treatment course of these two conditions based on weekly self-reports of high-risk indicators found lower levels of parental anger and physical discipline or force in CBT than family therapy (FT) families, although each group showed a reduction on these items from the early to late treatment sessions (Kolko, 1996a). Between 20% and 23% of all children and their parents independently reported high levels of physical discipline or force during the early and late phases of treatment and heightened parental anger and family problems.

In terms of treatment outcome data (Kolko, 1996c), CBT and FT were associated with improvements in child-to-parent violence and child externalizing behavior, parental distress and abuse risk, and family conflict and cohesion through a 1-year follow-up period, relative to those cases that received routine community service (RCS). At the same time, all three conditions reported numerous improvements across time (e.g., parental anger, parental practices, child fears). One parent participant each in CBT (5%) and FT (6%) and three in RCS (30%) had engaged in another incident of physical maltreatment, with similar percentages reported for child reabuse rates (10%, 12%, and 30%, respectively). No differences between CBT and FT were observed on consumer satisfaction or maltreatment risk ratings at termination. The findings of this evaluation provide additional, albeit qualified, support for the continued development of individual and family treatments involving child victims of physical abuse.

Parent-child interaction training. An additional treatment approach containing specific behavioral and systemic procedures, parent-child interaction training (PCIT) (Eisenstadt, Eyberg, McNeil, Newcomb, & Funderbunk, 1993), has been advocated for clinical application to the treatment of physical abuse (Urquiza & McNeil, 1996). As Urquiza and McNeil (1996) suggest, parent-child interactions in abusive families are often conflictual and problematic. Physically abused children show poor behavioral controls and heightened behavioral dysfunction. Social learning factors influence parental use of coercive discipline. PCIT addresses these issues by providing parents with opportunities to develop more positive relationships with their children and to learn appropriate parenting techniques through ongoing coaching efforts during observed interactions. Outcome evidence suggests the benefit of PCIT with behavior problem children. This approach is noteworthy for its attention to various stages in the treatment process, ranging from assessment and the training of behavioral play skills to the training of discipline skills and use of booster sessions.

Ecological, family-centered, and home-based intervention services. Other interventions have emphasized a more diverse set of procedures and methods applied in the home, on an individual, family, and intensive basis and directed toward multiple participants (see Corcoran, 2000). Such ecologically based and family-centered services generally have targeted contextual risk factors associated with abuse, specific skills deficits, or personal competencies. For example, some programs addressed problems such as excessive child care demands, financial and economic disadvantages, social isolation, marital discord, and substance abuse.

Early reports of in-home services that sought to promote family preservation and prevent placement used crisis-oriented, intensive, and brief services. By offering intensive counseling, casework, and concrete services to address multiple risk factors, programs such as Homebuilders are noteworthy for their individualized interventions, program intensity, flexible scheduling, small caseloads, goal orientation with time-limited services, and program evaluation efforts (Whittaker, Kinney, Tracy, & Booth, 1990). Indeed, this program has reported gains in family functioning (e.g., problem behaviors, communication skills), but the gains are difficult to interpret in the absence of comparison data (Amundson, 1989; Blythe, Jiordano, & Kelly, 1991), and other data fail to suggest the superiority of Homebuilders (vs. other services) in reducing child placements 6 to 12 months after termination of services (Nelson, 1990).

Other experimental evidence has demonstrated the superiority of intensive, family-based reunification services (vs. routine reunification services) in improving reunification rates after short-term treatment and 1-year follow-up (Fraser, Walton, Lewis, & Pecora, 1996; Walton, Fraser, Lewis, & Pecora, 1993). The provision of in vivo services and training in problem-solving and communication skills were identified as some of the contributors to service effectiveness.

Multicomponent clinical interventions targeting diverse individual, family, and systemic problems in the home and community have the potential to maximize client motivation and the durability of improvements across time (Ayoub, Willett, & Robinson, 1992; Brunk et al., 1987; Malinosky-Rummell et al., 1991; Willett, Ayoub, & Robinson, 1991). Brunk and colleagues (1987) compared behavioral group parent training in specific management principles with multisystemic family treatment in which various problems in child, parent, family, and social systems were targeted (e.g., peer training, child management, family communication). The multisystemic therapy (MST) approach is characterized by several principles (e.g., ecologically based, individualized, intensive). Whereas MST was more effective in improving parent-child relationships (parental efforts to control child, child compliance), parent

training was more effective in reducing identified social problems. The absence of follow-up data precludes any determination of the durability of these changes.

Related ecological programs, such as Project 12-Ways and Project SafeCare (see Lutzker, Bigelow, Doctor, Gershater, & Greene, 1998), have described numerous innovative services, often emphasizing the application of individualized skills-training methods to problems specific to the family (e.g., child management training, social support, assertion training, job training, home safety/finances training). Initial evaluation data have shown improvements in parent-identified goals and reduced reabuse rates relative to comparison cases after services (Lutzker & Rice, 1987), with less support for the maintenance of treatment effects, especially relative to comparison cases (Wesch & Lutzker, 1991).

Project SafeCare incorporates three primary interventions from several originally examined in Project 12-Ways designed to address the common behavioral deficiencies of abusive parents (infant and child health care, home safety, stimulation/bonding or parent-child interaction). Through the use of single-case experimental designs in much of this work, such interventions have been found to enhance parental skills and improve other general clinical problems (e.g., parental stress) (Lutzker et al., 1998). The strong emphasis on careful assessment and then individualized home-based training is a significant strength of this program. A similar program, described as an ecobehavioral approach, has been reported (see Donohue, Miller, Van Hasselt, & Hersen, 1998). Such comprehensive interventions underscore the need to provide multiple services to stabilize the home environment and promote improvements in parent-child relations with abusive families, many of which exhibit considerable family dysfunction.

Treatment Availability/ Access and Involvement

Beyond the description and evaluation of efficacious treatment approaches, issues related to treatment access and involvement are important to describe. Problems with engagement, compliance, and dropout have been identified for some time among abusive families (Cohn & Daro, 1987). One program evaluation report documented a 38% no-show rate at home, a 66% clinic no-show rate, and a 36% dropout rate among 45 families (Warner, Malinosky-Rummell, Ellis, & Hansen, 1990). Some studies have likewise reported high dropout rates from specialty treatment (Nicol et al., 1988).

A more fundamental concern is the fact that many cases fail to receive needed mental health services, as many victims of child physical abuse are not referred for treatment (Kaplan et al., 1999). As noted by English (1998), between 40% and 60% of cases in which maltreatment is substantiated are estimated to receive no subsequent services. A survey of practitioners found that child physical abuse victims received only 7 of 23 sessions of services generally conducted to reduce the negative consequences of this experience (Greenwald et al., 1997).

One study of families, referred to CPS following an incident of child physical or sexual abuse, examined the treatment experiences of the sample upon intake and at a second assessment following an initial service about 6 months later (Kolko, Selelyo, & Brown, 1999). On the basis of standardized clinical assessments conducted with child victims and their caregivers, several findings were reported. First, 30% of the caregivers and children had a past history of psychiatric hospitalization. Second, at the follow-up assessment, children and their caregivers reported high rates of family (47%, 39%) and parent counseling (33%, 48%) but lower rates for child treatment (17%, 19%), respectively. Four variables predicted overall family service use at intake: child is Caucasian, low child anxiety, parental distress, and parental abuse history as a child. The findings extend initial descriptions of the naturalistic service involvement of CPS families and may have implications for both practice and research on the delivery of services in CPS.

It is unclear how policies and practices within state social service agencies influence referral for and the availability of adequate clinical services. Findings from Kolko et al.'s (1999) study of families referred to CPS following an alleged incident of child physical or sexual abuse revealed considerable variability in the timeliness with which risk assessments were completed by accepted deadlines (see Kolko, 1998a, 1998b). Caseworkers' risk assessment reports for a subset of cases were not found to be related to several measures of clinical functioning collected by independent research assistants.

Not surprisingly, then, abuse recurrences have been reported in approximately one third of those receiving treatment and nearly half of those who complete treatment

(Daro, 1988; Malinosky-Rummell et al., 1991). Indeed, families characterized as multirisk and violent and who present with distressed parenting have shown the least improvement in family functioning during preventive intervention based on monthly therapist ratings (Ayoub et al., 1992). Many such families show no change at all, even after lengthy treatment (Willett et al., 1991). These and other obstacles to effective service delivery provide a significant challenge to the practitioner.

Practice Implications

Clinical Assessment

This section identifies some of the more important implications of recent developments in the design and evaluation of psychosocial interventions applied to this population. The heterogeneity in the clinical pictures of abused children and their parents has been well documented. Because this population is characterized by no specific syndrome or symptoms, it seems vital to conduct a comprehensive intake evaluation that incorporates multiple domains of functioning (e.g., behavior, social), using several informants (e.g., child, parent, siblings) and assessment methods (e.g., interviews, checklists, observations). Common foci of assessment include child and parent psychopathology, individual and family resources or strengths, and various aspects of the family environment (e.g., processes, relationships, interaction patterns). Several specialized assessment measures with adequate psychometric properties are available (see Hansen, Sedlar, & Warner-Rogers, 1999). In addition, investigators are encouraged to include in their evaluations semistructured diagnostic assessment instruments to document the presence of PTSD and other disorders, measures of individual impairment that include impact on health and behavior, and perceptions of the child's social competence and peer relationships.

Progress has been made in recent years in documenting the parameters of abusive interactions (e.g., frequency, severity, chronicity, situational context), using structured scales and objective definitions (e.g., Barnett, Manly, & Cicchetti, 1993; Chaffin, Wherry, Newlin, Crutchfield, & Dykman, 1997). The benefit of these tools is their ability to clearly articulate the nature of the abuse so that study samples can be better understood and more easily evaluated. Some evidence suggests that these parameters are correlated with clinical measures in victims of child physical abuse (e.g., Manly et al., 1994). Greater use of these and other operational criteria in defining a given sample is needed, however, to confirm any initial characterization of the sample by outside sources. From a research perspective, the use of operational criteria would help to establish the validity of the sample and permit needed cross-study comparisons.

Treatment Goals and Targets

One likely benefit of a thorough assessment and a coherent clinical formulation is the identification of concrete or objective, realistic, and individualized treatment goals. One primary consideration in articulating these goals is how to balance the child's needs with those of the parent or family and how much to emphasize a focus on individuals versus the family as a unit in treatment (Greenwald et al., 1997). In recent years, greater attention has been paid to identifying and then ameliorating children's mental health problems and related abuse sequelae (Carlson, 2000). Enhancing the child's welfare or functioning is a worthwhile goal commensurate with the need to prevent any further abuse. Still, studies that target both parental or family risk factors for reabuse and children's psychological reactions to abusive experiences have not been reported, with some exceptions (Kolko, 1996a, 1996c).

Discussion of and education regarding the abusive or traumatic incident are important to address in treatment (Cohen et al., 2000). Targets for child-focused intervention have included developmental competence, attributions about the abuse, behavioral self-control and emotional adjustment, social skills, and peer relations, among others. Targets for parents and families have included parent management skill, anger control, depression, developmental knowledge and expectations, and social support. Comprehensive treatments for several participants, incorporating both individual cognitive-behavioral treatment and family interventions, may be in the best position to integrate these targets (Kolko & Swenson, in press). The existing literature, however, still targets dysfunctional or deviant behavior more so than personal competencies or strengths, even though this dual focus is jus-

tified to address both behavioral deficiencies and excesses.

Treatment Preparation

Families recommended for services following investigation by CPS may struggle as much in handling the investigation experience as they do the sequelae of the abuse incident, although the reactions to both experiences may be exacerbated by the lack of a supportive process of referral for intervention. Cognizant of the various problems experienced at the individual and family levels, clinicians ought to consider ways to minimize any further frustration among the family and to promote a sense of concerned collaboration with them. Efforts to promote family rapport or engagement include the development of a client agreement that identifies all services, responsibilities, and goals; orientations to the agency and assigned therapists or counselors; and a short latency to establishing the first contact and conducting certain sessions (e.g., orientation meeting) in the family's home or a local community setting (see Swenson & Kolko, 2000).

Client participation during treatment may be enhanced by identifying and then addressing potential obstacles to attendance and providing assistance with specific needs, as well as offering incentives or contracts for meeting certain performance criteria.

Client participation during treatment may be enhanced by identifying and then addressing potential obstacles to attendance and providing assistance with specific needs (e.g., transportation, baby-sitting or child care, food and snacks), as well as offering incentives or contracts for meeting certain performance criteria (Azar & Wolfe, 1998). Certain families may express preferences for therapists with specific characteristics (e.g., gender, level of experience, religion) or backgrounds (e.g., ethnicity or cultural competence). Where available, advocacy services may help to promote parental autonomy or authority, prepare children for court or other high-stress meetings, hasten the receipt of requested materials or services, or establish an intermediary in special meetings or the legal arena. If multiple systems or agencies are involved in a case, maintenance of close communication among the various providers can maximize the likelihood that service goals and methods are consistent and complementary, contingent on family consent for such collaboration. Coordination of services is important to ensure in reality, not just on paper.

Abuse-Specific and Family-Centered Interventions

In addressing the broad clinical features of abusive families, integrated interventions that target child, parent, and family functioning may have the most potential to yield positive outcomes (Kolko, 1998a, 1998c; Stevenson, 1999). Although the most common treatment modality or component in prior studies has reflected some form of parent training, intervention studies in recent years have only recently begun to incorporate multiple participants, procedures, targets or treatment foci, and settings.

Although some interventions have included both children and parents in services, many studies have targeted either parents or children. In terms of clinical approaches, most interventions have applied CBT and skills-training procedures to specific competencies and clinical problems. This general focus is consistent with the four suggested CBT strategies recommended for the treatment of traumatized children and their parents: exposure to the traumatic event, stress management and coping skills training, exploration and correction of cognitive distortions related to the traumatic event, and interventions with parents (Cohen et al., 2000). Although many interventions have incorporated stress management or coping skills training, far less clinical attention has been paid to the child's (and, perhaps, even the parent's) perceptions and attributions related to an abusive experience or history. This focus may be important in influencing the level of psychological distress identified in child victims of physical abuse.

Treatment has gradually expanded to address an array of topics or targets (Wolfe et al., 1988). Such specific targets have included parental perceptions of their children's behavior and motives, developmentally appropriate expectations, self-control, cognitive distortion, the regulation of angry or anxious affect, stress management, positive discipline, and social support or activities. Child targets include teaching anger identification and control, relaxation, social skills and peer play activities, thinking errors or exaggerations, developmental and academic competencies, and understanding of the antecedents and consequences of individual problems.

For some time, intervention efforts have been conducted in multiple settings, especially the home (e.g., Lutzker et al., 1998; Swenson & Kolko, 2000). Providing treatment in the natural environment is generally beneficial if it provides access to all family members, permits accurate observations of existing family problems and interactions, and enables the therapist to select the most applicable and specific treatment techniques. Of course, it is not possible to determine the relative impact of community- versus clinic-based services for abusive families. Even if the choice of setting is left up to the family, therapists who can conduct home-based and family-centered treatment may acquire an enriched perspective on treatment.

Another aspect of service delivery bearing implications for practice concerns the degree to which programs integrate crisis intervention and support services into treatment (e.g., Homebuilders) (Whittaker et al., 1990). Given the varied risk factors and sequelae of physical abuse described earlier, there certainly are examples in which numerous interventions were administered on an intensive basis in an effort to modify multiple risk factors, bolster natural support systems, and identify other needed resources. Unfortunately, fewer studies in recent years have targeted contextual issues associated with abusive behavior (e.g., poverty, single parenthood, stress, marital discord, family instability, harsh child-rearing attitudes or practices, social insularity), thus making it difficult to know whether this diverse focus enhances family involvement and improvement. What has some empirical support, given the continuity of child and family problems following physical maltreatment, is the notion that follow-up services be considered an important extension of intervention (Daro, 1988). Especially because intervention studies have shown mixed evidence for the maintenance of treatment gains (e.g., Wesch & Lutzker, 1991; Wolfe et al., 1988), an examination of therapeutic methods that promote greater stability of improvements seems warranted (e.g., "checkups," service calls). Much work still needs to be done to promote the development, application, and evaluation of psychosocial interventions designed to modify both the sequelae of an abusive experience and the risk of reabuse (National Academy of Sciences, 1997).

Conclusion

This chapter has examined the findings of empirical studies examining the prevalence, measurement, risk factors, consequences, and treatment of child physical abuse. When taken together, developments achieved in each of these areas have provided greater evidence to support the impact and modification of this form of abusive experience, especially given recent studies on the long-term effects of physical abuse. Besides highlighting several gaps in our knowledge base, it is hoped that these collective findings provide some direction for future studies. Of course, continued research based on methodologically sound studies is needed to extend these findings and to address ongoing unresolved issues, particularly in the evaluation and dissemination of next-generation abuse assessment and abuse-specific procedures. These and other advances may contribute to the identification of effective methods to identify, treat, and, ultimately, prevent the experience of child physical abuse.

References

Aber, J. L., & Allen, J. P. (1987). Effects of maltreatment on young children's socioemotional development: An attachment theory perspective. *Developmental Psychology, 23*(3), 406-414.

Aber, J. L., Allen, J. P., Carlson, V., & Cicchetti, D. (1989). The effects of maltreatment on development during early childhood: Recent studies and their theoretical, clinical, and policy implications. In D. Cicchetti & V. Carlson (Eds.), *Child maltreatment: Theory and research on the causes and consequences of child abuse and neglect* (pp. 579-616). Cambridge, UK: Cambridge University Press.

Acton, R. G., & During, S. M. (1992). Preliminary results of aggression management training for aggressive parents. *Journal of Interpersonal Violence, 7,* 410-417.

Alessandri, S. M. (1991). Play and social behavior in maltreated preschoolers. *Development and Psychopathology, 3,* 191-205.

Alessandri, S. M. (1992). Mother-child interactional correlates of maltreated and nonmaltreated children's play behavior. *Development and Psychopathology, 4,* 257-270.

Allen, D. M., & Tarnowski, K. G. (1989). Depressive characteristics of physically abused children. *Journal of Abnormal Child Psychology, 17,* 1-11.

American Humane Association. (2000). *Physical abuse fact sheets* [Online]. Available: www.americanhumane.org.

Ammerman, R. T. (1990a). Etiological models of child maltreatment: A behavioral perspective. *Behavior Modification, 14,* 230-254.

Ammerman, R. T. (1990b). Predisposing child factors. In R. T. Ammerman & M. Hersen (Eds.), *Children at risk: An evaluation of factors contributing to child abuse and neglect* (pp. 199-221). New York: Plenum.

Ammerman, R. T. (1991). The role of the child in physical abuse: A reappraisal. *Violence and Victims, 6*(2), 87-101.

Amundson, M. J. (1989). Family crisis care: A home-based intervention program for child abuse. *Issues in Mental Health Nursing, 10*(3/4), 285-296.

Appel, A. E., & Holden, G. W. (1998). The occurrence of spouse and physical child abuse: A review and appraisal. *Journal of Family Psychology, 12,* 578-599.

Augoustinos, M. (1987). Developmental effects of child abuse: Recent findings. *Child Abuse & Neglect, 11*(1), 15-27.

Ayoub, C., Willett, J. B., & Robinson, D. S. (1992). Families at risk of child maltreatment: Entry-level characteristics and growth in family functioning during treatment. *Child Abuse & Neglect, 16,* 495-511.

Azar, S. T. (1989). Training parents of abused children. In C. E. Schaefer & J. M. Briesmeiste (Eds.), *Handbook of parent training* (pp. 414-441). New York: John Wiley.

Azar, S. T. (1997). A cognitive behavioral approach to understanding and treating parents who physically abuse their children. In D. Wolfe, R. J. McMahon, & R. D. Peters (Eds.), *Child abuse: New directions in prevention and treatment across the lifespan* (Vol. 4, pp. 79-101). Thousand Oaks, CA: Sage.

Azar, S. T., Barnes, K. T., & Twentyman, C. T. (1988). Developmental outcomes in abused children: Consequences of parental abuse or a more general breakdown in caregiver behavior? *Behavior Therapist, 11*(2), 27-32.

Azar, S. T., & Gehl, K. S. (1999). Physical abuse and neglect. In R. T. Ammerman & M. Hersen (Eds.), *Handbook of prescriptive treatments for children and adolescents* (pp. 329-345). Boston: Allyn & Bacon.

Azar, S. T., Robinson, D. R., Hekimian, E., & Twentyman, C. T. (1984). Unrealistic expectations and problem-solving ability in maltreating and comparison mothers. *Journal of Consulting and Clinical Psychology, 52,* 687-691.

Azar, S. T., & Siegel, B. R. (1990). Behavioral treatment of child abuse: A developmental perspective. *Behavior Modification, 14*(3), 279-300.

Azar, S. T., & Wolfe, D. A. (1998). Child physical abuse and neglect. In E. J. Mash & R. A. Barkley (Eds.), *Treatment of childhood disorders* (pp. 501-544). New York: Guilford.

Barahal, R. M., Waterman, J., & Martin, H. P. (1981). The social cognitive development of abused children. *Journal of Consulting and Clinical Psychology, 49,* 508-516.

Barnett, D., Ganiban, J., & Cicchetti, D. (1999). Maltreatment, negative expressivity, and the development of Type D attachments from 12 to 24 months of age. *Monographs of the Society for Research in Child Development, 64*(3), 97-118.

Barnett, D., Manly, J. T., & Cicchetti, D. (1993). Defining child maltreatment: The interface between policy and research. In D. Cicchetti & S. L. Toth (Eds.), *Child abuse, child development, and social policy* (pp. 7-73). Norwood, NJ: Ablex.

Barth, R. P., Blythe, B. J., Schinke, S. P., Stevens, P., & Schilling, R. F. (1983). Self-control training with maltreating parents. *Child Welfare, 62*(4), 313-324.

Beeghly, M., & Cicchetti, D. (1994). Child maltreatment, attachment, and the self system: Emergence of an internal state lexicon in toddlers at high social risk. *Development and Psychopathology, 6,* 5-30.

Belsky, J. (1993). Etiology of child maltreatment: A developmental-ecological analysis. *Psychological Bulletin, 114,* 413-434.

Belsky, J., & Vondra, J. (1989). Lessons from child abuse: The determinants of parenting. In C. D. Carlson & V. Carlson (Eds.), *Child maltreatment: Theory and research on the causes and consequences of child abuse and neglect* (pp. 153-202). New York: Cambridge University Press.

Berlin, I. N. (1997). Attachment theory: Its use in milieu therapy and in psychotherapy with children in residential treatment. *Residential Treatment for Children and Youth, 15*(2), 29-37.

Berliner, L., & Saunders, B. E. (1996). Treating fear and anxiety in sexually abused children: Results of a controlled 2-year follow-up study. *Child Maltreatment, 1,* 294-309.

Black, D. A., Heyman, R. E., & Smith-Slep, A. M. (2001). Risk factors for child physical abuse. *Aggression and Violent Behavior, 6*(2/3), 121-188.

Blythe, B. J., Jiordano, M. J., & Kelly, S. A. (1991). Family preservation with substance abusing families: Help that works. *Child, Youth, and Family Services Quarterly, 14,* 12-13.

Boney-McCoy, S., & Finklehor, D. (1995). Psychosocial sequelae of violent victimization in a national youth sample. *Journal of Consulting and Clinical Psychology, 63*(5), 726-736.

Bousha, D. M., & Twentyman, C. T. (1984). Mother-child interactional style in abuse, neglect, and control groups: Naturalistic observations in the home. *Journal of Abnormal Psychology, 93*(1), 106-114.

Brown, J., Cohen, P., Johnson, J. G., & Salzinger, S. (1998). A longitudinal analysis of risk factors for child maltreatment: Findings of a 17-year prospective study of officially recorded and self-reported child abuse and neglect. *Child Abuse & Neglect, 22*(11), 1065-1078.

Brown, J., Cohen, P., Johnson, J. G., & Smailes, E. M. (1999). Childhood abuse and neglect: Specificity of effects on adolescent and young adult depression and suicidality. *Journal of American Academy of Child and Adolescent Psychiatry, 38,* 1490-1505.

Browne, K. D., & Hamilton, C. E. (1998). Physical violence between young adults and their parents: Associations with a history of child maltreatment. *Journal of Family Violence, 13*(1), 59-79.

Brunk, M., Henggeler, S. W., & Whelan, J. P. (1987). Comparison of multisystemic therapy and parent training in the brief treatment of child abuse and neglect. *Journal of Consulting and Clinical Psychology, 55,* 171-178.

Bryant, S. L., & Range, L. M. (1997). Type and severity of child abuse and college students' lifetime suicidality. *Child Abuse & Neglect, 21*(12), 1169-1176.

Bugental, D. B., & Cortez, L. (1988). Physiological reactivity to responsive and unresponsive children as moderated by perceived control. *Child Development, 59*(3), 686-693.

Bugental, D. B., Mantyla, S. M., & Lewis, J. (1989). Parental attributions as moderators of affective communication to children at risk for physical abuse. In D. Cicchetti & V. Carlson (Eds.), *Child maltreatment: Theory and research on the causes and consequences of child abuse and neglect.* New York: Cambridge University Press.

Cadzow, S. P., Armstrong, K. L., & Fraser, J. A. (1999). Stressed parents with infants: Reassessing physical abuse risk factors. *Child Abuse & Neglect, 23*(9), 845-853.

Caliso, J. A., & Milner, J. S. (1992). Childhood history of abuse and child abuse screening. *Child Abuse & Neglect, 16*(5), 647-659.

Camras, L. A., Grow, J. G., & Ribordy, S. C. (1983). Recognition of emotional expression by abused children. *Journal of Clinical Child Psychology, 12*(3), 325-328.

Cantos, A. L., Neale, J. M., & O'Leary, K. D. (1997). Assessment of coping strategies of child abusing mothers. *Child Abuse & Neglect, 21*(7), 631-636.

Cappell, C., & Heiner, R. B. (1990). The intergenerational transmission of family aggression. *Journal of Family Violence, 5*(2), 135-151.

Carlson, B. E. (1986). Children's beliefs about punishment. *American Journal of Orthopsychiatry, 56,* 308-312.

Carlson, B. E. (1991). Emotionally disturbed children's beliefs and punishment. *Child Abuse & Neglect, 15,* 19-28.

Carlson, B. E. (2000). A conceptual framework for the impact of traumatic experiences. *Trauma, Violence and Abuse, 1*(1), 4-28.

Casanova, G. M., Domanic, J., McCanne, T. R., & Milner, J. S. (1991). Physiological responses to non-child-related stressors in mothers at risk for child abuse. *Child Abuse & Neglect, 16*(1), 31-44.

Caselles, C. E., & Milner, J. S. (2000). Evaluation of child transgressions, disciplinary choices, and expected child compliance in a no-cry and a crying infant condition in physically abusive and comparison mothers. *Child Abuse & Neglect, 24*(4), 477-491.

Caspi, A., & Elder, G. H. (1988). Emergent family patterns: The intergenerational construction of problem behaviour and relationships. In R. A. Hinde & J. Stevenson-Hinde (Eds.), *Relationships with families: Mutual influences* (pp. 218-240). Oxford, UK: Clarendon.

Chadwick, D. L. (1999). The message. *Child Abuse & Neglect, 23*(10), 957-961.

Chaffin, M., Kelleher, K., & Hollenberg, J. (1996). Onset of physical abuse and neglect: Psychiatric, substance abuse, and social risk factors from prospective community data. *Child Abuse & Neglect, 20*(3), 191-203.

Chaffin, M., Wherry, J. N., Newlin, C., Crutchfield, A., & Dykman, R. (1997). The abuse dimensions inventory: Initial data on a research measure of abuse. *Journal of Interpersonal Violence, 12*(4), 569-589.

Christman, A., Wodarski, J. S., & Smokowski, P. R. (1996). Risk factors for physical child abuse: A practice theoretical paradigm. *Family Therapy, 23,* 233-248.

Chu, J. A., Frey, L. M., Ganzel, B. L., & Matthews, J. A. (1999). Memories of childhood abuse: Dissociation, amnesia and corroboration. *American Journal of Psychiatry, 156*(5), 749-755.

Cicchetti, D., & Barnett, D. (1991). Toward the development of a scientific nosology of child maltreatment. In D. Cicchetti & W. Grove (Eds.), *Thinking clearly about psychology: Essays in honor of Paul E. Meehl* (pp. 346-377). Minneapolis: University of Minnesota Press.

Cicchetti, D., Toth, S. L., & Maughan, A. (2000). An ecologiocal-transactional model of child maltreatment. In A. J. Sameroff (Ed.), *Handbook of developmental psychopathology* (2nd ed., pp. 689-722). New York: Kluwer.

Claussen, A. H., & Crittenden, P. M. (1991). Physical and psychological maltreatment: Relations among types of maltreatment. *Child Abuse & Neglect, 15,* 5-18.

Cohen, J. A., Berliner, L., & Mannarino, A. (2000). Treating traumatized children. *Trauma, Violence and Abuse, 1,* 29-46.

Cohen, P., Cohen, J., & Brook, J. S. (1993). An epidemiological study of disorders in late childhood and adolescence: II. Persistence of disorders. *Journal of Child Psychology & Psychiatry & Allied Disciplines, 34*(6), 869-877.

Cohn, A. H., & Daro, D. (1987). Is treatment too late: What ten years of evaluative research tell us. *Child Abuse & Neglect, 11,* 433-442.

Conaway, L. P., & Hansen, D. J. (1989). Social behavior of physically abused and neglected children: A critical review. *Clinical Psychology Review, 9,* 627-652.

Coohey, C. (2000). The role of friends, in-laws, and other kin in father-penetrated child physical abuse. *Child Welfare, 79*(4), 373-402.

Coohey, C., & Braun, N. (1997). Toward an integrated framework for understanding child physical abuse. *Child Abuse & Neglect, 21*(11), 1081-1094.

Corcoran, J. (2000). Family interventions with child physical abuse and neglect: A critical review. *Children and Youth Services Review, 22,* 563-591.

Coster, W. J., Gersten, M. S., Beeghly, M., & Cicchetti, D. (1989). Communicative functioning in maltreated toddlers. *Development and Psychopathology, 25,* 777-793.

Courtney, M. E. (1999). The economics. *Child Abuse & Neglect, 23,* 975-986.

Crittenden, P. (1992). Children's strategies for coping with adverse home environments: An interpretation using attachment theory. *Child Abuse & Neglect, 16,* 329-343.

Culp, R. E., Heide, J. S., & Richardson, M. T. (1987). Maltreated children's developmental scores: Treatment versus nontreatment. *Child Abuse & Neglect, 11,* 29-34.

Culp, R. E., Little, V., Letts, D., & Lawrence, H. (1991). Maltreated children's self-concept: Effects of a comprehensive treatment program. *American Journal of Orthopsychiatry, 61,* 114-121.

Cummings, E. M., Hennessy, K. D., Rabideau, G. J., & Cicchetti, D. (1994). Responses of physically abused boys to interadult anger involving their mothers. *Development and Psychopathology, 6*(1), 31-41.

Daro, D. (1988). *Confronting child abuse: Research for effective program design.* New York: Free Press.

Davis, S., & Fantuzzo, J. W. (1989). The effects of adult and peer social initiations on social behavior of withdrawn and aggressive maltreated preschool children. *Journal of Family Violence, 4,* 227-248.

DeBellis, M. D., Baum, A., Birmaher, B., Keshavan, M., Eccard, C. H., Boring, A. M., Jenkins, F. J., & Ryan, N. D. (1999). A. E. Bennett Research Award. Developmental traumatology part I: Biological stress systems. *Biological Psychiatry, 45,* 1259-1270.

DeBellis, M. D., Keshavan, M. S., Clark, D. B., Giedd, J. N., Boring, A. M., Frustaci, K., & Ryan, N. D. (1999). A. E. Bennett Research Award: Developmental traumatology: Part II. Brain development. *Biological Psychiatry, 45*(10), 1271-1284.

Dodge, K. E., & Pettit, G. S. (1990). Mechanisms in the cycle of violence. *Science, 250,* 1678-1683.

Dodge, K. A., Pettit, G. S., & Bates, J. E. (1994). Effects of physical maltreatment on the development of peer relations. *Development and Psychopathology, 6*(1), 43-55.

Dodge, K. A., Pettit, G. S., & Bates, J. E. (1997). How the experience of early physical abuse leads children to become chronically aggressive. In *Developmental perspectives on trauma: Theory, research and intervention* (Vol. 8, pp. 263-288). Rochester, NY: University of Rochester Press.

Dolz, L., Cerezo, M. A., & Milner, J. S. (1997). Mother-child interactional patterns in high- and low-risk mothers. *Child Abuse & Neglect, 21*(12), 1149-1158.

Donohue, B., Miller, E. R., Van Hasselt, V. B., & Hersen, M. (1998). An ecobehavioral approach to child maltreatment. In V. B. Van Hasselt & M. Hersen (Eds.), *Handbook of psychological treatment protocols for children and adolescents* (pp. 279-356). Mahwah, NJ: Lawrence Erlbaum.

Dopke, C. A., & Milner, J. S. (2000). Impact of child compliance on stress appraisals, attributions, and disciplinary choices in mothers at high and low risk for child physical abuse. *Child Abuse & Neglect, 24,* 493-504.

Downs, W. R., & Miller, B. A. (1998). Relationships between experiences of parental violence during childhood and women's self-esteem. *Violence and Victims, 13*(1), 63-77.

Eckenrode, J., Laird, M., & Doris, J. (1993). School performance and disciplinary problems among abused and neglected children. *Developmental Psychology, 29*(1), 53-62.

Egan, K. (1983). Stress management and child management with abusive parents. *Journal of Clinical Child Psychology, 12,* 292-299.

Egeland, B., & Sroufe, L. A. (1981). Developmental sequelae of maltreatment in infancy. *New Directions for Child Development, 11,* 77-92.

Eisenstadt, T. H., Eyberg, S., McNeil, C. B., Newcomb, K., & Funderburk, B. (1993). Parent-child interaction therapy with behavior problem children: Relative effectiveness of two stages and overall treatment outcome. *Journal of Clinical Child Psychology, 22,* 42-51.

Emery, R. E., & Laumann-Billings, L. (1998). An overview of the nature, causes and consequences of abusive family relationships. *American Psychologist, 53,* 121-135.

English, D. J. (1998). The extent and consequences of child maltreatment. *Future of Children, 8,* 39-53.

Erickson, M. F., Egeland, B., & Pianta, R. (1989). The effects of maltreatment on the development of young children. In D. Cicchetti & V. Carlson (Eds.), *Child maltreatment: Theory and research on the causes and consequences of child abuse and neglect* (pp. 647-684). New York: Cambridge University Press.

Famularo, R., Fenton, T., Augustyn, M., & Zuckerman, B. (1996). Persistence of pediatric post traumatic stress disorder after 2 years. *Child Abuse & Neglect, 20*(12), 1245-1248.

Famularo, R., Fenton, T., & Kinscherff, R. T. (1992). Medical and developmental histories of maltreated children. *Clinical Pediatrics, 31,* 536-541.

Famularo, R., Fenton, T., Kinscherff, R., Ayoub, C., & Barnum, R. (1994). Maternal and child posttraumatic stress disorder in cases of child maltreatment. *Child Abuse & Neglect, 18,* 27-36.

Famularo, R., Kinscherff, R., & Fenton, T. (1990). Symptom differences in acute and chronic presentation of childhood posttraumatic stress disorder. *Child Abuse & Neglect, 14,* 439-444.

Famularo, R., Kinscherff, R., & Fenton, T. (1991). Posttraumatic stress disorder among children clinically diagnosed as borderline personality disorder. *Journal of Nervous and Mental Diseases, 179,* 428-431.

Fantuzzo, J., Sutton-Smith, B., Atkins, M., Meyers, R., Stevenson, H., Coolahan, K., Weiss, A., & Manz, P. (1996). Community-based resilient peer treatment of withdrawn maltreated preschool children. *Journal of Consulting and Clinical Psychology, 64*(6), 1377-1386.

Fantuzzo, J. W. (1990). Behavioral treatment of the victims of child abuse and neglect. *Behavior Modification, 14,* 316-339.

Fantuzzo, J. W., delGaudio, W. A., Atkins, M., Meyers, R., & Noone, M. (1998). A contextually relevant assessment of the impact of child maltreatment on the social competencies of low-income urban children. *Journal of American Academy of Child and Adolescent Psychiatry, 37*(11), 1201-1208.

Fantuzzo, J. W., DePaola, L. M., Lambert, L., Martino, T., Anderson, G., & Sutton, S. (1991). Effects of interparental violence on the psychological adjustment and competencies of young children. *Journal of Consulting & Clinical Psychology, 59,* 258-265.

Fantuzzo, J. W., Jurecic, L., Stovall, A., Hightower, A. D., & Goins, C. (1988). Effects of adult and peer social initiations on the social behavior of withdrawn, maltreated preschool children. *Journal of Consulting and Clinical Psychology, 56,* 34-39.

Fantuzzo, J. W., Stovall, A., Schachtel, D., Goins, C., & Hall, R. (1987). The effects of peer social initiations on the social behavior of withdrawn maltreated preschool children. *Journal of Behavior Therapy and Experimental Psychiatry, 18,* 357-363.

Feldman, R. S., Salzinger, S., Rosario, M., Alvarado, L., Caraballo, L., & Hammer, M. (1995). Parent, teacher, and peer ratings of physically abused and nonmaltreated children's behavior. *Journal of Abnormal Child Psychology, 23,* 317-334.

Feldman, R. S., Salzinger, S., Rosario, M., Hammer, M., Alvarado, L., & Caraballo, L. (1989). *Parent and teacher ratings of abused and non-abused children's behavior.* New York: American Academy of Child Psychiatry.

Fennell, D. C., & Fishel, A. H. (1998). Parent education: An evaluation of STEP on abusive parents' perceptions and abuse potential. *Journal of Child and Adolescent Psychiatric Nursing, 11*(3), 107-120.

Finkelhor, D., & Dziuba-Leatherman, J. (1994). Victimization of children. *American Psychologist, 49,* 173-183.

Flisher, A. J., Kramer, R. A., Hoven, C. W., Greenwald, S., Bird, H. R., Canino, G., Connell, R., & Moore, R. E. (1997). Psychosocial characteristics of physically abused children and adolescents. *Journal of American Academy of Child and Adolescent Psychiatry, 36*(1), 123-131.

Ford, J. D., Racusin, R., Daviss, W. B., Ellis, C., Thomas, J., Rogers, K., Reiser, J., Schiffman, J., & Sengupta, A. (1999). Trauma exposure among children with attention deficit hyperactivity disorder and oppositional defiant disorder. *Journal of Consulting & Clinical Psychology, 67,* 786-789.

Fraser, M. W., Walton, E., Lewis, R. E., & Pecora, P. J. (1996). An experiment in family reunification: Correlates of outcomes at one-year follow-up. *Children and Youth Services Review, 18*(4-5), 335-361.

Friedrich, W. N., Taylor, J. D., & Clark, J. A. (1985). Personality and psychophysiological variables in abusive, neglectful, and low-income control mothers. *Journal of Nervous and Mental Disease, 170,* 577-587.

Geen, R., Boots, S. W., & Tumlan, K. C. (1999). *The cost of protecting vulnerable children: Understanding federal, state, and local child welfare spending.* Washington, DC: Urban Institute.

Gelles, R. J., & Straus, M. A. (1987). Is violence toward children increasing? *Journal of Interpersonal Violence, 2,* 212-222.

Gelles, R. J., & Straus, M. A. (1990). The medical and psychological costs of family violence. In M. A. Straus & R. J. Gelles (Eds.), *Physical violence in American families: Risk factors and adaptations to violence in 8,145 families* (pp. 425-430). New Brunswick, NJ: Transaction.

Gillham, B., Tanner, G., Cheyne, B., Freeman, I., Rooney, M., & Lambie, A. (1998). Unemployment rates, single parent density, and indices of child poverty: Their relationship in different categories of child abuse and neglect. *Child Abuse & Neglect, 22*(2), 79-90.

Goldberg, R. T., Pachas, W. N., & Keith, D. (1999). Relationship between traumatic events in childhood and chronic pain. *Disability and Rehabilitation: An International Multidisciplinary Journal, 21*(1), 23-30.

Golub, J. S., Espinosa, M., Damon, L., & Card, J. (1987). A video-tape parent education program for abusive parents. *Child Abuse & Neglect, 11,* 255-265.

Graziano, A. M., & Mills, J. R. (1992). Treatment for abused children: When is a partial solution acceptable? *Child Abuse & Neglect, 16,* 217-228.

Greenwald, R. L., Bank, L., Reid, J. B., & Knutson, J. F. (1997). A discipline-mediated model of excessively punitive parenting. *Aggressive Behavior, 23,* 259-280.

Hansen, D. J., Pallotta, G. M., Tishelman, A. C., Conaway, L. P., & MacMillan, V. M. (1988). Parental problem-solving skills and child behavior problems: A comparison of physically abusive, neglectful, clinic, and community families. *Journal of Family Violence, 4,* 353-368.

Hansen, D. J., Sedlar, G., & Warner-Rogers, J. E. (1999). Child physical abuse. In R. T. Ammerman & M. Hansen (Eds.), *Assessment of family violence: A clinical and legal sourcebook* (2nd ed., pp. 127-156). New York: John Wiley.

Haskett, M. (1990). Social problem-solving skills of young physically abused children. *Child Psychiatry and Human Development, 21,* 109-118.

Haskett, M., & Kistner, J. A. (1991). Social interactions and peer perceptions of young physically abused children. *Child Development, 62,* 979-990.

Herrenkohl, E. C., Herrenkohl, R. C., Egolf, B. P., & Russo, M. J. (1998). The relationship between early maltreatment and teenage parenthood. *Journal of Adolescence, 21,* 291-303.

Herrenkohl, R. C. (1990). Research directions related to child abuse and neglect. In R. T. Ammerman & M. Hersen (Eds.), *Children at risk: An evaluation of factors contributing to child abuse and neglect* (pp. 85-105). New York: Plenum.

Herrenkohl, R. C., Egolf, B. P., & Herrenkohl, E. C. (1997). Preschool antecedents of adolescent assaultive behavior: A longitudinal study. *American Journal of Orthopsychiatry, 67,* 422-432.

Herrenkohl, R. C., Herrenkohl, E. C., & Egolf, B. P. (1983). Circumstances surrounding the occurrence of child maltreatment. *Journal of Consulting and Clinical Psychology, 51,* 424-431.

Herrenkohl, R. C., Herrenkohl, E. C., Egolf, B. P., & Wu, P. (1991). *The developmental consequences of child abuse: The Leigh longitudinal study* (Grant #MH41109). Washington, DC: National Center on Child Abuse and Neglect.

Hillson, J. M. C., & Kupier, N. A. (1994). A stress and coping model of child maltreatment. *Clinical Psychology Review, 14*(4), 261-285.

Holden, E. W., Willis, D. J., & Foltz, L. (1989). Child abuse potential and parenting stress: Relationships in maltreating parents. *Psychological Assessment: A Journal of Consulting and Clinical Psychology, 1,* 64-67.

Hotaling, G. T., Straus, M. A., & Lincoln, A. J. (1990). Intrafamily violence and crime and violence outside the family. In M. A. Straus & R. J. Gelles (Eds.), *Physical violence in American families: Risk factors and adaptations to violence in 8,145 families* (pp. 431-470). New Brunswick, NJ: Transaction.

Howes, C., & Espinosa, M. P. (1985). The consequences of child abuse for the formation of relationships with peers. *Child Abuse & Neglect, 9,* 397-404.

Howes, P. W., Cicchetti, D., Toth, S., & Rogosch, F. A. (2000). Affective, organizational, and relational characteristics of maltreating families: A system's perspective. *Journal of Family Psychology, 14*(1), 95-110.

Kaplan, S., Pelcovitz, D., Salzinger, S., Mandel, F. S., & Weiner, M. (1997). Adolescent physical abuse and suicide attempts. *Journal of American Academy of Child and Adolescent Psychiatry, 36*(6), 799-808.

Kaplan, S., Pelcovitz, D., Salzinger, S., Mandel, F. S., & Weiner, M. (1998). Adolescent physical abuse: Risk for adolescent psychiatric disorders. *American Journal of Psychiatry, 155*(7), 954-959.

Kaplan, S. J., Pelcovitz, D., & Labruna, V. (1999). Child and adolescent abuse and neglect research: A review of the past 10 years: Part I. Physical and emotional abuse and neglect. *Journal of the American Academy of Child and Adolescent Psychiatry, 38,* 1214-1222.

Kaplan, S., Pelcovitz, D., Salzinger, S., Mandel, F. S., & Weiner, M. (1997). Adolescent physical abuse and suicide attempts. *Journal of American Academy of Child and Adolescent Psychiatry, 36*(6), 799-808.

Kaufman, J., & Cicchetti, D. (1989). Effects of maltreatment on school-age children's socioemotional development: Assessments in day-camp setting. *Developmental Psychology, 25,* 516-524.

Kaufman, J., & Zigler, E. (1987). Do abused children become abusive parents? *American Journal of Orthopsychiatry, 57,* 186-192.

Kavanagh, K. A., Youngblade, L., Reid, J. B., & Fagot, B. I. (1988). Interactions between children and abusive versus control parents. *Journal of Clinical Child Psychology, 17,* 137-142.

Kazdin, A. E., Moser, J. T., Colbus, D., & Bell, R. (1985). Depressive symptoms among physically abused and psychiatrically disturbed children. *Journal of Abnormal Psychology, 94*(3), 298-307.

Kelleher, K., Chaffin, M., Hollenberg, J., & Fischer, E. (1994). Alcohol and drug disorders among physically abusive and neglectful parents in a community-based sample. *American Journal of Public Health, 84,* 1586-1590.

Kelley, S. J. (1992). Parenting stress and child maltreatment in drug-exposed children. *Child Abuse & Neglect, 16,* 317-328.

Kendall, P. C., Stark, K. D., & Adam, T. (1990). Cognitive deficit or cognitive distortion in childhood depression. *Journal of Abnormal Child Psychology, 18,* 255-270.

Kinard, E. M. (1980). Emotional development in physically abused children. *American Journal of Orthopsychiatry, 50,* 686-696.

Kinard, E. M. (1982). Experiencing child abuse: Effects on emotional adjustment. *American Journal of Orthopsychiatry, 52,* 82-91.

Kinard, E. M. (1996). Social support, self-worth, and depression in offending and nonoffending mothers of maltreated children. *Child Maltreatment, 1*(3), 272-283.

Klimes-Dougan, B., & Kistner, J. (1990). Physically abused preschoolers' response to peers' distress. *Developmental Psychology, 26,* 599-602.

Kolko, D. J. (1996a). Clinical monitoring of treatment course in child physical abuse: Psychometric characteristics and treatment comparisons. *Child Abuse & Neglect, 20,* 23-43.

Kolko, D. J. (1996b). Child physical abuse. In J. Briere, L. Berliner, J. A. Bulkley, C. Jenny, & T. Reid (Eds.), *The APSAC handbook on child maltreatment* (pp. 21-50). Thousand Oaks, CA: Sage.

Kolko, D. J. (1996c). Individual cognitive behavioral treatment and family therapy for physically abused children and their offending parents: A comparison of clinical outcomes. *Child Maltreatment, 1,* 322-342.

Kolko, D. J. (1998a). Integration of research and treatment. In J. R. Lutzker (Ed.)., *Handbook of child abuse research and treatment: Issues in clinical child psychology* (pp. 159-181). New York: Plenum.

Kolko, D. J. (1998b). Treatment and intervention for child victims of violence. In P. K. Trickett & C. J. Schellenbach (Eds.), *Violence against children in the family and in the community* (pp. 213-249). Washington, DC: American Psychological Association.

Kolko, D. J. (1998c). CPS operations and risk assessment in child abuse cases receiving services: Initial findings from the Pittsburgh Service Delivery System. *Child Maltreatment, 3,* 262-275.

Kolko, D. J., Moser, J. T., & Weldy, S. R. (1988). Behavioral/emotional indicators of child sexual abuse among child psychiatric inpatients: A comparison with physical abuse. *Child Abuse & Neglect, 12,* 529-541.

Kolko, D. J., Moser, J. T., & Weldy, S. R. (1990). Medical/health histories and physical evaluation of physically and sexually abused child psychiatric patients: A controlled study. *Journal of Family Violence, 5,* 249-267.

Kolko, D. J., Selelyo, J., & Brown, E. J. (1999). The treatment histories and service involvement of physically and sexually abusive families: Description, correspondence, and clinical correlates. *Child Abuse & Neglect, 23*(5), 459-476.

Kolko, D. J., & Swenson, C. C. (in press). *Cognitive-behavioral and family-system treatments for child physical abuse: Improving child welfare and reducing the risk of abuse.* Thousand Oaks, CA: Sage.

Langeland, W., & Hartgers, C. (1998). Child sexual and physical abuse and alcoholism: A review. *Journal of Studies on Alcohol, 59*(3), 336-348.

Lesserman, J., Li, Z., Drossman, D., Toomey, T. C., Nachman, G., & Glogau, L. (1997). Impact of sexual and physical abuse dimensions on health status: Development of an abuse severity measure. *Psychomatic Medicine, 59*(2), 152-160.

Levitan, R. D., Parikh, S. V., Lesage, A. D., Hegadoren, K. M., Adams, M., Kennedy, S. H., & Goering, P. N. (1998). Major depression in individuals with a history of childhood physical or sexual abuse: Relationship to neurovegatative features, mania and gender. *American Journal of Psychiatry, 155*(12), 1746-1752.

Lewis, D. O. (1992). From abuse to violence: Psychophysiological consequences of maltreatment. *Journal of the American Academy of Child and Adolescent Psychiatry, 31,* 383-391.

Lewis, D. O., Lovely, R., Yeager, C., & Femina, D. (1989). Toward a theory of the genesis of violence: A follow-up study of delinquents. *Journal of the American Academy of Child and Adolescent Psychiatry, 28,* 431-436.

Lopez, M. A., & Heffer, R. W. (1998). Self-concept and social competence of university student victims of childhood physical abuse. *Child Abuse & Neglect, 22*(3), 183-195.

Luiselli, J. K. (1996). Functional assessment and treatment of aggressive and destructive behaviors in a child victim of physical abuse. *Journal of Behavior Therapy and Experimental Psychiatry, 27*(1), 41-49.

Lung, C. T., & Daro, D. (1996). *Current trends in child abuse reporting and fatalities: The results of the 1995 annual fifty state survey.* Chicago: National Committee to Prevent Child Abuse.

Luntz, B., & Widom, C. S. (1994). Antisocial personality disorder in abused and neglected children grown up. *American Journal of Psychiatry, 151,* 670-674.

Lutzker, J. R., Bigelow, K. M., Doctor, R. M., Gershater, R. M., & Greene, B. F. (1998). An ecobehavioral model for the prevention and treatment of child abuse and neglect. In J. R. Lutzker (Ed.), *Handbook on child abuse research and treatment* (pp. 239-266). New York: Plenum.

Lutzker, J. R., & Rice, J. M. (1987). Using recidivism data to evaluate Project 12-Ways: An ecobehavioral approach to the treatment and prevention of child abuse and neglect. *Journal of Family Violence, 2,* 283-289.

Lynch, M., & Cicchetti, D. (1991). Patterns of relatedness in maltreated and nonmaltreated children: Connections among multiple representational models. *Development and Psychopathology, 3,* 207-226.

Lynch, M., & Cicchetti, D. (1998). An ecological-transactional analysis of children and contexts: The longitudinal interplay among child maltreatment, community violence, and children's symptomatology. *Development and Psychopathology, 10*(2), 235-257.

MacKinnon, C. E., Lamb, M. E., Belsky, J., & Baum, C. (1990). An affective-cognitive model of mother-child aggression. *Development and Psychopathology, 2,* 1-13.

Malinosky-Rummell, R., Ellis, J. T., Warner, J. E., Ujcich, K., Carr, R. E., & Hansen, D. J. (1991, November). *Individualized behavioral intervention for physically abusive and neglectful families: An evaluation of the family interaction skills project.* Paper presented at the 25th Annual Conference of the Association for the Advancement of Behavior Therapy, New York.

Malinosky-Rummell, R., & Hansen, D. J. (1993). Long-term consequences of childhood physical abuse. *Psychological Bulletin, 114,* 68-79.

Manly, J. T., Cicchetti, D., & Barnett, D. (1994). The impact of subtype, frequency, chronicity, and severity of child maltreatment on social competence and behavior problems. *Development and Psychopathology, 6*(1), 121-143.

Martin, J. A., & Elmer, E. (1992). Battered children grown up: A follow-up study of individuals severely maltreated as children. *Child Abuse & Neglect, 16,* 75-87.

Mash, E. J., & Johnston, C. (1990). Determinants of parenting stress: Illustrations from families of hyperactive children and families of physically abused children. *Journal of Clinical Psychology, 19,* 313-328.

Mason, W. A., Zimmerman, L., & Evans, W. (1998). Sexual and physical abuse among incarcerated youth: Implications for sexual behavior, contraceptive use, and teenage pregnancy. *Child Abuse & Neglect, 22*(10), 987-995.

Maxfield, M. G., & Widom, C. S. (1996). The cycle of violence: Revisited six years later. *Archives of Pediatrics and Adolescent Medicine, 150,* 390-395.

McCanne, T. R., & Milner, J. S. (1991). Physiological reactivity of physically abusive and at-risk subjects to child-related stimuli. In J. S. Milner (Ed.), *Neuropsychology of aggression* (pp. 147-166). Norwell, MA: Kluwer.

McFayden, R. G., & Kitson, W. J. H. (1996). Language comprehension and expression among adolescents who have experienced childhood physical abuse. *Journal of Child Psychology and Psychiatry and Allied Disciplines, 37,* 551-562.

Merrill, L. L., Hervig, L. K., & Milner, J. S. (1996). Childhood parenting experiences, intimate partner conflict resolution, and adult risk for child physical abuse. *Child Abuse & Neglect, 20*(11), 1049-1065.

Milner, J. S. (1998). Individual and family characteristics associated with intrafamilial child physical and sexual abuse. In P. K. Trickett & C. J. Schellenbach (Eds.), *Violence against children in the family and community* (pp. 141-170). Washington, DC: American Psychological Association.

Milner, J. S. (2000). Social information processing and child physical abuse: Theory and research. In D. J. Hansen (Ed.), *Nebraska symposium on motivation, Vol. 46, 1998: Motivation and child maltreatment* (pp. 39-84). Lincoln: University of Nebraska Press.

Mollerstrom, W. W., Patchner, M. M., & Milner, J. S. (1992). Family functioning and child abuse potential. *Journal of Clinical Psychology, 48*(4), 445-454.

Mulder, R. T., Beautrais, A. L., Joyce, P. R., & Fergusson, D. M. (1998). Relationship between dissociation, childhood sexual abuse, childhood physical abuse, and mental illness in a general population sample. *American Journal of Psychiatry, 155*(6), 806-811.

Murphy, J. M., Jellineck, M., Quin, D., Smith, G., Poitrast, F. G., & Goshko, M. (1991). Substance abuse and serious child maltreatment: Prevalence, risk, and outcome in a court sample. *Child Abuse & Neglect, 15,* 197-212.

National Academy of Sciences. (1993). *Understanding child abuse and neglect.* Washington, DC: National Academy Press.

National Academy of Sciences. (1997). *Violence in families: Assessing prevention and treatment programs.* Washington, DC: Author.

Nayak, M. B., & Milner, J. S. (1998). Neuropsychological functioning: Comparison of mother at high- and low-risk for child abuse. *Child Abuse & Neglect, 22,* 687-703.

Nelson, K. (1990). *How do we know that family-based services are effective?* Iowa City: University of Iowa, National Resource Center on Family Based Services.

Nicol, A. R., Smith, J., Kay, B., Hall, D., Barlow, J., & Williams, B. (1988). A focused casework approach to the treatment of child abuse: A controlled comparison. *Journal of Child Psychology and Psychiatry, 29,* 703-711.

Nuris, P. S., Lovell, M., & Edgar, M. (1988). Self-appraisals of abusive parents: A contextual approach to study and treatment. *Journal of Interpersonal Violence, 3,* 458-467.

Oates, R. K., & Bross, D. C. (1995). What have we learned about treating child physical abuse? A literature review of the last decade. *Child Abuse & Neglect, 19,* 463-473.

Oates, R. K., Forrest, D., & Peacock, A. (1985). Self-esteem of abused children. *Child Abuse & Neglect, 9,* 159-163.

Okun, A., Parker, J. G., & Levendosky, A. A. (1994). Distinct and interactive contributions of physical abuse, socioeconomic disadvantage, and negative life events to children's social, cognitive, and affective adjustment. *Development and Psychopathology, 6*(1), 77-98.

Oldershaw, L., Walters, G. C., & Hall, D. K. (1986). Control strategies and noncompliance in abusive mother-child dyads: An observational study. *Child Development, 57,* 722-732.

Parker, J. G., & Herrera, C. (1996). Interpersonal processes in friendship: A comparison of abused and nonabused children's experiences. *Developmental Psychology, 32*(6), 1025-1038.

Patterson, G. R., DeBaryshe, B. D., & Ramsey, E. (1989). A developmental perspective on antisocial behavior. *American Psychologist, 44*(2), 329-335.

Pelcovitz, D., Kaplan, S., Goldenberg, B., & Mandel, F. (1994). Posttraumatic stress disorder in physically abused adolescents. *Journal of American Academy of Child and Adolescent Psychiatry, 33*(3), 305-312.

Perez, C., & Widom, C. S. (1994). Childhood victimization and long term intellectual and academic outcomes. *Child Abuse & Neglect, 18,* 617-633.

Perry, B. (1997). Incubated in terror: Neurodevelopmental factors in the "cycle of violence." In J. D. Osofsky (Ed.), *Children in a violent society* (pp. 124-149). New York: Guilford.

Pianta, R., Egeland, B., & Erickson, M. F. (1989). The antecedents of maltreatment: Results of the mother-child interaction research project. In D. Cicchetti & V. Carlson (Eds.), *Child maltreatment: Theory and research on the causes and consequences of child abuse and neglect* (pp. 203-253). New York: Cambridge University Press.

Reid, J. B., Kavenaugh, K., & Baldwin, D. V. (1987). Abusive parents' perceptions of child problem behavior: An example of parental bias. *Journal of Abnormal Psychology, 15,* 457-466.

Rieder, C., & Cicchetti, D. (1989). Organizational perspective on cognitive control functioning and cognitive-affective balance in maltreated children. *Developmental Psychology, 25,* 382-393.

Riggs, S., Alario, A. J., & McHorney, C. (1990). Health risk behaviors and attempted suicide in adolescents who report prior maltreatment. *Journal of Pediatrics, 116,* 815-821.

Rogosch, F., Cicchetti, D., & Abre, J. L. (1995). The role of child maltreatment in early deviations in cognitive and affective processing abilities and later peer relationships problems. *Development and Psychopathology, 7*(4), 591-609.

Roth, S., Newman, E., Pelcovitz, D., van der Kolk, B., & Mandel, F. S. (1997). Complex PTSD in victims exposed to sexual and physical abuse: Results from the *DSM-IV* field trial for posttraumatic stress disorder. *Journal of Traumatic Stress, 10*(4), 539-555.

Salmon, P., & Calderbank, S. (1996). The relationship of childhood physical and sexual abuse to adult illness behavior. *Journal of Psychosomatic Research, 40*(3), 329-336.

Salzinger, S., Feldman, R. S., Hammer, M., & Rosario, M. (1991). Risk for physical child abuse and the personal consequences for its victims. *Criminal Justice and Behavior, 18,* 64-81.

Salzinger, S., Feldman, R. S., Hammer, M., & Rosario, M. (1993). The effects of physical abuse on children's social relationships. *Child Development, 64*(1), 169-187.

Salzinger, S., Kaplan, S., Pelcovitz, D., Samit, C., & Krieger, R. (1984). Parent and teacher assessment of children's behavior in child maltreating families. *Journal of the American Academy of Child Psychiatry, 23,* 458-464.

Salzinger, S., Samit, C., Krieger, R., Kaplan, S., & Kaplan, T. (1986). A controlled study of the life events of the mothers of maltreated children in suburban families. *Journal of the American Academy of Child Psychiatry, 25,* 419-426.

Sankey, C. C., Elmer, E., Halechko, A. D., & Schulberg, P. (1985). The development of abused and high-risk infants in different treatment modalities: Residential versus in-home care. *Child Abuse & Neglect, 9,* 237-243.

Schindler, F., & Arkowitz, H. (1986). The assessment of mother-child interactions in physically abusive and non-abusive families. *Journal of Family Violence, 1,* 247-257.

Schneider-Rosen, K., & Cicchetti, D. (1984). The relationship between affect and cognition in maltreated infants: Quality of attachment and the development of visual self-recognition. *Child Development, 55,* 648-658.

Sedlak, A. J., & Broadhurst, D. D. (1996). *Executive summary of the Third National Incidence Study of Child Abuse and Neglect.* Washington, DC: U.S. Department of Health and Human Services.

Shields, A., & Cicchetti, D. (1998). Reactive aggression among maltreated children: The contributions of attention and emotion dysregulation. *Journal of Clinical Child Psychology, 27*(4), 381-395.

Shields, A. M., Cicchetti, D., & Ryan, R. M. (1994). The development of emotional and behavioral self-regulation and social competence among maltreated school-age children. *Development and Psychopathology, 6,* 57-75.

Silovsky, J. F., Valle, L. A., & Chaffin, M. (1999, June). *Group treatment for children who have been physically abused or witnessed family violence.* Paper presented at the 7th Annual Colloquium of the American Professional Society on the Abuse of Children, San Antonio, TX.

Silverman, A. B., Reinherz, H. Z., & Giaconia, R. M. (1996). The long-term sequelae of child and adolescent abuse: A longitudinal community study. *Child Abuse & Neglect, 8*(8), 709-723.

Simons, R. L., Whitbeck, L. B., Conger, R. D., & Chyi-In, W. (1991). Intergenerational transmission of harsh parenting. *Developmental Psychology, 27,* 159-171.

Slade, B. B., Steward, M. S., Morrison, T. L., & Abramowitz, S. I. (1984). Locus of control, persistence, and use of contingency information in physically abused children. *Child Abuse & Neglect, 8,* 447-457.

Smith, C., & Thornberry, T. P. (1995). The relationship between childhood maltreatment and adolescent involvement in delinquency. *Criminology, 33,* 451-481.

Stevenson, J. (1999). The treatment of the long-term sequelae of child abuse. *Journal of Child Psychology and Psychiatry, 40*(1), 89-111.

Stovall, G., & Craig, R. J. (1990). Mental representations of physically and sexually abused latency-aged females. *Child Abuse & Neglect, 14,* 233-242.

Straus, M. A. (1994). *Beating the devil out of them: Corporal punishment in American families.* Lexington, MA: Lexington Books.

Straus, M. A., Gelles, R. J., & Steinmetz, S. K. (1980). *Behind closed doors.* New York: Doubleday.

Straus, M. A., Hamby, S. L., Finklehor, D., Moore, D. W., & Runyan, D. (1998). Identifications of child maltreatment with the parent-child conflict tactics scales: Development and psychometric data for a national sample of American parents. *Child Abuse & Neglect, 22*(4), 249-270.

Straus, M. A., & Smith, C. (1990). Family patterns and child abuse. In M. A. Straus & R. J. Gelles (Eds.), *Physical violence in American families: Risk factors and adaptations to violence in 8,145 families* (pp. 258-259). New Brunswick, NJ: Transaction.

Sullivan, P. M., & Knutson, J. F. (1998). The association between child maltreatment and disabilities in a hospital-based epidemiological study. *Child Abuse & Neglect, 22*(4), 271-288.

Susman, E. J., Trickett, P. K., Ianotti, R. J., Hollenbeck, B. E., & Zahn-Walker, C. (1985). Child rearing patterns in depressed, abusive and normal mothers. *American Journal of Orthopsychiatry, 55,* 237-251.

Swenson, C. C., & Kolko, D. J. (2000). Long-term management of the developmental consequences of child physical abuse. In R. M. Reece (Ed.), *Treatment of child abuse* (pp. 135-154). Baltimore: Johns Hopkins University Press.

Szykula, S. A., & Fleischman, M. J. (1985). Reducing out-of-home placements of abused children: Two controlled field studies. *Child Abuse & Neglect, 9*(2), 277-283.

Teicher, M. H., Ito, Y., Glod, C. A., Anderson, S. L., Dumont, N., & Ackerman, E. (1997). Preliminary evidence for abnormal cortical development in physically and sexually abused children using EEG coherence and MCI. In R. Yehuda & A. C. McFarlane (Eds.), *Psychobiology of posttraumatic stress disorder* (Vol. 821, pp. 160-175). New York: New York Academy of Sciences.

Terr, L. C. (1991). Childhood traumas: An outline and overview. *American Journal of Psychiatry, 148,* 10-20.

Trickett, P. K., & Kuczynski, L. (1986). Children's misbehaviors and parental discipline strategies in abusive and nonabusive families. *Developmental Psychology, 22*(1), 115-123.

Urquiza, A. J., & McNeil, C. B. (1996). Parent-child interaction therapy: An intensive dyadic intervention for physically abusive families. *Child Maltreatment: Journal of the American Professional Society on the Abuse of Children, 1*(2), 134-144.

U.S. Department of Health and Human Services. (2000). *Child maltreatment 1998: Reports from the states to the National Child Abuse and Neglect Data System*. Washington, DC: Government Printing Office.

Vondra, J. A., Barnett, D., & Cicchetti, D. (1990). Self-concept, motivation, and competence among pre-schoolers from maltreating and comparison families. *Child Abuse & Neglect, 14*, 525-540.

Walker, E., Downey, G., & Bergman, A. (1989). The effects of parental psychopathology and maltreatment on child behavior: A test of the diathesis-stress model. *Child Development, 60*, 15-24.

Walton, E., Fraser, M. W., Lewis, R. E., & Pecora, P. J. (1993). In-home family-focused reunification: An experimental study. *Child Welfare, 72*(5), 473-487.

Warner, J. D., Malinosky-Rummell, R., & Ellis, J. T., & Hansen, D. J. (1990, November). *An examination of demographic and treatment variables associated with session attendance of maltreating families*. Paper presented at the annual conference of the Association for the Advancement of Behavior Therapy, San Francisco.

Webster-Stratton, C. (1985). Comparison of abusive and nonabusive families with conduct-disordered children. *American Journal of Orthopsychiatry, 55*, 59-68.

Webster-Stratton, C. (1990). Stress: A potential disrupter of parent perceptions and family interactions. *Journal of Clinical Child Psychology, 19*(4), 302-312.

Wesch, D., & Lutzker, J. R. (1991). A comprehensive 5-year evaluation of Project 12-Ways: An ecobehavioral program for treating and preventing child abuse and neglect. *Journal of Family Violence, 6*, 17-35.

Westman, J. C. (1994). *Licensing parents: Can we prevent child abuse and neglect?* New York: Insight.

Whipple, E. E., & Richey, C. A. (1997). Crossing the line from physical discipline to child abuse: How much is too much? *Child Abuse & Neglect, 21*(5), 431-444.

Whipple, E. E., & Webster-Stratton, C. (1991). The role of parental stress in physically abusive families. *Child Abuse & Neglect, 15*, 279-291.

Whipple, E. E., & Wilson, S. R. (1996). Evaluation of a parent education and support program for families at risk of physical child abuse. *Families in Society, 77*(4), 227-239.

Whiteman, M., Fanshel, D., & Grundy, J. F. (1987). Cognitive-behavioral interventions aimed at anger of parents at risk of child abuse. *Social Work, 32*(6), 469-474.

Whittaker, J., Kinney, J., Tracy, E. M., & Booth, C. (1990). *Reaching high-risk families: Intensive family preservation in human services*. New York: Aldine.

Widom, C. S. (1989). Does violence beget violence? A critical examination of the literature. *Psychological Bulletin, 106*, 3-28.

Widom, C. S., Ireland, T. O., & Glynn, P. J. (1995). Alcohol abuse in abused and neglected children followed-up: Are they at increased risk? *Journal of Studies on Alcohol, 56*(2), 207-217.

Widom, C. S., & Kuhns, J. B. (1996). Childhood victimization and subsequent risk for promiscuity, prostitution, and teenage pregnancy: A prospective study. *American Journal of Public Health, 86*, 1607-1612.

Willett, J. B., Ayoub, C. C., & Robinson, D. (1991). Using growth modeling to examine systematic differences in growth: An example of change in the functioning of families at risk of maladaptive parenting, child abuse, or neglect. *Journal of Consulting and Clinical Psychology, 59*, 38-47.

Wolfe, D. (1987). *Child abuse: Implications for child development and psychopathology*. Newbury Park, CA: Sage.

Wolfe, D. (1999). *Child abuse: Implications for child development and psychopathology* (2nd ed.). Thousand Oaks, CA: Sage.

Wolfe, D., Edwards, B., Manion, I., & Koverola, C. (1988). Early intervention for parents at risk for child abuse and neglect: A preliminary report. *Journal of Consulting & Clinical Psychology, 56*, 40-47.

Wolfe, D., Fairbanks, J. A., Kelly, J. A., & Bradlyn, A. S. (1983). Child abusive parents' physiological responses to stressful and non-stressful behavior in children. *Behavioral Assessment, 5*, 363-371.

Wolfe, D., Werkele, C., Reitzel-Jaffe, D., & Lefebvre, L. (1998). Factors associated with abusive relationships among maltreated and monmaltreated youth. *Development and Psychopathology, 10*, 61-85.

Youngblade, L. M., & Belsky, J. (1990). Social and emotional consequences of child maltreatment. In R. T. Ammerman & M. Hersen (Eds.), *Children at risk: An evaluation of factors contributing to child abuse and neglect* (pp. 109-140). New York: Plenum.

Zingraff, M. T., Leiter, J., Myers, M. A., & Johnsen, M. C. (1993). Child maltreatment and youthful problem behavior. *Criminology, 31*, 173-202.

3

Sexual Abuse of Children

LUCY BERLINER

DIANA M. ELLIOTT

Incidents and Characteristics of Abuse

Sexual abuse involves any sexual activity with a child where consent is not or cannot be given (Berliner, 2000; Finkelhor, 1979). This includes sexual contact that is accomplished by force or threat of force, regardless of the age of the participants, and all sexual contact between an adult and a child, regardless of whether there is deception or the child understands the sexual nature of the activity. Sexual contact between an older and a younger child also can be abusive if there is a significant disparity in age, development, or size, rendering the younger child incapable of giving informed consent. The sexually abusive acts may include sexual penetration, sexual touching, or noncontact sexual acts such as exposure or voyeurism.

All states have laws prohibiting sexual abuse of children (Myers, 1998). Each state individually defines and labels prohibited activities, and thus criminal statutes vary from state to state. Child abuse statutes usually define sexually abusive behavior quite broadly but sometimes extend jurisdiction only to acts committed by caretakers. States identify an age that an individual can consent to sexual contact, usually between 14 and 18 years. Sexual contact between an adult and a minor under the age of consent is illegal. In addition, incest is generally illegal regardless of age or consent. Criminal statutes also apply to teenagers. Even younger children can be prosecuted for sexual abuse, but it must be established that the offending child was capable of forming the intent to commit a crime.

Rates of Sexual Abuse

The precise incidence and prevalence of sexual abuse in the general population are not known. It is difficult to establish incidence rates because most sexual abuse is not reported at the time it occurs (e.g., Finkelhor, Hotaling, Lewis, & Smith, 1990). In addition, it is impossible to know exactly how many cases of sexual abuse are reported on an annual basis nationwide. Because there is no national reporting system for crimes against children, official crime and child abuse statistics tend to be unreliable. Child abuse figures vary by state definitions and sometimes do not include sexual abuse committed by nonfamily members. Currently, the best mechanism for determining the scope of child sexual abuse is through retrospective surveys of adult nonclinical populations. Such surveys show considerable variability that can be best explained by differences in research methodology. The population surveyed, survey method, type and number of screening questions, and definitions of sexual abuse all influence the reported figures of abuse (Finkelhor, 1994).

Finkelor (1994) reviewed the various retrospective prevalence surveys with adults conducted in the United States and Canada and concluded that at least 20% to 25% of women and from 5% to 15% of men experience contact sexual abuse. Most studies of the impact of sexual abuse on adult populations find similar percentages. Two surveys of nationally representative samples of adolescents have been conducted that inquired about sexual and physical assault experiences (Finkelhor & Dziuba-Leatherman, 1994; Kilpatrick & Saunders, 1999). In these studies, relatively lower rates of sexual abuse were reported, but because the children were not yet 18, there was still an opportunity for victimization to occur. In addition, very few of these children reported intrafamilial abuse. It is quite possible that the research method of telephone interviews in which parents had to give the consent for children to participate inhibited them from reporting certain kinds of experiences.

Recent research on the impact of trauma on memory suggests that estimates of abuse rates based on self-report of adults may underestimate its prevalence. Two prospective longitudinal studies of adults with documented childhood sexual abuse histories found that more than 30% of the respondents did not report those early experiences when questioned (Widom & Morris, 1997; Williams, 1994). Although some of the nonreporting may be due to a reluctance to reveal remembered abuse, Williams's (1994) analysis of the responses of women who did not report documented abuse cases strongly suggests that they did not recall what had happened, given that more than half of these subjects reported *other* sexually abusive experiences in childhood.

Reporting of sexual abuse increased significantly in the late 1980s and the early 1990s. In recent years, however, there has been a substantial decline in reports to child abuse authorities (Jones & Finkelhor, 2001). A majority of states have seen decreases of up to 30% since 1994. The reasons for this change are unclear but may be the result of actual declines in the rate of sexual abuse or changes in policies and practices with regard to screening reports. Regarding the former, crime rates in general have been declining, and this trend may also be reflected in sexual abuse cases, or prevention efforts may have had an effect. Alternatively, given that "reported" cases reflect the number that has been accepted for investigation, the decrease in reported rates may reflect more stringent criteria applied to accepting cases for investigation.

Characteristics of Sexual Abuse Experiences

The reported characteristics of sexual abuse vary depending on the data source. For example, child abuse reporting systems and clinical programs tend to overrepresent intrafamilial cases. Based on general population surveys (e.g., Finkelhor, 1994; Saunders, Kilpatrick, Hanson, Resnick, & Walker, 1999), abuse by parent figures (parents and stepparents) constitutes between 6% and 16% of all cases, and abuse by any relative comprises more than one third of cases. In these nonclinical samples, teenagers represent up to 40% of offenders, and strangers account for a relatively small proportion (5%-15%), with the remainder of cases involving individuals known to the child or family. In clinical samples, parent figures comprise between a quarter and a third of the offenders and all relatives about one half (e.g., Elliott & Briere, 1994; Gomes-Schwartz, Horowitz, & Cardarelli, 1990; Ruggiero, McLeer, & Dixon, 2000). In both clinical and nonclinical samples, the vast majority of offenders are male, although boys are more likely than girls to be abused by women (20% vs. 5%) (Finkelhor & Russell, 1984), and 40% of the reported cases of day care sexual abuse involve female offenders (Finkelhor, Williams, & Burns, 1988).

Based on general population surveys, abuse by parent figures (parents and stepparents) constitutes between 6% and 16% of all cases, and abuse by any relative comprises more than one third of cases.

Multiple abuse episodes of sexual abuse are very common, occurring in up to half of the cases in nonclinical samples (e.g., Saunders et al., 1999) and in up to three fourths of children in clinical samples (Conte & Schuerman, 1987; Elliott & Briere, 1994; Ruggiero et al., 2000). Completed or attempted oral, anal, or vaginal penetration occurs in about one fourth of nonclinical subjects (Finkelhor, 1994) and in half or more of clinical samples (Elliott & Briere, 1994; Gomes-Schwartz et al., 1990; Ruggiero et al., 2000). The mean age for sexual abuse is approximately 9 years old, with a range from infancy to 17 years.

In clinical samples, both sex and race are associated with some differences in abuse experiences and circumstances. Compared with girls, boys are older at onset of victimization, more likely to be abused by nonfamily members, and more likely to be abused by women and by offenders who are known to have abused other children (e.g., Faller, 1989a, 1989b; Holmes & Slap, 1998). In the few available studies specifically examining ethnicity, differences in the type and length of abuse experience, offender relationship, family characteristics, and family response are associated with ethnic background (Huston, Parra, Prihoda, & Foulds, 1995; Mennen, 1995; Rao, DiClemente, & Ponton, 1992; Sanders-Phillips, Moisan, Wadlington, Morgan, & English, 1995). It is not entirely clear what accounts for these ethnic variations. They may be the result of reporting bias, differences in family configurations or cultural practices, or simply an ar-

tifact of the samples in these studies. Nonclinical African American and Caucasian women have similar rates of child sexual abuse (Wyatt, 1985). The rates for Asian women are somewhat lower, and Hispanic women are at increased risk for incestuous abuse (Russell, 1984).

Families with a child who has been sexually abused are thought to have certain characteristics. Empirical studies have found that families of both incest and nonincest sexual abuse victims are reported as less cohesive, more disorganized, and generally more dysfunctional than families of nonabused individuals (Elliott, 1994; Hoagwood & Stewart, 1989; Madonna, Van Scoyk, & Jones, 1991; Mannarino & Cohen, 1996a, 1996b). The areas most often identified as problematic in incest cases are problems with communication, a lack of emotional closeness and flexibility, and social isolation (e.g., Dadds, Smith, Weber, & Robinson, 1991). Although it appears that families in which incest has occurred do exhibit greater dysfunction, it is possible that the pathology is at least as much a result of the incest as the cause (Briere, 2000a; Briere & Elliott, 1993).

Nonclinical African American and Caucasian women have similar rates of child sexual abuse; the rates for Asian women are somewhat lower, and Hispanic women are at increased risk for incestuous abuse.

Some risk factors for sexual abuse have been identified. Girls are at higher risk for sexual abuse than boys. Both males and females are at increased risk if they have lived without one of their natural parents, have a mother who is unavailable, or perceive their family life as unhappy (Finkelhor & Baron, 1986a, 1986b; Finkelhor et al., 1990; Holmes & Slap, 1998). There is speculation that children who have a psychological or cognitive vulnerability also may be at increased risk for sexual abuse (e.g., Tharinger, Horton, & Millea, 1990). The reported incidence of sexual abuse among children with a disability is 1.75 times the rate for children with no disability (National

Center on Child Abuse and Neglect [NCCAN], 1993). However, there are insufficient data to confirm whether this is a reporting phenomenon or an actual increased vulnerability (Newman, Christopher, & Berry, 2000). Unlike other forms of child abuse, sexual abuse does not appear to be related to socioeconomic status.

Sexual abuse is accomplished in a variety of ways. In some cases, even though the offender has a relationship with the child, the victimization occurs without warning. More typically, offenders engage in a gradual process of sexualizing the relationship over time (Berliner & Conte, 1990). Offenders may conceal the sexual nature of the activity by characterizing it as nonsexual (e.g., sex education, hygiene) or may encourage the child to consider the relationship as mutual. Repeat offenders generally calculate and plan their approach to victimizing children, often employing elaborate strategies to involve the children, maintain their cooperation, and prevent reporting (Conte, Wolfe, & Smith, 1989; Elliott, Browne, & Kilcoyne, 1995; Lang & Frenzel, 1988). In a substantial percentage of cases, offenders use force, threaten the child, or induce fear of injury or death (e.g., Elliott & Briere, 1994; Gomes-Schwartz et al., 1990; Saunders et al., 1999). In other cases, the offender employs emotional coercion, offers tangible rewards, or misuses adult authority.

Disclosing and Reporting Sexual Abuse

Most sexual abuse is neither revealed immediately nor reported to authorities subsequent to disclosure. Studies of clinical and nonclinical populations of adults reveal that fewer than half of victims tell anyone at the time of the abuse, and a large percentage never reveal the victimization until asked for research purposes (Finkelhor et al., 1990; Smith, Elstein, Trost, & Bulkley, 1993). For example, Finkelhor et al. (1990) found that only about 40% of men and women had disclosed the abuse at the time it occurred, 24% of women and 14% of men told at a later time, and 33% of women and 42% of men had never told until the time of data collection. Similarly, Elliott (1993) found that among professional women who were abused as children, immediate disclosures occurred in only 20% of the cases, whereas 40% of the sample had not revealed the

abuse until completing the survey. In retrospective studies, only 6% to 12% of cases are reported to authorities (Elliott, 1993; Russell, 1984; Saunders et al., 1999).

Underreporting may be related to the nature of the acts, not just to the fact that the victims are children. In general, crimes against children are less likely to be reported to the criminal justice system than crimes against adults even when they are comparably serious in nature (Finkelhor, Wolack, & Berliner, 2001). However, the National Crime Victimization Survey, which includes children older than 12 years, found that although sexual assault was reported at the lowest rate of all crimes, the rate for adolescents was equivalent to that of adults, about 30% of acknowledged sexual assaults (Finkelhor & Olmrod, 2000).

Research conducted in clinical and forensic samples of children similarly suggests that there is typically a delay in disclosure. For example, Gomes-Schwartz et al. (1990) found that only 24% of victims reported within a week of the last episode, and some waited years. Many times the victimization comes to light because of an unintentional report from the child. Sometimes, for example, children confide in a friend without intending an official report. Abuse may also be uncovered because of suspicious behaviors or statements, medical findings of injury or infection, or because a witness interrupted the abuse, pornographic pictures were found, or an offender confessed.

When children do disclose, they are most likely to tell a parent, usually their mother (Sauzier, 1989). Overall, in 45% to 75% of all cases that come to the attention of authorities, the precipitating event is something other than the child's report of abuse (Elliott & Briere, 1995; Sauzier, 1989; Sorensen & Snow, 1991). It has been noted that even when children who have been abused are questioned directly, some may deny the abuse initially. Following an initial report, some children recant. Summit (1983, 1994) described a child sexual abuse accommodation syndrome (CSAAS) that consists of several dynamics that can affect children's ability to reveal their abuse. These dynamics (secrecy, helplessness, entrapment, and accommodation) can lead to delayed, unconvincing disclosure or retraction. In a study of children with sexually transmitted diseases, 43% did not acknowledge sexual contact when interviewed (Lawson & Chaffin, 1992), although eventually most children did reveal abuse. Similarly,

Elliott and Briere (1994) found that 10% of children in a forensic sample in which there was strong evidence of abuse denied it. Studies report that between 4% and 22% of children recant true allegations of sexual abuse at some point (Elliott & Briere, 1994; Jones & McGraw, 1987; Sorensen & Snow, 1991). Children are thought to recant either because they have been subjected to pressure from the offender or family members or because their report has produced negative consequences to themselves or others. Many children report fears about telling or regret the disclosure because of the outcome (Sauzier, 1989). Almost all children believe that telling is the right thing to do to stop abuse and to receive help (Berliner & Conte, 1995).

Although children sometimes do not report actual abuse when asked, it has been demonstrated in samples of children and adult women in treatment settings that they are more likely to report abuse if they are directly asked. A study of child outpatients showed a marked increase in the reported rate of sexual abuse (from 6%-31%) when the children were asked specifically about a possible abuse history (Lanktree, Briere, & Zaidi, 1991). Similarly, Briere and Zaidi (1989) found that the rate of sexual abuse history in adult female psychiatric emergency room patients increased from 6% to 70% after clinicians were instructed to screen for sexual abuse.

Effects of Sexual Abuse

Research conducted over the past two decades indicates that a wide range of psychological and interpersonal problems are more prevalent among those who have been sexually abused than among individuals with no such experiences (e.g., Wolfe & Birt, 1995). Because most studies are retrospective, a definitive causal relationship between such difficulties and sexual abuse cannot usually be established. In a prospective, longitudinal, general population study, however, Boney-McCoy and Finkelhor (1996) found that sexual abuse was associated with posttraumatic stress and depression. Boney-McCoy and Finkelhor controlled for prior symptoms and parent-child relationships. The aggregate of consistent findings in this literature has led many researchers and clinicians to conclude that childhood sexual abuse is a significant risk factor for a variety

of problems, both in the short term (e.g., Beitchman, Zucker, Hood, da Costa, & Akman, 1991; Kendall-Tackett, Williams, & Finkelhor, 1993) and in terms of later adult functioning (e.g., Beitchman et al., 1992; Fergusson, Horwood, & Lynskey, 1996; Mullen, Martin, Anderson, & Romans, 1994).

When sexual abuse causes harm, the harm can be attributed to the fact that sexual abuse is nonconsensual, is frequently developmentally inappropriate, and invariably alters the nature of the relationship within which it occurs. Sexual abuse can be painful, frightening, shame inducing, and confusing and can lead to responses in childhood that interfere with normal developmental processes and increase the risk for subsequent maladjustment in adult life.

Effects on Children

A body of empirical literature specifically describing the effects of sexual abuse on child victims has now accumulated. Unlike studies of adults that have been conducted with nonclinical as well as clinical samples, with few exceptions, information on children is derived from clinical samples, virtually all of which have some involvement with child protection or criminal justice authorities. Thus, what is discussed below regarding the effects of sexual abuse on children is based primarily on clinical data. Consistent with the clinical data, however, studies of nonclinical samples of teenagers find that victims of sexual abuse report higher rates of emotional and behavioral problems than their nonabused peers (Boney-McCoy & Finkelhor, 1995; Hibbard, Ingersoll, & Orr, 1990; Kilpatrick & Saunders, 1999).

Emotional distress and dysfunction. As a group, sexually abused children do not always self-report clinically significant levels of emotional distress. Most studies find, however, that they have more depressive symptoms and more anxiety or lower self-esteem than nonabused comparison children (Boney-McCoy & Finkelhor, 1995; Gidycz & Koss, 1989; McLeer et al., 1998; Mannarino & Cohen, 1996a, 1996b; Stern, Lynch, Oates, O'Toole, & Cooney, 1995). Emotional disturbance has been found on personality tests (e.g., Basta & Peterson, 1990; German, Habernicht, & Futcher, 1990) and projective measures (Stovall &

Craig, 1990). Projective measures may pick up aspects of functioning that children cannot or do not reveal symptomatically. For example, children who were reported by parents to have internalizing distress but did not themselves report depression revealed depressive symptomatology on their Rorschach responses (Shapiro, Leifer, Martone, & Kassem, 1990).

Sexually abused children in treatment settings, compared with their nonabused clinical cohorts, tend to have different kinds of problems. For example, they have been found to be more likely than their nonabused peers to be diagnosed with depression, exhibit suicidal behavior (Lanktree et al., 1991), have lower self-esteem (Cavaiola & Schiff, 1989; Wozencraft, Wagner, & Pellegrin, 1991), and have greater symptoms of anxiety (Kolko, Moser, & Weldy, 1988). When sexually abused girls from dysfunctional families are compared with nonabused girls from similarly disturbed families, the abused girls have lower self-esteem, more internalized aggression, and poorer relationships with their mothers (Hotte & Rafman, 1992).

Post-trauma effects. Trauma-specific symptoms are those associated with the diagnosis of posttraumatic stress disorder (PTSD) (American Psychiatric Association, 1994) and include reexperiencing, avoidance/numbing, and hyperarousal. Sexually abused children consistently report higher levels of these symptoms in both nonclinical and clinical samples (Boney-McCoy & Finkelhor, 1995; Briere, 1996a, 1996b; McLeer et al., 1998). More than one third of children meet diagnostic criteria for PTSD (Dubner & Motta, 1999; Kilpatrick & Saunders, 1999; McLeer et al., 1988; Ruggiero et al., 2000), and a majority exhibit some of the symptoms (McLeer, Deblinger, Henry, & Orvaschel, 1992; McLeer et al., 1998; Wolfe, Gentile, & Wolfe, 1989).

Sexually abused children appear more likely than other maltreated children to receive the diagnosis of PTSD (Deblinger, McLeer, Atkins, Ralphe, & Foa, 1989; Dubner & Motta, 1999).

Behavioral problems. On standard measures of child behavioral problems, sexually abused children are reported by their parents to have more behavioral problems than nonabused children, although the problems do not always reach clinically significant lev-
els (e.g., Gomes-Schwartz et al., 1990; Mannarino & Cohen, 1996a, 1996b; Stern et al., 1995). Maternal distress and lack of support for the child appear to be associated with reporting higher levels of child behavior problems (Everson, Hunter, Runyan, Edelsohn, & Coulter, 1989; Wind & Silvern, 1992). Adolescents who have been sexually abused are more likely than nonvictims to run away from home, use drugs, and be bulimic (Hibbard et al., 1990); report having trouble with a teacher (Boney-McCoy & Finkelhor, 1995); and have substance abuse disorders (Kilpatrick & Saunders, 1999). Teenage mothers with a history of sexual abuse are more likely to abuse their children or have them taken away by child protective services (Boyer & Fine, 1991).

A specific effect of sexual abuse is increased sexual behavior. Samples of sexually abused children are consistently reported to have more sexual behavior problems than samples of nonabused children (e.g., Friedrich et al., 2001; Mannarino & Cohen, 1996a, 1996b). In addition, the increased sexualized behavior appears more specifically related to sexual abuse, with sexually abused children reported to have more sexual behavior than clinical comparisons of neglected, physically abused, and psychiatrically disturbed children (Adams, McClellan, Douglass, McCurry, & Storck, 1995; Cosentino, Meyer-Bahlburg, Alpert, Weinberg, & Gaines, 1995; Friedrich, Jaworski, Huxsahl, & Bengston, 1997; Kendall-Tackett et al., 1993). Sexually abused children tend to engage in more sexual behavior that is associated with genital sexual activity, such as mimicking intercourse and inserting objects in the vagina or anus (Friedrich et al., 2001). In older children, girls are more likely to engage in hypersexual behavior, whereas boys are more likely to engage in genital exposure or sexual coercion, when compared with nonabused children (Adams et al., 1995). However, only a third of sexually abused children exhibit sexual behavior problems (Friedrich, 1993) and other variables, including family nudity, exposure to sexual activity, and family stressors, increase sexual behavior in nonabused children.

Interpersonal consequences. Sexually abused children tend to be less socially competent than nonabused children (Mannarino & Cohen, 1996a, 1996b; Stern et al., 1995). As a group, they perceive themselves as different from others and tend to be less trusting of those in their immediate environment (Mannarino, Cohen, & Berman, 1994). On projective measures, sexually abused children exhibit more disturbed object relations than their nonabused peers (Ornduff, Freedenfeld, Kelsey, & Critelli, 1994; Stovall & Craig, 1990).

Cognitive difficulties and distortions. Cognitive functioning may be affected by sexual abuse experiences. Einbender and Friedrich (1989) reported greater cognitive impairment in a sample of sexually abused girls, and Rust and Troupe (1991) found sexually abused children to have deficits in school achievement.

Negative or distorted attributions and perceptions have been frequently observed clinically, but the rates at which these symptoms occur in sexually abused children are not well documented. Contrary to a common clinical lore that self-blame is ubiquitous, empirical studies find that most children do not blame themselves for what happened but rather hold offenders responsible for the abuse (e.g., Hunter, Goodwin, & Wilson, 1992). There is evidence that sexually abused children as a group tend to perceive themselves as different from peers and have heightened self-blame for negative events and reduced interpersonal trust (Mannarino et al., 1994). Guilt, self-blame, shame, and negative attributional style, when present, are associated with more severe outcomes as discussed below.

Contrary to a common clinical lore that self-blame is ubiquitous, empirical studies find that most children do not blame themselves for what happened but rather hold offenders responsible for the abuse.

Course of symptoms. The few available studies that document children's symptoms over time reveal a general pattern of improvement for most children (e.g., Kendall-Tackett et al., 1993). However, in a study that followed children for 5 years following abuse, there were no significant changes in depression, self-esteem, or behavior problems; approximately equal numbers of children improved and deteriorated (Tebbutt, Swanston, Oates, & O'Toole, 1997). Over-

all, between 10% and 24% of child victims either do not improve or deteriorate (Berliner & Saunders, 1996; Kendall-Tackett et al., 1993). Gomes-Schwartz et al. (1990) found that abused children who were initially least symptomatic had more problems at 18 months than did their initially more highly symptomatic peers. Friedrich and Reams (1987) noted in a series of case studies that symptoms tended to fluctuate over time rather than improve in linear fashion. In a longitudinal study of children in abuse-focused therapy, Lanktree and Briere (1995) found that symptoms tended to subside at differential rates. Anxiety and depression abated fairly quickly; dissociation, sexual concerns, and posttraumatic stress took a longer time before significant attenuation in distress was reported by children. These data suggest that in many cases, even with intervention, many children continue to have significant symptomatology.

Effects on Adults

Sexual abuse appears to constitute a major risk factor for a variety of problems in adult life (Browne & Finkelhor, 1986; Finkelhor et al., 1990; Neumann, Houskamp, Pollock, & Briere, 1996; Polusny & Follette, 1996). The effects of abuse on adult living are not uniform, however. Some survivors report no or very few symptoms, whereas others experience life as overwhelming in many domains. Of the latter group, those who seek treatment often present with a complex array of difficulties and concerns (e.g., Briere, Woo, McRae, Foltz, & Sitzman, 1997; Gladstone, Parker, Wilhelm, Mitchell, & Austin, 1999; Lombardo & Pohl, 1997). Whether mild or severe, the symptoms evidenced by adult survivors are an extension of those found in children.

Although most studies find a relationship between childhood sexual abuse and psychological problems in adults, one recent meta-analysis of the literature (Rind, Tromovitch, & Bauserman, 1998) concluded that, among university students, this relationship was very small or nonexistent and could be accounted for by other, nonspecific family dysfunction. The authors also suggested that the term *child sexual abuse* should be rephrased as "adult-child sex" (p. 45) to eliminate the "negative value loadings" of the word *abuse*. Among the various criticisms of this article are as follows: (a) its generalization from (relatively high-functioning) university students to all sexual abuse survivors, (b) the use of statistical procedures that have been criticized by others as especially conservative in identifying possible abuse effects (e.g., Briere & Elliott, 1993), and (c) Rind et al.'s (1998) minimization of abuse effect sizes that are roughly equivalent to the relationship found between smoking and the development of lung cancer (Ondersma, Chaffin, & Berliner, 1999). What Rind et al. do appropriately emphasize is the complex relationship between dysfunctional family dynamics and childhood sexual abuse, such that the abuse may be more likely to occur in—and, potentially, influence the development of—disturbed families.

Research on the long-term effects of sexual abuse has tended to focus on the sequelae in women. Studies that include males suggest that sexual abuse has lasting impacts on adult adjustment for both genders, although a number of studies find more severe effects in females (e.g., Neumann et al., 1996; Rind et al., 1998). Some of this sex difference may reflect a tendency for males to cope with their abuse by denying it or externalizing their distress (e.g., increased anger and aggression toward others) and a tendency for females to express distress more directly and to employ greater internalization in coping (e.g., M. P. Mendel, 1995; S. Mendel, 1995; Rosen & Martin, 1998).

Emotional distress. As with sexually abused children, adult survivors report more dysphoria than do their nonabused peers. Depression is the most frequently reported symptom and has been documented in a variety of clinical and nonclinical samples (Briere & Runtz, 1993; Browne & Finkelhor, 1986; Polusny & Follette, 1996).

Sexual abuse victims may have as much as a fourfold greater lifetime risk for major depression than do individuals with no such abuse history (Stein, Golding, Siegel, Burnam, & Sorenson, 1988). The pervasiveness of depression among some survivors is thought to be the cumulative effects of chronic betrayal, disempowerment, feelings of guilt and helplessness, and low self-esteem (Finkelhor & Browne, 1985; Peters, 1988). Thus, it should not be surprising that increased suicidal behaviors have been linked to sexual abuse. In two studies of outpatient women, for example, patients with an abuse history were twice as likely to have attempted suicide as were their nonabused

peers (Briere & Runtz, 1987; Briere & Zaidi, 1989). In a community sample, approximately 16% of survivors had attempted suicide, whereas less than 6% of their nonabused cohorts had made a similar attempt (Saunders, Villeponteaux, Lipovsky, Kilpatrick, & Veronen, 1992). A number of other studies have demonstrated significant relationships between childhood sexual abuse and depression or depressive features (e.g., Levitan, Parikh, Lesage, Hegadoren, & Adams, 1998; Weiss, Longhurst, & Mazure, 1999).

Anxiety is a well-documented sequel of sexual abuse (Gold, Lucenko, Elhai, Swingle, & Sellers, 1999; Lombardo & Pohl, 1997). In the general population, survivors are more likely than nonabused individuals to meet the criteria for generalized anxiety disorder, phobias, panic disorder, or obsessive-compulsive disorder, with sexual abuse survivors having up to 5 times a greater likelihood of being diagnosed with at least one anxiety disorder than their nonabused peers (Saunders et al., 1992; Stein et al., 1988). Adults with child abuse histories may manifest their anxiety in multiple dimensions: (a) cognitively (e.g., through excessive preoccupation with and hypervigilance to danger) (Briere, 2000b; Jehu, 1988; Wenninger & Ehlers, 1998), (b) with classically conditioned responses (e.g., sexual dysfunction) (Jarvis & Copeland, 1997; McCabe & Cobain, 1998), and (c) somatically, as a natural extension of sympathetic nervous system hyperarousal (e.g., headaches, gastrointestinal problems, back and pelvic pain, and muscle tension) (Maynes & Feinauer, 1994; Salmon & Calderbank, 1996; Springs & Friedrich, 1992).

In addition to chronic anxiety and depression, problems with anger often are reported by adult survivors of child sexual abuse. Survivors frequently report chronic irritability, unexpected feelings of rage, and fear of their own anger (Briere & Runtz, 1987; Lisak, 1993; Scott & Day, 1996). Such feelings can be expressed internally through self-blame and self-injury (Briere & Gil, 1998) or externally, resulting in the perpetration of violence against others (Duncan & Williams, 1998). The rage experienced by some survivors can intensify when it is restimulated by interpersonal events reminiscent of the original abuse scenario.

Posttrauma effects. Psychological distress that occurs in reaction to a traumatic event often manifests itself through (a) nightmares, flashbacks, and intrusive thoughts of abuse; (b) avoidance and numbing; and (c) autonomic hyperarousal. Child sexual abuse has been shown to result in PTSD in as many as 36% of adult survivors, depending on whether they were in clinical or nonclinical samples (Rodriguez, Ryan, Van de Kemp, & Foy, 1997; Saunders et al., 1992; Saunders et al., 1999). PTSD rates for sexual abuse survivors appeared to increase when the abuse involved force or violence, when it included penetration, and when it involved multiple incidents of abuse over time (Briggs & Joyce, 1997; Rowan & Foy, 1994; Saunders et al., 1992). Although many adult survivors do not meet the *DSM-IV* (American Psychiatric Association, 1994) criteria for PTSD, the experience of both intrusive and avoidant symptoms associated with PTSD is common (Elliott & Briere, 1994). The reliving of the original abuse experience (whether through flashbacks, intrusive thoughts, or nightmares) often is not perceived as under the control of the adult survivor and is apt to reinforce the feelings of helplessness and victimization of the original experience.

Along with PTSD, dissociation appears to be a common response to highly traumatic events and often is seen in adult survivors of sexual abuse (Chu & Dill, 1990; Elliott & Briere, 1992; Zanarini, Ruser, Frankenburg, Hennen, & Gunderson, 2000). This relationship, however, is a complex one and may include physical abuse effects as well (Mulder, Beautrais, Joyce, & Fergusson, 1998). Dissociation is thought to be the psyche's defense against the complete awareness of abuse-related thoughts, feelings, and behaviors (Kluft, 1985; Putnam, 1990). For victims of especially severe abuse, the trauma may be overwhelming, making it difficult for the survivor to fully integrate the events cognitively and thus reinforcing a mechanism that reduces complete awareness of the trauma. The ability of the survivor to dissociate abuse-specific thoughts, affects, and memories allows for the reduction of the acute and continuing impacts of victimization by changing the nature or extent of abuse-related pain (Shengold, 1989).

Along with psychic numbing, depersonalization, and disengagement, dissociation may take the form of amnesia for the abuse. According to *DSM-IV* (American Psychiatric Association, 1994), amnesia refers to a memory disturbance "characterized by an inability to recall important personal information, usually of a traumatic or stressful nature, that is too extensive to be explained by ordinary forgetfulness" (p. 478). Recent research suggests that a substantial proportion of sexual abuse survivors report partial or complete loss of memory for their abuse experience (Elliott & Briere, 1995; Herman & Harvey, 1997; Williams, 1994). However, not all memory loss is necessarily due to dissociation (Berliner & Briere, 1999; Lindsay & Briere, 1997). It appears that incomplete or absent abuse-related memories may be correlated with maltreatment that began at a particularly early age, was long in duration, or was chronic or violent in nature (Briere & Conte, 1993; Herman & Schatzow, 1987). Incomplete memories for abuse also may be correlated with earlier abuse by a family member (Williams, 1994).

Dissociation of memories superficially may increase the survivor's level of behavioral and psychological functioning by numbing or partitioning off abuse-related affect and recollections (Putnam, 1990; van der Kolk & Kadish, 1987) and thus may be a valuable defense in the presence of acute trauma. However, dissociation may also have negative long-term consequences for adaptive functioning later in life and ultimately may decrease the survivor's capacity for self-care and interfere with adaptive cognitive processes (Briere, 1996a, 1996b, 1996c). Among sexual abuse survivors, for example, the use of avoidant and suppressing strategies as a means of coping with the abuse has been associated with poorer adult psychological adjustment (Leitenberg, Greenwald, & Cado, 1992).

Cognitive distortions. During childhood, internal templates for adult assumptions about self, others, and safety of the environment are created (Cole & Putnum, 1992). Sexual abuse survivors often are raised in intrusive and violent environments. As a result, abuse-related cognitions are common and reflect self-blame, low self-esteem, negative self-attributes, a disbelief in self-efficacy, and a perception of self as helpless and life as dangerous or hopeless (Gold, 1986; Jehu, 1988). Such cognitive disturbance is thought to arise from stigmatization associated with responses to the abuse and the victim's internalization of the assumptions regarding self, the abuser, and society at large (Finkelhor & Browne, 1985).

Clinical writers have stressed the role of the victim's need to make sense of his or her abuse as supporting the development of cognitive distortions (Briere, 1996a, 1996b). The child who is victimized by a caretaker can be thought of as forced into an "abuse dichotomy" when attempting to understand the perpetrator's behavior: "Either he or she is bad or I am the bad one." Because of children's developmental status and their acceptance of social messages regarding parent-child interactions (i.e., the caretaker is necessarily right in disagreements), children may assume that the abusive act is justifiable punishment for some misdeed. This conclusion logically leads to another: "It must be my fault that I am being hurt, and thus it follows that I am as bad as whatever was or is done to me" (Briere, 1989, p. 88). As a result, the survivor may internalize a sense of self-blame and inherent badness that lasts well into adulthood.

Externalized emotional distress. Child abuse can result in a constant challenge to the development and implementation of coping mechanisms because of the level of hyperarousal, emotional pain, and restimulation of abuse memories experienced by many survivors. Thus, any external activity that successfully reduces such internal tension (e.g., through distraction, self-soothing, or anesthesia) is reinforced. These activities include self-mutilatory activities, such as cutting, burning, or hitting oneself or pulling out hair (Briere & Gill, 1998; van der Kolk, Perry, & Herman, 1991; Walsh & Rosen, 1988); using sexual activity during times of intense negative abuse-related affect (Becker, Rankin, & Rickel, 1998; Briere, 1996a, 1996b, 1996c); bingeing and purging to deal with feelings of emptiness (Piran, Lerner, Garfinkel, Kennedy, & Brouillette, 1988; Steiger & Zanko, 1990); and alcohol or substance abuse (Briere et al., 1997; Epstein, Saunders, Kilpatrick, & Resnick, 1998).

These patterns, although potential problems for family members and therapists, are often the survivor's attempt to reduce overwhelming pain and reestablish a sense of internal balance. They are activated most frequently when feelings of anger, anxiety, guilt, intrusion, isolation, or sadness overwhelm the survivor's internal resources. Subsequent to engaging in tension reduction behaviors, survivors often report an initial sense of escape, pleasure, relaxation, or relief. This, however, may be followed by increased feelings of guilt or self-loathing and may precipitate a repeat of the tension re-

duction behavior (Briere, 1996a, 1996b, 1996c).

Interpersonal difficulties. Given the emotional distress, the tendency toward distorted beliefs regarding self and others, the intrusion and destabilization associated with posttraumatic stress, and the often maladaptive efforts to deal with such difficulties experienced by many survivors, interpersonal problems in adulthood are a predictable sequel of childhood sexual abuse. Because the victimization typically occurs in the context of human relationships, sexual abuse can cause a disruption in the normal process of learning to trust, act autonomously, and form stable, secure relationships (Courtois, 1988; Elliott, 1994). Furthermore, the violation and betrayal of boundaries in the context of developing intimacy can create interpersonal ambivalence in many adult survivors.

As adults, female survivors report a greater fear of both men and women (e.g., Briere & Runtz, 1987). Females are more likely to remain single, and once married, they are more likely to divorce or separate from their husbands than are nonabused women (e.g., Russell, 1986). They report having fewer friends (Gold, 1986), less satisfaction in their relationships, greater discomfort and sensitivity, and more maladaptive interpersonal patterns (Bartoi & Kinder, 1998; DiLillo & Long, 1999; Elliott, 1994).

Of the interpersonal sequelae, perhaps the most common complaint of sexual abuse survivors is in the sexual domain. This may take the form of sexual dysfunction (Sarwer & Durlak, 1996), sexual preoccupation (Black & DeBlassie, 1993), fantasies of forced sexual contact (Gold, 1991), or multiple brief, unsafe, or superficial sexual or romantic relationships (Bartoi & Kinder, 1998; Bensley, Eenwyk, & Simmons, 2000; Johnsen & Harlow, 1996). Some women experience revictimization in their adult lives (Messman & Long, 1996; Sorensen, Siegel, Golding, & Stein, 1991).

Mediating Factors

Although the literature summarized earlier is relatively unanimous with regard to the potential negative psychological impacts of childhood sexual abuse, such victimization does not necessarily have an inevitable or massive impact on victims. A careful examination of the data suggests that although child and adult survivors tend, as groups, to have more problems than their nonabused peers, there is no universal or uniform impact of sexual abuse and no guarantee that any given child will develop any posttraumatic responses to sexual abuse that are evident in childhood or adulthood. In a review of empirical studies, up to 40% of sexually abused children did not appear to have any of the expected abuse-related problems (Kendall-Tackett et al., 1993). In part, this reflects the fact that the term *sexual abuse* encompasses a range of abusive behaviors of varying intensity and duration. Children who experience one or a few incidents of less serious sexual abuse committed by a person who is not important in their lives, who then tell a supportive parent who takes protective action, may have only minor and transient distress. The absence of significant longer-term harm should not be taken as evidence that sexual abuse is innocuous, nor should absence of symptoms affect social or legal responses to the crime (Ondersma et al., in press).

Many studies have examined demographic and abuse characteristics as predictors of distress in children and reported surprisingly inconsistent findings. Older children tend to report more internalized distress, whereas parents report more sexual and nonsexual behavior problems in younger children (e.g., Ruggiero et al., 2000; Tebbutt et al., 1997; Wolfe, Sas, & Wekerle, 1994). Boys appear to have more externalizing problems than girls (Holmes & Slap, 1998). These results may be an artifact of the developmental stage and the manner of expressing distress. More serious abuse, involving penetration, longer duration or frequency, closer relationship to offender, or use of force, is sometimes but not always related to outcome (Ruggiero et al., 2000; Stern et al., 1995; Wolfe et al., 1994). The relationships between these variables and outcome appear to be more complex; different characteristics are associated with different outcomes, and some characteristics tend to be correlated with each other (e.g., longer duration with closer offender relationship). For example, Spaccarelli (1995) found that abuse seriousness (as indicated by type of sexual acts and offender relationship) was associated with depression but not anxiety, aggression, or social problems, whereas abuse stress (level of coerciveness, family upset following abuse and nonsupportive family reactions) was correlated only with

aggression. Attributional style and cognitive appraisal are considered among the most important factors in the development of problems in sexually abused children (Celano, 1992; Dalenberg & Jacobs, 1994; Fiering, Taska, & Lewis, 1996; Spaccarelli, 1994). Consistent with evidence that older children are more affected, higher levels of cognitive functioning are also correlated with greater distress (Shapiro, Leifer, Martone, & Kassem, 1992). This may be because older children or those with more sophisticated cognitive functioning are more likely to focus on the implications of having been abused. At least three types of attributions are relevant to abuse outcome: general attributional style, abuse-related attributions, and abuse-specific attributions.

Altered self and other perceptions that are abuse related but not abuse specific are also predictors of increased distress. Sexually abused girls with higher levels of shame have more depression and posttraumatic stress symptoms, as well as lower self-esteem.

A negative general attributional style is associated with poorer outcomes (Kress & Vandenberg, 1998; Mannarino & Cohen, 1996a, 1996b; Wolfe et al., 1989), as are negative appraisals for the abuse experience (Spaccarelli & Fuchs, 1997). As with nonabused children, negative attributions are primarily correlated with internalized distress. Altered self and other perceptions that are abuse related but not abuse specific are also predictors of increased distress. Sexually abused girls with higher levels of shame have more depression and posttraumatic stress symptoms, as well as lower self-esteem (Fiering, Taska, & Lewis, 1998). Mannarino and Cohen (1996a, 1996b) found that for sexually abused girls, feeling different from their peers, perceiving themselves to be less believed, and lacking interpersonal trust were correlated with more psychological distress over time. These relationships were not found in normal controls for whom general attributional style was a more important predictor. Abuse-specific attributions of self-blame or guilt have been associated with depression, lower self-esteem, and anxiety (Fiering et al., 1998; Manion et al., 1998; Morrow, 1991; Wolfe et al., 1989). Guilt and self-blame, when examined separately, have a different relationship to PTSD symptoms; guilt is positively correlated with PTSD symptoms, whereas self-blame is negatively correlated (Wolfe et al., 1994).

Coping style is another relevant variable in explaining differential outcomes (Spaccarelli, 1994). Victims who cope through wishful thinking and tension reduction have more internalized symptomatolgy (Johnson & Kenkel, 1991). Cognitive avoidance is associated with depression and anxiety (Spaccarelli & Fuchs, 1997). On the other hand, aggressive control is correlated with aggression and social problems (Spaccarelli & Fuchs, 1997). An angry coping style is associated with more behavior problems (Chaffin, Wherry, & Dykman, 1997). These results suggest that either internalizing or externalizing coping responses that are overdetermined can lead to maladaptive outcomes.

Family dysfunction not only may increase the likelihood of intrafamilial sexual abuse but also may exacerbate the effects of abuse once it occurs (Alexander, 1992; Courtois, 1988). Families of abused children often have multiple additional problems, including divorce, violence, psychiatric problems, and substance abuse (Elliott & Briere, 1994; Finkelhor & Baron, 1986a, 1986b). Families of sexually abused children have poorer functioning compared with nonabused controls (Mannarino & Cohen, 1997; Stern et al., 1995). Abused children are more distressed if their families have characteristics of negative family functioning (Conte & Schuerman, 1987; Faust, Runyon, & Kenny, 1995; Friedrich, Beilke, & Urquiza, 1987; Mannarino & Cohen, 1996a, 1996b; Tebbutt et al., 1997; Wind & Silvern, 1992). Maternal belief in the child's report of sexual abuse and support following the disclosure have a significant impact on later functioning. Most parents believe their children and take some protective action (Conte & Schuerman, 1987; Elliott & Briere, 1994; Gomes-Schwartz et al., 1990). Research suggests that higher levels of maternal support (Everson et al., 1989; Gomes-Schwartz et al., 1990; Leifer, Shapiro, & Kassem, 1993; Runyan, Hunter, & Everson, 1992; Spaccarelli & Fuchs, 1997) or the availability of a supportive relationship with another adult (Conte & Schuer-

man, 1987) are associated with decreased psychological distress and behavior problems.

In general, the closer the relationship of the offender to the mother, the more likely that support will be compromised. The highest risk of failure to support is found when the offender is a stepfather or the mother's live-in boyfriend (Elliott & Briere, 1994; Gomes-Schwartz et al., 1990). In incest cases, mothers are more likely to believe if the child is younger and has not also been physically abused and when the offender does not have a history of alcohol abuse (Sirles & Franke, 1989). Similarly, in combined incest and nonincest cases, lack of maternal support was predicted by physical abuse or neglect of the victim, spousal abuse, and substance abuse of the caretaker (Elliott & Briere, 1994).

Lack of maternal support also is associated with the impact of intervention. The most important variable predicting out-of-home placement is whether the mother believes and supports the child (Hunter, Coulter, Runyan, & Everson, 1990). Children who lack maternal support are more likely to recant the original allegation of abuse or refuse to report it, even in the face of clear evidence that the abuse occurred (Elliott & Briere, 1994; Lawson & Chaffin, 1992). Finally, maternal support is related to the impact of criminal court testimony on the abused child (Goodman et al., 1992; Whitcomb et al., 1991).

The various activities associated with professional intervention may affect the level of psychological distress. The most consistent finding is that multiple investigative interviews appear to increase symptoms (Berliner & Conte, 1995; Henry, 1997; Tedesco & Schell, 1987). Placement or separation per se is not always distressing (Berliner & Conte, 1995; Henry, 1997). The increased symptomatology noted in children who are taken into protective custody may be secondary to the lack of caretaker support that provoked placement (Runyan, Everson, Edelsohn, Hunter, & Coulter, 1988). Testifying in juvenile court has not been found to increase distress in child victims (Runyan et al., 1988). A small number of studies indicate that testimony in criminal court is associated with increased distress only when it occurs more than once or when cross-examination is lengthy and harsh (Goodman et al., 1992; Whitcomb et al., 1991). In studies, the outcome of the case or whether the children received psychotherapy was not associated with the impact of testifying on psychological distress. Children who are provided with a stress inoculation or other court preparation intervention have reduced psychological distress associated with providing court testimony (Sas, 1991). There is currently no evidence for long-term harm associated with testifying in criminal court per se (Quas, Redlich, Goodman, Ghetti, & Alexander, 1999).

Treatment Issues

Clinical Assessment

Children who have been sexually abused may exhibit both abuse-specific and general psychopathology. The disorder that occurs at the highest rates is PTSD, and the most specific behavior problems are sexual behaviors. These findings suggest that to capture the impact of abuse experiences, it is especially important to use abuse-specific assessment measures. Several standardized self-report checklists are commercially available to assess trauma symptoms in children and adults (Briere, 1997). Parent report checklists are available for sexual behavior (Friedrich, 1997) and trauma symptoms in children (Briere, 1996c). Assessment of attributional style, abuse-related and abuse-specific attributions, and coping styles is clinically relevant because these variables are associated with outcome and are potentially subject to alteration in treatment. Abuse-specific measures are increasingly available for assessing impact in adults (e.g., Briere, 1995). For children, clinical assessment should address the family context. Abuse-specific concerns such as level of support and maternal distress, as well as more general aspects of family functioning, have a direct impact on child functioning and may need to be a focus of clinical intervention.

Treatment for Children

Treatment approaches for sexually abused children have been extensively described in the clinical literature (e.g., Friedrich, 1992, 1995; Gil, 1991, James, 1989). There is also an accumulation of empirical evaluations of interventions with sexually abused and traumatized children. Reviews of the extant treatment outcome literature provide substantial evidence that abuse-specific cognitive behavioral treatment (CBT) is effective for posttraumatic stress reactions (American Academy of Child and Adolescent Psychiatry [AACAP], 1998; Cohen, Berliner, & Mannarino, 2000; Cohen, Berliner, & March, 2000; Finkelhor & Berliner, 1995; Saywitz, Mannarino, Berliner, & Cohen, 2000).

Abuse-specific CBT consists of interventions based on the principles of CBT that have been proven effective for a variety of conditions. Modifications of standard treatments for anxiety, depression, and behavior problems are applied to typical abuse reactions. The importance of targeting abuse-related perceptions and attributions derives from studies showing that they are important predictors for the course of symptoms and for treatment outcome, especially with school-age children (Cohen & Mannarino, 2000; Mannarino & Cohen, 1996a, 1996b).

The components of therapy include (a) psychoeducation, (b) anxiety management, (c) exposure, and (d) cognitive therapy (Cohen, Berliner, & Mannarino, 2000). Psychoeducation involves providing information about the nature of sexual abuse and offenders, as well as the principles of CBT and their application in therapy. Anxiety management refers to teaching children to identify emotional states and how to use various relaxation and emotional and cognitive coping strategies to reduce fearful and anxious responses to abuse memories and reminders. Gradual exposure via talking, drawing, or writing about the abuse experience is designed to decondition automatic negative emotional associations and reduce maladaptive avoidance. Cognitive therapy techniques are used to challenge and replace cognitive distortions about the event or generalized negative attributions about self and others. The goal of therapy is to assist children in successful emotional and cognitive processing of the abuse experience.

The majority of the most rigorous studies have included parents in the treatment protocol (e.g., Celano, Hazzard, Webb, & McCall, 1996; Cohen & Mannarino, 1998; Deblinger, Lippman, & Steer, 1996), although King et al. (2001) reported no additional value to the parental receipt of CBT. The treatment for parents usually contains similar abuse-focused elements as the children's treatments, with additional components designed to reduce parental distress and teach behavior management strategies. Parental involvement in CBT appears to be especially important in reducing behavior problems and in improving parental support and perceptions of the impact on their children. For example, one study compared outcomes if children only, parents only, or children and parents received abuse-specific CBT (Deblinger et al., 1996). Although children's PTSD symptoms improved more when they were the direct recipients of therapy, their depression and behavior problems abated more when the parents had treatment.

Approaches other than CBT have yet to be experimentally evaluated, although it is possible that they are also effective for sexually abused children. In addition, many children present for treatment with an array of problems beyond discrete posttrauma reactions. Children may have more pervasive disturbances in affect regulation, attachment style, and sense of self. An integrated, eclectic approach such as that developed by Friedrich (see Chapter 8, this volume) may be more appropriate in some cases or when CBT does not produce sufficient improvement. Because many children who have been sexually abused have had other adverse experiences and suffer from comorbid disorders, treatment should not exclusively focus on sexual abuse in these instances, and known effective treatments for other conditions should be incorporated into the treatment regimen. In randomized trials, CBT consistently outperforms nonspecific supportive therapy.

Parental involvement in CBT appears to be especially important in reducing behavior problems and in improving parental support and perceptions of the impact on their children.

It seems clear that participation in treatment does not always result in improvement. In one longitudinal study, for example, despite the fact that most children had treatment, 5 years later there were few changes in symptoms, and receiving therapy was not associated with children's status (Tebbutt et al., 1997).

Treatment modality does not appear to be an important factor. Early on, group therapy was considered the preferred approach because it afforded children an opportunity

to reduce stigmatization. The few studies that have compared group with individual or family therapy have not found an advantage to using groups (e.g., Hyde, Bentovim, & Monck, 1995), and individual therapy approaches have been shown to be effective. This does not mean that group therapy should be abandoned, only that it should not be seen as necessary or superior.

Pharmacological treatments are increasingly used with sexually abused and other traumatized children, but their effectiveness has not been shown (AACAP, 1998). A number of open-label trials with antidepressants and alpha-adrenergic or beta-blocker agents suggest these medicines may be helpful (e.g., Famularo, Kinscherff, & Fenton, 1988). However, there are no placebo-controlled trials of medication with abused children. Medication is not recommended as a primary treatment (AACAP, 1998), although it may be a useful adjunct to psychosocial interventions under carefully controlled conditions. Recommendations for decision making regarding medication are available (Donnelly, Amaya-Jackson, & March, 1999).

There are as yet unanswered questions about whether all children need treatment or if abuse-focused CBT is sufficient for those who have clinically significant symptomatology. Because many children exhibit few or moderate posttrauma symptoms, they may not need a full course of treatment, even though most of the tested treatments are relatively brief (10-16 sessions). It is possible that some children may receive adequate benefit from a few sessions that include psychoeducation, coping strategies, and anticipatory guidance about recognizing and responding to problems in the future (Saywitz et al., 2000). Of course, a careful assessment that screens for risk factors known to be associated with more serious outcomes and that considers the possibility that children are engaging in maladaptive avoidance should precede decisions not to engage in ongoing treatment.

At the other end of the spectrum are children who have multiple problems, some or all of which may not be abuse related. Many sexually abused children have comorbid conditions, including anxiety disorders, attention deficit hyperactivity disorder (ADHD), and disruptive behavior problems. Sexual abuse may co-occur with other forms of violence, abuse, and psychiatric conditions in parents. Abused children may have attachment problems. All of these conditions may very well need to be a focus of treatment.

Treatment Issues With Adults

Because of the complex array of symptoms evidenced by many adult survivors of sexual abuse, diagnosis and treatment of such individuals require careful attention to a variety of issues (see Chapter 10, this volume). Survivors in treatment may satisfy diagnostic criteria for several different forms of psychological disturbance, including various affective, dissociative, and somatization disorders; posttraumatic stress; and substance abuse or addiction (Pribor & Dinwiddle, 1992; Saunders et al., 1992; Stein et al., 1988). As a result of this complexity, clinicians run the risk of over- or underdiagnosing or of being distracted by diagnosis per se. A case in point is borderline personality disorder (BPD). The association between a childhood sexual abuse history and the diagnosis of BPD has received particular attention in the literature (Briere & Zaidi, 1989; Paris, Zweig, & Guzder, 1994) because many of the affective and interpersonal sequelae of chronic child abuse are contained in the diagnostic criteria for BPD. On the other hand, a number of studies suggest that childhood sexual abuse is probably not the only (or even the largest) etiological factor in borderline personality disorder (Fossati, Madeddu, & Maffei, 1999). The excessive or reflexive use of this diagnosis with abuse survivors demonstrates that the mere application of a diagnostic label is often not helpful without a contextual understanding of the specific dynamics and phenomenology of the childhood events that underlie it (Briere, 1992; Kroll, 1993).

Because of the many abuse-related problems cited earlier and the prevalence of childhood sexual abuse among clinical groups, a number of authors have elucidated abuse-specific treatment methodologies with adults (e.g., Briere, 1996a, 1996b; Courtois, 1988; Jehu, 1988; M. P. Mendel, 1995; S. Mendel, 1995; Roth & Batson, 1997). Only a few studies, however, have evaluated treatment interventions with adults sexually abused as children. These studies generally indicate that structured, empirically based approaches are helpful (Alexander, Neimeyer, & Follette, 1991; Chard, Weaver, & Resick, 1997; Follette, Alexander, & Follette, 1991; Smucker & Niederee, 1995). These treatment studies suggest that although there is significant benefit with an interpersonal group therapy approach in terms of reducing symptoms of depression and social anxiety, treatment effects are mitigated by the current support system and education of the survivor. Such treatment may be most helpful as an adjunct to individual therapy. Although clinical outcome data are limited at this time, abuse-specific treatment is probably more helpful in the resolution of postabuse trauma than are therapies that overlook the existence and impact of childhood molestation. Because the known effects of childhood sexual victimization are so varied (e.g., posttraumatic symptoms, cognitive distortions, problems with self-development, and disturbed relatedness), abuse-focused therapy must respond to a wide range of clinical problems and employ a variety of treatment interventions rather than rely on any single therapeutic approach or philosophy.

Conclusion

Sexual abuse is a relativity common experience in the lives of children, and sexually abused children typically suffer psychological aftereffects. Of great concern is the fact that such experiences not only produce immediate difficulties but also constitute a significant risk factor for the development of subsequent health, psychiatric, and life-functioning difficulties. Important mediating variables have been identified, including characteristics of the abuse and support from the family. Prospective studies are needed that will allow us to understand the processes and experiences that mitigate or exacerbate abuse effects. In the relative absence of such research, intervention efforts should be designed not only to ameliorate current symptoms but also to promote an emotional and cognitive resolution that may improve the likelihood of a positive outcome in later years.

References

Adams, J., McClellan, J., Douglass, D., McCurry, C., & Storck, M. (1995). Sexually inappropriate behaviors in seriously mentally ill children and adolescents. *Child Abuse & Neglect, 19,* 555-568.

Alexander, P. C. (1992). Application of attachment theory to the study of sexual abuse. *Journal of Consulting and Clinical Psychology, 60,* 185-195.

Alexander, P. C., Neimeyer, R. A., & Follette, V. M. (1991). Group therapy for women sexually abused as children: A controlled study and investigation of individual differences. *Journal of Interpersonal Violence, 6,* 218-231.

American Academy of Child and Adolescent Psychiatry (AACAP). (1998). Practice parameters for the assessment and treatment of children and adolescents with posttraumatic stress disorder. *Journal of the American Academy of Child and Adolescent Psychiatry, 37*(10, Suppl.), 4S-26S.

American Psychiatric Association. (1994). *Diagnostic and statistical manual* (4th ed.). Washington, DC: Author.

Bartoi, M. G., & Kinder, B. N. (1998). Effects of child and adult sexual abuse on adult sexuality. *Journal of Sex and Marital Therapy, 24,* 75-90.

Basta, S. M., & Peterson, R. F. (1990). Perpetrator status and the personality characteristics of molested children. *Child Abuse & Neglect, 14,* 555-566.

Becker, E., Rankin, E., & Rickel, A. U. (1998). *High-risk sexual behavior: Interventions with vulnerable populations.* New York: Plenum.

Beitchman, J. H., Zucker, K. J., Hood, J. E., da Costa, G. A., & Akman, D. (1991). A review of the short-term effects of child sexual abuse. *Child Abuse & Neglect, 15,* 537-556.

Beitchman, J. H., Zucker, K. J., Hood, J. E., da Costa, G. A., Akman, D., & Cassavia, E. (1992). A review of the long-term effects of child sexual abuse. *Child Abuse & Neglect, 16,* 101-118.

Bensley, L. S., Eenwyk, J. V., & Simmons, K. W. (2000). Self-reported childhood sexual and physical abuse and adult HIV-risk behaviors and heavy drinking. *American Journal of Preventive Medicine, 18,* 151-158.

Berliner, L. (2000). What is sexual abuse? In H. Dubowitz & D. DePanfilis (Eds.), *Handbook for child protection* (pp. 18-22). Thousand Oaks, CA: Sage.

Berliner, L., & Briere, J. (1999). Trauma, memory, and clinical practice. In L. M. Williams & V. L. Baynard (Eds.), *Trauma and memory* (pp. 3-18). Thousand Oaks, CA: Sage.

Berliner, L., & Conte, J. (1990). The process of victimization: The victim's perspective. *Child Abuse & Neglect, 14,* 29-40.

Berliner, L., & Conte, J. R. (1995). The effects of disclosure and intervention on sexually abused children. *Child Abuse & Neglect, 19,* 371-384.

Berliner, L., & Saunders, B. E. (1996). Treating fear and anxiety in sexually abused children: Results of a controlled 2-year follow-up study. *Child Maltreatment, 1,* 294-309.

Black, C. A., & DeBlassie, R. R. (1993). Sexual abuse in male children and adolescents: Indicators, effects, and treatments. *Adolescence, 28,* 123-133.

Boney-McCoy, S., & Finkelhor, D. (1995). Psychosocial sequelae of violent victimization in a national youth sample. *Journal of Consulting and Clinical Psychology, 63,* 726-736.

Boney-McCoy, S., & Finkelhor, D. (1996). *Is youth victimization related to PTSD and depression after controlling for prior symptoms and family relationships? A longitudinal, prospective study.* Unpublished manuscript, University of New Hampshire.

Boyer, D., & Fine, D. (1991). Sexual abuse as a factor in adolescent pregnancy and child maltreatment. *Family Planning Perspectives, 24,* 4-19.

Briere, J. (1989). *Therapy for adults molested as children: Beyond survival.* New York: Springer.

Briere, J. (1995). *Trauma Symptom Inventory.* Odessa, FL: Psychological Assessment Resources.

Briere, J. (1992). *Child abuse trauma: Theory and treatment of the lasting effects.* Newbury Park, CA: Sage.

Briere, J. (1996a). A self-trauma model for treating adult survivors of severe child abuse. In J. Briere, L. Berliner, J. Bulkley, C. Jenny, & T. Reid (Eds.), *APSAC handbook on child maltreatment* (pp. 140-157). Thousand Oaks, CA: Sage.

Briere, J. (1996b). *Therapy for adults molested as children* (2nd ed.). New York: Springer.

Briere, J. (1996c). *Trauma Symptom Checklist for Children (TSCC).* Odessa, FL: Psychological Assessment Resources.

Briere, J. (1997). *Psychological assessment of adult posttraumatic states*. Washington, DC: American Psychological Association.

Briere, J. (2000). Incest. In A. E. Kazdin (Ed.), *Encyclopedia of psychology*. Washington, DC: American Psychological Association and Oxford University Press.

Briere, J. (2000b). Cognitive Distortions Scale (CDS). Odessa, FL: Psychological Assessment Resources.

Briere, J. (in press). *Professional manual for the Trauma Symptom Checklist for Young Children (TSCYC)*. Odessa, FL: Psychological Assessment Resources.

Briere, J., & Conte, J. R. (1993). Self-reported amnesia for abuse in adults molested as children. *Journal of Traumatic Stress, 6,* 21-31.

Briere, J., & Elliott, D. M. (1993). Sexual abuse, family environment, and psychological symptoms: On the validity of statistical control. *Journal of Consulting and Clinical Psychology, 61,* 284-288.

Briere, J., & Gil, E. (1998). Self-mutilation in clinical and general population samples: Prevalence, correlates, and functions. *American Journal of Orthopsychiatry, 68,* 609-620.

Briere, J., & Runtz, M. (1987). Post-sexual abuse trauma: Data and implications for clinical practice. *Journal of Interpersonal Violence, 2,* 367-379.

Briere, J., & Runtz, M. (1993). Child sexual abuse: Long-term sequelae and implications for assessment. *Journal of Interpersonal Violence, 8,* 312-330.

Briere, J., Woo, R., McRae, B., Foltz, J., & Sitzman, R. (1997). Lifetime victimization history, demographics, and clinical status in female psychiatric emergency room patients. *Journal of Nervous and Mental Disease, 185,* 95-101.

Briere, J., & Zaidi, L. Y. (1989). Sexual abuse histories and sequelae in female psychiatric emergency room patients. *American Journal of Psychiatry, 146,* 1602-1606.

Briggs, L., & Joyce, P. R. (1997). What determines posttraumatic stress disorder syptomatology for survivors of childhood sexual abuse? *Child Abuse & Neglect, 21,* 575-582.

Browne, A., & Finkelhor, D. (1986). Impact of child sexual abuse: A review of the research. *Psychological Bulletin, 18,* 66-77.

Cavaiola, A. A., & Schiff, M. (1989). Self-esteem in abused, chemically dependent adolescents. *Child Abuse & Neglect, 13,* 327-334.

Celano, M. (1992). A developmental model of victims' internal attributions of responsibility for sexual abuse. *Journal of Interpersonal Violence, 7,* 57-69.

Celano, M., Hazzard, A., Webb, C., & McCall, C. (1996). Treatment of traumagenic beliefs among sexually abused girls and their mothers: An evaluation study. *Journal of Abnormal Child Psychology, 24,* 1-7.

Chaffin, M., Wherry, J. N., & Dykman, R. (1997). School age children's coping with sexual abuse: Abuse stresses and symptoms associated with four coping strategies. *Child Abuse & Neglect, 21,* 227-240.

Chard, K. M., Weaver, T. L., & Resick, P. A. (1997). Adapting cognitive processing therapy for child sexual abuse survivors. *Cognitive and Behavioral Practice, 4,* 31-52.

Chu, J. A., & Dill, D. L. (1990). Dissociative symptoms in relation to childhood physical and sexual abuse. *American Journal of Psychiatry, 147,* 887-892.

Cohen, J. A., Berliner, L., & Mannarino, A. P. (2000). Treating traumatized children: A research review and synthesis. *Trauma, Violence, and Abuse, 1,* 29-46.

Cohen, J. A., Berliner, L., & March, J. S. (2000). Treatment of children and adolescents. In E. B. Foa, T. M. Keane, & M. J. Friedman (Eds.), *Effective treatments for PTSD: Practice guidelines from the International Society for Traumatic Stress Studies* (pp. 106-138). New York: Guilford.

Cohen, J. A., & Mannarino, A. P. (1998). A treatment study for sexually abused preschool children: Outcome during a one-year follow-up. *Journal of the American Academy of Child and Adolescent Psychiatry, 36,* 1228-1235.

Cohen, J. A., & Mannarino, A. P. (2000). Predictors of treatment outcome in sexually abused children. *Child Abuse & Neglect, 24,* 983-994.

Cole, P. M., & Putnam, F. W. (1992). Effect of incest on self and social functioning: A developmental psychopathology perspective. *Journal of Consulting & Clinical Psychology, 60,* 174-184.

Conte, J. R., & Schuerman, J. R. (1987). Factors associated with an increased impact of child sexual abuse. *Child Abuse & Neglect, 11,* 201-212.

Conte, J. R., Wolfe, S., & Smith, T. (1989). What sexual offenders tell us about prevention strategies. *Child Abuse & Neglect, 13,* 293-302.

Cosentino, C. E., Meyer-Bahlburg, H. F. L., Alpert, J. L., Weinberg, S. L., & Gaines, R. (1995). Sexual behavior problems and psychopathology symptoms in sexually abused girls. *Journal of the American Academy of Child and Adolescent Psychiatry, 34,* 1033-1042.

Courtois, C. A. (1988). *Healing the incest wound: Adult survivors in therapy.* New York: Norton.

Dadds, M., Smith, M., Weber, Y., & Robinson, A. (1991). An exploration of family and individual profiles following father-daughter incest. *Child Abuse & Neglect, 15,* 575-586.

Dalenberg, C. J., & Jacobs, D. A. (1994). Attributional analyses of child sexual abuse episodes: Empirical and clinical issues. *Journal of Child Sexual Abuse, 3,* 37-50.

Deblinger, E., Lippmann, J. T., & Steer, R. (1996). Sexually abused children suffering posttraumatic stress symptoms: Initial treatment outcome findings. *Child Maltreatment, 1,* 310-321.

Deblinger, E., McLeer, S. V., Atkins, M. S., Ralphe, D., & Foa, E. (1989). Posttraumatic stress in sexually abused, physically abused, and nonabused children. *Child Abuse & Neglect, 13,* 403-408.

DiLillo, D., & Long, P. J. (1999). Perceptions of couple functioning among female survivors of child sexual abuse. *Journal of Child Sexual Abuse, 7,* 59-76.

Donnelly, C. L., Amaya-Jackson, L., & March, J. S. (1999). Psychopharmacology of pediatric posttraumatic stress disorder. *Journal of Child and Adolescent Psychopharmacology, 9,* 203-220.

Dubner, A. E., & Motta, R. W. (1999). Sexually and physically abused foster care children and posttraumatic stress disorder. *Journal of Consulting and Clinical Psychology, 67,* 367-373.

Duncan, L. E., & Williams, L. M. (1998). Gender role socialization and male-on-male vs. female-on-male child sexual abuse. *Sex Roles, 39,* 765-785.

Einbender, A. J., & Friedrich, W. N. (1989). Psychological functioning and behavior of sexually abused girls. *Journal of Consulting & Clinical Psychology, 57,* 155-157.

Elliott, D. M. (1993). *Disclosing sexual abuse: Predictors and consequences.* San Antonio, TX: International Society for Traumatic Stress Studies.

Elliott, D. M. (1994). Impaired object relations in professional women molested as children. *Psychotherapy, 21,* 79-86.

Elliott, D. M., & Briere, J. (1992). Sexual abuse trauma among professional women: Validating the Trauma Symptom Checklist-40 (TSC-40). *Child Abuse & Neglect, 16,* 391-398.

Elliott, D. M., & Briere, J. (1994). Forensic sexual abuse evaluations of older children: Disclosures and symptomatology. *Behavioral Sciences and the Law, 12,* 261-277.

Elliott, D. M., & Briere, J. (1995). Posttraumatic stress associated with delayed recall of sexual abuse: A general population study. *Journal of Traumatic Stress, 8,* 629-647.

Elliott, D., Browne, K., & Kilcoyne, J. (1995). Child sexual abuse prevention: What offenders tell us. *Child Abuse & Neglect, 19,* 579-584.

Epstein, J. N., Saunders, B. E., Kilpatrick, D. G., & Resnick, H. S. (1998). PTSD as a mediator between childhood rape and alcohol use in adult women. *Child Abuse & Neglect, 22,* 223-234.

Everson, M. D., Hunter, W. M., Runyan, D. K., Edelsohn, G. A., & Coulter, M. L. (1989). Maternal support following disclosure of incest. *American Journal of Orthopsychiatry, 59,* 197-207.

Faller, K. C. (1989a). Characteristics of a clinical sample of sexually abused children: How boy and girl victims differ. *Child Abuse & Neglect, 13,* 281-291.

Faller, K. C. (1989b). The myths of the "collusive mother": Variability in the functioning of mothers of victims of intrafamilial sexual abuse. *Journal of Interpersonal Violence, 3,* 190-196.

Famularo, R., Kinscherff, R., & Fenton, T. (1988). Propranolol treatment for childhood posttraumatic stress disorder, acute type. *American Journal of Diseases of Children, 142,* 1244-1247.

Faust, J., Runyon, M. K., & Kenny, M. C. (1995). Family variables associated with the onset and impact of intrafamilial childhood sexual abuse. *Clinical Psychology Review, 15,* 443-456.

Fergusson, D. M., Horwood, L. J., & Lynskey, M. T. (1996). Childhood sexual abuse and psychiatric disorder in young adulthood: II. Psychiatric outcomes of childhood sexual abuse. *Child & Adolescent Psychiatry, 34,* 1365-1374.

Fiering, C., Taska, L. S., & Lewis, M. (1996). Family self-concept: Ideas on its meaning. In B. Bracken (Eds.), *Handbook of self-concept: Developmental, social, and clinical considerations* (pp. 317-373). New York: John Wiley.

Fiering, C., Taska, L., & Lewis, M. (1998). The role of shame and attributional style of children's and adolescents' adaptation to sexual abuse. *Child Maltreatment: Journal of the American Professional Society on the Abuse of Children, 3,* 129-142.

Finkelhor, D. (1979). What's wrong with sex between adults and children? Ethics and the problem of sexual abuse. *American Journal of Orthopsychiatry, 49,* 692-697.

Finkelhor, D. (1994). Current information on the scope and nature of child sexual abuse. *Future of Children, 4,* 31-53.

Finkelhor, D., & Baron, L. (1986a). High-risk children. In D. Finkelhor (Ed.), *A sourcebook on child sexual abuse* (pp. 60-88). Beverly Hills, CA: Sage.

Finkelhor, D., & Baron, L. (1986b). Risk factors for child sexual abuse. *Journal of Interpersonal Violence, 1,* 43-71.

Finkelhor, D., & Berliner, L. (1995). Research on the treatment of sexually abused children: A review and recommendations. *Journal of the American Academy of Child and Adolescent Psychiatry, 34,* 1408-1423.

Finkelhor, D., & Browne, A. (1985). The traumatic impact of child sexual abuse: A conceptualization. *American Journal of Orthopsychiatry, 55,* 530-541.

Finkelhor, D., & Dziuba-Leatherman, J. (1994). Children as victims of violence: A national survey. *Pediatrics, 94,* 413-420.

Finkelhor, D., Hotaling, G., Lewis, I. A., & Smith, C. (1990). Sexual abuse in a national survey of adult men and women: Prevalence, characteristics, and risk factors. *Child Abuse & Neglect, 14,* 19-28.

Finkelhor, D., & Olmrod, R. (2000). *Reporting crimes against juveniles* (Special Report NCJ-178887, Juvenile Justice Bulletin, 1-7). Washington, DC: Government Printing Office.

Finkelhor, D., & Russell, D. E. H. (1984). Women as perpetrators: Review of the evidence. In D. Finkelhor (Ed.), *Child sexual abuse: New theory and research* (pp. 171-185). New York: Free Press.

Finkelhor, D., Williams, L. M., & Burns, N. (1988). *Nursery crimes: Sexual abuse in day care.* Newbury Park, CA: Sage.

Finkelhor, D., Wolack, J., & Berliner, L. (2001). Police reporting and professional help seeking for child crime victims: A review. *Child Maltreatment, 6,* 17-30.

Follette, V. M., Alexander, P. C., & Follette, W. C. (1991). Individual predictors of outcome in group treatment for incest survivors. *Journal of Consulting & Clinical Psychology, 59,* 150-155.

Fossati, A., Madeddu, F., & Maffei, C. (1999). Borderline personality disorder and childhood sexual abuse: A meta-analytic study. *Journal of Personality Disorders, 13,* 268-280.

Friedrich, W. N. (1992). *Psychotherapy of sexually abused children and their families.* New York: Norton.

Friedrich, W. N. (1993). Sexual victimization and sexual behavior in children: A review of recent literature. *Child Abuse & Neglect, 17,* 59-66.

Friedrich, W. N. (1995). *Treatment of sexually abused boys.* Thousand Oaks, CA: Sage.

Friedrich, W. N. (1997). Psychotherapy with sexually abused boys. In D. E. Wolfe (Ed.), *Child abuse: New directions in prevention and treatment across the lifespan* (pp. 205-223). Thousand Oaks, CA: Sage.

Friedrich, W. N., Beilke, R. L., & Urquiza, A. J. (1987). Children from sexually abusive families: A behavioral comparison. *Journal of Interpersonal Violence, 2,* 391-402.

Friedrich, W. N., Dittner, C. A., Action, R., Berliner, L., Butler, J., Damon, L., Davies, W. H., Gray, A., & Wright, J. (2001). Child Sexual Behavior Inventory: Normative, psychiatric and sexual abuse comparisons. *Child Maltreatment, 6,* 37-49.

Friedrich, W. N., Jaworski, T. M., Huxsahl, J. E., & Bengtson, B. S. (1997). Dissociative and sexual behaviors in children and adolescents with sexual abuse and psychiatric histories. *Journal of Interpersonal Violence, 12,* 155-171.

Friedrich, W. N., & Reams, R. A. (1987). Young school-age sexually aggressive children. *Professional Psychology, 19,* 155-164.

German, D. E., Habernicht, D. J., & Futcher, W. G. (1990). Psychological profile of the female adolescent incest victim. *Child Abuse & Neglect, 14,* 429-438.

Gidycz, C. A., & Koss, M. P. (1989). The impact of adolescent sexual victimization: Standardized measures of anxiety, depression and behavioral deviancy. *Violence & Victims, 4,* 139-149.

Gil, E. (1991). *The healing power of play.* New York: Guilford.

Gladstone, G., Parker, G., Wilhelm, K., Mitchell, P., & Austin, M. P. (1999). Characteristics of depressed patients who report childhood sexual abuse. *American Journal of Psychiatry, 156,* 812.

Gold, E. R. (1986). Long-term effects of sexual victimization in childhood: An attributional approach. *Journal of Consulting & Clinical Psychology, 54,* 471-475.

Gold, E. R. (1991). History of child sexual abuse and adult sexual fantasies. *Violence and Victims, 6,* 75-82.

Gold, S. N., Lucenko, B. A., Elhai, J. D., Swingle, J. M., & Sellers, A. H. (1999). A comparison of psychological/psychiatric symptomatology of women and men sexually abused as children. *Child Abuse & Neglect, 23,* 683-692.

Gomes-Schwartz, B., Horowitz, J. M., & Cardarelli, A. P. (1990). *Child sexual abuse: The initial effects.* Newbury Park, CA: Sage.

Goodman, G. S., Taub, E. P., Jones, D. P. H., England, P., Port, L. K., Rudy, L., & Prado, L. (1992). Emotional effects of criminal court testimony on child sexual assault victims. *Monographs of the Society for Research on Child Development, 57,* 1-163.

Henry, J. (1997). System intervention trauma to child abuse victims following disclosure. *Journal of Interpersonal Violence, 12,* 499-512.

Herman, J. L., & Harvey, M. R. (1997). Adult memories of childhood trauma: A naturalistic clinical study. *Journal of Traumatic Stress, 10,* 557-571.

Herman, J. L., & Schatzow, E. (1987). Recovery and verification of memories of childhood sexual trauma. *Psychoanalytic Psychology, 4,* 1-14.

Hibbard, R. A., Ingersoll, G. M., & Orr, D. P. (1990). Behavior risk, emotional risk, and child abuse among adolescents in a nonclinical setting. *Pediatrics, 86,* 896-901.

Hoagwood, K., & Stewart, J. M. (1989). Sexually abused children's perceptions of family functioning. *Child & Adolescent Social Work, 6,* 139-149.

Holmes, W. C., & Slap, G. B. (1998). Sexual abuse of boys: Definition, prevalence, correlates, sequelae, and management. *Journal of the American Medical Association, 280,* 1855-1862.

Hotte, J. P., & Rafman, S. (1992). The specific effects of incest on prepubertal girls from dysfunctional families. *Child Abuse & Neglect, 16,* 273-283.

Hunter, J., Goodwin, D. W., & Wilson, R. J. (1992). Attributions of blame in child sexual abuse victims: An analysis of age and gender influences. *Journal of Child Sexual Abuse, 1,* 75-90.

Hunter, W. M., Coulter, M. L., Runyan, D. K., & Everson, M. D. (1990). Determinants of placement for sexually abused children. *Child Abuse & Neglect, 14,* 407-418.

Huston, R. L., Parra, J. M., Prihoda, T. J., & Foulds, D. M. (1995). Characteristics of childhood sexual abuse in a predominantly Mexican-American population. *Child Abuse & Neglect, 19,* 165-176.

Hyde, C., Bentovim, A., & Monck, E. (1995). Some clinical and methodological implications of a treatment outcome study of sexually abused children. *Child Abuse & Neglect, 19,* 1387-1399.

James, B. (1989). *Treating traumatized children: New insights and creative interventions.* Lexington, MA: Lexington Books.

Jarvis, T. J., & Copeland, J. (1997). Child sexual abuse as a predictor of psychiatric co-morbidity and its implications for drug and alcohol treatment. *Drug and Alcohol Dependence, 49,* 61-69.

Jehu, D. (1988). *Beyond sexual abuse: Therapy with women who were childhood victims.* Chichester, UK: Wiley.

Johnsen, L. W., & Harlow, L. L. (1996). Childhood sexual abuse linked with adult substance use, victimization, and AIDS risk. *AIDS Education and Prevention, 8,* 44-57.

Johnson, B. K., & Kenkel, M. B. (1991). Stress, coping and adjustment in female adolescent incest victims. *Child Abuse & Neglect, 15,* 293-305.

Jones, D. P. H., & McGraw, J. M. (1987). Reliable and fictitious accounts of sexual abuse to children. *Journal of Interpersonal Violence, 2,* 27-45.

Jones, L., & Finkelhor, D. (2001). *The decline in child sexual abuse cases.* Washington, DC: U.S. Department of Justice.

Kendall-Tackett, K. A., Williams, L. M., & Finkelhor, D. (1993). Impact of sexual abuse on children: A review and synthesis of recent empirical studies. *Psychological Bulletin, 113,* 164-180.

Kilpatrick, D. G., & Saunders, B. E. (1999). *Prevalence and consequences of child victimization: Results from the national survey of adolescents* (No. 93-IJ-CX-0023). Charleston: National Crime Victims Research & Treatment Center, Department of Psychiatry & Behavioral Sciences, Medical University of South Carolina.

King, N. J., Tonge, B. J., Mullen, P., Myerson, N., Heyne, D., Rollings, S., Martin, R., & Ollendick, T. (2001). Treating sexually abused children with posttraumatic stress symptoms: A randomized trial. *Journal of the American Academy of Child and Adolescent Psychiatry, 39,* 1347-1355.

Kluft, R. P. (1985). *Childhood antecedents of multiple personality.* Washington, DC: American Psychiatric Press.

Kolko, D. J., Moser, J., & Weldy, S. R. (1988). Behavioral/emotional indicators of sexual abuse in psychiatric inpatients: A controlled comparison with physical abuse. *Child Abuse & Neglect, 12,* 529-541.

Kress, F., & Vandenberg, B. (1998). Depression and attribution in abused children and their nonoffending caregivers. *Psychological Reports, 83,* 1285-1286.

Kroll, J. (1993). *PTSD/borderlines in therapy: Finding the balance.* New York: Norton.

Lang, R. A., & Frenzel, R. R. (1988). How sex offenders lure children. *Annals of Sex Research, 1,* 303-317.

Lanktree, C., & Briere, J. (1995). Outcome of therapy for sexually abused children: A repeated measures study. *Child Abuse & Neglect, 19,* 1145-1156.

Lanktree, C., Briere, J., & Zaidi, L. (1991). Incidence and impact of sexual abuse in a child outpatient sample: The role of direct inquiry. *Child Abuse & Neglect, 15,* 447-453.

Lawson, L., & Chaffin, M. (1992). False negatives in sexual abuse disclosure interviews: Incidence and influence of caretaker's belief in abuse in cases of accidental abuse discovery by diagnosis of STD. *Journal of Interpersonal Violence, 7,* 532-542.

Leifer, M., Shapiro, J. P., & Kassem, L. (1993). The impact of maternal history and behavior upon foster placement and adjustment in sexually abused girls. *Child Abuse & Neglect, 17,* 755-766.

Leitenberg, H., Greenwald, E., & Cado, S. (1992). A retrospective study of long-term methods of coping with having been sexually abused during childhood. *Child Abuse & Neglect, 16,* 399-407.

Levitan, R. D., Parikh, S. V., Lesage, A. D., Hegadoren, K. M., & Adams, M. (1998). Major depression in individuals with a history of child physical or sexual abuse: Relationship to neurovegetative features, mania, and gender. *American Journal of Psychiatry, 155,* 1746-1752.

Lindsay, D. S., & Briere, J. (1997). The controversy regarding recovered memories of childhood sexual abuse: Pitfalls, bridges and future directions. *Journal of Interpersonal Violence, 12,* 631-647.

Lisak, D. (1993). Men as victims: Challenging cultural myths. *Journal of Traumatic Stress, 6,* 577-580.

Lombardo, S., & Pohl, R. (1997). Sexual abuse history of women treated in psychiatric outpatient clinic. *Psychiatric Services, 48,* 534-536.

Lwifer, M., Shapiro, J. P., & Kassem, L. (1993). The impact of maternal history and behavior upon foster placement and adjustment in sexually abused girls. *Child Abuse & Neglect, 17,* 755-766.

Madonna, P. G., Van Scoyk, S., & Jones, D. P. H. (1991). Family interactions within incest and nonincest families. *American Journal of Psychiatry, 148,* 46-49.

Manion, I., Firestone, P., Cloutier, P., Ligezinska, M., McIntyre, J., & Ensom, R. (1998). Child extrafamilial sexual abuse: Predicting parent and child functioning. *Child Abuse & Neglect, 22,* 1285-1304.

Mannarino, A. P., & Cohen, J. A. (1996a). Abuse-related attributions and perceptions, general attributions, and locus of control in sexually abused girls. *Journal of Interpersonal Violence, 11,* 162-180.

Mannarino, A. P., & Cohen, J. A. (1996b). A follow-up study of factors that mediate the development of psychological symptomatology in sexually abused girls. *Child Maltreatment, 1,* 246-260.

Mannarino, A. P., & Cohen, J. A. (1997). Family-related variables and psychological symptom formation in sexually abused girls. *Journal of Child Sexual Abuse, 5,* 105-120.

Mannarino, A. P., Cohen, J. A., & Berman, S. R. (1994). The Children's Attributions and Perceptions Scale: A new measure of sexual abuse-related factors. *Journal of Clinical Child Psychology, 23,* 204-211.

Maynes, L. C., & Feinauer, L. L. (1994). Acute and chronic dissociation and somatized anxiety as related to childhood sexual abuse. *American Journal of Family Therapy, 22,* 165-175.

McCabe, M. P., & Cobain, M. J. (1998). The impact of individual and relationship factors on sexual dysfunction among males and females. *Sexual and Marital Therapy, 13,* 131-143.

McLeer, S. V., Dixon, J. F., Henry, D., Ruggiero, K., Escovitz, K., Niedda, T., & Scholle, R. (1998). Psychopathology in non-clinically referred sexually abused children. *Journal of the American Academy of Child and Adolescent Psychiatry, 37,* 1326-1333.

McLeer, S. V., Deblinger, E., Henry, D., & Orvaschel, H. (1992). Sexually abused children at high risk for posttraumatic stress disorder. *Journal of the American Academy of Child and Adolescent Psychiatry, 31,* 875-879.

Mendel, M. P. (1995). *The male survivor: The impact of sexual abuse.* Thousand Oaks, CA: Sage.

Mendel, S. (1995). An adolescent group within a milieu setting. *Journal of Child and Adolescent Group Therapy, 5,* 47-51.

Mennen, F. E. (1995). The relationship of race/ethnicity to symptoms in childhood sexual abuse. *Child Abuse & Neglect, 19,* 115-124.

Messman, T. L., & Long, P. J. (1996). Child sexual abuse and its relationship to revictimization in adult women: A review. *Clinical Psychology Review, 16,* 397-420.

Morrow, K. B. (1991). Attributions of female adolescent incest victims regarding their molestation. *Child Abuse & Neglect, 15,* 477-483.

Mulder, R. T., Beautrais, A. L., Joyce, P. R., & Fergusson, D. M. (1998). Relationship between dissociation, childhood sexual abuse, childhood physical abuse, and mental illness in a general population sample. *American Journal of Psychiatry, 155,* 806-811.

Mullen, P. E., Martin, J. L., Anderson, J. C., & Romans, S. E. (1994). The effect of child sexual abuse on social, interpersonal and sexual function in adult life. *British Journal of Psychiatry, 165,* 35-47.

Myers, J. E. B. (1998). *Legal issues in child abuse and neglect practice* (2nd ed.). Thousand Oaks, CA: Sage.

National Center on Child Abuse and Neglect. (1993). *A report on the maltreatment of children with disabilities.* Washington, DC: U.S. Department of Health and Human Services.

Neumann, D. A., Houskamp, B. M., Pollock, V. E., & Briere, J. (1996). The long-term sequelae of childhood sexual abuse in women: A meta-analytic review. *Child Maltreatment, 1,* 6-16.

Newman, E., Christopher, S. R., & Berry, J. O. (2000). Developmental disabilities, trauma exposure, and posttraumatic stress disorder. *Trauma, Violence, and Abuse: A Review Journal, 1,* 154-170.

Ondersma, S., Chaffin, M., & Berliner, L. (1999). Comments on the Rind et al., meta-analysis controversy. *APSAC Advisor, 12,* 2-5.

Ondersma, S., Chaffin, M., Berliner, L., Cordon, Goodman, G. S., & Barnett. (in press). Sex with children is abuse: The Rind et al. controversy. *Psychological Bulletin.*

Ornduff, S. R., Freedenfeld, R. N., Kelsey, R. M., & Critelli, J. W. (1994). Object relations of sexually abused female subjects: A TAT analysis. *Journal of Personality Assessment, 63,* 223-238.

Paris, J., Zweig, F., & Guzder, J. (1994). Psychological risk factors for borderline personality disorder in female patients. *Comprehensive Psychiatry, 35,* 301-305.

Peters, S. D. (1988). Child sexual abuse and later psychological problems. In G. E. Wyatt & G. Powell (Eds.), *The lasting effects of child sexual abuse..* Newbury Park, CA: Sage.

Piran, N., Lerner, P., Garfinkel, P. E., Kennedy, S. H., & Brouillette, C. (1988). Personality disorders in anoretic patients. *International Journal of Eating Disorders, 7,* 589-599.

Polusny, M. A., & Follette, V. M. (1996). Remembering childhood sexual abuse: A national survey of psychologists' clinical practices, beliefs, and personal experiences. *Professional Psychology: Research and Practice, 27,* 41-52.

Pribor, E. F., & Dinwiddle, S. H. (1992). Psychiatric correlates of incest in childhood. *American Journal of Psychiatry, 149,* 52-56.

Putnum, F. W. (1990). Disturbance of "self" in victims of child sexual abuse. In P. R. Kluft (Ed.), *Incest-related syndromes of adult psychopathology* (pp. 113-132). Washington, DC: American Psychiatric Press.

Quas, J., Redlich, A., Goodman, G., Ghetti, S., & Alexander, K. (1999, May). *Long-term consequences on child sexual abuse victims of testifying in criminal court: Mental health and revictimization.* Paper presented at the biennial meeting of the Society for Research in Child Development, Albuquerque, NM.

Rao, K., DiClemente, R. J., & Ponton, L. E. (1992). Child sexual abuse of Asians compared with other populations. *Journal of the American Academy of Child & Adolescent Psychiatry, 31,* 880-886.

Rind, B., Tromovitch, P., & Bauserman, R. (1998). A meta-analytic examination of assumed properties of child sexual abuse using college samples. *Psychological Bulletin, 124,* 22-53.

Rodriguez, N., Ryan, S. W., Van de Kemp, H., & Foy, D. W. (1997). Posttraumatic stress disorder in adult female survivors of child sexual abuse: A comparison study. *Journal of Consulting and Clinical Psychology, 65,* 53-59.

Rosen, L. N., & Martin, L. (1998). Long-term effects of childhood maltreatment history on gender-related personality characteristics. *Child Abuse & Neglect, 22,* 197-211.

Roth, S., & Batson, R. (1997). *Naming the shadows: A new approach to individual and group psychotherapy for adult survivors of childhood incest.* New York: Free Press.

Rowan, A. B., & Foy, D. W. (1994). Posttraumatic stress disorder in a clinical sample of adults sexually abused as children. *Child Abuse & Neglect, 18,* 51-61.

Ruggiero, K. J., McLeer, S. V., & Dixon, J. F. (2000). Sexual abuse characteristics associated with survivor psychopathology. *Child Abuse & Neglect, 24,* 951-964.

Runyan, D. K., Everson, M. D., Edelsohn, G. A., Hunter, W. M., & Coulter, M. L. (1988). Impact of intervention on sexually abused children. *Journal of Pediatrics, 113,* 647-653.

Runyan, D. K., Hunter, W. M., & Everson, M. D. (1992). *Maternal support for child victims of sexual abuse: Determinants and implications* (Final Report No. Grant #90-CA-1368). Washington, DC: National Center on Child Abuse and Neglect.

Russell, D. E. H. (1984). *Sexual exploitation: Rape, child sexual abuse, and workplace harassment.* Beverly Hills, CA: Sage.

Russell, D. E. H. (1986). *The secret trauma: Incest in the lives of girls and women.* New York: Basic Books.

Rust, J. O., & Troupe, P. A. (1991). Relationships of treatment of child sexual abuse with school achievement and self-concept. *Journal of Early Adolescence, 11,* 420-429.

Salmon, P., & Calderbank, S. (1996). The relationship of childhood physical and sexual abuse to adult illness behavior. *Journal of Psychosomatic Research, 40,* 329-336.

Sanders-Phillips, K., Moisan, P. A., Wadlington, S., Morgan, S., & English, K. (1995). Ethnic differences in psychological functioning among Black and Latino sexually abused girls. *Child Abuse & Neglect, 19,* 691-706.

Sarwer, D. B., & Durlak, J. A. (1996). Childhood sexual abuse as a predictor of adult female sexual dysfunction: A study of couples seeking sex therapy. *Child Abuse & Neglect, 20,* 963-972.

Sas, L. (1991). *Reducing the system-induced trauma for child sexual abuse victims through court preparation, assessment, and follow-up* (No. #4555-1-125). Toronto: National Welfare Grants Division, Health and Welfare, Canada.

Saunders, B. E., Kilpatrick, D. G., Hanson, R. F., Resnick, H. S., & Walker, M. E. (1999). Prevalence, case characteristics, and long-term psychological correlates of child rape among women: A national survey. *Child Maltreatment: Journal of the American Professional Society on the Abuse of Children, 4,* 187-200.

Saunders, B. E., Villeponteaux, L. A., Lipovsky, J. A., Kilpatrick, D. G., & Veronen, L. J. (1992). Child sexual assault as a risk factor for mental disorders among women: A community survey. *Journal of Interpersonal Violence, 7,* 189-204.

Sauzier, M. (1989). Disclosure of child sexual abuse: For better or worse. *Psychiatric Clinics of North America, 12,* 455-469.

Saywitz, K. J., Mannarino, A. P., Berliner, L., & Cohen, J. A. (2000). Treatment of sexually abused children and adolescents. *American Psychologist, 55,* 1040-1049.

Scott, R. I., & Day, H. D. (1996). Association of abuse-related symptoms and style of anger expression for female survivors of childhood incest. *Journal of Interpersonal Violence, 11,* 208-220.

Shapiro, J. P., Leifer, M., Martone, M. W., & Kassem, L. (1990). Multimethod assessment of depression in sexually abused girls. *Journal of Personality Assessment, 55,* 234-248.

Shapiro, J. P., Leifer, M., Martone, M. W., & Kassem, L. (1992). Cognitive functioning and social competence as predictors of maladjustment in sexually abused girls. *Journal of Interpersonal Violence, 7,* 156-164.

Shengold, L. (1989). *Soul murder: The effects of childhood abuse and deprivation.* New Haven, CT: Yale University Press.

Sirles, E., & Franke, P. J. (1989). Factors influencing mothers' reactions to intrafamilial sexual abuse. *Child Abuse & Neglect, 13,* 131-139.

Smith, B. E., Elstein, S. G., Trost, T., & Bulkley, J. (1993). *The prosecution of child physical and sexual abuse cases.* Washington, DC: ABA Center on Children & the Law.

Smucker, M. R., & Niederee, J. (1995). Treating incest related PTSD and pathogenic schemas through imaginal exposure and rescripting. *Cognitive and Behavioral Practice, 2,* 63-92.

Sorensen, T., & Snow, B. (1991). How children tell: The process of disclosure in child sexual abuse. *Child Welfare, 70,* 3-15.

Sorenson, S. B., Siegel, J. M., Golding, J. M., & Stein, J. A. (1991). Repeated sexual victimization. *Victims & Violence, 91,* 299-308.

Spaccarelli, S. (1994). Stress, appraisal, and coping in child sexual abuse: A theoretical and empirical review. *Psychological Bulletin, 116,* 340.

Spaccarelli, S. (1995). Measuring abuse stress and negative cognitive appraisals in child sexual abuse: Validity data on two new scales. *Journal of Abnormal Psychology, 23,* 703-727.

Spaccarelli, S., & Fuchs, C. (1997). Variability in symptom expression among sexually abused girls: Developing multivariate models. *Journal of Clinical Child Psychology, 26,* 34-35.

Springs, F. E., & Friedrich, W. N. (1992). Health risk behaviors and medical sequelae of childhood sexual abuse. *Mayo Clinic Proceedings, 67,* 527-532.

Steiger, H., & Zanko, M. (1990). Sexual trauma among eating disordered, psychiatric, and normal female groups: Comparison of prevalences and defense styles. *Journal of Interpersonal Violence, 5,* 74-86.

Stein, J. A., Golding, J. M., Siegel, J. M., Burnam, M. A., & Sorenson, S. B. (1988). Long-term psychological sequelae of child sexual abuse: The Los Angeles Epidemiological Catchment Area Study. In G. E. Wyatt & G. Powell (Eds.), *The lasting effects of child sexual abuse.* Newbury Park, CA: Sage.

Stern, A. E., Lynch, D. L., Oates, R. K., O'Toole, B. I., & Cooney, G. (1995). Self esteem, depression, behaviour and family functioning in sexually abused children. *Journal of Child Psychology and Psychiatry, 36,* 1077-1089.

Stovall, G., & Craig, R. J. (1990). Mental representations of physically and sexually abused latency-aged females. *Child Abuse & Neglect, 14,* 233-242.

Summit, R. C. (1983). The child sexual abuse accommodation syndrome. *Child Abuse & Neglect, 7,* 177-192.

Summit, R. C. (1994). The dark tunnels of McMartin. *Journal of Psychohistory, 21,* 397-416.

Tebbutt, J., Swanston, H., Oates, R. K., & O'Toole, B. I. (1997). Five years after child sexual abuse: Persisting dysfunction and problems of prediction. *Child & Adolescent Psychiatry, 36,* 330-339.

Tedesco, J. F., & Schell, S. V. (1987). Children's reactions to sex abuse investigation and litigation. *Child Abuse & Neglect, 11,* 267-272.

Tharinger, D., Horton, C. B., & Millea, S. (1990). Sexual abuse and exploitation of children and adults with mental retardation and other handicaps. *Child Abuse & Neglect, 14,* 301-312.

van der Kolk, B. A., & Kadish, W. (1987). Amnesia, dissociation, and the return of the repressed. In B. A. van der Kolk (Ed.), *Psychological trauma*. Washington, DC: American Psychiatric Press.

van der Kolk, B. A., Perry, J. C., & Herman, J. L. (1991). Childhood origins of self-destructive behavior. *American Journal of Psychiatry, 148,* 1665-1671.

Walsh, B. W., & Rosen, P. M. (1988). *Self-mutilation: Theory, research, and treatment.* New York: Guilford.

Weiss, E. L., Longhurst, J. G., & Mazure, C. M. (1999). Childhood sexual abuse as a risk factor for depression in women: Psychosocial and neurobiological correlates. *American Journal of Psychiatry, 156,* 816-828.

Wenninger, K., & Ehlers, A. (1998). Dysfunctional cognitions and adult psychological functioning in child sexual abuse survivors. *Journal of Traumatic Stress, 11,* 281-300.

Whitcomb, D., Runyan, D. K., De Vos, E., Hunter, W. M., Cross, T. P., Everson, M. D., Peeler, N. A., Porter, C. Q., Toth, P. A., & Cropper, C. (1991). *Child victim as witness research and development program* (Executive Summary, Grant #87-MC-CX-0026). Washington, DC: Office of Juvenile Justice and Delinquency Prevention, Office of Justice Programs, U.S. Department of Justice.

Widom, C., & Morris, S. (1997). Accuracy of adult recollection of childhood victimization: Part 2. Childhood sexual abuse. *Psychological Assessment, 9,* 34-46.

Williams, L. (1994). Recall of childhood trauma: A prospective study of women's memories of child sexual abuse. *Journal of Consulting and Clinical Psychology, 62,* 1167-1176.

Wind, T. W., & Silvern, L. E. (1992). Type and extent of child abuse as predictors of adult functioning. *Journal of Family Violence, 7,* 261-281.

Wolfe, D. A., Sas, L., & Wekerle, C. (1994). Factors associated with the development of posttraumatic stress disorder among child victims of sexual abuse. *Child Abuse & Neglect, 18,* 37-50.

Wolfe, V. V., & Birt, J. (1995). The psychological sequelae of child sexual abuse. *Advances in Clinical Child Psychology, 17,* 233-263.

Wolfe, V. V., Gentile, C., & Wolfe, D. A. (1989). The impact of sexual abuse on children: A PTSD formulation. *Behavior Therapy, 20,* 215-228.

Wozencraft, T., Wagner, W., & Pellegrin, A. (1991). Depression and suicidal ideation in sexually abused children. *Child Abuse & Neglect, 15,* 505-510.

Wyatt, G. E. (1985). The sexual abuse of Afro-American and white women in childhood. *Child Abuse & Neglect, 9,* 507-519.

Zanarini, M. C., Ruser, T. F., Frankenburg, F. F., Hennen, J., & Gunderson, J. G. (2000). Risk factors associated with the dissociative experiences of borderline patients. *Journal of Nervous and Mental Disease, 188,* 26-30.

4

Psychological Maltreatment

STUART N. HART

MARLA R. BRASSARD

NELSON J. BINGGELI

HOWARD A. DAVIDSON

Psychological maltreatment has been conceptualized as consisting of psychological abuse or neglect occurring alone, occurring in association with other forms of abuse and neglect, and as the embedded psychological context behind other forms of abuse and neglect (Binggeli, Hart, & Brassard, 2001).

Empirical research suggests that the most common and lasting effects of physical abuse, sexual abuse, and neglect tend to be related to associated and embedded psychological experiences. In addition, several studies have indicated that emotional abuse or neglect, occurring alone, is associated with negative effects of a severity equal to or greater than other forms of abuse (Hart, Binggeli, & Brassard, 1998; also see "Evidence of Impact" section of this chapter).

Thus, psychological maltreatment may be thought of as a unifying concept that embodies many of the most significant components of child abuse and neglect.

The term *psychological maltreatment* is preferred because it denotes a category that is sufficiently broad to include both the cognitive and affective meanings of maltreatment (psychological) as well as perpetrator acts of both commission and omission (maltreatment). The American Psychological Association has designated psychological maltreatment as an area of priority for research and public policy (Garrison, 1987).

Although increased attention has been given to psychological maltreatment over the past two decades, this attention still lags substantially behind that given to other forms of maltreatment. For example, as one of many reforms in the response to child sexual abuse, it is now common for children's advocacy centers to take a lead role in coordinating the responses of many professionals for interventions with victims of sexual abuse. There has been no similar effort focused on coordination of services for psychological maltreatment victims.

Nevertheless, significant progress has been made in several relevant domains, including definitions, measurement strategies, and studies of prevalence and relationships to various forms of dysfunctional behavior. Particularly noteworthy is the fact that a broad consensus among child maltreatment experts has been achieved on evaluation standards for the suspected psychological maltreatment of children and adolescents (American Professional Society on the Abuse of Children [APSAC], 1995). Recent developments in this knowledge will be integrated in the following sections of this chapter.

Creating Definitions

The establishment of an adequate definition of psychological maltreatment has been perhaps the most fundamental challenge to advances in dealing with this topic. There are many inherent difficulties in producing such definitions, encompassing numerous complex philosophical, scientific, legal, political, and cultural issues. Despite these significant challenges, considerable progress has been made over the past 20 years in articulating rationally defensible definitions that appear to have substantial professional and public support.

In a landmark national law on child abuse, an aspect of psychological maltreatment was included under the category of "mental injury" (Public Law 93-247, originally passed in 1974). Following this, numerous attempts were made to elaborate this ambiguous category in national policy and state law (Hart, Germain, & Brassard, 1987). These early attempts to achieve widely accepted definitions were not very successful

(Holder, Newberger, & Loken, 1983). In the early 1980s, the lack of adequate definitions was recognized to be *the* major impediment to progress in research and practice in this area. In response, the International Conference on Psychological Abuse of the Child was held in 1983 to stimulate progress. This conference, with professionals representing virtually all the helping professions and major child advocacy groups as well as eight countries, produced the following definition:

> Psychological maltreatment of children and youth consists of acts of omission and commission, which are judged on the basis of a combination of community standards and professional expertise to be psychologically damaging. Such acts are committed by individuals, singly or collectively; who by their characteristics (e.g., age, status, knowledge, and organizational form) are in a position of differential power that renders a child vulnerable. Such acts damage immediately or ultimately the behavioral, cognitive, affective, or physical functioning of the child. Examples of psychological maltreatment include acts of rejecting, terrorizing, isolating, exploiting, and missocializing. (*Proceedings, 1983*)

Since the 1983 conference, significant conceptual and empirical progress has been made to further elaborate the definition of psychological maltreatment. Baily and Baily (1986) asked a large number of respondents from different protective service professions to rate and refine statements representing potential acts of "emotional maltreatment" and then organized these into 16 categories. Drawing on this research and previous conceptual work, Garbarino, Guttman, and Seeley (1986) and Hart et al. (1987) each produced similar sets of categorical systems.

From this base, Hart and Brassard (1986, 1989-1991; also see Brassard, Hart, & Hardy, 1993) conducted a federally funded research project, incorporating literature review, expert opinion, and empirical research, to produce operationally defined measures of emotional maltreatment that are now widely accepted. As a part of this research, a multidimensional scale was developed to rate parental behaviors in a videotaped interaction with their children. Psychological maltreatment was found to be reliably distinguished from appropriate caregiving and differentiated into distinct categories. Administered to a sample of 49 high-risk mother-child dyads, the scales enabled raters to differentiate between confirmed maltreating mothers and mothers from a demographically matched comparison group with a moderately high degree of accuracy. Raters were able to accurately identify nearly 82% of maltreating mothers with a sensitivity of .92 (proportion of maltreating mothers correctly identified) and a specificity of .71 (proportion of children not maltreated correctly excluded). In addition, this research provided further empirical support for the categories of *spurning, terrorizing, exploiting/corrupting,* and *denying emotional responsiveness.*

The present status of defining psychological maltreatment is best represented in the *Guidelines for the Psychosocial Evaluation of Suspected Psychological Maltreatment in Children and Adolescents* of the American Professional Society on Abuse of Children (APSAC, 1995). These guidelines were produced through a lengthy and rigorous process of development involving submission for review by child maltreatment experts, including the APSAC membership and board of directors. This document contains consideration of issues relating to forensic assessment. It includes the following broad conceptual statement and psychological maltreatment categories:

- *Psychological maltreatment* means a repeated pattern of caregiver behavior or extreme incident(s) that convey to children that they are worthless, flawed, unloved, unwanted, endangered, or only of value in meeting another's needs (APSAC, 1995, p. 2).
- Psychological maltreatment includes (a) spurning, (b) terrorizing, (c) isolating, (d) exploiting/corrupting, (e) denying emotional responsiveness, and (f) mental health, medical, and educational neglect.

Table 4.1, from the APSAC guidelines, presents the above six categories of psychological maltreatment with detailed subcategories that further clarify their meanings (Hart & Brassard, 1986, 1989-1991).

When considering the psychological maltreatment categories in Table 4.1, it is important to note that rejection does not have a category of its own but is represented, primarily, in two of the categories and is probably a factor in all categories. Rejection has been determined to embody two distinct patterns of caretaker behavior (Rohner & Rohner, 1980). In the first form, *spurning,* the mental attitude of hostility is expressed through caretaker acts of behavioral (including verbal) hostility and aggression toward a child (acts of commission). In the second form, *denying emotional responsiveness,* the mental attitude of indifference is manifested behaviorally in a caretaker's neglect of a child's emotional needs (acts of omission).

The above definitions have been subjected to additional empirical validation. This includes research that has developed measurement strategies and examined the correlates of psychological maltreatment, as well as studies that have surveyed professional and public opinion regarding definitions. Claussen and Crittenden (1991) investigated the parenting and child development outcomes for children averaging 4 years, 4 months of age for child populations of reported maltreatment, mental health treatment, and normative conditions. Drawing on the above definitional work, the researchers developed an instrument to measure parental psychological maltreatment. They found that although physical and psychological abuse were likely to occur together for the reported sample, (a) psychological maltreatment often occurred alone in the community sample, (b) parental psychological maltreating behavior was the strongest predictor of developmental outcomes, and (c) psychological maltreatment was more predictive of detrimental outcomes than the severity of physical injury. Crittenden, Claussen, and Sugarman (1994) found similar results in a related study that examined the functioning of adolescents who had been reported for suspected physical abuse, physical neglect, or psychological maltreatment.

The credibility of the spurning and denying emotional responsiveness categories has been further supported by the longitudinal research Minnesota Mother-Child Interaction Project, which followed at-risk children from before birth to adulthood (Egeland & Erickson, 1987; Erickson, Egeland, & Pianta, 1989). This research found that spurning may be as damaging to psychosocial development as physical abuse and that denying emotional responsiveness may be the most devastating of all forms of maltreatment (see Chapter 1, this volume).

Since the early 1990s, strategies and instruments designed to measure dimensions of psychological maltreatment have proliferated, most of them created with an explicit acknowledgment of the influence of the definitional work outlined earlier. Barnett, Manley, and Cicchetti (1991) described a

TABLE 4.1 Psychological Maltreatment Forms

SIX MAJOR TYPES OF PSYCHOLOGICAL MALTREATMENT ARE DESCRIBED BELOW AND FURTHER CLARIFIED BY IDENTIFICATION OF SUBCATEGORIES

A repeated pattern or extreme incidents of the conditions described in this table constitutes psychological maltreatment. Such conditions convey the message that the child is worthless, flawed, unloved, endangered, or only valuable in meeting someone else's needs.

SPURNING (hostile rejecting/degrading) includes verbal and nonverbal caregiver acts that reject and degrade a child. SPURNING includes the following: ■ Belittling, degrading, and other nonphysical forms of overtly hostile or rejecting treatment ■ Shaming and/or ridiculing the child for showing normal emotions such as affection, grief, or sorrow ■ Consistently singling out one child to criticize and punish, perform most of the household chores, or receive fewer rewards ■ Public humiliation	EXPLOITING/CORRUPTING includes caregiver acts that encourage the child to develop inappropriate behaviors (self-destructive, antisocial, criminal, deviant, or other maladaptive behaviors). EXPLOITING/CORRUPTING includes the following: ■ Modeling, permitting, or encouraging antisocial behavior (e.g., prostitution, performance in pornographic media, initiation of criminal activities, substance abuse, violence to or corruption of others) ■ Modeling, permitting, or encouraging developmentally inappropriate behavior (e.g., parentification, infantilization, living the parent's unfulfilled dreams) ■ Encouraging or coercing abandonment of developmentally appropriate autonomy through extreme overinvolvement, intrusiveness, or dominance (e.g., allowing little or no opportunity or support for child's views, feelings, and wishes; micromanaging child's life) ■ Restricting or interfering with cognitive development
TERRORIZING includes caregiver behavior that threatens or is likely to physically hurt, kill, abandon, or place the child or child's loved ones or objects in recognizably dangerous situations. TERRORIZING includes the following: ■ Placing a child in unpredictable or chaotic circumstances ■ Placing a child in recognizably dangerous situations ■ Setting rigid or unrealistic expectations with the threat of loss, harm, or danger if they are not met ■ Threatening or perpetrating violence against the child ■ Threatening or perpetrating violence against a child's loved ones or objects	DENYING EMOTIONAL RESPONSIVENESS (ignoring) includes caregiver acts that ignore the child's attempts and needs to interact (failing to express affection, caring, and love for the child) and show no emotion in interactions with the child. DENYING EMOTIONAL RESPONSIVENESS includes the following: ■ Being detached and uninvolved through either incapacity or lack of motivation ■ Interacting only when absolutely necessary ■ Failing to express affection, caring, and love for the child
ISOLATING includes caregiver acts that consistently deny the child opportunities to meet needs for interacting or communicating with peers or adults inside or outside the home. ISOLATING includes the following: ■ Confining the child or placing unreasonable limitations on the child's freedom of movement within his or her environment ■ Placing unreasonable limitations or restrictions on social interactions with peers or adults in the community	MENTAL HEALTH, MEDICAL, AND EDUCATIONAL NEGLECT includes unwarranted caregiver acts that ignore, refuse to allow, or fail to provide the necessary treatment for the mental health, medical, and educational problems or needs for the child. MENTAL HEALTH, MEDICAL, AND EDUCATIONAL NEGLECT includes the following: ■ Ignoring the need for, failing, or refusing to allow or provide treatment for serious emotional/behavioral problems or needs of the child ■ Ignoring the need for, failing, or refusing to allow or provide treatment for serious physical health problems or needs of the child ■ Ignoring the need for, failing, or refusing to allow or provide treatment services for serious educational problems or needs of the child

SOURCE: Office for the Study of the Psychological Rights of the Child, Purdue University, 902 West New York Street, Indianapolis, IN 46202-5155.

measurement strategy using child protective services records. Recognizing the limits of these records, McGee and Wolfe (1991a, 1991b) employed a protocol for interviewing both maltreated adolescents and their protective service caseworkers. In addition, several new instruments have been created to measure adults' retrospective perceptions of psychological and other maltreatment. The "Assessment" subsection of this chapter provides information on some of these.

Two studies have surveyed professional and public opinion regarding the definition of psychological maltreatment. These studies provide preliminary evidence of a broad societal consensus that psychological maltreatment is both recognizable and serious. Burnett (1993) surveyed the opinions of 452 social workers and 381 members of the general public regarding 20 vignettes of possible psychological abuse involving "latency age" children (ages 7-11). These vignettes were based largely on definitions that are similar to those above. Respondents were asked to state whether the vignette was abuse or not, how serious it was, and what should be done. Burnett found considerable agreement between both groups that 18 of the 20 vignettes constituted abuse, including behaviors representing isolating, spurning, corrupting/exploiting, terrorizing, and denying emotional responsiveness. The results of the seriousness scale showed that the mean for all vignettes was more than 3.52 (between "serious" and "quite serious"). The overall mean for the "what to do" scale was between "refer for counseling" and "refer to court." Citizen and social worker ratings were essentially the same, and when they differed, it was the citizens who wanted more drastic interventions.

Portwood (1999) surveyed 323 mental health, legal, and medical professionals as well as parents and adult nonparents regarding their opinions about rating the relative importance of various factors in deciding whether a specific caregiver act constitutes child maltreatment. A broad consensus resulted among the five respondent groups that the most important factors were actual physical or psychological harm to the child, possible physical or psychological harm to the child, and seriousness and frequency of the act. Each of these factors was rated above a 6 on a 7-point scale of importance by all respondent groups. Ratings indicated that respondents considered psychological harm to be as important as physical harm in defining maltreatment. Furthermore, all re-

spondent groups gave relatively high ratings to a vignette depicting a parent screaming at a child and calling a child names, indicating support for the view that this behavior constitutes maltreatment.

Complex and Controversial Conceptual Issues

The above work may be regarded as significant progress in establishing a broad foundation for definition and action. However, numerous complex and potentially controversial issues remain for further articulation, research, debate, and consensus building. These include

(a) articulation of the philosophical basis for definitions,

(b) sensitivity to the varied purposes that the definition is to serve,

(c) whether to define maltreatment in terms of perpetrator acts or in terms of the effects on the child or some combination of both,

(d) whether the criteria require evidence of actual harm or also include potential harm,

(e) the determination of levels of severity required for classification as maltreatment and distinguishing maltreatment from more general inadequate parenting,

(f) the likelihood that differing criteria are needed depending on the developmental stage of the child,

(g) the possibility of differential meaning and effects of acts depending on cultural context,

(h) differentiating from other forms of maltreatment.

A stimulating discussion and debate of many of these problems appeared in a special issue of *Development and Psychopathology* ("Psychological Maltreatment," 1991), which contained 14 articles representing a diversity of views from researchers and policy analysts. Next, we briefly address some of these issues.

Stated Purpose of the Definition

Maltreatment is defined in many diverse contexts, including the domains of research, mental health practice, law, and social policy. Many commentators have asserted that specific definitions must be sensitive to the needs of each context (Aber & Zigler, 1981; Haugaard, 1991; Wald, 1991). However, others have cautioned that unnecessarily divergent definitions may impair interdisciplinary collaboration (Toth, 1991).

Specific criteria for definitions and evaluation. Psychological maltreatment has been defined in terms of perpetrator acts, rather than effects on the child (APSAC, 1995). Acts are judged to be maltreatment based on their nature, including factors such as severity, frequency, and meaning. The potential for immediate and long-term harm may be an additional consideration. However, as maltreatment is defined in terms of perpetrator acts, many authors have argued that the definition should not require that children suffer demonstrable harm (e.g., Garbarino, 1991; Navarre, 1987). Acts must be assessed in their ecological context to determine if they place a child at a significant risk for harm or violate the standard of care. This context includes factors such as the nature of the relationship of the child to the perpetrator, the developmental stage of the child, and the culture in which the acts occur. The developmental stage of the child requires special consideration in the formation of specific definitions and in the evaluation of individual cases (APSAC, 1995). Although categories such as terrorizing and denying emotional responsiveness may be universally defined as maltreatment, the specific behaviors constituting each category may vary somewhat depending on the child's developmental stage. For research purposes, variables other than perpetrator acts (e.g., perpetrator intents, the child's subjective appraisals) may be conceptualized as moderator variables that are not part of the definition of maltreatment but are factors that determine whether harm will occur (Belsky, 1991).

Sensitivity to Cultural Context

Social ethics require the consideration of cultural differences in the acceptability and meaning of certain practices (see American Psychological Association, 1992; Sternberg & Lamb, 1991; see Chapter 23, this volume). Cultures vary in their values and their goals for human development (Belsky,

1991). In addition, superficially similar practices may have different meanings and effects in different cultural contexts. Thus, professionals in all fields must be sensitive to cultural factors in defining and evaluating maltreatment (APSAC, 1995).

Incidence and Prevalence

The concepts of incidence and prevalence are used in epidemiology to describe rates of phenomena in a population (Torrence, 1997). In the child maltreatment literature, incidence most often refers to the number of new cases that come to the attention of authorities during a particular year, whereas prevalence frequently represents the total number of people in a sample who have ever experienced abuse. The true incidence of psychological maltreatment is not known. In part, this is because previous studies have used inadequate definitions, measurement strategies, and recording procedures and because of the undoubtedly large number of unreported cases. However, there are now sufficient data from studies using definitions similar to those above to provide a rough estimate of the prevalence of childhood histories of psychological maltreatment in the adult general population of the United States. We believe that these studies provide a more accurate estimate of the true scope of psychological maltreatment than the more commonly cited official reports.

In 1997, 4.6% of all children were reported for child abuse and neglect to child protective services agencies in the United States.

According to the National Committee to Prevent Child Abuse (now called Prevent Child Abuse America), in 1997, 3,195,000 children (or 4.6% of all children) were reported for child abuse and neglect to child protective services (CPS) agencies in the United States (Wang & Daro, 1998). In the same year, CPS confirmed 1,054,000 children (or 1.5% of all children) as victims of child maltreatment. Of these confirmed cases, only 4% (or 42,160) represented specifically identified emotional maltreatment. These statistics are considered to be underestimates because it is generally accepted that only a small percentage of child maltreatment cases come to the attention of authorities during any particular year, and unless recognized psychological maltreatment co-occurs with other forms of abuse or neglect, it is likely to be unreported (Claussen & Crittenden, 1991; Egeland & Erickson, 1987).

The National Incidence Study, funded by the National Center on Child Abuse and Neglect (now the Federal Office on Child Abuse and Neglect), is generally considered to provide a more accurate estimate of the annual incidence of child abuse and neglect than reports from CPS agencies (Sedlak & Broadhurst, 1996). This study applies standardized definitions to all cases known to child welfare agencies as well as to local social service, health, and law enforcement professionals. The definitions incorporate a "harm standard," which only includes children who experienced documented harm, and an "endangerment standard," which includes children who experienced abuse or neglect that put them at risk of harm. More than 1.5 million children were estimated to be abused or neglected in the United States in 1993 under the harm standard and nearly 3 million under the endangerment standard. The latter standard also resulted in an estimate of approximately 532,200 children being emotionally abused and 585,100 children being emotionally neglected in that year.

In a telephone incidence survey of a nationally representative sample of 3,458 parents, Vissing, Straus, Gelles, and Harrop (1991) asked parents about their use of verbal or symbolic aggression with their children. Verbal or symbolic aggression was defined as "communication intended to cause psychological pain to another person, or a communication perceived as having that intent" (p. 224). Sixty-three percent of the parents reported one or more instances of verbal aggression occurring in the previous year. Children who were victims of verbal aggression experienced an average of at least 12.6 such attacks during that year. In the absence of standards of how frequent verbal aggression needs to be before it is considered abusive, the authors computed three thresholds to produce three estimates of the annual incidence of verbally abused children. If the criterion is set at 10 or more,

the rate is 267 per 1,000 children (or 26.7%). If the criterion is 20 or more, the rate is 138 per 1,000 children (or 13.8%). If the criterion is 25 or more (exceeding twice a month on average), the rate is 113 per 1,000 children (or 11.3%). The rates reported in this study are likely to be lower than the actual rates because they are based on the reports of parents who may be reluctant to report the full extent of verbal aggression they use with their children. In addition, it must be recognized that the survey dealt only with a limited set of the verbal behaviors that fall under the broader categories of psychological maltreatment.

A number of studies have collected data regarding the prevalence of childhood histories of one or more dimensions of psychological maltreatment by retrospectively surveying adults about their childhood experiences (e.g., Buntain-Ricklefs, Kemper, Bell, & Babonis, 1994; Gross & Keller, 1992; Hemenway, Solnick, & Carter, 1994; Moeller, Bachman, & Moeller, 1993). For example, Gross and Keller (1992) assessed for the presence of a history of childhood psychological and physical abuse in a sample of 260 college students. Of the total sample, 20.61% were classified as having histories of psychological abuse only, and an additional 16.67% reported histories of combined psychological and physical abuse, producing a total of 37.28% with psychological abuse histories. In another study, Moeller et al. (1993) assessed the rates of emotional, physical, and sexual abuse in a community sample of 668 women using a self-administered anonymous questionnaire. The subjects were predominantly White, well educated, and middle class. More than 37% (250) of the women reported experiences that met the criteria for emotional abuse, either alone or in combination with other forms, and 15% experienced it occurring alone. Physical abuse, in isolation or in combination, was indicated by the responses of 25.3% of the women, and nearly 20% reported experiences of sexual abuse.

Binggeli et al. (2001) reviewed this literature and estimated that psychological maltreatment may have been a significant presence in the childhood histories of more than one third of the general adult population of the United States. By examining the data and the definitions used to produce them, they estimated that approximately 10% to 15% of all people have experienced the more severe and chronic forms of this maltreatment. They also emphasized that the definitions used in these studies tended to be fairly conservative—they were based on behaviors that are generally agreed on by researcher and community opinion to be abusive (e.g., Burnett, 1993), and collectively these adults were not exaggerating their negative experiences because the most common human tendency seems to be to minimize one's own maltreatment history (e.g., Carlin, Kemper, Ward, Sowell, Gustafson, & Stevens, 1994; Femina, Yeager, & Lewis, 1990; Hemenway et al., 1994; Rausch & Knutson, 1991; Varia, Abidin, & Dass, 1996).

Psychological maltreatment, broadly defined, is associated with poor appetite, lying and stealing, encopresis and enuresis, low self-esteem or negative self-concept, emotional instability or emotional maladjustment, reduced emotional responsiveness, inability to become independent, incompetence or underachievement, inability to trust others, depression, prostitution, failure to thrive, withdrawal, suicide, and homicide.

Evidence of Impact

For more than 30 years, expert opinion and clinical findings have identified serious consequences to children associated with psychological maltreatment. The American Humane Association (Wald, 1991) and the National Center on Child Abuse and Neglect (Broadhurst, 1984) both published the following list of disorders as representative of possible psychological maltreatment consequences: habit disorders, conduct disorders, neurotic traits, psychoneurotic reactions, behavior extremes, overly adaptive behaviors, lags in development, and attempted suicide. A review of relevant literature by Hart et al. (1987) found psychological maltreatment, broadly defined, associated with the following problems: poor appetite, lying and stealing, encopresis and enuresis, low self-esteem or negative self-concept, emotional instability or emotional maladjustment, reduced emotional re-

sponsiveness, inability to become independent, incompetence or underachievement, inability to trust others, depression, prostitution, failure to thrive, withdrawal, suicide, and homicide.

In this section, the highlights of findings from more recent reviews of evidence of the known and probable effects of psychological maltreatment will be presented. The findings in this area have been reported in greater detail in Hart, Binggeli, and Brassard (1998) and in Binggeli et al. (2001). The available evidence will be presented under two major categories that support the position that psychological maltreatment is the core component in child abuse and neglect and that further illustrate accumulating knowledge of its destructive power.

Impact Evidence Supporting Core Component Status

Three bases of impact research exist in support of the position that psychological maltreatment is the core component of child abuse and neglect: (a) longitudinal (prospective) research, (b) cross-cultural research, and (c) studies allowing comparison of the impact of different forms of maltreatment. Highlights of studies of this nature are provided in the discussion that follows.

Longitudinal research focusing specifically on psychological maltreatment occurred in six studies that are reviewed briefly here. The Minnesota Mother-Child Interaction Project (Egeland & Erickson, 1987; Egeland, Sroufe, & Erickson, 1983; Erickson et al., 1989) followed from birth to adulthood the care and development of children born to mothers at risk for caretaking problems. The researchers identified five groups of families differentiated according to the presence or absence of five forms of treatment, including physical abuse, hostile or verbal abuse, physical and health care neglect, psychologically unavailable caretaking (i.e., denying emotional responsiveness), and adequate care. Comparisons with the control group have consistently shown that maltreatment, including psychological maltreatment, has serious consequences beyond simply being raised in a disadvantaged environment. Children of hostile or verbally abusive mothers were equally negatively affected as compared with children of physically abusive mothers. The negative impact on children of psychologically unavailable mothers (i.e., denying emotional responsiveness) was judged to be the most devastating.

The Lehigh longitudinal study (Herrenkohl, Egolf, & Herrenkohl, 1997; Herrenkohl, Herrenkohl, & Egolf, 1983; Herrenkohl, Herrenkohl, Egolf, & Wu, 1991; Herrenkohl, Herrenkohl, Toedter, & Yanushefski, 1984) investigated five parent-child interaction patterns to determine the developmental consequences of child maltreatment. Families of children were followed who were categorized as falling in five study groups: abuse families labeled by child welfare, protective-service families labeled neglectful but not abusive and served by child welfare, Head Start families, day care children, and middle-income families with children in private nursery school programs. Preschool children who experienced spurning and terrorizing in acts of criticizing, verbal rejection, and threats of punishment and physical abuse were likely to become school-age children who felt unloved, inadequate, and angry (i.e., with low self-esteem and likely to be aggressive). Levels of assaultive behavior in adolescence were judged to be influenced by their early childhood experiences, which exemplified terrorizing, spurning, or corrupting/exploiting.

Loeber and Strouthamer-Loeber (1986) conducted a meta-analysis of longitudinal research on delinquency and concluded that socialization variables, such as parental rejection and lack of parent-child involvement and supervision (i.e., spurning and denying emotional responsiveness), were among the most powerful predictors of juvenile delinquency.

The Cambridge-Somerville Youth Study, a 40-year investigation, followed 253 males to determine relationships between early conditions of psychological care and treatment and later adolescent or adult characteristics (McCord, 1983; McCord, McCord, & Zola, 1959). Discipline that is erratic and punitive or lax and parenting that is rejecting, neglectful, or cruel were found to particularly predispose children to crime. These conditions were also associated with child histories of emotional instability, substance abuse, and high mortality.

Lefkowitz, Eron, Walder, and Huesmann (1977) conducted a longitudinal study of the development of aggression, beginning with an extensive study of a nationally representative sample of 875 eight-year-old students of both genders and following them to young adulthood. Predictors of child aggression in the third grade were parental rejection, low parental nurturance, and punishment for aggression when the child had low or only moderate identification with parents (i.e., spurning and denying emotional responsiveness by caretakers). The strongest predictor of aggression at age 19 was the degree of aggression observed in third grade.

Ney, Fung, and Wickett (1994) followed 167 children, identified as experiencing five types of maltreatment, from years 7 through 18 of their development. Verbal abuse (i.e., spurning) and emotional neglect (i.e., denying emotional responsiveness) were judged to significantly influence the development of negative effects on feelings and perspectives about enjoyment of living, purpose in life, prospects for future life, chances of having a happy marriage, and expectations for being a good parent. In combination, verbal abuse and emotional neglect experiences were associated with the most devastating outcomes.

Cross-cultural research was conducted by Rohner and Rohner (1980) to investigate the impact of rejection in dozens of anthropological studies conducted in a wide variety of the world's cultures. They studied the antecedents and consequences of parental acceptance-rejection and emotional abuse. Two forms of rejection were found, one representing parental indifference and neglect (i.e., denying emotional responsiveness) and one representing parental hostility and aggression (i.e., spurning). Their research revealed that such rejection produced negative effects in children in every culture studied. Rejected children tended to have an impaired sense of self-esteem and self-adequacy; to be emotionally unstable, emotionally unresponsive, and aggressive; and to have a negative worldview.

Comparative research, making it possible to distinguish between the relative impact of different types of abuse and neglect, has been growing and now provides a large body of useful information. Some of the findings from the longitudinal studies already mentioned are helpful in this regard. Egeland and associates (Egeland & Erickson, 1987; Egeland et al., 1983; Erickson et al., 1989) found hostile verbal abuse to be similar to physical abuse in its negative impact on children and psychologically unavailable caretaking to be the most devastating of all maltreatment forms studied. McCord (1983) concluded that although child abuse and neglect seem to produce juvenile delinquency, parental rejection (spurning and denying emotional responsiveness) appears to be an even more powerful instigator of crime. Ney et al. (1994) found that verbal abuse and emotional neglect appeared frequently in combinations of abuse that tended to produce the most powerfully negative outcomes.

Other studies further clarify the differential impact of psychological maltreatment as compared with other forms of abuse and neglect. Claussen and Crittenden (1991), in studying young children averaging 4 years 4 months of age, found that psychological maltreatment was a better predictor of detrimental developmental outcomes than the severity of physical injury and that it usually co-occurred with physical abuse. They concluded that this "pervasive co-occurrence suggest[s] the need to assess systematically the evidence for psychological maltreatment for all reported cases of physical maltreatment" (p. 15). Crittenden et al. (1994), in studying physical neglect and psychological maltreatment experiences of children and adolescents 10 to 17 years of age, found that severity of psychological abuse was the only severity scale related to behavior problems. Vissing et al. (1991), through their national interview process described earlier, found that the more parents used verbal aggression, the more likely their children would be physically aggressive, delinquent, or experience interpersonal problems. In addition, they found that verbal aggression by parents was more strongly related to these negative child outcomes than was parental physical aggression and that physical aggression unaccompanied by verbal aggression was minimal in its impact on delinquency and interpersonal problems. Brown (1984) used a self-report survey to investigate the relationship between child maltreatment and juvenile delinquency. Results indicated that emotional abuse and neglect, targeted by questions on spurning, terrorizing, and denying emotional responsiveness, were correlated positively with all forms of delinquent behavior, but physical abuse was not positively correlated with any form.

Gross and Keller (1992), Briere and Runtz (1988, 1990), and Rorty, Yager, and Rossotto (1994) have investigated the maltreatment histories of adult populations. Respectively, their findings suggest that psychological abuse is a stronger predictor than physical abuse of both depression and low self-esteem; that psychological maltreatment bears a special relationship with maladjustment and is particularly strongly related to anxiety, depression, interpersonal sensitivity, dissociation, and low self-esteem; and that psychological maltreatment is the most prevalent form of abuse experienced by bulimics, occurring in more than 4 times the cases reported for physical abuse.

Main and colleagues (see George & Main, 1979; Main & Goldwyn, 1984) report on several studies in which they investigated the child-rearing experiences of mothers and their infants. The mother's history of being rejected by a parent was highly related to rejection of her own infant, particularly if the mother displayed cognitive distortions of idealization of the rejecting parent, difficulty in remembering childhood, and incoherency in discussing attachment issues. In addition, findings indicated that physical abuse and parental rejection (spurning and denying emotional responsiveness) produce quite similar negative effects on children, including display of unpredictable bouts of aggression and hostility, unsympathetic and sometimes violent responses to distress in others, and self-isolating behaviors.

The Broader Accumulating Findings Illustrating the Associates and Effects of Psychological Maltreatment

A wide range of studies, including many of those described so far in this chapter, have identified established or probable effects of psychological maltreatment within families. The impact evidence can be grouped in categories dealing with topics similar to those originally delineated in the section on "Serious Emotional Disturbance" in Public Law 94-142 and now included in the federal Individuals With Disabilities Act (i.e., problems with intrapersonal thoughts, feelings, and behaviors; emotional problem symptoms; social competency problems and antisocial functioning; learning problems; and physical health problems).

Problems with intrapersonal thoughts, feelings, and behaviors have been found to be caused by or associated with psychological maltreatment backgrounds investigated in research described earlier. The proven or possible negative effects identified have included anxiety, depression, low self-esteem, negative life views, and suicidal ideation (see Briere & Runtz, 1988, 1990; Claussen & Crittenden, 1991; Crittenden et al., 1994; Egeland & Erickson, 1987; Gross & Keller,

1992; Herrenkohl et al., 1983, 1984, 1991, 1997; Ney et al., 1994; Rohner & Rohner, 1980). Additional evidence exists. The impact on children of being exposed to the battering of women and spousal or family violence and thereby experiencing terrorizing, exploiting, and corrupting (Hughes, 1992; Hughes & Graham-Bermann, 1998) has been related to consistent differences of greater levels of anxiety, depression, and low self-esteem for these children when compared with other children. Terr (1981) studied 23 children who had been kidnapped from their school bus at gunpoint, driven in boarded-up vans for 11 hours, and buried underground for 16 hours (i.e., terrorized) but not harmed physically. Early symptoms included fears of further trauma, fearful misperceptions of innocuous situations, hallucinations, and "omen" formation; later, these victims exhibited posttraumatic symptoms and fears of being kidnapped again, thus establishing anxiety symptoms and negative life views as outcomes. Mullen, Martin, Anderson, Romans, and Herbison (1996) found outcomes associated with psychological maltreatment for a community sample of 610 women to include low self-esteem, depression, and enhanced risk for attempting suicide. Engels and Moisan (1994) studied 118 adult male and female clinical outpatients and found self-reports of parental hostile rejection (i.e., spurning) and emotional neglect (denying emotional responsiveness) related to a history lower self-efficacy or self-esteem for subjects. Braver, Bumberry, Green, and Rawson (1992) found that clients receiving services at a university counseling center who were more depressed than others reported emotional abuse histories (in addition to other forms of abuse) and that emotional abuse represented by far the largest proportion of abuse reported.

Emotional problem symptoms have been well established as being associated with psychological maltreatment in studies already identified in this chapter. The problems identified include emotional instability, impulse control problems, borderline instability, unresponsiveness, substance abuse, and eating disorder problems (see Braver et al., 1992; Briere & Runtz, 1988; Crittenden et al., 1994; Egeland & Erickson, 1987; Engels & Moisan, 1994; McCord, 1983; Mullen et al., 1996; Rohner & Rohner, 1980; Rorty et al., 1994).

Social competency problems and antisocial functioning, which have been found to be the probable results of psychological maltreatment in studies already noted, include attachment problems, self-isolating behavior, low social competency, low empathy, noncompliance, dependency, sexual maladjustment, aggression and violent behavior, and delinquency or criminality (see Briere & Runtz, 1988, 1990; Brown, 1984; Claussen & Crittenden, 1991; Crittenden et al., 1994; Egeland & Erickson, 1987; Herrenkohl et al., 1983, 1984, 1991, 1997; Hughes & Graham-Bermann, 1998; Lefkowitz et al., 1977; Loeber & Strouthamer-Loeber, 1986; Main & George, 1985; Main & Goldwyn, 1984; McCord, 1983; Mullen et al., 1996; Rohner & Rohner 1980; Rorty et al., 1994; Vissing et al., 1991).

Other studies add support to these relationships. The Hart and Brassard (1989-1991) research, which produced operationally defined measures of emotional maltreatment, found psychological maltreating behaviors of mothers to be strongly predictive of impaired social competence for their children, as measured by teachers. DeLozier (1982) found that mothers who physically assaulted their children were more likely than controls to have had child histories of being terrorized by threats of abandonment and violence (not acts of violence) and to have been spurned and denied emotional responsiveness. Dutton and Golant (1995), in reporting on the results of numerous studies, found that the recollections of the men who batter woman were characterized by memories of cold, rejecting, and abusive fathers. Numerous other studies have found psychological maltreatment histories related to the child victim's aggression, violence, delinquency, or criminality, indicating that parents of delinquents tended to be rejecting, cruel, and less affectionate (Bandura & Walters, 1959). Children ranked as "most delinquent" tended to have backgrounds of rejection (i.e., spurning and denying emotional responsiveness), whereas parental acceptance correlated with reduced chance of delinquency (Nye, 1958).

Numerous studies have shown that parents of delinquents tend in their discipline to be physically harsh, inconsistent, unfair, and nonobjective—in other words, likely to terrorize and spurn (Button, 1973; Glueck & Glueck, 1950; Shoemaker, 1984; Trojanowicz & Morash, 1983). Finally, research has indicated that a boy is twice as likely to commit a murder if his background includes being abused or being reared in a family environment of criminal violence (Zagar, Arbit,

Sylvies, & Busch, 1991), both of which are highly likely to be pervaded by psychological maltreatment.

Studies have shown that parents of delinquents tend in their discipline to be physically harsh, inconsistent, unfair, and nonobjective—in other words, likely to terrorize and spurn.

Learning problems or child characteristics likely to interfere with learning associated with psychological maltreatment backgrounds and found in studies already cited include decline in mental competence, lower measured intelligence, noncompliance, lack of impulse control, impaired learning, academic problems and lower achievement test results, and impaired development of moral reasoning (see Claussen & Crittenden, 1991; Crittenden et al., 1994; Egeland & Erickson, 1987; Hughes & Graham-Bermann, 1998; Main & George, 1985; Main & Goldwyn, 1984; Rohner & Rohner, 1980). Other studies have found rejected children to do less well than comparison children on achievement and intelligence tests (Manley, 1977), do less well in school in general (Sheintuch & Lewin, 1981; Starkey, 1980), and display impaired development of moral reasoning (Bilbro, Boni, Johnson, & Roe, 1979; Hoffman, 1970). Among economically disadvantaged children, psychologically maltreated children are significantly more likely to show school-related problems in ability and academic achievement (Hart & Brassard, 1989-1991).

Physical health problems of a variety of forms have been found to be related to psychological maltreatment backgrounds, including rejection (i.e., spurning and denying emotional responsiveness) and the psychophysiological problems of allergies (Miller & Baruch, 1948), asthma and other respiratory ailments (Jacobs, Spilken, & Noeman, 1972), and hypertension (McGinn, 1963); spurning, terrorizing, and denying emotional responsiveness and somatic complaints (Hughes, 1992; Krugman & Krugman, 1984); and spurning and high mortality rates (McCord, 1983). Denying emotional responsiveness has been found to be dramatically associated with negative physical health and development, including

high infant mortality rates (McCord, 1983; Spitz, 1945, 1946) and developmental delays in almost all areas of physical and behavioral development (Bowlby, 1951; Burlingham & Freud, 1944; Coleman & Provence, 1957; Goldfarb, 1945; Prugh & Harlow, 1962; Puckering et al., 1995). This relationship between inadequate emotional care and indicators of serious growth failure, despite adequate nutrition, became known during the 1960s as "nonorganic failure to thrive." Research on the effects of child maltreatment on brain development has reached a much higher level of sophistication progressed through the use of advanced technology. Recently reported results on brain-imaging studies (Joseph, 1999) suggest that severe, repeated sexual abuse in childhood (which includes psychological maltreatment, particularly spurning, terrorizing, isolating, and corrupting/exploiting) is the probable cause of damage to the brain structure related to memory and to significant reductions in the size of the hippocampus, which may predispose the victim to develop symptoms of posttraumatic stress disorder and experience dissociation. In addition, Moeller et al. (1993) found in a community sample of 668 women that for women maltreated in childhood, the greater the number of types of childhood abuse (including psychological maltreatment), the poorer the women's adult health tended to be.

Theoretical Perspectives

Psychological maltreatment is an extremely heterogeneous phenomenon, occurring in a great variety of contexts. As previously indicated, it embodies many major and minor categories of acts of commission and omission that are considered to be damaging to children. No two cases of psychological maltreatment will contain the same elements, and many will be quite different from others. Most of the major theories in psychology contain constructs that are meaningfully related to psychological maltreatment by the way they describe critical factors of the developmental process that are susceptible to the influences of various kinds of psychological experiences. Theories of recognized and strong relevance to psychological maltreatment include human needs theory, psychosocial theory, attachment theory, and acceptance-rejection theory. These and a few additional perspectives that help to clarify the nature of psychological maltreatment are briefly described here (for more a more detailed review, see Binggeli et al., 2001).

Human Needs Theory

Although all humanistic theories have relevance to child abuse and neglect, human needs theory has been recognized to have particularly strong explanatory and heuristic value for psychological maltreatment (Barnett, Manly, & Cicchetti, 1991; Binggeli et al., 2001; Hart et al., 1987; Hart, Brassard, & Karlson, 1996). Abraham Maslow (1970), an acknowledged leader in human needs theory, proposed that the human organism has certain needs to be met if it is to develop properly. The first set is the basic (or deficiency) needs, including physiological needs (such as food, clothing, and shelter) and the psychological needs of safety, love and belongingness, and esteem. The second set is the growth needs, including needs for aesthetic and cognitive knowledge and for what Maslow termed *self-actualization*. Self-actualization involves a process of making more complete use of one's talents and potentials and of becoming more self-motivating, self-directive, and self-reinforcing. If a child is thwarted in his or her healthy efforts to satisfy the basic needs, such as love and safety, the child may be forced to meet these needs in unhealthy ways, thus distorting development.

The various forms of psychological maltreatment can be seen as direct attacks on the basic human needs and as both direct and indirect attacks on the growth needs. For example, *spurning* would be in conflict with the needs for belongingness, love, and esteem. *Terrorizing* could affect each of these needs and seriously compromise a child's safety needs.

Psychosocial Stage Theory

Erik Erikson (1959) proposed that human development proceeds in the following series of stages, each with its own set tasks or conflicts:

infancy—trust versus mistrust (emphasis years 0-2) and autonomy versus shame and doubt (emphasis years 2-4),

childhood—initiative versus guilt (emphasis years 5-7) and industry versus inferiority (emphasis 8-12),

adolescence—identity versus identity confusion (emphasis years 13-17).

Each stage is seen as having its own period of ascendancy, although the tasks of each stage are present to some degree in preceding and later stages. The degree of success or failure an individual achieves at each stage is seen as affecting the quality and likelihood of success and failure at subsequent stages. Psychological maltreatment can be viewed as undermining the individual's efforts to successfully master the tasks of a developmental stage. Poor resolution at a previous stage can have direct effects on the individual's ability to successfully complete the tasks of later stages. For example, infants who are psychologically neglected (denied emotional responsiveness) or terrorized through direct assaults or chaotic and stressful surrounding interpersonal environments are likely to develop a basic sense of mistrust that will limit and distort their exploratory behavior and thwart development of a healthy autonomy. Without correction, this can erode a sense of self and a sense of self-worth and ultimately prevent the development of a strong sense of identity. Psychosocial stage theory has been used to clarify the influence of psychological maltreatment at different developmental points in children's lives (Cicchetti & Braunwald, 1984; Sroufe, 1996, 1979).

Attachment Theory

The human infant enters the world programmed with a set of behaviors designed to elicit appropriate caregiving, according to attachment theory (Ainsworth, 1969, 1989; Bowlby, 1973, 1980, 1982, 1988; Sroufe, 1979). Between 6 to 12 months of age, the infant begins forming attachments with one or a few individuals. The development of a secure attachment with a primary caregiver is the stage-salient task during this period. It is theorized that the quality of the attachment attained during these early stages affects subsequent attachment behavior. A growing body of evidence strongly suggests that the quality of attachment has profound implications for emotional health and interpersonal functioning. Two key ideas of attachment theory are the ideas of a "secure base" and "internal working models." It is thought that a secure attachment with a responsive caretaker provides a "secure base" for the infant to explore the environment, facilitating a basic sense of trust and growing autonomy. In addition, children form internal working models, or sets of expectations about the roles of themselves and others in social interactions, through their ongoing interactions with attachment figures.

Extensive research has been conducted on attachment issues (Ainsworth, Blehar, Waters, & Wall, 1978; Belsky, Rovine, & Taylor, 1984; Crittenden & Ainsworth, 1989; Goldberg, Perrota, Minde, & Corter, 1986; Grossman & Grossman, 1985; Main, 1996; Pearce & Pezzot-Pearce, 1994). Infant attachment patterns have been found to be systematically related to specific patterns of maternal caretaking behavior. Four attachment patterns have been identified: secure attachment, ambivalent-resistant attachment, avoidant attachment, and disorganized-disoriented attachment. Infants who display ambivalent-resistant attachment appear to have experienced inconsistent and insensitive care, which fits the denying emotional responsiveness category of psychological maltreatment. Avoidant attachment infants appear to have experienced insensitive caregiving, which alternates between rejecting, neglecting, and interfering and fits the spurning, denying emotional responsiveness, and exploiting/corrupting forms of psychological maltreatment. Disorganized-disoriented attachment infants appear to have experienced a confusing pattern of early consistent care and later inconsistent care that may include characteristics of spurning, terrorizing, isolating, and denying emotional responsiveness.

Parental Acceptance-Rejection Theory

This theoretical orientation was specifically developed by Rohner and Rohner (1980) to clarify the nature of "emotional maltreatment" and to guide cross-cultural research on rejection. In their theory, "acceptance" means parental warmth and affection, and "rejection" means emotional abuse that is embodied, principally, in parental hostility and aggression and parental indifference and neglect. These two forms of rejection are basically the equivalents of spurning and denying emotional responsiveness (see earlier section for the impact of rejection).

Additional Relevant Theories

The coercion model (Patterson, 1982, 1986) indicates that interpersonal relations problems frequently occur through a pattern of escalating negative interactions between persons, such that the negative action of one person stimulates a negative response by the other person, which stimulates another, possibly more severe, negative response by the first person, and so on. Many of the negative actions and responses would fall within psychological maltreatment categories.

The prisoner-of-war model contrasts the state of the child who experiences extended intrafamilial child abuse with that of the adult prisoner of war. It posits that a child victim of abuse may have greater vulnerability to harm because maltreatment occurs during critical developmental periods. It also recognizes that the influences of psychological maltreatment on the child may be strengthened due to the child (a) being discouraged from blaming adult perpetrators, (b) being encouraged to blame self, (c) having a relatively limited background of positive life experiences to ameliorate the experience, and (d) having a relatively limited ability to place the experience in a larger context of time and successful problem resolution to provide hope of and perseverance for respite (Benedek, 1985; Turgi & Hart, 1988).

Psychological Maltreatment and the Law

Psychological maltreatment (even at severe levels), when it has been unconnected to or not accompanied by physical abuse, sexual abuse, or serious neglect of a child's basic needs (e.g., food, clothing, shelter, education, health care), has rarely led to coercive or punitive governmental intervention—either by CPS agencies or the courts. Few reported appellate court decisions reviewing trial-level child protective judicial intervention actions address cases in which psychological maltreatment alone was the basis for a lower court's judgment. This makes it extremely difficult to identify or describe any general controlling judicial precedents to guide court actions in emotional or mental injury cases. As described below, the relevant language contained in the state's laws will most likely be the guidance that CPS workers and judges use in making determinations that a child has been the victim of psychological maltreatment.

The training that CPS workers, police, prosecutors, judges, and other professionals receive on the topic of child maltreatment focuses almost entirely on identifying and proving physical abuse, sexual abuse, or the tangible aspects of child neglect. The documentation of children's mental injuries related to psychological maltreatment has, regrettably, never been an important focus of professional training for those with legal responsibilities to intervene in cases of serious harm to children. Previously, there has not been an accepted and widely used set of specific "psychological maltreatment guidelines" designed for legal system professionals to either assess harm or make intervention decisions.

However, for more than 25 years, states receiving federal funding under the Child Abuse Prevention and Treatment Act have been required to include, within their laws, statutory language that incorporates the concept of "mental injury" within overall definitions of child abuse and neglect. This mental injury terminology has proven difficult for many state legislatures to define.

Some laws simply use the term *mental injury* (or some similar term) without any further explanation. Other state laws include a description of psychological maltreatment that incorporates one or more of the following legal requirements or aspects.

Some laws mandate that the child has suffered a serious psychological or emotional injury (or, in some states, merely a substantial threat of such an injury), caused by either overt acts (Minnesota adds that acts must be consistently and deliberately inflicted; Minn. Stat. Ann. § 260C.007) or omissions in care by a parent or other person responsible for the child's care.

Some states require that the child's injuries be evidenced by observable, substantial, sustained (either over a short term or long term), and identifiable impairments of the child's intellectual or psychological capacity or emotional stability (again, some laws permit intervention for a substantial "risk" of such impairment). Stated another way, these laws require that the "impairments" affect the child's ability to function in a developmentally appropriate manner or within a "normal range" of performance or behavior, with some states further requiring that the child's age, development, culture, and environment be taken into consideration.

Some laws use vague terms such as *failure to provide* for a child's "mental or emotional needs." Some laws use the term *emotional* or *psychological* abuse or injury, but most do not.

Some states focus on the child's problem-related symptoms to include evidence of the child's severe anxiety/agitation, depression, withdrawal, untoward aggressive behavior (toward self or others), seriously delayed development, psychosis, or similarly serious dysfunctional behavior. (Note: some state laws would permit intervention even if the parent's actions or omissions were not the *cause* of the child's problems but if the parent refused appropriate treatment for the child, really a form of "medical neglect.")

Some laws explicitly require that the above impairments or symptoms be supported by the opinion of an expert witness (e.g., a licensed physician or qualified mental health professional).

Several states take a different approach to defining *impairment* of emotional health/mental or emotional capacity to include a child's substantially diminished psychological or intellectual functioning in relation but not limited to factors such as failure to thrive (specifically mentioned in several state laws), control of aggressive or self-destructive impulses, ability to think and reason, or acting out or misbehavior, including incorrigibility, ungovernability, or habitual truancy, but only when the impairments are clearly attributable to the unwillingness or inability of the parent or caretaker to exercise a minimum degree of care toward the child.

A few state laws take unique approaches toward defining psychological maltreatment. Florida specifically recognizes *isolation* as a form of psychological maltreatment by including in the definition of *harm* the use of mechanical devices, unreasonable restraints, or extended periods of isolation to control a child (Fl. Stat. Ann. § 39.01); Hawaii includes evidence of the child's suffering "extreme mental distress" or "gross degradation" among its specifically enumerated categories of child maltreatment (Haw. Rev. Stat. § 350-1); Minnesota includes, as a defense in emotional maltreatment cases, that the parent or caretaker used a reasonable exercise of authority or used reasonable training and discipline (Minn. Stat. Ann. § 260C.007 Subd.8); and Vermont has a definition of emotional maltreatment that requires a pattern of malicious behavior, which results in a child's impaired psychological growth and development (Vt. Stat. Ann. tit. 33 § 4912).

One area of psychological maltreatment not yet incorporated into state laws but clearly affecting potential CPS agency mental injury-related actions involves situations in which children are exposed to domestic violence in the home but are not the direct victims of abuse themselves (see Chapter 6, this volume). There is increasing recognition that children who live in chronically violent homes can suffer great emotional harm, and we will likely see legislatures and child welfare agencies struggle to set proper limits on when intervention can occur on behalf of such *violence-exposed* children.

There are major legal concerns about classifying children exposed to domestic violence as per se victims of child maltreatment (not the least of which are the implications of having such a huge number of children who are so exposed become the focus of an already overburdened CPS system). Recently, California has taken an aggressive posture to work toward identifying and serving domestic violence-exposed children as abused. The experience of witnessing domestic violence was included as the first item in the "Emotional Abuse Decision Tree" of *California's Child Welfare Services Structured Decision Making Pilot Project* (Domestic Violence Unit, 1999). These developments followed the findings of *In re Heather A.* (1996), in which children were removed from their fathers' custody based on findings that "the minors were periodically exposed to violent confrontations between the father and the minors' stepmother that endangered their physical and emotional safety." These developments in California should be followed carefully to determine their implications for protecting children from psychological maltreatment. The question of government intervention in homes where children have witnessed or otherwise been affected by the domestic violence committed against a parent will undoubtedly continue to be debated among professionals and the public, and mental health professionals with expertise on this topic should be involved in these policy discussions.

In conclusion, despite all the potential statutory variations (and controversies) in approaching legal intervention due to emotional harm inflicted on children by their parents, there is no reason to believe that when evidence of psychological maltreatment and its serious impact on a child is clearly presented to the court, there cannot be active and appropriate judicial and CPS agency efforts to both protect the child from such continued harm and provide mental health services to the child to ameliorate the harm.

It is critical that psychologists and psychiatrists educate the bar and bench on the magnitude and long-term impact of parentally inflicted mental injuries to children, as well as on the likely prognosis for various child treatment interventions when children have suffered severe emotional harm.

It is particularly important for child welfare agency attorneys and juvenile court judges to receive education on the devastating effects on children of severe psychological maltreatment and why governmental intervention in these situations is important. CPS workers need practice-friendly guidelines for identifying cases of severe psychological maltreatment that warrant referral for possible judicial action. Given the continued focus of training on legal proof in the (more common) child sexual abuse and severe physical abuse cases, it is critical that psychologists and psychiatrists educate the bar and bench on the magnitude and long-term impact of parentally inflicted mental injuries to children, as well as on the likely prognosis for various child treatment interventions when children have suffered severe emotional harm. The APSAC (1995) practice guidelines provides a base that has the potential to be quite useful in the education and practice of the social service and legal professions' handling of psychological maltreatment cases.

Assessment of Psychological Maltreatment

The major challenge in assessing psychological maltreatment is answering the difficult question, "When does inadequate or poor parenting cross the line into psychological maltreatment?" Caregiver behavior is judged to be psychological maltreatment if one instance is highly likely to produce or has produced mental or developmental

TABLE 4.2 Developmental Tasks

Infancy	Attachment Assistance in the regulation of bodily states, emotion
Toddlerhood	Development of symbolic representation and further self-other discrimination Problem solving, pride, mastery motivation

Preschool	Development of self-control—the use of language to regulate impulses, emotions, store
	  information, predict, and make sense of the world
	Development of verbally mediated or semantic memory
	Gender identity
	Development of social relationships beyond immediate family and generalization of
	  expectations about relationships
	Moral reasoning

Latency age	Peer relationships Adaptation to school environment Moral reasoning
Adolescence	Regeneration of family roles Identity issues (sexuality, future orientation, peer acceptance, ethnicity) Moral reasoning
Young adult	Continued differentiation from family Refinement and integration of identity with particular focus on occupational choice and intimate partners Moral reasoning

harm (i.e., acts such as threatening to kill a pet if a child's grades don't go up, locking a young child in a tool shed overnight, failing to protect a child from another abusive adult) or if a continual pattern is likely to produce or has produced mental or developmental harm (e.g., making degrading or humiliating comments to a child several times a week, showing little or no interest in or love for a child).

Psychological maltreatment is identified through applying its definitions and descriptions as found in Table 4.1 and in relevant state laws to direct observations and reports of caregiver behavior by others. Some states also require that the caregiver's maltreating behavior has emotionally or mentally harmed a child. *Harm* means that there is clear evidence of related mental injuries (severe emotional disturbance under the federal Individuals With Disabilities Act or the *DSM-IV* [American Psychiatric Association, 1994]) or developmental harm (one or more areas of mastery have not occurred or have occurred in a strongly distorted manner; see Table 4.2).

The *Guidelines for the Psychosocial Evaluation of Suspected Psychological Maltreatment in Children and Adolescents* (APSAC, 1995) offer a framework for professionals evaluating children to determine whether they have been or are presently victims of psychological maltreatment. The guidelines were designed to assist in case planning, legal decision making, and treatment planning for psychological maltreatment that occurs in isolation as well as in conjunction with other forms of abuse and neglect. Because psychological maltreatment is often accompanied by or embedded in other forms of child abuse and neglect, its presence should be assessed when professionals are evaluating possible physical abuse, sexual abuse, or neglect, as well as when addressing family problems related to such maltreatment (e.g., initiating family therapy or beginning judicial intervention). Because many state laws require evidence of both acts of maltreatment and harm that have either occurred or are predicted to occur to make a case determination, the guidelines deal with both the assessment of maltreatment acts and of harm.

Psychological maltreatment consists of messages a child receives about himself or herself from important others in the social environment; therefore, professionals should observe the caregiver suspected of psychological maltreatment and the alleged child victim interacting over several occasions. Assessors may use the APSAC categories of psychological maltreatment to organize their observations and the reports of others familiar with the child-caregiver relationship. If a case involves younger children, they might also use one of the observational measures developed by researchers to help them screen, organize information, and

TABLE 4.3 Examples of Questions to Ask Caretakers, Neighbors, Relatives, and Older Children

How often have you done (or have you seen [name of caregiver] do) the following? Indicate if more than once a day, daily, several times a week, weekly, several times a month, once a month or less, or never.
Swore at the child or called the child a swear name
Called the child demeaning names such as "stupid," "loser," or "lazy"
Threatened to kick child out of the house or send child away or to foster care
Threatened to hit or spank a child or hurt the child's pet but didn't do it
Blamed an adult's drinking, family, marital, or mental health problem on the child
Ignored a child's request to be attended to when the child was crying, hurt, or frightened
Failed to show needed/desired affection to the child (kisses, hugs, playful gestures)
Made no attempt to monitor the child's whereabouts
Demonstrated no interest in or love for the child
Used extreme or humiliating forms of punishment (e.g., wearing a sign reading "slut," shaving a girl's hair)
Made fun of a child's feelings about something of importance to the child
Deliberately tried to terrify the child
Threatened to withdraw love from the child
Placed the child in position where he or she had to play a parental role

build a case that meets their state's requirements. These measures include the CARE Index (Crittenden, 1988), the Psychological Maltreatment Rating Scales (Brassard et al., 1993), and the MACRO (Louis, Condon, Shute, & Elzinga, 1997). The psychometric characteristics of these measures are not yet sufficient to use as the primary source of information to make a determination of maltreatment, but they could be used in conjunction with other information (see Binggeli et al., 2001, for a review of measures of psychological maltreatment and a discussion of assessment issues).

Although direct observation is desirable, it is not always necessary to form an opinion regarding whether psychological maltreatment has occurred. Other methods for assessing the child-caregiver relationship exist. These include interviews with the caregiver and the child (if old enough), review of pertinent records, consultation with other professionals, and collateral reports from siblings, grandparents, school and day care personnel, neighbors, and others. A suggested set of questions to ask these individuals is provided in Table 4.3.

Two screening measures, the Conflict Tactic Scales Parent-Child Form (Straus, Hamby, Boney-McCoy, & Sugarman, 1996; Straus, Hamby, Finkelhor, Moore, & Runyan, 1998) and the Record of Maltreatment Experiences (McGee, Wolfe, & Wilson, 1990; Wolfe & McGee, 1994), could be used with parents, other knowledgeable adults, and older children.

For the evaluator preparing forensic testimony, it will be important to document as precisely as possible the incidents of psychological maltreatment that have been observed, are present in the record, or were re-

ported by others. Evaluators will want to assess harm by conducting a thorough developmental assessment (a) through observation of child behavior, teacher interview/ratings, record review, and assessment of child or adolescent intellectual, academic, personality, and interpersonal functioning and moral development and (b) through the use of structured interviews with the child (if old enough) and informed others. In some cases, there is no evidence of harm. This does not mean that maltreatment has had or will have no effect. It may mean that the child has been able to cope with the developmental challenges experienced at a cost not easily recognized or detected. This may not hold true in the future. Evaluators should assess the likelihood of eventual harm through application of the research literature on child maltreatment and developmental and clinical psychology, psychiatry, and social work toward the goal of developing a coherent, empirically supported argument on the relationship between parental acts and child outcomes.

Interventions With Child Victims and Maltreating Families

In the 30 years since Kempe and his colleagues identified the battered child syndrome, clinicians and scholars have learned a great deal about the psychological impact of all forms of maltreatment, including psychological abuse and neglect, on children's emotional, social, and behavioral functioning (Kempe, Silverman, Steele, Droegemueller, & Silver, 1962). Unfortunately, identification of effective intervention approaches has not been as successful. At this point in time, few have been shown to effectively prevent or treat child abuse and neglect, and psychological maltreatment appears to be particularly resistant to intervention efforts (Daro, 1988). Although application of some intervention models has demonstrated improved client outcomes over those obtained by regular CPS (see MacLeod & Nelson, 2000, for a recent review), these intervention models require resources (e.g., reduced client load, highly trained and well-supervised therapists, many client contact hours) well beyond those typically available to CPS or contracting private agencies. If societal commitment can be achieved to fund high-quality intervention research (Thompson & Wilcox, 1995) and support effective programs at a level that maintains their treatment integrity, then the future looks hopeful.

The prevention of child maltreatment is clearly the top intervention priority. Prevention is discussed in detail in Chapter 21. For a recent review of the status of intervention efforts targeting psychological maltreatment in families, see Binggeli et al. (2001).

Studies of specific treatments for maltreated children are uncommon (Azar & Wolfe, 1998; Williams, 1983) despite compelling reasons to treat children. First and foremost is the ethical imperative: Providing therapeutic treatment for children who suffer mistreatment and trauma has been raised to the level of a universal imperative through the standards of the United Nations (UN) Convention on the Rights of the Child (see particularly article 39; United Nations General Assembly, 1989). Second, the evaluation of treatment programs indicates that children evidence far greater treatment gains than do maltreating adults (Daro, 1988). Yet another reason to target children for treatment is indisputable evidence of the intergenerational transmission of child maltreatment (Egeland, Jacobvitz, & Sroufe, 1988; Kaufman & Zigler, 1987; Youngblade & Belsky, 1990).

Treatment of children that provides trusting compensatory relationships, which model mutual respect and teach the behavioral skills necessary to relate to others, can not only ameliorate the psychosocial problems experienced by abused children but can also serve to truncate this intergenerational cycle of abuse (Youngblade & Belsky, 1990). Preschool and elementary schools can serve as important settings for both the prevention and treatment of psychological abuse and neglect. Preschool and elementary school teachers can serve as secure attachment figures for children and, at the same time, model appropriate child care skills for parents (see Crittenden, 1988; Pavenstedt, 1967; Sroufe, 1983) and, with peers, shape appropriate skills in children (Davis & Fantuzzo, 1989), thereby reducing aggression and social withdrawal. For older children and adolescents, group treatment and personal skill development classes have been recognized as important contexts in which to resolve relationship conflicts and develop social skills (Daro, 1988; Pittman, Wolfe, & Wekerle, 1998; Wolfe, et al., 1996). Research on the effectiveness of these programs is promising. School-based interventions that support the social and academic development of these children are as important as other treatments. Schools that give at-risk students a sense of competence through successful experience in academics, art, music, athletics, or social interaction and that teach them to plan and make conscious choices about important events in their lives have significantly better student outcomes than those that do not (Rutter & Rutter, 1993). This is an important area for future research.

Schools that give at-risk students a sense of competence through successful experience in academics, art, music, athletics, or social interaction and that teach them to plan and make conscious choices about important events in their lives have significantly better student outcomes.

Conclusion

Psychological maltreatment takes five forms—spurning, terrorizing, isolating, corrupting/exploiting, and denying emotional responsiveness—each of which can occur in isolation but more often occur in combination with other forms of maltreatment. Psychological maltreatment has been posited as the unifying concept in child abuse and neglect.

Knowledge about psychological maltreatment has expanded substantially during the past 20 years. Widely supported definitions have been established for the five basic forms of psychological maltreatment. The nature and extent of the problem have been clarified, producing credible evidence that psychological maltreatment produces devastating and long-lasting negative effects. Psychological maltreatment appears to be the most pervasive form of maltreatment, with approximately one third of the adult population having experienced it in childhood and 10% to 15% of all persons having experienced psychological maltreatment in its more severe and chronic forms.

Expert and lay opinion agree that psychological maltreatment is a recognizable and serious condition deserving attention. Although more research is needed, especially with regard to the interactions among various forms of maltreatment, enough is known to warrant renewed attention to legal policies and practices regarding psychological maltreatment.

References

Aber, J. L., & Zigler, E. (1981). Developmental considerations in the definition of child maltreatment. In R. Rizley & D. Cicchetti (Eds.), *Developmental perspectives on child maltreatment* (pp. 1-29). San Francisco: Jossey-Bass.

Ainsworth, M. D. S. (1969). Object relations, dependency, and attachment: A theoretical review of the infant-mother relationship. *Child Development, 40,* 969-1025.

Ainsworth, M. D. S. (1989). Attachments beyond infancy. *American Psychologist, 44,* 709-716.

Ainsworth, M. D. S., Blehar, M. C., Waters, E., & Wall, S. (1978). *Patterns of attachment: A psychological study of the strange situation.* Hillsdale, NJ: Lawrence Erlbaum.

American Professional Society on the Abuse of Children (APSAC). (1995). *Guidelines for the psychosocial evaluation of suspected psychological maltreatment in children and adolescents.* Chicago: Author.

American Psychiatric Association. (1994). *Diagnostic and statistical manual of mental disorders* (4th ed.). Washington, DC: Author.

American Psychological Association. (1992). Ethical principles of psychologists and code of conduct. *American Psychologist, 47,* 1597-1611.

Azar, S. T., & Wolfe, D. A. (1998). Child physical abuse and neglect. In E. J. Mash & R. A. Barkley (Eds.), *Treatment of childhood disorders* (pp. 501-544). New York: Guilford.

Baily, T. F., & Baily, W. H. (1986). *Operational definitions of child emotional maltreatment: Final report* (DHHD 90-CA-0956). Washington, DC: Government Printing Office.

Bandura, A., & Walters, R. H. (1959). *Adolescent aggression.* New York: Ronald.

Barnett, D., Manly, J. T., & Cicchetti, D. (1991). Continuing toward an operational definition of psychological maltreatment. *Development and Psychopathology, 3,* 19-29.

Belsky, J. (1991). Psychological maltreatment: Definitional limitations and unstated assumptions. *Development and Psychopathology, 3,* 31-36.

Belsky, J., Rovine, M., & Taylor, D. G. (1984). The Pennsylvania Infant and Family Development Project III: The origins of individual differences in infant-mother attachment: Maternal and infant contributions. *Child Development, 55,* 718-728.

Benedek, E. P. (1985). Children and psychic trauma: A brief review of contemporary thinking. In S. Eth & R. S. Pynoos (Eds.), *Posttraumatic stress disorder in children* (pp. 1-16). Washington, DC: American Psychiatric Association.

Bilbro, T., Boni, M., Johnson, B., & Roe, S. (1979). *The relationship of parental acceptance-rejection to the development of moral reasoning.* Unpublished manuscript, University of Connecticut, Center for the Study of Parental Acceptance-Rejection.

Binggeli, N. J., Hart, S. N., & Brassard, M. R. (2001). *Psychological maltreatment: A study guide.* Thousand Oaks, CA: Sage.

Bowlby, J. (1951). Maternal care and mental health. *Bulletin of the World Health Organization, 31,* 355-533.

Bowlby, J. (1973). *Attachment and loss: Vol. 2. Separation: Anxiety and anger.* New York: Basic Books.

Bowlby, J. (1980). *Attachment and loss: Vol. 3. Loss.* New York: Basic Books.

Bowlby, J. (1982). *Attachment and loss: Vol. 1. Attachment* (2nd ed.). New York: Basic Books.

Bowlby, J. (1988). *A secure base: Clinical applications of attachment theory.* London: Routledge Kegan Paul.

Brassard, M. R., Hart, S. N., & Hardy, D. B. (1993). The psychological maltreatment rating scales. *Child Abuse & Neglect, 17,* 715-729.

Braver, M., Bumberry, J., Green, K., & Rawson, R. (1992). Childhood abuse and current psychological functioning in a university counseling center population. *Journal of Counseling Psychology, 39*(2), 252-257.

Briere, J., & Runtz, M. (1988). Multivariate correlates of childhood psychological and physical maltreatment among university women. *Child Abuse & Neglect, 12,* 331-341.

Briere, J., & Runtz, M. (1990). Differential adult symptomatology associated with three types of child abuse histories. *Child Abuse & Neglect, 14,* 357-364.

Broadhurst, D. D. (1984). *The educator's role in the prevention and treatment of child abuse and neglect.* Washington, DC: National Center on Child Abuse and Neglect, U.S. Department of Health and Human Services.

Brown, S. E. (1984). Social class, child maltreatment, and delinquent behavior. *Criminology, 22,*259-278.

Buntain-Ricklefs, J. J., Kemper, K. J., Bell, M., & Babonis, T. (1994). Punishments: What predicts adult approval. *Child Abuse & Neglect, 18*(11), 945-955.

Burlingham, D., & Freud, A. (1944). *Infants without families.* London: Allen & Unwin.

Burnett, B. B. (1993). The psychological abuse of latency age children: A survey. *Child Abuse & Neglect, 17,*441-454.

Button, A. (1973). Some antecedents of felonious and delinquent behavior. *Journal of Child Clinical Psychology, 2,* 35-37.

Carlin, A. S., Kemper, K., Ward, N. G., Sowell, H., Gustafson, B., & Stevens, N. (1994). The effects of differences in objective and subjective definitions of childhood physical abuse in estimates of its incidence and relationship to psychopathology. *Child Abuse & Neglect, 18,* 393-399.

Cicchetti, D., & Braunwald, K. G. (1984). An organizational approach to the study of emotional development in maltreated infants. *Infant Mental Health Journal, 5,* 172-183.

Claussen, A. H., & Crittenden, P. M. (1991). Physical and psychological maltreatment: Relations among types of maltreatment. *Child Abuse & Neglect, 15,* 5-18.

Coleman, R., & Provence, S. A. (1957). Developmental retardation (hospitalism) in infants living in families. *Pediatrics, 19,* 285-293.

Crittenden, P. (1988). Family and dyadic patterns of functioning in maltreating families. In K. Brown, C. Davies, & P. Stratton (Eds.), *Early prediction and prevention of child abuse* (pp. 161-189). New York: John Wiley.

Crittenden, P. M., & Ainsworth, M. D. (1989). Child maltreatment and attachment theory. In D. Cicchetti & V. Carlson (Eds.), *Child maltreatment: Theory and research on the causes and consequences of child abuse and neglect* (pp. 432-463). New York: Cambridge University Press.

Crittenden, P. M., Claussen, A. H., & Sugarman, D. B. (1994). Physical and psychological maltreatment in middle childhood and adolescence. *Development and Psychopathology, 6,* 145-164.

Daro, D. (1988). *Confronting child abuse: Research for effective program design.* New York: Free Press.

Davis, S., & Fantuzzo, J. W. (1989). The effects of adult and peer social initiations on social behavior of withdrawn and aggressive maltreated preschool children. *Journal of Family Violence, 4,* 227-248.

DeLozier, P. P. (1982). Attachment theory and child abuse. In M. Parkes & J. Stevenson-Hinde (Eds.), *The place of attachment in human behavior* (pp. 95-117). New York: Basic Books.

Domestic Violence Unit. (1999). *It shouldn't hurt to go home: The domestic violence victim's handbook.* (Available: 3175 West 6th Street, Los Angeles, CA 90020)

Dutton, D. G., & Golant, S. K. (1995). *The batterer: A psychological profile.* New York: Basic Books.

Egeland, B., & Erickson, M. (1987). Psychologically unavailable caregiving. In M. R. Brassard, R. Germain, & S. N. Hart (Eds.), *Psychological maltreatment of children and youth* (pp. 110-120). New York: Pergamon.

Egeland, B., Jacobvitz, J., & Sroufe, L. A. (1988). Breaking the cycle of abuse. *Child Development, 59,* 1080-1088.

Egeland, B., Sroufe, L. A., & Erickson, M. (1983). The developmental consequences of different patterns of maltreatment. *Child Abuse & Neglect, 7,* 459-469.

Engels, M. L., & Moisan, D. (1994). The psychological maltreatment inventory: Development of a measure of psychological maltreatment in childhood for use in adult clinical settings. *Psychological Reports, 74,* 595-604.

Erickson, M. F., Egeland, B., & Pianta, R. (1989). The effects of maltreatment on the development of young children. In D. Cicchetti & V. Carlson (Eds.), *Child maltreatment: Theory and research on the causes and consequences of child abuse and neglect* (pp. 647-684). New York: Cambridge University Press.

Erikson, E. H. (1959). *Identity and the life cycle: Selected papers.* New York: International Universities Press.

Femina, D. D., Yeager, C. A., & Lewis, D. O. (1990). Child abuse: Adolescent records vs. adult recall. *Child Abuse & Neglect, 14,* 227-231.

Garbarino, J. (1991). Not all bad developmental outcomes are the result of child abuse. *Development and Psychopathology, 3,* 45-50.

Garbarino, J., Guttman, E., & Seeley, J. (1986). *The psychologically battered child: Strategies for identification, assessment and intervention.* San Francisco: Jossey-Bass.

Garrison, E. G. (1987). Psychological maltreatment of children: An emerging focus for inquiry and concern. *American Psychologist, 42*(2), 157-159.

George, C., & Main, M. (1979). Social interactions of young abused children: Approach, avoidance, and aggression. *Child Development, 50,* 306-318.

Glueck, S., & Glueck, E. (1950). *Unraveling juvenile delinquency.* New York: Harper & Row.

Goldberg, S., Perrota, M., Minde, K., & Corter, C. (1986). Maternal behavior and attachment in low birthweight twins and singletons. *Child Development, 57,* 34-46.

Goldfarb, W. (1945). Psychological privation in infancy and subsequent adjustment. *American Journal of Orthopsychiatry, 102,* 247-255.

Gross, A. B., & Keller, H. R. (1992). Long-term consequences of childhood physical and psychological maltreatment. *Aggressive Behavior, 18,* 171-185.

Grossman, K., & Grossman, K. E. (1985). Maternal sensitivity and newborns' orientation responses as related to the quality of attachment in northern Germany. *Monographs of the Society for Research in Child Development, 209*(50, Pts. 1 & 2).

Hart, S. N., Binggeli, N. J., & Brassard, M. R. (1998). Evidence of the effects of psychological maltreatment. *Journal of Emotional Abuse, 1*(1), 27-58.

Hart, S. N., & Brassard, M. R. (1986). *Developing and validating operationally defined measures of emotional maltreatment: A multimodal study of the relationship between caretaker behaviors and children characteristics across three developmental levels* (Grant No. DHHS90CA1216). Washington, DC: U.S. Department of Health and Human Services and National Center on Child Abuse and Neglect.

Hart, S. N., & Brassard, M. R. (1989-1991). *Developing and validating operationally defined measures of emotional maltreatment: A multimodal study of the relationship between caretaker behaviors and children characteristics across three developmental levels* (Grant No. DHHS90CA1216). Washington, DC: U.S. Department of Health and Human Services and National Center on Child Abuse and Neglect.

Hart, S. N., Brassard, M. R., & Karlson, H. C. (1996). Psychological maltreatment. In J. Briere, L. Berliner, J. A. Bulkley, C. Jenny, & T. Reid (Eds.), *The APSAC handbook on child maltreatment* (pp. 72-89). Thousand Oaks, CA: Sage.

Hart, S. N., Germain, R. B., & Brassard, M. (1987). The challenge: To better understand and combat psychological maltreatment of children and youth. In M. R. Brassard, R. Germain, & S. N. Hart (Eds.), *Psychological maltreatment of children and youth* (pp. 3-24). New York: Pergamon.

Haugaard, J. J. (1991). Defining psychological maltreatment: A prelude to research or an outcome of research? *Development and Psychopathology, 3,* 71-77.

Hemenway, D., Solnick, S., & Carter, J. (1994). Child-rearing violence. *Child Abuse & Neglect, 18*(12), 1011-1020.

Herrenkohl, R. C., Egolf, B. P., & Herrenkohl, E. C. (1997). Preschool age antecedents of adolescents assaultive behavior: Results from a longitudinal study. *American Journal of Orthopsychiatry, 67*(3), 422-432.

Herrenkohl, R. C., Herrenkohl, E. C., & Egolf, B. P. (1983). Circumstances surrounding the occurrence of child maltreatment. *Journal of Consulting and Clinical Psychology, 51,* 424-431.

Herrenkohl, R. C., Herronkohl, E. C., Egolf, V., & Wu, P. (1991). The developmental consequences of child abuse: The Lehigh longitudinal study. In R. H. Starr & D. A. Wolfe (Eds.), *The effects of child abuse and neglect: Issues and research* (pp. 57-80). New York: Guilford.

Herrenkohl, E. C., Herrenkohl, R. C., Toedter, L., & Yanushefski, A. M. (1984). Parent-child interactions in abusive and nonabusive families. *Journal of the American Academy of Child Psychiatry, 23*(6), 641-648.

Hoffman, M. L. (1970). Moral development. In P. H. Mussen (Ed.), *Carmichael's manual of child psychology* (Vol. 2). New York: John Wiley.

Holder, W., Newberger, E., & Loken, G. (1983). Child Abuse and Treatment and Adoption Reform Act Amendments of 1983. *Testimony in the Hearings before the Subcommittee on Family and Human Services of the Committee on Labor and Human Resources of the United States Senate* (pp. 219-304). Washington, DC: Government Printing Office.

Hughes, H. M. (1992). Impact of spouse abuse on children of battered women. *Violence Update, 2,* 8-11.

Hughes, H. M., & Graham-Bermann, S. A. (1998). Children of battered women: Impact of emotional abuse on adjustment and development. *Journal of Emotional Abuse, 1*(2), 23-50.

In re Heather A., 52 Cal. App. 4th 183; Cal. Rptr.2d (1996).

Jacobs, M., Spilken, A., & Noeman, M. (1972). Perception of faulty parent-child relationships and illness behavior. *Journal of Consulting and Clinical Psychology, 39,* 49-55.

Joseph, R. (1999). The neurology of traumatic "dissociative" amnesia: Commentary and literature review. *Child Abuse & Neglect, 23*(8), 715-727.

Kaufman, J., & Zigler, E. (1987). Do abused children become abusive parents? *American Journal of Orthopsychiatry, 57,* 186-197.

Kempe, C. H., Silverman, F. N., Steele, B. F., Droegemueller, W., & Silver, H. K. (1962). The battered-child syndrome. *Journal of the American Medical Association, 181*(17), 17-24.

Krugman, R. D., & Krugman, M. K. (1984). Emotional abuse in the classroom. *American Journal of Diseases of Children, 138,* 284-286.

Lefkowitz, M., Eron, L., Walder, L., & Huesmann, L. (1977). *Growing up to be violent: A longitudinal study of the development of aggression.* New York: Pergammon.

Loeber, R., & Strouthamer-Loeber, M. (1986). Family factors as correlates and predictors of juvenile conduct problems and delinquency. In M. Tonry & N. Morris (Eds.), *Crime and justice: An annual review of the research* (Vol. 7, pp. 29-149). Chicago: University of Chicago Press.

Louis, A., Condon, J., Shute, R., & Elzinga, R. (1997). The development of the Louis MACRO (mother and child risk observation) forms: Assessing parent-infant-child risk in the presence of maternal mental illness. *Child Abuse & Neglect, 21,* 589-606.

MacLeod, J., & Nelson, G. (2000). Programs for the promotion of family wellness and the prevention of child maltreatment: A meta-analytic review. *Child Abuse & Neglect, 24*(9), 1127-1149.

Main, M. (1996). Introduction to the special section on attachment and psychopathology 2: Overview of the field of attachment. *Journal of Consulting and Clinical Psychology, 64*(2), 237-243.

Main, M., & George, C. (1985). Responses of abused and disadvantaged toddlers to distress in agemates: A study in the day care setting. *Developmental Psychology, 21*(3), 407-412.

Main, M., & Goldwyn, R. (1984). Predicting rejection of her infant from mother's representation of her own experience: Implications for the abuse-abusing intergenerational cycle. *Child Abuse & Neglect, 8,* 203-217.

Manley, R. (1977). Parental warmth and hostility as related to sex differences in children's achievement orientation. *Psychology of Women Quarterly, 1,* 229-246.

Maslow, A. H. (1970). *A theory of human motivation.* New York: Harper & Row.

McCord, J. (1983). A forty year perspective on effects of child abuse and neglect. *Child Abuse & Neglect, 7,* 265-270.

McCord, W., McCord, J., & Zola, I. K. (1959). *Origins of crime: A new evaluation of the Cambridge-Somerville youth study.* New York: Columbia University Press.

McGee, R. A., & Wolfe, D. A. (1991a). Between a rock and a hard place: Where do we go from here in defining psychological maltreatment? *Development and Psychopathology, 3,* 119-124.

McGee, R. A., & Wolfe, D. A. (1991b). Psychological maltreatment: Toward an operational definition. *Development and Psychopathology, 3,* 3-18.

McGee, R. A., Wolfe, D. A., & Wilson, S. K. (1990). *A record of maltreatment experiences.* Unpublished manuscript, University of Western Ontario and the Institute for the Prevention of Child Abuse, Toronto.

Miller, H., & Baruch, D. W. (1948). Psychosomatic studies of children with allergic manifestations: I. Maternal rejection: A study of 63 cases. *Psychosomatic Medicine, 10,* 275-278.

Moeller, T. P., Bachman, G. A., & Moeller, J. R. (1993). The combined effects of physical, sexual, and emotional abuse during childhood: Long-term health consequences for women. *Child Abuse & Neglect, 17,* 623-640.

Mullen, P. E., Martin, J. L., Anderson, J. C., Romans, S. E., & Herbison, G. P. (1996). The long-term impact of the physical, emotional, and sexual abuse of children: A community study. *Child Abuse & Neglect, 20*(1), 7-21.

Navarre, E. L. (1987). Psychological maltreatment: The core component of child abuse. In M. R. Brassard, R. Germain, & S. N. Hart (Eds.), *Psychological maltreatment of children and youth* (pp. 45-56). New York: Pergamon.

Ney, P. G., Fung, T., & Wickett, A. R. (1994). The worst combinations of child abuse and neglect. *Child Abuse & Neglect, 18*(9), 705-714.

Nye, F. I. (1958). *Family relationships and delinquent behavior.* New York: John Wiley.

Patterson, G. R. (1982). *Coercive family process.* Eugene, OR: Castalia.

Patterson, G. R. (1986). Performance models for antisocial boys. *American Psychologist, 41,* 432-444.

Pavenstedt, E. (Ed.). (1967). *The drifters: children of disorganized lower-class families.* Boston: Little, Brown.

Pearce, J. W., & Pezzot-Pearce, T. D. (1994). Attachment theory and its implications for psychotherapy with maltreated children. *Child Abuse & Neglect, 18*(5), 425-438.

Pittman, A., Wolfe, D. A., & Wekerle, C. (1998). Prevention during adolescence: The Youth Relationship project. In J. R. Lutzker (Ed.), *Handbook of child abuse research and treatment: Issues in clinical psychology* (pp. 341-356). New York: Plenum.

Portwood, S. G. (1999). Coming to terms with a consensual definition of child maltreatment. *Child Maltreatment, 4*(1), 56-68.

Proceedings summary of the International Conference on Psychological Abuse of Children and Youth. (1983, August). Indianapolis: Office for the Study of the Psychological Rights of the Child, Indiana University.

Prugh, D. G., & Harlow, R. G. (1962). Masked deprivation in infants and young children. In M. D. Ainsworth (Ed.), *Deprivation of maternal care: A reassessment of its effects.* Geneva: World Health Organization.

Psychological maltreatment definitional issues [special issue]. (1991). *Development and Psychopathology, 3.*

Puckering, C., Pickels, A., Skuse, D., Heptinstall, E., Dowdney, L., & Zur-Szpiro, S. (1995). Mother-child interaction in the cognitive and behavioural development of 4 year old children with poor growth. *Journal of Child Psychology and Psychiatry and the Allied Disciplines, 36*(4), 573-595.

Rausch, K., & Knutson, J. F. (1991). The self-report of personal punitive childhood experiences and those of siblings. *Child Abuse & Neglect, 15,* 29-36.

Rohner, R. P., & Rohner, E. C. (1980). Antecedents and consequences of parental rejection: A theory of emotional abuse. *Child Abuse & Neglect, 4,* 189-198.

Rorty, M., Yager, J., & Rossotto, E. (1994). Childhood sexual, physical, and psychological abuse in bulimia nervosa. *American Journal of Psychiatry, 151*(8), 1122-1126.

Rutter, M., & Rutter, M. (1993). *Developing minds: Challenge and continuity across the life span.* New York: Basic Books.

Sedlak, A. J., & Broadhurst, D. D. (1996). *The Third National Incidence Study of child abuse and neglect.* Washington, DC: U.S. Department of Health and Human Services, Administration for Children, Youth, and Families.

Sheintuch, G., & Lewin, G. (1981). Parents' attitudes and children's deprivation: Child rearing attitudes of parents as a key to the advantaged-disadvantaged distinction in pre-school children. *International Journal of Behavioral Development 4*(125), 142.

Shoemaker, D. J. (1984). *Theories of delinquency.* New York: Oxford University Press.

Spitz, R. A. (1945). Hospitalism: An inquiry into the genesis of psychiatric conditions in early childhood. *The Psychoanalytic Study of the Child, 1,* 53-74.

Spitz, R. A. (1946). Hospitalism: A follow-up report. *The Psychoanalytic Study of the Child, 2,* 113-117.

Sroufe, L. A. (1979). The coherence of individual development: Early care, attachment, and subsequent developmental issues. *American Psychologist, 34,* 834-841.

Sroufe, L. A. (1983). Infant-caregiver attachment and patterns of adaptation in preschool: The roots of maladaption and competence. In M. Perlmutter (Ed.), *Development and policy concerning children with special needs: Minnesota symposium on child psychology* (Vol. 16, pp. 41-83). Hillsdale, NJ: Lawrence Erlbaum.

Sroufe, L. A. (1996). *Emotional development: The organization of emotional life in the early years.* New York: Cambridge University Press.

Starkey, S. L. (1980). The relationship between parental acceptance-rejection and the academic performance of fourth and fifth graders. *Behavior Science Research, 15,* 67-80.

Sternberg, K. J., & Lamb, M. E. (1991). Can we ignore context in the definition of child maltreatment? *Development and Psychopathology, 3,* 87-92.

Straus, M. A., Hamby, S. L., Boney-McCoy, S., & Sugarman, D. B. (1996). The revised Conflict Tactics Scales (CTS2): Development and preliminary psychometric data. *Journal of Family Issues, 17,* 283-316.

Straus, M. A., Hamby, S. L., Finkelhor, D., Moore, D. W., & Runyan, D. (1998). Identification of child maltreatment with parent-child Conflict Tactics Scales: Development and psychometric data for a national sample of American parents. *Child Abuse & Neglect, 22*(4), 249-270.

Terr, L. C. (1981). Psychic trauma in children: Observations following the Chowchilla school-bus kidnapping. *American Journal of Psychiatry, 138*(1), 14-19.

Thompson, R. A., & Wilcox, B. L. (1995). Child maltreatment research: Federal support and policy issues. *American Psychologist, 50,* 789-793.

Torrence, M. E. (1997). *Understanding epidemiology.* St. Louis, MO: Mosby.

Toth, S. L. (1991). Psychological maltreatment: Can an integration of research, policy, and intervention efforts be achieved? *Development and Psychopathology, 3,* 103-109.

Trojanowicz, R. C., & Morash, M. (1983). *Juvenile delinquency: Concepts and control* (3rd ed.). Englewood Cliffs, NJ: Prentice Hall.

Turgi, P., & Hart, S. N. (1988). Psychological maltreatment: Meaning and prevention. In O. C. S. Tzeng & J. J. Jacobsen (Eds.), *Sourcebook for child abuse and neglect* (pp. 287-317). Springfield, IL: Charles C Thomas.

United Nations (UN) General Assembly. (1989, November 17). *Adoption of a convention on the rights of the child.* New York: Author.

Varia, R., Abidin, R. R., & Dass, P. (1996). Perceptions of abuse: Effects on adult psychological and social adjustment. *Child Abuse & Neglect, 20*(6), 511-526.

Vissing, Y. M., Straus, M. A., Gelles, R. J., & Harrop, J. W. (1991). Verbal aggression by parents and psychosocial problems of children. *Child Abuse & Neglect, 15,* 223-238.

Wald, M. S. (1991). Defining psychological maltreatment: The relationship between questions and answers. *Development and Psychopathology, 3,* 111-118.

Wang, C. T., & Daro, D. (1998). *Current trends in child abuse reporting and fatalities: The results of the 1997 annual Fifty State Survey.* Chicago: National Committee to Prevent Child Abuse.

Williams, G. J. (1983). Child abuse reconsidered: The urgency of authentic prevention. *Journal of Clinical Child Psychology, 12,* 312-319.

Wolfe, D., & McGee, R. (1994). Dimensions of child maltreatment and their relationship to adolescent adjustment. *Development and Psychopathology, 6*(1), 165-182.

Wolfe, D., Wekerle, C., Gough, R., Reitsel-Jaffe, D., Grasley, C., Pittman, A. L., Lefebvre, L., & Stumpf, J. (1996). *The Youth Relationships manual: A group approach with adolescents for the prevention of woman abuse and the promotion of healthy relationships.* Thousand Oaks, CA: Sage.

Youngblade, L., & Belsky, J. (1990). Social and emotional consequences of child maltreatment. In R. Ammerman & M. Hensen (Eds.), *Children at risk* (pp. 109-146). New York: Plenum.

Zagar, R., Arbit, J., Sylvies, R., & Busch, K. G. (1991). Homicidal adolescents: A replication. *Psychological Reports, 67*(3), 1234-1242.

5

Child Maltreatment in the Context of Substance Abuse

SUSAN J. KELLEY

Recognition of the serious role that substance abuse plays in child maltreatment (CM) is growing, as evidenced by the emerging body of research linking substance abuse and CM. Numerous studies indicate that substance-abusing parents are at increased risk for abusing and neglecting their children, although the strength of the association varies due to methodological variations (Bennett & Kemper, 1994; Chaffin, Kelleher, & Hollenberg, 1996; Jaudes, Ekwo, & Voorhis, 1995; Kelleher, Chaffin, Hollenberg, & Fischer, 1994; Kelley, 1998; Murphy et al., 1991; Wasserman & Levanthal, 1993). Substance abuse includes the abuse of legal drugs (e.g., alcohol, prescription drugs, over-the-counter drugs) as well as the use of illegal drugs (including cocaine, heroin, marijuana, and methamphetamines). It is important to acknowledge that abuse of "legal" drugs, alcohol in particular, can be just as detrimental to parental functioning as so-called "illicit" drugs. Likewise, it is important to note that although most substance abusers may use a dominant drug, many are actually poly-substance abusers. This chapter examines various aspects of the relationship between substance abuse and CM, including the prevalence of substance abuse in cases of CM, prenatal exposure to substances of abuse, exposure to drugs after birth, child fatalities, and childhood history of abuse in substance abusers.

Substance Abuse as a Risk Factor for CM

Two national surveys shed light on the role of substance abuse in child protection. In the 1998 survey of the 50-state child protective services (CPS) agencies conducted by the National Committee to Prevent Child Abuse (now Prevent Child Abuse America), 85% of states reported substance abuse as one of the two leading problems exhibited by families reported for child maltreatment (Wang & Harding, 1999). Poverty was the other most frequently reported problem associated with child maltreatment.

In 1999, a national survey of 915 frontline professionals working in child welfare and in family courts was conducted to determine the extent of substance abuse as a factor in CM (Reid, Macchetto, & Foster, 1999). The survey resulted in findings consistent with the National Committee to Prevent Child Abuse survey. Eighty percent of respondents reported that substance abuse causes or contributes to most CM they encounter. Respondents cited substance abuse as a major cause for the dramatic rise in reports of CM since 1986. In addition, alcohol, usually in combination with other drugs, was identified as the leading substance of abuse. Almost half of all cases of illegal drugs were said to involve crack cocaine as the leading substance of abuse, with marijuana cited as the leading substance of abuse by 20% of respondents.

Reported rates of substance abuse among maltreating parents vary considerably due to methodological issues related to definitions used and the populations studied. In a study of 639 children who were removed from their homes for serious CM, evidence of caregiver substance abuse was found in 79% of the cases (Besinger, Garland, Litrownik, & Landsverk, 1999). However, in another group of children removed by CPS because of serious CM, a substance abuse rate of only 43% was reported (Murphy et al., 1991). The considerably lower rate of caregiver substance abuse found by Murphy et al. (1991) is most likely due to the more restrictive definition of substance abuse used by these researchers. Murphy and colleagues required that substance abuse be documented by a psychologist, a psychiatrist, or in a court-ordered screening, whereas Besinger et al. (1999) operationally defined substance abuse more broadly to include any known history of substance abuse.

Most studies conducted to date examining the relationship between substance abuse and CM have relied exclusively on families known to the CPS system, which results in an obvious bias. In a probabilistic survey of 11,662 adults, however, researchers determined through interviews that 169 had physically abused their children and 209 had neglected their children (Kelleher et al., 1994). Moreover, these researchers found a strong relationship between substance abuse and CM. Specifically, 40% of child abusers and 56% of neglectful parents were determined to be substance abusers compared with 16% of nonabusive and 17% of nonneglectful adults. This positive association between CM and substance abuse remained even after statistically controlling for other variables often associated with CM. Because this study uses a randomly selected community sample rather than relying on families known to CPS, it represents a major methodological advancement in the study of the role of substance abuse in CM.

Recurrence of CM. Not surprisingly, substance abuse is a major factor in the recurrence of CM. Researchers examined the characteristics and correlates of CM recurrences in referrals to CPS in Washington state over a period of 18 months (English, Marshall, Brummel, & Orme, 1999). Out of 12,329 original cases, 29% resulted in repeat referrals. Substance abuse was significantly associated with both rereferral and substantiated recurrence of CM. Other major risk factors for rereferral and recurrence included caregiver history of abuse or neglect as a child, domestic violence, and psychological or physical impairment of the caregiver. Wolock and Magura (1996) examined the relationship between parental substance abuse and subsequent rereports in 239 families in a longitudinal study of child maltreatment cases closed after investigation, with results consistent with English et al. (1999). Substance abuse of any kind, such as drugs, alcohol, or a combination of drugs and alcohol, greatly increased the likelihood of rereports of CM to CPS. When drugs and alcohol were used in combination, rereports were even more likely.

Child fatalities. Parental substance abuse has been linked to the most serious outcome of CM, fatalities. Substance abuse by parents and other caregivers is associated with as many as two thirds of all cases of child maltreatment fatalities (Reid et al., 1999). Half (51%) of these deaths involve physical abuse, 44% involve neglect, and 5% involve multiple forms of CM. Many deaths involve children who were born with signs that the mother had used drugs during pregnancy. For example, in New York City, more than 25% of child fatalities attributed to CM involved children prenatally exposed to alcohol and other drugs (New York City Child Fatality Review Panel, 1995).

Substance abuse in the past. Research published to date on substance abuse as a risk factor for CM has focused almost exclusively on caregivers who are currently active substance abusers. Several studies, however, indicate that past, as well as current, parental substance abuse increases the risk of child abuse. Researchers examined the impact of parental substance abuse on child abuse potential in a sample of mothers and fathers of 209 boys ages 10 to 12 years from intact families (Ammerman, Kolko, Kirisci, Blackson, & Dawes, 1999). Child abuse potential was measured using the Child Abuse Potential Inventory (Milner, 1995), an instrument widely used to measure those aspects of parental functioning associated with child abuse. A strong linkage was found between a lifetime history of substance abuse and child abuse potential in both mothers and fathers. No differences were found in abuse potential between those with a past (but not current) history of substance abuse and those with a current substance abuse disorder. Consistent with these findings, Famularo, Kinscherff, and Fenton (1992) found that mothers with either a current or past substance abuse history, when compared with a matched group of non-substance-abusing mothers, were more likely to abuse their children. The findings of these two studies go against the commonly held belief that if substance-abusing parents become "clean and sober," the risk of CM is substantially decreased.

The vast majority of studies linking perpetrators of CM and substance abuse have been retrospective, involving parents who have previously been reported for abuse, thus making it difficult to determine if substance abuse precedes the commission of CM. In a study of the relationship among CM, psychiatric disorders, substance abuse, and social risk factors, Chaffin et al. (1996)

overcame some of the methodological limitations of other studies. These researchers conducted a prospective study of parents from a probabilistic community sample of 7,103 parents to determine the risk factors associated with the onset of self-reported commission of physical abuse or neglect. Data were obtained from Waves I and II of the National Institute for Mental Health's Epidemiologic Catchment Areas Survey. Parents who did not self-report physical abuse or neglect of their children at Wave I were followed to determine risk factors associated with the onset of self-reported abuse or neglect of their children 1 year later. At Wave II, substance abuse was found to be strongly associated with the onset of both physical abuse and neglect. Furthermore, when other variables were statistically controlled, substance abuse tripled the risk of physical abuse and neglect. Depression was found to be a strong risk factor for physical abuse, but not neglect, once social factors and substance abuse were statistically controlled. The authors concluded that the relationship between depression and neglect may not be direct, as it appears to be for physical abuse, but instead may be mediated by substance abuse, a common complication of depression. The authors further reported that of the psychiatric disorders studied, substance abuse disorders were the most common and among the most powerfully associated with maltreatment.

Other studies have produced findings consistent with Chaffin et al. (1996) in regard to the role of substance abuse as a mediator of CM in persons with psychiatric disorders. Swanson, Holzer, Ganju, and Jono (1990), using a community-based sample, found that associations between psychiatric disorders and interpersonal violence, including child abuse, appear to be mediated by comorbid alcohol and drug abuse disorders. More specifically, they found that the risk of violence associated with many psychiatric disorders is not substantially increased unless a substance abuse disorder is also present. Using three large databases of community, clinical, and family study subjects, Dinwiddie and Bucholz (1993) found that self-reported child abusers have increased lifetime rates of major depression, antisocial personality disorders, and alcoholism. An association was also found between anxiety disorders and physical abuse, especially in alcohol-involved populations.

Childhood Maltreatment as Risk Factor for Substance Abuse

A childhood history of maltreatment dramatically increases the risk of becoming a substance abuser. Numerous retrospective studies have found that a disproportionately large number of adolescents and adults with substance abuse problems report having been physically or sexually abused in childhood (Bayatpour, Wells, & Holford, 1992; Bennett & Kemper, 1994; Boyd, 1993; Harmer, Sanderson, & Mertin, 1999; Kang, Magura, Laudet, & Whitney, 1999; Medrano, Zule, Hatch, & Desmond, 1999; Wallen & Berman, 1992). For instance, Kang and colleagues (1999) found that among 171 substance-abusing women with young children admitted to a substance abuse treatment program, 24% reported having been sexually abused during childhood. Forty-five percent reported physical abuse in childhood.

Because studying the link between childhood abuse and substance abuse in persons undergoing inpatient or outpatient substance abuse has obvious limitations, researchers have also examined the link between CM and substance abuse in samples obtained outside of substance abuse treatment programs. One study examined histories of CM in a community sample of 181 women who were actively using heroin and cocaine but who were not in substance abuse treatment at the time of the study. The prevalence of CM was found to be higher than reported in the general population in all five subsets of CM (emotional abuse or neglect, physical abuse or neglect, sexual abuse) (Medrano et al., 1999). In a study of mothers of young children receiving routine health care in five pediatric clinics, researchers found that 24% had histories of childhood physical abuse and that physical abuse during childhood was found to be a significant risk factor for substance abuse in adulthood, even after controlling for a family history of substance abuse (Bennett & Kemper, 1994). These findings suggest that when the link between childhood history of maltreatment and later substance abuse is studied in samples obtained outside of drug treatment programs, childhood maltreatment remains a significant risk factor for substance abuse.

Studies involving participants who abuse alcohol produce findings similar to those involving drug abusers. Using a national probability sample of 1,970 families, researchers found significant associations between current heavy drinking and childhood history of physical abuse (Kaufman & Asdigian, 1994). In a prospective study of 113 African American women with documented histories of child sexual abuse (CSA), researchers found a very high percentage of heavy drinkers compared with other general population surveys of African American women (Jasinski, Williams, & Siegel, 2000).

In another study, researchers examined the relationship between substance abuse and CM histories in 122,824 adolescent public school students (Harrison, Fulkerson, & Beebe, 1997). Physical and sexual abuse were associated with an increased likelihood of use of alcohol, marijuana, and almost all other drugs for both males and females. Rate of abuse of multiple substances was highly elevated among victims of abuse, with the highest rates among students who reported both physical and sexual abuse. Abuse victims also reported initiating substance use earlier than their nonabused peers and gave more reasons for using substances of abuse, including coping with painful emotions and escaping from problems. This study is particularly informative because it explores the relationship between CM and substance abuse closer in time to onset of substance abuse.

Psychiatric disorders. Childhood sexual abuse and physical abuse are associated with both short- and long-term psychological disturbances, including depression (Carlin et al., 1994; Hall, Sachs, Rayens, & Lutenbacher, 1993; Saunders, Villeponteauz, Lipovsky, & Kilpatrick, 1992), psychopathology, decreased self-esteem, and interpersonal problems (Mullen, Martin, Anderson, Romans, & Herbison, 1996). In cases of severe sexual and physical abuse, sequelae often include symptoms of posttraumatic disorder and dissociation. It has been hypothesized that individuals suffering from these disorders may use alcohol and illicit drugs to decrease or mitigate their psychological distress.

In a study exploring the relationship between posttraumatic stress disorder (PTSD) and substance abuse disorders (SUD), 30 women with SUD and PTSD and 25 women with SUD but without PTSD were compared on addiction severity, history of abuse, psychopathology, and aftercare compliance (Brady, Killeen, Saladin, Dansky, & Becker, 1994). The majority of women in both groups had experienced childhood abuse, although those with SUD *and* PTSD were more likely to have been victims of childhood sexual and physical abuse and to have more severe addictions. The authors concluded that screening for victimization and PTSD among women with substance abuse disorders may have important prognostic and treatment implications.

Problems common to substance abusers, including depression and inadequate social support, are also frequently observed with maltreating parents.

In a study involving 105 predominantly African American female crack cocaine users, 61% reported at least one childhood sexual abuse experience, and 70% reported depressive symptoms for more than 2 weeks of their lives, with 31% reporting depressive symptoms by age 15 (Boyd, 1993). Thus, a positive correlation was found between age of first sexual abuse experience, age of first depressive symptoms, and age of first use of illicit drugs. The findings suggest that for some individuals, sexual abuse is followed by the onset of depressive symptoms, which, in turn, is followed by the onset of drug abuse.

Substance Abuse as an Antecedent to CM

Several mechanisms by which alcohol and drug abuse have been hypothesized to undermine parenting and increase the risk of CM are proposed by Ammerman et al. (1999). First, substance abuse may contribute to low frustration tolerance and increased anger reactivity secondary to the acute effects of alcohol and other drugs or to the physical withdrawal symptoms associated with substance dependence. Second, substance abuse may cause disinhibition of aggressive impulses. Third, substance abuse may interfere with parenting judgment. Fourth, addiction may cause parents to focus primarily or exclusively on acquisition and use of drugs and alcohol, leading to neglect of a child's basic needs.

There are numerous overlaps in the characteristics of substance-abusing parents and maltreating parents. Problems common to substance abusers, including depression (Boyd, 1993; Hall et al., 1993) and inadequate social support (Harmer et al., 1999; Kelley, 1992), are also frequently observed with maltreating parents (Milner, 1995). Stress may also play an important role, given that substance-abusing women are often in situations characterized by high stress (Harmer et al., 1999; Kelley, 1992; Kelley, 1998; Mullen et al., 1996). According to Milner (1993), increased parental stress reduces the abuser's ability to implement and monitor the most effective response for dealing with children's behavior. Substance-abusing mothers may experience increased stress related to the parenting role due to insufficient internal resources, such as emotional stability and social support, which are needed to cope effectively with the demands of parenting young children. In a sample of 46 mothers undergoing residential treatment for drug and alcohol addiction, when compared with norming samples, these mothers reported significantly higher levels of psychological distress and parenting stress and lower levels of social support (Harmer et al., 1999).

Prenatal drug exposure. Prenatal drug exposure, although only one aspect of the link between substance abuse and CM, has, unfortunately, received disproportionate attention in both the professional literature and popular media. Much of the attention related to prenatal substance abuse has focused on the potential for biological harm to the developing fetus and whether prenatal exposure to illicit drugs, especially crack cocaine, in and of itself constitutes child abuse. When use of crack cocaine became epidemic in the 1980s, there was much concern, if not hysteria, regarding the supposedly devastating effects of prenatal exposure. However, research findings over time have failed to substantiate pervasive long-term adverse effects of cocaine exposure. In a systematic review of studies examining developmental outcomes in early childhood after prenatal cocaine exposure, Frank, Augustyn, Knight, Pell, and Zuckerman (2001) found no consistent negative association between prenatal cocaine exposure and physical growth, developmental test scores, or receptive or expressive language.

Although prenatal exposure to drugs is associated with increased risk for poor birth outcomes, in actuality it is difficult to disentangle the negative effects of prenatal substance abuse from the negative effects of confounding factors, such as poor prenatal care, poor prenatal nutrition, prematurity, and adverse postnatal environment, including postnatal passive exposure to cocaine fumes. Despite this knowledge, cocaine-exposed children continue to be labeled with the pejorative term *crack babies,* enabling society, teachers, social service, and health professionals to designate them as learning disabled, handicapped, and having behavioral problems. Another misconception is that cocaine-exposed infants are born "addicted." Neonatal withdrawal to drugs has been documented only in opiate-exposed infants, with methadone and heroin withdrawal being most prevalent. Thus, contrary to the beliefs of some, drug withdrawal has not been empirically validated in cocaine-exposed infants.

Neonatal withdrawal to drugs has been documented only in opiate-exposed infants, with methadone and heroin withdrawal being most prevalent.

Prenatal alcohol exposure appears to have the most dire consequences of all forms of prenatal substance abuse. It is the only prenatal substance of abuse that has been proven to have irreversible negative effects, including mental retardation, neurological deficits, facial malformations, and growth retardation. The term *fetal alcohol syndrome* (FAS) is used when these birth outcomes occur in combination with known prenatal exposure to large amounts of alcohol. An estimated 12,000 infants are born each year with FAS. A much greater number of infants suffer from more subtle effects of prenatal alcohol exposure, known as fetal alcohol effect (FAE).

Postnatal environment. In the 1980s and early 1990s, much more emphasis was placed on research determining harmful effects of prenatal exposure to substances of abuse than on the influence of parental substance abuse after birth. Recent research suggests that drug-exposed infants may be at greater risk of harm in the postnatal environment than in the prenatal environment. Several studies indicate that children prenatally exposed to substances of abuse are at increased risk for CM after birth. In a study examining parenting stress and child maltreatment in a sample of low-income women with one or more young children, those who had used cocaine alone or in combination with other substances of abuse during pregnancy reported significantly higher levels of parenting stress and were more likely to have abused or neglected their children than a carefully matched comparison group of mothers with no known history of drug use (Kelley, 1998). Almost half of the mothers who used cocaine prenatally scored in the clinical range on parenting stress. And almost a quarter of those in the substance abuse group had committed abuse or neglect serious enough to result in removal of one or more children by child protective services. It is important to note that the majority of mothers in the substance abuse group had never received any treatment for substance abuse, and the vast majority admitted current use of one or more illegal substances.

In another study examining prenatal substance abuse and subsequent CM, researchers compared baseline characteristics, service provision, and child placement for two groups of infants known to be prenatally exposed to cocaine: those who tested positive for cocaine at birth and those who tested negative for cocaine at birth (Byrd, Neistadt, Howard, Brownstein-Evans, & Weitzman, 1999). Although both groups had similar demographic characteristics and social problems, mothers of infants who tested positive for cocaine at birth were more likely than mothers of infants who tested negative at birth to have other children in foster care and to have previous involvement with CPS. Infants with positive cocaine screens were more likely than those with negative screens to have initial referrals to CPS (100% vs. 33%) and to have initial out-of-home placements (50% vs. 22%). By 1 year of age, infants with positive screens were more likely than those with negative screens to be in out-of-home placements (27% vs. 6%). One possible explanation for this is that women who continued to use cocaine throughout their entire pregnancy, including use at time of delivery, were more impaired by their substance abuse problem and, as a result, were at greater risk for CM.

In a retrospective study examining the CM experiences of 513 children born to women who used illicit drugs during pregnancy, researchers used the state registry of abuse and neglect to identify children who were subsequently maltreated (Jaudes et al., 1995). Of the drug-exposed children, 20% had CM substantiated, with neglect being the most common (73%) form of CM, followed by physical abuse (16%), drug exposure after the prenatal period (6%), sexual abuse (3%), and death (3%). The three fatalities—each around 3 months of age—died of neglect. The rate of substantiated CM was determined to be 2 to 3 times that of nondrug-exposed children living in the same geographic area of Chicago. Risk of CM was not significantly related to the infants' gender, race, and birth weight.

Rogers, Hall, and Muto (1991) found cocaine or its metabolites in 40% of 43 infants in Los Angeles who died at 2 or more days of age without an apparent cause of death at autopsy. In contrast, however, no evidence of higher rates of infant mortality due to prenatal drug exposure was found in a study by Ostrea, Ostrea, and Simpson (1997).

Postnatal drug exposure. An often overlooked consequence of parental substance abuse is the direct exposure of children to substances of abuse *after* birth. The literature contains numerous reports of children being exposed to illicit drugs beyond the neonatal period. Reports indicate that children living with substance-abusing parents are at risk for passive exposure to marijuana, methamphetamines, phencyclidine (PCP), and crack cocaine when these substances are smoked by caregivers in the presence of children (Bateman & Heagarty, 1989; Heidemann & Goetting, 1990; Mirchandani et al., 1991). Signs and symptoms of intoxication by passive inhalation of crack cocaine and PCP include lethargy, vomiting, seizures, apnea, coma, and death (Bays, 1994).

Several surveys provide disturbing evidence of the prevalence of cocaine exposure in children. A study examining 1,680 urine and blood toxicological screens from 1,120 patients, performed in a children's hospital over a 19-month period, revealed that 5% of these pediatric patients had specimens that contained cocaine or its metabolite (Shannon, Lacouture, Roa, & Woolf, 1989). In a study to determine the prevalence of cocaine exposure in pediatric patients with clinically unsuspected signs or symptoms of exposure, researchers examined the urine of 250 children ages 2 weeks to 5 years who were seen in an emergency department

(Kharasch, Vinci, Glotzer, Sargent, & Weitzman, 1990). Six (2.4%) of these urine screens were positive for cocaine metabolites. The authors determined the possible routes of exposure to be breastfeeding, intentional administration, accidental ingestion, and passive inhalation of crack cocaine vapors. In a follow-up study of prenatally exposed infants, 6% of children more than 3 months of age reported to CPS for CM had illicit drugs in their systems from either passive exposure or forced ingestion (Jaudes et al., 1995).

Infants have also been known to ingest dangerously high levels of alcohol and illegal drugs through breastfeeding when their mothers are active substance abusers (Chaney, Franke, & Wadlington, 1988; Chasnoff, Lewis, & Squires, 1987; Little, Anderson, Ervin, Worthington-Roberts, & Clarren, 1989; Shannon et al., 1989). Numerous negative effects from ingesting substances of abuse through breast milk have been reported in the literature. Researchers studying the effects of maternal alcohol use during breastfeeding found that even after controlling for potentially confounding variables, alcohol ingested through breast milk had a detrimental effect on infant motor development (Little et al., 1989). Seizures in breastfed infants have been reported in mothers who used cocaine as a topical anesthetic for sore nipples (Chaney et al., 1988). These findings raise the question of whether professionals should discourage substance-abusing mothers from breastfeeding.

Exposure to substances of abuse may also be intentional. Deliberate poisonings may occur when caretakers wish to amuse themselves or sedate a child (Bays, 1994). In a study of middle-class adolescent females enrolled in drug treatment, 11% reported deliberately intoxicating children they were baby-sitting by blowing marijuana smoke in the children's faces (Schwartz, Peary, & Mistretta, 1986). One case reported in the medical literature describes a 4-year-old girl whose parent inserted rock cocaine in her rectum to hide the drug (Reinhart, 1990). Initially, the father reported that a playmate had inserted marbles into his daughter's rectum but later reported that the mother had placed cocaine in her rectum (the mother later accused the father of this act). Toxicological evaluation of the child's urine was positive for cocaine.

Passive exposure to cocaine has been linked in several reports to deaths in otherwise healthy children. Mirchandani and colleagues (1991) report 16 cases of death in otherwise apparently healthy infants over a 2-year period in Philadelphia, in which toxicological analyses at autopsy revealed the presence of cocaine and/or its metabolite, benzoylecgonine. Investigations of the death scene documented that these infants had been exposed, shortly before death, to smoke from crack cocaine in crowded and poorly ventilated environments. Given the presence of cocaine in the infants at death and the fact that even low concentrations of cocaine may cause potentially fatal arrhythmias that are not detectable on autopsy, the authors concluded that the cocaine may have contributed to the death of these infants and that, therefore, the diagnosis of sudden infant death syndrome (SIDS) in such cases cannot be supported.

Impact of Substance Abuse on Kinship Care

Parental substance abuse is a driving factor in the tremendous increase in the number of abused and neglected children in out-of-home placements. Between 1980 and 1990, there was an increase of 44% in the number of children living with relatives in parent-absent households (U.S. Bureau of Census, 1990). More so than ever, children are placed formally or informally with relatives. The trend in use of kinship care placements is driven by two major factors. First is the lack of availability of nonrelative foster care homes to meet the burgeoning demand. The second factor is the shift in foster care policies toward a preference for placement with relatives over nonrelatives whenever feasible. In 1994, 2.1 million children were living with relative caregivers in the absence of either biological parent. With two thirds of these relative caregivers being grandparents (Feig, 1997), an examination of the growing phenomenon of grandparents raising children affected by substance abuse is warranted.

The percentage of children in grandparent-headed households increased from 4.9% in 1992 to 5.5% in 1997, resulting in 4.1 million children being raised by grandparents in approximately 2 million homes in 1997 (U.S. Bureau of the Census, 1998). Although this phenomenon affects all racial and economic groups, the most significant increases have been among African Americans (Feig, 1997). Studies consistently identify parental substance abuse as the major reason for grandparents having to assume the responsibility of parenting their grandchildren (Burton, 1992; Dowdell, 1995; Kelley, 1993; Minkler & Roe, 1993). Other interrelated factors include psychiatric disorders, AIDS, incarceration, and homicide.

The percentage of children in grandparent-headed households increased from 4.9% in 1992 to 5.5% in 1997, resulting in 4.1 million children being raised by grandparents in approximately 2 million homes in 1997.

Findings of an emerging body of research raise concerns over the challenges confronted by grandparents raising grandchildren. Numerous studies have found that assuming full-time parenting responsibilities for grandchildren is associated with increased psychological distress in grandparents (Burton, 1992; Dowdell, 1995; Kelley, 1993; Kelley & Damato, 1995; Minkler & Roe, 1993). Minkler and Roe (1993) found that 37% of grandmothers raising grandchildren reported that their psychological health had worsened since assuming full-time caregiving. Minkler, Fuller-Thompson, Miller, and Driver (1997) reported that caregiving grandmothers were almost twice as likely to be depressed as noncaregiving grandparents and that even after controlling for depression that preexisted the onset of caregiving, grandmothers had significantly higher rates of depression. In another study, researchers found that almost one third of the grandmother kinship care providers scored in the clinical range on a standardized measure of psychological distress (Kelley, Whitley, Sipe, & Yorker, 2000).

A number of factors have been identified as contributors to increased psychological distress in grandparent caregivers. Some of those most well documented include poor physical health, social isolation, and financial difficulties (Caliandro & Hughes, 1998; Kelley et al., 2000; Minkler & Roe, 1993). The events that led to the grandparents assuming care of their grandchildren can often be highly distressing and are typically linked to parental substance abuse (e.g., incarceration, CPS removal, abandonment). Other stressors experienced by grandparents raising grandchildren include concern regarding their own longevity, that is, living long enough to raise their grandchildren; concern over their adult children who are often incapacitated by drugs; and financial difficulties, social isolation, poor health, and the fact that most are raising multiple grandchildren (Burton, 1992; Kelley, 1993; Minkler & Roe, 1993). Grandparents raising grandchildren often experience feelings of anger and resentment related to their parenting role, which are likely to contribute to psychological distress (Burton, 1992; Kelley, 1993; Kelley & Damato, 1995; Minkler & Roe, 1993).

Assuming full-time parenting responsibilities for grandchildren is associated with increased psychological distress in grandparents.

Findings from studies examining the health status of grandparents raising grandchildren indicate that their health is often compromised and that, in many instances, advanced age may play a role. Consistently across available studies, regardless of race or socioeconomic status, the average age of grandparent caregivers is between 55 and 57 years (Dowdell, 1995; Kelley, 1993; Minkler, Roe, & Robertson-Beckley, 1994; Roy, Gordon, & Cohen, 1997). A national study of kinship caretakers, of which 66% were grandmothers, found that 57% of the caretakers were age 50 or older, including 29% over age 60 and almost 10% over age 70 (Feig, 1997). Undoubtedly, if the age of grandparent caretakers were reported separately from the other caretakers, the mean age of this subgroup of caregivers would be even higher.

In a study examining caregiver burden in grandparents raising grandchildren, Dowdell (1995) found that 45% of grandmothers identified themselves as having a physical problem or illness that seriously affected their health, with single grandmothers reporting more health problems than married grandmothers. Those who indicated their health had worsened after assuming parenting responsibilities also reported financial problems and lack of family support. In another study, more than one third of the participants reported heightened health problems since assuming full-time caregiving responsibilities for grandchildren (Burton, 1992). When Kelley (1993) examined caregiver stress in grandparents raising grandchildren, 22% of grandparent participants scored in what is considered the clinical range on the health problem scale of the Parenting Stress Index (Abidin, 1990).

The studies described earlier suggest the need for developing and testing interventions targeting this population. Kelley, Yorker, Whitley, and Sipe (2001) pilot tested a home-based nursing and social service intervention aimed at improving the well-being of 25 urban, African American grandparents raising grandchildren. The purpose of the intervention was to reduce psychological distress, improve physical and mental health, and improve the social support and resources of the grandparent. The 6-month intervention included home visitation by registered nurses and social workers, legal assistance, and support groups. Results included improved mental health, decreased psychological stress scores, and increased social support. The investigators have extended the duration of the intervention from 6 months to 1 year and are currently testing it with 250 families in a federally funded demonstration project.

Implications for Practice, Research, and Policy

The costs of parental substance abuse are enormous. Based on an extensive analysis of the impact of substance abuse on CM, the National Center on Addiction and Substance Abuse (CASA) at Columbia University concluded that parental substance abuse is the culprit in at least 70% and perhaps 90% of all child welfare spending (Reid et al., 1999). Using the more conservative 70% assessment, CASA found that substance abuse accounted for some $10 billion in federal, state, and local government spending in 1998 simply to maintain child welfare systems. This $10 billion figure does not include the costs of providing health care to abused and neglected children, operating law enforcement and judicial systems concerned with the problem, or treating the emotional and developmental problems these children encounter.

Given the high rates of substance abuse in society and its detrimental effect on parenting, professionals need to be prepared to screen parents, on a routine basis, for substance abuse. Although earlier substance screening tools were developed primarily to detect alcohol abuse, several brief measures are currently available to screen for use of illicit drugs (Kemper, Greteman, Bennett, & Babonis, 1993; McGovern & Morrison, 1992). Because parents who formerly abused alcohol and drugs are also at increased risk for committing CM, screening for a lifetime history of substance abuse is important. Routine screening for depression and other mental health disorders may lead to identification of those at increased risk for substance abuse and CM.

Although prenatal substance abuse does not constitute CM, empirical data clearly indicate that drug-exposed children are at very high risk for abuse and neglect in the future. Therefore, CPS agencies need to examine policies and practices that disallow accepting reports of positive toxicological screens as the sole basis for investigation. An assessment of the home environment, with emphasis on the caregiver's level of drug impairment, is necessary to determine the risk of subsequent CM.

Passive exposure to drugs *after* birth may be a more significant problem than previously realized. Children of substance-abusing parents need to be monitored for passive or deliberate exposure to substances of abuse. Passive exposure to the fumes from crack cocaine and methamphetamines smoked in confined spaces can have very serious health consequences, including death. Thus, in situations where children are deemed at risk for passive exposure, routine urine screening is indicated and can be incorporated into CPS treatment plans.

Increased access to substance abuse treatment is critical. In many communities, unfortunately, residential drug treatment programs are in high demand with long waiting periods. Because single women constitute the largest group of substance-abusing caregivers, more residential programs are needed that allow mothers to have their children with them while in residential treatment. In addition to treating addiction, such programs need to address parenting skills, the impact of CM and domestic violence, and comorbid psychiatric disorders, such as depression, anxiety, and posttraumatic stress disorder.

Because single women constitute the largest group of substance-abusing caregivers, more residential programs are needed that allow mothers to have their children with them while in residential treatment.

A major challenge in policy and practice relates to permanency planning. How long should children be allowed to languish in foster care while parents seek treatment? As stated by Reid et al. (1999), "There is an irreconcilable clash between the rapidly ticking clock of cognitive and physical development for the abused and neglected child and the slow motion clock of recovery for the parent addicted to alcohol or drugs" (p. iv). Even when parental rights are terminated in a timely manner, there are not nearly enough adoptive homes for abused and neglected children.

Based on the consistent findings indicating that survivors of childhood maltreatment are at increased risk for development of substance abuse problems, substance abuse prevention efforts should be targeted at this population. Because persons with psychiatric disorders are more likely to abuse children when using substances of abuse, such persons should also be targeted for substance abuse prevention efforts.

Further research is needed to examine the relationship between substance abuse and CM. The studies reviewed in this chapter indicate that the role of parental substance abuse in CM is difficult to disentangle from other factors associated with CM, such as poverty, a childhood history of maltreatment, and psychiatric disorders other than substance abuse. It appears that for many, serious maltreatment in childhood leads to such psychiatric disorders as depression, anxiety, and PTSD. These disorders, in turn, are often precursors to substance abuse, often at an early age. As substance abusers become parents, they are at increased risk of abusing and neglecting their own children. Without appropriate intervention, the cycle may very well continue. Longitudinal, intergenerational community-based studies examining the interaction of these variables are desperately needed.

Other research questions that need to be addressed include whether removal of a child by CPS is an incentive for mothers to seek drug treatment or whether it leads to increased stress, thereby increasing drug use and other maladaptive coping behaviors. How are extended family members—and grandmothers in particular—affected when they assume full-time parenting responsibilities for the children of substance-abusing mothers? What are the barriers to treatment for substance-abusing mothers?

Although the association between substance abuse and CM is well established, there appears to be minimal interaction between specialists in the fields of addiction and child maltreatment. The two fields can, undoubtedly, enlighten each other. Efforts should be made to facilitate a collaborative approach in addressing complex treatment, policy, and research issues of parents simultaneously trying to raise children and struggling with addiction.

In conclusion, the dramatic increase in parental substance abuse has essentially altered the challenge of protecting children. Although the financial cost of parental substance abuse is enormous, the human cost is immeasurable. Parental substance abuse presents, undoubtedly, one of the most difficult challenges to the field of child protection.

References

Abidin, R. R. (1990). *Parenting Stress Index*. Charlottesville, VA: Pediatric Psychology Press.

Ammerman, R. T., Kolko, D. J., Kirisci, L., Blackson, T. C., & Dawes, M. A. (1999). Child abuse potential in parents with histories of substance abuse disorder. *Child Abuse & Neglect, 23,* 1225-1238.

Bateman, D. A., & Heagarty, M. C. (1989). Passive freebase cocaine ("crack") inhalation in infants and toddlers. *American Journal of Diseases in Children, 143,* 25-27.

Bayatpour, M., Wells, R. D., & Holford, S. (1992). Physical and sexual abuse as predictors of substance use and suicide among pregnant teenagers. *Journal of Adolescent Health, 13,* 128-132.

Bays, J. (1994). Child abuse by poisoning. In R. M. Reece (Ed.), *Child abuse: Medical diagnosis and management* (pp. 69-106). Philadelphia: Lea & Febiger.

Bennett, E. M., & Kemper, K. J. (1994). Is abuse during childhood a risk factor for developing substance abuse problems as an adult? *Developmental and Behavioral Pediatrics, 15,* 426-429.

Besinger, B., Garland, A. F., Litrownik, A. J., & Landsverk, J. A. (1999). Caregiver substance abuse among maltreated children placed in out-of-home care. *Child Welfare, 78,* 221-239.

Boyd, C. J. (1993). The antecedents of women's crack cocaine abuse: Family substance abuse, sexual abuse, depression, and illicit drug use. *Journal of Substance Abuse Treatment, 10,* 433-438.

Brady, K. T., Killeen, T., Saladin, M. E., Dansky, B., & Becker, S. (1994). Comorbid substance abuse and posttraumatic stress disorder: Characteristics of women in treatment. *American Journal on Addictions, 3,* 160-164.

Burton, L. M. (1992). Black grandparents rearing children of drug-addicted parents: Stressors, outcomes and the social service needs. *Gerontologist, 32,* 744-751.

Byrd, R. S., Neistadt, A. M., Howard, C. R., Brownstein-Evans, C., & Weitzman, M. (1999). Why screen newborns for cocaine: Service patterns and social outcomes at age one year. *Child Abuse & Neglect, 23,* 523-530.

Caliandro, G., & Hughes, C. (1998). The experience of being a grandmother who is the primary caregiver for her HIV-positive grandchild. *Nursing Research, 47,* 107-113.

Carlin, A. S., Kemper, K., Ward, N. G., Sowell, H., Gustafson, B., & Stevens, N. (1994). The effect of differences in objective and subjective definitions of childhood physical abuse on estimates of its incidence and relationship to psychopathology. *Child Abuse & Neglect, 18,* 393-399.

Chaffin, M., Kelleher, K., & Hollenberg, J. (1996). Onset of physical abuse and neglect: Psychiatric, substance abuse, and social risk factors from prospective community data. *Child Abuse & Neglect, 20,* 191-203.

Chaney, N. E., Franke, J., & Wadlington, W. B. (1988). Cocaine convulsions in a breast-feeding baby. *Journal of Pediatrics, 112,* 134-135.

Chasnoff, I. F., Lewis, D. E., & Squires, L. (1987). Cocaine intoxication in a breast-fed infant. *Pediatrics, 80,* 836-838.

Dinwiddie, S. H., & Bucholz, K. K. (1993). Psychiatric diagnoses of self-reported child abusers. *Child Abuse & Neglect, 17,* 465-476.

Dowdell, E. B. (1995). Caregiver burden: Grandmothers raising their high risk grandchildren. *Journal of Psychosocial Nursing, 33,* 27-30.

English, D. J., Marshall, D. B., Brummel, S., & Orme, M. (1999). Characteristics of repeated referrals to child protective services in Washington state. *Child Maltreatment, 4,* 297-307.

Famularo, R., Kinscherff, R., & Fenton, T. (1992). Parental substance abuse and the nature of child maltreatment. *Child Abuse & Neglect, 16,* 475-483.

Feig, L. (1997). *Informal and formal kinship care: Findings from national and state data.* Washington, DC: U.S. Department of Health and Human Services, Office of the Assistant Secretary for Planning and Evaluation.

Frank, D. A., Augustyn, M., Knight, W. G., Pell, T., & Zuckerman, B. (2001). Growth, development, and behavior in early childhood following prenatal cocaine exposure: A systematic review. *Journal of the American Medical Association, 285,* 1613-1625.

Hall, L. A., Sachs, B., Rayens, M. K., & Lutenbacher, M. (1993). Childhood physical abuse and sexual abuse: Their relationship to depressive symptoms in adulthood. *Journal of Nursing Scholarship, 4,* 317-323.

Harmer, A. L. M., Sanderson, J., & Mertin, P. (1999). Influence of negative childhood experiences on psychological functioning, social support, and parenting for mothers recovering from addiction. *Child Abuse & Neglect, 23,* 421-433.

Harrison, P. A., Fulkerson, J. A., & Beebe, T. J. (1997). Multiple substance use among adolescent physical and sexual abuse victims. *Child Abuse & Neglect, 21,* 529-539.

Heidemann, S. M., & Goetting, M. G. (1990). Passive inhalation of cocaine by infants. *Henry Ford Hospital Medical Journal, 38,* 252-254.

Jasinski, J. L., Williams, L. M., & Siegel, J. (2000). Childhood physical and sexual abuse as risk factors for heavy drinking among African-American women: A prospective study. *Child Abuse & Neglect, 24,* 1061-1071.

Jaudes, P. K., Ekwo, E., & Voorhis, J. V. (1995). Association of drug abuse and child abuse. *Child Abuse & Neglect, 19,* 1065-1075.

Kang, S., Magura, S., Laudet, A., & Whitney, S. (1999). Adverse effect of child abuse victimization among substance-using women in treatment. *Journal of Interpersonal Violence, 14,* 657-670.

Kaufman, K., & Asdigian, N. (1994, June). *Socialization to alcohol-related family violence: Disentangling the effects of family history on current violence.* Paper presented at the American Society of Criminology Meetings, Phoenix, AZ.

Kelleher, K., Chaffin, M., Hollenberg, J., & Fischer, E. (1994). Alcohol and drug disorders among physically abusive and neglectful parents in a community-based sample. *American Journal of Public Health, 84,* 1586-1590.

Kelley, S. J. (1992). Parenting stress and child maltreatment in drug exposed children. *Child Abuse & Neglect, 16,* 317-328.

Kelley, S. J. (1993). Caregiver stress in grandparents raising grandchildren. *Image: Journal of Nursing Scholarship, 25*(4), 331-337.

Kelley, S. J. (1998). Stress and coping behaviors of substance-abusing mothers. *Journal of the Society of Pediatric Nursing, 3,* 103-110.

Kelley, S. J., & Damato, E. G. (1995). Grandparents as primary caregivers. *Maternal Child Nursing, 20,* 326-332.

Kelley, S. J., Whitley, D. M., Sipe, T. A., & Yorker, B. C. (2000). Psychological distress in grandmother kinship care providers: The role of resources, social support, and physical health. *Child Abuse & Neglect, 24,* 311-321.

Kelley, S. J., Yorker, B. C., Whitley, D. M., & Sipe, T. A. (2001). A multi-modal intervention for grandparents raising grandchildren: Results of a pilot study. *Child Welfare, 80*(1), 27-50.

Kemper, K. J., Greteman, A., Bennett, E., & Babonis, T. R. (1993). Screening mothers of young children for substance abuse. *Developmental and Behavioral Pediatrics, 14,* 308-312.

Kharasch, S., Vinci, R., Glotzer, D., Sargent, J., & Weitzman, M. (1990). Unsuspected cocaine exposure in young children. *American Journal of Diseases in Children, 144,* 441.

Little, R. E., Anderson, K. W., Ervin, C. H., Worthington-Roberts, B., & Clarren, S. K. (1989). Maternal alcohol use during breast-feeding and infant mental and motor development at one year. *New England Journal of Medicine, 321,* 425-430.

McGovern, M. P., & Morrison, D. H. (1992). The chemical use, abuse, and dependence scale: Rationale, reliability, and validity. *Journal of Substance Abuse Treatment, 9,* 27-38.

Medrano, M. A., Zule, W. A., Hatch, J., & Desmond, D. P. (1999). Prevalence of childhood trauma in a community sample of substance-abusing women. *American Journal of Drug and Alcohol Abuse, 25*(3), 449-462.

Milner, J. S. (1993). Social information processing and physical child abuse. *Clinical Psychology Review, 13,* 275-294.

Milner, J. S. (1995). Physical child abuse assessment: Perpetrator evaluation. In J. C. Campbell (Ed.), *Assessing for dangerousness: Violence by sexual offenders, batterers, and child abusers* (pp. 41-67). Thousand Oaks, CA: Sage.

Minkler, M., Fuller-Thompson, E., Miller, D., & Driver, D. (1997). Depression in grandparents raising grandchildren: Results of a national longitudinal study. *Archives of Family Medicine, 6,* 445-452.

Minkler, M., & Roe, K. M. (1993). *Grandmothers as caregivers: Raising children of the crack cocaine epidemic.* Newbury Park, CA: Sage.

Minkler, M., Roe, K. M., & Robertson-Beckley, R. J. (1994). Raising grandchildren from crack-cocaine households: Effects on family and friendship ties of African-American women. *American Journal of Orthopsychiatry, 64,* 20-29.

Mirchandani, H. G., Mirchandani, I. H., Hellman, F., English-Rider, R., Rosen, S., & Laposata, E. A. (1991). Passive inhalation of free-base cocaine ("crack") smoke by infants. *Archives of Pathological Laboratory Medicine, 115,* 494-498.

Mullen, P. E., Martin, J. L., Anderson, J. C., Romans, S. E., & Herbison, G. P. (1996). The long-term impact of the physical, emotional, and sexual abuse of children: A community study. *Child Abuse & Neglect, 20,* 7-21.

Murphy, J. M., Jellinek, M., Quinn, D., Smith, G., Poitrast, F. G., & Goshko, M. (1991). Substance abuse and serious child mistreatment: Prevalence, risk, and outcome in a court sample. *Child Abuse & Neglect, 15,* 197-211.

New York City Child Family Review Panel. (1995). *Annual report for 1994.* New York: New York City Child Fatality Review Panel.

Ostrea, E. M., Ostrea, A. R., & Simpson, P. M. (1997). Mortality within the first 2 years in infants exposed to cocaine, opiates, or cannabinoids during gestation. *Pediatrics, 100,* 79-83.

Reid, J., Macchetto, P., & Foster, S. (1999). *No safe haven: Children of substance-abusing parents.* New York: National Center on Addiction and Substance Abuse at Columbia University.

Reinhart, M. A. (1990). Child abuse: Cocaine absorption by rectal administration. *Clinical Pediatrics, 97,* 357.

Rogers, C., Hall, J., & Muto, J. (1991). Findings in newborns of cocaine-abusing mothers. *Journal of Forensic Sciences, 35,* 1074-1078.

Roy, G., Gordon, S. G., & Cohen, S. T. (1997). An innovative school-based intergenerational model to serve grandparent caregivers. *Journal of Gerontological Social Work, 28,* 47-61.

Saunders, B. E., Villeponteaux, L. A., Lipovsky, J. A., & Kilpatrick, D. G. (1992). Child sexual assault as a risk factor for mental disorder among women: A community survey. *Journal of Interpersonal Violence, 7,* 189-204.

Schwartz, R. H., Peary, P., & Mistretta, D. (1986). Intoxication of young children with marijuana: A form of amusement for pot-smoking teenage girls. *American Journal of Diseases in Children, 140,* 326.

Shannon, M., Lacouture, P. G., Roa, J., & Woolf, A. (1989). Cocaine exposure among children seen at a pediatric hospital. *Pediatrics, 83,* 337-341.

Swanson, J. W., Holzer, C. E., Ganju, V. K., & Jono, R. T. (1990). Violence and psychiatric disorder in the community: Evidence from the Epidemiologic Catchment Area surveys. *Hospital and Community Psychiatry, 41,* 761-770.

U.S. Bureau of the Census. (1998, May). *Current population reports: Coresident grandparents and grandchildren* (Series P-23, No. 198). Washington, DC: Author.

Wallen, J., & Berman, K. (1992). Possible indicators of childhood sexual abuse for individuals in substance abuse treatment. *Journal of Child Sexual Abuse, 1,* 63-74.

Wang, C. T., & Harding, K. (1999). *Current trends in child abuse reporting and fatalities: The results of the 1998 annual fifty state survey.* Chicago: National Committee to Prevent Child Abuse.

Wasserman, D. R., & Leventhal, J. M. (1993). Maltreatment of children born to cocaine-dependent mothers. *American Journal of Diseases in Children, 147,* 1324-1328.

Wolock, I., & Magura, S. (1996). Parental substance abuse as a predictor of child maltreatment re-reports. *Child Abuse & Neglect, 20,* 1183-1193.

6

Child Abuse in the Context of Domestic Violence

Historically, researchers in the areas of child abuse and domestic violence have occupied different spheres of inquiry, used disparate sources of data, received funding from different agencies, reported results at different conferences, and published their work in different journals (see Graham-Bermann & Edleson, 2001). Furthermore, the field of domestic violence research postdates the field of child abuse research by some 15 years. Differences can readily be seen in the ways in which data are collected and how violence is defined, as well as in the kinds of interventions available to ameliorate the problem. For example, there is mandated reporting of suspected cases of child abuse. This is not so for domestic violence. Statistics on child abuse are collected each year in all 50 states, whereas states do not routinely document the number of domestic violence cases. Yet, despite differences between the two domains, they share many similarities and concerns. For example, it is now well documented that much child abuse occurs in homes where domestic violence (i.e., woman abuse) is ongoing. These similarities and differences will be discussed in the pages that follow.

Defining Child Abuse in the Context of Domestic Violence

Observing Versus Being the Target of Violence

A number of differences are evident in the definitions of these two forms of violence. First, there is the distinction between being an observer of, as opposed to being the target of, violence. The standard definition of child abuse presumes that the child is the target of physical or sexual assault.

By definition, children's witnessing of domestic violence has relied on the child's observations of violence as the index of exposure. Yet, there is controversy as to exactly what the child may have observed. Furthermore, it is often difficult to sort out the abuse of the child from the abuse of the mother.

There are broad and narrow definitions of domestic violence. Domestic violence is generally defined as the intentional infliction of harm or injury by one intimate partner on another (National Research Council, 1998). We know from studies of multiple forms of abuse that severe physical violence against women rarely occurs in isolation (Graham-Bermann, 1998; Straus, Hamby, Boney-McCoy, & Sugarman, 1995; Tolman, 1989). Severe violence is often accompanied by other forms of maltreatment of the woman, to which children may be exposed. Some researchers have expanded the definition of domestic violence to include forms of emotional maltreatment and verbal and sexual abuse (Koss et al., 1994).

In research studies, the amount of violence reported varies by the sample source. The results of several studies illustrate the point. Graham-Bermann and colleagues used measures of conflict tactics (Straus, 1979) and psychological maltreatment of the woman (Marshall, 1992) to obtain the mean frequency of five kinds of domestic violence in three separate studies (Graham-Bermann, 1996, 1998; Levendosky & Graham-Bermann, 2000). Women were asked to self-report the number of times various kinds of maltreatment occurred. All of the women were mothers. One group came from shelters for battered women ($n = 60$). The second group consisted of battered women living in the community ($n = 60$). The third group was battered women who brought their child for treatment ($n = 119$). A comparison group of nonabused women

was included ($n = 61$). In Table 6.1, the mean frequencies of reported conflict tactics and abuse in the last year are displayed, including coercion tactics, threats to do physical harm, sexual assaults (from unwanted touching to rape), mild violence (pushing, shoving, slapping), and severe violence (hitting with an object, beating up, using or threatening to use a gun or knife).

Perhaps the most notable finding was that mild and severe violence to women was accompanied by threats to do greater harm to the women, such as sexual assault and acts of coercion. The children of these abused women were potentially exposed to different forms of psychological maltreatment several times a week, in addition to frequent mild and severe physical violence. Barnett, Manly, and Cicchetti (1993) emphasized that all maltreatment exists along a continuum and that less severe forms may be equally harmful if repeated often enough. Thus, when documenting children's exposure to domestic violence, the variables of interest should include a range of violence experiences, how often violence occurs, and whether the children experience violence directly or indirectly—whether they see it, hear it, or just know about it.

Intentionality of Violence That Is Observed or Experienced

It is presumed that batterers of women intend to harm their adult victims. It is less clear that batterers intend to victimize the children who witness battering. Children are sometimes used by batterers to coerce the other parent in some way in conjunction with a violent episode (Jaffe & Geffner, 1998; Jaffe, Poisson, & Cunningham, 2001). Battered women who are pregnant report that the target of violent assault is frequently the abdomen and, hence, the fetus (McFarlane, Parker, & Soeken, 1995; Seng et al., 2001). Physical violence against pregnant women has been calculated at 154 of every 1,000 pregnant women up to the 4th month and 170 of every 1,000 pregnant women from the 5th to 9th months (Seng et al., 2001).

We know that many children who observe interadult violence are injured either directly (intentionally) or indirectly (accidentally) during a violent episode. For example, in the study of 119 children of abused women shown in Table 6.1, 12% of

TABLE 6.1 Mean Frequencies of Five Kinds of Violence and Abuse Tactics for Four Sample Groups

	Coercion	Physical Threat	Sex Assault	Mild Violence	Severe Violence	Number
Shelter	106	57	32	36	27	60
Clinical	96	46	37	19	11	119
Community	51	22	13	14	9	60
Comparison	20	7	8	2	2	61

the children, .05% of the abusive partners, and 70% of the mothers received injuries as a result of the most recent violent episode (Graham-Bermann, 2000).

It is often difficult to sort out the abuse of the child from the abuse of the mother. One way of doing so is to identify the child's role in interparental violence, including whether the child tried to stop the violence, tried to call police, or attempted to protect family members. Hilberman and Munson (1977-1978) found that children were more likely to be abused when they tried to intervene and stop the abuse of their mothers. Older children and female children were most at risk for abuse by the father. As might be anticipated, efforts at intervention may not be well received by the abuser and could lead to escalating violence.

Variability in Definitions Across Studies and Across Settings

A range of terms is used to tease out the differences among various types and levels of violence against women and children, including mild violence as opposed to severe violence (Straus, 1979), everyday violence versus abusive violence (Jouriles, McDonald, Norwood, & Ezell, 2001), and soft aggression and hard aggression (Horowitz, 1992). Some argue that a distinction should be made between maltreatment and violence so that minimal endangerments can be differentiated from more serious levels of harm (Emery & Laumann-Billings, 1998).

Many labels have been used to describe interadult domestic violence, including woman abuse, spouse abuse, battering, and domestic assault (Graham-Bermann & Brescoll, 2000; Jouriles et al., 2001). Researchers are just beginning to differentiate among the various forms of family violence and distinguish domestic violence from

other forms of marital conflict (most usually verbal disagreement) (Porter & O'Leary, 1980; Rossman & Rosenberg, 1992). Unfortunately, this parsing effort leads to the categorization of some forms of violence as seemingly more harmful or worse than others. For example, "ordinary" family violence (Wauchope & Straus, 1990) has been defined as mild rather than severe violence. Mild violence has been defined as "maltreatment," as distinguished from severe violence that has been termed *abusive* (Emery & Laumann-Billings, 1998). In these categories, acts of violence appear to take precedence over the outcome (injuries) and the frequency and severity of acts of violence.

Distinctions are made as to whether domestic violence is bidirectional or unidirectional or results in injury that is mild or severe. Some studies show that women use violence as frequently as men (Wauchope & Straus, 1990). Researchers point out, however, that women who are assaultive may strike out peremptorily to defend themselves. In any event, women are significantly more likely to be injured as a result of violence than men (Koss et al., 1994; Saunders, 1986).

In some states, exposing children to adult domestic assault is considered a crime. In Utah, if domestic violence is perpetrated two or more times in the presence of a child, it is considered actionable.

Another pressing definitional issue is whether witnessing domestic violence itself is a reportable form of child maltreatment. In some states, exposing children to adult domestic assault is considered a crime. Specifically, in Utah, if domestic violence is perpetrated two or more times in the presence of a child, it is considered actionable (Utah Criminal Code § 76-5-109.1, 1997). Some researchers consider exposing a child to domestic assault to be a form of corrupting behavior and thus psychological maltreatment (Garbarino, Dubrow, Kostelny, & Pardo, 1992; Graham-Bermann, 1998). (For discussion of psychological maltreatment, see Chapter 4, this volume.) Whether a child's exposure to adult violence is intentional or not, witnessing domestic violence has deleterious consequences to the child. In sum, the task of studying overlapping child abuse and domestic violence is complicated by variability in definitions, problems in determining intentionality, and the difficulty inherent in measuring harm that derives from observing violence.

Prevalence and Incidence of Overlapping Domestic Violence and Child Abuse

Violence Against Women

Despite much attention to the problem since the 1970s, domestic violence has not abated (Bachman & Saltzman 1996). Abuse of women is a vastly underreported crime (Saunders & Azar, 1989). The overall rate of domestic violence in the United States is conservatively given at 28% of all married couples per year (Straus & Gelles, 1990).

Children's Exposure to Domestic Violence

Unfortunately, there is no national prevalence study of children's exposure to domestic violence. Many studies rely on data from women and children in shelters, in crisis, or both, and there is little by way of substantiation of violence reports. Rates of exposure to domestic violence for children ages 3 to 17 were first calculated at 3.3 million children per year (Carlson, 1984). This figure was derived from Straus, Gelles, and Steinmetz's (1980) estimate that violence occurs in 55% of American households and that there are approximately two children per family. Straus (1992) updated this esti-

mate to 10 million children witnessing domestic violence each year (based on data from 1975 and 1985 national surveys). These figures are broadly based and crude, deriving from reports of whether or not violence occurred, not its frequency, intensity, duration, or harm.

Child Physical Abuse

In their groundbreaking epidemiological survey in 1975, Straus et al. (1980) disclosed the extent of violence present in American families, challenging the myth that the family is a haven of safety. Straus and his colleagues reported that people are more likely to be assaulted, beaten, or killed by their own family members than by outsiders. This disturbing fact is particularly true for children. The prevalence of physical child abuse is discussed in Chapters 2 and 13, this volume.

Parental Kidnapping

A form of child abuse that sometimes occurs in the context of domestic violence is abduction or kidnapping. Parental kidnapping is particularly likely in the context of battles over child custody or visitation. More than 350,000 children are abducted by a parent each year (Finkelhor, Hotaling, & Sedlak, 1990). Although more than half of these abductions are short-lived, nearly half of the children are taken out of state and concealed. Fathers are most likely to abduct (Greif & Hagar, 1992). Just as battered women are at greater risk for abuse when they attempt to separate from the batterer, children are at greater risk for abduction following separation (Langen & Innes, 1986).

Overlapping Child Abuse and Domestic Violence

A meta-analysis by Appel and Holden (1998) of 42 studies containing data on the co-occurrence of domestic violence and physical child abuse found that the base rate of overlap varied by the origin of the sample. In studies that relied on clinical samples of either child physical abuse or domestic violence, the overlap ranged from 20% to 100%. By contrast, studies that used representative community samples had lower rates of overlapping violence, averaging 6%. Interestingly, these low figures reflect those found by Fantuzzo, Boruch, Beriama, Atkins, and Marcus (1997), who studied reported rates of child abuse and domestic violence in five cities. Only two cities—Atlanta and Miami—had complete data, and in those cities, the rates of overlap were 6% and 7%, respectively.

Another pathway to determining the overlap between domestic violence and child abuse is to calculate child abuse practices in families with domestic violence and to then compare these with national statistics derived from other studies. For example, Jouriles and Norwood (1995) demonstrated that the rate of aggression against children in families with domestic violence is 25% higher than rates reported in the national sample of Straus and Gelles (1990).

The Evolution of Child Abuse in the Context of Domestic Violence

To date, very little is known about the development and timing of child abuse in the context of domestic violence. Stark and Flitcraft (1996) found that woman abuse usually predates abuse to the child. Stark and Flitcraft identified conditions associated with a batterer's concomitant maltreatment of the child to include dissolution of the marriage, separation, or a husband committed to dominance and control over family members (see Bowker, Arbitell, & McFerron, 1988).

Age

Intimate partner violence and child abuse do not occur uniformly across the life span. Exposure to domestic violence may be greater for young children (Wolak & Finkelhor, 1996). In one study, domestic violence was found to occur more frequently during the early years of marriage (Suitor, Pillemer, & Straus, 1990). The Spouse Assault Replication Program collected data in five cities from police officers and from 2,402 female victims of misdemeanor domestic violence (Fantuzzo et al., 1997). Domestic violence occurred disproportionately in households with young children (< age 5). That is, young children (ages 0 to 5) were more likely to be exposed to multiple incidents of woman abuse than older children.

Given young children's limited capacity to understand domestic violence, it has been argued that the effects on them will be more severe (Graham-Bermann & Levendosky, 1998a). The effects may take a physiological form because young children lack the means to deal with the violence they see. Similarly, the coping mechanisms available to younger children (e.g., somatization, withdrawal) may leave them at risk for problems in attachment to significant figures in their lives. Older children are more independent and spend more time out of the home. Thus, young children may be most at risk from exposure to domestic violence.

Gender

Are men or women more abusive toward children in the context of domestic violence? Some studies find that abused women are twice as likely to abuse their children as nonabused women (Gayford, 1975; Walker, 1984). In the context of domestic violence, however, male batterers reportedly abuse their children twice as often as battered women (Giles-Sims, 1985; Jouriles & Norwood, 1995). In one study, girls whose mothers were battered were 6.5 times more likely to be sexually abused than were girls from nonviolent families (Bowker et al., 1988). Furthermore, the severity of abuse to the woman was directly linked to the severity of abuse to the child (Bowker et al., 1988; Straus & Gelles, 1990).

To date, there is no consistent evidence for gender differences in children victimized by exposure to domestic abuse (O'Keefe, 1994). Several studies on long-term outcomes suggest that boys from violent families have a higher risk of using abusive tactics in their teenage and young adult relationships (Jouriles & Norwood, 1995). A Massachusetts study showed that children exposed to the abuse of their mothers were more likely to engage in a variety of antisocial and criminal activities as adults (Hangen, 1994).

Substance Use and Abuse

Parental substance abuse or dependence is associated with increased risk for child abuse (Dore, Doris, & Wright, 1995). Although many batterers assault their partners without using alcohol, the temporal relationship between domestic violence and alcohol abuse has been amply demonstrated (Gondolf, 1993). Less is known about the relationship between illicit drug use and wife battering. In one study, the substance abuse of batterers was reported by women who received emergency treatment. Sixty-five percent of the batterers reportedly had used both cocaine and alcohol at the time of the assault.

Outcomes Associated With Exposure to Domestic Violence

The Carnegie report on "Saving Youth From Violence" (Carnegie Corporation of New York, 1994) identified the multiple stressors and traumas that contribute to the development of aggressive and anxious behavior in young children. Among these are violence in the home, including child abuse and exposure to domestic violence, and poverty. Poor children of all ages are disproportionately affected by violence.

School-age children raised in homes with domestic violence are at risk for developmental problems (for reviews, see Graham-Bermann, 1998; Fantuzzo & Lindquist, 1989; Margolin, 1998). Specifically, school-age children demonstrate high rates of internalizing and externalizing behavior problems, low self-esteem, and more difficulties in school than children raised in nonviolent families (Hughes & Graham-Bermann, 1998; Jaffe, Wolfe, & Wilson, 1990). Children raised in a violent home experience problems in interpersonal relationships, including heightened fear and worry about those in the home and difficulty establishing and maintaining friendships outside the home (Graham-Bermann, 1996).

Some children show symptoms of posttraumatic stress (Richters & Martinez, 1993). Thus, school-age children in domestic violence shelters are described as having clinical levels of trauma-related stress, such as repeated nightmares, exaggerated startle response, inability to focus attention, and intrusive thoughts (Graham-Bermann & Levendosky, 1998b; Rossman, 2001). Children can be traumatized by overhearing beatings (Peled, 2001) as well as by viewing them. Yet, children respond individually to witnessing repeated violence. Some children develop major psychological disorders. Others appear resilient and unaffected (Graham-Bermann, 1998; Hughes & Luke,

1998; Jaffe et al., 1990). Whether children who appear unaffected will become symptomatic later—the so-called "sleeper effect"—is unknown at this point.

Relatively little is known about the impact of domestic violence on preschoolers. The few studies on 3- to 5-year-olds who witnessed domestic violence found that most children exhibited behavior problems in the clinical range (74% of boys and 60% of girls) (Davis & Carlson, 1987) and that children had increased symptoms of trauma and dissociation (Rossman, 2001). These preschoolers were less empathic with others than were children from nonviolent homes (Hinchey & Gavelek, 1982). One study found that preschoolers living with battered mothers demonstrated restricted social problem-solving ability, but only if the mother was depressed (Tershak, 1982).

Preschool-age children exposed to domestic violence have difficulty regulating the expression of negative emotions and are more aggressive and violent in interpersonal play than children not so exposed.

Graham-Bermann and Levendosky (1998b) evaluated the social interaction and emotional adjustment of 3- to 5-year-olds, half of whom witnessed domestic violence. Children who experienced domestic violence had significantly more behavior problems (both externalizing and internalizing). Preschool-age children exposed to domestic violence had difficulty regulating the expression of negative emotions and were more aggressive and violent in interpersonal play than children not so exposed. On the other hand, children exposed to domestic violence were not less happy or less cooperative in play. Graham-Bermann and Levendosky found no differences in behavior due to gender or ethnic status.

Interventions

Programs have been designed to allay the negative effects of domestic violence on children, whether or not the child was directly assaulted. Many communities offer education, support, or intervention programs for children and battered women. Until recently, there has been little empirical evidence that these interventions help the children they serve (National Research Council, 1998). Rigorous intervention studies are just beginning to be reported. Some of these studies show promising, if preliminary, results in improving the social, cognitive, and emotional functioning of children who experience violence.

The Child Witnesses to Wife Abuse Program

Wilson, Cameron, Jaffe, and Wolfe (1989) evaluated a psychoeducational program called the Child Witnesses to Wife Abuse Program. The program emphasized knowledge about family violence and incorporated exercises designed to help children build social skills. The goals of the 10-week program included raising 8- to 13-year-old children's self-esteem while teaching positive conflict resolution strategies, changing attitudes regarding responsibility for violence, and changing attitudes about domestic violence. The children were living in shelters for battered women.

Wagar and Rodway (1995) tested the efficacy of the Child Witnesses to Wife Abuse Program with 38 children ages 8 to 13. Sixteen children received the intervention, and 22 served as a control (no treatment) group. Pre- and posttreatment evaluations included the Conflict Tactics Scale, as well as parent and child interviews. Although the study suffers from small sample size, unequal groups, and lack of systematic follow-up assessments, Wagar and Rodway reported positive effects of the program on children's attitudes and responses to anger and on reduction in children's self-blame for violence between parents. No statistically significant differences were found for improved knowledge of safety or enhanced coping through use of social support.

The Kid's Club: A Preventive Intervention Program

The Kid's Club was designed for children exposed to family violence (Graham-Bermann, 1992). This 10-week intervention targeted 6- to 12-year-old children's knowledge about family violence, their atti-

tudes and beliefs about families and family violence, their emotional adjustment, and their social behavior in a small group setting. A parenting program was created to empower mothers to discuss the impact of violence on various areas of the child's development, build parenting competence, reduce malparenting, provide a safe place to discuss fears and worries, and build self-esteem for the mother in the context of a supportive group (Graham-Bermann & Levendosky, 1994). The intervention was designed to improve parenting skills, including discipline strategies, as well as enhance social and emotional adjustment.

With a sample size of 221 families, The Kid's Club represents the largest intervention evaluation study to date for children of battered women (see Graham-Bermann, 2000). Pre- and postintervention and 8-month follow-up assessments were made of several areas of child functioning. Children exposed to high levels of domestic violence were randomly assigned to participate in a child-only intervention, a child-plus-mother intervention, or a comparison group that received "normal" services for 10 weeks.

For the children, significant change from baseline was found in knowledge about violence, safety planning, social skills, emotion regulation, and emotional/behavioral domains (internalizing and externalizing behaviors). When mothers and children received intervention, the effects in all areas were greater than when only the children were the focus of intervention. Children who received the intervention made more progress than did children in the control group (Graham-Bermann, 1998).

Focus on Parenting

Several programs address parenting, with an emphasis on managing the child's aggressive behavior (Jouriles et al., 1998). Jouriles and colleagues (1998) implemented a home-based program modeled on the work of Patterson (1986). The intervention was designed for battered women leaving shelters and their young children with high levels of conduct problems. Prescreening was used to identify children with clinical levels of aggression. Support and training were provided to the mother (e.g., problem-solving skills, parenting practices), and mentoring and support were given to the child. Preliminary outcome data for 18 families with 8-month follow-up indicate success in reducing conduct problems and enhancing mothers' parenting skills and coping.

Conclusion

More research is needed to help us understand the impact on children of witnessing domestic violence. Most studies to date rely on the mother's report to document both the violence in the home and the child's reaction. Yet, the mothers in most studies were recently traumatized by abuse. Many were depressed, anxious, or otherwise suffering from the effects of abuse. In such circumstances, mothers may not be the most reliable reporters of events.

Studies of domestic abuse that include the father's viewpoint are needed (Williams, Bogess, & Carter, 2001). There are few accounts of the child's own perception of events (Graham-Bermann, 1996; Peled,

2001). A national epidemiological study of children's exposure to domestic violence is needed.

As the respective fields of child abuse and children's exposure to domestic violence come together, regular and routine reporting of both forms of exposure should become the norm. To that end, we need longitudinal studies and studies that include more than one form of violence. We know, for instance, that some children who witness community violence also witness violence at home. The combination of these two forms of violence may play a significant role in predicting negative effects on children (DuRant, Cadenhead, Pendergrast, Slavens, & Linder, 1994; Singer, Miller, Guo, Slovak, & Frierson, 1998; Song, Singer, & Anglin, 1998). By studying a broader range of violence experiences, we can better document the problem and more clearly and effectively focus our solutions.

References

Appel, A. E., & Holden, G. W. (1998). The co-occurrence of spouse and physical child abuse: A review and appraisal. *Journal of Family Psychology, 12,* 578-599.

Bachman, R., & Saltzman, L. E. (1996). *Violence against women: Estimates from the redesigned survey* (Bureau of Justice Statistics special report: NJC No. 154348). Rockville, MD: US. Department of Justice.

Barnett, D., Manly, J. T., & Cicchetti, D. (1993). Defining child maltreatment: The interface between policy and research. In D. Cicchetti & S. L. Toth (Eds.), *Child abuse, child development, and social policy* (pp. 7-73). Norwood, NJ: Ablex.

Bowker, L. H., Arbitell, M., & McFerron, J. R. (1988). On the relationship between wife beating and child abuse. In K. Yllö and M. Bograd (Eds.), *Perspectives on wife abuse* (pp. 158-174). Newbury Park, CA: Sage.

Carlson, B. E. (1984). Children's observations of interpersonal violence. In A. Roberts (Ed.), *Battered women and their families* (pp. 147-167). New York: Springer.

Carnegie Corporation of New York. (1994). Saving youth from violence. *Carnegie Quarterly, 39,* 1-15.

Davis, L. V., & Carlson, B. E. (1987). Observation of spouse abuse: What happens to the children? *Journal of Interpersonal Violence, 2,* 278-291.

Dore, M. M., Doris, J., & Wright, P. (1995). Identifying substance abuse in maltreating families: A child welfare challenge. *Child Abuse & Neglect, 19,* 531-543.

DuRant, R. H., Cadenhead, C., Pendergrast, R. A., Slavens, G., & Linder, C. (1994). Factors associated with the use of violence among urban and Black adolescents. *American Journal of Public Health, 84,* 612-617.

Emery, R. E., & Laumann-Billings, L. (1998). An overview of the nature, causes and consequences of abusive family relationships: Toward differentiating maltreatment and violence. *American Psychologist, 53,* 121-135.

Fantuzzo, J. W., Boruch, R., Beriama, A., Atkins, M., & Marcus, S. (1997). Domestic violence and children: Prevalence and risk in five major cities. *Journal of the American Academy of Child and Adolescent Psychiatry, 36*(1), 116-122.

Fantuzzo, J. W., & Lindquist, C. U. (1989). The effects of observing conjugal violence on children: A review of research methodology. *Journal of Family Violence, 4,* 77-94.

Finkelhor, D., Hotaling, G. T., & Sedlak, A. (1990). *Missing, abducted, runaway, and thrownaway children in America: First report*. Washington, DC: Juvenile Justice Clearinghouse.

Garbarino, J., Dubrow, N., Kostelny, K., & Pardo, C. (1992). *Children in danger: Coping with the consequences of community violence*. San Francisco: Jossey-Bass.

Gayford, J. (1975). Wife battering: A preliminary survey of 100 cases. *British Medicine Journal, 1*.

Giles-Sims, J. (1985). A longitudinal study of battered children of battered women. *Family Relations, 34*, 205-207.

Gondolf, E. (1993). Treating the batterer. In M. Hansen & M. Harway (Eds.), *Battering and family therapy: A feminist perspective* (pp. 105-118). Newbury Park, CA: Sage.

Graham-Bermann, S. A. (1992). *The Kid's Club: A preventive intervention program for children of battered women*. Ann Arbor: Department of Psychology, University of Michigan.

Graham-Bermann, S. A. (1996). Family worries: The assessment of interpersonal anxiety in children from violent and nonviolent families. *Journal of Clinical Child Psychology, 25*(3), 280-287.

Graham-Bermann, S. A. (1998). The impact of woman abuse on children's social development. In G. W. Holden, R. Geffner, & E. N. Jouriles (Eds.), *Children and marital violence: Theory, research, and intervention* (pp. 21-54). Washington, DC: American Psychological Association.

Graham-Bermann, S. A. (2000). Evaluating interventions for children exposed to family violence. *Journal of Aggression, Maltreatment & Trauma, 4,* 191-216.

Graham-Bermann, S. A., & Brescoll, V. (2000). Gender, power, and violence: Assessing the family stereotypes of the children of batterers. *Journal of Family Psychology, 14*(4), 600-612.

Graham-Bermann, S. A., & Edleson, J. (Eds.). (2001). *Domestic violence in the lives of children: The future of research, intervention, and social policy*. Washington, DC: American Psychological Association.

Graham-Bermann, S. A., & Levendosky, A. A. (1994). *The Moms' Group: A parenting support and intervention program for battered women who are mothers*. Unpublished manuscript, University of Michigan.

Graham-Bermann, S. A., & Levendosky, A. A. (1998a). The social functioning of preschool-age children whose mothers are emotionally and physically abused. *Journal of Emotional Abuse, 1,* 59-84.

Graham-Bermann, S. A., & Levendosky, A. A. (1998b). Traumatic stress symptoms in children of battered women. *Journal of Interpersonal Violence, 13,* 111-128.

Greif, G., & Hagar, R. (1992). *When parents kidnap*. New York: Free Press.

Hangen, E. (1994). *D.S.S. Interagency Domestic Violence Team Pilot Project: Program data evaluation*. Boston: Massachusetts Department of Social Services.

Hilberman, E., & Munson, K. (1977-1978). Sixty battered women. *Victimology: An International Journal, 2*(3/4).

Hinchey, F. S., & Gavelek, J. R. (1982). Empathic responding in children of battered mothers. *Child Abuse & Neglect, 6,* 395-401.

Horowitz, T. (1992). Gender plus: Aggression, gender and other social variables. *Education and Society, 10,* 63-71.

Hughes, H., & Graham-Bermann, S. A. (1998). Impact of emotional abuse on development and adjustment. *Journal of Emotional Abuse, 1*(2), 23-50.

Hughes, H., & Luke, D. A. (1998). Heterogeneity in adjustment among children of battered women. In G. W. Holden, R. Geffner, & E. N. Jouriles (Eds.), *Children exposed to marital violence: Theory, research, and applied issues* (pp. 185-221). Washington, DC: American Psychological Association.

Jaffe, P., & Geffner, R. (1998). Child custody disputes and domestic violence: Critical issues for mental health, social services and legal professionals. In G. W. Holden, R. Geffner, & E. N. Jouriles (Eds.), *Children exposed to marital violence: Theory, research, and applied issues* (pp. 371-408). Washington, DC: American Psychological Association.

Jaffe, P., Poisson, S., & Cunningham, A. (2001). Domestic violence and high conflict divorce: Developing a new generation of research for children. In S. A. Graham-Bermann & J. L. Edleson (Eds.), *Domestic violence in the lives of children: The future of research, intervention, and policy* (pp. 189-202). Washington, DC: American Psychological Association.

Jaffe, P., Wolfe, D., & Wilson, D. (1990). *Children of battered women*. Newbury Park, CA: Sage.

Jouriles, E. N., McDonald, R., Stephens, N., Norwood, W., Spiller, L. C., & Ware, H. S. (1998). Breaking the cycle of violence: Helping families departing from battered women's shelters. In G. W. Holden, R. Geffner, & E. N. Jouriles (Eds.), *Children exposed to marital violence: Theory, research, and applied issues* (pp. 337-370). Washington, DC: American Psychological Association.

Jouriles, E. N., & Norwood, W. D. (1995). Physical aggression toward boys and girls in families characterized by the battering of women. *Journal of Family Psychology, 9,* 69-78.

Jouriles, E. N., McDonald, R., Norwood, W. D., & Ezell, E. (2001). Issues and controversies in documenting the prevalence of children's exposure to domestic violence. In S. A. Graham-Bermann &

J. L. Edleson (Eds.), *Domestic violence in the lives of children: The future of research, intervention, and social policy* (pp. 13-34). Washington, DC: American Psychological Association.

Koss, M. P., Goodman, L. A., Browne, A., Fitzgerald, L. F., Keita, G. P., & Russo, N. F. (1994). *No safe haven: Male violence against women at home, at work, and in the community.* Washington, DC: American Psychological Association.

Langen, P. A., & Innes, C. A. (1986). *Preventing domestic violence against women.* Washington, DC: Bureau of Justice Statistics Special Reports, Department of Justice.

Levendosky, A. A., & Graham-Bermann, S. A. (2000). Behavioral observations of parenting in battered women. *Journal of Family Psychology, 14,* 1-15.

Margolin, G. (1998). Effects of domestic violence on children. In P. K. Trickett & C. J. Schellenbach (Eds.), *Violence against children in the family and in the community* (pp. 57-102). Washington, DC: American Psychological Association.

Marshall, L. (1992). Development of the severity of violence against women scales. *Journal of Family Violence, 7,* 102-121.

McFarlane, J., Parker, B., & Soeken, K. (1995). Abuse during pregnancy: Frequency, severity, perpetrator, and risk factors of homicide. *Public Health Nursing, 12,* 284-289.

National Research Council, Institute of Medicine. (1998). *Violence in families: Assessing prevention and treatment programs.* Washington, DC: National Academy of Sciences.

O'Keefe, M. (1994). Linking marital violence, mother-child/father-child aggression, and child behavior problems. *Journal of Family Violence, 9,* 63-78.

Patterson, G. R. (1986). The contribution of siblings to training for fighting: A microsocial analysis. In D. Olweus, J. Block, & M. Radke-Yarrow (Eds.), *Development of antisocial and prosocial behavior* (pp. 235-261). New York: Academic Press.

Peled, E. (2001). Ethically sound research on children's exposure to domestic violence: A proposal. In S. A. Graham-Bermann & J. L. Edleson (Eds.), *Domestic violence in the lives of children: The future of research, intervention, and social policy* (pp. 111-132). Washington, DC: American Psychological Association.

Porter, B., & O'Leary, K. D. (1980). Marital discord and childhood behavior problems. *Journal of Abnormal Child Psychology, 8,* 287-295.

Richters, J., & Martinez, P. (1993). The NIMH community violence project: I. Children as victims of and witnesses to violence. *Psychiatry, 56,* 7-21.

Rossman, B. B. R. (2001). Longer-term effects of children's exposure to adult domestic violence. In S. A. Graham-Bermann & J. L. Edleson (Eds.), *Domestic violence in the lives of children: The future of research, intervention, and social policy* (pp. 35-66). Washington, DC: American Psychological Association.

Rossman, B. B. R., & Rosenberg, M. (1992). *Multiple victimization of children: Conceptual, developmental, research, and treatment issues.* New York: Haworth.

Saunders, D. G. (1986). When battered women use violence: Husband abuse or self defense? *Violence and Victims, 1,* 47-60.

Saunders, D. G., & Azar, S. T. (1989). Treatment programs for domestic violence. In L. Ohlin & M. Tonry (Eds.), *Family violence: Crime and justice, a review of research* (Vol. 11, pp. 481-546). Chicago: University of Chicago Press.

Seng, J. S., Oakley, D. J., Sampselle, C. M., Killion, C., Graham-Bermann, S., & Liberzon, I. (2001). Posttraumatic stress disorder and pregnancy complications. *Journal of Obstetrics and Gynecology, 97,* 17-22.

Singer, M. I., Miller, D. G., Guo, S., Slovak, K., & Frierson, T. (1998). *The mental health consequences of children's exposure to violence.* Cleveland, OH: Cayahoga County Community Mental Health Research Institute, Mandel School of Applied Social Sciences, Case Western Reserve University.

Song, L., Singer, M., & Anglin, T. (1998). Violence exposure and emotional trauma as contributors to adolescents' violent behavior. *Archives of Pediatric and Adolescent Medicine, 152,* 531-536.

Stark, E., & Flitcraft, A. (1996). *Women at risk: Domestic violence and women's health.* Thousand Oaks, CA: Sage.

Straus, M. A. (1979). Measuring family conflict and violence: The Conflict Tactics Scale. *Journal of Marriage and the Family, 41,* 75-88.

Straus, M. A. (1992). Children as witnesses to marital violence: A risk factor for lifelong problems among a nationally representative sample of American men and women. In D. F. Schwartz (Ed.), *Children and violence: Report of the Twenty-Third Ross Roundtable on Critical Approaches to Common Pediatric Problems* (pp. 98-109). Columbus, OH: Ross Laboratories.

Straus, M. A., & Gelles, R. J. (1990). *Physical violence in American families.* New Brunswick, NJ: Transaction.

Straus, M. A., Gelles, R. J., & Steinmetz, S. (1980). *Behind closed doors: Violence in the American family.* Garden City, NJ: Anchor.

Straus, M. A., Hamby, S. L., Boney-McCoy, S., & Sugarman, D. (1995). *The Revised Conflict Tactics Scales (CTS2).* Durham, NH: Family Research Laboratory.

Suitor, J. J., Pillemer, K., & Straus, M. A. (1990). Marital violence in a life course perspective. In M. A. Straus & R. J. Gelles (Eds.), *Physical violence in American families* (pp. 302-320). New Brunswick, NJ: Transaction.

Tershak, C. A. (1982). *The influence of domestic violence, psychological problems, and maternal parenting style upon interpersonal problem-solving ability in early childhood.* Unpublished doctoral dissertation, Oklahoma State University.

Tolman, R. (1989). The development of a measure of the psychological maltreatment of women by their male partners. *Violence and Victims, 4,* 159-177.

Utah Criminal Code § 76-5-109.1. (1997). Commission of domestic violence in the presence of a child.

Wagar, J. M., & Rodway, M. R. (1995). An evaluation of a group treatment approach for children who have witnessed wife abuse. *Journal of Family Violence, 10,* 295-306.

Walker, L. (1984). *The battered woman syndrome.* New York: Springer.

Wauchope, B. A., & Straus, M. A. (1990). Physical punishment and physical abuse of American children: Incidence rates by age, gender, and occupational class. In M. A. Straus & R. J. Gelles (Eds.), *Physical violence in American families: Risk factors and adaptations to violence in 8,145 families* (pp. 113-148). New Brunswick, NJ: Transaction.

Williams, O., Bogess, J., & Carter, J. (2001). Fatherhood and adult domestic violence: Exploring the role of men who batter in the lives of their children. In S. A. Graham-Bermann & J. L. Edleson (Eds.), *Domestic violence in the lives of children: The future of research, intervention, and social policy* (pp. 157-188). Washington, DC: American Psychological Association.

Wilson, S., Cameron, S., Jaffe, P., & Wolfe, D. (1989). Children exposed to wife abuse: An intervention model. *Social Casework, 70,* 180-192.

Wolak, J., & Finkelhor, D. (1996). Children exposed to partner violence. In J. L. Jasinski & L. M. Williams (Eds.), *Partner violence: A comprehensive review of 20 years of research* (pp. 73-112). Thousand Oaks, CA: Sage.

7

Munchausen by Proxy Syndrome

TERESA F. PARNELL

Sir Roy Meadow coined the term Munchausen Syndrome by Proxy in 1977 (Meadow, 1977). Meadow's original article described two cases. One case involved simulation of bloody urine in a 6-year-old. The other involved administration of sodium, causing vomiting and drowsiness with a high sodium level in a toddler. Both cases involved falsification of illness by the mother. Since Meadow's classic 1977 report, more than 700 cases of the syndrome have appeared in the literature (see Adshead & Brooke, 2001; Hall, Eubanks, Meyyazhagan, Kenney, & Johnson, 2000; Parnell & Day, 1998; Rosenberg, 1987, 2001; Sheridan, in press; Siegel & Fischer, 2001).

Munchausen by proxy syndrome[1] (MPS) is an uncommon form of child abuse in which a caretaker, usually the mother, fabricates, simulates, or induces symptoms of physical illness in a child. The perpetrator then presents the child for medical attention, all the while denying knowledge of the cause of the symptoms. The perpetrator is often quite ingenious in the methods used to deceive, and, as a result, the child may experience numerous unnecessary medical procedures. Perpetrators of MPS usually present in a very positive manner to medical professionals, exhibiting behavior that is viewed as attentive, caring, and nurturing. As a result, accusing a parent of this bizarre form of abuse is often met with resistance and disbelief by other professionals and by the perpetrator's family. Indeed, these accusations are sometimes turned against the professional, with an assertion that the professional is seeking to cover up medical mistakes or attempting to avoid acknowledging uncertainty regarding the child's condition. Even in the face of incontrovertible evidence, the perpetrator may deny responsibility and bolster her credibility with support from family, friends, attorneys, mental health professionals, and others.

The reasons for this deceptive form of abuse are diverse. In many cases, the adult uses the child as proxy to maintain the adult's relationship with the medical community to meet the adult's needs. Although the incidence of MPS appears to be relatively low, the short- and long-term implications for the child are serious, warranting immediate attention. Victims of MPS are usually infants and toddlers, although older children are occasionally victimized (McClure, Davis, Meadow, & Sibert, 1996; Rosenberg, 1987; Sheridan, in press). Cases exist in which older victims participate in the deception, are coached (Sanders, 1995), or falsify illness themselves (Libow, 2000).

Munchausen by proxy syndrome (MPS) is an uncommon form of child abuse in which a caretaker, usually the mother, fabricates, simulates, or induces symptoms of physical illness in a child.

When the perpetrator is the mother, male and female children are abused in relatively equal numbers. When the father is responsible, boys are more often victimized (Sheridan, in press). More than one child in a family may be abused (Alexander, Smith, & Stevenson, 1990; Sheridan, in press). Bools, Neale, and Meadow (1992) described a sample of 56 victims of MPS. In their sample, 11 siblings died of "unknown" causes. Perpetrators falsified illness in 39% of siblings. Seventeen percent of siblings suffered failure to thrive, nonaccidental injury, inappropriate medication, or neglect.

Victimization is often lengthy. Rosenberg (1987) reported a mean of 14.9 months from onset of symptoms to diagnosis. Sheridan (in press) reported an average of 21.7 months.

The impact of MPS on the victim is not fully understood. Clearly, the child may suffer unnecessary pain, either from the parent's actions or from medical procedures. The child may experience reduced social, educational, and emotional opportunities. Some children suffer long-term physical or developmental damage. Sadly, MPS is lethal for some children (Rosenberg, 1987; Sheridan, in press). Several articles describe the adverse consequences suffered by individual children (Boros & Brubaker, 1992; Byrk & Siegel, 1997; McGuire & Feldman, 1989; Parnell & Day, 1998; Porter, Heitsch, & Miller, 1994; Woollcott, Aceto, Rutt, Bloom, & Glick, 1982).

Bools, Neale, and Meadow (1993) reported on 54 victims of MPS. Data were obtained from 1 to 14 years after falsification of illness. At follow-up, 30 of the children were living with the offending parent. Twenty-four children were in out-of-home placements. Children who suffered more substantial abuse were more likely to be placed away from the parent. A range of problems, including significant conduct and emotional disorders and problems related to school, was reported for 13 of the children residing with the offending parent and for 14 of the children not residing with the parent. Fabrication of illness continued for 10 children placed with parents. Two of the children residing with abusive parents had questionable disabilities that restricted their lifestyles. One was confined to a wheelchair due to a supposed mobility problem. The other was restricted due to exaggeration of a genuine but mild congenital heart disease. There were a variety of concerns for an additional 8 children returned to their parent, including seeking opinions from specialists about symptoms for which no cause could be found, lying and fraud, problems with basic care of the child, overdependence on a social worker, and grossly overinvolved parenting. Bools et al. stated that 20 children (49%) of the sample had "unacceptable" outcomes. There were no child deaths during the follow-up period.

Libow (1995) completed an interesting study of the psychological outcome for 10 adults who identified themselves as victims of MPS during childhood. The adults reported significant emotional and physical problems during childhood, problems that continued in the form of posttraumatic symptoms, feelings of inadequacy, poor self-esteem, and relationship problems. For most of the subjects, the abuse continued a long time, sometimes until they left home. In several cases, the abuse continued with younger siblings. The subjects remembered being afraid to disclose their abuse and experiencing disbelief by others when they did tell.

Davis and colleagues (1998) reported on the outcome for 119 victims of MPS, nonaccidental poisoning, and nonaccidental suffocation in a 2-year period in the British Isles. Four children died from suffocation, and 5 died from nonaccidental poisoning. Forty-six children were allowed home without supervision. Children who suffered direct harm from induction of symptoms and those younger than age 5 were less likely to be returned home, although 11 children who suffered poisoning or suffocation were living at home without significant supervision. Twenty-four percent of the children who survived their abuse had resultant sequelae. Twelve percent of the children were disabled.

Continuing Definitional Uncertainty

Much discussion has occurred regarding Munchausen by proxy syndrome, including definition, parameters of behavior included within the syndrome, and proper nomenclature (Ayoub, Deutsch, & Kinscherff, 2000a; Ayoub & Alexander, 1998; Eminson & Postlethwaite, 2000; Jones, 1996; Kelly & Loader, 1997; Libow & Schreier, 1986; Masterson, Dunworth, & Williams, 1988; Meadow, 1982, 1993; Rand, 1993; Roth, 1990). At one level, there is disagreement about what we are labeling. Is it the perpetrator's mental illness? The child's experience? The adult's abusive behavior? The dynamics of the adult's relationship with the child and the medical community?

There is debate regarding whether this syndrome is best described and managed as a form of child abuse or as a psychiatric disorder. Many of the perpetrators manifest no psychiatric illness other than MPS, although some level of emotional disturbance is required to engage in such behavior (Bools, Neale, & Meadow, 1994; Sheridan, in press). Simply treating this as a psychiatric illness will not protect the victim. Attachment issues in these cases are complex. The extreme nature of the calculated deception must be considered. These perpetrators do more than lie. They impersonate a nurturing and attentive parent while secretly and intentionally harming their children.

There is a continuum of parent behavior regarding a child's physical condition. Arrayed along this continuum are different perceptions of the child's condition, differing levels of understanding of the need for health care, and various responses to a physician's actions. Where on this continuum does parental behavior cross the line into child abuse? Where do we assign the term *MPS*? If a parent is caught lying dramatically about the child's condition, or there is proof that the parent has induced illness, the diagnosis is relatively easy. More difficult is the case in which a parent mildly exaggerates symptoms, pays excessive attention to the child's physical condition, is overzealous in seeking specialist opinions for a child who is truly ill, or repeatedly misunderstands physician instructions. Perpetrator motivations, such as relieving parental anxiety, seeking help with parenting, and desiring to keep the child at home, may lead to further uncertainty regarding MPS. Most cases of MPS involve a mixture of exaggeration, false reporting, and symptom induction. It is clear that cases occur in which seemingly low-level exaggeration and excessive seeking of health care alone have adverse consequences (Parnell & Day, 1998). Rosenberg (1994) reminds us that "for those cases that seem to fall at the edges of MSBP, it is worth remembering that the name applied to the child's circumstances is not as material as a careful assessment of the threatened harm to the child" (p. 267).

The term *MPS* has been expanded beyond the realm of medicine to include false allegations of abuse and fabrication of psychological symptoms. This expands the perpetrator's audience to other professionals occupying positions of power in society, such as police investigators, child protection workers, lawyers, mental health professionals, and school personnel. The falsified problems include sexual and physical abuse, psychiatric symptoms, behavior difficulties, developmental delays, and learning disabilities (Meadow, 1993; Rand, 1993; Schreier, 1996, 1997; Schreier & Keller, 1996). The perpetrator engages in a pattern of deception similar to medical MPS, using fabrication, simulation, or induction. Once again, the child is used as an object to build a highly manipulative relationship in which the adult plays out psychological issues. Some cases involve medical as well as psychological illness or abuse falsification. Definitional expansion has gone even further to include one person using deception about another (child, adult, or even an animal) to bring him or her into a relationship with an authority figure (Levin & Sheridan, 1995; Sigal, Altmark, & Carmel, 1986; Sigal, Altmark, & Gelkopf, 1991; Smith & Arden, 1989). Obviously, there comes a time when expansion of the definition threatens to rob the syndrome of utility as a diagnostic concept.

Diagnostic Process

A major impediment to the diagnosis of MPS is failure to consider the possibility. When the issue is raised, it is usually met with skepticism. In many cases, no report is made, and no follow-up occurs. Many medical professionals are uncomfortable with the diagnosis. The thought that a parent could do something so awful is hard to fathom. For the professional who has been manipulated and duped into providing unnecessary medical care, it is difficult to accept the possibility of an elaborate deception (Blix & Brack, 1988; Sheridan, 1994).

Suspicion about the possibility of MPS is generally raised well before a firm diagnosis can be made. Diagnostic clarity may be obtained by review of present and past medical records, directed monitoring (with or without video surveillance), separation of the child from the suspected parent, and various testing procedures (Parnell & Day, 1998). Hospitalization may be necessary to protect the child and confirm the diagnosis (Rosenberg, 1987). Diagnostic guidelines for MPS typically identify victim features, perpetrator features, and family features.

Many medical professionals are uncomfortable with the diagnosis. The thought that a parent could do something so awful is hard to fathom.

Although the psychological aspects of MPS are important, diagnostic criteria lie primarily within the medical realm (Alexander, 2000). It can be misleading to place too much emphasis on the suspected parent's personality and interaction style (Rand & Feldman, 1999).

Once suspicion is aroused, it is advisable to proceed with a multidisciplinary team (Parnell & Day, 1998; Rosenberg, 1987). These cases are complex, and considerable information must be gathered. A thorough review of *all* medical records is essential. In addition, there are legal, mental health, and family systems issues to be pursued and coordinated. The multidisciplinary team should include a child protective services worker, law enforcement officer, psychologist or psychiatrist, prosecutor, hospital social worker, nurse, pediatrician, and other members of the child's medical team. It is good to include a physician with specialized knowledge of MPS. The team should be convened quickly. Immediately available medical information is reviewed. An action plan is developed, and investigatory responsibilities are delegated. The team determines what immediate steps are needed to ensure the child's safety, such as court involvement to remove the child from the parent's custody.

It is important to verify the history provided by the suspected parent by contacting prior health care providers. Person-to-person communication may be necessary because earlier medical records may simply repeat information provided by the suspected parent. Information regarding the parent's interaction with the child and others may be discovered in entries by nurses and social workers. Medical records may establish the temporal relationship between the child's symptoms and the parent's presence.

In some cases, thorough review of past and present medical records is sufficient to confirm or rule out MPS. There are times, however, when more information is needed. Directed monitoring of the child's environment may be necessary. Directed monitoring, generally possible only in the hospital, means controlling aspects of the child's environment, not simply watching what happens. The child can be closely monitored, with special focus on documenting times when any visitors, including the suspected parent, are present. At such times, a professional is in the room. No food or drink is allowed, except that provided by hospital staff. The suspected parent is not permitted to participate in the child's medical care. In some cases, it is necessary to partially or completely restrict the parent's access to the child. Restricting access generally requires a court order. If the child remains in the parent's custody, access to medical care must be controlled, perhaps through an aggressive primary care gatekeeper. Monitoring and controlling health care utilization are essential.

For some children, the best approach is covert video surveillance in the hospital. Covert video surveillance is controversial, requiring thorough assessment of ethical and legal issues (Epstein, Markowitz, Gallo, Holmes, & Gryboski, 1987; Foreman & Farsides, 1993; Hall et al., 2000; Kinscherff & Ayoub, 2000; Morrison, 1999; Southall, Plunkett, Banks, Falkov, & Samuels, 1997). Legal and ethical issues aside, however, there is no doubt that video surveillance is a powerful and effective tool in some cases.

If MPS abuse is confirmed, court involvement is usually needed to ensure the child's safety. Placement with extended family members is recommended only if the family will protect the child from the abusive parent. Case management issues are explored in Eminson and Postlethwaite (2000), Parnell and Day (1998), and Rosenberg (1994).

Psychological evaluation is used to gather information about the suspected parent and the parent's relationship with the child. Evaluation may provide insight into the parent's intent or motivation. The evaluator gathers pertinent psychosocial information. Family members are interviewed. The evaluator explores factors that lead to suspicion of MPS. The psychological evaluation helps elucidate issues that need to be addressed in the parent-child relationship. If MPS is ruled out, there may nevertheless be psychological issues that lead to the suspicion of the syndrome that must be pursued. The professional develops a prognosis and, where appropriate, a treatment plan. The professional may address placement of the child and the potential for reunification.

Psychotherapeutic Intervention

Psychotherapy with perpetrators of MPS is not yet well understood, although useful information is emerging (see Ayoub, Deutsch, & Kinscherff, 2000b); Berg & Jones, 1999; Chan, Salcedo, Atkins, & Ruley, 1986; Flynn, 1998; Leeder, 1994, 1990; Nicol & Eccles, 1985; Parnell & Day,

1998; Robins & Sessan, 1991; Sanders, 1996; Schreier & Libow, 1993; Waller, 1983). Successful treatment, including reunification, appears most likely with perpetrators who admit the abuse, willingly participate in treatment, and lack evidence of major psychopathology. Some therapists find success with intensive individual therapy (Parnell & Day, 1998). Other therapists prefer a family systems approach (Sanders, 1996).

Berg and Jones (1999) described an intensive inpatient therapeutic process. The authors reported on 17 children from 16 families selected for admission to the family unit of a psychiatric hospital in England. The biological mother was identified as the abuser, and the cases involved rather serious MPS. Four families were admitted for assessment and 13 for treatment to decide whether family reunification was feasible. Selection for admission was based on some degree of parental acknowledgment of the abuse and the likelihood for positive response to psychological intervention. There was variability in length of stay (3 days to 4 months; average $7\frac{1}{2}$ weeks). Treatments varied. One constant, however, was multidisciplinary team assessment and treatment based on attachment theory. Predictors of successful treatment included perpetrator acknowledgment of the abusive behavior; perpetrator insight into the personal context in which the abuse occurred; changes in the family system, including increased communication and openness about the abuse; increased parental sensitivity and responsiveness to the child's needs; and a plan to prevent relapse.

Berg and Jones (1999) obtained outcome data at a mean of 27 months following care. Of 13 cases, 10 children were reunited with parents. Only 1 child experienced further induced illness. In general, the children were developing and growing in a satisfactory manner. The authors concluded that psychiatric treatment had the desired effect.

Conclusion

Munchausen syndrome by proxy has both short- and long-term physical and psychological consequences for victims. Professionals continue to grapple with the proper definition for this phenomenon. Moreover, much remains to be learned about efficacious treatment. Despite the fact that much remains to be done, lack of definitive knowledge cannot deter us from protecting the victims of this bizarre and dangerous form of maltreatment.

Note

1. This form of child abuse has had many names, including Munchausen syndrome by proxy, Munchausen by proxy syndrome, Munchausen by proxy, Polle's syndrome, factitious illness by proxy, and factitious disorder by proxy. *Factitious disorder by proxy* is the term used by the *DSM-IV* (American Psychiatric Association, 1994). Other labels for particular types of presentation include doctor shopping, help seeking, extreme illness exaggeration, enforced invalidism, doctor addict, and other labels. In an attempt to clarify the constellation of behaviors and conditions currently described in the literature, the American Professional Society on the Abuse of Children Task Force on MPS developed a new definition—pediatric condition falsification. The task force identified a number of conditions that are abuse by pediatric condition falsification but are not considered to be factitious disorder by proxy (see Ayoub & Alexander, 1998).

References

Adshead, G., & Brooke, D. (Eds.). (2001). *Munchausen's syndrome by proxy: Current issues in assessment, treatmenth, and research.* London: Imperial College Press.

Alexander, R., Smith, W., & Stevenson, R. (1990). Serial Munchausen syndrome by proxy. *Pediatrics, 86*(4), 581-585.

Alexander, R. C. (2000). Medical treatment of Munchausen syndrome by proxy. In R. M. Reece (Ed.), *Treatment of child abuse* (pp. 236-241). Baltimore: Johns Hopkins University Press.

American Psychiatric Association. (1994). *Diagnostic and statistical manual of mental disorders* (4th ed.). Washington, DC: Author.

Ayoub, C. C., & Alexander, R. (1998). Definitional issues in Munchausen by proxy. *APSAC Advisor, 11*(1), 7-10.

Ayoub, C. C., Deutsch, R. M., & Kinscherff, R. (2000a). Munchausen by proxy: Definitions, identification, and evaluation. In R. M. Reece (Ed.), *Treatment of child abuse* (pp. 213-225). Baltimore: Johns Hopkins University Press.

Ayoub, C. C., Deutsch, R. M., & Kinscherff, R. (2000b). Psychosocial management issues in Munchausen by proxy. In R. M. Reece (Ed.), *Treatment of child abuse* (pp. 226-235). Baltimore: Johns Hopkins University Press.

Berg, B., & Jones, D. P. (1999). Outcome of psychiatric intervention in factitious illness by proxy (Munchausen's syndrome by proxy). *Archives of Disease in Childhood, 81*(6), 465-472.

Blix, S., & Brack, G. (1988). The effects of a suspected case of Munchausen's syndrome by proxy on a pediatric nursing staff. *General Hospital Psychiatry, 10*(6), 402-409.

Bools, C. N., Neale, B. A., & Meadow, S. R. (1992). Co-morbidity associated with fabricated illness (Munchausen syndrome by proxy). *Archives of Disease in Childhood, 67*(1), 77-79.

Bools, C. N., Neale, B. A., & Meadow, S. R. (1993). Follow up of victims of fabricated illness (Munchausen syndrome by proxy). *Archives of Disease in Childhood, 69*, 625-630.

Bools, C. N., Neale, B. A., & Meadow, S. R. (1994). Munchausen syndrome by proxy: A study of psychopathology. *Child Abuse & Neglect, 18*(9), 773-788.

Boros, S. J., & Brubaker, L. C. (1992). Munchausen syndrome by proxy case accounts. *FBI Law Enforcement Bulletin, 61*(6), 16-20.

Byrk, M., & Siegel, P. T. (1997). My mother caused my illness: The story of a survivor of Munchausan by proxy syndrome. *Pediatrics, 100*, 1-7.

Chan, D. A., Salcedo, J. R., Atkins, D. M., & Ruley, E. J. (1986). Munchausen syndrome by proxy: A review and case study. *Journal of Pediatric Psychology, 11*(1), 71-80.

Davis, P., McClure, R. J., Rolfe, K., Chessman, N., Pearson, S., Sibert, J. R., & Meadow, R. (1998). Procedures, placement, and risks of further abuse after Munchausen syndrome by proxy, non-accidental poisoning, and non-accidental suffocation. *Archives of Disease in Childhood, 78*(3), 217-221.

Eminson, M., & Postlethwaite, R. J. (2000). *Munchausen syndrome by proxy abuse: A practical approach.* Boston: Butterworth-Heinemann.

Epstein, M. A., Markowitz, R. L., Gallo, D. M., Holmes, J. W., & Gryboski, J. D. (1987). Munchausen syndrome by proxy: Considerations in diagnosis and confirmation by video surveillance. *Pediatrics, 80,* 220-224.

Flynn, D. (1998). Psychoanalytic aspects of inpatient treatment. *Journal of Child Psychotherapy, 24*(2), 283-306.

Foreman, D. M., & Farsides, C. (1993). Ethical use of covert videoing techniques in detecting Munchausen syndrome by proxy. *British Medical Journal, 307,* 611-613.

Hall, D. E., Eubanks, L., Meyyazhagan, S., Kenney, R. D., & Johnson, S. (2000). Evaluation of covert video surveillance in the diagnosis of Munchausen syndrome by proxy: Lessons from 41 cases. *Pediatrics, 105*(6), 1305-1312.

Jones, D. P. H. (1996). Commentary: Munchausen syndrome by proxy—Is expansion justified? *Child Abuse & Neglect, 20*(10), 983-984.

Kelly, C., & Loader, P. (1997). Factitious disorder by proxy: The role of child mental health professionals. *Child Psychology & Psychiatry Review, 2*(3), 116-124.

Kinscherff, R., & Ayoub, C. C. (2000). Legal aspects of Munchausen by proxy. In R. M. Reece (Ed.), *Treatment of child abuse* (pp. 242-267). Baltimore: Johns Hopkins University Press.

Leeder, E. (1990). Supermom or child abuser? Treatment of the Munchausen mother. *Women and Therapy, 9*(4), 69-88.

Leeder, E. (1994). *Treating abuse in families: A feminist and community approach.* New York: Springer.

Levin, A. V., & Sheridan, M. S. (1995). *Munchausen by proxy syndrome.* New York: Lexington.

Libow, J. A. (1995). Munchausen by proxy victims in adulthood: A first look. *Child Abuse & Neglect, 19,* 1131-1142.

Libow, J. A. (2000). Child and adolescent illness falsification. *Pediatrics, 105*(2), 336-342.

Libow, J. A., & Schreier, H. A. (1986). Three forms of factitious illness in children: When is it Munchausen syndrome by proxy? *American Journal of Orthopsychiatry, 56*(4), 602-611.

Masterson, J., Dunworth, R., & Williams, N. (1988). Extreme illness exaggeration in pediatric patients: A variant of Munchausen's by proxy? *American Journal of Orthopsychiatry, 58*(2), 188-195.

McClure, R. J., Davis, P. M., Meadows, S. R., & Sibert, J. R. (1996). Epidemiology of Munchausen syndrome by proxy, non-accidental poisoning, and non-accidental suffocation. *Archives of Disease in Childhood, 75*(1), 57-61.

McGuire, T. L., & Feldman, K. W. (1989). Psychologic morbidity of children subjected to Munchausen syndrome by proxy. *Pediatrics, 83*(2), 289-292.

Meadow, R. (1977). Munchausen syndrome by proxy: The hinterland of child abuse. *Lancet, 2,* 343-345.

Meadow, R. (1982). Munchausen syndrome by proxy. *Archives of Disease in Childhood, 57*(2), 92-98.

Meadow, R. (1993). False allegations of abuse and Munchausen syndrome by proxy. *Archives of Disease in Childhood, 68*(4), 444-447.

Morrison, C. A. (1999). Cameras in hospital rooms: The Fourth Amendment to the Constitution and Munchausen syndrome by proxy. *Critical Care Nursing Quarterly, 22*(1), 65-68.

Nicol, A. R., & Eccles, M. (1985). Psychotherapy for Munchausen syndrome by proxy. *Archives of Disease in Childhood, 60*(4), 344-348.

Parnell, T. F., & Day, D. O. (1998). *Munchausen by proxy syndrome: Misunderstood child abuse.* Thousand Oaks, CA: Sage.

Porter, G. E., Heitsch, G. M., & Miller, M. M. (1994). Munchausen syndrome by proxy: Unusual manifestations and disturbing sequelae. *Child Abuse & Neglect, 18,* 789-794.

Rand, D. C. (1993). Munchausen syndrome by proxy: A complex type of emotional abuse responsible for some false allegations of child abuse. In H. Wakefield & R. Underwager (Eds.), *Solomon's dilemma: False allegations in divorce and custody.* Springfield, IL: Charles C Thomas.

Rand, D. C., & Feldman, M. D. (1999). Misdiagnosis of Munchausen syndrome by proxy: A literature review and four new cases. *Harvard Review of Psychiatry, 7*(2), 94-101.

Robins, P. M., & Sessan, R. (1991). Munchausen syndrome by proxy: Another women's disorder? *Professional Psychology: Research & Practice, 22*(4), 285-290.

Rosenberg, D. (1987). Web of deceit: A literature review of Munchausen syndrome by proxy. *Child Abuse & Neglect, 11*(4), 547-563.

Rosenberg, D. A. (2001). Munchausen syndrome by proxy. In R. M. Reece & S. Ludwig (Eds.), *Child abuse: Medical diagnosis and management, 2nd ed.* (pp. 363-383). Philadelphia: Lippincott, Williams, & Wilkins.

Rosenberg, D. (1994). Munchausen syndrome by proxy. In R. M. Reece (Ed.), *Child abuse: Medical diagnosis and management* (pp. 266-278). Philadelphia: Lea & Febiger.

Roth, D. (1990). How "mild" is mild Munchausen syndrome by proxy? *Israel Journal of Psychiatry & Related Sciences, 27*(3), 160-167.

Sanders, M. J. (1995). Symptom coaching: Factitious disorder by proxy with older children. *Clinical Psychology Review, 15*(5), 423-442.

Sanders, M. J. (1996). Narrative family treatment of Munchausen by proxy: A successful case. *Families, Systems & Health, 14*(13), 315-329.

Schreier, H. A. (1996). Repeated false allegations of sexual abuse presenting to sheriffs: When is it Munchausen by proxy? *Child Abuse & Neglect, 20*(10), 985-991.

Schreier, H. A. (1997). Factitious presentation of psychiatric disorder: When is it Munchausen by proxy? *Child Psychology & Psychiatric Review, 2*(3), 1-8.

Schreier, H. A., & Keller, C. (1996). *Munchausen by proxy in special education.* Unpublished manuscript, Children's Hospital, Department of Psychiatry, Oakland, CA.

Schreier, H. A., & Libow, J. A. (1993). *Hurting for love: Munchausen by proxy syndrome.* New York: Guilford.

Sheridan, M. S. (1994). Parents' reporting of symptoms in their children: Physicians' perceptions. *Hawaii Medical Journal, 53,* 216-217, 221-222.

Sheridan, M. S. (in press). The deceit continues: An updated literature review of Munchausen by proxy syndrome. *Child Abuse & Neglect.*

Siegel, P. T., & Fischer H. (2001). Munchausen by proxy syndrome: Barriers to detection, confirmation, and intervention. *Children's Services: Social Policy, Research and Practice, 4,* 31-50.

Sigal, M. D., Altmark, D., & Carmel, I. (1986). Munchuasen syndrome by adult proxy: A perpetrator abusing two adults. *Journal of Nervous and Mental Disease, 174,* 696-698.

Sigal, M. D., Altmark, D., & Gelkopf, M. (1991). Munchausen syndrome by proxy revisited. *Israel Journal of Psychiatry and Related Services, 28*(1), 33-36.

Smith, N. J., & Arden, M. H. (1989). More in sickness than in health: A case study of Munchausen syndrome by proxy in the elderly. *Journal of Family Therapy, 11,* 321-324.

Southall, D. P., Plunkett, M. C. B., Banks, M. W., Falkov, A. F., & Samuels, M. P. (1997). Covert video recordings of life-threatening child abuse: Lessons for child protection. *Pediatrics, 100*(5), 735-760.

Waller, D. A. (1983). Obstacles to treatment of Munchausen by proxy syndrome. *Journal of the American Academy of Child Psychiatry, 22,* 80-85.

Woollcott, P., Aceto, T., Rutt, C., Bloom, M., & Glick, R. (1982). Doctor shopping with the child as proxy patient: A variant of child abuse. *Journal of Pediatrics, 101,* 297-391.

PART TWO

Psychosocial Treatment

William Friedrich's chapter on psychotherapy appeared in the first edition of the *APSAC Handbook* in 1996. In Chapter 8, Dr. Friedrich updates and expands his discussion of this vital subject. He notes that much has been learned since 1996, a truth that is evidenced by the fact that nearly half the references in Chapter 8 did not exist when Friedrich wrote the earlier version of his chapter. Dr. Friedrich describes an integrated, contextual model for psychotherapy with victims of child abuse, with particular emphasis on attachment theory, dysregulation theory, and self-perception theory.

Chapter 9 is an exciting examination of treatment for sexually abused adolescents. Debra Hecht, Mark Chaffin, Barbara Bonner, Karen Boyd Worley, and Louanne Lawson offer a wealth of information in this update from the first edition of the *Handbook*. The chapter provides a useful overview of adolescent development, followed by analysis of the prevalence and effects of sexual abuse of adolescents. With this background in place, the authors thoroughly discuss assessment and treatment issues.

John Briere contributes two ways to the second edition. First, Dr. Briere is one of the editors. Second, he has rewritten his chapter on treating adult survivors of severe child abuse. Chapter 10 is a stimulating, creative, theoretically sophisticated, enormously valuable contribution to the treatment literature.

Chapter 11 is new to the second edition. Mark Chaffin, Elizabeth Letourneau, and Jane Silovsky have produced an excellent analysis of adults, adolescents, and children who sexually abuse children. The authors bring a developmental perspective to their analysis of perpetration. They begin with a review of the literature on children with sexual behavior problems. From there, the authors move to discussion of adolescent sex offenders. Finally, they discuss adult offenders. Within each age group, the authors discuss characteristics of offenders, assessment, and treatment issues.

J.E.B.M.

8

An Integrated Model of Psychotherapy for Abused Children

WILLIAM N. FRIEDRICH

Special Issues in Psychotherapy With Children

It is heartening to revise this chapter and have many new findings to report. Shirk (1988) wrote that an average of only one child therapy outcome study has been published annually for the past 30 years, an enormous contrast with the burgeoning adult treatment literature. However, since the publication of the first edition of this book in 1996, the child maltreatment field alone has been responsible for an average of twice that number per year. Several outcome studies of sexually abused children have now been published (Berliner & Saunders, 1996; Cohen & Mannarino, 1997, 1998; Deblinger, Lippmann, & Steer, 1996),

and David Kolko's (1996) outcome study with physically abusive parents and their children is a welcome addition to a treatment literature that has long been dormant. In addition, the National Center on Child Abuse and Neglect (NCCAN) has funded two studies, now complete, on the treatment of sexually aggressive children (Bonner, Walker, & Berliner, 2000; Pithers, Gray, Busconi, & Houchens, 1998). Consequently, not only do we know considerably more about this subset of often maltreated children (sexual and/or physical abuse or neglect), but we also know that therapy can be helpful, at least in the short term. Pride in the work of our colleagues is clearly justified. The treatment research has been grounded in theory and has followed such research basics as the presence of a comparison group, a modicum of follow-up, random assignment to treatment modalities, and the assurance of the integrity of different treatment modalities. Consequently, I can now speak to the topic of psychotherapy for abused children with far more authority.

The most appropriate theoretical framework to guide the assessment and treatment of maltreated children is that provided by developmental psychopathology. A central feature of developmental psychopathology is the perspective that development proceeds in a relational context and is ongoing, not fixated at the point of the traumatic events (Rutter & Sroufe, 2000). Another key feature is its concern with the continuity and discontinuity between normalcy and pathology. Given that upwards of 40% of sexually abused children are not clinically symptomatic on initial assessment (Kendall-Tackett, Williams, & Finkelhor, 1993), theory that can illuminate why competence is demonstrated in the face of adversity is needed. Who are these asymptomatic children? Will they need therapy later? If we were better able to understand what features of the child, the maltreatment, and the child's ecosystem combine to create competence, then valid treatment guidelines could be developed for many children and their families.

Other central features of developmental psychopathology include the concept of causal processes and the concept of development. By the former, I mean an understanding of how risk and protective factors operate over time. For example, why is the onset of adolescent or adult sexuality a stumbling block for some sexual abuse victims? Why do some physically abused adults resort to physically abusive parenting strategies, but others do not?

The latter concept (i.e., of development) is central to any understanding of childhood problems yet is often ignored in treatment. For example, although insight is not useful to young children (Harter, 1999), the goal of much therapy with children and teens of all ages is the promotion of self-knowledge, something that is often called insight. Development implies change, but change that involves some degree of continuity with the past as well as the establishment of an increasingly integrated and coherent individual. Consequently, when we understand the causal processes inherent in the production of pathology in maltreated children, it will be critical to understand the key elements that help to bring about change. Some ex-

amples of key elements include a biological process, modification of affect regulation, and some change in cognitive set or processing (Rutter & Sroufe, 2000).

When we understand the causal processes inherent in the production of pathology in maltreated children, it will be critical to understand the key elements that help to bring about change.

An advantage of the developmental psychopathology framework is that the developing organism is viewed as a social creature. In fact, attachment research has a natural affinity to developmental psychopathology and is the theory that appreciates both *individual impact* and *family context* (Cassidy & Shaver, 1999). The salience of attachment to child maltreatment and its treatment is evidenced in the publication of Howe, Brandon, Hinings, and Schofield's (1999) excellent book, *Attachment Theory, Child Maltreatment, and Social Support.*

In addition, there have been advances in our understanding of how traumatic events can overwhelm normal cognitive processing of events, leading to disruptions in explicit memory (Siegel, 1999). An understanding of how this occurs points clearly to the need for the therapy of trauma to do more than simply reduce symptoms but to enhance the consolidation of these explicit memories of traumatic events so that they can be processed and not left to get activated randomly at key junctures in the person's life cycle. This chapter outlines an integrated model for psychotherapy with abused children that is derived from the field of developmental psychopathology.

The Need for a Treatment Model

My clinical practice involves daily contact with maltreated children and their families. These families are complex, and flexibility and creativity are needed to successfully intervene. How does any model enhance or foster the type of treatments that are needed in this often-difficult work? Can it provide the type of rigor and flexibility that are needed, or is it simply an artificial creation with a primarily intellectual rationale? An equally valid approach with this chapter would be to discuss a variety of treatment techniques and ignore any overarching theme.

Currently, the techniques are the ones with the empirical validation. However, most of them emerge from cognitive-behavioral theory, which by its very nature is an individual model of therapy. The efforts of Esther Deblinger (Deblinger et al., 1996) and David Kolko (1996) to make their cognitive-behavioral interventions more systemic only validate the need to include the larger system in any treatment approach.

Currently, most abused children do not receive treatment. Those who do are often seen by therapists who (a) may not appreciate the unique and differential impacts of physical and sexual abuse, (b) have little broad-based clinical training and are not aware of a wide variety of empirically validated treatment techniques, (c) have little idea of how and what to treat, (d) follow approaches that are too brief (or even traumatogenic), and (e) often are not attentive to the system the child is living in.

A model illustrates not only the ideal but also the essential considerations that are needed in sensitive and, it is hoped, successful treatment. The particular model that is outlined below starts with child/teen victims and their families. In addition, central features of the victims and often their parents warrant consideration to prevent further abuse and interrupt a pathological trajectory. Any model that appreciates only the child/family context is not sufficient if individual features are not also considered.

In the case of a physically abused child currently in "extended family foster care," a model should inform the therapist of typical symptoms, treatment targets, and who should be involved in treatment, and it should also provide a developmental view of the child and the child's system into the future.

The abused child exists in a family context. Research increasingly points to family variables (e.g., maternal distress) as being associated with the effect of abuse (Cohen & Mannarino, 1996). This is also true for long-term consequences of physical abuse, in which moderator variables, including individual, family, and environmental factors, are important (Malinosky-Rummell & Hansen, 1993). Thus, individually based models, such as the traumatogenic factors model and the posttraumatic stress disorder (PTSD) model, are not sufficient either to understand the impact of child abuse or to guide the type of broad-based treatment that is needed.

These impressions suggest the need for treatment that is contextual and derived from theoretical formulations that are more unifying and empirically validated than either of the two models mentioned earlier. Needed theoretical formulations should include specific and effective treatment techniques—both those unique to sexual and physical abuse and those that are widely applicable. Although many of the examples used in this chapter are particularly germane to sexual abuse, I believe that much of the theory and techniques discussed in this chapter is applicable to physical abuse as well. Sexually abusive and physically abusive families share some of the same features of inattention to children's needs and a multigenerational history of poor parenting. As a result, the treatment challenges can be significant, and a planful, sensitive approach clearly is needed.

An Integrated, Contextual Model

The integrated model outlined in the rest of this chapter borrows from attachment theory (Cassidy & Shaver, 1999), behavior/emotion regulation (Shipman, Zeman, Penza, & Champion, 2000), and self-perception/concept (Harter, 1999). The effects of abuse are reflected in each of these three broad domains. Treatment approaches specific to individual, group, and family treatment can be derived from this model.

The remainder of this chapter will outline the relevance of the three elements of this integrated model (attachment, dysregulation, and self-perception), identify specific treatment approaches that follow from each of these elements, and apply each approach to individual, group, and family therapy.

Attachment

The concept of attachment is a central element in almost all contemporary theories of child psychopathology and child treatment (Cassidy & Shaver, 1999). For example, children's prosocial inclinations are governed primarily by the quality of their relationships with their parents. This has implications for the emergence of peer relationships, aggression, and social skills.

Attachment is viewed as a biologically based bond with a caregiver (Cassidy, 1999). Attachment behavior, which ensures the child proximity with the caregiver, is most apparent during periods of early childhood distress. However, it also relates to reciprocal and mutual relationships across the life span.

An important aspect of attachment theory is the concept of the internal working model, a mental construction that forms the basis of the personality (Bretherton & Munholland, 1999). Early experiences with the attachment figure allow children to develop expectations about their role in relationships (e.g., worthy vs. unworthy) and others' roles in relationships (e.g., caring vs. uncaring). Because the development of this internal working model is so tied to the relationship, the child learns caregiving while receiving care.

Applying attachment theory to the onset and outcome of abuse necessitates examining the interactions of the whole family, a natural and logical focus of any trauma. Developmental psychologists argue strongly for the need to view family relations as part of an interrelated system, with each member affecting the others (Greenberg, 1999).

Children's attachment behavior can be sorted into four categories. The first and healthiest category is *secure* attachment. In addition, there are three types of insecure attachment: *resistant, avoidant,* and *disorganized* (Alexander, 1992). Securely attached children have an internal working model of caregivers as consistent, supportive in times of stress, attuned to their needs, and reciprocal. Insecurely attached children operate from the assumption that different levels of unpredictability, the absence of reciprocity, and punitiveness characterize interpersonal relationships. For example, the avoidantly attached child eventually may adopt a self-protective stance and hold back from caregivers, including therapists. The child who exhibits a disorganized pattern of attachment is inconsistent in dealing with relationships (e.g., simultaneously approaching and avoiding others). Given the frequent history of abuse in parents of abused children and the degree to which that history af-

fects their personal and parenting functioning (Friedrich, 1991), parents of children who exhibit disorganized attachment are thought to be characterized themselves by unresolved trauma (Solomon & George, 1999).

Harsh and abusive treatment by caregivers can inhibit the development of prosocial responses in children. Main and George (1985) found that physically abused preschoolers did not show responses of concern, sadness, or empathy when a peer was distressed. Physically abused children were consistently more aggressive in their social interactions, although there was between-child variability (George & Main, 1979).

There is evidence that sexual abuse is experienced by the child victim as betrayal. This is true not only in the perpetrator-child relationship but is also reflective of a preexisting, impaired level of attachment with one or more caregivers.

In general, child abuse of all types occurs in the context of low income, a chaotic and frequently disrupted lifestyle, and emotional deprivation (Friedrich, 1995). Thus, it is essential for the therapist to respect the child's entire history of victimization, including neglect.

Alexander (1992) has identified three organizing themes, pertaining to attachment, that have been observed in abusive and neglectful families, including sexually abusive families. The first theme is *rejection,* which is most often associated with subsequent avoidant attachment in the child. Parents' earlier attachment affects their subsequent attachment to their own children. For example, male children in the sexually abusive family may be rejected because of their representation as potential abusers by the mother, and female children may be rejected because of the intimacy threat that they represent to the abusive father. Another critical consequence of rejection is that preoccupied or dismissive parents selectively attune to the child's positive and negative expressions. Children learn that those affective experiences (e.g., distress) "fall outside the realm of shareable experience and [as a result they] deny or disavow such feelings" (Alexander, 1992, p. 188).

A second organizing theme outlined by Alexander (1992) pertains to *parentification and role reversal,* a process that has been shown to be particularly true in those families in which the mother's current relationship is unsatisfactory (Alexander, Teti, & Anderson, 2000). Empirical support for this phenomenon comes from the observation of sexually abusive families (Burkett, 1991). Children who have been elevated into a parental position may be more vulnerable to abuse and less likely to receive the support they need, both before and after the trauma.

The final organizing theme pertains to the *multigenerational transmission* of fear and unresolved trauma evident in families with a history of abuse. Thus, insecure attachment in the parents, as a result of their own abuse experiences, will precede insecure attachment in the child. This is consistent with evidence on risk factors contributing to sexual abuse (Friedrich, 1995).

The above themes pertain to preexisting attachment. However, the very act of abuse and the response of significant others to the disclosure of abuse may result in a sudden change in attachment. This may be true of a child with a previous history of reasonably secure attachment.

Although there are no studies specifically on the attachment behavior of sexually abused children, a great deal of research demonstrates the high frequency of insecure attachment in physically abused or neglected children (Cicchetti & Toth, 1995). The attachment model helps the therapist to appreciate (a) the origin and diversity of relationships between children and their parents, (b) the influence the internal working model plays on the formation of the treatment relationship and all other social relationships, and (c) the need to improve attachment relationships if the therapist is to alter basic assumptions children have about themselves.

Symptoms Reflecting Impaired Attachment

One advantage of theory is the potential for specificity in treatment goals. Potential targets of treatment include boundary problems, poor social skills, the recapitulation of victim or victimizing behavior in relationships, distrust of others, and the sexualizing of relationships. In addition, the relationship of insecure attachment to future psychopathology emphasizes the need to repair attachment problems within the family.

In the next three sections, attachment-related treatment suggestions are made in the areas of individual, group, and family therapy (see the appendix for a brief, selective synopsis of techniques in these areas).

Individual Treatment Techniques Derived From Attachment Theory

Formation of a therapeutic alliance is the first application of attachment theory and is critical in all three modes of treatment—individual, group, and family. Literature on treatment effectiveness routinely finds the therapeutic relationship to be of critical importance (Santostefano, 1998). The quality of the therapist-patient relationship may be central and more important than specific therapeutic techniques or approaches. From the beginning, it is the therapist's duty to determine how best to maximize the quality of the therapist-patient attachment relationship.

Therapists must ask themselves, "How can I best use myself as a therapeutic instrument that maximizes the child's ability to develop a good attachment relationship, not only with me but also with his or her current parents and caregivers?"

The therapist has the greatest control over factors that facilitate an alliance with the child. Therapists must ask themselves, "How can I best use myself as a therapeutic instrument that maximizes the child's ability to develop a good attachment relationship, not only with me but also with his or her current parents and caregivers?" In a wonderfully rich book, Santostefano (1998) described this process as the integration of "two subjective cultures." Such factors as the sex of the therapist, the emotional and behavioral style of the therapist, the ethnic match between child and therapist, and the therapist's current level of internal emotional resources should be considered to remove any overt roadblocks to this integration.

The therapist must avoid practices that interfere with acceptance by the child. Sexualized, aggressive, and physically unattractive children can elicit rejection from the therapist. At times, therapists can feel they have "lost control" of the therapy process and are playing out a script from a prior relationship the child has had with a caregiver. This illustrates the power of the internal working model of the child and the need for the therapist to provide a corrective experience.

Children's attachment histories will dictate their interactions with the therapist. For example, boundaryless children (those with disorganized attachment) will need therapists who are clear in their own boundaries so that they can tolerate and gradually alter the child's dependency, physical proximity seeking, and variability. On the other hand, a resistant child with a physical abuse history may expect aggression and work to provoke it. This child presents a challenge to the therapist, who will need to work differently with either this or an avoidant child than with the boundaryless child. The avoidant child may be very slow in forming an alliance, always anticipating rejection, and hypersensitive to therapist unavailability.

The sooner both therapist and child have a sense of "we-ness," or a dyad, the better. Therapists can start by being "fully present" and emotionally available in the session. Consultations with school personnel and occasional phone calls to the child can be important, along with small gifts to the child. Pictures of the therapist and child create a visual symbol of connection and can be given to the child and brought into sessions. Therapeutic triangulation allows the therapist-child dyad to ally with one another and be against a third party (e.g., a nonfamilial perpetrator), thus pushing the treatment alliance along (Friedrich, 1995). Finally, a sense of connection may be facilitated by closer attention to ethnic and gender matching of child and therapist.

If a child continues to be victimized at home, he or she will not feel safe and cannot turn his or her emotional energies to the formation of a therapeutic relationship. It is important early on in the therapy process to help children feel they have a "secure base" in their home and that their parent supports the disclosure of abuse. Unsupervised visitation by an abusive parent, foster placement that is nonsupportive, and other factors or combinations of factors may contribute to the absence of safety. One technique useful in helping to create a sense of safety in the child is to include the nonoffending parent early on in the therapy process for the purpose of giving the child permission to talk about the victimization.

Group Treatment Techniques Derived From Attachment Theory

It is important that the child identify with the group and its members. Although disclosure creates a sense of universality (Deblinger & Heflin, 1996) and also can foster a sense of connection, children who have few social skills are likely to find the group experience a rejecting one. Screening is critical to ensure a good mix of children, particularly if the group process is expected to be important.

Results from the FAST Track project with children at risk for conduct disorder seem to demonstrate that skill-based group interventions result in more sociable children by the end of first grade (Conduct Problems Prevention Research Group, 1999). The high level of oppositionality and reduced social skills in these group members is difficult to counter in groups that are not skillfully led and structured.

The creation of a group identity develops a sense of group attachment. This can be facilitated in a number of ways (e.g., members may select a name for the group that implies a common bond). The use of cotherapists is also important so that the availability of potential attachments is higher.

We sometimes forget that victims have directly experienced unempathic behavior from the offender and consequently are more likely to behave in a nonreciprocal, unempathic manner themselves. Group treatment provides an excellent setting in which to begin to address this often-neglected treatment need of victims.

Family Treatment Techniques Derived From Attachment Theory

The parents of abused children are often psychologically unavailable (Alexander, 1992). This is another type of rejection of the child, although it may be more passive. It is characterized by the absence of a reciprocal child-parent relationship and parental ambivalence toward the child. Goals for intervention in these neglectful systems include helping the parent understand the child's behavior and become better perspective takers (Deblinger & Heflin, 1996). The parent can then respond more effectively to the child's signals. The format outlined by Debligner and Heflin (1996) provides peer support to parents, meets many of the parents' emotional needs, and assists parents to learn how parental needs influence their perceptions of the child. This approach goes beyond traditional psychological services and actively brings parents and children together in a manner similar to that outlined in the parent-child interaction therapy (PCIT) model (Hembree-Kigin & McNeil, 1995).

PCIT deserves an entire section in this chapter, as fits a new and promising intervention with solid validation and one that respects the parent-child relationship and the need for skill instruction with parents of maltreated and problematic children. Although originally designed for younger children, PCIT has been extended to the early teen years and is now being specifically studied in families that are physically abusive (M. Chaffin, personal communication, November 21, 2000). The first aspect of PCIT focuses on repair of the parent-child relationship through the use of child-directed activities. The mother is instructed in the session in the use of praise and positive support of her child. Only after that process is under way is there a focus on discipline, an issue that may emerge in the context of parent-directed activities. The appeal of this intervention is that it specifically pays attention to the relationship, not simply on outfitting the parent with new cognitions or skills.

The various suggestions outlined earlier fit directly with the "constructionistic" approach to family therapy, which focuses on constructing a new set of perceptions, a new reality, or a new set of stories regarding the child and family (White, 1989). Rather than allowing the family to persist in its view of the problem, or residing "inside" the child, White (1989) actively "externalizes" the problem. For example, the family of the encopretic child would look for those times the child is "successful" at preventing the encopresis from "sneaking up on her." In addition, the therapist should highlight positive aspects of the child's behavior (Friedrich, 1995). In my own practice, I sometimes have had the impression that the family therapist actively must "market" the child to the parent.

Involvement of offending parents in their own therapy at this critical time is also important and can result in these parents becoming less rejecting and having more attuned attachment "prospects" for the child. Parallel group treatment for nonoffending parents is also useful at this point (Mandell & Damon, 1989). Cicchetti and Toth (1995) reviewed research suggesting that insecurely attached infants move toward secure attachment when mothers make friends with other adults and feel supported.

Finally, attachment is in part a function of reciprocity and acceptance. For families who feel misunderstood and for whom sessions in the therapist's office are foreign, home visits not only can facilitate a more accurate therapist perception of the family but also may impart a sense of acceptance and validation to the family that adds to the developing therapy alliance.

Regulation and Dysregulation

Children must face the core tasks of modulating arousal, developing the ability to maintain a psychological homeostasis, and differentiating the expression of a broad range of positive and negative affect. Maltreatment of all types interferes with this developing capacity of self-regulation, not only of feelings but also of thoughts and behaviors (Cicchetti, Ganiban, & Barnett, 1991).

Maltreatment is dysregulating for several reasons. Not only are there traumatic features of the abuse, but the abusive family itself is characterized by numerous other potentially dysregulating stressors, including marital conflict, domestic violence, frequent moves and losses, and higher levels of unpredictability and chaos. This is true for physically abusive (Malinosky-Rummell & Hansen, 1993) as well as incestuous and nonincestuous maltreating families (Kendall-Tackett et al., 1993). Given the heterogeneity of maltreatment, for many children, the major contributors to dysregulation are not abuse specific.

Katz and Gottman (1991) operationalized emotion regulation

> as consisting of children's ability to (1) inhibit inappropriate behavior related to strong negative or positive affect, (2) self-soothe any physiological arousal the strong affect has induced, (3) focus attention, and (4) organize themselves for coordinated action in the service of an external goal. (p. 130)

The authors go on to talk about a child's ability to coordinate play and manage conflict as being directly related to the child's ability to make friends. This relates directly to the attachment discussed earlier and indicates the linkage between these theoretical constructs.

Cicchetti and his colleagues (1991) argued that the development of emotional regulation in the child involves both physiological (e.g., central nervous system functioning) and psychological levels (e.g., growing cognitive and representational skills). In addition to these first two levels of intra-organismic factors, there are factors outside of the child (e.g., parental response to the child's affect, parental socialization of affective displays).

Research on how maltreated children differentiate and respond to affect is critical. How a child responds to strong feelings is part of self-regulation. Cicchetti et al. (1991) refer to four patterns of affect differentiation/response in children that presumably depend on caregiver experiences: (a) developmentally and affectively retarded, (b) depressed, (c) ambivalent and affectively labile, and (d) angry. For example, neglected children may fall into the first pattern more often, with physically abused children more often in the fourth pattern.

There is evidence also that prolonged abuse is related to physiological alterations. Siegel (1999) summarized several lines of research that have found consistently elevated cortisol levels in sexually abused girls when contrasted with closely matched, socioeconomically disadvantaged girls. The presence of PTSD symptoms in sexually abused children also reflects the dysregulating and overwhelming aspects of victimization and has been found in a significant minority of clinical cases (Kendall-Tackett et al., 1993).

Behaviorally, dysregulation in abused children is reflected in greater sleep problems in very young sexually abused children (Hewitt, 1999) and more aggressive behavior in physically abused children (Dodge, Pettit, & Bates, 1997). There is also evidence that attention deficit hyperactivity disorder (ADHD)-like symptoms are related to overstimulating types of parental interaction in the first 42 months of life (i.e., failure to soothe, maternal seductive behavior, frequent disruptions, etc.) (Jacobvitz & Sroufe, 1987). There is certainly a reason to find parallels to the above forms of parental interaction in the lives of sexually and physically abused children.

The attachment-related internal working model, referred to earlier, also carries with it "rules for the perception, display, and regulation of emotion" (Cicchetti et al., 1991, p. 31). Thus, when an abused child idealizes or is not given an opportunity to be honest about an abusive parent, a core of anger and hurt is sealed over, thus preventing the learning of new ways of dealing with painful affect.

There has been a recent focus on the role that verbal organization of experience exerts on the development of self-regulation of both emotions and behavior (Toth, Cicchetti, Macfie, Rogosch, & Maughan, 2000). This processing of experience helps children organize and make sense out of their world. Parents can be helpful in modeling narrative development, but children's experiences with maltreating parents do show up in their narratives. For example, Toth et al. (2000) found that maltreated children provided stories that contained more conflictual and fewer moral-affiliative themes. Conflictual narratives were related to externalizing behavior, suggesting that dysregulation is related to how children organize their life experiences.

Because the opportunity to disclose in a new setting and alter one's cognitions about the abuse is important, therapists should develop ways to allow the disclosure to proceed in a manner that does not create further dysregulation in the child.

A legitimate question for both therapists and parents of abused children is whether the therapy itself, particularly the disclosure of abuse, is dysregulating to the child by virtue of its negative and upsetting nature. In light of the above findings by Toth et al. (2000), my perspective is that narratives of dysregulated children need to be altered and made more useful to them. A child who is not given the opportunity to disclose or who is having a hard time disclosing uses the maladaptive technique of avoidance. Because the opportunity to disclose in a new setting and alter one's cognitions about the abuse is important, therapists should develop ways to allow the disclosure to proceed in a manner that does not create further dysregulation in the child.

Symptoms Reflecting Dysregulation

Again, theory can identify specific treatment targets, beginning with affective disruption, such as anxiety, and its related problems, sleep problems, and behavioral regression. In addition, victimized children may not have learned self-soothing behaviors and therefore may live in a heightened state of arousal, resulting in somatic symptoms. Other manifestations are inattentiveness or overactivity in class, akin to ADHD symptoms (Jacobvitz & Sroufe, 1987). In addition, sexualized behavior can add to the child feeling out of control. This problem should be addressed specifically in therapy.

The following discussion focuses on individual, group, and family therapy techniques designed to correct the dysregulatory affects of abuse on feelings, thoughts, and behaviors (see the appendix for a brief synopsis of relevant techniques).

Individual Treatment Techniques Derived From Dysregulation Theory

The therapist must remember that the child will not naturally associate uncovering painful aspects of abuse with an opportunity for support and feeling in control. This underscores the need for structure and predictability in the therapy process. This can prevent regression or decompensation in the child. When that happens, the therapist may be paired with this distress and be viewed by the child as negative and abusive.

Strategies to provide structure and predictability include a clear definition of the therapy process and the need for disclosure. Children can even schedule formally when and how they want to talk about their victimization experiences. The therapist and the child may also develop a word or phrase for the abuse that makes it easier to discuss.

Therapy with children can sometimes be psychoeducational and involve the use of didactic information (e.g., safety and sexual education). Psychoeducational techniques are not as dysregulating and may be more useful to extremely reactive children. It is also possible for the therapist to partition the session into working portions and play portions, with children provided an agreed-on amount of time to work on issues, followed by another period in which they are feeling less threatened. A part of the play portion can be placed at the end of the session to give the child a chance to reorganize and restabilize.

Other therapists have talked about "as-if" approaches to therapy (Friedrich, 1995). Children may never acknowledge having been molested directly, but they may talk to the therapist as if they had been or give the therapist advice for working with a similarly aged child who had a similar abuse experience. This particular technique underscores the need for the child to be given some element of control in the therapy.

It is in this area of therapy that some of the most empirically validated techniques are available from the cognitive-behavioral area (Stauffer & Deblinger, 1996). These are best described as anxiety reduction techniques. Using relaxation training and self-hypnosis instruction, the child can be assisted to develop a repertoire of strategies ranging from thought stopping to anxiety management strategies that are useful in a variety of settings.

It is important that the therapy become a reliable and predictable process for the child. This can prevent emotional and behavioral "spillover" from the therapy to the home and school situation, with the result that the child is ostracized. Other elements of the therapy process that can be difficult for the child to manage include the gender of the therapist, particularly when the therapist is the same sex as the child's perpetrator. However, at this time, nothing in the literature supports any particular therapist-child gender match.

Group Treatment Techniques Derived From Dysregulation Theory

Children should be screened for their appropriateness for group treatment because group therapy can be overwhelming and thus dysregulating. We should not view group therapy as automatic for every sexually abused child or as a panacea for every child. Children who have a history of poor peer relationships and frequent victimization may need to be involved either in individual or pair therapy (Selman & Schultz, 1990) before being involved in group treatment.

Here again, didactic and structured techniques lend themselves to preventing dysregulation in the group setting (Conduct Problems Prevention Research Group, 1999). The use of structured treatment modules, in which the child has the opportunity to work through a relevant segment (e.g., talking about feelings related to the abuse) and has a sense of closure by the end of it, can add a great deal to the child's sense of resolution and feeling in control.

There has been discussion of gender differences in group treatment, with boys presenting as more disruptive and prone to acting out and feeling dysregulated (Friedrich, Berliner, Urquiza, & Beilke, 1988). The clinical literature also supports this finding, suggesting that greater attention to regulation of affect and behavior be given to treatment groups for boy victims.

Family Treatment Techniques Derived From Dysregulation Theory

In the same way that individual therapy can be confusing and dysregulating to the child, family therapy can have the same effect on the child and family combination that is being seen by the therapist. Therapists must learn to help the families they see realize the purpose of therapy and focus on specific behavioral targets that provide the family with both a measure of success and an opportunity to learn to be more consistent with the child. Again, a psychoeducational component to the family therapy, mixed with liberal amounts of support, will be useful (Deblinger & Heflin, 1996).

For physically abusive families, one form of dysregulation is aggressive behavior. Therapists should attend to issues of anger management and self-control and suggest alternatives to physical punishment (Kolko, 1996).

An approach to therapy that provides the necessary structure to prevent dysregulation is the use of the goal attainment scaling system, as described in Friedrich (1995), for families of sexually abused children. With this goal-setting strategy, families are helped to identify a number of specific goals that have levels of accomplishment (e.g., acceptable level of outcome, optimal level of outcome). The family then can focus on these goals. A number of goals can be agreed on, with some related to attachment and others to dysregulation and self-perception. Dysregulation-based goals may include anger management for parents, the creation of predictable opportunities for family interaction, and the learning of more consistent parenting approaches.

The prescription of rituals, which can be regularly scheduled events in the family, also can go a long way toward increasing a sense of structure and order within the family. These rituals should be targeted around eating and bedtime, two naturally occurring occasions when families can become dysregulated. Empirical support for the use of rituals comes from research on the multigenerational transmission of alcoholism within families (Steinglass, 1987).

Finally, if family members do not feel safe from further victimization, the family setting itself is upsetting and potentially dysregulating to the child. The creation of a sense of safety in each family member is critical. Parents whose view of safety is skewed may not be able to answer the question, "Is your child safe from being revictimized or having his or her symptoms triggered by unsafe events in the home?" The therapist must help family members realize different ways that they are potentially victimizing to each other or excitatory in one way or another. Examples of the latter include family nudity, overt family sexuality, and other potential reminders to the child of sexuality or vulnerability. These are best assessed in a systematic manner (Friedrich, 1998).

Self-Perception

Children's accurate understanding of both their competencies and emotions follows a developmental course and reflects an integration of both cognitive and affective processes (Harter, 1999).

There are a number of developmental shifts in the child's self-understanding. Self-awareness begins with descriptions of one's physical self, and this transitions to the active self, then to the social self, and finally the psychological self, the latter containing one's emotions and cognitions. Findings of increased somatic symptoms in sexually abused children may be related to a heightened focus on the physical self in the young abused child (Friedrich & Schafer, 1995) and adult (Kendall-Tackett, 2000).

The accuracy of self-perception is a critical component of self-development. Young children are highly egocentric, and their self-assumptions often reflect wishes rather than accurate self-perceptions. Harter (1999) has written that accuracy in the judgment of one's abilities is often affected by changes in the child's environment, and maltreatment is certainly a major environmental variable. Harter also wrote that children who consistently view themselves inaccurately, either by over- or underestimating their competence, expose themselves to less challenging problems. For example, they may engage in avoidant coping.

There are some significant clinical implications for this finding. Supportive therapists who want to inflate an abused child's self-esteem should concentrate on the accuracy of the self-perception, not necessarily on the optimism of the perception. In fact, Harter (1999) stated that "relatively accurate self-evaluations are to be encouraged" (p. 318), and a therapy strategy doomed to failure involves categorically asserting to the child that he or she is not dumb but really is quite smart. This dictum should give pause to well-meaning therapists who emphasize blanket but untargeted and often insensitive support.

Numerous contributors to inaccurate self-perception exist in the world of the maltreated child. First, distorted self-perceptions are modeled by the parents. Not surprisingly, the maltreated child often engages in all-or-none thinking and overgeneralizations and shifts from one extreme self-perception to the other. Although these phenomena are seen in normal, nonabused children as well, the likelihood is that in the presence of increased stress and reduced support, an abused child is likely to persist in these immature self-perceptions.

Harter (1999) presented several clinical examples of all-or-none thinking (e.g., "all dumb") and her approach to its resolution (i.e., increase the accuracy of self-perception). Her approach is developmentally sensitive in that it takes into consideration how children think about feelings. In addition, it focuses not only on cognition but also on conflicting emotions.

Another phenomenon in the area of self-perception pertains to stability, or conservation of self, across settings or in the face of contradictions. Children will vary in whether changes are attributed to internal versus external forces, with internally focused children and adolescents not as likely to be bothered by these fluctuations (Harter, 1999). Because maltreatment is an external force, it takes a significant effort for the child to not blame himself or herself. In addition, the child's egocentricity increases the likelihood of self-blame.

Despite the centrality of self-perception in the establishment of the self, children have little interest in self-examination (Harter, 1999). This is likely to surprise child therapists who focus on self-awareness through play therapy. Because children are so deeply embedded in the family matrix, they most naturally will externalize their problems. The therapist may find it more useful working to alter the environmental influences on self-development (e.g., poor attachment) rather than help the child develop insight. Harter (1999) goes so far as to suggest that there are developmental reasons for the use of more didactic techniques and fewer attempts at insight with children. This suggestion supports the types of psychoeducational group interventions suggested in Mandell and Damon (1989).

In addition to the interpersonally related self-perception described earlier, it is useful to consider an intrapsychic self. Although behaviorally trained child psychotherapists may cringe at this suggestion, our new awareness about implicit memory and its influence on behavior (Siegel, 1999) and an appreciation of the internal working models' influence on current relationships (Feeney, 1999) strongly implicate the need to at least appreciate intrapsychic processes. The intrapsychic self is also reflected in the degree to which children's external behavior reflects their internal processing (e.g., are they superficially angry but yet terribly frightened and fearful?). Winnicott's (1965) term *false self* is apt, with many abused children who are precociously mature superficially but feel empty internally. Although seen more often in adolescents and adults, this can be seen in children as well.

Although adolescence brings the promise of greater maturity and coping capacities, it is also a critical developmental juncture that oftentimes magnifies the teen's internal distress related to maltreatment. This has been explored in a paper by Calverly, Fischer, and Ayoub (1994). They found that when children are severely maltreated, their developmental pathways are characterized by a shift in self-perception from a positivity bias to a negativity bias. They now see themselves as fundamentally bad, or as someone who does bad things or someone who deserves the bad that happens to them. This has profound implications for self-care in intimate relationships and the establishment of a genuine sense of self-efficacy.

Symptoms Reflecting Problems With the Self

Issues of self-perception are less tangible, and specific symptoms may not be as overt, particularly with younger children. Gender differences frequently will be evident as well, with girls reporting more depression (Zahn-Waxler, Cole, & Barrett, 1991). As mentioned earlier, somatic symptoms may reflect the abused child having a heightened focus on the physical self. However, disadvantaged children of all ages may have more than the usual difficulties with identifying their feelings or talking about how they feel about themselves (Beeghly & Cicchetti, 1994). Thus, a symptom focus may be less important than creating a therapy context in which the child can develop a greater sense of efficacy, learn about his or her feelings, and develop an increased capacity to talk about thoughts and feelings (i.e., can develop enriched narratives) (Toth et al., 2000).

The next portion of this chapter focuses on individual, group, and family therapy approaches that facilitate the development of an accurate self-perception (see the appendix for a brief synopsis of relevant techniques).

Individual Therapy Approaches Derived From Self-Perception Theory

Techniques from this perspective focus on helping children and teenagers correct their immature and inaccurate self-perceptions. A first strategy is typically to help children learn how to recognize and understand feelings. This can be facilitated through feeling exercises, the use of a feelings list, and related techniques. However, sending a newly verbal child into a home that is not prepared for his or her feelings identification is not a wise systems intervention.

Another approach emphasizes the need for the therapist first to understand the children's view of themselves and their world, before the therapist provides blanket reassurances about the children's worth as individuals. These overly positive reassurances (e.g., it's not your fault, you're a great kid, etc.) directed at the child might be confusing and unbelievable. One effect may be that the child's sense of connection to the therapist is undermined. For example, a child who had physiological arousal to the victimization and appreciated some of the support that came from the abuser may not understand the therapist's focus on the negative aspects of the abuse, particularly at the initial stage of treatment.

Harter (1999) has described excellent strategies to deal with the "good-bad" extremes that the victimized child frequently engages in. These techniques are strongly recommended for work with abused children so that they can make progressive approximations to a more accurate perception of themselves as having a combination of positive, neutral, and negative features.

For example, if a child initially reports a self-perception that is an extreme (e.g., "the best slut"), a developmentally sensitive approach is neither to affirm it nor offer reassurances. Rather, the therapist first realizes that extreme statements are inaccurate. Acceptance of what the child or teen offers, followed by systematic exploration of how this shows up in his or her life (e.g., a child says he or she is stupid, but you find out the child does well in math), opens the door to a corrective therapeutic experience. Although this superficially sounds like cognitive therapy, by respecting the child's needs and cognitive immaturity, it becomes developmentally informed cognitive therapy and facilitates the therapist-child connection (Santostefano, 1998).

It is also important in this area to increase a child's sense of efficacy. An example of this would be to "contract with the child for competency" (e.g., putting the sexually reactive child "in charge of his penis"). Cognitive approaches that address the physically abused child's self-defeating cognitions are also useful in enhancing a child's sense of mastery and competency (Stauffer & Deblinger, 1996).

For older children, particularly those who have some mastery of their feelings, it is also useful to "externalize the problem," which borrows from Michael White's (1989) constructionistic approach to therapy. Children are egocentric and assume blame for numerous things that happen to them. This is true for sexually abused children, who view themselves as bad, duplicitous, and guilty of the abuse. Reassurances to children of their goodness are not helpful. However, if you help children learn how to talk about the problem as "outside of them" and "sneaking up on them when they are unaware," they can learn to view themselves as having the potential for a more active role in keeping negative feelings outside of them. They also can learn to cope better with those times in which they are vulnerable to feeling poorly about themselves.

In addition, a maltreated child can be self-critical, creating the potential for depression and a reduced self-efficacy. This will show up more often in teenagers who are developmentally quite efficient but often inaccurate at comparing themselves with others. Calverly et al. (1994) developed a strategy that facilitates self-knowledge by systematically asking teenagers to describe features of themselves in their relationships with significant others (e.g., mother, father, boyfriend, best friend). The teen then arranges these attributes in order of importance to the self. Abused teen girls reflect the negativity bias, but the process opens them up to examining the why of this. This strategy has proven very helpful in my individual work with male and female teens.

Older latency and adolescent victims can be aided in the development of a "personal fable" regarding some unique aspect that helps in overcoming the abuse. This can be done in a cognitive therapy format, complete with a blackboard to facilitate the child's visual perception of the important concept that thoughts create feelings and direct behavior. For example, Cunningham and MacFarlane (1990) have written about the role of "vulture thoughts" in the thinking of sexually aggressive children. Although simply knowing that thoughts and feelings are connected will have a different effect on preteen children than teenagers, this concept can be the initial step toward learning how to think more accurately about oneself and how different moods or situations trigger them.

Finally, in keeping with Harter's (1999) suggestion, the therapist would do well to avoid focusing on insight in the child and concentrate on a developmentally simpler task (i.e., accuracy of self-perception).

Group Therapy Approaches Derived From Self-Perception Theory

The universality present in group therapy helps not only with attachment, which was described earlier, but also helps children view themselves more accurately (Yalom, 1995). Self-perception is constructed in part based on our understanding of other people's perceptions of us (Harter, 1999). Group therapy provides an excellent opportunity for peer perspectives to be incorporated into one's sense of self. In addition, the group format allows children to hear feedback from other people about gains they have made. Finally, by the use of structured treatment modules, children can realize that they are working gradually through the victimization, achieving closure, and, it is hoped, improving their sense of self-efficacy.

Family Therapy Techniques Derived From Self-Perception Theory

Abusive parents who have been victimized in the past and who now have a child whom they have abused, or who has been abused by someone else, may very well view themselves as inept. Countering that perspective will be very difficult, but family therapy is an appropriate arena to confront that parental perception (Deblinger & Heflin, 1996). This may be done by empowering parents and allowing them to see their effectiveness with small, easily attainable goals that are set in terms of their ability to parent their children in a less angry and nonvictimizing manner.

Some of the same all-or-nothing thinking that children have about themselves will be found in parents regarding their perceptions of their children. Parents can be encouraged to externalize their negative projections of their children (White, 1989). For example, parents do not always hate their children, although their abusive behavior suggests that. There are times, however, when their "dislike for the children gets the better of them." Discussion between the parents and children about these specific instances can go a long way toward developing a more positive sense of connection between them.

Need for Research

A review of the impact of sexual abuse (Kendall-Tackett et al., 1993) decried the atheoretical approach to assessing abuse impact. The theoretical model suggested in this chapter combines a number of developmentally sensitive theories that can guide both the assessment and treatment of sexually and physically abused children and their families. Child treatment clinicians, however, seem to view outcome research as daunting. The increasing volume of published research that exists on the treatment of sexually abused children suggests that treatment can be effective in the short term for anxiety and depression (Berliner & Saunders, 1996). It seems, however, that significantly longer periods of time are needed for the externalizing problems of aggression and sexual acting out (Berliner & Saunders, 1996). PTSD symptoms lend themselves to treatment with a cognitive-behavioral approach (Deblinger et al., 1996). These findings need to be replicated, and the treated children need to be followed for longer periods, preferably over a developmental transition (e.g., from childhood into adolescence), to determine long-term efficacy.

We need to know whether child treatment can be helpful with children who are in foster care, whose parents are not in treatment, or whose parental relationship faces termination.

The efficacy of the various treatment approaches with teenagers and their parents needs to be documented. Although we certainly have demonstrated short-term success with children and their internalizing problems, what about teenagers who are acting in self-destructive ways secondary to maltreatment? Or children with sexual behavior problems as they move into another developmental phase? Do parents of sexually abused children improve in their overall level of support, and to what degree is this contextual variable related to the children's adjustment?

Directive therapy, including disclosure of victimization, is strongly suggested by many clinicians (Friedrich, 1995), but its treatment value is being demonstrated only now. We need to know whether child treatment can be helpful with children who are in foster care, whose parents are not in treatment, or whose parental relationship faces termination. Finally, it may be that changing exter-

nal factors (e.g., poverty, maternal depression, and use of physical punishment) are as important to the child's long-term adjustment as any "internal" changes the child makes. However, we do not know that. These big questions must be answered before we can ask more narrow questions about the utility of specific techniques.

Conclusion

The theories and associated techniques identified in this chapter have the advantage of targeting specific symptoms presented by abused children. An equally valid approach to determine treatment effectiveness is goal attainment scaling, which is discussed specifically for sexually abused children in Friedrich (1995). This approach can be used to determine the therapy outcome for a diverse group of abused children with a broad range of presenting complaints. For example, treatment goals can be established in each of the domains suggested (e.g., an attachment-related goal of more positive interactions with their children, a dysregulation-related goal of no physical punishment, and a self-perception goal of improved school achievement by the children). Goal attainment scaling can enhance treatment and enable the therapist to measure outcome empirically.

Therapists owe it to the children they treat to do at least the following: (a) assess the presence of behavioral problems, using standard measures pretreatment and immediately after treatment and 3 to 6 months later; (b) document the interventions used in therapy; (c) document the amount of therapy and whether abuse was discussed; (d) invite other clinicians to collaborate to expand sample size and types of interventions; and (e) share findings. Not only will this inform the practice, but it can guide the treatment of other abused children as well.

APPENDIX

Synopsis of Selected Treatment Techniques

I. Attachment
  A. Individual Therapy
    1. Acceptance
    2. Alliance formation
    3. Correcting the internal working model
    4. Creating safety
  B. Group Therapy
    1. Developing cohesion
    2. Maintaining boundaries
    3. Creating safety
    4. Developing empathy
  C. Family Therapy
    1. Positive connotation
    2. Identifying similarities among family members
    3. Creating rapid treatment gains
    4. Goal setting
      Home visits
      Parent-Child Interaction Therapy

II. Dysregulation
  A. Individual Therapy
    1. Explaining the process of therapy
    2. Establishing specific goals
    3. Modulating treatment intensity
    4. Teaching self-soothing techniques
    5. Using psychoeducational approaches
    6. Using cognitive-behavioral strategies for PTSD and anxiety
  B. Group Therapy
    1. Creating safety
    2. Reducing agitation
    3. Practicing boundaries
    4. Interrupting victim-victimizer dynamics
  C. Family Therapy
    1. Creating safety
    2. Reducing sexualized behavior
    3. Behaviorally based family therapy
    4. Goal setting

III. Self-Perception Theory
  A. Individual Therapy
    1. Identifying and processing feelings
    2. Contracting for competency
    3. Externalizing the problem
    4. Confronting all-or-nothing thinking
    5. Encouraging relatively accurate self-representations
  B. Group Therapy
    1. Respecting the child's developmental level
      Using pair therapy
      Role-play
      Calverly et al.'s (1994) self-in-relationships exercise
  C. Family Therapy
    1. Normalizing unacceptable feelings
    2. Examining the parenting process
    3. Exploring parents' projections
    4. Examining parents who feel betrayed
    5. Creating new stories about the child

References

Alexander, P. C. (1992). Application of attachment theory to the study of sexual abuse. *Journal of Consulting and Clinical Psychology, 60,* 185-195.

Alexander, P. C., Teti, L., & Anderson, C. L. (2000). Childhood sexual abuse history and role reversal in parenting. *Child Abuse & Neglect, 24,* 829-838.

Beeghly, M., & Cicchetti, D. (1994). Child maltreatment, attachment, and the self system: Emergence of an internal state lexicon in toddlers at high social risk. *Developmental Psychopathology, 6,* 5-30.

Berliner, L., & Saunders, B. E. (1996). Treating fear and anxiety in sexually abused children: Results of a controlled 2-year follow-up study. *Child Maltreatment, 1,* 294-309.

Bonner, B. L., Walker, C. E., & Berliner, L. (2000). *Children with sexual behavior problems: Assessment and treatment* (Final report, Grant No. 90-CA-1469). Washington, DC: NCCAN, Administration for Children, Youth and Families, U.S. Department of Health and Human Services.

Bretherton, I., & Munholland, K. A. (1999). Internal working models in attachment relationships: A construct revisited. In J. Cassidy & P. R. Shaver (Eds.), *Handbook of attachment* (pp. 89-114). New York: Guilford.

Burkett, L. P. (1991). Parenting behaviors of women who were sexually abused in their families of origin. *Family Process, 30,* 421-434.

Calverly, R. M., Fischer, K. W., & Ayoub, C. (1994). Complex splitting of self-representations in sexually abused adolescent girls. *Development and Psychopathology, 6,* 195-213.

Cassidy, J. (1999). The nature of the child's ties. In J. Cassidy & P. R. Shaver (Eds.), *Handbook of attachment* (pp. 3-20). New York: Guilford.

Cassidy, J., & Shaver, P. R. (1999). *Handbook of attachment.* New York: Guilford.

Cicchetti, D., Ganiban, J., & Barnett, D. (1991). Contributions from the study of high risk populations to understanding the development of emotion regulation. In J. Garber & K. A. Dodge (Eds.), *The development of emotion regulation and dysregulation* (pp. 15-48). New York: Cambridge University Press.

Cicchetti, D., & Toth, S. L. (1995). Child maltreatment and attachment organization: Implications for intervention. In S. Goldberg, R. Muir, & J. Kerr (Eds.), *Attachment theory* (pp. 279-308). Hillsdale, NJ: Analytic Press.

Cohen, J. A., & Mannarino, A. P. (1996). Factors that mediate treatment outcome in sexually abused preschool children. *Journal of the American Academy of Child and Adolescent Psychiatry, 35,* 1402-1410.

Cohen, J. A., & Mannarino, A. P. (1997). A treatment study for sexually abused preschool children: Outcome during a one-year follow-up. *Journal of the American Academy of Child and Adolescent Psychiatry, 36,* 1228-1235.

Cohen, J. A., & Mannarino, A. P. (1998). Interventions for sexually abused children: Initial treatment outcome findings. *Child Maltreatment, 3,* 17-26.

Conduct Problems Prevention Research Group. (1999). Initial impact of the FAST Track prevention trial for conduct problems: I. High risk sample. *Journal of Consulting and Clinical Psychology, 67,* 631-647.

Cunningham, C., & MacFarlane, K. (1990). *When children molest children.* Orwell, VT: Safer Society Press.

Deblinger, E., & Heflin, A. H. (1996). *Treating sexually abused children and their parents.* Thousand Oaks, CA: Sage.

Deblinger, E., Lippman, J., & Steer, R. (1996). Sexually abused children suffering posttraumatic stress symptoms: Initial treatment outcome findings. *Child Maltreatment, 1,* 310-321.

Dodge, K., Pettit, G., & Bates, J. E. (1997). How the experience of early physical abuse leads children to become chronically aggressive. In D. Cicchetti & S. L. Toth (Eds.), *Rochester symposium on developmental psychopathology: Vol. 8. Trauma: Perspectives on theory, research and intervention* (pp. 263-288). Rochester, NY: University of Rochester Press.

Feeney, J. A. (1999). Adult romantic attachment and couple relationships. In J. Cassidy & P. R. Shaver (Eds.), *Handbook of attachment* (pp. 355-377). New York: Guilford.

Friedrich, W. N. (1991). Mothers of sexually abused children: An MMPI study. *Journal of Clinical Psychology, 47,* 778-783.

Friedrich, W. N. (1995). *Psychotherapy of sexually abused boys.* Thousand Oaks, CA: Sage.

Friedrich, W. N. (1998). *Safety checklist.* (Available from Mayo Clinic, Department of Psychiatry and Psychology, Rochester, MN 55905)

Friedrich, W. N., Berliner, L., Urquiza, A. J., & Beilke, R. L. (1988). Brief diagnostic group treatment of sexually abused boys. *Journal of Interpersonal Violence, 3,* 331-343.

Friedrich, W. N., & Schafer, L. C. (1995). Somatization in sexually abused children. *Journal of Pediatric Psychology, 20,* 661-670.

George, C., & Main, M. (1979). Social interactions of young abused children: Approach, avoidance, and aggression. *Child Development, 50,* 306-318.

Greenberg, M. (1999). Attachment and psychopathology in childhood. In J. Cassidy & P. R. Shaver (Eds.). *Handbook of attachment* (pp. 469-496). New York: Guilford.

Harter, S. (1999). *The construction of the self.* New York: Guilford.

Hembree-Kigin, T. L., & McNeil, C. B. (1995). *Parent-child interaction therapy.* New York: Plenum.

Hewitt, S. K. (1999). *Assessing allegations of sexual abuse in preschool children.* Thousand Oaks, CA: Sage.

Howe, D., Brandon, M., Hinings, D., & Schofield, G. (1999). *Attachment theory, child maltreatment, and social support.* Mahwah, NJ: Lawrence Erlbaum.

Jacobvitz, D., & Sroufe, L. A. (1987). The early caregiver-child relationship and attention-deficit disorder with hyperactivity: A prospective study. *Child Development, 58,* 1488-1495.

Katz, L. F., & Gottman, J. M. (1991). Marital discord and child outcomes: A social-psychophysiological approach. In J. Garber & K. A. Dodge (Eds.), *The development of emotion regulation and dysregulation* (pp. 129-155). New York: Cambridge University Press.

Kendall-Tackett, K. A. (2000). Physiological correlates of childhood abuse: Chronic hyperarousal in PTSD, depression, and irritable syndrome. *Child Abuse & Neglect, 24,* 799-811.

Kendall-Tackett, K. A., Williams, L. M., & Finkelhor, D. (1993). Impact of sexual abuse on children: A review and synthesis of recent empirical studies. *Psychological Bulletin, 113,* 164-180.

Kolko, D. (1996). Individual cognitive behavioral treatment and family therapy for physically abused children and their offending parents: A comparison of clinical outcomes. *Child Maltreatment, 1,* 322-342.

Main, M., & George, C. (1985). Responses of abused and disadvantaged toddlers to distress in age mates: A study in the day care setting. *Developmental Psychology, 21,* 407-412.

Malinosky-Rummell, R., & Hansen, D. J. (1993). Long-term consequences of childhood physical abuse. *Psychological Bulletin, 114,* 68-79.

Mandell, J. G., & Damon, L. (1989). *Group treatment for sexually abused children.* New York: Guilford.

Pithers, W. D., Gray, A., Busconi, A., & Houchens, P. (1998). Children with sexual behavior problems: Identification of five distinct child types and related treatment considerations. *Child Maltreatment, 3,* 384-406.

Rutter, M., & Sroufe, L. A. (2000). Developmental psychopathology: Concepts and challenges. *Development and Psychopathology, 12,* 265-296.

Santostefano, S. (1998). *A primer on integrating psychotherapies for children and adolescents.* Northvale, NY: Aronson.

Selman, R. L., & Schultz, L. H. (1990). *Making a friend in youth.* Chicago: University of Chicago Press.

Shipman, K., Zeman, J., Penza, S., & Champion, K. (2000). Emotion management skills in sexually maltreated and nonmaltreated girls: A developmental psychopathology perspective. *Development and Psychopathology, 12,* 47-62.

Shirk, S. R. (Ed.). (1988). *Cognitive development and child psychotherapy.* New York: Plenum.

Siegel, D. (1999). *The developing mind.* New York: Guilford.

Solomon, J., & George, C. (Eds.). (1999). *Attachment disorganization.* New York: Guilford.

Stauffer, L. B., & Deblinger, E. (1996). Cognitive-behavioral groups for nonoffending mothers and their young sexually abused children. *Child Maltreatment, 1,* 65-76.

Steinglass, P. (1987). *The alcoholic family.* New York: Basic Books.

Toth, S. L., Cicchetti, D., Macfie, J., Rogosch, F. A., & Maughan, A. (2000). Narrative representations of moral-affiliative and conflictual themes and behavioral problems in maltreated preschoolers. *Journal of Clinical Child Psychology, 29,* 307-318.

White, M. (1989). *Selected papers.* Adelaide, Australia: Dulwich Center.

Winnicott, D. W. (1965). *Maturational processes and the facilitating environment.* New York: International Universities Press.

Yalom, I. (1995). *The theory and practice of group psychotherapy* (4th ed.). New York: Basic Books.

Zahn-Waxler, C., Cole, P. M., & Barrett, K. C. (1991). Guilt and empathy: Sex differences and implications for the development of depression. In J. Garber & K. A. Dodge (Eds.), *The development of emotion regulation and dysregulation* (pp. 243-272). New York: Cambridge University Press.

9

Treating Sexually Abused Adolescents

DEBRA B. HECHT

MARK CHAFFIN

BARBARA L. BONNER

KAREN BOYD WORLEY

LOUANNE LAWSON

Adolescence is the period beginning at puberty and extending to a socially de-fined period of "adulthood." The end of adolescence tends to be defined more by legal statutes (e.g., voting and military age, the ability to get married without parental consent) than any developmental or physical milestones. The general populace and mental health professionals have a tendency to perceive adolescence as a time of *Sturm und Drang* (Levine, 1987; Offer, Ostrov, & Howard, 1981); the stereotypical picture of adolescence is one of moodiness, identity confusion, and rebelliousness. Yet, two reviews summarizing a decade of research conclude that approximately 80% of adolescents manage the transition from childhood to adulthood fairly smoothly, maintaining a positive self-image and adaptive coping (Offer & Boxer, 1991; Petersen, 1988). The stereotype of adolescent turmoil is more appropriately a description of an at-risk youngster whose problems may continue into adulthood (Jessor & Jessor, 1977).

The response of parents to adolescence often depends on the type of family structure that is present, and family response can affect the likelihood of maltreatment and its impact (Garbarino, 1989; Lourie, 1977; Ryan, 1991). Lourie (1977) hypothesized that for some adolescents, abuse can be a result of the failure of the family to readjust to the structural changes created by the youth's movement toward autonomy. Adolescence is a stage when the youth and the family need to accept that the child is moving out of the role of a "controlled and dependent" family member and is separating from the family (Lourie, 1977). The family and adolescent also have to adapt to physical changes and sexual maturity.

Just as it occurs in other stages of childhood, abuse begins during or continues into adolescence. Lourie (1977) outlined a typology describing the onset of adolescent maltreatment. Type I refers to abuse that began in childhood and continues into adolescence. Type II describes cases in which the nature and amount of abuse increase in severity during the adolescent years. Type II abuse is seen as the result of parents' inability or unwillingness to accept the adolescent's attempts at separation and individuation (Lourie, 1977; Williamson, Borduin, & Howe, 1991). Type III abuse describes instances when abuse begins in adolescence. With Type III, it is hypothesized that issues surrounding autonomy are a major contributing factor.

The actual pattern of abuse of adolescents is not as simple to delineate. According to 1997 data from 43 states, 440,944 youth were neglected, 197,557 experienced physical abuse, 98,339 experienced sexual abuse, and 49,338 experienced psychological abuse (U.S. Department of Health and Human Services, 1999). Of this total of 786,178 children, 18.6% (146,229) were between the ages of 12 and 15, and 6% (47,170) were 16 or older (U.S. Department of Health and Human Services, 1999). Older children and adolescents are less likely to be counted as neglected. Youth between the ages of 12 and 15 are as likely as younger children to be reported for physical abuse, but the rate drops dramatically for children older than age 16 (from approximately 27% to 8.1%) (U.S. Department of Health and Human Services, 1999). Rates of sexual abuse appear to be slightly higher in the 12- to 15-year-old range but again drop dramatically in youth age 16 and older. Psycho-

logical abuse is rarely reported in older adolescents.

Youth between the ages of 12 and 15 are as likely as younger children to be reported for physical abuse, but the rate drops dramatically for children older than age 16.

The incidence of adolescent abuse may be underreported for various reasons (Blythe, Hodges, & Guterman, 1990; Lourie, 1977). Adolescent victims often are not brought to the attention of the authorities. Abuse in adolescence may be harder to identify; there often is confusion between some of the telltale acting-out behaviors seen in child victims and the normal developmental changes seen in many adolescents (Blythe et al., 1990). This may be especially true with respect to sexual behaviors. It can be quite difficult to draw the line between normal experimentation and sexual behavior that might indicate an abuse history.

Adolescent Development

The transitional period of adolescence is characterized by changes and challenges that occur within and outside the individual. Many developmental events occur during adolescence that have a significant impact on an adolescent's functioning, including a variety of physical, cognitive, emotional, behavioral, and social changes. In addition, adolescents experience a variety of other important events, such as peer group changes, school moves, changes in family structure or functioning, and alterations in societal and community expectations (Hansen, Giacoletti, & Nangle, 1995; Petersen & Hamburg, 1986).

Physical/Sexual Development

Puberty signals the entrance into adolescence, although the age at which this occurs can vary. Data suggest that puberty is starting earlier and is somewhat earlier for girls than boys (Tanner, 1981, 1998). Although producing clear physical changes and increased sexual interest, the view that raging hormones impinge markedly on behavior does not appear to be completely justified. Most of the psychological impact of puberty appears to be interwoven with social or cultural standards. For example, boys have been found to report increased feelings of attractiveness during puberty, whereas girls express more dislike for their bodies, particularly regarding the more public aspects of their development, such as breasts, increased height, and loss of "thinness" (Crockett & Petersen, 1987; Petersen, 1988).

Adultlike sexuality, sexual identity issues, and romantic pairing make their debut during adolescence, and accommodating these physically derived psychological and social changes is a major developmental task of the period. Romantic intimacy, dating, and decisions (some would say preoccupations) about sexual activity quickly come to occupy a major part of the adolescent's concerns. By age 18, most adolescents have experienced intercourse, more so and earlier for boys than girls, for African Americans than for Caucasians, and for sexually abused than nonabused girls (Hayes, 1987; Wyatt, 1988). Unfortunately, most initial and later adolescent experiences with intercourse in the United States are unplanned and unprotected, putting young men and women at risk for unwanted pregnancies and diseases, including HIV (Brooks-Gunn & Furstenberg, 1989).

Changes in Dependency Status

Adolescence is characterized by increasing role competency, emphasis on peer relations, and independence from parental and adult control. The latter is often a regular focus of negotiation, if not conflict. Peer groups increase in size, complexity, and emotional intimacy, as increasing amounts of time are spent in contact with close friends, sharing thoughts, feelings, and activities (Petersen, 1988). Although this implies a different sort of relationship to family and parents than the dependency and relative exclusivity of earlier years, it would be a mistake to equate individuation or autonomy with freedom from parental attachments and influences. Rather, it appears that although most adolescents in Western cultures adhere to peer or idiosyncratic standards in dress, music, and other matters of fashion, they continue to hold fundamentally similar core values and beliefs with their parents (Kandel & Lesser, 1972).

Within different cultural groups, moving away from dependency may be manifested differently. For example, whereas most American culture values increased individualism and the pursuit of individual goals among adolescents, other cultures are more group or family oriented and value adolescents taking increasingly contributory or responsible roles within the group.

Parental ability to adjust to their adolescent's movement away from dependency appears to play a crucial role in determining the direction and character of this process. Having parents who are authoritative as opposed to authoritarian or restrictive and who combine context-specific limit setting and negotiation with an enabling, caring, and supportive attitude is associated with greater adolescent autonomy (Powers, Hauser, & Kilner, 1989). Unfortunately, parental styles that support autonomy are likely to be far from the experience of many abused adolescents (Claussen & Crittenden, 1991; Hart & Brassard, 1990).

Cognitive Development

Cognitive abilities, particularly the ability to think abstractly and introspectively, increase significantly during adolescence. Most teens develop the capacity to see things from the perspective of others, which often is paradoxically combined with a heightened self-consciousness and egocentrism that, gratefully, diminishes as adolescence progresses (Enright, Lapsley, & Shukla, 1979). Increased cognitive and self-reflective abilities and the ability to be sensitive to the plight of others can combine to produce an often philosophical and socially conscious perspective on life and the questions of identity and social justice.

Adolescent behaviors that can cause problems for adults are in part the result of the developmental shift from concrete operations to formal operations (Elkind, 1978). Youth who are beginning to think about other people's thinking, recognize general rules, and develop the capacity to hold more than one idea in mind at a time are approaching formal operations. At the same time, adolescents create a "personal fable" about their own beliefs, attitudes, and uniqueness that is designed to manage intense emotion (Elkind, 1967). Adolescents have peculiar ideas about universality and uniqueness. On one hand, they believe their thoughts and feelings are shared universally. At the same time, they feel special and thus not governed by the rules that govern others (Elkind, 1978).

Adolescents are often obsessed with their own behavior and appearance. They assume that other people are as obsessed with them as they are with themselves. They create an "imaginary audience" before which they play out their self-criticism and self-admiration. The imaginary audience is distinguished from locus of control; the youth do not feel as though they are being controlled by those outside, only that others are as concerned with the youths' thoughts, feelings, and behaviors as are the youth themselves.

Identity Development

The development of self-identity is a task associated with late adolescence (Marcia, 1994). The youth struggles to integrate a number of coexisting factors, including gender identity, physical capabilities, sexuality, reasoning ability, and social expectations. The result is an identity that is constructed rather than conferred by parents or society. Issues to be resolved in late adolescence include occupation, ideology, interpersonal values, and marital relationships. It is a process that requires that the youth explore alternatives in these areas, then commit to one among many choices or options. Identity at this stage of development goes beyond the ego ideal, which includes internalized goals and aspirations, and the self, which is a necessary but not sufficient condition for identity.

Developmental Victimatology

Developmental considerations are sometimes overlooked in understanding the dynamics of abuse, especially the risk of being abused and the impact of abuse. Finkelhor (1995) addressed these issues through a conceptualization of developmental victimology. Throughout childhood, individuals gain and lose characteristics that make them more or less vulnerable for various types of victimization. For example, sexual maturation may make children approaching puberty, especially girls, at increased risk for sexual abuse (Finkelhor, 1995). Alternatively, as children grow older, they are more likely to run away, fight back, and use their social networks to gain support. Thus, as children get older, they may be better able to protect themselves and prevent the recurrence of abuse.

There is a tendency to assume that adolescents, due to their increased control over their environment, are largely responsible for their own victimization (Finkelhor, 1995). This is not true; despite their increased independence and reasoning skills, adolescents are vulnerable to the factors that lead to victimization. In addition, adolescents may give in to social pressures and engage in behaviors (e.g., using drugs and alcohol) that do not facilitate self-protection (Finkelhor, 1995). As children grow older, victimization patterns become more like those of adults. For example, adolescents are more likely to be victims of rape, robbery, or assault than younger children or the adult population (Finkelhor & Dziuba-Leatherman, 1994).

The impact of abuse appears to be related to developmental level. For example, some evidence suggests that prepubescent abuse affects endocrine secretions, possibly resulting in the early onset of puberty (Finkelhor, 1995; Gil, 1996). On the other hand, physical and emotional stress may lead to a delayed onset of puberty (De Bellis & Putnam, 1994). Puberty brings about many uncomfortable feelings and issues related to body image, and an abusive experience during this time can have a wide-ranging impact (Gil, 1996). Cognitively, an important dimension appears to be how children understand the concept of victimization and the perception of responsibility for the event (Finkelhor, 1995). Older children may be more at risk in this respect because they are better able to understand the stigma associated with victimization. Also, the victims' sense of morality may be affected, which would affect the way they view their own abuse, as well as having possible consequences on their future behavior (Finkelhor, 1995). An adolescent's perception of power, right, wrong, and fairness may be shaped by abusive incidents, limiting the youth's moral development and paving the way toward the commission of an abusive act. Thus, knowledge of the developmental challenges and physical changes that occur during adolescence is necessary to fully understand the impact of abuse during this time.

Prevalence of Effects of Sexual Abuse of Adolescents

Sexual abuse causes serious problems for adolescents, just as it does for young children (see Chapter 3, this volume). Some adolescents are sexually abused for years, causing great harm. A number of studies indicate that onset of sexual abuse during adolescence is associated with greater symptomatology than onset earlier in life (Murphy et al., 1988; Sedney & Brooks, 1984; Sirles, Smith, & Kusama, 1989). Other studies point in the other direction, however, with early onset resulting in more profound problems (Russell, 1986). Still other studies suggest that onset between the ages of 7 and 13 is most harmful (Gomes-Schwartz, Horowitz, & Sauzier, 1985).

In contrast to their preschool and school-age counterparts, who are more likely to present with atypical sexualized behavior problems and anxiety, sexually abused adolescents often present with low self-esteem, depression, and suicidal ideation or behavior (Beitchman et al., 1992; Runtz & Briere, 1986). School problems, conflicts with authority, early sexual behavior, and eating disorders have been associated with sexual abuse in teenage girls (Hibbard, Ingersoll, & Orr, 1990; Runtz & Briere, 1986), although abused teens show lower problem levels than general adolescent psychiatric populations (Gomes-Schwartz, Horowitz, & Cardarelli, 1990). Many adolescents disclose their abuse out of anger (Sorenson & Snow, 1991), and angry accusations from an adolescent with nonspecific psychological symptoms must not be dismissed.

Adolescent victims of sexual abuse may exhibit substance abuse problems (Harrison, Hoffman, & Edwall, 1989; Kilpatrick et al., 2000; Singer, Song, & Ochberg, 1994). Research with substance-abusing victims of sexual abuse suggests that these adolescents perceive greater benefits (e.g., tension reduction, escape from family problems) in using substances, which leads to increased levels of intoxication and drug use (Harrison et al., 1989; Singer et al., 1994).

For males, an additional consideration may be their sexual self-concept (Richardson, Meredith, & Abbot, 1993). Sexual self-concept is defined as the sex-typed role with which a person identifies. Sexual self-concept is typically categorized as masculine, feminine, androgynous, or undifferentiated (Bem, 1974). Sexually abused adolescent males are more likely than nonabused males to report undifferentiated sexual self-concepts, suggesting an unresolved sense of sexual identity (Richardson et al., 1993). Correlates of this undifferentiated concept include poor adjustment, poor social relations, and lower self-esteem.

Assessment

Is Treatment Needed?

Not all teenagers who are sexually abused need treatment. It is often difficult to tell, however, which victims need help and which do not. Some teenage victims avoid dealing with their abuse, vacillating between intrusive thoughts about the experience and periods of avoidance and denial (Shapiro & Dominiak, 1990). Avoidant adolescents seldom welcome the therapist's invitation to remember what they are working to forget. Some adolescents interpret the referral for treatment as another unwelcome exposure of their most embarrassing secrets. Many teenagers tell us, "Look, there's nothing wrong with me. I just want to forget about it—OK?" This resistance can be compounded by the fact that the youngster's abuser often "escapes" without having to be involved in treatment, reinforcing the sense of unfairness and implicit blame in the referral to therapy. It is recommended that an experienced professional screen adolescents to differentiate youth who are not significantly adversely affected from those who may be avoidant or minimizing.

Not all teenagers who are sexually abused need treatment.

Although the experience of having to repeatedly tell strangers about abuse can be deleterious (Tedesco & Schnell, 1987), encouraging teenagers to rely on avoidant coping mechanisms is also risky. A study of a community sample found that denial and emotional suppression were the most common coping mechanisms used by adult survivors. Although rated as helpful by survivors, avoidant coping mechanisms were associated with poorer psychosocial adjustment (Leitenberg, Greenwald, & Cado, 1992). Among adolescent incest victims, avoidant coping strategies such as wishful thinking, detachment, distancing, or denial are associated with higher symptom levels (Johnson & Kenkel, 1991). A confounding issue is that some adolescent victims are involved in consensual sexual relationships and may have difficulty labeling the abusive experience as abusive.

In the absence of longitudinal data, it is difficult to determine whether avoidant coping styles actively contribute to a poorer resolution of abuse issues and consequently greater distress, as many trauma theorists suspect, or whether greater distress requires using more pronounced and primitive coping strategies to safeguard psychological integrity. In either case, the available evidence suggests that we cannot afford to neglect the needs of abused adolescents solely on the basis of their ambivalence or reluctance to seek help.

The Initial Interview

The initial interview should respect the youngster's boundaries and possible reluctance about therapy and should grant some sense of control over discussion of sensitive material. These youth may be afraid of exposing secrets and admitting feelings related to inferiority, sexual inadequacy, and drug and alcohol use (Azima & Dies, 1989). It is important, therefore, to be straightforward and honest, explaining confidentiality and stressing that honesty in the assessment process helps ensure better treatment. It is helpful to start with some of the more general, less threatening topics, such as measures of global adjustment, mood, or personality, before addressing the more intimate topics of substance abuse, sexual history, and sexual victimization. Often, it is helpful to give some choice over how much detail is talked about while holding out the possibility that talking about difficult topics may become less anxiety provoking in the future. In addition, it is important to convey respect for the victim's coping efforts and to devote time to detailing how well the adolescent has coped with the experience to date. The initial interview can highlight the teenager's strengths by de-pathologizing the mental status interview and separating the self from the problem. For example, it may be useful to say, "I've talked with a lot of people your age who have been through sexual abuse. We talk about the effects it has on them. Every-

one's different, but I want to find out if some of the things that have bothered other young people have bothered you. I'd also like to find out what sorts of things you've done that seem to help the most."

Given the wide range of possible consequences of sexual abuse, it can be helpful to gather information about the youth's functioning across domains (e.g., school, home, peers), as well as to obtain a thorough description of family dynamics and the victim's current complaints, symptoms, and level of functioning. Collateral interviews with parents and other significant people (e.g., teachers) are often useful. Before contacting others, however, discuss such meetings with the adolescent. Depending on the minor's age, it may be necessary to obtain the minor's consent before contacting others.

It is important to inquire into a range of abuse-specific effects and correlates, including a history of additional abuse, rape, or violent assault experiences beyond the referral report; posttraumatic stress disorder (PTSD) symptoms, including avoidance, numbing, intrusive thoughts, flashbacks, or sleep disturbance, including nightmares; triggers for fearfulness and anxiety; relationship issues, including with adults and peers of the same gender as the abuser; depression; suicidal or self-injurious tendencies; sexual behavior; substance use or abuse; eating problems; and difficulties with memory or other unusual experiences potentially suggestive of a dissociative disorder. Additional stressors include court involvement (Lipovsky, 1992), pressures from family members, or repeated unwanted "advice."

Clinicians should assess the youngster's social support network and ongoing stressors. Particularly critical is the belief or support of the nonoffending parent or parents, which is one of the most powerful predictors of recovery (Everson, Hunter, Runyon, Edelsohn, & Coulter, 1989; Wyatt & Mickey, 1987). Social stressors may arise from the tendency of many adolescents to be justifiably sensitive to the possibility that peers and schoolmates might discover the abuse and view them as responsible, disgraced, or stigmatized. Many teenage girls guard their reputations out of fear that they might be labeled "sluts," a term for which there appears to be no masculine equivalent. Boys may fear homophobic stigmatization and loss of their masculine status (Faller, 1991; Porter, 1986; Rew & Esparza, 1990). It is important for adolescents to turn to their peers and to experience close friendships and support without betrayal, which can be difficult if the youngster fears stigmatization. Clinical experience suggests that the presence of even a single trusted peer confidante can be helpful.

Assessing Attributions

Bright preteens or middle- late-phase adolescents are usually capable of abstractive and introspective thought required to discuss their own attributions about abuse (Celano, 1992; Offer & Boxer, 1991). Attribution theory holds that abuse effects are mediated not so much by the objective characteristics of the abuse as by how we subjectively explain it to ourselves. Attributions may be viewed as the internal "theory" we articulate about what caused and maintained the problem. Attributions of self-blame (internal attribution) lead to depression and distress (e.g., Fiering, Taska, & Lewis, 1998; Mannarino & Cohen, 1996). Morrow (1991) found that adolescent incest victims who tended toward internal attributions experienced more depression and lower self-esteem.

The relationship between attributions and outcome is complex. Celano (1992) suggested that internal attributions may be particularly damaging only when they refer to "characterological" (or global-stable) aspects of oneself rather than "situational" or behavioral aspects. Likewise, external attributions that are global-stable may lead to fearfulness or feelings that one is helpless in a world of ubiquitous danger and seemingly random and unavoidable victimization. Thus, it may be important for some abused adolescents to maintain some perception that they have the ability, at least in some situations, to control what happens to them.

Professionals should resist the temptation to challenge internal attributions, particularly at the time of assessment. It is more important at the outset to lay the groundwork for exploration of the adolescent's attributions, rather than attempting to change them. Efforts to press the point that "it wasn't your fault" may prohibit future disclosure and discussion. In our culture, adolescent sexual abuse victims are viewed as more causally and morally responsible for their abuse than are younger children, particularly if the assault was not violent or if they responded passively (Collings & Payne,

1991). Sensitive as they are to social exposure of "flaws," adolescents are keenly aware of the stigma that could await them on revealing reasons for their internal attributions. It is preferable for the clinician to accept the internal attributions and explore them nonjudgmentally before beginning to suggest that there may be other ways of thinking about what happened.

Psychological Testing

Many treatment programs make minimal use of standardized assessment tools (Friedrich, 1990). There is no profile to be found in psychological testing, which is typical or indicative of sexual abuse (American Professional Society on the Abuse of Children [APSAC], 1990). Nevertheless, testing can provide a broad range of information about how the teenager copes, the extent of current symptoms or discomfort, what resources are present, and what problems may lie ahead. Testing creates a baseline against which treatment can be assessed. Clinicians should de-pathologize testing.

The Trauma Symptom Checklist for Children (TSC-C) (Briere, 1996), for ages 8 to 15, is a self-report instrument with scales reflecting anxiety, depression, posttraumatic stress, sexual concerns, dissociation, and anger. The TSC-C is a standardized instrument with normative data and adequate reliability, validity, and sensitivity to changes across the course of treatment (Evans, Briere, Boggiano, & Barrett, 1994; Lanktree, 1994).

For younger adolescents, the Children's Attributions and Perceptions Scale (CAPS) (Mannarino, Cohen, & Berman, 1994) may be helpful, especially given the relationship between adjustment and the youth's attributions about the abuse (e.g., Fiering et al., 1998; Mannarino & Cohen, 1996). This instrument was specifically developed to measure abuse-related attributions and perceptions in children ages 7 to 14. The CAPS contains 18 items and assesses attributions related to feeling different from peers, personal attributions for negative events, perceived credibility, and interpersonal trust. Abuse-specific instruments share similarities in target areas with abuse-focused therapy, making them particularly well suited to assessing progress and documenting treatment outcome.

Treatment

Initial Treatment Plan

Friedrich (1990) emphasized the importance of viewing sexually abused children and adolescents as a heterogeneous population with correspondingly diverse treatment needs (see Chapter 8, this volume). There is no "one-size-fits-all" treatment model. It is important in therapy to recognize the idiosyncratic aspects of the client as well as the "typical teenager" that dwells within. With a thorough assessment in hand, the clinician is in a good position to suggest an individualized treatment plan and to understand the teenager's problem areas, strengths, and current family and social status. The first questions to be addressed are the following: Is the adolescent in a safe and appropriate environment? What is the least restrictive appropriate setting for treatment? Are there acute difficulties that require immediate relief?

Although not formally the responsibility of treatment professionals, safety issues cannot be ignored in assessment and treatment. Oftentimes, teenagers do not report additional abusers or continued exposure to their abuser until they reach the treatment setting. The therapist may be the first to find out about changes in status, changes that place the youngster at risk. It is important to work cooperatively with child protective services (CPS), the courts, and law enforcement to ensure adequate protection. The therapist is a mandated reporter and must report suspicions of new abuse. For discussion of the reporting law, see Chapter 22 (this volume).

Much of the literature on treating adolescent victims of sexual abuse focuses on females (e.g., Blick & Porter, 1982; Furniss, Bingley-Miller, & Van Elburg, 1988). The goals of therapy generally deal with helping adolescents communicate about the abuse experience, enhancing self-esteem, learning about and discussing normal sexuality, talking about appropriate family roles and boundaries, overcoming isolation, and developing healthy peer relationships (Blick & Porter, 1982; Furniss et al., 1988).

Special considerations have been suggested for boys (see Chapter 8, this volume). Specifically, males may need help opening up, especially in asking for help (Watkins & Bentovim, 1992). Boys need to discuss their fears and issues surrounding homosexuality and their attitudes toward women (Watkins & Bentovim, 1992).

Abuse-Focused Therapy

Abuse-focused treatment (AFT) is a dominant approach to treating abused children, adolescents, and adults. Emerging largely within the past two decades, AFT has generated book-length works that describe AFT and differentiate it from other approaches (Briere, 1989, 1992; Friedrich, 1990; Gil, 1991; Hunter, 1990; Meiselman, 1990; see Chapters 8 and 10, this volume). AFT is not affiliated with any particular theoretical perspective on the larger issues of human psychology. Neither is it wedded to any particular set of techniques or approaches. Indeed, AFT borrows from a wide variety of behavioral, cognitive, systemic, and reconstructive or dynamic therapy techniques.

The common threads of AFT are rooted in the perspective that abuse is a form of victimization by the powerful against the relatively powerless and that abuse sequelae are understandable—indeed, "normal"—adaptations to an abnormal experience. The common symptom presentation of abused adolescents and young adults has led in the direction of diagnostic conceptualizations based on full or partial PTSD, emphasizing the trauma of abuse (Coons, Bowman, Pellow, & Schneider, 1989; Deblinger, 1991; McCormack, Burgess, & Hartman, 1988). Because a variety of cognitive and behavioral techniques have been successfully applied to the treatment of PTSD in nonabuse contexts, AFT is able to borrow many of these techniques to target some of the more disruptive abuse sequelae such as severe anxiety/hyperarousal and avoidance symptoms (Deblinger, McLeer, & Henry, 1990; Lipovsky, 1991).

Early in therapy, it is important to address any acutely painful abuse sequelae such as panic attacks, sleep problems, severe anxiety, or fearfulness. These symptoms are often experienced as "ego-dystonic." In other words, they are not felt to be part of the self, and the person would gladly be rid of them. In addition to its face value, immediately targeting these symptoms is important for other reasons. First, AFT runs the risk of being experienced as aversive due to the repeated pairing of "coming to therapy" with "being reminded of things that make me feel bad." Finding relief early in treatment can immunize against later frustration. When "help feels like help," the therapeutic alliance is supported.

A number of behavioral or cognitive-behavioral techniques are employed, including relaxation training, distraction and self-control techniques, and procedures such as systematic desensitization and stress inoculation training (Lipovsky, 1991). These procedures have been shown to have the most empirical support and probably should be among the first tried (Cohen, Berliner, & March, 2000; Rothbaum, Meadows, Resnick, & Foy, 2000).

Short-term use of psychoactive medications may be considered when symptom relief is critical or when psychological remedies have been exhausted. Ideally, a psychiatrist who is well versed in abuse issues and abuse-focused therapy should supervise medication. The teenager should be included in the decision-making process if at all possible, and the level of medication should be adequately titrated to provide relief without numbing the affect and cognitive acuity needed to work through the trauma.

Education as Therapy

Given their intellectual capacities, teenagers can understand complex and detailed didactic information. Discussions, readings, and handouts can be particularly useful tools for understanding the victimization experience and normalizing many of the effects, such as PTSD symptoms (Lipovsky, 1991). Educative approaches are also appropriate for gaining a general explanation for why someone would commit sexual abuse (Berliner & Wheeler, 1987), a persistent question among adolescents.

Sex education helps neutralize anxiety, provide a language for discussing sexuality, facilitate a healthy body image, and correct misconceptions about sexuality (Cornman, 1989; Furniss et al., 1988; Meiselman, 1990). Sex education includes discussion of appropriate dating and sexual behavior (i.e., mutual consent, caring relationship, appropriate age/power/familial status, consistent with personal religious/moral values, safe sex, etc.). Some abused adolescents do not draw clear distinctions among types of sexual behavior, alternately feeling that it is either "all bad and forbidden" or "anything goes." Learning appropriate distinctions

helps teenagers separate abuse-related sexual experiences from normal sexuality.

Do not be misled by the pseudo-mature or "worldly" presentation of some youngsters into thinking that their sexual information is either accurate or consistent with healthy self-protection. Because of the risk of revictimization (Beitchman et al., 1992) or unwanted pregnancy, it is important to include information on rape and date rape, recognition and responses to unwanted advances, identification of signs of sexually dangerous situations, contraception, and prevention of sexually transmitted diseases.

Sex education helps neutralize anxiety, provide a language for discussing sexuality, facilitate a healthy body image, and correct misconceptions about sexuality.

Individual Therapy

The combination of individual therapy and group therapy is often seen as the optimal approach to treating adolescents who have been sexually abused. It is not always possible, however, to provide both, and decisions have to be made. There is no universal model for making this decision. Nor are there empirical data to drive decisions. In the end, clinical judgment is required, tempered by the realities of client need, staffing, and workload.

Individual therapy varies in duration and format. Deblinger et al. (1990) described a structured short-term cognitive-behavioral treatment for sexually abused children with PTSD, using parallel modules for children and their nonabusing parent. Coping skills, modeling, gradual exposure, education, and prevention are used to target specific PTSD-related symptoms. Patients showed significant decreases from baseline in anxiety, depression, and behavior problems. Similar treatment approaches involving anxiety reduction techniques, stress inoculation therapy, exploration of attributions, cognitive restructuring, and problem-solving techniques have been clinically described as useful (Berliner & Wheeler, 1987; Saunders, 1992; see Chapter 3, this volume).

As adolescents mature, their symptoms become similar to adults' (Cohen et al., 2000). Cognitive-behavioral therapies and procedures such as systematic desensitization and exposure therapy may be indicated to help reduce posttraumatic symptoms in adolescents. These procedures involve exposing the adolescent to thoughts, memories, or actual experiences reminiscent of the abuse while using techniques to relax the body. Challenging irrational thoughts is also involved.

Longer-term and less structured individual therapies are used with adolescents. Some treatment outcome data for younger victims suggest that longer-term treatment is required in many cases (Lanktree, 1994). Unfortunately, no data on adolescents have been reported that use clear control and comparison groups. In a study of hearing-impaired adolescents, clients receiving long-term individual treatment fared better than a treatment refusal group (Sullivan, Scanlan, Brookhouser, Schulte, & Knutson, 1992). It is unclear whether lengthy reconstructive treatment targeting in-depth issues offers advantages over short- or long-term symptomatically focused treatment.

In the absence of definitive studies of treatment efficacy and given the vast need and limited treatment resources, it is difficult to endorse a blanket recommendation for long-term, in-depth individual therapy for sexually abused adolescents. On the other hand, the extreme symptoms exhibited by some teens (e.g., self-mutilation, severe depression, dissociative disorders, etc.) justify intensive individual treatment for whatever period of time is needed.

Group Therapy

Few controlled studies have examined the efficacy of group therapy among adolescent victims of sexual abuse. Nevertheless, group therapy is widely endorsed for this age group (Blick & Porter, 1982; Cornman, 1989; Furniss et al., 1988; Gagliano, 1987; Goodwin & Talwar, 1989; Meiselman, 1990). Azima and Dies (1989) suggested that the group modality is advantageous because it reflects the shift adolescents make toward peers and away from parents. Teenagers will often accept comments and feedback from peers that they would reject from adults. Group therapy allows adolescents to see themselves in relation to other teens. Group treatment allows teens to work

through feelings of rebelliousness and hostility toward authority. Involvement in a group helps the members understand that they are not alone and that others understand what they are going through.

Groups offer numerous advantages. Group norms can have a powerful socializing impact (Phelan, 1987). Members of the group can vicariously benefit from the work of others, taking advantage of individual differences. Group therapy offers the opportunity to withdraw and listen without having to be "on the spot" throughout a session, thereby avoiding the silent "resistance" sometimes seen in individual work with teenagers. The empowering and meaningful experience of helping others is not limited to the therapist. Support, normalization, and validation of experiences are readily available. Interpersonal styles, social skills, and change can be observed and implemented in vivo. The sense of isolation and "differentness" can be diminished. Finally, in cases in which parental or family support is lacking, groups provide a context for youngsters to learn to rely on peers as an alternate support system.

Group therapy is not appropriate for all abused adolescents. Blanket referral of adolescents to group therapy is not recommended. Teenagers with severe depression, psychosis, or serious developmental delays, for example, may not only be overwhelmed or ostracized in a group but also may disrupt the progress of others. Groups may not be appropriate for youngsters with poor ability to tolerate limits and control impulses or who are psychologically fragile or in crisis. Likewise, severely shy or antagonistic youngsters may not fare well.

Assessment for the appropriateness of group therapy is not a luxury. With questionable candidates, it is sometimes useful to spend time in individual therapy preparing for the group experience. Despite this caution, it has been our experience that most teenagers who have been sexually abused are good candidates for group therapy and should participate if a group is available.

Abuse-focused groups can differ in duration (short term or long term), format (structured or unstructured), composition (coeducational vs. single gender), therapists (single vs. cotherapy; mixed vs. single gender), and membership (open-ended or closed). There is no accepted algorithm for selecting among these choices, leaving the matter to clinical judgment. The clinician must weigh the exigencies of the client population, overall treatment program, and strengths of available therapists. Our perspective is that shorter-term groups work well as an adjunct to individual therapy. We favor a set structure, closed membership, and a supportive and educative content. If the group is the core of the treatment program, however, there are advantages to longer-term, open-ended groups with looser structure and a more process-oriented format.

Teenagers will not tolerate too much structure for too long and will eventually usurp any efforts to constrain the topic of conversation or disallow time for free-form discussion of their day-to-day concerns. Nonetheless, nearly all groups benefit from some general boundaries (e.g., "We're mainly here to deal with sexual abuse") and a few established routines (Blick & Porter, 1982). Routines may be more important early in a group's life. Among adult survivors, less experienced patients have been found to do better in structured groups, whereas more experienced patients benefit from less structure (Alexander, Neimeyer, & Follette, 1991). A format we have found useful allows group members to define their own structure by selecting or requesting topics for sessions while generally maintaining a moderately unstructured framework.

There are minimal data to evaluate the efficacy of group therapy with adolescents. Particularly lacking are studies making adequate between-treatment and treatment/no-treatment comparisons. One study of adult survivors found that group treatment, irrespective of format, was superior to a waiting list control and that treatment gains were maintained at 6-month follow-up (Alexander, Neimeyer, Follette, Moore, & Harter, 1989).

Acute Inpatient Treatment

Sexually abused adolescents are generally admitted to inpatient psychiatric facilities for the same reasons nonabused teenagers are: suicide attempts, uncontrolled substance abuse, or severe behavior problems (Emslie & Rosenfeld, 1983). Unfortunately, some are inappropriately admitted simply on the basis of their history as abuse victims and the emotional upset that accompanies disclosure. Estimates vary regarding how many hospitalized teens have been abused. One survey of 110 inpatient facilities found histories of abuse in 48% of girls and 16% of boys (Kohan, Potheir, & Norbeck, 1986). Forty-two percent of teenage boys and 71% to 90% of teenage girls in inpatient substance abuse treatment report histories of childhood sexual abuse (Rohsenow, Corbett, & Devine, 1988). Findings suggest that for more than two thirds of physically and sexually abused teens in residential substance abuse treatment, abuse was not previously reported (Cavaiola & Schiff, 1988). It is common for disclosure to first occur during hospitalization.

In an acute inpatient setting, it is important to set realistic treatment goals due to the short amount of time available for treatment, often around 2 to 3 weeks. Working through abuse trauma and its associated defenses is generally not feasible in that limited time. It is a mistake to "work on" abuse issues before hospitalized youngsters can maintain self-control. The goal within this time frame is to assist the teenager with effective coping. Two goals that can be addressed during acute hospitalization are developing a feeling of personal safety and increased self-control (Hartman & Burgess, 1988). To restore some feeling of predictability and safety, it is critical that the inpatient unit maintain a reliable structure and provide calm, unintrusive nurturance and support. Once the young person feels safe, treatment can focus on self-regulation and problem-solving strategies to restore behavioral and emotional self-control (McCloskey & Bulechek, 1996). Structured teenage groups provide support, normalization, and information (Sturkie, 1983). Daily individual therapy can use any of the cognitive-behavioral techniques described earlier. In some cases, parent-child sessions help ensure that adequate support is maintained outside the hospital.

Two goals that can be addressed during acute hospitalization are developing a feeling of personal safety and increased self-control.

Once a safety plan is in place and adequate self-control achieved, it is usually time for discharge. If possible, the hospital should be involved in developing a multidisciplinary or multi-agency plan to ensure that gains are maintained and appropriate follow-up treatment for the adolescent and family is instituted.

Treatment Compliance

Not all teenagers who have been sexually abused comply with recommendations for treatment. The same is true for parents of victims. The reasons for lack of compliance are complex. Trauma avoidance for both the teenager and the parents undoubtedly plays a role in some cases. In incest cases, a court order for treatment is necessary in many cases (Chaffin, 1992; Ryan, 1986). Haskett and colleagues found that approximately 35% of sexually abused children and adolescents did not appear for their initial appointment (Haskett, Nowlan, Hutcheson, & Whitworth, 1991). In several studies, African American children were more likely not to appear at appointments than Caucasians (41% vs. 17%), a finding that is consistent with literature reflecting a trend for people of color to use informal helpers (i.e., ministers, neighbors, family) during times of crisis rather than the formal mental health system (Chatters, Taylor, & Neighbors, 1989; Neighbors, 1984). It is critical that treatment delivery systems for abused teenagers and their families become culturally competent and relevant to diverse groups of people.

When parents, typically mothers, have also been sexually abused, the parents may need to work through the effects of their own abuse so they can help their children (Damon & Waterman, 1986). There is sometimes an impaired relationship between victims and their mothers, especially in incest cases, and it is often unclear whether symptoms in these youth are directly a result of the abuse or more globally a by-product of family pathology (Berliner, 1991). Involvement of parents in treatment facilitates the identification and remediation of these issues.

Conclusion

We were continuously struck in writing this chapter with the lack of well-controlled treatment studies with regard to sexually abused adolescents. Beyond the global question, "Does treatment help?" unanswered questions abound. What treatments help with what sorts of youngsters in what sorts of settings and circumstances? How do cultural factors affect treatment outcomes? While we wait for answers to these questions, our hats are off to the thousands of professionals working with limited knowledge to help teenage victims of abuse.

References

Alexander, P., Neimeyer, R., & Follette, V. (1991). Group therapy for women sexually abused as children: A controlled study and investigation of individual differences. *Journal of Interpersonal Violence, 6,* 218-231.

Alexander, P., Neimeyer, R., Follette, V., Moore, M., & Harter, S. (1989). A comparison of group treatments of women sexually abused as children. *Journal of Consulting and Clinical Psychology, 57,* 479-483.

American Professional Society on the Abuse of Children (APSAC). (1990). *Guidelines for psychosocial evaluation of suspected sexual abuse in young children.* Chicago: Author.

Azima, F. J. C., & Dies, K. R. (1989). Clinical research in adolescent group psychotherapy: Status, guidelines, and directions. In F. J. C. Azima & L. H. Richmond (Eds.), *Adolescent group psychotherapy* (pp. 193-223). Madison, CT: International Universities Press.

Beitchman, J., Zucker, K., Hood, J., da Costa, G., Akman, D., & Cassavia, E. (1992). A review of the long-term effects of child sexual abuse. *Child Abuse & Neglect, 16,* 101-118.

Bem, S. L. (1974). The measurement of psychological androgeny. *Journal of Consulting and Clinical Psychology, 42,* 155-162.

Berdie, J., Berdie, M., Wexler, S., & Fisher, B. (1983). *An empirical study of families involved in adolescent maltreatment.* San Francisco: URSA Institute.

Berliner, L. (1991). Therapy with victimized children and their families. *New Directions for Mental Health Services, 51,* 29-46.

Berliner, L., & Wheeler, J. (1987). Treating the effects of sexual abuse on children. *Journal of Interpersonal Violence, 2,* 415-434.

Blick, L., & Porter, F. (1982). Group therapy with female adolescent incest victims. In S. Sgroi (Ed.), *Handbook of clinical intervention in child sexual abuse*. Lexington, MA: Lexington Books.

Blythe, B., Hodges, V., & Guterman, N. (1990). Intervention for maltreated adolescents. In M. Rothery & G. Cameron (Eds.), *Child maltreatment: Expanding our concept of helping* (pp. 33-47). Hillsdale, NJ: Lawrence Erlbaum.

Briere, J. (1989). *Therapy for adults molested as children: Beyond survival*. New York: Springer.

Briere, J. (1992). *Child abuse trauma: Theory and treatment of the lasting effects*. Newbury Park, CA: Sage.

Briere, J. (1996). *Trauma Symptom Checklist for Children: Professional manual*. Odessa, FL: Psychological Assessment Resources.

Brooks-Gunn, J., & Furstenberg, F. (1989). Adolescent sexual behavior. *American Psychologist, 44*, 249-257.

Cavaiola, A., & Schiff, M. (1988). Behavioral sequelae of physical and/or sexual abuse in adolescents. *Child Abuse & Neglect, 12*, 181-188.

Celano, M. (1992). A developmental model of victims' internal attributions of responsibility for sexual abuse. *Journal of Interpersonal Violence, 7*, 57-69.

Chaffin, M. (1992). Factors associated with treatment compliance and progress among intrafamilial sexual abusers. *Child Abuse & Neglect, 16*, 251-264.

Chatters, L., Taylor, R., & Neighbors, H. (1989). Size of informal helper network mobilized during a serious personal problem among Black Americans. *Journal of Marriage and the Family, 51*, 667-676.

Claussen, A. H., & Crittenden, P. M. (1991). Physical and psychological maltreatment: Relations among the types of maltreatment. *Child Abuse & Neglect, 15*, 5-18.

Cohen, J. A., Berliner, L., & March, J. S. (2000). Treatment of children and adolescents. In E. B. Foa, T. M. Keane, & M. J. Friedman (Eds.), *Effective treatments for PTSD: Practice guidelines from the International Society for the Traumatic Stress Studies* (pp. 106-138). New York: Guilford.

Collings, S., & Payne, M. (1991). Attribution of causal and moral responsibility to victims of father-daughter incest: An exploratory examination of five factors. *Child Abuse & Neglect, 15*, 513-521.

Coons, P., Bowman, E., Pellow, T., & Schneider, P. (1989). Posttraumatic aspects of the treatment of victims of sexual abuse and incest. *Psychiatric Clinics of North America, 12*, 325-335.

Cornman, B. (1989). Group treatment for female adolescent sexual abuse victims. *Issues in Mental Health Nursing, 10*, 261-271.

Crockett, L., & Petersen, A. (1987). Pubertal status and psychosocial development: Findings from the early adolescence study. In R. Lerner & T. Foch (Eds.), *Biological-psychosocial interactions in early adolescence: A life-span perspective* (pp. 173-188). Hillsdale, NJ: Lawrence Erlbaum.

Damon, L., & Waterman, J. (1986). Parallel group treatment of children and their mothers. In K. MacFarlane & J. Waterman (Eds.), *Sexual abuse of young children* (pp. 244-298). New York: Guilford.

De Bellis, M. D., & Putnam, F. W. (1994). The psychobiology of childhood maltreatment. *Child and Adolescent Psychiatric Clinics of North America, 3*, 663-678.

Deblinger, E. (1991). Diagnosis of posttraumatic stress disorder in childhood. *Violence Update, 2*, 9-11.

Deblinger, E., McLeer, S., & Henry, D. (1990). Cognitive behavioral treatment for sexually abused children suffering posttraumatic stress: Preliminary findings. *Journal of the American Academy of Child and Adolescent Psychiatry, 29*, 747-752.

Elkind, D. (1967). Egocentrism in adolescence. *Child Development, 38*, 1025-1034.

Elkind, D. (1978). Understanding the young adolescent. *Adolescence, 13*, 127-134.

Emslie, G., & Rosenfeld, A. (1983). Incest reported by children and adolescents hospitalized for severe psychiatric problems. *American Journal of Psychiatry, 140*, 708-711.

Enright, R., Lapsley, D., & Shukla, D. (1979). Adolescent egocentrism in early and late adolescence. *Adolescence, 14*, 687-696.

Evans, J., Briere, J., Boggiano, A., & Barrett, M. (1994, January). *Reliability and validity of the trauma symptom checklist for children in a normal child sample*. Paper presented at the San Diego Conference on Responding to Child Maltreatment, San Diego, CA.

Everson, M. D., Hunter, W. M., Runyon, D. K., Edelsohn, G. A., & Coulter, M. L. (1989). Maternal support following disclosure of incest. *American Journal of Orthopsychiatry, 59*, 197-207.

Faller, K. (1991). Treatment of boy victims of sexual abuse. *APSAC Advisor, 4*(4), 7-8.

Fiering, C., Taska, L., & Lewis, M. (1998). The role of shame and attributional style in children's and adolescents' adaptation to sexual abuse. *Child Maltreatment, 3*, 129-142.

Finkelhor, D. (1995). The victimization of children: A developmental perspective. *American Journal of Orthopsychiatry, 65*, 177-193.

Finkelhor, D., & Dziuba-Leatherman, J. (1994). Victimization of children. *American Psychologist, 49,* 173-184.

Fraiberg, S. (Ed.). (1983). *Clinical studies in infant mental health: The first year of life.* New York: Basic Books.

Friedrich, W. (1990). *Psychotherapy of sexually abused children and their families.* New York: Norton.

Furniss, T., Bingley-Miller, L., & Van Elburg, A. (1988). Goal-oriented group treatment for sexually abused adolescent girls. *British Journal of Psychiatry, 152,* 97-106.

Gagliano, C. (1987). Group treatment for sexually abused girls. *Social Casework, 68,* 102-108.

Garbarino, J. (1989). Troubled youth, troubled families: The dynamics of adolescent maltreatment. In D. Cicchetti & V. Carlson (Eds.), *Child maltreatment: Theory and research on the causes and consequences of child abuse and neglect* (pp. 685-706). New York: Cambridge University Press.

Gil, E. (1991). *The healing power of play: Working with abused children.* New York: Guilford.

Gil, E. (1996). *Treating abused adolescents.* New York: Guilford.

Gomes-Schwartz, B., Horowitz, J., & Cardarelli, A. (1990). *Child sexual abuse: The initial effects.* Newbury Park, CA: Sage.

Gomes-Schwartz, B., Horowitz, J., & Sauzier, M. (1985). Severity of emotional distress among sexually abused preschool, school-age, and adolescent children. *Hospital and Community Psychiatry, 36,* 503-508.

Goodwin, J., & Talwar, N. (1989). Group psychotherapy for victims of incest. *Psychiatric Clinics of North America, 12,* 279-293.

Hansen, D. J., Giacoletti, A. M., & Nangle, D. W. (1995). Social interactions and adjustment. In V. B. Van Hasselt & M. Hersen (Eds.), *Handbook of adolescent psychopathology: A guide to diagnosis and treatment* (pp. 102-129). New York: Macmillan.

Harrison, P. A., Hoffman, N. G., & Edwall, G. E. (1989). Sexual abuse correlates: Similarities between male and female adolescents in chemical dependency treatment. *Journal of Adolescent Research, 4,* 382-399.

Hart, S., & Brassard, M. (1990). Psychological maltreatment of children. In R. Ammerman & M. Hersen (Eds.), *Treatment of family violence* (pp. 77-112). New York: John Wiley.

Hartman, C., & Burgess, A. (1988). Information processing of trauma: Case application of a model. *Journal of Interpersonal Violence, 3,* 443-457.

Haskett, M., Nowlan, N., Hutcheson, J., & Whitworth, J. (1991). Factors associated with successful entry into therapy in child sexual abuse cases. *Child Abuse & Neglect, 15,* 467-476.

Hayes, C. (1987). *Risking the future: Adolescent sexuality, pregnancy, and childbearing.* Washington, DC: National Academy Press.

Hibbard, R., Ingersoll, G., & Orr, D. (1990). Behavioral risk, emotional risk, and child abuse among adolescents in a nonclinical setting. *Pediatrics, 86,* 896-901.

Hunter, M. (1990). *The sexually abused male: Application of treatment strategies* (Vol. 2). Lexington, MA: Lexington Books.

Jessor, R., & Jessor, L. (1977). *Problem behavior and psychological development.* New York: Academic Press.

Johnson, B., & Kenkel, M. (1991). Stress, coping and adjustment in female adolescent incest victims. *Child Abuse & Neglect, 15,* 293-305.

Kandel, D., & Lesser, G. (1972). *Youth in two worlds.* San Francisco: Jossey-Bass.

Kilpatrick, D., Acierno, R., Saunders, B., Resnick, H. S., Best, C. L., & Schnurr, P. P. (2000). Risk factors for adolescent substance abuse and dependence: Data from a national sample. *Journal of Consulting & Clinical Psychology, 68,* 19-30.

Kohan, M., Potheir, P., & Norbeck, J. (1986). Hospitalized children with history of sexual abuse: Incidence and care issues. *American Journal of Orthopsychiatry, 57,* 258-264.

Lanktree, C. (1994, January). *Therapy for sexually abused children: An outcome study.* Paper presented at the San Diego Conference on Responding to Child Maltreatment, San Diego, CA.

Leitenberg, H., Greenwald, E., & Cado, S. (1992). A retrospective study of long-term methods of coping with having been sexually abused during childhood. *Child Abuse & Neglect, 16,* 399-407.

Levine, S. (1987). The myths and needs of contemporary youth. *Adolescent Psychiatry, 14,* 48-62.

Lipovsky, J. (1991). Posttraumatic stress disorder in children. *Family and Community Health, 14,* 42-51.

Lipovsky, J. (1992, February). *Research in action: Children in court.* Paper presented at the Eighth Annual National Symposium on Child Sexual Abuse, Huntsville, AL.

Lourie, I. S. (1977). The phenomenon of the abused adolescent: A clinical study. *Victimology: An International Journal, 2,* 268-276.

Mannarino, A., & Cohen, J. A. (1996). Abuse-related attributions and perceptions, general attributions, and locus of control of sexually abused girls. *Journal of Interpersonal Violence, 11,* 162-180.

Mannarino, A., Cohen, J., & Berman, S. (1994). The children's attributions and perceptions scale: A new measure of sexual abuse-related factors. *Journal of Clinical Child Psychology, 23,* 204-211.

Marcia, J. E. (1994). The empirical study of ego identity. In H. A. Bosma (Ed.), *Identity and development: An interdisciplinary approach* (pp. 67-80). Thousand Oaks, CA: Sage.

McCloskey, J. C., & Bulechek, G. M. (1996). *Nursing interventions classification (NIC): Iowa intervention project.* St. Louis, MO: Mosby.

McCormack, A., Burgess, A., & Hartman, C. (1988). Familial abuse and posttraumatic stress disorder. *Journal of Traumatic Stress, 1,* 231-242.

Meiselman, K. (1990). *Resolving the trauma of incest: Reintegration therapy with survivors.* San Francisco: Jossey-Bass.

Morrow, K. (1991). Attributions of female adolescent incest victims regarding their molestation. *Child Abuse & Neglect, 15,* 477-483.

Murphy, S., Kilpatrick, D., Amick-McMullan, A., Veronen, L., Paduhovich, J., Best, C., Villeponteaux, L., & Saunders, B. (1988). Current psychological functioning of child sexual assault survivors. *Journal of Interpersonal Violence, 3,* 55-79.

Neighbors, H. (1984). Professional help use among Black Americans: Implications for unmet need. *American Journal of Community Psychology, 12,* 551-565.

Offer, D., & Boxer, A. (1991). Normal adolescent development: Empirical research findings. In M. Lewis (Ed.), *Child and adolescent psychiatry: A comprehensive textbook.* Baltimore: Williams & Wilkins.

Offer, D., Ostrov, E., & Howard, K. (1981). The mental health professional's concept of the normal adolescent. *Archives of General Psychiatry, 38,* 149-152.

Petersen, A. (1988). Adolescent development. *Annual Review of Psychology, 39,* 583-607.

Petersen, A. C., & Hamburg, B. A. (1986). Adolescence: A developmental approach to problems and psychopathology. *Behavior Therapy, 17,* 480-499.

Phelan, P. (1987). Incest: Socialization within a treatment program. *American Journal of Orthopsychiatry, 57,* 84-92.

Porter, E. (1986). *Treating the young male victim of sexual assault: Issues and intervention strategies.* Syracuse, NY: Safer Society Press.

Powers, S., Hauser, S., & Kilner, L. (1989). Adolescent mental health. *American Psychologist, 44,* 200-208.

Rew, L., & Esparza, D. (1990). Barriers to disclosure among sexually abused male children: Implications for nursing practice. *Journal of Child and Adolescent Psychiatric and Mental Health Nursing, 3,* 120-127.

Richardson, M. F., Meredith, W., & Abbot, D. A. (1993). Sex-typed role in male adolescent sexual abuse survivors. *Journal of Family Violence, 8,* 89-100.

Rohsenow, D., Corbett, R., & Devine, D. (1988). Molested as children: A hidden contribution to substance abuse? *Journal of Substance Abuse Treatment, 5,* 13-18.

Rothbaum, B. O., Meadows, E. A., Resnick, P., & Foy, D. W. (2000). Cognitive-behavioral therapy. In E. B. Foa, T. M. Keane, & M. J. Friedman (Eds.), *Effective treatments for PTSD: Practice guidelines from the International Society for Traumatic Stress Studies* (pp. 61-83). New York: Guilford.

Runtz, M., & Briere, J. (1986). Adolescent "acting-out" and childhood history of sexual abuse. *Journal of Interpersonal Violence, 1,* 326-334.

Russell, D. (1986). *The secret trauma: Incest in the lives of girls and women.* New York: Basic Books.

Ryan, T. (1991). The juvenile sex offender's family. In G. D. Ryan & S. L. Lane (Eds.), *Juvenile sexual offending: Causes, consequences, and correction* (pp. 143-160). Lexington, MA: Lexington Books.

Ryan, T. (1986). Problems, errors and opportunities in the treatment of father-daughter incest. *Journal of Interpersonal Violence, 1,* 113-124.

Saunders, B. (1992, March). *Treatment of child sexual assault: A family systems-multicomponent approach.* Paper presented at the annual meeting of the South Carolina Chapter of the National Association of Social Workers, Columbia, SC.

Sedney, M., & Brooks, B. (1984). Factors associated with a history of childhood sexual experience in a nonclinical female population. *Journal of the American Academy of Child Psychiatry, 23,* 215-218.

Shapiro, S., & Dominiak, G. (1990). Common psychological defenses seen in the treatment of sexually abused adolescents. *American Journal of Psychotherapy, 44,* 68-74.

Singer, M. I., Song, L., & Ochberg, B. (1994). Sexual victimization and substance abuse in psychiatrically hospitalized adolescents. *Social Work Research, 18,* 97-103.

Sirles, F., Smith, J., & Kusama, H. (1989). Psychiatric status of intrafamilial child sexual abuse victims. *Journal of the American Academy of Child and Adolescent Psychiatry, 28,* 225-229.

Sorenson, T., & Snow, B. (1991). How children tell: The process of disclosure in child sexual abuse. *Child Welfare, 70,* 3-15.

Sturkie, K. (1983). Structured group treatment for sexually abused children. *Health and Social Work, 8,* 299-308.

Sullivan, P., Scanlan, J., Brookhouser, P., Schulte, L., & Knutson, J. (1992). The effects of psychotherapy on behavior problems of sexually abused deaf children. *Child Abuse & Neglect, 16,* 297-307.

Tanner, J. (1981). *A history of the study of human growth.* Cambridge, MA: Harvard University Press.

Tanner, J. M. (1998). Sequence, tempo, and individual variation in growth and development of boys and girls aged twelve to sixteen. In R. E. Muus & D. H. Porton (Eds.), *Adolescent behavior and society: A book of readings* (5th ed., pp. 34-46). New York: McGraw-Hill.

Tedesco, J., & Schnell, S. (1987). Children's reactions to sex abuse investigation and litigation. *Child Abuse & Neglect, 11,* 267-272.

U.S. Department of Health and Human Services, Administration on Children, Youth and Families. (1999). *Child maltreatment 1997: Reports from the states to the National Child Abuse and Neglect Data System.* Washington, DC: Government Printing Office.

Watkins, B., & Bentovim, A. (1992). The sexual abuse of male children and adolescents: A review of current research. *Journal of Child Psychology and Psychiatry, 33,* 197-248.

Williamson, J. M., Borduin, C. M., & Howe, B. A. (1991). The ecology of adolescent maltreatment: A multilevel examination of adolescent physical abuse, sexual abuse, and neglect. *Journal of Consulting and Clinical Psychology, 59,* 449-457.

Wyatt, G. (1988). The relationship between child sexual abuse and adolescent sexual functioning in Afro-American and White American women. *Annals of the New York Academy of Sciences, 528,* 111-122.

Wyatt, G., & Mickey, M. (1987). Ameliorating the effects of child sexual abuse: An exploratory study of support by parents and others. *Journal of Interpersonal Violence, 2,* 403-414.

10

Treating Adult Survivors of Severe Childhood Abuse and Neglect

Further Development of an Integrative Model

JOHN BRIERE

his chapter outlines an integrated approach to the treatment of adults severely abused or neglected as children. The theory on which it is based, referred to as the *self-trauma model* (e.g., Briere, 1992, 1996), incorporates aspects of trauma theory as well as cognitive, behavioral, and self-psychology theory. Although this perspective is implicitly cognitive-behavioral, it also may be understood as an attempt to rework and reconceptualize psychodynamic therapy to encompass empirically based principles as they relate to child abuse victims. The current chapter especially expands the cognitive components of self-trauma theory, incorporating newer ideas in the areas of suppressed or "deep" cognitive activation (e.g., Wegner & Smart, 1997), relational schemas (e.g., Baldwin, Fehr, Keedian, Seidel, & Thompson, 1993), and the role of early attachment experiences on thoughts, feelings, and memories (e.g., Simpson & Rholes, 1998). In addition, this analysis takes as its foundation a growing awareness in cognitive-behavioral circles that implicit memories and processes are—at minimum—as important as explicit ones and that emotion is as important as cognition in understanding and treating anxiety-based disorders (Foa & Kozak, 1986; Samoilov & Goldfried, 2000; Westen, 2000). The implications of this model are presented in terms of the specific process, content, and goals of abuse-relevant psychotherapy.

The Phenomenology of Child Abuse and Neglect and Its Effects

As indicated in other chapters of this book, child abuse and neglect are unfortunately prevalent in North America. Beyond the moral and humanitarian objections that must be raised against child maltreatment, it is now becoming clear that childhood victimization is a substantial risk factor for the development of later mental health problems. The specific psychological impacts of early maltreatment experiences vary as a function of a number of variables, including temperament and other biopsychological factors, family environment, security of parent-child attachment, and previous history of support or abuse. In addition, it appears that the specific type of child abuse is, to some extent, related to the form of subsequent psychological distress or disorder.

Abuse Types

For the purposes of discussion here, these various types of maltreatment will be characterized as acts of *omission* and *commission*.

Acts of Omission

Most typically, child maltreatment in this category consists of psychological neglect. Psychological neglect of children generally refers to sustained parental nonresponsiveness and psychological or physical unavailability, such that the child is deprived of normal psychological stimulation, soothing, and support. One of the most obvious impacts of child neglect is its tendency to decrease the extent to which secure parent-child attachment can occur (see Chapter 1, this volume). As a result, the neglected child will not be as likely as others to encounter benign interactive experiences that teach self-awareness, self-security, positive views of others, and the development of regulated affective responses to interpersonal challenges.

In addition to the obvious effects of parental nonavailability on intra- and interpersonal learning, psychological neglect is thought to produce acute psychological distress (Bowlby, 1988). Because children are

social beings with profound biopsychological needs for contact comfort, nurturance, and love, sustained neglect can result in painful feelings of what appear to be deprivation and abandonment. This acute distress, in turn, may affect the child's development in many of the same ways described below for caretaker acts of commission. Also present, however, may be a growing sense of psychological emptiness and neediness and a general tendency later in life to be especially sensitive to the possibility of abandonment or rejection by others.

Acts of Commission

In contrast to acts of omission, acts of commission involve actual abusive behaviors directed toward the child. These acts, whether physical, sexual, or psychological, can produce longstanding interpersonal difficulties, as well as distorted thinking patterns, emotional disturbance, and posttraumatic stress.

When such acts occur early in life, they are especially likely to motivate the development of avoidance strategies that allow the child to function despite inescapable emotional pain (Putnam, 1997). Faced with parental violence, the child may develop a style of relating whereby he or she psychologically attenuates or avoids certain attachment interactions with a given abusive caretaker (Bowlby, 1988). Although this defense protects the child, to some extent, from overwhelming distress and distorted environmental input, it also tends to reduce his or her access to any positive attachment stimuli that might be available in the environment (Briere, 1992). This response, in turn, further deprives the child of normal attachment-related learning and development, reinforces avoidance as a primary response style, and may partially replicate the difficulties associated with neglect-related attachment deprivation.

Together, early acts of omission and commission serve as an etiologic reservoir for the development of later psychological disorder. Some of these responses are the direct result of psychological injury, whereas others appear to represent coping responses to the emotional pain associated with abuse and neglect. Based on the existing literature, recent scientific developments, and clinical experience, a hypothesized series of these traumagenic mechanisms are presented below.

Abuse-Related Symptom Development

For the purposes of this chapter, the primary impacts of childhood abuse and neglect on later (i.e., adolescent and adult) psychological functioning can be divided into six areas: (a) negative preverbal assumptions and relational schemas, (b) conditioned emotional responses (CERs) to abuse-related stimuli, (c) implicit/sensory memories of abuse, (d) narrative/autobiographical memories of maltreatment, (e) suppressed or "deep" cognitive structures involving abuse-related material, and (f) inadequately developed affect regulation skills. There are undoubtedly other major abuse effects, as noted throughout this volume, although many may be secondary to these six.

Preverbal Assumptions Regarding Self and Others

One of the earliest impacts of abuse and neglect is thought to be on the child's internal representations of self and others. These representations generally arise in the context of the early parent-child relationship, wherein the child makes inferences based on how he or she is treated by his or her caretakers. In the case of abuse or neglect, these inferences are likely to be negative. For example, the young child who is being maltreated often infers negative self- and other-characteristics from such acts. The child may conclude that he or she must be intrinsically unacceptable or malignant to deserve such "punishment" or neglect or may come to feel helpless, inadequate, or weak. In addition, the abused child may begin to view others as inherently dangerous, rejecting, or unavailable.

Although typically considered to be cognitive sequelae, these early inferences and perceptions appear to form basic beliefs that function more as a general model of self and others than as actual thought, per se. Instead, some theorists refer to such intrinsic self-other perceptions as *internal working models* (Bowlby, 1982) or core *relational schemas* (Baldwin, 1992), especially when they arise from child-caretaker attachment interactions in the early years of life. This notion of internalized models or schemas emphasizes the structural or organizing aspects of this

phenomenon, as opposed to the presence of discrete cognitions or episodic memories. These core beliefs and assumptions are often relatively nonresponsive to superficial verbal reassurance or the expressed alternate views of others later in life because they are not, in fact, verbally mediated. For example, the individual who believes, at a basic level, that he or she is unlikable or unattractive to others or that others are not to be trusted will not easily change such views based on others' declarations that the person is valued by them or that they can be relied on.

The quality and valence of these core schemas intrinsically affect the individual's later capacity to form and maintain meaningful attachments with other people. Such individuals may find themselves in conflictual or chaotic relationships later in life, have problems with forming intimate adult attachments, and engage in behaviors that are likely to threaten or disrupt close relationships with others (Collins & Read, 1990; Levy & Davis, 1988; Simpson, 1990). Generally, early childhood abuse and neglect have been associated with insecure attachment styles in adulthood (Alexander, 1992; Coe, Dalenberg, Aransky, & Reto, 1995; Styron & Janoff-Bulman, 1997). Insecure attachment, in turn, can be divided into three types: fearful (involving a high need for interpersonal acceptance and affirmation and yet avoidance of intimacy), preoccupied (involving similar high needs for validation and acceptance but with a tendency to be preoccupied with attaining such affirmation through relationships), and avoidant/dismissing (involving avoidance of interpersonal attachments and high needs for self-reliance). These patterns of relating are likely to represent, at least in part, behavioral outcomes of the implicit relational schemas or structures described earlier, wherein early life experiences (including child abuse and neglect) produce expectations about self and others that are played out in the interpersonal sphere (Baldwin et al., 1993). Interestingly, it appears that many individuals have different attachment styles in different situations, partially depending on what relational memories or schemas are cued or "primed" at any given period of time (Baldwin, Keelan, Fehr, Enns, & Koh-Rangarajoo, 1996).

In addition to attachment style–related schemas, it is clear that abuse and neglect early in life can produce more general relational disturbance. Pearlman and Saakvitne

(1995), for example, suggested that trauma during the early years can result in chronic, negative expectations and perceptions around issues of safety, trust/dependency, independence, power, esteem, and intimacy. These negative schemas, in turn, may be easily activated by interpersonal stimuli in the current environment, as noted earlier.

Because such disturbance is typically at the implicit, nonverbal level and is primarily based in safety and attachment needs, these relational schemas may not be evident except in negative or potentially threatening interactions with others, at which time these underlying cognitive structures may be cued and activated with resultant interpersonal difficulties (Simpson & Rholes, 1994). For example, an individual who—by virtue of early parental abandonment and rejection—has developed a preoccupied attachment style may relate relatively well in a given occupational or intimate context until he or she encounters stimuli that suggest some level of rejection or abandonment. At this point, he or she may respond in the context of an activated gestalt of archaic emotional responses and cognitions that, although excessive in the immediate context, are appropriate to the reactivated feelings and thoughts of an abused or neglected child. This gestalt, in turn, may motivate behavior that, although intended to ensure proximity and maintain the relationship, is so "primitive" (i.e., characterized by child-level responses and demands) and affect laden that it challenges or even destroys that relationship.

Conditioned Associations Between Abuse Stimuli and Emotional Distress

Perhaps the most basic learning that occurs during child maltreatment is that of classically conditioned associations between abuse stimuli and negative emotions. Children who are beaten, repetitively screamed at, sexually abused, or abandoned typically will come to associate aspects of the abuser (e.g., his or her sex, age, physical characteristics, or escalating behaviors) with fear and other emotional distress. These CERs may be embedded in generalized "fear structures" (Foa & Kozak, 1986), leading the child to experience distress in response to seeing any male, authority figure, angry person, and so on. In some cases, this generalization will result in negative CERs

to a variety of potential interpersonal relationships, especially those involving intimacy, closeness, or vulnerability.

These classically conditioned responses are not encoded as autobiographical memories but rather as simple associations between certain stimuli (e.g., the sudden raising of a hand) and certain responses (e.g., fear or flinching). As a result, they are not "remembered," per se, but rather are evoked or triggered by events that are similar to the original abuse context, including, as it turns out, sensory or autobiographical memories of that abuse. Later in life, exposure to such abuse-reminiscent stimuli and memories may produce strong, seemingly inappropriate, or "out-of-the-blue" negative affects that, given the nonverbal nature of the conditioning, may not even be understandable to the former victim, let alone others in his or her environment. When triggered CERs occur in the obvious context of a traumatic stressor (e.g., sudden fear when seeing a car similar to the vehicle that hit one in an accident), they are considered to be one of the "B" (reliving) criteria of PTSD. In other cases, however, the conditioned negative affect will be to early relational events that might not be definable as traumatic stressors.

Implicit/Sensory Memories

Frequently, memories of especially traumatic events, including severe child abuse, are reexperienced later in life on a sensory level, for example, as flashbacks. This is thought to be due, in part, to the fact that those brain and psychological systems responsible for directing the encoding and early organization and processing of explicit, narrative memory material may be flooded (or at least bypassed) by overwhelming emotional input during severe abuse or trauma—resulting in less integrated, primarily sensory (as opposed to verbally or autobiographically mediated) recollections on exposure to trauma-reminiscent stimuli (Metcalfe & Jacobs, 1996; Siegel, 1999; van der Kolk, McFarlane, & Weisaeth, 1996). In addition, traumatic experiences that occurred prior to the child's acquisition of language necessarily will be nonnarrative, typically sensorimotor in nature.

As opposed to narrative memories, implicit, sensory recollection is generally devoid of autobiographical material and is often experienced as an intrusion of unexpected sensation (e.g., sights or sounds of an event) rather than of remembering, per se. Although sensory reexperiencing is often accompanied by the associated emotions that were involved at the time of the abuse, the sensory memory of the maltreatment experience and the affects conditioned to the memory (i.e., CERs) are likely to be separate phenomena (Davis, 1992; LeDoux, 1995). In many cases, sensory memories become the stimuli that release strong CERs, which can, in turn, reinstate enough of the context of the original abuse to trigger additional reexperiencing. As will be described below, the combination of triggered sensory memories and associated negative affects is often characteristic of posttraumatic stress.

Narrative/Autobiographical Memories

Memories of abuse and trauma also may be encoded at the explicit, autobiographical level. In this instance, similar stimuli in the environment can trigger recall of autobiographical memories that, in turn, then activate negative emotional responses, cognitions, and other, more implicit memories. Thus, for example, a man may be criticized by his employer in a way that stimulates autobiographical memories of similar verbal abuse by his father when he was a child. These memories, in turn, may activate (a) anger and fear that remain conditioned to reminders of being repeatedly berated, (b) broader negative self-perceptions and schemas associated with these stimuli (e.g., of being bad or inadequate), and (c) intrusive, sensory/implicit recollections of aspects of the abuse experiences (e.g., his father's rageful face). These additional associations and responses may serve to reinstate the cognitive-emotional context of the original abuse, thereby providing additional stimuli that, in turn, activate further autobiographical, sensory, and cognitive reactions, each with its associated CERs.

Clinical experience suggests that for those with significant childhood trauma, autobiographically encoded memories are distressing primarily for their ability to activate related implicit memory intrusions, relational schemas, and CERs, as described earlier. In other words, explicit, verbally mediated memory material may be most aversive for its ability to activate associated nonverbal feelings, implicit/sensory memories, and abuse-related schemas. Although

this is distressing for the child abuse survivor, it will be suggested later in this chapter that the therapist can use this very phenomenon to activate otherwise less available implicit and schematic childhood memories during treatment.

Suppressed or "Deep" Cognitive Structures

Even some autobiographical, narrative memories may not be available to the survivor's surface awareness. In this regard, work in cognitive experimental psychology indicates that some verbally mediated, otherwise normally available cognitive material can be excluded from everyday "surface" thinking, instead operating at "deep" (i.e., nonconscious) levels (Wegner & Erber, 1992). These cognitions usually are negative and distress producing and are thought to be actively suppressed as a way to reduce dysphoria (Wegner & Smart, 1997). When suppressed thoughts are activated, such that they influence other thoughts or motivate behavior, the phenomenon is referred to as *deep cognitive activation*. For the purposes of this chapter, these suppressed but still influential thoughts—many of which appear to form associational networks and, on activation, trigger associated emotional responses (Wenzlaff, Wegner, & Klein, 1991)—will be referred to here as *deep cognitive structures*.

Thought suppression is a more difficult task than otherwise might be assumed, however. By virtue of what are called ironic processes (the mind's monitoring of whether it has successfully suppressed material ironically defeats suppression by keeping the material in mind), deep cognitive material typically presses for returned awareness (Wegner, 1994). It appears, however, that individuals with a history of continued avoidance (e.g., some abuse survivors) are able to suppress material for considerably longer periods of time (Kelly & Kahn, 1994; Wegner & Gold, 1995), probably through the use of distraction and—although not considered as such in the cognitive literature—dissociative compartmentalization of unwanted cognitive material. Even the defensive strategies of "expert" suppressors, however, can be relatively easily overwhelmed by exposure to stimuli in the environment that are reminiscent in some way of the suppressed material. This may be especially true for thoughts and memories of prior painful interpersonal experiences (i.e., those especially distressing to the individual and thus more likely to be suppressed) that are activated by later, similar stimuli in the interpersonal domain. For example, an individual whose parents were rejecting and discounting of him or her may have deep (not consciously perceived in the untriggered state) cognitive structures/memories of painful rejection experiences that, in turn, may be activated later in life by perceptions (real or otherwise) of criticism by significant others.

Because both tend to operate outside of conscious awareness, deep cognitive structures and the previously described relational schemas may appear similar. However, relational schemas are generally acquired much earlier in childhood, typically during the period of greatest parent-child attachment sensitivity, and involve memory that is intrinsically nonverbal, whereas deep cognitive structures are generally later, autobiographical memories that are actively suppressed for defensive reasons. Nevertheless, both operate as unconscious processes, and both can be triggered by environmental (typically relational) stimuli that are in some way similar to the original abusive context.

Interference in Development of Affect Regulation/Tolerance Skills

A final impact of severe childhood maltreatment appears to be that of insufficiently developed affect regulation (Pearlman, 1998). This concept refers to the individual's capacity to control and tolerate strong (especially negative) affect, without resorting to avoidance strategies, such as dissociation, substance abuse, or external tension-reducing behavior (Briere, 1992). This capacity is thought to develop in the early years of life (Bowlby, 1988), although it usually continues to develop thereafter. The normal development of affect regulation capacities is briefly described here, so that its misdevelopment in the severely abused can be more clearly appreciated. In addition, it will be suggested later in this chapter that affect regulation skills can be learned later in life, generally in ways parallel to their development in a healthy, normal childhood environment.

The child who develops in a generally positive environment is, nevertheless, likely to encounter a variety of surmountable ob-

stacles or challenges, ranging from small frustrations and minor discomfort to momentarily unavailable caretakers. In the context of sustained external security, the well-cared-for child is thought to learn to deal with the associated uncomfortable (but not overwhelming) internal states through trial and error, slowly building a progressively more sophisticated repertoire of internal coping strategies as he or she confronts increasingly more challenging and stressful experiences (Briere, 1996). At the same time, because the associated discomfort does not exceed the child's growing internal resources, he or she is able to become increasingly more at home with some level of distress and is able to tolerate greater levels of emotional pain. This process appears to be self-sustaining: As the individual becomes better able to modulate and tolerate distress or dysphoria, such discomfort becomes less destabilizing, and the individual is able to seek more challenging and complex interactions with the environment without being derailed by concomitant increases in stress and anxiety.

In contrast to those with good affect regulation skills, however, severely abused or neglected children have been exposed to *insurmountable* affective obstacles, such as extreme neglect, emotionally intolerable physical or sexual abuse, or chronic, invasive psychological maltreatment. In such instances, affect regulation skills are less likely to develop, given the danger and ongoing emotional pain that overwhelm and preclude trial-and-error skills development. Instead, as noted later, the abuse victim may become expert at using more powerful (but generally more primitive) dissociation, thought suppression, distraction, or other avoidance strategies that allow continued functioning in the face of otherwise potentially overwhelming distress. Unfortunately, however, these same defenses, by virtue of their effectiveness, further preclude the development of more sophisticated regulation capacities.

As a result of inadequate opportunities to develop affect regulation skills, the formerly abused adult may be subject to affective instability, problems in inhibiting the expression of strong affect, and difficulty terminating dysphoric states without externalization or avoidance. Because the individual is unable to adequately modulate his or her emotions, he or she may be seen as moody and emotionally hyperresponsive and as tending to overreact to negative or stressful events in his or her life. In the absence of sufficient internal affect regulation skills, the individual may respond to painful affect and activated negative cognitions with external behaviors that distract, soothe, numb, or otherwise reduce painful internal states, such as substance abuse, inappropriate or excessive sexual behavior, aggression, bingeing or purging, or even self-injury (Briere, 1992; Briere & Gil, 1998; McCann & Pearlman, 1990). In this regard, the survivor of extreme abuse and neglect may have to deal with two interacting sets of difficulties: the triggering of sudden abuse-related memories, cognitions, and painful affects in the interpersonal world and the relative absence of affect regulation capacities that might otherwise allow regulation and resolution of these triggered responses.

Posttraumatic Stress

The various cognitive, memory, and self-related difficulties noted earlier can contribute to the development of posttraumatic stress disorder (PTSD) in a significant proportion of those with severe child maltreatment histories. The major symptoms associated with abuse-related posttraumatic stress are (a) intrusive reliving experiences (such as sensory flashbacks, intrusive thoughts, and autobiographical memories of the abuse), nightmares, and heightened emotional reactions to events reminiscent of maltreatment stimuli; (b) avoidance and numbing (e.g., attempts to avoid people, places, and situations associated with the abuse), as well as reduced or constricted emotionality; and (c) autonomic hyperarousal, involving chronic activation of the sympathetic nervous system, with resultant heightened startle responses, sleep disturbance, muscle tension, irritability, and so on (American Psychiatric Association, 1994).

Not all people exposed to abuse or other upsetting events develop PTSD, however; nor do they necessarily exhibit significant posttraumatic symptoms short of PTSD (Blank, 1993). Various authors suggest that the extent to which a given event produces major posttraumatic stress is a function of a variety of pretrauma variables, such as temperament and biologically based vulnerability to stress, the presence of preexisting psychological difficulties that reduce stress tolerance, exposure to previous traumatic events that may be activated by current trauma exposure to produce even more

posttraumatic distress, and the individual's ability to regulate negative affect, as described earlier (Briere, 1997; March, 1993; Yehuda & McFarlane, 1995). Apropos of the last point, the self-trauma model suggests that a significant aspect of one's response to a potential trauma is the degree to which the stressor overwhelms one's capacity to handle its effects through self-capacities, especially affect regulation.

The relative mismatch between especially overwhelming trauma (i.e., severe child abuse) and inadequate affect regulation—whether by virtue of insufficient affective development or because the trauma was so severe that even normal affective capacities would fall short—is thought to produce extreme distress that, in turn, is classically conditioned to those stimuli present at the time of the trauma. As a result, phenomena that are reminiscent of the original traumatic event can activate sensory or narrative memories that, in turn, trigger negative emotional responses. When this memory is primarily sensory (e.g., suddenly seeing or hearing aspects of a childhood rape), it may be described as a flashback. When the triggered memory is more autobiographical (e.g., a less sensory, more narrative recollection of the rape), it is often referred to as a restimulated memory, per se. Finally, although not typically understood as such in this context, the release of deep or unmonitored, abuse-related relational memories and deep cognitive structures by reminiscent stimuli in interpersonal interactions can also be viewed as posttraumatic, as will be suggested later in this chapter. In many cases, different aspects of a memory (i.e., its sensory, narrative, emotional, and relational components) are triggered simultaneously, leading to an especially powerful reexperiencing of the original traumatic event. It is important to reiterate at this point that there appear to be two separate components of triggered memory: the memory itself, whether sensory or autobiographical, and the negative affective responses at the time of the abuse that are classically conditioned to the memory.

As a result of painful affects linked to trauma-related memory, remembering abuse (whether via a trigger or narrative recall) often is upsetting. In response, as noted earlier, many individuals engage in at least some level of avoidance when faced with a triggered feeling, memory, or cognition. This avoidance may be of one's thoughts, for example, by actively suppressing awareness of upsetting cognitions and memories of the trauma. Or, avoidance may be focused on reducing one's activated emotional responses to the memory of the trauma, for example, by numbing one's feelings with drugs and alcohol or by separating oneself from one's emotional experience through dissociation. Finally, avoidance may be of the triggers themselves, for example, by avoiding people, places, or situations that otherwise might activate a traumatic memory or, in some cases, by dissociating awareness of environmental stimuli that might otherwise serve as triggers. Such responses are superficially adaptive at the time they occur. However, avoidance also may disrupt normal psychological functioning and, as will be described later, can interfere with psychological recovery from traumatic events.

The intrusive and avoidant experiences associated with posttraumatic stress frequently interact with one another. For example, as described earlier, an abused or otherwise traumatized person may have flashbacks or intrusive cognitions that are triggered by a reminiscent event and then may try to suppress these thoughts and memories to avoid the associated conditioned responses. Such avoidance may involve distraction or other attempts to not think about or feel anything related to the traumatic event. However, also as noted earlier, suppression of thoughts or feelings is harder than it might seem—a number of researchers have found, for example, that trying not to think about something often results in a rebound effect; after initial suppression, the thought or feeling intrudes all the more (Wegner, 1994). In fact, it is likely that an important initiator of trauma-related intrusive thoughts is the very act of attempted suppression (Shipherd & Beck, 1999). As a result, although the original thought or memory might be triggered by an environmental stimulus and then suppressed, the subsequent reintrusion of the thought or memory may be due to, among other things, its unsuccessful continued suppression or avoidance.

Although these various intrusive experiences and avoidance responses are common in PTSD, they also may occur in people who have been traumatized but do not present with all the diagnostic criteria for this disorder. In contradistinction to more classical pathology models, the self-trauma model suggests that posttraumatic responses are not merely symptoms of dysfunction but

rather often are intrinsic mechanisms that serve an important psychological function—that of repetitive reactivation and processing of traumatic memories to the point that they lose their distress-producing characteristics and can be accommodated by existing self-capacities.

Intrusive Sensory and Cognitive Symptoms as Memory Processing

Given that overwhelming childhood maltreatment commonly produces repetitive and intrusive cognitive, sensory, and emotional experiences later in time, usually preceded and followed by avoidance activities, an important question is What psychological purpose, if any, do these phenomena serve? In other words, although it may be possible to establish that reexperiencing symptoms such as flashbacks, nightmares, or triggered trauma-related thoughts and feelings arise from triggered implicit or suppressed memories, an interesting question emerges: Could the cycles of intrusion and avoidance experienced by those exposed to traumatic events (e.g., child abuse) represent something more than just reciprocal effects? Could it be that posttraumatic intrusion represents an inherent tendency to *process* suppressed or intrinsic memory material, and could concomitant or subsequent avoidance activities represent the control or titration of this exposure function?

Apropos of this, and integrating Horowitz's (1976, 1986) ideas with behavioral exposure models (e.g., Foa & Rothbaum, 1998) and with Rachman's (1980) and others' notion of emotional processing, the self-trauma model suggests that posttraumatic intrusion and avoidance may be, in fact, an inborn self-healing activity. Specifically, symptoms such as flashbacks, intrusive cognitions, and nightmares may represent the mind's automatic attempt to desensitize affectively laden memories by repeatedly exposing itself to small "chunks" of such material in a safe environment. In this regard, similar to what may be the critical elements of cognitive-behavioral treatment for traumatic stress (see the "Treatment" section of this chapter), the ameliorative components of posttraumatic stress responses may be (a) *exposure* (i.e., to the triggered memory), (b) *activation* (i.e., of cognitive and emotional responses, as well as larger cognitive-emotional gestalts or structures), (c) *disparity* (i.e., the fact that reliving the memory means reliving danger and trauma, whereas, in reality, the current environment is not dangerous or traumatic), and (d) *processing* (habituation/extinction/counterconditioning in the case of conditioned emotional responses to the memory and restructuring/reconsideration of meaning in the case of negative cognitive schemas).

Thus, the repeated evocation (via internal or external triggers) of traumatic memory in the immediate absence of threat or danger may serve to habituate or extinguish conditioned emotional responses or prompt reconsideration of abuse- or trauma-related cognitive structures because these responses are no longer accurate in the current, nondangerous environment. The avoidant symptoms of posttraumatic stress, on the other hand, may serve to regulate or control the impact of intrusive cognitive-emotional memories by decreasing contact with posttraumatic triggers through dissociation of environmental stimuli and by reducing awareness of activated CERs. This avoidance mechanism would be most important in instances when early childhood maltreatment had precluded the development of sufficient affect regulation capacities, such that "normal" reexperiencing of memory would exceed the survivor's ability to regulate painful material, producing extreme distress and, ironically, eliminating the disparity requirement by making the current environment painful and subjectively dangerous.

From this perspective, the individual who was traumatized in the context of an otherwise relatively positive childhood history (e.g., in cases of isolated extrafamilial abuse or when the trauma occurred later in life) will have, on average, better affect regulation capacities than those with significant, ongoing childhood maltreatment (Briere, 2000a, 2000b; Elliott, 1994) and thus will need less avoidance of triggered traumatic memories. In such individuals, activated cognitive and emotional memories or schemas allow relatively rapid exposure, processing, and habituation/extinction of painful affects that were conditioned to the memory, leading to a more rapid resolution of posttraumatic distress.[1] In this regard, the CERs associated with the traumatic memory extinguish because they are repeatedly activated but not reinforced by current danger or pain. As, over time, the CERs be-

come less susceptible to activation, the traumatic memory becomes less distress producing. In addition, the diminution of abuse-era emotional responses means that the original abuse context is less fully reinstated and thereby is less able to activate additional sensory and autobiographical memories, leading to less reexperiencing.

Individuals from abusive or neglecting environments, however, have fewer affect regulation skills and thus are more easily overwhelmed by reexperienced traumatic memories and therefore require more avoidance to downregulate their distress to acceptable levels. The unfortunate but unavoidable result of this more extreme titration requirement, however, is less self-exposure and less activation—leading to a more delayed recovery. In the extreme case, very low affect regulation capacities in the face of especially painful childhood memories may result in chronic and extreme avoidance strategies (e.g., substance addiction, dissociative disorders) that, in fact, nullify the effects of intrusion and block recovery entirely.

From this perspective, flashbacks and related intrusive experiences, as well as avoidant symptoms such as numbing and cognitive disengagement, represent the mind's desensitization and processing activities more than they reflect underlying pathology, per se. This view of repetitive memory intrusion as a desensitization device is in some ways similar to Horowitz's (1976, 1986) cognitive stress response theory. Horowitz, however, suggested that posttraumatic intrusions represent the mind's ongoing attempt to integrate traumatic material into preexisting cognitive schemas that did not include the trauma or its implications. Horowitz hypothesized that the traumatized individual automatically cycles through periods of intrusion and avoidance in an attempt to cognitively process and accommodate new trauma-related material.

Although acknowledging the importance of reconfiguring cognitively unacceptable material via reexperiencing in a disparate environment (a concept similar but not equivalent to Horowitz's model—see Foa and Rothbaum [1998] for a critique of Horowitz's hypothesis), self-trauma theory suggests that these cycles also represent (perhaps more directly) the stepwise exposure and consolidation associated with an inborn form of systematic desensitization of *affect*. In this regard, many traumatic memories appear to be too anxiety producing to be cognitively processed prior to some reduction in their stress-producing capacity (Foa & Riggs, 1993) and therefore must be at least partially desensitized before equally important cognitive processes can occur.

Unfortunately, as noted earlier, some survivors of severe child maltreatment (and later adult traumas) are not able to fully desensitize and accommodate trauma through intrusive reexperiencing of affects, memories, or cognitions alone and hence present with chronic posttraumatic stress. This may occur because the severity of the trauma (or, perhaps more typically, the extent of impaired self-capacities) motivates excessive use of cognitive and emotional avoidance strategies. The presence of excessive dissociation or other avoidance responses lessens the survivor's self-exposure to traumatic material—and the availability of the associated emotional responses to habituation or extinction—and thus reduces the efficacy of the intrusion-desensitization process. In support of this notion, it appears that individuals who tend to avoid internal access to traumatic material, either through cognitive avoidance or dissociation, suffer more psychological distress than do those with less avoidant tendencies (e.g., Burt & Katz, 1987; Holen, 1993; Koopman, Classen, & Spiegel, 1994; Wirtz & Harrell, 1987). In contrast, even superficial exploration (exposure) and emotional expression (activation) of previous traumatic events in safe environments have been shown to significantly decrease psychological symptoms, as well as increase indices of physical health (Murray & Segal, 1994; Pennebaker, Kiecolt-Glaser, & Glaser, 1988; Petrie, Booth, Pennebaker, Davison, & Thomas, 1995). This seeming competition between two relatively automatic trauma-related processes, intrusion and avoidance, will be considered in the upcoming "Treatment" section.

Borderline Personality Disorder Reconsidered

If one considers posttraumatic stress to consist, in part, of intrusive feelings, thoughts, and memories that are triggered by some sort of reminiscent stimulus, often followed by attempts by the affected individual to avoid such triggers or their emotional effects, then a close cousin of PTSD may be borderline personality disorder. In addition to problems with identity and self-other boundaries, those diagnosed as borderline are often characterized as prone to sudden emotional outbursts, self-defeating cognitions, feelings of emptiness and intense dysphoria, and impulsive, tension-reducing behavior that are triggered by perceptions of having been abandoned, rejected, or maltreated by another person (American Psychiatric Association, 1994). The borderline person is often viewed as having problems in impulse control, such that he or she is seen as emotionally overreactive to perceived losses or maltreatment, responding with angry affect and sudden, ill-considered behavior.

As with PTSD, many severely abused people have a number of borderline traits but fail to meet all the diagnostic criteria for the disorder. And, as per PTSD, the self-trauma model holds that a fair portion of what is considered borderline behavior and symptomatology can be seen, instead, as triggered implicit memories, schemas, and feelings associated with early (in this instance, relational) traumas (e.g., abuse, abandonment, rejection, or lack of parental responsiveness/attunement) that the individual, in turn, tries to avoid via dysfunctional activities such as substance abuse, inappropriate proximity seeking, or involvement in distracting, tension-reducing behaviors (e.g., dramatic actions, sexual behaviors, or aggression). In this way, the impulsive acting-out behavior of borderline individuals parallels the experience of the PTSD individual, except that in the former, the triggers for reexperiencing are usually within some sort of relationship; the activated memories are often implicit, preverbal, and imbedded in attachment disturbance; and the reactions to the activated memories are often more relational and seemingly more "primitive" because they involve the reliving of unprocessed childhood-era events (see Jacobs & Nadel, 1985, regarding the infantile effects of some activated early childhood memories).

In a comparative example, a Vietnam veteran with PTSD might have intrusive sensory reexperiences of a combat scenario after being triggered by the sound of an automobile backfire and, on experiencing the Vietnam-era fear associated with the combat memory, engage in attempts to find safety. An individual with borderline personality disorder, after being triggered by a perceived slight in an intimate relationship, on the other hand, might experience sudden, intrusive thoughts and feelings of abandonment and betrayal associated with childhood maltreatment and reexperience abuse-era desperation and anger associated with that memory. The individual might then engage in dramatic negative tension-reducing or proximity-seeking behavior in the context of that relationship. Both are having posttraumatic reactions that involve reliving a previously traumatic event, although the relational components of the latter are often seen, instead, as evidence of a personality disorder.

Summary of the Self-Trauma Model

The self-trauma model suggests that, beyond its initial negative effects, early and severe child maltreatment interrupts normal child development, conditions negative affect to abuse-related stimuli, and interferes with the usual acquisition of self-capacities—perhaps especially the development of affect regulation skills. This reduced affect regulation places the individual at risk for being more easily overwhelmed by emotional distress associated with memories of the abuse or trauma, thereby motivating the use of dissociation and other methods of avoidance in adolescence and adulthood. In this way, impaired self-capacities lead to reliance on avoidance strategies, which, in turn, further preclude the development of self-capacities. This negative cycle is exacerbated by the concomitant need of the traumatized individual to process conditioned emotional responses and distorted cognitive schemas by repetitively reexperiencing cognitive-emotional memories of the original traumatic event—a process that can further overwhelm self-capacities and produce distress.

Unfortunately, if the individual is sufficiently dissociated or otherwise avoidant, the intrusion-desensitization process will not include enough direct exposure to upsetting material to significantly reduce the survivor's underlying conditioned emotional distress. As a result, the individual will continue to have flashbacks and other intrusive symptoms indefinitely and will continue to rely on avoidance responses, such as dissociation, tension reduction, or substance abuse, to deal with the negative emotions arising from such reexperiencing. This process may lead the abuse survivor in therapy to

present as chronically dissociated, besieged by overwhelming yet unending intrusive symptomatology, and as having "characterologic" difficulties associated with identity, relational, and affect regulation difficulties.

Treatment Implications of the Self-Trauma Model

The model outlined above has a number of implications for the treatment of adults severely abused as children. These include suggestions regarding (a) the correct focus, pace, and intensity of psychotherapy; (b) how one might intervene in the self and cognitive difficulties of abuse survivors; and (c) possible approaches to the resolution of the chronic posttraumatic symptomatology often found in this population.

Treatment Process Issues and the Therapeutic Window

A major implication of the self-trauma model is that many adult survivors of severe childhood abuse expend considerable energy addressing trauma-related distress and insufficient self-capacities with avoidance mechanisms. In other words, the survivor whose reexperienced CERs to traumatic memories generally exceeds his or her internal affect regulation capacities is forced to continually invoke dissociation, substance abuse, thought suppression, and other avoidance responses to maintain internal equilibrium. These avoidance strategies are used at several levels: (a) to reduce awareness of (and therefore susceptibility to) potential environmental triggers, (b) to lessen awareness of memories once they are triggered, and (c) to reduce cognitive and emotional activation once CERs to these memories are evoked. In the absence of such protective mechanisms, the individual is likely to become overwhelmed by anxiety and other negative affects on a regular basis—especially when exposed to triggers of traumatic memory in the environment. As a result, avoidance defenses are viewed as necessary survival responses by some survivors, and overly enthusiastic or heavy-handed attempts by a therapist to remove such resistance, denial, or dissociative symptoms may be seen as potential threats to the client's internal equilibrium. For this reason, the psychotherapeutic process must proceed carefully to avoid overwhelming the client and reinforcing the use of additional avoidance responses that otherwise would further impede therapeutic progress.

The process of effective psychotherapy may be conceptualized, in part, as taking place in the context of a *therapeutic window* (Briere, 1996). This window refers to that psychological location between overwhelming exposure and excessive avoidance wherein therapeutic interventions are most helpful. Such interventions are neither so nondemanding as to provide inadequate exposure and processing nor so evocative or powerful that the client's delicate balance between trauma activation and self-capacity is tipped toward the former. In other words, interventions that take the therapeutic window into account challenge and motivate psychological growth, desensitization, and cognitive processing but do not overwhelm internal protective systems and thereby retraumatize and motivate unwanted avoidance responses.

Interventions that undershoot the therapeutic window are those that either (a) completely and consistently avoid traumatic material, including any exploration of childhood abuse, or (b) are focused primarily on support and validation in a client who could, in fact, tolerate greater exposure and processing of traumatic material. Undershooting interventions are rarely dangerous; they can, however, waste time and resources at times when more effective therapeutic interventions might be possible.

Overshooting the window occurs when interventions provide too much exposure intensity or focus on material that requires additional work before it can be safely addressed. In addition, interventions that are too fast-paced may overshoot the window because they do not allow the client to adequately accommodate and otherwise process previously activated material before adding new stressful stimuli. When therapy consistently overshoots the window, the survivor must engage in avoidance maneuvers to keep from being overwhelmed by the therapy process. Most often, the client will increase his or her level of dissociation during the session or will interrupt the focus or pace of therapy through arguing, "not getting" obvious therapeutic points, or changing the subject to something less threatening. Although these behaviors may be seen as "resistance" by the therapist, they are often appropriate protective responses to,

among other things, therapist process errors. Unfortunately, the client's need for such avoidance strategies can easily impede therapy by decreasing her or his exposure to effective treatment components.

In the worst situation, therapeutic interventions that consistently exceed the window can harm the survivor. This occurs when the process errors are too numerous and severe to be balanced or neutralized by client avoidance or when the client is so impaired in the self-domain or intimidated by the therapist that he or she cannot adequately use self-protective defenses. In such instances, the survivor may become flooded with intrusive stimuli, "fragment" to the point that his or her thinking is less organized or coherent, or become sufficiently overwhelmed that more extreme dissociative behaviors emerge. Furthermore, in an attempt to restore a self-trauma equilibrium, she or he may have to engage in avoidance activities such as self-mutilation or substance abuse after an overstimulating session. Although these states and responses may not be permanent, they are stigmatizing or disheartening for many clients and may lead them to terminate treatment or become especially avoidant during subsequent sessions.

In contrast, effective therapy provides sufficient safety and containment that the client does not have to over rely on avoidance strategies. By carefully titrating therapeutic exposure so that the attendant emotional/CER activation does not exceed the survivor's internal affect regulation capacities, treatment in the therapeutic window allows the client to go where he or she may not have gone before without being retraumatized in the process. As is described below under "Intervening in Abuse-Related Posttraumatic Symptoms," this sense of safety and concomitant lower level of avoidance is a major prerequisite to the successful processing of posttraumatic stress in many individuals.

Clinical experience suggests that, at minimum, three aspects of therapeutic process should be considered in effective (window-centered) abuse-focused psychotherapy. These are the following: (a) exploration versus consolidation, (b) intensity control, and (c) goal sequence. Each represents the therapist's attempt to find the appropriate point between safety and processing, with the assumption that, when in doubt, the former is always more important than the latter.

Exploration
Versus Consolidation

This aspect of the therapeutic process occurs on a continuum, with one end anchored in interventions devoted to greater exposure to traumatic material, with subsequent nonoverwhelming activation of abuse-related CERs, and the other constrained to interventions that support and solidify previous progress and provide a secure base from which the survivor can operate without fear.

Exploratory interventions typically invite the client to verbally examine (and thereby implicitly reexperience) material related to his or her traumatic history. For example, an exploratory intervention might involve asking the client to approach the possibility of using slightly less cognitive avoidance (e.g., denial) or dissociative disengagement when describing a previously described painful subject. Or, the client may be asked about something that, although somewhat threatening or distress producing, is within his or her capacity to address. The key here is that the survivor—in the context of relative safety—attempts to do something new, whether it be thinking of something previously not completely considered or feeling something previously not fully experienced.

Consolidation, on the other hand, is less concerned with exposure or processing than it is with safety and foundation. Consolidative interventions may focus the client on potential imbalances between trauma-related activation and self-capacities at a given moment and invite the client to shore up the latter. Or, the therapist may choose to validate, sooth, or support the client at a point where he or she is experiencing significant distress. An important issue here is that the survivor is not necessarily being asked to avoid existing traumatic states but rather to more fully anchor himself or herself in such a way as to strengthen challenged self-capacities. Interventions in this domain may involve, in one instance, working to keep the agitated client from exceeding the therapeutic window. In another, it may involve reminding the client who is attempting to move too fast of how far he or she has come and of the need to honor his or her needs for safety and stability.

The decision to explore or consolidate at any given moment reflects the therapist's assessment of which direction the client's balance between stress and resources is tilting. The overwhelmed client, for example, typically requires less exposure and more consolidation, whereas the stable client may benefit most from the opposite. Furthermore, this assessment of the client's internal state may vary from moment to moment: At one point, exploration and exposure may be indicated, whereas at another point, consolidation may be required.

Intensity Control

Intensity control refers to the therapist's awareness and relative control of the level of activation occurring within the session. Most generally, it is recommended that—especially for those with impaired self-capacities—emotional intensity be highest at around mid-session, whereas the beginning and end of the session should be at the lowest intensity. At the onset of the session, the therapist should encourage the client to gradually enter the therapeutic domain of trauma and self-work, whereas by the end of the session, the clinician seeks to ensure that the client is sufficiently de-aroused and has sufficient closure that she or he can reenter the outside world without needing later tension reduction activities. In addition, the relative safety of the session may encourage some clients to become more affectively aroused than they normally would outside of the therapeutic environment. As a result, it is the therapist's responsibility to leave the client in as calm an affective state as is possible—ideally no more than the arousal level present initially—lest the client be left with more affective distress than he or she can reasonably tolerate on the session's end and termination of therapeutic support.

From the perspective offered in this chapter, intense affect during treatment may push the survivor toward the outer edge of the window, whereas less intensity (or a more "surface" cognitive focus) will represent movement toward the inner (safer) edge. The need for the client, at some point, to experience seemingly dangerous feelings and to think potentially distress-producing thoughts—not to dissociate them—during abuse-focused treatment requires that the therapist carefully titrate the level of affective activation the client experiences, at least to the extent this is under the therapist's control. The goal is for the client to neither feel too little (i.e., dissociate or otherwise avoid to the point that abuse-related CERs and cognitions cannot be processed) nor feel too much (become so flooded with previously avoided affect that he or she overwhelms available self-resources and is retraumatized).

Goal Sequence

As noted by various authors (Courtois, 1991; Linehan, 1993; McCann & Pearlman, 1990; van der Hart, Steele, Boon, & Brown, 1993), therapy for severe abuse-related difficulties should generally proceed in a stepwise fashion, with early therapeutic attention paid more to the assessment and development of self-resources and coping skills than to trauma per se. This notion of "self before trauma" takes into account the fact that those interventions most helpful in working through major traumatic stress (i.e., exposure and activation) may overwhelm the client who lacks sufficient internal resources (Linehan, 1993). Specifically, the process of accessing and affectively processing traumatic memories requires basic levels of affect tolerance and regulation skills. In the relative absence of such self-resources, exposure to traumatic material can easily exceed the therapeutic window and lead to fragmentation, increased dissociation, involvement in later tension reduction activities, and, potentially, therapy dropout.

Because of the need for adequate self-skills prior to intensive trauma work, the choice of therapeutic goals for a client must rely on detailed psychological assessment (Briere, 1997). Whether done with the assistance of psychological tests that tap self- and trauma domains or solely through careful attention to self- and trauma dynamics during early sessions, the therapist must determine if a given client has sufficient self-functioning to tolerate relatively quick progression to trauma-focused interventions or whether she or he requires extended therapeutic attention to identity, boundary, and affect regulation before significant trauma work can be undertaken (Linehan, 1993).

Due to the complex relationship between self-capacities and traumatic stress, assessment of readiness to do trauma work cannot be determined solely at one point in time and then assumed thereafter. Indeed, a client's affect regulation capacities may appear sufficient early in treatment, only to emerge as far less substantial later in therapy. For example, as therapy successfully reduces dissociative symptomatology, it may become clear that what originally appeared to be good affect regulation actually represents the effects of dissociative avoidance of painful affect or continued suppression of traumatic memories. Alternatively, a client who initially had superficially intact self-functioning may later experience a reduction in self-capacities as he or she addresses especially traumatic material or as the deepening therapeutic relationship triggers early attachment-related schemas. Although some of this fragmentation may be amenable to careful attention to the therapeutic window, it is also true that intense reexperiencing of traumatic events can temporarily reduce self-functioning (Linehan, 1993). Given these potential scenarios, it is strongly recommended that the therapist continue to evaluate the client's current affect regulation capacities and trauma level throughout treatment, so that he or she can adjust the type, focus, or intensity of intervention when necessary.

Intervening in Impaired Self-Functioning

As noted earlier, the availability and quality of self-resources are typically major determinants of the level of symptomatology and response to treatment. So important are such capacities to traumatic stress and therapeutic intervention that, as mentioned, some clients may require more "self-work" than trauma exposure early in treatment, although, as will be considered below, these two activities sometimes may be quite similar or even equivalent. For others, there may be sufficient self-skills available to allow some trauma-based interventions, yet continued attention to the development of further self-capacities will be required. Finally, for some clinical abuse survivors, self-issues may not require any significant intervention, and desensitization of traumatic material may occur relatively quickly (Linehan, 1993). Even in the latter case, however, it is possible for the processing of especially painful traumatic memory to briefly overwhelm normally sufficient self-capacities, thereby requiring some (typically temporary) self-level interventions.

Although the primary self-resource or capacity stressed thus far has been affect regulation, the survivor's ability to maintain a coherent sense of self is also important. Because early traumatic abuse typically pulls the child's attention away from internal experience and toward the external environment (where danger exists and must be assessed), the maltreated child may grow to become primarily "other-directed" (Briere, 1992, 1996). Although this adaptation is well suited for the hypervigilance required of endangered beings, it can easily interfere with optimal psychological functioning in later instances when self-awareness, internal security, and independence or self-directedness are necessary. Most relevant to this chapter, effective psychotherapy, abuse oriented or otherwise, requires that the client be able to attend to internal processes and dynamics and to develop a relationship to self—above and beyond his or her relationship with the therapist. For this reason, the self-trauma model attends not only to affect regulation but also to identity issues when working with maltreatment effects.

Safety and Support

Because, for many survivors, an early hazard to the development of self-resources was the experience of danger and lack of support or protection, thereby motivating hypervigilance and other-directness, these issues must receive continuing attention in abuse-focused psychotherapy. In the absence of continual and reliable safety and support during treatment, the survivor is unlikely to reduce his or her reliance on avoidance defenses or attempt the necessary work of forming a relatively open relationship with the psychotherapist. Because early neglect or abuse may have led to the development of an ambivalent or avoidant attachment pattern (Alexander, 1992), the client is, in some sense, being asked to go against lifelong learning and become dangerously vulnerable to a powerful relational figure. That he or she is willing to do so at all in such cases is testament to the investment and bravery that many abuse survivors bring to therapy.

Given the above, the clinician must work hard to provide an environment where the survivor can experience therapeutic nurturance and support. Just as the chronically avoidant, formerly abused child may reject a loving foster parent, the survivor of severe abuse may use similar defenses that, at least initially, preclude a working relationship with his or her therapist. As many clinicians will attest, there is no shortcut to the process of developing trust in such instances. Instead, the clinician must provide ongoing reliable data to the survivor that he or she is not in danger—neither from physical or sexual assaults, nor from rejection, domination, intrusion, or abandonment.

Beyond providing a secure base from which the client can explore his or her internal and interpersonal environment, therapeutic safety and support allow for the habituation of CERs associated with relatedness. As noted earlier, for activation of traumatic memories to be therapeutic, there must be a disparity between the contents of the traumatic memory (i.e., violence, danger, or violation) and the client's experience of the current environment (i.e., as safe and supportive). When this occurs, the emotional reactions conditioned to the traumatic memory slowly lose their power as they are unreinforced and, eventually, extinguished by the absence of current traumatic experience. In other words, as the client recalls, at sensory and autobiographical levels, his or her abusive experiences in childhood, the emotional experiences present at that time (e.g., fear or anger) also are evoked. However, these conditioned, abuse-era emotional responses are not relevant to the current safety of the therapy session, and so their association to the original abuse memory is not reinforced and eventually becomes attenuated. When this attenuation is complete, memories of the abuse cease to produce major abuse-era affects even when activated.

Facilitating Self-Awareness and Positive Identity

In the context of sustained and reliable support and acceptance, the survivor has the opportunity to engage in the relative luxury of introspection. Looking inward may have been punished by the survivor's early environment in at least two ways: It took attention away from hypervigilance and therefore safety, and greater internal awareness meant, by definition, greater pain. As a result, many untreated survivors of severe abuse are surprisingly unaware of their internal processes and individual identity and may, in fact, appear to have very little self-knowledge. This may present, for example, as reports of diminished access to an internal sense of self, the inability to predict one's own reactions or behavior in various situations, or little insight regarding the abuse or its effects.

By facilitating self-exploration and self-reference (as opposed to defining self primarily in terms of others' expectations or reactions), abuse-focused therapy potentially allows the survivor to gain a greater sense of personal identity. Increased self-awareness may be especially fostered by what cognitive therapists call Socratic questioning (Beck, 1995), wherein the client is asked primarily open-ended questions throughout the course of treatment. These include multiple, gentle inquiries about, for example, the client's early perceptions and experiences, the options that were and were not available to him or her at the time of the abuse, his or her feelings and reactions during and after victimization experiences, and what conclusions he or she might form about the abuse from the answers to these various questions. Equally important, however, is the need for the client to, literally, discover what he or she feels about current things, abuse related or otherwise. Because the external-directedness necessary to survive abuse generally works against self-understanding and identity, the survivor is encouraged to explore his or her own likes and dislikes, views regarding self and other, entitlements and obligations, and other aspects of self, in the context of the therapist's support and manifest acceptance. This more broad, less specifically abuse-focused intervention is, in some sense, "identity training": providing the survivor with the opportunity to discover what he or she thinks and feels, above and beyond what others think and feel.

In the process of self-exploration, many opportunities arise for the reworking of abuse-related, verbally mediated cognitive distortions and negative self-perceptions, as noted later in this chapter. These distortions typically involve harsh self-judgments of having caused, encouraged, or deserved the abuse (Briere, 2000a; Janoff-Bulman, 1992; Jehu, 1988). By exploring with the survivor the specifics of the abuse and the limits of his or her options as a child, the therapist can provide an environment wherein the client can reconsider the validity of any erroneous perceptions or assumptions he or she made as a child, thereby assisting in the development of a more positive sense of self. The reader is referred to Resick and Schnicke (1993); Chard, Weaver, and Resick (1997); and Jehu (1988) for further information on

interventions helpful with these cognitive sequels of interpersonal victimization.

Self-Other Entitlements and Boundary Issues

As noted earlier, many survivors of severe childhood abuse have difficulty distinguishing the boundary between self and others. This problem is thought to arise both from attachment disruption, wherein the child is deprived of the opportunity to learn normal self-other behaviors and demarcations, and from early intrusion by the abuser into the child's bodily space (McCann & Pearlman, 1990).

Effective abuse-focused therapy addresses both of these bases. The clinician is careful to honor the client's dignity, rights, and psychological integrity—even if the abuse survivor is unaware of his or her entitlement to such treatment. Over time, the therapist's consistent respect for the client's rights to safety and freedom from intrusion can be internalized by the client as evidence of his or her physical and psychological boundaries. Part of this learning process is overtly cognitive—during the client's recounting of his or her child abuse history and later adult experiences of violation or exploitation, the therapist actively reinforces the survivor's previous and current entitlement to integrity and self-determinism. Other aspects of this process are intrinsic and the learning implicit—as he or she is treated with compassion and respect by the therapist and slowly develops a growing sense of personal identity, the survivor begins to *assume* or understand that he or she has entitlements and intrinsic validity.

This latter, nonverbal component of self-trauma therapy is critical: Because early maltreatment leads to the formation of preverbal relational schemas, merely (verbally) insisting to a client that he or she is good, safe, or entitled to positive treatment will rarely be entirely effective. Instead, the client must be provided with the opportunity to learn (not just hear) that he or she is valued and is entitled to not be violated. In other words, much of distorted relational schemas are, by definition, nonverbal; as a result, their remediation must also be nonverbal—the clinician must show, not merely tell.

At the same time that the demarcation of his or her own psychological rights are being demonstrated and learned, the survivor in therapy may be exposed to important lessons regarding the boundaries of others. This may occur as the client impinges on the therapist, typically through inappropriate questions, requests, or behavior. As the therapist carefully repels such intrusions, he or she both teaches about the needs and rights of others to boundary integrity and models for the survivor appropriate limit-setting strategies the survivor can use in his or her own life (Elliott & Briere, 1995). In this way, the interpersonal give-and-take of psychotherapy tends to replicate some of the self-other lessons the survivor would have learned in childhood were it possible.

Affect Modulation and Affect Tolerance

Because affect tolerance and modulation are such important issues for adults severely abused as children, the self-trauma model addresses these issues in as many ways as possible. It stresses two general pathways to the development of what may be called affective competence: the acquisition of an affect regulation repertoire and the strengthening of inborn but underdeveloped affective capacities.

Skills training in this area is best outlined by Linehan (1993) in her outstanding manual on the cognitive-behavioral treatment of borderline personality disorder. She notes that distress tolerance and emotional regulation are internal behaviors that can be taught in clinical settings. Among the specific skills directly taught by Linehan's dialectical behavior therapy (DBT) for distress tolerance are distraction, self-soothing, "improving the moment" (e.g., through relaxation), and thinking of the "pros and cons" of behavior (p. 148). In the area of emotional regulation skills, Linehan teaches the survivor to (a) identify and label affect, (b) identify obstacles to changing emotions, (c) reduce vulnerability to hyperemotionality through decreased stress, (d) increase the frequency of positive emotional events, and (e) develop the ability to experience emotions without judging or rejecting them (pp. 147-148).

Self-trauma therapy makes use of these skills-training approaches, although it cannot replicate the formally programmatic, group-oriented aspects of DBT. Linehan's (1993) model, which has been shown in out-

come research to be effective for borderline personality disorder, stresses a central issue: Affect dysregulation does not reflect a structural psychological defect (as suggested by some analytic theories and approaches) as much as skills deficits arising from distorted or disrupted childhood development.

Affect regulation and tolerance are also learned implicitly during self-trauma therapy. Because, as outlined in the next section, trauma-focused interventions involve the repeated activation, processing, and resolution of distressing but nonoverwhelming affect, such treatment slowly teaches the survivor to become more "at home" with some level of distress and to develop whatever skills are necessary to de-escalate moderate levels of emotional arousal. This growing ability to move in and out of strong affective states, in turn, fosters an increased sense of emotional control and reduced fear of negative affect. In this regard, the nonoverwhelming exposure and processing of traumatic memories may intrinsically increase the client's affect regulation skills.

Finally, in the process of developing affect regulation capacities, the survivor is encouraged to identify and describe the intrusive and repetitive cognitions that often exacerbate or even trigger trauma-related affect. Thus, for example, the client's attention may be focused on childhood-era self-talk that occurs after memory activation and just before an intense negative emotional reaction (e.g., "They're trying to hurt me," or "I'm so disgusting"), as well as the catastrophizing cognitions triggered by strong emotion that produce panic and fears of being overwhelmed or inundated (e.g., "I'm out of control," or "I'm making a fool of myself"). As the client becomes more aware of these cognitive antecedents to overwhelming affect, he or she can also learn to lessen the impact of such thoughts by, in some sense, explicitly disagreeing with them (e.g., "Nobody's out to get me," "I look/sound fine," or "I can handle this") or merely by experiencing such cognitions as "old tapes" rather than accurate perceptions. In this regard, one of the benefits of what is referred to as *insight* in psychodynamic therapy is the realization that one is acting in a certain way by virtue of erroneous beliefs or perceptions—an understanding that often reduces the power of those cognitions to produce distress or motivate dysfunctional behavior. In other words, for distorted cognitions to be most affective, they probably need to act outside of full consciousness and to be agreed with or at least unchallenged.

Disturbed Relatedness

As noted earlier, many survivors of severe abuse and neglect suffer from significant difficulties in the interpersonal domain. Because relationships are of major importance to most people and are, in fact, the context in which much of human life unfolds, most therapies for abuse survivors devote considerable attention to this area. The self-trauma approach addresses relatedness problems by habituating negative CERs to powerful relational figures and the vulnerability associated with intimacy and connectedness, as well as by processing negative attachment-related schemas.

Because most disturbed relatedness appears to arise from reactions to maltreatment in early relationships, and these maltreatment effects are often triggered by later interpersonal stimuli, it is not surprising that the most effective interventions for relational problems appear to occur within a therapeutic relationship. As is discussed below in the section on abuse-related intrusive symptoms, the self-trauma model views the therapeutic relationship as directly and specifically curative, as opposed to being the nonspecific placebo effect or inert ingredient suggested by some cognitive-behavioral theorists. Among other things, the therapeutic relationship is a powerful source of interpersonal triggers—the give-and-take between client and clinician will almost always include phenomena that trigger abuse-related relational schemas (e.g., moments of decreased therapist empathy or attunement, or client perceptions or expectations of therapist abandonment or dangerousness) and affects (e.g., feelings of rage or despondency associated with these perceptions or expectations), as well as activating more complex attachment-level relational phenomena (e.g., preoccupied or ambivalent responses to the positive components of the therapeutic relationship). The therapeutic relationship, however, also is a powerful source of disparity and resolution—once activated by relational stimuli, cognitive-emotional responses can be examined and processed in the context of safety, soothing, and support, potentially leading to clinical improvement, including reduced abuse-specific difficulties in current and future relationships. The ac-

tual processing of traumatic memory, relational or otherwise, is described below.

Intervening in Abuse-Related Posttraumatic Symptoms

Assuming that the client either has sufficient self-skills or that these self-functions have been strengthened sufficiently, the treatment of intrusive trauma symptoms can be undertaken. The current model suggests at least five major steps in this process: identification of traumatic (i.e., abuse-related) events, gradual reexposure to memories (implicit or explicit) of the abuse, activation of associated CERs and cognitions, disparity between the original trauma and the current environment, and cognitive-emotional processing.

Identification of Traumatic Events

For traumatic material to be processed efficiently in treatment, it should be identified as such. Although this seems an obvious step, it is more difficult to implement in some cases than otherwise might be expected. The survivor's avoidance of abuse-related material may lead to suppression of abuse-specific thoughts, conscious reluctance to think about or speak of upsetting abuse incidents, or less conscious dissociation of such events. In the case of conscious avoidance, for example, survivors may believe that a detailed description of the abuse would be more painful than they are willing to endure or that exploration of the abuse would overwhelm their self-resources. Dissociation of abuse material, on the other hand, may present as incomplete or absent recall of the events in question.[2] In addition, those with an avoidant-dismissive adult attachment style (in which the individual tends to avoid close relationships and often does not acknowledge significant emotional distress) are hypothesized to have less access to painful childhood memories than those with a secure attachment style (Fraley, Davis, & Shaver, 1998).

Whether through suppression, denial, or dissociation, avoidance of abuse-related material should be respected because it indicates the survivor's implicit judgment that exploration in that area would challenge or exceed his or her capacity to regulate the associated negative affect. The role of the therapist at such junctures is not to overpower the client's defenses or in any way to convince him or her that abuse occurred, but rather to provide the conditions (e.g., safety, support, and a trustworthy environment) whereby avoidance is less necessary and exposure is more possible. Because this latter step can require significant time and skill, the specific enumeration and description of abusive events are far from a simple matter (Courtois, 1999).

In other instances, a specific traumatic event cannot be recalled for a different reason: The relevant material may not be an explicit or narratively encoded memory of a single traumatic event, but rather implicit, nonverbal, sensorimotor memories of abusive *processes* (e.g., sustained emotional neglect, repetitive boundary incursions, or parental narcissistic disattunement) that occurred early in childhood. Thus, for example, although specific instances of abandonment, rejection, or violation may or may not be recalled in the context of a painful childhood or may have occurred prior to language, the critical memory material may be of the general sense of not being loved, of being seen as bad, or of feeling entirely alone in the world. These latter reactions, as described earlier, may be incorporated into generalized working models of self and others, deep cognitive structures, or distorted relational schemas—much of which may be outside of the abuse survivor's conscious awareness, let alone describable/explicit memory. This issue may be especially relevant for abuse or neglect that occurred in the first 2 or 3 years of life, at which point, although implicit/sensory memory of maltreatment may be retained, explicit/verbal encoding did not occur and thus cannot be retrieved.

It might appear that, in the absence of explicit memory, early childhood maltreatment would have to go unprocessed. However, because such memory material is often triggered by reminiscent—often relational—stimuli, as described earlier, therapists are frequently able to work with the manifestations of childhood maltreatment that are activated in the therapy session. This may occur, in fact, without either client or therapist necessarily ever having a detailed, narrative understanding of the actual abuse or neglect that the client experienced. The actual process of treating implicit, as well as explicit, maltreatment memories is described below.

Gradual Exposure to Abuse-Related Material

For the purposes of this chapter, it is helpful to divide exposure activities into two kinds, based on what type of memory is being addressed. These will be referred to as *direct* exposure, involving conscious self-access to explicit, autobiographical memories, and *indirect* exposure, involving implicit memories that are activated in the context of the therapeutic relationship.

Direct exposure is the usual technique used by cognitive-behavioral therapy. According to Abueg and Fairbank (1992), this approach can be defined as "repeated or extended exposure, either in vivo or in imagination, to objectively harmless but feared stimuli for the purpose of reducing anxiety" (p. 127). Several types of direct exposure have been used to treat traumatic stress, one of which, prolonged exposure, has been shown to be effective in treating acute adult traumas, most notably sexual assault (Foa & Rothbaum, 1998). This approach typically eschews titrated or graduated access to traumatic memories and instead involves extended exposure to the full force of traumatic memories until the associated anxiety is habituated—an approach that may be most effective with those who were victimized as adults and who have the affect regulation capacities required for such activities.

In contrast, however, the direct exposure approach suggested here is a form of systematic desensitization (Wolpe, 1958), wherein the survivor is asked to recall nonoverwhelming but somewhat distressing abuse-specific experiences in the context of a safe therapeutic environment. The exposure is titrated according to the intensity of the recalled abuse, generally with less upsetting memories being recalled, verbalized, and desensitized before more upsetting ones are considered. However, the self-trauma approach does not adhere to a strict, preplanned series of extended exposure activities. This is because the survivor's ability to tolerate exposure may be quite compromised and may vary considerably from session to session as a function of outside life stressors; level of support from friends, relatives, and others; and, most important, the extent of self-capacities available to the abuse survivor at any given point in time.

As suggested earlier, for abuse-focused therapy to work well, there should be as little avoidance as possible during treatment. Specifically, the client should be encouraged to stay as "present" as he or she can during his or her verbalization and activation of abuse memories, so that exposure, per se, is maximized. The very dissociated survivor may have little true exposure to abuse material during treatment—despite what may be detailed renditions of a given memory. Of course, the therapist must keep the therapeutic window in mind and not interrupt survivor dissociation that is, in fact, appropriate in the face of therapeutic overstimulation. This might occur, for example, when the therapist requires or allows client access to memories whose associated CERs exceed the survivor's self-resources. On the other hand, it is not uncommon for avoidance responses to become so overlearned that they automatically (but unnecessarily) emerge during exposure to stress. In this case, some level of reduced dissociation during treatment is not only safe but also frequently imperative for significant desensitization to occur.

In contrast to direct exposure, indirect exposure relies on the therapeutic relationship to trigger—and thus provide exposure to—implicit or suppressed memory material. As described earlier, implicit memories of abuse and neglect are nonverbal in nature, composed primarily of sensory/perceptual material. Such memories are often encoded early in life, prior to the acquisition of language and the full development of certain brain structures. Later traumatic memories also may have implicit memory components, however, especially if the brain responds to incoming stress by selectively blocking explicit encoding (van der Kolk et al., 1996). Such memories cannot be "recalled," per se, but instead emerge when they are activated or triggered by reminiscent events in the environment. Thus, the therapeutic relationship, with its many triggering characteristics, emerges as a potent source of indirect exposure opportunities.

Interestingly, it is likely that classic psychodynamic interventions, because they typically focus on the recollection and discussion of early childhood trauma and the processing of cognitions and affects triggered by the therapeutic relationship, involve some degree of indirect exposure. In fact, as is addressed below, the psychodynamic notion of transference may be reconceptualized as the cued activation of implicit, relational memories in the context of therapy.

Activation

Once exposure has occurred, it is necessary that at least some degree of cognitive and emotional activation take place. Activation, in this context, refers primarily to triggered CERs to abuse memories, such as fear, sadness, or horror, or cognitive reactions such as the intrusion of negative self-perceptions or activation of negative relational schemas. Also activated may be other implicit or explicit memories associated with the triggering stimulus that are made more salient as the original abuse context becomes reinstated through increasingly detailed memory. For example, a woman who is asked to describe a childhood sexual abuse experience undergoes therapeutic exposure to the extent that she recalls aspects of that event during the therapy session. If these memories trigger further cognitive associations or self-schemas (e.g., "I am such a slut that I let that happen"), or emotional responses conditioned to the original abuse stimuli (e.g., fear or horror), or stimulate further memories (e.g., of other aspects of the abuse triggered by remembering certain aspects of it), therapeutic activation can be said to have taken place.

When activation is primarily of relational schemas, the process is quite similar to what is referred to psychodynamically as transference. For example, consider a 24-year-old woman with a long history of emotional abuse by her narcissistic father, who enters therapy with an older male clinician. Although the client initially views her therapist as supportive and caring, she soon comes to feel increasing distrust toward the therapist, begins to see subtle "put-downs" in his remarks, and eventually finds herself angry at the therapist's perceived lack of empathy, lapses in attunement and caring, and judgmental behavior. Although psychodynamic theory would hold that the client is experiencing a significant transference reaction, the self-trauma model suggests, not that dissimilarly, that the benign behaviors of the clinician nonetheless contains stimuli (e.g., the clinician's age and sex, the power differential between client and therapist, the growing feeling of emotional intimacy as treatment progresses) that cue and activate early, implicit abuse memories. As will be discussed, this phenomenon, whether described as transference or activation of implicit relational memories, is potentially a positive development, despite its distressing qualities for client and (on occasion) therapist.

Emotional activation is usually critical to recovery from trauma. Therapeutic interventions that consist solely of the narration of abuse-related memories, without also supporting (and allowing) emotional and cognitive activation, will not necessarily produce symptom relief (Foa & Kozak, 1986; Samoilov & Goldfried, 2000). As outlined in the next section, in most cases a conditioned emotional response to the trauma must be elicited before it can be extinguished or habituated. Probably for this reason, exposure that occurs in the presence of substance intoxication, significant dissociation, or emotional overcontrol is often relatively unsuccessful (Briere, 1996) because normal emotional activation is, to some extent, blocked.

Disparity

Although not always mentioned explicitly in cognitive-behavioral texts, it is not sufficient to have exposure and activation in trauma treatment; there also must be disparity. For conditioned emotional responses to traumatic memories to be extinguished, they must not be reinforced by similar danger (physical or emotional) in the current environment. Approximating the language of Foa and Kozak (1986), the fear structure associated with traumatic memory must be activated (i.e., the client must remember and experience fear conditioned to the memory) in the presence of information incompatible with that fear structure (i.e., experience safety in a relational context that originally was associated with danger).

To be effective, safety should be manifest in at least two ways. First, the client should come to realize that he or she is safe from the therapist. This safety should not be only from physical injury and sexual exploitation, of course, but also from harsh criticism, punitiveness, boundary violation, or narcissistic disregard for the client's experience. Because the survivor of interpersonal violence, maltreatment, or exploitation tends to perceive danger in interpersonal situations (Briere, 2000a; Janoff-Bulman, 1992), the absence of danger in the session must be experienced directly, not just promised. In other words, for the client's anxious associations to victimization memories to extinguish over time, they must not be rein-

forced by current maltreatment in the session, however subtle.

Second, safety in treatment should be from the client's own internal experience. The survivor whose recollection and activation of abuse memories produce overwhelmingly negative affect will not necessarily find therapeutic exposure to be substantially disparate from his or her original experience. Such overwhelming affect may occur because one or both of two things are present: (a) the memory is so traumatic and has so much painful affect (e.g., anxiety, rage) or cognitions (e.g., guilt or shame) conditioned to it that untitrated exposure produces considerable psychic pain, or (b) the survivor's affect regulation capacities are sufficiently compromised that any major reexperiencing is overwhelming. In each instance, however, safety—and therefore disparity—can be provided within the context of the therapeutic window. Because treatment within the window means that exposure to memories does not, by definition, exceed self-capacities, reexperiencing is not associated with the danger of overwhelming negative affect, identity fragmentation, or powerful feelings of loss of control.

Disparity is not just the absence of danger, however—in the best circumstances, it is the presence of positive phenomena that are antithetic to danger. Thus, in the example of the younger woman in therapy with the older man, her "transference" (triggered relational schemas) of therapist criticism, rejection, and abandonment are not merely met with the absence of those things in treatment but with the presence of therapist acceptance, validation, and reliable nurturance. In this regard, the most powerful disparity for many clients may be to expect hatefulness or disregard from their therapists and to get, instead, loving attention.

Processing and Resolution

It is likely that at least two types of activities take place when exposure activates memories (implicit or explicit) in the presence of safety: *emotional processing* and *cognitive processing*. However, because cognitions and emotions are often inextricably tied (Siegel, 1999), perhaps especially in response to activated traumatic material, both forms of processing may occur simultaneously.

Emotional Processing

Emotional processing occurs when painful memories of past trauma, whether implicit or explicit, are experienced in the presence of disparity and, as noted below, emotional expression. Processing during disparity, as discussed, probably involves habituation and desensitization, wherein the link between painful memory and conditioned emotional responses to that memory is weakened over time. For this to happen, painful affects must be repeatedly activated within and across sessions—a process that must be controlled by the constraints of the therapeutic window to be tolerable. Even under the best of circumstances, the CER activation that accompanies exposure activities in trauma treatment is seen by most clients as distressing and challenging. As a result, exposure must be carefully titrated to keep it from motivating unwanted avoidance behavior, including treatment dropout.

Recovery from abuse and other traumas also is facilitated by emotional expression and release during self-exposure. Teleologically speaking, for example, the biological "reason" for crying in response to upsetting events may be that such release engenders a relatively positive emotional state (i.e., relief) that can then countercondition the fear and related affects initially associated with the trauma. In other words, the lay suggestion that someone "have a good cry" or "get it off of your chest" may reflect support for ventilation and other emotional activities that naturally countercondition abuse-memory CERs. From this perspective, just as traditional systematic desensitization pairs a formerly distressing stimulus to a relaxed (anxiety-incompatible) state, in an attempt to neutralize the original anxious response over time, repeated emotional release during nondissociated exposure to painful memories is likely to pair the traumatic stimuli to the relatively positive internal states associated with emotional release. This process typically is facilitated in the session by gentle support for—and reinforcement of—emotional expression during exposure to traumatic memories. The level of emotional response in such circumstances will vary from person to person, partially as a function of his or her affect regulation and tolerance capacities. As a result, the therapist should not "push" for emotional response when the client is unable or unwilling to engage in such activities.

Cognitive Processing

In addition to emotional processing, it is clear that effective abuse- (or trauma-) focused treatment must facilitate *cognitive processing*. This domain includes at least the following activities: acquiring and integrating new information, developing a coherent narrative and deriving meaning, altering existing cognitive structures, and processing activated relational schemas.

New information. The acquisition of new information relates both to the psychoeducational component of trauma therapy and to the learning about self that typically arises during psychotherapy. The former may include the clinician providing information regarding, for example, the relative commonness of child abuse, frequent abuser justifications for maltreating children, and the fact that the client's symptoms are a frequent effect of such maltreatment. Such data may decrease the abuse survivor's sense of self-blame and stigma and may serve to de-pathologize, to some extent, the psychological symptoms that he or she experiences. Informational learning will be helpful, however, only to the extent that it is integrated (i.e., the client successfully applies it to his or her own specific experience). Therapists may assist in this integration by helping the client to see the personal applicability of this new information to memories of the abuse and the current model of self.

New information also arises from—and may be most powerful in—the process of self-exploration, as described earlier in the "Self-Capacities" section. As the client observes himself or herself in therapy; integrates feedback from the therapist; examines his or her thoughts, motives, and past behaviors; and considers previous abuse-related assumptions and cognitive distortions in light of current knowledge, a form of insight into one's past and one's self often develops. Such knowledge, in turn, may foster increased self-acceptance, as the client comes to reinterpret former "bad" behaviors, deserving of maltreatment, and presumed inadequacies in a more positive light. Self-knowledge and self-acceptance, almost by definition, can then serve as powerful antidotes to future negative self-thoughts and may interfere with the capacity of memories or misinterpreted environmental events to trigger painful affects, such as shame or self-hatred.

Developing a coherent narrative. Research (e.g., Amir, Stafford, Freshman, & Foa, 1998; Foa, Molnar, & Cashman, 1995) supports a common clinical impression that as the trauma survivor's rendition of his or her trauma experience becomes more coherent (i.e., is clearly articulated, well organized, and detailed), his or her trauma symptoms decrease. Although it is likely that narrative coherence intrinsically arises from trauma recovery, it is also likely that the development of a "story" of one's trauma is salutary. In this regard, it is probable that a coherent trauma (or abuse) narrative increases the survivor's sense of control over his or her experience, reduces feelings of chaos, and increases the sense that the universe is predictable and orderly, if not beneficent. Furthermore, deriving meaning from one's experiences may provide some degree of closure, in that it makes sense and fits into existing models of understanding. Finally, a more coherent trauma narrative, by virtue of its organization and complexity, may support more efficient and complete emotional and cognitive processing (Amir et al., 1998). In contrast, fragmented recollections of traumatic events that do not have an explicit chronological order and do not have obvious causes may easily lead to additional anxiety, insecurity, and the de-realization that sometimes occur in the presence of incomprehensible events and may ultimately inhibit trauma processing.

Narrative coherence typically arises from the detailed discussion and multiple revisitation of trauma or abuse memories during psychotherapy. In this regard, the tendency for exposure and activation to increase the details of traumatic memory (Foa & Rothbaum, 1998) and to reinstate awareness of the original context in which it occurred also supports the development of a detailed and logical story of what happened and, in some cases, why. As the client becomes more aware of the details of his or her victimization and of his or her own options and lack thereof at the time it occurred, it is also likely that the narrative will shift in valence, as described below.

Altering cognitive structures. An important part of cognitive processing is the modification of negative cognitive structures, as described earlier in this chapter. These structures may be divided into two types: consciously available cognitive distortions and "deep," less conscious negative cognitive structures. These cognitive phenomena often are interrelated, however, and a given cognitive sequel of abuse may contain aspects of both types.

Cognitive distortions refer to consciously available thoughts and assumptions about self and others that are inaccurate and typically detrimental to the individual, such as feelings of low self-esteem, helplessness, hopelessness, self-blame, shame, or perception of others as intrinsically dangerous or hurtful. Some of these distortions may reflect verbalized interpretations of less verbally mediated "core" schemas, as will be described later. Other distortions may arise from negative perceptions of self and others that occurred as a result of childhood psychological abuse, such as ongoing criticism, devaluation, and blaming verbalizations by parents or caretakers (Briere, 1992).

Intervention in conscious cognitive distortions often involves providing the client with opportunities to reconsider or reevaluate inaccurate self or other perceptions in light of new information. Clinical experience suggests that this process is less likely when the clinician merely disagrees (or argues) with the client about his or her cognitions. Rather, reconsideration may be most effective when it arises from disparity. Most typically, this will involve exposure and cognitive interventions that, in addition to addressing CERs, allow the client to experience both the original abuse-related phenomenon (e.g., memories of parental derogation for poor grades) and a concomitant, disparate, logical perspective (e.g., that the poor grades were due to explainable events [e.g., abuse] and that poor grades do not mean low intelligence or intrinsic inadequacy).

As is also true of deeper cognitive phenomena, reconsideration activities are often most effective when the abuse survivor realizes the disparity between early abuse-related messages and current, more accurate data about self or others. This is done not in a confrontational manner but rather through a series of gentle questions (i.e., via the Socratic approach mentioned earlier) that allow the client to examine questionable assumptions and interpretations that he or she has made about the abuse. The point here is to provide the client with an opportunity to explore his or her understanding, not to argue with the client regarding his or her thinking "errors." The reader is referred to the excellent treatment manual by Resick and Schnicke (1993) on cognitive processing therapy for additional coverage on cognitive (and a version of exposure) interventions in this area.

Suppressed or deep cognitive structures are similar to more surface cognitive distortions, except that the emotional associations to these cognitions are sufficiently distressing that the thoughts are consciously avoided. Although excluded from conscious awareness, suppressed cognitions, by virtue of their susceptibility to internal and external triggers, are often activated in therapy by the same processes used to address other cognitive distortions (i.e., during the process of recalling and describing childhood trauma). Such reemergence is typically brief, however, because the negative affect associated with—by definition—suppressed thoughts motivates their rapid resuppression. Experienced therapists often are alert to such intrusions, whether signaled by changed facial expressions, gaps in discourse, or sudden self-derogation, at which point the clinician supports conscious attention to—and verbalization of—the thought. Generally, clinical experience suggests that the verbal processing of previously suppressed material is associated with a temporary increase in distress (as found experimentally by Wenzlaff et al., 1991), which eventually decreases as the material is consciously addressed. This subsequent decrease, which may occur over several sessions, is probably due to both (a) the habituation and counterconditioning of anxiety associated with the suppressed thought once it has been processed and (b) the reduction in pressure to keep the thought suppressed. Regarding the former, although suppressed thoughts are often out of conscious awareness, their emotional sequels (e.g., anxiety, anger) may still be experienced consciously when activated by reminiscent stimuli (Wegner & Smart, 1997) and thus may be reduced as affective aspects of the thought are desensitized.

Once suppressed thoughts and memories of childhood maltreatment are verbalized and (through habituation and counterconditioning) stripped of some of their negative CERs, they can be cognitively processed in light of new information. For example, as an abuse survivor's previously suppressed thoughts (and associated feelings) of self-blame regarding her pseudoparticipation in incestuous contact with her father are accessed and discussed, she can more logically assess and seek feedback regarding the accuracy of her belief that she was to blame for her abuse—a process that

was impossible when this gestalt of thoughts and feelings were unavailable to conscious awareness. Similarly, intrusive negative self-talk associated with childhood psychological abuse may be suppressed from awareness, leading to a stream of unmonitored, negative self-perceptions and commentary that cannot be evaluated for its validity or fairness. As the clinician gently focuses attention on such statements or assumptions, further suppressed material is usually activated and potentially disclosed, allowing emotional and cognitive processing that otherwise might not occur.

Processing activated relational schemas. The final form of cognitive processing discussed in this chapter involves relational schemas. Although presented here as a cognitive phenomenon, thought per se is rarely involved, but rather a gestalt of interpersonal expectations and perceptions based on early, preverbal, childhood experience. In addition, concomitant emotional responses conditioned to the same maltreatment (e.g., feelings of loss, emptiness, and sadness) that produce negative relational schemas often mean that triggers of these cognitive structures will also activate associated strong negative affects.

As described earlier, negative relational schemas usually are triggered within the context of a close or significant relationship because the primary activators of such schemas are phenomena such as intimacy, interpersonal vulnerability, loss or abandonment, betrayal, or violation. Once triggered, negative relational schemas are often accompanied by intense negative affect and sudden, seemingly impulsive, often developmentally archaic behavior. This behavior may be proximity seeking (e.g., demanding or excessive dependency), punitive (e.g., verbal or physical aggression), or tension reducing (e.g., self-mutilation, sexual acting out). Most characteristically, such thoughts, feelings, and behaviors may be more relevant to the individual's childhood experiences than to the interpersonal context in which it is triggered.

Although such seemingly "borderline" responses are often immediately problematic during therapy, ultimately their emergence is both predictable and, to some extent, necessary for significant recovery to occur. Absent such relational triggers, therapy might be easier to conduct but would be unlikely to activate the very material that has to be processed before the client's relational life can improve. Thus, just as treatment for classic posttraumatic stress symptoms includes titrated exposure to traumatic memories and activation of conditioned emotional responses in the context of disparity, therapy for the relational aspects of severe childhood maltreatment must include similar components.

Specifically, per the earlier trauma-processing formulation, the client encounters *exposure* (i.e., to stimuli that are in some way similar between the original traumatic relationship and the current therapeutic one), *activation* (the client feels, on some level, suspicious, maltreated, unappreciated, or judged, thereby experiencing what can be considered a relational flashback), *disparity* (although the client feels this way, in reality the therapist is not doing any of these things to an appreciable extent and may be doing the opposite), and *processing* (the client's repeated expectation and perception of the therapist as, to some extent, abusive, in the presence of the therapist's manifest nonabusiveness and nondangerousness, eventually extinguish the original conditioned emotional responses through nonreinforcement).

As per the treatment for posttraumatic stress, these various components occur within the therapeutic window, except that instead of titrated exposure to sensory/autobiographical abuse memories, the titration is to the level of contact with the therapist. In this regard, the clinician is careful to be neither too close (running the risk of activating intrusion and boundary violation issues, as well as, paradoxically, reinforcing some clients' dependency needs) nor too distant (potentially triggering abandonment or rejection issues). Finally, therapists must monitor their behavior for evidence of their own activated relational schemas (e.g., punitiveness or rescuing behavior) in response to the client's schema-related behavior because such countertransference would eliminate the disparity requirement of trauma processing.

The frequent need for abuse survivors to process relational issues, in addition to cognitive distortions and posttraumatic stress, means that—as opposed to simple cognitive-behavioral therapy (CBT) for uncomplicated posttraumatic stress—successful therapy may require regular sessions over considerably longer periods of time. The actual length of treatment will vary according to the extent of the client's affect regulation difficulties, use of avoidance, degree and valence of deep cognitive disturbance, and the severity of his or her negative relational schemas.

Access to Previously Unavailable Material

Taken together, the self-trauma approach outlined in this chapter allows the therapist to address the impaired self-functioning, cognitive disturbance, and posttraumatic stress found in some adults who were severely abused as children. The activation and serial resolution of painful memories and intrusive cognitive states are likely to slowly reduce the survivor's overall level of posttraumatic stress and associated dysphoria—a condition that eventually lessens the general level of avoidance required by the survivor for internal stability. This process also increases self-resources—as noted earlier, progressive exposure to nonoverwhelming distress is likely to increase affect regulation skills and affect tolerance. As a result, successful ongoing treatment allows the survivor to confront increasingly more painful memories without exceeding the survivor's (now greater) self-capacities.

In combination, processing traumatic memory and increasing self-resources can lead to a relatively self-sustaining process: As the need to avoid painful material lessens with treatment, memories, affects, and cognitions previously too overwhelming to desuppress become more available for processing. As this new material is, in turn, desensitized and cognitively accommodated, self-capacity is further improved, and the overall stress level is further reduced—thereby permitting access to (and processing of) even more previously unavailable material. Ultimately, treatment ends when traumatic material is sufficiently desensitized and integrated, and self-resources are sufficiently learned and strengthened, that the survivor no longer experiences significant intrusive, avoidant, or dysphoric symptoms.

This progressive function of self-trauma therapy removes the need for any so-called memory recovery techniques. Instead of relying on hypnosis or drug-assisted interviews, for example, to increase access to unavailable material, the self-trauma approach allows these memories to emerge naturally as a function of the therapeutic relationship and the survivor's reduced need for avoidance. Whereas some memory recovery techniques might easily exceed the therapeutic window and flood the survivor with destabilizing memories and affects, the current approach allows access to trauma- or abuse-related material only when, by definition, the therapeutic window has not been exceeded.

Conclusions

This chapter has presented a synthesis of current dynamic, cognitive, and behavioral approaches that have been found helpful in the treatment of severe child abuse trauma. This model holds that postabuse symptomatology generally reflects the survivor's adaptive attempts to maintain internal stability in the face of potentially overwhelming abuse-related pain. It further suggests that many of these symptoms are, in actuality, inborn recovery algorithms that fail only when overwhelming stress or inadequate internal resources motivate the hyperdevelopment of avoidance responses.

It is argued here that successful treatment for abuse-related distress and dysfunction should not impose alien techniques and perspectives on the survivor but rather should help the client to do better what he or she is already attempting to do. Thus, like the survivor, the therapist should be especially concerned with balancing challenge with resource and growth with safety. The natural healing aspects of intrusion and avoidance are not countered in treatment but instead are refined to the point that they are maximally helpful and can be abandoned once successful.

In this way, the self-trauma model is ultimately optimistic; it assumes that much of abuse-related pathology and dysfunction are solutions in the making, albeit ones intrinsically more focused on survival than recovery. At the same time, unfortunately, the inescapable implication of abuse-focused therapy (and any other exposure-based treatment) is that to reduce posttraumatic pain and fear, both must be repeatedly confronted and experienced. As therapists, we should not forget what we are asking of our clients in this regard, lest we lose track of the courage and strengths that they inevitably must bring to the treatment process.

Notes

1. The actual recovery time is likely to vary considerably, according to the severity of the trauma and the presence of other predisposing factors.

2. Although this issue is a source of controversy, with some individuals claiming that psychological amnesia for childhood abuse is virtually impossible, the last three editions of the American Psychiatric Association's (1980, 1987, 1994) diagnostic manual and recent research (for reviews, see Courtois, 1999; Pezdek & Banks, 1996; Williams & Banyard, 1999) suggest that some level of dissociative amnesia for traumatic events is not especially rare.

References

Abueg, F. R., & Fairbank, J. A. (1992). Behavioral treatment of posttraumatic stress disorder and co-occurring substance abuse. In P. A. Saigh (Ed.), *Posttraumatic stress disorder: A behavioral approach to assessment and treatment* (pp. 111-146). Needham Heights, MA: Allyn & Bacon.

Alexander, P. C. (1992). Effect of incest on self and social functioning: A developmental psychopathology perspective. *Journal of Consulting and Clinical Psychology, 60,* 185-195.

American Psychiatric Association. (1980). *Diagnostic and statistical manual of mental disorders* (3rd ed.). Washington, DC: Author.

American Psychiatric Association. (1987). *Diagnostic and statistical manual of mental disorders* (3rd ed., rev.). Washington, DC: Author.

American Psychiatric Association. (1994). *Diagnostic and statistical manual of mental disorders* (4th ed.). Washington, DC: Author.

Amir, N., Stafford, J., Freshman, M. S., & Foa, E. B. (1998). Relationship between trauma narratives and trauma pathology. *Journal of Traumatic Stress, 11*, 385-393.

Baldwin, M. W. (1992). Relational schemas and the processing of social information. *Psychological Bulletin, 112*, 461-484.

Baldwin, M. W., Fehr, B., Keedian, E., Seidel, M., & Thompson, D. W. (1993). An exploration of the relational schemata underlying attachment styles: Self-report and lexical decision approaches. *Personality and Social Psychology Bulletin, 19*, 746-754.

Baldwin, M. W., Keelan, J. P. R., Fehr, B., Enns, V., & Koh-Rangarajoo, E. (1996). Social-cognitive conceptualization of attachment working models: Availability and accessibility effects. *Journal of Personality and Social Psychology, 71*, 94-109.

Beck, J. S. (1995). *Cognitive therapy: Basics and beyond.* New York: Guilford.

Blank, A. S. (1993). The longitudinal course of posttraumatic stress disorder. In J. R. T. Davidson & E. B. Foa (Eds.), *Posttraumatic stress disorder: DSM-IV and beyond* (pp. 3-22). Washington, DC: American Psychiatric Press.

Bowlby, J. (1982). *Attachment and loss: Vol. 1. Attachment* (2nd ed.). New York: Basic Books.

Bowlby, J. (1988). *A secure base: Parent-child attachment and healthy human development.* New York: Basic Books.

Briere, J. (1992). *Child abuse trauma: Theory and treatment of the lasting effects.* Newbury Park, CA: Sage.

Briere, J. (1996). *Therapy for adults molested as children* (2nd ed.). New York: Springer.

Briere, J. (1997). *Psychological assessment of adult posttraumatic states.* Washington, DC: American Psychological Association.

Briere, J. (2000a). *Cognitive Distortion Scales (CDS) professional manual.* Odessa, FL: Psychological Assessment Resources.

Briere, J. (2000b). *Inventory of Altered Self-Capacities (IASC) professional manual.* Odessa, FL: Psychological Assessment Resources.

Briere, J., & Gil, E. (1998). Self-mutilation in clinical and general population samples: Prevalence, correlates, and functions. *American Journal of Orthopsychiatry, 68*, 609-620.

Burt, M. R., & Katz, B. L. (1987). Dimensions of recovery from rape: Focus on growth outcomes. *Journal of Interpersonal Violence, 2*, 57-81.

Chard, K. M., Weaver, T. L., & Resick, P. A. (1997). Adapting cognitive processing therapy for child sexual abuse survivors. *Cognitive and Behavioral Practice, 4*, 31-52.

Coe, M. T., Dalenberg, C. J., Aransky, K. M., & Reto, C. S. (1995). Adult attachment style, reported childhood violence history and types of dissociative experiences. *Dissociation: Progress in the Dissociative Disorders, 8*, 142-154.

Collins, N. L., & Read, S. J. (1990). Adult attachment, working models, and relationship quality in dating couples. *Journal of Personality and Social Psychology, 58*, 644-663.

Courtois, C. (1991). Theory, sequencing, and strategy in treating adult survivors. In J. Briere (Ed.), *Treating victims of child sexual abuse* (pp. 47-60). San Francisco: Jossey-Bass.

Courtois, C. (1999). *Recollections of sexual abuse: Treatment principles and guidelines.* New York: Norton.

Davis, M. (1992). The role of the amygdala in fear and anxiety. *Annual Review of Neurosciences, 15*, 353-375.

Elliott, D. M. (1994). Impaired object relations in professional women molested as children. *Psychotherapy, 31*, 79-86.

Elliott, D. M., & Briere, J. (1995). Transference and countertransference. In C. Classen (Ed.), *Treating women molested in childhood* (pp. 187-226). San Francisco: Jossey Bass.

Foa, E. B., & Kozak, M. J. (1986). Emotional processing of fear: Exposure to corrective information. *Psychological Bulletin, 99*, 20-35.

Foa, E. B., Molnar, C., & Cashman, L. (1995). Change in rape narratives during exposure therapy for posttraumatic stress disorder. *Journal of Traumatic Stress, 8*, 675-690.

Foa, E. B., & Riggs, D. S. (1993). Posttraumatic stress disorder and rape. In R. S. Pynoos (Ed.), *Posttraumatic stress disorder: A clinical review* (pp. 133-163). Lutherville, MD: Sidran.

Foa, E. B., & Rothbaum, B. O. (1998). *Treating the trauma of rape: Cognitive-behavioral therapy for PTSD.* New York: Guilford.

Fraley, R. C., Davis, K. E., & Shaver, P. R. (1998). Dismissing-avoidance and the defensive organization of emotion, cognition, and behavior. In J. A. Simpson & W. S. Rholes (Eds.), *Attachment theory and close relationships* (pp. 249-279). New York: Guilford.

Holen, A. (1993). The North Sea oil rig disaster. In J. P. Wilson & B. Raphael (Eds.), *International handbook of traumatic stress syndromes* (pp. 471-478). New York: Plenum.

Horowitz, M. J. (1976). *Stress response syndromes.* New York: Aronson.

Horowitz, M. J. (1986). Stress-response syndromes: A review of posttraumatic and adjustment disorders. *Hospital and Community Psychiatry, 37*, 241-249.

Jacobs, W. J., & Nadel, L. (1985). Stress induced recovery of fears and phobias. *Psychological Review, 92*, 512-531.

Janoff-Bulman, B. (1992). *Shattered assumptions: Towards a new psychology of trauma*. New York: Free Press.

Jehu, D. (1988). *Beyond sexual abuse: Therapy with women who were childhood victims*. Chichester, UK: Wiley.

Kelly, A. E., & Kahn, J. H. (1994). Effects of suppression of personal intrusive thoughts. *Journal of Personality & Social Psychology, 66*, 998-1006.

Koopman, C., Classen, C., & Spiegel, D. (1994). Predictors of posttraumatic stress symptoms among survivors of the Oakland/Berkeley, Calif., firestorm. *American Journal of Psychiatry, 151*, 888-894.

LeDoux, J. E. (1995). Emotion: Cues from the brain. *Annual Review of Psychology, 46*, 209-235.

Levy, M. B., & Davis, K. E. (1988). Lovestyles and attachment styles compared: Their relations to each other and to various relationship characteristics. *Journal of Social and Personal Relationships, 5*, 439-471.

Linehan, M. M. (1993). *Cognitive-behavioral treatment of borderline personality disorder*. New York: Guilford.

March, J. S. (1993). What constitutes a stressor? The criterion issue. In J. R. T. Davidson & E. B. Foa (Eds.), *Posttraumatic stress disorder: DSM-IV and beyond* (pp. 37-54). Washington, DC: American Psychiatric Press.

McCann, I. L., & Pearlman, L. A. (1990). *Psychological trauma and the adult survivor: Theory, therapy, and transformation*. New York: Brunner/Mazel.

Metcalfe, J., & Jacobs, W. J. (1996). A "hot-system/cool system" view of memory under stress. *PTSD Research Quarterly, 7*, 1-6.

Murray, E. J., & Segal, D. L. (1994). Emotional processing in vocal and written expression of feelings about traumatic experiences. *Journal of Traumatic Stress, 7*, 391-405.

Pearlman, L. (1998). Trauma and the self: A theoretical and clinical perspective. *Journal of Emotional Abuse, 1*, 7-25.

Pearlman, L. A., & Saakvitne, K. W. (1995). *Trauma and the therapist: Countertransference and vicarious traumatization in psychotherapy with incest survivors*. New York: Norton.

Pennebaker, J. W., Kiecolt-Glaser, J. K., & Glaser, R. (1988). Disclosure of trauma and immune function: Health implications for psychotherapy. *Journal of Consulting and Clinical Psychology, 56*, 239-245.

Petrie, K. J., Booth, R. J., Pennebaker, J. W., Davison, K. P., & Thomas, M. G. (1995). Disclosure of trauma and immune response to a hepatitis B vaccination program. *Journal of Consulting and Clinical Psychology, 63*, 787-792.

Pezdek, K., & Banks, W. P. (Eds.). (1996). *The recovered memory/false memory debate*. New York: Academic Press.

Putnam, F. W. (1997). *Dissociation in children and adolescents: A developmental perspective*. New York: Guilford.

Rachman, S. (1980). Emotional processing. *Behavior, Research, and Therapy, 18*, 51-60.

Resick, P. A., & Schnicke, M. K. (1993). *Cognitive processing therapy for rape victims: A treatment manual*. Newbury Park, CA: Sage.

Samoilov, A., & Goldfried, M. R. (2000). Role of emotion in cognitive-behavior therapy. *Clinical Psychology: Science and Practice, 7*, 373-385.

Shipherd, J. C., & Beck, J. G. (1999). The effects of suppressing trauma-related thoughts on women with rape-related posttraumatic stress. *Behavior Research and Therapy, 37*, 99-112.

Siegel, D. J. (1999). *The developing mind: Toward a neurobiology of interpersonal experience*. New York: Guilford.

Simpson, J. A. (1990). Influence of attachment styles on romantic relationships. *Journal of Personality and Social Psychology, 59*, 971-980.

Simpson, J. A., & Rholes, W. S. (1994). Stress and secure base relationships in adulthood. In K. Bartholomew & D. Perlman (Eds.), *Advances in personal relationships* (Vol. 5, pp. 181-204). London: Jessica Kingsley.

Simpson, J. A., & Rholes, W. S. (Eds.). (1998). *Attachment theory and close relationships*. New York: Guilford.

Styron, T., & Janoff-Bulman, R. (1997). Childhood attachment and abuse: Long-term effects on adult attachment, depression and conflict resolution. *Child Abuse & Neglect, 21*, 1015-1023.

van der Hart, O., Steele, K., Boon, S., & Brown, P. (1993). The treatment of traumatic memories: Synthesis, realization, and integration. *Dissociation: Progress in the Dissociative Disorders, 6*, 162-180.

van der Kolk, B. A., McFarlane, A. C., & Weisaeth, L. (1996). *Traumatic stress: The effects of overwhelming experience on mind, body, and society*. New York: Guilford.

Wegner, D. M. (1994). Ironic processes of mental control. *Psychological Review, 10*, 34-52.

Wegner, D. M., & Erber, R. (1992). The hyperaccessibility of suppressed thoughts. *Journal of Personality and Social Psychology, 63*, 903-912.

Wegner, D. M., & Gold, D. B. (1995). Fanning old flames: Emotional and cognitive effects of suppressing thoughts of a past relationship. *Journal of Personality and Social Psychology, 68,* 782-792.

Wegner, D. M., & Smart, L. (1997). Deep cognitive activation: A new approach to the unconscious. *Journal of Consulting and Clinical Psychology, 65,* 984-995.

Wenzlaff, R. M., Wegner, D. M., & Klein, S. B. (1991). The role of thought suppression in the bonding of thought and mood. *Journal of Personality and Social Psychology, 60,* 500-508.

Westen, D. (2000). Commentary: Implicit and emotional processes in cognitive-behavioral therapy. *Clinical Psychology: Science and Practice, 7,* 386-390.

Williams, L. M., & Banyard, V. L. (Eds.). (1999). *Trauma and memory.* Thousand Oaks, CA: Sage.

Wirtz, P., & Harrell, A. (1987). Effects of post-assault exposure to attack-similar stimuli on long-term recovery of victims. *Journal of Consulting and Clinical Psychology, 55,* 10-16.

Wolpe, J. (1958). *Psychotherapy by reciprocal inhibition.* Stanford, CA: Stanford University Press.

Yehuda, R., & McFarlane, A. C. (1995). Conflict between current knowledge about posttraumatic stress disorder and its original conceptual basis. *American Journal of Psychiatry, 152,* 1705-1713.

11

Adults, Adolescents, and Children Who Sexually Abuse Children

A Developmental Perspective

MARK CHAFFIN

ELIZABETH LETOURNEAU

JANE F. SILOVSKY

When children are the objects of sexual aggression or sexual abuse, one of the images most readily brought to the public mind is that of the inveterate male predatory pedophile with a long history of abusive behaviors, perhaps beginning with his own sexual abuse as a child and leading from there into increasingly victimizing sexual behaviors during childhood, adolescence, and, finally, adulthood. Yet, despite generations of clinical acceptance of a "victim-to-victimizer cycle of sexual abuse" and notions that sexually abusive behavior toward children is inherently compulsive, progressive, and incurable, much of the best evidence available suggests that, although these assumptions may be true in particular cases, in general they are overstated or inaccurate. Even within developmental levels (i.e., childhood, adolescence, and adulthood), one sees enormous diversity in the types and patterns of behavior, in personality and demographic characteristics, and in environment and background. This diversity translates into critical differences in risk and prognosis, with differences becoming sharper between developmental levels. Yet, to a significant extent, our treatment and public policy efforts have underappreciated this diversity and these developmental differences.

In this chapter, we will examine sexually abusive behavior from a developmental perspective. We will begin with a short review of what is known about the developmental course of sexually abusive behavior, then move on to discuss characteristics, assessment, treatment, and public policy issues for each of three developmental groups: adult sex offenders, adolescent or juvenile sex offenders (JSOs), and children with sexual behavior problems (CSBPs). In reviewing the literature, we will focus primarily on the sexual abuse of children, where possible, rather than sex offenses or sexual behavior problems in general. We will argue that intervention models, whether emphasizing treatment or criminal justice, should generally view these three developmental groups as very different and very heterogeneous populations, and we suggest that separate and often qualitatively different interventions and policies need to be devised for each developmental level.

The Developmental Course of Sexually Abusive Behaviors

One of the more popular explanations for sexually abusive behavior is the so-called victim-to-victimizer cycle. This explanation holds that most individuals who molest children were themselves molested as children and go on to "complete the cycle" of abuse. Direct mechanisms (e.g., trauma reenactment, identification with the abuser, modeling, and social learning) or mediated mechanisms (e.g., abuse leads to low social competency and feelings of inadequacy that in turn lead to abusive behavior) can be postulated. The victim-victimizer link was originally based on retrospective self-reports of childhood sexual abuse among incarcerated adult sex offenders (e.g., Groth, 1979) and is still touted as a core tenet in many clinical models. However, in two studies reporting a high percentage (41% and 67%) of retrospectively self-reported child sexual abuse (CSA) among adult offenders, these rates decreased considerably (to 25% and 29%, respectively) when polygraph verification was employed or mentioned in the assessment of CSA history (Hindman, 1988; Letourneau, 1999). Across studies, the self-reported childhood sexual abuse rate for both adult offenders and JSOs has generally stabilized between 20% and 30%

(Hanson & Slater, 1988), suggesting that most adults or adolescents who have molested children were not themselves sexually victimized as children. Some data have suggested that the connection between sexual abuse victim and victimizer is greater among younger children and becomes progressively weaker through middle childhood and early adolescence. Johnson (1988) found that 72% of the 4- to 6-year-old CSBPs had a history of being sexually abused, compared with 42% of the 7- to 10-year-olds and 35% of the 11- and 12-year-olds.

Although sexual abuse histories are often clinically described as pandemic within prison or residential sex offender treatment settings, it should be noted that sexual abuse histories—and, indeed, histories of negative childhood events in general—are quite high among most groups of inmates and residentially placed juveniles and are not unique to sex offenders. If anything, these populations may be characterized more by pervasively negative histories in general than by their history of childhood sexual victimization in particular. Even among CSBPs in whom the connection between sexual behavior and sexual abuse history is more proximal and direct, a recent study found that family sexuality, the presence of other nonsexual behavior problems, and life stress are just as strongly associated with childhood sexual behavior problems as a history of previous sexual abuse (Friedrich, 1999). Childhood sexual abuse is not uniquely powerful in the etiology of childhood behavior problems, especially in the etiology of juvenile or adult sexual offending.

Studies using prospective methodologies, which are far superior to retrospective methodologies for determining risk and causal factors, document that very few sexual abuse victims go on to commit detected sex crimes and that childhood sexual abuse is not a large or uniquely powerful risk factor for adult sex crimes. In fact, a history of physical abuse or neglect may play a larger and more significant role (Widom & Ames, 1994).

Among offenders, a history of childhood sexual abuse may affect aspects of offending behavior. Sexual abuse histories are associated with a greater likelihood of younger and male victims (Kaufman, Hilliker, & Daleiden, 1996) and increased levels of deviant sexual arousal among some adolescents, particularly those who target young boys, although JSOs' arousal patterns are much more fluid than are those of adults (Becker, Hunter, Stein, & Kaplan, 1989; Hunter, Goodwin, & Becker, 1994). Sexual abuse histories also may be associated with an earlier onset of sexually abusive behavior (Burton, 2000; Richardson, Bhate, & Graham, 1997). Among adult offenders, a history of CSA may be related to arousal, but it does not appear to be strongly related to recidivism risk (Hanson & Bussière, 1998).

Although it seems clear that a sexual abuse history, if present, may be an important factor in some individual cases, it is overly simplistic and insufficient as a general causal explanation. It appears likely that the causes of abusive sexual behavior involve multiple complex pathways. The developmental trajectory of sexual acts toward children is not well known but is unlikely to be a single, clear, simple, deterministic pathway. In addition to pathways involving early sexualization or abuse, pathways may exist that closely parallel those for conduct disorder or serious violent offending in general. Sexual behavior that violates the rights of others is an inherent part of conduct disorder and antisocial personality disorder, both of which are prevalent among some subgroups of juvenile and adult offenders (Kavoussi, Kaplan, & Becker, 1988). Consequently, some pathways to sexually abusive behavior may be similar to pathways involved in serious violent behavior in general (e.g., early behavior problems, school failure, affiliation with delinquent peers, alcohol or drug use, etc.). Still other pathways might involve low social competency or loneliness. Some early data suggest that at least one pathway to juvenile sexual aggression may involve a combination of childhood sexual abuse by a male combined with physical abuse by fathers, mitigated to some extent by maternal bonding (Kobayashi, Sales, Becker, Figueredo, & Kaplan, 1995). Finally, sexually abusive behavior may simply arise out of opportunity or a confluence of individual circumstances. In some juvenile cases, for example, the behavior may be largely experimental or compensatory (O'Brien, 1994).

There are some sexual abusers whose abusive behavior begins early in life and is persistent across developmental transitions (i.e., child to juvenile and juvenile to adult), but this appears to be the exception rather than the rule. A minority of adult offenders report an early onset for their behavior (Abel et al., 1987; Marshall, Barbaree, & Eccles, 1991). However, these early-onset adult offenders may have larger numbers of victims and events (Abel, Osborne, & Twigg, 1993). Similarly, a minority of JSOs report beginning their behavior during childhood (Burton, 2000).[1] Thus, it appears that most adult offenders and JSOs did not develop their interests or behavior during an earlier developmental level. The prospective links between CSBP, JSO, and adult sex offender are even weaker than it might appear from the retrospective data. Recidivism is quite low for both CSBPs and JSOs (Alexander, 1999; Bonner, Walker, & Berliner, 1999a, 1999b, 1999c), and the large majority of CSBPs and JSOs do not appear to be destined to become continuous offenders.

Sexual behavior that violates the rights of others is an inherent part of conduct disorder and antisocial personality disorder, both of which are prevalent among some subgroups of juvenile and adult offenders.

Given the developmental discontinuities involved in sexually abusive behaviors and the differences between developmental groups (CSBPs, JSOs, and adults), we will summarize the research about each group separately, with an eye toward contrasting the populations and highlighting critical features relevant to treatment and public policy. The following sections will address characteristics, assessment, treatment, and public policy issues for each developmental group.

Children With Sexual Behavior Problems

Professionals in the child maltreatment and children's mental health fields have become increasingly aware of young children who demonstrate sexual behavior problems (American Academy of Child and Adolescent Psychiatry, 1999; Araji, 1997). The clinical literature describes childhood sexual behavior problems ranging from a preoccupation with sexual topics during play to serious aggressive sexual behaviors, including coercing other children into penetrative sexual acts (Araji, 1997; Cantwell, 1988; De Angelis, 1996; Gil & Johnson, 1993a, 1993b; Johnson, 1991). Children younger than 6 years of age have been found to exhibit sexually aggressive behaviors, including acts against other children such as fondling and oral sodomy (Burton, Nesmith, & Badten, 1997; Friedrich & Luecke, 1988; Johnson, 1988, 1989; Silovsky, Niec, & Hecht, 2000).

Sexual behaviors in children 12 years of age and younger are considered problematic when they are either potentially harmful or atypical. Definitions of what constitutes an atypical or concerning sexual behavior may vary between cultures. A general definition of sexual behavior problems within our culture involves behaviors that (a) occur at a frequency greater than would be developmentally expected; (b) interfere with children's development; (c) occur with coercion, intimidation, or force; (d) are associated with emotional distress; (e) occur between children of divergent ages or developmental abilities; or (f) repeatedly recur in secrecy after intervention by caregivers (adapted from Hall, Mathews, Pearce, Sarlo-McGarvey, & Gavin, 1996; Johnson, 1998).

Sexual behaviors and the children who exhibit them have been given a variety of labels (e.g., sexually reactive children, mini-"perps," children who molest, child perpetrators, or child offenders). In our opinion, criminal justice definitions or labels are inappropriate for young children because children are not usually held criminally liable for sexual misbehavior. The term *children with sexual behavior problems* was adapted because it labels the behavior and not the identity of the child (Araji, 1997; Bonner & Fahey, 1998; Bonner et al., 1999a, 1999b, 1999c; Gray & Pithers, 1997; National Task Force on Juvenile Sexual Offending, 1993). Terms such as *perpetrator* or *offender* when referring to children are not only legal malapropisms but also potentially psychologically damaging to the child's developing self-concept. How adults think about and respond to these children may in itself have a lasting impact on children's adjustment. Throughout childhood, children are developing an understanding of who they are. Responses from others that label or reinforce a belief that the child is deviant, perverted, or otherwise pathological have enormous potential to hinder children's developing sense of self. Children *do* need to

correct highly problematic behaviors. However, the goals of intervention should be to reduce and eliminate inappropriate sexual behavior without negatively labeling the child.

Characteristics. It is not unusual for young preschool children to engage occasionally in any of a wide range of sexualized behaviors, including exhibiting their genitals to others, being curious about their own bodies and those of other children, physically examining other children's or adults' bodies, and masturbating (Friedrich, Grambsch, Broughton, Kuiper, & Beilke, 1991). Many sexualized behaviors that are not unusual among preschool children might be considered problematic if exhibited by an older child or adolescent (Friedrich, 1997). Although we refer to these behaviors as sexual, it is important to note that the intentions and motivations for these behaviors may be unrelated to sexual gratification or sex drive as we adults understand it. Prepubertal children simply do not experience sexual arousal and drives comparable to those of adults or adolescents.

Cognitive and social aspects of child development have several important implications for understanding how to respond to childhood sexual behavior problems. Young children's cognitive development limits their repertoire of coping strategies. Self-soothing activities (e.g., masturbation) may occur more often among young children during times of stress (White, Halpin, Strom, & Santilli, 1988) than among older children who have developed the ability to use more sophisticated coping strategies. Young children's cognitive development also limits the types of cognitive processes involved in initiating and maintaining sexual misbehavior. Young CSBPs are not able to engage in complex cognitive processes such as planning, grooming, or rationalizing. Thus, typical adult sex offender or JSO concepts such as a "cycle of sexual behaviors" involving elaborate cognitive patterns or "thinking errors" may miss the mark with young children. Young children normally are self-focused, do not readily understand and experience others' perspectives of situations and emotions, and have only a rudimentary conceptualization of causes and consequences. Finally, short attention spans and limited impulse control are characteristic of young children. In contrast to many adult sex offenders, the modus operandi of CSBPs is more likely to involve impulsive rather than well-planned or rationalized acts, and many characteristics, such as failure to empathize, may be developmentally normal rather than pathological.

Several typologies of problematic childhood sexual behaviors have been proposed (Berliner, Manaois, & Monastersky, 1986; Bonner et al., 1999a, 1999b, 1999c; Hall et al., 1996; Hall, Mathews, & Pearce, 1998; Pithers, Gray, Busconi, & Houchens, 1998a, 1998b). Childhood sexual behaviors that are inappropriate but without interpersonal contact have been classified as "sexually inappropriate" (Bonner et al., 1999a, 1999b, 1999c). Subclassifying those behaviors into self-focused (e.g., excessive masturbation) and other-focused (e.g., sexual remarks and gestures) also may be relevant (Hall et al., 1996). "Sexually intrusive" behaviors have been described as sexual acts that are interpersonal but unplanned, impulsive, and nonaggressive (Bonner et al., 1999a, 1999b, 1999c; Hall et al., 1996). "Sexually aggressive" acts have been described as involving more serious sexual contact, often including threats, force, coercion, or aggression (Berliner et al., 1986; Bonner et al., 1999a, 1999b, 1999c; Hall et al., 1996; Hall et al., 1998). The effects of sexually intrusive or sexually aggressive behaviors by CSBPs on the children toward whom they are directed are unestablished. It is not known whether these behaviors carry the same potential degree of harm as sexual abuse committed by JSOs and adult offenders.

Children with sexual behavior problems are highly diverse, perhaps even more so than JSOs and adult offenders. Even the most prevalent characteristic found among JSOs and adult offenders—male gender—is not a defining feature among CSBPs. In fact, among preschool children with sexual behavior problems, the majority have been reported to be girls (65%) (Silovsky et al., 2000). There is no distinct CSBP profile or any clear pattern of demographic, psychological, or social factors. Empirical attempts to construct CSBP subtypes based on sexual behavior have not yielded clear or consistent results (Bonner et al., 1999a, 1999b, 1999c; Hall et al., 1996).

Attempts to construct empirically based typologies based on demographic, family, social, and abuse history characteristics have yielded tentatively better results (e.g., Bonner et al., 1999a, 1999b, 1999c; Pithers et al., 1998a, 1998b). Pithers et al. (1998a, 1998b) used cluster analysis to identify five subtypes labeled sexually aggressive, highly traumatized, abuse reactive, rule breaker, and nonsymptomatic. However, significant overlap in characteristics across the subtypes was found. Both the sexually aggressive and rule breaker groups demonstrated significant sexually aggressive behaviors. The rule breaker group may be a more severe subtype, with higher levels of general behavior problems, emotional problems, and related parental stress. Interestingly, although the sexually aggressive group was almost exclusively male (91%), 42% of the rule breaker group were girls. The highly traumatized and abuse-reactive groups both had extensive histories of maltreatment but differed from each other in occurrence of posttraumatic stress disorder (PTSD) (91% of the highly traumatized group; 5% of the abuse-reactive group) and in the occurrence of oppositional defiant disorder (18% of the highly traumatized group; 96% of the abuse-reactive group). The abuse-reactive group was also more likely to be male (96%) than the highly traumatized group. Other studies using cluster analysis have failed to find stable subtypes (Bonner et al., 1999a, 1999b, 1999c).

In addition, the child's age may be related to both the type and frequency of behavior. Preschool CSBPs may exhibit more frequent sexual behaviors than school-age children (Silovsky et al., 2000). Higher rates of child maltreatment, exposure to family violence, and general behavior problems have been found among preschool CSBPs (Silovsky et al., 2000). Preschoolers also are less likely to reside with their biological parents than samples of school-age CSBPs (Burton, 2000; Silovsky et al., 2000), often related to maltreatment.

Assessment. Most assessments of CSBPs are requested for clinical purposes, such as treatment planning. If there is CPS or law enforcement investigation, this should ordinarily be completed prior to beginning the clinical assessment. In those cases in which the child is actually a suspect rather than the victim in a law enforcement investigation, special safeguards are suggested. For example, children are more likely than adults or teens to produce false information in response to suggestion, reinforcement contingencies, confusion, manipulation, coercion, bias, or pressure. Law enforcement interrogations of suspect children should avoid highly suggestive techniques or the manipulative strategies designed to elicit confessions from adult sex crimes suspects, and children who are suspects in a law enforcement investigation should always have their parent or attorney present during questioning.

Clinical assessment of childhood sexual behavior problems is similar to the assessment of most other types of behavior problems in young children and should have both a general clinical and a sexual behavior-specific focus. The core of the assessment involves obtaining a thorough behavioral history of the problematic sexual behaviors (e.g., onset and precipitating events, types of behaviors involved, changes in the type or frequency of the behavior over time, responses to correction, etc.), child maltreatment history, a social history of the child and family, a history of the child's general psychological and social functioning, an assessment of the child's strengths and resources, a school history, an assessment of comorbid impulse control problems such as attention deficit hyperactivity disorder or oppositional defiant disorder, and an assessment of trauma-related conditions such as PTSD. With young children, environment is more important to assess than intrapersonal or psychological variables. It is important to gain a broad picture of the child's overall social ecology, identifying potential risk situations (such as unsupervised interactions with younger children) and resources (such as adult support and supervision). Information should be obtained from multiple sources (e.g., child self-report, caregiver report, interviews with family, teacher report, observation, CPS investigations). It is important to learn about how parents or other adults have responded to the child's behavior problems to date and what has helped and has not. Because the most effective interventions for childhood behavior problems often rely on teaching parents or caretakers effective behavior management skills (Brestan & Eyberg, 1998), it is important to learn about both the types and consistency of discipline approaches currently used. Finally, it is important to learn about any exposure to explicit sexuality that may have influenced the behavior. Many CSBPs have been exposed to some sort of explicit sexuality. This may be due to sexual abuse, living in a sexually explicit family, exposure to sexually explicit media, poor supervision or neglect, normal curiosity, or chance encounters with sexual behavior. Obtaining a frank, valid history of exposure to sexuality may be challenging due to children's or parents' reluctance to discuss the topic or parents' ignorance about their children's exposure. Interviewing children about a possible history of sexual abuse involves a range of complexities and is discussed in detail in Chapter 18 (this volume).

Although a thorough behavioral and social history is often sufficient for designing a good intervention plan, psychological testing may be added to answer specific questions, provide additional detail, or obtain a baseline against which to measure change. Assessment systems such as the Child Behavior Checklist (CBCL) (Achenbach, 1991) or the Behavior Assessment System for Children (BASC) (Reynolds & Kamphaus, 1992) are good choices because of their breadth, norms, and availability of self-report, parent-report, and teacher-report forms. The Child Sexual Behavior Inventory (CSBI) (Friedrich, 1997) is perhaps the most useful instrument for assessing sexual behaviors among children ages 2 to 12. The CSBI measures the frequency of common and atypical behaviors, self-focused and other-focused behaviors, and aggressive and nonaggressive behaviors and compares these with results found among a large normative sample. A shorter instrument appropriate for tracking week-to-week changes in behavior is the Weekly Behavior Checklist (WBC) (Cohen & Mannarino, 1996b). The WBC tracks sexual behaviors as well as other behaviors relevant for preschool children (e.g., sleep problems, regressive behaviors, and temper tantrums). Family environment, social history, and abuse history may be measured using instruments such as The Safety Checklist (Friedrich, 1996), and PTSD or other trauma-related symptoms, including sexual concerns, may be measured using instruments such as the Trauma Symptom Checklist for Children (TSCC) (Briere, 1996) or the Children's Impact of Traumatic Events Scale (CITES-R) (Wolfe, Gentile, Michienzi, Sas, & Wolfe, 1991).

Because interventions for CSBPs often focus on the child's environment and consequently must include caregivers, testing might include measures of parenting distress such as the Parenting Stress Index (Abidin, 1990) and, if the child has been sexually abused, the Parent Emotional Reaction Questionnaire or the Parent Support Questionnaire (Cohen & Mannarino, 1996a). Pithers et al. (1995) also recommend measures of caregiver psychological symptoms, such as the Brief Symptom Inventory (Derogatis & Melisaratos, 1983). Sexual deviancy assessment procedures sometimes used with adult offenders and older JSOs, such as polygraph, plethysmograph, and self-report sexual fantasy assessments, are not appropriate for CSBPs.

Assessing risk for repeated sexual behavior problems or risk to other children may be an important question, although it is arguably less forensically relevant than it is for adult sex offenders or JSOs. However, no empirically validated systems or instruments are currently available for this purpose. No long-term follow-up studies are available to suggest risk-relevant variables. Clinical estimation of risk may be employed, but its accuracy in general is notoriously poor.

Treatment. Several treatment protocols for CSBPs have been developed in recent years, including the Support Program for Abuse Reactive Kids (SPARK) (Cunnigham & MacFarlane, 1996), the STEP program (Gray & Pithers, 1993), the Harborview Sexual Assault Center Program (Berliner & Rawlings, 1991), and the Group Therapy Program for Children With Sexual Behavior Problems, developed by Bonner, Walker, and Berliner (1999b, 1999c, in press). Araji (1997) provides descriptions of several programs designed for children younger than age 12.

Although interventions for CSBPs are more recently developed than interventions for JSOs and adult offenders and the treatment research literature is smaller, two moderate-sized randomized clinical trials have been conducted. Both studies (Bonner, Walker, & Berliner, 1993; Pithers & Gray, 1993) compared two different treatments for CSBPs ages 6 to 12 years. Bonner et al. (1993) randomly assigned children to 12 sessions of either a structured sexual behavior-focused cognitive-behavioral treatment group or an unstructured and unfocused play therapy group, both with corresponding groups for parents. Equivalent reductions in sexual behavior problems were found among children in both types of treatment. Pithers and Gray (1993) compared the effectiveness of two 32-week group treatment programs: a structured sexual behavior focused relapse prevention program and a less structured or focused expressive therapy program. Parallel caregiver groups were provided in both treatments. Greater mid-treatment benefits were found with the relapse prevention program but only among the highly traumatized subgroup of children

(Pithers et al., 1998a, 1998b). However, this difference faded to statistical insignificance over time, with children in both conditions showing comparably reduced levels of sexual behavior problems (reported in Bonner & Fahey, 1998). At present, the most that can be suggested is that more structured treatments may have some initial advantages among more highly traumatized CSBPs. The tendency for traumatized children to benefit from more structured approaches is supported by randomized trials for sexually abused children, some of whom also had sexual behavior problems (Cohen & Mannarino, 1996a, 1996b), and by general clinical guidelines (American Academy of Child and Adolescent Psychiatry, 1999). Aside from this, however, there is little empirical evidence for preferring one approach to CSBP treatment over another, and no evidence suggests that "sex offender-specific" or specialized programs are the only acceptable option.

Both of the randomized trials to date have reported reductions in inappropriate sexual behaviors (both self-focused and other-focused) regardless of the treatment modality employed. Randomized trials with a no-treatment control group have not been conducted. Consequently, it is not possible to say whether the reduced levels of sexual behavior problems are actually due to the treatment. One consistency across both studies has been the direct involvement of caregivers in the treatment. The importance of involving caregivers is well supported in the general child treatment literature. The most effective treatments for general childhood behavior problems have included direct caregiver participation in treatment (Brestan & Eyberg, 1998; Deblinger, Lippmann, & Steer, 1996; Hembree-Kigin & McNeil, 1995), and it may be parent/caretaker involvement, rather than the modality of treatment used with the child, that is the critical ingredient for CSBP treatment. Children are more likely to practice and generalize new behaviors and skills learned in sessions when they are supported by their caregiver, and caregiver supervision can be critical in preventing an impulsive recurrence of inappropriate behavior. Parents or caretakers are also critical for establishing a safe and nonsexualized environment for the child. If a change in residential placement is anticipated, participation of the present and future caregivers in the treatment is recommended. For example, if a child is in a foster home and will be returning to his or her parents' home, then both the foster parents and parents should be involved.

Topics in structured or specialized CSBP treatment programs often include (a) acknowledging the sexual behaviors (except with preschoolers), (b) learning rules about sexual behavior, (c) learning age-appropriate sex education, (d) learning impulse control/self-control strategies, (e) learning sexual abuse prevention/safety skills, (f) learning social skills, and (g) learning simple emotional regulation/coping strategies. Topics for parents or caregivers often include

(a) learning the importance of supervision,
(b) communicating with other adults (such as day care personnel and teachers) about supervision needs of the children,
(c) reinforcing privacy and sexual behavior rules,
(d) learning what is normal sexual development and sexual play and how these differ from sexual behavior problems,
(e) learning how to maintain a nonsexualized environment,
(f) being guided in how to talk with children about sexuality,
(g) learning specific behavioral parenting strategies,
(h) supporting children's use of self-control strategies,
(i) communicating with children, and
(j) having appropriate nurturance and physical affection with children.

One frequently asked question is whether CSBPs need residential treatment or out-of-home placement. In making decisions about residential care, the potential benefits of residential treatment (e.g., controlled environment, daily treatment contacts, high levels of community protection) must be weighed against the potential liabilities (very high cost, difficulties in obtaining parent/caretaker involvement, exposure to other children with behavior problems, disruption of social attachments and normal activities, labeling and stigma, potential for victimization). In our opinion, childhood sexual behavior problems, by themselves, do not warrant residential treatment. Although sexually abusive adults should usually be required to leave the victim's home in cases of intrafamilial abuse, in our opinion, this need not be a routine rule in cases of abuse by a CSBP. In our experience, most cases of intrafamilial sexual abuse by a CSBP can be successfully managed on an

outpatient basis and without removal of any children from the home. Residential treatment or removal should be reserved for unusually severe and serious cases that may present with some of the following features: when highly aggressive sexual behavior problems continue to recur despite adequate treatment and close supervision, when the child is actively suicidal, when the child is actively homicidal, when the child has such severe behavioral and emotional problems that he or she is unable to function in the community, when adequate supervision cannot be realized, where demonstrable harm or emotional distress is being inflicted on an in-home victim, and when the child has severe symptoms that have not responded to adequate medication, outpatient treatment, or intensive in-home approaches. If children are residentially placed, it should be in a facility designed for children and with adequate supervision. Differences in maturity, size, and behavior severity should guide placement decisions. Under no circumstances should CSBPs be placed in the same residential unit with significantly older, larger, or more mature JSOs due to the differences in treatment needs, the risk of delinquent influences, and the risk of victimization.

If the primary difficulty appears to be lack of parental support and supervision, alternative home placements, such as therapeutic foster care, are preferable to inpatient, residential, shelter, or group home placements. Foster parents accepting CSBPs into their home should be fully informed of the problem, be willing and able to closely supervise and support the child, and be willing to participate in the child's treatment. If other children are in the foster home, appropriate steps should be taken to monitor behavior and ensure the safety of all children.

Public policy. Recent trends suggest increased levels of juvenile justice involvement for CSBPs (Burton et al., 1997). CSBPs as young as age 10 are now being adjudicated delinquent and entering the juvenile correctional system. Concerns about the negative impact of criminalization and viewing these children as "offenders" or "mini-perpetrators" rather than as children with behavior problems have been noted (Friedrich, 2000). The long-term ramifications of criminalization and being labeled as a sex-offender on young children's development have not been measured but are arguably likely to be negative and ultimately counterproductive. It is our opinion that the rights and welfare of the children must be foremost in the minds of professionals responding to CSBPs (Chaffin & Bonner, 1998a, 1998b; Friedrich, 2000), and these cases should be handled in ways qualitatively different from those of adult offenders and JSOs. Separate policies and practice parameters for adolescents and for children have been recommended (Bernet & Shaw, 2000; Friedrich, 2000). However, in many cases, CSBPs are subject to the same or similar policies as adult sex offenders. For example, some states place no lower age limit on sex offender registration and community notification procedures. Other states have maintained internal agency registries of sexually aggressive youth, including children as young as age 2. Once officially labeled as a sex offender or a sexually aggressive child, these youngsters may not have equal access to needed resources. Many of these policies are based on assumptions that CSBPs pose a unique danger and require highly specialized intervention and control procedures, similar to adult sex offenders. However, as we have reviewed earlier, the available evidence tends not to support these assumptions. Little evidence suggests serious long-term risk to the community from most CSBPs, and the available treatment outcome research suggests that a range of short-term outpatient interventions yield good results in most cases.

The long-term ramifications of criminalization and being labeled as a sex-offender on young children's development have not been measured but are arguably likely to be negative and ultimately counterproductive.

Juvenile Sex Offenders

Unlike CSBPs, in whom sexual behavior problems are best defined clinically, behavior that constitutes child sexual abuse by a teenager is usually defined as a crime by law, and consequently JSOs may correctly be labeled as legal offenders on the basis of their illegal sexual behavior. Over the past 15 to 20 years, it has become clear that a signifi-

cant number of sex crimes are attributable to adolescents (for a review, see Davis & Leitenberg, 1987). This is particularly the case for the sexual abuse of children. The percentage of sexual assaults attributable to juveniles is higher among younger victims. For example, according to data from the FBI's National Incident-Based Reporting System, only 5% of sexual assaults against victims older than age 25 are attributable to a juvenile offender. However, 43% of sexual assaults against children age 6 and younger are attributable to juvenile offenders (National Center for Juvenile Justice, 1999). Although accounting for a substantial portion of child sexual abuse, JSOs constitute a small percentage of the overall problem of juvenile delinquency. JSOs represent only 1% of all delinquency court cases and less than 6% of juvenile offenders of all kinds in juvenile correctional residential placements (National Center for Juvenile Justice, 1999). In response to increased awareness of the problem, specialized JSO treatment programs increased by around 40-fold between 1982 and 1992 (Knopp, Freeman-Longo, & Stevenson, 1992). Beginning in the late 1980s, research interest in juvenile sexual offending increased as well. Very little research was published in the years prior to 1980. Between 1985 and 1990, the average number of new articles abstracted in the PsycInfo database had reached 14 per year. Now, a decade later, this has increased to more than 35 new articles per year. However, very few large sample empirical studies have been published (Prentky, Harris, Frizell, & Righthand, 2000).

Characteristics. It is generally acknowledged that JSOs with child victims are a heterogeneous population (Becker, 1998; Knight & Prentky, 1993), often appearing to share little in common except the fact that that they have engaged in sexual behavior with a child. Adolescents who have molested children have no single defining profile and do not present with any single set of personality characteristics, family background, personal history, or comorbid conditions. Most of the published literature describing the characteristics of JSOs involves small-scale studies relying on convenience samples of clinical cases drawn from a single treatment program or correctional institution. In general, the characteristics reported in studies vary considerably with the source of the sample. Studies relying on adolescents from high-security correctional or residential institutions report higher levels of abuse, family dysfunction, and comorbid conditions. Studies relying on adolescents from outpatient programs present a healthier picture. The vast majority of studies have been limited to males who comprise 90% of the known population (Davis & Leitenberg, 1987).

Despite these limitations, a number of individual characteristics have been commonly reported across samples. Compared with nonoffending groups, juvenile sex offenders are found to have weak social skills, nonsexual behavior problems, learning disabilities, depression, and impulse dysregulation (for a review, see Becker, 1998). However, JSOs' levels of behavior problems and learning disabilities are not higher than those of other non-sex-offending juvenile delinquent groups (Blaske, Borduin, Henggeler, & Mann, 1989; Milloy, 1994).

In general, adolescents who molest children appear to be different from adolescents who rape peers, although the behaviors are not entirely mutually exclusive. Compared with peer rapists, adolescents who molest children have been found to be younger and have less social competency, less peer sexual activity, and fewer conduct problems (Krauth, 1998). Personality differences also have been found between these two groups, with adolescents who molest children appearing more submissively dependent, withdrawn, and self-belittling than peer rapists (Carpenter, Peed, & Eastman, 1995). JSOs also differ from adult sex offenders in several important ways. For example, JSOs have been found to engage in fewer abusive behaviors, over shorter periods of time, and less frequently involving penile penetration compared with adult offenders (Miranda & Corcoran, 2000).

Just as there is no profile for these adolescents, there also is no profile for their families. Family backgrounds are diverse and may or may not be dysfunctional. Graves, Openshaw, Ascione, and Ericksen (1996) conducted a meta-analysis of family characteristics, distinguishing between the family characteristics of youth who primarily target children and other types of sexual offenders. Youth involved primarily with children had higher levels of parental alcohol or substance abuse and higher levels of maternal depression. Extremes in family adaptability (chaotic or rigid) and family cohesion (disengaged or enmeshed) were also found in a high percentage of cases. Still, a significant number of families were described as

healthy. Again, extremes of family cohesion and communication problems among JSO families may not be greatly different than among the families of other non-sex-offending juvenile delinquent groups (Blaske et al., 1989).

A critical area in which adolescents who molest children may differ from adult sex offenders is in the role of deviant sexual interest patterns. The study of physical arousal in this population is compromised by a lack of data on normal adolescent male arousal patterns and by the fact that discriminating erectile responses in adolescent males is negatively correlated with age (Kaemingk, Koselka, Becker, & Kaplan, 1995). With the possible exception of some adolescents who target male children exclusively, it appears that there is less correspondence between measured arousal and offense histories than has been reported for adult offenders (Becker et al., 1989; Hunter et al., 1994). Also, screening instruments using reaction time in an attempt to identify individuals with deviant arousal patterns have not been completely successful in discriminating juvenile sex offenders and nonoffenders (Smith & Fischer, 1999). With regard to deviant fantasy activity, it appears that juvenile sex offenders are characterized not so much by an increased level of deviant fantasy as they are by decreased levels of nondeviant fantasy (Daleiden, Kaufman, Hilliker, & O'Neil, 1998). These findings suggest that routine use of "fantasy logs" and other sexual deviancy-oriented treatment approaches may miss the mark for most juveniles.

Adolescent sexual offenders, including adolescents who molest children, are a highly heterogeneous group possibly containing multiple coherent subtypes. To the extent that these subtypes might differ in characteristics, natural course of sexual behaviors, or treatment outcomes, examining only the omnibus group could obscure important facts. Work with adult sex offenders has suggested that empirically distinct subtypes may exist (Knight & Prentky, 1993), and early efforts have been made at identifying subtypes among young children with sexual behavior problems (Pithers et al., 1998a, 1998b). However, similar empirical work remains to be done with adolescents, although research in this area is under way.

Perhaps the simplest typology involves subdividing juvenile sex offenders by their type of offense (e.g., peer rapists vs. child molesters vs. mixed groups or others) or by characteristics of their victims (e.g., male vs.

female victims; incest vs. nonincest). These distinctions have been the most commonly used to date. As noted earlier, several significant differences have been noted among offense type and victim type groups, and this classification system has the advantage of simplicity. Other subdivisions have been made on the basis of background characteristics. For example, generally conduct-disordered versus non-conduct-disordered distinctions might be made, or abused versus nonabused distinctions.

Other typologies are clinically based. Clinical typologies are important because they can potentially guide interventions. Becker and Kaplan (1988) proposed differentiating between three groups of adolescents: one with emerging paraphilic interests, another with generalized conduct disorder, and a third with self-limited exploratory behavior. Perhaps the most detailed system is the PHASE typology developed by O'Brien and Bera (1986). This typology may be particularly useful for treatment providers because it is both descriptive (describing common characteristics, backgrounds, and motivations for each type) and prescriptive (suggesting core treatment targets and levels of care needed for each type). The categories include (a) naive experimenters, (b) undersocialized child molesters, (c) narcissistic child molesters, (d) sexual aggressives, (e) sexual compulsives, (f) disturbed impulsives, and (g) group influenced. To date, however, none of the clinical typologies have been empirically validated (Becker, 1998).

Assessment. Two main types of assessments are performed with adolescents who molest children. Clinical assessments are for purposes of determining strengths and weaknesses, identifying amenability and appropriateness for treatment, and understanding the youth's psychological status and social ecology. Risk assessments are for purposes of determining the likelihood of recidivism and are often related to placement and forensic decisions. Clinical assessments are ideally conducted after adjudication but prior to disposition in the juvenile court (Hunter & Lexier, 1998).

Clinical assessment typically begins by obtaining a multisource behavioral history, including a review of victim interviews, police and court records, and other data documenting the behavior involved in the current offense as well as prior known offenses. This is usually followed by an interview with the adolescent, his or her family members, and others involved in the adolescent's life. Clinical assessments typically obtain information regarding school, family history, drug and alcohol history, history of previous mental health and behavior problems, cognitive ability, social history, friendship patterns, and emotional status. In addition, the evaluation also should include taking a detailed sexual history. After establishing a clear understanding of the limits of confidentiality, the sexual behavior history should inquire into both normal nondeviant behavior and the behavioral details of the presenting offense and other known offenses, remaining cognizant of the ethical issues involved in discussing material that may be incriminating and subject to mandatory reporting laws (Hunter & Lexier, 1998).

Psychological testing may be useful for answering case-specific questions or for determining treatment baselines. Suggested instruments for specific target areas are described by Bonner, Marx, Thompson, and Michaelson (1998). These include instruments measuring general behavior problems such as Child Behavior Checklist (Achenbach, 1991), instruments measuring delinquent behavior patterns such as the Jesness Inventory (Jesness, 1988), and instruments measuring self-reported offense history, sexual behavior, interests, and knowledge, such as the Multiphasic Sex Inventory for Adolescents (Nichols & Molinder, 1986). Use of the plethysmograph in assessments with adolescents is controversial and should be limited to older teenagers in whom deviant arousal patterns are strongly suspected and will be specifically targeted in treatment. Plethysmograph assessment should only be conducted with voluntary informed consent and following published plethysmography and ethical guidelines (Association for the Treatment of Sexual Abusers [ATSA], 1997; National Task Force on Juvenile Sexual Offending, 1993).

Estimating risk for reoffense is often a major assessment question but can only be answered poorly at present. Mental health professionals relying on clinical impressions have a notoriously poor track record for predicting any type of future violent or sexually aggressive behavior in the absence of self-evident risk indicators (e.g., a client professing the intent to reoffend, a client exhibiting clearly uncontrolled sexual behavior, etc.). Clinicians tend to overpredict risk with juvenile sexual offenders, even when using lists of likely risk factors (Smith & Monastersky, 1986), and often perform little better than chance. For adult sexual offenders, actuarial risk prediction systems are currently considered the state of the art. Actuarial systems have numerous advantages over clinical impressions. Unfortunately, no actuarial systems exist for adolescents, and it has been difficult to establish risk predictors for adolescents due to the small samples studied combined with low reoffense rates and possible subtype diversity found in the population. A few preliminary steps toward developing JSO actuarial systems have been taken (Prentky et al., 2000). Some of the sexual reoffense risk factors that have been identified are similar to risk factors found in adult sex offender risk assessment systems, such as having a larger number of victims. However, other key adult risk factors may not have the same significance among JSOs. For example, Prentky et al.'s (2000) work suggests that deviant sexual interest is only weakly related to risk in JSOs, although it is a major risk domain among adults. Perhaps the strongest risk predictors for sexual and especially nonsexual reoffending are related to general delinquency, antisocial tendencies, or psychopathy (Becker, 1990; Gretton, McBride, O'Shaugnessy, & Hare, 2000; Prentky et al., 2000; Rasmussen, 1999). Still other factors included in adult actuarial risk prediction systems, such as being unmarried or young in age, clearly would be meaningless with adolescents. In our opinion, adult actuarial systems should not be applied to JSOs. The fact that JSOs have a very low base rate of known sexual recidivism (i.e., around 7%) (Alexander, 1999) further hampers risk prediction efforts. Even an actuarial system with good power to discriminate reoffenders from nonreoffenders would be subject to a high false-positive rate due to the low base rate of reoffenders in the treated JSO population.

Treatment. A large number of treatment programs have published single-group outcome data, but currently no published studies compare the outcomes for JSOs randomly assigned to treatment versus no-treatment conditions. Strictly speaking, we cannot empirically demonstrate whether treatment is beneficial or harmful or has no effect. However, there is evidence that JSOs who complete sex offender treatment fare better than a comparison group of those who do not, who drop out of treatment, or who are removed from treatment (Worling & Curwen, 2000). It is clear from multiple studies that known reoffense rates after treatment are not nearly as high as may be popularly assumed, and the overwhelming majority of adolescents enrolled in and being released from treatment programs do not have a known reoffense in the short to moderate term. Alexander (1999) combined the results of several published studies following more than a thousand juvenile sex offenders and calculated a mean overall reoffense rate of 7%. In most studies with adequate sample size, recidivism ranges between 5% and 15% across variable treatment approaches, treatment intensities, and follow-up times (Weinrott, 1996). The reoffense rates appear to be lower for the subgroup of adolescents who have molested children, as opposed to other types of sex offenses. This consistency of fairly positive outcomes across a diversity of approaches stands in contrast to the common opinion that only highly specialized and intensive approaches are effective, as well as to the general prognostic pessimism evident in some policies and practices with JSOs. Consistency of outcomes across a diversity of approaches might be explained in a number of ways, including an absence of treatment effects, equality of treatment effects, differential effectiveness of treatments across unspecified subgroups, strong effects from confounding variables (e.g., juvenile justice processing), insensitive outcome measures, or some combination of the above. Although JSO sexual reoffense rates are generally low, the rates of nonsexual recidivism are significantly higher (up to 50% or more), suggesting that sexual issues are not the sole problem for many of these adolescents (Weinrott, 1996).

A wide variety of clinical treatment approaches for JSOs have been described in the literature, including behavioral conditioning approaches (Kaplan, Morales, & Becker, 1993; Weinrott, Riggan, & Frothingham, 1997), pharmacological approaches (Bradford, 1993; Galli, Raute, McConville, & McElroy, 1998), family systems approaches (Bentovim, 1998), rational-emotive therapy (Whitford & Parr, 1995), music and art therapy (Gerber, 1994; Skaggs, 1997), "cycle"-based approaches (Ryan, Lane, Davis, & Issac, 1987), cognitive-behavioral approaches (Becker & Kaplan, 1993; Kahn, 1990), relapse prevention approaches (Gray & Pithers, 1993; Steen, 1993), and ecological multisystemic approaches (Swenson, Henggeler, Schoenwald, Kaufman, & Randall, 1998). Treatment programs often combine several different approaches. One of the current criticisms of the JSO treatment field is that treatment has been technique driven rather than theory driven, resulting in ad hoc combinations of potentially contradictory approaches.

Many current treatment programs are loosely based on a cognitive-behavioral model. These approaches focus on changing attitudes and belief systems in areas such as victim empathy and cognitive distortions or thinking errors. Cognitive-behavioral approaches also may focus on increasing social skills, improving anger management, and teaching self-control techniques. In some programs, these may be combined with a relapse prevention approach along with behavioral approaches focused on changing arousal patterns where this is indicated. Treatment is often carried out in a peer group environment (i.e., group homes, specialized residential units), although recent findings have raised concerns that programs that aggregate delinquent youth together may have negative effects due to the risks associated with increased delinquent peer influences and socialization into delinquent behavior and belief patterns (Chamberlain & Reid, 1998).

Many JSO treatment programs are derived directly from models developed for treating adult pedophiles. Some of these programs take a corrections-oriented approach, are highly confrontational, are punitive, or endorse unsupported tenets such as "offenders can never be cured" or assumptions that all juvenile offenders harbor deviant sexuality and deviant sexual fantasies and are inherently devious and dishonest about their sexual interests. Although application of adult models has been advocated by some (Valliant & Bergeron, 1997), there appear to be critical differences between adolescents who molest children and their adult counterparts, both in terms of motivational patterns and a lower prevalence of the types of sexual deviancy and psychopathic tendencies that are prevalent among the more high-risk subgroups of adult offenders (ATSA, 1997). This has led some observers to raise the issue of whether approaches developed for adult pedophiles are inappropriate or even potentially harmful when applied to the majority of JSOs (Becker, 1998; Chaffin & Bonner, 1998a, 1998b; Goocher, 1994).

One of the more promising approaches to treating adolescents with a wide range of delinquent behaviors, including sexually abusive behavior, is multisystemic therapy (MST). MST is an intensive community and home-based approach that has good empirical support with nonsexual delinquents, and preliminary data from two studies, one with a 10-year follow-up, supporting its effectiveness with juvenile sex offenders (Borduin, 2000; Borduin et al., 1995; Borduin, Henggeler, Blaske, & Stein, 1990). Rather than an exclusive focus on individual variables (e.g., sexual compulsions, denial, past trauma, etc.), MST focuses both on the youngster and the youngster's social ecology, including family supervision and involvement, school work, peer group affiliations, and so forth. These target areas more closely match the range of factors known to be correlates of severe antisocial behavior in adolescents (Swenson et al., 1998). An advantage for MST is its documented efficacy in reducing nonsexual recidivism, which, as noted earlier, is much more common than sexual recidivism among JSOs.

Levels of care employed for JSOs include outpatient treatment, intensive home-based approaches, therapeutic foster care, group homes, residential treatment facilities, and correctional institutions. Some states have invested large amounts of money in long-term institutional or group home facilities for juvenile sex offenders. Juvenile sex offenders account for around six times as many placements as they do cases in the system (National Center for Juvenile Justice, 1999). Reliance on institutional placement may be due to the pessimism of some clinicians about the risk posed by this population (Sapp & Vaughn, 1990), the complexities involved in cases with in-home victims, community safety concerns, lack of appropriate intermediate care resources such as therapeutic foster homes, or belief in institutional placement as a "just desert" for this type of emotionally evocative offense. There are no known data available on what percentage of JSO institutional placements are necessary or unnecessary as judged against some accepted criteria. In fact, there are no uniform accepted criteria. Although the need for residential care is clear for many JSOs, there is some professional consensus that most JSOs can be treated on an outpatient basis (ATSA, 1997), and many are seen in outpatient settings. Many more could probably be retained in community settings by using intensive ecologically based models, such as

MST, if these approaches were more widely available. Circumstances suggesting the need for residential placement are similar to those described earlier in this chapter for CSBPs. Where residential placement is indicated, facility standards are available to guide practitioners (Bengis et al., 1999), and placements often involve specialized JSO programming or segregated JSO units. Decisions about placement in restrictive settings should weigh not only community safety and treatment need issues but also must consider the possible negative effects of long-term aggregate placements, such as the increased risk of socialization into a delinquent lifestyle, negative peer influences, institutionalization, weakening of family ties, absence of parental involvement in treatment, and disruption of normal social development. In addition, placement decisions need to weigh the financial reality that residential placement is expensive and may divert funds away from other needed services.

Public policy. As we have discussed, generalizing adult sex offender characteristics, assumptions, and treatment models to most teenagers may be inappropriate. So may application of adult sex offender–oriented public policies, especially to younger and less severe adolescents. Particularly concerning are sex offender public notification laws. Although there is clear consensus in the treatment field that adolescents who molest children should be charged and processed through the juvenile justice system to ensure better supervision and accountability, as well as to establish an official record (ATSA, 1997; National Task Force on Juvenile Sexual Offending, 1993), treatment professionals have generally opposed including juveniles in sex offender public notification procedures (ATSA, 1997). Most issues arise in connection with public notification rather than with registries that are accessible only to law enforcement. States vary widely in their approach to registry and notification requirements. Some states apply notification laws only to adults (and often only to more severe adult cases), whereas other states have broad criteria and have established no lower age limit. Some states have placed young teenagers on public sex offender registries, including providing the names and addresses of JSOs as young as 12 or 13 years old on the Internet. Many of these actions have been fueled by what, in our opinion, are unduly negative perceptions of risk and

prognosis (see, e.g., Bureau of Justice Statistics, 1998, p. 88). These misperceptions are cause for concern, given the generally low known sexual recidivism rates for adolescents and the potential for public notification to have negative effects on normal social development. Routinely identifying JSOs to the public may potentially establish a self-fulfilling prophecy and may unnecessarily create social stigmatization, social isolation, peer rejection or violence, and expectations of failure. Finally, there is potential risk to the community if any benefits of selective notification are diluted by including low-risk populations, such as most JSOs, in community notification procedures. Notification about a few high-risk or predatory offenders may be much more valuable to the public than lists of thousands and thousands of primarily low-risk individuals.

Adult Sex Offenders

A great deal has been written about adult sex offenders against children, far outstripping what is known about CSBPs and JSOs. The purpose of this section is to condense this large body of information into a summary of what we do and do not know about adults who sexually molest children. This is a broad overview intended as a practical guide and not a comprehensive review of the literature. Although the literature on adult offenders is extensive, there are inherent biases in what we know. Sexual assaults in general, including childhood sexual assaults, usually go unreported (Smith et al., 2000). When reports of sexual assault are made, approximately 10% lead to arrests and 8% lead to convictions (Maguire & Pastore, 1998). We have gathered nearly all of our information about adult sex offenders from this 8% of incidents, and it seems unlikely that this is a representative sample.

Characteristics. Many early research efforts were aimed at identifying offender characteristics. At the very least, we wanted to know what a child molester looks like. The cover of an issue of *Sports Illustrated* (Nack & Yaeger, September, 1999) included mug shots of six convicted child molesters. The men are not smiling, and their pictures are dark and sinister. However, as the accompanying article pointed out, in real life these men were not dark and sinister-looking monsters—they were attractive, articulate, and socially skilled coaches. Adult child molesters may look like anyone else.

Efforts at identifying adult sex offenders based on demographic characteristics have consistently failed, with the single exception that they are far more likely to be male. However, a not insignificant number are women. One retrospective study of men sexually abused as children found that 17% of their offenders were female, and some surveys of sexually assaulted adolescents indicate that 20% or more of their offenders were female (Finkelhor, Hotaling, Lewis, & Smith, 1990). Unlike other adult criminals, adult child molesters are not necessarily characterized by youthfulness, aggressiveness, or impulsivity. Unfortunately, this also means that adult child molesters are not characterized by a "youthful" offending pattern that declines steeply after middle age, as is the case with nonsexual violent criminals. Although young adult male sex offenders are at a higher risk to reoffend than their older counterparts, a significant number of child molesters continue to molest children well into late adulthood. Relative to other adult criminal groups, child molesters are often found to be older, more likely to have been married, and to have attained higher economic status and education levels (Bard et al., 1987). There is wide variability within the population and between outpatient, prison, and civil commitment populations. For example, in a study involving civilly committed sex offenders with multiple offenses, Knight, Prentky, and Cerce (1994) found no differences between rapists and child molesters on IQ, achieved skill level, education, or marital status, differences that have been found in other settings. Thus, characteristics that have been reported for one population may not hold among another.

The most common psychological profile of a child molester is that of a psychiatrically nondisturbed individual.

It bears repeating that there is no child molester personality profile. There is no scientifically valid foundation for efforts either to include or exclude an individual from suspicion as an actual or potential child molester based on personal characteristics. In fact, the most common psychological profile of child molesters is that of a psychiatrically nondisturbed individual. Thus, in addition to having no defining set of demographic characteristics, most child molesters do not have specific comorbid psychological or personality disorders. The Minnesota Multiphasic Personality Inventory (MMPI) and other personality tests cannot identify child molesters, most of whom have normal profiles (Chaffin, 1992). When MMPI elevations do occur, they can include virtually every mathematically possible 2-point code type (Hall, Maiuro, Vitaliano, & Proctor, 1986). Likewise, social skills deficits, commonly thought to distinguish child molesters, are not consistently identified, although recent evidence suggests that loneliness, arising from poor attachment, may contribute to some types of child molestation (Ward, Hudson, & Marshall, 1996).

Despite the low frequency of most comorbid psychological disorders, some comorbid psychiatric or behavioral conditions are quite relevant to treatment planning and risk assessment. These include psychopathy and substance use disorders. Several studies have looked at the correlation between sexual offending and psychopathy. Psychopathy refers to a constellation of characteristics, including emotional shallowness, insincerity, callousness, interpersonal exploitation, lack of guilt or remorse, impulsiveness, pathological lying, proneness toward violence, and persistent violation of social norms. It is not equivalent to criminality or antisocial tendencies, although psychopaths often do engage in serious criminal acts. Although estimated to constitute only 1% or less of the general population, psychopaths may constitute 15% to 25% of the prison inmate population (Hare, 1996). Hart and Hare (1997) reviewed the research on psychopathy among adult sex offenders and concluded that sex offenders with adult victims have the highest rate of psychopathy, offenders with adolescent victims have the next highest rate, and offenders with child victims have the lowest rate of psychopathy (between 5% and 15%). This pattern of findings has been replicated (Seto & Barbaree, 1999). Despite generally low base rates, there are two compelling reasons why psychopathy is relevant to consider among adult child molesters. First, it is a strong predictor of violent recidivism and a significant predictor of sexual recidivism (Firestone et al., 1999; Hanson & Bussière, 1998). Second, treatment effects may be reversed among the minority of child molesters with high levels of psychopathy. That is, treatment may increase, rather than decrease, risk among psychopaths. Seto and Barbaree (1999) compared the sexual recidivism rates of child molesters grouped by level of psychopathy (low vs. high score) with clinicians' treatment ratings (poor vs. good). Psychopaths whose clinicians rated them as having done well in treatment were far *more* likely to reoffend sexually than any other group. In two earlier studies, Quinsey and his colleagues (Quinsey, Harris, Rice, & Cormier, 1998; Rice, Harris & Cormier, 1992) reported greater violent recidivism among treated versus untreated individuals scoring high on psychopathy.

Comorbid substance use problems also are potentially relevant among child molesters, although the evidence is mixed. Marshall (1997) has suggested that substance abuse may be the one reliable comorbid disorder contributing to child molestation. A substantial minority of child molesters (30%) self-report using substances (usually alcohol) immediately before offending against a child (Pithers, 1990), with a smaller but still noticeable percentage meeting diagnostic criteria for a substance use disorder (Langevin, 1990). Incest recidivists have been found to score higher on alcoholism screening tests (Firestone et al., 1999). However, in a comprehensive meta-analysis of sex offense recidivism, Hanson and Bussière (1998) did not find clear evidence of effects due to substance abuse. The role of substance abuse may be complex, and determining the role may be complicated by the efforts of offenders either to minimize their use, claim drunkenness as a justification for their behavior, or make improbable claims of substance-induced amnesia for their acts.

One characteristic that sets some child molesters apart from their non-sex-offending counterparts is a history of engaging in a variety of sexually anomalous (i.e., paraphilic) behaviors, behaviors that may or may not involve victimization of others. The percentage of child molesters who engage in other types of sexual offenses or in paraphilic behaviors varies greatly across studies. Using highly confidential and anonymous interviews with subjects meeting criteria for at least one paraphilia,[2] Abel and his colleagues (Abel, Becker, Cunningham-Rathner, Mittelman, & Rouleau, 1988) reported that many incest and extrafamilial child molesters (70% to 80%, respectively)

met lifetime prevalence criteria for multiple paraphilias. Using polygraph assessment, O'Connell (2000) has reported similar findings. However, Marshall et al. (1991), using clinical interviews, reported that only 8% of incest offenders and only 12% of extrafamilial offenders met criteria for any additional paraphilias. Regardless of the exact prevalence, it is clear that some significant number of child molesters will have engaged in other paraphilic behaviors, both victimizing and nonvictimizing. If present, these may need to be a focus of intervention. Sexual behaviors that are not directly targeted in treatment are likely to remain unchanged despite positive treatment effects on targeted behaviors (Brownell, Hayes, & Barlow, 1977).

Several systems have been developed for classifying child molesters into meaningful subgroups. Typologies may be geared to one or more of several different purposes, including determining appropriate interventions, identifying different etiological patterns, or predicting risk for recidivism. The basis for these methods may be either clinical or empirical. Early clinical typologies relied on clinical experience to make educated guesses about subgroups of offenders. The most frequently cited of the early clinical typologies was developed by Groth and his colleagues (Groth, 1979; Groth, Hobson, & Gary, 1982) and differentiated between fixated and regressed child molesters. Fixated child molesters were described as having a very high or exclusive sexual preference toward children (more commonly male children) accompanied by poor social skills that contributed to deviant sexual acting out. Although the distinctions based on sexual preference have subsequently held, research has suggested that levels of social competence are independent of the level of sexual preference (Knight, 1992).

Empirically based typologies have often emphasized factors associated with treatment outcome, including recidivism, in an attempt to derive formulas for classifying child molesters. Much work in this area has been conducted by Knight, Prentky, and their colleagues (Knight, 1989, 1992; Prentky, Knight, & Lee, 1997). These authors have developed a two-axis typological system currently in its third revision (MTC:CM3). The MTC:CM3 taxonomic system comprises rationally and empirically derived components and has two axes on which child molesters are assessed: degree of fixation (Axis I) and amount of contact with children (Axis II). Altogether, there are four Axis I subgroups and six Axis II subgroups of child molesters. The Axis I and II classifications have been tested for reliability, validity, and their ability to discriminate sex offenders from other groups (Knight, 1992; Prentky et al., 1997).

Assessment. A thorough assessment is important for planning appropriate interventions and monitoring change. Assessment procedures are far less useful or appropriate for determining whether accused individuals committed a particular offense, and information relevant to these determinations may be more appropriately sought through good detective work rather than through psychological assessment. Forensically speaking, assessment is more useful during the dispositional phase of legal proceedings, *after* a legal determination of guilt and with individuals who are admitting to illegal sexual behavior. Pretreatment assessments may assist in making risk predictions, determining the appropriate level of incarceration or supervision, and making specific treatment recommendations. It is also necessary as a baseline against which to measure outcomes or progress and to determine if a specific treatment actually produces its intended change. Outcome-oriented program evaluations may wish to assess whether clients are in fact deficient in a specific area and whether treatment in that area results in positive change. Posttreatment assessments also are important to determine whether treatment changes have been maintained over the often lengthy course of adult sex offender treatment and can be used when making recommendations about the posttreatment level of supervision.

As with assessment of CSBPs and JSOs, the core of the initial assessment is a thorough psychosocial history. With adult sex offenders, particular attention should be paid to sexual behavior history and criminal behavior history. Unlike assessment of CSBPs and JSOs, the assessment of adult child molesters is more focused on the individual offender's sexual interests and internal cognitions, rather than on the offender's broader social ecology. It is critical that the history be obtained from multiple sources and that information provided by the offender be corroborated, if realistically possible, by other sources. At a minimum, it is critical to examine victim statements, police records, and other official documents. Because parents or others may not be available

to provide background information, offender self-report may be the only available source for much information. Adult sex offenders may minimize the extent of their illegal sexual behavior or interests (Abel et al., 1988) and may overreport or fabricate their own history of childhood sexual abuse. Therefore, it is important to bear in mind that the history provided may or may not be accurate. For this reason, some programs have incorporated polygraph examinations into their assessment procedures (Ahlmeyer, Heil, McKee, & English, 2000), although the validity of polygraphs in general, as well as their use in sexual abuse cases in particular, has been strongly questioned (Cross & Saxe, 1992).

Common assessment areas include sexual fantasy activity, hostility, sex knowledge, social skills, cognitive distortions, and victim empathy. Several of the most frequently cited self-report measures used with adult sex offenders have been compiled in reference materials (see Davis, Yarber, Bauserman, Schreer, & Davis, 1998; Prentky & Edmunds, 1997; Salter, 1988). One of the most comprehensive self-report measures is the Multiphasic Sex Inventory II (Nichols & Molinder, 1986). Subscales indicate relative interest in children, rape, and exhibitionism as well as presence of cognitive distortions, other sexual disorders and dysfunction, sex knowledge, and treatment readiness. Abel, Huffman, Warberg, and Holland's (1998) assessment system includes both a visual response time measure of sexual interest along with a thorough self-report questionnaire assessing interests, behaviors, and paraphilias. A third comprehensive measure is the Clarke Sex History measure, currently under revision by its distributor company (Multi-Health Systems, personal communication, March 2000). Bear in mind that the validity and interpretation of all self-report tests, even those with validity scales, are limited by the honesty and accuracy of the test taker.

Although a range of assessment target areas can and should be considered, two particular areas are critical—psychopathy and sexual interest patterns. Psychopathy is most validly assessed using the revised Psychopathy Checklist (PCL-R) (Hare et al., 1990). This assessment combines information from a semistructured interview with file-based information and is completed by a professional based on criteria and a thorough client history. Sexual interest is most validly assessed using penile plethysmography, although data also support the use of a visual response time measure, particularly with adult child molesters (Abel et al., 1998; Letourneau, 1999). Penile plethysmography is a psychophysiologic technique used to assess sexual interests. No single standardized stimulus set or procedures have been established for plethysmography, and like other measures, plethysmography can be "faked" and is most accurate with individuals who are motivated to participate in the assessment in good faith. Established stimulus sets, guidelines for practice, and ethical guidelines are available and should be consulted (ATSA, 1997). It should be noted that the plethysmograph is a clinical assessment tool, not a criminal investigation tool (Murphy & Peters, 1992). In addition to the plethysmograph, there are card sort, self-report, and other procedures available to measure sexual interests.

Considerable recent progress has been made in assessing sexual or violent reoffense risk among adult sex offenders. The main advance has been the development of empirically validated actuarial risk prediction systems that represent a considerable improvement over unaided clinical judgment. Actuarial risk prediction is a rapidly advancing part of the field, and interested professionals are encouraged to remain abreast of changes to existing risk instruments and the development of new ones. At present, those risk scales that have moderate to high prediction strength for sexual recidivism include the Sex Offender Risk Appraisal Guide (SORAG) (Quinsey, Harris, et al., 1998), the Minnesota Sex Offender Screening Tool–Revised (MnSost-R) (Epperson, Kaul, & Hesselton, 1998), the Rapid Risk Assessment for Sexual Offense Recidivism, and the STATIC-99 (Hanson & Thornton, 1999). These and other measures of violent and general recidivism are all reviewed by Hanson (2000). Several systems have been developed, with considerable overlap in the main domains assessed and factors considered. Each instrument provides a weighting system for historical variables (e.g., presence of stranger victims, number of prior sexual offenses, history of male victims, alcohol problems, etc.). Weighted items are summed, and the total score is used to determine whether the individual presents low, medium, or high reoffense risk. Each score corresponds to a known level of probability for official recidivism for groups of men with that score. Most of these systems rely on static (i.e., un-

changing) historical factors. More recent research in the area of actuarial risk prediction has focused on expanding the static risk prediction systems by adding dynamic or changeable factors for measuring changes in risk over time, such as risk reduction related to treatment (Hanson & Harris, 2000).

Treatment. A substantial body of literature describes common adult sex offender treatment practices, and a growing body of literature presents treatment outcome findings. Marshall and his colleagues (Marshall, Fernandez, Hudson, & Ward, 1998) reviewed data from more than 30 sex offender treatment programs in different settings and for different offender populations worldwide. They concluded that despite the diversity of settings and clients, most programs operate from a cognitive-behavioral perspective and include relapse prevention (Pithers, 1990) as the connective theme running throughout the various treatment components. Most programs begin with the requirement that participants acknowledge at least some portion of their offense (e.g., Gordon & Hover, 1998). Some type of formal psychosexual assessment is then usually conducted and frequently includes actuarial-based risk assessment for establishing appropriate levels of incarceration or supervision (e.g., Moro, 1998). Once treatment begins, there is no single set order for the various treatment components. Most commonly, treatment includes behavioral or cognitive-behavioral techniques to increase victim empathy, change distorted thinking patterns, improve social skills, reduce deviant sexual arousal, and supplement sex education. Relapse prevention is a treatment model that may be implemented throughout the other treatment components. Relapse prevention is based on several core assumptions, including that risk for sexual offenses against children is long term and cannot be entirely eliminated, that offenses are planned in advance, and that triggers or warning signs for offending can be identified and then used to develop a plan to reduce the likelihood of recidivism. Many of these assumptions are well supported with adult sex offenders, especially among higher-risk subgroups. However, these assumptions may be inaccurate for most JSOs and CSBPs (Chaffin & Bonner, 1998a, 1998b). Most programs described in the literature involve group treatment, although no evidence suggests that group treatment is better than individual treatment or a combination of modalities.

Surgical and pharmacological interventions are occasionally used with select subgroups of adult offenders. Physical castration involves the removal of the testes and leads to a significant reduction of circulating testosterone (Hucker & Bain, 1990). Although this generally leads to reductions in sexual functioning, sex drive, and sexual fantasies, castration fails to eliminate erection in nearly 50% of patients (Heim, 1981). A less invasive procedure for reducing sex drive is to administer one of several pharmacological agents. Early efforts at "chemical castration" relied on estrogens. However, these caused extensive side effects and were replaced with antiandrogens, including medroxyprogesterone acetate and cyproterone acetate (Balon, 1998). These medications have been shown to reduce sex drive and sexual fantasy among selected offenders, but noncompliance with the drugs due to their side effects may be a problem (Balon, 1998). The latest class of drugs to be used with sex offenders includes the antidepressants setraline, clomiprimine, and fluoxetine. In most reported cases, subjects had comorbid mood disorders, and these medications were intended both to reduce deviant sex drive and to improve depressed mood. A potential advantage of these drugs is that their side effects are far less serious, and therefore noncompliance may be less of a problem. Although case reports and small, uncontrolled studies have been positive, larger-scale double-blind placebo-controlled trials remain to be done. Pharmacotherapy is almost always used in combination with cognitive-behavioral treatment programs and is typically used with small subgroups of offenders who have unusually strong and uncontrollable sexual interest in children (Marshall & Eccles, 1991). Medical or pharmacological treatment of sex offenders should be based on a careful individual assessment, be part of a comprehensive treatment plan, and be prescribed by a physician, not mandated by law for broad, legally defined groups (ATSA, 1997).

Does treatment of adult sex offenders work? The question is perhaps overly simplistic. Determining treatment outcomes is complicated by difficulties in constructing adequate comparison groups and by the diversity of offenders and treatment programs. To date, only one large-scale contemporary study has followed treatment outcomes of randomly assigned sex offenders (Marques, 1999; Marques, Day, Nelson, & West, 1994). Across studies, the emerging pattern of outcomes is variable and complex and may not yet lend itself to a clear synopsis. An earlier review of recidivism data (Furby, Weinrott, & Blackshaw, 1989) concluded there was "no evidence that treatment effectively reduces sex offense recidivism" (p. 25). However, most of the studies reviewed by Furby et al. (1989) were conducted prior to 1985 and prior to the use of cognitive-behavioral treatment techniques with sex offenders. A review of more current outcome literature concluded that, despite significant limitations in the available data, recidivism risk appears to be reduced for some offenders who complete cognitive-behavioral or hormonal treatment (Grossman, Martis, & Fichtner, 1999). Grossman et al. (1999) suggested that recidivism rates were reduced by 30% (over 7 years at risk) for treated versus untreated offenders. Across studies, recidivism rates ranged from 3% to 39% for treated offenders and between 12.5% and 57% for untreated offenders. Emerging data also suggest significant differences between offenders who complete treatment and those who do not, suggesting that offenders who meet specific skill goals have better outcomes (Day & Marques, 1998; Marques, Nelson, West, & Day, 1994; Studer & Reddon, 1998). However, the effects of therapy or the ability of therapists to judge success in therapy have not always been found to be positive (Quinsey, Khanna, & Malcolm, 1998).

Public policy. In the United States, our public policy on adults who sexually abuse children is heavily rooted in a criminal justice tradition, far more than our policy for perpetrators of other types of child maltreatment. Legal sanctions against sex offenders go back for centuries and are specifically designed to exercise social control over child molesters by subjecting them to criminal penalties similar to those for other criminals. More recently, criminal justice efforts aimed at child molesters have extended beyond incarceration to include specialized procedures, such as sex offender registration, public notification, and postincarceration civil commitment. Similarly, traditional criminal justice efforts have been amended by offering specialized sex offender treatment programs within correctional settings.

Civil commitment laws, otherwise known as sexual predator laws, have been enacted in 15 states with legislation pending in several others. These laws allow for involuntary postincarceration confinement and treatment of sex offenders. They most often apply to adult offenders with multiple convictions, although several states now have laws allowing for civil commitment of minors. Civil commitment is most appropriately used sparingly. For example, in Washington state, where civil commitment was first developed, it has been applied to less than 1% of all adult sex offenders released from prison (Washington State Institute for Public Policy, 1998). Civil commitment laws are consistent with the fact that a very small number of highly dangerous adult sex offenders appear to account for a large portion of offenses (Abel & Rouleau, 1986) and pose serious and long-term risks to the community. However, critics have held that predator laws amount to illegal incarceration masquerading as mental health treatment. Nonetheless, predator laws have passed the scrutiny of the U.S. Supreme Court (*Kansas v. Hendricks,* 1997).

Sex offender registries now exist in all states within the United States, although the particulars differ from state to state. Registries record demographic and locator information, photographs, and other information on adjudicated sex offenders. All registries are available for internal use by law enforcement agencies. In addition, many registries are made public on the Internet. States may proactively notify the public about the identity of some or all individuals on the registry. Some states have provisions for eventually removing a person from the registry in the absence of future convictions, but lifelong registration is often required. From a scientific perspective, it remains unclear whether registries and public notification actually reduce levels of future sexual offending or are useful in protecting children. What evidence is available suggests that although registration and notification may not achieve much in the way of actual abuse prevention, they may lead to faster apprehension of recidivists (Leib, cited in Bureau of Justice Statistics, 1998). It is not yet clear whether accelerated apprehension is attributable to registration, public notification, or a combination of the two.

All criminal justice approaches are necessarily reactive. They directly affect only the minority of sex offenders who are reported and convicted. These policies clearly achieve some measure of sexual abuse prevention via incapacitation, supervision, or mandated treatment, but to attack the broader problem, additional policy approaches will have to be considered. If new cases of child sexual abuse are actually to be prevented and not merely treated after the fact, then prevention must become a focus in our clinical, scientific, and funding initiatives. Very few prevention efforts target potential offenders or undetected offenders. Current policies have limited sexual abuse prevention to victimization prevention rather than the perpetration prevention approach used to prevent physical abuse. Victimization prevention programs educate young children about resisting abuse and urge disclosure. It is not clear that these approaches actually prevent abuse, although they may increase early detection (Finkelhor, Asdigian, & Dziuba- Leatherman, 1995a, 1995b). A more comprehensive public health prevention approach must include perpetration prevention as well as victimization prevention, and it must target adults and adolescents as well as potential child victims.

Several models focused on potential or undetected abusers exist. STOP IT NOW! is one of the few programs actively attempting to reduce sexual abuse by targeting adults, including at-large undetected sex offenders (Chasan-Taber & Tabachnick, 1999). Originators of this novel campaign reviewed the strategies of other successful public health initiatives and surveyed adults in a specific geographic region, including adult male sex offenders. Based on this information, three strategies were developed to intervene in sexually abusive behavior, including a toll-free hotline where offenders and potential offenders could confidentially call for help. Proponents of the public health approach to sexual offense prevention (e.g., Laws, 1996, 1999) have argued that any reduction in sexual abuse is a step in the right direction, even if complete abstinence for all sex offenders is not obtained and even if all sex offenders are not caught and subjected to criminal sanctions. Laws's (1996, 1999) controversial theory of harm reduction argues that services should be made readily available to potential and at-large undetected offenders without requiring legal involvement up front, similar to the policy currently used to treat users of illegal substances.

Policy attempts to augment criminal justice approaches with public health models will doubtlessly be controversial. The public generally wants to see all of these individuals locked up and off the streets (cf. McMahon & Puett, 1999). The reality, however, is that the vast majority of sex offenders will never go to prison, and nearly all of those who do will return to the community at some future point. It is neither economically nor legally practical for more than a small percentage of adult child molesters to be detected, prosecuted, convicted, and incarcerated for life. Adopting public health approaches does not mean decriminalizing sexual abuse, nor does it mean that we as a society no longer condemn this behavior as exploitive and corrupt. Many elements of a combined approach are already in place—for example, programs encouraging children to disclose abuse, multidisciplinary teams and advocacy centers to investigate reports, prosecution and incarceration of offenders, treatment programs inside and outside correctional institutions, civil commitment procedures, specialized probation and parole programs, and treatment for at-risk children and adolescents. However, other possible elements of a combined approach are yet to be fully developed, implemented, or tested—for example, perpetration prevention programs for youth, public education programs targeted at potential or actual abusers, treatment for undetected at-large abusers, and so on. Developing a comprehensive policy will require unprecedented cooperation between criminal justice, mental health treatment, public health professionals, and the public.

Conclusions

Child sexual abuse is a complex phenomenon, and individuals who engage in this behavior may do so in an almost infinite variety of ways and for a wide range of reasons. Sexually abusive behaviors may be committed by young children, teenagers, or adults. They may be limited and exploratory, or they may be extensive, violent, or compulsive. One individual may pose tremendous risk to the community and another very little. Much of what we know is from the small number of caught and convicted adult child molesters, a group that is unlikely to be representative of the full range of adult individuals who engage in sexually abusive behavior with children, let alone CSBPs or JSOs. Our efforts at assessing, intervening, preventing, and forming sensible public policies have yet to fully grapple with this heterogeneity. Sexual abusers have been and continue to be publicly characterized as misunderstood lovers, lonely sufferers, curious innocents, hurt victims, uncontrolled deviants, cruel exploiters, amoral psychopaths, or vicious predatory monsters. Each characterization may argue for its preeminence. Somewhere, each is right. We would argue that no single characterization fully grasps the whole. Our efforts to reduce the prevalence of child sexual abuse have been good and have met with success. Annual incidence rates for sexual abuse have been declining; between 1990 and 1998, they dropped from 2.3 to 1.6 per 1,000 children (U.S. Department of Health and Human Services, 2000). To extend this welcome trend, our continued efforts at intervention and prevention will need to evolve and become more discriminating, more developmentally attuned, more focused, and more open to a repertoire of solutions that respond to the full range of individuals who commit child sexual abuse.

Notes

1. The percentage was calculated from data published in this study.
2. Many adult sex offenders may not meet criteria for any paraphilia. Engaging in the behavior of molesting a child is not equivalent to meeting diagnostic criteria for pedophilia.

References

Abel, G. G., Becker, J. V., Cunningham-Rathner, J., Mittelman, M. S., & Rouleau, J. L. (1988). Multiple paraphilic diagnoses among sex offenders. *Bulletin of American Academy of Psychiatry and the Law, 16,* 153-168.

Abel, G. G., Becker, J. V., Mittelman, M. S., Cunningham-Rathner, J., Rouleau, J. L., & Murphy, W. D. (1987). Self-report sex crimes of nonincarcerated paraphiliacs. *Journal of Interpersonal Violence, 2,* 3-25.

Abel, G. G., Huffman, J., Warberg, B., & Holland, C. L. (1998). Visual reaction time and plethysmography as measures of sexual interest in child molesters. *Sexual Abuse: A Journal of Research and Treatment, 10,* 81-96.

Abel, G. G., Osborne, C. A., & Twigg, D. A. (1993). Sexual assault through the life span: Adult offenders with juvenile histories. In H. E. Barbaree, W. L. Marshall, & S. M. Hudson (Eds.), *The juvenile sex offender* (pp. 104-117). New York: Guilford.

Abel, G. G., & Rouleau, J. L. (2001, July). *The most recent data from the Abel Assessment.* Paper presented at the annual meeting of the International Academy of Sex Research, Montreal, Quebec, Canada.

Abidin, R. R. (1990). *Parenting Stress Index.* Odessa, FL: Psychological Assessment Resources.

Achenbach, T. M. (1991). *Manual for the Child Behavior Checklist/4-18 and 1991 Profile.* Burlington: University of Vermont, Department of Psychiatry.

Ahlmeyer, S., Heil, P., McKee, B., & English, K. (2000). The impact of polygraphy on admissions of victims and offenses in adult sexual offenders. *Sexual Abuse: Journal of Research & Treatment, 12,* 123-138.

Alexander, M. A. (1999). Sexual offender treatment efficacy revisited. *Sexual Abuse: A Journal of Research and Treatment, 11,* 101-116.

American Academy of Child and Adolescent Psychiatry. (1999). Practice parameters for the assessment and treatment of children and adolescents who are sexually abusive of others. *Journal of the American Academy of Child and Adolescent Psychiatry, 38*(Suppl.), 55-76.

Araji, S. K. (1997). *Sexually aggressive children: Coming to understand them.* Thousand Oaks, CA: Sage.

Association for the Treatment of Sexual Abusers (ATSA). (1997). *Ethical standards and principles for the management of sexual abusers.* Beaverton, OR: Author.

Balon, R. (1998). Pharmacological treatment of paraphilias with a focus on antidepressants. *Journal of Sex & Marital Therapy, 24,* 241-254.

Bard, L. A., Carter, D. L., Cerce, D. D., Knight, R. A., Rosenberg, R., & Schneider, B. (1987). A descriptive study of rapists and child molesters: Developmental, clinical and criminal characteristics. *Behavioral Sciences and the Law, 5,* 203-220.

Becker, J. V. (1990). Treating adolescent sexual offenders. *Professional Psychology: Research and Practice, 21,* 362-365.

Becker, J. V. (1998). What we know about the characteristics and treatment of adolescents who have committed sexual offenses. *Child Maltreatment: Journal of the American Professional Society on the Abuse of Children, 3,* 317-329.

Becker, J. V., Hunter, J. A., Stein, R. M., & Kaplan, M. S. (1989). Factors associated with erection in adolescent sex offenders. *Journal of Psychopathology & Behavioral Assessment, 11,* 353-363.

Becker, J. V., & Kaplan, M. S. (1988). The assessment of sexual offenders. *Advances in Behavioral Assessment of Children and Families, 4,* 97-118.

Becker, J. V., & Kaplan, M. S. (1993). Cognitive behavioral treatment of the juvenile sex offender. In H. E. Barbaree & W. L. Marshall (Eds.), *The juvenile sex offender* (pp. 264-277). New York: Guilford.

Bengis, S., Brown, A., Freeman-Longo, R. E., Matsuda, B., Ross, J., Singer, K., & Thomas, J. (1999). *Standards of care for youth in sex offense-specific residential programs.* Holyoke, MA: NEARI.

Berliner, L., Manaois, O., & Monastersky, C. (1986). *Child sexual behavior disturbance: An assessment and treatment model.* Seattle, WA: Harborview Medical Center.

Berliner, L., & Rawlings, L. (1991). *A treatment manual: Children with sexual behavior problems.* Seattle, WA: Harborview Sexual Assault Center.

Bernet, W., & Shaw, J. (2000). Children and adolescents who are sexually abusive of others [Letter to the editor]. *Journal of the American Academy of Child and Adolescent Psychiatry, 39,* 810.

Blaske, D. M., Borduin, C. M., Henggeler, S. W., & Mann, B. J. (1989). Individual, family, and peer characteristics of adolescent sex offenders and assaultive offenders. *Developmental Psychology, 25,* 846-855.

Bonner, B. L. (1991). Adolescent perpetrators: Adolescent sex offenders: Assessment and treatment. *APSAC Advisor, 4,* 13-14.

Bonner, B. L., & Fahey, W. E. (1998). Children with aggressive sexual behavior. In N. N. Singh & A. S. W. Winton (Eds.), *Comprehensive clinical psychology: Special populations* (Vol. 9). Oxford, UK: Elsevier Science.

Bonner, B. L., Marx, B. P., Thompson, J. M., & Michaelson, P. (1998). Assessment of adolescent sexual offenders. *Child Maltreatment: Journal of the American Professional Society on the Abuse of Children, 3,* 374-383.

Bonner, B. L., Walker, C. E., & Berliner, L. (1993). *Children with sexual behavior problems: Assessment and treatment.* Washington, DC: Administration for Children, Youth, and Families, Department of Health and Human Services.

Bonner, B. L., Walker, C. E., & Berliner, L. (1999a). *Children with sexual behavior problems: Assessment and treatment* (Final report, Grant No. 90-CA-1469). Washington, DC: Administration of Children, Youth, and Families, Department of Health and Human Services.

Bonner, B. L., Walker, C. E., & Berliner, L. (1999b). *Treatment manual for cognitive behavioral group treatment for parents/caregivers of children with sexual behavior problems* (Grant No. 90-CA-1469). Washington, DC: Administration of Children, Youth, and Families, Department of Health and Human Services.

Bonner, B. L., Walker, C. E., & Berliner, L. (1999c). *Treatment manual for dynamic group play therapy for children with sexual behavior problems and their parent/caregivers* (Grant No. 90-CA-1469). Washington, DC: Administration of Children, Youth, and Families, Department of Health and Human Services.

Bonner, B. L., Walker, C. E., & Berliner, L. (in press). Treatment of children with aggressive sexual behaviors. In L. Berliner & W. Friedrich (Eds.), *The APSAC compendium of treatment protocols.* Thousand Oaks, CA: Sage.

Borduin, C. M. (2000, May). *Multisystemic treatment of juvenile sexual offenders: A progress report.* Plenary address presented at the International Conference on the Treatment of Sexual Offenders, Toronto, Canada.

Borduin, C. M., Henggeler, S. W., Blaske, D. M., & Stein, R. J. (1990). Multisystemic treatment of adolescent sexual offenders. *International Journal of Offender Therapy and Comparative Criminology, 34,* 105-113.

Borduin, C. M., Mann, B. J., Cone, L. T., Henggeler, S. W., Fucci, B. R., Blaske, D. M., & Williams, R. A. (1995). Multisystemic treatment of serious juvenile offenders: Long-term prevention of criminality and violence. *Journal of Consulting and Clinical Psychology, 63,* 569-578.

Bradford, J. M. (1993). The pharmacological treatment of the adolescent sex offender. In H. Barbaree & W. Marshall (Eds.), *The juvenile sex offender* (pp. 278-288). New York: Guilford.

Brestan, E. V., & Eyberg, S. M. (1998). Effective psychosocial treatments of conduct-disordered children and adolescents: 29 years, 82 studies, and 5,272 kids. *Journal of Clinical Child Psychology, 27,* 180-189.

Briere, J. (1996). *Trauma Symptom Checklist for Children: Professional manual.* Odessa, FL: Psychological Assessment Resources.

Brownell, K. D., Hayes, S. C., & Barlow, D. H. (1977). Patterns of appropriate and deviant sexual arousal: The behavioral treatment of multiple sexual deviations. *Journal of Consulting and Clinical Psychology, 45,* 1144-1155.

Bureau of Justice Statistics. (1998). *National Conference on Sex Offender Registries: Proceedings of a BJS/SEARCH conference.* Washington, DC: U.S. Department of Justice.

Burton, D. L. (2000). Were adolescent sexual offenders children with sexual behavior problems? *Sexual Abuse: Journal of Research & Treatment, 12*(1), 37-48.

Burton, D. L., Nesmith, A. A., & Badten, L. (1997). Clinicians' views on sexually aggressive children and their families: A theoretical exploration. *Child Abuse & Neglect, 21,* 157-170.

Cantwell, H. B. (1988). Child sexual abuse: Very young perpetrators. *Child Abuse & Neglect, 12,* 579-582.

Carpenter, D. R., Peed, S. F., & Eastman, B. (1995). Personality characteristics of adolescent sexual offenders: A pilot study. *Sexual Abuse: Journal of Research & Treatment, 7,* 195-203.

Chaffin, M. (1992). Factors associated with treatment completion and progress among intrafamilial sexual abusers. *Child Abuse & Neglect, 16,* 251-264.

Chaffin, M., & Bonner, B. (1998a). "Don't shoot, we're children": Have we gone too far in our response to adolescent sexual abusers and children with sexual behavior problems? *Child Maltreatment, 3,* 314-316.

Chaffin, M., & Bonner, B. (1998b). Intervention with adolescent sexual abusers and children with sexual behavior problems [Special issue]. *Child Maltreatment: Journal of the American Professional Society on the Abuse of Children, 3*(4).

Chamberlain, P., & Reid, J. B. (1998). Comparison of two community alternatives to incarceration for chronic juvenile offenders. *Journal of Consulting & Clinical Psychology, 66,* 624-633.

Chasan-Taber, L., & Tabachnick, J. (1999). Evaluation of a child sexual abuse prevention program. *Sexual Abuse: A Journal of Research and Treatment, 11,* 279-292.

Cohen, J. A., & Mannarino, A. P. (1996a). Factors that mediate treatment outcome in sexually abused preschool children: Initial findings. *Journal of the American Academy of Child and Adolescent Psychiatry, 35,* 42-50.

Cohen, J. A., & Mannarino, A. P. (1996b). The Weekly Behavior Report: A parent-report instrument for sexually abused preschoolers. *Child Maltreatment, 1,* 353-360.

Cross, T. P., & Saxe, L. (1992). A critique of the validity of polygraph testing in child sexual abuse cases. *Journal of Child Sexual Abuse, 1,* 19-33.

Cunningham, C., & McFarlane, L. (1996). *When children abuse.* Brandon, VT: Safer Society Press.

Daleiden, E. L., Kaufman, K. L., Hilliker, D. R., & O'Neil, J. N. (1998). The sexual histories and fantasies of youthful males: A comparison of sexual offending, nonsexual offending, and nonoffending groups. *Sexual Abuse: Journal of Research & Treatment, 10,* 195-209.

Davis, C. M., Yarber, W. L., Bauserman, R., Schreer, G., & Davis, S. L. (1998). *Handbook of sexuality-related measures.* Thousand Oaks, CA: Sage.

Davis, G. E., & Leitenberg, H. (1987). Adolescent sexual offenders. *Psychological Bulletin, 101,* 417-427.

Day, D. M., & Marques, J. K. (1998). A clarification of SOTEP's method and preliminary findings: Reply to Nathaniel McConaghy [Letter to the editor]. *Sexual Abuse: A Journal of Research and Treatment, 10,* 162-166.

De Angelis, T. (1996). Project explores sexual misconduct among children. *American Psychological Association Monitor, 27,* 43.

Deblinger, E., Lippmann, J., & Steer, R. (1996). Sexually abused children suffering posttraumatic stress symptoms: Initial treatment outcome findings. *Child Maltreatment, 1,* 310-321.

Derogatis, L. R., & Melisaratos, N. (1983). The Brief Symptom Inventory: An introductory report. *Psychological Medicine, 13,* 595-605.

Epperson, D. L., Kaul, J. D., & Hesselton, D. (1998, October). *Final report on the development of the Minnesota Sex Offender Screening Tool–Revised (MnSOST-R).* Paper presented at the 17th Annual Conference of the Association for the Treatment of Sexual Abusers, Vancouver, British Columbia.

Finkelhor, D., Asdigian, N., & Dziuba-Leatherman, J. (1995a). The effectiveness of victimization prevention instruction: An evaluation of children's responses to actual threats and assaults. *Child Abuse & Neglect, 19,* 141-153.

Finkelhor, D., Asdigian, N., & Dziuba-Leatherman, J. (1995b). Victimization prevention programs for children: A follow-up. *American Journal of Public Health, 85,* 1684-1689.

Finkelhor, D., Hotaling, G., Lewis, I. A., & Smith, C. (1990). Sexual abuse in a national survey of adult men and women: Prevalence, characteristics, and risk factors. *Child Abuse & Neglect, 14,* 19-28.

Firestone, P., Bradford, J. M., McCoy, M., Greenberg, D. M., Larose, M. R., & Curry, S. (1999). Prediction of recidivism in incest offenders. *Journal of Interpersonal Violence, 14,* 511-531.

Friedrich, W. N. (1996). *Safety checklist.* Unpublished measure, Mayo Clinic, Rochester, MN.

Friedrich, W. N. (1997). *Child Sexual Behavior Inventory: Professional manual.* Odessa, FL: Psychological Assessment Resources.

Friedrich, W. N. (1999, October). *A treatment manual approach to working with sexually aggressive children and their parents.* Workshop presented at the 15th Annual Midwest Conference on Child Sexual Abuse and Incest, Madison, WI.

Friedrich, W. N. (2000). Children and adolescents who are sexually abusive of others [Letter to the editor]. *Journal of the American Academy of Child and Adolescent Psychiatry, 39,* 809-810.

Friedrich, W. N., Grambsch, P., Broughton, D., Kuiper, J., & Beilke, R. L. (1991). Normative sexual behavior in children. *Pediatrics, 88,* 456-464.

Friedrich, W. N., & Luecke, W. J. (1988). Young school-age sexually aggressive children. *Professional Psychology, 19,* 155-164.

Furby, L., Weinrott, M. R., & Blackshaw, L. (1989). Sex offender recidivism: A review. *Psychological Bulletin, 105,* 3-30.

Galli, V., Raute, N., McConville, B., & McElroy, S. L. (1998). An adolescent male with multiple paraphilias successfully treated with fluoxetine. *Journal of Child & Adolescent Psychopharmacology, 8,* 195-197.

Gerber, J. (1994). The use of art therapy in juvenile sex offender specific treatment. *Arts in Psychotherapy, 21,* 367-374.

Gil, E., & Johnson, T. C. (1993a). Current and proposed community response. In E. Gil & T. C. Johnson (Eds.), *Sexualized children: Assessment and treatment of sexualized children and children who molest* (pp. 121-135). Rockville, MD: Launch.

Gil, E., & Johnson, T. C. (1993b). *Sexualized children: Assessment and treatment of sexualized children and children who molest.* Rockville, MD: Launch.

Goocher, B. E. (1994). Some comments on the residential treatment of juvenile sex offenders. *Child & Youth Care Forum, 23,* 243-250.

Gordon, A., & Hover, G. (1998). The Twin Rivers sex offender treatment program. In W. L. Marshall, Y. M. Fernandez, S. M. Hudson, & T. Ward (Eds.), *Sourcebook of treatment programs for sexual offenders* (pp. 3-15). New York: Plenum.

Graves, R. B., Openshaw, D. K., Ascione, F. R., & Ericksen, S. L. (1996). Demographic and parental characteristics of youthful sexual offenders. *International Journal of Offender Therapy & Comparative Criminology, 40,* 300-317.

Gray, A., & Pithers, W. D. (1993). Relapse prevention with sexually aggressive adolescents and children: Expanding treatment and supervision. In H. E. Barbaree (Ed.), *The juvenile sex offender* (pp. 289-319). New York: Guilford.

Gray, A., & Pithers, W. D. (1997). Preface. In S. K. Araji (Author), *Sexually aggressive children: Coming to understand them.* Thousand Oaks, CA: Sage.

Gretton, H. M., McBride, M., O'Shaugnessy, R., & Hare, R. D. (2000, October). *The developmental course of offending in psychopathic and nonpsychopathic adolescent sexual offenders: A ten year follow up study.* Paper presented at the annual conference of the Association for the Treatment of Sexual Abusers, San Diego, CA.

Grossman, L. S., Martis, B., & Fichtner, C. G. (1999). Are sex offenders treatable? A research overview. *Psychiatric Services, 50,* 349-361.

Groth, A. N. (1979). Sexual trauma in the life histories of rapists and child molesters. *Victimology: An International Journal, 4,* 10-16.

Groth, A. N., Hobson, W. F., & Gary, T. S. (1982). The child molester: Clinical observations. *Social Work and Human Sexuality, 1,* 129-144.

Hall, G. C., Maiuro, R. D., Vitaliano, P. P., & Proctor, W. C. (1986). The utility of the MMPI with men who have sexually assaulted children. *Journal of Consulting and Clinical Psychology, 54,* 493-496.

Hall, D. K., Mathews, F., & Pearce, J. (1998). Factors associated with sexual behavior problems in young sexually abused children. *Child Abuse & Neglect, 22,* 1045-1063.

Hall, D. K., & Mathews, F., Pearce, J., Sarlo-McGarvey, N., & Gavin, D. (1996). *The development of sexual behavior problems in children and youth.* Ontario: Central Toronto Youth Services.

Hanson, R. K. (2000). *Risk assessment.* Beaverton, OR: Association for the Treatment of Sexual Abuse.

Hanson, R. K., & Bussière, M. T. (1998). Predicting relapse: A meta-analysis of sexual offender recidivism studies. *Journal of Consulting and Clinical Psychology, 66,* 348-362.

Hanson, R. K., & Harris, A. J. R. (2000). *The Sex Offender Need Assessment Rating (SONAR): A method for measuring change in risk levels.* Ottawa: Department of the Solicitor General of Canada.

Hanson, R. K., & Slater, S. (1988). Sexual victimization in the history of sexual abusers: A review. *Annals of Sex Research, 1*(4), 485-499.

Hanson, R. K., & Thornton, D. (1999). *Static-99: Improving actuarial risk assessments for sex offenders* (Users Report 99-02). Ottawa: Department of the Solicitor General of Canada.

Hare, R. D. (1996). Psychopathy: A clinical construct whose time has come. *Criminal Justice and Behavior, 23,* 25-54.

Hare, R. D., Harpur, T. J., Hakstian, A. R., Forth, A. E., Hart, S. D., & Newman, J. P. (1990). The Revised Psychopathy Checklist: Reliability and factor structure. *Psychological Assessments: A Journal of Consulting and Clinical Psychology, 2,* 338-341.

Hart, S. D., & Hare, R. D. (1997). Psychopathy: Assessment and association with criminal conduct. In D. M. Stoff, J. Breiling, & J. D. Maser (Eds.), *Handbook of antisocial behavior* (pp. 22-35). New York: John Wiley.

Heim, N. (1981). Sexual behavior of castrated sex offenders. *Archives of Sexual Behavior, 10,* 11-19.

Hembree-Kigin, T. L., & McNeil, C. B. (1995). *Parent-child interaction therapy.* New York: Plenum.

Hindman, J. (1988). Research disputes assumptions about child molesters. *NDAA Bulletin (National District Attorney's Association), 7,* 1-3.

Hucker, S. J., & Bain, J. (1990). Androgenic hormones and sexual assault. In W. L. Marshall, D. R. Laws, & H. E. Barbaree (Eds.), *Handbook of sexual assault: Issues, theories and treatment of the offender* (pp. 93-102). New York: Plenum.

Hunter, J. A., Goodwin, D. W., & Becker, J. V. (1994). The relationship between phallometrically measured deviant sexual arousal and clinical characteristics in juvenile sexual offenders. *Behavioral Research and Therapy, 32,* 533-538.

Hunter, J. A., & Lexier, L. J. (1998). Ethical and legal issues in the assessment and treatment of juvenile sex offenders. *Child Maltreatment: Journal of the American Professional Society on the Abuse of Children, 3,* 339-348.

Jesness, C. F. (1988). The Jesness Inventory Classification System. *Criminal Justice & Behavior, 15,* 78-91.

Johnson, T. (1988). Child perpetrators—children who molest other children: Preliminary findings. *Child Abuse & Neglect, 12,* 219-229.

Johnson, T. (1989). Female child perpetrators: Children who molest other children. *Child Abuse & Neglect, 13,* 571-585.

Johnson, T. C. (1991). Children who molest children: Identification and treatment approaches for children who molest other children. *APSAC Advisor, 4,* 9-11, 23.

Johnson, T. C. (1998). *Understanding children's sexual behaviors: What is natural and healthy.* South Pasadena, CA: Author.

Kaemingk, K. L., Koselka, M., Becker, J. V., & Kaplan, M. S. (1995). Age and adolescent sexual offender arousal. *Sexual Abuse: Journal of Research & Treatment, 7,* 249-257.

Kahn, T. J. (1990). *Pathways: A guided workbook for youth beginning treatment.* Orwell, VT: Safer Society.

Kansas v. Hendricks, 117 S.Ct. 2072 (1997).

Kaplan, M. S., Morales, M., & Becker, J. V. (1993). The impact of verbal satiation of adolescent sex offenders: A preliminary report. *Journal of Child Sexual Abuse, 2,* 81-88.

Kaufman, K. L., Hilliker, D. R., & Daleiden, E. L. (1996). Subgroup differences in the modus operandi of adolescent sexual offenders. *Child Maltreatment, 1,* 17-24.

Kavoussi, J., Kaplan, M. S., & Becker, J. V. (1988). Psychiatric diagnosis in adolescent sex offenders. *Journal of the Academy of Child Psychiatry, 23,* 241-243.

Knight, R. A. (1989). An assessment of the concurrent validity of a child molester typology. *Journal of Interpersonal Violence, 4,* 131-150.

Knight, R. A. (1992). A taxonomy for child molesters. In W. O'Donohue & J. H. Geer (Eds.), *The sexual abuse of children: Clinical issues* (Vol. 2, pp. 24-70). Hillsdale, NJ: Lawrence Erlbaum.

Knight, R. A., & Prentky, R. A. (1993). Exploring characteristics for classifying juvenile sex offenders. In H. E. Barbaree, W. L. Marshall, & S. M. Hudson (Eds.), *The juvenile sex offender* (pp. 45-83). New York: Guilford.

Knight, R. A., Prentky, R. A., & Cerce, D. D. (1994). The development, reliability, and validity of an inventory for the multidimensional assessment of sex and aggression. *Criminal Justice and Behavior, 21,* 72-94.

Knopp, F. H., Freeman-Longo, R., & Stevenson, W. F. (1992). *Nationwide survey of juvenile and adult sex-offender treatment programs and models.* Orwell, VT: Safer Society.

Kobayashi, J., Sales, B. D., Becker, J. V., Figueredo, A. J., & Kaplan, M. S. (1995). Perceived parental deviants, parent-child bonding, child abuse, and child sexual aggression. *Sexual Abuse: A Journal of Research and Treatment, 7,* 25-44.

Krauth, A. A. (1998). A comparative study of male juvenile sex offenders. *Dissertation Abstracts International: Section B: Sciences & Engineering, 58,* 4455.

Langevin, R. (1990). Sexual anomalies and the brain. In W. L. Marshall, D. R. Laws, & H. E. Barbaree (Eds.), *Handbook of sexual assault: Issues, theories, and treatment of the offender* (pp. 103-114). New York: Plenum.

Laws, D. R. (1996). Relapse prevention or harm reduction? *Sexual Abuse: A Journal of Research and Treatment, 8,* 243-247.

Laws, D. R. (1999). Harm reduction or harm facilitation? A reply to Maletzky. *Sexual Abuse: A Journal of Research and Treatment, 11,* 233-241.

Letourneau, E. J. (1999, October). *Comparison of sex offender disclosure prior to and during polygraph assessment.* Workshop presentation at the 15th Annual Midwest Conference on Child Sexual Abuse and Incest, Madison, WI.

Maguire, K., & Pastore, A. L. (Eds.). (1998). *Sourcebook of criminal justice statistics 1997.* Washington, DC: U.S. Department of Justice, Bureau of Justice Statistics.

Marques, J. K. (1999). How to answer the question "Does sexual offender treatment work?" *Journal of Interpersonal Violence, 14,* 437-451.

Marques, J. K., Day, D. M., Nelson, C., & West, M. A. (1994). Effects of cognitive-behavioral treatment on sex offender recidivism. *Criminal Justice and Behavior, 21,* 28-54.

Marques, J. K., Nelson, C., West, M. A., & Day, D. M. (1994). The relationship between treatment goals and recidivism among child molesters. *Behaviour Research & Therapy, 32,* 577-588.

Marshall, W. (1997). Pedophilia: Psychopathology and theory. In D. R. Laws & W. O'Donohue (Eds.), *Sexual deviance: Theory, assessment and treatment* (pp. 152-193). New York: Guilford.

Marshall, W., Barbaree, H. E., & Eccles, A. (1991). Early onset and deviant sexuality in child molesters. *Journal of Interpersonal Violence, 6,* 323-335.

Marshall, W., & Eccles, A. (1991). Issues in clinical practice with sex offenders. *Journal of Interpersonal Violence, 6,* 68-93.

Marshall, W., Fernandez, Y. M., Hudson, S. M., & Ward, T. (1998). *Sourcebook of treatment programs for sexual offenders.* New York: Plenum.

McMahon, P. M., & Puett, R. C. (1999). Child sexual abuse as a public health issue: Recommendations of an expert panel. *Sexual Abuse: A Journal of Research and Treatment, 11,* 257-266.

Milloy, C. D. (1994). *A comparative study of juvenile sex offenders and non-sex offenders.* Olympia: Washington State Institute for Public Policy.

Miranda, A. O., & Corcoran, C. L. (2000). Comparison of perpetration characteristics between male juvenile and adult sexual offenders: Preliminary results. *Sexual Abuse: A Journal of Research and Treatment, 12,* 179-188.

Moro, P. E. (1998). Treatment for Hispanic sexual offenders. In W. L. Marshall, Y. M. Fernandez, S. M. Hudson, & T. Ward (Eds.), *Sourcebook of treatment programs for sexual offenders* (pp. 445-456). New York: Plenum.

Murphy, W. D., & Peters, J. M. (1992). Profiling child sexual abusers: Psychological considerations. *Criminal Justice & Behavior, 19,* 24-37.

Nack, W., & Yaeger, D. (1999). Every parent's nightmare. *Sports Illustrated, 91*(10), 40-53.

National Center for Juvenile Justice. (1999). *Juvenile offenders and victims: 1999 national report.* Washington, DC: Office of Juvenile Justice and Delinquency Prevention.

National Task Force on Juvenile Sexual Offending. (1993). The revised report. *Juvenile and Family Court Journal, 44,* 1-120.

Nichols, H. R., & Molinder, I. (1986). *MSI II: Multiphasic sex inventory handbook.* (Available from H. R. Nichols & I. Molinder, 437 Bowes Drive, Tacoma, WA 98466)

O'Brien, M. J. (1994). *PHASE treatment manual.* (Available from Alpha PHASE, Inc., 1600 University Avenue, West, Suite 305, St. Paul, MN 55104-3825)

O'Brien, M. J., & Bera, W. (1986). Adolescent sexual offenders: A descriptive typology. *Newsletter of the National Family Life Education Network, 1,* 1-5.

O'Connell, M. A. (2000). Polygraphy: Assessment and community monitoring. In D. R. Laws, S. M. Hudson, & T. Ward (Eds.), *Remaking relapse prevention with sex offenders* (pp. 285-302). Thousand Oaks, CA: Sage.

Pithers, W. D. (1990). Relapse prevention with sexual aggressors: A method for maintaining therapeutic gain and enhancing external supervision. In W. L. Marshall & D. R. Laws (Eds.), *Handbook of sexual assault: Issues, theories, and treatment of the offender* (pp. 343-361). New York: Plenum.

Pithers, W. D., Becker, J. V., Kafka, M., Morenz, B., Schlank, A., & Leombruno, T. (1995). Children with sexual behavior problems, adolescent sexual abusers, and adult sex offenders: Assessment and treatment. *American Psychiatric Press Review of Psychiatry, 14,* 779-819.

Pithers, W. D., & Gray, A. S. (1993). *Pre-adolescent sexual abuse research project.* Washington, DC: National Center on Child Abuse and Neglect.

Pithers, W. D., Gray, A., Busconi, A., & Houchens, P. (1998a). Caregivers of children with sexual behavior problems: Psychological and familial functioning. *Child Abuse & Neglect, 22*(2), 129-141.

Pithers, W. D., Gray, A., Busconi, A., & Houchens, P. (1998b). Children with sexual behavior problems: Identification of five distinct child types and related treatment considerations. *Child Maltreatment, 3,* 384-406.

Prentky, R. A., & Edmunds, S. B. (1997). *Assessing sexual abuse: A resource guide for practitioners.* Brandon, VT: Safer Society.

Prentky, R. A., Harris, B., Frizell, K., & Righthand, S. (2000). An actuarial procedure for assessing risk with juvenile sex offenders. *Sexual Abuse: Journal of Research & Treatment, 12,* 71-93.

Prentky, R. A., Knight, R. A., & Lee, A. F. S. (1997). Risk factors associated with recidivism among extrafamilial child molesters. *Journal of Consulting and Clinical Psychology, 65,* 145-149.

Quinsey, V. L., Harris, G. T., Rice, M. E., & Cormier, C. E. (1998). *Violent offenders: Appraising and managing risk.* Washington, DC: American Psychological Association.

Quinsey, V. L., Khanna, A., & Malcolm, P. B. (1998). A retrospective evaluation of the regional treatment centre sex offender treatment program. *Journal of Interpersonal Violence, 13,* 621-644.

Rasmussen, L. A. (1999). Factors related to recidivism among juvenile sexual offenders. *Sexual Abuse: Journal of Research & Treatment, 11,* 69-86.

Reynolds, C., & Kamphaus, R. (1992). *Behavior assessment system for children manual.* Circle Pines, MN: American Guidance Service.

Rice, M. E., Harris, G. T., & Cormier, C. E. (1992). Evaluation of a maximum security therapeutic community for psychopaths and other mentally disordered offenders. *Law and Human Behavior, 16,* 399-412.

Richardson, G., Bhate, S., & Graham, F. (1997). Cognitive-based practice with sexually abusive adolescents. In M. Hoghughi, S. R. Bhate, & F. Graham (Eds.), *Working with sexually abusive adolescents* (pp. 128-143). London: Sage.

Ryan, G. (2000). Childhood sexuality: A decade of study. Part II–Dissemination and future directions. *Child Abuse & Neglect, 24,* 49-61.

Ryan, G., Lane, S., Davis, J., & Isaac, C. (1987). Juvenile sex offenders: Development and correction. *Child Abuse & Neglect, 11,* 385-395.

Salter, A. C. (1988). *Treating child sex offenders and victims: A practical guide.* Newbury Park, CA: Sage.

Sapp, A. D., & Vaughn, M. S. (1990). Juvenile sex offender treatment at state-operated correctional institutions. *International Journal of Offender Therapy & Comparative Criminology, 34,* 131-146.

Seto, M. C., & Barbaree, H. E. (1999). Psychopathy, treatment behavior, and sex offender recidivism. *Journal of Interpersonal Violence, 14,* 1235-1248.

Silovsky, J. F., Niec, L., & Hecht, D. (2000, January). *Clinical presentation and treatment outcome of preschool children with sexual behavior problems.* Paper presented at the San Diego Conference on Responding to Child Maltreatment, San Diego, CA.

Skaggs, R. (1997). Music-centered creative arts in a sex offender treatment program for male juveniles. *Music Therapy Perspectives, 15,* 73-78.

Smith, G., & Fischer, L. (1999). Assessment of juvenile sexual offenders: Reliability and validity of the Abel Assessment for Interest in Paraphilias. *Sexual Abuse: Journal of Research & Treatment, 11,* 207-216.

Smith, D. W., Letourneau, E. J., Saunders, B. E., Kilpatrick, D. G., Resnick, H. S., & Best, C. (2000). Delay in disclosure of childhood rape: Results from a national survey. *Child Abuse & Neglect, 24,* 273-287.

Smith, W. R., & Monastersky, C. (1986). Assessing juvenile sexual offenders' risk for reoffending. *Criminal Justice & Behavior, 13,* 115-140.

Steen, C. (1993). *The relapse prevention workbook for youth in treatment.* Orwell, VT: Safer Society.

Studer, L. H., & Reddon, J. R. (1998). Treatment may change risk prediction for sexual offenders. *Sexual Abuse: A Journal of Research and Treatment, 10,* 175-182.

Swenson, C. C., Henggeler, S. W., Schoenwald, S. K., Kaufman, K. L., & Randall, J. (1998). Changing the social ecologies of adolescent sexual offenders: Implications of the success of multisystemic therapy in treating serious antisocial behavior in adolescents. *Child Maltreatment: Journal of the American Professional Society on the Abuse of Children, 3,* 330-338.

U.S. Department of Health and Human Services. (2000, April). *Child maltreatment 1998: Reports from the states to the National Child Abuse and Neglect Data System.* Washington, DC: Government Printing Office.

Valliant, P. M., & Bergeron, T. (1997). Personality and criminal profile of adolescent sexual offenders, general offenders in comparison to nonoffenders. *Psychological Reports, 81,* 483-489.

Ward, A., Hudson, S. M., & Marshall, W. L. (1996). Attachment style in sex offenders: A preliminary study. *Journal of Sex Research, 33,* 17-26.

Washington State Institute for Public Policy. (1998). *Sex offenders in Washington state: 1998 update.* Olympia, WA: Author.

Weinrott, M. R. (1996). *Sexual aggression: A critical review.* Boulder: Center for the Study and Prevention of Violence, Institute for Behavioral Sciences, University of Colorado, Boulder.

Weinrott, M. R., Riggan, M., & Frothingham, S. (1997). Reducing deviant arousal in juvenile sex offenders using vicarious sensitization. *Journal of Interpersonal Violence, 12,* 704-728.

White, S., Halpin, B. M., Strom, G. A., & Santilli, G. (1988). Behavioral comparisons of young sexually abused, neglected, and nonreferred children. *Journal of Clinical Child Psychology, 17,* 53-61.

Whitford, R., & Parr, V. (1995). Uses of rational emotive behavior therapy with juvenile sex offenders. *Journal of Rational-Emotive & Cognitive Behavior Therapy, 13,* 273-282.

Widom, C. S., & Ames, M. A. (1994). Criminal consequences of childhood sexual victimization. *Child Abuse & Neglect, 18*(4), 303-318.

Wolfe, V. V., Gentile, C., Michienzi, T., Sas, L., & Wolfe, D. A. (1991). The Children's Impact of Traumatic Events Scale: A measure of post-sexual-abuse PTSD symptoms. *Behavioral Assessment, 13,* 359-383.

Worling, J. R., & Curwen, T. (2000). Adolescent sexual offender recidivism: Success of specialized treatment and implications for risk prediction. *Child Abuse & Neglect, 24,* 965-982.

PART THREE

Medical Aspects of Child Maltreatment

In Chapter 12, Carole Jenny updates her chapter in the first edition of the *APSAC Handbook* with a useful analysis of medical aspects of child sexual abuse. Dr. Jenny begins with discussion of the roles of health care professionals in responding to sexual abuse. From there, she discusses the physical examination for sexual abuse. Although Chapter 12 discusses the complexities of medical diagnosis, including analysis of sexually transmitted diseases, Jenny's primary goal is to make the technical world of medicine comprehensible to nonmedical professionals.

In Chapter 13, Charles Johnson thoroughly analyzes the medical aspects of physical abuse. Dr. Johnson's chapter provides a readable and interesting road map to physical abuse. Social workers, mental health professionals, law enforcement officers, and others will find the information in Chapter 13 particularly helpful to their efforts to understand and investigate allegations of physical abuse. Dr. Johnson's chapter appeared in the first edition, and is thoroughly updated for the second edition.

Howard Dubowitz and Maureen Black's chapter in the second edition offers a comprehensive examination of neglect of children's health. Chapter 14, which updates Dubowitz and Black's contribution to the first edition, defines neglected health. The authors discuss the incidence and prevalence of medical neglect. Next, the authors analyze the etiology of medical neglect, with emphasis on society and community, the family, and the child. The chapter concludes with in-depth discussion of effective prevention, evaluation, and treatment of medical neglect.

Chapter 15 is new to the second edition. Robert Block discusses fatal child abuse, with particular emphasis on child death review teams, the importance of autopsies, and death scene investigation.

J.E.B.M.

12

Medical Issues in Child Sexual Abuse

CAROLE JENNY

Medical practitioners play an important role in the diagnosis and treatment of child sexual abuse. Physicians and nurses are in a good position to detect early signs of sexual abuse during medical history-taking and examinations of children and during interactions with children and members of their families. Unfortunately, medical personnel are not always trained in diagnosing child sexual abuse. However, with appropriate training, doctors, nurses, and other health care providers can become more alert to this problem and more comfortable in initiating steps to resolve it (Socolar, Champion, & Green, 1996).

As professionals committed to the well-being of their patients, health care providers have a duty to identify sexually abused children and ensure their safety (see Finkel & Giardino, 2002; Reece & Ludwig, 2001; and Reece, 2000).

Overview of Roles for Health Care Professionals

Primary identification. Because most children obtain "well-child care" throughout childhood and adolescence, medical care providers have regular and repeated contact with children. For infants and young children who are not in schools or day care, medical visits may provide the only opportunity for an adult outside of the family to interact with the child. Therefore, the medical office is an important setting for the primary identification of child abuse. Screening for abuse should be a regular feature of well-child visits (Jenny, Sutherland, & Sandahl, 1986).

Reporting. Physicians and nurses are mandated reporters of child abuse in every state (see Chapters 20 and 22, this volume, for detailed discussion of the reporting law). However, physician reports from primary care settings are uncommon (Flaherty, Sege, Binns, Mattson, & Christoffel, 2000).

Talking to children. Pediatricians, family practitioners, nurse practitioners, physicians' assistants, and nurses have extensive experience talking to children. Medical practitioners should feel comfortable asking children about adverse experiences, including abuse. Although medical professionals are at ease questioning children, most professionals have little training in the forensic implications of interviewing. For detailed discussion of interviewing, see Chapter 18 (this volume). For discussion of the legal importance of documenting children's statements describing abuse, see Chapter 16 (this volume) (see also Myers, 1997, 2000, 2001, 2002).

Physical examination and diagnosis. Children who are sexually abused sometimes have physical complaints and findings that can help make the diagnosis of abuse. After abuse has been disclosed, examination of the child is important to document evidence and reassure the child. Although not frequently found in sexually abused children (Berenson et al., 2000), physical evidence can be powerful confirmation of a child's history and is one of the few ways abuse can be diagnosed in preverbal children.

Diagnosis and treatment of sexually transmitted diseases. During medical examinations of sexually abused children, physicians can identify sexually transmitted diseases. All sexually transmitted diseases that are found in adults can also be transmitted to children. These diseases can affect children's physical and psychological health and the health of their reproductive systems, and they can even threaten their lives.

Diagnosis and management of pregnancy. Sexual abuse or assault of adolescent girls may result in conception. The management of these pregnancies is complicated by the severe psychological stress of the pregnant adolescent. Timely diagnosis increases the options available to the pregnant teenager.

Collection of forensic evidence. Particularly in the emergency care setting, the practitioner may see a child who has been sexually assaulted within hours to days prior to the visit. In these cases, the examiner can collect specimens for forensic analysis to help identify the abuser.

Recognizing psychological, behavioral, and psychosomatic problems resulting from abuse. Sexual abuse often leads to emotional or physical illness (see Chapter 3, this volume). Depression, dissociative states, posttraumatic stress disorder, and sexual behavior disorders can be recognized by the medical practitioner, leading to psychopharmacologic treatment or appropriate referral for psychotherapy. Psychosomatic disorders such as enuresis, encopresis, and chronic pain syndromes can be diagnosed and treated.

Documenting the medical record. Accurate and complete documentation of medical aspects of sexual abuse cases is imperative to preserve verbal and physical evidence of abuse. Documentation should include drawings, descriptions, and photographs or videotapes of physical findings, as well as carefully documented histories of and statements by the child. For discussion of the legal implications of children's statements describing abuse, see Chapters 16 and 18 (this volume).

The diagnosis of sexual abuse in the medical setting can be difficult; it is rarely made because of obvious physical signs.

Participating in the multidisciplinary teams addressing child abuse. Many communities assemble multidisciplinary teams to protect children from abuse and neglect. These teams offer physicians and nurses important opportunities to coordinate children's care with other agencies and to participate in community efforts to ensure children's safety. Medical input into these teams is critical to transmit information about cases and to explain the significance of medical findings (Hoshstadt & Harwicke, 1985).

Primary Identification of Sexually Abused Children

The diagnosis of sexual abuse in the medical setting can be difficult; it is rarely made because of obvious physical signs. Oc-

TABLE 12.1 Guidelines for Making the Decision to Report Sexual Abuse of Children

	Data Available		Response	
History	Physical Examination	Laboratory Findings	Level of Concern About Sexual Abuse	Report Decision
None	Normal	None	None	No report
Behavioral changes[a]	Normal	None	Variable depending on behavior	Possible report;[b] follow closely (possible mental health referral)
None	Nonspecific findings	None	Low (worry)	Possible report;[b] follow closely
Nonspecific history by child or history by parent only	Nonspecific findings	None	Intermediate	Possible report;[b] follow closely
None	Specific findings[c]	None	High	Report
Clear statement	Normal	None	High	Report
Clear statement	Specific findings	None	High	Report
None	Normal, nonspecific, or specific findings	Positive culture for gonorrhea; positive serologic test for HIV; syphilis; presence of semen, sperm, acid phosphatase	Very high	Report
Behavior changes	Nonspecific findings	Other sexually transmitted diseases	High	Report

SOURCE: American Academy of Pediatrics (1999).

a. Some behavioral changes are nonspecific, and others are more worrisome (Krugman, 1986).

b. A report may or may not be indicated. The decision to report should be based on discussion with local or regional experts or child protective services agencies.

c. Other reasons for findings ruled out (Bayes & Jenny, 1990).

casionally, the parent or child presents with a complaint of abuse, but more likely the diagnosis is "masked," and the child presents with behavioral disturbances, physical illness caused by abuse, or psychosomatic or emotional problems (Hunter, Kilstrom, & Loda, 1985; Massie & Johnson, 1989).

Sexual abuse of children is associated with a wide variety of emotional and behavioral problems (Kendall-Tackett, Williams, & Finkelhor, 1993). For discussion of the psychological sequelae of sexual abuse, see Chapters 3 and 4 (this volume). However, none of these abuse-related problems are specifically diagnostic of abuse, and all can occur in nonabused children. Understanding the effect of base rates of these symptoms in the general population is important for weighing the significance of any of these symptoms (Wood, 1996). For discussion of base rates, see Chapter 19 (this volume).

With greater public awareness of sexual abuse, medical practitioners often are confronted by parents who are concerned about abuse. It can be difficult to know when and how to reassure parents, how to talk to and assess the child, when to refer to a medical subspecialist for evaluation, when to refer for psychotherapy, and when to report to child protection authorities. The American Academy of Pediatrics has published general guidelines for reporting abuse (see Table 12.1). Chapter 22 (this volume) provides in-depth discussion of the duty to report suspected maltreatment.

Interviewing

The type and extent of interviewing abused children depend on many factors. When forensic interviewing teams are available, children ideally will need to relate the details of their abuse on only one occasion. In some communities, however, this type of interview team does not exist, and the medical practitioner examining the child may be the most experienced interviewer at hand. It

TABLE 12.2 Guidelines for a Medical Interview With the Caretakers of a Sexually Abused Child

---

Interview the child's caretakers about suspected abuse:

Elicit details of concerning incidents or behaviors. Ask about past episodes of sexual abuse.

Determine relationships in the family constellation (genogram).

Screen for history of other types of abuse and neglect, as well as history of family violence or inappropriate sexuality.

Obtain a list of agencies and people involved in investigation or treatment.

Obtain a developmental history, including level of functioning in school and quality of peer relationships.

Obtain menstrual history, if indicated.

Ask about behavioral symptoms, depression, or posttraumatic stress disorder.

Take a history of physical problems related to abuse, including vaginal and anal pain, bleeding, discharge, or inflammation; enuresis or encopresis; chronic pain syndromes; sexually transmitted diseases; and pregnancy.

Obtain child's past medical history, growth history, and diet history and ask about immunization status, allergies, and medications.

Take a family history of physical and mental illness.

Screen for risk factors for sexually transmitted diseases in the perpetrator, including drug use, sexual preference, promiscuity, and history of known sexually transmitted diseases. If perpetrator unknown or only suspected or in preverbal children, further protocols are suggested (e.g., see Hewitt, 1998).

Assess child's current safety and level of protection and support.

---

is important for medical practitioners to be aware of the interviewing resources and policies in their communities. If medical care providers will be talking with children about abuse, they need to be educated about forensically valid questions and approaches to the interview.

A more complete interview may be indicated if the child is giving an initial, spontaneous disclosure to the practitioner. It is not helpful to tell a child who has just told you about sexual abuse that you do not want to know any details about the abuse. A unique opportunity to obtain important information may be lost if the child becomes reluctant to talk at a later date or in a different setting. Some children will relate details of abuse spontaneously during a physical examination. A child may be more likely to talk about abuse to a medical practitioner who has had a relationship with the child over time rather than talk to a stranger about abuse.

The child's response to the interview will depend on the child's cognitive, emotional, and behavioral development; the nature of the abuse experienced; and the response received after previous disclosures. Tasks for the interviewer are to establish rapport; ask open-ended, nonleading questions rather than "yes-no" questions; ask about pain, bleeding, dysuria, or other physical symptoms; and give the child a chance to ask questions. For detailed discussion of interviewing, see Chapter 18 (this volume).

Table 12.2 provides a list of subjects to cover when interviewing the caretakers of a child who has been sexually abused. Interviews with involved adults should not be done in the presence of the child.

Physical Examinations

When abuse is suspected, the physical examination of the child should be done with maximum sensitivity to the child's feelings of vulnerability and embarrassment. The examination will be less stressful if the examiner prepares the child by explaining procedures, uses drapes to protect the child's modesty, and uses distraction techniques during the examination. A child should not be physically forced to be examined. Sedation is sometimes used in cases in which the child is unable to cooperate.

Genital and anal examinations can be accomplished with the child supine in a frog-leg position or prone in a knee-chest position (Herman-Giddens & Frothingham, 1987). In the frog-leg position, the child lays on her back. The knees are bent and the heels are brought together in the midline. The knees are then pressed down toward the exam table, allowing the genitals to be seen. The knee-chest position requires the child to be prone, that is, face down. The child's knees are drawn up against the child's chest, raising the buttocks. The examiner separates the buttocks, exposing the genitals.

The labia are separated with gentle lateral traction or with traction toward the examiner. An excellent light source is needed to see internal structures, and magnification is also helpful. In adolescents, a Foley catheter can be inserted into the vagina, and then the catheter balloon is inflated and gently pulled back to delineate hymenal structures (Starling & Jenny, 1997). The use of both the frog-leg and knee-chest positions is important. Sometimes, the child's exam will appear abnormal in the frog-leg position, only to normalize in the knee-chest position. Although the knee-chest position is more difficult for the child to assume, it should be used to confirm any abnormal findings.

A common misconception is that child sexual abuse examinations involve vaginal or anal instrumentation, such as use of a speculum or anoscope. In most cases, the examination in prepubertal children is noninvasive and not painful. When instrumentation is required, sedation or anesthesia can be offered to decrease the child's discomfort. A sexual abuse evaluation does not have to be traumatic for the child. One study found that children's fear of the examination was related to past negative experiences in the health care setting (Lazebnik et al., 1994). Children's anxiety can be ameliorated by careful preparation and sensitivity.

The physical examination for sexual abuse is often entirely normal, even in cases of proven abuse (Adams, Harper, & Revilla, 1994; Muram, 1989). The absence of physical signs of trauma does not mean that abuse did not occur. Many types of abuse, such as fondling or oral-genital contact, will not cause anal, genital, or oral trauma. Other types of trauma may heal completely (Finkel, 1989).

Gross trauma to the genital or anal tract generally is not difficult to diagnose (Pokorny, Pokorny, & Kramer, 1992), but healed or subtle trauma may be more problematic. Studies of genital and anal anatomy in normal, nonabused children have elucidated a wide range of normal findings previously attributed to abuse (Berenson et al., 2000; Emans, Woods, Flagg, & Freeman, 1987; Gardner, 1992b; McCann, Voris, Simon, & Wells, 1989; McCann, Wells, Simon, & Voris, 1990). Normal findings in prepubertal girls include hymenal redundancy, hymenal ridges, hymenal bumps, and tissue tags. V-shaped hymenal notches that do not extend to the vestibule are considered normal when located superiorly and laterally on the hymen. However, notches found on the posterior aspect of the hymen are considered abnormal and have been found to be associated with trauma.

Normal anal findings include erythema (redness), increased or decreased pigmentation, venous engorgement, midline skin tags, and anal dilatation in the presence of stool (McCann et al., 1989). Anal abrasions, lacerations, hematomas, and extreme anal dilatation in the absence of stool are considered signs of possible abuse.

The diameter of the hymenal opening previously has been used as a diagnostic criterion for abuse. More recent studies have shown this to be undependable (McCann, Wells, et al., 1990; Paradise, 1989). Factors affecting hymenal and anal diameter include the examination position (McCann, Voris, et al., 1990) and the degree of relaxation of the child. The anal diameter is also affected by the presence of stool in the ampulla. Hymenal diameter can increase with age and with the onset of pubertal development.

Sexual abuse of boys is less frequently reported than sexual abuse of girls. Physical examination of boys is more likely to reveal anal abnormalities than genital abnormalities (Holmes & Slap, 1998). Anal findings reported after male abuse include erythema, abrasions, or fissures (Spencer & Dunklee, 1986).

Many physical conditions not related to abuse have been confused with sexual abuse trauma. The most commonly mistaken diagnoses include lichen schlerosis, vaginal and anal streptococcal infections, and accidental trauma such as straddle injuries (Bayes & Jenny, 1990). Physicians who are experts in forensic pediatrics have been trained to recognize illness and conditions that mimic sexual abuse trauma (Jenny, 1997). In many cases, referral to subspecialists in the field can avoid unnecessary psychological trauma for parents and children who have not been abused.

Sexually Transmitted Diseases

The presence of sexually transmitted diseases and microorganisms in children may or may not be diagnostic of sexual abuse. The epidemiology, diagnosis, and modes of transmission of sexually transmitted diseases in children differ from adults. Physicians should be aware of the biological differences in children's genital tracts that affect infectivity of organisms. They also need to differentiate sexual acquisition of organisms from perinatal transmissions. Finally, screening procedures need to reflect the fact that the sensitivity and specificity of diagnostic tests for sexually transmitted microorganisms used in adults may not be adequate for use in children.

A variety of pathogenic organisms may be sexually transmitted from adult to child:

Neisseria gonorrhoeae. Gonorrhea infections outside the immediate neonatal period can be attributed to sexual abuse. The organism is very fastidious and unlikely to be transmitted through casual contact (Neinstein, Goldenring, & Carpenter, 1984). *Neisseria gonorrhoeae* can be misidentified using rapid diagnostic tests (Whittington, Rice, Biddle, & Knapp, 1988). The use of at least two different confirmatory tests is indicated in cases of childhood gonorrhea. Although the U.S. Centers for Disease Control and Prevention recommends using cultures to diagnose gonorrhea in children (Centers for Disease Control and Prevention, 1998), nucleic acid amplification methods have shown great promise (Embree et al., 1996). When adequately tested, they could offer greater sensitivity and would be readily available to areas without easy access to laboratory services (Lindsay, Williams, Morris, & Embree, 1995).

Recent studies have shown that cultures for *Neisseria gonorrhoeae* are rarely positive in prepubertal children without signs and symptoms of vaginitis or in children who have not been exposed to perpetrators with documented infections (Ingram, Everett, Flick, Russell, & White-Sims, 1997; Muram, Speck, & Dockter, 1996; Sicoli, Losek, Hudlett, & Smith, 1995; Siegel, Schubert, Myers, & Shapiro, 1995). The use of routine screening for *Neisseria gonorrhoeae* in asymptomatic prepubertal children being evaluated for sexual abuse is probably not indicated.

Neisseria gonorrhoeae has been shown to be sensitive to a single-dose therapy with oral cefixime in adults (Handsfield et al., 1991). This offers a simple treatment for children that avoids an intramuscular injection. Because the effectiveness of this treatment in children has not been proven, follow-up cultures for "test of cure" are imperative if this regimen is used.

Chlamydia trachomatis. Chlamydia trachomatis can be acquired perinatally and carried by the child without symptoms after birth. The longest documented cases remained asymptomatically infected for 12.5 months after birth in the anus and 12.2 months in the vagina (Bell et al., 1992). Infections after the second year of life and/or symptomatic infections are more likely to be sexually acquired.

Rapid diagnostic tests for *C. trachomatis* have not been proven to be sensitive or specific for infections in children (Hammerschlag, Ajl, & Laraque, 1999), although newer nucleic acid amplification tests are being tested and show promise for future use in children (Embree et al., 1996).

Trichomonas vaginalis. Trichomonal vaginal infections in children are likely to be caused by sexual abuse (Jones, Yamauchi, & Lambert, 1985). Diagnosis by saline wet preparation of vaginal fluids may miss trichomonal infections (Krieger et al., 1988).

Herpes simplex virus (HSV). Genital herpes virus infections can be difficult to differentiate from other genital infections and conditions by clinical appearance (Nahmias, Dowdle, Zuher, Josey, & Luce, 1968; Simon & Steele, 1995). Cultures can be helpful if positive and if viral typing is available. Reliable commercial type-specific serum antibody tests also have recently become available (Ashley & Wald, 1999) and are useful in documenting infection.

The presence of Type I herpes genital infection does not rule out sexual abuse, even though Type I infections are less likely to be transmitted by sexual contact.

Bacterial vaginosis. Bacterial vaginosis (a mixed gram-negative infection associated with *Gardnerella vaginalis*) is found more commonly in sexually abused girls than in controls (Gardner, 1992a). The presence of bacterial vaginosis or *Gardnerella vaginalis* is not diagnostic of abuse. The accuracy of the diagnostic criteria for bacterial vaginosis used in adults has not been clinically evaluated in children (Hammerschlag, 1998).

Human papillomavirus infections (HPV). Genital and anal warts are caused by infections with human papillomavirus. In adults, anal or genital warts are sexually transmitted. Fomite transmission is not likely (Koutsky, Galloway, & Holmes, 1988). In infants, perinatal exposure to the wart virus is well documented (Puranen, Yliskoski, Saarikoski, Syrjanen, & Syrjanen, 1997). However, recent research indicates that perinatal HPV infection is extremely rare in infants of infected mothers (Watts et al., 1998), and the risk of the children developing obvious clinical warts is even more rare (Puranen, Yliskoski, Saarikoski, Syrjanen, & Syrjanen, 1996).

Most cases of genital and anal warts in children are caused by one of the types of human papillomavirus known to cause sexually transmitted condylomata acuminata in adults rather than by the virus types that cause common nongenital skin warts (Craighill, O'Connell, McLachlin, Kozakewich, & Crum, 1993; Gibson, Gardner, & Best, 1990). Many cases of genital and anal warts in children have been shown to be sexually acquired (Gutman, St. Claire, Herman-Giddens, Johnston, & Phelps, 1992; Hanson, Glasson, McCrossin, & Rogers, 1989). Two studies have compared the isolation of human papillomavirus from genital specimens obtained from sexually abused and nonabused girls. In both, the virus was found only in the abused girls (Gutman et al., 1994; Stevens-Simon, Nelligan, Breese, Jenny, & Douglas, 2000).

Multiple questions remain unanswered concerning the epidemiology of human papillomavirus infections in children. Differences between children and adults that could affect modes of transmission might include the differences between genital mucosa and genital and anal skin of children and adults, as well as differences in the clinical presentation of primary viral infection versus reinfection (Moscicki, 1996). Although caution is advised in interpreting the implications of genital or anal warts, in every case occurring outside the neonatal period, sexual abuse should be considered as a possible etiology (Gutman, Herman-Giddens, & Phelps, 1993).

Syphilis. Infections with *Treponema pallidum* have been documented in sexually abused children (Starling, 1994). Syphilis should be considered proof of sexual abuse unless it is shown to be acquired congenitally. The clinical diagnosis of syphilis in children may be missed. Most medical practitioners have a low "index of suspicion," and syphilitic rashes and lesions can mimic other common childhood diseases (Christian, Lavelle, & Bell, 1999).

Human immunodeficiency virus (HIV). Children have contracted HIV and acquired immunodeficiency syndrome (AIDS) from sexual abuse (Lindegren et al., 1998). A history of sexual abuse in childhood has been found to be a risk factor for HIV infection in adults (Zierler et al., 1991).

The Centers for Disease Control and Prevention recommends individualizing the screening for sexually transmitted diseases (STDs) in abused children. When deciding which tests for sexually transmitted diseases are to be done, the following factors should be considered (Sirotnak, 1994):

- How likely is it that abuse has occurred?
- What type of sexual contact is alleged? STDs are more likely to be transmitted after contact with the offender's penis or vagina than after fondling or contact with the offender's mouth.
- What are the risk factors for STDs in the offender's history? If the offender is known to be promiscuous, a frequenter of prostitutes, a man known to have sex with other men, or an intravenous drug user, screening for STDs definitely would be indicated.
- Is the child symptomatic? In any case in which sexual abuse is suspected and the child has symptoms of sexually transmitted diseases, diagnostic testing for STDs should be done.
- Does the child have one proven sexually transmitted disease? If so, complete screening for other diseases is indicated.
- Does the child live in a high-risk geographic area? Sexually transmitted diseases are much more prevalent in some communities than in others. If the child lives in an area where disease rates are high, screening is more likely to yield positive results.
- Is the patient an adolescent who has had sexual intercourse? Adolescents are at higher risk for STDs than adults, and screening for STDs should be part of their routine gynecological care.

The ideal work-up for sexually transmitted diseases when abuse is suspected may vary, depending on the above factors, the cost of pursuing unlikely diagnoses, and the ability of the child to cooperate with and tolerate testing.

Prevention, Diagnosis, and Management of Pregnancy

Pregnancy resulting from abuse or rape can be emotionally devastating to an adolescent girl. One national incidence study estimated that more than 32,000 pregnancies result from rape each year in the United States, and 48% of victims are younger than age 18 (Holmes, Resnik, Kilpatrick, & Best, 1996). In 17% of the rape-related pregnancies in adolescents, the perpetrator is a father, stepfather, or other relative.

If an acute sexual assault is immediately reported, effective medication for the prevention of pregnancy can be offered. Since 1998, a Food and Drug Administration (FDA)-approved ethinyl estradiol/levonorgestrel product has been available specifically for postcoital contraception (Preven®, Gynetics, Somerville, NJ). When used as prescribed, it results in a 75% reduction in the likelihood of pregnancy occurring (Grow, 2000). If pregnancy occurs after postcoital contraception, the possibility of harm to the fetus cannot be ruled out. However, the risk of fetal malformation is probably less than would be encountered if the mother took birth control pills early in pregnancy (Yuzpe & Kubba, 1989). It is important to rule out preexisting pregnancy by obtaining a serum pregnancy test before using the medication. If the serum pregnancy test is negative and a postcoital contraceptive is prescribed, the pregnancy test should be repeated weekly until the test is positive or until menstruation occurs.

When a pregnancy is the result of incest, the likelihood of serious genetic disease in the offspring is greatly increased. Each person is thought to carry between five and eight deleterious genes, most of which are recessive and not expressed. When mating occurs between related individuals, the likelihood of a serious genetic disease occurring in the resulting infant increases dramatically (Cotran, Kumar, & Collins, 1999). In matings of first-degree relatives (father-daughter or brother-sister), the chance of serious malformation and/or mental retardation in the offspring has been found to be 50% to 69% (Baird & McGillivray, 1982). In matings of second-degree relatives (brother/half-sister, uncle/niece), chance of malformed and/or mentally retarded offspring is half that of first-degree relative matings. In matings of cousins, the risk is one fourth that of first-degree matings.

When pregnancy results from incest, abuse, or assault, options for management include abortion, term pregnancy leading to adoption, or term pregnancy without placement. In any case, psychological counseling for the pregnant adolescent is imperative.

A history of sexual abuse can increase the risk and complications of pregnancy. Pregnant teens have been shown to have a high prevalence of sexual abuse histories (Boyer & Fine, 1992; McCullough & Scherman, 1991; Rainey, Stevens-Simon, & Kaplan, 1995). In addition, pregnant teens with a history of abuse are more likely to abuse drugs and alcohol, are less likely to use contraception, and had their first intercourse at a younger age than pregnant teens without a history of abuse. Teens with a history of abuse may be at a higher risk for complications of pregnancy, including preterm labor and bleeding early in pregnancy, than adolescents without a history of abuse (Stevens-Simon & Reichert, 1994). Abused teens also are more likely than nonabused teens to try to conceive purposefully (Rainey et al., 1995). Medical practitioners caring for adolescent abuse victims should provide information and counseling on pregnancy prevention, contraception, and sexuality to these "high-risk" young people.

Pregnant teens with a history of abuse are more likely to abuse drugs and alcohol, are less likely to use contraception, and had their first intercourse at a younger age than pregnant teens without a history of abuse.

Collection of Forensic Evidence

Good forensic examination of acutely sexually assaulted children and adolescents can facilitate effective police investigation of these crimes. Most physicians do not receive training in forensic examinations of sexual assault victims. Thus, many opportunities to collect important evidence are missed.

Any facility offering medical care to victims of sexual assault should use a sexual assault examination protocol to guide evidence collection. Forensic examination is usually offered if the victim is seen within 72 hours of any assault. However, the yield from physical specimen collection in prepubertal children is slight after 24 hours post assault (Christian et al., 2000). After 24 hours, clothing and linens are more likely to be positive for forensic evidence of assault than specimens collected from the bodies of children. The importance of collecting evidence on inanimate objects should be emphasized (Christian et al., 2000). Any evidence collected should be processed, labeled, and stored carefully to ensure its integrity and quality (Jenny, 2000).

Forensic examinations can be traumatic for young children. If multiple swabs and tests are to be collected, the use of sedation or anesthesia should be considered. The value of collecting good forensic evidence should be compared to the emotional cost of the procedure to the child or to the risk of sedation.

Psychological and Psychosomatic Sequelae

The medical evaluation of abused children includes an assessment of the child's general physical and mental health. Abuse is a stressful experience for a child, often leading to health problems. Abused children are sometimes neglected as well. A health assessment can uncover untreated illnesses, risk factors for future illnesses, psychological problems such as depression or dissociation, or psychosomatic problems.

Psychosomatic diseases and conditions associated with abuse are varied. Enuresis, encopresis, chronic pain syndromes, and other psychosomatic disorders are frequently encountered in sexual abuse victims.

Enuresis and encopresis. Many children experience urinary tract or anal inflammation and pain after episodes of abuse (Klevan & DeJong, 1990; Morrow, Yeager, & Lewis, 1997). This can lead to urinary incontinence, fecal impaction, or fecal soiling. Behavioral problems and the inability to deal with psychologically charged body areas cause persistence of the enuresis and encopresis.

Enuretic and encopretic children often are ridiculed by peers and punished by adults. The child gets into a downward spiral of shame and denial, leading to further bowel and bladder dysfunction. Although the treatment of enuresis and encopresis is difficult in children dealing with abuse issues, medical diagnosis and management are associated with decreased behavioral problems and increased self-esteem (Long-staffe, Moffatt, & Whalen, 2000; Young, Brennen, Baker, & Baker, 1995).

Chronic pain syndromes and psychosomatic conditions. Abused children and adult survivors of sexual abuse often express their emotional discomfort in physical symptoms. Chronic abdominal pain, headaches, anal or pelvic pain, vocal cord dysfunction, premenstrual syndrome, pseudo-seizures, fibromyalgia, and other psychosomatic complaints may be related to abuse (Felitti, 1991; Freedman, Rosenberg, & Schmaling, 1991; Harrop-Griffiths et al., 1988; Paddison et al., 1990; Walker, Gelfand, Gelfand, Koss, & Katon, 1995; Walker et al., 1997).

The symptoms of discomfort are not feigned but result from a somatic response to stress and psychological pain. These symptoms may be related to actual physical changes in the hypothalamic-pituitary-adrenal axis caused by chronic stress and trauma (Heim, Ehlert, Hanker, & Hellhammer, 1998). Treatment of psychosomatic conditions includes ruling out pathologic causes of pain, reassuring the patient, controlling pain without overreliance on pain medications, and referring the patient for psychotherapy.

Accurate Medical Record

In child abuse cases, the medical record is a legal document. Careful recording of the children's histories can help protect both victims and the accused. Factors to consider when preparing the medical record include the following:

- When recording history, note the source. Is the child reporting abuse, or is it another person telling you what the child said?
- Write legibly or dictate the record for readability.
- Use direct quotes from the child. Include in the history what question you asked to elicit the child's response and record details, such as the child's affect, developmental level, and use of language.
- Use careful descriptors of physical examination findings, both normal and abnormal (American Professional Society on the Abuse of Children, 1998).
- Visual images of physical findings are helpful in abuse cases. If a camera or video recorder is not available, careful drawings by the examiner should be done, particularly if trauma or abnormalities exist (American Academy of Pediatrics, 1999).

Conclusion

Medical practitioners perform essential services in the evaluation and treatment of abuse victims. Training in the management of abuse cases should be part of every primary care physician's education. The competent medical practitioner functions as a member of the larger team of professionals protecting children and their families. In addition to primary care providers, medical specialists in the field of child maltreatment are available to consult, teach, and advance the field (Jenny, 2000).

References

Adams, J. A., Harper, K., & Revilla, J. (1994). Examination findings in legally confirmed child sexual abuse: It's normal to be normal. *Pediatrics, 94,* 310-317.

American Academy of Pediatrics, Committee on Child Abuse and Neglect. (1999). Guidelines for the evaluation of sexual abuse of children: Subject review. *Pediatrics, 103,* 186-191.

American Professional Society on the Abuse of Children (APSAC), Committee on the Interpretation of Physical Findings in Sexual Abuse. (1998). *Glossary of terms and interpretation of findings for child sexual abuse evidentiary examinations.* Chicago: Author.

Ashley, R. L., & Wald, A. (1999). Genital herpes: Review of the epidemic and potential use of type-specific antibody. *Clinical Microbiology Reviews, 12,* 1-8.

Baird, P. A., & McGillivray, B. (1982). Children of incest. *Journal of Pediatrics, 101,* 854-857.

Bayes, J., & Jenny, C. (1990). Genital and anal conditions confused with child sexual abuse trauma. *American Journal of Diseases of Children, 144,* 1319-1322.

Bell, T. A., Stamm, W. E., Wang, S. P., Kuo, C. C., Holmes, K. K., & Grayson, J. T. (1992). Chronic chlamydia trachomatis infections in infants. *Journal of the American Medical Association, 15,* 400-402.

Berenson, A. B., Chacko, M. R., Wiemann, C. M., Mishaw, C. O., Friedrich, W. N., & Grady, J. J. (2000). A case-control study of anatomic changes resulting from sexual abuse. *American Journal of Obstetrics and Gynecology, 182,* 820-834.

Boyer, D., & Fine, D. (1992). Sexual abuse as a factor in adolescent pregnancy and child maltreatment. *Family Planning Perspectives, 24,* 4-11.

Centers for Disease Control and Prevention. (1998). 1998 guidelines for the treatment of sexually transmitted diseases. *Morbidity and Mortality Weekly Review, 47,* 1-118.

Christian, C. W., Lavelle, J., & Bell, L. M. (1999). Preschoolers with syphilis. *Pediatrics, 103,* E4.

Christian, C. W., Lavelle, J. M., DeJong, A. R., Loiselle, J., Brenner, L., & Joffe, M. (2000). Forensic evidence findings in prepubertal victims of sexual assault. *Pediatrics, 1086,* 100-104.

Cotran, R. S., Kumar, V., & Collins, T. (1999). *Pathological basis of disease* (6th ed.). Philadelphia: W. B. Saunders.

Craighill, M., O'Connell, B., McLachlin, C., Kozakewich, H., & Crum, C. (1993). HPV PCR analysis of prepubertal genital lesions. *Adolescent and Pediatric Gynecology, 6,* 183-189.

Emans, S. J., Woods, E. R., Flagg, N. T., & Freeman, A. (1987). Genital findings in sexually abused, symptomatic and asymptomatic girls. *Pediatrics, 79,* 778-785.

Embree, J. E., Lindsay, D., Williams, T., Peeling, R. W., Wood, S., & Morris, M. (1996). Acceptability and usefulness of vaginal washes in premenarcheal girls as a diagnostic procedure for sexually transmitted diseases. *Pediatric Infectious Disease Journal, 15,* 662-667.

Felitti, V. J. (1991). Long-term medical consequences of incest, rape, and molestation. *Southern Medical Journal, 84,* 328-331.

Finkel, M. A. (1989). Anogenital trauma in sexually abused children. *Pediatrics, 84,* 317-322.

Finkel, M. A., & Giardino, A. P. (Eds.). *Medical evaluation of child sexual abuse: A practical guide.* Thousand Oaks, CA: Sage.

Flaherty, E. G., Sege, R., Binns, H. J., Mattson, C. L., & Christoffel, K. K. (2000). Health care providers' experience reporting child abuse in the primary care setting. *Archives of Pediatric & Adolescent Medicine, 154,* 489-493.

Freedman, M. R., Rosenberg, S. J., & Schmaling, K. B. (1991). Childhood sexual abuse in patients with paradoxical vocal cord dysfunction. *Journal of Nervous & Mental Disease, 179,* 295-298.

Gardner, J. J. (1992a). Comparison of the vaginal flora in sexually abused and nonabused girls. *Journal of Pediatrics, 120,* 872-877.

Gardner, J. J. (1992b). A descriptive study of the genital variation in healthy, nonabused premenarcheal girls. *Journal of Pediatrics, 120,* 251-257.

Gibson, P. E., Gardner, S. D., & Best, S. J. (1990). Human papillomavirus types in anogenital warts of children. *Journal of Medical Virology, 30,* 142-145.

Grow, D. R. (2000). New contraception methods. *Obstetrics and Gynecology Clinics, 27,* 817-839.

Gutman, L. T., Herman-Giddens, M. E., & Phelps, W. C. (1993). Transmission of human genital papillomavirus disease: Comparison of data from adults and children. *Pediatrics, 91,* 31-38.

Gutman, L. T., St. Claire, K. K., Everett, V. D., Ingram, D. L., Soper, J., Johnston, W. W., Mulvaney, G. G., & Phelps, W. C. (1994). Cervical-vaginal and intra-anal human papillomavirus infection of young girls with external genital warts. *Journal of Infectious Diseases, 170,* I339-I344.

Gutman, L. T., St. Claire, K., Herman-Giddens, M. E., Johnston, W. W., & Phelps, W. C. (1992). Evaluation of sexually abused and nonabused young girls for intravaginal human papillomavirus infection. *American Journal of Diseases of Children, 146,* 694-699.

Hammerschlag, M. R. (1998). Sexually transmitted diseases in sexually abused children: Medical and legal implications. *Sexually Transmitted Infections, 74,* 167-174.

Hammerschlag, M. R., Ajl, S., & Laraque, D. (1999). Inappropriate use of nonculture tests for the detection of *Chlamydia trachomatis* in suspected victims of child sexual abuse. *Pediatrics, 104,* 1137-1139.

Handsfield, H. H., McCormack, W. M., Hook, E. W., Douglas, J., Covino, J. M., Verdon, M. S., Richart, C. A., Ehret, J. M., & the Gonorrhea Treatment Study Group. (1991). A comparison of single dose cefixime with ceftriaxone as treatment for uncomplicated gonorrhea. *New England Journal of Medicine, 325,* 1337-1341.

Hanson, R. M., Glasson, M., McCrossin, I., & Rogers, M. (1989). Anogenital warts in childhood. *Child Abuse & Neglect, 13,* 225-233.

Harrop-Griffiths, J., Katon, W., Walker, E., Holm, L., Russo, J., & Hickok, D. E. (1988). The association between chronic pelvic pain, psychiatric diagnoses, and childhood sexual abuse. *Obstetrics & Gynecology, 71,* 589-594.

Heim, C., Ehlert, U., Hanker, J. P., & Hellhammer, D. H. (1998). Abuse-related posttraumatic stress disorder and alterations of the hypothalamic-pituitary-adrenal axis in women with chronic pelvic pain. *Psychosomatic Medicine, 60,* 309-318.

Herman-Giddens, M. E., & Frothingham, T. E. (1987). Prepubertal female genitalia: Examination for evidence of sexual abuse. *Pediatrics, 80,* 203-208.

Hewitt, S. K. (1998). *Assessing allegations of sexual abuse in preschool children: Understanding small voices.* Thousand Oaks, CA: Sage.

Holmes, M. M., Resnick, H. S., Kilpatrick, D. G., & Best, C. L. (1996). Rape-related pregnancy: Estimates and descriptive characteristics from a national sample of women. *American Journal of Obstetrics & Gynecology, 175,* 320-324.

Holmes, W. C., & Slap, G. B. (1998). Sexual abuse of boys: Definitions, prevalence, correlates, sequelae, and management. *Journal of the American Medical Association, 280,* 1855-1862.

Hoshstadt, N. J., & Harwicke, N. J. (1985). How effective is the multidisciplinary approach? A follow-up study. *Child Abuse & Neglect, 9,* 365-372.

Hunter, R. S., Kilstrom, N., & Loda, F. (1985). Sexually abused children: Identifying masked presentation in a medical setting. *Child Abuse & Neglect, 9,* 17-25.

Ingram, D. L., Everett, V. D., Flick, L. A. R., Russell, T. A., & White-Sims, S. T. (1997). Vaginal gonococcal cultures in sexual abuse evaluations: Evaluation of selective criteria for preteenaged girls. *Pediatrics, 99,* E8.

Jenny, C. (1997). Pediatric fellowships in child abuse and neglect: The development of a new subspecialty. *Child Maltreatment, 2,* 356-361.

Jenny, C. (2000). Forensic examination: The role of the physician as "medical detective." In A. Heger, S. J. Emans, D. Muram, C. Jenny, C. Koverola, C. J. Levitt, & S. Pokorny (Eds.), *Evaluation of the sexually abused child* (2nd ed., pp. 79-93). New York: Oxford University Press.

Jenny, C., Sutherland, S. E., & Sandahl, B. B. (1986). A developmental approach to the prevention of child sexual abuse. *Pediatrics, 78,* 1034-1038.

Jones, J. G., Yamauchi, T., & Lambert, B. (1985). *Trichomonas vaginalis* infestation in sexually abused girls. *American Journal of Diseases of Children, 139,* 846-847.

Kendall-Tackett, K., Williams, L. M., & Finkelhor, D. (1993). Impact of sexual abuse on children: A review and synthesis of recent empirical studies. *Psychological Bulletin, 13,* 164-180.

Klevan, J. L., & DeJong, A. R. (1990). Urinary tract symptoms and urinary tract infection following sexual abuse. *American Journal of Diseases of Children, 144,* 242-244.

Koutsky, L. A., Galloway, D. A., & Holmes, K. K. (1988). Epidemiology of genital human papillomavirus infection. *Epidemiologic Reviews, 10,* 122-163.

Krieger, J. N., Tam, M. R., Stevens, C. E., Nielsen, I. O., Hale, J., Kaviat, N. B., & Holmes, K. K. (1988). Diagnosis of trichomoniasis: Comparison of conventional wet mount examinations with cytologic studies, cultures and monoclonal antibody staining of direct specimens. *Journal of the American Medical Association, 259,* 1223-1227.

Krugman, R. D. (1986). Recognition of sexual abuse in children. *Pediatrics in Review, 8,* 25-30.

Lazebnik, R., Zimet, G. D., Ebert, J., Anglin, T. M., Williams, P., Bunch, D. L., & Krowehuk, D. P. (1994). How children perceive the medical evaluation for suspected sexual abuse. *Child Abuse & Neglect, 18,* 739-745.

Lindegren, M. L., Hanson, I. C., Hammett, T. A., Beil, J., Fleming, P. L., & Ward, J. W. (1998). Sexual abuse of children: Intersection with the HIV epidemic. *Pediatrics, 102,* E46.

Lindsay, D., Williams, T., Morris, M., & Embree, J. E. (1995). Pediatric gonococcal infection: Case report demonstrating diagnostic problems in remote populations. *Child Abuse & Neglect, 19,* 265-269.

Longstaffe, S., Moffatt, M. E., & Whalen, J. C. (2000). Behavioral and self-concept changes after six months of enuresis treatment: A randomized, controlled trial. *Pediatrics, 105,* 935-940.

Massie, M. E., & Johnson, S. M. (1989). The importance of recognizing a history of sexual abuse in female adolescents. *Journal of Adolescent Health Care, 10,* 184-191.

McCann, J., Voris, J., Simon, M., & Wells, R. (1989). Perianal findings in prepubertal children selected for nonabuse. *Child Abuse & Neglect, 13,* 179-193.

McCann, J., Voris, J., Simon, M., & Wells, R. (1990). Comparison of genital examination techniques in prepubertal girls. *Pediatrics, 85,* 182-187.

McCann, J., Wells, R., Simon, M., & Voris, J. (1990). Genital findings in prepubertal girls selected for nonabuse: A descriptive study. *Pediatrics, 86,* 428-439.

McCullough, M., & Scherman, A. (1991). Adolescent pregnancy: Contributing factors and strategies for prevention. *Adolescence, 26,* 809-816.

Morrow, J., Yeager, C. A., & Lewis, D. O. (1997). Encopresis and sexual abuse in a sample of boys in residential treatment. *Child Abuse & Neglect, 21,* 11-18.

Moscicki, A. B. (1996). Genital HPV infections in children and adolescents. *Obstetrics & Gynecology Clinics of North America, 23,* 675-697.

Muram, D. (1989). Child sexual abuse: Relationship between sexual acts and genital findings. *Child Abuse & Neglect, 13,* 211-216.

Muram, D., Speck, P. M., & Dockter, M. (1996). Child sexual abuse examination: Is there a need for routine screening for *N. gonorrhoeae*? *Journal of Pediatric & Adolescent Gynecology, 9,* 79-80.

Myers, J. E. B. (1997). *Legal issues in child abuse and neglect practice.* Thousand Oaks, CA: Sage.

Myers, J. E. B. (2000). Medicolegal aspects of child abuse. In R. M. Reece (Ed.), *Treatment of child abuse: Common ground for mental health, medical, and legal practitioners* (pp. 313-335). Baltimore: Johns Hopkins University Press.

Myers, J. E. B. (2002). Legal issues in the medical evaluation of child sexual abuse. In M. A. Finkel & A. P. Giardino (Eds.), *Medical evaluation of child sexual abuse: A practical guide* (pp. 233-250). Thousand Oaks, CA: Sage.

Myers, J. E. B. (2001). Mediolegal aspects of child abuse. In R. M. Reece & S. Ludwig (Eds.), *Child abuse: Medical diagnosis and management* (2nd ed.). Philadelphia: Lippincott, Williams & Wilkins.

Nahmias, A. J., Dowdle, W. R., Zuher, M. N., Josey, W., & Luce, C. F. (1968). Genital infection with herpes virus hominis types 1 and 2 in children. *Pediatrics, 42,* 659-666.

Neinstein, L. S., Goldenring, J., & Carpenter, S. (1984). Nonsexual transmission of sexually transmitted diseases: An infrequent occurrence. *Pediatrics, 74,* 67-76.

Paddison, P. L., Gise, L. H., Lebovits, A., Strain, J. J., Cirasole, D. M., & Levine, J. P. (1990). Sexual abuse and premenstrual syndrome: Comparison between a lower and higher socioeconomic group. *Psychosomatics, 31,* 265-272.

Paradise, J. E. (1989). Predictive accuracy and the diagnosis of sexual abuse: A big issue about a little tissue. *Child Abuse & Neglect, 13,* 169-176.

Pokorny, S. F., Pokorny, W. J., & Kramer, W. (1992). Acute genital injury in the prepubertal girl. *American Journal of Obstetrics & Gynecology, 166,* 1461-1466.

Puranen, M. H., Yliskoski, M. H., Saarikoski, V. S., Syrjanen, K. J., & Syrjanen, S. M. (1996). Vertical transmission of human papillomavirus from infected mothers to their newborn babies and persistence of the virus in childhood. *American Journal of Obstetrics & Gynecology, 174,* 694-699.

Puranen, M. H., Yliskoski, M. H., Saarikoski, V. S., Syrjanen, K. J., & Syrjanen, S. M. (1997). Exposure of an infant to cervical human papillomavirus infection of the mother is common. *American Journal of Obstetrics & Gynecology, 176,* 1039-1045.

Rainey, D. Y., Stevens-Simon, C., & Kaplan, D. W. (1995). Are adolescents who report prior sexual abuse at higher risk for pregnancy? *Child Abuse & Neglect, 19,* 1283-1388.

Reece, R. M. (Ed.). (2000). *Treatment of child abuse: Common ground for mental health, medical, and legal practitioners.* Baltimore: Johns Hopkins University Press.

Reece, R. M., & Ludwig, S. (Eds.). (2001). *Child abuse: Medical diagnosus and management, 2nd ed.* Philadelphia: Lippincott, Williams, & Wilkins.

Sicoli, R. A., Losek, J. D., Hudlett, J. M., & Smith, D. (1995). Indications for *Neisseria gonorrhoeae* cultures in children with suspected sexual abuse. *Archives of Pediatric & Adolescent Medicine, 149,* 86-89.

Siegel, R. M., Schubert, C. J., Myers, P. A., & Shapiro, R. A. (1995). The prevalence of sexually transmitted diseases in children and adolescents evaluated in Cincinnati: Rationale for limited STD testing in prepubertal girls. *Pediatrics, 96,* 1090-1094.

Simon, H. K., & Steele, D. W. (1995). Varicella: Pediatric genital/rectal vesicular lesions of unclear origin. *Annals of Emergency Medicine, 25,* 111-114.

Sirotnak, A. P. (1994). Testing sexually abused children for sexually transmitted diseases: Whom to test, when to test, and why? *Pediatric Annals, 23,* 370-374.

Socolar, R. R., Champion, M., & Green, C. (1996). Physicians' documentation of sexual abuse of children. *Archives of Pediatrics & Adolescent Medicine, 150,* 191-196.

Spencer, M. J., & Dunklee, P. (1986). Sexual abuse of boys. *Pediatrics, 78,* 133-138.

Starling, S. P. (1994). Syphilis in infants and young children. *Pediatric Annals, 23,* 334-340.

Starling, S. S., & Jenny, C. (1997). Forensic examination of adolescent female genitalia: The Foley catheter technique. *Archives of Pediatrics & Adolescent Medicine, 151,* 102-103.

Stevens-Simon, C., Nelligan, D., Douglas, J. M., Jr., Breese, P., & Jenny, C. (2000). The prevalence of genital human papillomavirus infections in abused and nonabused preadolescent girls. *Pediatrics, 106,* 645-649.

Stevens-Simon, C., & Reichert, S. (1994). Sexual abuse, adolescent pregnancy, and child abuse: A developmental approach to an intergenerational cycle. *Archives of Pediatrics & Adolescent Medicine, 148,* 23-27.

Walker, E. A., Gelfand, A. N., Gelfand, M. D., Koss, M. P., & Katon, W. J. (1995). Medical and psychiatric symptoms in female gastroenterology clinic patients with histories of sexual victimization. *General Hospital Psychiatry, 17,* 85-92.

Walker, E. A., Keegan, D., Gardner, G., Sullivan, M., Bernstein, D., & Katon, W. J. (1997). Psychosocial factors in fibromyalgia compared with rheumatoid arthritis: II. Sexual, physical, and emotional abuse and neglect. *Psychosomatic Medicine, 59,* 572-577.

Watts, D. H., Koutsky, L. A., Holmes, K. K., Goldman, D., Kuypers, J., Kiviat, N. B., & Galloway, D. A. (1998). Low risk of perinatal transmission of human papillomavirus: Results from a prospective cohort study. *American Journal of Obstetrics & Gynecology, 178,* 365-373.

Whittington, W. L., Rice, R. J., Biddle, J. W., & Knapp, J. S. (1988). Incorrect identification of *Neisseria gonorrhoeae* from infants and children. *Pediatric Infectious Disease Journal, 7,* 3-10.

Wood, J. M. (1996). Weighing evidence in sexual abuse evaluations: An introduction to Bayes's theorem. *Child Maltreatment, 1,* 25-36.

Young, M. H., Brennen, L. C., Baker, R. D., & Baker, S. S. (1995). Functional encopresis: Symptom reduction and behavioral improvement. *Journal of Developmental & Behavioral Pediatrics, 16,* 226-232.

Yuzpe, A., & Kubba, A. (1989). Postcoital contraception. In M. Filshie & J. Guillebaud (Eds.), *Contraception science and practice* (pp. 126-143). Boston: Butterworth.

Zierler, S., Feingold, L., Laufer, D., Velentgas, P., Kantorwitz-Gordon, I., & Mayer, K. (1991). Adult survivors of childhood sexual abuse and subsequent risk of HIV infection. *American Journal of Public Health, 81,* 572-575.

13

Physical Abuse

Accidental Versus Intentional Trauma in Children

CHARLES F. JOHNSON

Accidents and Child Abuse: Common Childhood Experiences

Children suffer a wide variety of injuries. In 1967, it was estimated that 1,750,000 children aged less than 1 year sustained an injury from a fall (Kravitz, Driessen, Gomberg, & Korach, 1969), and approximately 15,000,000 children of all ages were injured annually in the United States (Izant & Hubay, 1966). One study has found that 10% of children seen in an emergency department have been abused (Holter & Friedman, 1968). Determining which children have suffered nonaccidental injury and should be reported to proper authorities requires diligence (Johnson, 1990). A wise approach is to routinely determine the cause of all injuries to answer the following question: Is this injury in keeping with the history offered and the child's level of development?

Tissue and Trauma

Because state laws require all professionals dealing with children to report suspect child maltreatment (CM), professionals must become familiar with the manifestations of accidental and nonaccidental trauma. Tissues have a limited repertory of responses to trauma. Although a variety of orderly and complex activities take place at the microscopic and biochemical levels, relatively few *observable* changes take place when the integrity of a tissue has been disrupted by heat, force, infection, or chemical insult. The visible manifestations of tissue trauma depend on one or more of the following: (a) the amount and vectors of force delivered to the tissue (Spivak, 1992); (b) the type of injurious agent applied to the tissues (chemical, electrical, thermal, etc.); (c) the strength of the agent applied, such as temperature, concentration, amperage, or wavelength; (d) the length of time of the exposure; and (e) how and where these are distributed on and

249

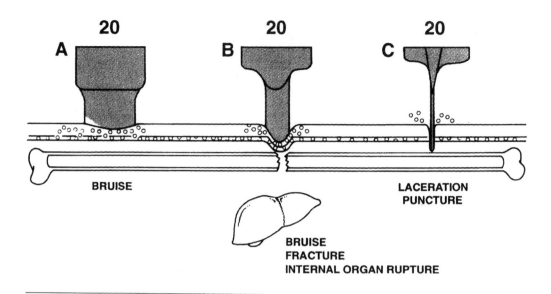

Figure 13.1. Concentration of Force and Injury Consequences

into the body. Darker skin color may hide the consequences of mild trauma. What appears to be "easy bruising" may be the normal manifestations of trauma to a fair-skinned child. Underlying fat and muscle may dissipate the force of a blow. The shape and size of an instrument also may dissipate or concentrate the force of a blow. For example, a blow from a large, flat surface may dilate superficial blood vessels. This results in a visible and temporary erythema or redness (see Figure 13.1a). With more force to the same area, blood vessels under the skin will rupture. Having escaped the blood vessels, the red blood cells are seen as a prolonged discoloration or bruise. The time of appearance of a bruise may be delayed if the trauma is to deeper tissues, such as that of the buttocks or thighs (Wilson, 1977).

If unyielding bone is close to the surface, the skin is more likely to be crushed between the striking object and the bone, with more visible and extensive tissue damage. In one study of infants younger than 12 months of age, all bruises were found on the front of the body over bony prominences (Carpenter, 1999). A blunt impact to the hand is more likely to cause bruising than a similar impact to the buttocks or thighs. Thick tissue of the buttocks and thighs may dissipate and conceal the consequences of certain injuries. The pelvic bones and femurs lie deep below the surface and are difficult to fracture, but hand bones are superficial and more easily fractured.

A blow of similar force to the same body area from a smaller object is likely to cause more concentrated, more serious, and deeper damage (Wheeler & Shope, 1997) (see Figure 13.1b). Underlying and inflexible bone is more likely to be fractured. If the blow is to the chest, the relatively flexible ribs may escape damage; however, if the blow is low on the right side of the chest, the underlying liver can be ruptured. If the blow is to the mid-abdomen unprotected by ribs, the part of the duodenum that is bound to the back of the abdomen against the spine is not free to move and may be crushed against the spine. Because of these anatomic features, blows to the abdomen are the second leading cause of death due to CM. If the object striking the body is narrow or pointed, the force is concentrated further, and the skin and underlying tissue are lacerated or punctured. Little bruising may be seen because blood cells are not trapped in the skin, but they escape to the skin surface as bleeding (see Figure 13.1c). This type of trauma results from electric cords, switches, picks, screwdrivers, nails, knives, and bullets.

It is not ethically possible to research the force that is required to cause a specific injury to the tissues of living children. The applicability of trauma research done on adult robots may be challenged in court. Surveys have been conducted to analyze the consequences of falls from windows and fire escapes (Barlow, Niemirska, & Gandhi, 1983; Sieben, Leavitt, & French, 1971; Smith,

Burrington, & Woolf, 1975), from beds in hospitals (Helfer, Slovis, & Black, 1977; Lyons & Oates, 1993), from elevated surfaces and down stairs in homes (Joffe & Ludwig, 1988), and from observed falls in playgrounds. A fall from a 36- to 48-inch height (3 to 4 feet) may rarely fracture the skull, clavicle, or femur, but central nervous system damage is highly unlikely (Helfer et al., 1977). Falls from greater heights are not invariably associated with injury (Lehman & Schonfeld, 1993; Smith et al., 1975). In one study of infants and children, 14 died who fell four or more stories, but 47 others survived with few permanent sequelae (Barlow et al., 1983). The determination of the cause of an injury requires familiarity with the manifestations and locations of *common* accidental and nonaccidental injuries of children, the common objects that injure children (Johnson & Showers, 1985), and the pattern of healing of bruises (Sugar, Taylor, & Feldman, 1999; Wilson, 1977), fractures (Swischuk, 1992), and burns. Bruises are rare in children prior to the time they walk with support and are most common over the anterior tibia and knee and unusual on the back and trunk.

Caretakers' Responses to Injuries

Although caretakers may readily admit to spanking or slapping their children, it is unlikely that perpetrators of a serious intentional injury readily will admit their role. If caretakers could be depended on to give an accurate and truthful history, there would be no need to evaluate whether their explanations accounted for a child's injury. Children may be too young, frightened, confused, or intimidated to give an accurate or truthful history of an injury. They may repress memory of the event (Chu, Frey, Ganzel, & Matthews, 1999).

If caretakers could be depended on to give an accurate and truthful history, there would be no need to evaluate whether their explanations accounted for a child's injury.

Caretakers may not have witnessed an injury. In this instance, it is necessary to ap-

ply the term *unexplained injury*. This circumstance may raise concern about appropriate supervision or safety neglect (Johnson & Coury, 1992). In their efforts to escape culpability and ire, caretakers who accidentally injure a child may concoct a story that is improbable or impossible and thereby create suspicion of intentional injury. For example, the caretaker may blame the child or a sibling when neither is developmentally able to have caused the injury. When the true details finally are related, the explanation may seem defensive and therefore likely to be false. A caretaker's delay in seeking help for an injury is considered a risk factor for abuse. The delay may be the result of ignorance, failure to comprehend the seriousness of the injury, lack of transportation, or fear of reprisal. In addition, a burn may progress from what appears to be first-degree erythema at bedtime to a serious vesiculated (blistered) second-degree burn by morning.

Professional Attitudes and Practices: Reporting of Suspected Abuse

Professionals who believe that certain caretakers are unlikely to be perpetrators of physical abuse because of age, sex, race, or socioeconomic status may neglect to consider the possibility (Drake & Zuravin, 1998; Morris, Johnson, & Clasen, 1985). A young child with a history of previous or severe abuse, whose parents are perceived as lazy, angry, and poor, is more likely to be reported (Zellman, 1992).

The physician's examinations or medical records may be incomplete in cases of injury to children. The records of emergency department physicians in a hospital for children have been studied to determine if they routinely ask and record the answers to basic questions that can help determine the cause of an injury. Missing information included the place in which the injury occurred, notation of previous injuries, chart review, and size, color, and age of the injury (Johnson, Apollo, Joseph, & Corbitt, 1986). A complete examination was recorded only 22.3% of the time.

When interpreting injury, knowledge about normal child development is necessary; however, some children may be capable of physical activity that is beyond what is expected. It may be necessary to question noninvolved adults about the child's capabilities. For example, accidents to children in walkers are common. The speed with which preambulating children in a walker can travel and the trunk support given by the walker seat may facilitate accidents expected to occur only in an older child (Johnson, Erickson, & Caniano, 1990).

What Constitutes Reportable Abuse?

Despite state mandates, professionals may fail to report suspected abuse (Finkelhor & Zellman, 1991; see Chapter 22, this volume). Physicians asked to rate the appropriateness of various types of child discipline also were asked if they would report those actions that they considered to be inappropriate discipline (Morris et al., 1985). There were disparities about what constituted appropriate discipline. Instances of inappropriate discipline were not considered uniformly reportable as abuse until the consequences were serious. Other reasons why general pediatricians and practitioners have failed to consider abuse and failed to report included seriousness of the injury, familiarity with the family, presence of other injuries, single versus repeated injury, affect or attitude of the caretakers, personal experience, child's affect, legal requirements, trust of social and legal agencies, and legal and economic consequences (American Academy of Pediatrics, 1998).

The History of the Injury From the Child

Children routinely should be asked about the cause of any injuries they suffer. This practice will (a) increase the opportunities for children to tell about the causes of their injuries, (b) improve the professional's techniques for questioning children of various ages about trauma, (c) increase the interviewer's knowledge about the manifestations of various types of injury in children, and (d) teach children and their caretakers that it is likely and proper for adults to be concerned about children's injuries (for guidance on interviewing children, see Chapter 18, this volume).

TABLE 13.1 Risk Factors Associated With Physical Abuse

Factors in the child: premature, twin, chronic illness, delayed development, retarded, hyperactive, seen as different, previous severe injury, poor health care, unkempt.

Factors in the caretaker: unplanned or unwanted pregnancy, single parent, closely spaced children, abused as child, stressed, substance abuse, isolated, limited support system, limited knowledge of child rearing and child development, known to child protective services, chronic or acute illness, emotional disturbance, developmentally delayed, lack of empathy, lack of control.

Factors in the injury or injuries: no history, not in keeping with history, different histories, different ages, different types of injuries, symmetrical, geometric, silhouette of object, outline of object, mirror or bilateral, not in keeping with child's development, delay in seeking attention, protected area (genitalia, buttocks), nonleading surface (back, back of legs, ears, neck, underarms), nonexploratory surface (top of hands), bands, tattoos.

Medical and Social History

The presence of risk factors involving the child, the caretaker, and the injury increases concerns that an injury is not accidental (Dubowitz, Hampton, Bithoney, & Newberger, 1987; Johnson, 1983). Risk factors are summarized in Table 13.1.

Social factors associated with risk for abuse may begin in the past of a parent with inadequate or no preparation for pregnancy, drug use (Langeland & Hartgers, 1998; Taylor et al., 1991), lack of child-rearing and accident prevention knowledge (Johnson, 1999a, 1999b, 1999c; Johnson, Loxterkamp, & Albanese, 1982; Showers & Johnson, 1985), and a history of being abused (Cadzow, Armstrong, & Fraser, 1999; Coohey, 1997). Poverty, with its associations with substance abuse, teen pregnancy, unemployment, and single parenthood, is a well-documented risk factor (Gillham, Tanner, & Cheyne, 1998). Other risk factors or recent stresses include illness, divorce, death in the family, and loss of employment (Johnson & Cohn, 1990). Many of the social risk factors for nonaccidental injuries are the same for accidental injuries (Aber, Bennett, Conley, & Li, 1997; Bourguet & McArtor,

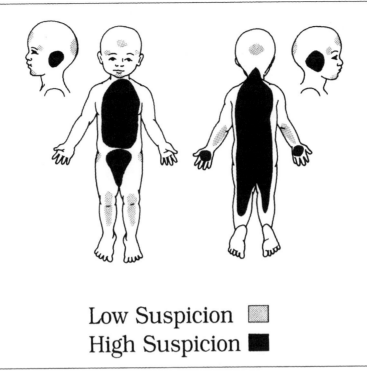

Low Suspicion ▨

High Suspicion ■

Figure 13.2. Bruises and Abuse: Bruise Location in Accidental and Nonaccidental Injury

1989; Dubowitz et al., 1987; Gregg & Elmer, 1969). Caretakers under stress may not be able to provide for the safety of their children or may react to stress with violence.

When an injury appears to be nonaccidental, it is essential to obtain a detailed past medical and social history to guide approaches to management. The charts of children with injuries who are seen in the emergency room should be reviewed for records of previous injuries (Olney, 1988).

The question, "What caused this mark here?" should be directed to the communicating child and parent for all injuries. The answers to the question should include details about what object(s) caused the injury or came in contact with the child. If the history given is that the child fell, it is important to know the distance involved and the characteristics of the surface(s) contacted. When the injury is highly suggestive of abuse, additional questions must be asked to determine (a) when the injury occurred; (b) where the injury occurred; (c) who witnessed the injury; (d) the child's developmental abilities for rolling, crawling, reaching, grasping, turning faucets and door handles, climbing, walking, running, and riding; and (e) clothing worn by the child. This information should be recorded carefully. The record *for all injuries* should in-

clude the following statement: "This injury is/is not compatible with the history given and the child's development."

Examination of the Injury

Complete examination requires determination of the location, size, shape, and age of all external and internal injuries. Bruises are the most common injury to the skin of children who are abused and seen in a hospital setting (Johnson & Showers, 1985). Bruises are also common in accidental injuries. Accidental bruises occur on surfaces over bones that are close to the surface and "the leading edges" of the body as the child interacts with the environment (see Figure 13.2). The location of the injury may be incompatible with an accident. Bilateral or mirror nonintentional injuries are uncommon (Lasing & Buchan, 1976). It is unlikely that a child will injure both thumbs, both ears, both eyes, or more than one side of the body in a fall onto one surface or from a single impact with an instrument.

To determine if the age of a bruise is in keeping with the history given, one must determine the color of the bruise. Bruises go through a series of color changes as the blood cells ruptured from the vessel walls

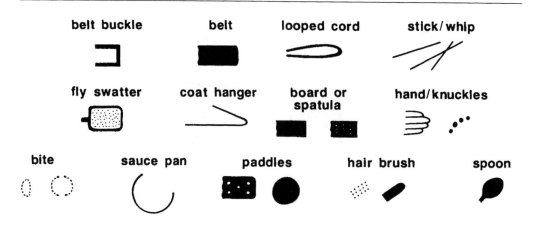

Figure 13.3. Marks From Instruments
SOURCE: Johnson (1990). Reprinted by permission of W. B. Saunders.

disintegrate and undergo chemical transformations (Wilson, 1977). The *exact* number of days that have transpired since the injury cannot be determined with certainty, especially if the bruise is deep (Schwartz & Ricci, 1996). The shape of a bruise often presents as a silhouette or outline of the shape of the object that caused it (see Figure 13.3).

The marks from a slap to the cheeks or buttocks appear as an outline of the hand, as if the fingers have pressed the blood from underlying vessels to vessels underlying the periphery of the fingers where the vessels subsequently rupture. If the perpetrator is right handed, the marks are expected on the left cheek of the child and the outline of the fingers is angled toward the ear. Because the face is a common target for discipline and is in proximity to delicate structures, such as the eyes, eardrums, and brain, slap marks on the face should be recognized by all individuals dealing with children and should be considered pathognomonic for child abuse (see Photo 13.1). Although the hand (22%) and belt strap (23%) have been found to be the most common objects to cause injury to the abused child seen in a hospital setting, a variety of other instruments or objects may be used (see Table 13.2) (Showers & Johnson, 1985). The choice of object is likely to be a matter of convenience and availability. For example, older homes have a limited number of electric outlets, and families living in such homes may have greater access to extension cords. Of course, access does not mean misuse. Culture may influence the choice of instrument. Extremities may be bound by a cord to restrain a child during a beating or sexual abuse (Johnson, Kaufman, & Callendar, 1990). Human bite marks have

elliptical or oval patterns. Teeth marks can be matched against dental impressions from suspected perpetrators (Wagner, 1986).

Not all serious internal injuries have external markers; the child who is thrown against a soft surface, such as a bed, may have extensive brain damage and no external marks (Johnson & Showers, 1985).

The Laboratory and X-Rays

Parents, especially of a fair-skinned child, may claim that their child bruises more readily than normal. It is important to rule out this possibility by performing clotting studies, including a prothrombin time (PT), partial thromboplastin time (PTT), a platelet count, and a complete blood count. It is possible that the child with a bleeding problem, such as hemophilia, may be abused (Johnson & Coury, 1988).

A skeletal survey should be considered in the evaluation of children younger than 2 years of age who have unusual bruises or other signs of abuse. In addition, because newly fractured bones, especially ribs (Spivak, 1992), may not be seen on a bone survey, a bone scan should be considered (Merten, Radkowski, & Leonidas, 1983). Follow-up X-rays may reveal fractures that were not seen on the original survey but become more visible as the result of callus formation during healing. Skull fractures may not be seen on bone scans (Howard, Barron, & Smith, 1990).

When the abdomen has been injured, liver function studies should be ordered to rule out trauma to the liver (Coant, Kornberg, Brody, & Edwards-Holmes,

TABLE 13.2 Primary Injury by Cause Among 616 Children Reported for Physical Abuse by
Children's Hospital of Columbus, Ohio, 1980-1982[a]

Known Cause of Injury	Frequency	%
Belt or strap	124	23
Hand open (choked, grabbed, pinched, slapped)	120	22
Fist	60	11
Propelled (thrown, dropped, pushed, pulled, or dragged)	41	8
Other (e.g., hit by toy, telephone, kitchen fork, bottle, household item, etc.; shot with gun; dunked in ice water, etc.)	41	8
Switch or stick	33	6
Paddle or board	32	6
Cord	19	4
Hot liquid	17	3
Foot	11	2
Grid, heater, or stove	11	2
Cigarette	8	1
Shoe	5	1
Knife	4	1
Mouth	4	1
Shaking	3	< 1
Iron	3	< 1

SOURCE: Adapted from Johnson and Showers (1985).
a. Cause unknown = 157 (23% of total).

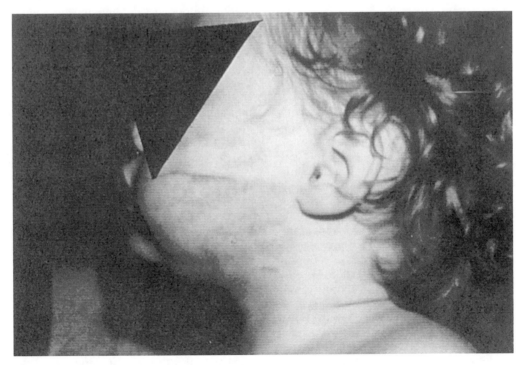

Photo 13.1. Slap Mark

1992). Although creatine phosphokinase (CPK) elevations are seen in damage to the muscle or brain, there are no standards for using the laboratory results to quantify severity or date the injury in children. Fractionation of the CPK will determine if the source is muscle or brain tissue. The computerized tomography (CT) scan and magnetic resonance imagery (MRI), used in the evaluation of head trauma, are also of value in investigating trauma to the lungs or abdominal organs in crushing injuries. Because head injuries are reported in 10% to 44% of abused children (Alexander, Kao, & Ellerbroek, 1989), a head CT scan or MRI has been recommended for all children younger than 2 years of age with external signs of abuse, especially if there is a past history of abuse (Alexander et al., 1990). On the other hand, a child with a normal neurological examination and a normal head circumference is unlikely to have significant injury on a CT scan or MRI of the head.

Shaking or Impact Injuries to the Brain

The highest morbidity and mortality from child abuse are caused by central nervous system injuries (Caniano, Beaver, & Boles, 1986). The term *shaken baby syndrome* (SBS) has been applied to acceleration-deceleration injuries to the brains of infants that result from vigorous shaking. Because the injuries may be due to impact or shaking, the terms *intentional head injury* (IHI) and *abusive head trauma* (AHT) have been proposed (Jenny, Hymel, Ritzen, Reinert, & Hay, 1999). These infants, generally younger than 1 year of age, present with seizures, failure to thrive, vomiting associated with lethargy or drowsiness, hypothermia, bradycardia, hypotension, respiratory irregularities, coma, or death (Spaide, Swengel, Scharre, & Mein, 1990). The common histories given are that the infant (a) spontaneously stopped breathing, and marks about the face are explained as the results of slapping the child to initiate respiration; (b) went to sleep and could not be aroused; (c) was dropped by a sibling; and (d) rolled from an elevated surface to the floor. The condition also can result if the infant is thrown against an object or surface.

When babies are shaken, their relatively large and poorly supported heads whip back and forth—hence the term *whiplash*

shaken baby syndrome, which was originally coined by Caffey (1972, 1974). As the head moves back and forth, the brain moves in the opposite direction. Brain tissue is sheared, and blood vessels are ruptured. A spinal tap will reveal fresh bleeding if the injury is recent. Physicians who obtain a bloody tap when investigating central nervous system problems in young children should not conclude that the bleeding was iatrogenic (Apollo, 1978). The term *tin ear syndrome* has been applied to a variant of SBS in which there is unilateral ear bruising, ipsilateral cerebral edema with obliteration of basilar cisterns, and hemorrhagic retinopathy (Hanigan, Peterson, & Njus, 1987).

CT scan or MRI and eye examination help make the diagnosis of intentional head injury (IHI). Other causes of brain hemorrhage, such as arteriovenous malformation or aneurysm, and trauma resulting from resuscitation usually can be excluded. Skull fractures may or may not be present. CT scan or MRI reveals intracranial hemorrhages. MRI has been shown to be the better technique for demonstrating cortical contusions, subdural hematomas, and shearing injuries, but CT scan is superior in detecting subarachnoid hemorrhage (Alexander et al., 1989). Eye-ground examination by an experienced examiner reveals retinal hemorrhage in 50% to 80% of cases (Levin, 1990). Although retinal hemorrhage should suggest the diagnosis of IHI, other causes must be considered. For example, retinal hemorrhages are seen in 40% of newborns after vaginal delivery (Smith, Alexander, Jurisch, Sato, & Kao, 1992). These hemorrhages usually clear in 2 weeks. The type, number, and location of hemorrhages are important to document.

Follow-up laboratory, hearing, vision, and developmental studies are necessary because the full extent of brain injury may not be apparent for several months or years. Developmental assessments should be videotaped for presentation in court to aid in demonstrating the extent of functional central nervous system damage. The coroner should be notified if an abused child's condition is deteriorating so that a properly detailed autopsy can be performed soon after the death. In addition, it is helpful if the coroner is provided with a written or verbal summary of the case in addition to a copy of the hospital record. The police and social service agencies may be impatient for a definitive diagnosis. It is appropriate to suggest firmly that they remove any children remaining in the home, until a suspicion of IHI can be verified.

Other Injuries to the Face and Head

When the face is the target of intentional trauma, careful examination of the mouth (Tate, 1971), eyes (Levin, 1990), and ears (Manning, Casselbrant, & Lammers, 1990) is necessary. A blow to the face or a fall may fracture teeth or put them through the lips. The shape of the bruise overlying the mouth may be consistent with a blow from a hand. The eardrum may be ruptured by a blow to the ear from a hand or object (Obiako, 1987). The frenulum between the tongue and base of the mouth or from the lips to the jaw may be torn as the result of forced feeding. The nasal septum may be eroded by intentional trauma (Grace & Grace, 1987). Because the internal structures of the eye may be injured when the face is struck, an ophthalmoscopic examination is necessary when a child suffers a black eye.

Bruised Abdomens and Internal Injuries in Child Abuse

Marks on the body routinely should raise the question of what anatomic structures lie inside that may have been damaged by force (see Figure 13.1b). A blow that results in trauma to the internal abdominal organs can lead to consequent bowel evisceration (Press, Grant, Thompson, & Milles, 1991), organ contusion, or rupture (Grosfeld & Ballantine, 1976; McCort & Vaudagna, 1964; Philipart, 1977; Vasundhara, 1990).

In one study, abdominal or lower thoracic visceral injury was found in 14 of 69 children (20.3%) suffering blunt trauma suspected as being due to CM. The abdominal organs injured included liver (5), spleen (3), kidney, adrenal glands, pancreas, and duodenum. Thoracic injuries included pulmonary contusion or laceration in 2 children. Four of the children died (Sivit, Taylor, & Eichelberger, 1989). Traumatic pancreatitis has resulted from intentional injury to the abdomen; CT scan is recommended in suspected abdominal trauma, with ultrasound as a supplemental diagnostic tool. Knuckle marks from a blow to the abdomen by a fist will appear as a row of three or four circular or teardrop shaped bruises, whose geometry approximates that of the imprint from the metacarpal-phalangeal joints of an adult, but serious internal injury can also occur in the absence of external marks (see Figure 13.3).

Misdiagnosis of Child Maltreatment

Any injury that results from *accidental* contact with an object through a fall also can result from the object being wielded carelessly or intentionally by an assailant. Injuries can be self-inflicted. In addition, a variety of metabolic (Hurwitz & Castells, 1987) infectious diseases, hematologic bleeding disorders (Brown & Melinkovich, 1986; Johnson & Coury, 1988; McRae, Ferguson, & Lederman, 1973; O'Hare & Eden, 1984), allergic skin reactions (Adler & Kane-Nussen, 1983), and birthmarks may be mistaken for child abuse (see Table 13.3).

Cigarette burns may be difficult to distinguish from a similar sized circular lesion of impetigo on the face or hand (Raimer, Raimer, & Hebeler, 1981). The primary lesion of impetigo is a small pustule (a bump with pus). Autoinoculation from scratching will spread the lesions of impetigo, and when surfaces contact each other, such as between the buttocks, underarms, or thighs, "kissing" lesions may result. Mongolian spots, present at birth, are more likely to be seen on the buttocks of dark-skinned infants. The spots, which are slate-blue color, may appear on any body surface and can be confused with bruises; however, Mongolian spots will not clear over a few weeks.

Children may discolor their skin with various temporary pigments, or they may tattoo or brand themselves permanently with pigments or objects. A tattoo by a caretaker may be considered a form of abuse. Self-mutilation is most likely to involve the hands in retarded or emotionally disturbed children (Putnam & Stein, 1985). Accidental and self-mutilation may be seen when sensation is lost in Cornelia-DeLange syndrome, familial dysautonomia, and Lesch-Nyhan syndrome. Banding, with the possible consequence of amputation or circular scarring, of a digit or the penis may be accidental or intentional (Johnson, 1988). Ringworm (tinea corporus) may resemble a human bite (see Photo 13.2). The ringworm lesion that is typified by raised red papules with a scale

TABLE 13.3 Conditions That May Mimic Child Abuse Injuries

SKIN CONDITIONS

Coagulopathies
Congenital:
  Hemophilia
Acquired:
  Vitamin K deficiency
  liver disease
  binding by resins
  malnutrition

Toxic:
  Salicylate poisoning

Other vascular-hematologic conditions
Schonlein-Henoch purpura
Platelet aggregation disorders
Disseminated intravascular coagulation
Blood dyscrasias

Connective tissue disorders
Type I Ehlers-Danlos syndrome

Chromosomal disorders

Birthmarks
Stork bites (bruises, pinchmarks)
Mongolian spots (bruises)
Pigmented nevi (bruises)
Strawberry hemangiomas

Infectious diseases
Chicken pox scars (cigarette burns)
Impetigo (cigarette burns)
Monilia (burn)
Scalded skin syndrome (burn)
Purpura fulminans of meningococcemia
Endocarditis

Hypersensitivity vasculitis
Stephens-Johnson syndrome
Hives
Phytophotodermatitis (burn)

Self-inflicted or factitial injury
Sucker-bites/hickies (pinchmarks)
Bruise, burn, puncture
Banding
Self-stimulation in retarded child
Cornelia de Lange syndrome
Lesch-Nyhan syndrome
Familial disautonomia

Self-inflicted skin coloration
Tattoo
Paint, crayons, dyes

Neglect/accident
Car restraint belt buckle burn (geometric burn)

Folk medicine practices
Cia Gao/coin rubbing (linear bruise or burn)
Moxibustion (burn)
Cupping (geometric burn)

Parasite
Pediculosis (maculae ceruleae mimic bruises)
Crab louse (maculae ceruleae mimic bruises)

Miscellaneous
Lichen sclerosis (in genital area may suggest
  trauma)
Valsalva (bilateral ecchymosis of eyes)
Forceful vomiting or coughing (petechial
  lesions on face)

FRACTURES

Congenital
Osteogenesis imperfecta (old and new fractures)
Chromosomal disorders
Schmid-like metaphyseal chondrodysplasia
  (corner fractures)
Wilson's disease (rib fractures)

Infections
Syphilis

Accidental
Fatigue fracture from exercise

Iatrogenic
Cardiopulmonary resuscitation
Restraint
Physical therapy

Acquired
Vitamin C or D deficiency
Prostaglandin use in newborn (subperiosteal
  hemorrhage)

RETINAL HEMORRHAGES

Folk medicine practices
Caida de Mollera/fallen fontanelle

Normal birth[a]

Coagulopathies[a]

Blood dyscrasias[a]

Infectious[a]
Meningitis
Endocarditis

Miscellaneous
Severe hypertension
CPR (Purtscher retinopathy) (very rare)
Accidental (very, very rare)

SHAKEN BABY SYNDROME

Congenital anomalies
Arterio-venous fistula
Ruptured aneurysm

Coagulopathies
Hemophilia[b]

a. These are possible causes of retinal hemorrhage in children younger than 3 years of age.
b. Children with any acute or chronic disease also may be abused.

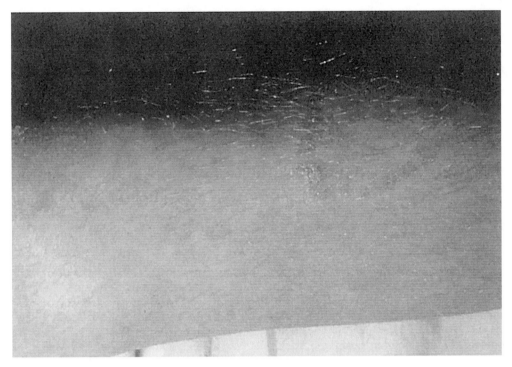

Photo 13.2. Tinea Corporus (Ringworm)

is likely to be more irregular in shape and spacing than the mark from a human bite. Because injuries to the skin may heal as scars, the examination of a child should include an inquiry into the etiology of all scars. Stria on the back, buttocks, upper thighs, breasts, lower abdomen, and back, not uncommon in adolescents, may be mistaken for scars from lacerations (Cohen, Matalon, Mezger, Ben, & Barzilai, 1997; Heller, 1995).

Professionals who are uncertain about the cause of a mark on a child or internal injuries should seek consultation from individuals experienced in child abuse or trauma investigation. A staff that involves all professionals participating in the investigation—including nurses, physicians, emergency medicine technicians, laboratory technicians, and radiologists—can reduce the likelihood of error. The group can clarify the etiology of an unusual injury and increase credibility and understanding of a report to protective agencies or the police.

Fractures in Child Abuse

After skin lesions, fractures are the second most common presentation of physical abuse (Kocher & Kasser, 2000). In one study, 17% of abused children presented with a fracture (Sinal & Stewart, 1998). The consequences of force to a bone will depend on the bone's location and resiliency. Growing children suffer types of fractures that are not seen in adults. The growing portion of the bone is an anatomically distinct area from the bone shaft. Classic metaphyseal lesions (CML) in infants are highly suspicious for abuse (Carty, 1993; Swischuk, 1992). Healing CML may mimic scurvy, leukemia, or congenital syphilis. Spiral fractures, in which a bone is fixed at one end and twisted at the other, are unusual in small children but not restricted to intentional injury (Mellick & Reesor, 1990). If a history of accidental fixation and twisting is not obtained, one should consider the likelihood that one end of the extremity was held and the other end twisted. Direct blows to an extremity are most likely to fracture the shaft of the bone; however, it is difficult to fracture the relatively resilient ribs, even during cardiopulmonary resuscitation (Feldman & Brewer, 1984). Nonaccidental rib fractures of infants occur when the chest is squeezed or crushed by a caretaker's hands, arms, or feet (Leonidas, 1983). Other fractures with a high specificity for abuse include scapular fractures, vertebral

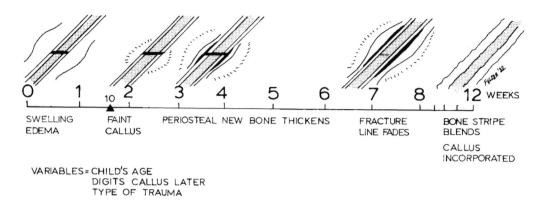

Figure 13.4. Dating Longbone Fractures

fractures or subluxations, finger injuries in nonambulating children, bilateral fractures, and complex skull fractures (Carty, 1993). Isolated fracture and dislocation of the lumbar spine with cord compression have been reported as due to abuse, although such cases are rare (Gabos, 1998).

In considering the cause of a fracture, it must be ascertained if the mass and speed of the child were sufficient to result in a fracture. It is possible to fracture the clavicle, skull, or humerus in a fall from 36 inches or more (Helfer et al., 1977). Fractures of the ribs, skull, clavicles, cervical spine, and extremities can occur during birth (Rizzolo, 1989). In children younger than 2 years of age, multiple, complex, depressed, wide, or growing skull fractures; fractures that involve more than a single cranial bone; and fractures of skull bones other than the parietal bone are more likely to be due to abuse (Hobbs, 1984; Meservy, Towbin, McLaurin, Myers, & Ball, 1987). It is important to recognize that 50% of all intracranial injuries are not associated with skull fractures (Merten, Osborne, Radkowski, & Leonidas, 1984). If a child falls onto a small object that concentrates the force on a small area, surface and deep injury, including a fracture, are more likely. One would expect visible tissue damage overlying a fracture caused by a fall onto an object (Figure 13.1b).

Fractures heal in a regular sequence (Swischuk, 1981). Dating the age of a fracture, like that of a bruise, is necessary to determine the credibility of the injury history. The first radiological signs of healing appear as periosteal elevation, followed by callus in 10 to 14 days (see Figure 13.4) (Swischuk, 1981). As with any tissue, this timing may be modified by individual variations, the specific bone(s) involved, and the existence of repetitive injuries. Early peak and late time ranges have been described, with the earliest periosteal new bone formation visible at 4 days and late appearance at 21 days (O'Connor & Cohen, 1987).

If an infant who is more than 2 weeks old presents with a fracture that shows no signs of healing, it is *unlikely* that this was due to an injury at birth. Rib fractures are rare. Even in difficult deliveries, no rib fractures were found in one series of 34,946 live births (Bhat, Kuman, & Oumachiqui, 1994). Fractures that show various stages of healing at one point in time are not compatible with a single injury. Children with osteogenesis imperfecta (Gahagan & Rimsza, 1991), a genetic disease with several types and manifestations, have bones that fracture easily. In Type II, the fractures may appear at birth. Blue sclerae, a common finding in Type I, may not be obvious, especially in fair-skinned children. After genetics consultation, the diagnosis can be made in most cases by analysis of Type I collagen obtained by biopsy. Not all cases of multiple fractures of differing ages will require this analysis. There is no scientific basis to "temporary brittle bone disease" (Block, 1999).

Trauma Resulting From Folk Medicine Practice

In an effort to treat illness, the caretaker may resort to a variety of home or folk remedies. Although the merits of chicken soup are familiar to most people in the United States, other folk practices may not be readily recognized. If folk practices leave a mark, they are likely to be mistaken for CM. For example, in *Cao Gio* (Gellis &

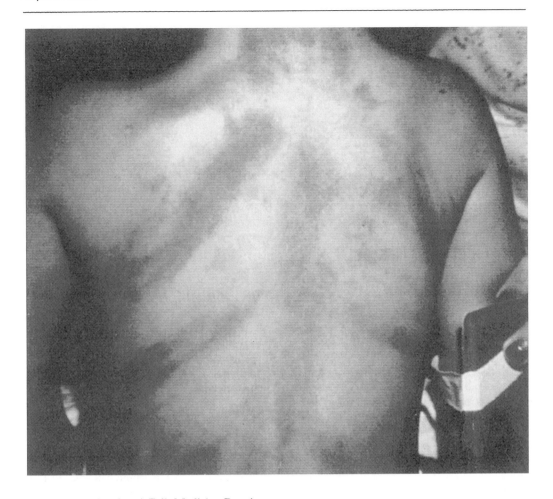

Photo 13.3. *Cao Gio*–A Folk Medicine Practice
SOURCE: Johnson (1990). Reprinted by permission of W. B. Saunders.

Feingold, 1976; Yeatman, 1976, 1980), a folk medicine practice among certain East Asians, the skin is rubbed with a spoon or coin that may be dipped in heated oil. The skin of the area is reddened in a linear pattern. On the chest, the marks follow the directions of the ribs (see Photo 13.3). In *Cao Gio,* the injury is intentional, and visible trauma results; however, the parents readily will describe what they have done. Their intent, although of no proven medical benefit, is not to vent anger or influence the child's behavior but to elicit a cure. Treatment should be guided toward minimizing tissue damage and ensuring that prescribed "Western medicine" is given to the child.

Physicians should familiarize themselves with the folk practices of immigrants to their communities. The practice of *Caida de Mollera* (fallen fontanelle) may be used by Hispanics. In an attempt to treat diarrhea and vomiting, in which the anterior fontanelle has sunken from dehydration, the child is held upside down. Retinal hemorrhages, which may result, mimic those re-sulting from shaken baby syndrome (Guarnaschelli, Lee, & Pitts, 1972). A lack of professional sensitivity to these issues may result in families avoiding the medical system. It may be as difficult to change these behaviors.

If a healing practice is performed by a recognized religious organization, the state laws defining child abuse and neglect may not allow an abuse report to be processed or acted on. Parents who repeatedly fail to follow medical advice that has been accompanied by adequate instruction and that endangers the child should be reported for medical neglect (Johnson & Coury, 1992; see Chapter 14, this volume).

Thermal Injuries in Child Abuse

Any instrument that is capable of containing or generating heat can be intention-

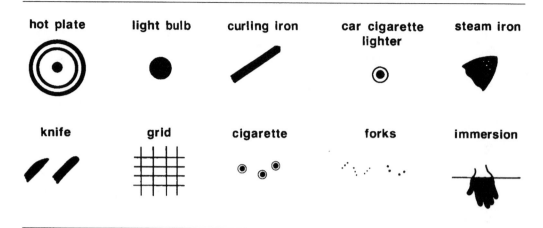

Figure 13.5. Marks From Burns
SOURCE: Johnson (1990). Reprinted by permission of W. B. Saunders.

ally applied to a child's skin. A hot object will imprint or brand the skin with its mark. Underlying structures, such as a bony prominence, can distort the shape of the mark (see Figure 13.5). Pressure from clothing, restraints, and restraining objects, such as furniture, can result in marks that suggest contact burns (Feldman, 1995).

If a child is immersed in hot water, all body surfaces in contact with the water will be burned except for areas that are protected by flexion. For example, when a child is placed in hot water feet first, legs may be flexed onto the abdomen, and the skin in the antecubital fossa, groin, and abdominal folds will be spared from heat injury. Because the palm and sole skin are thicker than other areas of skin, these surfaces may not be burned as severely, and the resulting burn pattern may suggest that hot water was poured on the top of the hand or foot. A stocking or glovelike pattern, without evidence of burns from splashing, should suggest an immersion burn. The degree of burn injury depends on the temperature of the object, the amount of time the object remains on the skin, and the peculiarities of children's skin on various parts of the body. Caretakers may not be aware of the short amount of time required to inflict a first- or second-degree burn on a child. Studies of adults have indicated that if water temperature is 64°C (147°F), a 1-second contact will result in a second- or third-degree burn (Moritz & Henriques, 1947) (see Table 13.4). Burns from hot grease can be more severe than burns from hot water. Water cannot be heated beyond 100°C (220°F).

Hot water heater thermostats may be set at dangerously high temperatures. Parents living in rental units may not be able to change the hot water heater thermostat. Intentional immersion burns usually occur during the toilet training ages of 6 to 24 months. Inexperienced parents may begin toilet training as early as 6 months (Johnson et al., 1982). Diaper changing, which takes place in the bathroom where hot water is accessible, may provide the opportunity to "teach the baby not to mess the diaper." Alternatively, hot water is run and the child is placed in the water to be cleansed, without the water temperature being tested. The caretaker may try to escape culpability for a nonintentional burn by blaming the child victim or a sibling. Caretakers also may create a history that is incompatible with the burn.

In determining the feasibility of the history of a burn, it is important to visit the accident site and measure water temperature,

TABLE 13.4   Time Required for Water to Cause First- or Second-Degree Burns on Human Skin

Water Temperature (°C/°F)	Time of Exposure (seconds)
52 (125.6)	70
54 (129.2)	30
56 (132.8)	14
58 (136.4)	6
60 (140.0)	3
62 (143.6)	1.6
64 (147.2)	1

SOURCE: Johnson (1990). Reprinted by permission of W. B. Saunders.

height and style of control knobs, tub depth, tub sill height, and location of spouts. These measurements can be compared to the child's height and reach measurements and motor capacity. Turning a round faucet is considered to be possible after 24 months of age. The height of the sill of the tub may preclude feet first entry into water. Small children entering a tub will generally slide in sideways or head first. In addition, one would expect a child who enters hot water, at any angle, to move and splash as they attempt to escape. When the cause of an immersion burn cannot be diagnosed as intentional, filing for safety neglect is necessary. A home safety inspection should be performed with education in accident prevention.

Determining the cause of burns from hot irons is especially perplexing. If the palm of the hand is involved, an exploratory or self-inflicted burn is probable. Burns to the dorsum of the hand or to multiple body surfaces decrease the likelihood of an accident. Iron burns may involve the curved edge of the iron or the flat surface. Steam holes may be seen in the burn pattern. Young infants may pull hot irons or hot liquids into strollers (Johnson et al., 1990).

Accidental splash burns from containers on tables or stoves are most severe on the upper body and under insulated clothing; the burn pattern "feathers" as the hot liquid runs down the body and cools. A plastic diaper may spare the diaper area in a splash burn or contain the hot water in a pour burn.

Cigarette burns can occur when the child explores the ignited end or runs into it. Burns that are complete circles, indicating prolonged contact, on the dorsum of the hand or on other protected surfaces suggest an intentional burn. Flame burns are likely to be more serious and accidental. Thumbs may be burned with cigarette lighters in response to thumb sucking, and children have been held over flames and pressed to hot grids. Two children who were placed in a microwave oven sustained third-degree burns. In one, the pattern involved the abdomen, thorax, and left thigh, with circumferential burns on the left hand and right foot. Another suffered second- and third-degree burns to the mid-back. The burn location was influenced by proximity to the microwave-emitting device (Alexander, Surrell, & Cohle, 1987). Cattle prods have been applied to the skin of children, which may cause symmetrical burns.

Children Who Die: Child Abuse or Accident?

Children who die in the hospital are most likely to have an autopsy to confirm the cause of death (see Chapter 15, this volume). Children who die from CM in the community may be signed out as sudden infant death syndrome or death due to accidental cause without an autopsy. Abuse or neglect may be the cause of 7% to 27% of deaths considered to be due to unintentional injury (McClain, Sachs, Froehlke, & Ewigman, 1993). When the cause of death is uncertain, the law requires that the coroner be notified, and it is imperative that an autopsy be performed. The examination of the child who has died from unknown causes should be as detailed and extensive as the child who has survived trauma and include external and internal examination, with radiological studies and toxicology screening by the coroner (Norman, Newman, Smialek, & Horembala, 1984). The police department routinely should investigate the death scene and interview the caretakers and witnesses. If CM is indicated, it is important that the welfare agency be notified immediately to obtain a court order to protect other children who may be at risk in the home. Active surveillance of infant deaths, with review of the child abuse registry, has been recommended as a way to monitor the success of efforts to prevent child abuse fatalities (Schloesser, Pierpont, & Poertner, 1992). Controversies continue to exist in the diagnosis and treatment of child physical abuse. Research will help to resolve these controversies (Block, 1999).

The training required in child abuse recognition and reporting should begin in undergraduate school and continue throughout the professional's career.

Summary

A high degree of skepticism about the possible causes of all injuries, as well as knowledge of the many ways CM can be manifested, is mandatory if children are to be protected from further abuse through reports to the law enforcement and social service systems. Reporting should be guided by an ethical and moral responsibility to serve children rather than personal bias, state mandates, lack of confidence in agencies (Marshall & Locke, 1997; Van Haeringen, 1998), or fear of court or legal actions. The training required in child abuse recognition and reporting (Dubowitz, 1988; Johnson, 1989) should begin in undergraduate school (Bar-on, 1998) and continue throughout the professional's career (Offer-Shechter, Tirosh, & Cohen, 2000; Warner-Rogers, 1996). Training must continue to emphasize documentation using standardized forms (Limbos & Berkowitz, 1998), audiovisual materials (Ricci & Finkle, 1997), professional stress reduction (John-son, 1999a, 1999b, 1999c), and preparation for court (Johnson, 1999a, 1999b, 1999c). Familiarity with the training and language of the various professionals involved in serving the needs of abused children and the sharing of detailed legible information about diagnosis, treatment, and outcome are necessary for continued improvement in the motivation of mandated reporters to report and appear in court to testify in cases of abuse. It is imperative that present and future parents, caretakers, and vulnerable infants and children be screened and flagged for abuse risk so that appropriate prevention services can be offered (Alvarez, Doris, & Larson, 1988; Caldwell, Bogat, & Davidson, 1988; Dubowitz, 1989; Fischler, 1985; Zuravin, 1989).

References

Aber, J. L., Bennett, N. G., Conley, D. C., & Li, J. (1997). The effects of poverty on child health and development. *Annual Review of Public Health, 18,* 463-483.

Adler, R., & Kane-Nussen, B. (1983). Erythema multiform: Confusion with child battering syndrome. *Pediatrics, 72,* 718-720.

Alexander, R., Altemeier, W. A., O'Connor, S., Crabbe, L., Sato, Y., Smith, W., & Bennett, T. (1990). Serial abuse in children who are shaken. *American Journal of Diseases of Children, 144,* 58-60.

Alexander, R., Kao, S. C. S., & Ellerbroek, C. J. (1989). Head injury in child abuse: Evaluation with MR imaging. *Radiology, 17*(3), 653-657.

Alexander, R., Surrell, J. A., & Cohle, S. D. (1987). Microwave oven burns to children: An unusual manifestation of child abuse. *Pediatrics, 79,* 255-260.

Alvarez, W. F., Doris J., & Larson, O. (1988). Children of migrant farm families are at high risk for maltreatment: New York State study. *American Journal of Public Health, 78*(8), 934-936.

American Academy of Pediatrics, Committee on Psychosocial Aspects of Child and Family Health. (1998). Guidance for effective discipline. *Pediatrics, 101*(4), 723-728.

Apollo, J. O. (1978). Bloody cerebrospinal fluid: Traumatic tap or child abuse? *Pediatric Emergency Care, 3,* 93-95.

Barlow, B., Niemirska, M., & Gandhi, R. P. (1983). Ten years of experience with falls from a height in children. *Journal of Pediatric Surgery, 18,* 509-511.

Bar-on, M. E. (1998). Teaching residents about child abuse and neglect. *Academic Medicine, 73,* 573-574.

Bhat, B. V., Kuman, A., & Oumachiqui, A. (1994). Bone injuries during delivery. *Indian Journal of Pediatrics, 61,* 401-405.

Block, R. W. (1999). Child abuse: Controversies and imposters. *Current Problems in Pediatrics, 29,* 251-276.

Bourguet, C. C., & McArtor, R. E. (1989). Unintentional injuries. *American Journal of Diseases of Children, 143,* 556-559.

Brown, J., & Melinkovich P. (1986). Shoenlein-Henoch purpura misdiagnosed as suspected child abuse: A case report and literature review. *Journal of the American Medical Association, 256,* 617-618.

Cadzow, S. P., Armstrong, K. L., & Fraser, J. A. (1999). Stressed parents with infants: Reassessing physical abuse risk factors. *Child Abuse & Neglect, 23,* 845-853.

Caffey, J. (1972). On the theory and practice of shaking infants. *American Journal of Diseases of Children, 124,* 161.

Caffey, J. (1974). The whiplash shaken infant syndrome: Manual shaking by the extremities with whiplash induced intracranial and intraocular bleedings, linked with residual permanent brain damage and mental retardation. *Pediatrics, 54,* 396.

Caldwell, R. A., Bogat, G. A., & Davidson, W. S. (1988). The assessment of child abuse potential and the prevention of child abuse and neglect. *American Journal of Community Psychology, 16,* 609-624.

Caniano, D. A., Beaver, B. L., & Boles, E. T. (1986). An update on surgical management in 256 cases. *Annals of Surgery, 203,* 219-224.

Carpenter, R. F. (1999). The prevalence and distribution of bruising in babies. *Archives of Disease in Childhood, 80,* 363-366.

Carty, H. M. (1993). Fractures caused by child abuse. *Journal of Bone and Joint Surgery, 75,* 849-857.

Chu, J. A., Frey, L. M., Ganzel, B. L., & Matthews, J. A. (1999). Memories of childhood abuse: Dissociation, amnesia, and corroboration. *American Journal of Psychiatry, 156,* 749-755.

Coant, P. N., Kornberg, A. E., Brody, A. S., & Edwards-Holmes, K. (1992). Markers for occult liver injury in cases of physical abuse in children. *Pediatrics, 89,* 274-278.

Cohen, H. A., Matalon, A., Mezger, A., Ben, A. D., & Barzilai, A. (1997). Striae in adolescents mistaken for physical abuse. *Journal of Family Practice, 45,* 84-85.

Coohey, C. (1997). Toward an integrated framework for understanding child physical abuse. *Child Abuse & Neglect, 21,* 1081-1094.

Drake, B., & Zuravin, S. (1998). Bias in child maltreatment reporting: Revisiting the myth of classlessness. *American Orthopsychiatric Association, 68,* 295-304.

Dubowitz, H. (1988). Child abuse programs and pediatric residency training. *Pediatrics, 82*(Suppl.), 477-480.

Dubowitz, H. (1989). Prevention of child maltreatment: What is known. *Pediatrics, 83,* 570-577.

Dubowitz, H., Hampton, R. L., Bithoney, W. G., & Newberger, E. H. (1987). Inflicted and non-inflicted injuries: Differences in child and familial characteristics. *American Journal of Orthopsychiatry, 57,* 525-535.

Feldman, K. W. (1995, February). Confusion of innocent pressure injuries with inflicted dry contact burns. *Clinical Pediatrics,* pp. 114-115.

Feldman, K. W., & Brewer, D. K. (1984). Child abuse, cardiopulmonary resuscitation, and rib fractures. *Pediatrics, 73,* 339-342.

Finkelhor, D., & Zellman, G. L. (1991). Flexible reporting options for skilled child abuse professionals. *Child Abuse & Neglect, 15,* 335-341.

Fischler, R. S. (1985). Child abuse and neglect in American Indian communities. *Child Abuse & Neglect, 9,* 99-106.

Gabos, P. G. (1998). Fracture-dislocation of the lumbar spine in an abused child. *Pediatrics, 102*(3), 473-476.

Gahagan, S., & Rimsza, M. E. (1991). Child abuse or osteogenesis imperfecta: How can we tell? *Pediatrics, 88,* 987-992.

Gellis, S., & Feingold, M. (1976). Cao Gio: Pseudobattering in Vietnamese children. *American Journal of Diseases of Children, 130,* 857-858.

Gillham, B., Tanner, G., & Cheyne, B. (1998). Unemployment rates, single parent density, and indices of child poverty: Their relationship to different categories of child abuse and neglect. *Child Abuse & Neglect, 22,* 79-90.

Grace, A., & Grace, S. (1987). Child abuse within the ear, nose & throat. *Journal of Otolaryngology, 16,* 111.

Gregg, G. S., & Elmer, E. (1969). Infant injuries: Accident or abuse? *Pediatrics, 44,* 434-439.

Grosfeld, J. L., & Ballantine, T. V. (1976). Surgical aspects of child abuse (Trauma-X). *Pediatrics, 5,* 106-120.

Guarnaschelli, J., Lee, J., & Pitts, F. W. (1972). Fallen fontanelle (Caida de Mollera): A variant of the battered child syndrome. *Journal of the American Medical Association, 222,* 1545.

Hanigan, W. C., Peterson, R. A., & Njus, G. (1987). Tin ear syndrome. *Pediatrics, 80,* 618-622.

Helfer, R. E., Slovis, T. L., & Black, M. (1977). Injuries resulting when small children fall out of bed. *Pediatrics, 60,* 533-535.

Heller, D. (1995). Lumbar physiological striae in adolescence suspected to be non-accidental injury. *British Medical Journal, 311,* 738.

Hobbs, C. J. (1984). Skull fracture and the diagnosis of abuse. *Archives of Disease in Childhood, 59,* 246-252.

Holter, J. C., & Friedman, S. B. (1968). Child abuse: Early case finding in the emergency department. *Pediatrics, 42,* 128-138.

Howard, J. L., Barron, B. J., & Smith, G. G. (1990). Bone scintigraphy in the evaluation of extraskeletal injuries from child abuse. *Radio Graphics, 10,* 67-81.

Hurwitz, A., & Castells, S. (1987). Misdiagnosed child abuse and metabolic disorders. *Pediatric Nursing, 13,* 33-36.

Izant, R. J., & Hubay, C. (1966). The annual injury of 15,000,000 children: A limited study of childhood accidental injury and death. *Journal of Trauma, 6,* 65-74.

Jenny, C., Hymel, K., Ritzen, A., Reinert, S. E., & Hay, T. C. (1999). Analysis of missed cases of abusive head trauma. *Journal of the American Medical Association, 281,* 621-626.

Joffe, M., & Ludwig, S. (1988). Stairway injuries in children. *Pediatrics, 82,* 457-461.

Johnson, C. F. (1983). Sudden infant death syndrome vs. child abuse: The teenage connection. *Journal of Pedodontics, 7,* 196-208.

Johnson, C. F. (1988). Constricting bands: Manifestations of possible child abuse. *Clinical Pediatrics, 27,* 439-444.

Johnson, C. F. (1989). Residency and child abuse [Letter to the editor]. *Pediatrics, 83,* 805-806.

Johnson, C. F. (1990). Inflicted injury versus accidental injury. *Pediatric Clinics of North America, 37,* 791-814.

Johnson, C. F. (1999a). Child abuse as a stressor of pediatricians. *Pediatric Emergency Care, 15,* 84-89.

Johnson, C. F. (1999b). Child abuse prevention: Actions that pediatricians can take to prevent child maltreatment. *Newsletter of the American Academy of Pediatrics Section on Child Abuse and Neglect, 11,* 1-2.

Johnson, C. F. (1999c). The use of charts and models to facilitate a physician's testimony in court. *Child Maltreatment, 4,* 228-241.

Johnson, C. F., Apollo J., Joseph, J. A., & Corbitt, T. (1986). Child abuse diagnosis and the emergency department chart. *Pediatric Emergency Care, 2,* 6-9.

Johnson, C. F., & Cohn, D. S. (1990). The stress of child abuse and other family violence. In L. E. Arnold (Ed.), *Childhood stress* (pp. 268-295). New York: John Wiley.

Johnson, C. F., & Coury, D. L. (1988). Bruising and hemophilia: Accident or child abuse? *Child Abuse & Neglect, 12,* 409-415.

Johnson, C. F., & Coury, D. L. (1992). Child neglect: General concepts and medical neglect in child abuse. In S. Ludwig & A. E. Kornberg (Eds.), *Child abuse: A medical reference* (2nd ed., pp. 321-331). New York: Churchill Livingstone.

Johnson, C. F., Erickson, K. A., & Caniano, D. (1990). Walker-related burns in infants and toddlers. *Pediatric Emergency Care, 6,* 58-61.

Johnson, C. F., Kaufman, K. L., & Callendar, C. (1990). The hand as a target organ in child abuse. *Clinical Pediatrics, 29,* 66-72.

Johnson, C. F., Loxterkamp, D., & Albanese, M. (1982, May). Effect of high school students' knowledge of child development and child health on approaches to child discipline. *Pediatrics, 69,* 559-563.

Johnson, C. F., & Showers, J. (1985). Injury variables in child abuse. *Child Abuse & Neglect, 9,* 207-215.

Kocher, M. S., & Kasser, J. R. (2000). Orthopaedic aspects of child abuse. *Journal of the American Academy of Orthopaedic Surgeons, 8,* 10-20.

Kravitz, H., Driessen, G., Gomberg, R., & Korach, A. (1969). Accidental falls from elevated surfaces in infants from birth to one year of age. *Pediatrics, 44,* 869-876.

Langeland, W., & Hartgers, C. (1998). Child sexual and physical abuse and alcoholism: A review. *Journal of Studies on Alcohol, 59,* 336-348.

Lasing, S. A., & Buchan, A. R. (1976). Bilateral injuries in childhood: An alerting sign? *British Medical Journal, 2,* 940-941.

Lehman, D., & Schonfeld, N. (1993). Falls from heights: A problem not just in the northeast. *Pediatrics, 92,* 121-124.

Leonidas, J. C. (1983). Skeletal trauma in the child abuse syndrome. *Pediatrics Annual, 12,* 875-881.

Levin, A. V. (1990). Ocular manifestations of child abuse. *Pediatric Ophthalmology, 3,* 249-264.

Limbos, M. A., & Berkowitz, C. D. (1998). Documentation of child physical abuse: How far have we come? *Pediatrics, 102,* 53-58.

Lyons, T., & Oates, R. K. (1993, July). Falling out of bed: A relatively benign occurrence. *Pediatrics, 92,* 125-127.

Manning, S. C., Casselbrant, M., & Lammers, D. (1990). Otolaryngologic manifestations of child abuse. *International Journal of Pediatric Otorhinolaryngology, 20,* 7-16.

Marshall, W. N., & Locke, C. (1997). Statewide survey of physician attitudes to controversies about child abuse. *Child Abuse & Neglect, 21,* 171-179.

McClain, P. W., Sachs, J. J., Froehlke, B. G., & Ewigman, B. G. (1993). Estimates of fatal child abuse and neglect, United States, 1979 through 1998. *Pediatrics, 91,* 338-343.

McCort, J., & Vaudagna, J. (1964). Visceral injuries in battered children. *Radiology, 88,* 424-428.

McRae, K. N., Ferguson, C. A., & Lederman, R. S. (1973). The battered child syndrome. *Canadian Medical Association Journal, 108,* 859-860.

Mellick, L. B., & Reesor, K. (1990, May). Spiral tibial fractures of children: A commonly accidental spiral long bone fracture. *American Journal of Emergency Medicine, 8,* 234-237.

Merten, D. F., Osborne, D. R. S., Radkowski, M. A., & Leonidas, J. L. (1984). Craniocerebral trauma in the child abuse syndrome: Radiological observations. *Pediatric Radiology, 14,* 272-277.

Merten, D. F., Radkowski, M. A., & Leonidas, J. C. (1983). The abused child: A radiological reappraisal. *Radiology, 146,* 377-381.

Meservy, C. J., Towbin, R., McLaurin, R. L., Myers, P. A., & Ball, W. (1987). Radiographic characteristics of skull fractures resulting from child abuse. *American Journal of Neuroradiology, 8,* 455-457.

Moritz, A. R., & Henriques, F. C. (1947). Studies of thermal injury: Pathology and pathogenesis of cutaneous burns experimental study. *American Journal of Pathology, 23,* 915-941.

Morris, J. L., Johnson, C. F., & Clasen, M. (1985). To report or not to report: Physicians' attitudes toward discipline and child abuse. *American Journal of Diseases of Children, 139,* 194-197.

Norman, M. G., Newman, D. E., Smialek, J. E., & Horembala, E. J. (1984, Winter). The postmortem examination on the abused child. *Perspectives in Pediatric Pathology, 8,* 313-342.

Obiako, M. N. (1987). Eardrum perforation as evidence of child abuse. *Child Abuse & Neglect, 11,* 149-151.

O'Connor, J. F., & Cohen, J. (1987). Dating fractures. In P. K. Kleinman (Ed.), *Diagnostic imaging of child abuse* (pp. 103-113). Baltimore: Williams & Wilkins.

Offer-Shechter, S., Tirosh, E., & Cohen, A. (2000). Physical abuse: Physicians' knowledge and reporting attitude in Israel. *European Journal of Epidemiology, 16,* 53-58.

O'Hare, A. E., & Eden, B. (1984). Bleeding disorders and non-accidental injury. *Archives of Diseases of Childhood, 50,* 860-864.

Olney, D. B. (1988). Patterns of presentation of abused children to the accident and emergency department. *Archives of Emergency Medicine, 5,* 228-232.

Philipart, A. I. (1977). Blunt abdominal trauma in childhood. *Surgical Clinics of North America, 57,* 151-163.

Press, S., Grant, P., Thompson, V. T., & Milles, K. L. (1991). Small bowel evisceration. *Pediatrics, 88,* 807-809.

Putnam, N., & Stein, M. (1985). Self-inflicted injuries in childhood: A review and diagnostic approach. *Clinical Pediatrics, 24,* 514-518.

Raimer, B. G., Raimer, S. S., & Hebeler, J. R. (1981). Cutaneous signs of child abuse. *Journal of the American Academy of Dermatology, 5,* 203-214.

Ricci, L. R., & Finkle, M. A. (1997). Documentation of preservation of visual evidence in child abuse. *Child Maltreatment, 2,* 322-330.

Rizzolo, P. J. (1989). Neonatal rib fracture: Birth trauma or child abuse? *Journal of Family Practice, 29,* 561-563.

Schloesser, P., Pierpont, J., & Poertner, J. (1992). Active surveillance of child abuse fatalities. *Child Abuse & Neglect, 16,* 3-10.

Schwartz, A. J., & Ricci, L. R. (1996). How accurately can bruises be aged in abused children? *Pediatrics, 97,* 254-257.

Showers, J., & Johnson, C. F. (1985). Students' knowledge of child health and development: Effects on approaches to discipline. *Journal of School Health, 54,* 122-125.

Sieben, R. L., Leavitt, J. D., & French, J. H. (1971). Falls as childhood accidents: An increasing urban risk. *Pediatrics, 47,* 886-892.

Sinal, S. H., & Stewart, C. D. (1998). Physical abuse of children: A review for orthopedic surgeons. *Journal of the Southern Orthopaedic Association, 7,* 264-276.

Sivit, C. J., Taylor, G. A., & Eichelberger, M. R. (1989). Visceral injury in battered children: A changing perspective. *Radiology, 173,* 659-661.

Smith, M. D., Burrington, J. D., & Woolf, A. D. (1975). Injuries in children sustained in free falls: An analysis of 66 cases. *Journal of Trauma, 15,* 987-991.

Smith, W. L., Alexander, R. C., Jurisch, F. G., Sato, Y., & Kao, S. C. S. (1992). Magnetic resonance imaging evaluation of neonates with retinal hemorrhage. *Pediatrics, 89,* 332-333.

Spaide, R. F., Swengel, R. M., Scharre, D. W., & Mein, C. E. (1990, April). Shaken baby syndrome. *American Family Physician, 41,* 1145-1152.

Spivak, B. S. (1992). Biomechanics of non-accidental trauma in child abuse. In S. Ludwig & A. E. Kornberg (Eds.), *Child abuse: A medical reference* (2nd ed., pp. 61-78). New York: Churchill Livingstone.

Sugar, N. F., Taylor, J. A., & Feldman, K. W. (1999). Bruises in infants and toddlers: Those who don't cruise rarely bruise. *Archives of Pediatrics and Adolescent Medicine, 153,* 399-403.

Swischuk, L. E. (1981). Radiology of the skeletal system in child abuse and neglect. In N. S. Ellerstein (Ed.), *Child abuse and neglect: A medical reference* (pp. 253-273). New York: John Wiley.

Swischuk, L. E. (1992). Radiologic signs of skeletal trauma. In S. Ludwig & A. E. Kornberg (Eds.), *Child abuse and neglect: A medical reference* (2nd ed., pp. 151-174). New York: Churchill Livingstone.

Tate, R. J. (1971). Facial injuries associated with the battered child syndrome. *British Journal of Oral Surgery, 9,* 41-45.

Taylor, C. G., Norman, D. K., Murphy, M. J., Jellinek, M., Quinn, D., Poitrast, F. G., & Goshko, M. (1991). Diagnosed intellectual and emotional impairment among parents who seriously mistreat their children. *Child Abuse & Neglect, 15,* 389-401.

Van Haeringen, A. R. (1998). The child abuse lottery: Will the doctor suspect and report? Physician attitudes towards and reporting of suspected child abuse and neglect. *Child Abuse & Neglect, 22,* 159-169.

Vasundhara, T. (1990). Pancreatic fracture secondary to child abuse: The role of computed tomography in its diagnosis. *Clinical Pediatrics, 29,* 667-668.

Wagner, G. (1986). Bitemark identification in child abuse cases. *Pediatric Dentistry, 8,* 96-100.

Warner-Rogers, J. E. (1996). The influence of case and professional variables on identification and reporting of physical abuse: A study with medical students. *Child Abuse & Neglect, 20,* 851-866.

Wheeler, D. S., & Shope, T. R. (1997). Depressed skull fracture in a 7-month-old who fell from bed. *Pediatrics, 100,* 1033-1034.

Wilson, E. F. (1977). Estimation of the age of cutaneous contusions in child abuse. *Pediatrics, 60,* 750-752.

Yeatman, G. W. (1976). Pseudobattering in Vietnamese children. *Pediatrics, 58,* 617-618.

Yeatman, G. W. (1980). Cao Gio (coin rubbing): Vietnamese attitudes toward health care. *Journal of the American Medical Association, 244,* 2748-2749.

Zellman, G. L. (1992). The impact of case characteristics on child abuse reporting decisions. *Child Abuse & Neglect, 16,* 57-74.

Zuravin, A. J. (1989). The ecology of child abuse and neglect: Review of the literature and presentation of data. *Violence Victims, 4,* 101-120.

14

Neglect of
Children's Health

HOWARD DUBOWITZ

MAUREEN BLACK

Health care providers and others have focused on child physical and sexual abuse, paying less attention to child neglect (Wolock & Horowitz, 1984). There are several reasons why neglect has not received the attention it deserves (Dubowitz, 1994). First, the typically vague definitions of neglect have made it an amorphous phenomenon; many are understandably unclear about what constitutes neglect, how to identify neglect, or what course of action is appropriate and effective. Second, health care providers are under demands to screen for multiple conditions and also to be aware of cost containment, thus limiting the time they spend with individual families to detect problems such as neglect. Third, the strong association between child neglect and poverty (Giovannoni & Becerra, 1979) often evokes a sense of hopelessness and helplessness among professionals, deterring them from becoming involved in the complex issues common among very low-income families. Finally, ne-

AUTHORS' NOTE: This work was partially supported by a grant (90CA1401/01) from the National Center on Child Abuse and Neglect to study child neglect.

glect does not evoke the horror and outrage that abuse does. However, more than half the reports for child maltreatment made in the United States each year are for neglect (U.S. Department of Health and Human Services [DHHS], 1999), and the morbidity and mortality associated with child neglect are substantial, as severe as those associated with abuse (Bonner, Crow, & Logue, 1999; Gaudin, 1999).

This chapter focuses on one major form of child neglect: neglect of children's health. In the following sections, we discuss (a) definitional issues concerning neglected health, (b) incidence, (c) etiology, (d) major manifestations, (e) general principles for evaluation, and (f) intervention.

Defining Neglected Health

Our interest in defining neglect is to adequately protect children and to help ensure their health, safety, and well-being. Neglected health care can thus be conceptualized as occurring when children's basic health care needs are not met. This relatively broad definition is based on basic needs of children that are not met, rather than on parental omissions in care (Dubowitz, Black, Starr, & Zuravin, 1993). A basic health care need is one in which there is adequate evidence that health is harmed or jeopardized by the specific need not being addressed (e.g., death of a child with diabetes due to lack of attention to recommendations) (Geffken, Johnson, Silverstein, & Rosenbloom, 1992). Many situations may not rise to this standard of actual or potential harm (e.g., a missed follow-up appointment for an ear infection in a healthy child). Implicit in this definition is the likelihood that the care or treatment will significantly benefit the child. If the benefit is equivocal (e.g., an experimental treatment for cancer), not receiving the treatment should not be construed as neglect. This definition of neglect is based on a child's unmet needs and does not include the issues of cause(s) or contributory factor(s). From the child's perspective, not receiving necessary care is neglect, regardless of the reasons why such care is not provided. The causes, however, are important when considering how best to intervene.

This broad definition of neglect of children's health differs from the narrow framework embodied in federal and state laws that limit neglect to omissions in care by a parent or primary caregiver (U.S. Congress, 1996). Child protective services (CPS) accordingly confines its involvement to a narrow view. A broad, child-focused definition has many advantages over a narrow one. By examining the role of all the contributory factors, the broad definition should lead to more varied and appropriate interventions. Potentially, this broad approach should be more effective in preventing or ameliorating neglectful situations. The broad definition more accurately reflects the array of possible causes, not just parental behavior. However, clarification of the parental role remains important; parents are primarily responsible for their children's care. But professionals, community agencies, and social policies also influence the health of children and therefore share responsibility.

There are several other important issues in conceptualizing neglect: actual versus potential harm, short- versus long-term harm, concern with physical and psychological outcomes, and a continuum of care. The following case helps illustrate many of the issues pertaining to neglect.

Case example. Amy is a 6-year-old girl with severe asthma. She has been hospitalized four times in the past 2 years, twice in the intensive care unit. She was discharged from the hospital a week ago and given prescriptions for two medications. She comes to the office for follow-up and appears to be doing well. However, the prescription was not filled, and Amy has not received the recommended medications. Amy's mother explains that she was waiting to get her paycheck to fill the prescription. Amy is an only child who lives with her mother. After school, Amy's grandmother cares for her until her mother returns from work. There has been no contact with her father in the past 3 years, and he makes no financial contributions to Amy or to her mother.

Actual versus potential harm. Does there need to be actual harm in defining neglect, or is the risk of harm sufficient? Most states' laws include potential harm in their definitions of child abuse and neglect. Most CPS agencies, however, often overwhelmed by the number of reports, prioritize the more serious cases, and actual harm is usually viewed as more serious than potential harm. Consequently, reports involving only mild or moderate potential harm often are screened out or not substantiated. Excluding cases of potential harm is especially problematic because the sequelae of neglect are often not immediate. In the above case, even though Amy appears to be healthy, her history of recent hospitalizations indicates her vulnerability. Without the prescribed medications, her risk for recurrent asthmatic attacks is substantial. Amy is a child with severe asthma, a condition that may be lethal, and nonadherence to the recommended medications constitutes neglect. If the purpose of defining neglect is to ensure children's health, and if we are interested in preventing neglect, a limited focus on actual harm is too narrow, too late. The inclusion of potential harm in defining neglect facilitates prevention.

Short- versus long-term harm. As indicated in the above paragraph, in many cases, the impact of neglect is not immediately apparent but manifests in the long term. Amy may do well this week, but persistent failures in following recommendations to prevent asthma attacks can contribute to significant morbidity with repeated hospitalizations. Tied to a goal of prevention, long-term outcomes need to be considered in assessing whether a child has experienced neglect.

Physical and psychological outcomes. Our concern with children's health and well-being is a broad one. Accordingly, medical, dental, and mental health are all important aspects of health. For instance, Amy would also be experiencing neglect if she had a history of hospitalizations associated with severe dental or psychiatric problems, rather than asthma, and was not receiving prescribed medication that had been effective in the past.

A continuum of care. We artificially categorize cases as "neglect" or "not neglect" when the adequacy of basic needs being met clearly falls on a continuum from optimal to grossly inadequate. The child welfare system is involved when we encounter situations that cross a threshold into "grossly inadequate." For example, few pediatricians would report Amy to CPS for neglect if the

lapse in treatment occurred once or twice. More typically, neglect is construed when there is a pattern of repeated episodes that persist despite efforts to help and where harm clearly results.

Operationalizing the Definition of Neglect of Children's Health

There are challenges in implementing the above conceptual definition of neglect. How do we determine that a child's health is being neglected? Determining the adequacy of basic needs being met is at the core of assessing whether neglect exists. Epidemiological data guide us in some instances. For example, the risks associated with not using a car seat or seat belt have been determined (Stewart, 1993), justifying a safety standard that children should wear seat belts in cars. Not doing so can be construed as a form of neglect (in the United States). In other instances, the child's history is informative, such as Amy's repeated hospitalizations for severe asthma, partly due to her not receiving prescribed medications. Also, in some areas, common sense indicates that children's needs are being neglected (e.g., homelessness, hunger, lack of health insurance, and young children left alone). There remain instances when it is difficult to determine whether care is adequate to meet basic needs (e.g., emotional support, parental monitoring, care provided by a health professional, quality of education at school). The quality of care can be judged, but it is difficult to specify the threshold of adequacy. In general, neglect is construed only when there are gross inadequacies in these areas. Although intermediate inadequacies may not meet a "neglect threshold," they may nevertheless invite some intervention. For example, the family of a child who has repeated hospitalizations for asthma may benefit from specific recommendations regarding strategies to maintain a smoke-free environment, avoid other environmental risks, and identify early warning signs of asthma attacks.

Neglect should be considered when a child's condition could reasonably be attributed to a basic need not being met. For example, a child may have problems with diabetes control despite careful adherence to treatment. The specific condition may be inherently difficult to manage. Another issue concerns our knowledge (or lack thereof) as to what constitutes adequate care. For example, missing some doses of a course of antibiotics may still be adequate; 80% adherence to treatment for a streptococcal sore throat appears to be adequate (Olson, Zimmerman, & Reyes de la Rocha, 1985). Assessing neglect becomes still more complex when we recognize the variability among children and their needs. For example, one 10-year-old may be mature enough to be left alone briefly, but another may not. Similarly, one 10-year-old may be left alone with a neighbor nearby, but another may not. The determination of neglect involves an understanding of the context in which the event or condition occurred. Thus, evaluations of possible neglect should include consideration of family and contextual issues.

How do we determine that a child's health is being neglected? Determining the adequacy of basic needs being met is at the core of assessing whether neglect exists.

Severity. Severity is generally rated in terms of the actual or estimated potential harm as well as the degree of harm involved. For example, Amy's untreated asthma that results in an admission to the intensive care unit would be rated as most severe, a regular hospital admission less so, a visit to the emergency department still less so, followed by mild symptoms not requiring professional attention, and, finally, no symptoms. Regarding potential harm, some risks entail only minor consequences, but others might be life threatening. The likelihood of the harm occurring is also important to consider. Missing a follow-up appointment for a child with eczema is very different from not seeking care for an infant who has had frequent vomiting and diarrhea for several days. Both the potential medical and psychological ramifications should be considered. Although longitudinal research may help estimate the likelihood and nature of long-term outcomes associated with specific lapses in care (e.g., prenatal drug exposure), many situations are complicated by ongoing environmental challenges, such as poverty (Lester, LaGasse, & Brunner, 1997). Consideration of severity includes assessing the

number of times the condition has occurred or its duration.

Frequency/chronicity. Neglect is usually inferred when the condition is chronic or there is a pattern of unmet needs. A dilemma arises regarding single or rare incidents that may constitute neglect. In some instances, omissions in care are unlikely to be harmful unless they are recurrent. For example, there may be serious risks for a child with a seizure disorder who repeatedly does not get anticonvulsant medication, but not if there is an occasional lapse in medication adherence. However, an infant left unattended in a bath once, for a few minutes, could drown. Thus, this single lapse could be a significant instance of neglect. In Amy's case, it is important to clarify the frequency of her not receiving medications. The intervention is likely to be different if there is a persistent pattern of neglect.

Measuring the frequency or chronicity of a problem is difficult. In some instances, medical or pharmacy records can help in showing appointments not kept or the filling of prescriptions. At times, parents or children may disclose for how long they have had food shortages or problems accessing health care. Careful monitoring allows providers to establish the chronicity of problems prospectively.

In summary, we propose a definition of neglected health care, focusing on basic needs of children that are not met. Actual and potential harm are both of concern, although neglect is more likely to be inferred when there is actual harm. Actual or potential harm that is severe should be considered more seriously. Although chronic or recurrent neglectful situations are especially worrisome, a single exposure to harmful conditions may constitute neglect, particularly if severe harm is involved.

Incidence/Prevalence Data

It is difficult to estimate the extent of neglected health care. Health care providers do not identify many cases of neglect, and they may not report identified cases to CPS. The most recent report from the National Child Abuse and Neglect Data System (NCANDS) on the Detailed Case Data Component indicated that 2% of all maltreatment reports were for medical neglect (U.S. DHHS, 1999). Fifty-two percent of

TABLE 14.1 Incidence of Child Abuse and Neglect in the United States in 1993

Category	Number of Children	Rate Per 1,000 Children
Physical abuse	614,100	9.1
Sexual abuse	300,200	4.5
Emotional abuse	532,200	7.9
Total abuse	1,221,800	18.2
Physical neglect	1,335,100	19.9
Emotional neglect	584,100	8.7
Educational neglect	397,300	5.9
Total neglect	1,961,300	29.2

SOURCE: Third National Incidence Study of Child Abuse and Neglect.

the 5,984 children identified were younger than 4 years of age; 14% were teenagers.

The best, most recent effort to circumvent the limitations of relying on reported cases was the Third National Incidence Study in 1993 (NIS-III) (U.S. DHHS, 1996). In addition to reports made to CPS, professionals in the community (e.g., physicians, workers in child care centers, teachers) served as sentinels to identify cases that met the study definitions. Neglected health care was defined by two categories. *Delay in health care* is the failure to seek timely and appropriate medical care for a serious health problem that any reasonable layperson would have recognized as needing professional medical attention. *Refusal of health care* is the failure to provide or allow needed care in accordance with recommendations of a competent health care professional for a physical injury, illness, medical condition, or impairment (U.S. DHHS, 1996). These definitions applied to both medical and mental health care. Professionals in selected health care facilities were recruited into the study and asked to record each case of suspected child abuse or neglect that they encountered over a 3-month period. The distribution of different types of maltreatment is presented in Table 14.1. Children were classified in each category that applied, so the rows are not additive. Physical neglect was by far the most common type, including abandonment, inadequate nutrition, clothing or hygiene, and leaving a young child unattended in a motor vehicle, as well as medical neglect. The incidence rate of 19.9 per 1,000 children in the general population per year was double that estimated in 1986. Approximately 25% of the children identi-

fied with physical neglect had evidence of harm; the remainder were considered "endangered." These findings are probably gross underestimates because neglected health care is often difficult to determine, and it is likely that many situations do not come to the attention of health care professionals.

The data on child fatalities due to abuse or neglect reveal that approximately half of the estimated 2,000 deaths each year result from neglect, mostly unsupervised children dying in fires or drowning (U.S. Advisory Board on Child Abuse and Neglect, 1995). Few deaths appear to be due to neglected health care, although sympathy for a grieving family makes it difficult to assess how health care may have prevented a death (e.g., a teen suicide). Since 1975, there have also been 172 known deaths of children in the United States in which medical care was withheld on religious grounds (Asser & Swan, 1998).

Many American children lack access to mental health services. For example, one major study of youth ages 9 to 17 years found that only 38% to 44% of those meeting stringent criteria for a psychiatric disorder received some mental health-related contact in the year prior to the interview (Leaf et al., 1996). Most of those contacts occurred in schools, and the qualifications of the providers were not reported.

Dental care is also not accessible to many American children, particularly those from low-income families. Eighty-five percent of U.S. schoolchildren have obvious caries or fillings affecting, on average, more than eight surfaces of their permanent teeth (Edelstein & Douglass, 1995). A study of preschoolers found that 49% of 4-year-olds had caries, and fewer than 10% were fully treated (Tang et al., 1997).

Other forms of neglected health care extend beyond the family's domain. If access to health care and health insurance are basic needs in the United States, then 15.5% or 9 million children have their health care neglected by our society (U.S. DHHS, 2000). In addition, there are the problems of underinsurance and limited access to health care if health professionals do not accept medical assistance. Children younger than age 5 reported to be in poor health and living above the poverty level are two and a half times more likely to have seen a physician, compared with those living below poverty levels (U.S. DHHS, 1989). Less access to health care is associated with less use of health care, and, frequently, poor children in poor health are most affected. A study of asthmatic children found that being insured was associated with increased use of primary care and parental perceptions of diminished asthma severity (Szilagyi et al., 2000). Malnutrition, lead poisoning, increased injuries, and other health problems that often are associated with poverty are symptoms of neglected health care.

Etiology

There is no single cause of child neglect. Belsky (1980) has proposed an ecological theory of multiple and interacting factors at the individual (parent and child), familial, community, and societal levels. A toddler with a chronic, toxic blood lead level illustrates this theory. This child's health is being neglected by a lack of protection from lead and a lack of satisfactory treatment. Contributory factors may include the parents' unwillingness to allow treatment, the parents' inability to move to a lead-free home, a landlord's refusal to have the home de-leaded, a city's inability to ensure an adequate lead abatement program, and society's limited investment in low-income housing. An understanding of a neglectful situation demands an appreciation of the contributory factors to plan the optimal interventions. Regardless of which contributory factors are responsible, a child with a high lead level experiences neglect. Different neglectful situations may involve different contributory factors. Although few studies of the etiology of neglected health care

are available, many of the risk factors for neglect in general may also apply to medical neglect. There have been few prospective studies of neglect; most of the research has been conducted on families already identified through CPS records as neglectful. Therefore, much of the following section may represent characteristics and manifestations of neglect as well as contributory factors. We will focus on issues especially germane to neglected health care.

Context (Society and Community)

Context refers to the environment or society, including poverty, culture, and religion, as well as aspects of the community. The context shapes the attitude, knowledge, and behavior of parents and the quality of health care children receive. Poverty has been strongly associated with neglect (Sedlak & Broadhurst, 1996). For example, in the NIS-III, neglect was identified 44 times more often in families with annual incomes under $15,000 compared with those earning above $30,000. These families are the poorest of the poor, concluded one study of families of neglected children (Giovannoni & Billingsley, 1970). It should be noted, however, that most children raised in poor families do not experience child neglect. They do, however, experience the adverse effects of poverty (Black & Krishnakumar, 1999). The effects of poverty may result from stress, compromising the functioning of families and parents. Poverty may also directly harm children via increased exposure to environmental hazards (e.g., lead, violence) and the risk of hunger and malnutrition (Cutts, Pheley, & Geppert, 1998; Klerman, 1991; Parker, Greer, & Zuckerman, 1988; Wise & Meyers, 1988). Poverty is also associated with diminished access to health care, particularly for the "near poor" who do not qualify for Medical Assistance and who lack health insurance.

Another aspect of the context concerns culture and religion. Different cultures may differ in their beliefs regarding health care. For example, children from Southeast Asia may receive the folkloric remedy of *Cao Gio* for a fever (Yeatman & Dang, 1980). A hard object is vigorously rubbed over the chest and may cause bruising. It is unclear whether this practice results in any benefit or significant harm, but there is the risk of not receiving appropriate care for a serious illness (e.g., meningitis). Cultural differences may be less dramatic, such as segments of the population that have little interest in psychotherapy. These variations in beliefs pose sensitive dilemmas as health care providers strive to avoid an ethnocentric approach ("My way is right") and cultural relativism (cultures differ and all should be accepted) (Korbin & Spilsbury, 1999). When a practice clearly harms children and when good alternatives exist, intervention should ensure that children's needs for health care are adequately met. Similarly, parents may hold religious views that are antithetical to Western medicine, believing in alternative approaches to health and healing. Accordingly, sick children may receive, for example, prayer from a Christian Scientist faith healer. Many illnesses (e.g., colds) are self-limiting, and satisfactory outcomes result regardless of treatment; others can lead to serious harm without effective health care.

The community and neighborhood and their resources influence parent-child relationships and are strongly associated with child maltreatment (Garbarino & Crouter, 1978). A community with a rich array of services, such as parenting groups, child care, and good public transportation, enhances the ability of families to nurture and protect children. Informal support networks, safety, and recreational facilities are important in supporting healthy family functioning. Families in a high-risk environment are less able to give and share and might be mistrustful of neighborly exchanges. In this way, a family's problems may be aggravated rather than helped when surrounded by other needy families (Garbarino & Sherman, 1980). Neglect has been strongly associated with social isolation (Polansky, Ammons, & Gaudin, 1985). In one large controlled study, mothers of neglected children perceived themselves as isolated and as living in unfriendly neighborhoods (Polansky, Gaudin, Ammons, & Davis, 1985). Indeed, their neighbors saw these mothers as deviant and avoided social contact with them. In summary, communities can offer valuable support to families, or they may add to the stresses that families experience.

Family

Poor organization of the home has characterized families of neglected children

(Gaudin & Dubowitz, 1997). Kadushin (1988) described chaotic families of neglected children with impulsive mothers who repeatedly showed poor planning. Deficient problem-solving skills, poor parenting skills, and inadequate knowledge of children's needs have been associated with neglect (Azar, Robinson, Hekemian, & Twentyman, 1984; Herrenkohl, Herrenkohl, & Egolf, 1983; Jones & McNeely, 1980). The absence of fathers or their limited involvement in their children's lives may be factors in neglect. Several studies have found more negative interactions between mothers and their young children in families of neglected children (e.g., Crittenden, 1988). Some cases of failure to thrive might be rooted in "a poor fit" between mother and child (Black, Feigelman, & Cureton, 1999). A child's passive or lively temperament may displease a parent. In addition, family problems, such as spousal violence or a lack of social support, may contribute to a difficult parent-child relationship and failure to thrive (Giovannoni & Billingsley, 1970; Polansky, Ammons, & Gaudin, 1985; Wolock & Horowitz, 1979). In contrast, a supportive family can buffer the stresses that impair parenting, illustrating the importance of considering both risk and protective factors in assessing families and possible neglect.

Stress also has been associated with child maltreatment. One study found the highest level of stress—concerning unemployment, illness, eviction, and arrest—among families of neglected children, compared with abusive and control families (Gaines, Sangrund, Green, & Power, 1978). Lapp (1983) found stress to be frequent among parents reported to CPS for neglect, particularly regarding family relationships and financial and health problems.

Parents

Many of the characteristics of mothers of neglected children may also contribute to children's health care needs not being met. Maternal problems concerning emotional health, intellectual abilities, and substance abuse have been associated with neglect. Emotional disturbances, especially depression, have frequently been found among mothers of neglected children (e.g., Polansky, Chalmers, Williams, & Buttenwieser, 1981; Zuravin, 1988). Intellectual impairment, including severe mental retardation and a lack of education, has also been associated with neglect (Kadushin, 1988; Martin & Walters, 1982; Wolock & Horowitz, 1979). High rates of alcoholism and drug addiction have been found among families of neglected children; Jones (1987) reported rates of 28% and 25%, respectively. Maternal drug use during pregnancy has become a pervasive problem (Gomby & Shiono, 1991; Lester et al., 1997; Singer, 1999). Most illicit drugs pose definite risks to the fetus and child, and the compromised caregiving abilities of drug-abusing parents are a major concern.

Most decisions regarding children's health are made by parents, including when to seek professional care. Crittenden's (1993) model helps refine our understanding of parental difficulties by considering four steps: (a) perception of the child's problem, (b) interpretation of the problem, (c) response, and (d) implementation. Difficulties with any of these steps may lead to health needs not being met. The parent first needs to perceive the problem. Subtle signs such as decreased urination or gradually falling grades may go undetected. Inadequate knowledge about children and health and inappropriate expectations contribute to neglect. For example, parents may not know that a baby with diarrhea risks becoming dehydrated. Parents may not appreciate such needs, particularly if they are cognitively limited (Kadushin, 1988). At times, parents may be in denial, an unconscious defense mechanism, about a child's condition. Parents of neglected children are less knowledgeable about developmental milestones (Twentyman & Plotkin, 1982) and have limited knowledge about parenting, poor skills, and low motivation to be a good parent (Herrenkohl et al., 1983).

Parents may perceive the problem but interpret it incorrectly. For example, based on the parent's prior experience, a child's poor growth may be seen as normal. Lack of knowledge is again an obstacle. A parent may feel moodiness is common in children, unaware that children can be depressed. For these conditions, parents may be unaware treatment exists. Popular or folk interpretations of a symptom, such as an infant crying frequently because "he's spoiled," may lead to a problem being missed. Again, parents with limited cognitive abilities or emotional problems may have difficulty interpreting their child's cues, determining the care needed, and understanding and implementing the treatment plan. In addition, parents

may not appreciate the seriousness of the problem or the importance of the treatment, perhaps due to inadequate communication with health care providers.

Parents with limited cognitive abilities or emotional problems of their own may have difficulty interpreting their child's cues, determining the care needed, and understanding and implementing the treatment plan.

After recognizing and interpreting the problem, parents choose their response. Initially, they may hope the problem will resolve spontaneously or with a home remedy. For example, parents may hope a small burn will heal without professional care—a reasonable response. If the condition deteriorates, only then may it be clear that medical care is needed. Such delays have been viewed suspiciously, but it is important that reasonable delays be seen as such. Sometimes a delay in seeking care can have dire consequences. In considering neglect, the context should be considered. If care was obtained at a point when a reasonable layperson could be expected to have recognized the need for professional help, then it is not a neglectful situation. On the other hand, if the child did not receive care when a "reasonable" person would seek care, then it is a neglectful situation. An inappropriate response may also result from inadequate knowledge, parental distress, and cultural or religious beliefs. For example, a depressed youngster may not receive psychotherapy if the parents hold such treatment in disdain.

Finally, the problem may be with implementing recommendations the family has received from health care providers. A parent's inaction may be due to being distracted by other priorities (e.g., an eviction notice, obtaining drugs), depression, or difficulty accessing health care.

Other influences on parents' behavior may be useful for health care providers to consider. Confidence in the remedy or in one's ability to implement the treatment is important (Liptak, 1996). For example, a parent's belief that a medicine works will enhance compliance. Motivation to address a health problem is important and may be influenced by the chronicity of the problem (there may be complacency with longstanding problems) and competing demands. For all parents and families, there is a need to balance many needs and to prioritize. For example, paying an electricity bill before filling a prescription may be appropriate in some circumstances. However, in other circumstances, such as Amy's asthma prescription not being filled, the decision to delay in implementing recommendations may place the child at risk, thereby constituting neglect.

Child

Children may contribute to their health being neglected, directly and indirectly. A direct example is an adolescent's denial of diabetes, refusing to adhere to the treatment plan, despite excellent efforts by caring parents. Some children give no or few cues that they need help, not revealing the problem. Children's age may influence perceptions of their vulnerability and neglect, with more concern directed to younger children; almost two thirds of neglect reports are made on children younger than age 8 (U.S. DHSS, 1996). The unmet needs of adolescents may not evoke the same concern.

Belsky and Vondra (1989) described how children's health status could affect their parents' ability to provide care. For example, premature infants may require extended care in neonatal intensive care units, which may impair bonding and the attachment with their parents. Caring for a child born with low birth weight can be challenging; at least two studies have found low birth weight to be a risk factor for neglect (Brayden, Altemeier, Tucker, Dietrich, & Vietze, 1992; Kotch et al., 1989).

Children with chronic health problems or disabilities have special needs that put them at added risk for those needs not being met (Klerman, 1985). Many parents of such children are dedicated caregivers; others may be so stressed that they are unable to provide adequate care. Diamond and Jaudes (1983) found cerebral palsy to be a risk factor for neglect, but another study found no increase in maltreatment among 500 moderately to profoundly retarded children (Benedict, White, Wulff, & Hall, 1990). Sullivan and Knutson (2000) found in a population-based study that disabled children were 3.4 times more likely to be identified as maltreated than were nondisabled peers (9% vs.

31%). Families of children with special health care needs are often involved with multiple professionals, and increased surveillance may bias reports for neglect. Overall, it appears that the special health care needs of children with disabilities may overwhelm some caring and competent parents, thus contributing to neglect (Klerman, 1985; Sullivan & Knutson, 2000).

The Disorder and the Treatment

The nature of the disorder may influence children's and parents' responses to recommendations or treatment (e.g., Liptak, 1996). For example, a disorder that is highly visible (e.g., an ugly rash) often evokes more of a response than a disorder that is invisible (e.g., lead poisoning). Children and parents who do not perceive that the disorder is serious or do not have confidence in the effectiveness of the treatment are at risk because they are less likely to adhere to recommendations. In contrast, children and parents who are concerned about the disorder and have confidence in the recommended treatment are likely to follow through. Thus, health care providers can prevent neglect by ensuring that children and families are well informed about the nature of the disorder and the effectiveness of treatment.

The severity of symptoms makes an understandable difference. Chronic health problems may be accepted without much alarm. For example, Amy's mother may believe that her daughter is a severe asthmatic who will periodically need to be hospitalized. This may be a valuable coping strategy, but undue complacency may result. Alternatively, a chronic and severe disease may evoke great distress, contributing to denial, such as is sometimes seen in adolescent diabetics.

Neglect is also more likely to occur if the goals of treatment are not consistent with the goals of the child or family. For example, improving pulmonary function tests (a health care provider goal) may mean little to Amy, compared with being able to play sports (a family goal). Thus, communication about the goals of the child and family and the impact of the disorder and treatment on those goals should help health care providers reframe the reason for the treatment recommendations to be consistent with the goals of the child and family.

Concerns about side effects of treatment or doubts of its effectiveness may dissuade a parent from seeking care. Obesity is an example in which a parent may recognize the problem but be reluctant to engage in treatment that is seen as burdensome.

In addition to questions about the efficacy of the treatment, families may doubt their ability to implement recommended treatments. For example, the likelihood of neglect may be increased if a parent is reluctant to give injections to a child with insulin-dependent diabetes. Health care providers should evaluate parents' ability to implement the treatment, and, when they detect a hesitation or lack of confidence, they should institute additional steps to ensure that parents have both the competence and confidence to follow through with the treatment.

The cost of treatment is another consideration that may contribute to the likelihood of neglect. For example, Amy's mother had not filled the prescription because she was waiting to receive her weekly paycheck. Sensitive questioning is necessary to determine if families have the financial resources to purchase recommended medications or to implement recommendations. When financial resources are a problem, health care providers may consider less expensive options or look for strategies to offset costs associated with treatment.

Poor communication may be a problem, with the treatment not being clearly conveyed or understood. Finally, simply remembering to take a medication several times in a busy day may be an obstacle and may contribute to neglect. Working with families to help them incorporate recommended treatment into their daily routine is one way to help families adhere to recommendations and avoid child neglect.

The Nature of Health Care

The nature of health care includes the relationship between a health professional and family (Gorski, 2000). Ideally, there is a relationship of mutual trust and respect. Families are more likely to follow recommendations if they have confidence that the recommendations are sound, will be beneficial, and are possible to implement. Without a trusting relationship, families may be discouraged from seeking help or from following recommendations. Managed care requires that a primary care provider coordinate most aspects of health care. One of the benefits of a primary care system is to

strengthen the relationship between families and health professionals, thereby promoting continuity of care. In an ideal system, primary care providers focus on prevention to avoid serious health problems (including neglect). However, low reimbursement rates and pressures to conserve costs may lead providers to spend less time on prevention and psychosocial issues. In addition, changing participation of providers and families in managed care plans may be an obstacle to developing the rapport needed for prevention and optimal health care. If the clinic or office is not perceived as friendly and supportive, families may feel discouraged from seeking care. Families may be more compliant and experience less medical neglect when they have positive relationships with their primary care providers.

Manifestations of Neglected Health

This section will address the more common forms of neglected health.

Noncompliance With Health Care Recommendations

The most common form of neglected health care involves a lack of adherence with health care appointments or recommendations, resulting in actual or potential harm (e.g., Amy, a severe asthmatic, not getting or taking prescribed treatment). Adherence with medical recommendations is a relatively common concern. For example, one study found that approximately half of adolescents have been estimated to be nonadherent with medical regimens (Litt & Cuskey, 1980). Another study found only 25% of parents of children with attention deficit disorder adhered to the treatment plan, and fewer than 10% consulted the physician before stopping medication (Firestone & Witt, 1982). The pervasiveness of noncompliance does not minimize its importance. Noncompliance is not restricted to patients. Studies of physicians' management of clinical problems with clear professional guidelines as to appropriate treatment have found rates between 48% and 72% of failure to adhere to those guidelines (i.e., physician noncompliance) (Meichenbaum, 1989).

Failure or Delay in Seeking Health Care

Consider the following case:

Case example. Joe is a 10-month-old infant brought to the emergency department following 4 days of vomiting, diarrhea, decreased appetite, lethargy, and fever. On the second day, his father spoke with their pediatrician, who recommended an electrolyte solution, fever management, and follow-up if Joe's condition should worsen. The pediatrician mentioned that he would be leaving town for the holiday weekend, but a partner would be on call. Joe had had this problem once before, and it resolved after a few days. The emergency department staff found Joe to be at least 10% dehydrated and in need of admission to the intensive care unit. The staff were concerned that medical care had not been obtained earlier, raising a question of neglect.

Another form of neglect is a delay in seeking health care. Parents or primary caregivers generally decide on the appropriate care for minor problems (e.g., a scrape, cold, sadness at the death of a pet). As conditions become more serious, the need for professional care increases, and parents are responsible for seeking such care. Neglect occurs when necessary health care is not obtained or when the delay is so significant that a child's health is harmed or jeopardized (e.g., a child with serious mental health problems not receiving help, or the above case of Joe). Again, the challenge is to understand what may be contributing to health care not being sought.

Joe's case highlights the importance of clear communication between providers and caregivers. Although Joe's father contacted the pediatrician on the second day of his symptoms, Joe's prior recovery from similar symptoms, together with the holiday weekend, may have led to the decision to recommend home management without the need for an office visit. Although there is no assurance that an office visit could have prevented the worsening of Joe's symptoms, vomiting and diarrhea in a 10-month-old can progress rapidly to dehydration, and daily phone contact may have alerted the pediatrician to Joe's worsening condition prior to his need for hospitalization. Thus, although Joe's symptoms worsened and his health was in jeopardy, he did not experience neglect because his parents and pediatrician made reasonable efforts to ensure his care.

Religiously Motivated Medical Neglect

Medical neglect might occur when parents actively refuse medical treatment. In some cases, parents believe that an alternative treatment is preferable, perhaps because the prescribed approach is prohibited by their religion. For example, Jehovah's Witnesses, with their prohibition of blood transfusions, routinely refuse surgery when the need for transfusions is anticipated. Other religions, such as Christian Scientists, rely on their own faith healers and reject Western medicine.

Situations involving religious beliefs and children's health care needs can be difficult because they can constitute neglect. How do we balance a concern with civil liberties and respect for varying beliefs in a pluralistic society with an interest in protecting children? The principle of *parens patriae* establishes the state's right and duty to protect the rights of its younger citizens; if a child's parents cannot or will not provide adequate care, for any reason, then society and the state must do so. However, 44 states have religious exemptions from their child abuse statutes, stating, for example, "that a child is not to be deemed abused or neglected merely because he or she is receiving treatment by spiritual means, through prayer according to the tenets of a recognized religion" (American Academy of Pediatrics, 1988, p. 169). These exemptions have been based on the arguments of religious groups that the U.S. Constitution guarantees the protection of religious practice. This interpretation of the Constitution is challenged by court rulings prohibiting parents from martyring their children based on parental beliefs (*Prince v. Massachusetts,* 1944) and from denying them essential medical care (*Jehovah's Witnesses of Washington v. King County Hospital,* 1968). The separation of church and state in the First Amendment does not sanction harming individuals in the practice of religion. The American Academy of Pediatrics has strongly opposed these religious exemptions, arguing that the

opportunity to grow and develop safe from physical harm with the protection of our society is a fundamental right of every child. . . .

The basic moral principles of justice and of protection of children as vulnerable citizens require that all parents and caretakers must be treated equally by the laws and regulations that have been enacted by State and Federal governments to protect children. (American Academy of Pediatrics, 1988, pp. 169-171)

Inadequate Food

Inadequate food may manifest as repeated hunger and may place a child at risk for impaired growth, including failure to thrive. Data from the National Health and Nutrition Examination Survey (NHANES III) conducted from 1988 through 1994 indicate that the national prevalence of food insufficiency is approximately 4.1% (Alaimo, Briefel, Frongillo, & Olson, 1998). Although food insufficiency is related to poverty, more than half of food-insufficient individuals live in employed families. Hunger remains remarkably prevalent in the United States and may adversely affect children's growth and their ability to participate in school. Inadequate access to food constitutes a serious form of neglect, and health care providers should screen for food insufficiency by asking families if they have adequate food for themselves and their children.

Hunger remains remarkably prevalent in the United States and may adversely affect children's growth and their ability to participate in school.

The etiology of failure to thrive (FTT) is multifactorial. The traditional classification of "organic" (i.e., medical) and "nonorganic" (i.e., psychosocial) has limited usefulness; more often, there is a mixed etiology. Children who have medical explanations for their poor growth (e.g., gastrointestinal problems such as gastroesophageal reflux or celiac disease) often experience discomfort while eating and develop feeding problems along with their growth deficiency. Health care providers who limit their attention to the medical explanations often miss the feeding problems and psychosocial disorders that have developed along with poor growth. The diagnosis of a psycho-

social contribution should be considered regardless of the presence of a medical condition. In addition, psychosocial conditions should be diagnosed with reasonable justification, not simply by excluding medical causes (Black, Feigelman, & Cureton, 1999).

Serious, long-term consequences can occur when growth deficiency occurs together with neglect. Young children with both FTT and neglect have lower scores on standardized measures of cognitive development than children with neither condition or only one of the conditions (Mackner, Starr, & Black, 1997). The problems persist even when children recover from FTT. By age 6, children with a history of FTT and neglect are more likely to have behavior problems at home and school and to have lower scores on standardized assessments of cognitive performance than children with neither condition or only one of the conditions (Kerr, Black, & Krishnakumar, 2000). These findings illustrate the long-lasting negative consequences when neglect co-occurs with other problems, such as FTT.

Obesity

Pediatric obesity (body mass index > 95th percentile) is a serious public health problem that is increasing in prevalence and has been associated with adult obesity and multiple health problems (Troiano & Flegal, 1998; Whitaker, Wright, Pepe, Seidel, & Dietz, 1997), particularly among children from low-income families. Although obesity is a chronic disease that is influenced by genetic, metabolic, and physiologic factors, family dietary and activity practices (food selection, food quantity, and frequency of eating) have long been associated with obesity (Lau, Quadrell, & Hartman, 1990). At least two family dietary patterns are associated with pediatric obesity. The first pattern includes parents who provide irregular diets of high-fat foods with little or no nutritional value. Without healthy role models, many children live on snack foods that contribute to obesity and do not provide needed vitamins and minerals (Picciano et al., 2000). The second pattern includes parents who attempt to control their children's feeding behavior through dietary restraint (Birch & Fisher, 2000). When parents are very controlling and limit their children's access to specific foods, there may be a rebound effect whereby children crave those foods and overeat. Because there are environmental and family contributions to obesity, some cases of morbid obesity may be a form of neglect in that the child's need for healthy food and physical activity is not being met. In addition, obesity without attempts to address the problem is neglectful.

Exposure to Environmental Hazards

The health risks associated with several environmental hazards have been firmly established. Hence, exposure to these hazards, in or outside the home, is a form of neglect. Examples in the home include poisonous substances and dangerous objects within easy reach of young children, smoking around children with pulmonary conditions (Gergen, Fowler, & Maurer, 1998), exposure to domestic violence (Sternberg, 1998; see Chapter 6, this volume), and access to a loaded gun. Hazards outside the home include riding a bike without a helmet (Wesson, Spence, Hu, & Parkin, 2000), failure to use a car seat or seat belt (Stewart, 1993), and neighborhood violence (Osofsky, 1999). Exposure to lead may be a problem both in and out the home (Tong, von Schirnding, & Prapamontol, 2000).

Drug-Exposed Newborns and Older Children

More than a million infants are born each year following prenatal exposure to alcohol or illicit drugs (Chasnoff & Lowder, 1999), and the association between prenatal drug exposure and children's health and development has attracted much attention. Several illicit drugs, such as cocaine and heroin, cross the placental barrier and influence the developing fetus, jeopardizing growth, health, and behavior (e.g., Eyler, Behnke, Conlon, Woods, & Wobie, 1998; Frank et al., 1990). The impact of illicit drugs on long-term development is controversial, primarily because it is difficult to disentangle prenatal drug exposure from the negative environment that often accompanies drug use (Chasnoff, 1997; Lester & Tronick, 1994; Shriver & Piersel, 1994; Singer, 1999). In contrast, in utero exposure to alcohol has been found to impair long-term growth and development (Streissguth, Sampson, & Barr, 1989).

Parental drug use increases the risk for abuse and neglect. Approximately 20% of children exposed to drugs prenatally are subsequently reported for abuse or neglect (Illinois Department of Children and Family Services, 1997; Kelly, 1992). Chaffin, Kelleher, and Hollenberg (1996) found that approximately half of maltreating parents had had a substance abuse disorder. Postnatal substance abuse can place children at risk by exposing them to the violence that often accompanies such activity, providing a negative example of illegal activity, and denying them access to necessary services and stimulation. Cigarettes can expose children to secondary smoke and can be particularly damaging to children with respiratory problems, such as asthma (Gergen et al., 1998).

Core Principles of Evaluation

Do the circumstances indicate that the child's health care needs are not being adequately met, resulting in actual or potential harm? This is the first question to answer. For example, Amy's not receiving her asthma medications places her at risk for another episode of her disease.

Interview the child, if possible. Children are a valuable source of information, and their perceptions are important for guiding the evaluation and subsequent intervention.

Is there a pattern of neglect? For how long has there been a problem? Are there other forms of neglect? There is greater concern if the lapse in health care represents a chronic pattern, rather than a single incident. By reviewing the child's medical record and talking with other health care providers, it is often possible to identify whether there is a pattern of neglect. It is also important to know whether problems with health care are an exception or are associated with other basic needs not being met (i.e., other types of neglect). Health professionals can assess whether a child is receiving adequate medical, mental, and dental health care. The professional can evaluate nutrition and appropriate growth. The child's clothing and hygiene can be assessed, and primary care providers should have a sense of whether a child's educational needs are being met. Once the emergency department workers spoke with Joe's pediatrician, they were assured that his parents had provided adequate care and that Joe's symptoms had accelerated faster than anticipated. Thus, there was not a pattern of neglect.

What is the overall seriousness of the situation? Is immediate intervention needed? Practitioners should evaluate the severity of the situation and the immediacy of harm or endangerment because the health and safety of the child are paramount. Immediacy hinges on the specific circumstances requiring emergency treatment or intervention. A dehydrated infant faces immediate harm, whereas an inadequate diet in an older child entails longer-term risks. At times, regular medical care is delayed due to religious beliefs, and care is sought at a very late stage when a child might be terminally ill. At that point, physicians should make every effort to provide necessary treatment, including court authorization for treatment if parents refuse permission. Beyond attending to the child's immediate needs, there is concern with the risk of continued or recurrent neglect and possible long-term ramifications. The assessment of severity is based on the frequency and nature of prior and current circumstances and their effect on the child, results of past interventions, and the family's recognition of the problem and ability to address it.

What is contributing to the neglect? Consider each of the categories discussed under etiology. A comprehensive understanding is essential to help tailor the intervention to the specific needs of the individual child and family.

What strengths or resources are available to the family? What goals do the child and family express? Consider the following:

Child—for example, child wants to play sports, requiring better health; child would like to stop wetting his or her bed

Parent—for example, parent interested to know more about child's condition, parent would like to stop having to wash sheets from child wetting the bed

Family—for example, other family members willing to help

Community—for example, programs for parents, families; religious affiliation

What interventions have been tried, and with what results? Knowing the details of the interventions can be useful, including agency name, nature of the intervention, frequency of contacts, duration, and satisfaction with the service. What interventions have health professionals and others tried?

Were efforts made to modify the approach when one strategy did not work?

An interdisciplinary approach is optimal (e.g., Berkowitz, 1984). It is often difficult for one professional to evaluate possible neglected health care. A social work assessment addresses problems and resources within the family and the community. For hospitalized children, a primary nurse may have helpful observations of the child and family. A mental health evaluation can assess a child's developmental and emotional status and parents' abilities to nurture and protect children. Teachers can report on school behavior and performance. Health professionals can review the medical record for prior conditions and observations as well as compliance with appointments and recommendations. Specific problems, such as failure to thrive, may call for nutritional or other consultation. Interdisciplinary teams, including medical, nursing, social work, and psychology or psychiatry, enable optimal assessment of these often-complex situations.

Does the parental or professional behavior meet reasonable expectations? Efforts to identify neglect should be driven by an interest in ensuring children's adequate care, rather than assigning blame. In our current child welfare system, however, the question is whether a parental omission in care was unreasonable. A "reasonableness test" is whether the desired behavior (e.g., taking a child to a dentist) can reasonably be expected of an average layperson. A child with a very high blood lead level may appear healthy, for example, and one would not expect a parent to recognize the problem unless there were changes in the child's behavior.

Core Principles for the Management of Neglected Health Care

Professionals need to convey concerns to family in a respectful but forthright manner. It is important to focus on the child's needs and to ensure that the child's health care needs are adequately met before moving to the discussion of why the problem is occurring. Families are more likely to be cooperative when the professional adopts a supportive and constructive stance rather than a blaming stance.

State clearly your interest in helping. Such statements develop the rapport and trust on which successful interventions depend. Professionals often find it frustrating to work with families where neglect is a problem because change can be hard to achieve. In fact, some health care providers harbor negative feelings about such families. Consultation between the family and a social worker or mental health colleague may be valuable. For example, Amy's mother confided to the clinic social worker that she had been feeling "really down." She agreed to a mental health referral, and since being treated for depression, she has developed several strategies for securing Amy's medication (saving money in a medical fund, reviewing the benefits package where she works).

Address contributory factors, prioritizing those most important and amenable to being remedied (e.g., recommending treatment for Amy's mother's depression, rather than focusing on neighborhood violence). There are issues that health care providers may feel competent to manage or prefer to refer elsewhere. It is important to consider the need for help from other community resources (e.g., Women, Infants, and Children [WIC] program, mental health clinics).

Begin with the least intrusive approach. The approach needs to fit the underlying problems and risks, but, in general, it is advisable to respect the importance of a family's privacy and to start with the least intrusive intervention. For example, when faced with a child failing to thrive, an initial strategy might be to provide guidance on feeding and a suitable diet while closely monitoring the child's growth. If the child's growth does not improve, referral to an interdisciplinary program is recommended (Bithoney & Newberger, 1987; Black, Cureton, & Berenson Howard, 1999). Health professionals need to be cognizant of their state laws regarding the reporting of child neglect (see Chapter 22, this volume). Clearly, many situations of neglect, even when recognized as such, are not reported to CPS (U.S. DHHS, 1996). In low-risk situations, it may be appropriate to begin with less intrusive approaches and to advance to more intrusive approaches only if less intrusive ones are not successful. CPS may have resources such as parent aides that would not otherwise be available. Thus, options need to be carefully weighed in deciding the optimal approach. One option is to report suspected neglect to CPS and, recognizing the limitations of any one agency, facilitate necessary referrals.

Recognize that neglect often requires long-term intervention, support, and follow-up. Clinicians may wish to see improvement quickly, so it is frustrating when problems are recalcitrant. Many neglectful families need long-term, ongoing support, akin to those with a chronic medical condition.

Try to ensure continuity of care as a primary health care provider. For all children, but especially when neglect is a concern, continuity of health care with a single clinic or primary care provider is important. Continuity of care fosters a relationship that may be instrumental in preventing neglect and in facilitating the coordination of health care. Primary care providers have an important liaison role between the family and others involved in their care; managed care usually requires a primary care provider relationship.

Help the family identify specific objectives that they can implement (e.g., family will always use a car seat), with measurable proximal, intermediate, and distal outcomes (e.g., family reports routine use of car seat at next visit). The objectives should be relevant to the family, reasonable (attainable), and clearly identified, preferably in writing.

Engage the family in developing the plan and solicit their input and agreement. Successful intervention requires working in collaboration with families. Positive rapport and mutual respect between professionals and families are critical components of effective interventions. Helping parents resolve a problem they identify as important to them can help establish rapport and trust.

The needs of parents, children, and families should be considered. Effective programs focus on basic problem-solving skills and concrete family needs (Daro, 1988; Sudia, 1981), provide behavior management strategies, and address environmental factors (Gambrill, 1983). Parents may benefit from a therapeutic relationship that includes nurturance, support, empathy, encouragement to express feelings, and motivation to change behavior. Parents of children who have been neglected often require attention to their own emotional needs to adequately nurture their children. However, insight-oriented therapy that is abstract, verbal, time-consuming, and expensive may be inappropriate for many parents of neglected children (Howing, Wodarski, Gaudin, & Kurtz, 1989).

Although a family-level approach generally is needed, neglected children may require individual attention. The focus of CPS has been mostly on parents, and few maltreated children have received direct services (Daro, 1988). Treatment of neglected children may reduce the psychological harm and possibly the intergenerational transmission of neglect. There are few treatment programs specifically for neglected or maltreated children. Nevertheless, a number of interventions appear useful, including therapeutic day care for younger children and group therapy for older children and adolescents (Howing et al., 1989). It is important that parents be included in their children's treatment and that therapeutic strategies also be implemented at home.

Build on family strengths. Too often, health care providers focus on problems and ignore strengths. This deficit approach impedes more constructive approaches to working with families. For example, parents' concern for their children's well-being can be used to encourage them to comply with treatment recommendations. Other strengths may include coping abilities, intelligence, determination, and religious faith.

Encourage the use of informal supports (i.e., family, friends). Professionals often think of professionals to provide services, overlooking informal help from family and friends. Families who are resistant to interventions from a public agency or a mental health professional may accept support from someone they trust and with whom they have a relationship. Health professionals can, for example, encourage a father's involvement in child rearing by inviting him to office visits. Similarly, other kin or supports may be included as we make pediatric care more family focused.

Families who are resistant to interventions from a public agency or a mental health professional may accept support from someone they trust and with whom they have a relationship.

Consider support through a family's religious affiliation. Professionals too often overlook this important source of support and guidance to many families.

Consider need for concrete services (e.g., medical assistance, Temporary Assistance to Needy Families [TANF], food stamps, and WIC).

Be knowledgeable about community resources, and facilitate referrals. Primary care providers serve as an important conduit to other services in the community, particularly when families may benefit from specialized services. Thus, it is important to know the resources in the community. Primary care providers are in a good position to encourage reluctant or ambivalent families to accept or try other services.

Consider the need to involve CPS, particularly when there is serious harm or risk or when less intrusive interventions have failed. Even when a CPS report is substantiated, most children remain in the care of their parents and are not placed in foster care. Constructive efforts to work with families are thus needed. Clinicians often face the dilemma of whether to report a family to CPS. State laws typically mandate that suspected neglect (and abuse) be reported, but there are varying levels of suspicion. Health professionals may feel discouraged if CPS does not respond, but many CPS agencies are overwhelmed and are forced to focus on the most serious cases. However, CPS often has valuable resources, including the ability to assess the home situation.

Provide support, follow-up, review of progress, and adjustment of the plan if needed. Recent changes in the reimbursement for health care make it increasingly difficult to provide the more frequent or longer appointments that neglect often requires. Thus, there is an increasing need for collaboration with other professionals and community agencies.

Interventions should be based on existing knowledge and theory (DePanfilis, 1999). Interventions known to be effective should be favored whenever possible. For example, because neglectful families often lack basic parenting skills, a behavioral approach may be preferable to insight-oriented psychotherapy. Similarly, if poverty is a major factor, the treatment plan should try to address this problem (e.g., helping a family secure benefits they are eligible to receive).

To provide a child adequate health care and prevent neglect, health care providers need to be familiar with the family structure, beliefs regarding health care, the stresses and strengths, barriers to care, and community resources. This understanding requires time and is also an ongoing process; circumstances change. In addition to the child's needs, it is necessary to consider those of the parents and family. It is especially important to identify the family strengths and resources on which to build.

Risk factors for neglect need to be addressed. The section on etiology included risk factors associated with neglect, including maternal depression, cognitive limitations, and substance abuse; families who are stressed and with few supports; and children with chronic disabilities. Families at risk for neglect often require social and mental health services, and health care providers should facilitate referrals. For example, help may be offered in securing health insurance, or a depressed mother may be encouraged to seek treatment. Health care providers can also help by scheduling more frequent visits to provide counseling, support, and monitoring and to anticipate and address barriers to care. Table 14.2 offers some suggested areas for routine screening, either by observation or direct questioning.

Some risk factors are unlikely to be detected unless specific screening efforts are made. For example, depression, although highly prevalent, is often not obvious and is frequently not recognized by pediatricians (Zuckerman & Beardslee, 1987). Domestic violence is often a well-kept family secret. Food shortages and hunger are seldom part of health professionals' screening during pediatric health maintenance visits. Even parents' ability to obtain a medication may not be clarified. An approach to address these possible problems is to universally screen all families at selected pediatric visits (e.g., initially and then once a year) with a brief questionnaire, which can be completed while waiting or be incorporated into the visit interview. An additional option is to inquire about potential barriers to recommendations (e.g., "This is an expensive medication. Are you going to be able to fill the prescription today?"). Couching questions regarding adherence and environmental conditions in the context of environmental problems being widespread and pediatric concern for children's environment and safety helps introduce sensitive questions. Health professionals need to be able to assess identified problems briefly, provide initial management, and facilitate appropriate referrals. Pediatricians also need to recognize what is known about the prevalence of these conditions (e.g., substance abuse) and of the risk for children.

TABLE 14.2 A Neglect Checklist for Health Professionals

Are the child's clothing and hygiene adequate?

Are the child's affect and interaction relationship with parent appropriate for the situation? For example, a child may be apprehensive of a health care visit, particularly if the child is in discomfort. Is the relationship between the child and parent nurturing and supportive?

Is there a problem having enough food available?

Is the child's growth satisfactory?

Are health problems (physical, mental, and dental) adequately identified, evaluated, and treated?

Are there problems accessing health care and filling prescriptions?

Are the child's educational needs being adequately met?

Is the child being exposed to hazards in the home (e.g., gun, cigarette smoke, domestic violence) or outside (e.g., no bike helmet, not wearing car seat belt)?

Is there a pattern of multiple injuries/ingestions suggesting the need for closer supervision?

Are major risk factors jeopardizing the child's basic needs being met (e.g., maternal depression, substance abuse, domestic violence, father absence)?

Anticipatory guidance is offered in routine pediatric care when advice is offered on potential problems. For example, when physicians explain the natural curiosity of toddlers and recommend safety precautions, they help prevent injuries from inadequate supervision. For children with identified health problems (e.g., allergies), families should be educated about the condition, what to expect, when to seek help, and what they can do at home. It is then necessary to monitor the child's course, assess the success of the recommended approach, and make modifications when necessary.

Advocacy Is Much Needed

Returning to the context in which neglect occurs, advocacy is needed at different levels: the individual child, parent, family, community, and society. Helping parents improve their children's treatment is advocacy on behalf of the children who are unable to express or meet their own needs. Acknowledging the stress a parent feels and facilitating help are also advocacy. Health care providers are often in the position to recognize service gaps in the community. By partnering with advocacy groups, they can work to secure additional resources for families to reduce the likelihood of neglect or to provide services for children who have experienced neglect. Efforts to strengthen families and support the development of community resources are also forms of advocacy. Enhancing access to health care illustrates advocacy at the broadest level. Each of these levels of advocacy is valuable in addressing the problems underpinning the neglect of children's health care. In summary, health care providers can play a pivotal role in ensuring that children receive adequate health care and that they do not experience neglect.

Special Considerations in the Assessment and Management of Specific Types of Neglected Health Care

Nonadherence to Health Care Recommendations

Assessment

Screening questions: "With the increasing costs of medical care and medicines, many parents have difficulty getting care and medicine for their children. Is this an issue for you? Will you be able to fill Amy's prescription?"

Is the child's condition clearly attributable to the lack of care? Alternatively, the condition may be inherently severe (e.g., brittle diabetes) or the treatment inadequate.

What are the possible barriers to care? Lack of health insurance, inability to afford medication, transportation, ignorance, parental health beliefs, child's feelings or attitude (e.g., denial of a chronic disease), poor skills to implement treatment (e.g., use inhaler), and difficult treatment regimen are some examples.

Has the doctor-family communication been clear? Were the recommendations in writing? Was the plan agreed on? Were concerns addressed? Is there continuity and trust in the doctor-family relationship? Is there a backup plan for emergencies or when the physician is unavailable?

Management

Make treatment practical, set priorities, simplify the regimen, and provide cues (e.g., take one tablet with breakfast and one at bedtime).

Involve the family from the beginning. Consider developmental, family, and individual differences in choosing recommendations and in discussing them with the family. Reassure the family that the treatment should work, review the medication schedule, check for concerns, anticipate problems (e.g., not being able to afford the medicine), stress the importance of completing the treatment course, repeat critical points, and check parents' comprehension. Providing recommendations in writing and to more than one family member should increase the likelihood of adherence. Communicate clearly, avoid jargon, give oral and written instructions, and emphasize the importance of the treatment. For chronic illnesses (e.g., diabetes), help children learn self-management skills.

Follow-Up

Facilitate phone, office, or in the home follow-up (e.g., visiting nurse) to help ensure treatment is implemented. Consider the timing of follow-up; the longer the period, the lower the likelihood of follow-up occurring. If the treatment plan is not being followed, assess why and consider alternative strategies.

Delay or Failure in Getting Health Care

Assessment

Screening questions: "When did you suspect your child had a problem? What did you do? Were there reasons that you did not bring your child to the emergency room sooner?"

Is the treatment deemed necessary and likely to have a significant benefit compared with the alternative being used or no treatment? (If not, neglect is not a serious concern.)

Does the family hold religious or cultural views that led to the child not receiving medical care? What exactly are these views and practices? Do they conform to their group as suggested? What efforts have been made in the past to convey concerns and negotiate an acceptable compromise regarding health care? Would a reasonable layperson have recognized the need for treatment by a parent (i.e., the health care parents usually provide) or by a professional? (The "reasonableness" standard is particularly important to CPS and the judicial system.)

Management

Health education of families and children will help them recognize the conditions that require health intervention. Children and families can benefit from education related to both acute and chronic conditions (e.g., acute gastroenteritis and potential dehydration). Sensitivity, respect, and humility are important in addressing religious or cultural differences. Some knowledge of the religion and culture is needed. There should be clear harm or risk of harm and a significantly preferable alternative to the parents' course of action to justify intervening.

Avoid two approaches: ethnocentrism (the belief that one's own culture is best) and cultural relativism (the view that all cultural practices should be accepted, precluding any judgment of another's approach). Sometimes, a practice that is accepted in some cultures may be clearly damaging (e.g., female genital mutilation).

Seek compromise, where appropriate (e.g., arrangements with Jehovah's Witnesses to have bloodless surgery). If the risks are serious and an acceptable compromise cannot be reached, public agencies should be immediately involved, and custody may need to be transferred to the state (i.e., CPS) for treatment to occur.

Rather than limiting intervention to an individual case, it often helps to approach community leaders. This broader approach diminishes the risk of being ostracized if the family deviates from cultural practices and may help avoid further instances of neglect.

With regard to neglect based on religious beliefs, Fost (1988) has noted that "standard medical practice isn't always effective, and some conditions are helped by nontraditional approaches, but this should not be confused with life-threatening illnesses for which there is effective, established medical treatment" (p. 99). The refusal of medical treatment must be evaluated in light of potential benefits and potential harm. Bross

(1982) has presented criteria for legal involvement in this form of medical neglect:

1. The treatment refused by the parents should have definite and substantial benefits over the alternative. Therefore, if the treatment has only a modest chance of success or if there is a risk of major complications, neglect may not be an issue, and legal intervention is not recommended.
2. Not receiving the recommended treatment could result in serious harm. Most cases that have been decided in court have involved the risk of death or severe impairment, although a number of court decisions have mandated treatment for less serious conditions.
3. The child is likely to enjoy a "high-quality" or "normal" life. This reflects the court's reluctance to mandate treatment for severely handicapped and terminally ill children. Indeed, the Baby Doe law concerning treatment of severely impaired newborns has had little impact on the management of these cases.
4. In the case of teenagers, the youth consents to treatment. This criterion reflects the increasingly recognized right of youth to participate in decisions regarding their health.

The legal route should be the last resort if serious neglect exists and attempts to provide adequate treatment have not succeeded.

Obesity

Assessment

Plot the child's weight for age, height for age, and weight for height (or body mass index [BMI]). Growth charts have been updated recently and include standards for BMI (www.cdc.gov). If the child's BMI is increasing (crosses two major percentiles) or is above the 85th percentile, the provider should express concern about the child's weight.

Management

Review the child's growth chart with the child and family to explain how the child's pattern of growth differs from what is expected of children of the same age. Parents often fail to recognize growth problems in their children. Explain the risks associated with pediatric obesity, the need to consider ways to prevent obesity, and the effectiveness of prevention strategies.

Is there a family history of obesity, diabetes, or cardiovascular problems?

Encourage the family to focus on prevention of obesity as a family, rather than as the child's problem. When high-fat foods are available and children see others eating them, these foods are difficult to resist.

Review the family's dietary patterns. Who determines what food is offered and when it is offered? The family may benefit from consultation with a dietitian to identify ways to decrease the fat content in their diet and to increase consumption of fruits and vegetables.

Review mealtime structure. Are mealtimes structured and pleasant? Is there tension around meals? When parents and children do not eat together, children are more likely to eat snack foods with little nutritious value.

Review the child's access to foods. Parents have the responsibility to provide healthy foods on a predictable schedule, and children should determine the amount of food they eat. If children are in charge of the food they eat, they may not be receiving an adequate diet.

In many cases, pediatric obesity is related to sedentary behavior. Review the amount of time the child spends watching television or engaged in other sedentary activities. Review the availability of opportunities for physical activity. Encourage the child and family to look for school or neighborhood opportunities for physical activity.

Exposure to Environmental Hazards

Assessment

Screening questions: "Are all poisons and dangerous things out of reach? If your child rides a bike, does he or she wear a helmet? Do you have a smoke alarm that's working? Does anyone smoke at home? Is there a gun in your home? Is anyone harassing you, making you afraid, or physically hurting you?"

What is the history with injuries and ingestions? What is the parents' and child's understanding of the hazard(s) and of prevention strategies? What is parents' understanding of the child's developmental capabilities and limitations? What efforts have been made to educate the family and help access resources?

Management

Convey the importance of preventing injuries and other conditions from environmental hazards, a major health problem for children. Children who are "injury prone" may be at the extreme of risk-taking behavior and need extra guidance and supervision.

Provide appropriate educational materials, reinforcing two or three key, developmentally timed (e.g., walkers and gates for infants/toddlers) recommendations. American Academy of Pediatrics leaflets on the prevention of poisonings, bike helmets, smoke alarms, guns, and domestic violence have useful information for assessing and managing these issues. Refer to community resources (e.g., car seat, smoke alarm, bike helmet programs).

Exposure to Drugs

Assessment

Screening questions: "Does anyone in the household smoke? Does anyone in the household drink alcohol? Smoke marijuana? Use drugs, such as cocaine or heroin? How often does this occur? Is the primary caregiver involved in these activities?"

Does the caregiver perceive of the smoking, alcohol, or drug use as a problem? Is the caregiver motivated to make changes?

Management

Explain the risk of the specific substance to the child (e.g., smoking for a child with asthma). Ask the caregivers how they would feel if the child started to smoke, use drugs, and so on. Explain that by permitting these activities in the household, the caregiver is modeling these behaviors as appropriate. Help the caregiver identify appropriate strategies for intervention. Refer to community resources (e.g., smoking cessation, drug treatment). Refer to CPS if the child is at risk for abuse and neglect.

Conclusion

Medical neglect is a serious threat to children's well-being. Medical care providers have an opportunity to collaborate with families and with other providers and agencies to ensure that children and families have access to adequate care. Preventing neglect by educating families about children's health care needs and working with them to develop strategies for meeting those needs are critical roles for pediatricians and other health care providers.

References

Alaimo, K., Briefel, R. R., Frongillo, E. A., Jr., & Olson, C. M. (1998). Food insufficiency exists in the United States: Results from the third National Health and Nutrition Examination Survey (NHANES III). *American Journal of Public Health, 88,* 419-426.

American Academy of Pediatrics, Committee on Bioethics. (1988). Religious exemptions from child abuse statutes. *Pediatrics, 81,* 169-171.

Asser, S., & Swan, R. (1998). Child fatalities from religion-motivated medical neglect. *Pediatrics, 101,* 625-629.

Azar, S., Robinson, D., Hekemian, E., & Twentyman, C. (1984). Unrealistic expectations and problem solving ability in maltreating and comparison mothers. *Journal of Consulting and Clinical Psychology, 52,* 687-691.

Belsky, J. (1980). Child maltreatment: An ecological integration. *American Psychologist, 35,* 320-335.

Belsky, J., & Vondra, J. (1989). Lessons from child abuse: The determinants of parenting. In D. Cicchetti & V. Carlson (Eds.), *Child maltreatment: Theory and research on the causes and consequences of child abuse and neglect* (pp. 153-202). New York: Cambridge University Press.

Benedict, M. I., White, R. B., Wulff, L. M., & Hall, B. J. (1990). Reported maltreatment in children with multiple disabilities. *Child Abuse & Neglect, 14,* 207-217.

Berkowitz, C. (1984). Comprehensive pediatric management of failure to thrive: An interdisciplinary approach. In D. Drotar (Ed.), *New directions in failure to thrive* (pp. 193-210). New York: Plenum.

Birch, L. E., & Fisher, J. O. (2000). Mothers' child-feeding practices influence daughters' eating and weight. *American Journal of Clinical Nutrition, 71,* 1054-1061.

Bithoney, W. G., & Newberger, E. H. (1987). Child and family attributes in failure to thrive. *Journal of Developmental and Behavioral Pediatrics, 8*(1), 32-36.

Black, M. M., Cureton, P., & Berenson Howard, J. (1999). Behavior problems in feeding. In P. B. Kessler & P. Dawson (Eds.), *Pediatric undernutrition: Failure to thrive in young children: A transdisciplinary approach* (pp. 151-172). Baltimore: Brookes.

Black, M. M., Feigelman, S., & Cureton, P. (1999). Evaluation and treatment of children with failure to thrive: An interdisciplinary perspective. *Journal of Clinical Outcomes Management, 6*(5), 60-73.

Black, M. M., & Krishnakumar, A. (1999). Predicting height and weight longitudinal growth curves using ecological factors among children with and without early growth deficiency. *Journal of Nutrition, 129,* 539S-543S.

Bonner, B. L., Crow, S. M., & Logue, M. B. (1999). Fatal child neglect. In H. Dubowitz (Ed.), *Neglected children: Research, practice, and policy* (pp. 156-173). Thousand Oaks, CA: Sage.

Brayden, R., Altemeier, W., Tucker, D., Dietrich, M., & Vietze, P. (1992). Antecedents of child neglect in the first two years of life. *Journal of Pediatrics, 120,* 426-429.

Bross, D. C. (1982). Medical care neglect. *Child Abuse & Neglect, 6,* 375-381.

Chaffin, M., Kelleher, K., & Hollenberg, J. (1996). Onset of physical abuse and neglect: Psychiatric, substance abuse and social risk factors from prospective community data. *Child Abuse & Neglect, 20,* 191-200.

Chasnoff, I. J. (1997). Prenatal exposure to cocaine and other drugs: Is there a profile? In P. H. Accardo, B. K. Shapiro, & A. J. Capute (Eds.), *Behavior belongs in the brain.* Baltimore: York.

Chasnoff, I. J., & Lowder, L. A. (1999). Prenatal alcohol and drug use and risk for child maltreatment: A timely approach to intervention. In H. Dubowitz (Ed.), *Neglected children: Research, practice, and policy* (pp. 132-155). Thousand Oaks, CA: Sage.

Crittenden, P. M. (1988). Family and dyadic patterns of functioning in maltreating families. In K. Browne, C. Davies, & P. Stratton (Eds.), *Early prediction and prevention of child abuse* (pp. 161-189). Chichester, UK: John Wiley.

Crittenden, P. M. (1993). Characteristics of neglectful parents: An information processing approach. *Criminal Justice and Behavior, 20,* 27-48.

Cutts, D. B., Pheley, A. M., & Geppert, J. S. (1998). Hunger in mid-western inner-city young children. *Archives of Pediatrics & Adolescent Medicine, 152*(5), 589-593.

Daro, D. (1988). *Confronting child abuse.* New York: Free Press.

DePanfilis, D. J. (1999). Intervening with families when children are neglected. In H. Dubowitz (Ed.), *Neglected children: Research, practice, and policy* (pp. 211-236). Thousand Oaks, CA: Sage.

Diamond, L. J., & Jaudes, P. K. (1983). Child abuse and the cerebral palsied patient. *Developmental Medicine and Child Neurology, 25,* 169-174.

Dubowitz, H. (1994). Neglecting the neglect of neglect. *Journal of Interpersonal Violence, 9*(4), 556-560.

Dubowitz, H., Black, M., Starr, R., & Zuravin, S. (1993). A conceptual definition of child neglect. *Criminal Justice and Psychology, 20*(1), 8-26.

Edelstein, B., & Douglass, C. (1995). Dispelling the myth that 50% of U.S. school children have never had a cavity. *Public Health Reports, 110,* 522-530.

Eyler, F. D., Behnke, M., Conlon, M., Woods, N. S., & Wobie, K. (1998). Birth outcome from effects on health and growth. *Pediatrics, 101,* 229-237.

Firestone, P., & Witt, J. E. (1982). Characteristics of families completing and prematurely discontinuing a behavioral parent-training program. *General Pediatric Psychology, 7,* 209-222.

Fost, N. (1988, March 14). Loopholes permit child abuse. *Medical World News,* p. 99.

Frank, D. A., Bauchner, H., Parker, S., Huber, A. M., Kyei-Aboagye, K., Cabral, J., & Zuckerman, B. (1990). Neonatal body proportionality and body composition after in-utero exposure to cocaine and marijuana. *Journal of Pediatrics, 177,* 622-626.

Gaines, R., Sangrund, A., Green, A. H., & Power, E. (1978). Etiological factors in child maltreatment: A multivariate study of abusing, neglecting, and normal mothers. *Journal of Abnormal Psychology, 87,* 531-540.

Gambrill, E. D. (1983). Behavioral interventions with child abuse and neglect. *Progress in Behavior Modification, 15,* 1-56.

Garbarino, J., & Crouter, A. (1978). Defining the community context of parent-child relations. *Child Development, 49,* 604-616.

Garbarino, J., & Sherman, D. (1980). High-risk neighborhoods and high-risk families: The human ecology of child maltreatment. *Child Development, 51*(1), 188-198.

Gaudin, J. M. (1999). Child neglect: Short-term and long-term outcomes. In H. Dubowitz (Ed.), *Neglected children: Research, practice, and policy* (pp. 89-108). Thousand Oaks, CA: Sage.

Gaudin, J. M., & Dubowitz, H. (1997). Family functioning in neglectful families: Recent research. In J. Duerr Berick & N. Barth (Eds.), *Child welfare research* (Vol. 2). New York: Columbia University Press.

Geffken, G., Johnson, S. B., Silverstein, J., & Rosenbloom, A. (1992). The death of a child with diabetes from neglect: A case study. *Clinical Pediatrics, 31,* 325-330.

Gergen, P. J., Fowler, J. A., & Maurer, K. R. (1998). The burden of environmental tobacco smoke exposure on the respiratory health of children 2 months through 5 years of age in the United States, 3rd National Health and Nutrition Examination Survey, 1988-1994. *Pediatrics, 101,* E8.

Giovannoni, J. M., & Becerra, R. M. (1979). *Defining child abuse.* New York: Free Press.

Giovannoni, J. M., & Billingsley, A. (1970). Child neglect among the poor: A study of parental adequacy in families of three ethnic groups. *Child Welfare, 49.*

Gomby, D. S., & Shiono, P. H. (1991). Estimating the number of substance-exposed infants. In Center for the Future of Children (Ed.), *The future of children: Drug exposed infants.* Los Altos, CA: Center for the Future of Children.

Gorski, P. A. (2000). Caring relationships: An investment in health? *Public Health Reports, 115,* 144-150.

Herrenkohl, R., Herrenkohl, E., & Egolf, B. (1983). Circumstances surrounding the occurrence of child maltreatment. *Journal of Consulting and Clinical Psychology, 51,* 424-431.

Howing, P., Wodarski, J., Gaudin, J., & Kurtz, P. D. (1989). Effective interventions to ameliorate the incidence of child maltreatment: The empirical base. *Social Work, 34,* 330-338.

Illinois Department of Children and Family Services, Office of the Inspector General. (1997). *Recommendations for improving the state's child welfare response to families affected by parental substance abuse.* Springfield, IL: Author.

Jehovah's Witnesses of Washington v. King County Hospital, 278 F. Supp. 488 (Washington, DC, 1967), aff'd per curiam 390 US 598 (1968).

Jones, J. M., & McNeely, R. L. (1980). Mothers who neglect and those who do not: A comparative study. *Social Casework, 61,* 559-567.

Jones, M. A. (1987). *Parental lack of supervision: Nature and consequence of a major child neglect problem*. Washington, DC: Child Welfare League of America.

Kadushin, A. (1988). Neglect in families. In E. W. Nunnally, C. S. Chilman, & F. M. Cox (Eds.), *Mental illness, delinquency, addictions, and neglect* (pp. 147-166). Newbury Park, CA: Sage.

Kelly, S. J. (1992). Parenting stress and child maltreatment in drug-exposed children. *Child Abuse & Neglect, 16*, 317-328.

Kerr, M., Black, M. M., & Krishnakumar, A. (2000). Failure-to-thrive, maltreatment and the behavior and development of 6-year-old children from low-income urban families: A cumulative risk model. *Journal of Child Abuse & Neglect, 24*, 587-598.

Klerman, L. V. (1985). Interprofessional issues in delivering services to chronically ill children and their families. In N. Hobbs & J. M. Perrin (Eds.), *Issues in the care of children with chronic illness: A sourcebook on problems, services, and policies* (pp. 420-440). San Francisco: Jossey-Bass.

Klerman, L. V. (1991). The health of poor children: Problems and programs. In A. C. Huston (Ed.), *Children in poverty: Child development and public policy* (pp. 79-104). New York: Cambridge University Press.

Korbin, J. E., & Spilsbury, J. C. (1999). Cultural competence and child neglect. In H. Dubowitz (Ed.), *Neglected children: Research, practice, and policy* (pp. 69-88). Thousand Oaks, CA: Sage.

Kotch, J., Browne, D., Symons, M., Ringwalt, C., Bentz, W., Evans, G., Rosebloom, L., Glenn, W., Cheng, N., & Park, M. (1989). *Stress, social support, and abuse and neglect in high risk infants*. Springfield, VA: U.S. Department of Commerce, National Technical Information Service.

Lapp, J. (1983). A profile of officially reported child neglect. In C. M. Trainer (Ed.), *The dilemma of child neglect: Identification and treatment*. Denver, CO: American Humane Association.

Lau, R. R., Quadrell, M. J., & Hartman, K. A. (1990). Development and change of young adults' preventive health beliefs and behavior: Influence from parents and peers. *Journal of Health and Social Behavior, 31*, 240-259.

Leaf, P., Alegria, M., Cohen, P., Goodman, S., McCue Horwitz, S., Hoven, C., Narro, W., Vaden-Kiernan, M., & Regier, D. (1996). Mental health service use in the community and schools: Results from the four-community MACA Study. *Journal of the American Academy of Child Adolescent Psychiatry, 35*(7), 889-897.

Lester, B. M., LaGasse, L., & Brunner, S. (1997). Data base of studies on prenatal cocaine exposure and child outcome. *Journal of Drug Issues, 27*, 487-499.

Lester, B. M., & Tronick, E. Z. (1994). The effects of prenatal cocaine exposure and child outcome. *Infant Mental Health Journal, 15*, 107-120.

Liptak, G. S. (1996). Enhancing patient compliance in pediatrics. *Pediatrics in Review, 17*(4), 128-134.

Litt, I. F., & Cuskey, W. R. (1980). Compliance with medical regimens during adolescence. *Pediatric Clinics of North America, 27*, 3-15.

Mackner, L. M., Starr, R. H., & Black, M. M. (1997). The cumulative effect of neglect and failure to thrive on cognitive functioning. *Child Abuse & Neglect, 21*, 691-700.

Martin, M., & Walters, S. (1982). Familial correlates of selected types of child abuse and neglect. *Journal of Marriage and the Family, 44*, 267-275.

Meichenbaum, D. (1989). Non-compliance. *Feelings and Their Medical Significance, 31*(2), 4-8.

Olson, R. A., Zimmerman, J., & Reyes de la Rocha, S. (1985). Medical adherence in pediatric populations. In N. Arziener, D. Bendell, & C. E. Walker (Eds.), *Health psychology treatment and research issues*. New York: Plenum.

Osofsky, J. (1999). The impact of violence on children. *Future Child, 9*(3), 33-49.

Parker, S., Greer, S., & Zuckerman, B. (1988). Double jeopardy: The impact of poverty on early child development. *Pediatric Clinics of North American, 35*, 1227-1240.

Picciano, M. F., Smiciklas-Wright, H., Birch, L. L., Mitchell, D. C., Murray-Kolb, L., & McConahy, K. L. (2000). Nutritional guidance is needed during dietary transition in early childhood. *Pediatrics, 106*(1), 109-114.

Polansky, N., Ammons, P. W., & Gaudin, J. M., Jr. (1985). Loneliness and isolation in child neglect. *Social Casework, 66*(1), 38-47.

Polansky, N., Chalmers, M. E., Williams, D., & Buttenwieser, E. (1981). *Damaged parents: An anatomy of child neglect*. Chicago: University of Chicago Press.

Polansky, N., Gaudin, J. M., Jr., Ammons, P. W., & Davis, K. B. (1985). The psychological ecology of the neglectful mother. *Child Abuse & Neglect, 9*, 265-275.

Prince v. Massachusetts, 3/21 U.S. 158 (1944).

Sedlak, A. J., & Broadhurst, D. D. (1996). *Third national incidence study of child abuse and neglect: Final report*. Washington, DC: National Center on Child Abuse and Neglect.

Shriver, M. D., & Piersel, W. (1994). The long-term effects of intrauterine drug exposure: Review of recent research and implications for early childhood special education. *Topics in Early Childhood Special Education, 14*(2), 161-183.

Singer, L. T. (1999). Advances and redirections in understanding effects of fetal drug exposure. *Journal of Drug Issues, 29,* 253-262.

Sternberg, K. J. (1998). Violent families. In M. E. Lamb (Ed.), *Parenting and child development in "nontraditional" families.* Mahwah, NJ: Lawrence Erlbaum.

Stewart, J. R. (1993). Seat belt use and accident involvement: A comparison of driving behavior before and after a seat belt law. *Accident Analysis & Prevention, 25,* 757-763.

Streissguth, A., Sampson, P., & Barr, H. (1989). Neurobehavioral dose-response effects of prenatal alcohol exposure in humans from infancy to adulthood. *Annals of the New York Academy of Sciences, 562,* 145-158.

Sudia, C. (1981). What services do abusive families need? In L. Pelton (Ed.), *The social context of child abuse and neglect.* New York: Human Sciences Press.

Sullivan, P. M., & Knutson, J. F. (2000). Maltreatment and disabilities: A population-based epidemiological study. *Child Abuse & Neglect, 24*(10), 1257-1273.

Szilagyi, P. G., Holl, J. L., Rodewald, L. E., Yoos, L., Zwanziger, J., Shone, L. P., Mukamel, D. B., Trafton, S., Dick, A. W., & Raubertas, R. F. (2000). Evaluation of New York state's Child Health Plus: Children who have asthma. *Pediatrics, 105,* 719-727.

Tang, J., Altman, D., Robertson, D., O'Sullivan, D., Douglass, J., & Tinanoff, N. (1997). Dental carries prevalence and treatment levels in Arizona preschool children. *Public Health Reports, 112,* 319-331.

Tong, S., von Schirnding, Y. E., & Prapamontol, T. (2000). Environmental lead exposure: A public health problem of global dimensions. *Bull World Health Organization, 78*(9), 1068-1077.

Troiano, R. P., & Flegal, K. M. (1998). Overweight children and adolescents: Description, epidemiology, and demographics. *Pediatrics, 101,* 497-504.

Twentyman, C., & Plotkin, R. (1982). Unrealistic expectations of parents who maltreat their children: An educational deficit that pertains to child development. *Journal of Clinical Psychology, 38,* 497-503.

U.S. Advisory Board on Child Abuse and Neglect. (1995). *A nation's shame: Fatal child abuse and neglect in the United States.* Washington, DC: Government Printing Office.

U.S. Congress, Child Abuse Prevention and Treatment Act, Pub. L. 93-247, 42 U.S.C. 5101 (as revised in 1996).

U.S. Department of Health and Human Services (DHHS). (1996). *Study findings: Study of national incidence and prevalence of child abuse and neglect—1993.* Washington, DC: Government Printing Office.

U.S. Department of Health and Human Services (DHHS). (2000). *Child health USA 2000.* Washington, DC: Government Printing Office.

U.S. Department of Health and Human Services, National Center on Child Abuse and Neglect. (1999). *Child abuse and neglect case-level data 1996: Working paper I.* Washington, DC: Government Printing Office.

U.S. Department of Health and Human Services, Office of Maternal and Child Health. (1989). *Child Health USA '89.* Washington, DC: Government Printing Office.

Wesson, D., Spence, L., Hu, X., & Parkin, P. (2000). Trends in bicycling-related head injuries in children after implementation of a community-based bike helmet campaign. *Journal of Pediatric Surgery, 35*(5), 688-689.

Whitaker, R. C., Wright, J. A., Pepe, M. S., Seidel, K. D., & Dietz, W. H. (1997). Predicting obesity in young adulthood from childhood and parental obesity. *New England Journal of Medicine, 337*(13), 869-873.

Wise, P. H., & Meyers, A. (1988). Poverty and child health. *Pediatric Clinics of North America, 35,* 1169-1186.

Wolock, I., & Horowitz, H. (1979). Child maltreatment and maternal deprivation among AFDC recipient families. *Social Services Resource, 53,* 175-194.

Wolock, I., & Horowitz, H. (1984). Child maltreatment as a social problem: The neglect of neglect. *American Journal of Orthopsychiatry, 54,* 530-543.

Yeatman, G. W., & Dang, V. V. (1980). Cao Gia (coin rubbing): Vietnamese attitudes toward health care. *Journal of American Medical Association, 244,* 2748-2749.

Zuckerman, B. S., & Beardslee, W. R. (1987). Maternal depression: A concern for pediatricians. *Pediatrics, 79,* 110-117.

Zuravin, S. (1988). Child abuse, child neglect, and maternal depression: Is there a connection? In National Center on Child Abuse and Neglect (Ed.), *Child neglect monograph: Proceedings from a symposium.* Washington, DC: Clearinghouse on Child Abuse and Neglect Information.

15

Child Fatalities

ROBERT W. BLOCK

It only hurts for a while,
But you killed me.
The blanket of guilt lies upon you
Now . . .
And now we are separated
Because of you.
I am all alone.
All I wanted was love.

"All I Wanted Was Love"
Andrea Block (1999)

A century ago, children usually died from infectious diseases. With our great success in subduing infectious diseases, however, children in the United States at the beginning of the 21st century are most likely to die from injury. Almost all the major causes of death (motor vehicle crashes, fires, drowning, firearm deaths, and homicide) are preventable. Over the past several years, there has been increasing interest in the causes of child fatalities and accompanying efforts to review child fatalities to more accurately determine the cause and manner of these deaths. This formal review can lead to systems changes necessary to protect children from both unintentional and intentional injury and eventually to reduce other causes of sudden, unexpected deaths.

Research is needed to shed light on our ability to detect inflicted injuries and resolve controversies on the pathophysiology and biomechanics of intentional versus unintentional trauma. The continuing activities of child fatality review teams will increase the frequency and accuracy of child death reporting, investigation, diagnosis, and case resolution. All professionals who care for children must be prepared to recognize violence in the lives of children. Trauma and neglect may be caused by ignorance, accident, or intent. In all cases, trauma and neglect warrant the full attention of child welfare professionals, law enforcement, medical examiners, physicians, district attorneys, elected and appointed officials, and other professionals interested in protecting children.

Data on Child Fatalities

In 1997, 18,524 neonatal deaths were recorded in the United States. Congenital anomalies, disorders related to short gestation and low birth weight (LBW), respiratory distress syndrome, and maternal complications of pregnancy were leading causes of death. There was a dramatic overrepresentation of Black neonates dying from LBW or short gestation (288 per 100,000 live births vs. 99.6 for all races and 66.3 for White babies). An additional 9,521 infants 28 days to 11 months old died in 1997 in the United States, with Black babies' mortality rates about double that of Whites for most leading causes. Infants died most commonly from sudden infant death syndrome (SIDS), congenital anomalies, injuries, and pneumonia or influenza (U.S. Department of Health and Human Services, 1999). In the year ending June 30, 1997, the infant mortality rate in the United States was 7.1 per 1,000 live births (White 6.0, Black 13.8) (National Center for Health Statistics, 1997). Among the leading causes of death was the category "unintentional injury and adverse effects," ranking eighth with 765 deaths.

> Suffocation was the leading cause of injury death among infants, followed by motor vehicle traffic injuries. Seventy percent of the suffocations among infants were due to mechanical means (such as in a bed or cradle, by a plastic bag, or due to a lack of air in an enclosed space) rather than due to respiratory obstruction. (U.S. Department of Health and Human Services, 1997)

The prevailing belief is that approximately 2,000 infants and children die in the United States each year from abuse and neglect (McClain, Sacks, Sroehlke, & Ewigman, 1993). Most deaths from known events are due to neglect. In 1994, 42% of 1,271 officially reported deaths from abuse and neglect were due to neglect (Daro & Wiese, 1995). In 1997, children in age groups from 0 to 4 years, 5 to 9 years, and 10 to 14 years experienced homicide incidences of 692, 174, and 283 deaths, respectively (National Center for Health Statistics, 1997). Among causes of death in older age groups, injuries rank first, followed by congenital anomalies and malignant neoplasm. Suicide appears initially in the 10- to 14-year-old age group, presenting dramatically for the first time on the chart of the 10 leading causes of death, ranking third. For ages 1 to 14 years, homicide is consistently ranked fourth. Other common causes of death among children younger than age 15 include heart disease, respiratory problems (pneumonia, influenza, bronchitis, asthma), and others (HIV, septicemia, neoplasms, anemias, and cerebrovascular conditions) (Web-Based Injury Statistics Query and Reporting System [WISQARS], 1997).

The most dramatic point emerging from a review of statistical literature is the variance among data sets. Most of the problem is likely due to problematic differences in two areas: definitions and data collection methods. An example is the review of surveys published by the National Center for Child Abuse and Neglect; in its report for 1994, only 47 states and the District of Columbia reported data for abuse and neglect, and only 43 states reported 1,111 deaths (U.S. Department of Health and Human Services, 1994). Yet another example is from the U.S. Department of Health and Human Services (DHHS) data books, in which the coding default for uncoded etiologies of injury deaths was "unintentional" until 1996, when it was changed to "undetermined."

In 1992, child abuse fatalities from Kansas were published (Schloesser, Pierpont, & Portner, 1992). There were 64 deaths between 1983 and 1988, broken into age groups of < 1 year (42), 1 to 2 years (12), 2 to 3 years (8), and 3 to 4 years (2). Causes of death included head injury (35), asphyxiation (12), and failure to thrive (5), consistent with literature indicating that head trauma is the leading cause of death among children who have been abused (Smith, 1994). A report from Oklahoma documents child abuse and neglect deaths between 1987 and 1995 (Bonner, Crowe, & Testa, 1997). There was an average of 27 deaths per year (range = 18-38/year). Deaths in this study were more likely to be from abuse (60%) than from neglect. Age groups were also analyzed in this report, which found that 40% of the deaths were among infants < 1 year of age, 13% between 1 and 2 years, 14% between 2 and 3 years, and 10% between 3 and 4 years.

A compilation of state vital statistics reports lists infant homicides for the years 1993 to 1997. The five jurisdictions with the highest average infant homicides per total births (prevalence rate) were Nevada, Washington, D.C., Missouri, Arkansas, and Oklahoma. The five states with the lowest prevalence rates were Delaware, Hawaii, New Hampshire, Vermont, and Montana. The ratio between the highest ranking and lowest ranking states is 9.3/1.0 (Durfee, 2000). The DHHS has also reported child maltreatment fatalities for 1998 by state. Based on fatalities per 100,000 children, the five highest-ranking jurisdictions were Oklahoma (5.1), Indiana (4.3), Texas (3.1), District of Columbia (2.9), and Nevada (2.8). Two states reported no child maltreatment fatalities—Vermont and North Dakota. Also low ranking were West Virginia (0.2), California (0.3), and New Hampshire (0.3) (U.S. Department of Health and Human Services, 1999).

The autopsy and death scene investigation, along with radiologic studies and toxicology, are important tools in the process of distinguishing between SIDS and child abuse homicides.

Reviews have documented causes of death other than intentional injuries. An 11-year autopsy review in Kentucky revealed causes of death, including asphyxiation in unsafe environments, overlying, drowning, scald burns, plastic bag suffocation, house fires, motor vehicle collisions, aspiration of foreign bodies, hypothermia, accidental blunt head trauma, and alcohol toxicity (Corey, McCloud, Nichols, & Buchino, 1992). The authors correctly concluded that "the majority of deaths in this se-

ries could have been prevented by minor changes in the household environment."

The findings in Kentucky were corroborated by a more extensive review of infant injury deaths in the United States from 1983 to 1991 (Brenner, Overpeck, Trumbel, DerSimonlan, & Berendes, 1999). In this report, leading causes of death were homicide, suffocation, motor vehicle crashes, and inhalation of foreign bodies. During the study years, there was an alarming 6.4% per year increase in homicides. The leading causes of unintentional deaths were the same as had been previously reported, but this report also included intentional deaths (homicides) that totaled 22.6% of all infant deaths over the 9-year period.

The same authors also reported a concern that the incidence of child homicide is underascertained (Overpeck & Brenner, 1999). For the years 1983 to 1991, there were 2,345 homicide deaths, 7,594 unintentional injury deaths, and 431 deaths with undetermined intent (4.2% of injury deaths among infants). In this study, deaths listed as undetermined had case risk profiles more closely resembling homicide than accidental death profiles. A previous study also concluded that child homicide is underreported in the United States by at least 20% (Schloesser et al., 1992).

In a pivotal paper, Robert Reece (1993) pointed out that child death review teams were established in many states to correct "an egregious omission in the conduct of the medical, social, and legal stewardship of our children." Reece thoroughly discussed sudden infant death syndrome (SIDS), including a definition, the clinical presentation of SIDS, the incidence and epidemiology of SIDS, and the importance of autopsy and death scene investigation. The autopsy and death scene investigation, along with radiologic studies and toxicology, are important tools in the process of distinguishing between SIDS and child abuse homicides. Reece and Krous (2001) provided a useful summary (see Table 15.1).

The Child Death Review Process

Over the past several years, there has been considerable interest in review processes to analyze child fatalities. Although most states have one or more child fatality

TABLE 15.1 Criteria for Distinguishing SIDS From Fatal Child Abuse and Other Medical
Conditions

	Consistent With SIDS	Less Consistent With SIDS	Suggestive or Diagnostic of Child Abuse
History surrounding death	Apparently healthy infant fed, put to bed. Found lifeless. Silent death. EMS resuscitation unsuccessful.	Infant found apneic. EMS transports to hospital. Infant lives hours to days. Substance abuse. Family illness.	Atypical history for SIDS. Discrepant history. Unclear history. Prolonged interval between bedtime and death.
Age at death	Most common age of death: 2 to 4 months. Range: 1 to 12 months. Ninety percent of SIDS die before age 7 months.	8 to 12 months of age	> 12 months
Physical examination and laboratory studies	Pinkish frothy nasal discharge. Postmortem lividity in dependent areas of body. Possible marks on pressure points of body. No skin trauma. Well-cared-for baby.	Enlarged organs. Evidence of disease process in organs.	Skin injuries. Traumatic lesions on body or body cavities. Malnutrition. Physical signs of neglect. Fractures.
History of pregnancy, labor, delivery, and infancy	Normal. Prematurity or low birth weight. Multiple births (twins, triplets). History of cigarette smoking. Prone sleeping position. Overdressing leading to hyperthermia.	Recurrent illnesses. Multiple hospitalizations. "Sickly" or "weak" baby. Specific diagnosis of organ system disease.	Unwanted pregnancy. Failed attempt at abortion. Little or no prenatal care. Out-of-hospital birth. Late arrival for delivery. No well-baby visits. No immunizations. Use of drugs/alcohol and tobacco during and after pregnancy. Baby described as hard to care for or to "discipline." Unusual feeding practices.

review teams, there is no uniform system in place in the United States. Recommended fatality review procedures have been published (Anderson & Wells, 1991; Granik, Durfee, & Wells, 1991; Kaplan & Granik, 1991), but widely disparate levels of functioning continue to exist. In 1999, the American Academy of Pediatrics (1999) published an updated policy statement, titled "Investigation and Review of Unexpected Infant and Child Deaths." This statement highlights several important issues:

- Appropriately functioning multidisciplinary fatality review teams may accelerate understanding of SIDS, reduce the number of missed cases of child homicide, increase the detection of familial and metabolic diseases, identify public health threats, and identify medical care systems in need of remediation.
- An adequate death investigation should include a scene investigation and interviews with caregivers.
- Cooperation and sharing of records among agencies involved with the fatality or investigation of the death are essential.
- Consistent retrospective review of child deaths will promote quality in death investigations.

Several models of functioning child death review teams have been reviewed in the literature. The American Academy of Pediat-

TABLE 15.1 Continued

	Consistent With SIDS	Less Consistent With SIDS	Suggestive or Diagnostic of Child Abuse
Death scene investigation	Crib or bed in good repair. No dangerous bedclothes, toys, plastic sheets, pacifier strings, lamb's wool, or pellet pillows. No cords or bands for possible entanglement. No apparent head/neck entrapment. Normal room temperature. No toxins, insecticides. Good ventilation. Heating system functioning normally.	Defective crib/bed. Use of inappropriate sheets, pillows, sleeping clothes. Presence of dangerous toys, plastic sheets, pacifier cords, pellet pillows, lamb's wool. Poor ventilation, heat control. Presence of toxins, insecticides. Unsanitary conditions.	Chaotic, unsanitary, crowded living conditions. Evidence of drugs/alcohol. Signs of terminal struggle in crib, bedclothes. Bloodstains. Hostility, discord, accusations of caretakers. Admission of harm.
Previous infant deaths in family	First unexplained infant death in family.	One previous unexplained death in family.	More than one previous unexplained death.
Autopsy findings	No adequate cause for death. Normal: skeletal survey, toxicology, blood chemistries, microscopic examination of tissues, metabolic screen. Presence of intrathoracic petechiae. Presence of dysmorphic, dysplastic, or anomalous lesions. Presence of gliosis of brainstem. Anal sphincter dilation.		Traumatic cause of death. Intracranial or visceral bleeding. External bruises, abrasions, or burns. No intrathoracic petechiae. Malnutrition. Fractures. Subgaleal hematoma. Abnormal blood chemistries. Abnormal blood toxicology.
Previous child protective services or law enforcement involvement	None	One	Two or more. One or more family members arrested for violent behavior. Restraining orders against a partner. History of domestic violence.

SOURCE: Adapted from Reece (1993) with permission.
NOTE: SIDS = sudden infant death syndrome; EMS = emergency medical services.

rics' (1999) policy statement on investigation and review of unexpected deaths makes seven recommendations. First, pediatricians should advocate for proper death certification, which requires a thorough investigation. Second, autopsies should be required in all deaths of children younger than 18 years resulting from trauma or that are unexpected, suspicious, obscure, or otherwise unexplained. Third, state legislation should be enacted to establish comprehensive child death investigation and review at state and local levels. Fourth, pediatricians should be involved with local and state review teams.

Fifth, public health, medical societies, and other groups should be involved in the child fatality review process. Sixth, death scene investigators should be trained by physicians knowledgeable about SIDS, child development, pediatric disease, and child abuse. Seventh, public health initiatives aimed at death prevention can be developed using review team data and should be supported.

One of the first nationwide reports on child death review teams was published in the *Journal of the American Medical Association*. Written by Durfee, Gellert, and Tilton-

Durfee (1992), the paper reviewed the origins and status of child death review teams in the 21 states that reported having teams in place at that time. Among the states with either or both local and state teams, only 10 had been in place prior to 1990. The first team originated in Los Angeles in 1978, and 7 years passed before a second team emerged in South Carolina. Child death review developed as a response to child abuse and neglect fatalities. Today, however, many teams include review of deaths due to suicide, accidents, SIDS, and other causes and manners of death (Durfee, 2000).

The term *child death (or child fatality) review team* will be familiar to many who work in child abuse or child advocacy fields. Others, however, may not be familiar with the composition, mission, or procedures of a team. Most teams are now operating as a result of a state statute creating them and documenting their purpose. Most teams consist of volunteers from several disciplines who meet regularly to review some or almost all deaths of children younger than age 18 that occur in their state. Some states have local teams (cities or counties) that limit their review to their communities. The disciplines represented on a typical team may include but are not limited to the following:

- a physician, optimally one with experience, knowledge, training, and ongoing involvement with child abuse;
- a forensic pathologist from the medical examiner's office;
- a representative from the state child welfare organization;
- a representative from the state health department;
- a prosecutor;
- a representative from the state Bar Association;
- representatives from local and state law enforcement agencies;
- an emergency medical technician (EMT), paramedic, or similar "first responder";
- a mental health professional;
- a representative from social work;
- representatives of groups such as CASA (court-appointed special advocates), foster care review boards, and other child-related organizations involved in child protection;
- appropriate staff.

The common goal of child fatality review teams is to prevent child death or serious injury by identifying appropriate system changes; protecting siblings of children who died from sudden, unexplained causes; and increasing awareness among professionals and citizens of the causes of children's deaths.

The Importance of Autopsies

Reece (1993) emphasized the importance of an autopsy in the diagnosis of SIDS and in the critical diagnostic decisions that must be made in many unexpected or sudden child deaths. Other publications, including the policy statement from the American Academy of Pediatrics (1999), reinforce the critical importance of autopsies in child deaths (R. W. Block, 1999; Durfee et al., 1992; Thigpen & Bonner, 1994; U.S. Advisory Board on Child Abuse and Neglect, 1995). A model protocol for child death autopsies was published in 1987 by the Illinois Department of Children and Family Services and the Office of the Cook County Medical Examiner (Task Force for the Study of Non-Accidental Injuries and Child Deaths, 1987).

An appropriate autopsy is necessary to answer several important questions, including the following: Was the death due to injury, neglect, or complications of injury or neglect? If the death was related to injury, what was the mechanism of injury? Was the injury consistent with the alleged history or circumstances of injury? If not, why not? When did the injury occur in relation to the time of death? Did a delay in seeking medical care contribute to death? If so, was this an "unreasonable" delay? Did death result from a single episode of injury or as the result of multiple episodes of injury? Were drugs or poisons involved in the death? If neglect was involved, what form did it take? If there is evidence of failure to thrive, was this due to metabolic disorder, other disease, or neglect? To what extent did environmental, nutritional, and social factors contribute to death (Kirschner, 1998)?

There are four important reasons for insisting on autopsies on all child deaths (Valdes-Dapena, 1995). First, the autopsy is important for parents and their peace of mind. Second, the autopsy may be able to detect an unusual disease. Third, in cases of apparent sudden death in an infant, the autopsy may be able to differentiate between infanticide and several recognizable causes of sudden death: Examples include viral myocarditis, the cardiac rhabdomyomas of tuberous sclerosis, intracranial arteriovenous malformations, and sepsis. A fourth and critically important reason for autopsies is research. Only by linking careful and credible medical histories with meticulous death scene investigations and interviews, assessing laboratory and radiologic imaging information and then combining that information with detailed autopsy findings, and collecting valid data will we ultimately have secure and accurate information to couple with biomechanical theories of child death.

Death Scene Investigation

One of the major contributions of child fatality review teams has been a new emphasis on the importance of a good death scene investigation. When a child is seriously injured or dies at home, the emphasis of the moment is usually on resuscitation attempts and transportation of the child, as well as the panic of the parents. First responders can contribute a great deal to subsequent case analysis by properly securing the death scene and coordinating an appropriate investigation by law enforcement and others, including, where available, investigators from the office of the medical examiner. The Oklahoma Child Death Review Board, for example, has developed a pocket guide for police, fire, EMT, and other professionals called to a child death or injury scene. It is reproduced by permission at the end of this chapter.

Conclusion

Misidentification of deaths might occur after poor medical diagnosis, incomplete law enforcement investigation, incomplete child protection investigation, or flawed death certification (Grayson, 2000; Griest & Zumwalt, 1989). Properly organized and functioning child fatality review teams should be able to improve the accuracy of child death reporting. Teams make important recommendations to state agencies and legislatures concerning methods to protect children. For example, after reviewing 277 deaths in 1998, the Oklahoma Child Death Review Board found that 13% of the reviewed deaths were due to natural causes other than SIDS, 11% were due to SIDS, 17% were traffic related, 35% were other accidents, 5% were suicides, and 6% were unknown at time of review. Thirty-two (11%) of the deaths were homicides attributable to child abuse and neglect. Following the 1998 review, several recommendations were made to the Oklahoma legislature, including improvements in laws regarding seat belts and smoke detectors, increased funding for child protective services, and stable funding for the Child Fatality Review Board and the Office of the Medical Examiner.

Misidentification of deaths might occur after poor medical diagnosis, incomplete law enforcement investigation, incomplete child protection investigation, or flawed death certification.

In a little more than a decade, child death (and "near-death") cases have come under greater scrutiny. We are learning to be more skeptical about sudden, unexpected deaths, and we are learning the sad lesson that more deaths than once anticipated are due to maltreatment. We are also learning how to sway policy to protect children from preventable accidental causes of significant injury and death. However, a great deal of work remains to be done.

CHILD DEATH/INJURY INTERVIEW AND DOCUMENTATION GUIDE

This is just a guide. Not all information may be obtainable. FOLLOW LOCAL PROCEDURES AND MEDICAL DIRECTION! **INTERVIEW GUIDELINES** Mini interview at scene if treating patient or by 3rd on scene or follow up at hospital. Be non-judgmental, non-confrontational, compassionate, observant, and composed. *"These questions will help evaluate what precipitated your loss."* *"The history you provide helps evaluate the cause of your loss."*	**INTERVIEW QUESTIONS** ■ Time found ■ Last seen alive ■ Who found child ■ Caregiver at time of death ★ **ELAPSED TIME BETWEEN DISCOVERY AND CALL** ■ Hx surrounding death ■ Last feeding ■ Hx of apnea or cyanosis ■ Recent illness ■ ER/physician visit last 2 weeks ■ Physician's name ■ Medications ■ Other med. hx ■ Prenatal care ■ Labor problems ■ Premature or multiple births ■ Prenatal smoking ■ Low birth weight

■ Address ■ How long lived there ■ Parent married ★ **OTHER INFANT DEATHS** ***PRESERVE THE SCENE!*** **HOME OBSERVATIONS** ★ **UNSANITARY CONDITIONS** ■ Crib conditions ■ Bedding ■ Room tmp ■ Outside tmp ■ Odors/toxins ■ Smoking ■ Ventilation ■ Heating ■ Alcohol/drugs ■ Freq. calls to home by PD, FD, EMS ■ Adequate food ■ Meds in home ***PD ON SCENE? IF NOT CALL!***	**CHILD OBSERVATIONS** ★ **BODY MOVED** ★ **INJURIES/ MARKS** ★ **DISCOLORATION** ■ Appearance ■ Cleanliness and type of clothing ■ Clothing soiled ■ Cleanliness of child ■ Body position ■ Head ■ Neck ■ Sweaty ■ Tmp: cold, cool, warm ■ Rigor ■ Diaper ■ Bedding over baby ■ Bedding under baby ■ Objects in bed **PARENT/CAREGIVER OBSERVATIONS** (or anyone in home) ■ Demeanor ■ Physical appearance ■ Alcohol/Drug use ■ Resuscitative effort

CHARACTERISTICS OF SIDS

	Consistent With SIDS	Red Flags
History of death	Healthy infant; fed; put to bed; silent death	Unclear history; prolonged interval between bedtime and discovery
Age at death	90% 2-4 months most common; 1-12 month range	Greater than 12 months
Physical exam at death	Pink watery frothy fluid from nose/mouth; post mortem dependent lividity; no skin trauma; well cared for	Injuries; trauma; bruises; malnutrition; neglect; fractures
History of pregnancy	Cigarette use; premature or low birth weight; multiple births; illness requiring hospitalization	Unwanted pregnancy; no health checks; drug/alcohol use during pregnancy
Death scene	Crib in good condition; firm sleep surface; no dangers or toxins; good ventilation	Chaotic, unsanitary, crowded living conditions; drugs/alcohol; struggle in crib; blood-stained bedclothes; hostility by caretakers; discord; accusations
Previous deaths	First unexplained infant death	More than one unexplained infant death
Previous CPS or Law Enf. involvement	None	Prior CPS calls; family members arrested for violent behavior

★ **HISTORY INCONSISTENT WITH DEATH OR INJURY**
★ **DELAY IN SEEKING TREATMENT**
 	
ABBREVIATIONS
★ **RED FLAG!**
ER = Emerg. Room
Hx = History
Med = Medical
Tmp = Temperature
 	
Phone numbers
Police
Sheriff
Medical Examiner
OKC 405-239-7141
Tulsa 918-582-0985
OSBI 405-848-6724
Child/Adult Abuse Hotline
  1-800-522-3511
Child Death Review
  Board 405-271-8858
Domestic Violence Hotline
  1-800-522-7233
SIDS Hotline
  1-800-248-7437
	These guidelines were developed for use in those cases in which there is a child death or injury. In addition to the items listed on this guide, please make a note of any other information that may be relevant.
	
	For additional resources and training information, please contact the Child Death Review Board, 405-271-8858.
	
	These guidelines were produced in 1997 by the Oklahoma Child Death Review Board. Printing costs were paid through funds from the Federal Children's Justice Act and the Oklahoma EMT Association.

References

American Academy of Pediatrics, Committees on Child Abuse and Neglect and Community Health Services. (1999). Investigation and review of unexpected infant and child deaths. *Pediatrics, 104,* 1158-1159.

Anderson, T. L., & Wells, S. J. (1991). *Data collection for child fatalities: Existing efforts and proposed guidelines.* Chicago: American Bar Association.

Block, A. (1999). All I wanted was love. *Journal of the Oklahoma State Medical Association, 92,* 142.

Block, R. W. (1999). Child abuse: Controversies and imposters. *Current Problems in Pediatrics, 29,* 251-272.

Bonner, B. L., Crow, S. M., & Testa, J. A. (1997). *Child abuse & neglect fatalities in Oklahoma, 1987-1995.* Oklahoma City: Center on Child Abuse & Neglect, University of Oklahoma Health Sciences Center.

Brenner, R. A., Overpeck, M. D., Trumbel, A. C., DerSimonlan, R., & Berendes, H. (1999). Deaths attributable to injuries in infants, United States, 1983-1991. *Pediatrics, 103,* 968-974.

Corey, T. S., McCloud, L. C., Nichols, G. R., II, & Buchino, J. J. (1992). Infant deaths due to unintentional injury: An 11-year autopsy review. *American Journal of Diseases of Control, 146,* 968-971.

Daro, D., & Wiese, D. (1995). *NCPCA annual fifty-state survey.* Chicago: National Committee to Prevent Child Abuse.

Durfee, M. (2000). *State incident homicide data: A comparison by population* [Online]. Available: www.ican-ncfr.org.

Durfee, M. J., Gellert, G. A., & Tilton-Durfee, D. (1992). Origins and clinical relevance of child death review teams. *Journal of the American Medical Association, 267,* 3173-3175.

Granik, L. A., Durfee, M., & Wells, S. J. (1991). *Child death review teams: A manual for design and implementation.* Chicago: American Bar Association.

Grayson, J. (Ed.). (2000). Child fatalities: An update. *Virginia Child Protection Newsletter, 58,* 1-5.

Griest, K. F., & Zumwalt, R. E. (1989). Child abuse by drowning. *Pediatrics, 83,* 41-46.

Kaplan, S. R., & Granik, L. A. (Eds.). (1991). *Child fatality investigative procedures manual.* Chicago: American Bar Association.

Kirschner, R. H. (1998). The pathology of child abuse. In M. E. Helfer, R. S. Kempe, & R. D. Krugman (Eds.), *The battered child* (5th ed., pp. 248-295). Chicago: University of Chicago Press.

McClain, P. W., Sacks, J., Sroehlke, R. G., & Ewigman, B. G. (1993). Estimates of fatal child abuse and neglect, United States, 1979 through 1988. *Pediatrics, 91,* 338-343.

National Center for Health Statistics (NCHS). (1997). *Vital statistics system.* Atlanta, GA: Centers for Disease Control and Prevention.

Overpeck, M. D., & Brenner, R. A. (1999). Infant injury deaths with unknown intent: What else do we know? *Injury Prevention, 5,* 272-275.

Reece, R. M. (1993). Fatal child abuse and sudden infant death syndrome: A critical diagnostic decision. *Pediatrics, 91,* 423-429.

Reece, R. M., & Krous, H. F. (2001). Fatal child abuse and sudden infant death syndrome. In R. M. Reece & S. Ludwig (Eds.), *Child abuse: Medical diagnosis and management* (2nd ed.). Philadelphia: Lippincott, Williams & Wilkins.

Schloesser, P., Pierpoint, J., & Poertner, J. (1992). Active surveillance of child abuse fatalities. *Child Abuse & Neglect, 16,* 3-10.

Smith, W. L. (1994). Abusive head injury. *APSAC Advisor, 7,* 16-19.

Task Force for the Study of Non-Accidental Injuries and Child Deaths. (1987). *Protocol for child death autopsies.* Chicago: Illinois Department of Child and Family Services.

Thigpen, S. M., & Bonner, B. L. (1994). Child death review teams in action. *APSAC Advisor, 7,* 5-8.

U.S. Advisory Board on Child Abuse and Neglect. (1995). *A nation's shame: Fatal child abuse and neglect in the United States.* Washington, DC: Author.

U.S. Department of Health and Human Services. (1994). *National Center for Child Abuse and Neglect System.* Washington, DC: Author.

U.S. Department of Health and Human Services. (1997). *Health, United States, 1996-1997: Injury chartbook.* Washington, DC: Author.

U.S. Department of Health and Human Services. (1999). Web site [Online]. Available: www.acf.dhhs.gov/news.stats.fatalities.htm.

Valdes-Dapena, M. (1995). The postmortem examination. *Pediatric Annals, 24,* 365-372.

Web-Based Injury Statistics Query and Reporting System (WISQARS). (1997). *10 leading causes of death, U.S. 1997, all races, both sexes; CDC, 1997* [Online]. Available: www.cdc.gov/ncipc/wisqars.

PART FOUR

Legal Aspects

The law impacts child protection in myriad ways. The chapters in Part Four address legal issues in child abuse practice. Chapter 16 is new to the second edition and introduces nonlawyers to the American legal system. The chapter begins with a broad overview of the legal system, including the role of the federal, state, and local governments in child protection. In the United States, criminal and civil litigation are adversarial, and many professionals find the adversary system quite off-putting. In Chapter 16, I explain the rationale for the adversary system in the hope nonlawyers will have greater patience with their legal colleagues. The chapter describes criminal prosecution of child abuse, family court proceedings, and the juvenile court. Chapter 16 also covers confidentiality and privilege, responding to subpoenas, and hearsay.

Kenneth Lanning employs Chapter 17 to thoroughly discuss criminal investigation of child sexual abuse. An update of Lanning's superb contribution to the first edition of the *Handbook,* Chapter 17 offers valuable insight into the perspective of law enforcement on child abuse and neglect. Lanning discusses interviews, including the benefits and drawbacks of videotaping. His long years as the F.B.I.'s leading expert on child sexual exploitation come through in this chapter, which is a must-read for anyone who investigates child abuse.

During the past decade, few subjects have caused greater controversy than interviewing children about possible abuse. In Chapter 18, three of the leading authorities analyze this important topic from the ground up. Karen Saywitz, Gail Goodman, and Tom Lyon review the enormous literature on children's memory and suggestibility, emphasizing, among other things, the impact of trauma on memory, the relationship between age and suggestibility, and the impact of suggestive questions. Saywitz, Goodman, and Lyon provide practical guidance for professionals who interview children. In addition, the authors provide valuable information on children's developing ability to communicate. Children sometimes have to testify in court, and the authors comprehensively describe what we know about children's competence as witnesses, their effectiveness on the witness stand, and the psychological impact of testifying. Drs. Saywitz and Goodman contributed to the first edition of the *Handbook*. With the valuable addition of Dr. Lyon, the three produce a tour de force for the second edition.

Expert testimony plays an important role in litigation to protect children. In Chapter 19, Paul Stern and I discuss expert testimony in physical and sexual abuse cases. We begin by explaining the differences between expert and lay witnesses. From there, we set forth metaprinciples to guide expert testimony, including honesty, objectivity, willingness to acknowledge the limits of one's expertise, and preparation. We discuss who is qualified to testify as an expert witness, the forms taken by expert testimony, the information experts are permitted to rely on, the reasonable certainty standard, and the special rules governing novel scientific evidence. This chapter is a revised version of a chapter that appeared in the first edition of the *Handbook*.

Chapter 20 is new to the second edition. Unfortunately, professionals working to protect abused and neglected children sometimes face the threat or the reality of legal action, usually brought by angry parents. In this chapter, I discuss risk management for professionals working with abused children and adult survivors. Topics covered include basics of malpractice, lawsuits by nonclients against mental health professionals, the duty to report child abuse, the emerging world of e-health, informed consent, dual relationships, the importance of documentation, and constitutional rights.

J.E.B.M.

16

The Legal System and Child Protection

JOHN E. B. MYERS

Whether in the courtroom, the interview room, the classroom, or the clinic, law influences practice with abused and neglected children. Legal issues are discussed throughout this volume. The present chapter introduces the legal system. In addition, this chapter discusses (a) confidentiality and privilege, (b) subpoenas, and (c) hearsay.

Overview of the Legal System

This section provides an introduction to the American legal system as it pertains to child maltreatment.

The Federal Government's Role in Child Protection

In the United States, lawmaking authority is divided between federal, state, and lo-cal governments. This division of authority is accomplished in the first instance by the U.S. Constitution, which creates the federal government and defines its relationship to the states. Under the U.S. Constitution, the authority of the federal government is limited to matters delegated to the federal government by the Constitution. Matters not delegated to the federal government are reserved to the states or the people (U.S. Constitution, Amendment X, 1798). Among the matters delegated to the federal government

305

are the authority to regulate interstate commerce, coin money, operate a postal service, provide for the common defense, declare war, and provide for the general welfare (U.S. Constitution, Art. I, Section 8, 1787).

The U.S. Constitution divides the federal government into three branches: Congress, federal courts, and the executive branch. The U.S. Congress passes laws on a host of subjects within Congress's delegated authority. The U.S. Supreme Court is at the pinnacle of the federal courts. Below the Supreme Court are federal trial and appellate courts. The president heads the executive branch of the federal government, including agencies such as the departments of health and human services, justice, and education.

The U.S. Constitution does not delegate to the federal government responsibility for child protection. Yet, federal legislation has a tremendous impact on child abuse policy and practice at state and local levels. In 1974, Congress passed the landmark Child Abuse Prevention and Treatment Act (CAPTA). CAPTA authorizes millions of federal dollars to support state child protection efforts. To receive CAPTA funds, states are required, among other things, to conform their child abuse reporting laws to federal standards. In 1980, Congress passed the Adoption Assistance and Child Welfare Act, which requires states to make reasonable efforts to prevent removal of children from their parents and to reunify children following removal. Congress clarified the reasonable efforts requirement in 1997 with passage of the Adoption and Safe Families Act, which provides that "in making reasonable efforts, the child's health and safety shall be the paramount concern" (42 U.S. Code § 671(a)(15)(A)). The Iowa Supreme Court noted that state "laws relating to the welfare of children have been driven for the last twenty-five years by policies and laws generally developed at the national level" (*In re C.B.*, 2000).

If child abuse is not among the subjects delegated to Congress by the Constitution, then what gives Congress authority to pass laws that have such a profound impact on child protection at state and local levels? The answer lies in Congress's "spending power." Congress has constitutional authority to spend federal funds on programs that further national welfare. "Spending power" laws do *not* have to relate to matters specifically delegated to Congress. Under spending power laws, Congress influences policy and practice by making federal funds available to states that agree to abide by condi-

tions established by Congress. In child protection, the federal laws described above are spending power laws. CAPTA, for example, provides millions of federal dollars to states that are willing to comply with CAPTA's requirements. The Adoption and Safe Families Act requires states receiving federal funds to move children toward reunification or permanent placement within federally established time frames.

States are not required to accept federal funds under spending power laws such as CAPTA. Theoretically, a state could say "no thanks" to CAPTA and the federal money that accompanies it. Given the extraordinary cost of child protection, however, all 50 states accept federal child protection dollars and the strings that come with it. Thus, Congress's spending power gives the federal government a large say in child abuse policy and practice at state and local levels.

It should be added that Congress has direct authority rather than spending power authority to pass laws regarding child protection in Indian territory, on military reservations, and on federal land.

The State Government's Role in Child Protection

Every state has its own constitution, which divides state government into three branches: the legislature, state courts, and the executive branch, led by the governor.

The Legislature

Two sources of government authority authorize state legislatures to pass laws regarding child maltreatment: the police power and *parens patriae* authority. The police power clothes the government with authority to protect the health, safety, and welfare of the people. The legislature employs the police power to pass laws defining and punishing child abuse. *Parens patriae* authority is the authority of government to protect people who cannot protect themselves. *Parens patriae* authority is the source of laws permitting involuntary hospitalization of the mentally ill. The juvenile court is a product of the state's *parens patriae* authority and the police power. State legislatures pass hundreds of laws directly and indirectly related to child protection.

The Executive Branch
of State Government

The executive branch of state government is divided into numerous agencies. Although agency names vary from state to state, every state has an agency responsible for transportation, fish and game, agriculture, environment, education, corrections, and so on. When it comes to child protection, the state agencies with greatest responsibility are the departments of social services, health, mental health, and justice.

State agencies promulgate regulations designed to implement laws passed by the legislature. Thus, the state social services agency may promulgate regulations regarding foster care, child protective services (CPS), and other matters. Although regulations are promulgated by state agencies rather than the legislature, agency regulations are law.

It is easy to see why law relating to child protection is complex. First, there are federal laws such as CAPTA. In addition, federal agencies, especially the U.S. Department of Health and Human Services, promulgate *volumes* of regulations implementing federal laws. These federal laws and regulations apply to the states. At the state level, the legislature passes numerous laws. In addition to laws passed by the legislature, state agencies promulgate regulations. But there is more. State agencies issue countless memos, policies, and procedures, many of which are binding on professionals in child protection. But we are not done yet. At the local level, county agencies issue their own memos, policies, and procedures. Sometimes it takes a bevy of lawyers just to *find* the law, let alone figure out what it *means*.

The Courts

State courts are divided into trial and appellate courts. Trial courts are located throughout the state. In rural areas, there may be one trial judge for two or three counties. In large urban centers, there are many trial judges. Trial courts handle hundreds of thousands of cases each year, including criminal prosecutions, divorce cases, personal injury matters, commercial litigation, and juvenile court actions. Most cases do not end in a trial. In both criminal and noncriminal matters, the vast majority of cases settle. When a case does go to trial, the losing party may appeal. The most important exception to the right to appeal is in criminal cases. When the defendant in a criminal case is found not guilty, the prosecution may not appeal. On the other hand, if the defendant is found guilty, the defendant may appeal.

The role of an appellate court is to determine whether the trial judge made mistakes that warrant a new trial. Depending on the appellate court, anywhere from three to nine appellate judges participate in the appeal. Generally, the appellate court does not listen to witnesses or take new evidence. Each appellate judge reads the record of the trial and considers the lawyers' legal briefs. The lawyers may appear before the appellate judges for oral argument. The appellate judges vote on how the case should be decided. If all judges agree, one judge writes the opinion for the unanimous court. If one or more judges disagree with the majority, one judge writes the majority opinion, and a member of the minority writes a dissent.

In the United States, the decision of an appellate court does two things. First, the appellate court decides the case before it. Second, the decision of an appellate court *makes* law. Law created by appellate courts is called "common law." Thus, in the United States, law is created by legislatures *and* appellate courts.

The Local Government's
Role in Child Protection

In America, states are divided into counties or, in Louisiana, parishes. Every county is governed by local elected officials. Counties contain cities, towns, and villages, each with its own elected officials. In many states, each county or parish has an agency that is directly responsible for child protection. The local child protection agency (CPS) is usually part of the county department of social services. In some states, CPS is a statewide agency with local offices. CPS social workers collaborate with law enforcement officers from several agencies and with professionals in medicine, mental health, education, law, and other disciplines.

Litigation in American Courts

This section briefly describes litigation in American courts.

Criminal and Civil Litigation

Litigation is divided into civil and criminal. Criminal litigation is the prosecution of an individual accused of crime. The parties to a criminal case are the defendant, on one hand, versus the people of the state, on the other. The people are represented by a prosecutor. Civil litigation is of many kinds, including divorce and child custody litigation, child protection proceedings in juvenile court, adoption, parental rights termination, and guardianship. Juvenile delinquency cases in juvenile court are similar in many respects to criminal litigation in adult court. One important difference is that in most states, there is no jury in juvenile court delinquency cases. In addition, in delinquency cases, there is a greater emphasis on rehabilitation than one finds in adult criminal proceedings.

Standards of Proof

American law employs three standards of proof: (a) beyond a reasonable doubt, (b) clear and convincing, and (c) preponderance. The higher the standard of proof, the more difficult it is to prove a case. The highest standard of proof–beyond a reasonable doubt–applies in criminal and juvenile delinquency cases. In criminal and delinquency cases, the defendant is presumed innocent. The prosecution must overcome this presumption with evidence that convinces the jury beyond a reasonable doubt of the defendant's guilt (*In re Winship*, 1970). Criminal litigation uses the highest standard of proof to reduce the likelihood that innocent people are convicted.

Reasonable doubt is difficult to define. The definition that is read to jurors in federal criminal cases provides insight. Jurors are told that

> it is not required that the [prosecution] prove guilt beyond all possible doubt. The test is one of a reasonable doubt. A reasonable doubt is a doubt based upon reason and common sense–the kind of doubt that would make a reasonable person hesitate to act. Proof beyond a reasonable doubt must, therefore, be proof of such a convincing character that a reasonable person would not hesitate to rely and act upon it in the most important of his or her affairs. (O'Malley, Grenig & Lee, 2000, § 12.10)

If the prosecution fails to meet this demanding burden, the defendant *must* be found not guilty.

Clear and convincing evidence is required to psychiatrically hospitalize individuals against their will, to permanently terminate the parent-child relationship, and, in some states, to remove a child from an abusive home for a substantial time.

Most civil litigation uses the preponderance of evidence standard of proof, which is the least demanding of the three standards. With the preponderance standard, the totality of the evidence need only tip slightly in favor of the party offering the evidence. Child custody cases in family court are decided under the preponderance standard. The judge decides what custodial arrangement will serve the best interests of the child. If the evidence preponderates, for example, slightly in favor of the mother, the judge awards custody to her.

Clear and convincing proof lies somewhere between a preponderance and proof beyond a reasonable doubt. A small number of civil cases require clear and convincing evidence. For example, clear and convincing evidence is required to psychiatrically hospitalize individuals against their will. Clear and convincing evidence is needed to permanently terminate the parent-child relationship. Finally, some states require clear and convincing evidence to remove a child from an abusive home for a substantial time.

Burden of Proof

The *burden* of proof is not the same as the *standard* of proof. The standard of proof is determined by the kind of litigation–beyond a reasonable doubt in criminal cases, preponderance in most civil litigation. The burden of proof is the responsibility imposed on one side of a lawsuit–civil or criminal–to produce enough evidence to meet the applicable standard of proof. In criminal cases, the prosecution has the burden to prove the defendant's guilt beyond a reasonable doubt. In juvenile court cases alleging abuse or neglect, the state has the burden of proof to establish that the child was abused or neglected. In family court child custody litigation, both parents have the burden of proof. Each parent tries to convince the judge to give custody to him or her.

Although the burden of proof is technical, it is far from irrelevant to professionals outside law. Parents often ask medical and mental health professionals questions about the legal system. It is particularly important for parents contemplating custody litigation in family court to understand the implications of the burden of proof. When one parent accuses the other of abusing his or her child, for example, the *accusing* parent has the burden of proof to prove the abuse. Failure to produce enough evidence to carry the burden of proof means the judge will rule against the parent on that issue. In a disturbing number of cases, a parent's failure to meet the burden of proof has led to countercharges that the parent fabricated the charges and is an unfit parent. For detailed discussion of custody litigation involving allegations of abuse and what can go terribly wrong in family court, see Myers (1997).

Evidence

Cases are won with evidence. But what is evidence? Six-year-old Eric defined evidence as "the stuff bad guys drop." Not bad for a 6-year-old. Basically, evidence is anything that helps prove a point. Lilly (1996) defines evidence as "any matter, verbal or physical, that can be used to support the existence of a factual proposition" (p. 2). Evidence includes testimony from lay and expert witnesses (see Chapter 19, this volume), written documents, photographs, and objects such as the gun used in a bank robbery. In child abuse cases, the child's testimony is often the most critical evidence. Professionals provide testimony on a range of subjects, from the results of physical examination to the prospects for successful psychotherapy. Complex rules govern the use of evidence in court.

The Adversary Nature of Litigation

Litigation in America is based on the adversary system developed long ago in England. The adversary system is founded on the idea that the most effective way to arrive at just results in court is for each side of the controversy to present the evidence that is most favorable to its position and to let a neutral judge or jury sift through the conflicting evidence and decide where the truth lies. In other words, the truth emerges from a clash of opposing evidence in the controlled environment of a courtroom.

One component of adversary litigation is the effort to undermine the opponent's evidence. Attorneys use several devices to accomplish this objective. For example, if one side offers evidence to prove Z, the other side may offer evidence to prove non-Z. In a physical abuse case, the prosecutor offers evidence to prove that the child's injuries were deliberately inflicted by the defendant. The defense attorney may offer evidence that the injuries were accidental. Alternatively, the defense may admit that the injuries were inflicted but offer evidence that someone else is responsible.

The most common method used to undermine testimony is cross-examination. The cross-examiner may test the witness's memory. The cross-examiner may discredit the witness by pointing out inconsistencies in the witness's testimony, drawing attention to the witness's motivation for testifying, or otherwise asking questions to convince the jury to disbelieve the witness. For detailed analysis of cross-examination, see Myers (1998) and Stern (1997).

Cross-examination is the aspect of the adversary system that professionals find least appealing, especially when the cross-examiner targets a child. Professionals are also uncomfortable with taking the witness stand themselves to be subjected to the microscope of cross-examination. Although cross-examination is seldom pleasant, it serves an essential role in the adversary system of justice. A leading authority on litigation wrote that

> for two centuries, common law judges and lawyers have regarded the opportunity for cross-examination as an essential safeguard of the accuracy and completeness of testimony, and they have insisted that the opportunity is a right and not a mere privilege. (Cleary, 1984, p. 47)

Another leading authority asserted that cross-examination "is beyond any doubt the greatest legal engine ever invented for the discovery of truth" (Wigmore, 1904/1974, § 1367). Difficult though cross-examination is, history is littered with cases in which cross-examination served the truth.

The Juvenile Court

The juvenile court was an outgrowth of the Progressive Era of the late 19th century. Idealistic reformers in Chicago and Denver created the juvenile court, believing it would save troubled youth. The juvenile court was responsible not only for abused, neglected, and dependent children but also for children in trouble with the law. As the creators of the juvenile court saw it, the judge takes boys and girls under his protective wing and prescribes just the right "social medicine" to set them on the path to productive adulthood (Hurley, 1907; Mack, 1909).

The juvenile court was immediately popular and spread across the country (Fox, 1996). Although the creators of the juvenile court were naive about the ability of judges to ameliorate the deep-seated social and psychological reasons for juvenile delinquency, child abuse, neglect, and poverty, the juvenile court was a brilliant humanitarian idea and continues to play an important and positive role (Sagatun & Edwards, 1995).

The juvenile court is generally a department or division of the trial court that is responsible for all criminal and civil matters. In rural areas with one or two judges for an entire county, judges wear multiple hats. In the morning, the judge dons her juvenile court hat. After lunch, she presides over a criminal case. The next day, the judge handles divorces in the morning and empanels a jury for a land dispute in the afternoon.

In urban areas, especially large cities, the juvenile court is usually housed in its own building, along with the detention facility for children accused of delinquency, and the court's probation staff. Judges are assigned to the juvenile court for a number of years, after which they rotate back to the main courthouse. A small number of judges choose to devote many years to the juvenile court. In many communities, judges of the juvenile court are assisted by lawyers serving as referees or commissioners.

A few states have an integrated family court that incorporates into one court all matters related to divorce, child custody, delinquency, child protection, adoption, guardianship, and other issues related to children and families (e.g., Hawaii, Nevada, New Jersey, New York).

Most child abuse and neglect cases do not find their way to juvenile court. Social workers and other professionals cooperate with families to alleviate stress, provide resources, and improve parenting. When maltreatment is serious, however, juvenile court intervention may be necessary. The first step in many cases is for the police or CPS to take the child into emergency protective custody. Proceedings are then commenced in juvenile court by filing a document called a petition. The petition is delivered to the parents so they know what they are accused of. CPS is represented in juvenile court by a government attorney. The parents may hire their own attorney, although most parents cannot afford counsel, and so the judge appoints an attorney for the parents. Increasingly, the child has an attorney too. In many communities, trained volunteers called court-appointed special advocates (CASA) are assigned to children. CASAs do an effective job ensuring that children do not fall between the cracks of the child protection system.

Most juvenile court cases are settled without a formal trial. In settled cases, the parents agree to accept services. If the child remains at home, the parents agree that CPS may monitor the child's safety. If the child is removed, a plan for reunification is created unless the abuse is so severe that CPS moves directly to terminate parental rights. If there is a trial in juvenile court, CPS has the burden of proof to establish the allegations of maltreatment contained in the petition. If CPS's attorney does not produce sufficient evidence to meet the burden of proof, the judge dismisses the petition and the case is closed. If sufficient evidence is produced, the judge rules in CPS's favor and enters an order designed to protect the child and strengthen the family or move toward termination. The juvenile court conducts periodic hearings to keep things on track.

Family Court

Divorce and child custody are handled by the trial court with responsibility for such matters. In a small community, the judge who decides child custody matters one day may preside over a criminal trial the next. In urban areas, divorce and child custody cases are assigned to a department of the court called "domestic relations" or "family court."

A divorce accomplishes five things. First, the divorce ends the marriage. Second, a divorce divides property, including the family home, cars, investments, pensions, and so on. Third, the judge decides whether one spouse must pay spousal support—formerly called alimony—to the other. The fourth component of divorce concerns child support. When a marriage ends, both parents remain financially responsible for the children. This is so whether or not the parents ever married. If one parent receives primary or sole custody of the children (see below), the noncustodial parent typically is ordered to make monthly child support payments to the custodial parent. In marriages where there is a biological parent and a stepparent, both "parents" pool their resources to support the family. When such marriages end, however, the stepparent has no further financial obligation to the stepchildren unless the stepparent adopted the children or agreed to provide continuing support. For financial purposes, an adopted child is the same as a biological child.

The fifth aspect of divorce concerns child custody and visitation. The legal rules on custody and visitation are similar whether or not parents marry. The word *custody* is used in several ways to describe postdivorce child rearing: "Sole *legal* custody" means that one parent has the primary right to make important decisions for the child. For example, the parent with sole legal custody has authority to decide where the child goes to school and whether the child should receive medical care. "Sole or primary *physical* custody" means that one parent has the primary right to physical control of the child. The parent with sole physical custody—the custodial parent—is the parent with whom the child lives most of the time. The custodial parent does most of the day-to-day parenting. The parent with sole physical custody often, although not invariably, has legal custody as well. "Joint *legal* custody" means that the parents share the right and the responsibility to make decisions relating to the health, education, and welfare of their child. "Joint *physical* custody" means that each parent has significant periods of physical custody. "Joint *legal and physical* custody" means that the parents share physical custody and legal custody. Although the words used to describe custody vary from state to state, the custodial arrangements described above are available across the United States.

Some form of joint custody is a good solution for parents who are able to work cooperatively. When there is serious acrimony between parents, however, joint custody seldom works. When one parent accuses the other of child abuse, the chances for successful joint custody are low.

In many divorces, one parent gets primary custody and the other gets visitation. Visitation is a legally enforceable right, not a mere privilege. Visitation is granted automatically unless the noncustodial parent has engaged in serious misbehavior such as child abuse. The divorce decree usually describes the visitation schedule of the noncustodial parent, and the custodial parent has no right to unilaterally change the schedule. If for some reason the custodial parent believes visitation should stop, the custodian must return to court and ask a judge to modify the visitation schedule.

Most divorcing parents work out a custody and visitation arrangement that suits their needs and the needs of their children. So long as the parents' agreement is in the best interest of the children, the judge approves it. When parents cannot agree on custody or visitation, however, a trial may be necessary, and the judge determines who should have custody and what visitation is appropriate.

Contested custody and visitation litigation is extremely difficult for parents and children alike. Most divorcing couples are not on the best terms anyway, and when child custody becomes an issue, things can get extremely ugly. The degree of hostility in some custody battles beggars description. In an effort to reduce friction, many courts encourage or require parents to consult a professional mediator who is trained to help parents work out their differences and reach a friendly—or at least not openly hostile—custody and visitation arrangement. When mediation succeeds, there is no need for an adversarial custody battle.

To determine custody, the judge applies the "best interest of the child" standard.

In custody litigation, the judge may order the parents to undergo a custody evaluation by a mental health professional. In some cases, one mental health professional evaluates both parents and the children. In other cases, each parent obtains a separate evaluator. In some communities, custody evaluations are performed by professionals working directly for the court. In other communities, parents select a custody evaluator from among mental health professionals in private practice.

To determine custody, the judge applies the "best interest of the child" standard. Under this standard, the judge evaluates all available evidence about the parents and the child and makes the custody decision that serves the child's best interests. The following factors play a role in the judge's decision:

Tender years presumption. Until 20 years ago, many states had custody laws that favored mothers of young children. This maternal preference was called the "tender years presumption." The belief was that young children—children of tender years—are usually better off with their mothers. Today, the law has changed. The rule of modern custody litigation is that a child's parents have equal rights.

Primary caretaker presumption. In many families, one parent does most of the day-to-day parenting. For example, the father may be a full-time homemaker while the mother holds down a 40-hour-a-week job. When young children are involved, and the mother and the father are both good parents, judges often award custody to the primary caretaker.

Which is the better parent? Most contested custody cases boil down to this: Who is the better parent? Which parent is more likely to provide the love, guidance, discipline, support, and nurturance children need to develop into happy and well-adjusted adults?

After divorce, which parent is most likely to encourage the child's relationship with the other parent? When parents divorce, it is usually in the child's best interest to have regular contact with the parent who does not receive custody. Of course, this in not the case when child abuse is involved. Contact with the abuser may be unwise. Apart from abuse cases, however, judges deciding custody consider which parent is more likely to encourage the child's relationship with the other parent.

Mental illness. The fact that a person has mental health problems does not make him or her a bad parent. Many people struggling with mental illness are wonderful parents. There is no gainsaying, however, that some parents with serious mental illness are not up to the demands of parenting. Judges consider the mental health and stability of both parents, and if one parent has a mental illness that could seriously interfere with the ability to care for children, the judge may decide that the other parent should have custody.

Alcohol and drugs. Drinking in moderation is generally not important in custody cases. Problem drinking and alcoholism, on the other hand, are definite black marks. Drug abuse is illegal, and judges frown on such behavior. For many judges, so-called "recreational" drug use is a clear indication of irresponsibility.

A parent who has an extramarital affair. Some marriages end because one spouse is unfaithful. An extramarital affair does not necessarily make someone a bad parent. Thus, the affair itself is usually not very important, especially if it is over. The impact of marital infidelity depends on the impact on the children.

Domestic violence. Judges take domestic violence seriously in determining child custody. States increasingly have laws that require judges to consider domestic violence. In California, for example, a finding of domestic violence raises a presumption that the perpetrator is unfit for custody. For discussion of the impact of domestic violence on children, see Chapter 6 (this volume).

Child abuse. Physical or sexual abuse of a child indicates serious deficits in parenting and is likely to determine the outcome of a custody case.

Child's wishes. The law in most states requires the judge to consider the wishes of older children. Judges give little weight to the wishes of young children. Indeed, some judges do not consider young children's wishes at all. By the time children approach adolescence, most judges consider their preference. Although judges listen to older children, they are not required to go along with the children's wishes.

In the final analysis, the judge considers everything that sheds light on parenting and strives to serve the child's short- and long-term best interests.

Criminal Prosecution

Child abuse is a crime, and thousands of criminal prosecutions are commenced annually. The criminal justice process begins with notification to the police that a child may have been abused or killed. The police investigate and determine whether there is enough evidence to refer the matter to a prosecutor. Prosecutors have considerable discretion in deciding whether to bring criminal charges. Among the factors that weigh heavily in the prosecutor's decision are the strength of the evidence against the suspect, the seriousness of the crime, and the likelihood of successful prosecution.

A prosecutor's decision not to file charges can be frustrating for parents and professionals. No one should "get away" with child abuse. There are cases, however, in which the prosecutor believes abuse occurred but nevertheless concludes that the evidence is not sufficient to prove guilt beyond a reasonable doubt. Prosecutors are ethically prohibited from filing charges on insufficient evidence, and child abuse, particularly sexual abuse, is often difficult to prove. The U.S. Supreme Court noted that "child abuse is one of the most difficult crimes to detect and prosecute, in large part because there often are no witnesses except the victim" (*Pennsylvania v. Ritchie,* 1987, p. 60). Some children are too young to testify. Although most children older than age 4 have the cognitive capacity to testify (see Lyon, 2000; Lyon & Saywitz, 1999; Myers, 1997), many children find the courtroom forbidding. When a child is asked to testify against a familiar person, especially a loved one or someone who has threatened the child, the experience can be overwhelming. Consequently, some children's testimony is ineffective. The problem of ineffective testimony is compounded by the paucity of medical evidence in many sexual abuse cases. The sad fact is that the criminal justice system cannot provide justice for all victims of child abuse. On the other hand, prosecution plays an important role in punishing offenders and in sending a clear message that child abuse is intolerable.

Confidentiality and Privilege

Confidentiality is important to every professional working with victims of maltreatment. There are three primary sources of confidentiality: (a) the ethical duty to protect confidential client information, (b) laws making certain records confidential, and (c) privileges that apply in legal proceedings.

The Ethical Duty to Protect Confidential Client Information

The ethics codes of all professional organizations place a premium on confidentiality. For example, the *Code of Ethics* of the American Professional Society on the Abuse of Children (APSAC, 1997) states that "the right of clients to confidentiality, which is the assurance that nothing about an individual is revealed except under agreed-upon conditions, is fundamental to professional relationships with clients" (p. 3). The *Code of Ethics* of the National Association of Social Workers (1997) provides that "social workers should protect the confidentiality of all information obtained in the course of professional services, except for compelling professional reasons" (Standard 1.07(c)). The "Ethical Principles of Psychologists and Code of Conduct" of the American Psychological Association (1992) states that "psychologists have a primary obligation to take reasonable precautions to respect the confidentiality rights of those with whom they work or consult" (Standard 5.02).

Laws Making Clients' Records Confidential

Every state has a plethora of laws making records confidential. Confidentiality laws differ slightly from state to state, and professionals should be aware of the requirements in their state.

Privileges in Legal Proceedings

Confidential communications between certain professionals and their clients are privileged from disclosure in legal proceedings. Privileges protect confidential communications between psychotherapists and clients and between physicians and patients. Some states have a privilege for confidential communications between social workers and clients.

What kinds of communication are covered by privilege? The client's confidential verbal statements to the professional are covered, as are the professional's notes documenting a client's words. In addition, a professional's verbal statements *to* a client are covered by the privilege. Gestures that are communicative are covered. The privilege covers confidential written, telephone, and e-mail communication between a client and a professional.

Privileges apply only in legal proceedings such as court testimony and depositions. By contrast, the ethical duty to protect confidential information applies everywhere–at the clinic, at home, over dinner with friends, *and* in legal proceedings. Because the ethical duty to preserve confidentiality applies in legal proceedings, it is reasonable to ask, "What protection for confidentiality is added by a privilege like the psychotherapist-client privilege? In court, the professional is ethically bound to protect confidential information. Isn't the ethical duty sufficient?" The answer is no. In legal proceedings, professionals generally must answer questions that require disclosure of information covered by the ethical obligation to protect confidential information. If a privilege applies, however, the professional does not have to reveal privileged information. Thus, in legal proceedings, a privilege provides protection for confidentiality that is not available under the ethical duty.

Privileges generally belong to the client, not the professional. In legal parlance, the client is the "holder" of the privilege. As the privilege holder, the client can prevent the professional from disclosing privileged communications in legal proceedings. For example, suppose a psychotherapist is subpoenaed to testify about a client. While the therapist is on the witness stand, the attorney who subpoenaed the therapist asks questions that call for disclosure of privileged information. At that point, the client's attorney should object. The client's attorney asserts the privilege on behalf of the client. The judge then decides whether a privilege applies and whether the professional must answer the question. If the client's attorney failed to object to a question calling for privileged information, or if a client is not represented by an attorney, a professional may assert a privilege on behalf of a client. Indeed, a professional is ethically obliged to assert a privilege if no one else does (see *Runyon v. Smith*, 1999).

Generally, privileged communications remain privileged after termination of the professional relationship. Death of the client generally does not end a privilege.

The law of privilege is complex. Professionals should know whether they are covered by a privilege and should get legal advice before disclosing possibly privileged information in court or in response to a subpoena.

Liability for Unauthorized Release of Confidential Client Information

Unauthorized release of confidential information can lead to three types of proceedings against professionals. First, a member of a professional organization who violates the organization's ethical principles regarding confidentiality may be disciplined by the organization. Second, state licensing authorities may institute disciplinary proceedings against the professional. Third, a client whose confidentiality is breached may sue the professional.

Professionals should not release confidential information without client consent. Professionals must be particularly sensitive when communicating with attorneys. It is good practice to decline communication regarding confidential information–whether in writing, over the phone, or in person–until client consent is obtained.

Confidentiality When the Client Is a Child

The ethical obligation to protect confidentiality applies regardless of age. Who, then, consents to release of confidential information on a child? Generally, parents have the right to consent to the release of confidential information, especially when the child is young. For teenage clients, the issue is more complex. If the teen has legal authority to consent to treatment, as teens do in some states for some kinds of treatment, then the teen probably has the sole right to consent to the release of confidential information regarding the treatment. In other situations, the parents have the "legal" right to make decisions about confidentiality, but the therapist takes the teenage client's wishes into consideration. Indeed, in many cases, the teen's wishes should prevail.

Do parents have the right to read their child's record? What if parents are paying for psychotherapy? Again, answers are not always clear. The fact that parents pay for therapy does not automatically give them the right to confidential information. Much depends on the age and maturity of the child. The potential for disagreement can be reduced by clarifying issues of confidentiality at the outset of treatment.

Confidentiality in Group Therapy

The ethical duty to protect confidential information applies to professionals conducting group therapy. Members of the group, however, are not ethically bound to respect confidentiality (Roback, Moore, Waterhouse, & Martin, 1996). It is advisable to engage the group in discussion of the importance of confidentiality. Appelbaum and Greer (1993) stated that "it seems clear that group leaders should alert their patients that the sanctity of the communications depends on the goodwill of their fellow patients" (p. 312). The *Code of Ethics* of the National Association of Social Workers (1997) suggests that

> when social workers provide counseling services to families, couples, or groups, social workers should seek agreement among the parties involved concerning each individual's right to confidentiality and obligation to preserve the confidentiality of information shared by others. Social workers should inform participants in family, couples, or group counseling that social workers cannot guarantee that all participants will honor such agreements. (Principle 1.07(f))

Bennett, Bryant, VandenBos, and Greenwood (1990) suggest that therapists have group members sign a form that "1. states that members will hold in confidence all matters discussed in the group, 2. indicates the limit of legal protection of privilege within group therapy, . . . [and] 3. provides for signatures of all group members" (p. 54).

Although there is relatively little law addressing the application of privileges to confidential communications during group treatment, existing law suggests that privileges do apply.

Reviewing Client Records Before Testifying

When a professional prepares to testify, it is often useful to review the client's file. Such review refreshes the professional's memory about pertinent details. Some professionals take files to court. Although reviewing files is usually proper, a word of caution is in order. Information in a client's file is confidential, and some of the information may be privileged. If a professional refers to a file *while* testifying in court, the cross-examining attorney may have a right to inspect the file, including privileged information. Thus, by referring to a client's file while testifying, a professional may unwittingly allow an attorney to gain access to sensitive information that would otherwise be privileged from disclosure.

When a professional reviews a client file *before* going to court, there is less likelihood the opposing attorney will seek the file. File review before testifying is not entirely without risk, however. Once a professional is in court on the witness stand, the cross-examining attorney may ask whether the professional reviewed files before coming to court. If the answer is yes, the attorney may ask questions about the files or may ask the judge to order the files produced in court.

Because reviewing client files could lead to disclosure of privileged information, professionals should consult an attorney to determine the best practice regarding file review.

Confidentiality of Progress Reports on Children in Court-Ordered Treatment

When a juvenile court judge orders therapy for a child, the typical procedure is for a social worker to make the treatment referral. The judge and the social worker expect periodic reports from the child's therapist. Yet, information obtained from the child during court-ordered treatment is confidential and may be privileged. On one hand, the therapist wants to cooperate with the court and social services, both of which are endeavoring to help the child. On the other hand, the therapist is obliged to protect confidentiality. Is there an escape from this dilemma? With a little planning and good will, the answer can be yes. When possible, resolve the issue before therapy begins. In many cases, the judge can be asked to specify in the court order that the therapist will provide periodic progress reports. Place a copy of the court order in the child's clinical file. Unless contraindicated, inform the child's parents of the court order and obtain their written consent. Progress reports generally do not have to reveal all that goes on during therapy. In many cases, a report can keep the court informed without disclosing sensitive information. Finally, the therapist may ask that progress reports that become part of the court record be shielded from inappropriate disclosure.

Disclosure of Confidential and Privileged Client Information

This section discusses disclosure of confidential and privileged information.

Client Consent

Client consent plays the central role in release of confidential information (American Psychological Association, 1992). As Gutheil and Appelbaum (1982) observed, "With rare exceptions, identifiable information [about clients] can be transmitted to third parties only with the [client's] explicit consent" (p. 5). A competent adult client may consent to release of information to attorneys, courts, and anyone else selected by the client. The professional should explain any disadvantages of disclosing confidential information. For example, the client should be told that release to third persons might waive any privilege that would apply. Client consent should be in writing.

When the client is a child, parents typically have authority to make decisions about confidential and privileged information regarding the child. If the child is not living with parents, if the child is under the protection of the juvenile court, or if parents are divorced, laws and practices vary regarding who has authority to consent to the release of confidential information (for detailed discussion of California law, see Myers, 2001).

Client Inspection and Copying of Records

In most if not all states, clients have a right to inspect and copy their records. A professional may deny inspection if there is a substantial risk that seeing the record will have significant detrimental consequences for the client. When the client is a child, the parents normally have the right to inspect and copy the child's records. Parents may be denied access to their child's records when a professional determines that parental access would be detrimental to the professional's relationship with the child or when parental access would jeopardize the child's physical safety or psychological well-being. When a minor is legally authorized to consent to care, the minor has the right to inspect her or his records. The law regarding client access to records varies slightly from state to state.

Parents may be denied access to their child's records when a professional determines that parental access would be detrimental to the professional's relationship with the child or when parental access would jeopardize the child's physical safety or psychological well-being.

A Criminal Defendant's Constitutional Right to Confidential Records

In criminal cases, the defendant has a limited constitutional right to inspect confidential records on the victim (*Pennsylvania v. Ritchie,* 1987; *People v. Hammon,* 1997). This right extends in some cases to files of the CPS agency and records maintained by professionals in private practice. The defense attorney must request the child's file and convince the judge that the file could contain information helpful to the defense. The judge may review the file in private—called *in camera review*—and decide whether the file contains information that could help the defense. If so, the judge releases portions of the file to the defense and the prosecution. If the file contains nothing useful to the defense, the file remains confidential.

Child Abuse Reporting Laws

Child abuse reporting laws require professionals to report suspected maltreatment. The child abuse reporting law overrides privilege and the ethical duty to maintain confidentiality. When complying with the reporting law, however, professionals should disclose only as much confidential information as is needed to comply with the reporting obligation. Information that is not needed for the report remains confidential. Kalichman (1999) stated,

> Once the information that is needed to report is collected or organized, the next step is to contact the social service agency responsible for taking reports. There are, however, additional ethical considerations to make when determining what to include in a report. The level of detail released in a report should be limited to an amount that minimizes breaches of confidentiality while maximizing child protection. It is not necessary to release information in a report unless it will assist the social service agency in making determinations of abuse or will help the agency to take action on behalf of the child and family. As stated in the *Ethical Principles of Psychologists and Code of Conduct,* "In order to minimize intrusions on privacy, psychologists include in written and oral reports, consultations, and the like, only information germane to the purpose for which the communication is made" (Standard 5.03a). In reporting suspected child abuse, the purpose of the information released is to protect children. Information should therefore be limited to the degree to which child protection will be achieved.
>
> Professionals should be aware that including more information than is necessary in a mandated report, and providing additional information after a report is filed, can violate privacy rights and can raise issues of liability. Circumstances unrelated to the suspicion of abuse, such as details of family life and family relationships that are peripheral to the abuse, need not be included in a report. (p. 148)

The Dangerous-Client Exception to Confidentiality

In 1976, the California Supreme Court ruled in the famous *Tarasoff* case that a psychotherapist has a legal duty to take steps to protect the potential victim of a client who threatens the victim (*Tarasoff v. Regents of the University of California,* 1976). In *Tarasoff,* a disturbed young man murdered the woman he professed to love. The parents of the murdered woman sued the murderer's therapist, alleging that the therapist knew that his client posed a danger to their daughter but did not warn the victim or her parents. The California Supreme Court ruled that

> when a therapist determines, or pursuant to the standards of his profession should deter-

mine, that his patient presents a serious danger of violence to another, he incurs an obligation to use reasonable care to protect the intended victim against such danger. (p. 334)

Following *Tarasoff,* it was unclear how far a psychotherapist's duty to warn extended (Kaufman, 1991; Leong, Eth, & Silva, 1992, 1994). Whom does a psychotherapist have to warn? Must a psychotherapist warn the public at large if a patient seems dangerous even though the patient has not made specific threats? Or is the duty to warn limited to individuals specifically threatened by the patient? In *Thompson v. County of Alameda* (1980), the California Supreme Court ruled that the duty to warn does not extend to the general public. The duty to warn arises only when a patient threatens a readily identifiable and foreseeable victim.

In the years since *Tarasoff,* courts that have considered the dangerous-patient scenario have, for the most part, agreed with the California Supreme Court (see *Emerich v. Philadelphia Center for Human Development,* 1998; Lake, 1994). Courts generally state that "the relationship between the psychotherapist and the outpatient constitutes a special relation that imposes upon the psychotherapist an affirmative duty to protect against or control the patient's violent propensities" (*Estate of Morgan,* 1997, p. 1320). In 1997, the Ohio Supreme Court summarized the law:

> Recognizing that the duty is imposed by virtue of the relationship, these courts acknowledge that the duty can be imposed not only upon psychiatrists, but also on psychologists, social workers, mental health clinics and other mental health professionals who know, or should have known, of their patient's violent propensities. The courts do not impose any single formulation as to what steps must be taken to alleviate the danger. Depending upon the facts and the allegations of the case, the particular psychotherapist-defendant may or may not be required to perform any number of acts, including prescribing medication, fashioning a program for treatment, using whatever ability he or she has to control access to weapons or to persuade the patient to voluntarily enter a hospital, issuing warnings or notifying the authorities and, if appropriate, initiating involuntary commitment proceedings. (*Estate of Morgan,* 1997, pp. 1320-1321)

A *Tarasoff*-style duty to warn can arise if a psychotherapist learns that a client plans to sexually abuse a particular child (*Bradley v. Ray*, 1995; see also *Gritzner v. Michael R.*, 2000). Although less certain, a judge might extend the duty to warn to a case in which no particular child was targeted but in which a sexually dangerous client had access to readily identifiable children (see *Barry v. Turek*, 1990). The *Tarasoff* duty to warn overrides the ethical duty to protect confidential information *and* the psychotherapist-client privilege.

Occasionally, a client threatens a therapist (*Menendez v. Superior Court*, 1992). Perhaps the client reveals criminal activity during therapy and threatens the therapist to maintain secrecy. Leong, Eth, and Silva (1994) noted that "if a patient offers a deadly secret and then threatens the psychotherapist to ensure silence, the patient has sacrificed any claim to confidentiality (privacy) in the psychotherapist-patient (and physician-patient) relationship" (p. 241).

Emergencies

In emergencies, professionals may release confidential information without client consent. For example, there may be no time to contact the client, or contacting the client may be contraindicated because the *client* is dangerous.

Court-Ordered Psychological Evaluation

A judge may order an individual to submit to a psychological *evaluation* for use in legal proceedings. The evaluation will be read by the judge, the attorneys, and, perhaps, others. The ethical obligation to protect confidentiality is correspondingly limited. Yet, the evaluator should protect confidentiality within the constraints imposed by the judge. As for privileges such as the psychotherapist-client privilege, the effect of most court-ordered psychological evaluations is that privileges do not apply.

Court-ordered *treatment* is another matter. The expectation in treatment is confidentiality, even when treatment is court ordered. There are times, however, when confidentiality is limited. Consider, for example, a case in which a juvenile court judge orders psychotherapy for a sexually abused child living in foster care. Very likely, the judge will request progress reports from the thera-

pist. The therapist may be asked to testify about the child's condition. Such requests may be appropriate and in the child's best interest. Thus, with court-ordered therapy, limits on confidentiality should be clarified at the outset. The judge might discuss the issue in the court order. The therapist should discuss the issue with relevant parties, including the child if the child is sufficiently mature.

Boards, Commissions, and Administrative Agencies

Certain boards, commissions, and administrative agencies can compel disclosure of client information.

Search Warrant

A professional must disclose client information in response to a lawful search warrant.

Consultation and Supervision

Client information may be shared with colleagues for purposes of supervision and consultation (see Reid, 1999). The American Psychological Association's (1992) "Ethical Principles of Psychologists and Code of Conduct" provides, however, that "in order to minimize intrusions on privacy, psychologists include in written and oral reports, consultations, and the like, only information germane to the purpose for which the communication is made" (Standard 5.03(a)). The National Association of Social Worker's (1999) *Code of Ethics* provides that "social workers should not disclose identifying information when discussing clients with consultants unless the client has consented to disclosure of confidential information or there is a compelling need for such disclosure" (Standard 1.07(q)). Hilliard (1998) stated,

Often a consultation on a difficult issue is in keeping with the standard of care. Therapists do not have to reveal the identity of their patient in order to seek a consultation. Under these circumstances, no breach of confidentiality occurs. When it is necessary to reveal the identity of a patient for a consultation, the patient's permission is necessary. A note in the patient's chart that permission was granted is usually sufficient. In all cases, whether the patient's identity is or is not revealed, a note of the consultation should be made. (p. 53)

It is generally a good idea, at the outset of therapy, to inform the client that consultation may be obtained and to obtain permission.

In his book on legal issues in psychotherapy, Reid (1999) noted,

From the treater's or evaluator's point of view, when important doubts about assessment or care arise, there are almost always ways to reduce them, and one of the best is to get advice from a peer or subspecialist. You do not need the patient's permission to do this. I cringe when I hear a psychiatrist or psychotherapist try to convince a jury that he or she couldn't ask for a second opinion about a patient's suicidal behavior because of "confidentiality." No state, so far as I know, limits clinical consultation intended in the patient's interest. (p. 53)

Insurers

To the extent necessary to secure payment, client information may be released to insurers and other third-party payers (Brant & Brant, 1998). The professional should release only so much information as is necessary for payment. Sensitive therapy notes usually are not necessary for this purpose and should not be revealed. Behnke, Preis, and Bates (1998) advise that "a mental health professional should never release information to a third party payor over a patient's explicit objection; a patient retains the prerogative to pay out of pocket or to stop treatment" (p. 38).

The Patient-Litigant Exception to Privilege

Privileges do not apply when a client deliberately makes his or her mental or physical condition an issue in a lawsuit (see *Johnson v. Trujillo*, 1999; *Reda v. Advocate Health Care*, 2000). To use a simple illustration, suppose an individual consults a physician to treat a broken leg suffered in an auto accident. Later, the patient sues the other driver, seeking money for the leg injury. The patient has made the injury an issue in the case. The other driver has a right to subpoena the doctor and ask not only about the broken leg but also about what the patient

said to the doctor about the injury. Ordinarily, the physician-patient privilege would protect the patient's words. In this case, however, the patient made a legal issue of the injury, and the privilege is waived. This is the so-called "patient-litigant exception to privileges."

The patient-litigant exception to privilege sometimes arises in child custody litigation in family court. In custody battles, parents accuse each other of all sorts of things, from mild malfeasance to raging psychosis. A parent who claims that the other parent is mentally ill may subpoena privileged mental health records to prove the illness. Should the patient-litigant exception apply in this situation? To put the question differently: Does contesting custody place both parents' mental health in issue, waiving privileges? On one hand, the judge who decides the child's future needs to know as much as possible about the parents, and mental health records may shed valuable light. On the other hand, stripping away privilege could undermine therapy. There is no easy answer to this dilemma, and judges reach different decisions depending on the facts of each case. The New Jersey Supreme Court wrote that

most courts do not pierce the psychotherapist-patient privilege automatically in disputes over the best interests of the child, but may require disclosure only after careful balancing of the policies in favor of the privilege with the need for disclosure in the specific case before the court. (*Kinsella v. Kinsella*, 1997, p. 581; see also *Laznovsky v. Laznovsky*, 2000)

Subpoenas

The impact of a subpoena for confidential and privileged information is discussed elsewhere in this chapter.

Raw Psychological Test Data

Psychologists who administer psychological tests are aware of their ethical responsibility regarding release of raw test data. According to the "Ethical Principles of Psychologists and Code of Conduct" of the American Psychological Association (1992),

Psychologists refrain from misuse of assessment techniques, interventions, results, and interpretations and take reasonable steps to prevent others from misusing the information these techniques provide. This includes refraining from releasing raw test results or raw data to persons, other than to patients or clients as appropriate, who are not qualified to use such information. (Standard 2.02(b))

Raw psychological data include "standardized scores, including IQ's and percentiles," as well as "test scores, stimuli, and responses" (Tranel, 1994, pp. 34, 37). In some cases, the psychologist's ethical duty to protect raw data collides with a legal duty to disclose client information. Tranel (1994) analyzed such conflicts and offered practical advice:

> The APA Ethical Principles prohibit the release of raw data to unqualified individuals, and with rare exceptions, attorneys are not qualified individuals. A viable course of action if an attorney should request raw data from psychologist (A), would be to advise the attorney to engage the consultation of another psychologist (B), who is qualified, by virtue of licensure, training, and experience, to receive the data. Psychologist A then could send the raw data to Psychologist B (provided the client or patient has given appropriate consent). Psychologist B could then interpret the data to the attorney. Needless to say, Psychologist B must operate under the same rules and standards of ethics and confidentiality as Psychologist A. (p. 35)

Responding to Subpoenas

This section discusses subpoenas. Before defining *subpoena,* however, it is necessary to define another word, *process.* In law, process is the method courts use to assert their authority. A subpoena is one type of legal process. The person who delivers a subpoena is usually called a "process server" (i.e., process deliverer). In some cases, a subpoena is served by a law enforcement officer. Some subpoenas are served by mail.

There are two primary types of subpoenas: (a) a subpoena that requires a person to testify as a witness (called a subpoena *ad testificandum*) and (b) a subpoena that requires a person to produce records (called a subpoena *duces tecum*). Sometimes, a subpoena requires testimony *and* production of records. Subpoenas are used to compel attendance of witnesses and production of records in criminal cases, civil cases, juvenile court cases, and divorce and child custody proceedings. A subpoena may be issued by a judge, a court clerk, or, in many cases, an attorney.

Responding to a Subpoena

A subpoena is a court order and cannot be ignored. Disobedience of a subpoena can be punished as contempt of court. Although a subpoena cannot be ignored, neither should a subpoena be unthinkingly obeyed. Tranel (1994) stated that "psychologists need not automatically translate the serving of a subpoena into prompt acquiescence to legal demands without regard for the ethics of the matter" (p. 36). Some subpoenas, after all, are partially or completely invalid.

Before complying with a subpoena, consider the following:

Should I contact the client before I respond to a subpoena? A client cannot override a professional's duty to respond to a subpoena. Nevertheless, the client should be consulted before responding to a subpoena. If the client is a child, communicate with the child's parent or the adult with legal responsibility for the child. If the child is sufficiently mature, consult the child. If the child has an attorney, the attorney should be consulted.

When discussing a subpoena with a client or the client's attorney, describe what information has been requested through the subpoena and by whom. The client should understand what, if any, confidential information may be released. The client should also understand that the release of information that meets the requirements of a privilege such as the psychotherapist-patient privilege could jeopardize future application of the privilege. The client needs to know who will have access to released information and where the information will be stored. "Following such a discussion, a legally competent client or the client's legal guardian may choose to consent in writing to production of the data" (Committee on Legal Issues, 1996, p. 246). Getting the client's consent in writing "may avoid future conflicts or legal entanglements with the client over the release of confidential [information]" (Committee on Legal Issues, 1996, p. 246).

When the client is a child, the discussion described above typically takes place with an adult. The child's therapist owes it to the child to make sure the adult's decision about the subpoena is in the child's best interest.

As stated earlier, professionals cannot ignore subpoenas. Yet, blind obedience to subpoenas can cause problems. Consider the unusual case in which a psychologist was disciplined for *complying* with a subpoena (*Rost v. State Board of Psychology*, 1995). The psychologist supervised an unlicensed therapist who provided treatment to a child suffering chronic headaches. The headaches were allegedly caused by a fall at a community center. The child's mother sued the community center. Some time later, the attorney for the community center mailed a subpoena to the supervising psychologist requesting the child's treatment records. Without contacting the child, the child's mother, or the child's attorney, the psychologist gave the child's treatment records to the community center's attorney. Although the mother had previously given permission to disclose the child's records to the *child's* attorney, no permission had been given to disclose the records to anyone else. The state board of psychology disciplined the psychologist. The psychologist appealed to a court, but the judges agreed with the board of psychology. The judges wrote that the psychologist

> had a duty to either obtain written permission to release the records from [the child] or challenge the propriety of the subpoena before a judge. [The psychologist] did neither. Instead, she unilaterally gave [the child's] records to [the attorney for the community center] without consulting with [the child] or her attorney. (*Rost v. State Board of Psychology*, 1995, p. 629)

Moral of the story? Consult the client, the client's attorney, and, if you have an attorney, your attorney *before* responding to a subpoena.

Should I get legal advice? If you have any doubt about what to do, consult an attorney *before* you comply with a subpoena. Do not accept "legal" advice from someone who is not an attorney. If you work for a government agency, consult legal counsel for the agency. Hospitals and some clinics have an attorney on staff or on retainer. Professionals in private practice should retain an attorney, talk to an attorney they know, or contact their malpractice insurance carrier. Behnke et al. (1998) advise that

> it is wise to consult your malpractice carrier any time you testify, to determine whether

presence of a lawyer is indicated. If you receive a subpoena, be sure to check with your malpractice carrier and follow their advice on whether you should have legal representation. (p. 62)

If the child has an attorney, consult the child's attorney. In criminal cases, the prosecutor handling the child's case is sometimes a good source of information on responding to a subpoena. Keep in mind, however, that prosecutors are not always interested in protecting the confidentiality of records. Indeed, the prosecutor may wish to inspect the child's record. If the prosecutor does so, the defense attorney may have the right to do the same. In juvenile court cases, the attorney handling the child's case may be consulted. In many juvenile court cases, the child has an attorney of her or his own.

Professional organizations such as the American Psychological Association and the National Association of Social Workers dispense useful information. So do government agencies such as the State Board of Psychology. Generally speaking, however, these organizations and agencies do not give legal advice on specific cases.

Should I talk to the attorney who issued the subpoena? The one attorney who is not in a position to give objective advice about a subpoena is the attorney who issued the subpoena. Do not get the impression, however, that you should never talk to the attorney who issued the subpoena. Before doing so, get the client's consent. When the client is a child, obtain consent from the child's parent or the person with legal authority to consent. When the child is sufficiently mature, get the child's consent. If the child has an attorney, consult the attorney.

When you talk to the attorney who issued the subpoena, it is usually possible to avoid revealing confidential information. The Committee on Legal Issues (1996) of the American Psychological Association recommends that discussions with the attorney who issued the subpoena "explore whether there are ways to achieve the requesting party's objectives without divulging confidential information, for example, through disclosure of nonconfidential materials or submission of an affidavit by the psychologist disclosing nonconfidential information" (p. 246). In some cases, discussion between a therapist and an attorney helps the attorney realize that the therapist has nothing useful, and the subpoena is withdrawn. In other cases, discussion narrows the information requested.

What if my client does not want me to respond to the subpoena? As stated earlier, a client cannot override the duty to respond to a subpoena. At the same time, however, some subpoenas are invalid and can be resisted. For example, a subpoena may seek disclosure of information that is protected by the psychotherapist-patient privilege. A subpoena does *not* override this privilege. Sometimes, the client is too young to decide, yet the adults in the child's life are not making responsible decisions. What to do? If the client wants to resist the subpoena, or if resistance is in a child's best interest, the appropriate action is to file a motion in court to quash the subpoena. A motion to quash a subpoena may be filed by the child's attorney, a prosecutor, or the professional's attorney.

When a motion to quash is filed, a judge decides whether the subpoena is valid. The professional may have to testify at the hearing on the motion to quash. If the judge quashes the subpoena, the professional does not have to respond. The judge may decide, for example, that records sought by the subpoena are privileged. On the other hand, if the judge rules that the subpoena is valid, the professional must comply or risk being held in contempt of court.

Instead of a motion to quash, the Committee on Legal Issues (1996) of the American Psychological Association suggests that the professional may wish to write to the judge, sending a copy of the letter to the lawyers. The committee stated,

> The simplest way of proceeding, and perhaps the least costly, may be for the psychologist (or his or her attorney) to write a letter to the court, with a copy to the attorneys for both parties, stating that the psychologist wishes to comply with the law but that he or she is ethically obligated not to produce the confidential records or test data or to testify about them unless compelled to do so by the court or with the consent of the client. In writing such a letter, the psychologist (or his or her lawyer) may request that the court consider the psychologist's obligations to protect the interests of the client, the interests of third parties (e.g., test publishers or others), and the interests of the public in preserving the integrity and continued validity of the tests themselves. This letter may help sensitize the court about the potential adverse effects of dissemination. The letter might also attempt

to provide suggestions, such as the following, to the court on ways to minimize the adverse consequences of disclosure if the court is inclined to require production at all:

1. Suggest that, at most, the court direct the psychologist to provide test data only to another appropriately qualified psychologist designated by the court or by the party seeking such information.

2. Suggest that the court limit the use of client records or test data to prevent wide dissemination. For example, the court might order that the information be delivered, be kept under seal, and be used solely for the purposes of the litigation and that all copies of the data be returned to the psychologist under seal after the litigation is terminated. The order might also provide that the requester may not provide the information to any third parties.

3. Suggest that the court limit the categories of information that must be produced. For example, client records may contain confidential information about a third party, such as a spouse, who may have independent interests in maintaining confidentiality, and such data may be of minimal or no relevance to the issues before the court. The court should limit its production order to exclude such information.

4. Suggest that the court determine for itself, through in camera proceedings (i.e., a nonpublic hearing or a review by the judge in chambers), whether the use of the client records or test data is relevant to the issue before the court or whether it might be insulated from disclosure, in whole or in part, by the therapist-client privilege or another privilege. (p. 247)

What if my client receives a subpoena and calls me for advice? Needless to say, mental health and medical professionals do not give legal advice. For legal advice, the client is referred to a lawyer. The professional may work with the lawyer. Of course, the professional helps the client deal with the psychological aspects of testifying.

Verbal Evidence of Abuse: Hearsay

A child's statements to professionals, parents, and others may be powerful evidence of abuse. Yet, such statements are hearsay and cannot be repeated in court unless an exception to the rule against hearsay applies. Although there are numerous exceptions to the hearsay rule, only four play a day-to-day role in child abuse cases: (a) the excited utterance exception, (b) the medical diagnosis or treatment exception, (c) the exception for prior consistent statements, and (d) the child hearsay exception.

Excited Utterance Exception

An excited utterance is a hearsay statement that relates to a startling or traumatic event. To be admissible in court, the excited utterance must be made while the child is still upset. To determine whether the child was sufficiently upset, the judge considers the following:

1. *Nature of the event.* The more startling and traumatic the event, the more likely a child's statement describing the event is an excited utterance.
2. *Lapse of time.* The more time that goes by between the startling event and the child's statement relating to the event, the less likely the statement qualifies.
3. *Emotional and physical condition.* If the child is upset, crying, or in pain when the statement is made, the odds increase that it is an excited utterance. On the other hand, if the child is calm, the odds decrease.
4. *Speech pattern.* The way the child speaks may indicate excitement. The words themselves may evidence excitement.
5. *Spontaneity and questioning.* The more spontaneous the child's statement, the more likely it is an excited utterance. Open-ended questions such as "What happened?" do not destroy spontaneity. As questions become suggestive, spontaneity may suffer.

Medical Diagnosis or Treatment Exception

Most states have an exception to the hearsay rule for certain statements to professionals providing diagnostic or treatment services. This exception includes statements of medical history, past and present symptoms, pain, and the cause of injury or illness. The exception applies to statements to medical professionals such as nurses and physicians. In most states, the exception applies to statements to mental health professionals.

To increase the probability that the medical diagnosis or treatment exception applies, professionals should document the following: (a) the child's understanding of the clinical purpose of the interview or examination, (b) the child's awareness of the importance of providing accurate and complete information, (c) why information provided by the child is pertinent to diagnosis or treatment, and (d) if the child identifies the perpetrator, why knowing identity is pertinent to the ability to treat or diagnose the child.

Child Hearsay Exception

Most states have a hearsay exception for reliable statements that do not meet the requirements of traditional exceptions such as excited utterances and statements for medical diagnosis or treatment. The key issue under the child hearsay exception is reliability. Document anything that sheds light on reliability, including the following:

1. *Spontaneity and questioning.* The more spontaneous the child's statement, the better. Spontaneity is related to the suggestiveness of questioning.
2. *Consistency.* Consistency within and across interviews is a barometer of reliability, although complete consistency is not required.
3. *Developmentally unusual sexual knowledge.* Young children lack the knowledge to fabricate detailed and anatomically correct accounts of sexual acts (see Chapter 19, this volume). Of course, care is taken to rule out alternative explanations for a child's developmentally unusual sexual knowledge.
4. *Motive to lie.* Does the child or an adult have a motive to lie?

Prior Consistent Statements

When a child testifies, the defense may cross-examine the child to undermine the child's credibility. When the cross-examiner's questions leave the impression that the child's testimony is fabricated, the judge may allow adults to describe the child's earlier statements that are consistent with the child's testimony in court.

Documentation

Professionals who interview and treat children should do two things: First, professionals should record children's hearsay statements. Do not paraphrase. Exact quotes are preferred. In addition to recording the child's words, it is important to document the questions that elicited the child's statements. Second, professionals should document the factors judges use to determine whether children's hearsay statements meet the requirements of an exception to the rule against hearsay. The Verbal Evidence Checklist provided in Figure 16.1 can be used to document the necessary information.

Conclusion

Child abuse and neglect are complex problems requiring complex solutions. The past 30 years have taught us that no single profession has all the answers. Interdisciplinary cooperation is indispensable. Yet, professional jealously and narrow-mindedness ("My way is the best way") are facts of life. To bridge the gap between professions, we need to "sit around the same fire," spend time with each other, and learn about each other. Greater understanding leads to greater appreciation. It is hoped that this chapter sheds a little light on the legal system for readers who had the good sense not to go to law school.

Child's Name: Date: Your Name: Case No.:

____ Document your questions. Don't paraphrase.

____ Document child's *exact* words. Don't paraphrase.

____ Did child tell anyone else? Who? When? Why? What?

All Professionals Document:

____ *What happened?* According to the child, what happened?

____ *Elapsed time:* How much time elapsed between the event and the child's description? (Be precise; minutes count)

____ *Emotional condition:* Child's emotional condition when child described what happened. (Crying? Upset? Calm? Excited? Traumatized?)

____ *Physical condition:* Was child hurt, injured, in pain?

____ *Spontaneous?* Was the child's description spontaneous?

____ *Consistency:* If child described the event more than once, are there consistencies across descriptions?

____ *Developmentally unusual sexual knowledge or conduct:* Document any developmentally unusual sexual knowledge or behavior, including idiosyncratic details (e.g., smells or tastes).

____ *Motive to lie:* Does anyone—child or adult—have a motive to lie?

____ *Reliability:* Document **anything** that sheds light on the reliability of the child's statement.

Ask Questions About and Document:

____ Child's memory for simple events (e.g., Breakfast this morning? What was on TV today?)

____ Child's ability to communicate.

____ Child's understanding of the difference between the truth and lies. *Don't* ask children under age 9 to define "truth" and "lie." *Don't* ask kids to give examples of truth or lies. *Don't* ask kids to explain the difference between a truth and a lie. *Do* give simple examples of something that is true and something that is a lie. Then ask the child to identify which it is. (e.g., Hold up a blue pen and say "If someone said this is red, would that be the truth or a lie?" Or, "If someone said this is blue, would that be the truth or a lie?")

____ Child's understanding of the importance of telling the truth to you.

Clinical Professionals Providing Medical or Psychological Diagnosis or Treatment

____ Inform child of your clinical purpose. (e.g., "I'm going to give you a checkup to make sure you are healthy." "My job is talking to kids to help them with their problems.")

____ Inform child of the clinical reasons why it is important for the child to tell the truth to you. (e.g., "I need you to tell me only true things, only things that really happened. I need you to tell me only true things so I can help you.")

____ Document anything indicating the child understood your clinical role, the clinical nature of what you did or said, and why it was clinically important for the child to tell the truth to you.

____ Document why what the child told you was pertinent to your ability to diagnose or treat the child.

____ If child identified the perpetrator, document why knowing identity was pertinent to your ability to diagnose or treat the child.

Figure 16.1. Verbal Evidence Checklist
SOURCE: Copyright © by John E. B. Myers. Permission is given to copy and distribute this checklist.

References

American Professional Society on the Abuse of Children (APSAC). (1997). *Code of ethics*. Chicago: Author.

American Psychological Association. (1992). Ethical principles of psychologists and code of conduct. *American Psychologist, 47,* 1597-1611.

Appelbaum, P. S., & Greer, A. (1993). Confidentiality in group therapy. *Law and Psychiatry, 44,* 311-312.

Barry v. Turek, 267 Cal. Rptr. 553 (Ct. App. 1990).

Behnke, S. H., Preis, J., & Bates, R. T. (1998). *The essentials of California mental health law: A straightforward guide for clinicians of all disciplines.* New York: Norton.

Bennett, B. E., Bryant, B. K., VandenBos, G. R., & Greenwood, A. (1990). *Professional liability and risk management.* Washington, DC: American Psychological Association.

Bradley v. Ray, 904 S. W. 2d 302 (Mo. Ct. App. 1995).

Brant, R. T., & Brant, J. (1998). Child and adolescent therapy. In L. E. Lifson & R. I. Simon (Eds.), *The mental health practitioner and the law: A comprehensive handbook.* Cambridge, MA: Harvard University Press.

Cleary, E. W. (Ed.). (1984). *McCormick on evidence* (3rd ed.). St. Paul, MN: West.

Committee on Legal Issues, American Psychological Association. (1996). Strategies for private practitioners coping with subpoenas or compelled testimony for client records or test data. *Professional Psychology: Research and Practice, 27,* 245-251.

Emerich v. Philadelphia Center for Human Development, 720 A. 2d 1032 (Pa. 1998).

Estate of Morgan, 673 N. E. 2d 1131 (Ohio 1997).

Fox, S. J. (1996). The early history of the court. *Future of Children, 6,* 29-39.

Gritzner v. Michael R., 611 N. W. 2d 906 (Wis. 2000).

Gutheil, T. G., & Appelbaum, P. S. (1982). *Clinical handbook of psychiatry and law.* New York: McGraw-Hill.

Hilliard, J. (1998). Liability issues with managed care. In L. E. Lifson & R. I. Simon (Eds.), *The mental health practitioner and the law: A comprehensive handbook* (pp. 50-53). Cambridge, MA: Harvard University Press.

Hurley, T. (1907). *Origin of the Illinois juvenile court law* (3rd ed.). Chicago: Visitation and Aid Society.

In re C. B., 2000 WL 76338 (Iowa 2000).

In re Winship, 397 U.S. 358 (1970).

Johnson v. Trujillo, 977 P. 2d 152 (Colo. 1999).

Kalichman, S. C. (1999). *Mandated reporting of suspected child abuse: Ethics, law, & policy* (2nd ed.). Washington, DC: American Psychological Association.

Kaufman, M. (1991). Post-*Tarasoff* legal developments and the mental health literature. *Bulletin of the Menninger Clinic, 55,* 308-322.

Kinsella v. Kinsella, 696 A. 2d 556 (N.J. 1997).

Lake, P. F. (1994). Revisiting *Tarasoff. Albany Law Review, 58,* 97-173.

Laznovsky v. Laznovsky, 745 A. 2d 1054 (Md. 2000).

Leong, G. B., Eth, S., & Silva, J. A. (1992). The psychotherapist as witness for the prosecution: The criminalization of *Tarasoff. American Journal of Psychiatry, 149,* 1001-1015.

Leong, G. B., Eth, S., & Silva, J. A. (1994). Silence or death: The limit of confidentiality is threatened by the patient. *Journal of Psychiatry and Law, 22,* 235-244.

Lilly, G. C. (1996). *An introduction to the law of evidence* (3rd ed.). St. Paul, MN: West.

Lyon, T. D. (2000). Child witnesses and the oath: Empirical evidence. *Southern California Law Review, 73,* 1017-1074.

Lyon, T. D., & Saywitz, K. J. (1999). Young maltreated children's competence to take the oath. *Applied Developmental Science, 3,* 16-27.

Mack, J. W. (1909). The juvenile court. *Harvard Law Review, 23,* 104-122.

Menendez v. Superior Court, 834 P. 2d 786 (Cal. 1992).

Myers, J. E. B. (1997). *A mother's nightmare—incest: A practical legal guide for parents and professionals.* Thousand Oaks, CA: Sage.

Myers, J. E. B. (1997). *Evidence in child abuse and neglect cases* (3rd ed.). New York: Aspen Law and Business.

Myers, J. E. B. (1998). *Legal issues in child abuse and neglect practice* (2nd ed.). Thousand Oaks, CA: Sage.

Myers, J. E. B. (2001). Legal issues. In M. Winterstein & S. R. Scribner (Eds.), *Mental health care for child crime victims: Standards of care task force guidelines*. Sacramento: California Victim Compensation and Government Claims Board, Victims of Crime Program.

National Association of Social Workers. (1997). *Code of ethics*. Washington, DC: Author.

O'Malley, K. F., Grenig, J. E., & Lee, W. C. (2000). *Federal jury practice and instructions* (5th ed.). St. Paul, MN: West.

Pennsylvania v. Ritchie, 480 U.S. 39 (1987).

People v. Hammon, 938 P. 2d 986 (Cal. 1997).

Reda v. Advocate Health Care, 738 N. E. 2d 153 (Ill. Ct. App. 2000).

Reid, W. H. (1999). *A clinician's guide to legal issues in psychotherapy: Or proceed with caution*. Phoenix, AZ: Zeig, Tucker & Co.

Roback, H. B., Moore, R. F., Waterhouse, G. J., & Martin, P. R. (1996). Confidentiality dilemmas in group psychotherapy with substance-dependent physicians. *American Journal of Psychiatry, 153,* 125-126.

Rost v. State Board of Psychology, 659 A. 2d 626 (Pa. Commonwealth Ct. 1995).

Runyon v. Smith, 730 A. 2d 881 (N.J. Super. App. Div. 1999), *aff'd,* 749 A. 2d 852 (N.J. 2000).

Sagatun, I. J., & Edwards, L. P. (1995). *Child abuse and the legal system*. Chicago: Nelson-Hall.

Stern, P. (1997). *Preparing and presenting expert testimony in child abuse litigation: A guide for expert witnesses and attorneys*. Thousand Oaks, CA: Sage.

Tarasoff v. Regents of the University of California, 551 P. 2d 334 (Cal. 1976).

Thompson v. County of Alameda, 614 P. 2d 728 (Cal. 1980).

Tranel, D. (1994). The release of psychological data to nonexperts: Ethical and legal considerations. *Professional Psychology: Research and Practice, 25,* 33-38.

Wigmore, J. H. (1974). *Evidence in trials at common law*. Boston: Little, Brown. (Original work published 1904)

17

Criminal Investigation of Sexual Victimization of Children

KENNETH V. LANNING

Overview

The goal of this chapter is to describe the investigational process in language understandable to a multidisciplinary audience. It is not intended as a detailed, step-by-step investigative manual, nor does it offer rigid standards for investigation of child sexual abuse cases. The material presented here may not be applicable to every case or circumstance. Many real-world constraints, including lack of time and personnel, make following all the steps discussed here impossible. In the interest of readability, children alleging abuse or who are suspected of being abused will sometimes be referred to as "victims," even though their victimization may not have been proven. This shorthand should not blur the fact that investigators are expected to maintain complete objectivity.

The information in this chapter and its application are based on my education, training, and more than 27 years of experi-

ence studying the criminal aspects of deviant sexual behavior and interacting with investigators and prosecutors. Its legal acceptance and application, however, must be carefully evaluated by investigators and prosecutors based on departmental policy, rules of evidence, and current case law. This chapter is not intended to be a precise legal analysis with technical legal definitions. The use of terms also used in mental health (e.g., pedophilia) is not meant to imply a psychiatric diagnosis or lack of legal responsibility.

It commonly is accepted that child sexual abuse is a complex problem requiring the efforts and coordination of many agencies and disciplines. No one agency or discipline possesses the personnel, resources, training, skills, or legal mandate to deal effectively with every aspect of child maltreatment. In this context, law enforcement interacts with a variety of professions and agencies during the investigation process. For example, some offenders cross jurisdictional boundaries, and many violate a variety of laws when abusing children. This often will mean working with other local, state, and federal law enforcement agencies in multijurisdictional investigative teams and with prosecutors, social services, and victim assistance in multidisciplinary teams. This can be done as part of informal networking or as part of a formal task force.

The multidisciplinary approach not only is advantageous in avoiding duplication and making cases but also is in the best interests of the child victim. It may minimize the number of interviews and court appearances and provide the victim with needed support. The team approach also can help investigators to deal with the stress and isolation of this work by providing peer support. The multidisciplinary approach is mandated statutorily or authorized in the majority of states and under federal law (U.S. Department of Justice, 1993).

Working together as part of a multidisciplinary team means coordination, not abdication. Each discipline performs a function for which it has specific resources, training, and experience. Although each discipline must understand how its role contributes to the team approach, it is equally important that it understands the respective responsibilities and limitations of that role. For example, child protection agencies usually do not get involved in cases in which the alleged perpetrator is not a parent or caretaker.

The team approach is a two-way street. Just as medical and psychological professionals are charged with evaluating and treating the abused or neglected child, law enforcement investigators are responsible for conducting criminal investigations. Just as law enforcement officers need to be concerned that their investigation might further traumatize a child victim, therapists and physicians need to be concerned that their treatment techniques might hinder the investigation.

The Law Enforcement Perspective

The law enforcement perspective deals with criminal activity and legally defensible fact finding. Therefore, the process must focus more on admissible evidence of *what* happened than on emotional belief that *something* happened, more on the accuracy

than on the existence of a memory, more on objective than on subjective reality, and more on neutral investigation than on child advocacy.

In their desire to convince society that child sexual abuse exists and children rarely lie about it, some professionals interpret efforts to seek corroboration for alleged abuse as a sign of denial or disbelief. Corroboration, however, is essential. When the only evidence offered is the word of a child against the word of an adult, child sexual abuse can be difficult to prove in a court of law. Moreover, many factors combine to make testifying in court difficult and possibly traumatic for children (see Chapter 18, this volume, for a fuller discussion of this issue). Despite some recent advances that make such testimony easier for the child victim or witness, a primary objective of every law enforcement investigation of child sexual abuse and exploitation should be to prove a valid case without child victim testimony in court. More often than many investigators realize, there *is* corroborative evidence. It is not the job of law enforcement officers to believe a child or any other victim or witness. Instead, law enforcement must listen, assess and evaluate, and then attempt to corroborate any and all aspects of a victim's statement. Obviously, in a valid case, the best and easiest way to avoid child victim testimony in court is to build a case that is so strong that the offender pleads guilty. Failing that, most children can testify in court if necessary.

Emotion Versus Reason

Regardless of intelligence and education and often despite evidence to the contrary, adults tend to believe what they want or need to believe. The greater the need, the greater the tendency. The extremely sensitive and emotional nature of child sexual abuse makes this phenomenon a potential problem in these cases. Investigators must evaluate this tendency in other interveners and minimize it in themselves by trying to do their job in a rational, professional manner.

To be effective interviewers, investigators must be both aware of and in control of their own feelings and beliefs about victims and offenders of child sexual abuse. Americans tend to have stereotypical concepts of the innocence of children and the malevolence of those who sexually victimize them. Most investigators now know that a child molester can look like anyone else and may even be someone we know and like. The stereotype of the child victim as a completely innocent little girl, however, is still prevalent and is unlikely to be addressed by laypeople and even by professionals. In reality, child victims of sexual abuse and exploitation can be boys as well as girls, and not all victims are "angels" or even "little." The idea that some children might enjoy some sexual activity or behave like human beings and engage in sexual acts as a way of receiving attention, affection, gifts, and money is troubling for society and for many investigators.

Before beginning an interview, the investigator must understand that the victim may have many positive feelings for the offender and may even resent law enforcement intervention. The investigator must be able to discuss a wide variety of sexual activities, understand the victim's terminology, and avoid being judgmental. Not being judgmental is much more difficult with a delinquent adolescent engaged in homosexual activity with a prominent clergyman than with a sweet 5-year-old girl abused by her "low-life" father. Investigators often nonverbally communicate their judgmental attitude through gestures, facial expressions, and body language. Some investigators do a poor job of interviewing children because deep down inside they really do not want to hear the answers.

Another emotion-related problem that occurs during subject and suspect interviews is the inability of some investigators to control or conceal their anger and outrage at the offender's behavior. They often want to spend as little time as possible with the offender. Occasionally, investigators have the opposite problem and are confused that they have sympathetic feelings for the offender. Many investigators also find it difficult to discuss deviant sexual behavior calmly, nonjudgmentally, and in detail with anyone, much less an alleged child molester.

An officer who gets too emotionally involved in a case is more likely to make mistakes and errors in judgment. He or she might wind up losing a case and allowing a child molester to go free because the defendant's rights were violated in some way. The officer is also less likely to interview and assess a child victim properly and objectively. Investigators must learn to recognize and control these feelings. If they cannot, they should not be assigned to child sexual abuse cases or, at least, not to the interview phase.

Maligned Investigator

Any law enforcement officer assigned to the investigation of child sexual abuse should be a volunteer, even if reluctant at first, who has been carefully selected and trained in this highly specialized work. This kind of work is not for everyone. Investigators must decide for themselves if they can deal with it. Just as important, the investigators working these cases must monitor themselves continually. The strong emotional reactions evoked by this work and the isolation and prejudice to which they may expose the investigator can make this work "toxic" psychologically and socially.

Police officers investigating the sexual victimization of children must learn to cope with the residual stigma within law enforcement attached to sex crime and child sexual abuse investigation. Because there is so much ignorance about sex in general and deviant sexual behavior specifically, fellow officers frequently joke about sex crime and vice investigators. This phenomenon is often most problematic for officers working child sexual abuse cases, especially in medium or small departments. Investigators frequently become isolated from their peer group because fellow officers do not want to hear about child sexual abuse. This is a problem that supervisors as well as individual investigators must recognize and address. Investigators must be alert to the early warning signs of overexposure or stress. By using appropriate humor, limiting exposure, maintaining good physical fitness, nurturing and seeking peer support, and feeling a sense of self-accomplishment, the investigator can turn a job perceived as "dirty" into a rewarding assignment (Lanning & Hazelwood, 2001).

The "Big-Picture" Approach

Law enforcement officers must recognize that the sexual victimization of children involves more than father-daughter incest. The sexual victimization of children involves varied and diverse dynamics. Types of cases investigated can range from one-on-one intrafamilial abuse to multioffender/ multivictim extrafamilial sex rings and from stranger abduction of toddlers to prostitution of teenagers (Lanning, 1992b). The child victim can range in age from birth to almost 18 years of age. Cases also may involve the interview and investigation of allegations from adult survivors reporting delayed memories of sexual abuse. Although this chapter cannot cover in detail the investigation of all types of cases, it can serve to alert investigators to the "big-picture" approach to the sexual victimization of children. Rather than focusing only on one act by one offender against one victim on one day, investigators also must consider offender typologies, patterns of behavior, multiple acts, multiple victims, child pornography, proactive techniques, and so on.

The big-picture approach starts with recognizing four basic but often ignored facts about child molesters:

1. Child molesters sometimes molest multiple victims.
2. Intrafamilial child molesters sometimes molest children outside their families.
3. Sex offenders against adults sometimes molest children.
4. Other criminals sometimes molest children.

These elements are not always present or even usually present; nevertheless, their possibility must be incorporated into the investigative strategy. Neat categories of offenders and crime are, unfortunately, often ignored by offenders. A window peeper, an exhibitionist, or a rapist also can be a child molester. "Regular" criminals also can be child molesters. A child molester put on the FBI "Ten Most-Wanted" list was later arrested for burglarizing a service station. Although most professionals now recognize that an intrafamilial child molester might victimize children outside his or her family and that identifying other victims can be an effective way to corroborate an allegation by one victim, few seem to incorporate a search for additional victims into their investigative approaches.

In numerous cases, offenders have operated for many years after first being identified because no one took the big-picture approach. Convicting a child molester who is a "pillar of the community" is almost impossible based only on the testimony of one confused 5-year-old girl or one delinquent adolescent boy. To stop the offender, law enforcement must be willing to evaluate the allegation, do background investigation, document patterns of behavior, review records, identify other acts and victims, and, as soon as possible, develop probable cause for a search warrant. Simply interviewing the child (or obtaining the results of someone else's interview), asking the offender if he did it, polygraphing him, and then closing the case does not constitute a thorough investigation and is certainly not consistent with the big-picture approach.

The big-picture investigative process consists of three phases: (a) interview, (b) assess and evaluate, and (c) corroborate. These three phases do not always happen in this sequence and even may occur simultaneously.

Interview

A detailed discussion of the latest research and techniques for interviewing children is contained in Chapter 18 (this volume). Therefore, only the law enforcement perspective of child victim interviewing and some general guidelines will be discussed here.

Law Enforcement Role

For some, the criminal investigation of child sexual abuse has evolved into using newly acquired interviewing skills to get children to communicate and then believing whatever they say. For others, it has become letting someone else do the interview and then blindly accepting the interviewer's opinions and assessments. Law enforcement officers should take advantage of the skills and expertise of other disciplines in the interviewing process. If the primary purpose of an interview of a child is to gain investigative information, however, law enforcement must be involved. This involvement can range from actually doing the interview to carefully monitoring the process. Although there is nothing wrong with admitting shortcomings and seeking help, law enforcement should *never* abdicate its control over the investigative interview.

The solution to the problem of poorly trained investigators is better training, not therapists and physicians independently conducting investigative interviews. Even if, for good reasons, an investigative interview is conducted by or with a social worker or therapist, law enforcement must be in control.

The Disclosure Continuum

Before applying interviewing research, training, and skills, investigators first must attempt to determine where the child is on the disclosure continuum. This determination is essential to developing a proper interview approach that maximizes the amount of legally defensible information and minimizes allegations of leading and suggestive questioning. The disclosure process is set forth as a continuum because there can be many variations, combinations, and changes in situations involving the disclosure status of child victims. Training material and presentations often fail to consider and emphasize the determination of this disclosure status prior to conducting a child victim interview.

1. At one end of the continuum are children who already have made voluntary and full disclosures to one or more people. These are generally the easiest children to interview. The child has made the decision to disclose and has done so at least once. It is, of course, important to determine the length of time between the abuse and the disclosure.

2. At another point along the continuum are children who have voluntarily decided to disclose but it appears have made incomplete or partial reports. For understandable reasons, some children fail to reveal the full story, minimize, or even deny all or part of their victimization; however, not every child who reports sexual abuse has more details not yet revealed.

3. Further down the continuum are children whose abuse was discovered rather than disclosed (e.g., medical evidence of abuse; recovered child pornography). These interviews can be more difficult because the child has not decided to report and may not be ready to make a statement. They also can be easier, however, because the investigator knows with some degree of certainty that the child was abused. The interview can now focus more on determining additional details.

4. At the far end of the continuum are children whose abuse is only suspected. These may be the most difficult, complex, and sensitive interviews. The investigator must weigh a child's understandable reluctance to talk about sexual abuse against the possibility that the child was not abused. The need to protect the child must be balanced with concern about leading or suggestive questioning.

Establishing Rapport and Clarifying Terms

The interviewer's first task, with any age child, is to establish rapport. Investigators should ask primarily open-ended questions that encourage narrative responses. It is hoped that this will set the stage for more valid responses to investigative questions that follow.

Part of developing rapport is to subtly communicate the message that the child is not at fault. Victims need to understand that they are not responsible even though they did not say no, did not fight, actively cooperated, did not tell, accepted gifts and money, or even enjoyed the sexual activity. If they think they are going to be judged, some children may exaggerate their victimization by alleging threats and force that did not occur to make the crime more socially acceptable. When the victim comes to believe that the investigator understands, he or she is more likely to talk.

Although many of the same interview principles apply to the interview of adolescent victims, it can be far more difficult to develop rapport with a streetwise 13-year-old boy than with an appealing 5-year-old girl. The investigator must recognize and sometimes allow the child to use face-saving scenarios when revealing victimization. For example, victims might claim they were drugged, or drunk, or forced into a car when they were not. These face-saving devices are used most often by adolescents, who pose special challenges for the interviewer.

Another critical task in the interview is to clarify the suspected victim's terminology for various body parts and sexual activities. If this clarification is not achieved, misunderstanding can occur. Although it is just as important to find out exactly what the adolescent victim means by the terms he or she uses for sexual activity, terms such as "head job" and "rim job" are not as readily acceptable as the 5-year-old's "pee-pee" and "nina."

The interview of an adolescent boy can be extremely difficult. The stigma of homosexuality and the embarrassment over victimization greatly increase the likelihood that the boy victim will deny or misrepresent the sexual activity. Even if such a victim discloses, the information may be incomplete, minimizing the boy's involvement and responsibility and, in some cases, exaggerating the offender's.

Videotaping

The taping of victim interviews was once thought to be the ultimate solution to many of the problems involving child victim interviews and testimony. Many legislatures rushed to pass special laws allowing it. Aside from the constitutional issues, *there are advantages and disadvantages to videotaping or audiotaping child victims' statements.*

The advantages include the following:

1. knowing exactly what was asked and answered,
2. the potential ability to reduce the number of interviews,
3. the visual impact of a videotaped statement,
4. the ability to deal with recanting or changing statements,
5. the potential to induce a confession when played for an offender who truly cares for the child victim.

The disadvantages include the following:

1. An artificial setting is created when people "play" to the camera instead of concentrating on communicating.
2. The investigator must determine which interviews to record and explain variations between them.
3. Tapes must be accounted for after the investigation. Copies are sometimes furnished with little control to defense attorneys and expert witnesses. Many are played at training conferences without concealing the identity of victims.
4. Because there are conflicting criteria on how to conduct such an interview, each tape is subject to interpretation and criticism by "experts."

Many experts now feel that child victim interviews must be videotaped to be assessed and evaluated properly. Some judges and courts now require videotaping of child victim interviews. Many people in favor of taping argue, "If you are doing it right, what do you have to hide?" When you videotape a victim interview, however, you create a piece of evidence that did not previously exist, and that evidence can becomes the target of a great deal of highly subjective scrutiny. Every word, inflection, gesture, and movement becomes the focus of attention rather than whether or not the child was molested. Unreliable information and false denials can be obtained even from "perfect" interviews, and reliable information and valid disclosures can be obtained even from highly imperfect interviews. This fact can be lost in excessive focus on how the interview is conducted. This in no way denies the fact that repetitive, suggestive, or leading interviews are real problems and can produce false or inaccurate information.

Many videotaping advocates do not seem to recognize the wide diversity of circumstances and dynamics comprising sexual victimization of children cases. Interviewing a 12-year-old boy who you only suspect may have been molested by his coach is far different from interviewing a 9-year-old girl who has disclosed having been sexually abused by her father. Interviewing a runaway 15-year-old inner-city street prostitute is far different from interviewing a middle-class 5-year-old kidnapped from her backyard by a child molester. Interviewing a Native American child in a hogan without electricity on a remote reservation is far different from interviewing a White child in a specially designed interview room at a child advocacy center in a wealthy suburb. In addition, videotape equipment can be expensive, and it can and does malfunction.

Many experienced child sexual abuse prosecutors oppose the taping of child victim statements, although special circumstances may alter this opinion on a case-by-case basis. One such special situation might be the interview of children younger than age 6. Departments should be careful of written policies concerning taping. It is potentially embarrassing and damaging to have to admit in court that you usually tape such interviews but you did not in this case. It is better to be able to say that you usually do not tape such interviews, but you did in a certain case because of some special circumstances you can articulate. In this controversy over videotaping, investigators should be guided by their prosecutors' expertise and preferences, legal or judicial requirements, and their own common sense.

Although some of the disadvantages can be reduced if the tapes are made during the medical evaluation, it is my opinion that the disadvantages of taping generally outweigh the advantages.

General Rules and Cautions

Investigative interviews always should be conducted with an open mind and the assumption that there are multiple hypotheses or explanations for what is being described or alleged. Investigative interviews should emphasize open-ended, age-appropriate questions that are designed to elicit narrative accounts of events. All investigative interaction with victims must be documented carefully and thoroughly.

The interview of an alleged or potential child victim as part of a criminal investigation should be conducted as quickly as possible. It is important to interview as many potential victims as is legally and ethically possible. This is especially important in cases involving adolescent boy victims, most of whom will deny their victimization no matter what the investigator does. Unfortunately for victims, but fortunately for the investigative corroboration, men who victimize adolescent boys appear to be among the most persistent and prolific of all child molesters (Abel et al., 1987). The small percentage of their victims who disclose still may constitute a significant number of victims.

The investigation of allegations of recent activity from multiple young children should begin quickly, with interviews of all potential victims being completed as soon as possible. The investigation of adult survivors' allegations of activity 10 or more years earlier presents other problems and should proceed, unless victims are at immediate risk, more deliberately with gradually increasing resources as corroborated facts warrant. Children rarely get the undivided attention of adults, even their parents, for a long period of time. Investigators must be cautious about subtly rewarding a child by allowing this attention to continue only in return for furnishing additional details. The investigator should make sure this necessary attention is unconditional.

Interviews of young children under age 6 are potentially problematic and should be done by investigators trained and experienced in such interviews. Because suggestibility is potentially a bigger problem in younger children, the assessment and evaluation phase is especially important in cases

involving these young victims, and videotaping is more justified.

Assess and Evaluate

Assessing the validity of a child sexual abuse report is an essential component of a complete investigation. Is the victim describing events and activities that are consistent with law enforcement-documented criminal behavior, or are they more consistent with distorted media accounts and erroneous public perceptions of criminal behavior? Investigators should apply the "template of probability." Accounts of child sexual victimization that are more like books, television, and movies (e.g., big conspiracies, child sex slaves, organized pornography rings) and less like documented cases should be viewed with skepticism but still *thoroughly investigated.* It is the investigator's job to consider and investigate all possible explanations of events. In addition, the information learned will be invaluable in counteracting the defense attorneys when they raise alternative explanations.

The so-called "backlash" has had both a positive and negative impact on the investigation and prosecution of child sexual abuse cases. In a positive way, it has reminded criminal justice interveners of the need to do their jobs in a more professional, objective, and fact-finding manner. Most of the damage caused by the backlash actually is self-inflicted by well-intentioned child advocates. In a negative way, it has cast a shadow over the validity and reality of child sexual abuse and has influenced some to avoid properly pursuing cases.

For many years, the statement, "Children never lie about sexual abuse. If they have the details, it must have happened," was rarely questioned or debated at training conferences. During the 1970s, there was a successful crusade to eliminate laws requiring corroboration of child victim statements in child sexual abuse cases. It was believed that the way to convict child molesters was to have the child victims testify in court. If we believe, them, the jury will believe them. Any challenge to this basic premise was viewed as a threat to the progress made and a denial that the problem existed. Both parts of this statement—"Children never lie about sexual abuse" and "If they have the details, it must have happened"—are receiving much-needed reexamination today—a process that is critical to the investigator's task of assessing and evaluating the alleged victim's statements.

"Children Never Lie"

The available evidence suggests that children rarely lie about sexual abuse, if a lie is defined as a statement deliberately and maliciously intended to deceive. If children in sexual victimization cases do lie, it may be because factors such as shame or embarrassment over the nature of the victimization increase the likelihood that they misrepresent the sexual activity. Seduced victims sometimes lie to make their victimization more socially acceptable or to please an adult. Occasionally, children lie because they are angry and want to get revenge on somebody. Some children, sadly, lie about sexual victimization to get attention and forgiveness. A few children may even lie to get money or as part of a lawsuit. This can sometimes be influenced by pressure from their parents. Objective investigators must consider and evaluate all these possibilities. It is extremely important to recognize, however, that because children might lie about part of their victimization does not mean that the entire allegation is necessarily a lie and they are not victims. Sexual victimization of children cases often involve complex dynamics and numerous incidents that often make it difficult to say "it" is all true or all false.

In addition, just because a child is not lying does not mean he or she is making an accurate statement. Children might be telling you what they have come to believe happened to them, even though it might not be literally true. Other than lying, there are many possible alternative explanations for why victims might allege things that do not seem to be accurate:

- The child might be exhibiting distortions in traumatic memory.
- The child's account might reflect normal childhood fears and fantasy.
- The child's account might reflect misperception and confusion caused by deliberate trickery or drugs used by perpetrators.
- The child's account might be affected by suggestions, assumptions, and misinterpretations of overzealous interveners.
- The child's account might reflect urban legends and shared cultural mythology.

Such factors, alone or in combination, can influence a child's account to be inaccurate without necessarily making it a "lie." Children are not adults in little bodies. Children go through developmental stages that must be evaluated and understood. In many ways, however, children are no better and no worse than other victims or witnesses of a crime. They should not be automatically believed or automatically dismissed. Some of what victims allege may be true and accurate, some may be misperceived or distorted, some may be screened or symbolic, and some may be "contaminated" or false. The problem and challenge, especially for law enforcement, is to determine which is which. This can only be done through evaluation and active investigation.

The investigator must remember, however, that almost anything is possible. Just because an allegation sounds farfetched or bizarre does not mean it did not happen. The debate over the literal accuracy of grotesque allegations of ritual abuse has obscured the well-documented fact that there are child sex rings, bizarre paraphilias, and cruel sexual sadists. Even if only a portion of what these victims allege is factual, it still may constitute significant criminal activity.

"If They Have the Details, It Must Have Happened"

The second part of the basic statement also must be evaluated carefully. The details in question in some cases have little to do with sexual activity. Investigators must do more than attempt to determine how a child could have known about sex acts. Some cases involve determining how a child could have known about a wide variety of bizarre activity. Young, nonabused children usually know little about sex, but they might know more than you realize about monsters, torture, kidnapping, and even murder.

In evaluating reported details, it is important to consider that victims might supply details of sexual or other acts using information from sources other than their own direct victimization. Such sources must be evaluated carefully and may include the following:

Personal knowledge. The victim might have personal knowledge of the activity, but not as a result of the alleged victimization. The knowledge could have come from participating in cultural practices; viewing pornography, sex education, or other pertinent material; witnessing sexual activity in the home; or witnessing the sexual abuse of others. It also could have come from having been sexually or physically abused by someone other than the alleged offender(s) and in ways other than the alleged offense.

Other children or victims. Young children today interact socially more often and at a younger age than ever before. Many parents are unable to provide possibly simple explanations for their children's stories or allegations because they were not with the children when the events occurred. They do not know what videotapes their children might have seen, what games they might have played, and what stories they might have been told or overheard. Some children are placed in day care centers for 8, 10, or 12 hours a day, starting as young as 6 weeks of age. The children share experiences by playing house, school, or doctor. Bodily functions such as urination and defecation are a focus of attention for these young children. To a certain extent, each child shares the experiences of all the other children. Children of varying ages are also sharing information and experiences on the Internet. The possible effects of the interaction of such children prior to the disclosure of the alleged abuse must be evaluated.

Media. The amount of sexually explicit, bizarre, or violence-oriented material available to children in the modern world is overwhelming. This includes movies, videotapes, music, books, games, and CD-ROMs. Cable television, computers, the Internet, and the home VCR make all this material readily available to even young children. There are numerous popular toys on the market with bizarre or violent themes.

Suggestions and leading questions. This problem is particularly important in cases involving children under the age of 6 and especially those stemming from custody/visitation disputes. This is not to suggest that custody/visitation disputes usually involve sex abuse allegations, but when they do and when the child in question is young, such cases can be very difficult to evaluate.

It is my opinion that most suggestive, leading questioning of children by interviewers is done inadvertently as part of a good-faith effort to learn the truth. Not all interviewers are in equal positions to potentially influence allegations by children.

Parents and relatives are in the best position to subtly cause their young children to describe their victimization in a certain way. They sometimes question children in a suggestive and accusatory style that casts doubt on the child's statements. In most cases, parents and relatives are well-meaning and do not realize that their style of questioning might influence their child to make inaccurate or false statements. Family members sometimes misinterpret innocuous or ambiguous statements as evidence of sexual abuse. Children also might overhear their parents discussing the details of the case. They might be trying to prolong the rarely given undivided attention of an adult. Children often tell their parents what they believe their parents want or need to hear. In one case, a father gave the police a tape recording to "prove" that his child's statements were spontaneous disclosures and not the result of leading, suggestive questions. The tape recording indicated just the opposite. Why, then, did the father voluntarily give it to the police? Probably because he truly believed he was not influencing his child's statement—but he was.

Some victims have been subtly as well as overtly rewarded by usually well-meaning interviewers for furnishing details. Some "details" of a child's allegation even might have originated as a result of interviewers making assumptions about or misinterpreting what the victim actually said. The interviewers then repeat and possibly embellish these assumptions and misinterpretations, and eventually the victims come to agree with or accept this "official" version of what happened.

Therapists can influence the allegations of children and adult survivors. Types and styles of verbal interaction useful in therapy sometimes create problems for a criminal investigation. Some therapists may have beliefs about sexual abuse or may be overzealous in their efforts to help children in difficult circumstances. It should be noted, however, that when a therapist does a poor investigative interview as part of a criminal investigation, it is the fault of the criminal justice system that allowed it—not the therapist who did it.

Misperception and confusion by the victim. Sometimes, what seems unbelievable has a reasonable explanation. In one case, for example, a child's description of the apparently impossible act of walking through a wall turned out to be the very possible act of walking between the studs of an unfinished wall in a room under construction. In another case, pennies in the anus turned out to be copper foil-covered suppositories. The children might describe what they believe happened. It is not a lie, but neither is it an accurate account. It might be due to confusion deliberately caused by the offender or to misperception inadvertently caused by youthful inexperience.

Many young and some older children have little experience or frame of reference for accurately describing sexual activity. They might not understand the difference between "in" and "on" or the concept of "penetration." Drugs also might be used deliberately to confuse the victims and distort their perceptions.

Education and awareness programs. Some well-intentioned awareness and sex education programs designed to prevent child sex abuse and child abduction or provide children with information about human sexuality may, in fact, unrealistically increase fears and provide some of the details that children are telling interveners. The answer to this potential problem, however, is to evaluate the possibility, not to stop education and prevention programs.

When considering a child's statement, remember that lack of sexual detail does not mean abuse did not happen. Some children are reluctant to discuss the details of what happened.

Areas of Evaluation

As part of the assessment and evaluation of victim statements, it is important to determine how much time elapsed between the time the disclosure was first made and the time the incident was reported to the police or social welfare. The longer the delay, the greater the potential for problems. The next step is to determine the number and purpose of all prior interviews of the victim concerning the allegations. The more interviews conducted before the investigative interview, the greater the potential difficulties. Problems also can be created by interviews conducted by various interveners after the investigative interview(s).

The investigator must closely and carefully evaluate events in the victim's life be-

fore, during, and after the alleged abuse. Events occurring before the alleged abuse to be evaluated might include the following:

1. Background of the victim
2. Abuse or drugs in the home
3. Pornography in the home
4. Play, television, VCR, computer, and Internet habits
5. Attitudes about sexuality in the home
6. Religious beliefs and training
7. Extent of sex education in the home
8. Cultural and subcultural attitudes and practices
9. Activities of siblings
10. Need or craving for attention
11. Childhood fears
12. Custody/visitation disputes
13. Victimization of or by family members
14. Family disputes and discipline problems
15. Interaction between victims

Events occurring during the alleged abuse to be evaluated include the following:

1. Use of fear or scare tactics
2. Degree of trauma
3. Use of magic, deception, or trickery
4. Use of rituals
5. Use of drugs
6. Use of pornography
7. Use of grooming and seduction

Events occurring after the alleged abuse to be evaluated include the following:

1. Disclosure sequence
2. Number and type of interviews of the child
3. Background of prior interviewers
4. Background of parents
5. Commingling of victims
6. Type of therapy received
7. Contact by offender
8. Shame or guilt
9. Lawsuits

Contagion

Investigators must also evaluate possible contagion. Consistent statements obtained from different interviews and from multiple victims are powerful pieces of corroborative evidence—that is, as long as those statements were not "contaminated." Investigation must evaluate both pre- and postdisclosure contagion and both victim and intervener contagion carefully. Are the different victim statements consistent because they describe common experiences or events or because they reflect contamination or shared cultural mythology?

The sources of potential contagion are widespread. Victims can communicate with each other both prior to and after their disclosures. Interveners can communicate with each other and with victims. The team or cell concepts are attempts to deal with potential investigator contagion in multivictim cases. All the victims are not interviewed by the same individuals, and interviewers do not necessarily share information directly with each other (Lanning, 1992b).

Documenting existing contagion and eliminating additional contagion are crucial to the successful investigation and prosecution of many cases. There is no way, however, to erase or undo contagion. The best you can hope for is to identify and evaluate it and attempt to explain it. Mental health professionals requested to evaluate suspected victims must be carefully selected and evaluated.

Once a case is contaminated and out of control, little can be done to salvage what might have been a prosecutable criminal violation. A few cases have even been lost on appeal after a conviction because of contamination problems.

To evaluate the contagion element, investigators must investigate these cases meticulously and aggressively. Whenever possible, personal visits should be made to all locations of alleged abuse and the victims' homes. Events prior to the alleged abuse must be evaluated carefully. Investigators might have to view television programs, movies, computer games, and videotapes seen by the victims. In some cases, it might be necessary to conduct a background investigation and evaluation of everyone who, officially or unofficially, interviewed the victims about the allegations prior to and after the investigative interview(s).

Investigators must be familiar with information about sexual abuse of children being disseminated in magazines, books, television programs, conferences, the Internet, and so on. Every alternative way that a victim could have learned about the details of the abuse must be explored, if for no other reason than to eliminate them and counter defense arguments. There may be validity to these contagion factors, however. They might explain some of the "unbelievable" aspects of the case and result in the successful prosecution of the substance of the case.

Consistency of statements becomes more significant if contagion is identified or disproved by independent investigation.

Munchausen syndrome and Munchausen syndrome by proxy are complex and controversial issues in child abuse cases (see Chapter 7, this volume). No attempt will be made to discuss them in detail, but they are well-documented facts. Most of the literature about them focuses on their manifestation in the medical setting as false or self-inflicted illness or injury. They are also manifested in the criminal justice setting as false or self-inflicted crime victimization. If parents would poison their children to prove an illness, they might sexually abuse their children to prove a crime. These are the unpopular but documented realities of the world. Recognizing their existence does not mean that child sexual abuse and sexual assault are any less real and serious.

Many mental health professionals might be good at determining that something traumatic happened to a child, but determining exactly what happened is another matter.

Summary of Evaluation and Assessment

As much as investigators might wish otherwise, there is no simple way to determine the accuracy of a victim's allegation. Investigators cannot rely on therapists, evaluation experts, or the polygraph as shortcuts to determining the facts. Many mental health professionals might be good at determining that something traumatic happened to a child, but determining exactly *what* happened is another matter. Mental health professionals are now more willing to admit that they are unable to determine, with certainty, the accuracy of victim statements in these cases. There is no test or statement analysis formula that absolutely will determine how or whether a child was sexually abused. Although resources such as expert opinion, statement validity analysis, and the polygraph might be potentially useful as part of the evaluation process, none of them should ever be the sole criterion for pursuing or not pursuing an allegation of child sexual abuse. Law enforcement must proceed with the investigation and rely primarily on the corroboration process.

The criminal justice system must identify (or develop) and use fair and objective criteria for evaluating the accuracy of allegations of child sexual abuse and for filing charges against the accused. Just because it is possible does not mean it happened. The lack of corroborative evidence *is* significant when there should be corroborative evidence. Blindly believing everything despite a lack of logical evidence or simply ignoring the impossible or improbable and accepting the possible is *not* good enough. If some of what the victim describes is accurate, some misperceived, some distorted, and some contaminated, what is the court supposed to believe? Until we come up with better answers, the court should be asked to believe what a thorough investigation can corroborate, understanding that physical evidence is only one form of corroboration. In those cases in which there simply is no corroborative evidence, the court may have to make its decision based on carefully assessed and evaluated victim testimony and the elimination of alternative explanations.

Corroborate

As a general principle, valid cases tend to get better and false cases tend to get worse with investigation. The following techniques are offered as ways to corroborate allegations of child sexual abuse and avoid child victim testimony in court. If child victim testimony cannot be avoided, at least the victim will not bear the total burden of proof if these techniques are used. These techniques can, to varying degrees, be used in any child sexual abuse case. The amount of corroborative evidence available might depend on the type of case, type of sexual activity, and type of offender(s) involved. Corroboration might be more difficult in an isolated one-on-one case perpetrated by a situational sex offender and easier in a sex ring case perpetrated by a preferential sex offender (Lanning, 1992a).

Document Behavioral
Symptoms of Sexual Abuse

Because the behavioral symptoms of child sexual abuse are described elsewhere in this book, they will not be presented here

in detail (see Chapters 3 and 19, this volume). Developmentally unusual sexual knowledge and behavior seem to be the strongest symptoms. The documentation of these symptoms can be of assistance in corroborating child victim statements. It must be emphasized, however, that these are only symptoms, and their significance must be carefully evaluated in context by objective experts. Many behavioral symptoms of child sexual abuse are actually symptoms of trauma, stress, and anxiety that could be caused by other events in the child's life. Almost every behavioral indicator of sexual abuse can be seen in nonabused children. Because of variables such as the type and length of abuse, the resiliency of the child victim, and society's response to the abuse, not all children react to being abused in the same way. Therefore, just as the presence of behavioral symptoms does not prove that a child was sexually abused, the absence of them does not prove that a child was not abused.

The use of expert witnesses to introduce this evidence into a court of law is a complex legal issue that is discussed in Chapter 19 (this volume). Mental health professionals, social workers, child protective services workers, and law enforcement investigators can be the source of such expert testimony regarding symptoms of sexual abuse. Experts might not be allowed to testify about the guilt and innocence of the accused but might be able to testify about the nature of the offense and "offender/victim" behavior. The most commonly acceptable use of such expert testimony is to impeach defense experts and to rehabilitate prosecution witnesses after their credibility has been attacked by the defense. An expert might be able to testify concerning such symptoms to rebut defense allegations that the prosecution has no evidence other than the testimony of a child victim or that the child's disclosure is totally the result of leading and improper questioning.

These and other possible uses of expert testimony should be discussed with the prosecutor. Even if not admissible in court, the symptoms of sexual abuse still can be useful as part of investigative corroboration, particularly when symptoms predate any disclosure. Ongoing research reveals that sexually abused girls also may experience physiological changes and symptoms (DeBellis, Lefter, Trickett, & Putnam, 1994). The investigative and prosecutive significance of these findings is unknown at this time.

Document Patterns of Behavior

Two patterns of behavior should be documented: victim patterns and offender patterns.

Victim patterns. By far the most important victim pattern of behavior to identify and document is the disclosure process. Investigators must verify through active investigation the exact nature and content of each disclosure, outcry, or statement made by the victim. Second-hand information about disclosure is not good enough. To whatever extent humanly possible, the investigator should determine exactly when, where, to whom, in precisely what words, and why the victim disclosed. A well-documented, convincing report, especially a spontaneous one with no secondary gain, may be the most convincing evidence.

The fact that a victim does not reveal the abuse for years or recants previous disclosures might be part of a pattern of behavior that in fact helps to corroborate sexual abuse. The documentation of the secrecy, the sequence of disclosures, the recantation of statements, the distortion of events, and so on can all be part of the corroboration process.

Offender patterns. There is one answer to the questions investigators most commonly ask about child molesters, such as, "What is the best way to interview them?" "Do they collect child pornography?" "How many victims do they have?" "Can they be reliably polygraphed?" "Can they be treated?" The answer to these questions is, "It depends." It depends on what kind of child molester you have. Documenting offender patterns of behavior is one of the most important and most overlooked steps in the corroboration process. Investigators must make every reasonable effort to document offender patterns of behavior and attempt to determine the type of offender involved.

I have previously developed and published an investigative typology of child molesters that distinguishes between "preferential" and "situational" offenders (Lanning, 1992a). Situational offenders have no true sexual preference for children but might molest them for a wide variety of situational reasons. In many cases, children might be targeted because they are weak, vulnerable, or available. Situational offenders' patterns of behavior are more likely to involve the concept of *method of operation* (MO) that is

well known to most police officers. MO is something done by offenders because it works and will help them get away with the crime. MO is fueled by thought and deliberation. Most offenders change and improve their MO over time and with experience.

Preferential child molesters (i.e., pedophiles), on the other hand, have specific sexual preferences. Their sexual fantasies and erotic imagery can focus on children. The patterns of behavior of preferential offenders are more likely to involve the concept of sexual ritual that is less known to most police officers. Sexual ritual is nothing more than repeatedly engaging in an act or series of acts in a certain manner because of a sexual need. To become aroused or gratified, a person must engage in the act in a certain way. Unlike the situational offender's MO, ritual is necessary to the offender but not to the successful commission of the crime. In fact, instead of facilitating the crime, it often increases the odds of identification, apprehension, and conviction. Ritual is fueled by erotic imagery and fantasy and can be bizarre in nature. Most offenders find it difficult to change and modify ritual, even when their experience tells them they should. Understanding sexual ritual is the key to investigating preferential sex offenders.

You cannot accurately determine the type of offender with whom you are dealing unless you have the most complete, detailed, and accurate information possible. Doing a background investigation on a suspect means more than obtaining the date and place of birth and credit and criminal checks. School, juvenile, military, medical, driving, employment, bank, sex offender and child abuse registry, sex offender assessment, computer, and prior investigative records can all be valuable sources of information about an offender. Knowing the kind of offender with whom you are dealing can go a long way toward learning where and what kind of corroborative evidence might be found. It can be helpful in determining the existence and location of other victims and child pornography or erotica (Lanning, 1992a).

Because their molestation of children is part of a long-term persistent pattern of behavior, preferential sex offenders are like human evidence machines. During their lifetime, they leave behind a string of victims and a collection of child pornography and erotica. Therefore, the preferential child molester is easier to convict if investigators understand how to recognize him and how he operates and if their departments give them the time and resources.

Identify Adult Witnesses and Suspects

Not all sexual abuse is "one-on-one." There are cases with multiple offenders and accomplices. One benefit of a multioffender case is that it increases the likelihood that there is a weak link in the group. Do not assume that accomplices will not cooperate with the investigation. The conspiracy model of building a case against one suspect and then using that suspect's testimony against others can be useful. Because of the need to protect potential child victims, however, the conspiracy model of investigation has limitations in child sexual abuse cases. You cannot knowingly allow children to be molested as you build your case by turning suspects. Corroboration of a child victim's statement with adult witness testimony, however, is an important and valuable technique.

Medical Evidence

Whenever possible, all children suspected of having been sexually victimized should be afforded a medical examination by a trained and competent physician. This examination is covered in detail in Chapter 12 (this volume). The primary purpose of this examination is to assess potential injury and the need for treatment and to reassure the patient. A secondary purpose is to determine the presence of any corroborating evidence of acute or chronic trauma. The ability and willingness of medical doctors to corroborate child sexual abuse has improved greatly in recent years, primarily due to better training and the use of protocols, rape kits, the colposcope, toluidine blue dye, ultraviolet light photography, and other techniques.

When used with a camera, the colposcope can document the trauma without additional examinations of the child victim. Positive laboratory tests for sexually transmitted diseases can be valuable evidence, especially in cases involving very young children. Statements made to doctors by the child victim as part of the medical examination might be admissible in court without the child testifying.

Law enforcement investigators should be cautious of doctors who have been identified as child abuse crusaders or who always find—or never find—medical evidence of sexual abuse. Medical doctors should be objective scientists doing a professional examination. The exact cause of any anal or vaginal trauma needs to be evaluated carefully and scientifically. It also should be noted that most acts of child sexual abuse do not leave any physical injuries that can be identified by a medical examination. In addition, children's injuries can heal rapidly. Thus, lack of medical corroboration does not mean that a child was not sexually abused or that it cannot be proven in court.

Other Victims

The simple understanding and recognition that a child molester might have other victims is one of the most important steps in corroborating an allegation of child sexual abuse. There is strength in numbers. If an investigation uncovers one or two victims, each will probably have to testify in court. If an investigation uncovers multiple victims, the odds are that none of them will testify because there will not be a trial. With multiple victims, the only defense is to allege a flawed investigation.

Because of the volume of crime and limited resources, many law enforcement agencies are unable to continue an investigation to find multiple victims. If that is the case, they must try to identify as many victims as possible. Other victims are sometimes identified through publicity about the case. Consistency of statements obtained from multiple victims, independently interviewed, can be powerful corroboration.

Search Warrants

The major law enforcement problem with the use of search warrants in child sexual abuse cases is that they are not obtained soon enough. In many cases, investigators have probable cause for a search warrant but do not know it. Because evidence can be moved or destroyed so quickly, search warrants should be obtained as soon as legally possible. Waiting too long and developing, in essence, too much probable cause also might subject investigative agencies to criticism or even lawsuits that this delay allowed additional victims to be molested. The value and significance of child erotica (pedophile paraphernalia) often are not recognized by investigators (Lanning, 1992a).

The expertise of an experienced investigator and well-documented behavior patterns of preferential offenders sometimes can be used to add to the probable cause, expand the scope of the search, or address the legal staleness problem of old information. Such "expert" search warrants should be used only when necessary and only when there is probable cause to believe the alleged offender fits the preferential pattern of behavior (Lanning, 1992a).

Physical Evidence

Physical evidence can be defined as any object that corroborates anything a child victim said, saw, tasted, smelled, drew, and so on. It can be used to prove offender identity and type and location of activity. It could be bed sheets, articles of clothing, sexual aids, lubricants, fingerprints, documents, and so on. It also could be an object or sign on the wall described by a victim. If the victim says the offender ejaculated on a doorknob, ejaculate on the doorknob becomes physical evidence if found. If the victim says the offender kept condoms in the nightstand by his bed, they become physical evidence if found. A pornography magazine with the back page missing described by the victim is physical evidence. Satanic occult paraphernalia is evidence if it corroborates criminal activity described by the victim. Positive identification of a subject through DNA analysis of trace amounts of biological evidence left on a child or at a crime scene might result in a child victim not having to testify because the perpetrator pleads guilty.

Child Pornography and Child Erotica

Child pornography, especially that produced by the offender, is one of the most valuable pieces of corroborative evidence of child sexual abuse that any investigator can have. Many collectors of child pornography do not molest children, and many child molesters do not possess or collect child pornography. However, investigators should always be alert for it. Child pornography can be present in intrafamilial cases. Preferential child molesters, especially those operating

child sex rings, almost always collect child pornography and/or child erotica. If situational child molesters possess child pornography, they usually have pictures of their own victims.

Today, child pornography often is found in videotape format and, with rapidly increasing frequency, in digital format on computers. In addition to viewing any homemade videotapes seized from the offenders, investigators also must listen to them carefully. The voices and sounds might reveal valuable corroborative or intelligence information. If necessary, photographic enhancement can be used to help identify individuals, locations, and dates on newspapers and magazines otherwise unrecognizable in the child pornography. In one case, a subject was identified from his fingerprint, which was visible in a recovered child pornography photograph. The computer of any suspected child molester must be considered for justified and legal search and seizure. Child pornography is increasingly being found on home computer hard drives and disks.

Child erotica can be defined as any material, relating to children, that serves a sexual purpose for a given individual (Lanning, 1992a). Some of the more common types of child erotica include drawings, fantasy writings, diaries, souvenirs, letters, books about children, psychological books on pedophilia, and ordinary photographs of children. It must be evaluated in the context in which it is found, using good judgment and common sense. Child erotica is not as significant as child pornography, but it can be of value. It can help prove intent. It can be a source of intelligence information, identifying other offenders or victims. It can be used to deny bond if it indicates the offender is a risk to the community. Child erotica can be instrumental in influencing the offender to plead guilty, and it also can be used at the time of sentencing to demonstrate the full scope of the offender's activity. This is consistent with the big-picture approach.

Computers

Investigators must be alert to the rapidly increasing possibility that a child molester with the intelligence, economic means, or employment access might use a computer in a variety of ways as part of his sexual victimization of children. The computer could be a stand-alone system or one using online service capability. Whether a system at work, at a library, at a cyber café, or at home, the computer provides sex offenders with an ideal means of filling their needs to (a) organize their collections, correspondence, and fantasy material; (b) communicate with potential victims and other offenders; (c) store, transfer, manipulate, and create child pornography; and (d) maintain financial records. Therefore, legally searching and seizing such a computer potentially could provide almost unbelievable amounts of corroborative evidence. Investigators need to be careful about evaluating computer communications. Because of perceived anonymity and immediate feedback, many child molesters greatly exaggerate their sexual exploits when communicating by computer. As computers have become less expensive, more sophisticated, and easier to operate, the potential for this abuse will grow rapidly.

Consensual Monitoring

Consensual monitoring is a valuable but often underused investigative technique. It includes the use of body recorders and pretext phone calls. Because of the legal issues involved and variations in state laws, use of this technique should always be discussed with prosecutors and police department legal advisers. It is important to remember that children must never be endangered by investigators in the service of the investigation. The use of this technique with child victims presents ethical issues as well as legal considerations. Pretext phone calls are more suitable than body recorders with child victims but are obviously not appropriate in all cases. They might not be suitable for use with very young victims or victims with a strong bond with the offender. The use of this technique should be discussed with the parents or guardians of a victim who is a minor. The parent, however, might not be trusted to be discreet about the use of this technique or might even be a suspect in the investigation. Although there is the potential for further emotional trauma, many victims afterward describe an almost therapeutic sense of empowerment or return of control through their participation in pretext phone calls.

Investigators using the pretext phone call should ensure that they have a telephone number that cannot be traced to the police and that they have a method to verify the date and time of the calls. In addition to victims, investigators also can make such calls themselves by impersonating a wide variety of potentially involved or concerned individuals. Sometimes victims or their relatives or friends do the monitoring and recording on their own. Investigators need to check appropriate laws concerning the legality of such citizen taping and the admissibility of the material obtained.

Consensual monitoring with body recorders is probably best reserved for use with undercover investigators and adult informants. Under no circumstance should an investigative agency produce a videotape or audiotape of the actual molestation of a child victim as part of an investigative technique. However, the victim might be used to introduce the undercover investigator to the subject.

Inappropriate responses obtained through consensual monitoring can be almost as damaging as outright admissions. When told by a victim over the phone that the police or a therapist wants to discuss the sexual relationship, "Let's talk about it later tonight" is a suspicious response.

Subject Confessions

Getting a subject to confess obviously can be an effective way to corroborate child sexual abuse and avoid child victim testimony in court. Unfortunately, many investigators put minimal effort into subject interviews. Simply asking an alleged perpetrator if he molested a child does not constitute a proper interview. Any criminal investigator needs effective interviewing skills. In view of the stakes involved, child sexual abuse investigators must do everything reasonably possible to improve their skills in this area. Entire books and chapters have been written about interview techniques and strategies (Macdonald & Michaud, 1987; Machovec, 1989; Rutledge, 1987). In this limited space, only a brief review of interviewing issues will be offered.

Investigators need to collect background information and develop an interview strategy before conducting a potentially very important discussion with the alleged offender. Many sexual offenders against children really want to discuss either their behavior or at least their rationalization for it. If treated with professionalism, empathy, and understanding, many of these offenders will make significant admissions. If the offender is allowed to rationalize or project some of the blame for his behavior onto someone or something else, he is more likely to confess. Most sex offenders will admit only that which has been discovered and that which they can rationalize. If you do not confront the subject with all your evidence, he might be more likely to minimize his acts rather than totally deny them. Many child molesters admit their acts but deny the intent. A tougher approach can always be tried if the softer approach does not work.

Investigators should consider noncustodial (i.e., no arrest), nonconfrontational interviews of the subject at home or work. Interviews during the execution of a search warrant also should be considered. Investigators should not overlook admissions made by the offender to wives, girlfriends, neighbors, friends, and even the media.

The polygraph and other lie detection devices can be valuable tools when used as part of the interview strategy by skilled interviewers. Their greatest value is in the subject's belief that they will determine the truth of any statement he makes. Once used, their value is limited by their lack of legal admissibility. The polygraph (or any lie detection device) should never be the sole criterion for discontinuing the investigation of child sexual abuse allegations.

Surveillance

Surveillance can be a time-consuming and expensive investigative technique. In some cases, it also can be a very effective technique. Time and expense can be reduced if the surveillance is not open-ended but is based on inside information about the subject's activity. One obvious problem, however, is what to do when the surveillance team comes to believe that a child is being victimized. How much reasonable suspicion or probable cause does an investigator on physical or electronic surveillance need to take action? If a suspected child molester simply goes into a residence with a child, does law enforcement have the right to intervene? What if the offender is simply paying the newspaper boy or watching television with a neighborhood child? These are important legal and ethical issues to consider when using this surveillance technique. Despite these potential problems, surveillance is a valuable technique, especially in the investigation of child sex rings.

> *A combination of federal and state charges for different aspects of his criminal sexual behavior might convince the subject to plead guilty.*

Creative Prosecution

Another effective way to avoid child victim testimony is to prosecute the offender for violations that might not require such testimony. This is limited only by the imagination and skill of the prosecutor. One effective technique, when appropriate, is to file federal or local child pornography charges, which usually do not require victims to testify. A combination of federal and state charges for different aspects of his criminal sexual behavior might convince the subject to plead guilty. Some offenders might plead guilty in order to do their time in the federal penitentiary. Because the sexual abuse of children sometimes involves the commission of other crimes, charges involving violations of child labor laws, involuntary servitude, bad checks, drugs, or perjury also can be filed. Valuable information also can be introduced in court without child victim testimony if the prosecutor is familiar with the use of out-of-court statements and the exceptions to the hearsay rule.

Proactive Approach

Because this book is available to the general public, specific details of proactive investigative techniques will not be set forth. In general, however, proactive investigation involves the use of surveillance, mail covers, undercover correspondence, "sting" operations, reverse "sting" operations, online computer operations, and so on. For example, when an offender who has been communicating with other offenders is arrested, investigators can assume his identity and continue the correspondence.

It is not necessary for each law enforcement agency to "reinvent the wheel." Federal law enforcement agencies such as the U.S. Postal Inspection Service, U.S. Customs, the FBI, and some state and local departments have been using these techniques for years. Because the production and distribution of child pornography and child prostitution frequently involve violations of federal law, the U.S. Postal Inspection Service, U.S. Customs, and the FBI all have intelligence information about such activity. It is recommended that any law enforcement agency about to begin the use of these proactive techniques, especially those involving online Internet activity, contact nearby federal, state, and local law enforcement agencies to determine what is already being done. Many areas of the country have organized task forces on sexual abuse, exploitation, and computer exploitation of children. Law enforcement agencies must learn to work together in these proactive techniques, or else they may wind up "investigating" each other. Some child molesters also are actively trying to identify and learn about these proactive techniques.

The proactive approach also includes the analysis of records and documents obtained or seized from offenders during an investigation. In addition to possibly being used to convict these offenders, such material can contain valuable intelligence information about other offenders and victims. This material must be evaluated carefully in order not to overestimate or underestimate its significance.

Establish Communication With Parents

The importance and difficulty of this technique in extrafamilial cases cannot be overemphasized. An investigator must maintain ongoing communication with the parents of victims. Not all parents react the same way to the alleged abuse of their children. Some are very supportive and cooperative. Others overreact and some even deny the victimization. Sometimes there is animosity and mistrust among parents with differing reactions.

Once the parents lose faith in the police or prosecutor and begin to interrogate their children and conduct their own investigation, the case might be lost forever. Parents from one case communicate the results of their "investigation" with each other, and some have even contacted the parents in other cases. Such parental activity, however understandable, is an obvious source of potential contamination.

Parents must be reminded that their child's credibility will be jeopardized when and if the information obtained turns out to be unsubstantiated or false. To minimize this problem, within the limits of the law and without jeopardizing investigative techniques, parents must be told on a regular basis how the case is progressing. Parents also can be assigned constructive things to do (e.g., lobbying for new legislation, working on awareness and prevention programs) to channel their energy, concern, and guilt.

Conclusion

It is the job of the professional investigator to listen to all victims, assess and evaluate the relevant information, and conduct an appropriate investigation. Corroborative evidence exists more often than many investigators realize. Investigators should remember that not all childhood trauma is abuse, and not all child abuse is a crime. There can be great frustration when, after a thorough investigation, you are convinced that something traumatic happened to the child victim but do not know with any degree of certainty exactly what happened, when it happened, or who did it. That is sometimes the price we pay for a criminal justice system in which people are considered innocent until proven guilty beyond a reasonable doubt.

APPENDIX

The Investigator's Basic Library

The following 10 publications are recommended for inclusion in the basic reference library of a law enforcement investigator of *sexual* victimization of children:

Goodman, G. S., & Bottoms, B. L. (Eds.). (1993). *Child victims, child witnesses: Understanding and improving testimony.* New York: Guilford.

Heger, A., & Emans, S. J. (1992). *Evaluation of the sexually abused child: A medical textbook and photographic atlas.* New York: Oxford University Press.

Lanning, K. (1992). *Child molesters: A behavioral analysis.* Arlington, VA: National Center for Missing and Exploited Children.

Lanning, K. (1992). *Child sex rings: A behavioral analysis.* Arlington, VA: National Center for Missing and Exploited Children.

Myers, J. E. B. (1998). *Legal issues in child abuse and neglect practice* (2nd ed.). Thousand Oaks, CA: Sage.

Ney, T. (Ed.). (1995). *True and false allegations of child sexual abuse.* New York: Brunner/Mazel.

Office of Juvenile Justice and Delinquency Prevention. (1996-1999). *Portable guides to investigating child abuse.* Washington, DC: U.S. Department of Justice.

Pence, D., & Wilson, C. (1994). *Team investigation of child sexual abuse: The uneasy alliance.* Thousand Oaks, CA: Sage.

Poole, D., & Lamb, M. (1998). *Investigative interviews of children.* Washington, DC: American Psychological Association.

Stern, P. (1997). *Preparing and presenting expert testimony in child abuse litigation.* Thousand Oaks, CA: Sage.

References

Abel, G., Becker, J., Mittelman, M., Cunningham-Rathner, J., Rouleau, J., & Murphy, W. (1987). Self-reported sex crimes of nonincarcerated paraphiliacs. *Journal of Interpersonal Violence, 2*(1), 3-25.

DeBellis, M., Lefter, L., Trickett, P., & Putnam, F. (1994). Urinary catecholamine excretion in sexually abused girls. *Journal of the American Academy of Child and Adolescent Psychiatry, 33,* 320-327.

Lanning, K. (1992a). *Child molesters: A behavioral analysis.* Arlington, VA: National Center for Missing and Exploited Children.

Lanning, K. (1992b). *Child sex rings: A behavioral analysis.* Arlington, VA: National Center for Missing and Exploited Children.

Lanning, K., & Hazelwood, R. (2001). The maligned investigator of criminal sexuality. In R. R. Hazelwood & A. W. Burgess (Eds.), *Practical aspects of rape investigation* (3rd ed., pp. 243-257). Boca Raton, FL: CRC.

Machovec, F. (1989). *Interview and interrogation.* Springfield, IL: Charles C Thomas.

Macdonald, J., & Michaud, D. (1987). *The confession.* Denver, CO: Apache.

Rutledge, D. (1987). *Criminal interrogation.* Sacramento, CA: Custom.

U.S. Department of Justice. (1993). *Joint investigations of child abuse: Report of a symposium.* Washington, DC: Author.

18

Interviewing Children in and out of Court

Current Research and Practice Implications

KAREN J. SAYWITZ

GAIL S. GOODMAN

THOMAS D. LYON

What do we know about children's abilities to provide accurate eyewitness testimony? Until recently, scientific data were surprisingly sparse. However, beginning in the mid-1980s, the study of child victims/witnesses grew at an astounding rate; now it is a worldwide endeavor. When Melton (1981) published one of the first modern reviews of psychological research on children's testimony, only one contemporary empirical study directly addressing children's eyewitness memory was cited. Today, entire books and journal issues are devoted to research on this topic (e.g., Ceci & Bruck, 1995; Dent & Flin, 1992; Goodman, 1984; Goodman & Bottoms, 1993; Perry & Wrightsman, 1991; Poole & Lamb, 1998; Spencer & Flin, 1993). Important research currently is being undertaken not only in the United States but also in England (e.g., Davies, Westcott, & Horan, 2000), Scotland (e.g., Flin, 1993), New Zealand (e.g., Priestly, Roberts, & Pipe, 1999), Australia (e.g., Brennan & Brennan, 1988; Bussey, Lee, & Grimbeek, 1993), Canada (e.g., Bala, Lee, Lindsay, & Talwar, 2000; Peterson, Dowden, & Tobin, 2000; Sas, Hurley, Austin, & Wolfe, 1991), Israel (Hershkowitz & Elul, 1999), Sweden (Cederborg, Orbach, Sternberg, & Lamb, 2000), and elsewhere.

AUTHORS' NOTE: Support for the writing of this chapter was provided in part by grants from the National Center on Child Abuse and Neglect.

There are several reasons why understanding children's testimony is important and worthy of investigation. For example, exploration of children's testimony provides us with new insights into memory development. But aside from theoretical reasons, pressing practical issues motivate the study of child witnesses; these practical issues add urgency and consequence to research endeavors.

Perhaps the most salient of the practical reasons concerns reports of child abuse. It is estimated that in 1998 in the United States alone, more than 2.8 million cases of maltreatment were reported. Among these, approximately 903,000 cases either were substantiated or showed some evidence indicating maltreatment (Golden, 2000). More than 50% of these cases focused on neglect, 25% on physical abuse, and nearly 12% on sexual abuse. Many of these cases are likely to involve interviews of children; the children's statements will influence whether they receive protection or whether the case is deemed unfounded. In addition, an unknown number of children are questioned each year more informally by parents, relatives, therapists, teachers, doctors, and others about suspicions of abuse. The results of these interviews also determine the number of children who receive protection and strongly influence the number of cases that come to the attention of social service and legal authorities. The study of children's testimony concerns in large part the accuracy and completeness of children's reports during such interviews.

In addition, although children are questioned more often in forensic investigations than in court, children take the stand at times. When they do, their testimony can influence whether justice prevails. National statistics concerning the number of child abuse victims who testify in criminal or family court do not exist, but relevant information is available, at least in regard to criminal court. Such information indicates considerable variability across jurisdictions in the number of child sexual abuse cases prosecuted and the number of children who testify. For example, Smith (1993) conducted a national telephone survey of 530 district attorneys' offices; she uncovered a large range (1 to 800; $M = 66$) in the number of child sexual assault cases prosecuted by each office. In a study of child sexual assault prosecutions in eight jurisdictions around the United States, Gray (1993) found that in several jurisdictions, children usually testi-

fied at grand jury hearings or preliminary hearings, but in other jurisdictions, they did not. Sas et al. (1991) substantiated that 50% of the nearly 150 children involved in research on preparing children for court later testified either at trial or in some type of preliminary hearing. Finally, in every child sexual abuse trial studied by Myers, Redlich, Goodman, Prizmich, and Imwinkelreid (1999), the child victim/witness testified.

These studies remind us that children do testify in court, and that even if a case never reaches the trial stage, children may be required to provide eyewitness reports during investigative interviews or during competency examinations, grand jury hearings, or preliminary hearings. A focus on the number of children who testify at trial underestimates the number of children who provide information in forensic interviews and who serve as witnesses in courts of law at pretrial stages. At least in some jurisdictions, a relatively large percentage of children involved as victim/witnesses in sexual assault prosecutions take the stand.

In sum, there are important theoretical and practical reasons to study children's testimony. Given the complexities and seriousness of child sexual abuse charges and the fact that the case may boil down to a child's word against an adult's, the accuracy of children's testimony and the best way to obtain children's statements become matters of substantial societal concern. When one considers that the terms *children's eyewitness memory* and *children's testimony* apply as much to children who are interviewed in a forensic, social service, therapeutic, school, or family setting as to children who testify in court, the importance of the topic is magnified.

In this chapter, we provide readers with a survey of some of the recent findings from child-witness research. We also draw practical *implications* of the studies for professionals who interview and evaluate children. Although our review is not comprehensive, we trust that it will acquaint readers with the flavor of current empirical work and inform readers of child witnesses' abilities and needs. We first discuss research concerning children's memory and suggestibility, particularly as they relate to child sexual abuse investigations. We next consider children's communicative competence—that is, their language and communication abilities—as they relate to children's testimony. We turn then to the topic of children in the legal system, focusing special attention on ways to improve the investigative and courtroom process for children. Finally, we discuss practical implications of current research.

Memory and Suggestibility

The ability to provide accurate testimony depends on being able to remember and communicate memories to others. Research consistently indicates that the amount of information a witness reports about an event generally increases with age (e.g., Peterson & Bell, 1996), and young children (e.g., preschoolers) are usually more suggestible than older children and adults (Ceci & Bruck, 1993; Goodman & Aman, 1991). Nevertheless, even young children do not necessarily have poor memories, and they are not necessarily highly suggestible (Eisen, Quas, & Goodman, 2001). Memory abilities and the ability to resist suggestion typically vary at any age, be it childhood or adulthood, depending on situational and personality factors. These abilities are not stable even within a particular person but instead can change depending on a number of factors, including (a) the type of event experienced, (b) the type of information to be recounted, (c) the conditions surrounding an interview, (d) the strength of the memory, (e) the language used, and (f) postevent influences. It is precisely because memory and suggestibility are such complex, variable processes that researchers have devoted so much time and energy to studying them.

The ability to provide accurate testimony depends on being able to remember and communicate memories to others.

One robust finding from the research literature is that free recall (a narrative provided in response to an open-ended question, such as "What happened?") is typically the most accurate form of memory report (e.g., Dent & Stephenson, 1979; Stern, 1910). One problem, however, is that such reports predictably are the most circumscribed, especially when young children are questioned (List, 1986). In comparison to their limited recall, children's recognition memory is fairly good (Jones, Swift, & Johnson, 1988; List, 1986; Todd & Perlmutter, 1980).

The amount of information one obtains is increased when children are asked specifically about information of interest (e.g., "Did you go to Uncle Bob's house?") (e.g., Baker-Ward, Gordon, Ornstein, Larus, & Clubb, 1993; Gordon, Ornstein, Clubb, Nida, & Baker-Ward, 1991; Ornstein, Gordon, & Larus, 1992) or when their recognition memory is triggered by physical cues (e.g., a picture of the child's home or preschool) (e.g., Priestly et al., 1999; Salmon & Pipe, 2000). Although cues and specific questions elicit accurate information not otherwise reported, this may come at a cost. Inaccuracies tend to increase as well, and children make errors they would not otherwise have made (e.g., Dent & Stephenson, 1979).

Free Recall and Open-Ended Questions

One area of vigorous research has been examination of the effects of different question types. When an interviewer asks a broad, open-ended question, the information provided by the witness must come mainly, if not completely, from the witness's own mind and, ideally, from the witness's own experience. At times, however, children say relatively little in response to free recall and open-ended questions. A rather frustrating form of circumscribed free recall is evinced commonly by timid 2- or 3-year-olds: It is not atypical for a very young child to answer "Nothing" to the question "What happened?" even though the child can demonstrate memory of an incident when asked more specifically about it. Some young children will even respond "Nothing" when interviewed about very significant real-life events that clearly happened (e.g., the child almost died after attempted murder). The problem for the interviewer, then, is that it can be difficult to determine, based solely on young children's free recall, whether something major or inconsequential occurred.

Although open-ended questions typically are recommended at least for the initial interview queries, studies indicate that open-ended questions are not a panacea. They can elicit very inaccurate reports from a small number of children. For example, in a study by Goodman and Aman (1991), one young boy who had played games with a man later reported, in response to a free-recall question, a wild adventure story of how the man and he had played cowboys and Indians, how he had been tied up, and so on. Thus, although free recall is most likely to lead to an accurate, albeit limited, statement, it is not guaranteed to do so. Moreover, studies also indicate that the free recall of young children can be distorted if preceded by repeated misleading questions asked in a multiply suggestive context, especially if negative expectations about a person have been created in the child's mind (Leichtman & Ceci, 1995; Poole & Lindsay, 1995; Thompson, Clarke-Stewart, & Lepore, 1997). Even in the absence of previous questioning, an accusatory context may lead to inaccuracies in free recall and spontaneous statements by some preschool children (Tobey & Goodman, 1992).

Free recall and open-ended questions relevant to abuse. One other problem with the use of open-ended questions is that they may fail to elicit reports of genuine abuse when it has occurred. Such questions may be so vague and general that young children fail to discern the significance or relevance of potential topics for discussion (e.g., "Tell me about what happened." "Is there anything you want to tell me?"). When content is embarrassing, such questions fail to convey that the interview is an appropriate place to violate social conventions that normally restrict conversations with strangers about private matters. In a study by Saywitz, Goodman, Nicholas, and Moan (1991), children who had experienced genital touch by a doctor during a medical examination omitted the fact that they had experienced vaginal touch more than 60% of the time *unless* asked directly about it. On the other hand, for children who did not experience genital contact during the doctor examination, there was an 8% false-report rate when asked a single leading, anatomical doll-aided question. Such findings highlight the difficult cost-benefit analysis facing interviewers regarding the phrasing of questions. In addition, age of the witness appears to be a critical factor for consideration. In two studies of younger children using more strongly leading techniques, 2- to 4-year-olds acquiesced to leading questions about a similar medical exam at much higher rates (Bruck, Ceci, & Francoeur, 2000; Bruck, Ceci, Francouer, & Renick, 1995).

Fortunately, there has been some success in ways to help children respond to free-recall questions regarding reports of abuse. For example, Saywitz, Snyder, and Lamphear (1996), Dorado and Saywitz (2001), as well as Sternberg, Lamb, Esplin, Orbach, and Hershkowitz (in press) have explored training children to provide narrative reports, with some positive results. Such training techniques are described later in this chapter. These training programs are promising because, notwithstanding some potential problems with free recall, disclosures of abuse elicited in this way are likely to have the greatest credibility and to be particularly accurate.

Specific Questions

Despite demonstrations that young children's free recall can be inaccurate at times, typically, young children's responses to free-recall and open-ended questions provide accurate but overly succinct information rather than error-ridden information. How can one obtain more information from children? The obvious answer is to ask children specific or directive questions. Unfortunately, children's accuracy declines when asked yes-no questions (Brady, Poole, Warren, & Jones, 1999; Garven, Wood, Malpass, & Shaw, 1998; Ornstein, Baker-Ward, Myers, Principe, & Gordon, 1995; Peterson & Biggs, 1997; Poole & Lindsay, 1996, 1997). Fortunately, the accuracy of responses to such questions increases dramatically with age. Analyzing children's memories for traumatic experiences, Peterson and Biggs (1997) argued that yes-no questions should be avoided altogether with preschoolers (p. 288), whereas 5-year-olds were 89% accurate in responding to such questions (Peterson & Bell, 1996).

When children are asked specific questions, it is often useful to return to open-ended questions (Poole & Lamb, 1998). For example, after a child answers the question, "Did he put the chair anywhere?" the interviewer follows up with questions such as, "Tell me more about where the chair was." or "Then what happened?"

Specific questions relevant to abuse. Similar results have been obtained in asking children specific questions about genital touch; in two studies, Bruck has found near-chance performance among 2- to 4-year-olds (Bruck et al., 2000; Bruck, Ceci, Francouer, &

Renick, 1995), whereas Saywitz and colleagues found much better (near-ceiling) performance among 5- to 7-year-olds (Saywitz et al., 1991). Under some conditions, even 4-year-olds maintain substantial accuracy in answering specific questions relevant to abuse (Rudy & Goodman, 1991). False "yes" responses among younger children to abuse-related questions tend to be unelaborated monosyllabic or nonverbal affirmations (Goodman & Aman, 1991), although some children provide false detail (Saywitz et al., 1991). Ultimately, the choice between completeness and accuracy when deciding whether to increase or decrease one's use of specific questions is a value judgment *informed* by, rather than *dictated* by, research on children's memory.

Suggestibility, Implanting False Memories

There has been a flurry of research on children's suggestibility in the past 10 years, much of it focused on the special vulnerabilities of preschool children (for reviews, see Ceci & Bruck, 1998; Goodman, Emery, & Haugaard, 1998; Lyon, 1999). The results of this research, coupled with basic empirical findings in developmental psychology, provide at least three reasons why young children are particularly susceptible to suggestion. First, young children have special difficulty in producing narratives without relying on cues provided by an adult questioner. Because cues are potentially misleading, the risk of inaccuracy increases. Second, young children are especially deferential to adults' perceptions and interpretations of prior events. If an adult communicates to a child that an event happened in a particular way, either explicitly or implicitly through the kinds of questions asked, the younger child is more inclined to believe it than an older child. Third, young children have difficulty in identifying the sources of their beliefs. They are more prone to confuse what they have been told with what they actually remember.

Children's difficulty producing narratives in response to free-recall questions was addressed earlier. Thus, we turn next to a discussion of children's deference to authority and children's source-monitoring errors.

Deference to adults and source-monitoring errors. Children's errors are increased by their tendency to defer to adults. Young children often defer to adults' interpretations of prior events, even if those adults did not personally witness the events. Young children are less likely to infer that an adult questioner does not know what occurred because the adult was not present. In part, this is attributable to preschool children's lack of understanding about how we come to know things (Saywitz & Lyon, in press). Preschool children's suggestibility can be heightened when questions presuppose misleading information. Preschool children are also particularly susceptible to accepting adults' moral interpretation of others' actions, making children vulnerable to suggestions that innocuous actions were immoral (Lepore & Sesco, 1994; Thompson et al., 1997).

Another source of suggestibility is the preschool child's difficulty remembering the specific source of his or her beliefs—a task called source monitoring. Preschool children exhibit difficulties in recalling how they know some fact: because of something they saw, something they inferred, or something they were told (Gopnik & Graf, 1988; O'Neill & Gopnik, 1991; Woolley & Bruell, 1995). This difficulty is most pronounced with 3- to 4-year-olds, who performed not much better than chance in one simple source-monitoring study, whereas 5-year-olds were almost 100% correct on the same simple task (Gopnik & Graf, 1988). Researchers have documented relations between young children's source-monitoring abilities and their suggestibility (Leichtman, Morse, Dixon, & Spiegel, 2000; Welch-Ross, 2000; but see Quas, Schaaf, Alexander, & Goodman, 2000). Young children may therefore confuse what they have been told with what they have actually perceived.

Deference to authority may underlie situations in which researchers have found some dramatic rates of elaborated affirmations of nonevents among preschool children, such as when interviewers move beyond simple yes-no questions to ask questions that are more leading. Questions can be made highly leading by turning them into tag questions (e.g., "He touched you, *didn't he?*"), negative term questions (e.g., "*Didn't* he touch you?"), or suppositional questions, in which details are presupposed (e.g., "Where did he touch you?" when the child has not acknowledged touching) (Lyon, in press).

Children's deference to adult interpretation can also be exploited by giving the child negative information regarding the person about whom questions are asked.

Children's source-monitoring difficulties can be heightened by telling them that the asked-about events have in fact occurred, giving them the means to visualize the nonevents. Lepore and Sesco (1994) found, for example, that repeating yes-no questions about potentially sexual activities did not elicit errors among 4- to 6-year-old children, but labeling every action as "bad" and asking suppositional, tag, and negative term questions led to false affirmations that were subsequently repeated in 30% to 40% of the responses to yes-no questions, one third of which were elaborated with additional details. In a study of 3- to 4-year-olds' memories for an uneventful visit to their school by Sam Stone (Leichtman & Ceci, 1995), four suggestive interviews were employed, composed of forced-choice suppositional questions (e.g., "Did Sam Stone rip the book with his hands, or did he use scissors?") that not only told participants that Sam Stone had in fact committed misdeeds that never occurred but also assisted the preschool children in developing elaborated narratives of how he had done so. Children were visited by research assistants once a week for 4 weeks before Sam Stone's visit. The research assistants narrated 12 clumsy mishaps caused by Sam Stone. Potential errors were generated by presenting children with physical evidence of Sam's fictitious misdeeds in the first two interviews: They were shown a ripped book and a soiled teddy bear. Asked a free-recall question 10 weeks after Sam's visit, 46% of the 3- and 4-year-old children spontaneously reported that Sam had performed one or both misdeeds.

Bruck and her colleagues (Bruck, Ceci, Francouer, & Barr, 1995; Bruck, Ceci, Francouer, & Renick, 1995) attempted to convince 4- and 5-year-olds that a research assistant rather than their pediatrician had given them a shot 11 months previously. The researchers employed two suggestive interviews, including forced-choice suppositional questions such as those used in the Sam Stone study (e.g., "When Laurie [the research assistant] gave you the shot, was your mom or your dad with you?"). Other aspects of the interviews were more blunt. The interviewer told the child that the research assistant "gives kids their shots. She gave you your shot. Laurie said that she remembered when she gave you your shot." Moreover, the interviewers pointed to pictures of the research assistant and the pediatrician when misidentifying who had performed the various checkup procedures. Forty to 60% of the children subsequently misidentified who had performed various actions during the checkup.

Other research has similarly demonstrated that preschool children's vulnerabilities make it possible to produce false narratives and high rates of error through suppositional questions, denigrating the target adult, telling children that nonevents occurred, and encouraging source-monitoring errors (Bruck, Hembrooke, & Ceci, 1997; Ceci, Loftus, Leichtman, & Bruck, 1994; Poole & Lindsay, 1995; Tobey & Goodman, 1992). More recently, Garven, Wood, and colleagues have shown that positive and negative reinforcement are also effective in distorting young children's reports (Garven, Wood, & Malpass, 2000; Garven et al., 1998). Space prevents a more complete discussion of this research, which can be found elsewhere (Lyon, 1999).

Suggestibility relevant to abuse. Despite the dramatic findings just reviewed, it is also true that suggestibility varies considerably across individuals and situations, even within a specific age group. Children, like adults, are more likely to give incorrect reports and to be more suggestible about peripheral or poorly retained information than about more salient, memorable information. Abusive genital contact is likely to be a fairly salient event for a child; therefore, children are likely to be less suggestible about such actions. Nevertheless, young children (e.g., 3-year-olds) appear to conform to suggestive questions relating to abuse more often than older children, at least under the types of situations often studied in child testimony research (e.g., Goodman & Aman, 1991). Perhaps young children do not yet fully realize the impropriety of most genital touch and thus are not as taken aback by such questions as older children seem to be. Even by age 4 or 5, many nonabused children show signs of surprise or embarrassment when asked whether a stranger removed the child's clothes or was naked.

Intimidation can add to young children's suggestibility about abuse-related events, and younger children appear to be more easily intimidated. A supportive context may be especially important in bolstering young children's resistance to suggestive misinformation about abuse (Carter, Bottoms, & Levine, 1996; Goodman, Bottoms, Schwartz-Kenney, & Rudy, 1991).

Recently, children who have suffered maltreatment have been included in studies of children's suggestibility about abuse. The studies address the likelihood of false reports of abuse in children with a previous history of maltreatment. The research to date indicates that maltreated children appear to evince similar levels of suggestibility as nonmaltreated children (Eisen, Goodman, Davis, & Qin, 1999). However, there are hints in the data that greater psychopathology may be associated with inaccuracies (Eisen, Goodman, Qin, & Davis, 1998).

Overall, the research counsels extreme caution in questioning young children, lest an overzealous interviewer suggest false information, including about abuse. At the same time, three positive implications can be drawn as well: (a) implanting false memories, even in young children, has often required researchers to move beyond simple yes-no questions (although false affirmations to abuse-related yes-no questions can be obtained in young preschool children); (b) just as younger children are substantially more suggestible than older children, older children are substantially less suggestible than younger children; and (c) there are ways to reduce the suggestiveness of interviews, given what the research has taught us (discussed in a later section on practical implications).

Trauma and Memory

Many would agree that sexual abuse can be a traumatic experience for a child, yet most studies of children's testimony do not concern the effects of trauma on memory. A number of researchers are studying children's and adults' memories for stressful events. Whereas the psychological lore used to be that stress had a debilitating effect on memory (e.g., Loftus, 1979), and some researchers still adhere to that view (Ceci & Bruck, 1993), some work with adults supports the notion that core features of highly emotional events are retained in memory with particular durability, although peripheral details may or may not be as strongly encoded or retained (Christiansson, 1992).

Nevertheless, research findings are quite mixed when it comes to studying children's memory and suggestibility for stressful events. On one hand, findings from several studies of children's memory for stressful events are consistent with the view that core features of stressful events are retained espe-

cially well in memory. For example, Goodman and her colleagues (Goodman, Hepps, & Reed, 1986; Goodman, Hirschman, Hepps, & Rudy, 1991) found that distress was associated with children's more complete recall and greater resistance to suggestion. On the other hand, some researchers (e.g., those who test children's memory for information not integral to the stressor) report decrements in memory (Bugental, Blue, Cortez, Fleck, & Rodriguez, 1992; Peters, 1991). At times, the decrements may reflect a lack of willingness to report memories associated with stressful events, as reflected in less complete free recall (Quas et al., 1999). Some researchers find mixed results even within the same study (Merritt, Ornstein, & Spicker, 1994; Peterson & Bell, 1996). An example of the mix of particularly enduring but not infallible memory for stressful events comes from Peterson and Rideout's (1998) research, in which 2.5- to 3-year-old children who suffered trauma injuries demonstrated largely accurate verbal recall 2 years later, although some errors were made. Interestingly, in that research, a subset of younger children (e.g., 20-25 months at time of injury) could verbally recall the stressful event 18 months later, even though they were not very verbal at the time of the event.

Thus, stressful events may be associated with particularly strong memories, but memories that are in certain ways inaccurate. In a series of clinical studies (Bidrose & Goodman, 2000; Pynoos & Eth, 1984; Pynoos & Nader, 1988; Terr, 1991) concerning children's memories for such horrifying events as homicides of loved ones, kidnappings, sexual abuse, and sniper attacks on schools, both accuracies and inaccuracies were noted. Moreover, certain children may remember stressful events more accurately than others. Important individual differences in children's processing of a stressful event have been uncovered (Goodman, Batterman-Faunce, Quas, Riddlesberger, & Kuhn, 1994; Ornstein, Baker-Ward, Gordon, & Merritt, 1993). Emotional forces, as yet not fully understood, may affect memory for highly traumatic events.

By adulthood, lost memory of traumatic events such as sexual abuse experienced in childhood may occur, although it is difficult to differentiate lost memory from unwillingness to disclose traumatic information (Goodman, Ghetti, Quas, Redlich, & Alexander, 1999; Williams, 1994). Younger age and less legal involvement are associated with greater likelihood of lost memory of sexual abuse (Ghetti et al., 2000).

By adulthood, lost memory of traumatic events such as sexual abuse experienced in childhood may occur, although it is difficult to differentiate lost memory from unwillingness to disclose traumatic information.

False memories of traumatic events are also possible in children and adults. Many have concluded that the flurry of reports in the 1980s and 1990s of satanic cult ritual abuse involved false memories (see Bottoms, Shaver, & Goodman, 1996). False memories in children are more likely, however, for positive events than for negative events (Ceci et al., 1994; Schaaf, Goodman, & Alexander, 1999).

Summary

In summary, research indicates that even young children can, under certain conditions, provide accurate testimony, especially when interviewed in a supportive manner that does not involve highly or multiply suggestive accusatory questions. However, young children can be expected on average to make more errors in their statements than older children and adults. Substantial individual differences exist at all ages. Children may have particularly vivid memories for traumatic events, such as invasive genital touch, but may need to be asked specifically about such touch to reveal that it occurred. False memories, misperceptions, and errors in reporting of traumatic events also can occur. Preschoolers are often more susceptible to error and pose greater challenges for interviewers in attempts to obtain accurate and complete reports.

Children's Communicative Competence

It is through the spoken word that children typically are required to express their memories. Even when a child's memory is accurate and strong, efforts to elicit reliable reports from children may be frustrated by developmental limitations on communication. Only gradually do children master articulation, vocabulary, grammar, and conversational rules of everyday speech. From birth to 10 years of age, children learn to discriminate and articulate sounds, comprehend increasingly more complicated questions, and produce increasingly more complex and intelligible responses. Hence, much of the difficulties posed by child witnesses can be a function of children misunderstanding adult questions and adults misinterpreting children's answers.

To learn to communicate, children rely on familiar adults to structure conversations. They depend on familiar environments to glean meaning from context. With age, children learn to communicate effectively, regardless of the familiarity of the listener or setting. Initially, language serves only a limited number of functions, such as identifying objects and locations. With maturation and experience, language comes to serve a wide array of functions, including the exchange of information via question answering.

In the forensic context, the exchange of information follows unique and unfamiliar rules for sociolinguistic interaction in an unfamiliar setting. Given these conditions, the communication demands of the legal system can be poorly matched to the child's stage of language development. Even older children may not communicate at their optimal level of functioning under such conditions. Recent studies have begun to examine children's abilities to communicate in the forensic setting. The linguistic complexity, vocabulary, and content of questions have been investigated, as have children's comprehension skills.

Linguistic Complexity

Recent studies suggest that many types of grammatical constructions are not mastered by young children but are common in the courtroom. In one study, children's abilities to repeat questions drawn from the transcripts of same-age child witnesses were tested (Brennan & Brennan, 1988). Repetitions were categorized by the degree to which error in repetition (e.g., rephrasing) captured the sense of the original question. Results revealed that children misunderstand many common courtroom question types. Such question types often are referred to as *legalese*. Legalese contains lengthy compound sentences fraught with independent and embedded clauses and grammatical constructions that are beyond the comprehension and memory of many children under 8 years of age. Serious miscommunications can result. When children are asked abuse-related questions in legalese, for example, error rates increase substantially (Carter et al., 1996).

Vocabulary

Researchers have tested children's knowledge of legal terminology. Results suggest that children younger than ages 8 to 10 misunderstand or fail to comprehend many legal terms commonly used with children in and out of court (Flin, Stevenson, & Davies, 1989; Saywitz, Jaenicke, & Camparo, 1990). For example, young children tend to make auditory discrimination errors, mistaking an unfamiliar legal term for a similar-sounding familiar word—for example, interpreting *jury* as *jewelry* ("that stuff my mom wears around her neck and on her finger") or *journey* (a trip) (Saywitz et al., 1990). Children also make errors by assuming that a familiar nonlegal definition is the operative definition in the forensic context. For example, children have maintained that a "court is a place to play basketball," "a hearing is something you do with your ears," and "charges are something you do with a credit card" (Saywitz et al., 1990). Word choice and grammatical construction are critical factors in eliciting accurate reports from children, whether in the courtroom or in an investigative interview.

The vocabulary of the competence examination. To qualify as competent to take the oath, most courts still require that child witnesses have some understanding of the meaning of *truth* and *lie* and appreciate the importance of telling the truth (Lyon, 2000). The ways in which attorneys and judges routinely question children often lead to underestimation of children's competence (Bala et al., 2000; Cashmore & Bussey, 1996). Children find it much easier to identify true and false statements than to explain the difference between the truth and lies or to define the terms (Lyon & Saywitz, 1999).

To demonstrate their understanding of the immorality of lying, children are fre-

quently asked what would happen to them if they lied. Because young children have difficulty in responding to hypothetical questions about negative events, they may refuse to answer such questions because of their fears of the consequences of lying. Children find it easier to describe what will happen to story characters who lie than to imagine themselves lying (Lyon, Saywitz, Kaplan, & Dorado, 2001).

Drawing from research on children's difficulties with traditional competency questions, an oath-taking competency picture task has been developed to sensitively assess young children's basic understanding of the meaning and morality of lying (Lyon & Saywitz, 2000). Using a version of the task, Lyon and Saywitz (1999) found that most maltreated children exhibit a good understanding of truth and lies by 5 years of age, despite serious delays in receptive vocabulary.

The oath itself can also be made more child-friendly. Many elementary schoolchildren do not understand what it means to "swear" to tell the truth (Saywitz et al., 1990). It is recommended that children be asked, "Do you *promise* that you *will* tell the truth?" (Lyon, 2000), although even the word *promise* is not well understood by many preschool children.

Content

Researchers are beginning to examine children's abilities to respond to questions that contain particular content and thus require specific cognitive skills or learning experiences. For example, forensic questions often require witnesses to pinpoint time or location and estimate height or weight by using conventional systems of measurement (e.g., minutes, hours, dates, feet, inches, pounds). Studies suggest that these skills are learned gradually over the course of the elementary school years (Brigham, Vanverst, & Bothwell, 1986; Davies, Stevenson, & Flin, 1988; Friedman, 1982; Saywitz et al., 1991). As discussed later, children may try to answer questions that require skill they have not yet developed. For example, young witnesses might be asked the time or day of an occurrence before they have learned to tell time, skills typically mastered around 7 to 8 years of age (Freidman, 1982). The type of information requested in a question can be an important determinant of the accuracy of children's responses.

Comprehension

Children's abilities to monitor their comprehension and identify misunderstandings are taxed heavily in the forensic context. Recent studies suggest that children being questioned about a past event may try to answer questions they do not fully understand (Saywitz, Snyder, & Nathanson, 1999). Children respond to a part of the question that they understand, typically the beginning or the end of a lengthy question, knowing that it is their turn in the conversation. Their response, however, is not necessarily the answer to the intended question. They follow the everyday rules of being a "good" conversational partner instead of the unique sociolinguistic rules for exchanging evidentiary information.

Although preschoolers have been shown to recognize comprehension difficulties and implement strategies for resolving them, they do so mainly in naturalistic settings on simple, familiar, nonverbal tasks (Gallagher, 1981; Revelle, Wellman, & Karabenik, 1985). In contrast, when settings, tasks, and stimuli are complex, unfamiliar, and verbal, young children may not know when they have failed to understand. In such situations, they rarely request clarification from adults (Asher, 1976; Markman, 1977; Patterson, Massad, & Cosgrove, 1978). Because the forensic context typically represents a complex, unfamiliar situation that relies heavily on verbal exchange, children can be expected to display comprehension-monitoring difficulties.

Currently, researchers are beginning to develop techniques for improving children's abilities to respond accurately to forensic questions (Bull, 1995; Camparo, Wagner, & Saywitz, 2001; Dorado & Saywitz, 2001; Fisher & McCauley, 1995; Saywitz, Geiselman, & Bornstein, 1992; Saywitz et al., 1999; Saywitz & Moan-Hardie, 1994; Saywitz & Snyder, 1996; Saywitz et al., 1996; Sternberg et al., 1997). One recent study suggests that through instruction and preparation, children can be taught to indicate their lack of comprehension and ask for rephrasing of questions, thus improving the resulting accuracy of their reports (Saywitz et al., 1999). After participating in a scripted school activity, 6- to 8-year-olds were interviewed with questions that varied in comprehensibility from easy to difficult. One group of children was instructed, prior to the interview, to tell the interviewer when they did not understand a question. Their

interview responses were significantly more accurate than those of children in a control group who were given only motivating instructions to do their best. A third group of children was prepared for the interview by explicitly teaching them to ask for a rephrase when confronted with incomprehensible questions and then practicing this skill with feedback. This third group provided significantly more accurate reports than children in the other two groups. They told the interviewer they did not understand linguistically complex questions, asked for rephrasing, and, in debriefing after the interview, attributed their success to this strategy.

In summary, studies suggest that the quality of a child's report depends on the competence of the questioner to ask questions in language children can comprehend about concepts they can understand. Communication also depends on the child's ability to detect and cope with noncomprehension, a skill that may be enhanced through instruction and preparation.

Children in Court

Children's increased participation in legal settings has brought considerable public and legislative attention not only to children's eyewitness memory but also to children's emotional capability to withstand legal proceedings. Courtrooms are austere, formal settings capable of intimidating adults, not to mention children. What do children know about the legal system, how does participation in it affect them, and what can be done to aid children while still protecting the rights of the accused?

Children's Legal Knowledge

Research adds to our understanding of children's expectations and fears of the legal system. Children have limited legal knowledge. Children possess misunderstandings and unrealistic as well as realistic fears of the legal process (Cashmore & Bussey, 1990; Flin et al., 1989; Melton, Limber, Jacobs, & Oberlander, 1992; Saywitz, 1989; Warren-Leubecker, Tate, Hinton, & Ozbek, 1989). As might be expected, with age, children show increasing knowledge of legal terms. One might suspect increasing knowledge comes from greater exposure to legal concepts. Although this is undoubtedly true, developmental differences in legal knowledge are not just a matter of exposure. Two studies indicate that children who were involved directly in the legal system showed *less* accurate knowledge and *more* confusion than age mates without legal experience (Melton et al., 1992; Saywitz, 1989).

By 10 years of age, most children understand the basics of the investigative and judicial process. Ten-year-olds grasp the functions of the various court personnel, and they have rudimentary notions of legal representation and the adversarial process. Younger children, 4 to 7 years of age, are aware of court personnel, but their conceptualizations are based on observations of overt behavior (e.g., "The judge is there to sit at a high desk and bang the hammer. He wears a black gown; I don't know why."). These younger children may not be aware that the judge is in charge of the courtroom. Young children have little conception of invisible abstractions, such as laws, rules of evidence, or trial procedures. Children younger than age 10 do not fully understand the decision-making role of the jury or judge, often assuming that jurors are mere spectators (Saywitz, 1989; Warren-Leubecker et al., 1989). On the other hand, children as young as 5 years of age understand the need to tell the truth in court (Cashmore & Bussey, 1990; Saywitz, 1989). Although younger children cite fear of punishment as the reason for telling the truth, older children understand the fact-finding purpose of the trial.

Many authors speculate that lack of knowledge can adversely affect the quality of children's evidence because anxiety associated with fear of the unknown disrupts memory performance (Cashmore & Bussey, 1990; Flin, 1993; Melton & Thompson, 1987; Sas et al., 1991; Saywitz, 1989; Saywitz & Snyder, 1996). Even when age is taken into account, children with less legal knowledge express more anxiety about testifying in mock trials (Goodman, Tobey, et al., 1998). However, studies have not shown a definitive link between lack of legal knowledge and poor memory performance in the forensic setting, although at least one study uncovered a positive correlation between legal knowledge and accurate answers to specific questions posed in a mock trial (Goodman, Tobey, et al., 1998).

Other support for the hypothesis that court-related fear disrupts memory performance comes from experimental studies that concern eyewitness testimony when children are questioned in a courtroom (involving a simulated trial environment) compared with a school or a private room (Hill & Hill, 1987; Saywitz & Nathanson, 1993; Saywitz, Nathanson, Snyder, & Lamphear, 1993). These studies show impaired recall and greater physiological correlates of anxiety (heart rate variability) when children are questioned in a courtroom atmosphere. It is unclear, however, from these studies if knowledge of courtroom procedures mediates the results.

Also germane are studies showing inhibited performance on identification tasks associated with confrontational stress at the time of questioning (Dent, 1977; Peters, 1991).

It is possible that in actual trials, children who are more knowledgeable about the legal system will show greater anxiety than less knowledgeable age mates because the more knowledgeable children would know, for example, that an attempt would be made to discredit their testimony in court. Older children and girls have been found to express greater negativity about testifying than younger children and boys (Goodman, Pyle-Taub, et al., 1992), and older children who experience harsh cross-examination in court fare less well emotionally (Whitcomb et al., 1992). Further research is needed to address the relation between legal knowledge, the stress of testifying, and eyewitness performance.

Fears of court expressed by both child witnesses and peers with little or no legal experience include fears of public speaking, losing self-control on the stand, and not being believed (Cashmore & Bussey, 1990; Sas et al., 1991; Saywitz & Nathanson, 1993). Children also express concern that as a witness they would have to prove their own innocence in court. Some children fear they will be punished or sent to jail for making a mistake. In addition, child witnesses express fear of facing the accused in court, retaliation, and physical harm to self or loved ones, especially if threatened not to tell. In intrafamilial cases of abuse, children express fear of angering family members if negative consequences are anticipated, such as loss of income. Although many of these fears also are expressed by adult rape victims (Katz & Mazur, 1979), children's emotional immaturity is likely to make them more vulnerable than adults to these fears.

In summary, as might be expected, children are relatively naive about the intricacies of the legal system and even about common legal terms that are used in court. Children have fears about testifying. One could well question the adequacy of the courtroom as an ideal setting for obtaining complete and accurate testimony from children. Although the courtroom is also less than an ideal setting for adult victim/witnesses, children's emotional and cognitive immaturity places them at an even greater risk of adverse effects.

Effects on Children of Legal Participation

What are the effects on children of participation in the legal system? A number of studies suggest that at least for a subset of children, involvement as witnesses in the criminal justice system is associated with the prolonging of emotional distress (e.g., DeFrancis, 1969; Goodman, Pyle-Taub, et al., 1992; Oates & Tong, 1987; Runyan, Everson, Edelsohn, Hunter, & Coulter, 1988). In contrast, involvement as a witness in the juvenile justice system has not been found to be associated with increased emotional problems (Runyan et al., 1988). Next, we review research on some of the stressors for children who become involved as victim/witnesses in prosecutions of child sexual abuse.

One stressor for children that is inherent in the criminal justice system concerns repetition of interviews by different persons. When children are involved in forensic investigations and prosecutions, the children may be interviewed more than once. Police, social workers, investigators, clinicians, attorneys, and judges may all have occasion to interview the child. Concerns about multiple interviews revolve around possible adverse effects on children's emotional well-being (e.g., by forcing them, in effect, to reexperience the trauma multiple times by having to describe it over and over), intensification of children's feelings of self-blame and guilt about the abuse experience (Runyan et al., 1988), and promotion of inaccuracies in children's memory (Ceci & Bruck, 1995). On the other hand, repeated interviewing can help consolidate accurate memory (Brainerd & Ornstein, 1991). Research reveals that a greater number of interviewers or interviews is associated with lower ratings of perceived helpfulness of the legal system and higher scores on measurers

of traumatization (Henry, 1997; Tedesco & Schnell, 1987). Fortunately, many jurisdictions have established children's advocacy centers (also called multidisciplinary interview centers) to reduce the number of times children are interviewed.

Perhaps the quintessential stressor for children is testifying face-to-face with the defendant in court and submitting to cross-examination.

Perhaps the quintessential stressor for children is testifying face-to-face with the defendant in court and submitting to cross-examination. Several studies confirm that testifying face-to-face with the accused in criminal court is associated with continued distress in a subset of children (Goodman, Pyle-Taub, et al., 1992; Whitcomb et al., 1992). Factors such as facing the defendant, harsh cross-examination, and lack of corroborative evidence have been identified as contributing to the distress testifiers often experience. However, even anticipation of testifying in criminal court is associated with children's increased distress and anxiety (Berliner & Conte, 1995). Feelings of helplessness and fear may increase as the scheduled day for testifying approaches, even though only a subset of children subpoenaed to court actually take the stand. (Defendants frequently accept plea bargains at the last minute, relieving the child of the need to testify.)

Another stressor concerns the length of the legal process. Research reveals that when legal cases are prolonged and unresolved, children are likely to continue to score relatively high on measures of depression. These findings are maintained regardless of whether children testify, their age, and the abuse characteristics (Runyan et al., 1988).

These are just some of the stressors for children in the legal system (for reviews, Edelstein et al., in press; Spencer & Flin, 1993). Research has concentrated more on the stressors than on factors that can buffer the distress. Nevertheless, one factor has consistently emerged as a buffer for child witnesses. Specifically, maternal support can moderate the potentially adverse effects of children's legal involvement. Maternal support at the time of disclosure of abuse is a predictor of children's well-being (Everson, Hunter, Runyan, Edelsohn, & Coulter, 1989; Sas, 1993), and maternal support is also important throughout the legal case. Lack of maternal support is associated with adverse mental health outcomes for children who testify and is a predictor of children feeling negative about legal involvement more generally (Goodman, Pyle-Taub, et al., 1992).

Clearly, participation as a victim/witness can at times be a stressful experience for many children. However, research findings on the effects of legal involvement are likely to vary over time because of changes in legal procedures affecting children. For instance, in the United States, use of children's advocacy centers may affect children's reactions to legal involvement. In some European countries, such as England, dramatic legal reforms for child victim/witnesses include use of videotaped forensic interviews in place of in-court direct examination and use of closed-circuit (live-link) television during cross-examination, both of which limit or prevent face-to-face confrontation. Several such reforms are discussed in the next section of this chapter.

Improving the Process

Given that children may be required to become involved in legal investigations and testify, are there ways we can improve the current system? Are there ways we can help prepare children for the experience?

Researchers are investigating the efficacy of legal reforms thought to improve the investigative and judicial process (e.g., Goodman, Quas, Bulkley, & Shapiro, 1999; Whitcomb et al., 1992). The goal of these reforms is to elicit the most accurate information from children in the least stressful manner. The reforms include scientifically based techniques for interviewing children, special methods to prepare children for court, implementation of multidisciplinary interviewing teams, and use of innovative courtroom procedures, such as closed-circuit television. Here we discuss the results of these initial efforts to improve the quality of children's testimony and reduce their stress.

Interview Instructions

Researchers are beginning to examine the effects of giving children instructions before the interview. For example, techniques for increasing children's resistance to suggestive questions are being studied. Researchers have warned children that questions might be tricky (Warren, Hulse-Trotter, & Tubbs, 1991) or that admitting lack of knowledge ("I don't know") is preferable to acquiescence (e.g., Saywitz & Moan-Hardie, 1994). Initially, researchers found no effects of simple instructions giving children permission to say "I don't know" before a memory interview (Moston, 1987). More recently, however, three sets of researchers have increased children's use of "I don't know" in response to misleading questions when children are given reminders during the interview or practice with feedback before the interview (Howie & O'Neill, 1996; Mulder & Vrij, 1996; Saywitz & Moan-Hardie, 1994).

For example, in two preparation studies, children were warned that when an interviewer was not present at the event in question, he or she could not know what really happened, but he or she might inadvertently put a guess into the question. Then children were discouraged from "going along" with the interviewer's guess and encouraged to admit lack of knowledge ("I don't know") or to tell the answer if known (Saywitz & Moan-Hardie, 1994). Before the interview, children practiced resisting misleading questions about unrelated events in the waiting room. The children received positive feedback when appropriate. Children prepared in this manner resisted significantly more misleading questions than children in control groups.

Some evidence suggests that instructions might promote children's motivation and effort in the interview (e.g., "Do your best" and "Try your hardest to listen carefully and tell everything you remember."). Children may not always recognize that the forensic interview is a situation demanding high levels of attention and effort. Impulsive or careless answering might heighten rates of acquiescence to adult suggestion. In fact, children who have experienced traumatic events and losses may show symptoms of depression or posttraumatic stress, which could include indifference, hopelessness, helplessness, fatigue, avoidance, or poor concentration, that could affect effort and motivation. Compared with a no-instructions scenario, motivating instructions were associated with more complete free recall of a staged event for preschoolers and school-age children (Dorado & Saywitz, 2001; Saywitz & Snyder, 1996; Saywitz et al., 1996).

Innovative Questioning Formats

Recently, a number of innovative interview formats and protocols have been developed. Several have been tested empirically. The *cognitive interview* has received considerable attention because of its potential as a possible means of obtaining detailed information from children in a nonleading format. The cognitive interview is a collection of memory enhancement techniques based on principles of cognitive psychology. It has been shown to elicit 35% more information from adults than standard police interviews (Geiselman & Fisher, 1989). The four basic retrieval aids that comprise the bulk of the cognitive interview are (a) mentally reconstructing the context at the time of the crime; (b) reporting even partial information, regardless of perceived importance; (c) recounting events in a variety of orders; and (d) reporting events from a variety of perspectives. The cognitive interview has been revised for use with children (Fisher & McCauley, 1995; Saywitz et al., 1992; for a review, see Fisher, Brennan, & McCauley, in press).

Studies of children have revealed positive results when comparing the cognitive interview to standard police interview techniques (better recall without increased error) or no differences in one study when compared to motivating instructions in a brief interview by college students (Memon, Cronin, Eaves, & Bull, 1996, Experiment 2).

In one study, the revised cognitive interview was tested with 7- to 12-year-olds who were interviewed by experienced, off-duty police officers, resulting in a 26% improvement over standard police interviews and a 45% improvement over standard police interviews when children were given practice using the retrieval aids prior to the interview (Saywitz et al., 1992). Researchers find one component of the cognitive interview, the change-perspective task, difficult for young children. Some recommend that it be reserved for adults until there is further study of its effects with children (Fisher &

McCauley, 1995; Saywitz & Geiselman, 1998).

Another new questioning technique, *narrative elaboration,* is designed to increase the detail and relevance of information children provide without the use of leading questions (Camparo et al., 2001; Dorado & Saywitz, 2001; Saywitz & Snyder, 1996; Saywitz et al., 1996). In line with the notion that interviewers should use the least leading approaches first, the narrative elaboration procedure is intended as an interim step between free recall and leading questions to help children elaborate on free recall in their own words. Children learn that the interviewer expects them to provide the most independent, detailed, and forensically relevant report possible in their own words with the fewest number of questions asked by the interviewer. Before the interview, children practice reporting the details of an unrelated event (e.g., morning routine for getting up, dressed, fed, and transported to school) with feedback. They are taught to provide a high level of detail regarding four categories of forensically relevant information (the participants, setting, actions, conversations). Children use four cards that depict an unbiased reminder of each category (e.g., participants card depicts a stick figure; setting card depicts a line drawing of a house and yard).

When children are questioned about the event under investigation, they are asked an open-ended free-recall question after which they are shown each card and asked simply, "Does this card remind you to tell something else?" In four separate studies of recall for staged events, children (ages 4-12) responded to the cards with additional accurate details and without generating more error than comparison groups. In one study, 6- to 11-year-olds using this technique evinced a 53% greater increase in accurate information about a past school activity than did children in a control group who received no intervention (Saywitz & Snyder, 1996).

These studies begin to suggest that relatively unbiased retrieval aids can be developed to help children overcome the incompleteness of their spontaneous free recall without resorting to leading questions. However, if these aids encourage elaboration and increase children's productivity when children are questioned about fictitious events, false reporting could increase as well. One study of staged and fictitious events compared standard interview formats (free recall followed by specific questions) to the narrative elaboration format (free recall followed by an opportunity for elaboration using reminder cards before specific questions) (Camparo et al., 2001). The results suggest that when children report an event in free recall but provide few details, narrative elaboration is successful at helping children report additional accurate detail without generating any more error than standard interview formats. However, when children who deny that an event occurred in free recall continue to be vigorously questioned about the fictitious event nonetheless, a small number of children may respond to the cards with false information that would not otherwise have occurred, although the majority do not.

Another team of researchers (see Sternberg et al., 1996) has developed a *structured interview protocol* derived from the results of laboratory research but tested with investigative interviews in actual cases. The impetus for the protocol derives from the fact that several studies have found that even trained interviewers tend to abandon open-ended questions too quickly and resort prematurely to suggestive questions (Aldridge & Cameron, 1999; Craig, Scheibe, Kircher, Raskin, & Dodd, 1999; Sternberg et al., in press; Warren et al., 1999). Research indicates that the structured protocol helps interviewers ask more open-ended questions, and these questions elicit more details per question than option posing (yes-no and forced choice) and suggestive questions (Hershkowitz, Lamb, Sternberg, & Esplin, 1997; Lamb, Hershkowitz, Sternberg, Boat, & Everson, 1996; Lamb, Hershkowitz, Sternberg, Esplin, et al., 1996). Although the overall number of details does not appear to increase with use of the structured protocol (Orbach et al., 2000; Sternberg et al., 1999), the researchers point out that because a higher proportion of the details are elicited through open-ended questions, they are likely to be more accurate. The researchers are currently testing whether the structured protocol indeed improves accuracy, which requires a laboratory setting in which the accuracy of the child's statements can be objectively measured.

Sternberg, Lamb, and colleagues' structured interview protocol includes rapport building and instructions that teach children to indicate when they do not understand a question, acknowledge when they do not know the answer to a question, and resist suggestive questions. The abuse-specific portion of the interview introduces the topic by asking the child why he or she came to talk to the interviewer. If the child does not reveal abuse, the interviewer asks a series of increasingly focused questions but avoids naming the alleged perpetrator or specifying the alleged act. These questions include the following: "I heard that you saw a policeman last week. Tell me what you talked about" and "Tell me why you think your mom brought you here today."

If the child discloses abuse, the interviewer responds, "Tell me everything that happened to you, from the beginning to the end, as best as you can remember." The interviewer prompts the child to provide more information through open-ended questions regarding the order of events, such as, "Tell me what happened next," and then open-ended questions regarding specific details, such as, "Tell me more about [a detail mentioned by the child]." If the interviewer does feel compelled to ask a more focused question (e.g., "Where were your clothes?"), he or she would follow up with an open-ended question (Child: "He took them off." Interviewer: "Tell me everything about how they got off."). After the initial free narrative is complete, the interviewer asks, "Did that happen one time or more than one time?" and if the child responds "more than one time," the interviewer asks the child to describe the "last time something happened," the best-remembered time, the first time something happened, and any other time the child remembers.

As mentioned earlier, interviewers trained in use of the protocol ask more open-ended questions and fewer option-posing questions, and children interviewed under the protocol produce more details in response to open-ended questions (Orbach et al., 2000; Sternberg, Lamb, Esplin, & Baradaran, 1999).

There is some evidence, however, to suggest that this protocol is less useful with preschoolers (Hershkowitz, Orbach, Lamb, Sternberg, & Horowitz, 2001; Lamb, Hershkowitz, Sternberg, Boat, & Everson, 1996; Lamb, Hershkowitz, Sternberg, Esplin, et al., 1996; Sternberg et al., 1996; Sternberg et al., 1997) and reticent children (Hershkowitz & Elul, 1999). This evidence is consistent with findings from a study in England by Davies et al. (2000). In that study, researchers analyzed videotapes from 36 forensic interviews of 4- to 14-year-olds in child sexual abuse cases. Longer answers were elicited from 12- to 14-year-olds in response to open-ended questions versus closed and specific (but not highly leading) questions, but this pattern was basically reversed for the younger two age groups. Further research is under way to better understand the conditions in which highly structured protocols are most beneficial.

Reforming the Investigative Process

Studies have identified characteristics of the investigative process that can compromise memory for detail and interfere with a child's psychological recovery from trauma (Ceci & Bruck, 1993; Goodman, Pyle-Taub, et al., 1992; Tedesco & Schnell, 1987). These include protracted investigations, developmentally insensitive personnel, repeated interviews or court appearances, and multiple interviewers. Investigations conducted by multidisciplinary teams with a high level of coordination among law enforcement and social service agencies are thought to produce more accurate and complete information with less stress placed on children. When such teams are employed, a single interviewer (e.g., a police officer) may question the child, having consulted first with officials from relevant agencies (e.g., social services) on important questions to ask. In some settings, such officials watch behind a one-way mirror to reduce the need for subsequent interviews.

One field study examined the effectiveness of such a team approach on the investigative process (California Attorney General's Office, 1994). Cases before and after the implementation of a multidisciplinary child interview center (MDIC) were examined: 177 consecutive cases of suspected child sexual abuse reported to police in Sacramento County, California, were compared with 212 cases investigated after institution of a countywide MDIC. The center was associated with significantly fewer interviews, interviewers, and interview settings per case. Furthermore, children themselves rated the center-based interviews more positively than standard practices. Unfortunately, data were not collected on the number of additional interviews during the judicial phase of cases. Therefore, it is not possible to know how the MDIC affected interview patterns at later stages. There was no evidence that the MDIC affected the rates at which charges were filed in courts. Hence, factors thought to be associated with stress and contamination (repeated inter-

views) were reduced, but the costs associated with these benefits remain unknown.

Preparing Children for Court

Preparation is one of many factors that can influence children's testimony and their subjective experience of the process (see Spencer & Flin, 1993). Attorneys who prepare children for court typically include a tour of the courtroom and perhaps a cursory review of the facts of the case. Although preliminary studies suggest a tour of the courtroom is indeed beneficial for children in reducing anxiety (Goodman, Sachsenmaier, et al., 1992), these steps alone are not sufficient to prepare children for the communicative, cognitive, and emotional challenges witnesses face (Saywitz & Snyder, 1996). Moreover, young children's limited knowledge of the legal system leaves them ill equipped to understand the context and function of their testimony. They possess a limited repertoire of coping strategies to prevent anxiety from interfering with ability to testify optimally.

Recently, court schools designed to prepare children for the judicial process have appeared around the country. Some are operated by prosecutors and are approved by the judicial administration. Others are operated by social service or mental health agencies. Typically, the content is focused on educating children about courtroom personnel and their functions. Sometimes, programs include anxiety reduction techniques as well. The degree to which the facts of individual cases are discussed during court school sessions seems to vary widely. However, some programs prepare children in groups and prohibit discussion of individual cases to avoid contamination of testimony.

By and large, the efficacy of such programs has not been tested empirically. Because there is little systematic evaluation of these programs, it is difficult to determine which, if any, of the components of these programs actually improve children's performances and reduce stress. Also, there is insufficient evidence that such efforts are free of side effects that could influence children's testimony in unintended ways.

One preparation program has been subjected to systematic evaluation (Sas et al., 1991). In Canada, alleged victims of abuse received either status quo services from the Victim Witness Assistance Program or individual preparation focused on demystifying the process with education and anxiety reduction techniques such as relaxation training. Children receiving the experimental preparation gained more knowledge of the legal system and showed less generalized fear and less abuse-specific fear (e.g., fears of revictimization). Nevertheless, group differences in fear of testifying or fear specific to court were not found.

From this study, the effects of preparation on the accuracy of children's testimony could not be evaluated because there was no record of the crime under investigation against which to compare the accuracy of the children's memory. When children from the preparation program testified in court, however, the case was more likely to be associated with a conviction than when children from the regular services group testified. Whether this can be linked to children's performance on the stand requires further investigation. Attorneys rated children from the preparation program as better witnesses; unfortunately, the attorneys were not blind raters and may have been invested in the success of the program to which they referred their clients. Despite the limitations in this study, it is the first of its kind and an important springboard for future research.

In addition to field studies of ongoing programs, there is a need for experimental analog studies that examine the effects of preparation on children's reports of previously staged events. In this way, children's reports with and without preparation can be compared to a record of the event in question to examine both positive and negative effects on accuracy. Researchers have begun to examine the effects of legal education and anxiety reduction techniques on accuracy (Saywitz et al., 1993). Preliminary results suggest that although children learn a great deal about the system and appear less anxious when prepared, increased accuracy and reduced fear of testifying have been difficult to document. This is partially due to the lack of sensitive measurement instruments, young children's limited ability to report anxiety, and differences between "normal" research subjects and abused children (e.g., in levels of motivation and anxiety).

Many of the clinical approaches to anxiety reduction are thought to be helpful to child witnesses. Techniques such as deep breathing, guided imagery, self-monitoring, and self-statements ("I can do it") are found to have beneficial effects in other contexts.

Examinations of their effects on memory are a fruitful area for further research.

Special Court Procedures

At present, most child witnesses are not given the benefits of special programs to prepare them to testify. What measures can be taken to make the courtroom more "child friendly"? Goodman, Pyle-Taub, et al. (1992) found that when children testified in criminal court, they were better able to answer questions and looked less frightened when a parent or loved one was permitted to stay in the courtroom with them. The children also cried less when the courtroom was closed to spectators. In contrast, children who were more frightened of the defendant had more difficulty answering the prosecutor's questions and later expressed greater negativity about having been involved in the prosecution.

In an attempt to shelter children from the intimidation of facing the defendant and from testifying in open court, closed-circuit television can be used in certain child sexual abuse cases (*Maryland v. Craig,* 1990). Such technology is being employed in England with encouraging results. For example, children appear as more fluent, confident, relaxed, and consistent witnesses when they testify via closed-circuit television (Davies & Noon, 1991; see also Cashmore, 1992). However, there is also an indication that jurors are more likely to mistrust a child's statements and that the child's testimony will have less impact on them when it is presented via closed-circuit television (Davies & Noon, 1991; Goodman, Sachsenmaier, et al., 1992; Goodman, Tobey, et al., 1998). District attorneys claim that the maximum impact is from the child testifying live (Goodman et al., in press). For this and other reasons, Israel is considering reverting back to increased use of live testimony for children rather than having child interviewers testify in children's place (I. Hershkowitz, personal communication, 2000).

It is possible that other formats for obtaining children's testimony will be even more beneficial to justice and to children; in the United States, there is evidence of public support for a variety of alternative means of gathering testimony from children (Batterman-Faunce & Goodman, 1993; Goodman et al., 1994), such as using children's courtrooms and having a neutral clinician rather than an attorney take the child's testimony, the latter of which is permitted in some countries such as Norway. Strong empirical evidence that such procedures improve the fact-finding process are needed before the U.S. courts will be likely to consider them because they represent drastic changes to traditional procedures.

Practice Implications

The results of child witness research have a number of implications for children's performance in pretrial interviews and legal proceedings. Below, we discuss implications for interviewing children in forensic settings and for presenting their testimony in court.

Questioning Children

Studies suggest important age differences in children's responses to questioning. Different techniques will be required to elicit accurate information from children of different age groups. Interviewing protocols are needed that are sensitive to developmental differences in free recall, suggestibility, communicative competence, and socioemotional concerns (e.g., intimidation, embarrassment). Protocols also must be sensitive to individual differences among children and to different cultural expectations across ethnic groups.

Preschool children. Preschool children's special deficiencies—limited free recall, deference to adults, and source-monitoring errors—make them vulnerable to suggestion through coercive questioning. What is the interviewer to do? Interviewers must carefully consider the form, content, and context of their questions. Clearly, studies suggest there are question types to be avoided altogether such as tag questions (e.g., "He hurt you, didn't he?"), negative term questions (e.g., "Didn't he hurt you?"), or suppositional questions (e.g., "Where did he hurt you?" if the child has not mentioned hurting). Strongly worded accusatory questions and accusatory contexts should be avoided as well (e.g., "John hurt you, didn't he?" "Tell me about the bad things that bad man did to you."). They can affect the child's memory and the child's credibility adversely.

Although leading questions are to be avoided whenever possible, preschoolers are likely to benefit from specific questions to trigger memory for additional information not provided spontaneously. Open-ended questions (questions that cannot be answered in a single word) that focus the child's attention on particular aspects of an event (e.g., "Tell me everything that you *heard*"; "Where did it happen?") can increase the completeness of young children's reports without decreasing accuracy (Hamond & Fivush, 1991; Hudson, 1990; Poole & Lindsay, 1995), even if repeated over interviews (see reviews in Fivush & Schwarzmueller, 1995; Poole & White, 1995).

> *Although leading questions are to be avoided whenever possible, preschoolers are likely to benefit from specific questions to trigger memory for additional information not provided spontaneously.*

Children are often most resistant to leading questions about central actions, but at times, even statements concerning central actions can be contaminated through the use of leading questioning. Important individual differences exist in children's responses, with many children retaining accuracy in the face of specific questioning, especially in regard to salient abuse-related actions such as nakedness. The majority of false reports that do occur in research studies are often limited to false affirmations of misleading yes-no questions (e.g., "He touched your private parts, didn't he?"), although some children will provide false detail as well, perhaps especially if multiply suggestive, repeated questioning occurs. If interviewers use yes-no questions with children, follow-up questions that require children to explain their answer in their own words (e.g., "What makes you think so?") could be critical to untangling the meaning of children's answers. Interviewers must remain as open-minded as possible rather than pursue an "agenda," especially when corroborative evidence is lacking.

To bolster the reliability of preschoolers' reports, interviewers should carefully consider the language, content, and suggestiveness of questions. Interviewers can keep misunderstandings to a minimum by keeping questions short, grammatical constructions simple, and vocabulary familiar. Accuracy is also promoted when questions concern events that are salient and meaningful to children and when question content is matched closely to children's knowledge and experience. Accuracy can be facilitated when hesitant preschoolers are not pressured, coerced, or bullied into answering questions by authority figures. Inconsistencies can be probed by professing confusion, not by challenging children. Suggestibility may be reduced when interviewers are neutral or supportive of children's efforts but do not praise them for providing specific content. Interviewer bias can be reduced when interviewers take an objective, nonjudgmental stance on both nonverbal and verbal levels (e.g., tone of voice, facial expression, wording of questions). This does not preclude empathic comments to overcome children's anxiety. It does imply that an accusatory climate must be avoided, for example, one in which suspects are labeled as "bad" and assumed to have done "bad things."

Preschoolers can be inconsistent in their retelling of past events across multiple interviews (Fivush, 1993; Fivush & Shukar, 1995). Different settings and different questioning styles can result in disclosure of different pieces of information at different points in time. More complete and detailed renditions can be expected from children in familiar and informal settings than in unfamiliar, formal, and anxiety-provoking settings (Ceci, Bronfenbrenner, & Baker, 1988; Saywitz & Nathanson, 1993; Saywitz et al., 1993). The practice of equating inconsistency with false information should be reevaluated in light of these findings.

On one hand, a generic or general question may be best for avoiding any hint of suggestion. On the other hand, such questions can elicit irrelevancies and inconsistencies from preschoolers. For example, when asked, "Did he put *something in* your mouth?" a young child is likely to answer no. If asked more specifically, "Did he put *a thermometer* in your mouth?" the same child is likely to say yes, responding accurately about a physical examination (Saywitz et al., 1991). When asked if he or she saw a weapon after witnessing a shooting, a preschooler is likely to answer no. If asked more specifically, "Did you see a gun?" the same child is likely to respond yes. Hierarchical, conceptual categories, such as *weapon,* may not be understood, but concrete, familiar objects, such as *gun,* may be

understood well. Although the more general term is less leading, it can create inconsistencies and errors. Preschoolers reason on the basis of what they can see and visualize (specifics) rather than on abstract concepts and principles (generalities).

Sexual abuse investigators will probably find it difficult to elicit complete narratives from genuinely abused children without resorting to some specific questions. To determine the appropriate charges, prosecutors need to know certain specific information (e.g., was force involved, was the abuse repeated). Children who are reluctant to disclose embarrassing experiences are more likely to acknowledge those experiences if asked specific questions than if asked for free recall (Saywitz et al., 1991). Similarly, specific questions are more effective than recall questions in eliciting reports of wrongdoing that children have been told to keep secret (Wilson & Pipe, 1989). Specific questions may also help to overcome younger children's limited productive vocabulary, particularly for sexual topics (Schor & Sivan, 1989), and younger children's limited understanding of what information is important or expected (Fivush, 1993).

Obtaining the most complete and accurate reports from preschoolers remains a challenge. Sandra Hewitt (1998) devotes an entire book to the subject. Practitioners can anticipate an expanding body of relevant research that can inform decision making in the field. No doubt, today's techniques will need to be revised and updated tomorrow.

Elementary-age children. Elementary-age children (5 to 11 years of age) show both strengths and weaknesses. Under certain conditions, their performance may exceed that of adults (e.g., reporting details that go unnoticed by grown-ups). Under many other conditions, elementary-age children show noteworthy limitations. Individual practitioners need to conduct a cost-benefit analysis on a case-by-case basis, combining clinical judgment with knowledge of the dangers of leading questions.

Because children within this age range often can provide detailed narratives of events, inquiry can begin with open-ended questions to elicit free recall. Then, children can be prompted to elaborate on their narratives in a nonbiased manner with comments such as, "Tell me a little more," "What happened next?" or repeating the end of their last sentence with a rising intonation. Although capable of providing accurate narratives, free recall is still likely to be incomplete, and specific follow-up questions may be necessary. Research and clinical literature have suggested that interviewers proceed from narrative elaboration to open-ended questions ("What was the weather like that night?" "What kinds of clothes was she wearing?") and then to specific, short-answer questions ("What color was her scarf?"), reserving closed questions (yes-no, multiple choice) for the end, if used at all (Lamb, 1994; Lamb, Hershkowitz, Sternberg, Boat, & Everson, 1996; Lamb, Hershkowitz, Sternberg, Esplin, et al., 1996; *Memorandum of Good Practice,* 1992; Saywitz, 1994, 1995; Saywitz & Geiselman, 1998). Research results suggest that yes-no questions must be dealt with cautiously but need not be avoided totally (Peterson & Bell, 1996; Saywitz et al., 1991). Such questions can be followed by attempts to elicit elaboration ("Tell me more") or justification ("What makes you think so?") to avoid misinterpretation. The ensuing explanation helps determine how much or how little weight to place on a child's response.

Some interviewers deem it necessary to ask specific questions about information that may not otherwise be reported (e.g., sexual or injurious contact) for a variety of reasons (e.g., the child's embarrassment or fear of retaliation). Research on elementary-age children's accuracy in the face of leading or misleading questions suggests that elementary-age children are more resistant than preschool children (e.g., Goodman & Reed, 1986). Interviewers also need to be aware of the possibility of lying or coaching.

School-age children may benefit from learning about the investigative and judicial process (Sas et al., 1991; Saywitz et al., 1993). These children have a better understanding of the broader context in which the interview occurs, the purpose of questioning, the role of the interviewer, and the limits on confidentiality. This could facilitate increased familiarity and decreased anxiety, resulting in improved interview performance.

School-age children benefit from a warning that they might not understand all the questions and from instructions to announce when they do not understand (Saywitz & Snyder, 1996). As discussed earlier, studies suggest that children benefit from preinterview practice with strategies for detecting and coping with noncomprehension (Saywitz & Snyder, 1996).

Inconsistencies or contradictions in children's statements can result from a variety of interview-induced sources, such as developmentally inappropriate wording of questions. These can be reduced or eliminated when questions are well matched in vocabulary and linguistic complexity to the school-age child's stage of language acquisition. For example, elementary-school children's knowledge of common legal terms cannot be assumed. Children may think they understand a term's meaning when, in fact, they and the adult interviewer have a different meaning in mind. When asked, "Do you know what testify means?" a child may answer yes but may be thinking about taking a test. In general, interviewers need to avoid or compensate for linguistic forms that are slow to develop.

If children have to testify, elementary-school children should be helped to reduce the gap between everyday rules of conversation and the language of the courtroom. For example, interview questions often jump from one topic to another without the necessary transition for children to switch frames of reference (Brennan & Brennan, 1988). Children become disoriented. They require transitional comments to signal a change of topic that may be rare in the courtroom context. For example, "Before, we were talking about school. Now I want to ask you about your vacation."

Adolescents. For many forensic purposes, the interview performance of children older than age 11 can be expected to be comparable to that of a large number of adults, at least in terms of quantity and quality of memory, resistance to suggestion, legal knowledge, comprehension of questions, and formulation of verbal responses. Unfortunately, few studies directly concern teenagers' testimony about sexual matters (but see Bidrose & Goodman, 2000; Eisen et al., 2001). Therefore, developmental differences in interview performance due to the effects of emotions (e.g., embarrassment), self-image, and coping strategies have not been well researched. Likewise, the interaction between interview performance and individual differences in expressions of stress and psychological disturbance (e.g., posttraumatic stress disorder) has yet to be understood fully. Even older children may differ substantially from adults in these respects. Because research on adolescents' testimony in regard to sexual abuse allegations is lacking, we hesitate to provide many guidelines concerning the interviewing of adolescents.

Limits of current knowledge. Despite the age-related trends described earlier, there is danger in generalizing to individual cases using research studies based on averages and probabilities. It is important to note that a given child may be delayed or advanced for his or her age in one or more domains of development. A child with excellent verbal skills for his or her age may nevertheless have poor retrieval strategies and inferior recall of details, especially if the child is intimidated or frightened more easily. Moreover, the ecological validity of research studies is limited. Much of the most recent research on suggestibility examines the effects of highly leading techniques on preschool-age children and is of questionable applicability to grade-school children questioned in a more routine manner. Moreover, the research on suggestibility rarely takes account of factors such as fear, loyalty, and embarrassment, which make children less likely to make false claims of sexual abuse and make truly abused children reluctant to reveal (Lyon, 1999).

Studies have not produced a single, proper method for interviewing child victim witnesses that can be held out as the standard by which all questioning should be conducted. The proper balance between open-ended and specific questions is in part a question for researchers but also entails value judgments regarding the trade-offs between false affirmations and false denials. Even with more research, the judgment of experienced professionals is needed to apply one or more of a variety of interviewing strategies.

It seems fair to conclude that when children are questioned as if they were adults, their testimony can be contaminated and their credibility undermined; children misunderstand complex questions, adults misinterpret children's responses, and children fail to clarify their meaning. An accepting, unbiased environment that poses understandable questions in an objective yet empathic climate should be created to maximize reliability and minimize suggestibility. The interviewer builds a bridge between the world of the child and the world of the adult to create the best opportunity for the discovery of truth.

Court Appearances

Research permits implications to be drawn in regard to children's courtroom testimony. Special approaches for preparing children to testify and for reducing their anxiety hold promise in bolstering children's abilities to withstand the lengthy and stressful criminal justice system. However, such programs and approaches must be considered carefully in each jurisdiction to ensure that they meet with attorneys' approval so that challenges to children's credibility are minimized.

Factors such as lack of maternal support, the need to testify multiple times, harsh cross-examination, victim age, and fear of the defendant should be considered in predictions that children may suffer stress from the legal process.

Legal professionals need to be aware that a certain subset of children who testify may be particularly vulnerable witnesses. Research indicates that such factors as lack of maternal support, the need to testify multiple times, harsh cross-examination, victim age, and fear of the defendant should be considered in predictions that children may suffer stress from the legal process (Goodman, Pyle-Taub, et al., 1992). For children who are at risk of stress from legal involvement, protective measures, such as testifying via closed-circuit television, may prove particularly important (Cashmore, 1992; Davies & Noon, 1991). Although such techniques may reduce children's credibility in jurors' eyes, they may be, at times, the only reasonable and fair way of obtaining the testimony of a frightened child.

It should also be kept in mind that in the long run, the final outcome of the case—that is, whether the defendant is found guilty and whether the defendant receives a light or tough sentence—may be of particular importance to child victim/witnesses. A court appearance may be empowering or devastating in the end, depending on the verdict and the sentence (Ghetti, 2000).

Conclusion

Research on children's testimony has provided valuable insights regarding children's abilities and needs as witnesses. Although many pressing questions still need to be explored, the research base has grown substantially and provides a number of consistent findings. Perhaps the most important finding is that age alone is not a measure of a child's ability to provide accurate testimony or withstand court appearances. Instead, the context in which a child is questioned and in which the child testifies can help bolster or undermine a child's performance as well as a child's emotional resilience. The task is to find optimal interview techniques and contexts to help children be as accurate and resilient as possible.

References

Aldridge, J., & Cameron, S. (1999). Interviewing child witnesses: Questioning strategies and the effectiveness of training. *Applied Developmental Science, 3,* 136-147.

Asher, S. (1976). Children's ability to appraise their own and other person's communication performance. *Developmental Psychology, 12,* 24-32.

Baker-Ward, L., Gordon, B. N., Ornstein, P. A., Larus, D. M., & Clubb, P. A. (1993). Young children's long-term retention of a pediatric examination. *Child Development, 64,* 1519-1533.

Bala, N., Lee, K., Lindsay, R., & Talwar, V. (2000). A legal & psychological critique of the present approach to the assessment of the competence of child witnesses. *Osgoode Hall Law Journal, 38,* 409-451.

Batterman-Faunce, J. M., & Goodman, G. S. (1993). Effects of context on the accuracy and suggestibility of child witnesses. In G. S. Goodman & B. L. Bottoms (Eds.), *Child victims, child witnesses* (pp. 301-330). New York: Guilford.

Berliner, L., & Conte, J. (1995). The effects of disclosure and intervention on sexually abused children. *Child Abuse & Neglect, 19,* 371-384.

Bidrose, S., & Goodman, G. S. (2000). Testimony and evidence: A scientific case study of memory for child sexual abuse. *Applied Cognitive Psychology, 14,* 197-214.

Bottoms, B. L., Shaver, P. R., & Goodman, G. S. (1996). Allegations of ritualistic and religion-related child abuse. *Law and Human Behavior, 20,* 1-34.

Brady, M. S., Poole, D. A., Warren, A. R., & Jones, H. R. (1999). Young children's responses to yes-no questions: Patterns and problems. *Applied Developmental Science, 3,* 47-57.

Brainerd, C., & Ornstein, P. (1991). Children's memory for witnessed events: The developmental back drop. In J. Doris (Ed.), *The suggestability of children's recollections* (pp. 10-20). Washington, DC: APA.

Brennan, M., & Brennan, R. (1988). *Strange language: Child victims under cross examination.* Riverina, Australia: Charles Stuart University.

Brigham, J., Vanverst, M., & Bothwell, R. (1986). Accuracy of children's eyewitness identifications in a field setting. *Basic and Applied Social Psychology, 7,* 295-306.

Bruck, M., Ceci, S. J., & Francoeur, E. (2000). Children's use of anatomically detailed dolls to report genital touching in a medical examination: Developmental and gender comparisons. *Journal of Experimental Psychology: Applied, 6,* 74-83.

Bruck, M., Ceci, S. J., Francouer, E., & Barr, R. (1995). "I hardly cried when I got my shot!": Influencing children's reports about a visit to their pediatrician. *Child Development, 66,* 193-208.

Bruck, M., Ceci, S. J., Francouer, E., & Renick, A. (1995). Anatomically detailed dolls do not facilitate preschoolers' reports of a pediatric examination involving genital touching. *Journal of Experimental Psychology: Applied, 1,* 95-109.

Bruck, M., Hembrooke, H., & Ceci, S. J. (1997). Children's reports of pleasant and unpleasant events. In D. Read & S. Lindsay (Eds.), *Recollections of trauma: Scientific research and clinical practice* (pp. 199-213). New York: Plenum.

Bugental, D. B., Blue, J., Cortez, V., Fleck, K., & Rodriguez, A. (1992). Influences of witnessed affect on information processing in children. *Child Development, 63,* 774-786.

Bull, R. (1995). Innovative techniques for the questioning of child witnesses, especially those who are young and those with learning disabilities. In M. Zaragoza, J. R. Graham, G. C. N. Hall, R. Hirschman, & Y. S. Ben-Porath (Eds.), *Memory and testimony in the child witness* (pp. 179-194). Thousand Oaks, CA: Sage.

Bussey, K., Lee, K., & Grimbeek, E. (1993). Lies and secrets: Implications for children's reporting of sexual abuse. In G. S. Goodman & B. L. Bottoms (Eds.), *Child victims, child witnesses* (pp. 147-168). New York: Guilford.

California Attorney General's Office. (1994, July). *Child victim witness investigation pilot project: Research and evaluation, final report.* Sacramento, CA: Author.

Camparo, L., Wagner, J., & Saywitz, K. (2001). Interviewing children about real and fictitious events: Revisiting the narrative elaboration procedure. *Law and Human Behavior, 25* (1), 63-80.

Carter, C., Bottoms, B. L., & Levine, M. (1996). Linguistic and socioemotional influences on the accuracy of children's reports. *Law and Human Behavior, 20,* 335-358.

Cashmore, J. (1992). *The use of closed circuit television for child witnesses in the act.* Sydney: Australian Law Reform Commission.

Cashmore, J., & Bussey, K. (1990). Children's conceptions of the witness role. In J. Spencer, G. Nicholson, R. Flin, & R. Bull (Eds.), *Children's evidence in legal proceedings: An international perspective* (pp. 177-188). Cambridge, UK: Cambridge University Faculty of Law.

Cashmore, J., & Bussey, K. (1996). Judicial perceptions of child witness competence. *Law & Human Behavior, 3,* 313-334.

Ceci, S. J., Bronfenbrenner, U., & Baker, J. C. (1988). Memory in context: The case of prospective remembering. In F. E. Weinert & M. Perlmutter (Eds.), *Universal changes and individual differences* (pp. 243-256). Hillsdale, NJ: Lawrence Erlbaum.

Ceci, S. J., & Bruck, M. (1993). Suggestibility of the child witness: A historical review and synthesis. *Psychological Bulletin, 113,* 403-439.

Ceci, S. J., & Bruck, M. (1995). *Jeopardy in the courtroom: A scientific analysis of children's testimony.* Washington, DC: American Psychological Association.

Ceci, S. J., & Bruck, M. (1998). Children's testimony: Applied and basic issues. In D. Kuhn & R. S. Siegler (Eds.), *Handbook of child psychology: Vol. 2. Cognition, perception, and language* (5th ed., pp. 713-774). New York: John Wiley.

Ceci, S. J., Loftus, E. F., Leichtman, M. D., & Bruck, M. (1994). The possible role of source misattribution in the creation of false beliefs among preschoolers. *International Journal of Clinical and Experimental Hypnosis, 62,* 304-320.

Cederborg, A. C., Orbach, Y., Sternberg, K. J., & Lamb, M. E. (2000). Investigative interviews of child witnesses in Sweden. *Child Abuse & Neglect, 24,* 1355-1361.

Christiansson, S. A. (1992). Emotional stress and eyewitness memory: A critical review. *Psychological Bulletin, 12,* 284-309.

Craig, R. A., Scheibe, R., Kircher, J. C., Raskin, D. C., & Dodd, D. H. (1999). Interviewer questions and content analysis of children's statements of sexual abuse. *Applied Developmental Science, 3,* 77-85.

Davies, G., & Noon, E. (1991). *An evaluation of the live link for child witnesses.* London: Home Office.

Davies, G., Stevenson, Y., & Flin, R. (1988). Telling tales out of school: Children's memory for an unexpected event. In M. Gruenberg, P. Morris, & R. Sykes (Eds.), *Practical aspects of memory* (pp. 122-127). New York: John Wiley.

Davies, G. M., Westcott, H. L., & Horan, N. (2000). The impact of questioning style on the content of investigative interviews with suspected child sexual abuse victims. *Psychology, Crime & Law, 6,* 81-97.

DeFrancis, V. (1969). *Protecting the child victim of sex crimes committed by adults.* Denver, CO: American Humane Association.

Dent, H. (1977). Stress as a factor influencing person recognition in identification parades. *Bulletin of the British Psychological Society, 30,* 339-340.

Dent, H., & Flin, R. (1992). *Children as witnesses.* London: Wiley.

Dent, H., & Stephenson, G. (1979). An experimental study of the effectiveness of different techniques of questioning child witnesses. *British Journal of Social and Clinical Psychology, 18,* 41-51.

Dorado, J., & Saywitz, K. (2001). Interviewing preschoolers from low- and middle-SES communities: A test of the narrative elaboration recall improvement techniques. *Journal of Clinical Child Psychology, 30* (4), 566-578.

Edelstein, R., Goodman, G. S., Quas, J., Redlich, A., Ghetti, S., & Alexander, K. (in press). Emotional effects on children on legal involvement. In G. Davies, H. Westcott, & R. Bull (Eds.), *Evaluating children as witnesses.* London: Wiley.

Eisen, M., Goodman, G. S., Davis, S., & Qin, J. (1999). Individual differences in maltreated children's memory and suggestability. In L. Williams (Ed.), *Trauma and memory* (pp. 31-46). Thousand Oaks, CA: Sage.

Eisen, M., Goodman, G. S., Qin, J., & Davis, S. (1998). Memory and suggestability in maltreated children: New research relevant to evaluating allegations of abuse. In S. Lynn & K. McConkey (Eds.), *Truth in memory* (pp. 163-189). New York: Guilford.

Eisen, M. L., Quas, J. A., & Goodman, G. S. (2001). *Memory and suggestibility in the forensic interview.* Mahwah, NJ: Lawrence Erlbaum.

Everson, M. D., Hunter, W. M., Runyan, D. K., Edelsohn, G. A., & Coulter, M. L. (1989). Maternal support following disclosure of incest. *American Journal of Orthopsychiatry, 59,* 197-227.

Fisher, R., Brennan, K. H., & McCauley, M. R. (in press). The cognitive interview. In M. Eisen, J. A. Quas, & G. S. Goodman (Eds.), *Memory and suggestibility in the forensic interview.* Mahwah, NJ: Lawrence Erlbaum.

Fisher, R., & McCauley, M. (1995). Improving eyewitness testimony with the cognitive interview. In M. Zaragoza, J. R. Graham, G. C. N. Hall, R. Hirschman, & Y. S. Ben-Porath (Eds.), *Memory and testimony in the child witness* (pp. 141-159). Thousand Oaks, CA: Sage.

Fivush, R. (1993). Developmental perspectives on autobiographical recall. In G. S. Goodman & B. L. Bottoms (Eds.), *Child victims, child witnesses* (pp. 1-24). New York: Guilford.

Fivush, R., & Schwarzmueller, A. (1995). Say it once again: Effects of repeated questions on children's event recall. *Journal of Traumatic Stress, 8,* 555-580.

Fivush, R., & Shukar, J. (1995). What young children recall: Issues of content, consistency, and coherence. In M. Zaragoza, J. R. Graham, G. C. N. Hall, R. Hirschman, & Y. S. Ben-Porath (Eds.), *Memory and testimony in the child witness* (pp. 5-23). Thousand Oaks, CA: Sage.

Flin, R. (1993). Hearing and testing children's evidence. In G. Goodman & B. Bottoms (Eds.), *Child victims, child witnesses* (pp. 279-299). New York: Guilford.

Flin, R., Stevenson, Y., & Davies, G. (1989). Children's knowledge of court proceedings. *British Journal of Psychology, 80,* 285-297.

Friedman, W. (1982). *The developmental psychology of time.* New York: Academic Press.

Gallagher, T. (1981). Contingent query sequences within adult-child discourse. *Journal of Child Language, 8,* 51-62.

Garven, S., Wood, J. M., & Malpass, R. S. (2000). Allegations of wrongdoing: The effects of reinforcement on children's mundane and fantastic claims. *Journal of Applied Psychology, 85,* 38-49.

Garven, S., Wood, J. M., Malpass, R. S., & Shaw, J. S. (1998). More than suggestion: The effect of interviewing techniques from the McMartin preschool case. *Journal of Applied Psychology, 83,* 347-359.

Geiselman, E., & Fisher, R. (1989). The cognitive interview technique for victims and witnesses of crime. In D. Raskin (Ed.), *Psychological methods in criminal investigation and evidence.* New York: Springer.

Ghetti, S., Goodman, G. S., Quas, J., Redlich, A., Alexander, K., & Edelstein, R. (2000, March). *Child sexual abuse victims' perceptions and experiences years after legal involvement.* Symposium presented at the American Psychology-Law Society Convention, New Orleans, LA.

Golden, O. (2000). The federal response to child abuse and neglect. *American Psychologist, 55*(9), 1050-1053.

Goodman, G. S. (1984). The child witness. *Journal of Social Issues, 40,* 1-175.

Goodman, G. S., & Aman, C. J. (1991). Children's use of anatomically detailed dolls to recount an event. *Child Development, 61,* 1859-1871.

Goodman, G. S., Batterman-Faunce, J. M., Quas, J. A., Riddlesberger, M. M., & Kuhn, J. (1994). Predictors of accurate and inaccurate memories of traumatic events experienced in childhood. *Consciousness and Cognition, 3,* 269-294.

Goodman, G. S., & Bottoms, B. L. (Eds.). (1993). *Child victims, child witnesses.* New York: Guilford.

Goodman, G. S., Bottoms, B. L., Rudy, L., Davis, S., Port, L. P., Schwartz-Kenney, B. M., & England, P. (in press). Effects of past abuse experiences on children's eyewitness memory. *Law and Human Behavior.*

Goodman, G. S., Bottoms, B. L., Schwartz-Kenney, B., & Rudy, L. (1991). Children's memory for a stressful event: Improving children's reports. *Journal of Narrative and Life History, 1,* 69-99.

Goodman, G. S., Emery, R. E., & Haugaard, J. J. (1998). Developmental psychology and law: Divorce, child maltreatment, foster care, and adoption. In I. Siegel & A. Renninger (Eds.), *Handbook of child psychology: Vol. 4. Child psychology in practice* (5th ed., pp. 775-876). New York: John Wiley.

Goodman, G. S., Ghetti, S., Quas, J. A., Redlich, A., & Alexander, K. (1999, April). *Memories of abuse 12 years after legal involvement.* Symposium presented at the Society for Research on Child Development Meetings, Albuquerque, NM.

Goodman, G. S., Hepps, D., & Reed, R. S. (1986). The child victim's testimony. In A. Haralambie (Ed.), *New issues for child advocates* (pp. 167-177). Phoenix: Arizona Council of Attorneys for Children.

Goodman, G. S., Hirschman, J., Hepps, D., & Rudy, L. (1991). Children's memory for stressful events. *Merrill-Palmer Quarterly, 37,* 109-158.

Goodman, G. S., Pyle-Taub, E. P., Jones, D. P. H., England, P., Port, L. K., Rudy, L., & Prado, L. (1992). Testifying in court: The effects on child sexual assault victims. *Monographs of the Society for Research in Child Development, 57*(Serial No. 229), 1-163.

Goodman, G. S., Quas, J., Bulkley, J., & Shapiro, C. (1999). Innovations for child witnesses: A national survey. *Psychology, Public Policy, and Law, 5,* 255-281.

Goodman, G. S., & Reed, R. (1986). Age differences in eyewitness testimony. *Law and Human Behavior, 10,* 317-332.

Goodman, G. S., Sachsenmaier, T., Batterman-Faunce, J., Tobey, A., Thomas, S., Orcutt, H., & Schwartz-Kenney, B. (1992, August). *Impact of innovative court procedures on children's testimony.* Symposium presented at the annual meeting of the American Psychological Association, Washington, DC.

Goodman, G. S., Tobey, A., Batterman-Faunce, J., Orcutt, H., Thomas, S., Shapiro, C., & Sachsenmaier, T. (1998). Face-to-face confrontation: Effects of closed-circuit technology on children's eyewitness testimony and jurors' decisions. *Law and Human Behavior, 22,* 165-203.

Gopnik, A., & Graf, P. (1988). Knowing how you know: Young children's ability to identify and remember the sources of their beliefs. *Child Development, 59,* 1366-1371.

Gordon, B. N., Ornstein, P. A., Clubb, P. A., Nida, R. E., & Baker-Ward, L. E. (1991, October). *Visiting the pediatrician: Long-term retention and forgetting.* Paper presented at the annual meeting of the Psychonomic Society, San Francisco.

Gray, E. (1993). *Unequal justice.* New York: Free Press.

Hamond, N. R., & Fivush, R. (1991). Memories of Mickey Mouse: Young children recount their trip to Disneyworld. *Cognitive Development, 6,* 433-448.

Henry, J. (1997). System intervention trauma to child sexual abuse victims following disclosure. *Journal of Interpersonal Violence, 12,* 499-512.

Hershkowitz, I., & Elul, A. (1999). The effects of investigative utterances on Israeli children's reports of physical abuse. *Applied Developmental Science, 3,* 28-33.

Hershkowitz, I., Lamb, M. E., Sternberg, K. J., & Esplin, P. W. (1997). The relationships among interviewer utterance types, CBCA scores and the richness of children's responses. *Legal and Criminological Psychology, 2,* 169-176.

Hershkowitz, I., Orbach, Y., Lamb, M. E., Sternberg, K. J., & Horowitz, D. (2001). The effects of mental context reinstatement on children's accounts of sexual abuse. *Applied Cognitive Psychology, 15,* 235-248.

Hewitt, S. K. (1998). *Assessing allegations of sexual abuse in preschool children: Understanding small voices.* Thousand Oaks, CA: Sage.

Hill, P., & Hill, S. (1987). Videotaping children's testimony: An empirical view. *Michigan Law Review, 85,* 809-833.

Howie, P., & O'Neill, D. K. (1996). *Monitoring and reporting lack of knowledge: Developmental changes in the ability to say "I don't know" when appropriate.* Paper presented at the annual conference of the Australian Psychological Society, Sydney, Australia.

Hudson, J. A. (1990). Constructive processing in children's event memory. *Developmental Psychology, 26,* 180-187.

Jones, D. C., Swift, D. J., & Johnson, M. A. (1988). Nondeliberate memory for a novel event among preschoolers. *Developmental Psychology, 24,* 641-645.

Katz, S., & Mazur, M. A. (1979). *Understanding the rape victim.* New York: John Wiley.

Lamb, M. (1994). The investigation of child sexual abuse: An interdisciplinary consensus statement. *Journal of Child Sexual Abuse, 3*(4), 93-106.

Lamb, M. E., Hershkowitz, I., Sternberg, K. J., Boat, B., & Everson, M. D. (1996). Investigative interviews of alleged sexual abuse victims with and without anatomical dolls. *Child Abuse & Neglect, 20,* 1251-1259.

Lamb, M. E., Hershkowitz, I., Sternberg, K. J., Esplin, P. W., Hovav, M., Manor, T., & Yudilevitch, L. (1996). Effects of investigative utterance types on Israeli children's responses. *International Journal of Behavioral Development, 19,* 627-637.

Leichtman, M., & Ceci, S. J. (1995). Effects of stereotypes and suggestions on preschoolers' reports. *Developmental Psychology, 31,* 568-578.

Leichtman, M. D., Morse, M. B., Dixon, A., & Spiegel, R. (2000). Source monitoring and suggestibility: An individual differences approach. In K. P. Roberts & M. Blades (Eds.), *Children's source monitoring* (pp. 257-287). Mahwah, NJ: Lawrence Erlbaum.

Lepore, S. J., & Sesco, B. (1994). Distorting children's reports and interpretations of events through suggestion. *Journal of Applied Psychology, 79,* 108-120.

List, J. A. (1986). Age and schematic differences in the reliability of eyewitness testimony. *Developmental Psychology, 22,* 50-57.

Loftus, E. F. (1979). *Eyewitness testimony.* Cambridge, MA: Harvard University Press.

Lyon, T. D. (1999). The new wave of suggestibility research: A critique. *Cornell Law Review, 84,* 1004-1087.

Lyon, T. D. (2000). Child witnesses and the oath: Empirical evidence. *Southern California Law Review, 73,* 1017-1074.

Lyon, T. D. (in press). Applying suggestibility research to the real world: The case of repeated questions. *Law and Contemporary Problems.*

Lyon, T. D., & Saywitz, K. J. (1999). Young maltreated children's competence to take the oath. *Applied Developmental Science, 3,* 16-27.

Lyon, T. D., & Saywitz, K. J. (2000). *Qualifying children to take the oath: Materials for interviewing professionals.* Unpublished manuscript [Online]. Available: hal-law.usc.edu/users/tlyon/articles/competency.PDF.

Lyon, T. D., Saywitz, K. J., Kaplan, D. L., & Dorado, J. S. (2001). Reducing maltreated children's reluctance to answer hypothetical oath-taking competency questions. *Law & Human Behavior, 25,* 81-92.

Markman, E. M. (1977). Realizing that you don't understand: A preliminary investigation. *Child Development, 48,* 986-992.

Maryland v. Craig, 110 S. Ct. 3157, 3169 (1990).

Melton, G. (1981). Children's competence to testify. *Law and Human Behavior, 5,* 73-85.

Melton, G., Limber, S., Jacobs, J., & Oberlander, L. (1992). *Preparing sexually abused children for testimony: Children's perceptions of the legal process* (Grant No. 90-CA-1274). Lincoln: University of Nebraska–Lincoln.

Melton, G., & Thompson, R. (1987). Getting out of a rut: Detours to less traveled paths in child-witness research. In S. Ceci, M. Toglia, & D. Ross (Eds.), *Children's eyewitness memory* (pp. 209-229). New York: Springer-Verlag.

Memon, A., Cronin, O., Eaves, R., & Bull, R. (1996). An empirical test of the mnemonic components of the cognitive interview. In G. Davies, S. Lloyd-Bostock, M. McMuran, & C. Wilson (Eds.), *Psychology, law and criminal justice: International developments in research and practice* (pp. 135-145). New York: Aldine.

Memorandum of good practice on video-recorded interviews with child witnesses for criminal proceedings. (1992). London: Her Majesty's Stationery Office.

Merritt, K. A., Ornstein, P. A., & Spicker, B. (1994). Children's memory for a salient medical procedure: Implications for testimony. *Pediatrics, 94,* 17-23.

Moston, S. (1987). The suggestibility of children in interview studies. *First Language, 7,* 67-78.

Mulder, M., & Vrij, A. (1996). Explaining conversations rules to children: An intervention study to facilitate children's accurate responses. *Child Abuse & Neglect, 10*(7), 623-631.

Myers, J. E. B., Redlich, A., Goodman, G. S., Prizmich, L., & Imwinkelreid, E. (1999). Jurors' perceptions of hearsay in child sexual abuse cases. *Psychology, Public Policy, and Law, 5,* 388-419.

Oates, K., & Tong, L. (1987). Sexual abuse of children: An area with room for professional reform. *Medical Journal of Australia, 147,* 544-548.

O'Neill, D. K., & Gopnik, A. (1991). Young children's ability to identify the sources of their beliefs. *Developmental Psychology, 27,* 390-397.

Orbach, Y., Hershkowitz, I., Lamb, M. E., Sternberg, K. J., Esplin, P. W., & Horowitz, D. (2000). Assessing the value of structured protocols for forensic interviews of alleged child abuse victims. *Child Abuse & Neglect, 6,* 733-752.

Ornstein, P., Baker-Ward, L., Gordon, B., & Merritt, R. (1993, March). *Children's memory for medical procedures.* Symposium presented at the Society for Research in Child Development Meetings, New Orleans, LA.

Ornstein, P. A., Baker-Ward, L., Myers, J., Principe, G. F., & Gordon, B. N. (1995). Young children's long-term retention of medical experiences: Implications for testimony. In F. E. Weinert & W.

Schneider (Eds.), *Memory performance and competencies: Issues in growth and development* (pp. 349-371). Mahwah, NJ: Lawrence Erlbaum.

Ornstein, P. A., Gordon, B. N., & Larus, D. M. (1992). Children's memory for a personally experienced event: Implications for testimony. *Applied Cognitive Psychology, 6,* 49-60.

Patterson, C., Massad, C., & Cosgrove, J. (1978). Children's referential communication: Components of plans for effective listening. *Developmental Psychology, 14,* 401-406.

Perry, N., & Wrightsman, L. (1991). *The child witness.* Newbury Park, CA: Sage.

Peters, D. (1991). The influence of stress and arousal on the child witness. In J. Doris (Ed.), *The suggestibility of children's recollections* (pp. 60-76). Washington, DC: American Psychological Association.

Peterson, C., & Bell, M. (1996). Children's memory for traumatic injury. *Child Development, 67,* 3045-3070.

Peterson, C., & Biggs, M. (1997). Interviewing children about trauma: Problems with "specific" questions. *Journal of Traumatic Stress, 10,* 279-290.

Peterson, C., Dowden, C., & Tobin, J. (2000). Interviewing preschoolers: Comparisons of yes/no and wh- questions. *Law & Human Behavior, 23,* 539-555.

Peterson, C., & Rideout, R. (1998). Memory for medical emergencies experienced by 1- and 2-year-olds. *Developmental Psychology, 34,* 1059-1072.

Poole, D. A., & Lamb, M. E. (1998). *Investigative interviews of children: A guide for helping professionals.* Washington, DC: American Psychological Association.

Poole, D. A., & Lindsay, D. S. (1995). Interviewing preschoolers: Effects of nonsuggestive techniques, parental coaching, and leading questions on reports of nonexperienced events. *Journal of Experimental Child Psychology, 60,* 129-154.

Poole, D. A., & Lindsay, D. S. (1996, June). *Effects of parental suggestions, interviewing techniques, and age on young children's event reports.* Paper presented at the NATO Advanced Study Institute, Recollections of Trauma, Port de Bourgenay, France.

Poole, D. A., & Lindsay, D. S. (1997, April). *Misinformation from parents and children's source monitoring: Implications for testimony.* Paper presented at the Biennial Meeting of the Society for Research in Child Development, Washington, DC.

Poole, D. A., & White, L. T. (1995). Tell me again and again: Stability and change in the repeated testimony of children and adults. In M. S. Zaragoza, J. R. Graham, G. C. N. Hall, R. Hirschman, & Y. S. Ben-Porath (Eds.), *Memory and testimony in the child witness* (pp. 24-43). Thousand Oaks, CA: Sage.

Priestly, G., Roberts, S., & Pipe, M. E. (1999). Returning to the scene: Reminders and context reinstatement enhance children's recall. *Developmental Psychology, 35,* 1006-1019.

Pynoos, R., & Eth, S. (1984). The child as witness to homicide. *Journal of Social Issues, 40,* 87-108.

Pynoos, R., & Nader, K. (1988). Children's memory and proximity to violence. *Journal of the American Academy of Child and Adolescent Psychiatry, 27,* 567-572.

Quas, J., Goodman, G. S., Bidrose, S., Pipe, M. -E., Craw, S., & Ablin, D. (1999). Emotion and memory: Children's remembering, forgetting, and suggestability. *Journal of Experimental Child Psychology, 72,* 235-270.

Quas, J. A., Schaaf, J., Alexander, K., & Goodman, G. S. (2000). Do you *really* remember it happening or do you only remember being asked about it happening? Children's source monitoring in forensic contexts. In K. Roberts & M. Blades (Eds.), *Memory development and source monitoring.* Mahwah, NJ: Lawrence Erlbaum.

Revelle, G., Wellman, H., & Karabenik, J. (1985). Comprehension monitoring in preschool children. *Child Development, 56,* 654-663.

Rudy, L., & Goodman, G. S. (1991). Effects of participation on children's reports: Implications for children's testimony. *Developmental Psychology, 27,* 1-26.

Runyan, D. K., Everson, M. D., Edelsohn, G. A., Hunter, W. M., & Coulter, M. L. (1988). Impact of legal intervention on sexually abused children. *Journal of Pediatrics, 113,* 647-653.

Salmon, K., & Pipe, M. -E. (2000). Recalling an event one year later: The impact of props, drawing and a prior interview. *Applied Cognitive Psychology, 14,* 99-120.

Sas, L. (1993). *Three years after the verdict.* London, Ontario: London Family Court.

Sas, L., Hurley, P., Austin, G., & Wolfe, D. (1991). *Reducing the system-induced trauma for child sexual abuse victims through court preparation, assessment and follow-up.* Final report for the National Welfare Grants Division, Health and Welfare (Project #4555-1-125), Canada.

Saywitz, K. (1989). Children's conceptions of the legal system: Court is place to play basketball. In S. Ceci, M. Toglia, & D. Ross (Eds.), *Perspectives on children's testimony* (pp. 131-157). New York: Springer-Verlag.

Saywitz, K. (1994). Questioning child witnesses. *Violence Update, 4*(7), 3-10.

Saywitz, K. (1995). Improving children's testimony: The question, the answer, and the environment. In M. S. Zaragoza, J. R. Graham, G. C. N. Hall, R. Hirschman, & Y. S. Ben-Porath (Eds.), *Memory and testimony in the child witness* (pp. 113-140). Thousand Oaks, CA: Sage.

Saywitz, K., & Geiselman, E. (1998). Interviewing the child witness: Maximizing completeness and minimizing error. In S. Lynn (Ed.), *Memory and truth*. New York: Guilford.

Saywitz, K., Geiselman, R., & Bornstein, G. (1992). Effects of cognitive interviewing and practice on children's recall performance. *Journal of Applied Psychology, 77*(5), 744-756.

Saywitz, K., Goodman, G. S., Nicholas, E., & Moan, S. (1991). Children's memories of physical examinations involving genital touch: Implications for reports of child sexual abuse. *Journal of Consulting and Clinical Psychology, 59,* 682-691.

Saywitz, K., Jaenicke, C., & Camparo, L. (1990). Children's knowledge of legal terminology. *Law and Human Behavior, 14*(6), 523-535.

Saywitz, K., & Lyon, T. D. (in press). Coming to grips with children's suggestibility. In M. Eisen, G. Goodman, & J. Quas (Eds.), *Memory and suggestibility in the forensic interview*. Mahwah, NJ: Lawrence Erlbaum.

Saywitz, K., & Moan-Hardie, S. (1994). Reducing the potential for distortion of childhood memories. *Consciousness and Cognition, 3,* 257-293.

Saywitz, K., & Nathanson, R. (1993). Children's testimony and their perceptions of stress in and out of the courtroom. *Child Abuse & Neglect, 17,* 613-622.

Saywitz, K., Nathanson, R., Snyder, L., & Lamphear, V. (1993). *Preparing children for the investigative and judicial process: Improving communication, memory, and emotional resiliency* (Grant No. 90-CA-1179). Torrance: University of California, Los Angeles, Harbor–UCLA Medical Center, Department of Psychiatry.

Saywitz, K., & Snyder, L. (1996). Narrative elaboration: Test of a new procedure for interviewing children. *Journal of Consulting and Clinical Psychology, 64,* 1347-1357.

Saywitz, K., Snyder, L., & Lamphear, V. (1996). Helping children tell what happened: A follow up study of the narrative elaboration procedure. *Child Maltreatment, 1*(3), 200-212.

Saywitz, K., Snyder, L., & Nathanson, R. (1999). Facilitating the communicative competence of the child witness. *Applied Developmental Science, 3*(1), 58-68.

Schaaf, J. M., Goodman, G. S., & Alexander, K. (1999, April). *Effects of repeated interviewing on children's memory and suggestibility for true and false events.* Symposium presented at the Society for Research on Child Development Meetings, Albuquerque, NM.

Schor, D. P., & Sivan, A. B. (1989). Interpreting children's labels for sex-related body parts of anatomically explicit dolls. *Child Abuse & Neglect, 13,* 523-531.

Smith, B. (1993). *The prosecution of child sexual and physical abuse cases.* Final report to the National Center on Child Abuse & Neglect, Washington, DC.

Spencer, J., & Flin, R. (1993). *The evidence of children: The law and the psychology.* London: Blackstone.

Stern, W. (1910). Abstracts of lectures on the psychology of testimony and on the study of individuality. *American Journal of Psychology, 21,* 270-282.

Sternberg, K., Lamb, M. E., Esplin, P. W., & Baradaran, L. (1999). Using a scripted protocol to guide investigative interviews: A pilot study. *Applied Developmental Science, 3,* 70-76.

Sternberg, K. J., Lamb, M. E., Esplin, P. W., Orbach, Y., & Hershkowitz, I. (in press). Using a structured protocol to improve the quality of investigative interviews. In M. Eisen, G. Goodman, & J. Quas (Eds.), *Memory and suggestibility in the forensic interview*. Mahwah, NJ: Lawrence Erlbaum.

Sternberg, K. J., Lamb, M. E., Hershkowitz, I., Esplin, P. W., Redlich, A., & Sunshine, N. (1996). The relation between investigative utterance types and the informativeness of child witnesses. *Journal of Applied Developmental Psychology, 17,* 439-451.

Sternberg, K. J., Lamb, M. E., Hershkowitz, I., Yudilevitch, L., Orbach, Y., Esplin, P. W., & Hovav, M. (1997). Effects of introductory style on children's abilities to describe experiences of sexual abuse. *Child Abuse & Neglect, 21,* 1133-1146.

Tedesco, J., & Schnell, S. (1987). Children's reactions to sex abuse investigation and litigation. *Child Abuse & Neglect, 11,* 267-272.

Terr, L. (1991). Childhood traumas: An outline and overview. *American Journal of Psychiatry, 148,* 10-20.

Thompson, W. C., Clarke-Stewart, A., & Lepore, S. J. (1997). What did the janitor do? Suggestive interviewing and the accuracy of children's accounts. *Law & Human Behavior, 21,* 405-426.

Tobey, A., & Goodman, G. S. (1992). Children's eyewitness memory: Effects of participation and forensic context. *Child Abuse & Neglect, 16,* 779-796.

Todd, C. M., & Perlmutter, M. (1980). Reality recalled by preschool children. In M. Perlmutter (Ed.), *New directions for child development: No. 10. Children's memory* (pp. 69-85). San Francisco: Jossey-Bass.

Warren, A., Hulse-Trotter, K., & Tubbs, E. (1991). Inducing resistance to suggestibility in children. *Law and Human Behavior, 15*(3), 273-285.

Warren, A. R., Woodall, C. E., Thomas, M., Nunno, M., Keeney, J. M., Larson, S. M., & Stadfield, J. A. (1999). Assessing the effectiveness of a training program for interviewing child witnesses. *Applied Developmental Science, 3,* 128-135.

Warren-Leubecker, A., Tate, C., Hinton, I., & Ozbek, I. (1989). What do children know about the legal system and why do they know it? In S. Ceci, M. Toglia, & D. Ross (Eds.), *Perspectives on children's testimony* (pp. 158-184). New York: Springer-Verlag.

Welch-Ross, M. (2000). A mental-state reasoning model of suggestibility and memory source monitoring. In K. P. Roberts & M. Blades (Eds.), *Children's source monitoring* (pp. 227-255). Mahwah, NJ: Lawrence Erlbaum.

Whitcomb, D., Runyan, D., De Vos, E., Hunter, W., Cross, T., Everson, M., Peeler, N., Porter, C., Toth, P., & Gropper, C. (1992). *Child victim as witness research and development program* (Grant No. 87-MC-CX-0026). Final report to the National Institute of Justice Educational Development Center, Boston.

Williams, L. M. (1994). Recall of childhood trauma: A prospective study of women's memories of child sexual abuse. *Journal of Consulting and Clinical Psychology, 62,* 1167-1176.

Wilson, J. C., & Pipe, M. (1989). The effects of cues on young children's recall of real events. *New Zealand Journal of Psychology, 18,* 65-70.

Woolley, J. D., & Bruell, M. J. (1995, February). *Young children's awareness of the origins of their mental representations.* Poster presented at Current Directions in Theories of Mind Research, Eugene, OR.

19

Expert Testimony

JOHN E. B. MYERS

PAUL STERN

C hild abuse is often difficult to prove in court (*In re Cindy L.,* 1997; *Pennsylvania v. Ritchie,* 1987). Abuse occurs in secret, and the child is usually the only eyewitness. Although many children are excellent witnesses, some are too young to testify, and others are ineffective on the witness stand. Because evidence of abuse is often difficult to find, expert testimony sometimes plays an important role in child abuse litigation. This chapter describes the scope and limits of expert testimony.

Experts testify in criminal court, juvenile court, family court, and other legal arenas. In most criminal cases, there is a jury. Juries are not universal in criminal court, however, and when there is no jury, the judge fulfills the fact-finding responsibility normally entrusted to jurors. In juvenile and family court cases, there usually is no jury. In this chapter, the word *jury* is used for convenience to describe the fact finder, whether that is a jury or a judge.

Lay and Expert Witnesses

Two types of witnesses testify in court: lay witnesses and experts. A lay witness is someone with personal knowledge of relevant facts. Examples of lay witnesses are an eyewitness to a bank robbery and the victim in a child abuse case. A lay witness tells the jury what the witness saw or heard.

An expert witness is a person with special knowledge who helps the jury understand technical, clinical, or scientific issues. Depending on the type of case, an expert may or may not need personal knowledge of the facts of the case. An example of an expert witness is a mental health professional who helps the jury understand that some sexually abused children recant following disclosure.

In child abuse and neglect litigation, professionals provide both lay and expert testimony. For example, suppose a child discloses sexual abuse to a psychotherapist. The child's disclosure is evidence, and the therapist is an eyewitness *to the disclosure*. In court, the psychotherapist may testify as a lay witness to repeat the child's disclosure for the jury. In another case, the same therapist might testify as an expert. Indeed, in some cases, the professional testifies as both a lay witness *and* an expert. Suppose, for example, that a child discloses sexual abuse to a nurse practitioner who examines the child for possible sexual abuse. In court, the nurse practitioner testifies as a lay witness when repeating the child's disclosure. The nurse offers expert testimony when interpreting the results of the physical examination.

Two Categories of Evidence: Substantive and Rehabilitative

Cases are won and lost with evidence, which is defined as "any matter, verbal or physical, that can be used to support the existence of a factual proposition" (Lilly, 1996, p. 2). Thus, evidence includes testimony from lay and expert witnesses, written documents, photographs, and objects such as the gun used to hold up a bank. The admissibility of evidence is governed by complex rules administered by the judge.

Substantive evidence. Evidence offered in court to prove that a child was abused is called substantive evidence. In a physical abuse case, the substantive evidence might consist of the child's hospital record plus expert testimony on battered child syndrome. In a sexual abuse case, the substantive evidence might be the findings of a physical examination, the child's disclosure statement to a social worker, lay testimony from the child, lay testimony from the child's mother, and expert testimony from a mental health professional. In the physical and the sexual abuse cases, the expert testimony is substantive evidence, that is, evidence that abuse occurred.

Rehabilitation. There is a second category of expert testimony. Testimony in the second category is *not* offered as substantive evidence of abuse but serves the more limited role of rehabilitating a child witness's credibility after the defense attorney attacks it. The two categories of expert testimony—substantive evidence and rehabilitation—are discussed later in this chapter.

Expert Testimony in Criminal Versus Noncriminal Proceedings

On paper, similar rules govern expert testimony in criminal and noncriminal proceedings. In practice, however, judges often allow experts greater latitude in noncriminal cases, such as juvenile court proceedings and family court litigation regarding child custody or visitation. Thus, in a juvenile court proceeding, a judge might allow an expert to give an opinion the judge would not allow in a criminal case. Judges are most likely to limit or disallow expert testimony when there is a jury. Judges worry that some jurors defer too quickly to experts, abdicating the juror's responsibility to decide the case.

Metaprinciples of Expert Testimony

Expert testimony is allowed when members of the jury need help to understand technical, clinical, or scientific issues (Chadwick, 1990; Myers, 1997a; Stern, 1997). In many physical abuse cases, for example, the defendant claims that the child's injuries were accidental. The jury lacks the knowledge required to differentiate accidental from inflicted injuries. Thus, to help the jury, a physician testifies as an expert. In essence, the physician is a teacher, helping the jury understand complex medical evidence.

In the case of sexual abuse, some children recant. Many jurors do not understand that recantation occurs among abused children (Morison & Greene, 1992). The defense attorney may attack the child's credibility in an effort to convince the jury that the only explanation for recantation is that abuse did not occur. In light of this attack on the child's credibility, an expert may rehabilitate the child by explaining that recantation occurs among sexually abused children.

Thus, expert witnesses help jurors understand technical, clinical, and scientific issues. With help for the jury as the loadstar for expert testimony, the acronym HELP is useful to organize the metaprinciples underlying expert testimony:

H–honesty
E–evenhandedness
L–limits of expertise
P–preparation

Honesty. Expert witnesses must be honest with the jury, the judge, the attorneys, and, in the final analysis, themselves (Committee on Ethical Guidelines for Forensic Psychologists, 1991). The duty to provide honest testimony derives in part from the oath. Honesty, however, has deeper roots. Honesty lies at the core of professionalism and personal integrity. Experts who allow half-truths to go unchecked or who shade the truth to favor one side in the litigation undermine the purpose of the law. Half-honest experts seldom help the jury.

Evenhandedness. In our legal system, an expert witness plays a very different role from an attorney. The attorney's job is to win the case for the client. To be sure, the ultimate goal of the legal system is truth, but the theory of our adversary system of justice is that the truth emerges through the courtroom confrontation of adversaries. Thus, attorneys are advocates for their clients and are not supposed to be objective.

Unlike attorneys, expert witnesses are not–or, at least, should not be–partisan advocates. The expert's responsibility is not to win the case but to help the jury understand clinical, technical, or scientific issues. The expert's responsibility is to educate, not to claim victory. Experts who view litigation through advocate's eyes lose their bearings and sink to the level of "hired gun."

In the effort to avoid becoming an advocate, must experts aspire to complete objectivity? Is an expert irreparably sullied if the expert's sympathies lean toward one side or the other? Although it may be possible in theory to attain unqualified objectivity, such purity is rare in the "real world" of litigation (Saks, 1990). Moreover, in a system

where each side retains its own expert, it is unrealistic to expect professionals to be completely dispassionate about the outcome. What is important is not unconditional evenhandedness but the degree of objectivity that is compatible with honesty and professionalism.

Just as important as reasonable objectivity is a willingness to acknowledge one's biases and recognize the shaping influence bias can exert on one's testimony. Finally, experts should not represent themselves as objective when, in fact, they are not. The latter requirement relates, of course, to the metaprinciple of honesty.

Limits of expertise. During the past 30 years, much has been learned about child abuse, yet many questions remain. With sexual abuse in particular, our knowledge is in the formative stage of development. For example, controversy continues about the meaning of various genital and anal findings (American Academy of Pediatrics, 1999; Wells, McCann, Adams, Voris, & Dahl, 1997; see Chapter 12, this volume). Even more uncertainty surrounds the diagnostic importance of behaviors such as nightmares, regression, and acting out (see below).

> *In addition to understanding the limits of knowledge in the field, experts should have a clear fix on the limits of their own knowledge.*

Expert witnesses should be familiar with relevant literature and appreciate the limits of current knowledge. While on the witness stand, experts should acknowledge these limits and refuse to exceed them, even in the face of pressure from attorneys or the judge (Melton, Petrila, Poythress, & Slobogin, 1997). In addition to understanding the limits of knowledge in the field, experts should have a clear fix on the limits of their own knowledge (Saks, 1990).

Preparation. Preparation is the key to effective expert testimony. The expert should evaluate all relevant information and should be intimately familiar with the case. The expert should fully review pertinent records. The attorneys will use the records as a basis for questions, and the opposing attorney will look for inconsistencies between the records and the expert's testimony.

Before testifying, the expert should meet with the attorney who solicited the testimony. Chadwick (1990) emphasizes that such meetings "are always desirable, and rarely impossible" (p. 963).

Who Qualifies to Testify as an Expert Witness?

Before a person may testify as an expert witness, the judge must be convinced that the person possesses sufficient "knowledge, skill, experience, training, or education" to qualify as an expert (Fed. R. Evid. 702). Normally, proposed experts take the witness stand and answer questions about their educational accomplishments, specialized training, and relevant experience. A professional does not have to be a well-known authority to testify as an expert witness. For example, publication of books or articles is not required. The important question is whether the jury will be helped by the professional's testimony (Wigmore, 1974). The type and degree of expertise required depend on the testimony.

The Form of Expert Testimony

Expert testimony usually takes one of the following forms: (a) an opinion, (b) an answer to a hypothetical question, (c) a lecture providing background information on a pertinent subject, or (d) some combination of the above.

Opinion Testimony

Lay witnesses generally confine their testimony to a description of what they saw or heard and refrain from offering opinions. Experts, by contrast, are permitted to offer opinions. For example, in a physical abuse case, a physician could testify that, in the doctor's opinion, the child has battered child syndrome, and the child's injuries are not accidental. Experts must be reasonably confident of their opinions. Lawyers and judges use the term *reasonable certainty* to describe the necessary degree of confidence (Lewin, 1998). Thus, the question to an ex-

pert might be, "Do you have an opinion, based on a reasonable degree of certainty, about whether the child's injuries were accidental?"

Unfortunately, the reasonable certainty standard is not self-defining, and the law does little to elucidate the term. It is clear that expert witnesses may not speculate or guess (Wigmore, 1974). It is equally clear that experts do not have to be completely certain before offering opinions (Mueller & Kirkpatrick, 1994). Thus, the degree of certainty required for expert testimony lies between guesswork and certainty. Unfortunately, locating reasonable certainty somewhere between guesswork and certainty adds little to the concept, and, in the end, the reasonable certainty standard fails to provide a meaningful tool to evaluate the helpfulness of expert testimony. With the insight that has graced his brilliant career, David Chadwick once remarked, "Reasonable medical certainty means that despite various possible diagnoses, the doctor is 'certain enough' to take out the patient's appendix" (personal communication, 2001).

A more productive approach to assessing the helpfulness of expert testimony looks beyond the rubric of reasonable certainty and asks questions such as the following:

1. In formulating an opinion, did the expert consider all relevant facts?
2. How much confidence can be placed in the facts underlying the expert's opinion?
3. Does the expert have an adequate understanding of pertinent clinical and scientific principles?
4. To the extent the expert's opinion rests on scientific principles, have the principles been subjected to testing?
5. Have the principles or theories relied on by the expert been published in peer-reviewed journals?
6. Are the principles or theories relied on by the expert generally accepted as reliable by experts in the field?
7. Did the expert employ appropriate methods of assessment?
8. Are the inferences and conclusions drawn by the expert defensible?
9. Is the expert reasonably objective?

In the final analysis, the important question is whether the expert's opinion is logical, consistent, explainable, objective, and defensible. The value of the expert's opinion depends on the answers to these questions (Black, 1988).

The Hypothetical Question

In bygone days, expert testimony often was elicited in response to a lengthy hypothetical question asked by an attorney. Such a question contains hypothetical facts that closely parallel the actual facts of the case. The hypothetical question is an awkward device and is falling into disuse. Today, experts are more likely to be asked hypothetical questions by the cross-examining attorney. The cross-examiner's hypothetical question might be, "Would your opinion change if facts A, B, and C were different?" So long as A, B, and C are reasonable, the expert might agree, with the proviso that, "Of course we should keep in mind that when I evaluated the child, I found no evidence of A, B, or C, which is why my opinion is what it is."

Expert Testimony in the Form of a Lecture

Rather than offer an opinion, an expert may testify in the form of "a dissertation or exposition of scientific or other principles relevant to the case, leaving to the [jury] to apply them to the facts" (Fed. R. Evid. 702, 1975, Advisory Committee Note). A common example of this form of expert testimony occurs in child sexual abuse cases in which an expert helps the jury understand that delayed reporting and recantation occur among sexually abused children.

Types of Information on Which Expert Witnesses May Rely to Form Opinions Offered in Court

Professionals draw from many sources of information to reach conclusions about child abuse. When it comes to expert testimony in court, the law generally allows professionals to base their testimony on the same sources of information they rely on in their normal, day-to-day practice outside the courtroom. Thus, in a sexual abuse case, an expert may base expert testimony on the child's disclosure, the results of a child protective services (CPS) investigation, and consultation with colleagues. In a physical abuse case, the physician may form an opinion on the basis of an interview and physical examination of the child, statements of the parents, results of laboratory tests, X-rays, and the literature. Many other combinations of data are possible.

Expert Testimony Based on Scientific Principles or Techniques

A special rule governs the admissibility of expert testimony that is based on scientific principles or techniques. The purpose of the special rule is to exclude expert testimony based on unreliable scientific principles or techniques. In the United States, the rule takes two forms: (a) the general acceptance rule, commonly known as *Frye,* and (b) relevance analysis, commonly known as *Daubert.* The two rules are described briefly below.

General Acceptance—*Frye*

The general acceptance rule takes its name from a 1923 case called *Frye v. United States.* In *Frye,* the court ruled that expert testimony based on a novel scientific principle is admissible only when the principle gains "general acceptance in the field in which it belongs" (p. 1014). An attorney offering expert testimony based on a novel scientific principle must convince the judge that the principle is generally accepted as reliable in the relevant professional community.

The general acceptance rule was once the dominant rule in the United States. In recent years, however, a majority of states have rejected the general acceptance rule because the rule sometimes excludes expert testimony that could help the jury.

Relevance Analysis—*Daubert*

In 1993, the U.S. Supreme Court adopted relevance analysis for the federal courts, rejecting *Frye*'s general acceptance rule (*Daubert v. Merrell Dow Pharmaceuticals, Inc.,* 1993). Although the Supreme Court's *Daubert* ruling is not binding on state court judges, *Daubert* has influenced an increasing number of state court judges to switch from *Frye* to *Daubert.*

With relevance analysis, the judge conducts a searching inquiry into the reliability of scientific principles supporting expert testimony. To assess reliability, the judge considers the following:

- Whether the principle "can be (and has been) tested" to determine its reliability and validity (*Daubert,* p. 581).
- How often the principle yields accurate results.
- Existence of standards governing use of the principle to ensure accurate results (e.g., clear diagnostic criteria).
- Degree to which expert testimony is based on subjective analysis, as opposed to objective analysis. Expert testimony based on subjective analysis may be of unverifiable reliability if it is difficult to evaluate the expert's subjective decision-making process.
- Publication in the peer-reviewed literature. The Supreme Court wrote that

  another pertinent consideration is whether the theory or technique has been subjected to peer review and publication. Publication (which is but one element of peer review) is not a *sine qua non* of admissibility; it does not necessarily correlate with reliability, . . . and in some instances well-grounded but innovative theories will not have been published. . . . Some propositions, moreover, are too particular, too new, or of too limited interest to be published. But submission to the scrutiny of the scientific community is a component of "good science," in part because it increases the likelihood that substantive flaws in methodology will be detected. . . . The fact of publication (or lack thereof) in a peer-reviewed journal thus will be a relevant, though not dispositive, consideration in assessing the scientific validity of a particular technique or methodology on which an opinion is premised. (*Daubert,* pp. 593-594)

- Whether the scientific or clinical principle is generally accepted by experts in the field (the *Frye* rule). The *Daubert* Court wrote that "widespread acceptance can be an important factor in ruling particular evidence admissible" (p. 594).
- Whether the principle or technique is consistent with established and proven modes of analysis (Black, Francisco, & Saffran-Brinks, 1994).

When Does the Special Rule Governing Scientific Evidence Apply?

The special rule governing scientific evidence does not apply every time an expert's testimony is based in whole or in part on scientific principles. Many scientific principles are sufficiently well established that the judge takes what is called judicial notice of the reliability of the principles. For example, battered child syndrome is an accepted medical diagnosis. Judges take judicial notice of the reliability of the syndrome, and expert testimony based on the syndrome is not subject to *Frye* or *Daubert.*

The Supreme Court's 1993 *Daubert* decision dealt with scientific evidence. Following *Daubert,* it was uncertain whether *Daubert* applied to nonscientific and partially scientific expert testimony. For example, is *Daubert* applicable to expert testimony based on psychological and clinical principles? Is *Daubert* applicable to medical testimony based on scientific knowledge coupled with clinical judgment? Much of the uncertainty was erased with the Supreme Court's 1999 decision in *Kumho Tire Co. v. Carmichael,* in which the Court ruled that *Daubert* applies not only to scientific knowledge but also to "technical" and "other specialized" knowledge. In the final analysis, the special rule for scientific evidence can apply whenever expert testimony is based on scientific or clinical principles that are of unknown or untested reliability. That said, however, it should be added that many courts apply neither *Frye* nor *Daubert* to clinical judgments and diagnoses by medical and mental health professionals. The upshot is that it is often difficult to tell in advance whether a judge will apply *Frye* or *Daubert* to particular testimony. When *Frye* or *Daubert* does apply, the attorney offering expert testimony must convince the judge that the scientific or clinical principles underlying the testimony are sufficiently reliable.

Expert Testimony in Physical Abuse and Neglect Cases

Expert testimony regarding nonaccidental injury is a complex subject. Limitations of space preclude extended discussion of this interesting and important subject, and the reader is referred to other sources (Helfer, Kempe & Krugman, 1997; Reece,

2000; Reece & Ludwig, 2001; see Chapter 13, this volume).

Briefly, in physical child abuse litigation, accused individuals usually raise one of two defenses. The most common defense is that the child's injuries were accidental. Alternatively, the accused may acknowledge that the child was abused but claim someone else did it.

Expert testimony from medical professionals plays a key role in proving nonaccidental injury (Chadwick, 1990; Myers, 1997a). Physicians regularly provide testimony about bruises, bites, head injuries, abdominal injuries, burns, and fractures.

Expert Medical Testimony on Cause of Injury

A properly qualified medical professional may testify that a child's injuries were probably not accidental. In general, experts are allowed to describe the means used to inflict injury (Myers, 1997a). In *People v. Jackson* (1971), for example, the court wrote that "an expert medical witness may give his opinion as to the means used to inflict a particular injury, based on his deduction from the appearance of the injury itself" (p. 921). In *State v. Wilding* (1999), a physician "testified that the injuries that had caused Cassandra's death seemed consistent with the infant's having been struck by a human hand" (p. 1238). An expert may offer an opinion on "whether the explanation given for the injuries is reasonable" (*Gideon v. State,* 1986, p. 1336). Finally, an expert may offer an opinion on the cause of death or the potential harm of injuries inflicted on certain parts of the body (Myers, 1997a). In *People v. Sargent* (1999), Dr. John McCann stated that

> shaking Michael was a circumstance likely to result in great bodily injury or death. For a fall to have caused the injuries sustained, Michael would have to fall out a second story window, not off the couch or from his father's arms. (p. 838)

Battered Child Syndrome

In their landmark article, Kempe and his colleagues coined the term *battered child syndrome* (Kempe, Silverman, Steele, Droege-mueller, & Silver, 1962). Kempe et al. describe the battered child:

> The battered child syndrome may occur at any age, but, in general the affected children are younger than 3 years. In some instances the clinical manifestations are limited to those resulting from a single episode of trauma, but more often the child's general health is below par, and he shows evidence of neglect, including poor skin hygiene, multiple soft tissue injuries, and malnutrition. One often obtains a history of previous episodes suggestive of parental neglect or trauma. A marked discrepancy between clinical findings and historical data as supplied by the parents is a major diagnostic feature of the battered-child syndrome.... Subdural hematoma, with or without fracture of the skull . . . is an extremely frequent finding even in the absence of fractures of the long bones.... The characteristic distribution of these multiple fractures and the observation that the lesions are in different stages of healing are of additional value in making the diagnosis. (p. 17)

Not all victims of physical abuse have injuries in various stages of healing. Kempe et al. (1962) noted that abusive injury sometimes results from "a single episode of trauma" (p. 17). Many child abuse fatalities lack a pattern of repeated injury.

Expert testimony on battered child syndrome is routinely admitted. Physicians are permitted to state that a child has the syndrome and probably suffered nonaccidental injury. As stated earlier, battered child syndrome is generally accepted as a reliable diagnosis and is not subject to *Frye* or *Daubert.*

Shaken Baby Syndrome

Frustrated caretakers sometimes grasp young children by the shoulders or under the arms and shake them. Neurological damage caused by violent shaking is called shaken baby syndrome or shaken impact syndrome (Duhaime, Christian, Rorke, & Zimmerman, 1998; see Chapter 13, this volume). Expert testimony on shaken baby syndrome is admissible and is not subject to *Frye* or *Daubert* (e.g., *Steggall v. State,* 2000).

Munchausen Syndrome by Proxy

Munchausen syndrome in adults is "a condition characterized by habitual presentation for hospital treatment of an apparent acute illness, the patient giving a plausible and dramatic history, all of which is false" (*Dorland's Illustrated Medical Dictionary,* 1994, p. 1635). Munchausen syndrome by proxy occurs when adults use a child as the vehicle for fabricated illness (see Chapter 7, this volume). Zumwalt and Hirsch (1987) write that

> Munchausen syndrome by proxy occurs when a parent or guardian falsifies a child's medical history or alters a child's laboratory test or actually causes an illness or injury in a child in order to gain medical attention for the child which may result in innumerable harmful hospital procedures. (p. 276)

Courts allow expert testimony describing Munchausen syndrome by proxy (*Reid v. State,* 1998). In *People v. Phillips* (1981), for example, the court approved expert psychiatric testimony on the syndrome to establish the defendant's motive to poison her baby by putting large quantities of salt in the baby's food. The court ruled that the syndrome was not scientific evidence subject to *Frye.*

Neglect Cases

Neglect is a broad concept, covering several types of maltreatment. Expert testimony plays a role in numerous neglect cases. For example, expert testimony is the norm in medical neglect cases (Dubowitz, 1999; see Chapter 14, this volume). Expert testimony is needed to diagnose nonorganic failure to thrive, Munchausen syndrome by proxy, and other matters. Mental health professionals are called on in neglect cases to evaluate the parenting skills and the mental condition of parents and children.

Expert Testimony in Sexual Abuse Litigation

Expert testimony plays an important role in some child sexual abuse litigation (Bulkley, 1992; Myers, 1997a). At the outset, expert testimony regarding sexual abuse can be divided into four categories: (a) testimony describing medical evidence, (b) testimony based largely on the psychological effects of abuse, (c) testimony regarding

interviewing, and (d) testimony regarding the defendant.

Medical Evidence

The first category of expert testimony concerns medical evidence of sexual abuse, such as genital injury and sexually transmitted disease (Bays & Chadwick, 1993; Finkel & Giardino, 2002; see Chapter 12, this volume). Although medical evidence is found in only a small percentage of cases, when medical evidence exists, judges allow physicians and other qualified medical professionals to describe it.

Testimony Based Largely on the Psychological Effects of Sexual Abuse

Expert testimony regarding psychological effects falls into two categories: (a) substantive evidence and (b) rehabilitation.

Substantive Evidence

Substantive expert testimony from mental health professionals takes several forms. The expert may offer an opinion that the child has a diagnosis of sexual abuse. There is some disagreement about whether diagnostic terminology should be employed to describe the determination of sexual abuse by mental health professionals. Opponents argue that sexual abuse is an event, not an illness or injury that can be diagnosed. For example, an emergency room physician does not diagnose "car accident." The doctor diagnoses "broken leg" caused by the accident. Sexual abuse, like a car accident, is an event, and diagnostic terminology should not be employed. On the other hand, professionals are comfortable using diagnostic terminology with physical abuse. Battered child syndrome is an accepted medical diagnosis despite the fact that physical abuse is an event. It seems the word *diagnosis* is sufficiently elastic to describe a mental health finding of sexual abuse. This position finds support in the American Psychiatric Association's (2000) *Diagnostic and Statistical Manual of Mental Disorders* (Technical Revision), which lists child sexual abuse as a diagnosis.

The expert may eschew diagnostic terminology and offer an opinion that the child was abused. The expert may state that the child's symptoms are consistent with sexual abuse. Alternatively, the expert may state that the child demonstrates sexual knowledge that is unusual for children of that age. Finally, the expert may avoid mention of the child in the case at hand and confine testimony to a description of symptoms observed in sexually abused children as a group. Whatever the form, the objective is the same: to prove abuse. Thus, the testimony is substantive evidence.

Controversy in the literature. There is disagreement regarding whether mental health professionals have the knowledge required to determine whether abuse occurred (see *State v. Konechny,* 2000). Melton and Limber (1989) assert that "under no circumstances should a court admit the opinion of [a mental health professional] about whether a particular child has been abused" (p. 1230). Melton et al. (1997) reiterate this position in *Psychological Evaluations for the Courts,* where they write the following:

> There is no reason to believe that clinicians' skill in determining whether a child has been abused is the product of specialized knowledge. The conclusions to be drawn from a child's graphic description of a sexual encounter, for example, are a matter of common sense, not scientific knowledge or even clinical acumen.
>
> Because testimony by an expert involves an implicit representation that the opinions presented are grounded in specialized knowledge, a mental health professional should decline on ethical grounds to offer an opinion about whether a child told the truth or has been "abused." By the same token, under the rules of evidence, such an opinion should never be admitted. (p. 463)

Although Melton et al.'s (1997) position commands respect and is the law in some states, Melton probably speaks for a minority of mental health professionals. Many professionals believe mental health professionals can provide useful substantive evidence in some cases. Of course, a mental health professional cannot "know" whether abuse occurred because the professional did not witness the crime. Many professionals believe, however, that it is possible to draw on the literature and on clinical judgment to

interpret symptoms, behavior, statements, and other evidence to help the jury.

Oberlander (1995) surveyed 31 Massachusetts mental health professionals who evaluate children for possible sexual abuse:

> Evaluators were asked whether it was possible to determine whether a child's behavior and symptoms were consistent with typical responses to sexual abuse. . . . In this sample, 67.7% said they believed it was possible to make such a determination, 9.7% said they were unsure or that it depends on the case, and 22.5% said they believed it was not possible to make such a determination. (p. 482)

Professionals were asked to indicate their opinion about whether psychosocial assessment could establish that a child was sexually abused:

> In this sample, 58.1% said they believed evaluation results could establish abuse, 12.9% said they were unsure or that it depends on the case, and 29.0% said they believed evaluation results could not establish abuse. (Most evaluators drew a distinction between "establish" and "prove," suggesting that their opinions are probabilistic). (Oberlander, 1995, pp. 482-483)

This Massachusetts sample illustrates the diversity of opinion among knowledgeable mental health professionals. In response to both questions, however, the majority believed mental health professionals can reach reasoned decisions about abuse.

In 1996, the American Professional Society on the Abuse of Children issued guidelines for the psychosocial evaluation of sexual abuse in young children. The guidelines state that an "evaluator may state an opinion that abuse did or did not occur, an opinion about the likelihood of the occurrence of abuse, or simply provide a description and analysis of the gathered information" (p. 2).

Symptoms and behaviors shared by abused and nonabused children—base rates. A mental health professional who provides substantive evidence of child sexual abuse must have a firm grip on the literature describing symptoms and behaviors in sexually abused and nonabused children (Kendall-Tackett, Williams, & Finkelhor, 1993). There is no single set of symptoms observed in all sexually abused children. Nevertheless, the presence of certain symptoms can provide evidence of abuse. Stress-related symptoms are rela-

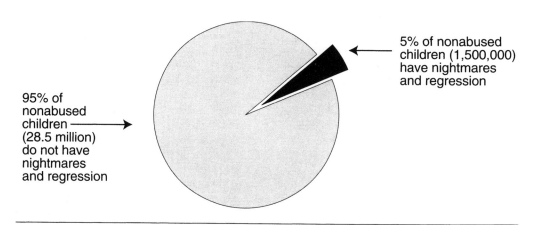

Figure 19.1. Thirty Million Nonabused Children, 5% of Whom Have Nightmares and Regression

tively common, including fear, sleep disturbance and nightmares, flashbacks, startle reactions, hypervigilance, regression, bedwetting, phobic behavior, withdrawal from usual activities, nervousness, and clinginess (Browne & Finkelhor, 1986; Kendall-Tackett et al., 1993; Mannarino & Cohen, 1986; see Chapter 3, this volume). Some sexually abused children are depressed (Lanktree, Briere, & Zaidi, 1991).

The fact that a child has nightmares and regression says little about sexual abuse because other circumstances cause such symptoms. In fact, if all we know about a child is that the child has nightmares and regression, it is more likely, statistically speaking, that the child is nonabused than abused.

The fact that a child has nightmares and regression says little about sexual abuse because other circumstances cause such symptoms. In fact, if all we know about a child is that the child has nightmares and regression, it is more likely, statistically speaking, that the child is *non*abused than abused. Consider 4-year-old Sally. Until a month ago, Sally was a happy-go-lucky preschooler living with her happily married mom and dad. Sally attends day care while her parents work. Quite suddenly, a month ago, Sally started experiencing terrifying nightmares

three or four times a week. She wakes up crying and is very difficult to soothe back to sleep. In addition, Sally started wetting the bed, something she has not done in years. Sally has no prior history of nightmares or regression, nor is there a family history of such problems. Clearly, something is going on, but what? Sally's parents wonder if something happened to their daughter at day care. Is it possible Sally was abused at day care? Do Sally's symptoms help answer that question? The clinical literature tells us that nightmares and regression are observed in some sexually abused children. Yet, if all we know about Sally is that she has nightmares and regression, the odds are Sally is a nonabused child. This conclusion flows from the base rate at which nightmares and regression occur in the total population of nonabused children (Melton & Limber, 1989). The base rate of a symptom or behavior is essentially the prevalence of the symptom or behavior (for detailed analysis of base rates, see Koehler, 1993; Lyon & Koehler, 1996; Wood, 1996; Wood & Wright, 1995).

To illustrate the base rate effect, consider the following hypothetical case. The population figures in this hypothetical case are for illustration only and are not accurate. Assume there are 30 million nonabused children in the United States, and 5% of these nonabused children experience serious nightmares and regression. Thus, in the total population of nonabused children, 1.5 million have nightmares and regression. Figure 19.1 illustrates the number of nonabused children with nightmares and regression.

Now, shift your attention away from nonabused children and concentrate on sex-

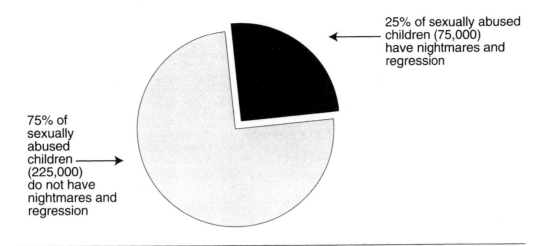

Figure 19.2. Total of 300,000 Sexually Abused Children With Nightmares and Regression

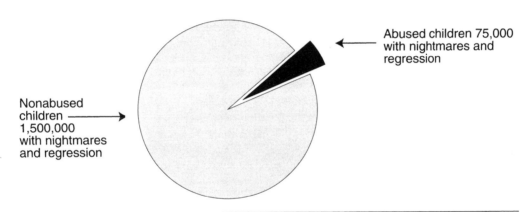

Figure 19.3. There Are 1,575,000 Children–Abused *and* Nonabused–With Nightmares and Regression

ually abused children. Assume there are 300,000 sexually abused children in the United States, and 25% of them have serious nightmares and regression. Why the higher percentage for sexually abused children? Because we accept for purposes of this illustration that sexual abuse does cause nightmares and regression in quite a few victims. Thus, among sexually abused children, 75,000 experience nightmares and regression. Figure 19.2 illustrates the number of sexually abused children with nightmares and regression.

When the abused and the nonabused children with nightmares and regression are combined, the total number of children with these symptoms is 1,575,000. Figure 19.3 illustrates the important point that in the *total* population of children with night-

mares and regression, the great majority are nonabused.

Figure 19.3 is deceptive, however, because the sexually abused children are clearly distinguishable from the nonabused children. In reality, of course, abused and nonabused children look alike. Thus, to bring home the effect of base rates, it is necessary to intermingle the 1.5 million symptomatic nonabused children and the 75,000 abused children to form one large, undifferentiated group of children. Figure 19.4 illustrates the point.

Now, suppose we transport all 1,575,000 children with nightmares and regression to your hometown and turn them loose. With all those kids running around, you reach outside and grab the first child who runs past your door. Did you pick an abused

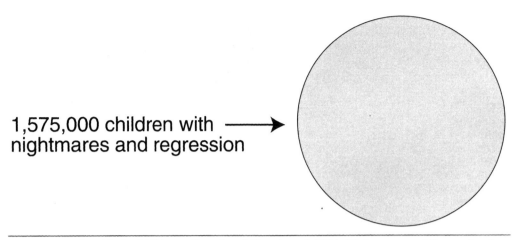

1,575,000 children with ⟶
nightmares and regression

Figure 19.4. Put All the Children—Abused and Nonabused—With Nightmares and Regression Into One Large, Undifferentiated Group (the nonabused children vastly outnumber the abused children)

child or a nonabused child? It is easy to see that the odds are tremendous you picked a nonabused child. Among the total population of children with nightmares and regression, the vast majority are not sexually abused. This illustration helps us understand why Sally's nightmares and regression tell us so little about abuse. If all you know about Sally is that she has nightmares and regression, the odds are Sally is not abused.

The base rate phenomenon is complex. Indeed, the foregoing example is an oversimplification. For readers like the authors of this chapter, who are as likely to be bemused as enlightened by pie charts, there is another way to think about base rates: Beans! Yes, beans. Imagine a paper bag filled with 1,000 red beans. The red beans represent nonabused children with nightmares and regression. Now, imagine another bag containing 25 beans of another color, say white. The white beans represent sexually abused children with nightmares and regression. The number of red beans (nonabused) is much larger than the number of white beans (abused) because the number of nonabused children in the total population (abused *and* nonabused) far exceeds the number of abused children. You can see the effect of base rates by pouring the white beans into the bag of red beans, shaking the two together, and picking one bean at random. The odds are you will pick a red (nonabused) bean. The first author has performed this demonstration many times, and only once has a white bean been picked. Whether it is pie charts or beans, the lesson is simple: If all you know about a child is

that the child has symptoms shared to a considerable degree by abused and nonabused children, then, statistically, the child is probably not abused. Clearly, professionals should not make judgments about sexual abuse primarily on symptoms that overlap considerably between abused and nonabused children.

Developmentally unusual sexual knowledge and behavior. Although quite a few symptoms and behaviors observed in sexually abused children are found in nonabused children, some behaviors are much more frequently observed in sexually abused children. Behaviors that appear to have a closer connection to sexual abuse include developmentally unusual sexual knowledge and sexualized play in young children (Davies, Glaser, & Kossoff, 2000; Friedrich, 1993; Friedrich, Brambsch, Broughton, & Beilke, 1991; Friedrich, Fisher, Broughton, Houston, & Shafran, 1998; Kolko & Moser, 1988; Mannarino & Cohen, 1986).

In 1991, Friedrich reported on normative sexual behavior in American children (Friedrich et al., 1991), noting that

[a] relatively clear finding is that despite the fact that 2- through 12-year-old children exhibit a wide variety of sexual behaviors at relatively high frequencies, e.g., self-stimulatory behavior and exhibitionism, there are a number of behaviors that are quite unusual. . . . These tend to be those behaviors that are either more aggressive or more imitative of adult sexual behavior. (p. 462)

In Friedrich et al.'s (1991) study, the sexual behaviors observed *least* often in nonabused children were placing the child's mouth on a sex part, asking to engage in sex acts, masturbating with an object, inserting objects in the vagina/anus, imitating intercourse, making sexual sounds, French kissing, undressing other people, asking to watch sexually explicit television, and imitating sexual behavior with dolls. From his research on nonabused and abused children, Friedrich developed the Child Sexual Behavior Inventory (CSBI), which is a useful tool to evaluate the possibility of sexual abuse (Friedrich, 1993; Friedrich et al., 1992).

In 1998, Friedrich and his colleagues reported further data on normative sexual behavior. Sexual behavior observed in young children reaches a peak at roughly age 5. After that age, children begin to understand the social restrictions placed on behaviors such as touching private parts in public. Friedrich et al. found that the following factors increase the likelihood of sexual behavior in children: (a) family violence, (b) hours per week in day care, (c) stressful life circumstances, and (d) family attitudes about sexual matters, including nudity, co-sleeping, co-bathing, and pornography. Friedrich et al. write that

> the results were extremely consistent with earlier research, and clearly indicate that children exhibit numerous sexual behaviors at varying levels of frequency. Sexual behaviors that appear to be the most frequent include self-stimulating behaviors, exhibitionism, and behaviors related to personal boundaries. Less frequent behaviors are clearly the more intrusive behaviors. . . . Although sexual behavior is normative, excessive sexual behavior appears related to other behavioral problems including sexual abuse. (pp. 6-8)

Schoentjes, Deboutte, and Friedrich (1999) studied normal sexual behavior in a sample of Dutch-speaking children living in Antwerp. The authors write that "our results confirmed that the 2- to 5-year-old children are relatively sexual compared with the 10- to 12-year-old children and this is true for both genders" (p. 892). The authors conclude that

> this description of sexual behavior in a normative sample of Dutch-speaking 2- to 12-year-old children confirms earlier findings in this field. A variety of sexual behaviors seems to be normal and their occurrence tends to be age-dependent. . . . Unusual sexual behaviors like intrusive or aggressive sexual behaviors, or highly increased sexual behavior, should warn the pediatrician of the possibility of other behavioral or emotional problems, including the possibility of sexual abuse. (p. 893)

Lindblad and colleagues (Lindblad, Gustafsson, Larsson, & Lundin, 1995) examined the frequency of sexual behaviors in a sample of Swedish preschool children attending day care centers. The following behaviors are of interest: 99.6% of the children never attempted to make an adult at day care touch the child's genitals, 91.2% never attempted to touch a female staff member's breasts, 99.6% never attempted to touch an adult's genitals at day care, 91.6% of the children never exhibited their genitals at day care, 92.0% never played sexually explorative games such as "doctor," and 96.8% never initiated games simulating adult sexual activity.

Davies et al. (2000) interviewed 58 English preschool staff about sexualized behavior in children. The authors write,

> The behaviors most rarely observed were a child attempting to, or inserting a penis or finger into, or oral contact with, another child's genitalia, a child putting their mouth on a doll's genital area, and a child asking to be touched in their genital area. . . . Our findings in regard to rarer and more commonly observed behaviors are very similar to those reported by Friedrich and colleagues and Lindblad and colleagues. (p. 1340)

Phipps-Yonas and her colleagues (Phipps-Yonas, Yonas, Turner, & Kauper, 1993) surveyed 564 licensed family day care providers in Minnesota regarding the providers' "observations of children's behavior and apparent sexual knowledge" (p. 2). Phipps-Yonas et al. (1993) write,

> We are all sexual creatures and sexual learning begins in early infancy. . . . Among preschoolers there is often considerable freedom regarding their bodies as well as touching of themselves, their peers, and family members. Children at this stage engage in games such as playing doctor or house which involve explorations through touch and sight of each other's so-called private parts.
>
> We asked people to answer how children aged one to three behave and how children aged four to six behave. . . . Older children

were viewed as much more curious than the younger ones regarding the mechanics of sexual activities and reproduction. They were also much more likely to engage in exploratory "sexual" games such as "I'll show you mine, if you show me yours" or doctor or house.

As other investigators have reported, touching of other children's genitals is relatively common.... Certain behaviors were reported as having a very low probability by the day care providers, especially for children under age four. These include: efforts to engage in pretend sexual intercourse; French-kissing; requests to have another suck, lick, or kiss their genitals; and attempts to insert objects into their own or another's buttocks or vaginas. (pp. 1, 3-4)

Conte and his colleagues surveyed 212 professionals who regularly evaluate children for possible sexual abuse (Conte, Sorenson, Fogarty, & Dalla Rosa, 1991). The evaluators were asked to rank the importance of 41 indicators of sexual abuse. The following indicators were thought to be important by more than 90% of the evaluators: medical evidence of abuse, age-inappropriate sexual knowledge, sexualized play during the interview, precocious or seductive behavior, excessive masturbation, consistency in the child's description over time, and the child's report of pressure or coercion.

Conte et al. (1991) cautioned against placing undue confidence in the findings, noting that consensus among professionals "does not ensure that professional practice or professional beliefs are knowledge-based, and agreement among these respondents should not be assumed to validate various practices as reliable and effective" (p. 433). Indeed, professional judgment based on clinical experience alone is sometimes a poor foundation for decision making (Dawes, Faust, & Meehl, 1989; Garb, 1989; Wood, 1996).

Wells and colleagues studied symptoms in three groups of prepubescent females: nonabused, confirmed abuse, and suspected but unconfirmed abuse (Wells, McCann, Adams, Voris, & Ensign, 1995). The authors write,

Children with known or suspected sexual abuse were significantly more likely to have sudden emotional and behavioral change, to be fearful of being left with a particular person, to know more about sex and to be more

interested and curious about sex matters or private parts. There were no differences between the groups on bed-wetting, headaches, constipation, or vaginal bleeding. Significant problems in concentration and changes in school performance were noted in those children with suspected sexual abuse, but there were no significant differences regarding bath habits, truancy or extracurricular involvement. No children in the nonabused sample were described as acting overly mature or adult like for age, while 33% of children in the other groups had this reported by a parent. Similarly, there were no parents in the nonabused groups who reported that their child had become fearful of males or unusually self-conscious about her body. In contrast, 27% of children with suspected sexual abuse were reportedly fearful of males and 28% had become unusually self-conscious about their bodies.... Children with a perpetrator confession had significantly greater rates of reported fearfulness of being left alone, fearfulness of males, and of being self-conscious about her body.... Nightmares, crying easily, and being fearful of being left alone were common symptoms in the nonabused sample, as were difficulties with bed-wetting, headaches and stomach aches. These symptoms do not appear to be necessarily reflective of abuse. In contrast, specific fears of a particular person, self-consciousness about her body and fearfulness of males appear to be questions that discriminate amongst abused and nonabused samples.... Sudden changes in children's behaviors and particularly increased and specific fears and heightened interest and curiosity regarding sexual matters appear to happen relatively infrequently in the nonabused sample, but are present in 30 to 66% of children who are suspected victims of abuse. (pp. 159-161)

Brilleslijper-Kater and Baartman (2000) studied 63 Dutch children ranging in age from 2 to 7 years. The research demonstrates that very young children ask about genital differences, pregnancy, and birth. Young children typically do not ask about adult sexual behavior such as sexual intercourse. In this study, children younger than age 5 had very little knowledge of sexuality. By age 5 or 6, children begin learning some aspects of sexuality, although most children in this study had very little, if any, idea of sexual intercourse or other adult sexual conduct.

Heiman, Leiblum, Esquilin, and Pallitto (1998) studied "what professionals believe constitutes normal sexual development" in children (p. 298). Heiman et al. write that

> adults' beliefs about what constitutes normal childhood sexual behavior revealed trends and patterns that replicate past research. The most consistent finding was that sexual acts involving oral, vaginal, or anal penetration were judged to be abnormal in children younger than 12 years of age. (p. 298)

Heiman et al. (1998) sought to determine whether professionals who work with sexually abused children "overpathologize sexual behaviors" (p. 300). Heiman et al. found little evidence "to support the view that sexual abuse experts overpathologize all childhood sexual behaviors" (p. 300).

The Child Behavior Checklist (CBC) (Achenbach, 1991) is a well-known questionnaire used to rate the frequency of behaviors over a 6-month period. Six items on the CBC concern sexual behavior. Friedrich (1997) developed the Child Sexual Behavior Inventory (CSBI) as a measure of sexual behavior in children. Neither the CBC nor the CSBI are "tests" for sexual abuse. Nor can these instruments be used in isolation to diagnose sexual abuse. Rather, the CBC and the CSBI can play a role in the overall assessment of possible abuse. Drach, Wientzen, and Ricci (2001)

> found no significant relationship between sexual abuse diagnosis and sexual behavior problems as measured by the Child Sexual Behavior Inventory among children assessed for sexual abuse in a multidiciplinary forensic evaluation setting. Similarly, the study found no significant relationship between sexual abuse diagnosis and behavior problems as measured by the Child Behavior Checklist. (p. 498)

Drach et al.'s (2001) study examined only summary scores on the CSBI and CBC. The study did not examine the possible relationship between sexual abuse and specific sexual behaviors. In particular, the study did not examine the relationship between sexual abuse and sexual behaviors that is very seldom observed in nonabused children.

Current research has limitations. Nevertheless, the findings described above lay an empirical foundation for the conclusion that the presence of sexual behaviors that are seldom observed in nonabused children can provide evidence of sexual abuse. Of course, the fact that a child displays one or

more uncommon sexual behaviors is not conclusive evidence of sexual abuse. Friedrich et al. (1991) remind us that "sexual behavior in children is related to the child's family context, most specifically the sexual behavior in the family" (p. 462). A nonabused child may acquire sexual knowledge watching pornography or witnessing adults engage in sexual conduct. Finally, base rate issues arise even with uncommon sexual behaviors. Melton et al. (1997) point out that "because a large proportion of a small population still may be smaller than a small proportion of a large population and because sexualized behavior is exhibited by only a minority of the sexually abused population, the base-rate problem still applies" (p. 758, note 211).

In the final analysis, there is no behavior or set of behaviors—sexual or nonsexual—that is pathognomonic of abuse.

In the final analysis, there is no behavior or set of behaviors—sexual or nonsexual—that is pathognomonic of abuse. Nor is there a psychological "test" for sexual abuse. What is more, there is no psychological syndrome that detects sexual abuse. Despite these limitations, developmentally unusual sexual knowledge can be a "marker" for sexual abuse and an important piece of an overall psychosocial assessment.

When can one place the most confidence in evidence a child was sexually abused? The greatest confidence is sometimes warranted when there is a coalescence of five types of data:

1. developmentally unusual sexual behavior, knowledge, or symptoms providing relatively strong evidence of sexual experience (e.g., 4-year-old with detailed knowledge of fellatio, including ejaculation);
2. nonsexual behavior or symptoms commonly observed in sexually abused children (e.g., symptoms such as nightmares and regression);
3. medical evidence of sexual abuse;
4. convincing report by the child;
5. evidence that corroborates the abuse (e.g., incriminating statements by the alleged perpetrator).

Confidence in the evidence typically (although not invariably) grows as the amount and quality of evidence increases. For example, confidence may grow as the number or persuasiveness of developmentally unusual sexual behaviors increases, the types of nonsexual symptoms expand, the strength of medical evidence increases, the corroborating evidence becomes more convincing, and when there is evidence that the professionals who interviewed the child used proper technique.

Confidence in the evidence often (although, again, not invariably) declines as the amount and quality of evidence decreases. The decline in confidence may be particularly precipitous when evidence providing relatively strong evidence of abuse is lacking. For example, there may be no medical evidence, the child may demonstrate none of the developmentally unusual sexual behaviors that are related to sexual abuse, and there may be no corroborating evidence. In such a case, the evidence of sexual abuse consists of nonsexual symptoms and the child's disclosure. To take the process one step further, suppose a case in which there is no medical evidence, no developmentally unusual sexual behavior, no corroboration, and no convincing disclosure. In this case, the only evidence of abuse is nonsexual symptoms observed in sexually abused and nonabused children. Of course, we can have *no* confidence in this evidence because of base rates.

One should not conclude from the foregoing that the *quantity* of evidence is a satisfactory basis for decision making. Rather, sound decisions rest on careful assessment of the quantity, quality, and context of the evidence.

Do American judges allow mental health professionals to offer substantive evidence of child sexual abuse? Although judges do not question the ability of mental health professionals to make *clinical* decisions about sexual abuse, the level of certainty that suffices for clinical judgment may not suffice in court. As discussed earlier, mental health professionals continue to debate whether current knowledge is adequate to support expert testimony offered as substantive evidence. With considerable oversimplification, it is possible to say that American judges take three positions regarding expert testimony from mental health professionals offered as substantive evidence of sexual abuse: yes, no, and maybe.

One group of courts allows properly qualified professionals to offer *some forms* of substantive evidence of sexual abuse in some cases. A second group of courts rejects most or all forms of substantive evidence from mental health professionals. A third group of courts—the maybe courts—adopt a middle position. The maybe courts treat substantive evidence from mental health professionals as scientific evidence subject to *Frye* or *Daubert*. Under the maybe approach, the court leaves the door open to such testimony *if and when* it is established as reliable (see *State v. Konechny,* 2000).

Rehabilitation Expert Testimony

Expert mental health testimony offered as substantive evidence is complex, controversial, and evolving. By contrast, expert testimony offered to rehabilitate a child's damaged credibility is straightforward and uncontroversial. Such testimony serves the limited purpose of rehabilitating a child's credibility *after* it is attacked by the defense attorney. When expert testimony is limited to rehabilitation, the testimony is *not* offered as substantive evidence.

How does the defense attorney attack the child's credibility? The defense attorney may assert that the child cannot be believed because the child did not report the abuse for a substantial period of time, because the child was inconsistent, or because the child recanted. When the defense concentrates on delay, inconsistency, and recantation, judges in most states allow the prosecutor to respond with expert testimony to inform jurors that such behavior is not uncommon in sexually abused children (Myers, 1997a). Courts generally hold that expert rehabilitation testimony is not subject to *Frye* or *Daubert*.

The following guidelines are offered to help professionals keep rehabilitation testimony within proper bounds:

1. In some states, the prosecutor must tell the judge and the defense attorney which behavior(s) the expert will discuss (*People v. Bowker,* 1988). For example, if the defense attorney limits the attack on the child's credibility to delayed reporting, the prosecutor lets the judge and defense counsel know that the expert's testimony will be limited to helping the jury understand delay. The expert should limit testimony to the behavior emphasized by the defense attorney and should not offer a broad-ranging lecture on children's reactions to sexual abuse.

2. In most cases, expert rehabilitation testimony is limited to a description of behaviors seen in sexually abused children *as a group*. Unless asked to do so, it is generally wise to avoid describing any particular child and, in particular, the child in the present case.

3. If it is necessary to refer to the child in the present case, the expert should avoid using the word *victim*. Referring to the child as a victim sends the jury a message that the expert believes the child was abused. Remember, however, when expert testimony is limited to rehabilitation, the expert is *not* there to give the jury substantive evidence on whether the child was abused.

4. In most sexual abuse cases, the expert should avoid reference to syndromes, such as child sexual abuse accommodation syndrome (Summit, 1983). An expert does not need to use the loaded word *syndrome* to help the jury understand that delayed reporting, recantation, and inconsistency occur in sexually abused children.

The Continuum of Expertise Regarding Child Sexual Abuse

Professionals with relatively little experience and training can provide expert testimony to rehabilitate a child's credibility. Rehabilitation is typically limited to explaining recantation or delay. The expert does not venture an opinion that the child was abused. Indeed, with rehabilitation, it is usually unnecessary to refer to the child. Rehabilitation testimony is straightforward and simple. To provide such testimony, the only requirement is knowledge of relevant literature.

Unlike the *limited* knowledge required for rehabilitation testimony, an *extraordinary* level of expertise is required to offer substantive evidence of sexual abuse. Only a small fraction of professionals working with sexually abused children know enough to provide substantive evidence.

Expert Testimony About Psychological Syndromes

Psychological syndromes sometimes play a role in child sexual abuse litigation. For detailed analysis of the use and abuse of syndromes, see Myers (1993, 1997a) and Richardson, Ginsburg, Gatowski, and Dobbin (1995).

Child sexual abuse accommodation syndrome. In 1983, Summit described child sexual abuse accommodation syndrome (CSAAS). Summit noted five characteristics commonly observed in sexually abused children: secrecy; helplessness; entrapment and accommodation; delayed, conflicted, and unconvincing disclosure; and retraction. Summit's purpose in describing the accommodation syndrome was to provide a "common language" for professionals working to protect sexually abused children. Summit did not intend the syndrome as a diagnostic device (Summit, Miller, & Veltkamp, 1998). The accommodation syndrome does *not* detect sexual abuse. Rather, CSAAS assumes that abuse occurred and explains the child's reactions to it. Thus, the accommodation syndrome does not prove abuse and does not constitute substantive evidence.

The accommodation syndrome helps explain why some sexually abused children delay reporting their abuse and why some children recant allegations of abuse and deny that anything happened. When the syndrome is confined to these rehabilitative purposes, the syndrome serves a useful forensic function.

Rape trauma syndrome. Rape trauma syndrome (RTS) was described by Burgess and Holmstrom (1974) as "the acute phase and long-term reorganization process that occurs as a result of forcible rape or attempted forcible rape. This syndrome of behavioral, somatic, and psychological reactions is an acute stress reaction to a life-threatening situation" (p. 982). Although expert testimony on RTS is used most often in litigation involving adult victims, RTS is useful in child sexual abuse litigation involving older children and adolescents.

Expert testimony on RTS has been offered by prosecutors for two purposes: (a) as substantive evidence to prove lack of consent to sexual relations and (b) as rehabilitation evidence to explain behavior such as delay in reporting rape, which jurors might misconstrue as evidence the rape did not occur. Courts are divided on the admissibility of RTS to prove lack of consent. When it comes to rehabilitation, however, most courts allow expert testimony on RTS to explain delayed reporting and related matters. In *People v. Bledsoe* (1984), the California Supreme Court wrote that "expert testimony on rape trauma syndrome may play a particularly useful role by disabusing the jury of some widely held misconceptions about rape and rape victims, so that it may evaluate the evidence free of the constraints of popular myths" (p. 475). In *People v. Taylor* (1990), New York's highest court approved expert testimony that explains why a rape victim might not appear upset following the assault.

Posttraumatic stress disorder. Symptoms of posttraumatic stress disorder (PTSD) are observed in more than half of sexually abused children (Kendall-Tackett et al., 1993). Briere and Elliott (1994) write that "although most child sexual abuse victims do not meet the full diagnostic criteria for PTSD, more than 80% are reported to have some posttraumatic symptoms" (p. 56). Famularo, Fenton, Augustyn, and Zuckerman (1996) add that "the type, duration, and frequency of trauma determines the likelihood of PTSD development, and as such Post Traumatic Stress Disorder may result from a single or repeated traumatic event exposure" (p. 1248). Although PTSD does not directly prove sexual abuse, the disorder means *something* traumatic occurred, and sexual abuse is one possibility.

Expert testimony on PTSD is sometimes admissible in court as substantive evidence of abuse. In addition, evidence of PTSD is sometimes admissible to rehabilitate a victim's credibility.

Parental alienation syndrome. The term *parental alienation syndrome* was coined by Gardner (1992) to describe a parent who alienates a child from the other parent. The syndrome finds play most often in family court. Of course, the idea that a parent embroiled in custody litigation might use a child as a pawn is hardly revolutionary. Unfortunately, Gardner's syndrome has had an unfairly negative impact on parents who raise allegations of sexual abuse in family court (see Myers, 1997b). Parental alienation syndrome has been cogently criticized (Bruch, in press; Faller, 1998; Myers, 1998, 1993). On balance, the search for truth about abuse would be better served if parental alienation syndrome went the way of the dinosaur.

Expert Testimony That Judges Do Not Allow

American courts agree that expert witnesses should not comment directly on the credibility of individual children or on the credibility of sexually abused children as a group. Thus, expert witnesses should not say that a child told the truth or was believable when describing abuse. The Oregon Supreme Court did not mince words in its condemnation of expert testimony on the truthfulness of children. The court wrote,

> We have said before, and we will say it again, but this time with emphasis—we really mean it—*no psychotherapist may render an opinion on whether a witness is credible in any trial conducted in this state.* The assessment of credibility is for the trier of fact and not for psychotherapists. (*State v. Milbradt*, 1988, p. 624)

Courts reject expert testimony on credibility because judges firmly believe that assessment of credibility is the exclusive province of the jury. As one court put it, "The jury is the lie detector in the courtroom" (*United States v. Barnard*, 1973, p. 912). Judges also do not permit expert witnesses to testify that a particular person perpetrated abuse.

This is an appropriate juncture to mention criterion-based content analysis (CBCA) and statement validity analysis (SVA). CBCA is a technique designed to assess the validity of a child's statement describing abuse. CBCA is the key element of an overall assessment process called SVA. A verbatim written record of a child's statement is analyzed in light of a set of predetermined criteria. At present, there are serious doubts about the validity of SVA (see Anson, Golding, & Gully, 1993; Berliner & Conte, 1993; Lamb et al., 1997; Ruby & Brigham, 1997). Lamb et al. (1997) write that

> overall, the results reported here are quite sobering, particularly when viewed from the perspective of forensic application. . . . The level of precision [with CBCA] clearly remains too poor to permit the designation of CBCA as a reliable and valid test suitable for use in the courtroom. . . . CBCA should not yet—and perhaps should never—be used in forensic contexts to evaluate individual statements. (pp. 262-263)

Expert Testimony Regarding Interviewing

Defense attorneys in child sexual abuse cases increasingly offer expert testimony to attack the way children were interviewed (e.g., *Commonwealth v. LeFave,* 1999; *State v. Michaels,* 1994). Judges generally permit such testimony. As the Georgia Supreme Court put it in *Barlow v. State* (1998), "The defendant in a child molestation case is entitled to introduce expert testimony for the limited purpose of providing the jury with information about proper techniques for interviewing children and whether the interviewing techniques actually utilized were proper" (p. 417). For in-depth discussion of expert testimony regarding suggestability, see Ceci and Friedman (2000) and Lyon (1999).

Expert Testimony Regarding the Defendant

In the effort to prove that a person sexually abused a child, is the prosecutor allowed to offer evidence that the person fits the psychological profile of a sex offender or pedophile? For psychological as well as legal reasons, the answer should be no.

From the psychological perspective, the clinical and scientific literature indicate that persons who sexually abuse children are a heterogeneous group with few shared characteristics apart from a predilection for deviant sexual behavior with children. Furthermore, no psychological test or device reliably detects persons who have or will sexually abuse children (Becker & Murphy, 1998; Murphy, Rau, & Worley, 1994). Thus, under the current state of scientific knowledge, there is no profile of a "typical" child molester (see Chapter 11, this volume).

From the legal perspective, the inappropriateness of profile testimony is supported by one of the basic rules of American law. A prosecutor generally is not allowed to establish a person's guilt through evidence that the person has a particular character trait or propensity. Thus, evidence of the defendant's bad character is not allowed to prove that the defendant committed a crime. In a bank robbery case, for example, the prosecutor may not offer evidence that the defendant robbed other banks and therefore probably robbed this bank "because he is the kind of guy who sticks up banks." Such character evidence is forbidden. The law may allow the jury to hear about the other bank jobs for some other reason but not to prove the defendant's bad character or propensity for bank robbery.

In the effort to prove that a person sexually abused a child, is the prosecutor allowed to offer evidence that the person fits the psychological profile of a sex offender or pedophile? No.

The rule against character evidence applies in sex abuse litigation. The prosecutor is not allowed to prove that because the defendant abused other children in the past, he probably abused this child "because he is the kind of guy who molests children." Expert testimony that the defendant fits the profile of a "typical" sex offender is essentially character evidence and is inadmissible for that reason.

In 1994, Congress abolished the time-honored rule against character evidence in sex offense cases in federal court. Thus, in federal court, a prosecutor who is attempting to prove sexual abuse may offer evidence that the defendant abused other children in the past. From the evidence of earlier abuse, the jury is allowed to infer that the defendant is guilty in the present case because "he is the kind of guy who molests children." California adopted the federal position. A small number of other states have for a long time allowed some character evidence in sex abuse cases. Most states, however, continue to enforce the rule against character evidence in sex offense cases.

May a prosecutor offer expert testimony that there is *no* profile of a "typical" child molester? In *People v. McAlpin* (1991), the California Supreme Court said yes, at least in some cases. Such expert testimony helps the jury understand that child molesters come from all walks of life and backgrounds.

Unlike the prosecutor, the defendant in a criminal case *is* allowed to offer evidence of the defendant's good character to prove that the defendant is innocent. With this rule in mind, should a person accused of child sexual abuse be allowed to offer expert testimony that the person does *not* fit the profile or share the character traits of child molesters? From the scientific perspective, the answer should be no (*Flanagan v. State,* 1993; *State v. Person,* 1989). Despite the lack of a reliable profile, however, some mental health professionals are willing to describe profiles or testify that a person does not share the characteristics of individuals who typically abuse children, and a few courts allow such testimony (e.g., *People v. Stoll,* 1989). Once the defendant offers expert testimony that the defendant does not share the characteristics of child molesters, the prosecutor is allowed to offer expert testimony to contradict the defendant's expert witness.

Conclusion

Expert testimony plays an important role in child abuse litigation. As long as experts realize the limits of their knowledge and keep their testimony within those limits, they will continue to help juries decide these difficult cases.

References

Achenbach, T. (1991). *Manual for the Child Behavior Checklist/4-18 and 1991 profile.* Burlington: University of Vermont, Department of Psychiatry.

American Academy of Pediatrics, Committee on Child Abuse and Neglect. (1999). Guidelines for the evaluation of sexual abuse of children: Subject review. *Pediatrics, 103,* 187-191.

American Professional Society on the Abuse of Children (APSAC). (1996). *Guidelines for psychosocial evaluation of suspected sexual abuse in young children.* Chicago: Author.

American Psychiatric Association. (2000). *Diagnostic and statistical manual of mental disorders* (Technical rev.). Washington, DC: Author.

Anson, D. A., Golding, S. J., & Gully, K. J. (1993). Child sexual abuse allegations: Reliability of criteria-based content analysis. *Law and Human Behavior, 17,* 331-341.

Barlow v. State, 507 S.E. 2d 416 (Ga. 1998).

Bays, J., & Chadwick, D. L. (1993). Medical diagnosis of the sexually abused child. *Child Abuse & Neglect, 17,* 91-110.

Becker, J. V., & Murphy, W. D. (1998). What we know and do not know about assessing and treating sex offenders. *Psychology, Public Policy and Law, 4,* 116-137.

Berliner, L., & Conte, J. R. (1993). Sexual abuse evaluations: Conceptual and empirical obstacles. *Child Abuse & Neglect, 17,* 111-125.

Black, B. (1988). A unified theory of scientific evidence. *Fordham Law Review, 56,* 595-695.

Black, B., Francisco, J., & Saffran-Brinks, C. (1994). Science and the law in the wake of *Daubert:* A new search for scientific knowledge. *Texas Law Review, 72,* 715-802.

Briere, J. N., & Elliott, D. M. (1994). Immediate and long-term impacts of child sexual abuse. *Future of Children, 4,* 54-69.

Brilleslijper-Kater, S. N., & Baartman, H. E. M. (2000). What do young children know about sexuality? Research on the knowledge of children between the age of 2 and 7. *Child Abuse Review, 9,* 166-182.

Browne, A., & Finkelhor, D. (1986). Impact of child sexual abuse: A review of the research. *Psychological Bulletin, 99,* 66-77.

Bruch, C. S. (in press). Parental alienation syndrome: Junk science in child custody determination. *European Journal of Law Reform.*

Bulkley, J. A. (1992). The prosecution's use of social science expert testimony in child sexual abuse cases: National trends and recommendations. *Journal of Child Sexual Abuse, 1,* 73-93.

Burgess, A., & Holmstrom, L. (1974). Rape trauma syndrome. *American Journal of Psychiatry, 131,* 981-986.

Ceci, S. J., & Friedman, R. D. (2000). The suggestability of children: Scientific research and legal implications. *Cornell Law Review, 86,* 33-108.

Chadwick, D. L. (1990). Preparation for court testimony in child abuse cases. *Pediatric Clinics of North America, 37,* 955-970.

Committee on Ethical Guidelines for Forensic Psychologists. (1991). Specialty guidelines for forensic psychologists. *Law and Human Behavior, 15,* 655-665.

Commonwealth v. LeFave, 714 N.E. 2d 805 (Mass. 1999).

Conte, J. R., Sorenson, E., Fogarty, L., & Dalla Rosa, J. (1991). Evaluating children's reports of sexual abuse: Results from a survey of professionals. *American Journal of Orthopsychiatry, 61,* 428-437.

Daubert v. Merrell Dow Pharmaceuticals, Inc., 509 U.S. 579 (1993).

Davies, S. L., Glaser, D., & Kossoff, R. (2000). Children's sexual play and behavior in pre-school settings: Staff's perceptions, reports, and responses. *Child Abuse & Neglect, 24,* 1329-1343.

Dawes, R. M., Faust, D., & Meehl, P. E. (1989). Clinical versus actuarial judgment. *Science, 243,* 1668-1674.

Dorland's illustrated medical dictionary (28th ed.). (1994). Philadelphia: W. B. Saunders.

Drach, K. M., Wientzen, J., & Ricci, L. R. (2001). The diagnostic utility of sexual behavior problems in diagnosing sexual abuse in a forensic child abuse evaluation clinic. *Child Abuse & Neglect, 25*(4), 489-503.

Dubowitz, H. (Ed.). (1999). *Neglected children: Research, practice, and policy.* Thousand Oaks, CA: Sage.

Duhaime, A., Christian, C. W., Rorke, L. B., & Zimmerman, R. A. (1998). Nonaccidental head injury in infants: The "shaken baby syndrome." *New England Journal of Medicine, 338,* 1822-1829.

Faller, K. C. (1998). The parental alienation syndrome: What it is and what data support it? *Child Maltreatment, 3,* 100-115.

Famularo, R., Fenton, T., Augustyn, M., & Zuckerman, B. (1996). Persistence of pediatric post traumatic stress disorder after 2 years. *Child Abuse & Neglect, 20,* 1245-1248.

Federal rules of evidence. United States Code. Title 28.

Finkel, M. A., & Giardino, A. P. (Eds.). (2002). *Medical evaluation of child sexual abuse: A practical guide.* Thousand Oaks, CA: Sage.

Flanagan v. State, 625 So. 2d 827 (Fla. 1993).

Friedrich, W. N. (1993). Sexual victimization and sexual behavior in children: A review of recent literature. *Child Abuse & Neglect, 17,* 59-66.

Friedrich, W. N. (1997). *Child Sexual Behavior Inventory: Professional manual.* Odessa, FL: Psychological Assessment Resources.

Friedrich, W. N., Brambsch, P., Broughton, K., & Beilke, R. L. (1991). Normative sexual behavior in children. *Pediatrics, 88,* 456-464.

Friedrich, W. N., Fisher, J., Broughton, D., Houston, M., & Shafran, C. R. (1998). Normative sexual behavior in children: A contemporary sample. *Pediatrics, 101,* section E9.

Friedrich, W. N., Grambsch, P., Damon, L., Hewitt, S., Koverola, C., Lang, R., Wolfe, V., & Broughton, D. (1992). The child sexual behavior inventory: Normative and clinical findings. *Psychological Assessment, 4,* 303-311.

Frye v. United States, 293 F. 1013 (D.C. Cir. 1923).

Garb, H. N. (1989). Clinical judgment, clinical training, and professional experience. *Psychological Bulletin, 105,* 387-396.

Gardner, R. A. (1992). *The parental alienation syndrome and the differentiation between fabricated and genuine child sex abuse.* Cresskil, NJ: Creative Therapeutics.

Gideon v. State, 721 P.2d 1336 (Okla. Crim. App. 1986).

Heiman, M. L., Leiblum, S., Esquilin, S. C., & Pallitto, L. M. (1998). A comparative study of beliefs about "normal" childhood sexual behaviors. *Child Abuse & Neglect, 22,* 298-304.

Helfer, R. E., Kempe, R. S., & Krugman, R. D. (Eds.). (1997). *The battered child* (5th ed.). Chicago: University of Chicago Press.

In re Cindy L., 947 P.2d 1340 (Cal. 1997).

Kempe, C. H., Silverman, F. N., Steele, B. F., Droegemueller, W., & Silver, H. K. (1962). The battered child syndrome. *Journal of the American Medical Association, 181,* 17-24.

Kendall-Tackett, K. A., Williams, L. M., & Finkelhor, D. (1993). Impact of sexual abuse on children: A review and synthesis of recent empirical studies. *Psychological Bulletin, 113,* 164-180.

Koehler, J. J. (1993). The normative status of base rates at trial. In N. J. Castellan (Ed.), *Individual and group decision making: Current issues* (pp. 137-149). Hillsdale, NJ: Lawrence Erlbaum.

Kolko, D. J., & Moser, J. T. (1988). Behavioral/emotional indicators of sexual abuse in child psychiatric inpatients: A controlled comparison with physical abuse. *Child Abuse & Neglect, 12,* 529-541.

Kumho Tire Co. v. Carmichael, 526 U.S. 137 (1999).

Lamb, M. E., Sternberg, K. J., Esplin, P. W., Hershkowitz, I., Orbach, Y., & Hovav, M. (1997). Criterion-based content analysis: A field validation study. *Child Abuse & Neglect* 255-264.

Lanktree, C., Briere, J., & Zaidi, L. (1991). Incidence and impact of sexual abuse in a child outpatient sample: The role of direct inquiry. *Child Abuse & Neglect, 15,* 447-453.

Lewin, J. L. (1998). The genesis and evolution of legal uncertainty about "reasonable medical certainty." *Maryland Law Review, 57,* 380-504.

Lilly, G. C. (1996). *An introduction to the law of evidence* (3rd ed.). St. Paul, MN: West.

Lindblad, F., Gustafsson, P. A., Larsson, I., & Lundin, B. (1995). Preschoolers' sexual behavior at daycare centers: An epidemiological study. *Child Abuse & Neglect, 19,* 569-577.

Lyon, T. D. (1999). The new wave in children's suggestibility research: A critique. *Cornell Law Review, 84,* 1004-1087.

Lyon, T. D., & Koehler, J. J. (1996). The relevance ratio: Evaluating the probative value of expert testimony in child sexual abuse cases. *Cornell Law Review, 82,* 43-78.

Mannarino, A. P., & Cohen, J. A. (1986). A clinical-demographic study of sexually abused children. *Child Abuse & Neglect, 10,* 17-23.

Melton, G. B., & Limber, S. (1989). Psychologists' involvement in cases of child maltreatment. *American Psychologist, 44*(9), 1225-1233.

Melton, G. B., Petrila, J., Poythress, N., & Slobogin, C. (1997). *Psychological evaluations for the courts* (2nd ed.). New York: Guilford.

Morison, S., & Greene, E. (1992). Juror and expert knowledge of child sexual abuse. *Child Abuse & Neglect, 16,* 595-613.

Mueller, C. B., & Kirkpatrick, L. C. (1994). *Federal evidence* (2nd ed.). Rochester, NY: Lawyers Cooperative.

Murphy, W., Rau, T., & Worley, P. (1994). The perils and pitfalls of profiling child sex abusers. *APSAC Advisor, 7,* 3-4, 28-29.

Myers, J. E. B. (1993). Expert testimony regarding psychological syndromes. *Pacific Law Journal, 24,* 1449-1464.

Myers, J. E. B. (1997a). *Evidence in child abuse and neglect cases* (3rd ed.). New York: Aspen Law and Business.

Myers, J. E. B. (1997b). *A mother's nightmare: Incest: A practical legal guide for parents and professionals.* Thousand Oaks, CA: Sage.

Myers, J. E. B. (1998). *Legal issues in child abuse and neglect* (2nd ed.). Thousand Oaks, CA: Sage.

Oberlander, L. B. (1995). Psycholegal issues in child sexual abuse evaluations: A survey of forensic mental health professionals. *Child Abuse & Neglect, 19,* 475-490.

Pennsylvania v. Ritchie, 480 U.S. 39 (1987).

People v. Bledsoe, 681 P.2d 291 (Cal. 1984).

People v. Bowker, 249 Cal. Rptr. 886 (1988).

People v. Jackson, 95 Cal. Rptr. 919 (Ct. App. 1971).

People v. McAlpin, 812 P.2d 563 (Cal. 1991).

People v. Phillips, 175 Cal. Rptr. 703 (Ct. App. 1981).

People v. Sargent, 970 P.2d 409 (Cal. 1999).

People v. Stoll, 783 P.2d 698 (Cal. 1989).

People v. Taylor, 552 N.E.2d 131 (1990).

Phipps-Yonas, S., Yonas, A., Turner, M., & Kauper, M. (1993). Sexuality in early childhood: The observations and opinions of family day care providers. *University of Minnesota CURA Reporter, 23,* 1-5.

Reece, R. M. (Ed.). (2000). *Treatment of child abuse: Common ground for mental health, medical, and legal practitioners.* Baltimore: Johns Hopkins University Press.

Reece, R. M., & Ludwig, S. (2001). *Child abuse: Medical diagnosis and management.* Philadelphia: Lippincott.

Reid v. State, 964 S.W.2d 723 (Tex. Ct. App. 1998).

Richardson, J. T., Ginsburg, G. P., Gatowski, S., & Dobbin, S. (1995). The problems of applying *Daubert* to psychological syndrome evidence. *Judicature, 79,* 10-16.

Ruby, C. L., & Brigham, J. C. (1997). The usefulness of the criteria-based content analysis technique in distinguishing between truthful and fabricated allegations: A critical review. *Psychology, Public Policy, and Law, 3,* 705-737.

Saks, M. J. (1990). Expert witnesses, nonexpert witnesses, and nonwitness experts. *Law and Human Behavior, 14,* 291-313.

Schoentjes, E., Deboutte, D., & Friedrich, W. (1999). Child sexual behavior inventory: A Dutch-speaking normative sample. *Pediatrics, 104,* 885-893.

State v. Konechny, 3 P.3d 535 (Idaho Ct. App. 2000).

State v. Michaels, 642 A.2d 1372 (N.J. 1994).

State v. Milbradt, 756 P.2d 620 (Or. 1988).

State v. Person, 564 A.2d 626 (Conn. Ct. App. 1989).

State v. Wilding, 740 A.2d 1235 (R.I. 1999).

Steggall v. State, 8 S.W.3d 538 (Ark. 2000).

Stern, P. (1997). *Preparing and presenting expert testimony in child abuse litigation.* Thousand Oaks, CA: Sage.

Summit, R. C. (1983). The child sexual abuse accommodation syndrome. *Child Abuse & Neglect, 7,* 177-193.

Summit, R. C., Miller, T. W., & Veltkamp, L. J. (1998). The child sexual abuse accommodation syndrome: Clinical and forensic implications. In T. W. Miller (Ed.), *Children of trauma: Stressful life events and their effects on children and adolescents* (pp. 43-60). Madison, CT: International Universities Press.

United States v. Barnard, 490 F.2d 907 (9th Cir. 1973).

Wells, R. D., McCann, J., Adams, J., Voris, J., & Dahl, B. (1997). A validation study of the structured interview of symptoms associated with sexual abuse (SASA) using three samples of sexually abused, allegedly abuse, and nonabused boys. *Child Abuse & Neglect, 21,* 1159-1167.

Wells, R. D., McCann, J., Adams, J., Voris, J., & Ensign, J. (1995). Emotional, behavioral, and physical symptoms reported by parents of sexually abused, nonabused, and allegedly abused prepubescent females. *Child Abuse & Neglect, 19,* 155-163.

Wigmore, J. (1974). *Evidence in trials at common law.* Boston: Little, Brown.

Wood, J. (1996). Weighing evidence in sexual abuse evaluations: An introduction to Bayes' theorem. *Child Maltreatment, 1,* 25-36.

Wood, J. M., & Wright, L. (1995). Evaluation of children's sexual behaviors and incorporation of base rates in judgments of sexual abuse. *Child Abuse & Neglect, 19,* 1263-1273.

Zumwalt, R. E., & Hirsch, C. S. (1987). Pathology of fatal child abuse and neglect. In R. E. Helfer & R. S. Kempe (Eds.), *The battered child* (4th ed., pp. 247-285). Chicago: University of Chicago Press.

20

Risk Management for Professionals Working With Maltreated Children and Adult Survivors

JOHN E. B. MYERS

The thought of being sued sends chills down your spine, and getting a subpoena is sure to ruin your day. Twenty years ago, the only mental health professionals who worried about getting sued were those who worked with dangerous or suicidal clients. Today, however, America is more litigious than ever, and lawsuits and ethics complaints to licensure boards are on the rise against mental health professionals. Although the number of lawsuits is growing, the likelihood that a competent professional will be sued remains small. Montgomery, Cupit, and Wimberley (1999) write that "malpractice statistics released from the [American Psychological Association] Insurance Trust indicated there was less than one half of 1% chance of being sued for malpractice" (p. 402). Regarding ethics complaints, professionals who perform child custody evaluations in divorce cases are at higher risk. Kirkland and Kirkland (2001) write that "practitioners who work in the area of child custody evaluation should expect to encounter a formal board complaint" (p. 173).

Although the number of lawsuits is growing, the likelihood that a competent professional will be sued remains small.

This chapter has two goals. First, the chapter introduces principles of malpractice liability. Second, integrated with these principles, the chapter outlines steps professionals can take to lower the probability they will be sued or have an ethics complaint filed against them.

Basic Legal Principles Regarding Liability

This section outlines the basic contours of professional liability, with the emphasis on malpractice and negligence. The section begins with a brief description of the legal settings in which professionals find themselves on the defensive.

Settings for Legal Action Against Professionals

Legal action against professionals working with abused children and adult survivors occurs in three settings: (a) civil actions, (b) administrative law proceedings, and, rarely, (c) criminal prosecutions. Civil actions against professionals usually assert negligence or malpractice. In the typical negligence/malpractice action, the plaintiff seeks monetary compensation (called *damages*) from the professional or the professional's employer. Civil damages actions are brought against professionals in private practice and government service.

Administrative law is a complex branch of civil (i.e., noncriminal) law. "Administrative law is the law concerning the powers and procedures of administrative agencies" (Davis, 1972, p. 2). Administrative law affects two critical aspects of child abuse: (a) licensure of day care, foster care, and other institutional child care and (b) licensure of professionals.

Principles of administrative law govern the granting, suspension, and revocation of licenses to foster parents, day care facilities, and other providers of child care. When abuse or neglect occurs in a licensed home or facility, government attorneys invoke the machinery of administrative law to suspend or revoke the license.

Licensed professionals must abide by the requirements of licensure. A professional who engages in serious misconduct or who is unable due to illness or incapacity to practice competently may be subjected to administrative law proceedings to limit, suspend, or revoke the professional's license. Such proceedings are commenced by government attorneys.

In rare cases, professionals commit acts that violate criminal law. For example, child abuse reporting statutes generally provide that it is a crime to fail to report suspected abuse. In *State v. Hurd* (1986), a school administrator was convicted of willfully failing to report suspected child abuse.

Malpractice and Negligence

Malpractice means, literally, bad practice. Malpractice covers a wide range of wrongdoing, from *in*tentional acts such as sexual relations with clients to *un*intentional acts that injure clients. Most malpractice claims are based on the legal theory called negligence. A person is negligent when the person fails to act in accordance with the degree of care required in the circumstances, injuring someone else.

Negligence is not limited to professionals. Everyone has a legal duty to exercise reasonable care to avoid foreseeable harm to others. For example, drivers have a legal duty to exercise reasonable care in the operation of motor vehicles. Suppose you drive your car at such an excessive speed that you fail to negotiate a curve, cross the centerline, and collide with Ruth. You were negligent. You failed to conform your conduct to the standard of reasonable care required of drivers. In legal parlance, you breached the duty of care you owed other drivers, including Ruth. Your breach of duty constitutes negligence, rendering you financially liable for Ruth's injuries. (It is hoped that your auto insurance will foot the bill.)

Professional negligence (i.e., malpractice) occurs when a professional fails to live up to the standard of care required of competent professionals in that discipline and when the failure injures someone (*Johnson v. Rogers Memorial Hospital,* 2000). The standard of care is shaped in significant measure by the ethics codes promulgated by organizations such as the National Association of Social Workers, the American Psychological Association, and the American Medical Association. Failure to abide by the applicable ethics code can be evidence of malpractice.

Professionals are not required to measure up to unrealistically high standards. Nor must generalists possess the knowledge of specialists, unless, of course, the generalists hold themselves out as or practice as specialists. Professionals "do not warrant, guarantee, or insure a good result or that they will effect a cure, or that their diagnosis will be correct or even that their treatment will be beneficial" (*Corpus Juris Secundum,* 1987, Vol. 70, p. 465). Again, however, professionals who promise a particular result or outcome commit themselves to that end, and failure to deliver can lead to liability for malpractice or breach of contract. It is a good idea as part of the informed consent process to inform prospective clients about the limitations of diagnosis and treatment.

Honest mistakes and errors in judgment are not malpractice. All professionals make mistakes. As is true with much in life, mistakes are a matter of degree. Except for the occasional easy case, it is difficult to say precisely when an error in judgment crosses the line into negligence. In our legal system, we let a jury decide.

Returning to the issue of duty, the duty to act carefully does not extend to the entire world. A duty of care exists only between certain persons in certain circumstances. Suppose, for example, that A is careless and injures B. It does not automatically follow that A is liable to B. In negligence law, A is liable to B *only* if A had a legal duty to act carefully toward B. If A had no duty of care toward B, then B cannot sue A for negligence, no matter how careless A's behavior.

In most cases, a legal duty of care is obvious. Thus, automobile drivers owe a duty of care to other drivers and pedestrians. A surgeon owes a duty of care to the patient under the knife. A psychotherapist owes a duty of care to the client. In some situations, however, the existence of a duty of care is disputed. For example, does a psychotherapist owe a duty to care to nonclients? The answer is, sometimes yes, usually no (Slovenko, 1996). Consider the scenario in which an adult enters psychotherapy for treatment of anxiety, depression, or other problems. During therapy, the client recovers memories of child sexual abuse by a family member, often the father. The client then confronts the father, who denies the allega-

tion and sues the therapist for "manufacturing false memories." In such lawsuits, the critical first question is whether the psychotherapist owed a duty of care to the nonclient father. If the answer is no, then the father's lawsuit dies without reaching the issue of the therapist's alleged negligent treatment. If, however, the therapist owed a duty of care to the nonclient father, then the father's lawsuit proceeds. This is not to say that the father will win. The point is that if the therapist owed a duty of care to the nonclient father, then the father is allowed to press the lawsuit in the hope of proving that the therapist breached the duty of care owed *to him.*

Nonclient Lawsuits Against Mental Health Professionals: Where Are the Courts Headed?

This is a logical place to discuss the small but worrisome number of lawsuits by nonclients against psychotherapists working with abused children and adult survivors (see Appelbaum & Zoltek-Jick, 1996; Bowman & Mertz, 1996). The courts are still sorting out this litigation. A brief description of several cases gives an idea of the issues involved and where the courts appear to be headed.

Court Decisions Finding There Is a Duty to a Nonclient

In *Hungerford v. Jones* (1998), the New Hampshire Supreme Court ruled that a mental health professional owed a duty of care to the father of the therapist's adult client. In his lawsuit against the therapist, the nonclient father alleged that the therapist (a) lacked training and experience needed to work with recovered memories of abuse, (b) incorrectly represented herself as qualified to treat such issues, (c) failed to inform the client of the controversy regarding repressed memories and the uncertainty of some of the therapeutic techniques employed to uncover such memories, (d) used controversial techniques such as body memories and guided imagery, (e) encouraged the client to cut off contact with the father, and (f) communicated with the police to validate the daughter's accusations against her father.

In concluding that the therapist owed a duty of care to the nonclient father, the New

Hampshire court emphasized the harm caused by false accusations of child sexual abuse:

> It is undisputable that "being labeled a child abuser [is] one of the most loathsome labels in society" and most often results in grave physical, emotional, professional, and personal ramifications. This is particularly so where a parent has been identified as the perpetrator. Even when such an accusation is proven to be false, it is unlikely that social stigma, damage to personal relationships, and emotional turmoil can be avoided. In fact, the harm caused by misdiagnosis often extends beyond the accused parent and devastates the entire family. (*Hungerford v. Jones*, 1998, p. 480)

The court ruled that the likelihood of harm to the accused increases when the accused is the client's parent, when the therapist lacks proper qualifications, when the therapist uses techniques that are not generally accepted as reliable, and when the accusations are made public. On the latter point, the court wrote,

> The likelihood of harm to an accused parent is exponentially compounded when treating therapists take public action based on false accusations of sexual abuse or encourage their patients to do so. Public action encompasses any effort to make the allegations common knowledge in the community. In this situation, the foreseeability of harm is so great that public policy weighs in favor of imposing on therapists a duty of care to the accused parent throughout the therapeutic process. (*Hungerford v. Jones*, 1998, p. 481)

In *Sawyer v. Midelfort* (1999), the Wisconsin Supreme Court agreed with the New Hampshire court that therapists sometimes owe a duty of care to nonclients. In *Sawyer*, the nonclient parents of the adult client sued two therapists, alleging that the therapists (a) failed to properly diagnose and treat the client's condition, (b) produced false memories of abuse through negligent use of hypnosis, (c) mishandled transference and countertransference, and (d) failed to recognize that the client's memories were false. Like the New Hampshire court in *Hungerford*, the Wisconsin court in *Sawyer* emphasized the "great harm that accompanies an accusation of sexual abuse of a child" (p. 433). The Wisconsin court wrote that "we are quite confident that negligent treatment which encourages false accusa-

tions of sexual abuse is highly culpable for the resulting injury" (p. 433).

Finally, in *Montoya v. Bebensee* (1988), the Colorado Court of Appeal found a duty to the nonclient father of a child in a child custody case in family court. The child's mother reported to child protective services (CPS) that the father molested their 4-year-old daughter. CPS could not confirm the mother's accusation. The mother retained a therapist to determine whether abuse occurred and to provide treatment. The therapist concluded abuse had occurred and reported to CPS. Following further investigation, CPS concluded there were serious doubts about the alleged abuse. Nevertheless, the therapist advised the mother to limit the father's visitation despite a court order allowing visitation. The father sued the therapist, and the court of appeal ruled that the therapist owed a duty of care to the father. The court was particularly perturbed that the therapist advised the mother to disobey a court order.

Court Decisions
Finding No Duty to Nonclients

In *Zamstein v. Marvasti* (1997), the Connecticut Supreme Court ruled that a psychiatrist owed no duty to the nonclient father of two children.[1] The psychiatrist was hired by the children's mother to evaluate the children regarding possible sexual abuse by the father. Thus, the psychiatrist's clients were the children. The father sued the psychiatrist, claiming that mental health professionals who evaluate children for sexual abuse owe a duty of care to the individual suspected of abuse. The Connecticut Supreme Court rejected the father's claim, writing,

> We conclude that imposing upon mental health professionals, who have been engaged to evaluate whether there has been sexual abuse, a duty of care running to the benefit of the alleged sexual abuser would be contrary to the public policy of this state. . . . Imposing a duty on mental health professionals . . . would carry with it the impermissible risk of discouraging such professionals in the future from performing sexual abuse evaluations of children altogether, out of a fear of liability to the very persons whose conduct they may implicate. Such a result would necessarily run contrary to the state's policy of encouraging the reporting and investigation of suspected child abuse. . . . In addition, imposing such a

duty creates too high a risk that, in close cases, mental health professionals would conclude that no sexual abuse had occurred because they feared potential liability to the suspected abusers, rather than because of their professional judgment that, in all likelihood, no abuse had occurred. Because "rules of law have an impact on the manner in which society conducts its affairs," we conclude that the sounder judicial ruling is to hold that no such duty exists. (*Zamstein v. Marvasti,* 1997, pp. 786-787)

In *Doe v. McKay* (1998), Jane Doe, an adult, was in treatment with a psychologist. During therapy, Jane recovered memories of child sexual abuse by her father. During several therapy sessions, the father was present in the psychologist's office. According to the father, the psychologist told him his daughter's memories of abuse were repressed until she entered therapy. Also according to the father, the psychologist recommended that he get treatment from one of the psychologist's colleagues. The father denied he abused his daughter. The father sued the psychologist, asserting two claims. First, the father claimed that the psychologist's allegedly negligent treatment of Jane Doe made the psychologist liable *to the father.* Second, the father claimed that because he attended a few of his daughter's therapy sessions, *he* had a psychologist-client relationship with the psychologist. The Illinois Supreme Court rejected the first claim. The court ruled that the psychologist's treatment of the daughter did not create a duty of care to the nonclient father. According to the court, "The duty of due care owed by a health care professional runs only to the patient, and not to third parties" (p. 1022). The Illinois Supreme Court did not address the father's second claim—that sessions attended by the father created a psychologist-client relationship directly with the father. In all likelihood, the father was correct on that score, in which case the psychologist owed a duty of care to the father. This case illustrates the point that professionals should consider the legal implications of meeting with nonclients. Such meetings may transform a nonclient into a client, especially if the professional gives advice to the "nonclient" during the meeting.

In *Althaus v. Cohen* (2000), the Pennsylvania Supreme Court ruled that a professional treating a child does not owe a legal duty to the child's nonclient parents. In *Cohen,* the 15-year-old adolescent began seeing a counselor to help her deal with the emotional impact of the death of the child's grandmother and her mother's cancer. During sessions with the counselor, the child revealed that her father had touched her inappropriately. The counselor notified CPS, the child was removed from her home, and criminal charges were filed against the father and the mother. The child was referred to Dr. Cohen, a psychiatrist. During 16 months of treatment, Dr. Cohen attended several court hearings at the child's request. Over time, the child's descriptions of abuse became progressively bizarre. Eventually, Dr. Cohen testified in the criminal proceedings that the child could not distinguish fact from fantasy, and the criminal charges were dismissed.

Following dismissal of the criminal charges, the parents and the child filed a medical malpractice case against Dr. Cohen, claiming that she negligently diagnosed and treated the child. A jury found against Dr. Cohen and returned a judgment in excess of $270,000. Dr. Cohen appealed the judgment in favor of the parents. The Pennsylvania Supreme Court reversed the judgment in favor of the parents and wrote,

> The special nature of the relationship between a therapist and a child patient in cases of alleged sexual abuse weighs against the imposition of a duty of care beyond that owed to the patient alone. To hold otherwise would create a conflict of interest for the treating therapist, a conflict which would necessarily hinder effective treatment of the child. Therefore, we hold that the non-patient parents cannot sustain a medical malpractice cause of action against their child's psychiatrist under the circumstances of this case. . . .
>
> There are certainly compelling arguments that a person falsely accused of child abuse should have a remedy in law and our decision today would not prevent all such actions against liable parties. However, the societal interest in encouraging treatment of child abuse victims and maintaining the trust and confidentiality within the therapist-patient relationship dictates against the imposition of a duty of care beyond that owed to the patient. (*Althaus v. Cohen,* 2000, pp. 552, 556-557)

The court indicated that under different circumstances, a nonclient might be allowed to sue. For example, the court pointed out that this is not a case where "false memories" were implanted by a therapist. We note that other jurisdictions that have imposed a duty of care upon therapists that extends to parents accused of sexual abuse have done so in "false memory" cases. (pp. 555, 557)

In addition to Connecticut, Illinois, and Pennsylvania, courts in several other states have ruled against imposing on therapists a duty of due care to nonclients (see California, *Trear v. Sills,* 1999; Iowa, *J.A.H. v. Wadle & Associates,* 1999; Maine, *Flanders v. Cooper,* 1998; Texas, *Bird v. W.C.W.,* 1994).

Risk Management Regarding Nonclients—Keeping Nonclients Nonclients

Therapists working with abused children and adult survivors can reduce the likelihood they will owe a legal duty of care to nonclients. Direct contact with a nonclient can transform the nonclient into a client even though the nonclient does not formally enter treatment. As mentioned earlier, therapists should consider the legal implications of therapy sessions that include a nonclient. Written, telephonic, and person-to-person communication with a nonclient may, depending on what is said, create a therapist-client relationship. The line is likely crossed when the therapist offers professional advice to the nonclient. On the other hand, the therapist is probably safe saying, "Because you are not my client, I cannot give you advice, treatment, or counseling on how to proceed apart from advising you that you may wish to consult a professional on your own." Any such statement should be carefully documented.

Professionals who work with survivors of abuse often see themselves as advocates for their clients. In the context of individual therapy, professionals advocate competent treatment, client self-actualization, and recovery. On a broader scale, professionals advocate for programs to prevent child abuse and provide treatment for survivors. When does client advocacy raise the potential of a legal duty to a nonclient? Although there is no simple answer to this question, certain behaviors stand out, among them advising a client to take action that *directly and adversely* affects a third person. Examples include advising a client to sue a suspected perpetrator or to go to the police. Certainly, therapists should be free to discuss the psychological implications of such actions. Apart from

psychological issues, however, advising a client about a lawsuit is beyond the competence of the mental health professional.

Advocacy on behalf of clients is often entirely appropriate. Professionals do well, however, to pause a moment and ask themselves, "What impact, if any, will my conduct have on people who are not my clients?" Knapp and VandeCreek (1996) caution psychotherapists about "aligning too closely with patients. Psychotherapists who become strong advocates for the rights of victims risk losing their objectivity and critical judgment" (p. 455).

The possibility of a legal duty to a nonclient increases when a therapist causes suspicions about a nonclient to come to public attention. Certainly, therapists should not discuss clients or nonclients with members of the press or with the general public.

Although this is largely uncharted legal territory, a judge is more likely to find that a therapist acted negligently when the therapist knew or should have known that the client's memories were false but the therapist nevertheless advised the client to take direct action against a specific individual.

A nagging question is whether a therapist has a responsibility to inquire into the validity of a client's memories of abuse. For many clinicians, the factual accuracy of a client's memories is not terribly relevant. A therapist, after all, is not an investigator. The therapist is not expected to go into the community to corroborate or refute a client's memories of abuse. Does this mean professionals are entirely free to ignore the validity of a client's memories, especially when the client proposes direct action against the person he or she believes committed the abuse and when the therapist has serious doubts about the accuracy of the client's memories? Although this is largely uncharted legal territory, a judge is more likely to find that a therapist acted negligently when the therapist knew or should have known that the client's memories were false but the therapist nevertheless advised the client to take direct action against a specific individual. Whenever a client has memories of abuse, the therapist should evaluate the circumstances in which the accuracy of those memories could affect the client or others.

In addition to the specific steps outlined above, therapists should (a) possess the training and experience required to work with abuse survivors, (b) employ sound therapeutic techniques, (c) refuse to exceed the limits of their expertise, (d) maintain proper therapeutic boundaries, (e) diagnose clients carefully, (f) understand laws and ethical rules governing practice, and (g) obtain informed consent, especially for experimental or untested techniques.

Knapp and VandeCreek (1996) point out the dangers of "questionable techniques used to retrieve lost memories" such as "age regression, body memory interpretation, suggestive questioning, guided visualization, sexualized dream interpretation, high-pressure survivor groups, aggressive sodium amytal interviews, and misleading bibliotherapy" (p. 456). Knapp and Vande-Creek note that

> many experienced clinicians believe that it is therapeutically indicated, under certain circumstances, to seek to retrieve (or "de-repress") memories of abuse through hypnotherapy or sodium amytal interviews. According to Gold, Hughs, and Hohnecker (1994); Terr (1994); and Herman (1992), these techniques may be justified when hidden trauma is strongly suspected on the basis of objective criteria and the patient's suffering is severe. We would add that they are justified only when more prosaic techniques of memory recovery (e.g., talking) have failed and the patient has been informed of the limitations of these techniques and the potential for creating false memories.
>
> To minimize the possibility that therapist bias could influence the content of the memory, contextual cues should be kept as neutral as possible. Psychologists should record in detail the patient's statements about possible past abuse ahead of time and should video- or audio-tape the sessions to protect against possible allegations that they, the psychologists, implanted false memories. (p. 456)

Working with survivors is complex and enormously important. The forensic implications of the work add another layer of complexity, but one that does not have to impede therapy.

Hypnosis

Hypnosis has important legal implications (Myers, 1997). In some states, individuals who have been hypnotized are not allowed to testify about events remembered during or after hypnosis. "Many courts have held or recognized that testimony concerning matters consciously recalled for the first time through pretrial hypnosis is inadmissible" (Fleming, 1990, p. 934). A professional whose client may someday serve as a witness should seek legal advice *before* using hypnosis, sodium amytal, or similar methods.

Child Abuse Reporting Laws

The law requires professionals to report suspected child abuse and neglect to the authorities (see Chapter 22, this volume). For many professionals, the question, "What level of suspicion triggers a report?" is the most perplexing issue under the reporting law. Essentially, the duty to report is triggered when a professional possesses a prescribed level of suspicion. The phrases used to describe the triggering level of suspicion vary slightly from state to state and include "cause to believe," "reasonable cause to believe," "known or suspected abuse," and "observation or examination that discloses evidence of abuse." Despite shades of difference, the basic thrust of the reporting laws is the same across the United States. Reporting is required when a professional has evidence that would lead a competent professional to believe abuse or neglect is reasonably likely. In the final analysis, the decision to report depends on the facts of each case, interpreted through experience and judgment.

It is important to emphasize that the duty to report does not require the professional to "know" abuse or neglect occurred. All that is required is reasonable *suspicion* of maltreatment. The law requires reporting of suspicion, not certainty. A professional who delays reporting until all doubt is eliminated probably violates the reporting law. The law deliberately leaves the ultimate decision about maltreatment to investigating officials, not professionals. Thus, Kalichman (1999) advises that professionals "should avoid acting as investigators and restrict their actions within proper roles" (p. 117).

This is not to say that professionals ask no questions and consider no alternatives to maltreatment. The point is that in-depth investigation is the domain of law enforcement and child protective services, not professionals who diagnose and treat maltreatment.

Getting Sued for Failure to Report

If a professional fails to report suspected abuse and a child is abused or killed as a result, the professional can be sued for malpractice (*Stecker v. First Commercial Trust,* 1998). The leading case addressing liability for failure to report is *Landeros v. Flood* (1976). Gita Landeros was born on May 14, 1970. In Gita's lawsuit against Dr. Flood, Gita's lawyer claimed that Gita was brutally beaten by her mother and stepfather. On April 26, 1971, when Gita was 11 months old, her mother took her to a hospital, where Gita was examined by Dr. Flood. The child was suffering from spiral fractures of both bones in her lower right leg, for which the mother had no explanation. Gita's back was covered with bruises, and she had scratches on other parts of her body. In addition, Gita had a healing skull fracture. Gita had the classic signs of battered child syndrome.

Unfortunately, Dr. Flood failed to diagnose child abuse. Because he did not diagnose abuse, Dr. Flood did not report to the authorities. Gita was released from the hospital and taken home, where she was further brutalized. On July 1, 1971, a little more than 2 months after her examination by Dr. Flood, Gita was taken to a different hospital, where a different physician immediately diagnosed battered child syndrome and notified authorities. Gita was rescued.

Gita sued Dr. Flood, claiming that his failure to diagnose and report the abuse was medical malpractice. Essentially, Gita's lawyer argued that if Dr. Flood had properly diagnosed battered child syndrome and reported to authorities, Gita would not have suffered the second round of abuse. Thus, according to Gita's claim, even though Dr. Flood did not inflict the second round of abuse, he was legally obligated to compensate Gita for the second round of injuries.

The lesson of *Landeros v. Flood* is clear. Professionals who fail to diagnose and report suspected maltreatment may be financially liable if a child suffers further abuse. The same type of liability is possible when a professional fails to diagnose and report suspected sexual abuse or neglect.

In addition to civil liability along the lines of *Landeros v. Flood,* failure to report may spur licensing officials to take administrative action against a professional. In *Matter of Schroeder* (1988), for example, a psychologist's license was restricted because he failed to report known child sexual abuse of two of his clients.

Deliberate failure to report suspected abuse is a crime.

Getting Sued for Reporting

Occasionally, an angry parent sues the professional who reported suspected abuse or neglect. In the typical case, the parent claims that the report was baseless and that reporting triggered an unwarranted investigation. Most lawsuits for reporting are dismissed because the professional has immunity from liability.

Immunity From Liability for Reporting Suspected Maltreatment

All reporting laws provide professionals with some form of immunity from liability. Immunity clearly covers the act of reporting. In many states, immunity extends beyond the report to include acts leading up to the report and, after the report is filed, to communication with investigators and to testifying in court. In *Nosbaum v. Martini* (2000), the court ruled that the immunity of the reporting act did not cover a physician's negligent diagnosis of child sexual abuse that contributed to a report. The court explained that the reporting act was not "meant to immunize doctors from liability for any medical malpractice simply because it might have a link to a child abuse report" (p. 91). As explained later in this chapter, immunity does not prevent an angry parent from suing. What immunity does is give the professional a way out of a lawsuit *after* it is filed.

Kalichman's Guidelines

In the first edition of his excellent book on reporting, Kalichman (1993) offers the following guidelines:

- Knowledge of state laws regarding requirements to report suspected child maltreatment is necessary for all mandated reporters.
- Treatment and research professionals need standard informed-consent procedures that clearly detail the conditions under which confidentiality is limited.
- Disclosures of child abuse can be interpreted as evidence of maltreatment and should surpass reporting thresholds.
- Suspicions of child maltreatment based on behavioral or physical indicators that do not appear to warrant reporting require close evaluation before reporting can be completely dismissed.
- Professionals operate within their areas of competence and defined professional roles and should not overstep their limitations to verify the occurrence of child abuse.
- It is necessary to inform parents or guardians of a report before it is filed unless doing so would endanger the welfare of the child or children.
- Professionals should keep thorough and detailed records of information released in a report.
- Professionals are expected to follow up on reports to the child protection system.
- When professionals do not report suspected child maltreatment because they have caused a report to be filed by someone else, it is necessary to follow up on the case and verify that a report was filed with the child protection system.
- Cases of suspected child abuse that do not surpass reporting criteria should be discussed with a colleague to achieve some degree of objective reliability in reporting decisions.
- Training in recognizing signs of child maltreatment should be obtained by all human service professionals to the degree to which they have potential contact with abused children or abusive adults. (pp. 149-151)

Negligent Hiring or Supervision

A professional can be liable for negligent hiring, retention, or supervision of employees or students. Consider, for example, a psychologist who owns a clinical practice. The owner hires a clinician to treat clients. The owner does not check the references of the prospective employee. Nor does the owner inquire about the employee's license. Six months later, during a therapy session, the employee sexually assaults a client. As it turns out, the employee has a history of similar offenses in other communities. Moreover, the employee's license was revoked in another state. A background check would have revealed the problem. There is no doubt that the victim can sue the perpetrator. In addition, the victim is likely to sue the employing psychologist for negligent hiring. It is clear that failure to conduct any form of background check was negligent. The victim will probably win *both* lawsuits.

A professional can be liable for negligent supervision of unlicensed practitioners, students, and others. A supervising professional must exercise the degree of oversight that a competent supervisor would exercise in similar circumstances. Bennett, Bryant, VandenBos, and Greenwood (1990) emphasize the importance of adequate training, support, guidance, and procedures for students. Bennett et al. also remind supervisors to document supervision.

Negligent Failure to Refer

Malpractice occurs when a professional negligently fails to refer a client to a specialist or a practitioner in a more appropriate discipline (Smith, 1996). For example, a psychologist or social worker may be liable for failing to refer a client who needs medical treatment to a physician.

Abandoning a Client

Termination of therapy is a delicate and important part of treatment. Professionals may not simply abandon clients. Smith (1996) observes that "the therapist must not 'dump' or suddenly stop seeing a patient. After treatment has begun, the professional's failure to attend to the patient or to make reasonable provision for the patient to see another competent professional may constitute abandonment" (p. 82). Bennett et al. (1990) recommend active planning for the termination of the therapeutic relationship. The professional and the client should openly discuss the termination process, including the possibility of referral to another therapist. Bennett et al. suggest that professionals "consider sending a follow-up letter providing names of individuals for referral"

(p. 56). The client should be told what to do if further therapy is needed.

The Internet and the Emerging World of eHealth

The Internet and other means of electronic communication create exciting opportunities for mental health and medical professionals. Yet, the new technology raises a plethora of ethical and legal issues. For example, suppose a psychotherapist communicates via e-mail with an individual in a state where the therapist is not licensed. Is the therapist practicing without a license? Suppose a therapist learns that a "client" on the other side of the world is abusing a child. Can confidentiality be protected online? Guidance on these and other issues is just emerging.

Humphreys, Winzelberg, and Klaw (2000) provide useful information for professionals who participate in "online groups," which the authors define as

> bulletin boards, chat rooms, news and discussion groups operated within health-related web pages (e.g., rdkoop.com, ivillage.com), listservs (groups in which each individual message is copied and E-mailed to all subscribers), and other electronic forums focused on social, health, and psychological issues. (p. 493)

Humphreys et al. (2000) write that "our definition of on-line groups intentionally excludes group psychotherapy, which we believe cannot be conducted in an ethical manner over the Internet except in very limited circumstances" (p. 493).

In an article titled "Counseling and Therapy on the Internet," Maheu and Gordon (2000) write,

> Psychologists who use E-mail in their practices should ensure patients' confidentiality by maintaining high levels of electronic security. Encryption should be used to protect both E-mail and electronic records. Furthermore, all E-mail exchanges with patients should be printed and placed in the patients' permanent patient records. (p. 487)

Koocher and Morray (2000) discuss regulation of telepsychology and provide useful interim guidelines:

1. Before engaging in the remote delivery of mental health services via electronic means, practitioners should carefully assess their competence to offer the particular services and consider the limitations of efficacy and effectiveness that may be a function of remote delivery.

2. Practitioners should consult with their professional liability insurance carrier to ascertain whether the planned services will be covered. Ideally, a written confirmation from a representative of the carrier should be obtained.

3. Practitioners are advised to seek consultation from colleagues and to provide all clients with clear written guidelines regarding planned emergency practices (e.g., suicide risk situations).

4. Because no uniform standards of practice exist at this time, thoughtful written plans that reflect careful consultation with colleagues may suffice to document thoughtful professionalism in the event of an adverse incident.

5. A careful statement on limitations of confidentiality should be developed and provided to clients at the start of the professional relationship. The statement should inform clients of the standard limitations (e.g., child abuse reporting mandates), any state-specific requirements, and cautions about privacy problems with broadcast conversations (e.g., overheard wireless phone conversations or captured Internet transmissions).

6. Clinicians should thoroughly inform clients of what they can expect in terms of services offered, unavailable services (e.g., emergency or psychopharmacology coverage), access to the practitioner, emergency coverage, and similar issues.

7. If third parties are billed for services offered via electronic means, practitioners must clearly indicate that fact on billing forms. If a third-party payer who is unsupportive of electronic service delivery is wrongly led to believe that the services took place in vivo as opposed to online, fraud charges may ultimately be filed.

Informed Consent

Informed consent is a legal requirement for most medical and mental health treatment, and failure to obtain informed consent can be malpractice (American Psychological Association, 1992). The requirement for informed consent grows out of respect for autonomy (Faden & Beauchamp, 1986; Smith, 1986). Client consent should be in writing and should be included in the client's record.

Informed consent is obtained before therapy begins (Ebert, 1993). In the usual case, consent is a one-time event. In some cases, however, informed consent is a process, and the clinician revisits consent at appropriate times during therapy (Reaves, 1998; Younggren, 1995). Harris (1995) writes that

> both the substance and the timing of certain information has to be tailored to the particular dynamics of the patient and the dynamics of the therapy. Even when the therapist knows the particular risks and benefits of treatment of a specific client, the client may not be able to tolerate their explication until there is a firmer alliance. With trauma victims in particular, informed consent is not a one-shot event, but rather an ongoing process of mutual information sharing and evaluation of risk. (pp. 252-253)

The information required for informed consent is described in the *Code of Ethics* of the National Association of Social Workers (1997):

> Social workers should use clear and understandable language to inform clients of the purpose of the services, risks related to the services, limits to services because of the requirements of a third-party payer, relevant costs, reasonable alternatives, clients' right to refuse or withdraw consent, and the time frame covered by the consent. Social workers should provide clients with an opportunity to ask questions. (Standard 1.03(a))

Ebert (1993) recommends that professionals inform clients of the limits of confidentiality; the clinician's record-keeping system; the clinician's training, experience, and areas of practice; nature of treatment; probable length of treatment; limitations of service; risks of proposed treatment; alternatives to proposed treatment (including no treatment); fees and billing practices; the client's right to stop treatment; and the procedure for after-hours and emergency consultation.

Explaining the meaning of confidentiality and its limits is an important part of informed consent (Deed, 1993; Ebert, 1993). The American Psychological Association (1992) states that "unless it is not feasible or

is contraindicated, the discussion of confidentiality occurs at the outset of the relationship and thereafter as new circumstances may warrant" (Standard 5.01(b)). The duty to report suspected child abuse limits confidentiality, and "it is advisable at the outset of treatment to inform your clients that the usual rule concerning confidentiality does not apply when the duty to report child abuse arises" (Committee on Professional Practice and Standards, 1995, p. 378).

In addition to the information described earlier, the informed consent process includes discussion of client access to records. Professionals who plan to use experimental or controversial methods such as hypnosis, sodium amytal, age regression, or guided visualization should inform clients of any clinical or legal issues raised by such techniques. Professionals working in a managed care setting should explain any limitations imposed by the managed care system.

Is informed consent required for purely forensic evaluation, where treatment is not provided? Because informed consent is based on respect for autonomy, the answer should normally be yes. In certain court-ordered evaluations, however, informed consent may not be necessary. Even in court-ordered cases, however, professionals are encouraged to inform clients of the nature of services to be provided and, where possible, to obtain informed consent. The National Association of Social Workers' (1997) *Code of Ethics* provides that "in instances when clients are receiving services involuntarily, social workers should provide information about the nature and extent of services and about the extent of clients' right to refuse services" (Standard 1.03(d)). The American Academy of Psychiatry and the Law's (1995) "Ethical Guidelines for the Practice of Forensic Psychiatry" provides that

> the informed consent of the subject of a forensic evaluation is obtained when possible. Where consent is not required, notice is given to the evaluee of the nature of the evaluation. If the evaluee is not competent to give consent, substituted consent is obtained in accordance with the laws of the jurisdiction. (Guideline III)

Along similar lines, the American Psychological Association's (1992) guidelines provides that forensic psychologists have an obligation to ensure that prospective clients are informed of their rights with respect to the anticipated forensic service, of the purposes of any evaluation, of the nature of procedures to be employed, of the intended uses of any product of their services, and of the party who has employed the forensic psychologist. Unless court ordered, forensic psychologists obtain informed consent of the client or party, or their legal representative, before proceeding with such evaluations and procedures. (Guideline IV.E)

Finally, the American Psychological Association's (1992) "Guidelines for Child Custody Evaluations in Divorce Proceedings" states that "the psychologist obtains informed consent from all adult participants and, as appropriate, informs child participants" (Guideline III, paragraph 8).

Informed consent should be documented in writing, and the client should sign and receive a copy of the informed consent form. "Consent to treatment can be part of a written treatment contract" (Bennett et al., 1990, p. 49).

Can Children Give Informed Consent?

Children are legally incapable of consenting to most forms of medical and mental health treatment. Thus, informed consent is obtained from parents or caretakers (American Psychological Association, 1992). It should be noted, however, that children older than specified ages (e.g., 14) are allowed to consent to certain types of treatment, including, in many states, testing for venereal disease or pregnancy, abortion, and some kinds of mental health care (for California law, see Myers, 2001).

Therapy Versus Forensic Evaluation: Avoiding Dual Relationships

Should mental health professionals providing psychotherapy also perform forensic evaluations of their therapy clients (see Appelbaum, 1997; Bennett et al., 1990)? For example, should the psychotherapist for a woman who is divorcing her husband agree to perform a court-ordered child custody evaluation of the entire family? Should a

psychotherapist who is treating a child for the effects of sexual abuse agree to conduct a formal forensic assessment of abuse and testify in court regarding the findings of the assessment? (For general guidance on accepting forensic referrals, see Hess, 1998.)

Before attempting to answer these questions, it is useful to define *forensic psychology*. The "Speciality Guidelines for Forensic Psychologists," prepared by the Committee on Ethical Guidelines for Forensic Psychologists (1991), provides the following definition:

> Forensic psychology means all forms of professional psychological conduct when acting, with definable foreknowledge, as a psychological expert on explicitly psycholegal issues, in direct assistance to courts, parties to legal proceedings, correctional and forensic mental health facilities, and administrative, judicial, and legislative agencies acting in an adjudicative capacity. (p. 657)

Examples of forensic psychology include a court-ordered evaluation by a mental health professional to determine whether a person charged with a crime is competent to stand trial, expert testimony in criminal cases regarding the insanity defense, and expert testimony in various types of civil proceedings, including involuntary civil commitment for psychiatric treatment, capacity to make a will, and guardianship. Finally, a mental health professional who conducts a child custody evaluation for use in family court acts as a forensic evaluator.[2]

In a useful article, Greenberg and Shuman (1997) write that "a role conflict arises when a treating therapist also attempts to testify as a forensic expert addressing the psycholegal issues in the case" (p. 50). Melton, Petrila, Poythress, and Slobogin (1997) add that "forensic assessment differs from a therapeutic assessment on a number of dimensions" (p. 42). The American Professional Society on the Abuse of Children (1996) notes that "forensic evaluations are different from clinical evaluations in generally requiring a different professional stance and additional components" (Statement of Purpose).

Ethics codes of professional organizations emphasize the potential conflict between therapeutic and forensic roles. The "Ethical Principles" of the American Psychological Association (1992) states that "in most circumstances, psychologists avoid performing multiple and potentially conflicting roles in forensic matters" (Principle 7.03). The "Speciality Guidelines for Forensic Psychologists" states the following:

> Forensic psychologists recognize potential conflicts of interest in dual relationships with parties to legal proceedings, and they seek to minimize their effects. Forensic psychologists avoid providing professional services to parties in a legal proceeding with whom they have personal or professional relationships that are inconsistent with the anticipated relationship. When it is necessary to provide both evaluation and treatment services to a party in a legal proceeding (as may be the case in small forensic hospital settings or small communities), the forensic psychologist takes reasonable steps to minimize the potential negative effects of these circumstances on the rights of the party, confidentiality, and the process of treatment and evaluation. (Committee on Ethical Guidelines for Forensic Psychologists, 1991, p. 659)

The ethical guidelines of the American Academy of Psychiatry and the Law (1995) provide that

> treating psychiatrists should generally avoid agreeing to be an expert witness or to perform evaluations of their patients for legal purposes because a forensic evaluation usually requires that other people be interviewed and testimony may adversely affect the therapeutic relationship. (p. xiv)

The Committee on Psychiatry and Law (1991) states that "while, in some areas of the country with limited numbers of mental health practitioners, the therapist may have the role of forensic expert thrust upon him, ordinarily, it is wise to avoid mixing the therapeutic and forensic roles" (p. 44). The *Code of Ethics* of the American Professional Society on the Abuse of Children (1997) provides the following:

> Clear definitions of professional roles, responsibilities, duties, and tasks and the limits of professional conduct provide clients with maximal information upon which to base their own decisions and actions. The nature of child maltreatment, in which boundaries are blurred or broken, relationships are disturbed, and social positions such as parent, caregiver, and helper are perverted, makes the maintenance of clear professional relationships all the more critical for client protection and in creating the optimal conditions for

growth and development. . . . When a professional is called upon to engage in more than one professional role, such as therapist and advocate, investigator and therapist, assessor and healer, investigator and concerned citizen, the professional must be clear about the different responsibilities and tasks required for each role; take appropriate steps to guard against role conflict; and make sure that the client understands the nature and different responsibilities of each role. Assuming more than one professional role in a given case at a given time does not necessarily represent an unethical multiple-role relationship. (p. 3)

Ethical guidelines for mental health professionals performing child custody evaluations in family court are quite specific regarding the potential conflict between forensic and treatment roles. The "Model Standards of Practice" of the Association of Family and Conciliation Courts (1994) provides that

> a person who has been a mediator or a therapist for any or all members of the family should not perform a custody evaluation because the previous knowledge and relationships may render him or her incapable of being completely neutral and incapable of having unbiased objectivity. (Principle VI.B)

The "Guidelines for Child Custody Evaluations in Divorce Proceedings" of the American Psychological Association (1994) provides that

> psychologists generally avoid conducting a child custody evaluation in a case in which the psychologist served in a therapeutic role for the child or his or her immediate family or has had other involvement that may compromise the psychologist's objectivity. (Guideline 7)

Glassman (1998) writes that "changing roles from therapist to custody evaluator will most likely be interpreted as an ethics violation" (p. 123).

Kirkland and Kirkland (2001) offer good advice for mental health professionals who perform custody evaluations:

> The best defense against what may be an eventual and inevitable complaint would include the following steps: (a) conduct only court-appointed evaluations; (b) ensure that your work reflects a thorough compliance with all specific state and national guidelines

for conducting such evaluations; (c) stay on top of the developing ethical and procedural literature in this area; (d) avoid any role conflicts or even possible sources of perceived bias; (e) use multiple data sources for conclusions, particularly interviews with third-party sources; (f) avoid ultimate issue testimony; (g) have parties sign releases and agreements about notification of rights and parameters of limited confidentiality; (h) do not under- or overinterpret test data; (i) document billing practices thoroughly; and (j) create a file that is composed with the assumption that it be subject to board review. (p. 174)

Treating professionals do not transgress ethical boundaries when they testify as lay witnesses. For example, a child's psychotherapist may testify as a lay witness to repeat the child's abuse statements uttered during therapy. Before testifying, however, the therapist should discuss the impending testimony with the attorney requesting the testimony and, assuming the child is old enough to understand, with the child and the child's caretakers.

Consultation and Peer Review

Regular consultation and peer review decrease the likelihood of being sued (Harris, 1995). If a lawsuit or ethics complaint is filed, a written record of consultation and peer review constitutes powerful evidence of proper care. Knapp and VandeCreek (1996) write that

at times, it may be desirable to seek consultation with an expert who has a different perspective. . . . The consultation should be documented and include responses to specific questions, including, but not limited to, the diagnosis or presenting problem, specific treatment plans, and alternative treatment strategies. (p. 458)

Documentation

Documentation is critical to risk management (Moline, Williams, & Austin, 1998). "An axiom among malpractice defense attorneys is 'If it isn't written down, it didn't occur' " (Knapp & VandeCreek, 1996, p. 458). Rivas-Vazquez, Blais, Rey, and Rivas-Vazquez (2001) write that "deficient

documentation can draw attention away from the appropriateness of an intervention" (p. 194). Thorough, accurate, ongoing documentation is convincing evidence of proper practice (Harris, 1995). Avoid "humorous" remarks in client records. What seemed funny at the time may appear callous and unprofessional when an attorney reads the professional's notes aloud in court. Never alter records. "This is particularly true once litigation involving the records is anticipated" (Smith, 1996, p. 92). Of course, records can be corrected. Corrections, however, should be noted as such.

How long should records be retained? The American Psychological Association's Committee on Professional Practice and Standards (1993) states

The psychologist is aware of relevant federal, state and local laws and regulations governing record retention. Such laws and regulations supersede the requirements of these guidelines. In the absence of such laws and regulations, complete records are maintained for a minimum of 3 years after the last contact with the client. Records, or a summary, are then maintained for an additional 12 years before disposal. If the client is a minor, the record period is extended until 3 years after the age of majority. (p. 985)

***Documentation is
critical to risk management.***

Constitutional Rights

When professionals working with abused and neglected children think of liability, they usually do not have the Constitution in mind. Yet, the Constitution plays a central role in some litigation against professionals, especially professionals employed by government. The Constitution bestows important rights on individuals, and when a government employee violates the constitutional rights of a citizen, the employee can be sued. Two examples illustrate the point. First, a police officer who uses excessive force to make an arrest violates the constitutional rights of the arrestee. Second, a social worker who unlawfully removes a child from home may violate the parents' constitutional right of family autonomy (see *Troxel v. Granville,* 2000).

As early as 1923, the U.S. Supreme Court ruled in *Meyer v. Nebraska* that the U.S. Constitution protects "the right of the individual . . . to marry, establish a home and bring up children" (p. 399). In *Pierce v. Society of Sisters* (1925), the Court added that "the child is not the mere creature of the State; those who nurture him and direct his destiny have the right, coupled with the high duty, to recognize and prepare him for additional obligations" (p. 535). In *Prince v. Massachusetts* (1944), the Court stated that "it is cardinal with us that the custody, care and nurture of the child reside first in the parents, whose primary function and freedom include preparation for obligations the state can neither supply nor hinder" (p. 166). Thus, the Constitution creates a "private realm of family life which the state cannot enter" (p. 166).

Although the decisions of the U.S. Supreme Court provide strong support for parental rights, the Court has made clear that parental rights are not absolute. The Court wrote in *Prince v. Massachusetts* (1944) that the state has a "wide range of power for limiting parental freedom and authority in things affecting the child's welfare" (p. 167). The Court added in *Wisconsin v. Yoder* (1972) that the state may intervene "if it appears that parental decisions will jeopardize the health or safety of the child" (p. 234). In *Watterson v. Page* (1993), the U.S. Court of Appeals for the First Circuit wrote that "the right to family integrity clearly does not include a constitutional right to be free from child abuse investigations" (p. 8). The First Circuit added in *Wojcik v. Town of North Smithfield* (1996) that "there is no way for the government to protect children without making inquiries that in many cases do turn out to be baseless" (p. 3). Finally, a different federal circuit court wisely observed that "the only way that a state can ensure that parents have not exceeded the limits of their responsibility to discipline their children is to permit public officers to investigate alleged incidents of child abuse" (*Sweaney v. Ada County, Idaho,* 1997, p. 1392).

To ensure that rights guaranteed by the U.S. Constitution are vindicated, Congress passed laws authorizing lawsuits against government employees who violate rights protected by the Constitution. The most notable of these federal laws is Section 1983 of Title 42 of the U.S. Code, which provides that government workers who deprive citizens of constitutional rights—including constitutionally protected parental rights—can be sued. Section 1983 figures prominently in lawsuits by angry parents against social workers who investigate reports of abuse, remove children from parental custody, refuse to return children, or terminate parental rights.

Can an Abused Child Sue the State for Failing to Protect the Child? *DeShaney v. Winnebago County Department of Social Services*

Can an abused child sue government employees for failing to protect him or her? The answer depends on the facts of the case and the applicable law. Quite a few states have laws allowing such lawsuits (see, e.g., *Rodriguez v. Perez,* 2000). The issue came before the U.S. Supreme Court in the famous—many would say infamous—case of *DeShaney v. Winnebago County Department of Social Services* (1989). Joshua DeShaney was born in 1979 in Wyoming. In 1980, his parents divorced and Joshua's father moved with him to Winnebago County, Wisconsin. CPS became involved in 1982, when the father's second wife complained to the police that Joshua was abused by his father. CPS investigated, but the father denied the charges, and Joshua was left in the home. A year later, Joshua was admitted to a hospital with numerous bruises. CPS obtained a juvenile court order temporarily placing Joshua in the custody of the hospital. After further investigation, CPS decided there was not enough evidence to warrant further action. The juvenile court dismissed the case, the father agreed to cooperate with CPS, and Joshua was returned home. Over the next 6 months, CPS was aware of a strong likelihood of continued abuse but did not intervene. Eventually, Joshua was beaten so savagely by his father that he suffered permanent brain damage.

Joshua's mother sued Winnebago County CPS, claiming that Joshua had a constitutional right under the due process clause of the Fourteenth Amendment to protection, and that CPS's inaction violated that right. The U.S. Supreme Court rejected Joshua's lawsuit. The Court ruled that the due process clause "generally confer[s] no affirmative right to governmental aid, even when such aid may be necessary to secure life, liberty, or property interests of which the government itself may not deprive the individual" (p. 196). The Court explained,

> Nothing in the language of the Due Process Clause itself requires the State to protect the life, liberty, and property of its citizens against invasion by private actors. The Clause is phrased as a limitation on the State's power to act, not as a guarantee of certain minimal levels of safety and security. It forbids the State itself to deprive individuals of life, liberty, or property without "due process of law," but its language cannot fairly be extended to impose an affirmative obligation on the State to secure that those interests do not come to harm through other means. (*DeShaney v. Winnebago County Department of Social Services,* 1989, p. 195)

The Supreme Court conceded that in limited circumstances, the state has a constitutional duty to protect. Thus, the state must provide medical care to incarcerated prisoners and must afford reasonable safety to involuntarily committed mental patients. These precedents did not help Joshua, however, because

> taken together, they stand only for the proposition that when the State takes a person into its custody and holds him there against his will, the Constitution imposes upon it a corresponding duty to assume responsibility for his safety and general well-being. (pp. 199-200)

Joshua was *not* in state custody when his father abused him. Thus,

> while the State may have been aware of the dangers that Joshua faced in the free world, it played no part in their creation, nor did it do anything to render him any more vulnerable to them. That the State once took temporary custody of Joshua does not alter the analysis, for when it returned him to his father's custody, it placed him in no worse position than that in which he would have been had it not acted at all; the State does not become the permanent guarantor of an individual's safety by having once offered him shelter. Under these circumstances, the State had no constitutional duty to protect Joshua. (p. 201)

In the years since *DeShaney,* lower courts have struggled to determine when the state

has a constitutional duty to protect abused children. In *S.S. v. McMullen* (2000), the court relied on *DeShaney* to conclude that social workers were not liable for returning a child to her father, although the social workers knew the father allowed the child to have contact with a pedophile who subsequently molested her. On the other hand, when a child is in state custody pursuant to a court order (e.g., in foster care), the Constitution usually imposes a duty to protect. A number of courts hold that "state officials can be liable for the acts of third parties where those officials 'created the danger' that caused the harm" (*Seamons v. Snow,* 1996). Thus, in *Currier v. Doran* (2001), the court found a duty to protect when CPS removed two children from their mother and placed them with their father, who abused them. The court wrote that "when the state affirmatively acts to remove a child from the custody of one parent and then places the child with another parent, *DeShaney* does not foreclose constitutional liability" (p. 919). Another court wrote that "if the [social workers] knowingly placed [the child] in a position of danger, they would not be shielded from liability by the decision in *DeShaney*" (*Bank of Illinois v. Over,* 1995, p. 78).

Immunity From Liability

When a professional is sued, the professional may have absolute or qualified immunity from liability. Five kinds of immunity are described below. Before discussing types of immunity, however, it is important to distinguish between absolute and qualified immunity and to explain what immunity does *not* do. *Immunity does not prevent a lawsuit from being filed against a professional.* For example, an angry parent may file suit against a CPS social worker even though a judge eventually determines that the social worker has immunity. One may ask, "If immunity does not prevent a lawsuit from being filed, what good is it?" The answer is that immunity is very good indeed. If a lawsuit is filed against a professional, the professional's attorney can ask the judge to declare that the professional has immunity and to dismiss the suit—that is, throw the suit out of court. Basically, immunity gives professionals an escape hatch from a lawsuit. Moreover, in many cases, escape comes quite early in the process, well before a trial.

A professional who lacks immunity—qualified or absolute—will not necessarily lose a lawsuit. After all, the professional may have done nothing wrong (see *Renn v. Garrison,* 1996). If the professional lacks immunity, however, the professional's exposure to the possibility of money damages increases. The case may settle for a specified dollar amount or go all the way to trial.

What is the difference between absolute and qualified immunity? With absolute immunity, the professional is nearly always entitled to early dismissal from the lawsuit. So long as the professional's conduct was covered by the immunity, the conduct cannot form the basis for a successful lawsuit for money damages (*Hodorowski v. Ray,* 1988).

Qualified immunity provides less protection than absolute immunity. Nevertheless, qualified immunity is a powerful shield, and most professionals with qualified immunity escape lawsuits filed against them.

I. Qualified Immunity of Government Employees

As mentioned earlier, when a government professional working with an abused child is sued by angry parents, the suit is often filed under Section 1983 of federal law. A Section 1983 lawsuit can be filed in state or federal court. Many Section 1983 suits accuse professionals of improperly removing children from the home. In other suits, professionals are sued because they left a child in the home and the child was later abused.

In Section 1983 cases, it is important to determine whether the professionals have qualified immunity. The law of qualified immunity is enormously complex, and we can do little more than scratch the surface. Qualified immunity extends to a broad range of government employees, including social workers, police officers, educators, and mental health workers. Qualified immunity extends to certain private practice professionals working with the government. "Immunity serves as a shield to protect officials from undue interference with their duties and from potentially disabling threats of liability" (*Austin v. Borel,* 1987, p. 1358). With specific reference to CPS social workers, the court in *Millspaugh v. County Department of Public Welfare of Wabash County* (1991) observed that

social workers often act on limited information; those who tarry, or resolve all doubts in favor of the parents, chance enduring damage to the children. Immunity helps social workers put their private interests aside and concentrate on the welfare of children. Unfortunately, immunity also may embolden social workers to pursue their private agendas. . . . One effect is inseparable from the other. (pp. 1176-1177)

When does qualified immunity apply? In *Wooley v. City of Baton Rouge* (2000), the court addressed this issue:

We conduct a bifurcated analysis to determine whether a [professional] is entitled to qualified immunity. The first step is to determine whether the [parent who is suing] has alleged a violation of a clearly established constitutional right. A right is clearly established if its contours are sufficiently clear that a reasonable [professional] would understand that what he is doing violates that right. This is not to say that [professional] action is protected by qualified immunity unless the very action in question has previously been held unlawful, but it is to say that in the light of pre-existing law the unlawfulness must be apparent. Further, the applicable law that binds the conduct of the [professional] must be clearly established at the very moment that the allegedly actionable conduct was taken. . . .

The second step is to determine whether the [professional's] conduct was objectively reasonable. Objective reasonableness is assessed in light of legal rules clearly established at the time of the incident. [A professional's] conduct is not objectively reasonable when all reasonable [professionals] would have realized the particular challenged conduct violated the constitutional provisions sued on. (p. 919, internal quote marks omitted)

What constitutional rights are "clearly established"? Parents have a clearly established constitutional right to the care, custody, and control of their children (*Michael H. v. Gerald D.,* 1989). Parental rights are not absolute, however, and the state has ample authority to intervene in the family to protect children from imminent harm (*Prince v. Massachusetts,* 1944). In *Bartell v. Lohiser* (2000), a federal court wrote that despite a parent's fundamental right to raise her child, "the State has a concomitant interest in the welfare and health of children in its jurisdiction, and in certain narrowly-defined circumstances, the State's interest in a child's well-being may supersede that of a parent" (p. 558). In *Watterson v. Page* (1993), the court added that "the right to family integrity clearly does not include a constitutional right to be free from child abuse investigations" (p. 8).

Although it is clear that parents have constitutionally protected rights, it is not always clear when those rights are infringed. Professionals "are not liable for bad guesses in gray areas; they are liable for transgressing bright lines" (*Maciariello v. City of Lancaster,* 1992, p. 298). Qualified immunity "provides ample protection to all but the plainly incompetent or those who knowingly violate the law" (*Malley v. Briggs,* 1986, p. 341). In *Kia P. v. McIntyre* (2000), the court wrote

> No matter how important the right to family integrity, it does not automatically override the sometimes compelling governmental interest in the protection of minor children, particularly in circumstances where the protection is considered necessary as against the parents themselves. Though a decision to remove a child from parental custody implicates the constitutional rights of the parents, it obliges protective services caseworkers to choose between difficult alternatives in the context of child abuse. If they err in interrupting parental custody, they may be accused of infringing the parents' constitutional rights. If they err in not removing the child, they risk injury to the child and may be accused of infringing the child's rights.
>
> Recognizing the need for unusual deference in the abuse investigation context, we have held that an investigation will pass constitutional muster provided simply that case workers have a reasonable basis for their findings of abuse. (pp. 758-759)

On a different matter, the Constitution clearly prohibits state employees from intentionally presenting false or perjured evidence in court. In *Snell v. Tunnell* (1990), professionals were not entitled to qualified immunity when they were accused of deliberately fabricating allegations of child prostitution and pornography to have a judge order removal of children from a foster home.

The Fourth Amendment to the U.S. Constitution protects against unreasonable search and seizure by the government. Removing a child from his or her home against the parents' wishes is a "seizure" for Fourth Amendment purposes (*Wooley v. City of Baton Rouge,* 2000). "The Fourth Amendment applies in the context of the seizure of a child by a government-agency official during a civil child-abuse or maltreatment investigation" (*Kia P. v. McIntyre,* 2000, p. 762). In *Brokaw v. Mercer County* (2000), a federal court wrote that

> in the context of removing a child from his home and family, a seizure is reasonable if it is pursuant to a court order, if it is supported by probable cause, or if it is justified by exigent circumstances, meaning that state officers have reason to believe that life or limb is in immediate jeopardy. (p. 1010, internal quotes removed)

In *Wallis v. Spencer* (2000), the court explained that the "state may not remove children from their parents' custody without a court order unless there is specific, articulable evidence that provides reasonable cause to believe that a child is in imminent danger of abuse" (p. 1138). The *Wallis* court added that

> the police cannot seize children suspected of being abused or neglected unless reasonable avenues of investigation are first pursued, particularly where it is not clear that a crime had been—or will be—committed. Whether a reasonable avenue of investigation exists, however, depends in part upon the time element and nature of the allegations. (p. 1138)

Not every report of abuse constitutes exigent circumstances (*Darryl H. v. Coler,* 1986). "*Imminent* danger of future harm is required to show exigency" (*Mabe v. San Bernardino County,* 2001, p. 1108). Absent an emergency, professionals must obtain a warrant or a court order to remove a child. The court wrote in *Brokaw v. Mercer County* (2000) that

> courts have recognized that a state has no interest in protecting children from their parents unless it has some definite and articulable evidence giving rise to a reasonable suspicion that a child has been abused or is in imminent danger of abuse. (p. 1019)

The subject of qualified immunity is complex and evolving. When government professionals act competently, they usually enjoy this important shield from liability.

2. Absolute Immunity for Prosecutors and, by Analogy, CPS Social Workers

Prosecutors engaged in normal prosecutorial activities such as courtroom advocacy, preparing cases for trial, and filing criminal charges enjoy absolute immunity for such acts (*Hughes v. Long,* 2001). "It is clear that prosecutorial immunity from liability for damages attaches to those acts of the prosecutor performed in the role of advocate" (Nahmod, 1991, p. 67). Absolute immunity does not extend to everything prosecutors do, however. For example, a prosecutor conducting a criminal investigation has much in common with a police officer, and, like the police officer, the investigating prosecutor enjoys only qualified immunity (*Kalina v. Fletcher,* 1997). So too, a prosecutor engaged in purely administrative activities has qualified immunity (*Holloway v. Brush,* 2000). It is sometimes difficult to tell when a prosecutor crosses the line separating advocacy (absolute immunity) from investigation or administration (qualified immunity).

In some circumstances, CPS social workers have absolute prosecutorial immunity (*Ernst v. Child and Youth Services of Chester County,* 1997). Absolute immunity is most likely to apply when a CPS professional files or participates in filing child protection proceedings in juvenile court (*Hughes v. Long,* 2001). In *Ernst v. Child and Youth Services of Chester County* (1997), the court wrote that "child welfare workers and attorneys who prosecute proceedings on behalf of the state are entitled to absolute immunity from suit for all of their actions in preparing for and prosecuting such dependency proceedings" (pp. 488-489). The court added that absolute immunity extends to "the formulation and presentation of recommendations to the court in the course of [child protection] proceedings" (p. 495). In a similar vein, the court in *Mabe v. San Bernardino County* (2001) wrote that

> social workers are entitled to absolute immunity for the initiation and pursuit of dependency proceedings, including their testimony offered in such proceedings.... Moreover, social workers enjoy absolute quasi-judicial immunity when making post-adjudication custody decisions pursuant to a valid court order. (p. 1109)

In *Holloway v. Brush* (2000), the court wrote that "absolute immunity extends to social workers only when they are acting in the capacity of *legal advocates*" (p. 775). A professional who lacks absolute may have qualified immunity.

It is sometimes difficult to tell whether a judge will grant absolute prosecutorial immunity to CPS social workers. Thus, in *Austin v. Borel* (1987), the court ruled that social workers were "not entitled to absolute immunity for their conduct in filing an allegedly false verified complaint seeking the removal of two children" (p. 1363). By contrast, in *Salyer v. Patrick* (1989), the court granted absolute immunity to social workers for filing a petition in juvenile court. The judge's decision depends on the facts of the specific case.

Absolute immunity does not extend to CPS social workers conducting investigations (*Gilliam v. Department of Social and Health Services,* 1998). Nor does absolute immunity protect purely administrative activities. Absolute immunity is restricted to conduct that is intimately associated with the judicial process (*Achterhof v. Selvaggio,* 1989). Thus, when a judge evaluates a social worker's claim of absolute immunity, the judge looks to "the distinction between prosecutorial ... duties and duties which are administrative or investigatory" (*Achterhof v. Selvaggio,* 1989, p. 829).

3. Absolute Judicial Immunity and Its Application to Court-Appointed Professionals

Judges enjoy absolute immunity for most judicial activities. A judge lacks absolute immunity only "where the challenged conduct is accompanied by a clear absence of jurisdiction or where the challenged conduct is not a judicial act but is, for example, administrative in nature. Otherwise, absolute judicial immunity applies" (Nahmod, 1991, p. 23).

A mental health professional who is *appointed by a judge* to conduct a psychological assessment *for the judge* is typically protected by absolute judicial immunity (sometimes called quasi-judicial immunity). In *Delcourt v. Silverman* (1996), for example, parents battled in family court over custody of their young child. The judge appointed Dr. Silverman to evaluate the parents and the child and to file a written report with the court. Eventually, the mother sued Dr. Silverman. In ruling that the doctor was absolutely immune from liability, the Texas Court of Appeals stated,

> A party is entitled to absolute immunity when the party is acting as an integral part of the judicial system or an "arm of the court."
>
> A psychologist who is appointed by the court is entitled to absolute immunity if he or she is appointed to fulfill quasijudicial functions intimately related to the judicial process.
>
> Numerous courts have extended absolute immunity to psychiatrists and other mental health experts assisting the court in criminal cases.
>
> We believe this reasoning also applies to mental health experts appointed to provide psychological expertise in child custody suits. Many courts recognize that psychiatrists and psychologists performing court-ordered custody evaluations perform a judicial function and enjoy absolute immunity. (pp. 782-783)

Thus, in child custody litigation, a professional who is appointed by the judge to perform a custody evaluation is normally protected by absolute judicial immunity (*Diehl v. Danuloff,* 2000; *Lythgoe v. Guinn,* 1994; *Parker v. Dodgion,* 1998; *Stone v. Glass,* 2000). Immunity extends to the evaluation, the resulting report, and testimony in court. Generally speaking, however, a professional who is retained by one or both parents to conduct a custody evaluation does not enjoy absolute judicial immunity (see *Politi v. Tyler,* 2000). Judicial immunity attaches only when a judge formally appoints the professional to conduct an evaluation for the court. Some professionals require one or both parents to agree in advance that the professional will be court appointed. The parents' agreement is put in writing and submitted to the judge. The judge signs the agreement, converting the agreement into a court order appointing the professional. Absolute judicial immunity accompanies the appointment.

4. Absolute Witness Immunity

In most if not all states, witnesses, including expert witnesses, have absolute immunity for testimony (American Law Institute, 1977; *California Civil Code,* 2000, § 47; *Franklin v. Terr,* 2000). Thus, the court in *General Electric Co. v. Sargent and Lundy* (1990) wrote that "courts have long recognized that statements in judicial proceedings, if relevant to the issues involved, are absolutely privileged, even though it may be claimed that

they are false and alleged with malice" (p. 1126). The California Supreme Court defined the public policy that supports absolute witness immunity, writing that "the principal purpose of [the privilege] is to afford litigants and witnesses the utmost freedom of access to the courts without fear of being harassed subsequently by derivative court actions" (*Silberg v. Anderson,* 1990, p. 642). The California Court of Appeals added, with particular emphasis on expert witnesses, that

> freedom of access to the courts and encouragement of witnesses to testify truthfully will be harmed if neutral experts must fear retaliatory lawsuits from litigants whose disagreement with an expert's opinions perforce convinces them the expert must have been negligent in forming such opinions. (*Gootee v. Lightner,* 1990, p. 700)

Absolute witness immunity applies to testimony at a trial or hearing in court. It also applies to testimony given at a deposition (*Darragh v. Superior Court,* 1995). Moreover, absolute witness immunity extends to "preparatory activity leading to the witnesses' testimony" (*Gootee v. Lightner,* 1990, p. 701). Thus, a report prepared by an expert who is retained to testify falls within the absolute privilege so long as the report has some relation to the litigation (*Adams v. Peck,* 1979; *Bruce v. Byrne-Stevens & Associates,* 1989; *Durand Equipment Co. v. Superior Carbon Products, Inc.,* 1991; *Kahn v. Burman,* 1987; *Rainier's Dairies v. Rairtan Valley Farms,* 1955; *Woodward v. Weiss,* 1996). In *Darragh v. Superior Court* (1995), the court wrote that

> courts have agreed that reports, consultations, and advice, which are relevant to litigation as preliminary steps in the institution or defense of a case, are a part of the preparation for trial and are therefore within the absolute privilege accorded communications in judicial proceedings. (p. 1218)

Even when litigation is not under way, absolute witness immunity may attach to experts who are retained to evaluate potential litigation or to work on issues that are likely to end up in court (*Mershon v. Beasley,* 1993).

Although absolute witness immunity protects expert witnesses from nearly all types of civil liability, an occasional allegation slips past the protective shield. For example, absolute witness immunity may not protect an expert against allegations of malicious prosecution (*Silberg v. Anderson,* 1990) or conspiracy (*Darragh v. Superior Court,* 1995). In *Deatherage v. State Examining Board of Psychology* (1997), the Washington Supreme Court ruled that absolute witness immunity does not apply in disciplinary proceedings against professionals. Thus, the state board of psychology could maintain a disciplinary action against a psychologist for work that the psychologist did in a child custody case (see also *Moses v. McWilliams,* 1988; *Moses v. Parwatikar,* 1987; *Silberg v. Anderson,* 1990).

The case of *Gootee v. Lightner* (1990) is a useful example of absolute witness immunity. Irene and Michael Gootee were divorced and had three children. In 1985, Irene went to family court requesting a change in custody. Irene and Michael agreed to undergo psychological testing and evaluation regarding custody. They further agreed to retain Marshall Lightner, a mental health professional, to perform the testing and to evaluate the family. Lightner prepared a report and testified in court, recommending that Irene have custody of the children, with visitation for Michael. Upset with Lightner's report and testimony, Michael sued Lightner, alleging professional negligence. The trial judge threw out Michael's lawsuit, ruling that Lightner's evaluation, report, and testimony were protected by absolute witness immunity. On appeal, the California Court of Appeals endorsed the trial judge, writing,

> It is undisputed that [Lightner's] role was a limited one: to evaluate the partisans in the custody matter for purposes of testifying concerning the custody dispute. Because the gravamen of [Michael's] claim relies on negligent or intentional tortious conduct committed by [Lightner] in connection with the testimonial function, we conclude the absolute privilege bars civil lawsuits (other than for malicious prosecution) seeking to impose liability on [Lightner]. (p. 699)

The court further concluded that "the protective mantle of the privilege embraces not only the courtroom testimony of witnesses, but also protects prior preparatory activity leading to the witnesses' testimony" (p. 701).

5. Child Abuse Reporting Laws

As explained earlier in this chapter, the child abuse reporting laws extend immunity to professionals who report suspected maltreatment. In most states, the reporting law provides qualified immunity. So long as the professional reported in good faith, immunity prevents liability. In a small number of states (e.g., California), the reporting law provides absolute immunity.

Malpractice Insurance

Professionals are advised to obtain malpractice insurance. Read the policy carefully and make sure you understand all exclusions from coverage. The insurance company is only required to cover the professional if the professional gives "timely" notice to the company of claims or lawsuits. Notify the company immediately. If a lawsuit is filed, Bennett et al. (1990) advise professionals

> not to attempt to work it out by contacting the client or conducting more therapy. Once a suit is filed, your relationship with the client is supplanted by a relationship with the client's attorney, who is not interested in "therapeutically" working out the problem with you. (p. 97)

Bennett et al. (1990) go on to advise against contacting the client or the client's attorney. Let your attorney communicate for you. If documents are requested by the client or the client's attorney, do not provide them directly. Again, allow your attorney to respond to requests for documents and to subpoenas. Finally, Bennett et al. write, "Do not make self-incriminating statements to staff, to the client, or to the client's lawyers. Do not discuss the case with anyone, including your own family, other than your attorney" (p. 98).

The best way to avoid a lawsuit is to practice competently and compassionately.

Reaves (1998) provides insight into the care that should be taken when speaking with attorneys:

> It is a favorite ploy of successful plaintiffs' lawyers to file an action against a rather innocuous defendant, such as a state, county, or hospital, and then take a series of depositions from individuals who readily submit because

they are not defendants. Following the series of depositions, chances are the pleadings will be amended and all "unknowing" deponents added as parties defendant. A [professional] should not go to such a deposition alone, even if this means he or she has to retain his or her own counsel. The same admonition applies to records. [Professionals] should not respond to a subpoena without consulting counsel. (p. 45)

Conclusion

Professionals can reduce the likelihood of being sued. The best way to avoid a lawsuit is to practice competently and compassionately. Smith (1996) suggests that professionals "promote an atmosphere of concern for patients and respect for their legal rights" (p. 91). Reaves (1998), an expert on risk management for mental health professionals, provides sound advice:

1. Be as open and honest as possible with patients regarding the parameters of the provider-patient relationship.
2. Set out your qualifications, area of practice, and expectations, including limitations on confidentiality and the fee-for-service arrangement in writing, and have patients sign the document.
3. Practice within areas of competence for which you can demonstrate you are competent.
4. Maintain competence in your areas of practice.
5. Maintain complete records.
6. Treat your patients with respect, the way you would expect your therapist to treat you.
7. Terminate treatment properly and in writing.
8. Know the laws that affect your practice.
9. Maintain an ongoing consultative relationship with other respected colleagues.
10. When in doubt, seek competent advice (pp. 62-63).

Notes

1. In *Jacoby v. Brinkerhoff* (1999), the Connecticut Supreme Court ruled that a psychiatrist did not owe a duty of care to the psychiatrist's client's husband. The court wrote,

> The psychotherapists whom the spouse chose to consult for treatment owed a duty of undivided loyalty to her and not to him. Our common-law cases have shielded professional decision making from the complaints of third parties when third party intervention carried with it a substantial risk of interference with the primary purpose of the professional consultation. . . . When it is foreseeable that marital differences may become a subject for therapeutic analysis, sound public policy counsels that a psychiatrist's treatment of a troubled spouse should not be burdened by accountability to the other spouse. (p. 353)

2. Mental health professionals who perform custody evaluations are at increased risk of being sued (see Montgomery et al., 1999).

References

Achterhof v. Selvaggio, 886 F.2d 826 (6th Cir. 1989).

Adams v. Peck, 403 A.2d 840 (Md. Ct. App. 1979).

Althaus v. Cohen, 756 A.2d 1166 (Pa. 2000).

American Academy of Psychiatry and the Law. (1995). Ethical guidelines for the practice of forensic psychiatry. In *Membership directory of American Academy of Psychiatry and the Law* (pp. xi-xiv). Bloomfield, CT: Author.

American Law Institute. (1977). *Restatement of the law of torts.* St. Paul, MN: Author.

American Professional Society on the Abuse of Children. (1997). *Code of ethics.* Chicago: Author.

American Professional Society on the Abuse of Children. (1996). *Guidelines for psychosocial evaluation of suspected sexual abuse in young children.* Chicago: Author.

American Psychological Association. (1992). Ethical principles of psychologists and code of ethics. *American Psychologist, 47,* 1597-1611.

American Psychological Association. (1994). Guidelines for child custody evaluations in divorce proceedings. *American Psychologist, 49,* 677-680.

Appelbaum, P. S. (1997). A theory of ethics for forensic psychiatry. *Journal of the American Academy of Psychiatry and the Law, 25,* 233-246.

Appelbaum, P. S., & Zoltek-Jick, R. (1996). Psychotherapists' duties to third parties: *Ramona* and beyond. *American Journal of Psychiatry, 153,* 457-465.

Association of Family and Conciliation Courts. (1994). Model standards of practice. *Family and Conciliation Courts Review, 32,* 504-513.

Austin v. Borel, 830 F.2d 1356 (5th Cir. 1987).

Bank of Illinois v. Over, 65 F.3d 76 (7th Cir. 1995).

Bartell v. Lohiser, 215 F.3d 550 (6th Cir. 2000).

Bennett, B. E., Bryant, B. K., VandenBos, G. R., & Greenwood, A. (1990). *Professional liability and risk management.* Washington, DC: American Psychological Association.

Bird v. W. C. W., 868 S.W.2d 767 (Tex. 1994).

Bowman, C. G., & Mertz, E. (1996). A dangerous direction: Legal intervention in sexual abuse survivor therapy. *Harvard Law Review, 109,* 549-639.

Brokaw v. Mercer County, 235 F.3d 1000 (7th Cir. 2000).

Bruce v. Byrne-Stevens & Associates, 776 P.2d 666 (Wash. 1989).

California Civil Code. (2000). St Paul, MN: West.

Committee on Ethical Guidelines for Forensic Psychologists. (1991). Speciality guidelines for forensic psychologists. *Law and Human Behavior, 15,* 655-665.

Committee on Professional Practice and Standards, a Committee of the Board of Professional Affairs of the American Psychological Association. (1993). Record keeping guidelines. *American Psychologist, 48,* 984-986.

Committee on Professional Practice and Standards, a Committee of the Board of Professional Affairs of the American Psychological Association. (1995). Twenty-four questions (and answers) about professional practice in the area of child abuse. *Professional Psychology: Research and Practice, 26,* 377-385.

Committee on Psychiatry and Law, Group for the Advancement of Psychiatry. (1991). *The mental health professional and the legal system* (Rep. No. 131). New York: Brunner/Mazel.

Corpus Juris Secundum. (1987). St. Paul, MN: West.

Currier v. Doran, 242 F. 3d 905 (10th Cir. 2001).

Darragh v. Superior Court, 900 P.2d 1215 (Ariz. Ct. App. 1995).

Darryl H. v. Coler, 801 F.2d 893 (7th Cir. 1986).

Davis, K. C. (1972). *Administrative law.* Boston: Little, Brown.

Deatherage v. State Examining Board of Psychology, 948 P.2d 828 (Wash. 1997).

Deed, M. L. (1993). Mandated reporting revisited: *Roe v. Superior Court. Law and Policy, 14,* 219-239.

Delcourt v. Silverman, 919 S.W.2d 777 (Tex. Ct. App. 1996).

DeShaney v. Winnebago County Department of Social Services, 489 U.S. 189 (1989).

Devereauz v. Perez, 218 F.3d 1045 (9th Cir. 2000).

Diehl v. Danuloff, 618 N.W.2d 83 (Mich. Ct. App. 2000).

Doe v. McKay, 700 N.E.2d 1018 (Ill. 1998).

Durand Equipment Co. v. Superior Carbon Products, Inc., 591 A.2d 987 (N.J. Super. A.D. 1991).

Ebert, B. W. (1993). Informed consent. In *Board of psychology update.* Sacramento: California Department of Consumer Affairs.

Ernst v. Child and Youth Services of Chester County, 108 F.3d 486 (3rd Cir. 1997).

Faden, R. R., & Beauchamp, T. L. (1986). *A history and theory of informed consent.* New York: Oxford University Press.

Flanders v. Cooper, 706 A.2d 589 (Me. 1998).

Fleming, T. J. (1990). Admissibility of hypnotically refreshed or enhanced testimony. *American Law Reports 4th, 77,* 927-983.

Franklin v. Terr, 201 F.3d 1098 (9th Cir. 2000).

General Electric Co. v. Sargent and Lundy, 916 F.2d 1119 (6th Cir. 1990).

Gilliam v. Department of Social and Health Services, 950 P.2d 20 (Wash. Ct. App. 1998).

Glassman, J. B. (1998). Preventing and managing board complaints: The downside risk of custody evaluation. *Professional Psychology: Research and Practice, 29,* 121-124.

Gootee v. Lightner, 274 Cal. Rptr. 697 (Ct. App. 1990).

Greenberg, S. A., & Shuman, D. W. (1997). Irreconcilable conflict between therapeutic and forensic roles. *Professional Psychology: Research and Practice, 28,* 50-57.

Harris, E. A. (1995). The importance of risk management in a managed care environment. In M. B. Sussman (Ed.), *A perilous calling: The hazards of psychotherapy practice*. New York: John Wiley.

Hess, A. K. (1998). Accepting forensic case referrals: Ethical and professional considerations. *Professional Psychology: Research and Practice, 29,* 109-114.

Hodorowski v. Ray, 844 F.2d 1210 (5th Cir. 1988).

Holloway v. Brush, 220 F.3d 767 (6th Cir. 2000).

Hughes v. Long, 242 F.3d 121 (3d Cir. 2001).

Humphreys, K., Winzelberg, A., & Klaw, E. (2000). Psychologists' ethical responsibilities in Internet-based groups: Issues, strategies, and a call for dialogue. *Professional Psychology: Research and Practice, 31,* 493-496.

Hungerford v. Jones, 722 A.2d 478 (N.H. 1998).

Jacoby v. Brinkerhoff, 735 A.2d 347 (Conn. 1999).

J. A. H. v. Wadle & Associates, 589 N.W.2d 256 (Iowa 1999).

Johnson v. Rogers Memorial Hospital, 616 N.W.2d 903 (Wis. Ct. App. 2000).

Kahn v. Burman, 673 F. Supp. 210 (E.D. Mich. 1987).

Kalichman, S. C. (1993). *Mandated reporting of suspected child abuse: Ethics, law, and policy.* Washington, DC: American Psychological Association.

Kalichman, S. C. (1999). *Mandated reporting of suspected child abuse: Ethics, law, and policy* (2nd ed.). Washington, DC: American Psychological Association.

Kalina v. Fletcher, 522 U.S. 118 (1997).

Kia P. v. McIntyre, 235 F.3d 749 (2nd Cir. 2000).

Kirkland, K., & Kirkland, K. L. (2001). Frequency of child custody evaluation complaints and related disciplinary action: A survey of the Association of State and Provincial Psychology Boards. *Professional Psychology: Research and Practice, 32,* 171-174.

Knapp, S., & VandeCreek, L. (1996). Risk management for psychologists: Treating patients who recover lost memories of childhood abuse. *Professional Psychology: Research and Practice, 27,* 452-459.

Koocher, G. P., & Morray, E. (2000). Regulation of telepsychology: A survey of state attorneys general. *Professional Psychology: Research and Practice, 31,* 503-508.

Landeros v. Flood, 551 P.2d 389 (Cal. 1976).

Lythgoe v. Guinn, 884 P.2d 1085 (Alaska 1994).

Mabe v. San Bernardino County, 237 F3d 1101 (9th 2001).

Maciariello v. City of Lancaster, 973 F.2d 295 (4th Cir. 1992).

Maheu, M. M., & Gordon, B. L. (2000). Counseling and therapy on the Internet. *Professional Psychology, Research and Practice, 31,* 484-489.

Malley v. Briggs, 475 U.S. 335 (1986).

Matter of Schroeder, 415 N.W.2d 436 (Minn. Ct. App. 1988).

Melton, G. B., Petrila, J., Poythress, N., & Slobogin, C. (1997). *Psychological evaluations for the courts* (2nd ed.). New York: Guilford.

Mershon v. Beasley, 994 F.2d 449 (8th Cir. 1993).

Meyer v. Nebraska, 262 U.S. 390 (1923).

Michael H. v. Gerald D., 491 U.S. 110 (1989).

Millspaugh v. County Department of Public Welfare of Wabash County, 937 F.2d 1172 (7th Cir. 1991).

Moline, M. E., Williams, G. T., & Austin, K. M. (1998). *Documenting psychotherapy: Essentials for mental health practitioners.* Thousand Oaks, CA: Sage.

Montgomery, L. M., Cupit, B. E., & Wimberley, T. K. (1999). Complaints, malpractice, and risk management: Professional issues and personal experiences. *Professional Psychology: Research and Practice, 30,* 402-410.

Montoya v. Bebensee, 761 P.2d 285 (Colo. Ct. App. 1988).

Moses v. McWilliams, 549 A.2d 950 (Pa. Super. 1988).

Moses v. Parwatikar, 813 F.2d 891 (8th Cir. 1987).

Myers, J. E. B. (1997). *Evidence in child abuse and neglect cases.* New York: Aspen Law and Business.

Myers, J. E. B. (2001). Legal issues. In M. Winterstein & S. Scribner (Eds.), *Mental health care for child crime victims: Standards of Care Task Force guidelines* (pp. 13.1-13.52). Sacramento: California Victim Compensation and Government Claims Board.

Nahmod, S. H. (1991). *Civil rights and civil liberties litigation: The law of Section 1983.* Colorado Springs, CO: Shepards/McGraw-Hill.

National Association of Social Workers. (1997). *Code of ethics.* Washington, DC: Author.

Nosbaum v. Martini, 726 N.E.2d 84 (Ill. Ct. App. 2000).

Parker v. Dodgion, 971 P.2d 496 (Utah 1998).

Pierce v. Society of Sisters, 268 U.S. 510 (1925).

Politi v. Tyler, 751 A.2d 788 (Vt. 2000).

Prince v. Massachusetts, 321 U.S. 158 (1944).

Rainier's Dairies v. Rairtan Valley Farms, 117 A.2d 889 (N.J. 1955).

Reaves, R. P. (1998). *Avoiding liability in mental health practice.* Association of State and Provincial Psychology Boards.

Renn v. Garrison, 100 F.3d 344 (4th Cir. 1996).

Rivas-Vazquez, R. A., Blais, M. A., Rey, G. J., & Rivas-Vazquez, A. A. (2001). A brief reminder about documenting the psychological consultation. *Professional Psychology: Research and Practice, 32,* 194-199.

Rodriguez v. Perez, 994 P.2d 874 (Wash. App. 2000).

Salyer v. Patrick, 874 F.2d 374 (6th Cir. 1989).

Sawyer v. Midelfort, 595 N.W.2d 423 (Wis. 1999).

Seamons v. Snow, 84 F.3d 1226 (10th Cir. 1996).

Silberg v. Anderson, 786 P.2d 365 (Cal. 1990).

Slovenko, R. (1996). The duty of therapists to third parties. *Journal of Psychiatry and Law, 23,* 383-410.

Smith, J. T. (1986). *Medical malpractice: Psychiatric care.* New York: McGraw-Hill.

Smith, S. R. (1996). Malpractice liability of mental health professionals and institutions. In B. D. Sales & D. W. Shuman (Eds.), *Law, mental health, and mental disorder.* Pacific Grove, CA: Brooks/Cole.

Snell v. Tunnell, 920 F.2d 673 (10th Cir. 1990).

S. S. v. McMullen, 225 F.3d 960 (8th Cir. 2000).

State v. Hurd, 400 N.W.2d 42 (Wis. Ct. App. 1986).

Stecker v. First Commercial Trust, 962 S.W.2d 792 (Ark. 1998).

Stone v. Glass, 35 S.W.3d 827 (Ky. Ct. App. 2000).

Sweaney v. Ada County, Idaho, 119 F.3d 1385 (9th Cir. 1997).

Trear v. Sills, 82 Cal. Rptr. 2d 281 (Ct. App. 1999).

Troxel v. Granville, 530 U.S. 57 (2000).

Wallis v. Spencer, 202 F.3d 1126 (9th Cir. 2000).

Watterson v. Page, 987 F.2d 1 (1st Cir. 1993).

Wisconsin v. Yoder, 406 U.S. 205 (1972).

Wojcik v. Town of North Springfield, 76 F.3d 1 (1st Cir. 1996).

Woodward v. Weiss, 932 F. Supp. 723 (D.S.C. 1996).

Wooley v. City of Baton Rouge, 211 F.3d 913 (5th Cir. 2000).

Younggren, J. N. (1995). Informed consent: Simply a reminder. *Register Report,* 21.

Zamstein v. Marvasti, 692 A.2d 781 (Conn. 1997).

PART FIVE

Prevention and Service Delivery

The second edition of the *APSAC Handbook* concludes with five interesting and important chapters. In Chapter 21, Deborah Daro and Anne Cohn Donnelly update their first edition chapter on prevention. A great deal has been learned since 1996, and Daro and Cohn Donnelly bring us up to date on the latest research and developments.

Chapter 22 focuses on the important issue of reporting suspected child abuse and neglect. Gail Zellman and Christine Fair provide a comprehensive description of the literature on reporting. They trace the history of the reporting laws and analyze the impact of these laws on identification of abuse and neglect. Zellman and Fair examine the literature on professional compliance with reporting laws, including the reasons professionals fail to report. Chapter 22 is an update of the Zellman and Faller chapter from the first edition.

In Chapter 23, Veronica Abney reminds us of the importance of cultural competency in the field of child maltreatment. Updating her contribution to the first edition, Ms. Abney provides an overview of research on cultural competency. She provides valuable practical guidance on approaching culturally different clients.

Chapter 24 is new to the second edition. John Landsverk, Ann Garland, and Laurel Leslie provide an extremely interesting analysis of the organization and delivery of mental health services to abused and neglected children. The authors document the need for mental health services among victims of abuse. The authors note that few studies have actually examined the use of mental health services by maltreated children. Pulling together the existing literature, Landsverk, Garland, and Leslie paint a picture of the use of mental health services. The chapter concludes with recommendations to improve the delivery of services to abused and neglected children.

The final chapter in the second edition is by David Chadwick, one of the senior statesmen of the modern era of child protection. Dr. Chadwick's chapter in the first edition of the *Handbook* outlined a plan to more effectively cope with child abuse. In his chapter for the second edition, Chadwick takes the next step and outlines a bold plan to end child abuse.

J.E.B.M.

21

Child Abuse Prevention

Accomplishments and Challenges

DEBORAH DARO

ANNE COHN DONNELLY

Overview

Child abuse prevention, at its most basic level, is about strengthening the capacity of parents and societies to care for their children's health and well-being. Over the past 30 years, prevention advocates have designed and implemented hundreds of interventions to resolve parents' lack of knowledge and skills, create extended networks of formal support, and alter normative and societal standards for child rearing and education. Whether one talks about the family support movement, the early childhood movement, or child abuse prevention, these and similar efforts have created a plethora of programs that have, in the eyes of many, significantly improved conditions for children (Daro, 1988; Schorr & Schorr, 1985; Willis, Holden, & Rosenberg, 1992). Recent declines in the number of child abuse reports and a sustained reduction in many indicators of childhood distress provide hope that prevention efforts can be effective in reducing maltreatment rates and minimizing those conditions that place children at risk.

> *Some 3 million children are still reported annually for suspected maltreatment, and roughly one third of these children require formal child protective services.*

Not all families, however, have equal access to or benefit from primary and secondary prevention efforts, so not all children are being helped (Daro, 1993; U.S. Department of Health and Human Services, 1990). Although gains have been realized, some 3 million children are still reported annually for suspected maltreatment, and roughly one third of these children require formal child protective services (Chalk & King, 1998; Sedlak & Broadhurst, 1996). And once identified, many of these young victims are not well served by existing tertiary prevention efforts. Among the failings in the current response system are the inability to provide adequate assessments for all reports, inappropriate and insufficient therapeutic resources, burgeoning foster care roles, high reincidence rates among those children remaining with their families, and foster care options that perpetuate mistreatment and poor child outcomes (Bartholet, 1999). These and similar problems underscore the simple fact that "fixing" a broken parent-child relationship is neither a self-evident nor routine procedure. The complications and interdependence of various factors conspire to foil the best of intentions.

This mixed performance record stems from some prevention services not being as available as necessary and other prevention programs not being implemented with sufficient attention to quality and purpose. On balance, most prevention programs target and successfully serve parents who recognize their limitations and seek out the resources necessary to compensate for these limitations. Far fewer resources exist for families who may not know they need assistance or, if they recognize their shortcomings, do not know how to gain access to help. Parents may be unable or unwilling to integrate the social, emotional, and cognitive competencies needed for healthy parenting (Daro, 1993). This mismatch between what is being offered and what is needed is reflected in the 30% to 50% attrition rate observed in most child abuse prevention and family support services (Gueron & Pauly, 1991; Johnson & Walker, 1991; McCurdy, Hurvis, & Clark, 1996; Quint, Polit, Bos, & Cave, 1994; St. Pierre et al., 1995).

The absence of consistent and sustained outcomes also reflects the inability of current prevention strategies to be as comprehensive as necessary in their conceptual frameworks and programmatic reach. Dramatic changes in family structure, community cohesiveness, and public social welfare and health care delivery have expanded the gap between what many parents need to safely rear their children and what society is willing to offer.

The purpose of this chapter is to summarize the collective strengths of current prevention efforts and to highlight new avenues that prevention advocates might pursue if they are to keep pace with changes in family dynamics and social policy. The chapter begins by briefly outlining the theoretical frameworks that have shaped the development of child abuse prevention programming. Specific attention is paid to the impact different forms of maltreatment have had on the design and replication of specific prevention strategies. We then summarize the key program models emerging in this field and the empirical evidence regarding their relative effectiveness. Finally, the chapter outlines the challenges facing prevention advocates and offers suggestions on how new strategies might be developed.

The Theoretical Context Shaping Prevention Efforts

Broad causal theories have been used to explain the general relationship between specific individual or environmental conditions and child abuse. The theories most commonly found in the literature range from interpersonal functioning theories, such as psychodynamic and learning theories, to systemic and social explanations of maltreatment, suggested by theories of stress and poverty (Newberger & Newberger, 1982). For the purpose of identifying the program design implications of this body of work, Daro (1988, 1993) has classified these theoretical frameworks into four general groups:

- Psychodynamic theory suggests that parents would be less abusive if they better understood themselves and their role as parents.
- Learning theory suggests that parents would be less abusive if they knew more specifically how best to care for their children.
- Environmental theory suggests that parents would be less abusive if they had greater resources available to them in terms of material support or social support for a given set of actions.
- Ecological theory suggests that parents would be less abusive if a network of services or supports existed to compensate for individual, situational, and environmental shortcomings.

Over the years, the child maltreatment field has evolved from reliance on "linear or main effect" frameworks into models that recognize the interdependence or interaction of multiple causal agents (Belsky, 1980; Bronfenbrenner, 1979; Cicchetti & Rizley, 1981; Garbarino, 1977). Despite this theoretical understanding of the interaction among the personal and the environmental, most prevention efforts have focused on a fairly limited range of causal agents in designing and delivering services. Furthermore, possible differences in the etiology across types of maltreatment also have fragmented the prevention field, often resulting in a plethora of prevention activities with limited scope and limited resources (Daro, 1988, 2000).

The bulk of the literature on prevention has focused on the development and assessment of strategies aimed at reducing the prevalence of physical abuse and neglect. To a large extent, this pattern reflects the field's major emphasis for the past 30 years. Until recently, professionals and public alike perceived maltreatment to involve problematic or damaging parenting practices. Excessive physical discipline, failure to provide children with basic necessities and care, and mismatches between a parent's expectations and a child's abilities have long been recognized as precursors to maltreatment. Whether these failures stemmed from limitations within the parent or within the surrounding social system, the most prevalent and best-researched methods to prevent child abuse have been efforts to enhance parental capacity.

Beginning in the late 1970s, this singular focus was altered with the long overdue recognition of child sexual abuse. Reports of child sexual abuse increased from 6,000 in 1976 to an estimated 490,000 in 1992, with the bulk of this increase occurring between 1976 and 1984 (McCurdy & Daro, 1994). Prevalence studies on this problem estimate that as many as 20% of all females and 7% of all males will experience at least one episode of sexual abuse during their childhood (Peters, Wyatt, & Finkelhor, 1986; see Chapter 3, this volume). Furthermore, sexual abuse victims are a far more heterogeneous population than physical abuse or neglect victims. Risk factors with respect to perpetrator characteristics, victim characteristics, and sociodemographic variables are far from universal (Melton, 1992). Consequently, prevention advocates have had limited information to use in formulating effective

prevention strategies targeted to potential perpetrators or communities.

Driven by a sense of urgency to respond to the sexual abuse problem, prevention advocates have focused their energies on educating children who may be potential victims (Finkelhor, 1984). These efforts, generally identified under the rubric of child assault prevention education, provide classroom-based instruction for children of all ages on how to protect themselves from sexual assault and what to do if they experience actual or threatened abuse. Although in most cases these strategies include informational sessions for parents and school personnel, their primary focus is strengthening a child's ability to resist assault.

Both the historic pool of prevention services (parent enhancement efforts) and the more recent efforts to strengthen potential victims (child assault prevention education) have undergone numerous evaluations. As noted elsewhere, most of these evaluation and prevention programs are not controlled experiments, and many are fraught with serious methodological problems (Daro, 1994, 2000; Gomby, Culross, & Behrman, 1999; Howing, Wodarski, Kurtz, & Gaudin, 1989). Criticism of existing efforts is justified and underscores the need for more sophisticated and consistent evaluation efforts. However, limiting the pool of useful program evaluations to only those efforts that meet strict standards of scientific purity is impractical. Although the present pool of evaluative research has its limitations, it does offer preliminary guidelines for shaping programs and systems.

Interventions to Assist Parents—What Do We Know?

The number of parent support programs in the United States is staggering (Bryant, 1993). At least one national survey estimates that more than 100,000 groups of parents meet every year in the United States to attend parent education classes, provide mutual support to other parents, and advocate for better services or policy options for their children (Carter, 1995). Similarly, numerous home visitation programs have been established throughout the United States since 1993. Considering only the six most common of these models, as many as 550,000 children are reached annually by home visiting programs for pregnant women and families with young children (Gomby et al., 1999).

In investigating the features of successful programs, many have written about the need for programs to establish clear, coherent linkages among participant needs, program goals, program structure, and staff skills (Berlin, O'Neal, & Brooks-Gunn, 1998; Fulbright-Anderson, Kubisch, & Connell, 1998; Olds et al., 1999; Weiss, 1995). Others have emphasized the need for greater attention to the role community values and resources play in a child's development (Earls, 1998; Melton & Berry, 1994; Schorr, 1997) and the importance of continuous adherence to quality standards in both structuring programs and hiring and supervising staff (Dunst, 1995; Schorr, 1997; Wasik, Bryant, & Lyons, 1990). Within these parameters, child abuse prevention advocates have designed and implemented a number of diverse and effective prevention efforts. Concerns over parental rights and family privacy have led prevention advocates to frame these efforts in terms of those risk factors identified in the literature as resulting in a higher probability of abuse or neglect. Such factors include both demographic characteristics (e.g., poverty, single-parent status, young maternal age, etc.) as well as psychosocial characteristics (e.g., low frustration tolerance, substance abuse, limited knowledge of child development, situational stress, etc.).

Efforts to enhance parental capacity fall into three broad categories—public education and awareness efforts; home visitation programs, primarily directed to new parents; and parenting education and support services targeted to at-risk populations. Although sometimes offered in concert, these three approaches more commonly operate in parallel universes, reflecting different conceptualizations of the child abuse problem and different belief systems as to how to maximize program impact. The following discussion summarizes the key findings that have emerged from evaluative work on each approach.

Public Education and Awareness Through the Media

Using the media to mobilize the public in efforts to prevent child abuse has long been regarded as a vital component of a comprehensive child abuse prevention strategy (Cohn Donnelly, 1997). The values and attitudes that a people hold about children and how to raise them, the behaviors they engage in as parents toward their own and other children, and the degree to which they support or fail to support certain public policies all help to explain the existence of child abuse and its increase or decrease over time. The media (e.g., television, radio, newspapers and magazines, billboards, and now even the Internet) allow one to reach out to large numbers of individuals in a consistent manner. These strategies allow advocates to educate the public about the existence and dimensions of a given problem and, more important, how every individual can take action to foster abuse prevention. As such, media strategies are embraced as relatively nonintrusive options to delivering the prevention message. Regrettably, they also are widely regarded as the "softest" or least important elements of a comprehensive approach to prevention. In truth, however, research suggests that public education and awareness efforts may be among the most critical strategies to pursue when seeking to implement broad-scale change in behaviors or to widely implement a service innovation. Anecdotally, we have learned that parents take prevention programs more seriously when they have heard them described on TV or when they are recognized throughout the community as a high-quality program.

Public education efforts can accomplish a variety of goals, including creating awareness of a problem, improving knowledge about a problem (its extent, its causes, its consequences), changing attitudes (or values) regarding the problem, and changing the behavior of those directly affected by or causing the problem and of the public more generally. Creating and sustaining awareness of a given problem are most commonly thought of and typically sequenced first in a series of public education prevention efforts. For example, in the mid-1970s, as child abuse prevention efforts were just developing across the country, the general public was largely unaware of the problem and thus not disposed to helping stop it (e.g., reporting cases, helping stressed parents, supporting prevention policies, etc.). One study showed that fewer than 10% of the American public was aware of the child abuse problem during this period (National Committee to Prevent Child Abuse [NCPCA], 1976).

During the late 1970s and early 1980s, the NCPCA, now known as Prevent Child

Abuse America (PCAA), and other national public and private entities undertook efforts to explicitly raise the public's level of awareness. These efforts, primarily public service announcements on TV and radio, were supplemented by extensive news coverage of particularly atrocious cases. By the early 1980s, a national public opinion survey showed that more than 90% of the public was not only aware of the problem but also understood that there were different types of child maltreatment, that the causes of maltreatment were rooted in a variety of individual and societal conditions, and that people needed to take action if the problem was to be resolved (Daro & Gelles, 1992). During this period, reports to public agencies of suspected child abuse rose dramatically, increasing from fewer than 100,000 in 1976 to more than one million in the early 1980s (McCurdy & Daro, 1994). Many of these reports came from the general public. Whether a primary cause or an additive one, deliberate use of the media to make the public aware of child abuse appears to have had a substantial impact on awareness, knowledge, and behavior.

Targeting parents themselves with the intent of changing their attitudes and behaviors regarding how they parent has long been seen as a more ambitious and difficult and thus less popular use of public education tools—even though these efforts undoubtedly are more closely tied to actual prevention. The theory has been that changing parental attitudes about such behaviors as spanking and other forms of hitting or constant yelling creates an environment in which the more targeted prevention programs (such as home visitation services for new parents) have a better chance to succeed (e.g., the home visitor can more successfully support new parents in developing positive parenting practices when negative ones are not abundant in the environment).

This theory had been tested in the child abuse field in relatively narrow ways. Most notably, the PCAA conducted a series of educational campaigns using TV, print, radio, and billboard public service announcements (PSAs) with editorial assistance from the media (e.g., op-ed pieces, columns in Dear Abby) targeted sequentially at physical abuse/hitting, verbal abuse/yelling, and emotional neglect/ignoring. In conjunction with the Advertising Council, full-service campaigns were developed, pilot tested, and distributed to all major media outlets across the country. With the assistance of PCAA state chapters and their local affiliates, the combined campaigns garnered between $20 to $60 million a year worth of exposure in donated time and space. The impact from the first two of these three waves has been monitored, and the findings are encouraging. Since 1988, parents participating in an annual public opinion poll conducted for PCAA have reported a steady reduction in the use of both corporal punishment and verbal forms of aggression in disciplining their children (Daro & Gelles, 1992).

Researchers are quick to point out that it is not certain if the changes measured reflect changes in attitude (and thus a greater reluctance to admit certain behaviors) or an actual change in behavior. Also encouraging and somewhat more clear, however, are the results of the public education efforts of the National Campaign to Prevent Teen Pregnancy. This campaign has sought to reduce the teen pregnancy rate in the United States by one third by 2005 by supporting values and stimulating actions consistent with pregnancy-free adolescence. The centerpiece of this work has been building a strong, ongoing, widespread public education campaign with support from top-level politicians, entertainment and news powerhouses, and corporate leaders. The efforts include extensive editorial coverage of teen pregnancy (particularly in materials that teens read and view, using ideas that teens have suggested), story lines in popular TV shows, PSAs, briefings for TV writers and producers, videos for use on TV and in schools, and posters and booklets that have been distributed widely. In other words, every conceivable media outlet that could be used to communicate with the target audiences (teens, their parents, and grandparents) has been used. These efforts appear to have contributed to a 12% decline in teen pregnancy rates from 1990 to 1996. In studying this experience, it becomes clear what an important role the media play in prevention efforts, how extensive and intensive and deliberate those efforts must be, and how little the child abuse field has done to capitalize on these strategies.

Home Visitation Programs for New Parents

Strong theoretical and empirical arguments exist for initiating parent education services at the time a child is born or early in the mother's pregnancy. Most important is the belief that such early initiation of services facilitates the development of a secure, positive attachment between the parent and child and establishes a cornerstone for later development (Bowlby, 1969, 1973, 1980). Recently, particular attention has been paid to the impact of early attachment on patterns of brain development:

> Infants thrive on one-to-one interactions with parents. Sensitive, nurturing parenting is thought to provide infants with a sense of basic trust that allows them to feel confident in exploring the world and forming positive relationships with other children and adults. (Carnegie Task Force, 1994, p. 5)

By initiating parent education programs at birth or earlier, these interventions are in a position to help shape these early parent-child interactions.

Early intervention efforts have been found to produce significant and substantial impacts on parenting behavior and child health and well-being (Daro, 1993; Gutterman, 1997; Infant Health and Development Program, 1990; Karoly et al., 1998; Ramey & Ramey, 1998; Seitz, Rosenbaum, & Apfel, 1985). Home visitation has been cited by several policy analysts and advocates as offering a particularly promising service delivery approach for educating parents and reducing abuse potential (Government Accounting Office [GAO], 1990; U.S. Department of Health and Human Services, 1990, 1991, 1993; Zero to Three, 1999). Offering services in a parent's home has a number of distinct advantages, particularly if the objective is to reduce the likelihood of maltreatment. Such services offer the provider an excellent opportunity to assess the safety of the child's living environment and to work with the parent in a very concrete way to improve parent-child interactions. The method also affords the participant a degree of privacy and the practitioner a degree of flexibility that is difficult to achieve in center-based programs.

In addition to the strong theoretical and clinical evidence supporting home visitation strategies, empirical evidence suggests that this strategy can achieve initial and lasting effects on parental behavior, particularly with young single mothers. The work of David Olds, Harriet Kitzman, and their colleagues suggest that repeated home visits initiated during pregnancy have both initial positive effects on abuse potential and maternal health behavior (Kitzman et al., 1997; Olds, Henderson, Chamberlin, & Tatelbaum, 1986; Olds et al., 1999), as well as long-term impacts on the child's development (Olds et al., 1997; Olds et al., 1998). Repeated evaluations of other national home visitation models also suggest that these efforts, when delivered in a prevention as well as treatment context, can produce positive outcomes for at least a subgroup of program participants (Baker, Piotrkowski, & Brooks-Gunn, 1999; Daro & Harding, 1999; Gray, Cutler, Dean, & Kempe, 1979; Heinicke et al., 1998; Lutzker & Rice, 1984, 1987; Wagner & Clayton, 1999). For example, a summary of 29 evaluations of the Healthy Families America (HFA) home visitation programs documented notable change among participant families, particularly in the area of parent-child interaction and parental capacity. Most families receiving these services appear better able to care for their children; access and effectively use health care services; resolve many of the personal and familial problems common among low-income, single-parent families; and avoid the most intrusive intervention into their parenting, namely, being reported for child abuse or neglect (Daro & Harding, 1999).

At least three longitudinal studies suggest not only that comprehensive parenting services provided over 2 years produce initial gains but also that these gains are strengthened over time (Olds et al., 1997; Seitz et al., 1985; Wieder, Poisson, Lourie, & Greenspan, 1988). Again, the major areas showing improvement include parenting skills, parent-child relationships, educational achievement, employment rates, and economic well-being (Daro, 1993; Karoly et al., 1998; Ramey & Ramey, 1998).

By initiating parent education programs at birth or earlier, these interventions are in a position to help shape these early parent-child interactions.

Positive outcomes, however, are neither universal nor consistent, leading some to rethink the utility of home visitation (Abt Associates, 1997; Barnard, 1998; Gomby et al., 1999). For example, none of the major home visitation models being replicated across the country have produced consistent, main effects in important domains such as social support and child development. In part, the absence of significant gains in these areas might reflect the limited time period during which these programs have worked with families (i.e., a maximum in most cases of 2 years). Altering a child's developmental trajectory or solidifying social networks may well require multiple years of directed intervention. On the other hand, home visitation, in and of itself, may not be the most effective strategy to accomplish a broad array of outcomes. Rather than view this lack of consistency as an indication of program failure, this pattern of results underscores the inevitable limitation of any single intervention, no matter how well designed and delivered. Additional analysis of this method is needed to better articulate the unique role home visitation might play within a broad, diversified system of parent education and support.

Group- and Center-Based Interventions

Altering parental knowledge, skills, and capacity also has been the goal of numerous group-based educational and support efforts. In contrast to home visitation services, a unique strength of this service modality is the opportunities it provides parents for sharing experiences, concerns, and solutions. "The universal parental search for normalcy and support—something most readily available from other parents—can often find its fullest expression through this process" (Carter & Harvey, 1996, p. 3). In addition, group-based efforts provide a natural vehicle for continuing the help-seeking process over time. Parents remain committed and engaged in this intervention because they have now formed a connection or friendship to a specific group of parents, not simply a sense of loyalty to an individual provider. When these connections are established, parent groups begin building the type of reciprocity and mutual support viewed by many as essential to achieving a higher standard of care for children (Melton & Berry, 1994).

Numerous experimental and quasi-experimental evaluations of parenting education and center-based services have documented positive gains in overall parenting skills and in the use of community resources (Daro, 1988, 1993). Many of these programs are school based or use community-based organizations, thereby increasing their availability to high-risk populations (Furstenburg, 1970, 1980; Polit & White, 1988; Rodriguez & Cortez, 1988). The most notable outcomes of these efforts include an increase in positive parent-child interactions, more extensive use of social supports, less use of corporal punishment, and higher self-esteem and personal functioning. For teen mothers, positive outcomes also include fewer subsequent births, higher employment rates, and less welfare dependency (Ellwood, 1988).

As in the case of home visitation services, positive outcomes are not consistent (Chalk & King, 1998; Videka-Sherman, 1989). Efforts to educate abusive or neglectful families or parents facing significant personal obstacles such as severe depression, substance abuse, and domestic violence have produced limited success (Daro & Cohn, 1988). On the other hand, educational and support efforts that work with new parents or parents whose behaviors have not yet resulted in an official report of maltreatment have found more promising results (Baker, Piotrkowski, & Brooks-Gunn, 1999; Carter & Harvey, 1996; Daro, 1988, 1993; Wolfe, 1994).

Repeated process and outcome evaluations of at least one national group-based model have identified a set of program characteristics more highly associated with positive outcomes. An assessment of MELD (formerly the Minnesota Early Learning Design) found the following service features central to achieving positive outcomes: group facilitation by parents who have experienced life situations similar to those of group members, long-term service availability (e.g., 2 or more years), persistent focus on parent strengths, emphasis on making decisions that produce long-term solutions to problems rather than achieving a "quick fix," and a commitment to ongoing staff training and supervision (Ellwood, 1988; Hoelting, Sandell, Letourneau, Smerlinder, & Stranik, 1996).

In working with the most dysfunctional families, one successful approach has been to combine parenting instruction with a therapeutic approach (Gambrill, 1983). These types of group-based programs have proven a useful addition to more individualized interventions generally offered to families being served through the mental health and child protective services systems (Hogue & Liddle, 1999). In these cases, an individual provider or therapist may attend group meetings with the parent, accompany the parent on service referrals, and serve as an interpreter of the information the parent receives in the group-based program. This dual strategy allows these parents to benefit from the mutual support inherent in a group setting while still retaining access to more individualized methods focusing on the parent's complex psychosocial and emotional needs.

Testing this notion, Wolfe, Edwards, Manion, and Koverola (1988) achieved notable success by combining group-based family support services with individual training in child management for families referred by local child protective services agencies. Three months following the intervention, mothers who received individual parent training in addition to group services for an average of 20 weeks reported fewer and less intense child behavior problems and indicated fewer adjustment problems associated with the risk of maltreatment than did the controls who attended only the group services for an average of 18 weeks. This pattern was supported by caseworker ratings at 1-year follow-up, which showed greater improvement and a lowered risk of maltreatment among clients who received both interventions.

Summary

Collectively, these three strategies offer parents a variety of opportunities to enhance their parenting knowledge and skills. For some parents, these interventions will offer them an enhanced awareness of the need to reach out and ask for assistance. For other parents, these programs offer a more promising beginning with their newborns or an opportunity to improve relationships with older children. For still others, these interventions will help them successfully manage chronic or episodic personal or situational stress. In those cases in which abuse or neglect has occurred, parents may find in this constellation of programs the parenting information and support needed to avoid continued or more serious maltreatment.

The empirical evidence suggests that each strategy has the potential to alter parenting knowledge, attitudes, and skills, but that such potential is far from universal. Taken in isolation, each strategy leaves a sizable percentage of families unserved. None of the methods works for all families, and none of the methods will be universally ac-

cepted in all communities. The ultimate strength of each, therefore, depends on its own quality and the vitality, quality, and local availability of other options.

Several service features or components have been identified as increasing the probability of reducing physical abuse and neglect within diverse populations. The program evaluation literature reviewed earlier suggests the following promising design features:

- Supporting parents in their child-rearing responsibilities is best done by initiating services prior to or as close to the birth of the first child as possible.
- Parenting enhancement services need to be tied to a child's specific developmental level and recognize the unique challenges involved in caring for and disciplining children of various ages.
- Regardless of service location, it is important to provide opportunities for parents to model the interactions or discipline methods being promoted through the intervention.
- Although child development knowledge can be transferred to parents in a relatively brief period of time (i.e., 6-12 weeks), changing attitudes and strengthening parenting and personal skills often require a longer time commitment (i.e., more than 6 months).
- An emphasis on social supports and the ability to obtain needed assistance is a critical element of programs seeking to ensure the safety of children beyond the immediate intervention period.
- A balance of home-based and group-based alternatives for parents is needed to address those isolated and uncomfortable in group settings as well as those who appreciate opportunities to share problems with other parents.
- Programs need to recognize cultural differences in how families function and in the nature of parent-child interactions.

Child Assault Prevention Programs: What Do We Know?

In contrast to the evolution of prevention efforts to reduce rates of physical abuse and neglect, efforts to prevent child sexual abuse followed a different developmental path in two critical respects—the targeting of the potential victim rather than the potential perpetrator and an emphasis on primary rather than secondary or tertiary prevention. Specifically, the prevention of child sexual abuse has largely focused on altering the behavior of children through group-based instruction to children on how to protect themselves from or respond to sexual assault or abuse. In many instances, this education is provided through elementary and secondary schools, although several national youth organizations have developed their own curricula, such as those developed by the Boy Scouts of America and Camp Fire, Inc. (Boy Scouts of America, 1991; Lutter & Weisman, 1985). Although these programs do include information for parents and teachers, their primary focus is on strengthening the potential victim's capacity to resist assault.

Concern over the advisability of this strategy is widespread (Gilbert, 1988; Melton, 1992; Reppucci & Haugaard, 1989). Despite the theoretical limitations of these programs, evaluations in this area have become more rigorous over time and have influenced the content and focus of child sexual abuse prevention programs. At least six major review articles on child sexual assault and victimization programs have concluded that, on balance, most evaluations find significant, if not always substantial, gains in a child's knowledge of sexual abuse and how to respond (Carroll, Miltenberger, & O'Neill, 1992; Daro, 1991, 1994; Finkelhor & Strapko, 1992; Hazzard, 1990; Reppucci & Haugaard, 1989; Wurtele & Miller-Perrin, 1992). Furthermore, a meta-analysis that reviewed the findings from 30 such evaluations concluded that these programs produce a small but statistically significant gain in knowledge (Berrick & Barth, 1992). Although some of these gains have been noted following repeated presentation of the concepts over a 10- to 15-week period (Downer, 1984; Fryer, Kraizer, & Miyoski, 1987; Woods & Dean, 1986; Young, Liddell, Pecot, Siegenthaler, & Yamagishi, 1987), most of these gains have been realized after less than five brief presentations (Borkin & Frank, 1986; Conte, Rosen, Saperstein, & Shermack, 1985; Garbarino, 1987; Kolko, Moser, Litz, & Hughes, 1987; Harvey, Forehand, Brown, & Holmes, 1988; Nibert, Cooper, Fitch, & Ford, 1988; Plummer, 1984; Swan, Press, & Briggs, 1985).

As with all prevention efforts, these gains are unevenly distributed across concepts and participants. On balance, children have greater difficulty in accepting the idea that abuse can occur at the hands of someone they know than at the hands of strangers (Finkelhor & Strapko, 1992). Among younger participants, the more complex concepts such as secrets and dealing with ambiguous feelings often remain misunderstood (Gilbert, Duerr-Berrick, LeProhn, & Nyman, 1990). Although most children learn something from these efforts, a significant percentage of children fail to show progress in every area presented. For example, Conte et al. (1985) noted that even the best performers in their study grasped only 50% of the concepts taught. Retention of the gains noted immediately following these instructions also varies. At least one evaluator discovered that although children have been found to retain increased awareness and knowledge of safety rules several months after receiving instruction, they retain less information with respect to such key concepts as who can be a molester, the difference between physical abuse and sexual abuse, and the fact that sexual abuse, if it occurs, is not the victim's fault (Plummer, 1984).

In addition to having a potential for primary prevention, child assault prevention instructions create environments in which children can more easily disclose ongoing maltreatment. In other words, independent of the impact these programs may have on future behavior, they offer an opportunity for present victims to reach out for help, thereby preventing continued abuse (Leventhal, 1987). Even those who have little faith that any useful prevention strategy can be developed with respect to sexual abuse admit that child assault prevention programs hold strong promise in obtaining earlier disclosures (Melton, 1992).

The few studies that have measured the extent to which these interventions result in increased disclosures have been promising. Kolko, Moser, and Hughes (1989) reported that in five of six schools in which prevention programs were offered, school guidance counselors received 20 confirmed reports of inappropriate sexual or physical touching in the 6 months following the intervention. In contrast, no reports were noted in the one control school in their study. Similarly, Hazzard, Webb, and Kleemeier (1988) found that 8 children reported ongoing sexual abuse and 20 others reported past occurrences within 6 weeks of receiving a three-session prevention program.

Summary

The generally positive findings from the evaluations conducted to date suggest that some form of child-focused education is an important component in our efforts to reduce the likelihood a child will submit to ongoing sexual abuse. Equally true, however, is the reality that preventing child abuse requires much more than simply educating the next generation of children on how to avoid abuse. Rather than offering definitive conclusions on the merits of these programs, the current pool of evaluative data suggests that positive outcomes can be maximized if programs include the following features:

- providing children with behavioral rehearsal of prevention strategies and offering feedback on their performance to facilitate children's depictions of their involvement in abusive as well as unpleasant interactions;

- developing curricula with a more balanced developmental perspective and tailoring training materials to a child's cognitive characteristics and learning ability;

- for young children, presenting the material in a stimulating and varied manner to maintain their attention and reinforce the information learned;

- teaching generic concepts such as assertive behavior, decision-making skills, and communication skills that children can use in everyday situations, not just to fend off abuse;

- repeatedly stressing the need for children to tell every time someone continues to touch them in a way that makes them uneasy;

- developing longer programs that are better integrated into regular school curricula and practices;

- creating more formal and extensive parent and teacher training components, particularly when targeting young children;

- developing extended after-school programs and more in-depth discussion opportunities for certain high-risk groups (e.g., former victims, teen parents).

Prevention's New Frontier

Limitations in the existing prevention system call for new thinking. Specifically, these reflections suggest that future prevention efforts need to be built on three key principles. First, such efforts need to offer community planners flexible, empirically based criteria for building their own prevention programs. Simply adopting predetermined, monolithic intervention strategies has not produced a steady expansion of high-quality, effective interventions (Brookings Institute, 1998; Schorr, 1997). Replication efforts need to include a specific planning phase in which local stakeholders (e.g., potential participants, local service providers, funders, the general public, etc.) assess the scope of maltreatment in their community, identify local human and social service resources, and craft a service delivery system in keeping with local realities.

The most powerful theories of explaining human behavior have drawn on the interdependency of the individual, family, and social context.

Second, intensive efforts for those families facing the greatest challenges need to be nested within a more broadly defined network of support services. Successfully engaging and retaining those parents facing the greatest challenges will not result from more stringent efforts to identify and serve only these parents. Until systems are established that normalize the parent support process by assessing and meeting the needs of all new parents, prevention efforts will continue to struggle with issues of stigmatization and deficit-directed imagery.

Finally, prevention programs need to focus not merely on changing individual behaviors but also on using these services as a springboard for systemic reforms in health and social service institutions. Establishing a series of solid, well-implemented direct service programs is one level of change. Integrating these efforts into a coherent system of support that can be used to leverage broader, institutional change is a more challenging and less obvious process. Although many private and public agencies have engaged in efforts to alter the way major institutions interface with families, few consistent success stories exist (Kagan, 1996; Schorr, 1997; St. Pierre, Layzer, Goodson, & Bernstein, 1997). Developing and sustaining such systemic success stories are essential.

The varied success of all prevention efforts—those directed at parents and those designed to reduce a child's vulnerability to violence—has led many to broaden their service focus to include the communities in which parents live. The importance of creating a more positive context for parents has been a longstanding goal of child abuse prevention. Indeed, the most powerful theories of explaining human behavior have drawn on the interdependency of the individual, family, and social context (Bronfenbrenner, 1979; Cicchetti & Rizley, 1981). Commenting on the positive results from targeted early intervention programs noted by Olds et al. (1998), Felton Earls (1998) emphasized this point by speculating on

> how much stronger the effects of this early intervention would have been if the program had continued beyond the child's second year of life or if efforts had been made to engage the wider social settings in which the families lived. (p. 1272)

Over the past 10 years, a growing body of work has developed that attempts to measure and better articulate the mechanisms by which neighborhoods influence child development and support parents. In summarizing this work, the Working Group on Communities, Neighborhoods, Family Process, and Individual Development (Brooks-Gunn, Ducan, & Aber, 1997) concluded that neighborhood mattered both directly (e.g., schools, parks, other primary supports) and indirectly in shaping parental attitudes and behaviors and in affecting a parent's self-esteem and motivational processes.

Explicit recognition of the continuous interplay between individual and environment in addressing the problem of child maltreatment was central in a series of reports issued by the U.S. Advisory Board on Child Abuse and Neglect between 1990 and 1993 (U.S. Department of Health and Human Services, 1990, 1991, 1993). Berry (1994) has articulated this interplay in terms of four basic assumptions:

- Child abuse and neglect result in part from stress and social isolation.
- The quality of neighborhoods can either encourage or impede parenting and social integration of the families who live in them.
- Both external and internal forces influence the quality of life in neighborhoods.
- Any strategy for preventing child maltreatment should address both internal and external dimensions and should focus on both strengthening at-risk families and improving at-risk neighborhoods.

Neighborhood has long been viewed as an important mediating variable in explaining differential levels of maltreatment among residents who share a common socioeconomic profile. A study of contrasting neighborhoods in Omaha, Nebraska, by Garbarino and Sherman (1980) found that the communities with the same predicted but different observed rate of child maltreatment reports differed dramatically in terms of their human ecology. Specifically, the community with a higher rate of reported maltreatment was less socially integrated, had less positive neighboring, and represented more stressful day-to-day interactions. Replicating this methodology with two economically comparable neighborhoods in Spokane, Washington, Deccio, Horner, and Wilson (1991) found reported rates of child maltreatment more than two times higher in the community with the lower rate of social integration, as evidenced by higher unemployment rates, greater residential mobility, and fewer telephones.

Although these single-point-in-time studies are insightful, Garbarino and Kostelny (1992) demonstrated that the concepts were equally true in a dynamic model. Examining child abuse reports at three points in time (e.g., 1980, 1983, and 1986) in four economically disadvantaged Chicago communities, the authors found significant differences in the relative ratings of neighborhoods over time. To explain this pattern, the authors interviewed a sample of community residents regarding their perceptions of their neighborhood as a social environment, characteristics of neighboring, and morale. On all dimensions, the community that demonstrated the greatest increase in maltreatment rates was the community where residents expressed the most negative views of their community, knew little about existing community services or agencies, and demonstrated little evidence of a formal or informal social support network.

More recently, researchers have begun examining the mechanisms through which neighborhoods might explicitly support parents and children. One particularly promising research strategy has been the concept of social capital (Coleman, 1988). Korbin and Coulton and their colleagues at Case Western Reserve University have implemented a series of studies examining the role of neighborhood in shaping parental practices and influencing child outcomes. Using census and administrative agency data for 177 urban census tracts in Cleveland, variation in rates of officially reported child maltreatment was found to be related to structural determinants of community social organization: economic and family resources, residential instability, household and age structure, and geographic proximity of neighborhoods to concentrated poverty. Children who live in neighborhoods that are characterized by poverty, excessive number of children per adult resident, population turnover, and the concentration of female-headed families are at highest risk of maltreatment (Coulton, Korbin, Su, & Chow, 1995).

Consistent with the multimethod approach adopted by Garbarino's research, Korbin and Coulton (1997) developed an ethnographic study component that focused on 13 of the original 177 census tracts. The ethnographic component included interviews with neighborhood residents and with owners and mangers of local businesses. In addition, informal observations were made and structured discussions were held with various personnel at churches, libraries, recreation centers, and other organizations such as block clubs in the neighborhoods. These interviews extended the authors' understanding of how the constructs identified in the aggregate analysis (e.g., child care burden, neighborhood impoverishment, and residential mobility) influenced parental behaviors and attitudes.

Residents of neighborhoods with high rates of child maltreatment reports and other adverse outcomes perceived their neighborhoods as settings where they and their neighbors were the least able to intervene in or control the behavior of neighborhood children. In justifying their lack of action, residents in the high maltreatment communities were more likely to express concerns that the child or adolescent being corrected would verbally or physically retaliate. In contrast, residents in low maltreatment communities were more likely to monitor the behavior of local children because they saw such action as part of their responsibility to "protect" children from violent or dangerous neighborhood conditions (traffic, broken glass, etc.) (Korbin & Coulton, 1997).

In examining the impacts of neighborhood on levels of violence, Sampson, Raudenbush, and Earls (1997) found lower crime rates in those neighborhoods where residents were able to achieve a level of shared values and demonstrate a willingness to intervene on behalf of the collective good. Using the term *social cohesion,* the authors hypothesized that social and organizational characteristics of neighborhoods explained variations in crime rates that were not solely attributable to the aggregated demographic characteristics of individuals. The sample included personal interviews with some 8,782 Chicago residents living in one of 343 distinct "neighborhood clusters" that differed in terms of race and socioeconomic status (SES). Interviews were used to construct a measure of "informal social control" (i.e., the degree to which residents expressed a likelihood that their neighbors could be counted on to help in various ways, such as correcting adolescent behavior, advocating for necessary services, or intervening in fights) and "social cohesion" (i.e., the degree to which respondents felt their neighbors could be counted on to help each other or could be trusted). Together, three dimensions of neighborhood stratification— concentrated disadvantage, immigration concentration, and residential stability— explained 70% of the neighborhood variation in collective efficacy. Collective efficacy, in turn, mediates a substantial portion of the association of residential stability and disadvantage with multiple measures of violence. In other words, although large structural issues play a critical role in establishing the social milieu in neighborhoods, neighborhoods that are able to establish a sense of community and mutual reciprocity develop a unique and potentially powerful tool to reduce violence and support parents.

Major Policy and Program Challenges

Collectively, this body of research suggests several advantages in both our conceptualization and ability to deliver effective prevention services. As our thinking continues to evolve, however, researchers, practitioners, and policymakers are faced with several challenges. Some of these challenges include the following:

Operating at scale. Small, targeted programs unevenly scattered across communities, although having some empirical support, will never engage the number of people necessary to achieve a substantial impact on aggregate indicators of distress. Accomplishing this type of broad-scale change will require far-reaching prevention systems that offer meaningful assistance to all new parents. The effort will require policymakers, program managers, and the public to share a common vision of what these efforts can mean for a child's welfare and the society's common good. For many, this shared vision is one in which normative standards encourage parents to seek and receive the support they need to care for their children. It is a vision where parents understand that their child's ability to develop his or her full potential depends on not only their actions as parents but also the supportive efforts of others such as school teachers, coaches, ministers, youth leaders, and the parents of their child's peers. To take prevention "to scale" is more than simply replicating a single strategy or promising reform. It is infusing the society with this vision of responsibility and mutual reciprocity.

Integrating across institutions and issues. The rapid expansion of a variety of prevention services and institutional reforms in child welfare, health, and educational institutions presents both an opportunity and challenge. Although many of these efforts share a common rhetoric peppered with terms such as *individualized services, collaboration,* and *service integration,* altering policy and practice behaviors will require more than eloquent rhetoric. Left to their own design, interventions are unlikely to group themselves in some logical sequence the way the human cells coordinate their efforts during fetal development. Such coordination, if it is to occur, will require explicit and continuous planning among all parties. "History clearly shows," Kagan (1996) writes, "that focusing on isolated inventions breeds problems of scaling up which have rarely been successfully addressed. Normalization suggests an alternative strategy; it focuses on envisioning a wholly reconstituted system and suggests incremental strategies toward its accomplishment" (p. 163).

Efforts to achieve this type of fundamental change face immense obstacles (Kagan, 1996; Schorr, 1997). Public provision of services is most commonly characterized by mandatory, not voluntary, service provision in which the relationship between caregiver and recipient is perceived as paternalistic, not egalitarian. Whereas community-based agencies seek to differentiate services based on an individual's need and cultural standards, institutional care is best organized in predefined, uniform "packages" or options. And as noted in the current debate over welfare reform, public systems of care may foster continued dependency rather than offer a realistic path toward independence. Future partnerships across programs and institutions will need to challenge existing paradigms of service delivery and organizational structure if they are to realize true system reform. Public entities will need to adopt new interpretations of standards and management, forestalling centralized control and adopting flexible, locally defined quality indicators. Private organizations and corporate entities will need to accept greater responsibility for supporting families within their sphere of influence. Public-private partnerships will be needed to forge strong, durable, and universal support networks ultimately attractive to all new parents.

Implementing diversified research methods. Research and policy development are circular, not linear, processes. Research informs practice, and practice informs research. The challenge the field faces is how best to accomplish this partnership in a manner that is equally respectful of science and practice. This balance is particularly difficult to achieve when the interventions under study target a complex and multicausal problem such as child maltreatment. It is difficult to follow predetermined protocols with scientific rigor when a service provider is encouraged to be responsive to local norms, standards, and cultural realities. More important, if a provider faithfully adheres to a protocol in all instances, maintaining a narrow vision, he or she may miss the very opportunity necessary to be effective. By assuming a consistency in the intervention, randomized trials may easily overstate or understate an intervention's potential efficacy.

In addition, those seeking to develop effective interventions need to know a wide range of information—how families view the service they are being offered, why they accept a given service, why they do not, what other options they see in their community to support them, and how they view their relationship with their service provider. To the extent every intervention with a family is unique, evaluation data need to provide guidance as to the specific change mechanisms operating with specific families, under specific conditions. Such information can only be achieved through the careful application of differential assessment methods.

Critical research findings are not limited to those that result in statistically significant changes on various standardized measures of narrow constructs. Useful knowledge also is gleaned from the stories that participants and providers tell in response to structured interviews, well-developed single-case studies, and theories of change models. To capture these diverse data, researchers need to implement diverse strategies. In this learning process, researchers need to implement multiple research designs, including randomized trials, but not exclusively randomized trials; use multiple methods of assessment, including standardized measures, but not exclusively standardized measures; and learn from multiple standards of evidence, relying on statistically significant findings, but not exclusively relying on statistically significant findings.

In short, the standard toolbox of research techniques and principals may not be sufficient to get the job done. Researchers cannot simply rely on randomized trials as the "gold standard." They need to integrate new standards of evidence into their traditional thinking. Rather than being hierarchical, in which one method is always considered superior, they will need to be more democratic, more participatory. Although challenging, this imagery—being democratic and participatory—is better suited to determining the ultimate utility of implementing complex programs within a community context and at a scale sufficient to prevent child abuse.

References

Abt Associates. (1997). *National impact evaluation of the Comprehensive Child Development Program: Final report.* Cambridge, MA: Author.

Baker, A., Piotrkowski, C., & Brooks-Gunn, J. (1999). The Home Instruction Program for Preschool Youngsters (HIPPY). *Future of Children, 9*(1), 116-133.

Barnard, K. (1998). Developing, implementing and documenting interventions with parents and young children. *Zero to Three, 18*(4), 23-29.

Bartholet, E. (1999). *Nobody's children: Abuse and neglect, foster drift and the adoption alternative.* Boston: Beacon.

Belsky, J. (1980). Child maltreatment: An ecological integration. *American Psychologist, 35,* 320-335.

Berlin, L., O'Neal, C., & Brooks-Gunn, J. (1998). What makes early intervention programs work? The program, its participants and their interaction. *Zero to Three, 18*(4), 4-15.

Berrick, J., & Barth, R. (1992). Child sexual abuse prevention training: What do they learn? *Child Abuse & Neglect, 12,* 543-553.

Berry, F. (1994). A neighborhood-based approach: What is it? In G. Melton & F. Berry (Eds.), *Protecting children from abuse and neglect: Foundations for a new national strategy* (pp. 14-39). New York: Guilford.

Borkin, J., & Frank, L. (1986). Sexual abuse prevention for preschoolers: A pilot program. *Child Welfare, 65,* 75-82.

Bowlby, J. (1969). *Attachment.* New York: Basic Books.

Bowlby, J. (1973). *Attachment and loss: Vol. 2. Separation.* New York: Basic Books.

Bowlby, J. (1980). *Loss.* New York: Basic Books.

Boy Scouts of America (BSA). (1991). How to protect your children from abuse and drug abuse. Insert into the *Boy Scout handbook* (10th ed.). Irving, TX: Author.

Bronfenbrenner, U. (1979). *The ecology of human development: Experiments by nature and design.* Cambridge, MA: Harvard University Press.

Brookings Institute. (1998). *Learning what works: Evaluating complex social interventions: Report on the symposium held October 22, 1997.* Washington, DC: Author.

Brooks-Gunn, J., Ducan, G., & Aber, J. L. (1997). *Neighborhood poverty: Vol. 2. Policy implications in studying neighborhoods.* New York: Russell Sage.

Bryant, P. (1993). *Availability of existing statewide parent education and support programs and the need for these programs nationwide.* Chicago: National Committee to Prevent Child Abuse.

Carnegie Task Force on Meeting the Needs of Young Children. (1994). *Starting points: Meeting the needs of our youngest children.* New York: Carnegie Corporation of New York.

Carroll, L., Miltenberger, R., & O'Neill, K. (1992). A review and critique of research evaluating child sexual abuse prevention programs. *Education and Treatment of Children, 15,* 335-354.

Carter, N. (1995). *Parenting education in the United States: An investigative report.* Philadelphia: Lew Charitable Trusts.

Carter, N., & Harvey, C. (1996). Gaining perspective on parenting groups. *Zero to Three, 16*(6), 1, 3-8.

Chalk, R., & King, P. (Eds.). (1998). *Violence in families: Assessing prevention and treatment programs.* Washington, DC: National Academy Press.

Cicchetti, D., & Rizley, R. (1981). Developmental perspectives on the etiology, intergenerational transmission, and sequelae of child maltreatment. *New Directions for Child Development, 11,* 31-55.

Cohn Donnelly, A. (1997). An overview of prevention of physical abuse and neglect. In M. E. Helfer, M. Kempe, & R. Krugman (Eds.), *The battered child* (5th ed., pp. 579-593). Chicago: University of Chicago Press.

Coleman, J. (1988). Social capital in the creation of human capital. *American Journal of Sociology, 94*(Suppl.), S95-S120.

Conte, J., Rosen, C., Saperstein, L., & Shermack, R. (1985). An evaluation of a program to prevent the sexual victimization of young children. *Child Abuse & Neglect, 9,* 329-334.

Coulton, C., Korbin, J., Su, M., & Chow, J. (1995). Community level factors and child maltreatment rates. *Child Development, 66,* 1262-1276.

Daro, D. (1988). *Confronting child abuse.* New York: Free Press.

Daro, D. (1991). Prevention programs. In C. Hollin & K. Howells (Eds.), *Clinical approaches to sex offenders and their victims* (pp. 285-306). New York: John Wiley.

Daro, D. (1993). Child maltreatment research: Implications for program design. In D. Cicchetti & S. Toth (Eds.), *Child abuse, child development, and social policy* (pp. 331-367). Norwood, NJ: Ablex.

Daro, D. (1994). Prevention of childhood sexual abuse. *Future of Children, 4*(2), 198-223.

Daro, D. (2000). Child abuse prevention: New directions and challenges. *Journal on Motivation, 46,* 161-220.

Daro, D., & Cohn, A. (1988). Child maltreatment evaluation efforts? What have we learned? In G. Hotaling, D. Finkelhor, J. Kirkpatrick, & M. Straus (Eds.), *Coping with family violence: Research and policy perspectives* (pp. 275-287). Newbury Park, CA: Sage.

Daro, D., & Gelles, R. (1992). Public attitudes and behaviors with respect to child abuse prevention. *Journal of Interpersonal Violence, 7*(4), 517-531.

Daro, D., & Harding, K. (1999). Healthy Families America: Using research in going to scale. *Future of Children, 9*(1), 152-176.

Deccio, G., Horner, B., & Wilson, D. (1991). *High-risk neighborhoods and high-risk families: Replication research related to the human ecology of child maltreatment.* Unpublished manuscript, Eastern Washington University, Cheney.

Downer, A. (1984). *An evaluation of talking about touching.* (Unpublished manuscript available from author, P.O. Box 15190, Seattle, WA 98115)

Dunst, C. (1995). *Key characteristics and features of community-based family support program.* Chicago: Family Resource Coalition.

Earls, F. (1998). Positive effects of prenatal and early childhood interventions. *Journal of the American Medical Association, 280*(14), 1271-1273.

Ellwood, A. (1988). Prove to me that MELD makes a difference. In H. Weiss & F. Jacobs (Eds.), *Evaluating family programs* (pp. 303-314). New York: Aldine.

Finkelhor, D. (1984). *Child sexual abuse: New theory and research.* New York: Free Press.

Finkelhor, D., & Strapko, N. (1992). Sexual abuse prevention education: A review of evaluation studies. In D. Willis, E. Holder, & M. Rosenberg (Eds.), *Child abuse prevention* (pp. 150-167). New York: John Wiley.

Fryer, G., Kraizer, S., & Miyoski, T. (1987). Measuring actual reduction of risk to child abuse: A new approach. *Child Abuse & Neglect, 11,* 173-179.

Fulbright-Anderson, K., Kubisch, A., & Connell, J. (Eds.). (1998). *New approaches to evaluating community initiatives: Vol. 2. Theory, measurement and analysis.* Queenstown, MD: Aspen Institute.

Furstenburg, F. (1970). *Unplanned parenthood.* New York: Free Press.

Furstenburg, F. (1980). Burdens and benefits: The impact of early childbearing on the family. *Journal of Social Issues, 36,* 64-87.

Gambrill, E. (1983). Behavioral interventions with child abuse and neglect. *Progress in Behavior Modification, 15,* 1-56.

Garbarino, J. (1977). The human ecology of child maltreatment: A conceptual model for research. *Journal of Marriage and the Family, 39,* 721-735.

Garbarino, J. (1987). Children's response to a sexual abuse prevention program: A study of the Spiderman comic. *Child Abuse & Neglect, 11,* 143-148.

Garbarino, J., & Kostelny, K. (1992). Child maltreatment as a community problem. *International Journal of Child Abuse and Neglect, 16,* 455-464.

Garbarino, J., & Sherman, D. (1980). High-risk neighborhoods and high-risk families: The human ecology of child maltreatment. *Child Development, 51,* 188-198.

Gilbert, N. (1988). Teaching children to prevent sexual abuse. *The Public Interest, 93,* 3-15.

Gilbert, N., Duerr-Berrick, J., LeProhn, N., & Nyman, N. (1990). *Protecting young children from sexual abuse: Does preschool training work?* Lexington, MA: Lexington Books.

Gomby, D., Culross, P., & Behrman, R. (1999). Home visiting: Recent program evaluations—analysis and recommendations. *Future of Children, 9*(1), 4-26.

Government Accounting Office (GAO). (1990). *Home visiting: A promising early intervention strategy for at-risk families* (GAO/HRD-90-83). Washington, DC: Author.

Gray, J. D., Cutler, C. A., Dean, J. G., & Kempe, C. H. (1979). Prediction and prevention of child abuse and neglect. *Journal of Social Issues, 35*(2), 127-139.

Gueron, J. M., & Pauly, E. (1991). *From welfare to work.* New York: Russell Sage.

Gutterman, N. (1997). Early prevention of physical abuse and neglect: Existing evidence and future directions. *Child Maltreatment, 2*(1), 12-34.

Harvey, P., Forehand, R., Brown, C., & Holmes, T. (1988). The prevention of sexual abuse: Examination of the effectiveness of a program with kindergarten-age children. *Behavior Therapy, 19,* 429-435.

Hazzard, A. (1990). Prevention of child sexual abuse. In R. Ammerman & M. Hersen (Eds.), *Treatment of family violence* (pp. 354-384). New York: John Wiley.

Hazzard, A., Webb, C., & Kleemeier, C. (1988). *Child sexual assault prevention programs: Helpful or harmful?* Unpublished manuscript, Emory University School of Medicine, Atlanta, GA.

Heinicke, C., Goorsky, M., Moscov, M., Dudley, K., Gordon, J., & Gurthrie, D. (1998). Partner support as a mediator of intervention outcome. *American Journal of Orthopsychiatry, 68*(4), 534-541.

Hoelting, J., Sandell, E., Letourneau, S., Smerlinder, J., & Stranik, M. (1996). The MELD experience with parent groups. *Zero to Three, 16*(6), 9-18.

Hogue, A., & Liddle, H. (1999). Family-based preventive intervention: An approach to preventing substance use and antisocial behavior. *American Journal of Orthopsychiatry, 69*(3), 278-293.

Howing, P., Wodarski, J., Kurtz, P., & Gaudin, J. (1989). Methodological issues in child maltreatment research. *Social Work Research and Abstracts, 25*(3), 3-7.

Infant Health and Development Program. (1990). Enhancing outcomes of low-birth weight preterm infants. *Journal of the American Medical Association, 263*(22), 3035-3042.

Johnson, D. L., & Walker, T. (1991). A follow-up evaluation of the Houston Parent-Child Development Center: School performance. *Journal of Early Intervention, 15*(3), 226-236.

Kagan, S. L. (1996). America's family support movement: A moment of change. In E. Zigler, S. Kagan, & N. Hall (Eds.), *Children, families & government: Preparing for twenty-first century* (pp. 156-170). Cambridge, UK: Cambridge University Press.

Karoly, L. A., Greenwood, P. W., Everingham, S. S., Hoube, J., Kilburn, M. R., Rydell, C. P., Sanders, M., & Cheisa, J. (1998). *Investing in our children: What we know and don't know about the costs and benefits of early childhood interventions.* Santa Monica, CA: RAND.

Kitzman, H., Olds, D., Henderson, C., Hanks, C., Cole, R., Tatelbaum, R., McConnochie, K., Sidora, K., Luckey, D., Shaver, D., Engelhart, K., James, L., & Barnard, K. (1997). Effects of prenatal and infancy home visitations by nurses on pregnancy outcomes, childhood injuries and repeated childbearing. *Journal of the American Medical Association, 278*(22), 644-652.

Kolko, D., Moser, J., & Hughes, J. (1989). Classroom training in sexual victimization awareness and prevention skills: An extension of the Red Flag/Green Flag people program. *Journal of Family Violence, 4*(1), 25-45.

Kolko, D., Moser, J., Litz, J., & Hughes, J. (1987). Promoting awareness and prevention of child sexual victimization using the Red Flag/Green Flag program: An evaluation with follow-up. *Journal of Family Violence, 2,* 11-35.

Korbin, J., & Coulton, C. (1997). Understanding the neighborhood context for children and families: Combining epidemiological and ethnographic approaches. In J. Brooks-Gunn, G. Ducan, & J. L. Aber (Eds.), *Neighborhood poverty: Vol. 2. Policy implications in studying neighborhoods* (pp. 65-79). New York: Russell Sage.

Leventhal, J. (1987). Programs to prevent sexual abuse: What outcomes should be measured? *Child Abuse & Neglect, 11,* 169-171.

Lutter, Y., & Weisman, A. (1985). *Sexual victimization prevention project: Campfire Girls.* Unpublished final report to the National Institute of Mental Health, Grant R18 MH39549.

Lutzker, J., & Rice, J. (1984). Project 12-Ways: Measuring outcome of a large in-home service for treatment and prevention of child abuse and neglect. *Child Abuse & Neglect, 18*(4), 519-524.

Lutzker, J., & Rice, J. (1987). Using recidivism data to evaluate Project 12-Ways: An ecobehavioral approach to the treatment and prevention of child abuse and neglect. *Journal of Family Violence, 2*(4), 283-290.

McCurdy, K., & Daro, D. (1994). Current trends in child abuse reporting and fatalities. *Journal of Interpersonal Violence, 9*(4), 75-94.

McCurdy, K., Hurvis, S., & Clark, J. (1996). Engaging and retaining families in child abuse prevention programs. *APSAC Advisor, 9*(3), 1-8.

Melton, G. (1992). The improbability of prevention of sexual abuse. In D. Willis, E. Holden, & M. Rosenberg (Eds.), *Child abuse prevention* (pp. 168-192). New York: John Wiley.

Melton, G., & Berry, F. (1994). *Protecting children from abuse and neglect: Foundations for a new national strategy.* New York: Guilford.

National Committee to Prevent Child Abuse (NCPCA). (1976). *Preventing child abuse and neglect: The role of public education.* Chicago: Author.

Newberger, C., & Newberger, E. (1982). Prevention of child abuse: Theory, myth and practice. *Journal of Prevention Psychiatry, 1*(4), 443-451.

Nibert, D., Cooper, S., Fitch, L., & Ford, J. (1988). *Prevention of abuse of young children: Exploratory evaluation of an abuse prevention program.* Columbus, OH: National Assault Prevention Center.

Olds, D., Eckenrode, J., Henderson, C. R., Jr., Kitzman, H., Powers, J., Cole, R., Sidora, K., Morris, P., Pettitt, L., & Luckey, D. (1997). Long-term effects of home visitation on maternal life course, child abuse and neglect and children's arrests: Fifteen-year follow-up of a randomized trial. *Journal of the American Medical Association, 278*(8), 637-643.

Olds, D., Henderson, C., Chamberlin, R., & Tatelbaum, R. (1986). Preventing child abuse and neglect: A randomized trial of nurse home visitation. *Pediatrics, 78*(1), 65-78.

Olds, D., Henderson, C., Cole, R., Eckenrode, J., Kitzman, H., Luckey, D., Pettitt, L., Sidora, K., Morris, P., & Powers, J. (1998). Long-term effects of nurse home visitation on children's criminal and antisocial behavior. *Journal of the American Medical Association, 280*(14), 1238-1244.

Olds, D., Henderson, C., Kitzman, H., Eckenrode, J., Cole, R., & Tatelbaum, R. (1999). Prenatal and infancy home visitation by nurses: Recent findings. *Future of Children, 9*(1), 44-65.

Peters, S. D., Wyatt, G. E., & Finkelhor, D. (1986). Prevalence. In D. Finkelhor (Ed.), *A sourcebook on child sexual abuse* (pp. 15-59). Beverly Hills, CA: Sage.

Plummer, C. (1984, July). *Preventing sexual abuse: What in-school programs teach children.* Paper presented at the Second National Conference on Family Violence, University of New Hampshire.

Polit, D., & White, C. (1988). *The lives of young, disadvantaged mothers: The five year follow-up of the project redirection sample.* Saratoga Springs, NY: Human Analysis.

Quint, J. C., Polit, D. F., Bos, H., & Cave, G. (1994). *New chance: Interim findings on a comprehensive program for disadvantaged young mothers and their children.* New York: Manpower Demonstration Research Corporation.

Ramey, C., & Ramey, S. (1998). Early intervention and early experience. *American Psychologist, 53*(2), 109-120.

Reppucci, N., & Haugaard, J. (1989). Prevention of child sexual abuse: Myth or reality? *American Psychologist, 44*(10), 1266-1275.

Rodriguez, G., & Cortez, C. (1988). The evaluation experience of the Avanc, Parent-Child Education Program. In H. Weiss & F. Jacobs (Eds.), *Evaluating family programs* (pp. 287-302). New York: Aldine.

Sampson, R., Raudenbush, S., & Earls, F. (1997). Neighborhoods and violent crime: A multilevel study of collective efficacy. *Science, 277*, 918-924.

Schorr, L. (1997). *Common purpose: Strengthening families and neighborhoods to rebuild America.* New York: Anchor.

Schorr, L., & Schorr, D. (1985). *Within our reach.* New York: Anchor/Doubleday.

Sedlak, A., & Broadhurst, D. (1996). *Third national incidence study of child abuse and neglect (NIS-3): Executive summary.* Washington, DC: U.S. Department of Health and Human Services, ACYF, NCCAN.

Seitz, V., Rosenbaum, L. K., & Apfel, N. H. (1985). Effects of family support intervention: A ten-year follow-up. *Child Development, 56*, 376-391.

St. Pierre, R. G., Layzer, J. I., Goodson, B. D., & Bernstein, L. S. (1997). *National impact evaluation of the Comprehensive Child Development Program: Final report.* Cambridge, MA: Abt Associates.

St. Pierre, R. G., Swartz, J., Gamse, B., Murray, S., Deck, D., & Nickel, P. (1995). *National evaluation of the comprehensive child development program: Interim report.* Cambridge, MA: Abt Associates.

Swan, H., Press, A., & Briggs, S. (1985). Child sexual abuse prevention: Does it work? *Child Welfare, 64,* 395-405.

U.S. Department of Health and Human Services, U.S. Advisory Board on Child Abuse and Neglect. (1990). *Child abuse and neglect: Critical first steps in response to a national emergency.* Washington, DC: Government Printing Office.

U.S. Department of Health and Human Services, U.S. Advisory Board on Child Abuse and Neglect. (1991). *Creating caring communities: Blueprint for an effective federal policy for child abuse and neglect.* Washington, DC: Government Printing Office.

U.S. Department of Health and Human Services, U.S. Advisory Board on Child Abuse and Neglect. (1993). *The continuing child protection emergency: A challenge to the nation.* Washington, DC: Government Printing Office.

Videka-Sherman, L. (1989, October). *Therapeutic issues for physical and emotional child abuse and neglect: Implications for longitudinal research.* Paper presented at a research forum titled "Issues in the longitudinal study of child maltreatment," Institute for the Prevention of Child Abuse, Toronto, Canada.

Wagner, M., & Clayton, S. (1999). The Parents as Teachers program: Results from two demonstrations. *Future of Children, 9*(1), 91-115.

Wasik, B. H., Bryant, D. M., & Lyons, C. M. (1990). *Home visiting: Procedures for helping families.* Newbury Park, CA: Sage.

Weiss, C. (1995). Nothing as practical as good theory: Exploring theory-based evaluation for comprehensive community initiatives for children and families. In J. Connell, A. Kubisch, L. Schorr, & C. Weiss (Eds.), *New approaches to evaluating community initiatives: Concepts, methods and contexts* (pp. 65-92). Washington, DC: Aspen Institute.

Wieder, S., Poisson, S., Lourie, R., & Greenspan, S. (1988). Enduring gains: A five-year follow-up report on the Clinical Infant Development Program. *Zero to Three, 8*(4), 6-11.

Willis, D., Holden, E. W., & Rosenberg, M. (Eds.). (1992). *Prevention of child maltreatment: Developmental and ecological perspectives.* New York: John Wiley.

Wolfe, D. (1994). The role of intervention and treatment services in the prevention of child abuse and neglect. In G. Melton & F. Berry (Eds.), *Protecting children from abuse and neglect: Foundations for a new national strategy* (pp. 224-303). New York: Guilford.

Wolfe, D., Edwards, B., Manion, I., & Koverola, C. (1988). Early intervention for parents at risk of child abuse and neglect: A preliminary investigation. *Journal of Consulting and Clinical Psychology, 56*(1), 40-47.

Woods, S., & Dean, K. (1986). *Community-based options for maltreatment prevention: Augmenting self-sufficiency.* Prepared under contract to the U.S. Department of Health and Human Services, National Center on Child Abuse and Neglect.

Wurtele, S., & Miller-Perrin, C. (1992). *Preventing child sexual abuse: Sharing the responsibility.* Lincoln: University of Nebraska Press.

Young, B., Liddell, T., Pecot, J., Siegenthaler, M., & Yamagishi, M. (1987). *Preschool sexual abuse prevention project: Executive summary.* Report prepared under a research grant funded by the U.S. Department of Heath and Human Services, Office of Human Development Services, Washington, DC.

Zero to Three. (1999). *Home visiting: Reaching babies and families "where they live."* Washington, DC: Author.

Preventing and Reporting Abuse

GAIL L. ZELLMAN

C. CHRISTINE FAIR

The incidence and prevalence of child maltreatment are continuing concerns for those who advocate for children, those who provide services, and those who make funding and other relevant policies. And, as with other social problems that occur behind closed doors and often in families, determining the incidence and prevalence of child maltreatment is a difficult task.

A number of sources have been tapped to yield incidence and prevalence figures; as we shall see, each is flawed in its own way, and jointly the picture remains clouded. Official reports, which are mandated under state laws, provide an important national source of incidence and prevalence data. Their aggregation was facilitated by a provision of the Child Abuse Prevention Adoption and Family Service Act of 1988 (P.L. 100-294), which required the National Cen-

ter on Child Abuse and Neglect (NCCAN) to establish a national data collection and analysis program on child maltreatment.[1]

Large, rigorous incidence studies funded by the federal government track cases and estimate the percentage that result in formal reports. Findings from these studies indicate that many cases do not eventuate in formal reports. Such findings emphasize the need for studies of would-be reporters who are required because of their professional position to report suspected maltreatment to appropriate authorities. Such studies validate the widespread failures to report found in the incidence studies and suggest the importance of a final type of prevalence indicator—surveys of adults about their experiences with maltreatment, either as perpetrators or as victims.

This chapter presents findings from each of these very different indicators and attempts to integrate their findings. Because officially reported cases have the clearest implications for the child protective system, we focus particularly on several important issues related to outcomes for officially reported cases.

History of Reporting Laws

Concerns about child maltreatment in the 1960s revivified an issue that had disappeared from the public policy agenda some 40 years before (Gordon, 1988). An article published in 1962 by Dr. C. Henry Kempe and his associates (Kempe, Silverman, Steele, Droegemueller, & Silver, 1962) at the University of Colorado Medical Center marked the beginning of modern interest in child maltreatment.

Their paper argued that much of the accidental injury seen by pediatricians was in fact the result of intentional abuse. Kempe et al. (1962) relied on radiographic evidence of fractures in various stages of healing (e.g., Caffey, 1957, cited in Williams, 1983, p. 240) to shatter the widely held belief that abuse of children was a practice of the past (Williams, 1983, p. 240). By labeling the phenomenon the *battered child syndrome,* the paper convinced people that child maltreatment was a "disease" that could afflict anyone (Pleck, 1987, p. 172). The focus on physical abuse implied in the use of radiographic evidence served as well to reframe the meaning of child maltreatment: Long associated with neglect arising out of or in concert with poverty, physical abuse seemed far less tied to social class.

Kempe et al.'s (1962) arguments found an immediate and responsive audience. In an era marked by a growing concern for individual rights, increased sensitivity to injustice, and a belief that government had the means and the obligation to improve the prospects of individuals and families, the paper stimulated a tremendous response in both professional and lay media.

This response was different from earlier ones. The older "cruelty" model of child maltreatment viewed perpetrating parents as miscreants; their crimes invoked criminal sanctions under cruelty laws. The reframing of child maltreatment as a medical condition implied more humane treatment. The battered child syndrome accorded parents greater compassion, care, and treatment by helping professionals and implied the possibility of a "cure." A number of agencies organized to make this response.

In 1962, Dr. Kempe discussed the battered child syndrome at meetings held by the U.S. Children's Bureau, which had become interested in child abuse as a natural extension of its mission (Nelson, 1984). One product of these meetings was a model child abuse statute requiring certain types of persons to report known cases of child abuse and neglect to social services agencies (Nelson, 1984). Soon thereafter, the American Humane Association, the American Medical Association, and the Council of State Governments developed their own model statutes (Fraser, 1986).

The motivation for these laws was simple: Protection and services could be provided only when cases of child maltreatment became known. Reporting laws would provide the incentive to make such identification. The medicalizing of child maltreatment pointed to physicians as the obvious group to bring such cases to light. Physicians possessed expert skill and judgment, and they saw injured children regularly. The model laws would require physicians to report cases of suspected maltreatment. Statutory provisions would free them of any civil or criminal liability for doing so (Paulsen, Parker, & Adelman, 1966).

Implicit in the identification focus of the model laws was the assumption that child abuse only had to be identified to be "cured." Moreover, it was assumed that very few "cures" would be required: Child abuse, although serious, was believed to be rare. These two assumptions contributed to the unprecedented support garnered for the reporting legislation. Legislators in every state saw the reporting laws as an opportunity to demonstrate "no-cost rectitude" (Nelson, 1984, p. 75). No one thought at that time that the reporting laws would become a driving force for the expansion of child welfare services (Nelson, 1984).

No legislation in the history of the United States had been so widely adopted in so little time. Within a 5-year span, every state had passed a child abuse reporting law, which required specified professionals likely to come in contact with children in the course of their work to report suspected maltreatment to child protective agencies. The framers of these laws, not unmindful of the ignorance, denial, and confidentiality concerns that had made such laws necessary, devised a number of provisions designed to remove legal impediments to reporting. These provisions included statutory immunity for good-faith reporting, abolition of doctor-patient privilege in situations of suspected maltreatment, language that required only reasonable suspicion or belief and that precluded investigation on the part of the reporting professional, anonymity provisions for reporters in some states, and assessment of criminal or civil penalties for failure to report as required by law (Davidson, 1988).

As knowledge and understanding of child maltreatment increased over time, it became evident that professionals other than physicians also might be in a position to identify maltreatment. Indeed, the framers of reporting legislation became aware that members of other professions might be able to detect maltreatment and bring it to the attention of authorities at an earlier juncture—before the occurrence of the severe injuries that often brought abuse to the attention of physicians (Fraser, 1986).

These new understandings led to a substantial increase in the number of professional groups designated in state laws as mandated reporters. In 1974, for example, all state reporting laws mandated physicians to report suspected abuse and neglect, but only 25 states required social workers to report, and only 9 states required that police officers do so. By 1986, virtually every state included nurses, social workers, other mental health professionals, teachers, and school staff in the category of mandated reporters (Fraser, 1986).

The expansion of the ranks of mandated reporters was accompanied by a broadening of the concept of reportable maltreatment in the 1970s to include sexual abuse, emotional maltreatment, and neglect. Both of these changes were strongly influenced by the Child Abuse Prevention and Treatment Act (CAPTA) (P.L. 93-247) passed in 1974. In addition to the establishment of the National Center on Child Abuse and Neglect, CAPTA included a small state grant program. To obtain a grant, a state had to meet specified eligibility requirements. Key were

the establishment of procedures for reporting and investigating child abuse reports and the assurance of treatment availability. These provisions speeded the creation of specialized child protective services (CPS) agencies and gave state child welfare agencies the power to remove a child if investigation suggested that the child was in danger (Pleck, 1987).

Impact of Laws on Identification of Maltreatment

The reporting laws clearly succeeded in encouraging the identification of abuse and neglect. The reporting rate—10.1 per 1,000 children in 1976—had climbed to 45.0 by 1992. More than 2 million reports were made in 1987, representing a 225% increase since 1976, when 669,000 reports were estimated to have been received.[2] In 1993, almost 3 million reports of suspected maltreatment were received by state agencies (Daro & McCurdy, 1994). Beginning in the mid-1990s, the number of reports gradually declined in many states (Jones & Finkelhor, 2001). Reports of child sexual abuse declined 26% from 1991 to 1998. Among victims of substantiated or indicated reports collected from state sources by NCCAN (1993), neglect was the most frequently reported kind of maltreatment. Forty-four percent of these children suffered deprivation of necessities. Physical injury accounted for 24% of all substantiated or indicated cases reported in that year; the figure for sexual abuse was 15%. Emotional maltreatment accounted for 6% of these cases; other maltreatment accounted for 11% of children (NCCAN, 1993). The relative rankings of types of abuse have not changed in recent years.

Reporting laws clearly succeeded in encouraging the identification of abuse and neglect.

As a direct result of reporting statutes, medical and mental health professionals, school staff, police, and other mandated reporters have reported suspected incidents of abuse to official agencies in growing numbers. Since 1984, professionals have accounted for the majority (mean = 53%) of reports (American Humane Association, 1988; NCCAN, 1993).

Recent data reveal that among professional reporters, school personnel were responsible for the largest number of reports (30% of all reports from professional sources). Law enforcement accounted for 22% of reports made by professionals. Medical personnel and social services workers accounted for 20% and 24% of reports, respectively. Child care providers accounted for the remaining 4% of reports made by professionals (American Humane Association, 1988; NCCAN, 1993). Again, these figures have changed little in recent years.

Impact of Laws on Protective Agencies

The success of the reporting laws created substantial and unanticipated problems for the protective agencies designated to receive those reports. Most simply lacked the capacity to respond adequately to a large share of the cases that flooded in. As Newberger (1983) notes, "No one could have foreseen that the prevalence of child abuse, however narrowly defined, was far greater than was believed at the time of the publication of the 'Battered Child Syndrome' paper or the signing of Public Law 93-247" (p. 308).

As idealists succeeded in expanding both the definition of child abuse and the numbers of professional groups required to make reports, the inability of protective agencies to respond occasioned a crisis. As the optimism of the 1960s and 1970s faded and government support for CPS programs failed to keep pace with increasing numbers of reports, the ability of CPS agencies to materially assist children and families identified through child abuse reports was called into question.

Observers and actors from all points on the political spectrum began to worry publicly about the state of CPS. Agencies were forced to cope with unmanageable caseloads by defining maltreatment more narrowly, screening out less severe reports, and setting priorities that precluded the provision of help to large numbers of children and families (Kamerman & Kahn, 1990; Rose, Talbert, & Sullivan, 1993; Zellman & Antler, 1990).

Professional Compliance With Reporting Laws

Although the number of reports increased dramatically, a sure sense that not all professionals were meeting the reporting mandate continued, and not all of even the most serious cases of child maltreatment were being reported. Such failures to report suspected maltreatment undermine the child abuse reporting system and its ability to help children in need of protection in many ways. Most important, failure to report may deny children in need of protection any opportunity to receive it. This is particularly true when the abuse is severe and the harm imminent.

Widespread violation of the reporting mandate reduces wholehearted professional support for it and may undermine the credibility of professionals in the eyes of the public (Kalichman, 1999). It is impossible for professionals to endorse fully to the public and to other professionals a law that many have knowingly violated (Finkelhor & Zellman, 1991). In addition, widespread failure to report actually may punish those professionals who do make reports by driving people who wish to avoid being reported to professionals known to violate the reporting law.

Failure to report also exposes professionals to anxiety and liability. Nevertheless, some knowledgeable professionals take this risk when they believe that a report threatens their relationship with a child and when they are fairly certain that the report will not result in any benefit to the child or the family, as discussed below.

Finally, cases handled covertly and outside the system do not come into the data collection process. Unreported cases distort the aggregate picture of child abuse and may reduce funding and policy support for children in need.

A number of studies using different methods consistently have confirmed widespread concerns that mandated reporter compliance with the reporting laws is far from complete (e.g., Bensen, Swann, O'Toole, & Turbet, 1991; Finkelhor, Gomes-Schwartz, & Horowitz, 1984; James, Womack, & Stauss, 1978; Kalichman & Brosig, 1993; Kalichman, Craig, & Follingstad, 1990; Morris, Johnson, & Clasen, 1985; Saulsbury & Campbell, 1985). Two studies in particular, described in detail below, address this important issue and provide national data concerning the degree of compliance with the reporting mandate and the reasons that professionals may not report.

National Incidence Studies

The National Incidence Studies of Child Abuse and Neglect (NIS) collect comprehensive data on the current incidence of child abuse and neglect in the United States. The NIS is a congressionally mandated effort conducted under the auspices of the NCCAN. To date, there have been three surveys. The first, the NIS-1, was conducted in 1979 and 1980 as mandated under Public Law (P.L.) 93-247. This effort was followed by the NIS-2, which was conducted in 1986 and 1987, as called for by P.L. 98-457. Finally, the NIS-3 was conducted in 1993 and 1995, as mandated under P.L. 100-294.

Each of the three studies employs similar methodologies to yield comparable national estimates of the incidence of child abuse and neglect. The consistent methodology also permits analysis of how the severity, frequency, and character of child maltreatment have changed across the study years (Sedlak & Broadhurst, 1996).

Each survey is based on a nationally representative sample of counties from all regions of the country, which vary in terms of degree of urbanization. Community professionals in the sampled counties reported cases of child maltreatment to the study from their positions in schools, hospitals, police departments, juvenile probation, and other child-serving agencies. CPS provided information about all reported cases accepted for investigation during the study period. Participating professionals at other agencies served as "sentinels," looking for and reporting to the study cases of maltreatment that met the study's definitions (Sedlak, 1991; Sedlak & Broadhurst, 1996).

One of the substantial contributions of the NIS methodology is the imposition of specific definitional standards. Such a uniform standard mitigates some of the problems in assessing prevalence and incidence that result from the variation across states in definitions of abuse and neglect. All cases included in the NIS studies have been screened by project staff so that only those cases that conform to specific definitional standards are countable toward incidence

estimates. Moreover, efforts are made to minimize duplicated cases that may arise in the event that the same maltreatment event was reported by more than one source (Sedlak & Broadhurst, 1996). This also represents a significant advance over efforts to aggregate state-level reports, few of which are unduplicated.

Another important contribution of the NIS is the promulgation of workable definitions of maltreatment. In the NIS-1, the "harm standard" requirement was developed and stringently employed. To be included under this standard, the child had to have experienced demonstrable harm from maltreatment. In both the NIS-2 and NIS-3, a broader, more inclusive standard was developed and employed, the "endangerment standard." This standard includes all of those cases that are countable under the harm standard but also includes those children who have not yet been harmed as a result of maltreatment, provided that, in the opinion of the community professional or CPS agency, the experienced maltreatment puts them at risk for harm. Although only the stricter standard was used in the NIS-1, both the NIS-2 and NIS-3 measures are employed to assess maltreatment incidence. Thus, we have 3 years of data based on the harm standard across which to compare and 2 years for the endangerment standard (Sedlak & Broadhurst, 1996).

The NIS methodology is based on a model that depicts five levels of official recognition or public awareness of maltreatment:

1. Children reported to CPS.
2. Children not known to CPS but who are known to other "investigatory" agencies, such as police, courts, or public health departments. Although such children are known officially, they are not necessarily known as maltreated.
3. Maltreated children who are not known to CPS or to any investigatory agency but who have been recognized as maltreated by professionals in other major community institutions, such as schools, hospitals, day care centers, and social services agencies.
4. Maltreated children known to people in the community, such as neighbors or other family members; these people have not reported the maltreatment to any agency.
5. Children whose maltreatment has not been recognized by anyone.

TABLE 22.1 Percentage of Cases Investigated Under the Harm and Endangerment Standards

	NIS-3: 1993	NIS-2: 1986	NIS-1: 1980
All maltreatment under the harm standard	28	44[a]	33
All maltreatment under the endangerment standard	33	51[a]	NA

SOURCE: Adapted from Sedlak and Broadhurst (1996, Table 7-5 and Table 7-6).
NOTE: NA = not available.
a. The difference from the NIS-3 estimate is statistically significant at the $p < .5$ level.

The NIS surveys collected data relevant to Levels 1 through 3 using both of the maltreatment definitions described above.

Another unique contribution of the NIS studies is their ability to determine what proportion of cases known to professionals in non-CPS agencies were investigated by CPS. Thus, these data illuminate professional reporting practices, particularly compliance with the reporting laws. One serious limitation of these data is that it is not clear whether a case was not investigated by CPS because the case was not known to CPS or because CPS concluded that the case did not merit investigation. Thus, the analysis of these data focuses on cases *investigated* by CPS rather than cases *known* to CPS.

In Table 22.1, we present data on the percentage of cases known to professionals in a non-CPS agency that were investigated by CPS. Findings under the harm standard appear for all three surveys; findings using the broader endangerment standard are presented for the NIS-2 and NIS-3.

As is apparent in Table 22.1, under both standards, CPS generally investigated fewer than 50% of the countable cases known to non-CPS professionals or agencies. CPS investigated more than half (51%) of these cases only in 1986, under the endangerment standard.

The data in Table 22.1 also demonstrate that in 1993, under both standards, CPS investigated a smaller percentage of cases than in previous surveys. The decline from 44% in 1986 to 28% in 1993 under the harm standard was statistically significant; the decline from 33% in 1980 under the same standard was not. Under the endangerment standard, the decline from 51% in 1986 to 33% in 1993 was statistically significant as well.

One interesting finding in the NIS-3 (Sedlak & Broadhurst, 1996) is that although the percentage of cases investigated by CPS under the harm standard declined from the previous study, the incidence of cases investigated was nearly equivalent to the NIS-2 level (roughly 6.5 children per 1,000). The decrease in the percentage of cases investigated may be attributed to the large increase in the numbers of children who fit the harm standard. Thus, overall, although CPS investigated more children in the 1993 survey than it did in either of the two previous ones, it is clear that CPS has not been able to keep up with the growth in cases as defined by the harm standard.

Similarly, under the endangerment standard, although the percentage of cases investigated declined between the NIS-2 and NIS-3 studies, the incidence of children whose maltreatment was investigated by CPS actually increased from 11.6 children per 1,000 to 13.7 per 1,000.

In Table 22.2, we present data on the sources recognizing maltreated children under the harm standard in the three studies. In all years, noninvestigatory agencies, including schools, hospitals, social services, and mental health agencies, recognized many more child victims than did investigatory agencies such as probation departments, courts, and law enforcement. According to Sedlak and Broadhurst (1996), in 1993, police/sheriff agencies, hospitals, and mental health agencies had the highest proportion of cases reported to cases investigated by CPS (45%, 40%, and 39%, respectively) under the harm standard. Rates for other agencies were far lower (Sedlak & Broadhurst, 1996).

The percentage of reports investigated by CPS differed significantly between NIS-3 and NIS-2. For example, in the NIS-2, under the harm standard, 100% of the cases known to hospitals were investigated by CPS, and 82% and 78% of the cases known to mental health agencies and law enforcement agencies, respectively, were investigated. The NIS-3 results more closely resemble those for the NIS-1; 56% of the cases known to hospitals were investigated, as were 31% and 42% of cases known by mental health agencies and law enforcement agencies, respectively (Sedlak & Broadhurst, 1996).

TABLE 22.2 Sources Recognizing Children Maltreated Under the Harm Standard

Source	NIS-3: 1993		NIS-2: 1986		NIS-1: 1980	
	Total Number of Children	Rate Per 1,000 Children	Total Number of Children	Rate Per 1,000 Children	Total Number of Children	Rate Per 1,000 Children
Investigatory agencies						
Juvenile probation	36,600	0.5	44,100	0.7	41,600	0.7
Police/sheriff	111,500	1.7	76,100	1.2	52,100	0.8[a]
Public health	27,500	0.4	26,100	0.4	8,900	0.1[a]
Investigatory agencies total	175,600	2.6	146,300	2.3	102,500	1.6[a]
Noninvestigatory agencies						
Hospitals	113,200	1.7	32,700	0.5[a]	35,300	0.6[a]
Schools	920,000	13.7	507,400	8.1[a]	348,300	5.5[a]
Day care centers	59,700	0.9	24,300	0.4	NA	NA
Mental health agencies	50,900	0.8	13,400	0.2[b]	27,900	0.4
Social service agencies	96,000	1.4	77,000	1.2[a]	21,500	0.3[a]
Noninvestigatory agencies total	1,239,800	18.5	654,700	10.4[a]	433,100	6.8[a]

SOURCE: Adapted from Sedlak and Broadhurst (1996, Table 7-1).
NOTE: NA = not available.
a. Result is statistically significant from the NIS-3 finding at the $p < .5$ level.
b. Result is statistically significant at the $10 > p > .5$ level.

It is not entirely clear what conclusions should be drawn from the differences in proportions across these various types of agencies. There is some evidence that CPS agencies have tightened substantiation standards since 1980; some cases that would have been accepted for investigation in 1980 would not be pursued in subsequent years (see Ards & Harrell, 1993, for further discussion). The impact of such changes may differ across agencies. For example, if an agency tends to report milder abuse (e.g., schools), more restrictive substantiation standards might disproportionately affect the proportion of cases investigated by CPS. Conversely, institutions that tend to report more severe cases (e.g., hospitals, law enforcement agencies) might be less affected by changes in substantiation criteria.

Despite ambiguities with regard to some of the data, NIS findings in all years clearly show that most children who are recognized as abused or neglected by mandated reporters do not enter the CPS report base. Most cases of suspected maltreatment known to professionals are not reported or investigated. With support from NCCAN, Zellman and her colleagues undertook a national survey of mandated reporters to understand why.

Mandated Reporter Study

Professionals in 15 states, sampled from directories of their various professional organizations, were mailed a questionnaire in the spring of 1987 that surveyed their reporting behavior and the nature of their professional work. At the very beginning of the survey form, each respondent read and responded to five vignettes, each of which briefly described a case of possible abuse or neglect. The vignettes provided common stimuli across respondents and permitted the exploration of the independent contributions of case characteristics to intended reporting and to other decisions that bear on reporting intentions.

A total of 1,196 general and family practitioners, pediatricians, child psychiatrists, clinical psychologists, social workers, public school principals, and heads of child care centers responded to the survey (59% response rate).

Reporting behavior. More than three fourths of respondents (77%) indicated that they had made a child abuse report at some time in their professional career. Rates of ever reporting varied considerably by profession. Nearly all elementary school principals had reported at some time (92%). Rates of ever reporting were nearly as high for child psychiatrists (90%) and pediatricians (89%). Rates for secondary school principals, social workers, and clinical psychologists were 84%, 70%, and 63%, respectively. The majority of these reporters (56%) had made a report in the past year. Reporting rates in the past year by profession followed a pattern similar to that for ever reporting.

Failure to report. Almost 40% of respondents admitted that at some time in their career they had suspected abuse or neglect but had decided not to make a report. There were substantial differences across professional groups in failure-to-report (FTR) rates, with child psychiatrists most likely to have failed to report (58%) and child care providers and pediatricians least likely to have done so (24% and 30%, respectively). The majority of respondents (56%) who had ever failed to report had done so at least once in the past year, suggesting that failure to report was not simply an artifact of the lack of awareness about the reporting mandate that characterized the reporting environment as recently as 10 or 15 years ago.

Patterns of reporting behavior. To provide a clearer picture of reporting behavior, two variables that measured lifetime reporting behavior were combined into a single variable with four categories that described the respondents' reporting history: (a) never reported and never failed to report (outside system), (b) reported at least once and never failed to report (consistent reporting), (c) reported at least once and failed to report at least once (discretionary reporting), and (d) never reported but failed to report at least once (consistent failure to report). The most common lifetime reporting pattern in our sample was consistent reporting, which is what the law requires. Forty-four percent of respondents indicated that they had reported at some time and had never failed to do so when they suspected maltreatment. The second most common pattern was discretionary reporting. One third of the sample fell into this category. Seventeen percent had neither reported nor failed to report and thus remained outside the child abuse reporting system. Finally, 6% of respondents

had a lifetime pattern that included no reporting but at least one instance of FTR.

Reasons for making reports. Those respondents who had ever reported rated the importance of a series of reasons for doing so. Ninety-two percent indicated that stopping maltreatment was a very important reason for past reporting; 89% indicated that getting help for the family was a very important motivator. The reporting law was cited as a strong reason for past reporting by 71%. Differences across professions revealed that family/general practitioners were less influenced by the reporting mandate and were less likely to cite workplace reporting policy as an important motivator for reports, in part because of their tendency to practice in private group or solo settings. Child psychiatrists and psychologists were less likely to believe that a report would help the child or family, help the family see the seriousness of the problem, or stop maltreatment. They were least likely of all professional groups to rate "bringing CPS expertise to bear" as an important reason for past reporting.

Analysis of the vignette data reveals additional factors that enter into professionals' reporting decisions (Zellman, 1992).[3] Respondents were significantly more likely to intend a report in cases of serious abuse (e.g., when there were physical injuries or intercourse had occurred), when the child was young rather than an adolescent, and when there was a history of previous maltreatment. When a teenager recanted an allegation of physical or sexual abuse after confrontation by an adult, respondents were significantly less likely to intend a report, despite growing awareness that recantation is not uncommon in sexually abused children and should not be taken at face value (Summit, 1983). Many of these findings have been confirmed in later studies. O'Toole, O'Toole, Webster, and Lucal (1994) and Crenshaw, Crenshaw, and Lichtenberg (1995) also found that severity of abuse was an important factor in decisions to report. Hansen et al. (1997), employing a vignette analysis, also found that vignettes of younger children are more likely to raise suspicion and precipitate reporting than those depicting older children.

Reasons for Failing to Report

Using factor analysis, we identified three clusters of reasons for failure to report. One cluster, which we labeled "bad for me," focuses on the perceived costs of reporting to the reporter. A second cluster, "I can do better than the system," includes a range of criticisms of CPS agencies *and* respondent beliefs that he or she could do more for the child than CPS could. The third cluster, "not reportable," includes a number of evidence-based reasons for not reporting.

Table 22.3 indicates levels of support by profession for several reasons from each of the three clusters. Reasons in the "not reportable" category were endorsed most commonly; reasons in the "bad for me" category received limited support. The most frequently endorsed reason for failing to report was a lack of sufficient evidence that maltreatment had occurred. This finding is consistent with the work of Delaronde, King, Bendel, and Reece (2000), who found that insufficient evidence and lack of certainty were the predominant motivation not to report among mandated reporters in their study. One third of respondents ascribed great importance to their judgment that the maltreatment that they suspected or had observed was not serious enough to report, a result also found by Ashton (1999).

Nineteen percent considered the fact that a report would disrupt treatment to be an important reason for not having reported suspected maltreatment. A similar percentage ascribed considerable importance to the belief that they could help the child better themselves. Sixteen percent considered the poor quality of CPS services an important reason for not having reported.

The levels of endorsement of these reasons for FTR provide some important insights into how mandated professionals view the reporting laws. Reporting laws ask professionals to be reasonably vigilant and to report their suspicions or beliefs that maltreatment has occurred or is occurring. The laws are clear that no more is required. Indeed, professionals are precluded explicitly from conducting any further investigation, a prohibition reinforced by the short latency period before a report is required (Maney & Wells, 1988). Furthermore, they are not to exercise professional discretion in choosing which cases to report. The laws are mute regarding the efficacy of making reports, but it is clear in the prohibitions on professional discretion that the potential benefits of reports are not to be considered in the reporting decision.

These data reveal, however, that issues of efficacy are of considerable concern to would-be reporters. As noted earlier, a common reporting pattern among mandated reporters is discretionary reporting—reporting in some instances and deciding not to report in others. Indeed, discretionary reporters accounted for four fifths of all those who admitted having ever failed to report.

Discretionary reporters did not lack knowledge and experience. Unlike consistent nonreporters, who tended to have little child abuse training and limited child abuse knowledge, discretionary reporters were just as knowledgeable about and just as well trained in child abuse as the consistent reporters, a finding supported in subsequent work (e.g., Kalichman & Brosig, 1993). Discretionary reporters also expressed more confidence than other reporters in their own ability to treat child abuse. Moreover, the discretionary reporters were more likely than even consistent reporters to indicate that they served as their agency's child abuse resource person.

The most frequently endorsed reason for failing to report was a lack of sufficient evidence that maltreatment had occurred.

What most distinguished discretionary reporters from other groups was their negative opinion of the professionalism and capability of CPS staff and their beliefs that reports often had negative consequences for the children involved (Finkelhor & Zellman, 1991). Their experience and attitudes led them to conclude that it was better for the child not to make a report in some cases. These cases often involved mild abuse or neglect that they knew would not receive adequate attention from overburdened CPS staff. At the same time, such reports would risk termination of treatment and loss of the opportunity to continue to monitor the family and perhaps provide the support or education that might reduce the likelihood of further maltreatment.

Perceived efficacy was a significant contributor to reporting intentions. When respondents believed that the child would be unlikely to benefit from a report, they were significantly less likely to intend to make one (Zellman, 1990). Despite the fact that the usefulness of an intended report is raised only rarely in law or training, would-be re-

TABLE 22.3 Ratings of Reasons for Failing to Report by Those Who Had Ever Failed to Report by Profession (in percentages)

Reasons for Failure to Report	PROFESSIONAL GROUP								
	Family/General Practitioners (n = 34)	Pediatricians (n = 90)	Child Psychiatrists (n = 54)	Clinical Psychologists (n = 75)	Social Workers (n = 100)	Child Care Providers (n = 28)	Elementary Principals (n = 61)	Secondary Principals (n = 40)	Total Sample (N = 482)
Bad for me									
Reports take too much time	2.9	2.3	0.0	0.0	1.0	4.2	1.6	0.0	1.2
Fear of lawsuit for reporting	0.0	2.3	1.7	2.7	3.0	9.5	1.6	2.4	2.5
Discomfort with family	0.0	3.4	0.0	1.4	2.0	15.0	5.1	0.0	2.6
I can do better									
CPS overreacts to reports	5.9	11.5	7.1	12.2	12.0	4.8	0.0	8.0	8.0
CPS services are of poor quality	9.1	11.6	23.2	19.2	22.5	10.0	8.2	7.3	15.5
Could help the child better myself	2.9	18.4	21.1	24.0	29.1	14.8	13.3	10.0	19.3
Treatment was already accepted	12.1	16.3	33.3	32.9	40.2	5.3	6.7	20.0	24.2
Report would disrupt treatment	11.8	20.7	28.1	23.2	27.5	4.8	8.6	2.4	19.0
Not reportable									
Lacked sufficient evidence that abuse has occurred	67.6	63.6	57.9	55.1	49.5	76.0	59.7	73.8	59.9
Abuse or neglect not serious enough to report	25.7	35.6	38.6	28.4	36.3	28.0	37.3	27.5	33.4
Situation resolved itself	18.2	19.3	10.7	21.3	29.3	26.1	13.6	20.0	20.3
Case already reported	18.2	21.8	35.1	16.0	22.0	9.5	11.7	24.4	20.7

NOTE: Sample numbers reflect the exclusion of respondents who indicated that they had never failed to report. Cell entries represent the mean percentage of professionals in the specified group who rated the reason as "very important" in their decisions not to report suspected abuse or neglect.

458

porters clearly consider it when they decide whether to report suspected maltreatment.

Protective system incapacity increases concerns about the usefulness of reports. When the protective system becomes increasingly burdened as agency budgets fail to keep pace with reports, attention needs to be paid to this issue, as we do below.

Victim and Offender Disclosure of Maltreatment

Gathering information about maltreatment and its disclosure directly from the persons involved represents another way to learn about the extent of the problem. Population surveys have two particular advantages. First, they provide information about cases that may not come to professional attention. Second, they yield better data than incidence studies about the extent and effects of child abuse (Peters, Wyatt, & Finkelhor, 1986).

Most prevalence studies involve surveys of adults who are asked about victimization during their childhood. These may be studies of volunteers, community samples, or special populations (e.g., college students). There are far fewer surveys of offenders. Most of this research focuses on sexual abuse, although there are some important findings regarding physical abuse as well. The little work that investigates neglect and emotional maltreatment generally does so with clinical populations.

Prevalence of Physical Abuse

Research that addresses the prevalence of physical abuse examines both the use of violence by parents and victimization experiences of special populations—specifically, college students and health care professionals. Prevalence data are also available from state reports to the National Child Abuse and Neglect Data System.

Straus and colleagues (Gelles & Straus, 1988; Straus, Gelles, & Steinmetz, 1978) investigated rates of parental violence in national samples of adults in two-parent families in two surveys 10 years apart. Parents were asked about their use of tactics for resolving conflicts with their children, ranging from nonabusive to severely abusive. Conflict tactics characterized as "severe violence" and thus physically abusive included kicking, biting, punching, hitting or trying to hit the child with an object, beating up, threatening with a gun or knife, and using a gun or knife.

In 1975, 14% of 1,428 parents reported using severe violence, and in 1985, 11% of 1,146 parents did so. The difference in these two rates is small but statistically significant. The researchers have argued that this represents a decrease in parental abuse of children over the decade. An alternative explanation posits that differences in methodology and changes in reporting norms account for the decrease in rate. In the first study, data were collected using face-to-face interviews and in the second using telephone interviews. Moreover, adverse publicity about child abuse may have discouraged disclosure by parents by the time of the second survey.

Three studies that questioned college students about being abused as children (Graziano & Namaste, 1990; Henschel, Briere, & Morlau-Magallanes, 1990; Wiemers & Petretic-Jackson, 1991) focused on spankings, observable injury, and physical abuse. Findings suggest that the vast majority of the study populations experienced spankings, and 10% to 20% were victims of behaviors that we now would label physical abuse.

Nuttall and Jackson (1994) surveyed 646 health care professionals (169 social workers, 128 pediatricians, 176 psychologists, and 173 psychiatrists) about their own abuse victimization during childhood. Among their findings was that 7.1% reported physical abuse as children. Psychiatrists reported significantly lower rates of physical abuse than did the other three disciplines.

Every year, child maltreatment prevalence estimates are published from the National Child Abuse and Neglect Data System. These data are compiled through both an annual survey that asks states to report relevant statistics and case-level data collection efforts. According to *Child Maltreatment 1998* (U.S. Department of Health and Human Services [DHHS], 2000), the rate for physically abused children was 1.9 per thousand in 1998. This represented a considerable decline from 1990, when the comparable rate was 3.5 per thousand. Because of differences in policy, law, and stage of implementation of state reporting systems, these data may not be entirely accurate estimates of prevalence. Readers are referred to Appendix F of the report for more detail or cross-state differences in reporting of these data.

Prevalence of Sexual Abuse

No researcher has directly questioned adults in nonclinical populations about their sexual abuse *of* children. However, Briere and Runtz (1989) surveyed college males about their sexual attraction to children and reported that 21% endorsed items indicating such arousal.

In contrast, the number of studies of victims of sexual abuse is considerable. The findings from these studies are quite varied. This variability derives from methodological differences in the various studies—specifically, definitions of sexual abuse, the number and structure of questions about sexual abuse, data collection strategies, populations studied, and sample selection. All of these influence prevalence rates. As might be expected, the broader the definition, the higher the rates of sexual abuse. Studies that focus largely on sexual abuse and ask more questions about it yield more disclosures. Face-to-face interviews, as opposed to telephone surveys or questionnaires, tend to result in increased rates, as do studies of "high-risk" populations, such as psychiatric patients, convicted felons, prostitutes, and abusive parents. Finally, higher proportions of females than males report sexual victimization.[4]

The rates for male sexual victimization range from as low as 3% when a single question about sexual abuse or forced sexual contact is asked (Burnam, 1985, personal communication, as cited in Finkelhor, 1986; Kercher & McShane, 1984; Murphy, 1987) to 30% in a survey of college students, using a nonspecific definition (Landis, 1956). Of particular interest is a study by Risin and Koss (1987) involving 2,972 male college students who were asked about their sexual experiences before age 14. The importance of this study is not so much its prevalence rate (7.3%) but its finding that close to half of the offenders were females and that almost 40% of the men reported that they did not feel victimized by the experience.

Prevalence rates across studies vary more dramatically for women. The study with the lowest rate involved 1,623 women, interviewed face-to-face by nonprofessional interviewers about issues of mental health. They were asked a single question about

sexual assault prior to age 16; 6% indicated they had been assaulted (Burnam, 1985, personal communication, as cited in Finkelhor, 1986). The highest rate is reported by Wyatt in a study of 248 women focusing on their sexual experiences and using a broad definition of sexual abuse (Wyatt, 1985). Sixty-two percent of respondents reported sexual victimization; this figure was 45% when only contact behavior was considered. Wyatt's research involved face-to-face extended interviews, and the interviewers were matched with respondents on gender and race.

A larger study than Wyatt's, conducted about the same time with similar methodology and a slightly more restricted definition, yielded similar results (Russell, 1983, 1986). Fifty-four percent of 930 San Francisco–area women reported being sexually abused before age 18; this figure was 35% when only contact behavior was considered.

Data on sexual abuse of women come from two surveys by Saunders and colleagues (Saunders et al., 1991; Saunders, Villeponteaux, Lipovsky, Kilpatrick, & Veronen, 1993). Both employed the same broad definition of sexual abuse but differed in data collection methods. One involved a representative national sample surveyed by trained female telephone interviewers. The second was a probability sample of women in Charleston County, South Carolina, interviewed face-to-face by trained female research assistants. The 4,008 (weighted) respondents in the national study reported a rate of child sexual abuse of 13.3%. In contrast, the 391 women in the Charleston study reported a rate of 33.5%.

A survey conducted by Vogeltanz et al. (1999) on a national sample of women used a highly structured format and trained female interviewers. The authors found prevalence rates for childhood sexual abuse that ranged from 15% to 32%, depending on whether a broader or narrower definition was applied. A survey of women in Los Angeles County that compared prevalence rates with those from a 1984 data set found that 34% of the contemporary sample reported at least one incident of sexual abuse before age 18; this figure was comparable to the prevalence rate in the 1984 data set (Wyatt, Loeb, Solis, & Carmona, 1999). This lack of change over time is consistent with the findings of Feldman et al. (1991), who reviewed the Kinsey Report and 19 prevalence studies conducted in the 1980s. They found that prevalence rates in more recent studies with the strongest methodology were similar to those of Kinsey in the 1940s; 10% to 12% of girls younger than age 14 had been victimized.

Prevalence data about sexual abuse are also reported by the above-noted National Child Abuse and Neglect Data System. According to *Child Maltreatment 1998* (U.S. DHHS, 2000), in 1998, the rate for sexual abuse was 1.6 per thousand, compared with 2.3 per thousand in 1990.

The Relationship of Victim and Offender Reports to Official Reports

An important but not extensively studied issue is the relationship between estimates of the prevalence of maltreatment derived from victims and offenders in response to surveys and those derived from official reports. Limited data illuminate this issue.

Some prevalence researchers have asked respondents whether their cases were ever reported. Russell (1986), who, as noted earlier, surveyed 930 women in the San Francisco area, obtained 648 disclosures of child sexual abuse. Of these, respondents indicated that only 30 cases (5%) were ever reported to the police. Saunders and colleagues (Saunders et al., 1991; Saunders et al., 1993) asked participants in both the Charleston, South Carolina, community survey and the national survey of adult women whether their sexual abuse was ever reported to the police or to other authorities. In the former study, only 5.7% of the 139 incidents described to researchers were ever reported. The proportion was a little higher for the national study: 12% of the 699 sexual assaults. But these data are less than illuminating in terms of reporting rates because many of the incidents described probably occurred before the advent of the mandatory reporting laws. In addition, victim studies usually ask about abuse during childhood, as opposed to, for example, abuse during a given year, which might more readily allow comparisons with official reporting data.

However, Straus and his colleagues (Gelles & Straus, 1988; Straus et al., 1978) asked in their surveys of parents not only if they had *ever* used severe violence tactics with their children but whether they had done so during the *previous year.* They found that when data from that same year were compared, the rates reported by parents were 50% higher than official estimates from NCCAN. Moreover, the authors contend that these parental reports are themselves underestimates, because parents may not remember or reveal abuse. They conclude that if parents reported *all* abuse, these rates would be two to three times higher than the 3.6% of parents surveyed in 1975 who reported using severe violence during the previous year and the 1.9% making such disclosures in 1985 (Gelles & Straus, 1988, p. 104).

Thus, both victim and offender surveys suggest that most abuse does not come to the attention of officials. Moreover, many researchers, including Straus and colleagues (e.g., Gelles & Straus, 1988; Peters et al., 1986), regard findings from general population prevalence surveys to be underestimates because respondents may be unwilling to disclose maltreatment, may not remember, or may not view these events as abuse. These findings indicate that failure to report by mandated professionals, as revealed by the National Incidence Studies and the Mandated Reporter Study, is not the only reason child maltreatment cases elude official identification and intervention.

When Should I Report?

If you are a mandated reporter, you are obligated to report suspected maltreatment when you encounter it in the course of carrying out your professional obligations. Although the language of the reporting statute varies slightly from state to state, the child abuse reporting laws require that a report be made when you have "cause to believe" or "reasonable cause to believe" that child maltreatment is occurring or may have occurred or that a child is at risk of such victimization. You do not need to *know* that maltreatment has occurred, but your suspicions should be "reasonable." The standard is a "reasonable professional" standard, meaning that the suspicion should be reasonable based on your professional training and experience. A member of the general public might not be suspicious when you are; the best comparison group is your own colleagues.

As Myers (1998) notes, the duty to report does not require the professional to be certain that abuse or neglect has occurred. Indeed, the reporting laws clearly divide responsibilities for identification and investigation between mandated reporters and CPS, with mandated reporters responsible only for identification. This limited responsibility is structured into the reporting laws by the short time frame permitted between the time maltreatment is first suspected and a report must be made. Often, mandated reporters are required to make a report within a specified period.

But what is *reasonable* suspicion? The law is of limited help in answering this question. As discussed earlier, the reporting laws were written to cast a wide net so that children would be protected from maltreatment and social welfare agencies would be alerted to situations in which maltreatment might be occurring *before* obvious injury occurred.

The flood of reports that the laws precipitated, as well as the inability of CPS to keep up, has led some reporters to tighten up their own standards for making a report. Indeed, Zellman (1990) found that some mandated reporters decide not to report cases that they believe should be reported under the law because they know from experience that CPS will be unlikely to respond with services. In such cases, professionals sometimes decide that through frequent contact with the family, they will be able to educate and guide the parents away from maltreatment and keep watch over the child.

As noted earlier, your colleagues' views form the standard of what is reasonable. Consequently, consulting with one or more colleagues is often the best way to answer that question (Deisz, Doueck, & George, 1996; Kalichman, 1999). Some professional organizations are attempting to address these concerns for professionals. Recently, for example, the Committee on Child Abuse and Neglect of the American Academy of Pediatrics updated its 1991 guidelines for physicians (American Academy of Pediatrics, 1999). These guidelines specifically address the evaluation of suspected cases of child sexual abuse. The guidelines also provide guidance on obtaining histories, interviewing children, and performing physical exams and laboratory data collection. These guidelines encourage physicians to seek consultation from child abuse consultants or local agencies.

Yet, your colleagues' views may not be consistent or definitive. Deisz et al. (1996) found substantial variation among the therapists in their study in the way in which they interpreted the "reasonable cause" standard. Some reported "inklings" to CPS; others reported only when the evidence convinced

them that a report needed to be made. Kalichman and Brosig (1993) found that most psychologists considered disclosure of abuse or apparent physical signs, such as bruises, to meet the reasonable cause standard; far fewer relied on behavioral indicators alone.

But what should you do when you begin to have an "inkling"? Although investigation is precluded, Kalichman (1999) urges mandated reporters to pursue reasonable questions consistent with their own professional duties. Make sure you really understand the situation. Be very aware of your own goals and how they mesh with those of CPS. For example, some reports are made because a child and family are perceived by the mandated reporter to need help, and the mandated reporter hopes CPS will provide it. But absent significant indicators of maltreatment, the family will probably not receive help through this approach. The time and effort involved in making a report might be better spent networking a family into other services (Zellman, 1990). Know your own state's law, and seek training on reporting procedures. If you decide a report is in order, present the situation as precisely as possible. CPS fails to investigate many reports due to imprecise or missing information (Wells, Stein, Fluke, & Downing, 1989). If you decide the situation currently does not meet your own reporting standard, continue to monitor the situation in case things take a turn for the worse. For further discussion of reporting, see Chapter 20, this volume.

Case Management and Disposition After Reporting

The purpose of child abuse reports is to bring potential abuse to the attention of CPS and to precipitate some CPS response when appropriate. The type and intensity of that response depend on the characteristics of the report and on the receiving agency's approach to organizing, classifying, and deploying its resources.

The nature of the reporting mandate and the state of child welfare services result in the receipt of some reports outside the CPS mandate. Because mandated reporters must act only on "reasonable suspicions" or "reasonable beliefs," some reports may be found not to constitute child maltreatment. Insufficient staffing of child welfare services in many communities has caused some reports that might have been accepted to be screened out (Wells, 1987). Such practices increase the number of uninvestigated or unsubstantiated reports. Given demand for investigation and services that far outstrips available resources, CPS must act to preserve and allocate these resources appropriately. Gatekeeping activities help CPS agencies do this. Gatekeeping in CPS agencies takes place at three points: the decision to investigate a report, the decision to substantiate a report after investigation, and the decision to provide agency service (Wells, 1987).

Screening is the first gatekeeping point. It occurs when a report is received; its final outcome is a decision about whether to conduct an official investigation. The decision to investigate hinges on whether a report of suspected maltreatment that the agency has received is determined to be a "valid report of abuse or neglect" (Wells, 1987, p. 2). This determination is a function of law, agency policies and procedures, local conditions, and practice (Wells, 1987, p. 2).

Screening serves several purposes for CPS agencies. First, screening is a tool to reduce investigative caseloads to a point that at least approaches, if not matches, available resources (Zellman & Antler, 1990). If the number of reports increases and agency budgets do not increase accordingly, caseload management approaches take on increased urgency (Downing, Wells, & Fluke, 1990).

Second, screening may identify non-abusive families who are in need of support and preventive services; CPS can make referrals to agencies that can provide those services. As Wells et al. (1989) note, many reports to CPS may be made in the belief that child welfare services are accessible only through an allegation of maltreatment. Often, reports motivated for this reason are unfounded on investigation. If screening occurs prior to investigation, nonabusive families in need of services may be referred without the potential stigma of an investigation to an agency that can provide needed services, although the availability of such services is far from certain.

Third, screening may help CPS agencies to manage caseloads and deploy limited investigational staff and resources to those cases in which the threat of harm is greatest. This third purpose is problematic for many: A triage approach to investigation institu-

tionalizes the movement of CPS agencies away from the preventive goals that motivated the expansion of the reporting laws to include additional mandated reporter groups (Wells et al., 1989). Others applaud this more limited purview. Besharov (1988), for example, argues that because our ability to predict future danger to the child is so limited, agencies are best advised to focus resources on cases in which harm already has occurred or past parental behavior could have been harmful. This approach avoids the subjectivity implicit in responding to "threatened harm."

All jurisdictions are required to investigate all bona fide reports (Van Voorhis & Gilbert, 1998). This stance complies with the federal statute that requires all reports of child abuse and neglect to be investigated (P.L. 93-247). Nevertheless, the screening function is implicit in most of the reporting laws. Some laws circumscribe the investigatory responsibility of CPS through their definitions of maltreatment. For example, most states limit investigatory responsibility to reports of children age 18 and younger by defining child maltreatment as something that occurs only to those in this age group. The identity and role of the alleged perpetrator vis-à-vis the child often figure into definitions of maltreatment as well. In most states, the alleged perpetrator must be a caretaker; in some states, alleged maltreatment in out-of-home care is explicitly a matter for the police rather than for CPS. In at least one state, the level of seriousness of the allegations figures into the definition of child abuse. Reports in which alleged physical or mental injury is not serious are not subject to investigation because nonserious injuries are not defined as child maltreatment (Wells, 1987).

In some states, complaints from reporters who refuse to give their name need not be investigated.

Other legislative criteria may permit CPS not to investigate. For example, in some states, complaints from reporters who refuse to give their name need not be investigated (Wells, 1987). Complaints may be rejected if the same person has made three previous unfounded reports concerning the same child and alleged perpetrator (Wells et al.,

1989). Policies permit screen-out on the basis of incomplete information, outdated reports, absence of a specific incident or pattern of incidents, and "inappropriate referrals" (Wells, 1987, p. 6). Indeed, Wells's analysis of 45 state policies revealed that more than two thirds appear to allow some screening (Wells, 1987). Such widespread acknowledgment and acceptance of screening contrast with the lack of discussion or permission to screen in the state reporting laws.

Other empirical data confirm the prevalence of screening policies. In a survey of CPS administrators and intake supervisors in 100 local agencies in eight states, respondents revealed to Downing et al. (1990) that most agencies have written policies that delimit the nature of reports considered appropriate for investigation. At least half of each group reported that the policy permitted screen-outs when the alleged perpetrator was not a caregiver or when the complaint concerned the parents' behavior (e.g., parental drug use with no specific act of abuse or neglect alleged). Another common reason for screening out complaints is that the problem reported is not appropriate for CPS and is better handled by another agency. Alleged school truancy, failure to provide medical care, and a mother's psychiatric problems were examples frequently cited in this latter category.

Some state policies prohibit screening: All reports are to be investigated. Zellman and Antler (1990) found, however, that even when screening is not permitted, it may occur by default. Using formal or informal risk assessment tools, cases are assigned to be investigated urgently, immediately, or as soon as possible. Because of the press of new, more emergent cases, those cases in the last, least serious category may never be investigated at all.

California data confirm that de facto screening is rampant. Van Voorhis and Gilbert (1998) cite several studies in which the percentage of reports that were investigated was well under 100%. In one county, 53.7% of official child abuse reports were closed after the initial telephone intake. Of these, 40% did not meet legal definitions of maltreatment, but 60% were screened out because of insufficient evidence, a judgment that the child was not in immediate danger, or because of information that the police were already involved (Barth, Courtney, Needell, & Jonson-Reid, 1994; Gilbert, Karski, & Frame, 1996).

Although an agency's intent may be to respond to all reported cases, prioritization or risk assessment schemes may screen out the lowest-priority cases effectively (Wells, 1987). The danger in this, notes Giovannoni (1989), is that the ability to predict risk is "in its infancy"; therefore, screen-outs based on risk are ill advised at this time.

Given the reality that screening does occur, many argue that the process should be formalized and regulated (e.g., Barone, Adams, & Tooman, 1981). Besharov (1988) urges child protective agencies to develop policies that specify the kinds of reports that will be accepted for investigation. Daniel, Newberger, Reed, and Kotelchuck (1978) note that the use of screening tests focuses program efforts on high-risk populations and is thus a useful approach. Screening would be more acceptable if there were links to other services, so that screened-out cases might be referred elsewhere, as appropriate. This approach seems particularly important given evidence that families that teachers described as near but below their own reporting threshold were found to be troubled; reported cases would likely be more so (Gracia, 1995). But, as Wells (1987) notes, unless agencies have limitless funding, they cannot serve every child whose life is troubled or traumatic. Consequently, CPS can and should limit definitions of abuse and neglect.

Classification of Cases After Investigation

CPS ultimately must determine whether reports of suspected abuse and neglect describe valid maltreatment. The purpose of the investigation is to make this determination. Whether CPS will intervene in the family, refer to another agency for voluntary services, or withdraw completely depends on whether the investigation process determines that maltreatment has occurred.

The labels applied to this determination vary by child protection agency. The terms *substantiation, founded,* and *indicated* all describe similar but not identical decisions. Essentially, the decision following investigation is whether to process the case further into the system. "Substantiated" cases are opened for service after investigation; "unsubstantiated" cases are closed (Giovannoni, 1989).

The Substantiation Decision

States require a report to be substantiated with either "some credible evidence" or a sufficient reason to conclude that the child has been abused or neglected. Involuntary court-ordered services can be imposed, but state laws require either a "preponderance of the evidence" or "clear and convincing evidence" that maltreatment has occurred (Besharov, 1988, p. 9).

Unsubstantiated cases indicate only that CPS has decided to take no further action after investigation. "Unsubstantiated" is not synonymous with "false report" (Giovannoni, 1989). Cases may be unsubstantiated for a variety of reasons. Many of the reasons (e.g., inability to locate the address) are unrelated to the validity of the case. The many reasons for failure to substantiate are important to keep in mind because substantiation rates have become a source of controversy, as discussed below.

Giovannoni (1989) argues that cases dismissed after investigation without further CPS involvement should be described using three categories:

- No maltreatment or other evidence of family dysfunction found
- No maltreatment found, but some evidence of family dysfunction or need for service found
- Maltreatment found, but further CPS activity not indicated

The use of such categories would clarify what sorts of cases CPS is not pursuing and why. These data also would focus attention on an important group of cases—those in which service needs exist in the absence of maltreatment. Such cases should but rarely do receive social welfare services (e.g., Besharov, 1994). New approaches to structuring the system, discussed below, have been proposed to enable nonabusive families in need of help to receive social welfare services.

A limited number of studies have attempted to understand the process of making substantiation decisions. The studies have relied on a range of methodologies, including case review, interviews with decision makers, and responses of CPS workers to case vignettes (Eckenrode, Powers, Doris, Munsch, & Bolger, 1988; Giovannoni, 1989).

Giovannoni (1989) reviewed 1,156 reports made to CPS. Several report variables significantly discriminated between cases that were and were not substantiated on investigation. A higher number of specific incidents of maltreatment alleged in the report were associated with substantiation. The availability of the address of the child and the alleged perpetrator increased the likelihood of a finding of maltreatment. Reports from absent spouses and reports of alleged drug or alcohol abuse by caretakers were less likely to be substantiated on investigation. Finally, reports from schools, law enforcement, and responsible caretakers were more likely to have had some maltreatment on investigation than reports from other sources.

Eckenrode et al. (1988) reviewed a total of 1,974 cases in the New York State Registry, looking for factors that predicted substantiation. Multiple-regression analyses revealed that the source of report, particularly whether the reporter was a professional or not, was a significant predictor of substantiation, with reports from professionals more likely to be substantiated. However, there were some important interactions between source of report and report type. For example, when sexual abuse was alleged by a caretaker mother, the likelihood of substantiation was the same as if the report had been made by a professional. Cases involving court action were more likely to be substantiated. The nature of the investigatory process also influenced substantiation probability, with the number of official contacts with the subjects of the report and the length of the investigation significantly contributing to substantiation probability. However, as Eckenrode et al. note, these process variables may reflect caseworker assessment of risk based on evidence available in the case, which complicates their meaning for the substantiation decision.

Substantiation Rates

The rate at which cases are substantiated is an issue among those concerned with protecting children. Some argue that when large numbers of cases that are investigated are not substantiated, this represents a significant waste of limited CPS resources and poses a significant burden on the families that are investigated. Although there is consensus that some level of failure to substantiate is legitimate in a reporting system that accords mandated reporters no discretion and insists that reports be made on the basis of suspicions only, the amount that will or should be tolerated and the implications of higher rates are in considerable dispute.

Besharov (1986, 1988) has been among those most active in raising these concerns. Relying heavily on data reported by states (e.g., American Humane Association, 1988), he argues that there has been a steady increase in the percentage of "unfounded" reports since 1976 and finds these statistics troubling on several counts.

First, Besharov (1985) argues, investigations are "unavoidably traumatic" (p. 557). Second, conducting investigations of "minor" cases diverts inadequate resources from children in danger of serious maltreatment. These latter cases get more cursory investigation and less intensive supervision than they require because resources are being used to pursue "minor" cases. Third, would-be reporters may decide not to make reports to agencies that they know to be overtaxed.

Besharov (1985) argues that society's overambitious expectations about the ability of social agencies to identify and protect endangered children must be changed. He urges that state action should be limited to situations in which the parents have "already engaged in abusive or neglectful behavior" (p. 580) or done something that was capable of causing serious injury—in short, limited to situations in which seriously harmful behavior has occurred. These narrowed definitions should be accompanied by increased screening authority in CPS agencies. Implementation of rigorous screening policies by experienced caseworkers would reduce the number of investigations initiated, raise the substantiation rate, and help more families receive services on a voluntary basis.

The other side of this political coin is probably best represented by David Finkelhor (1990). He notes that the American Humane Association and state-level data that Besharov (1985) cites as evidence of declining substantiation rates are rife with methodological problems that make estimates difficult at best. Citing the methodologically far more rigorous NIS data, which indicate that substantiation rates significantly increased (from 43% in 1980 to 53% in 1986), Finkelhor suggests that substantiation rates may be largely unchanged over time or actually may be increasing.

More important, he argues, the very different ways that substantiation rates are measured over jurisdictions and over time render these measures inappropriate bases for policy decisions. Revised definitions or screening policies can change reported substantiation rates in the absence of any other change.

Finkelhor (1990) makes a larger and more significant point about substantiation as well. He notes that the U.S. public repeatedly has demonstrated its willingness to tolerate some considerable inefficiency and intrusion in the pursuit of important policy goals. He points to the criminal justice system as an example of a system that demonstrates considerable inefficiency, with only about half of all arrests leading to convictions. Yet public opinion polls repeatedly indicate that Americans want more—not fewer—people arrested. And limited studies suggest that the mandated reporters who must interact with CPS most frequently, although sometimes frustrated with CPS (Zellman & Antler, 1990), are not totally dissatisfied (Compaan, Doueck, & Levine, 1997). Even those families who are the subjects of maltreatment investigations seem to understand the need for such activity. For example, Fryer, Bross, Krugman, Denson, and Baird (1990) conducted a consumer satisfaction survey of parents who had been investigated by CPS. The majority (more than 70%) rated the quality of services as excellent or good and felt that their family was better off as a result of CPS involvement.

Reasons for Failure to Substantiate

Politicization of substantiation statistics obscures a complex process that is not well understood. There are many reasons why reports of child maltreatment are not substantiated; little research has been conducted on this issue. Major studies that produce substantiation rates (e.g., American Humane Association, 1988; Sedlak, 1991) provide no data concerning reasons for lack of substantiation. Clinical data and anecdotal information suggest a range of reasons why cases that are investigated are not substantiated.

Insufficient information. Many cases are not substantiated because there is insufficient information to make a determination about child maltreatment. In a substantial number of these cases, no contact is ever made with the family; most often this happens when families cannot be located. However, cases also may not be investigated because the allegations are too vague or no injury was reported (Finkelhor, 1990).

Cases also are denied after investigation because of insufficient information. Without clear-cut medical or other physical evidence, firsthand observations of home conditions or neglectful behavior, or a credible eyewitness, the CPS worker may not have enough information to conclude that the child has been maltreated, or it may not be possible to know whether the parent is responsible for the child's condition.

Data from one of the few studies that examined reasons for failing to substantiate (Jones & McGraw, 1987) revealed that 24% of the 576 sexual abuse cases examined were unfounded because of insufficient information.

Inappropriate referral. A case may be classified as unsubstantiated because the referral was not an appropriate one. A substantial number of these cases are in fact cases of child maltreatment. The referral may be inappropriate for jurisdictional reasons. For example, the maltreatment occurred in one county, but the victim resides in another. A case may be denied because the parties are not subject to the child protection act. Children may be too young or too old. Reports on unborn children or those older than age 16 may not be substantiated. Cases involving juvenile offenders or adults who are not the alleged victim's primary caretaker may be considered inappropriate referrals. A case may be denied because services already are being received. These include cases subject to duplicate report (Finkelhor, 1990), new reports on already open cases, cases already receiving service from another agency, and cases already active in court (e.g., divorce court). In addition, some states only classify cases as substantiated if protective action is taken in the juvenile court (Finkelhor, 1990).

The problem does not constitute child maltreatment. Two kinds of cases fall into this category: those in which the cause of the child's condition is not maltreatment and those in which the problem is a resource issue.

Designated professionals are mandated to report cases when they have "reasonable cause to suspect" child maltreatment. CPS investigation may determine that the suspicion was warranted but the child's problem was not caused by maltreatment. For example, an injury may be determined to have resulted from an accidental fall.

The failure of social and welfare services to keep pace with reports has resulted in both inappropriate referrals and inappropriate denials. In the first instance, there has been increased use of CPS reports to address problems that really do not constitute child maltreatment—for example, situations involving severely impaired children. Similarly, a family problem may be characterized as maltreatment in hopes that CPS will provide the family services that are not available elsewhere in the community.

In the second instance, scarce resources within CPS and increased referrals have led to a higher threshold for opening cases. CPS may decide that the standard of care in the family meets "minimum sufficient level," even though other community professionals and certainly the mandated reporter may perceive neglect (Johnson, 1993). Cases in which there is a risk of maltreatment, but no maltreatment has been found on investigation, also may be denied.

Because of scarce resources, some CPS agencies tend to substantiate only when the maltreatment is severe enough to warrant removal of the child. Intensive, short-term, home-based services to prevent placement of children in foster care may reverse this pattern.

Because of scarce resources, some CPS agencies tend to substantiate only when the maltreatment is severe enough to warrant removal of the child.

Child no longer at risk. Several types of cases are not substantiated because the child is deemed no longer at risk. These include cases in which maltreatment occurred too long ago (Finkelhor, 1990), family circumstances have changed, and the maltreatment is deemed minor and not likely to recur.

False allegations. Despite widespread concern about false allegations, little empirical data exist concerning them. Almost all of the available research on false allegations has been conducted on sexual abuse cases. These studies confront a range of difficult methodological problems, including defining and validating the falsity of reports and determining whether the reporter has made a knowingly false report.

False allegations appear to be rare (Faller, 1988; Goodwin, Sahd, & Rada, 1979; Horowitz, Salt, Gomes-Schwartz, & Sauzier, 1984; Jones & McGraw, 1987). Jones and McGraw (1987) concluded that such reports represented only 6% of the sexual abuse cases that they examined. State data collected by NCCAN (1993) suggest that the number of intentionally false reports is very low. The percentage of intentionally filed false reports was less than 1% of all reports. However, with only four states reporting in this category, these data must be considered with caution.

False allegations are more likely to be made by adults than children. Jones and McGraw (1987) determined that only 1% of their reports represented false accounts by children. The comparable figure reported by Oates et al. (2000) was 2.5%. But of their 14 cases in this category, only 8 (1.5% of the sample) involved a fabricated allegation that was made independent of parental coaching or collusion. When children make intentionally false accusations, they are usually older children (Faller, 1988; Horowitz et al., 1984; Jones & McGraw, 1987; Olds et al., 2000).

False allegations appear to be more common surrounding divorce than in other contexts. However, even in divorce cases, between 50% and 75% of allegations of maltreatment appear to be valid (Faller, 1991; Faller, Corwin, & Olafson, 1993; Green, 1986; Thoennes & Tjaden, 1991). Those who report higher rates of false allegations either present no data (Blush & Ross, 1986; Gardner, 1989) or rely on small, biased samples (Benedek & Schetky, 1985; Green, 1986; Kaplan & Kaplan, 1981). Moreover, most of these authors do not differentiate between cases involving calculated lies and those in which parents' mental functioning led to a false accusation.

Even in divorce situations, calculated false allegations appear to be rare. Thoennes and Tjaden (1991), in a sample of 9,000 divorces from 12 states with disputed custody or visitation, found that 169 (less than 2%) involved child sexual abuse allegations, and only 8 were judged to be knowing lies. Faller (1991), using a clinical sample of 136 sexual

abuse allegations in divorce, found only 3 cases that were judged to be calculated lies.

Proposals to Improve CPS Operations

A range of approaches have been suggested to improve CPS's handling of reports and allocation of limited resources. These include the implementation of risk assessment systems, closer coordination between mandated reporters and CPS regarding substantiation criteria, modifications to the reporting process, and restructuring of services to families in need. Each of these approaches is discussed briefly below.

Risk assessment systems. Risk assessment systems (RAS) are "formalized methods that provide a uniform structure and criteria for determining risk" (Baird, Wagner, Healy, & Miles, 1999, p. 724) and are designed to help CPS workers decide what to do with a family at the conclusion of a maltreatment investigation. Key to these decisions is an assessment of risk of future harm (Baird et al., 1999). These decisions are inherently difficult to make, and the consequences of a wrong decision can be catastrophic. RAS incorporate empirical data on case outcomes and direct the decision-making process to help workers more accurately estimate risk. As individual workers presumably improve their ability to assess risk, RAS should reduce variations in decisions across workers, which vary greatly, even among experts (Rossi, Schuerman, & Budde, 1996).

RAS are relatively new. A 1996 American Public Welfare Association survey revealed that of 44 responding states and jurisdictions, 38 had some RAS in place; 26 had first been implemented after 1987 (Tatara, 1996). RAS are largely untested. One reason is that assessment of RAS requires longitudinal research, in which families are followed to determine whether the RAS predictions proved accurate (Baird et al., 1999). However, a large body of research in psychology and corrections finds that decision making based on empirical data and actuarial predictions can more accurately predict future behavior than clinical assessments alone (e.g., Dawes, Faust, & Meehl, 1989; Meehl, 1954; Sawyer, 1966), a conclusion that applied as well to Baird et al.'s

(1999) comparison of clinical and actuarial decision making in CPS.

RAS are not a panacea either. DePanfilis (1996) notes considerable questioning of the empirical basis for many of these systems and discusses at length the inadequate and inconsistent implementation of these models in CPS agencies. Brissett-Chapman (1997) argues that the "simplistic linear models" incorporated in RAS poorly serve minority families, as they fail to account for individual, family, and community assets in minority communities.

Closer coordination between CPS and mandated reporters. Many argue that, along with informing professionals about their responsibility to report suspected maltreatment, training sessions also should include information about what levels of maltreatment constitute abuse that is likely to be acted on by CPS (e.g., that CPS is less likely to respond to reports from mental health professionals who rely solely on the child's behavior) (Deisz et al., 1996). Mandated reporters should be acquainted with decision-making models and assessment tools used by CPS (Ashton, 1999). This way, training would not necessarily increase the number of reports but would likely increase the percentage of pursuable ones. Zellman (1990) argues that feedback from CPS to reporters on individual cases would serve a similar purpose. Such feedback also might increase professionals' sense that their reports would benefit the child or family, a key factor in reporting intentions (Zellman & Bell, 1990).

Kalichman and Brosig (1992) and Giovannoni (1989) warn that such efforts could be misdirected. Although clearer decision rules would likely increase substantiation rates, this might well occur at the cost of missing cases of maltreatment. Asking would-be reporters to use categories such as "serious" may inappropriately transfer some of the investigative function from CPS to them (Giovannoni, 1989).

Modifications to the reporting process. Finkelhor and Zellman (1991) suggest that some level of professional discretion be built formally into the reporting system. They argue for the creation of a category of registered reporters, who by dint of their previous reporting history and child maltreatment expertise are accorded carefully bounded discretion in their reporting behavior. As Thompson-Cooper, Fugere, and Cormier (1993) note, Finkelhor and Zell-

man's proposal contains some of the essential elements of the "confidential doctor" system operating in the Netherlands since 1971 (Marneffe & Bruce, 1997; Roelofs & Baartman, 1997). Under this system, there is no reporting mandate, and in most cases, no child protection measures are imposed. Instead, once a notification is made, a trusted professional meets with those involved with the family to determine whether abuse has in fact taken place. According to Thompson-Cooper et al. (1993), the system has resulted in more notifications, including a sharp rise in the number of parents and children applying for help. At the same time, the number of removals of children from their homes has dropped.

There has been limited study of such options in this country. Delaronde et al. (2000) asked mandated reporters whether they preferred the current system or a system in which less severe cases could be referred to a critical intervention specialist who would work with the mandated reporter to determine a strategy for dealing with the case, including coming to a decision about whether a report should be made to CPS. The researchers found slightly more support for the current policy, although those who had ever failed to report preferred the alternative system.

System Restructuring

Under the current system, access to services largely depends on a finding of maltreatment after investigation and a court referral (Van Voorhis & Gilbert, 1998). Several designs have been proposed that seek to unlink the provision of services from the investigatory and coercive aspects of CPS. Pelton (1989, 1992), for example, suggests that CPS be restructured into three agencies with responsibility for family preservation, out-of-house placements, and investigation of maltreatment, respectively. Another approach devolves some or all responsibility for serious cases to the police, leaving the child welfare system to deliver services, in combination with other agencies, to low-risk families (Clark Foundation, 1996; Lindsey, 1994). Delaronde et al. (2000) note that there have been some efforts in this country to create such differentiated systems (e.g., Siegel & Loman, 1998; Zimmerman, 1996) and that early reports are encouraging.

Besharov (1994) argues that significant barriers exist to approaches that increase families' access to social services, either as part of CPS or independent of it, as discussed earlier. These barriers include inertia, a lack of political will to advocate for expensive ongoing services that might prevent more harm, and lack of funds. Bergmann (1994) notes that the contentions of those who claim that we "can't afford" such services often obscure insufficient desire or will:

> The $150-500 billion savings and loan crisis has illuminated the lack of seriousness of the "can't afford" argument against child welfare programs. The public money to make the S&L depositors whole was forthcoming with no debate at all. . . . Until we change our notions of how desirable adequate child welfare programs are, the public purse, which opens so easily and lavishly for other purposes, will not be available for them. (p. 18)

Conclusion

Contemporary concerns about child maltreatment were expressed in the development of model reporting laws in the 1960s, which were adopted rapidly by every state. These laws succeeded in increasing both public awareness of child maltreatment and the number of maltreatment reports.

The success of the reporting laws has created substantial and unanticipated problems for the protective agencies that receive those reports. Most simply have lacked the capacity to respond adequately to a large share of the reports that have flooded in. This reality has resulted in calls to narrow the basis for reporting, increase the amount of screening in CPS agencies, and increase the availability of both protective and other child welfare services.

Although concerns about too many reports recently have dominated discussions of reporting, prevalence studies of victims and offenders indicate that official reports do not reflect the full extent of child maltreatment. In addition, there continues to be a sure sense supported by empirical data that not all professionals are meeting the reporting mandate and not all of even the most serious cases of child maltreatment are reported. The inability of protective agencies to respond to many reports has been implicated as a significant factor in professional decisions to withhold reports.

Few efforts have been made to do more than lament inadequacies in the current system. Proposals to limit reporting (e.g., Besharov, 1985; Hutchison, 1993; Thompson-Cooper et al., 1993) or to increase professional discretion in reporting (e.g., Crenshaw, Bartell, & Lichtenberg, 1994; Finkelhor & Zellman, 1991) are of concern to those who have worked hard to create a system in which individual, idiosyncratic decisions would be replaced by professional, universalistic ones. Proposals to increase the funding and reach of protective agencies have concerned those who worry about unwarranted intrusion into families and have disheartened those who realize that such expansion is very difficult when need exceeds resources. A broader perspective on the delivery of all types of services to needy families that transfers many services from protective agencies back to social welfare agencies might help both families and the systems that attempt to serve them, as Besharov (1994) suggests. But the lack of political will to sell long-term programs with limited outcomes and, to a smaller extent, lack of funds (Bergmann, 1994) reduce the chances of substantial change any time soon.

From a longer historical perspective, however, there is reason for encouragement and self-congratulation. Although some reports do not receive the attention they deserve, and many maltreated children remain unidentified to protective agencies, the reporting laws have brought attention and services to many others. Research aimed at identifying rates of child maltreatment in national and community samples and in special populations has raised public and professional awareness about the pervasiveness of this problem. These studies and requirements for reporting and intervention also have established child maltreatment as an important policy concern that is not likely to be eclipsed in the near future.

Notes

1. The Child Abuse, Domestic Violence, Adoption, and Family Services Act of 1992 (P.L. 102-295) retained the provisions of the 1988 act and also required NCCAN to develop a program that analyzes available state child abuse and neglect reporting information that is, to the extent possible, universal and case specific.

2. The numbers prior to 1976 are even lower but are available for only a limited number of states. American Humane statistics are obtained from state-level CPS programs that voluntarily provide data on officially reported child abuse and neglect. Differences across states in policy, definitions, and information collection procedures limit the comparability of data across states. Moreover, data on specific case measures are not available from many states. The reauthorized Child Abuse Prevention and Treatment Act, now called the Child Abuse, Domestic Violence, Adoption, and Family Services Act of 1992 (P.L. 102-295), mandated collection of state child abuse reports by NCCAN. This mandate, including its technical assistance provision, already has improved the quality of data about reported cases.

3. We were unable to measure reporting behavior in the vignettes but used reporting intentions as a reasonably proxy. Such intentions have been found to be significant predictors of actual behavior in a number of studies across a broad range of behaviors (e.g., Ajzen & Fishbein, 1980; Sheppard, Hartwick, & Warshaw, 1988).

4. For a thorough review of the studies of prevalence of sexual abuse and methodological issues, see Peters et al. (1986).

References

Ajzen, I., & Fishbein, M. (1980). *Understanding attitudes and predicting social behavior.* Englewood Cliffs, NJ: Prentice Hall.

American Academy of Pediatrics, Committee on Child Abuse and Neglect. (1999). Guidelines for the evaluation of sexual abuse of children: Subject review. *Pediatrics, 103,* 187-191.

American Humane Association. (1988). *Highlights of official child neglect and abuse reporting, 1986.* Denver, CO: Author.

Ards, S., & Harrell, A. (1993). Reporting of child maltreatment: A secondary analysis of the national incidence surveys. *Child Abuse & Neglect, 17*(3), 337-344.

Ashton, V. (1999). Worker judgements of seriousness about and reporting of suspected child maltreatment. *Child Abuse & Neglect, 23*(6), 539-548.

Baird, C., Wagner, D., Healy, T., & Miles, M. (1999). Risk assessment in child protective services: Consensus and actuarial model reliability. *Child Welfare, 78*(6), 723-748.

Barone, N., Adams, W., & Tooman, P. (1981). The screening unit: An experimental approach to child protective services. *Child Welfare, 60*(3), 198-204.

Barth, R., Courtney, M., Needell, B., & Jonson-Reid, M. (1994). *Performance indicators for child welfare services in California.* Berkeley: University of California at Berkeley, Child Welfare Research Center.

Benedek, E., & Schetky, D. (1985). Allegations of sexual abuse in child custody and visitation disputes. In E. Benedek & D. Schetky (Eds.), *Emerging issues in child psychiatry and the law* (pp. 145-156). New York: Brunner/Mazel.

Bensen, D., Swann, A., O'Toole, R., & Turbet, J. (1991). Physicians' recognition of and response to child abuse: Northern Ireland and the USA. *Child Abuse & Neglect, 15,* 5-67.

Bergmann, B. (1994, May). *Child care: The key to ending child poverty.* Paper presented at the Conference on Social Policies for Children, Princeton University, Woodrow Wilson School of Public and International Affairs, Princeton, NJ.

Besharov, D. (1985). Doing something about child abuse: The need to narrow the grounds for state intervention. *Harvard Journal of Law & Public Policy, 8*(3), 539-589.

Besharov, D. (1986). Unfounded allegations: A new child abuse problem. *The Public Interest, 83,* 18-33.

Besharov, D. (1988). Child abuse and neglect reporting and investigation: Policy guidelines for decision making. *Family Law Quarterly, 22,* 1-15.

Besharov, D. (1994, May). *Don't call it child abuse if it's really poverty.* Paper presented at the Conference on Social Policies for Children, Princeton University, Woodrow Wilson School of Public and International Affairs, Princeton, NJ.

Blush, G., & Ross, K. (1986). *SAID syndrome: Sexual allegations in divorce.* Unpublished manuscript, Baker College, MI.

Briere, J., & Runtz, M. (1989). University males' sexual interest in children: Predicting potential indices of "pedophilia" in a non-forensic sample. *Child Abuse & Neglect, 13*(1), 65-75.

Brissett-Chapman, S. (1997). Child protection risk assessment and African American children: Cultural ramifications for families and communities. *Child Welfare, 76*(1), 45-63.

Caffey, J. (1957). Some traumatic lesions in growing bones other than fractures and dislocations: Clinical and radiological features, the Mackenzie Davidson Memorial Lecture. *British Journal of Radiology, 30,* 225-238.

Clark Foundation. (1996). *Program for children strategy statement.* New York: Author.

Compaan, C., Doueck, H., & Levine, M. (1997). Mandated reporter satisfaction with child protection: More good news for workers? *Journal of Interpersonal Violence, 12*(6), 847-857.

Crenshaw, W., Bartell, P., & Lichtenberg, J. (1994). Proposed revisions to mandatory reporting laws: An exploratory survey of child protective service agencies. *Child Welfare, 73*(1), 15-27.

Crenshaw, W., Crenshaw, L., & Lichtenberg, J. (1995). When educators confront child abuse: An analysis of the decision to report. *Child Abuse & Neglect, 19*(9), 1095-1133.

Daniel, J., Newberger, E., Reed, R., & Kotelchuck, M. (1978). Child-abuse screening: Implications of the limited predictive power of abuse discriminants from a controlled family study of pediatric social illness. *Child Abuse & Neglect, 2*(4), 247-259.

Daro, D., & McCurdy, K. (1994). *Current trends in child abuse reporting and fatalities: The results of the 1993 annual fifty-state survey.* Chicago: National Committee for the Prevention of Child Abuse.

Davidson, H. (1988). Failure to report child abuse: Legal penalties and emerging issues. In A. Maney & S. Wells (Eds.), *Professional responsibility in protecting children* (pp. 93-103). New York: Praeger.

Dawes, R., Faust, D., & Meehl, P. (1989). Clinical versus actuarial judgment. *Science, 243,* 1668-1674.

Deisz, R., Doueck, H., & George, N. (1996). Reasonable cause: A qualitative study of mandated reporting. *Child Abuse & Neglect, 20*(4), 275-287.

Delaronde, S., King, G., Bendel, R., & Reece, R. (2000). Opinions among mandated reporters toward child maltreatment reporting policies. *Child Abuse & Neglect, 27*(7), 901-910.

DePanfilis, D. (1996). Implementing child mistreatment risk assessment systems: Lessons from theory. *Administration in Social Work, 20*(2), 41-59.

Downing, J., Wells, S., & Fluke, J. (1990). Gatekeeping in child protective services: A survey of screening policies. *Child Welfare, 69*(4), 357-369.

Eckenrode, J., Powers, J., Doris, J., Munsch, J., & Bolger, N. (1988). Substantiation of child abuse and neglect reports. *Journal of Consulting and Clinical Psychology, 56,* 9-16.

Faller, K. C. (1988). *Child sexual abuse: An interdisciplinary manual for diagnosis, case management, and treatment.* New York: Columbia University Press.

Faller, K. C. (1991). Possible explanations for sexual abuse allegations in divorce. *American Journal of Orthopsychiatry, 61*(1), 86-91.

Faller, K. C., Corwin, D., & Olafson, E. (1993). Research on false allegations of sexual abuse in divorce. *APSAC Advisor, 6*(3), 1-10.

Feldman, W., Feldman, E., Goodman, J., McGrath, P., Pless, R., Corsini, L., & Bennett, S. (1991). Is childhood sexual abuse really increasing in prevalence? An analysis of the evidence. *Pediatrics, 88*(1), 29-33.

Finkelhor, D. (1986). *A sourcebook on child sexual abuse.* Beverly Hills, CA: Sage.

Finkelhor, D. (1990, Winter). Is child abuse overreported? *Public Welfare,* pp. 22-29.

Finkelhor, D., Gomes-Schwartz, B., & Horowitz, J. (1984). Professionals' responses. In D. Finkelhor (Ed.), *Child sexual abuse: New theory and research* (pp. 200-220). New York: Free Press.

Finkelhor, D., & Zellman, G. (1991). Flexible reporting options for skilled child abuse professionals. *Child Abuse & Neglect, 15,* 335-341.

Fraser, B. (1986). A glance at the past, a gaze at the present, a glimpse at the future: A critical analysis of the development of child abuse reporting statutes. *Journal of Juvenile Law, 10,* 641-686.

Fryer, G., Bross, D., Krugman, R., Denson, D., & Baird, D. (1990, Winter). Good news for EPS workers. *Public Welfare,* pp. 39-41.

Gardner, R. (1989). Differentiating between bona fide and fabricated allegations of sexual abuse of children. *Journal of the American Academy of Matrimonial Lawyers, 5,* 1-26.

Gelles, R., & Straus, M. (1988). *Intimate violence: The causes and consequences of abuse in the American family.* New York: Simon & Schuster.

Gilbert, N., Karski, R., & Frame, L. (1996). *The emergency response system: Screening and assessment of child abuse reports: A report to the California policy seminar.* Berkeley: University of California at Berkeley, Center for Social Services Research.

Giovannoni, J. (1989). Substantiated and unsubstantiated reports of child maltreatment. *Children and Youth Services Review, 11*(4), 299-318.

Goodwin, J., Sahd, D., & Rada, R. (1979). Incest hoax. In W. Holder (Ed.), *Sexual abuse of children* (pp. 37-46). Denver, CO: American Humane Association.

Gordon, L. (1988). *Heroes of their own lives: The politics and history of family violence.* Boston: Viking.

Gracia, E. (1995). Visible but unreported: A case for the "not serious enough" cases of child maltreatment. *Child Abuse & Neglect, 19*(9), 1083-1093.

Graziano, A., & Namaste, K. (1990). Parental use of physical force in child discipline. *Journal of Interpersonal Violence, 5*(4), 449-453.

Green, A. (1986). True and false allegations of sexual abuse in child custody disputes. *Journal of the American Academy of Child Psychiatry, 25*(4), 449-456.

Hansen, D., Bumby, K., Lundquist, L., Chandler, R., Le, P., & Futa, K. (1997). The influence of case and professional variables on the identification and reporting of child maltreatment: A study of licensed psychologists and certified masters social workers. *Journal of Family Violence, 12*(3), 313-332.

Henschel, D., Briere, J., & Morlau-Magallanes, D. (1990, August). *Multivariate long-term correlates of childhood physical, sexual, and psychological abuse.* Paper presented at the annual meeting of the American Psychological Association, Boston.

Horowitz, J., Salt, P., Gomes-Schwartz, B., & Sauzier, M. (1984). Unconfirmed cases of sexual abuse. In Tufts New England Medical Center (Ed.), *Sexually exploited children* (pp. 231-244). Washington, DC: Office of Juvenile Justice and Delinquency Prevention.

Hutchison, E. (1993). Mandatory reporting laws: Child protective case finding gone awry? *Social Work, 38*(1), 56-63.

James, J., Womack, W., & Stauss, F. (1978). Physician reporting of sexual abuse of children. *Journal of the American Medical Association, 181,* 17-24.

Johnson, C. (1993). Physicians and medical neglect: Variables that affect reporting. *Child Abuse & Neglect, 17,* 605-612.

Jones, D., & McGraw, E. (1987). Reliable and fictitious accounts of sexual abuse to children. *Journal of Interpersonal Violence, 2*(1), 27-45.

Jones, L., & Finkelhor, D. (2001). The decline in child sexual abuse cases. In *Juvenile justice bulletin.* Washington, DC: U.S. Department of Justice, Office of Juvenile Justice and Delinquency Prevention.

Kalichman, S. (1999). *Mandated reporting of suspected child abuse: Ethics, law, and policy* (2nd ed.). Washington, DC: American Psychological Association.

Kalichman, S., & Brosig, C. (1992). Mandatory child abuse reporting laws: Issues and implications for policy. *Law and Policy, 14*(2/3), 153-168.

Kalichman, S., & Brosig, C. (1993). Practicing psychologists' interpretations of and compliance with child abuse reporting laws. *Law and Human Behavior, 17,* 83-93.

Kalichman, S., Craig, M., & Follingstad, D. (1990). Mental health professionals and suspected cases of child abuse: An investigation of factors influencing reporting. *Community Mental Health Journal, 24,* 43-51.

Kamerman, S., & Kahn, A. (1990). If CPS is driving child welfare, where do we go from here? *Public Welfare, 48*(1), 9-13.

Kaplan, S. L., & Kaplan, S. J. (1981). The child's accusation of sexual abuse during a divorce and custody struggle. *Hillside Journal of Clinical Psychiatry, 3,* 81-95.

Kempe, C., Silverman, F., Steele, B., Droegemueller, W., & Silver, H. (1962). The battered child syndrome. *Journal of the American Medical Association, 181,* 17-24.

Kercher, G., & McShane, M. (1984). *The prevalence of child sexual abuse victimization in an adult sample of Texas residents.* Huntsville, TX: Sam Houston State University.

Landis, J. (1956). Experiences of 500 children with adult sexual deviants. *Psychiatric Quarterly Supplement, 30,* 91-109.

Lindsey, D. (1994). *The welfare of children.* New York: Oxford University Press.

Maney, A., & Wells, S. (1988). *Professional responsibilities in protecting children.* New York: Praeger.

Marneffe, C., & Bruce, P. (1997). Belgium: An alternative approach to child abuse reporting and treatment. In N. Gilbert (Ed.), *Combining child abuse: International perspectives and trends* (pp. 167-191). New York: Oxford University Press.

Meehl, P. (1954). *Clinical versus statistical prediction: A theoretical analysis and a review of the evidence.* Minneapolis: University of Minnesota Press.

Morris, J., Johnson, C., & Clasen, M. (1985). To report or not to report: Physicians' attitudes toward discipline and child abuse. *American Journal of Diseases of Children, 139,* 195-197.

Murphy, J. (1987, July). *Reports of sexual abuse in a community sample.* Paper presented at the National Family Violence Research Conference, Durham, NH.

Myers, J. (1998). *Legal issues in child abuse and neglect practice* (2nd ed.). Thousand Oaks, CA: Sage.

National Center on Child Abuse and Neglect (NCCAN). (1993). *National child abuse and neglect data systems* (Working Paper No. 2, 1991 summary data component). Washington, DC: Government Printing Office.

Nelson, B. (1984). *Making an issue of child abuse.* Chicago: University of Chicago Press.

Newberger, E. (1983). The helping hand strikes again: Unintended consequences of child abuse reporting. *Journal of Clinical Child Psychology, 2,* 307-311.

Nuttall, R., & Jackson, H. (1994). Personal history of childhood abuse among clinicians. *Child Abuse & Neglect, 18,* 455-472.

Oates, R. K., Jones, D., Denson, D., Sirotnak, A., Gray, N., & Krugman, R. (2000). Erroneous concerns about child sexual abuse. *Child Abuse & Neglect, 24,* 149-157.

O'Toole, A., O'Toole, R., Webster, S., & Lucal, B. (1994). Nurses' responses to child abuse. *Journal of Interpersonal Violence, 9*(2), 194-206.

Paulsen, M., Parker, G., & Adelman, L. (1966). Child abuse reporting laws: Some legislative history. *George Washington Law Review, 34,* 482-506.

Pelton, L. (1989). *For reasons of poverty: A critical analysis of the public child welfare system in the United States.* New York: Praeger.

Pelton, L. (1992). A functional approach to reorganizing family and child welfare interventions. *Children and Youth Services Review, 14,* 289-303.

Peters, S. D., Wyatt, G. E., & Finkelhor, D. (1986). Prevalence. In D. Finkelhor (Ed.), *A sourcebook on child sexual abuse* (pp. 15-59). Newbury Park, CA: Sage.

Pleck, E. (1987). *Domestic tyranny: The making of social policy against family violence from colonial times to the present.* New York: Oxford University Press.

Risin, L., & Koss, M. (1987). The sexual abuse of boys. *Journal of Interpersonal Violence, 2*(3), 309-323.

Roelofs, M., & Baartman, H. (1997). The Netherlands: Responding to abuse, compassion or control. In N. Gilbert (Ed.), *Combating child abuse: International perspectives and trends* (pp. 192-211). New York: Oxford University Press.

Rose, J., Talbert, W., & Sullivan, P. (1993). Screening, risk assessment, and case planning. In T. Tatara (Ed.), *Sixth national roundtable on CPS risk assessment.* Washington, DC: American Public Welfare Association.

Rossi, P., Schuerman, J., & Budde, S. (1996). *Understanding child maltreatment decisions and those who make them.* Chicago: University of Chicago, Chapin Hall Center for Children.

Russell, D. E. H. (1983). The incidence and prevalence of intrafamilial and extrafamilial sexual abuse of female children. *Child Abuse & Neglect, 7*(2), 133-146.

Russell, D. E. H. (1986). *The secret trauma: Incest in the lives of girls and women.* New York: Basic Books.

Saulsbury, F., & Campbell, R. (1985). Evaluation of child abuse reporting by physicians. *American Journal of Diseases, 139,* 393-395.

Saunders, B., Kilpatrick, D., Lipovsky, J., Resnick, H., Best, C., & Sturgis, E. (1991, March). *Prevalence, case characteristics, and long-term psychological effects of sexual assault: A national survey.* Paper presented at the annual meeting of the American Orthopsychiatric Association, Toronto.

Saunders, B., Villeponteaux, L., Lipovsky, J., Kilpatrick, D., & Veronen, L. (1993). Child sexual abuse as a risk factor for mental disorders among women: A community survey. *Journal of Interpersonal Violence, 7*(2), 189-204.

Sawyer, J. (1966). Measurement and prediction, clinical and statistical. *Psychological Bulletin, 66*(3), 178-200.

Sedlak, A. (1991). *National incidence and prevalence of child abuse and neglect: Revised 1988 report.* Rockville, MD: Westat.

Sedlak, A., & Broadhurst, D. (1996). *Third national incidence study of child abuse and neglect.* Washington, DC: U.S. Department of Health and Human Services.

Sheppard, B., Hartwick, J., & Warshaw, P. (1988). The theory of reasoned action: A meta-analysis of past research with recommendations of modifications and future research. *Journal of Consumer Research, 15,* 325-343.

Siegel, G., & Loman, A. (1998). *Child protection services, family assessment and response demonstration: Impact evaluation.* St. Louis, MO: Institute of Applied Research.

Straus, M., Gelles, R., & Steinmetz, S. (1978). *Behind closed doors.* New York: Free Press.

Summit, R. (1983). The child abuse accommodation syndrome. *Child Abuse & Neglect, 7,* 177-193.

Tatara, T. (1996). *A survey of states on CPS risk assessment practice: Preliminary findings.* Paper presented at the American Public Welfare Association 10th National Roundtable on CPS Risk Assessment, Washington, DC.

Thoennes, N., & Tjaden, P. (1991). The extent, nature, and validity of sexual abuse allegations in custody/visitation disputes. *Child Abuse & Neglect, 14,* 151-163.

Thompson-Cooper, I., Fugere, R., & Cormier, B. (1993). The child abuse reporting laws: An ethical dilemma for professionals. *Canadian Journal of Psychiatry, 38,* 557-562.

U.S. Department of Health and Human Services (DHHS), Administration on Children, Youth and Families. (2000). *Child maltreatment 1998: Reports from the states to the National Child Abuse and Neglect Data System.* Washington, DC: Government Printing Office.

Van Voorhis, R., & Gilbert, N. (1998). The structure and performance of child abuse reporting systems. *Children and Youth Services Review, 20*(3), 207-221.

Vogeltanz, N., Wilsnack, S., Harris, T., Wilsnack, R., Wonderlich, D., & Kristjanson, E. (1999). Prevalence and risk factors for childhood sexual abuse in women: National survey findings. *Child Abuse & Neglect, 23*(6), 579-592.

Wells, S. (1987). *Screening practices in child protective services.* Washington, DC: National Legal Resource Center for Child Advocacy and Protection.

Wells, S., Stein, T., Fluke, J., & Downing, J. (1989). Screening in child protective services. *Social Work, 34*(1), 45-48.

Wiemers, K., & Petretic-Jackson, P. (1991, August). *Defining physical child abuse: Ratings of parental behaviors.* Paper presented at the annual meeting of the American Psychological Association, San Francisco.

Williams, G. (1983). Child protection: A journey into history. *Clinical Child Psychology, 12,* 236-243.

Wyatt, G. (1985). The sexual abuse of Afro-American and white women in childhood. *Child Abuse & Neglect, 9,* 507-519.

Wyatt, G., Loeb, T., Solis, B., & Carmona, J. (1999). The prevalence and circumstances of child sexual abuse: Changes across a decade. *Child Abuse & Neglect, 23*(1), 45-60.

Zellman, G. (1990). Linking schools and social services: The case of child abuse reporting. *Educational Evaluation and Policy Analysis, 12,* 41-56.

Zellman, G. (1992). The impact of case characteristics on child abuse reporting decisions. *Child Abuse & Neglect, 16,* 57-74.

Zellman, G., & Antler, S. (1990). Mandated reporters and child protective agencies: A study in frustration. *Public Welfare, 48*(1), 30-37.

Zellman, G., & Bell, R. (1990). *The role of professional background, case characteristics, and protective agency response in mandated child abuse reporting.* Santa Monica, CA: RAND.

Zimmerman, F. (1996). Community partnerships for protecting children. *Safekeeping, 1*(1), 4-5.

23

Cultural Competency in the Field of Child Maltreatment

VERONICA D. ABNEY

Stolorow and Atwood's (1992) theory of intersubjectivity holds that the individual's subjective world evolves "organically from the person's encounter with the critical formative experiences that constitute his unique life history" (p. 202). These critical formative experiences include not only child maltreatment but also the effects of the culture in which the individual lives.

Culture is a set of beliefs, attitudes, values, and standards of behavior that are passed from one generation to the next. Culture includes language, worldview, dress, food, styles of communication, notions of wellness, healing techniques, child-rearing patterns, and self-identity. Human beings create culture, and each group develops its own over time. Culture is dynamic and changing, not static; it changes as the condition of the people changes and as their interaction with the larger society changes. Every culture has a set of assumptions made up of beliefs that are so completely accepted by the group that they do not need to be stated, questioned, or defended.

Cultural identification has a crucial impact on an individual's response to traumatic stress because of its effect on the organization of experience (Parson, 1985). Therefore, cultural identification must be considered carefully when addressing practice issues in the field of child maltreatment. Cultural identification affects the individual's perception of the trauma, disclosure of the trauma, expression of symptoms, and attitude toward treatment and recovery.

Discussions of cultural differences and issues regarding our competence as professionals in a cross-cultural context often evoke strong emotions that cause us considerable stress. This seems related in part to our nation's long history of racial and ethnic turmoil. These discussions also are stressful because there are certain risks inherent in such a pursuit. We risk disclosing that we have prejudices or may not have the knowledge or skill required to work cross-culturally. This leads to embarrassment and feelings of inadequacy. The greatest risk is that of change, moving from what we thought was a comfortable space to one filled with uncertainty and ambiguity.

This chapter explores how to improve therapeutic and professional interactions with those from other cultures. It will address *cultural competency* from a generic perspective, presenting a brief historical overview of human science's attempts to look at the role of culture, a rationale for cultural competency, and a tripartite approach to the culturally different client. Although the focus will be primarily at the practice level, what will be discussed can be generalized to the organizational level.

Throughout the chapter, there is frequent use of the term *ethnic group,* the modern definition of which is "large groups of people classed according to common racial, national, tribal, religious, linguistic, or cultural origin or background (Merriam Webster online, 2001). In medieval times, the noun *ethnic* originally meant heathen or pagan. This meaning has most certainly contributed to the pathologizing of various ethnic groups. In common usage, ethnicity mistakenly is used to refer only to race, nationality, and land of origin, ignoring the important variable of culture.

In this chapter, the term *people of color* is used to describe those viewed as culturally different in our society or those who are members of a "visible minority group" (Yamamoto, James, & Palley, 1968, p. 45). This term has largely political significance, focuses on color as a significant social factor in the United States, and is meant by me to include African Americans, American Indians/Alaska Natives, Latinos, and Asian/Pacific Islanders in terms of their experience of oppression and discrimination. These experiences have an impact on virtually all of our intercultural interactions.

Historical Overview

Historically, there has been a tendency to explore cultural differences from either a perspective of cultural deviance or cultural relativism. Regarding the former, we are prone to view others from our own cultural perspective, either seeing our culture as superior or "normal." From the perspective of cultural relativism, we see everything that is different in others as related to culture and therefore acceptable. Both perspectives can be counterproductive when assessing child maltreatment and can function as barriers to the delivery of culturally competent services.

The cultural deviance perspective is ethnocentric. It blinds us to the strengths of a particular culture and alienates us in a way that limits our ability to help and empower. It also can cause us to view culturally based child-rearing practices as inappropriate or dangerous when they may well reflect parents' ways of protecting their children.

The perspective of cultural relativism is based on the philosophical theory of relativism that holds that judgment criteria are relative and vary with each individual and his or her environment. This presents a difficulty because it suggests that if a practice is sanctioned culturally, it is devoid of negative impact. Thus, practitioners may ignore the danger or destructiveness inherent in certain culturally approved child-rearing practices (e.g., infibulation, coining, foot binding, physical discipline, discouragement of displays of "weakness" in male children) and consequently leave children at risk for physical or psychological harm.

The "culturally diverse" or "culturally different" model (Sue & Sue, 1990, p. 20) offers a potentially more valid and pluralistic perspective. It brings together the subjective worldview of a particular culture and that from a broader cross-cultural base (Korbin, 1981), avoiding both ethnocentrism and cultural relativism. It accepts that cultures vary and does not use one culture as the ideal norm. It also accepts that some cultural practices, despite having evolved to meet universal human needs, may be destructive. Such a model has particular significance in the field of child maltreatment. It offers us a theoretical basis to assess cultural practices with an understanding and appreciation of cultural variations. It is the core of cultural competency.

Rationale for Cultural Competency

In brief, cultural competency is the ability to understand, to the best of one's ability, the worldview of our culturally different clients (or peers) and adapt our practice accordingly. Cultural competency is good practice. To best meet the needs of a client, the professional must understand the world from the client's point of view and provide the help needed in a manner in which it can be used. Contemporary urgency regarding cultural competency by child treatment professionals is a response to three factors in the United States: (a) increasing cultural diversity, (b) the underrepresentation of professionals from diverse backgrounds, and (c) inadequate delivery of social and mental health services to maltreated children of color.

If our policies and clinical practices are not culturally proficient, the needs of maltreated children will be neglected.

Increasing Cultural Diversity in the United States

The United States has seen a tremendous increase in ethnic diversity over the past decade as immigration from Asia, Europe, and Central and South America has increased and birthrates among cultural minorities have risen rapidly. The U.S. census estimates that nearly 28% of Americans are people of color (U.S. Bureau of the Census, 2000a, 2000b, 2000c). By the year 2050, the U.S. Bureau of the Census projects that the Anglo population will decrease from its current 72% to 53%, and people of color will constitute 48% of the U.S. population (U.S. Bureau of the Census, 2000a, 2000b, 2000c). Given this rate of growth in U.S. ra-

cial and ethnic diversity, the likelihood of intercultural problems in service delivery may increase. If our policies and clinical practices are not culturally proficient, the needs of maltreated children will be neglected.

Underrepresentation of Professionals From Diverse Backgrounds

Although people of color are overrepresented in child protective services (CPS) populations, professionals of color appear to be underrepresented in the fields of social work and psychology. In 1993, only 9.1% of the National Association of Social Work (NASW) members (Gilbelman & Schervish, 1993) and 5.1% of the American Psychological Association (APA) members (APA Education Directorate, 1993) were identified as people of color. These figures only indicate how many professionals of color are members of these organizations and therefore do not offer an exact percentage of professionals of color in the field. However, they do suggest a substantial shortage when looked at in conjunction with statistics such as those of the Council for Social Work Education, which reports that in 1991-1992, only 17.1% of those receiving a master's degree in social work were people of color (Lennon, 1993). These shortages may reflect a number of factors: Undergraduate and graduate programs in relevant areas may not recruit and retain students of color adequately, hiring and promotion practices may be discriminatory, and qualified candidates of color may be lured away by increased opportunities (Gilbelman & Schervish, 1993). The current decline in affirmative action programs, designed to *level the playing field* and set aside monies for financial aid, will only increase this shortage.

The relative scarcity of professionals of color in the fields is not a problem that can be solved easily or quickly, and recruiting more professionals of color is not the entire solution. Although there always will be clients who desire ethnic match, it is not always feasible, nor is it always a client's choice. The idea that being a member of a particular ethnic group makes one automatically cognizant of and sensitive to cultural issues is a myth. Within each cultural group, there is much heterogeneity resulting from varying levels of assimilation, acculturation, and socioeconomic status. The match or fit that we must aim for derives from expanding our worldview and increasing our empathy for those who are different from us. As increasing numbers of people of color enter the social service system, an increasing percentage of professionals of all colors must be able to respond to their needs in a culturally competent and sensitive manner.

Inadequate Delivery of Social and Mental Health Services

The failure of professionals to be culturally competent is reflected in a number of ways in the delivery of social and mental health services. One consequence of this failure, although not immediately seen as such, is the overrepresentation of children of color in the child protection system. This is clearly indicated in the National Child Abuse and Neglect Data System (NCANDS) report for 1996 (U.S. Department of Health & Human Services, 1998). Forty-one states provided data on the race/ethnicity of a total of 254,613 children. The report indicates that African American and American Indian/Alaska Native children represent 15% and 1% of the nation's total child population, respectively, yet represent almost 30% and 2% of substantiated or indicated child abuse reports—double their representation in the general population. In sharp contrast, White and Asian/Pacific Islander children represent close to 67% and 4% of the population, respectively, but only 56% and 1% of substantiated child maltreatment reports. Hispanic children are about equally represented in substantiated reports and in the general population.

Gathering data on the incidence and prevalence of child maltreatment in various ethnic groups is a methodological challenge, and, to date, our attempts have been flawed. This may be due, in part, to the difficulty of disentangling social class and cultural difference in a society in which people of color are more likely than Whites to hold lower socioeconomic status and lack access to powerful institutions (Garbarino & Ebata, 1983). In addition, substantiation rates may be affected by factors such as sampling biases and professionals' perceptions of the behavior of those being reported. Racial and ethnic stereotypes, poverty, drug availability, and the culturally sanctioned use of physical discipline may leave African Americans and Native Americans more vulnerable to reporting and subsequent substantiation. In contrast, lower rates of substantiated reports for Asian American children may be due not only to the lower incidence of child abuse in these communities but also to professional stereotypes regarding Asian "passivity" and the view of Asians as the "model minority" (Sue & Sue, 1990, p. 192).

Although not definitive evidence, these disproportionate substantiation rates raise concerns about the cultural competence of professionals in the field of child protection. One could speculate that if professionals understood the worldview of their clients and had adequate awareness of their own stereotyped ideas and biases, these rates might be a closer approximation of the prevalence of child abuse in communities of color. Concern about the cultural competence of professionals is only heightened by the data on the delivery of social and mental health services.

As child abuse professionals, we are all concerned that social and mental health services be delivered in the most efficacious manner. Unfortunately, much evidence indicates that services for clients of color are inadequate. In a series of research studies done by Sue and associates in 1974 and 1975, it was revealed that 50% of people of color terminate treatment after just one contact with the mental health system as compared to a rate of 30% for Whites. The primary reasons cited were the lack of non-White staff, the traditional way in which services were delivered, poor response to education and vocational needs of clients, and an antagonistic response to culture, class, and language-bound variables (Sue & Sue, 1990).

Reviewing the evidence on the fate of families of color in public social service systems, one researcher concluded, "Once children and families of color enter child welfare systems, there is evidence which indicates differential treatment with regard to what services are provided, both in terms of quantity and quality" (Harris, 1990). Assessment and intervention are more severe for families of color. One study cited higher rates of out-of-home placements for children of color than for Anglo children, different and more restrictive referral and diagnostic patterns for African American children, and a disproportionate number of these children in less desirable placements (Stehno, 1982). In Los Angeles County, the rate of African American children going into the child protective services (CPS) system is four times higher than that for Whites (Swinger, 1993). Nationally, 50% of children in out-of-home care are children of color, even though they comprise only 20% of the population (Keys, 1991). These statistics suggest a link between inadequate service delivery and placement of children of color in more restricted levels of care.

These higher rates cannot be explained simply by a higher incidence or greater severity of child abuse in communities of color, but, more likely, they appear to be a consequence of greater poverty in communities of color. Impoverished people depend more on publicly funded social and mental health systems that, when not culturally competent, result in overscrutiny and misunderstanding of people of color. In addition, poverty leaves people powerless to deal with these massive governmental systems, so parents are less able to challenge removal of children from their homes.

Approaching Culturally Different Clients

Culture affects all levels of service delivery. Practitioners and administrators must take into account the culture of their service populations and the impact of their response to these populations to ensure effective service delivery. The challenges to service delivery encompass variables of culture, class, and language (Sue & Sue, 1990). For instance, White professionals in the field usually have Western world beliefs that are brought into the treatment room. As a result, their focus tends to be on the individual: They tend to stress cause and effect; value insight, openness, and verbal expressiveness; and believe that the best family is a nuclear family. As professionals, many of us, from all cultures, share middle-class values such as long-range planning and strict adherence to time schedules; we have a high tolerance for ambiguity and use only Standard English.

What happens when the professional encounters the culturally different client? A poor working-class client often does not view self-disclosure as healthy or safe, due to numerous experiences with racism and oppression. These clients are more likely to believe in collectivism, have an intuitive approach to life, have a great reliance on extended family, think more about today than tomorrow, and have little time for insight because they must figure out how to feed the children and pay the rent. Used to waiting endlessly at public institutions, clients arrive at the agency an hour late expecting to be seen and then do not speak a language or dialect the professional can understand easily. Because professional behavior is mediated by client behavior and vice versa (Ridley, 1985), the fit needed to work effectively may not be possible.

Subtle or unconscious, stereotypical or value-laden attitudes of the professional and client may be communicated and responded to verbally or nonverbally, precipitating a potentially negative and destructive interactive dynamic. The subjective worldviews of client and professional, reflective of each individual's cultural experience, can collide and result in what Stolorow and Atwood (1992, p. 103) describe as "intersubjective dysjunction." Professional or client may assimilate the other's communications in such a way that the meaning of these communications can be altered grossly and lead to misunderstandings.

So how do we address the cultural needs of our clients in a culturally sensitive and competent fashion? There are three aspects to cultural competency that, when addressed at all levels of service, will improve cross-cultural interactions and enable professionals to better provide services to the culturally different client: value base, knowledge, and methods.

Value Base

Value base describes the ideals, customs, attitudes, practices, and beliefs that one deems worthy and useful and that stimulate within that individual a strong emotional response. Each of us sees the world through culture-colored glasses. We compare others and process events based on our own value systems. A professional's value base should have an earnest appreciation of three factors: (a) the dynamics of difference and a belief in multiculturalism, (b) the existence of individual and institutional biases and the sometimes subtle but immense power of myths and stereotypes in our interactions, and (c) the essential need to empower the disenfranchised. An appropriate value base is the most important aspect to culturally competent practice. Without it, our knowledge and methods mean little.

Dynamics of Difference

Difference can create dynamics that lead to negative learning experiences. Individuals become hostile when faced with someone different. Freud (1918) termed this "the narcissism of minor differences" and saw it as a result of narcissistic injury: "It is precisely the minor differences in people who are otherwise alike that form the basis of feelings of strangeness and hostility between them" (p. 199). Martin Luther King, Jr. (1964) linked this hostility to fear of the unknown. History is full of accounts depicting the inhumane treatment of those deemed by society as different (e.g., the Salem witch trials, the Holocaust, the lynching of African Americans, the treatment of Muslims in Bosnia).

In the field of mental health, difference too often becomes synonymous with pathology. When the behavior of a culturally different client is not understood, it may be labeled as a negative transference response or viewed as indicative of pathology. The following is a fictitious case example that is not atypical.

G is an 8-year-old African American female who had been physically abused by her mother. She was referred by a White clinical social worker for educational and psychological assessment after completion of the initial intake. The social worker reported that during the interview, G was timid and shy, offered little verbal communication, and did not play. G was described as "immature and possibly, developmentally delayed." A week later, an African American child welfare worker did a home visit and within this setting saw a very different child. He arrived to find G crossing the street, laundry basket and siblings in tow. The worker accompanied G to the Laundromat, where he observed her counting money, washing the family's clothes, and disciplining her siblings. He was able to engage her in a lengthy conversation about home and school. On reading the first social worker's evaluation, the second worker was puzzled.

These contrasting pictures of G can be explained by looking more closely at the different contexts within which these observations were made. The first view of G was from a White social worker in a university clinic staffed primarily by Whites and displaying artwork and media from the White culture. At best, this had to be alienating, frightening, and overwhelming for G, who was undoubtedly already anxious about having to disclose her mother's abusive behavior of her. The second view of G was from an African American worker in an environment familiar to G, an environment she negotiated daily and within which she proved herself to be competent.

Research findings on the diagnosis of the culturally different client suggest increased pathologizing of these groups (Baskin, Bluestone, & Nelson, 1981). Non-Whites are given more severe diagnoses than middle-class Whites (Adebimpe, 1981; Marsella & Pedersen, 1981; Rayburn & Stonecypher, 1996). Non-White children (ages 10-17) are hospitalized at a rate three times higher than that for Whites (Shiloh & Selavan, 1974), and non-Whites (ages 11-43) are almost twice as likely as Whites to be given a diagnosis of schizophrenia (U.S. Department of Health, Education, and Welfare, 1977). In addition, the culturally different patient is at high risk to receive inferior and biased treatment because many hold a lower socioeconomic status (Learner, 1972; Lorion, 1973, 1974; Pavkov, Lewis, & Lyons, 1989; Powell & Powell, 1983; Yamamoto et al., 1968).

Culturally different clients are faced with the fact of their difference from the moment they enter most treatment facilities or child welfare offices, which tend to display media from the White culture and may require interactions with workers outside their particular culture. This makes a very powerful statement to clients, communicating a sense of their invisibility in this society and triggering feelings of alienation and hostility as described clearly in Ellison's (1947) *Invisible Man.* It is the professional's role to explore such feelings empathically and attempt to understand the patient's subjective reality rather than to respond by pathologizing or defensively assuming no responsibility for the patient's response. It is here that believing and valuing multiculturalism come into play. The University of Maryland's *Diversity Dictionary* (2000) defines *multiculturalism* as "the practice of acknowledging and respecting the various cultures, religions, races, ethnicities, attitudes and opinions within an environment." If professionals do not value multiculturalism, then their work with the culturally different will at best be inadequate.

Differences between client and professional can lead to positive learning experiences for professionals and a curative experience for the client, if responses of ignorance, fear, antagonism, and hostility are avoided. The culturally different client can enhance professional growth and development, and, if approached with *sustained empathic inquiry,* the mutually decided on goals of treatment can be attained (Stolorow, Brandchaft, & Atwood, 1987).

Accepting the Existence of Biases, Myths, and Stereotypes

The professional's value base must include room for the fact that individual and institutional biases do exist and that these biases slant toward the worldview, well-being, and desires of the majority culture. Accepting this fact will positively influence the care delivered at two levels. It allows the clinician to better meet particular needs of an individual client and offers the treating institution an opportunity to explore its own biases that directly affect a community's use of the facility.

> *The child maltreatment professional must accept the power of myths and stereotypes in the field and in our society.*

The biases of the White culture affect the lives of people of color on a daily basis and at numerous levels (e.g., housing access, job availability, educational and social opportunities). Regardless of the presenting complaint, the culturally different client will bring this issue into treatment, at some point, on a manifest or latent level. As with other reality-based issues, the client will require support. For instance, a Latina mother in a Parent's United program may complain that it is taking her longer than Anglo mothers in similar situations to regain custody of her children. She believes this is the result of discrimination, and consequently she becomes depressed at what she views as the hopelessness of her predicament. The well-meaning clinician, who does not believe such biases exist today and knows that this patient tends to project, may, without malicious intent, invalidate the patient's complaint by ignoring it and encouraging her to look at her defensive behavior as the *real* cause of the problem. A more effective

response is to first investigate the possibility of bias and, if needed, advocate for the woman. If, after some investigation, it appears bias is not the cause of delayed reunification, exploration and interpretation of the issue are appropriate.

The child maltreatment professional must accept the power of myths and stereotypes in the field and in our society. All of us are affected in some way by these myths and stereotypes. Sue and Sue (1990) define *stereotypes* as "rigid preconceptions we hold about *all* people who are members of a particular group, whether it be defined along racial, religious, sexual, or other lines" (p. 47). Myths and stereotypes are perpetrated in a variety ways, most particularly by mass media and flawed research. For instance, studies have documented that White counselors often believe African Americans are paranoid and angry and more likely to suffer from character disorders (Evans, 1985; Jones, 1985; Willie, Kramer, & Brown, 1973) and schizophrenia (Pavkov et al., 1989). The list of racial and ethnic myths and stereotypes is long and cannot be explored fully here, but no one can escape exposure to them. One of the most destructive beliefs is the assumption of homogeneity within minority ethnic groups. A mistake often is made in believing that all Asians, Native Americans, African Americans, or Latinos are alike, despite the fact that individuals within minority ethnic groups vary as much as those in majority ethnic groups.

Empowerment

The child maltreatment professional must value the notion of empowerment as a treatment goal. Empowerment is a goal that has been recognized for more than a decade by the child welfare system as a crucial aspect of family preservation. Empowerment is a process that enables clients to exert their personal power to obtain needed emotional, physical, or social resources. Sue and Sue (1990) understand empowerment as a worldview that embraces the belief that the *locus of control* rests with the individual rather than an external force. Most clinicians would agree that this worldview is one that offers clients greater ability to master the environment and function in healthy ways.

Powerlessness is an ever-present and well-accepted effect of child abuse trauma. Powerlessness is also a feeling that people of color often are faced with because of their minority group status and overrepresentation in the poverty class. Research has documented that the poor and people of color tend to believe more in an external locus of control (Sue & Sue, 1990). Frequent discrimination, decreased employment and educational opportunities, racial and ethnic stereotypes, and poverty make it difficult for an individual to feel powerful, especially when combined with the effects of childhood trauma. Feelings of powerlessness are increased further when paternalistic public agencies intervene in one's life.

Empowerment skills offer clients an opportunity to negotiate the various systems that affect their lives in ways that may provoke feelings of frustration and helplessness. A professional can model and teach the client how to use power by advocating openly for the client. In addition, however, the professional needs to help the client move out of the passive role by sharing power with him or her. This means involving the client in the advocacy process that enables use of the client's power as an individual. Without the client's involvement, the professional risks becoming a patron and perpetuating client powerlessness (Pinderhughes, 1983). Solomon (1985) argues that an empowerment-based practice recognizes client strengths. It is a practice in which the client and clinician collaborate as peers in solving problems. Instead of telling a client how to change, the professional might better ask how the client would like to change and work toward that goal mutually.

Heger and Hunzeker (1988) point out the complexity of teaching empowerment skills to children whose "powerlessness is unavoidable because they lack experience, maturity, and the resources to meet their own needs" (p. 501). They suggest offering children experiences that encourage mastery and a sense of belonging:

> These include association with valued adults who demonstrate empowerment; strong ties with sources of identity, including biological kin, ethnic heritage, and religious tradition; age-appropriate participation in decisions; and involvement in building a network of relationships and institutional supports that will sustain children into adulthood. (p. 501)

Knowledge

The second key aspect of cultural competency requires that professionals be informed from a phenomenological point of view and have knowledge of several factors. First, it is important to understand the influence of culture on perceptions (including those formed in transference and countertransference responses), behaviors, sex roles, interactions, expectations, and modes of communication (verbal and nonverbal). Second, professionals should study the history of racism and oppression to gain an understanding of the individual's response and adaptation to it. Membership in an oppressed group has a profound effect on the individual's identity and life experience.

Third, the professional should gain knowledge of the client's culture by becoming familiar with its child-rearing practices, sex roles, family structure, religious beliefs, worldview, community characteristics, and levels of acculturation or assimilation. This knowledge should be used cautiously, with an assumption that such information is only a generalization and should not be used to stereotype.

Fourth, understanding social class and its impact is also crucial. Many factors that appear related to culture are better correlated with socioeconomic status, but separating the two is difficult.

Fifth, professionals must work from an unbiased theoretical base. Contemporary relational theories, such as those of the interpersonal/cultural school, social constructivists, or intersubjectivity and cultural variance theory, lend themselves to working cross-culturally.

Last, although there never may be agreement on a set of universal criteria of child abuse, Korbin (1981) suggests that in determining what constitutes child maltreatment, professionals must take into account the physical and emotional harm done to a child, parental intent, and socialization goals of the culture.

Methods

The third aspect of cultural competency concerns the methods used in professional practice, research, and the development of human resources. Professionals must develop their ability to diagnose, determine, and adapt clinically to culturally based values, viewpoints, attitudes, and behavior patterns. Researchers often assume that the methods they use are *objective* and do not understand that the methods they employ are influenced by their own cultural background and experience. Current research practices and databases must be improved and expanded. It cannot be assumed that what is true for one culture is true for another culture; such an assumption is ethnocentric. Research undertaken on one cultural group is only valid for that group. Journals in the field must begin to require that the research results published meet the basic guidelines for culturally competent research, such as those presented by Urquiza and Wyatt (1994) and Fontes (1998).

Resource development is needed within the workforce, in the community, and at the funding level. For example, support systems and informal helping networks can be created through consultation with various individuals at different community levels. Finally, we must view cultural competency as an integral part of professional training programs and practice standards. It is important to develop culturally sensitive tools like that developed by Roizner (1996) for the Judge Baker Children's Center in Boston.

Conclusion

Although knowing all there is to know about a particular culture is not possible from an outsider's vantage point, it is possible to work effectively in a cross-cultural context if certain givens are accepted. The trauma of abuse and neglect is experienced and organized from the subjective viewpoint of the individual. It is a viewpoint derived from the individual's entire life experience, which includes cultural identification. The child maltreatment professional approaches clients from a viewpoint organized by similar factors. Both client and professional come to the interaction with values derived from cultural experience. The space in which the viewpoint of professional and client meets holds the potential for meaningful work and change. Through "sustained empathic inquiry" (Stolorow et al., 1987) and an appreciation of subjectivity and interactive dynamics, the professional can work competently with the culturally different client.

Social and mental health delivery for children and families of color has suffered from a lack of cultural awareness, acceptance, and professional competence. The increased diversity within the United States presents a challenge that can only be met if cultural competency is regarded as a standard professional skill supported by a valid theory, knowledge, and methods.

References

Adebimpe, V. (1981). Overview: White norms and psychiatric diagnosis of Black patients. *American Journal of Psychiatry, 138,* 279-285.

APA Education Directorate. (1993). *1993 APA directory survey.* Washington, DC: American Psychological Association.

Baskin, D., Bluestone, H., & Nelson, M. (1981). Ethnicity and psychiatric diagnosis. *Journal of Clinical Psychology, 137,* 529-537.

Ellison, R. (1947). *Invisible man.* New York: Random House.

Evans, D. A. (1985). Psychotherapy and Black patients: Problems of training, trainees, and trainers. *Psychotherapy, 22,* 457-460.

Fontes, L. A. (1998). Ethics in family violence research: Cross-cultural issues. *Family Relations, 47*(1), 53-61.

Freud, S. (1918). The taboo of virginity. *Standard Edition, 11,* 191-208.

Garbarino, J., & Ebata, A. (1983). The significance of ethnic and cultural differences in child maltreatment. *Journal of Marriage and the Family, 45*(4), 773-783.

Gilbelman, M., & Schervish, P. H. (1993). *Who we are: The social work labor force as reflected in the NASW membership.* Washington, DC: NASW.

Harris, N. (1990). Dealing with diverse cultures in child welfare. *Protecting Children, 7*(3), 6-7.

Heger, R. L., & Hunzeker, J. M. (1988). Moving toward empowerment-based practice in public child welfare. *Social Work, 33,* 499-502.

Jones, A. C. (1985). Psychological functioning in Black Americans: A conceptual guide for use in psychotherapy. *Psychotherapy, 22,* 363-369.

Keys, H. (1991). The CWLA cultural responsiveness initiative: A status report. *APSAC Advisor, 4*(3), 12-13.

King, M. L., Jr. (1964). *Why we can't wait.* New York: Penguin.

Korbin, J. (1981). *Child abuse and neglect: Cross-cultural perspectives.* Berkeley: University of California Press.

Learner, B. (1972). *Therapy in the ghetto.* Baltimore: Johns Hopkins University Press.

Lennon, T. M. (1993). *Statistics of social work education in the United States: 1992.* Alexandria, VA: Council on Social Work Education.

Lorion, R. P. (1973). Socioeconomic status and treatment approaches reconsidered. *Psychological Bulletin, 79,* 263-280.

Lorion, R. P. (1974). Patient and therapist variables in the treatment of low-income patients. *Psychological Bulletin, 81,* 344-354.

Marsella, A., & Pedersen, P. (Eds.). (1981). *Cross-cultural counseling and psychotherapy.* Elmsford, NY: Pergamon.

Parson, E. R. (1985). Ethnicity and traumatic stress: The intersecting point in psychotherapy. In C. R. Figley (Ed.), *Trauma and its wake: The study and treatment of posttraumatic stress disorder* (Vol. 1, pp. 315-337). New York: Brunner/Mazel.

Pavkov, T. W., Lewis, D. A., & Lyons, J. S. (1989). Psychiatric diagnosis and racial bias: An empirical investigation. *Professional Psychology: Research & Practice, 20,* 364-368.

Pinderhughes, E. (1983). Empowerment for our clients and for ourselves. *Social Casework, 64,* 331-338.

Powell, G., & Powell, R. (1983). Poverty: The greatest and severest handicapping condition in childhood. In G. Powell (Ed.), *The psychosocial development of minority group children* (pp. 573-580). New York: Brunner/Mazel.

Rayburn, T. M., & Stonecypher, J. F. (1996). Diagnostic differences related to age and race of involuntarily committed psychiatric patients. *Psychological Reports, 79,* 881-883.

Ridley, C. R. (1985). Pseudo-transference in interracial psychotherapy: An operant paradigm. *Journal of Contemporary Psychotherapy, 15*(1), 29-36.

Roizner, M. (1996). *A practical guide for the assessment of cultural competence in children's mental health organizations.* Boston: Judge Baker Children's Center.

Shiloh, A., & Selavan, I. C. (Eds.). (1974). *Ethnic groups in America: Their morbidity, mortality and behavior disorders: Vol. 2. The blacks.* Springfield, IL: Charles C Thomas.

Solomon, B. B. (1985). How do we really empower families? New strategies for social work practitioners. *Family Resource Coalition—FRC Report, 3,* 2-3.

Stehno, S. M. (1982). Differential treatment of minority children in service systems. *Social Work, 27*(1), 39-46.

Stolorow, R. D., & Atwood, G. E. (1992). *Contexts of being: The intersubjective foundations of psychological life.* Hillsdale, NJ: Analytic Press.

Stolorow, R. D., Brandchaft, B., & Atwood, G. E. (1987). *Psychoanalytic treatment: An intersubjective approach.* Hillsdale, NJ: Analytic Press.

Sue, D. W., & Sue, D. (1990). *Counselling the culturally different: Theory and practice.* New York: John Wiley.

Swinger, H. (1993, January). *Cross cultural considerations in working with African-American families.* Paper presented at the San Diego Conference on Responding to Child Maltreatment, La Jolla, CA.

University of Maryland. (2000). *Diversity database: Diversity dictionary* [Online]. Available: www.inform. umd.edu/edRes/Topic/Diversity/Reference/divdic.html

Urquiza, A., & Wyatt, G. (1994). Culturally relevant violence research with children of color. *APSAC Advisor, 7*(4), 17-20.

U.S. Bureau of the Census. (2000a). *NP-D1-A projections of the population by age, sex, race, Hispanic origins for United States, 1999-2001.* Washington, DC: Government Printing Office.

U.S. Bureau of the Census. (2000b). *Projections of the resident population by race, Hispanic origin, & nativity: Middle series, 1999-2001.* Washington, DC: Government Printing Office.

U.S. Bureau of the Census. (2000c). *Projections of the resident population by race, Hispanic origin, & nativity: Middle series, 2050-2070.* Washington, DC: Government Printing Office.

U.S. Department of Health and Human Services, Children's Bureau. (1998). *Child maltreatment 1996: Reports from the states to the national child abuse and neglect data system.* Washington, DC: Government Printing Office.

U.S. Department of Health, Education, and Welfare. (1977). *Psychiatric services and the changing institutional scene, 1950-1975* (Pub. No. [ADM] 717-433, NIMH Series B, No. 12). Washington, DC: Government Printing Office.

Willie, C. V., Kramer, B. M., & Brown, B. S. (1973). *Racism and mental health.* Pittsburgh: University of Pittsburgh Press.

Webster, Merriam. (2001) Online dictionary.

Yamamoto, J., James, J. C., & Palley, N. (1968). Cultural problems in psychiatric therapy. *Archives of General Psychiatry, 19,* 45-59.

24

Mental Health Services for Children Reported to Child Protective Services

JOHN LANDSVERK

ANN F. GARLAND

LAUREL K. LESLIE

Few policymakers, advocates, and treatment specialists would disagree about the need to provide mental health services for children who have experienced maltreatment, especially those whose experience has come to the attention of the child protective services system. Yet, considerable debate could be expected regarding what type of services should be provided to which children at what time in their lives, how services are to be organized and funded, and how services should be monitored for quality and effectiveness. These issues have become especially visible in public policy discourse during the 1990s for several reasons. Along with the general health care system, the service system for mental health care delivery has changed at an unprecedented rate, as managed care models have replaced the prior fee-for-service delivery system in both commercial and publicly funded arenas. Parity issues have

AUTHORS' NOTE: Portions of this chapter are adapted with permission from Landsverk, J., & Garland, A. F. (1999). Foster care and pathways to mental health services. In P. A. Curtis, G. Dale, Jr., & J. C. Kendall (Eds.), *The foster care crisis: Translating research into practice and policy* (pp. 193-210). Lincoln: University of Nebraska Press.

been debated as policymakers have considered whether mental health conditions should be covered with the same benefits as physical health conditions. In children's mental health services, beneficial outcomes have not been observed in community settings despite considerable evidence for the efficacy of treatments observed in university-based clinical trials. These are the types of issues addressed by mental health services research.

This chapter addresses a selected set of issues regarding the organization and delivery of mental health services to children whose child maltreatment experience has been reported to child protective services, including (a) the level and type of needs for mental health services shown by children entering the child welfare system, (b) the use of mental health services by these children, (c) factors that predict mental health referral and service use patterns, (d) what is known about the effectiveness of these services, and (e) special issues in the organization and funding of mental health services for this population in an era of rapid change from fee-for-service to managed care models.

The chapter focuses primarily on services delivered within the public mental health system because most services studies have been conducted on samples of maltreated children involved with the child welfare system and served by the public system. In addition, the child welfare system has special linkages to public funding for mental health services, especially because states traditionally have used Medicaid funds to provide medical, developmental, and mental health services for children adjudicated to the foster care system. Public mental health is defined as services funded through Medicaid or by state and local public mental health agencies. Most studies relevant to this topic have been carried out with children and families involved with the child welfare/child protective services system. In fact, most of the extant research literature involves children who have been adjudicated to the foster care system. Little information is available about the need for and use of mental health services for children whose families receive in-home services from the child welfare system. Even less information is available about the use of mental health services by maltreated children whose families have private insurance available for funding mental health services.

The child welfare system (CWS) is charged with protecting children, preserving families, and providing permanency for children whose protective needs have required disposition to out-of-home care. En-

suring the well-being of children is usually considered a part of these three mission elements. However, providing services for the amelioration of problems in psychosocial or developmental functioning is most often seen as at the discretion of the child welfare agency. Therefore, most service delivery for mental health and developmental problems is done through linkages to mental health and other agencies outside of child welfare.

As indicated earlier, child welfare investigates maltreatment and other protective risk allegations, places children in foster care, and finds permanent families for children (either their biological families or adoptive families) as part of the mission to protect children at risk for further maltreatment. This means that child welfare services for "open cases" (i.e., open for services) are usually delivered in two settings: (a) in the home of origin in an attempt to preserve families and improve families' functioning and (b) in out-of-home foster care or other settings to which children are court-ordered in an effort to ensure safety. Child welfare research has consistently shown that although involved children may come from all ethnic groups, family types, and income levels, they are disproportionately from poor, single-parent, and ethnic minority families. For example, Barth, Courtney, Berrick, and Albert (1994) report that 80% of foster children in California come from single-parent homes, two out of three from Aid for Families With Dependent Children (AFDC)-eligible families, and three of five from minority families.

Both types of open cases in the CWS have increased exponentially over the past decade. The rise in open, in-home cases reflects the growing number of child abuse and neglect reports requiring investigation as well as the increased efforts to maintain children in their own homes through family maintenance and family preservation services mandated through the Adoption Assistance and Child Welfare Act of 1980 (P.L. 96-272) and the Adoption and Safe Families Act of 1997 (ASFA). Yet, despite a heightened focus on in-home services and preservation of children with their families of origin, there has also been tremendous growth in the number of children in out-of-home foster care, with 547,000 children in foster care reported in 1999, a 95% increase from 1986, when the total was 280,000 children (Petit & Curtis, 1997; U.S. Department of Health and Human Services [DHHS], 2000). This increase in children in out-of-home care is thought to reflect an excess of entrances into foster care as compared with exits and the impact of escalating poverty, family violence, mental illness, drug and alcohol abuse, and AIDS (Barbell, 1997). Children entering foster care today differ from those entering during the late 1980s, as there are "growing numbers of seriously handicapped infants at one end of the spectrum, and a preponderance of emotionally disabled teenagers at the other end" (American Public Welfare Association, 1990, p. 35).

Research studies over the past two decades have firmly established what practitioners have known for considerably longer—namely, that children in child welfare and especially those who enter foster care represent a high-risk population for maladaptive outcomes, including socioemotional, behavioral, and psychiatric problems warranting mental health treatments. The major risk factors for maladaptive outcomes include the maltreatment experiences that lead to child welfare involvement, the stresses involved with processes of child protective services (CPS) investigation and judicial decision making, and, for those who are placed in foster fare, the stress of removal from home. Given this increased risk for maladaptive outcomes, one would assume that most children in child welfare and especially foster care are referred for mental health services. However, although studies document the urgent need for treatment, only recently have researchers begun to describe the patterns of mental health service use by children who have experienced child maltreatment. This chapter describes this new research and addresses its policy and practice implications.

Need for Mental Health Services

Costello, Burns, Angold, and Leaf (1993) outlined four ways to estimate need for mental health services—namely, "need as service use," "need as diagnosis," "need as functional impairment," and "need as exposure to risk." The first definition fails to distinguish between need for services and use of services. For children involved in the child welfare system, the fourth type, "need as exposure to risk," would require universal mental health treatment because almost all these children have experienced maltreatment, which is a clear risk for development of problems in psychosocial functioning. It is likely that the fourth type, "need as exposure to risk," is the usual framework used by mental health service providers working with children in the child welfare system. However, because this definition assumes that need for services is based solely on exposure to risk rather than a clear indication of need based on problems in symptoms or functioning, it has not been seen by researchers in the services field as the definition of choice for research purposes that require demonstrable need. Therefore, for the purposes of this chapter, *need for mental health services* is defined according to the second and third types—namely, as need derived from either diagnosis or functional impairment, especially as established by standardized measures.

Estimates of the need for mental health services for children and adolescents, as indicated by standardized measures, range widely for both community and special populations. In community studies, estimates of this need range from 10% to 22% (Costello et al., 1988; Gould, Wunsch-Hitzig, & Dohrenwend, 1981; Offord et al., 1987; Zahner, Pawelkiewicz, DeFrancesco, & Adnopoz, 1992). Most recent meta-analytic and epidemiological studies have narrowed the estimate for the prevalence of psychiatric disorders among community youth to a range of 5% to 8% for serious emotional disturbance (both psychiatric diagnosis and moderate to severe level of impairment) (Costello, 1999; Friedman, Katz-Leavy, Manderscheid, & Sondheimer, 1996) and approximately 20% for any diagnosis with functional impairment (Costello et al., 1996; Shaffer, Fisher, Lucas, Dulcan, & Schwab-Stone, 2000).

Almost all studies of children in the child welfare system have focused on those who were placed in foster care. Most studies of children living in foster care have shown that they exhibit problems requiring mental health assessment or intervention at a considerably higher rate than what would be expected from either normative data or from community studies. Pilowsky's (1995) recent review of studies published from

1974 through 1994 supports this conclusion, noting that externalizing disorders in particular may be more prevalent than internalizing in the foster care population.

Eleven studies not included in Pilowsky's (1995) review also confirm this widely accepted conclusion. In the state of Washington, Trupin and colleagues (Trupin, Tarico, Benson, Jemelka, & McClellan, 1993) compared children receiving protective services from child welfare with a criterion group of children in the state's most intensive mental health treatment programs and found that 72% of the children in child welfare exhibited profiles of severe emotional disturbance indistinguishable from the criterion group. In a study of children residing in kinship care in Baltimore, Dubowitz et al. (1994) found that 32% were in the clinical range on behavior problems as reported by the caretaker on the Achenbach Child Behavior Checklist. This study is especially important because of the increasing proportion of foster care children living in this type of placement and the paucity of studies of their psychosocial functioning. In a Tennessee study of children older than age 4 entering state custody, of whom 64% were under the supervision of child welfare, Glisson (1994, 1996) found that 52% were in the clinical range of the Child Behavior Checklist, as determined by both the parent and teacher informant, with 82% scoring in the clinical range of at least one of the three scales of internalizing, externalizing, and total behavior problems. In another Tennessee study of children in custody, Heflinger, Simpkins, and Combs- Orme (2000) have shown elevated rates of aggressive, delinquent, and withdrawn behavior. In a study of 272 children entering foster care in Connecticut before age 8, Horwitz, Simms, and Farrington (1994) found that 53% showed developmental delays as determined by either the Connecticut Infant/Toddler Developmental Assessment or the Battelle Developmental Inventory.

Six of 11 recent studies were conducted with children entering foster care or having resided in foster care in California. Urquiza, Wirtz, Peterson, and Singer (1994) conducted a comprehensive screening and evaluation of 167 children between ages 1 and 10 who were made dependents of the juvenile court in Sacramento for reasons of child abuse and neglect. They found that 68% of the children displayed significant problems in one of four psychosocial domains, as operationalized by a score one and a half

standard deviations below national norms on one or more of four standardized assessment instruments.

Halfon, Mendonca, and Berkowitz (1995) reported on 213 young children with a mean age of 3 years who were referred to a comprehensive health clinic after entering foster care in Oakland and found that more than 80% had developmental, emotional, or behavior problems. They also found that children who were placed after 2 years of age exhibited a higher rate of these problems than children placed at an earlier age.

Clausen, Landsverk, Ganger, Chadwick, and Litrownik (1998) examined 140 children between the ages of 4 and 16 entering foster care in three California counties and found that 54.4% met clinical or borderline criteria on one or more of the narrow-band, broad-band, or total behavior problem scales of the Achenbach Child Behavior Checklist–Parent Report Form, and 62.6% met clinical or borderline criteria on one or more of the narrow-band and social competency scales as well. Only 23.0% were determined to fall in the nonclinical or borderline range on both the behavior problem and social competency dimensions.

Landsverk, Litrownik, Newton, Ganger, and Remmer (1996) conducted a study in San Diego County, California, comparing children entering kinship care with children entering nonrelative foster care through the Parent Report Form of the Achenbach Child Behavior Checklist. For children between the ages of 4 and 16, the investigators determined that 32.9% in the kinship group and 39.8% in the nonrelative foster care group were in the clinical range on total behavior problems. Using the borderline cut-point, the respective percentages were 43.2% and 51.9%. In the same study, they found that 60% of the children younger than age 6½ and residing in kinship care were in the questionable or abnormal range on the Denver Developmental Screening Test, Version Two (DDST II), as compared with 72% of same-age children residing in nonrelative foster placements.

A more recent study of 791 consecutive children in San Diego County entering the emergency shelter/receiving facility found that 61.2% were in the questionable or abnormal range (currently termed the *suspect range*) on the DDST II (Leslie, Gordon, Ganger, & Gist, in press). More than two thirds of these children (69%) received a developmental evaluation using the Bayley Scales of Infant Development II (Bayley II), with 34% scoring more than two standard deviations below the standard score on at least one component of the Bayley II. Comparable with the findings from the earlier study, children entering nonrelative foster care placement were more likely to score in the suspect range (67%) as compared with children ending up in kinship care (56%) or reunified with their biological parents (58%).

Two separate studies conducted in San Diego have used the National Institute of Mental Health (NIMH) Diagnostic Interview Schedule for Children (DISC) for estimating rate of psychiatric disorder based on separate versions of the *Diagnostic and Statistical Manual* (*DSM*). In a study from the early 1990s, Madsen (1992) used the Diagnostic Interview Schedule for Children (DISC), Version 3.2, with 59 children between the ages of 11 and 16 in the early months of foster care and found that 60% met criteria for one or more *DSM-III-R* (American Psychiatric Association, 1987) diagnoses, as determined by reports from either the parent or the youth. In a more recent study conducted from 1997 through 1999 in San Diego, Garland et al. (2000) reported on estimates for selected diagnoses using Version IV of the DISC (Shaffer et al., 2000), with weighted samples drawn from five different sectors of care, including 426 youth who had been declared dependents of the court between the ages of 6 and 18. More than 40% of these youth (41.8%) met criteria for one or more *DSM-IV* (American Psychiatric Association, 1994) diagnoses with at least one moderate level of diagnostic-specific functional impairment. The largest proportion met criteria for the disruptive disorders, with 22.2% meeting criteria for oppositional defiant disorder, 16.1% for conduct disorder, and 20.8% for attentional deficit with hyperactivity disorder. Considerably smaller proportions met criteria for mood disorders (5.2%) and anxiety disorders (8.6%).

The knowledge base is much smaller regarding need for mental health services within "in-home" cases. However, given the poverty and low family functioning consistent with referral to the child welfare system, it can be hypothesized that these children will show significantly greater need for mental health services than children not involved with the system. Two community studies (New York and North Carolina), addressing the impact of poverty on need, provide empirical support for this hypothesis. Cohen and Hesselbart (1993) and Costello et al. (1996) found that youth in families with incomes at or below the poverty line were at increased risk for diagnosable mental health disorders as compared with youth in families above the poverty line. In a reanalysis of the Great Smoky Mountains study data (Costello et al., 1996), Farmer et al. (2001) compared three subgroups of children (ages 9, 11, or 13 at baseline) who were randomly selected into their community sample: (a) children who had ever been in foster care (*n* = 132), (b) children who had been in contact with child welfare but who had never been placed in out-of-home care (*n* = 234), and (c) children living in poverty with no known contact with child welfare (*n* = 413). More than three of four children met criteria for a *DSM-III-R* diagnosis, functional impairment, or both, using the Child and Adolescent Psychiatric Assessment (CAPA) measurement, with only small differences between the three groups (78% for the foster care group, 80% for the child welfare contact group, and 74% for the poverty group). These data suggest that children provided services by child welfare while remaining in their biological home may evidence high rates of mental health problems comparable to those observed in children placed in foster care.

Children with developmental problems were almost two times more likely to remain in foster care than be reunified.

Two of the studies reported findings suggesting that decisions about reunification may be affected by the psychosocial functioning of the child in foster care. Horwitz et al. (1994) found that children with developmental problems were almost two times more likely to remain in foster care than be reunified. Landsverk, Davis, Ganger, Newton, and Johnson (1996) found that children with significant behavior problems, especially externalizing problems, were one half as likely to be reunified with their birth parent within 18 months of foster care entry as were those without significant behavior problems.

In summary, the research literature based on studies across several states suggests that between one half and three fourths of the children entering foster care exhibit behavior or social competency problems warranting mental health services, with preliminary evidence that this high rate may also be anticipated for children served by child welfare while remaining in their biological home. The rate of problems is significantly higher than what would be expected in community populations although more comparable for children living below the poverty level within these communities. Furthermore, these maladaptive outcomes range across a number of domains, rather than being concentrated in only broad behavior problems. An especially noteworthy finding includes developmental problems in the large number of children entering foster care prior to ages 7 and 8. In addition, evidence suggests that the rate of problems may be somewhat less in children who end up in kinship care as compared with children who are placed in nonrelative foster care, although this relationship remains open to further, more definitive, research. Finally, psychosocial functioning of the children in foster care may not only affect their long-term functioning outcomes but also basic decisions regarding their continuity or exit from living in foster care.

Policy and Practice Implications

The high rate of need for mental health services in the foster care population and possibly in the full child welfare population indicates that full assessment protocols rather than screening protocols may constitute the most appropriate strategy for identifying children with maladaptive problems and linking them to specific interventions. Screening programs are only appropriate when low base rates prevail. The data from a number of studies in diverse states and child welfare systems suggest a very high base rate for children and adolescents entering foster care. Therefore, assessment for a wide range of problems in psychosocial functioning should be taken as a routine first step in determining appropriate interventions for specific problems. Although assessment protocols for children entering out-of-home care have been implemented in a number of agencies, these protocols are not likely to cover children served by child welfare but not placed in out-of-home care. Given the comparable rates of problems in both out-of-home and in-home settings, full coverage for all children involved with the

child welfare system should be seriously considered.

The data from recent studies suggest that assessment protocols need to be comprehensive in scope and specific in a wide range of developmentally appropriate domains to facilitate better treatment planning. This policy recommendation implies that broad-based behavioral problem checklists, such as the Achenbach Child Behavior Checklist, may not be sufficient for developing the detailed clinical profiles critical for good treatment planning. Examples of a comprehensive assessment strategy for children entering foster care have been published by Simms (1989) and Halfon, Mendonca, and Berkowitz (1995). These protocols cover a wide range of domains relevant to psychosocial functioning and constitute an excellent foundation for future work. Nevertheless, there is a need for assessment referral practice guidelines with wide support from experienced clinicians and clinical settings that can be implemented by most child welfare systems. The development of these guidelines will require extensive collaboration between the child welfare system, the mental health system, and the medical care system (Knitzer & Yelton, 1990).

Findings from both the California and Connecticut studies underscore the importance of developmental assessment for all children entering foster care prior to age 7. Furthermore, assessment rather than screening protocols would be most appropriate, given the high base rate of developmental problems found in this population. These findings suggest that routine use of standardized assessment measures for developmental delays across multiple areas should be considered rather than broad screening instruments such as the Denver Developmental Screening Test or the Battelle Developmental Inventory.

One study in California and one study in Connecticut have shown the possible impact of a foster child's psychosocial functioning on case decision making. These preliminary investigations suggest that the policy imperatives undergirding reunification and family preservation may be undercut by case workers' perceptions regarding the psychosocial functioning of the child. More research needs to be conducted to understand how case workers and courts are using information about psychosocial problems to affect their decisions about exits from foster care. Practice guidelines need to be developed to provide direction for case workers on the most appropriate use of information about the child's psychosocial functioning in making recommendations to dependency courts regarding reunification.

Use of Mental Health Services

In contrast to the psychosocial functioning of children in child welfare, fewer studies have examined the use of mental health services for this special population. Although studies of psychosocial functioning have been published for more than two decades, studies of mental health service use have been conducted only since 1988. This section discusses findings from six studies that provide estimates of service use for five states—namely, California, North Carolina, Pennsylvania, Tennessee, and Washington. These rates are compared to rates found in community samples.

Estimates regarding rates of mental health service use are difficult to ascertain given the variations in definitions of mental health services, ranging from the traditional outpatient and inpatient modalities to the less traditional services such as case management and therapeutic group homes. Despite these definitional variations, a number of community studies using survey reports by parents and youth have estimated that between 4% and 12% of children in community samples have received mental health services (Koot & Verhulst, 1992; Offord et al., 1987; Zahner et al., 1992).

Three studies of mental health service use by the specialized population of children in foster care have used Medicaid program claims data: one in the state of California (Halfon, Berkowitz, & Klee, 1992a, 1992b), one in the state of Washington (Takayama, Bergman, & Connell, 1994), and a recently published study in the state of Pennsylvania (Harman, Childs, & Kelleher, 2000). The Medicaid data from these three states are especially relevant because these states have made all children in foster care categorically eligible for the Medicaid program regardless of the eligibility status of their biological parents.

In the California study conducted by Halfon et al. (1992a, 1992b), Medi-Cal data (the name for the Medicaid program in California) were examined for all paid claims involving children younger than age 18 in the fee-for-service program in 1988. Rates of health care use and associated costs were compared between the 50,634 children identified in foster care and the 1,291,814 total program-eligible children. Although the children in foster care represented less than 4% of the population of Medi-Cal-eligible users, they represented 41% of the users of reimbursed mental health services and incurred 43% of all mental health expenditures. This overrepresentation among mental health service users held for all age groups within the foster care population, ranging from rates of 31% for children younger than age 6, 32% for children between the ages of 6 and 11, and 49% for all users between the ages of 12 and 17. The investigators further determined that children in foster care had an age-adjusted rate of mental health service use that was 15 times the overall Medi-Cal population that served as the reference group. The investigators found that this pattern of greater use was also true across many different types of mental health services, with children in foster care accounting for 53% of all psychologist visits, 47% of psychiatry visits, 43% of public hospital inpatient hospitalizations, and 27% of all psychiatric inpatient hospitalizations.

The second study using Medicaid claims form data compared the health care use rates of 1,631 children in foster care with those of a sample of 5,316 children from the population of children who were AFDC recipients but not in foster care in 1990 (Takayama et al., 1994). This research focused on children younger than age 8 in Washington state, making it less inclusive than the California study. Despite the younger age cohort studied, the findings were comparable to those reported by Halfon et al. (1992a, 1992b) for California, with 25% of the children in Washington foster care using mental health services as compared with only 3% of the AFDC comparison group children. When the diagnoses were examined for high-cost children whose 1990 health care expenditures exceeded $10,000 (8% of foster children and 0.4% of AFDC children), the prominent diagnoses for the children in foster care were mental disorders and neurological conditions.

The third study compared use and costs of mental health services between children in foster care and children identified under the Supplemental Security Income (SSI) program (children qualify for SSI if there is a medically determinable physical or mental impairment that results in marked and severe functional limitations) in western Pennsylvania. This research team found that

> children in foster care were 3 to 10 times more likely to receive a mental health diagnosis, had 6.5 times more mental health claims, were 7.5 times more likely to be hospitalized for a mental health condition, and had mental health expenditures that were 11.5 times greater ($2082 vs. $181) than children in the Aid to Families With Dependent Children (AFDC) program. Overall, utilization rates, expenditures, and prevalence of psychiatric conditions for children in foster care were comparable with those of children with disabilities. (Harman et al., 2000, p. 1114)

Further insight into the use of mental health services by children in foster care is provided by two additional studies that shared important design features. The foster care investigations in Tennessee (Glisson, 1994, 1996) and San Diego County, California (Garland, Landsverk, Hough, & Ellis-Macleod, 1996; Landsverk, Litrownik, et al., 1996; Leslie et al., 2000), both studied children entering foster care, and both used the Achenbach Child Behavior Checklist to determine the need for mental health services.

The San Diego County study examined the need for mental health services in a cohort of 662 children between the ages of 2 and 17 at the first out-of-home interview (approximately 5-8 months after entry into foster care). Need for services was determined by a behavior problems score above the borderline cut-point on the Parent Report Form of the Child Behavior Checklist (Achenbach, 1991). Mental health service use was based on reports by the substitute parent regarding any service use for help with behavioral, social, school, or other adjustment problems. In addition, the type of provider and frequency of visits were elicited from the same informant. The study found that 56% of the children between the ages of 2 and 17 had used mental health services within the period between entry into foster care and the first interview. The proportion using mental health services ranged from 21% of the children ages 2 to 3, 41% of the children ages 4 to 5, 61% of the children ages 6 to 7, and more than 70% for children and adolescents older than age 7. These rates contrast sharply with less than 10% of the same foster children for whom there was evidence of mental health care use prior to

entry into out-of-home placement (Blumberg, Landsverk, Ellis-Macleod, Ganger, & Culver, 1996). By far the largest proportion (60%) were being seen by a clinical psychologist. The frequency of outpatient visits for all subjects receiving services (except those in residential care) was relatively high, with an estimated mean of 15.4 visits in 6 months. This suggests that most subjects who received outpatient services were in some type of ongoing treatment as opposed to an initial evaluation.

The Tennessee study followed a cohort of 600 children between the ages of 5 to 18 who were randomly selected from approximately 2,000 children who entered state custody in 24 Tennessee counties over the course of 1 year. Two thirds of the sample children were placed in the custody of the child welfare system. The social workers for all of the 600 sample children reported that 14% had been referred for mental health treatment after being placed in custody. No information was included on the actual use of services.

Only one study has generated information about the use of mental health services for children in both in-home and out-of-home settings. Farmer et al. (2001), in a reanalysis of North Carolina community youth in the Great Smoky Mountain study (described in the prior section), found that 90% of youth reported use of mental health services in both the group who had experienced foster care and the group who had contact with child welfare but had not entered foster care. This was significantly higher than the 70% rate of use reported by youth living in families with incomes below the poverty line.

In summary, two California studies, a state of Washington study, and a North Carolina study demonstrate a very high rate of use of mental health services for children in foster care across all age groups, with the highest rate of 70% shown in children older than age 7. The studies using Medicaid data confirmed this much higher rate for children in foster care in contrast to the relatively low rates seen in AFDC children. The Tennessee studies showed a considerably lower rate of mental health referral, a surprising finding given the older age of the study cohort and the very high rate of behavior problems reported in the Tennessee special population. This lower rate may result in part from the predominantly rural counties in the Tennessee studies compared with the urban counties in the California and Washington state studies. The rates of use of mental health services observed in the North Carolina study were considerably higher than rates observed in the other states but did indicate that children in both the in-home and out-of-home settings were significantly more likely to receive mental health services than children in families with incomes below the poverty line.

Policy and Practice Implications

The high rate of mental health service use observed for children in foster care suggests that the child welfare system and the mental health system may be more strongly linked than commonly thought. In California, Washington state, and Pennsylvania, there is consistent evidence that the foster care system may serve as a large gateway into the mental health service system for children who have been abused or neglected. The data from North Carolina suggest that this gateway may also serve for children in contact with child welfare who do not enter out-of-home settings. Because these two systems share many child and adolescent clients, more explicit collaborative ties need to be forged, directed at improving the efficiency of service delivery.

In California, Washington, and Pennsylvania, there is consistent evidence that the foster care system may serve as a large gateway into the mental health service system for children who have been abused or neglected.

It appears that the Medicaid program, as categorically applied to children in foster care, provides a powerful impetus to the provision of mental health services to this population. Medicaid is currently undergoing a major transition to a managed care form of service delivery. We do not know how this shift in the organization and financing of mental health care will affect the mental health treatment of children in foster care. The policy implication is that leaders of the child welfare system and foster care systems need to be proactive in developing managed care contracting within the Medicaid program in collaboration with the managers of public mental health systems. This issue is addressed in more detail in the final section of this chapter.

There is little information available about the impact of exits from foster care on the continuity of mental health care for these children. Further study is necessary to determine whether children are receiving only mental health services when they are within the foster care system or whether treatment services continue across the major permanency plans of reunification and adoption as well as exit at majority. The potential negative impact of developmental problems and behavior problems on exits from foster care would suggest the continued need for mental health services when exits are considered or completed.

The widespread use of mental health services for this population is not accompanied by systematic monitoring of service outcomes for the children receiving these services. No studies have been published to date that have examined either the quality of care being provided through mental health services or the outcomes of those services. We do not know whether the services are effective in ameliorating the mental health and developmental problems observed in children entering the foster care system. There is a clear need for efficient monitoring of developmental, behavioral, social, and adaptive functioning for children in foster care who are receiving mental health services. In short, systems of accountability need to be developed to determine the course of treatment at the level of the individual foster child.

Collaborators across the child welfare and mental health systems need to develop and test best practice models for the delivery of mental health treatment services. The San Diego County study found that almost all mental health services were being delivered in 1-hour office visits, with little evidence of the use of group services, family therapy, or other modalities of treatment. No specialized models exist for determining what services to provide for what children within the context of what types of maladaptive functioning. An excellent example of the type of discussion needed for the development of service delivery models for high-risk children and adolescents has been provided by Halfon, Inkelas, and Wood (1995). The authors go back to the Aday and Anderson (1974) model of health care use that describes financial and nonfinancial barriers to care for children. Case studies of immunization delivery, children with chronic illness, and mobile populations of children are used to argue for integrated service models for high-risk populations of children that coordinate the delivery of medical, developmental, educational, and social services.

Pathways Into Mental Health Services

This section considers what is known about the pathways into mental health services for children who experience an episode of placement in foster care. Rogler and Cortes (1993) introduced the concept of pathways to assist in the description of ways in which people seek help for mental health problems and how these help-seeking strategies interact with responses from help-giving organizations. They defined *pathways* as "a sequence of contacts with individuals and organizations prompted by the distressed person's efforts, and those of his or her significant others, to seek help as well as the help that is applied in response to such efforts" (p. 555). In the context of children in child welfare, this definition is translated into the following question: How do children and adolescents with need for help with mental health problems come to the attention of service providers and receive treatment? Mental health services research generally addresses this question with studies of factors that predict either referral for mental health care or use of mental health care. These studies distinguish between those factors that concern the clinical condition of the help seeker, such as the presence of behavior problems or psychiatric diagnoses, and nonclinical aspects of the help seeker or the organizations that structure the help seeking, such as demographic status (i.e., age, gender, race/ethnicity) and the availability of treatment services. An explicit assumption in this discussion is that a rational system of mental health service delivery would emphasize clinical factors rather than nonclinical factors as the major predictors of referral and use.

The problem with epidemiologic research that simply reports rates of need for service and rates of service use is that there is no analysis of the relationship between need and use and the factors that may confound that relationship. Research with community and clinical samples indicates that there is a relationship between need and use of children's mental health services, but the relationship may not be as strong as expected. A range of factors other than severity of emotional or behavioral problems are likely to predict service use patterns, including demographic, behavioral, attitudinal, family, service system (service availability and financing), and policy-level factors (Bui & Takeuchi, 1992; Cohen & Hesselbart, 1993; Costello & Janiszewski, 1990; Koot & Verhulst, 1992; Zahner et al., 1992).

Only two studies have reported on the relationship between need, referral, and use of mental health services for children in foster care. In his studies of children entering state custody in Tennessee, Glisson (1994, 1996) found no relationship between the child's mental health status, as measured by the Achenbach Child Behavior Checklist, and the decision to refer for mental health services. No information about actual use of mental health services was provided in the published reports.

In the San Diego County study (Garland et al., 1996; Landsverk, Litrownik, et al., 1996; Leslie et al., 2000), investigators found that there was a significant relationship between need for services, as defined by clinically significant total behavior problems on the Achenbach Child Behavior Checklist (CBCL), and the child's use of services, as reported by the foster parent. Using the reports of service use from the foster parents (Garland et al., 1996; Landsverk, Litrownik, et al., 1996), subjects with clinically significant total behavior problem scores were three times as likely to receive services as those without clinically significant scores, even with the effects of other variables controlled. Using linked Medicaid claims data (Leslie et al., 2000), children above one standard deviation on total behavior problems for the CBCL were significantly more likely to receive mental health services (55.4% vs. 44.6%) and used twice as many outpatient visits (4.13 annual visits vs. 2.14 annual visits). These findings for children in the San Diego foster care system are consistent with community studies that indicate that children and adolescents with clinically significant problems are significantly more likely to receive services (e.g., Koot & Verhulst, 1992).

However, community research on children not in the foster care system also shows that factors other than need for services can be significant predictors of use, including child, family, and service delivery system characteristics (Bui & Takeuchi, 1992; Cohen & Hesselbart, 1993; Costello & Janiszewski, 1990; Koot & Verhulst, 1992; Zahner et al., 1992). An especially pertinent factor for studies of mental health service delivery in the child welfare system is the type of maltreatment for which the child has been placed in foster care. This factor was the special focus of Garland and colleagues in their analysis of data from the San Diego County study (Garland et al., 1996). The investigators found that the subject's type of maltreatment was a significant predictor of use of mental health services, even when the effects of severity of total behavior problems, gender, and age were controlled. Logistic regression analysis revealed that children who were in foster care due to sexual abuse were almost four and a half times more likely to receive mental health services as were children who were not placed for this reason, whereas children who were in placement due to neglect or caretaker absence were only half as likely to receive mental health services as compared with children not placed for reason of neglect. Type of maltreatment was also observed to affect intensity of services, as measured by the number of outpatient visits in the past 6 months. The frequency of visits for sexually abused children was significantly higher than the frequency for children placed because of neglect or caretaker absence. A later analysis from the same study (Leslie et al., 2000) using administrative data on service use found that children with an allegation of physical abuse showed a significantly higher mean number of visits as compared with children without such an allegation. This analysis did not find statistically significant differences on number of visits for allegations of sexual abuse or neglect, suggesting that the relationship of service use to type of maltreatment may be sensitive to how the service use is measured.

A possible explanation for the increased rates of service use among sexually and physically abused youth may include a general perception by case workers, judges, and caretakers that these types of "active" maltreatment have a more negative effect on a child's psychosocial adjustment than do the more "passive" types of maltreatment such as neglect. However, there is very little research to support or refute these perceptions. In one study of the impact of various types and dimensions of maltreatment on children's psychosocial functioning, Manly, Cicchetti, and Barnett (1994) found that dimensions of maltreatment, such as severity and chronicity, were more significant predictors of the global severity of behavior problems than was the type of maltreatment. Nothing in their results suggests that sexually or physically abused children have increased need for mental health services compared with children who were neglected.

The observed differences in service use rates may also reflect the availability of specific types of mental health services. In San Diego, there are established treatment programs for sexually abused children, and the programs receive referrals directly from child protective services. This linkage may help explain why children who were sexually abused were very likely to have received mental health services, regardless of the severity of behavior problems observed by the caretaker. There is no identified treatment program for neglected children. However, this differential in the availability of mental health services may also reflect the underlying perception by system managers that sexually and physically abused children are in greater need of services than neglected children.

In addition to detecting the effect of maltreatment on mental health service use, the San Diego County study also examined the effects of age and gender on service use. Increased age was associated with a significantly greater likelihood of service use, whereas gender did not exert a significant effect when the effect of other variables was controlled. The age effect for children in foster care was also reported by Halfon et al. (1992b) in their study of Medi-Cal data from California. Studies with community samples did not report an increase in service use associated with age, but the samples were generally older, with a more restricted age range (Costello & Janiszewski, 1990; Koot & Verhulst, 1992; Offord et al., 1987; Zahner et al., 1992).

The lack of a significant effect of gender on service use is consistent with some community studies (Koot & Verhulst, 1992; Zahner et al., 1992). The San Diego County study also found that there were no significant interaction effects of age or gender by type of maltreatment, suggesting that the effects of type of maltreatment on service use operate regardless of the age or gender of the child.

Garland et al. (2000) examined the impact of racial and ethnic background of children in the San Diego County foster care system on their use of mental health services. Even after controlling for age, gender, and total behavior problems, African American and Latino children in foster care were significantly less likely to receive mental health services. In addition, the frequency of outpatient visits was significantly predicted by race and ethnic background. This finding is consistent with a review of research on race and child welfare services that found that minority families and children were likely to experience fewer services than their majority counterparts involved with the child welfare system (Courtney et al., 1996).

Garland and Besinger (1997) examined the court records for 142 children between the ages of 2 and 16 who entered foster care in San Diego County and found significant differences by race and ethnicity for mental health service use both prior to foster care entry and after entry. Caucasian youth were more likely to receive court orders for psychotherapy than were African American and Hispanic youth, even when the potential confounding effects of age and type of maltreatment were controlled.

Finally, later analyses by Leslie et al. (2000) in the San Diego study, using administrative mental health services data, replicated the earlier findings using parent report service use data on the impact of race/ethnicity. In addition, the later analyses found an impact of type of placement, with children living only in nonrelative foster care showing significantly greater use of outpatient services than children living in kinship care.

In summary, there is limited recent evidence that both clinical and nonclinical factors affect mental health referral and use patterns for children in foster care. The nonclinical factors implicated in one California study are type of maltreatment, racial/ethnic background, age, and type of placement.

Policy and Practice Implications

Further research is clearly needed to examine the available service systems for maltreated children and to address implicit and explicit policies that may result in the inequitable distribution of service resources based on factors other than need. This work cannot be conducted without parallel lines of research investigating the effectiveness of services for children with different types of maltreatment so that greater specificity in the delivery of appropriate services can be achieved. Specific pathways into services and the barriers to service use must be identified, including an examination of the roles of various gatekeepers and decision makers, such as case managers, judges, and caretakers. Concurrently, advances in developmental psychopathology studies of the sequelae of maltreatment may inform us more specifically about the mental health service needs of children who have been maltreated.

There is a need to develop explicit guidelines to be used in systematically linking children who show need with clinically effective and appropriate services. In particular, these guidelines need to address the issue of nonclinical factors affecting service use in terms such as access to services, acceptability of services, and perception of need for services by "gatekeepers." The guidelines also need to address the type and severity of maladaptive behaviors warranting referral for mental health services. Eventually, models need to be developed that both recommend specific treatment services based on specific emotional and behavioral problems and allow for some flexibility and creativity in treatment choices for children in child welfare.

There is a need to develop explicit guidelines to be used in systematically linking children who show need with clinically effective and appropriate services.

There is a need to develop models for family participation in mental health treatment for children in foster care within the context of dual families. Both biological families in the process of negotiating with child protective services regarding the issues of risk for maltreatment, family functioning, and reunification and foster care/kinship families who are standing in for the biological parent need to be included in models of family participation. This will be necessary so that the policy impetus of family preservation and family empowerment will be better served while children are receiving mental health services to ameliorate their emotional, behavioral, and social problems.

Effectiveness of Mental Health Services

The prior sections of this chapter used results from a growing body of empirical research to suggest that there is substantial evidence for a high rate of need for mental health services and a high rate of use of mental health services for children reported to child protective services, especially in the out-of-home setting of foster care. A reasonable question to ask is whether the use of mental health services results in ameliorating the mental health problems of this high-risk group. Unfortunately, no studies have been conducted that provide an answer to this question. We do not know whether these services are effective in reducing behavioral and emotional symptoms or enhancing functional outcomes in children reported to child protective services.

However, other bodies of research suggest there may not be measurable beneficial effects of mental health services delivered in the type of community settings to which children reported to child protective services are referred. This section briefly discusses the overall research findings from these research areas.

A large body of efficacy trial research supports the conclusion that psychotherapeutic interventions can produce large improvements in children's symptomatology and functioning. Similar evidence exists for the efficacy of psychotropic medications for certain conditions such as attention deficit hyperactivity disorder (ADHD), but that research will not be addressed here. Evidence to support this claim comes from meta-analytic studies that review a broad range of psychotherapeutic interventions in the research literature and from criterion-based reviews of interventions for specific kinds of mental health disorders.

Extensive meta-analytic reviews of clinical trial studies (Casey & Berman, 1985; Kazdin, Bass, Ayers, & Rodgers, 1990; Kazdin & Weisz, 1998; Weisz, Weiss, Alicke, & Klotz, 1987; Weisz, Weiss, & Donenberg, 1992; Weisz, Weiss, Han, Granger, & Morton, 1995), conducted by different investigators and using somewhat different review methodologies, have examined the effects of psychotherapeutic interventions on symptomatology and functioning across a large number of published studies. Uniformly, these reports conclude that psychotherapies for children result in improved clinical outcomes. Depending on the meta-analytic methodology employed (weighted or unweighted least squares), the average treatment effect size (defined as the difference between treatment and control groups, after treatment or at follow-up, divided by the standard deviation of the outcome measure) falls between .5 and .8. These effects are similar to those reported in the meta-analytic literature on adult psychotherapeutic outcomes (Weisz et al., 1992; Weisz et al., 1995). The conclusions of these meta-analyses remain, even when subjected to extensive reanalyses. For example, the positive effects of psychotherapy exist across years within the same meta-analyses and in meta-analyses spanning different years. Outcomes are more positive for domains related to the target of the intervention but are not due to the use of outcome measures that are unnecessarily close to the actual treatment process. Effects of treatment are not limited to immediate post-treatment improvements but remain relatively constant across follow-up periods of a year or more. Positive outcomes appear across different problem categories and across different kinds of potential outcome measures, including parental report and child self-report (Casey & Berman, 1985; Kazdin et al., 1990; Weisz et al., 1995). The conclusions of meta-analytic studies are thus quite robust.

Whereas meta-analytic studies and review papers typically examine the impact of psychotherapies generally or a class of treatments (e.g., Baer & Nietzel, 1991; Grossman & Hughes, 1992), alternative methods have been established to determine whether specific psychotherapeutic interventions result in improved outcomes for children. These methods involve establishing a set of criteria for deciding whether sufficient evidence exists to label a psychotherapeutic treatment as empirically supported (e.g., Chambless & Hollon, 1998). In a series of reviews, a number of different psychotherapies fulfilled the criteria to be judged either "probably efficacious" or "well established" (American Academy of Child and Adolescent Psychiatry, 1998; Birmaher, Ryan, Williamson, Brent, & Kaufman, 1996; Brestan & Eyberg, 1998; Chambless & Williams, 1996; Kaslow & Thompson, 1998; Kazdin & Weisz, 1998;

Pelham, Wheeler, & Chronis, 1998; Ollendick & King, 1998; Rogers, 1998), including treatments for depression and conduct disorders, two of the most common problems presenting for care in public mental health service systems (Rosenblatt & Rosenblatt, 2000).

From both the meta-analytic perspective and the criterion-based perspective, relatively clear evidence exists that psychotherapeutic interventions can result in moderate to large improvements in client outcomes both at the close of treatment and over follow-ups of 1 year or more.

In contrast to the strong evidence demonstrating the efficacy of psychotherapeutic interventions generally and of specific treatments in particular, evidence supporting the effectiveness of mental health treatment delivered in community settings is quite weak. In a meta-analytic review of studies that compared children receiving treatment in a community setting with children receiving no treatment, Weisz et al. (1995) identified nine studies sufficiently well designed for sound conclusions to be drawn. Across the nine studies reviewed, effect sizes for treatment relative to a no-treatment control ranged from −.4 to +.29, with an overall mean effect size of .01. Not surprisingly, this was not significantly different from zero and amounted to no clinically important impact. A closer review of the studies included in this meta-analysis reveals that a number of studies provided relatively good tests of the impact of care delivered in community treatment settings (e.g., Jacob, Magnussen, & Kemler, 1972; Levitt, Beiser, & Robertson, 1959). The studies generally compared children receiving no treatment to children receiving extensive treatment. Tests were conducted to confirm the comparability of groups at baseline; in some cases, quite large sample sizes were employed.

The same conclusions were reached in two studies by Bickman and colleagues that involved relatively similar designs to those employed in the studies reviewed by Weisz et al. (1995). The two studies were follow-up analyses from two major systems of care experiments: the Fort Bragg Evaluation Project (Bickman, 1997) and the Stark County system of care evaluation (Bickman, Noser, & Summerfelt, 1999). As part of the Fort Bragg system-of-care experiment, an analysis was conducted comparing children who received treatment with children who dropped out of treatment early. Andrade, Lambert, and Bickman (2000)

found that over the course of 12 months, outcomes for children receiving care did not differ from outcomes of children who did not receive care. As part of the Stark County system of care experiment, similar analyses were conducted to determine whether children who received care experienced greater improvement than children who never entered care. Results of these analyses replicated the findings of those from the Fort Bragg study, revealing that children who received treatment did not have a trend for greater levels of improvement over time than children who did not receive treatment, nor was there a dose-response effect for children who received extensive treatment relative to those who received less treatment (Bickman et al., 1999). The striking finding about results from both the Fort Bragg and Stark County studies is the fact that services within the systems had been enhanced as part of the original system-of-care experiments. This means that in both studies, evidence to support the effectiveness of "usual care" in the community did not appear despite the presence of a relatively rich service environment.

Policy and Practice Implications

Based on the evidence to date from studies of general public mental health service systems, the effectiveness of mental health services for children referred to child protective services cannot be assumed. In short, good access to care, as inferred from the high proportion of such children receiving mental health services, does not guarantee that the receipt of these services will result in beneficial outcomes. This suggests that practitioners, managers, and policymakers from both the child welfare and the public mental health service systems need to focus on strategies that will increase the effectiveness of ameliorative services, such as increasing the use of evidence-based interventions and improving the quality of mental health care.

A relatively strong empirical and theoretical case can be made for focusing attention on the quality of mental health treatment that children receive (Bickman & Noser, 1999; Hoagwood, Hibbs, Brent, & Jensen, 1995; Noser & Bickman, 2000; Weisz, Han, & Valeri, 1997). This argument can be established on the following grounds. First, a large body of work shows that psychotherapeutic treatments delivered in highly controlled studies can produce improved clinical and functional outcomes for children receiving care. Second, the weight of evidence suggests that care provided in community treatment settings does not result in outcomes significantly better than normal improvements occurring over time. Third, large system-level interventions have failed to improve clinical and functional outcomes over the short or long term. Finally, there is some evidence that many therapists do not regularly adopt empirically based treatments as part of their normal treatment practice. Taken together, these points suggest that attention to treatment process (quality of care) in community treatment settings could have substantial effects on the outcomes achieved by children receiving mental health care. The importance of developing methods for improving treatment quality within community treatment contexts is highlighted by the NIMH reports, *Bridging Science and Service* and *Translating Behavioral Science Into Action* (National Institute of Mental Health, 1999, 2000), which suggest specific directions for improving the translation of effective practices to broader treatment environments.

Organization and Financing in an Era of Managed Care

Patterns of mental health service delivery to children and adolescents involved with the child welfare system are strongly influenced by service system changes at the macro level of health care organization and financing. Over the past decade, particularly large-scale changes in organization and financing have taken place, including the development of managed care technologies, the delinking of AFDC/Temporary Assistance to Needy Families (TANF) from Medicaid, the development of the State Child Health Insurance Program (SCHIP), and the expansion of the Early and Periodic Screening, Diagnosis, and Treatment (EPSDT) program under Medicaid. This section briefly discusses these changes and their likely impact on mental health care for children and adolescents involved with the child protective services system.

Over the past decade, the health care system in the United States has changed in the direction of the rapid employment of managed care and privatization strategies to organize medical care and specialty mental health care systems. Related to the types of families involved in the child welfare system, managed care technologies such as cost sharing, utilization review, and preferred provider networks are increasingly used in health care delivery for poor families covered under the federal Medicaid program. Perhaps the major appeal of managed care to policymakers is its cost-cutting potential.

A particular feature of managed care that emerged in the 1990s is the development of specialized approaches to the delivery of mental health services under managed care. Often, mental health benefits are administered separately from physical health benefits under "carve-out" arrangements, frequently by a small number of national behavioral health companies. In addition, these mental health benefits have been very limited in comparison with the physical health care benefits, leading to important policy debates about "parity." Sturm et al. (1999) observed that the growth of carve-outs "was accompanied by a change in managed care itself, which now often represents intensive concurrent utilization review of specialty care, compared to primary care gate-keeping mechanisms that remain common for other medical care" (p. 222). Strum and colleagues also suggest that mental health care (along with care for alcohol and drug disorders) under managed care arrangements is further differentiated from general medical care in that

> a large and substantially funded public delivery sector has evolved to provide care to the Medicaid and uninsured populations. These public systems today are a complex array of state and locally directed ADM services that include significant contracting with privately owned firms. (p. 222)

The development of capitation models, with their emphasis on the selection of relatively healthy and low-cost target populations, and managed care quality assurance mechanisms such as prior review, single point of entry, utilization review, and practice guidelines have been seen to potentially sacrifice mental health systems of care values in the interests of cost cutting and cost-effectiveness (Jerrell, 1998; Ogles, Trout, Gillespie, & Penkeert, 1998), especially in regard to the care necessary for the more seriously emotionally disturbed who require more expensive care. Related to this growth of managed care models has been the marked policy enthusiasm for the development and implementation of outcome monitoring systems. These systems generally have been characterized as initiatives to make service systems more "accountable" (e.g., performance outcome requirements in California and Texas) (Rosenblatt, Wyman, Kingdon, & Ichinose, 1998). These initiatives are now appearing as state-level mandated systems and are also being driven by the consumer movement in health care.

Related to the rapid deployment of managed care has been the recent shift in Medicaid financed systems from fee-for-service to managed care models. This may have serious implications for youth systems that serve high-risk populations who have been provided mental health care under Medicaid funding, such as children involved in the foster care portion of the child welfare system.

A second major source of change came about through welfare reform and the changes from AFDC eligibility requirements to the more restrictive TANF eligibility requirements. As part of welfare reform, application for social welfare and Medicaid was delinked, and separate TANF and Medicaid applications must be submitted. Although it is unclear how these major policy changes in social welfare may affect the provision of mental health services for children and adolescents in the future, it is reasonable to hypothesize that these changes may reduce Medicaid coverage of child and adolescent specialty mental health services, especially for high-risk children who are involved in the child welfare sector of care. It is likely that some proportion of TANF-eligible families will not take the second required action of applying for Medicaid. In addition, restrictions on the number of years for which TANF will provide support likely will have an impact on insurance coverage for children and adolescents under the Medicaid funding system. Finally, changes in SSI (Supplemental Security Income—demonstrated medical disability as an eligibility requirement) that came about through welfare reform may also affect high-risk children by making it more difficult to meet medical necessity requirements for eligibility.

A third source of change has been the enactment in 1997 of the State Children's Health Insurance Program (SCHIP), which is potentially the largest expansion of health insurance in more than three decades. SCHIP is intended to extend insurance to currently uninsured children in families with up to 200% of poverty-level income. SCHIP operates through block grants to states to expand their Medicaid coverage, establish new programs that subsidize private insurance for children, or combine the two approaches. Approximately equal numbers of states are adopting each of the three options. Published state plans are showing tremendous variability in their decisions regarding eligibility with respect to a child's age and parental income (Rosenbach et al., 2001). Seventeen states are covering all children ages 0 to 18 years at a single percentage of federal poverty level (FPL), ranging from 150% to 300% of the FPL depending on the states. Two states have elected to not cover children from ages 0 to 18 years but have limited ages of children covered to 0 to 14 years (Oklahoma) and 0 to 16 years (Pennsylvania). The other 7 states have chosen to provide enhanced coverage to younger children with respect to income eligibility. States also have considerable flexibility in terms of the benefit packages chosen. Advocates caution that, depending on the state, mental health benefits under the SCHIP plan could be minimal (Bazelon Center for Mental Health Law, 1997). Early reports suggest that enrollment of children and adolescents into SCHIP programs is proving to be difficult and slow (Rosenbach et al., 2001). The impact of SCHIP on the funding and organization of mental health service systems is unknown.

The Early Periodic Screening, Diagnosis, and Treatment (EPSDT) program under Medicaid was originally added to Medicaid in 1967 to ensure that children enrolled in Medicaid would have coverage for a comprehensive range of preventive, primary, and specialized health services (Rosenbach & Gavin, 1998). The 1989 amendments to EPSDT expanded the program, allowing for "interperiodic" screening and requiring that all of the care and services eligible for federal financial assistance under federal law be made available to children younger than age 21 to treat problems revealed on an EPSDT exam. Despite Medicaid's mandate to provide comprehensive care through the EPSDT program, most states have failed to meet this requirement. The percentage of children receiving services through EPSDT is low; of the 22.9 million children eligible for EPSDT in 1996, only 37% received a screening exam through EPSDT (Olson, Perkins, & Pate, 1998). States vary in their outreach programs, number of children receiving services through EPSDT, and their definition of "medically necessary" services. A report by Fox, McManus, Almeida, and Lesser (1997) demonstrated variable inclusion of EPSDT services in managed care contracts; 38 states had a program in place that specifies and explains EPSDT benefits, and an additional 6 states had a plan for implementation of such a program in the future. Of the 38 states, 26 required services to correct or ameliorate identified defects or conditions, 29 required services for both physical and mental health problems, and only 20 states required all federally allowable diagnostic, treatment, and other health care services.

There are signs that states are increasing mental health services to low-income children through Medicaid's EPSDT program. For example, in 1994, California substantially increased such services through the EPSDT program following legal pressure to comply with federal EPSDT guidelines (Lonnie Snowden, personal communication, 2001).

The expansion of resources for children's mental health services through the SCHIP program and the EPSDT program is especially important to children and adolescents involved with the child welfare system because they are likely to come from poor families that meet eligibility requirements for these programs. Therefore, the expansion of these programs is likely to widen access to ameliorative services for this high-risk population.

Policy and Practice Implications

The implementation of managed care mechanisms, especially in Medicaid-funded services, presents a critical challenge to the delivery of health and mental health services to children and adolescents reported to child protective services and served by the child welfare system. Children in the child welfare system, especially the foster care system, are typically dependent on the Medicaid program for financing health care. However, the health and mental health care needs of children in child welfare are more complex than those of the typical child receiving Medicaid benefits (Leslie, Kelleher, Burns, Landsverk, & Rolls, 2001). In addition, children in foster care have unique needs because of their circumstances. Most states have implemented mandatory managed care programs for some or all of their Medicaid populations as a way to control escalating medical costs while providing necessary medical services. The implications of the Medicaid transition to managed care for child welfare and especially for foster care need to be carefully considered by practitioners, managers, and policymakers. Especially crucial is the need for a clearly identified care coordinator under managed care because of the need for comprehensive and coordinated care for this vulnerable population and the frequent placement changes experienced by children in foster care.

The implementation of SCHIP and the expansion of the Medicaid EPSDT program mean that there is a current window of opportunity for greater access to ameliorative services for children and adolescents reported to child protective services. Greater availability of resources also may mean that service systems have greater freedom in developing mechanisms for increasing the quality of care provided, such as the incorporation of more evidence-based treatments in community settings. Advocates for services that target children in the child welfare system need to focus their attention on using the increased access and resources to gain the level of services and coordination of care needed for this population.

References

Achenbach, T. M. (1991). *Integrative guide for the 1991 CBCL/4-18, YSR, and TRF profiles*. Burlington: University of Vermont, Department of Psychiatry.

Aday, L. A., & Andersen, R. M. (1974). A framework for the study of access to medical care. *Health Services Research, 9,* 208-220.

American Academy of Child and Adolescent Psychiatry. (1998). Practice parameters for the assessment and treatment of children and adolescents with depressive disorders. *Journal of the American Academy of Child & Adolescent Psychiatry, 37*(Suppl.), S63-S83.

American Psychiatric Association. (1987). *Diagnostic and statistical manual of mental disorders* (3rd ed., rev.). Washington, DC: Author.

American Psychiatric Association. (1994). *Diagnostic and statistical manual of mental disorders* (4th ed.). Washington, DC: Author.

American Public Welfare Association (APWA). (1990). *A commitment to change: Report of the National Commission on Child Welfare and Family Preservation.* Washington, DC: Author.

Andrade, A. R., Lambert, E. W., & Bickman, L. (2000). Dose effect in child psychotherapy: Outcomes associated with negligible treatment. *Journal of the American Academy of Child and Adolescent Psychiatry, 39*(2), 161-168.

Baer, R. A., & Nietzel, M. T. (1991). Cognitive behavioral treatment of impulsivity in children: A meta-analytic review of the outcome literature. *Journal of Clinical Child Psychology, 20,* 400-412.

Barbell, L. (1997). *Foster care today: A briefing paper.* Washington, DC: Child Welfare League of America.

Barth, R. P., Courtney, M., Berrick, J. D., & Albert, V. (1994). *From child abuse to permanency planning.* New York: Aldine.

Bazelon Center for Mental Health Law. (1997). *Child health block grant program approved* [Online]. Available: www.bazelon.org/bazelon/blkgrant.html.

Bickman, L. (1997). Resolving issues raised by the Fort Bragg evaluation: New directions for mental health services research. *American Psychologist, 52,* 562-565.

Bickman, L., & Noser, K. (1999). Meeting the challenges in the delivery of child and adolescent mental health services in the next millennium: The continuous quality improvement approach. *Applied & Preventive Psychology, 8,* 247-255.

Bickman, L., Noser, K., & Summerfelt, W. T. (1999). Long-term effects of a system of care on children and adolescents. *Journal of Behavioral Health Sciences Research, 26,* 185-202.

Birmaher, B., Ryan, N. D., Williamson, D. E., Brent, D. A., & Kaufman, J. (1996). Childhood and adolescent depression: A review of the past 10 years: Part II. *Journal of the American Academy of Child and Adolescent Psychiatry, 35,* 1575-1583.

Blumberg, E., Landsverk, J., Ellis-Macleod, E., Ganger, W., & Culver, S. (1996). Use of the public mental health system by children in foster care: Client characteristics and service use patterns. *Journal of Mental Health Administration, 23*(4), 389-405.

Brestan, E. V., & Eyberg, S. M. (1998). Effective psychosocial treatments of conduct-disordered children and adolescents: 29 years, 82 studies, 5272 kids. *Journal of Clinical Child Psychology, 27,* 180-189.

Bui, K. T., & Takeuchi, D. T. (1992). Ethnic minority adolescents and the use of community mental health care services. *American Journal of Community Psychology, 20,* 403-417.

Casey, R. J., & Berman, J. S. (1985). The outcome of psychotherapy with children. *Psychological Bulletin, 98,* 388-400.

Chambless, D. L., & Hollon, S. D. (1998). Defining empirically supported therapies. *Journal of Consulting and Clinical Psychology, 66,* 7-18.

Chambless, D. L., & Williams, K. E. (1996). An update on empirically validated therapies. *The Clinical Psychologist, 49,* 5-18.

Clausen, J. M., Landsverk, J., Ganger, W., Chadwick, D., & Litrownik, A. (1998). Mental health problems of children in foster care. *Journal of Child and Family Studies, 78,* 221-239.

Cohen, P., & Hesselbart, C. S. (1993). Demographic factors in the use of children's mental health services. *American Journal of Public Health, 83,* 49-52.

Costello, E. J. (1999). Commentary on prevalence and impact of parent-reported disabling mental health conditions among U.S. children. *Journal of the American Academy of Child and Adolescent Psychiatry, 38,* 610-613.

Costello, E. J., Angold, A., Burns, B., Stangl, D. K., Tweed, D. L., Erkanli, A., & Worthman, C. M. (1996). The Great Smoky Mountains study of youth: Goals, design, and prevalence of *DSM-III-R* disorders. *Archives of General Psychiatry, 53,* 1129-1136.

Costello, E. J., Burns, B. J., Angold, A., & Leaf, P. J. (1993). How can epidemiology improve mental health services for children and adolescents? *Journal of the American Academy of Child and Adolescent Psychiatry, 32,* 1106-1113.

Costello, E. J., Costello, A. J., Edelbrock, C., Burns, B. J., Dulcan, M. K., Brent, D., & Janiszewski, S. (1988). Psychiatric disorders in pediatric primary care. *Archives of General Psychiatry, 45,* 1107-1116.

Costello, E. J., & Janiszewski, S. (1990). Who gets treated? Factors associated with referral in children with psychiatric disorders. *Acta Psychiatrica Scandanavica, 81,* 523-529.

Courtney, M. E., Barth, R. P., Berrick, J. D., Brooks, D., Needell, B., & Park, L. (1996). Race and child welfare services: Past research and future directions. *Child Welfare, 75,* 99-137.

Dubowitz, H., Feigelman, S., Harrington, S., Harrington, D., Starr, R., Zuravin, S., & Sawyer, R. (1994). Children in kinship care: How do they fare? *Children and Youth Services Review, 16*(2).

Farmer, E. M. Z., Burns, B. J., Chapman, M. V., Phillips, S. D., Angold, A., & Costello, E. J. (2001). *Use of mental health services by youth in contact with social services.* Manuscript under review.

Fox, H. B., McManus, M. A., Almeida, R. A., & Lesser, C. (1997). Medicaid managed care policies affecting children with disabilities: 1995 and 1996. *Health Care Financing Review, 18*(4), 23-36.

Friedman, R. M., Katz-Leavy, J. W., Manderscheid, R. W., & Sondheimer, D. L. (1996). Prevalence of serious emotional disturbance in children and adolescents. In Center for Mental Health Services (Ed.), *Mental Health, United States 1996* (DHHS Pub. No. SMA 96-3098). Washington, DC: Government Printing Office.

Garland, A. F., & Besinger, B. A. (1997). Racial/ethnic differences in court referred pathways to mental health services for children in foster care. *Children and Youth Services Review, 19,* 1-16.

Garland, A. F., Hough, R. L., Landsverk, J. A., McCabe, K. M., Yeh, M., Ganger, W. C., & Reynolds, B. J. (2000). Racial/ethnic variations in mental health care utilization among children in foster care. *Children's Services: Social Policy, Research, and Practice.*

Garland, A. F., Landsverk, J. A., Hough, R. L., & Ellis-Macleod, E. (1996). Type of maltreatment as a predictor of mental health service use in foster care. *Child Abuse & Neglect, 20,* 675-688.

Glisson, C. (1994). The effects of services coordination teams on outcomes for children in state custody. *Administration in Social Work, 18,* 1-23.

Glisson, C. (1996, June). Judicial and service decisions for children entering state custody: The limited role of mental health. *Social Service Review,* pp. 257-281.

Gould, M. S., Wunsch-Hitzig, R., & Dohrenwend, B. (1981). Estimating the prevalence of childhood psychopathology. *Journal of the American Academy of Child and Adolescent Psychiatry, 20,* 462-476.

Grossman, P. B., & Hughes, J. N. (1992). Self-control interventions with internalizing disorders: A review and analysis. *School Psychology Review, 21,* 229-245.

Halfon, N., Berkowitz, G., & Klee, L. (1992a). Children in foster care in California: An examination of Medicaid reimbursed health services utilization. *Pediatrics, 89,* 1230-1237.

Halfon, N., Berkowitz, G., & Klee, L. (1992b). Mental health service utilization by children in foster care in California. *Pediatrics, 89,* 1238-1244.

Halfon, N., Inkelas, M., & Wood, D. (1995). Nonfinancial barriers to care for children and youth. *Annual Review of Public Health, 16,* 447-472.

Halfon, N., Mendonca, A., & Berkowitz, G. (1995). Health status of children in foster care: The experience of the Center for the Vulnerable Child. *Archives of Pediatric and Adolescent Medicine, 149,* 386-392.

Harman, J. S., Childs, G. E., & Kelleher, K. J. (2000). Mental health care utilization and expenditures by children in foster care. *Archives of Pediatric and Adolescent Medicine, 154,* 1114-1117.

Heflinger, C. A., Simpkins, C. G., & Combs-Orme, T. (2000). Using the CBCL to determine the clinical status of children in state custody. *Children and Youth Services Review, 22*(1), 55-73.

Hoagwood, K., Hibbs, E., Brent, D., & Jensen, P. (1995). Introduction to the special section: Efficacy and effectiveness in studies of child and adolescent psychotherapy. *Journal of Consulting and Clinical Psychology, 63,* 683-687.

Horwitz, S. M., Simms, M. D., & Farrington, R. (1994). Impact of developmental problems on young children's exits from foster care. *Journal of Developmental and Behavioral Pediatrics, 15,* 105-110.

Jacob, T., Magnussen, M. G., & Kemler, W. M. (1972). A follow-up of treatment terminators and remainers with long-term and short-term symptom duration. *Psychotherapy: Theory, Research and Practice, 9,* 139-142.

Jerrell, J. M. (1998). Utilization management analysis for children's mental health services. *Journal of Behavioral Health Services & Research, 25,* 35-42.

Kaslow, N. J., & Thompson, M. P. (1998). Applying the criteria for empirically supported treatments to studies of psychosocial interventions for child and adolescent depression. *Journal of Clinical Child Psychology, 27,* 146-155.

Kazdin, A. E., Bass, D., Ayers, W. A., & Rodgers, A. (1990). Empirical and clinical focus of child and adolescent psychotherapy research. *Journal of Consulting and Clinical Psychology, 58,* 729-740.

Kazdin, A. E., & Weisz, J. R. (1998). Identifying and developing empirically supported child and adolescent treatments. *Journal of Consulting and Clinical Psychology, 66,* 19-36.

Knitzer, J., & Yelton, S. (1990). Collaborations between child welfare and mental health: Both systems must exploit the program possibilities. *Public Welfare, 48,* 24-33.

Koot, H. M., & Verhulst, F. C. (1992). Prediction of children's referral to mental health and special education services from earlier adjustment. *Journal of Child Psychology and Psychiatry, 33,* 717-729.

Landsverk, J., Davis, I., Ganger, W., Newton, R., & Johnson, I. (1996). Impact of child psychosocial functioning on reunification from out-of-home care. *Children and Youth Services Review, 18,* 447-462.

Landsverk, J., Litrownik, A., Newton, R., Ganger, W., & Remmer, J. (1996). *Psychological impact of child maltreatment.* Final report to National Center on Child Abuse and Neglect, Washington, DC.

Leslie, L. K., Gordon, J. N., Ganger, W., & Gist, K. (in press). Developmental delay in young children in child welfare by initial placement type. *Infant Mental Health Journal.*

Leslie, L. K., Kelleher, K., Burns, B. J., Landsverk, J., & Rolls, J. A. (2001). *Managed care: Making it work for children in foster care.* Manuscript under review.

Leslie, L. K., Landsverk, J., Ezzet-Lofstrom, R., Tschann, J. M., Slymen, D. J., & Garland, A. F. (2000). Children in foster care: Factors influencing outpatient mental health services use. *Child Abuse & Neglect, 24,* 465-476.

Levitt, E. E., Beiser, H. R., & Robertson, R. E. (1959). A follow-up evaluation of cases treated at a community child guidance clinic. *American Journal of Orthopsychiatry, 29,* 337-347.

Madsen, J. (1992). *Mental health assessment of children in foster care.* Doctoral dissertation submitted to the University of California, San Diego and San Diego State University.

Manly, J. T., Cicchetti, D., & Barnett, D. (1994). The impact of subtype, frequency, chronicity, and severity of child maltreatment on social competence and behavior problems. *Development and Psychopathology, 6,* 121-143.

National Institute of Mental Health. (1999). *Bridging science and service: A report by the National Advisory Mental Health Council's Clinical Treatment and Services Research Workgroup.* Rockville, MD: Author.

National Institute of Mental Health. (2000). *Translating behavioral science into action: Report of the National Advisory Mental Health Council Behavioral Science Workgroup.* Rockville, MD: Author.

Noser, K., & Bickman, L. (2000). Quality indicators of children's mental health services: Do they predict client outcomes? *Journal of Emotional and Behavioral Disorders, 8,* 9-18.

Offord, D. R., Boyle, M. H., Szatmari, P., Rae-Grant, N. I., Links, P. S., Cadman, D. T., Byles, J. A., Crawford, J. W., Blum, H. M., Byrne, C., Thomas, H., & Woodword, C. A. (1987). Ontario child health study: II. Six month prevalence of disorder and rates of service utilization. *Archives of General Psychiatry, 44,* 832-836.

Ogles, B. M., Trout, S. C., Gillespie, D. K., & Penkeert, K. S. (1998). Managed care as a platform for cross-system integration. *Journal of Behavioral Health Services & Research, 25,* 252-268.

Ollendick, T. H., & King, N. J. (1998). Empirically supported treatments for children with phobic and anxiety disorders: Current status. *Journal of Clinical Child Psychology, 27,* 156-167.

Olson, K., Perkins, J., & Pate, T. (1998). *Children's health under Medicaid: A national review of early and periodic screening, diagnosis, and treatment.* Washington, DC: National Health Law Program.

Pelham, W. E., Wheeler, T., & Chronis, A. (1998). Empirically supported psychosocial treatments for attention deficit hyperactivity disorder. *Journal of Clinical Child Psychology, 27,* 190-205.

Petit, M. R., & Curtis, P. A. (1997). *Child abuse and neglect: A look at the states.* Washington, DC: Child Welfare League of America Press.

Pilowsky, D. (1995). Psychopathology among children placed in family foster care. *Psychiatric Services, 46,* 906-910.

Rogers, S. J. (1998). Empirically supported comprehensive treatments for young children with autism. *Journal of Clinical Child Psychology, 27,* 168-179.

Rogler, L. H., & Cortes, D. E. (1993). Help-seeking pathways: A unifying concept in mental health care. *American Journal of Psychiatry, 150,* 554-561.

Rosenbach, M., Ellwood, M., Czajka, J., Irvin, C., Coupe, W., & Quinn, B. (2001). *Implementation of the state children's health insurance program: Momentum is increasing after a modest start.* Cambridge, MA: Mathematica Policy Research.

Rosenbach, M., & Gavin, N. I. (1998). Early and periodic screening, diagnosis, and treatment and managed care. *Annual Review of Public Health, 19,* 507-525.

Rosenblatt, A., & Rosenblatt, J. (2000). Demographic, clinical, and functional characteristics of youth enrolled in six California systems of care. *Journal of Child and Family Studies, 9,* 51-66.

Rosenblatt, A., Wyman, N., Kingdon, D., & Ichinose, C. (1998). Managing what you measure: Creating outcome-driven systems of care for youth with serious emotional disturbances. *Journal of Behavioral Health Services & Research, 25,* 177-193.

Shaffer, D., Fisher, P., Lucas, C. P., Dulcan, M. K., & Schwab-Stone, M. E. (2000). NIMH Diagnostic Interview Schedule for Children version IV (NIMH DISC-IV): Description, differences from previous versions, and reliability of some common diagnoses. *Journal of the American Academy of Child and Adolescent Psychiatry, 39,* 28-38.

Simms, M. D. (1989). The foster care clinic: A community program to identify treatment needs of children in foster care. *Journal of Developmental and Behavioral Pediatrics, 10,* 121-128.

Sturm, R., Gresenz, C. R., Sherbourne, C. D., Minnium, K., Klap, R., Bhattacharya, J., Farley, D., Young, A. S., Burnam, M. A., & Wells, K. A. (1999). The design of Health Care for Communities: A study of health care delivery for alcohol, drug abuse, and mental health conditions. *Inquiry, 36*(2), 221-233.

Takayama, J. I., Bergman, A. B., & Connell, F. A. (1994). Children in foster care in the state of Washington: Health care utilization and expenditures. *Journal of the American Medical Association, 271,* 1850-1855.

Trupin, E. W., Tarico, V. S., Benson, P. L., Jemelka, R., & McClellan, J. (1993). Children on child protective service caseloads: Prevalence and nature of serious emotional disturbance. *Child Abuse & Neglect, 17,* 345-355.

Urquiza, A. J., Wirtz, S. J., Peterson, M. S., & Singer, V. A. (1994). Screening and evaluating abused and neglected children entering protective custody. *Child Welfare, 123,* 155-171.

U.S. Department of Health and Human Services, Children's Bureau Administration on Children Youth and Families. (2000). *The AFCARS report: Current estimates as of January, 2000* [Online]. Available: www.afc.dhhs.gov/programs/cb.

Weisz, J. R., Han, S. S., & Valeri, S. M. (1997). More of what? Issues raised by the Fort Bragg study. *American Psychologist, 52,* 541-545.

Weisz, J. R., Weiss, B., Alicke, M. D., & Klotz, M. L. (1987). Effectiveness of psychotherapy with children and adolescents: A meta-analysis for clinicians. *Journal of Consulting and Clinical Psychology, 55,* 542-549.

Weisz, J. R., Weiss, B., & Donenberg, G. R. (1992). The lab versus the clinic: Effects of child and adolescent psychotherapy. *American Psychologist, 47,* 1578-1585.

Weisz, J. R., Weiss, B., Han, S. S., Granger, D. A., & Morton, T. (1995). Effects of psychotherapy with children and adolescents revisited: A meta-analysis of treatment outcome studies. *Psychological Bulletin, 117,* 450-468.

Zahner, G. E. P., Pawelkiewicz, W., DeFrancesco, J. J., & Adnopoz, J. (1992). Children's mental health service needs and utilization patterns in an urban community: An epidemiological assessment. *Journal of the American Academy of Child and Adolescent Psychiatry, 31,* 951-960.

25

Community Organization of Services to Deal With and End Child Abuse

DAVID L. CHADWICK

The recognition and the increasingly sophisticated definition of child abuse over the past 30 years have revealed a large number of needs and a growing list of services and interventions. However, resources have failed to grow along with the professionally perceived needs and the knowledge of presumably helpful remedies. Most communities now recognize abused children at a rate between 2% and 3% of all children in the community each year (U.S. Department of Health and Human Services [DHHS], 1996), and most provide a number of interventions and services that attempt to interrupt abuse, prevent it, or deal appropriately with its consequences. Although the services and interventions tend to be quite similar from one locale to another in the United States, the manner in which they are provided, the organization of services, and the ways in which they relate vary considerably. Services and interventions have developed as *responses* to the problems of abuse as the problems have been recognized. Most are described in detail elsewhere in this book; the connections between them and the ways of improving outcomes are the subject of this chapter.

Despite 40 years of more or less organized efforts, no political jurisdiction in the United States has reported that child abuse has ceased. Neither has any other country in the world, although international comparisons are difficult and rare. Sweden appears to have less physical abuse than the United States (Gelles & Edfeldt, 1986) and has essentially eliminated the homicide of infants between birth and 1 year (Durrant, 1999). However, sexual abuse persists there (Edgardh & Ormstad, 2000; Edgardh, von Krogh, & Ormstad, 1999).

Very recently, some speakers, authors, and thinkers have begun to discuss the possibility that most child maltreatment as we now recognize it could be ended (Chadwick, 1999; Sadler, Chadwick, & Hensler, 1999). Such explicit goals were largely unstated in the past, and the implicit goals of most programs and individual professionals were to identify and interrupt ongoing maltreatment, institute criminal proceedings in serious and provable cases, and treat the problems that resulted from the abuse. At the time of this writing, the new initiative is called "The National Call to Action to End Child Abuse" (Hensler, 2000). Widespread discussion of the new goal is designed to bring about a radical paradigm shift. If the goal can be adopted nationally, we will be looking at a major, long-term, and expensive effort that will achieve a goal at some definable point in the future in place of a never-ending, expensive struggle against an intractable problem. If the goal becomes a national goal, it would also necessarily become the goal of states, counties, cities, "communities," and most individuals. This would be a cultural sea change.

The activities required will need to be located very close to children and families. However, roles exist for the larger "communities" (meaning states and the nation). These will be the following:

- to improve knowledge and practice through research,
- to discover uniform and valid ways to measure success,
- to disseminate improved practices,
- to fund what may be some very significant costs,
- to design overarching policies that will facilitate dealing with abuse in the field,
- to develop and sustain the political will that is needed to bind the effort together at all levels.

The actual services to prevent abuse and the interventions that interrupt it must be delivered to families by persons in their communities and close to them. Success will be achieved (and measured) in counties, cities, neighborhoods, parks and streets, work sites, schools, and homes. However, general acceptance of the goal and its feasibility requires a multicentric political process that diffuses in all directions until it becomes confluent.

The "child abuse movement" has a substantial political history that is beyond the scope of this chapter. A recent and important component is the work of the U.S. Advisory Board on Child Abuse and Neglect. This has been summarized (Krugman, 1996). Many of the necessary steps to the ending of child abuse are described in these reports.

In the past, the political component of the movement was largely initiated and managed by professionals who were dealing with abuse and looking for better policies to support their work. Despite the fact that about 25% of U.S. citizens are abused during childhood, the massive potential constituency of persons who can speak with "authentic voices" has never been mobilized in support of the needed policy changes. One vital part of the call to action to end child abuse will be an attempt to bring such persons to the table for all discussions of policy and to develop the political strength that will be needed. In the process of developing community plans for dealing with child abuse, it will be essential to involve the authentic voices locally and to use their experiences in the process of improving services and policies.

Another belief that has dominated past efforts was that most of the work to interrupt child abuse would be performed by governmental agencies at the state or county level. Although the role of governmental agencies remains important, they will not be able to end child abuse without the cultural change that makes that achievement valuable to everyone. The role of the private sector is likely to be much more important in the future.

The concept of interdisciplinary work in child abuse is well accepted, and communication between different agencies and individuals who are attempting to manage individual cases is not a new idea (Bross, Ballo, & Korfmacher, 2000; Bross, Krugman, Lenherr, Rosenberg, & Schmitt, 1988; Hochstadt & Harwicke, 1985; Krugman,

1984). However, the notion that political jurisdictions, definable neighborhoods, or regions might consciously attempt to organize the services that deal with violence against children and other vulnerable family members in a coherent way is still not standard. Organization of services follows traditional patterns in which professional sectors such as social services, justice, education, health, and their contained disciplines generally operate independently. The quantity and quality of coordination are highly variable, and the services are determined by the education of the providers rather than the human problems that exist. However, there appears to be an increase in both co-location of services and collaboration between traditional agencies, and these interesting changes will be discussed.

Because many disciplines must contribute skills to the assessment and management of child abuse cases, most communities have informal or formal networks of professionals who participate in these processes. An effect of these contacts is the development of a shared body of knowledge about child abuse that is regularly applied and allows the promulgation of guidelines and standards. Knowledge about child abuse was very limited a few decades ago and at present is growing rapidly as a result of increased clinical experience and formal research. Moving and sharing this new knowledge are vital. Any form of community organizational plan must include a plan for the continuing education of the participating professionals.

Goals and Objectives

The Goal Is to End Child Abuse in a Generation or So

The goal of ending child abuse in a generation must be endorsed by most persons and by all that play professional roles in dealing with the problem if it is to be achieved. Because child abuse is often an ongoing phenomenon, an important component of ending it is the interruption of ongoing abuse and prevention of recurrence. Three 20-year objectives are the following:

1. Children younger than age 5 do not experience abuse.

2. No abused child carries the problems associated with his or her abuse into his or her adulthood.

3. Our nation's child protection systems are reconstituted to deliver the highest quality response in every community.

These are not the only possible objectives, but if these were achieved, a claim could be made that the major goal of ending the problem was proven to be achievable. The focus of prevention on the early years stems from both practical and sound theoretical factors. The delivery of preventive services can best be initiated during the perinatal period when most families have lots of contact with health providers and such services fit in well with other sorts of care. In addition, the rewards of prevention of early abuse and neglect are likely to be greater because the developmental imperatives in the early months and years make these young children more vulnerable and the effects of maltreatment are more damaging and prolonged (Glaser, 2000).

Despite the fact that about 25% of U.S. citizens are abused during childhood, the massive potential constituency of persons who can speak with "authentic voices" has never been mobilized in support of the needed policy changes.

Principles and Values for Organization

Effective organization of local services and interventions to interrupt and end child abuse is more likely to occur if there is general agreement on a number of principles and values. Some of these are listed in categories as follows.

A. Definition of Goals and Objectives

The bold goal of ending child abuse must remain constant. Objectives will change from time to time as progress is made.

B. Equitable Delivery and Complete Access to Services for All Children and Families

1. Organization should provide services and interventions in an equitable, culturally competent manner to all children and families.
2. Discrimination in the application of interventions based on ethnicity or economic status is unfair and must be identified and stopped whenever it occurs.
3. Demonstrably serious harmful actions affecting children are not culturally acceptable in the United States, although they may be tolerated in other countries.
4. Organization must ensure access to interventions and services by all children and families.

C. Highest Standards of Professional Performance in All Cases and All Programs

1. The practices required for the successful protection of children by the interruption of ongoing abuse are well described but very exacting. Errors are costly, and present error rates tend to be high. The resources needed for these interventions are very great. These resources will be needed for a number of years to come.
2. The practices required for criminal prosecution of child abuse in appropriate cases are also very demanding and require major resources. These activities are also likely to be needed for many years to come but not indefinitely.
3. Interventions to protect children and activities to investigate serious abuse must often be available very promptly, and such capabilities must be available at all times with very short response times.
4. The practices required to protect children by improving overall care of children in families are still under development but are sufficiently advanced to justify universal, voluntary application together with ongoing evaluation. It is efficient and sensible to initiate these services in the perinatal period. If this becomes universal, the youngest children will be protected first and older children later.
5. The practices required to achieve healing for abused children and to minimize generational violence are quite well developed,

and such services should be universally available as long as children are abused. Treatment services must also be available for adults abused as children.
6. Organization requires definition of best practices for all services and interventions (by any and all disciplines) affecting abused children, children at risk for abuse, and all involved family members. Frequent updating of best-practices documents based on new evidence is essential. Best practices are likely to be nationally applicable with some local adaptation.
7. Organization requires application of quality assurance and quality improvement processes for *all* activities.

D. Governmental Powers and Responsibilities

1. Legislators at all levels must know about child abuse. They must work toward its ending, its interruption, and its treatment in their political jurisdictions. Developing knowledge and movement toward the goal will bring about needs for frequent legislative change.
2. Vital executive branch functions include public social services, public safety (law enforcement and prosecution), public health, and public education at all levels. Improved practice in many specific areas is needed, and almost all jurisdictions need to improve the coordination of activities.
3. The judiciary currently plays a vital role in dealing with child abuse after it occurs, and these activities will be required for many years to come but at a steadily decreasing level as prevention becomes effective. No major change in this role is proposed; however, knowledge of child abuse issues in the judiciary must be increased.
4. The governments of states and the nation must support research and development to improve knowledge and practice and to provide the science and technology that allow a high level of certainty about the incidence and prevalence of abuse and the changes over time.

E. Duties and Relationships of Governmental and Private Providers

1. Interventions that require the use of the authority to make arrests, enter homes, detain or restrain persons against their will,

or assume the responsibility for the care of children can be carried out only by agencies of the government reporting ultimately to elected officials and supervised by judicial decisions.

2. Public child protective services and law enforcement agencies based in state and local governments should generally limit their work to the functions requiring authority.

3. Services that require the development of "therapeutic alliances" and ongoing relationships should generally be provided by the private sector, and children and families should be able to exercise choice in their selection.

4. Many services provided by the private sector may be supported by public funds. The governmental payer can and should set standards and guidelines for such care based on expert recommendations and peer acceptance.

F. Coordinating the Work of Multiple Organizations and Professions

1. The interruption and the ending of child abuse require involvement of many organizations, persons, professions, and activities. A form of local authority that can oversee this work is required at the state, county, city, and possibly the neighborhood level.

2. "Sectors" that must cooperate in this work include (at least) social services, justice, health, and education. All of these sectors exist in public and private settings. None is more important than the others, and all are less important than the problem.

3. Co-location of activities markedly increases the likelihood of coordination and cooperation.

4. Dealing with child abuse and ending it both require the careful management of a number of related activities. Management structures need to be developed, and a corps of managers who understand the problems must be trained. "Generic" management skill and experience are not sufficient.

5. The organization of interventions and services must be planned. The complexity in the activities described earlier creates an absolute requirement for planning at all levels, especially at the levels of intervention or service delivery.

G. Authentic Voices Are Heard

1. Persons whose lives have been more or less directly affected by child abuse must be involved in dealing with the problem. Although such participation must be voluntary, it must be encouraged by professionals and governmental entities. It should be developed on a very large scale, and substantial resources must be applied to this development.

2. Identified authentic voices should participate in many ways but, most important, in mutual support, policy development, advocacy, and, in professional education, the development of standards and oversight. Given that about 25% of U.S. adults experienced abuse as children, many such persons are also likely to be engaged as professionals. Although disclosure of a history of abuse may be encouraged in the professions, it cannot ethically be required.

H. Privacy, Confidentiality, and Communication

1. Organization should facilitate communication between agencies and individuals that work with abused children and their families. Confidentiality needs of affected persons must be respected, but confidentiality should never be used as an excuse for a failure to communicate essential information between professionals who are making decisions that may affect the lives of abused children and their families. The use of contemporary communications technologies is essential to this work.

2. Interactions and demonstration by grandparents and relatives to mothers, fathers, and children may be the best ways to diffuse knowledge, skill, and attitude about child nurture and family safety. However, home visitors can substitute for natural teachers and can bring increasing knowledge about infant and child development. Prevention work should always include attempts to link families and children in ways that promote good parenting. Whenever possible, communal forms of infant and child care should be encouraged.

3. Although privacy is valued in many ways, its overemphasis leads to isolation and loss of social restraints that tend to prevent child abuse. Programs that encourage all adults to assist in protecting children in

their neighborhoods may be valuable in prevention.

I. A Cultural Change Is Required

1. In the culture to be created, most adults will be aware of child abuse and will know their own roles in prevention and family support.
2. Work sites and schools will do what they can to prevent abuse. Businesses and corporations will be family friendly and child friendly.
3. Children's rights, as defined in the United Nations Convention on the Rights of the Child (United Nations High Commissioner for Human Rights, 1989), will be taken for granted in the United States.

J. Ending Child Abuse Requires Ending Violence Against Women and the Elderly in the Home

1. Violence against intimate partners, the elderly, the disabled, and other vulnerable persons in the presence of children is actually a form of emotional child abuse even though the child may not have been directly assaulted (see Chapter 6, this volume). Programs that focus on these violence forms must be coordinated with work on child abuse. The ending of child abuse will probably involve the ending of other violence in the home.

The Organization of Services and Interventions

A. Recognition and Reporting of Maltreatment

Reporting child abuse is reviewed in Chapter 22 of this volume. The reporting function requires a level of knowledge and awareness among persons who encounter children as a result of their work (mandated reporters) and a consciousness of abuse in the population at large. The needed level of knowledge and awareness usually has been sought by the provision of continuing education programs for professionals who deal with children and through publication of

standards and guidelines for these professionals. More guidance for the public at large is needed.

Mandated reporters of child abuse are professional persons whose work makes it likely that they will see abused children. The professions involved are health care (almost all types), education, child care, welfare, law enforcement, and a few others. In most states, workers in these professions are required to report the "reasonable suspicion" of child abuse to a law enforcement or child protective agency.

Mandated reporters often are experienced with children and families and capable of performing preliminary assessments of the cases they see so that their reports may express more than "suspicion." They also are often connected to the families of abused children in ways that give them valuable insights into what sort of interventions may be appropriate in the cases they report. Often (although not always) they want to be in a position to recommend further steps in investigation or intervention. Whenever it is feasible, they should be offered opportunities to participate in interdisciplinary discussions about the cases they have reported, and, in almost all cases, they should be provided with feedback about the case they have reported as the case moves forward. Two major reasons for professional disenchantment with reporting are the lack of feedback and the perceived high error rates in protective interventions.

Education for mandated reporters will be needed as long as mandated reporting is in place.

B. Detailed Assessment of Children Suspected of Being Abused

The process requires a sufficient amount of investigation to determine, at some level of certainty, that the child in question has (or has not) been abused and to acquire as much information as possible about the abuse. A number of different sorts of assessment techniques may be needed, depending on the individual case; however, interviewing of children who are old enough to describe their experiences and medical examination of children of all ages are essential components for almost all cases involving all maltreatment forms. Both of these functions are well described (see Chapters 12,

13, and 18, this volume; see also Feldman, 1997; Saywitz & Goodman, 1996).

Most of the investigative processes are described in considerable detail elsewhere in this text. The various functions performed by different professional disciplines overlap. Without cooperation among professionals and agencies, dealing with a child abuse case that calls for criminal investigation, child protective action, and medical care for a serious condition of the child will quickly become chaotic. Communities must have protocols that describe the roles of different agencies and professionals in these processes, and this is a part of organizational planning.

C. An Emerging Model: The Child Advocacy Center

In 1985, the first children's advocacy center (CAC) opened in Huntsville, Alabama. This program was initiated by a prosecutor seeking a safe, competent, and reliable service for the interviewing of children who were suspected of having been sexually abused. The Huntsville Center soon expanded its services and became known as the National Children's Advocacy Center (2000).

The model became popular and gained national support from Justice Department resources. A national network of children's advocacy centers evolved into the National Children's Alliance (2000), an umbrella organization that provides standard setting, accreditation, and education for the CACs that now number over 400. To be accredited, all CACs must offer all forms of assessment services (except perpetrator interviews and exams), and they may also provide mental health care. CACs may be based in any of a number of community institutions, including hospitals, and many hospitals with child abuse programs have developed qualifying CACs. CACs now concern themselves with all child abuse forms, and they strive to co-locate child protective services (CPS), law enforcement and health services, and intervention capabilities to improve coordination and provide one-stop functionality.

More than any other professional group, the National Children's Alliance and the component CACs are building a national model for coordinated and competent child abuse interventions and services. Although the system grew from a justice orientation using a justice-funding stream, it is fully committed to the interdisciplinary concepts that are needed for all competent professional work affecting child abuse.

D. The Assessment of Hospitalized Children

The most serious cases of physical abuse surface in hospitals, and a majority of children who die from abuse do so after a period or resuscitation and intensive hospital care. In the past two decades, a system for the accreditation of designated hospitals as "trauma centers" has been developed by the American College of Surgeons (2000). The best care for injured patients is provided in such centers, and many jurisdictions have "trauma systems" that encourage or require their use for major injuries.

Suspected abused children in hospitals must have specialized assessment by physicians familiar with the syndromes of inflicted injury. At present, most of the physicians who are qualified in this area are pediatricians. However, special contributions in the objective determination of injury mechanisms often can be provided by radiologists, neurosurgeons, neurologists, and critical care physicians.

The most serious cases of physical abuse surface in hospitals, and a majority of children who die from abuse do so after a period or resuscitation and intensive hospital care.

Communities with organized trauma systems that admit children must include physical abuse diagnostic and substantiation services at the sites of care. All primary health care providers that see children must have basic knowledge and skill for the recognition of abuse.

E. Fatal Child Abuse Cases

Fatal child abuse cases require that communities establish "medical examiner" systems for the investigation of unexplained or suspicious deaths. Autopsies of such cases by forensic pathologists should be mandatory in all cases, including those infant deaths that appear to be related to sudden infant death syndrome (SIDS).

An infant death cannot be classified as SIDS unless an autopsy is performed (American Academy of Pediatrics, 1994). Forensic pathologists need to be very familiar with the syndromes of child physical abuse and with the knowledge that differentiates unintentional from inflicted injury after death (Kirschner & Wilson, 1994).

Systematic review of all child fatalities is an excellent method for ensuring that deaths from inflicted injury are discovered. However, it will not work well in the absence of competent forensic pathology and training of pathologists about child abuse. Communities that still operate fatality review systems under the direction of "lay coroners" should reexamine their systems carefully and attempt to secure the services of forensic pathologists through shared arrangements with neighboring communities or with statewide medical examiner systems. In addition, the training programs for forensic pathology generally need to provide more emphasis on child abuse.

The review of fatal cases that may be due to inflicted injuries also requires the participation of physicians and other health personnel who had contact with the case prior to death. Although this is most important in relationship to observations and care during the period immediately preceding death, medical data also may be needed going back to the time of birth. The observations of emergency medical providers who go into homes in response to calls from caretakers may be valuable, as may be the observations of nurses from the bedside care of hospitalized children. Scene data collected by law enforcement or protective service workers who visit the home also are valuable in many cases. Fatal case review has become standard in many states and communities (Durfee, Gellert, & Tilton-Durfee, 1992). This process enhances the recognition of child abuse deaths in communities that have such teams (see Chapter 15, this volume).

F. The Assessment Site(s)

The CAC model has been described earlier and constitutes the only site type with an organized system of accreditation and quality control. Designated assessment sites for abused children and their families are now the standard in most communities. Large cities often have several sites, and the number that the city needs and can support varies. Rural areas and small communities often must share assessment sites. A single assessment site can serve a total population of 2 or 3 million comfortably. However, the ability to reach the site within 1 hour is a desirable feature. Small communities in lightly populated areas should have sites that serve smaller populations.

Sites are based in a variety of different facilities. Hospitals with emergency departments and with pediatric services often house assessment sites. Children's emergency shelters must be capable of providing basic health assessment to children at the site, and definitive evidential assessments also may be provided in emergency shelters. Ideally, an assessment site provides a focal point in which many child abuse-related services can be offered.

G. Definitive Decision Making: Organization of the Courts

Criminal and protective interventions in child abuse cases often are contested by affected parties, resulting in litigation or bargaining in the face of litigation. The courts provide the means for decision making in such cases. Depending on the nature of the child abuse case, any of a number of forms of litigation may occur. The most common and the most important are the protective action in the juvenile (or sometimes family) court and the criminal case brought against a suspected abuser in a criminal court. Domestic (divorce) courts also are involved in many child abuse cases, and the determination of jurisdiction sometimes may cause problems. Competence of judges themselves and of the supporting investigative staffs is an important issue, and courts must avail themselves of the opportunities for learning that are available (National Council of Juvenile and Family Court Judges, 2000).

For the courts also, planning and developing protocols are essential in avoiding unnecessary conflict and inefficiency. Courts also can set standards and guidelines for the participation of various professionals (especially attorneys and expert witnesses) in child abuse work. The courts themselves must develop special knowledge and skills to provide competent judgments in child maltreatment cases.

The most controversial aspect of the litigation of child abuse cases may be that of determining who is and who is not qualified to provide expert testimony. Many courts still allow testimony by physicians whose only involvement with child abuse cases is in connection with litigation (Chadwick & Krous, 1997).

H. Ongoing Interventions and Services to Families

After child abuse has been reported, investigated, and proven, any one or a large array of interventions, services, and treatments may be put in place. Some of these are voluntary for the persons affected, and some are court mandated.

Some of the interventions are incompatible with others—for example, a long period of confinement for an abusing parent may be incompatible with family preservation or with a reunification plan.

There also may be a tendency to consider a case as solved once the court actions are over and decisions made. However, regardless of the short-term dispositions, the underlying problems that led to the abuse are unlikely to be solved quickly. In the ongoing management of such cases, coordinated efforts are needed especially from social services, personal health services, preventive family support services, and mental health services. The same is true for families whose children have been removed and placed in foster care or kinship care and for whom reunification is planned, as well as for those children and families in which parental rights have been terminated and adoption or guardianship is being sought.

Community protocols describing the participation and responsibilities of the various agencies and professionals also should be developed for these later phases of care. Except for criminal sanctions, most of what is done after the proof of abuse is the promotion of healing, and these therapeutic and supportive services are best provided by the private sector.

Foster care is beset with problems as a result of chronic and severe governmental neglect of the system (Simms, 1999). However, exemplary care can be and sometimes is provided to foster children, and good models exist (Casey Family Program, 2000). Repair or replacement of this and other damaged components of the system formerly known as "child welfare" is essential to ending child abuse.

I. Provision of Abuse-Focused Mental Health Services

The long-term effects of child abuse on the mental and physical health of survivors constitute a serious personal and public health issue (Briere, Woo, McRae, Foltz, & Sitzman, 1997; Felitti et al., 1998). Although it is not yet certain that mental health services provided to abused children can avert all of the long-term problems, it is reasonable to attempt to provide such care in every identified case of child abuse in which the child or adult has symptoms. The treatment of asymptomatic persons is not of proven value; however, survivors with histories of very severe events need careful mental health assessments and an "open door" to future care because symptoms may appear after intervals and as a result of developmental or life events.

Crisis counseling and sensitive support services should be available at the "assessment site." More definitive and prolonged services will be needed by many victims, perpetrators, and family members, and very few, if any, communities have the resources to provide these at the levels that are needed. Depending on community size, population distribution, and many other factors, these services may be organized or provided in a variety of ways. Because mental health services typically require frequent visits to the therapist over long periods of time, long travel times for access are likely to result in difficulties for families. Therefore, decentralization of these services is essential.

Mental health services for the persons affected by child abuse require that providers have specialized training or experience that provides familiarity with the problems that are likely to develop as a result of abuse and the therapies that are effective for them. A first principle in abuse-focused therapy is that the abusive acts should stop if a good outcome is to be achieved. The use of insight therapy in the face of ongoing abuse may do more harm than good.

Mental health services must be tailored to the mental health problems presented by clients who have a wide range of symptoms, behaviors, and degrees of severity. Services should meet these needs to the maximum extent that is compatible with available resources. The tendency for persons abused as children to repeat these behaviors as they grow up (Kaufman & Zigler, 1987) imposes a social mandate for treatment beyond the individual needs to relieve distressing symptoms. It also imposes a mandate for sufficient follow-up to determine the long-term outcome of as many cases as possible.

All of the conventional settings for mental health care are likely to be needed by certain abuse survivors, including outpatient care, day care, residential and group home care, and inpatient and intensive care.

In addition, specialized services that focus on the needs of preschool children and infants also are needed badly, although rarely available. Many very young children are physically abused or neglected, and some are sexually abused as well. The long-term disabling effects of early abuse are potentially profound but not inevitable. Therapeutic preschool settings appear to have great value in ameliorating these effects (Kempe, 1987), but mental health professionals with training and experience in treating abused infants and preschool children are in short supply. Most communities now settle for a system that attempts to interrupt the abuse and attempts to place the infant in a caring and supportive environment (typically foster or kinship care).

Mental health providers in the public and private sectors should work with the agencies involved in child abuse services to develop community protocols to ensure the provision of the best possible care to the largest number of children in a climate of scarcity.

Prevention Programs

A. Home-Based Programs

Prevention of child maltreatment is addressed in detail in Chapter 21. Research (Brust, Heins, & Rheinberger, 1998; Guterman, 1997) has demonstrated the feasibility and probable cost-effectiveness of some home-based services for the prevention of child abuse. Hawaii has developed a statewide program based on a combination of risk assessment and home-based services for high-risk families. The program is sponsored and funded by the state, but the provision of services is contracted to nonprofit entities, including a hospital. The close relationship of the home-based service program to the clients is an important feature of this program. At present, many models and best practices are still under study. Olds (Olds, 1992; Olds et al., 1997; Olds et al., 1998; Olds, Hill, Robinson, Song, & Little, 2000) maintains that the use of nurses as home visitors plus high intensity and fairly long duration are all essential to success; however, many other programs use less expensive supports. Guterman (1997) argues for universal visiting for all new parents, but risk-based models appear to be much more common because of lower costs. In fact in the superb 1998 review (Brust et al., 1998), the Health Care Coalition on Violence found no publications about programs serving all new parents.

Home-based programs appear to focus on the prevention of physical abuse and neglect while enhancing parent-infant attachment and interaction to encourage development. An important question relates to the extent to which they might (or might not) prevent child sexual abuse. To the extent that these programs reduce the isolation of families and increase the time that children spend with caring adults, they might be expected to reduce sexual abuse. However, this effect has not been studied.

B. Sexual Abuse Prevention

Sexual abuse prevention programs have a long history (Wurtele, 1992) and usually have employed educational methods in which children and parents are informed about the definitions of sexual abuse and the methods of avoiding or deterring it. Finkelhor, Asdigian, and Dziuba-Leatherman (1995) have demonstrated the effectiveness of some of these prevention programs, although a number of problems remain. One of these is that this form of prevention is not available to many children. Schools probably best provide preventive education. However, for many school districts, the development of this service is not financially feasible despite its relatively low cost. Under these conditions, any provider willing and capable of meeting standards for the provision of prevention education should be encouraged to do so.

C. Organization of Preventive Services

A very wide range of organizational structures exists that support and provide preventive services. Possibly the most common form involves a relatively small nonprofit agency contracting with an agency of county or state government to provide services to a defined population. A few programs operate out of county or local health departments. Few, if any, are linked to primary health care despite the apparent advantages of such linkages. No programs except the one in Hawaii (with a total population of about 1 million) serve the entire population of a state, and most serve rather small fractions of the populations that might be at risk. At present, child abuse prevention can properly be described as a promising cottage industry.

In theory, at least, it would appear important to link child abuse prevention to perinatal health care and to initiate it with all new families soon after the first prenatal visit for health care. It also appears wise to make it universal for all new parents. The requirement of screening for risk is inevitably stigmatizing, and the screening processes are likely to have fairly high numbers of false-negative reports. Other countries appear able to sustain such programs, and they have good public acceptance. Linkage to personal and public health systems is probably wiser than attempting to link prevention to the organizations providing interventions and services that follow a report of abuse.

Political and Economic Considerations

A. Problem Orientation

Communities and political jurisdictions are organized using historically defined departmental structures. The problems that present themselves to communities (such as child abuse) require the participation of many public and private components, and no political structure exists that can commit these components to common courses of action. This creates the need for interdisciplinary and interagency councils and other such bodies that provide for communication and the development of protocols, guidelines, and standards. Such councils are commonplace and essential in child abuse work, but they require constant nurturing by their communities if they are to be effective.

The political structures of state and local government must look to child abuse councils and to the private sector for much of the work that can ameliorate the problem of child abuse.

This does not mean that state and local governments can forget about the problem. It must, in fact, remain on their "problem list" for generations to come, along with such items as crime, family violence, homelessness, and unemployment. Elected leaders must expect regular reports from their law enforcement agencies, courts, children's services departments, and health departments about progress in dealing with child abuse. A component of these reports must be an analysis of long-term outcomes for children and families that have been reported. The reports from agencies to their executives and legislatures also should contain documentation of interdisciplinary activity and of public-private initiatives and ongoing work.

B. Better Information

State and local governmental entities also need to develop more accurate ways in which to assess the seriousness of the child abuse problem in their communities and determine trends. The gross confounding of statistics, based solely on counting child abuse reports, requires that this method be supplemented by hospital samples and by ongoing retrospective surveys using the memories of older children and adults about abusive events in their childhoods, as well as other methods. Governmental entities should use the epidemiological skills available in the health sector in the development of their statistical methodologies.

Governments must adopt methods for counting the costs of child abuse.

Along with more accurate and standardized methods of assessing the numbers of cases, governments must adopt methods for counting the costs of child abuse. Unless this is done, the cost-benefit ratios for various interventions cannot be known, and the government will continue to make policies in a whimsical fashion based on the latest anecdote to emerge in the press.

Large jurisdictions need to improve the information systems that store and report data about child abuse cases. Although initiatives to accomplish this have begun in several states, most cities and counties remain unaffected and uninformed about what really is going on. Most managers in government would prefer to have very accurate information, although some of them recognize that these data may present an unflattering view of the governmental response to child abuse. The initial development of effective information systems is costly. However, a system developed in a single large jurisdiction probably can be exported to many others and to small jurisdictions at fairly low costs, so there is no longer any excuse for political leaders to remain in a state of ignorance about child abuse.

C. Specific Actions: Protocol Development

Throughout this chapter, a recurrent recommendation has been for planning and development of protocols. These serve as both guidelines and commitments by and for the various involved agencies and professionals to carry out their work in ways that will meet high standards of practice and still provide an efficient and coordinated response to the occurrence of child abuse. Many communities already have done so, but most of these documents are not published formally, nor are they easily available for reference. Although the child abuse problem is similar in most parts of the United States, the resources available to deal with it differ considerably, so most communities are better advised to develop their own than to adopt one developed in another area.

In addition, the process of developing the protocol has great value because it brings managers together from the involved agencies and organizations. In the course of communication during multiple meetings and over considerable time, the habit of working together and communicating freely about problems can become established.

It is possible to define a list of common elements that should be a part of most or all protocols for dealing with child abuse after

the fact. This list should contain at least the following items:

1. a statement of goals and a statement of objectives containing quantitative, time-limited, measurable reductions in child abuse and the problems that it causes;
2. definition of the agencies receiving child abuse reports;
3. description of cross-reporting procedures between law enforcement and children's services agencies;
4. definition of types of cases to be investigated by law enforcement, by children's services, and by both agencies;
5. designation of providers of services such as interviews of children, medical assessments and care, mental health assessments and care, and preventive services;
6. description of the communication links between agencies and providers that are to be used to move information quickly in the course of an investigation;
7. commitments of the agencies and providers to follow certain procedures and to communicate about cases;
8. reference to any contractual arrangements between agencies involving the provision of child abuse-related services;
9. description of the precise roles of all participants in the process, including child advocacy centers, law enforcement, public children's services, private health care institutions and providers, mental health professionals, public health agencies, prosecutors, attorneys representing children and families, and the various courts that are involved in child abuse cases;
10. designation (by position and by name) of the persons responsible for carrying out the provisions of the protocol.

D. Commitment of Resources

At present, the costs of dealing with child abuse are difficult to track because they are merged with operating budgets of agencies that deal with many sorts of problems, and they may not be easily identifiable. Precise knowledge of the expenditures for the problem would be useful in policy development, and it is worthwhile to develop means for teasing out these costs. The knowledge, in a given community, that the expenditures for this purpose were dramatically higher or lower than a national average would be valuable. If accurate cost information became available, political decision making might improve substantially as a result of guidance by accurate programmatic and financial data.

Although few child advocates believe that the resources for dealing with child abuse are sufficient, even fewer can calculate what is being spent and what needs to be spent or in what way. The process of consciously organizing community efforts and documenting organization with written protocols might lead to far greater knowledge and better decision making in the allocation of resources for this pervasive and debilitating societal problem.

Conclusion

Ending child abuse requires a cultural change in which most persons recognize the problem and wish to see it ended. After that, it requires political will and then a carefully designed and effective combination of prevention activity, interventions, and services for recognized cases. Better measurements are needed to know when progress is being made. Communities need to organize services with the goal in mind and to give the work a very high priority. The impetus to bring about this change must come from the work and the public statements of persons who have been affected by the problem in their personal lives as well as from involved professionals.

The organization of services at the level of counties, cities, and neighborhoods may be somewhat idiosyncratic and related to local needs and resources; however, communities can use a number of useful principles and guidelines to assure their citizens and the body politic that everything is being done that can and should be done.

To define a community's organization, a responsible group of providers from public and private sectors and from multiple disciplines must meet together and develop community protocols that describe how the different forms of abuse are to be handled in the given community. Minimally, the participants in this process must include public social service and law enforcement agencies, hospitals, health providers who frequently provide services to abused children, public health services, schools, preschools, infant development programs, and services for developmentally disabled people, mental health service providers, foster parents, resi-

dential and group home care providers, and others.

The organization and the content of community protocols may vary considerably from one community to another, but all protocols should emphasize provision of services at the best level of quality that is possible, based on best-practice statements developed by a large list of professional societies whose members do this work with substantial input from affected persons.

Community protocols may require fairly frequent review and updating as scientific and professional knowledge affecting child maltreatment continues to advance.

Glossary

The purpose of this glossary is to ensure that the meanings of the words and "terms of art" used in the text can be precisely understood.

Child abuse Physical abuse, sexual abuse, emotional abuse, or neglect affecting a person younger than age 18.

Child maltreatment Child abuse.

Community A body of persons having a common history or common social, economic, intellectual, religious, political, ethnic, or regional interests.

Developmental imperative A need of an infant or child that, if unmet at a particular age or stage, results in a deficit that is much harder to repair later.

Emotional abuse Avoidable emotional or psychological harm to a child resulting from acts of omissions of a caretaker.

Ending child abuse A scientifically validated reduction of the occurrence of abuse to less than 5% of the overall incidence and to less than 1% of forms that result in serious long-term harm to the child.

Family preservation Social services or interventions designed to keep abused children in their existing families while making them safe from further abuse.

Family violence Violent acts or seriously neglectful events that take place in the home. Includes abuse of children, abuse of intimate partners, and abuse of the elderly.

Goal A really major accomplishment defined in general terms.

Intervention An action performed to come between events for the purpose of hindrance or modification.

Investigation Observation and study by close examination and systematic inquiry. (Investigation is not a service or an intervention, but both of those functions may use the acquired information.)

Neglect Omission of needed care of a child by a caretaker.

Neighborhood A defined area, usually small and typically without a government.

Objective An achievement that is subsidiary to a goal. Usually expressed in quantitative terms and with a time imposed.

Permanency planning Providing stable, long-term nurturing homes for abused children.

Physical abuse Physical injury inflicted on a child by a caretaker.

Political jurisdiction A defined area with a government.

Protocol A detailed plan of a procedure.

Reunification Returning abused children to the original homes while keeping them safe from further abuse.

Service A helpful act performed by one person for another and perceived by both to be helpful.

Sexual abuse Any sexual act involving a child committed by an adult or a much older child.

References

American Academy of Pediatrics. (1994). Distinguishing sudden infant death syndrome from child abuse fatalities. *Pediatrics, 94*(1), 124-126.

American College of Surgeons. (2000). Web site [Online]. Available: www.facs.org.

Briere, J., Woo, R., McRae, B., Foltz, J., & Sitzman, R. (1997). Lifetime victimization history, demographics, and clinical status in female psychiatric emergency room patients. *Journal of Nervous Mental Disorders, 185*(2), 95-101.

Bross, D. C., Ballo, N., & Korfmacher, J. (2000). Client evaluation of a consultation team on crimes against children. *Child Abuse & Neglect, 24*(1), 71-84.

Bross, D. C., Krugman, R. D., Lenherr, M. R., Rosenberg, D. A., & Schmitt, B. D. (1988). *The new child protection team handbook.* New York: Garland.

Brust, J., Heins, J., & Rheinberger, M. (1998). *A review of the research on home visiting.* (Available from Health Care Coalition on Violence, 2829 Verndale Avenue, Anoka, MN 55303)

Casey Family Program. (2000). Web site [Online]. Available: www.casey.org/whatworks/index.htm.

Chadwick, D. L. (1999). Convening a national call to action: Working toward the elimination of child maltreatment. *Child Abuse & Neglect, 23*(10), 851-1018.

Chadwick, D. L., & Krous, H. F. (1997). Irresponsible testimony by medical experts in cases involving the physical abuse and neglect of children. *Child Maltreatment, 2*(4), 313-321.

Durfee, M. J., Gellert, G. A., & Tilton-Durfee, D. (1992). Origins and clinical relevance of child death review teams. *Journal of the American Medical Association, 267*(23), 3172-3175.

Durrant, J. E. (1999). Evaluating the success of Sweden's corporal punishment ban. *Child Abuse & Neglect, 23,* 435-448.

Edgardh, K., & Ormstad, K. (2000). Prevalence and characteristics of sexual abuse in a national sample of Swedish seventeen-year-old boys and girls. *Acta Paediatrica, 89*(3), 310-319.

Edgardh, K., von Krogh, G., & Ormstad, K. (1999). Adolescent girls investigated for sexual abuse: History, physical findings and legal outcome. *Forensic Science International, 104*(1), 1-15.

Feldman, K. W. (1997). Evaluation of physical abuse. In M. E. Helfer, R. S. Kempe, & R. F. Krugman (Eds.), *The battered child* (pp. 175-220). Chicago: University of Chicago Press.

Felitti, V. J., Anda, R. F., Nordenberg, D., Williamson, D. F., Spitz, A. M., Edwards, V., Koss, M. P., & Marks, J. S. (1998). Relationship of childhood abuse and household dysfunction to many of the leading causes of death in adults. *American Journal of Preventive Medicine, 14*(4), 245-258.

Finkelhor, D., Asdigian, N., & Dziuba-Leatherman, J. (1995). The effectiveness of victimization prevention instruction: An evaluation of children's responses to actual threats and assaults. *Child Abuse & Neglect, 19*(2), 141-153.

Gelles, R. J., & Edfeldt, A. W. (1986). Violence towards children in the United States and Sweden. *Child Abuse & Neglect, 10*(4), 501-510.

Glaser, D. (2000). Child abuse and neglect and the brain: A review. *Journal of Child Psychology and Psychiatry, 41*(1), 97-116.

Guterman, N. (1997). Early prevention of physical child abuse and neglect: Existing evidence and future directions. *Child Maltreatment, 2*(1).

Hensler, D. J. (2000). *The national call to action to eliminate child abuse* [Online]. Available: www.nationalcalltoaction.com.

Hochstadt, N. J., & Harwicke, N. J. (1985). How effective is the multidisciplinary approach? A follow-up study. *Child Abuse & Neglect, 9*(3), 365-372.

Kaufman, J., & Zigler, E. (1987). Do abused children become abusive parents? *American Journal of Orthopsychiatry, 57,* 186-192.

Kempe, R. S. (1987). A developmental approach to the treatment of the abused child. In R. E. Helfer & R. S. Kempe (Eds.), *The battered child* (4th ed., pp. 360-381). Chicago: University of Chicago Press.

Kirschner, R., & Wilson, H. L. (1994). Fatal child abuse: The pathologist's perspective. In R. M. Reece (Ed.), *Child abuse medical diagnosis and management.* Philadelphia: Lee & Febiger.

Krugman, R. (1984). The multidisciplinary treatment of abusive and neglectful families. *Pediatric Annals, 13*(10), 761-764.

Krugman, R. (1996). Epilogue. In J. Briere, L. Berliner, J. Bulkley, C. Jenny, & T. Reid (Eds.), *The APSAC handbook on child maltreatment* (pp. 420-422). Thousand Oaks, CA: Sage.

National Children's Advocacy Center. (2000). Web site [Online]. Available: www.ncac-hasv.org.

National Children's Alliance. (2000). Web site [Online]. Available: www.nncac.org/index.html.

National Council of Juvenile and Family Court Judges. (2000). Web site [Online]. Available: www.ncjfcj.unr.edu.

Olds, D. (1992). Home visitation for pregnant women and parents of young children. *American Journal of Diseases of Children, 146*(6), 704-708.

Olds, D., Eckenrode, J., Henderson, C. R., Jr., Kitzman, H., Powers, J., Cole, R., Sidora, K., Morris, P., Pettitt, L. M., & Luckey, D. (1997). Long-term effects of home visitation on maternal life course and child abuse and neglect: Fifteen-year follow-up of a randomized trial. *Journal of the American Medical Association, 278*(8), 637-643.

Olds, D., Henderson, C. R., Jr., Cole, R., Eckenrode, J., Kitzman, H., Luckey, D., Pettitt, L., Sidora, K., Morris, P., & Powers, J. (1998). Long-term effects of nurse home visitation on children's criminal and antisocial behavior: 15-year follow-up of a randomized controlled trial. *Journal of the American Medical Association, 280*(14), 1238-1244.

Olds, D., Hill, P., Robinson, J., Song, N., & Little, C. (2000). Update on home visiting for pregnant women and parents of young children. *Current Problems in Pediatrics, 30*(4), 107-141.

Sadler, B. L., Chadwick, D. L., & Hensler, D. J. (1999). The summary chapter: The national call to action: Moving ahead. *Child Abuse & Neglect, 23*(10), 1011-1008.

Saywitz, K. J., & Goodman, G. S. (1996). Interviewing children in and out of court: Current research and practice implications. In J. Briere, L. Berliner, J. Bulkley, C. Jenny, & T. Reid (Eds.), *The APSAC handbook on child maltreatment* (pp. 297-318). Thousand Oaks, CA: Sage.

Simms, M. (1999). Delivering health and mental health care services to children in family foster care after welfare and health care reform. *Child Welfare, 78*(1).

United Nations High Commissioner for Human Rights. (1989). *Convention on the rights of the child.* Geneva: Author.

U.S. Department of Health and Human Services. (1996). *The third national incidence study of child abuse and neglect.* Washington, DC: Government Printing Office.

Wurtele, S. (1992). *Preventing child abuse: Sharing the responsibility.* Lincoln: University of Nebraska Press.

Name Index

Subject Index

About the Editors

John E. B. Myers, JD, is Professor of Law at the University of the Pacific, McGeorge School of Law in Sacramento, California. He has written or edited seven books, including *Legal Issues in Child Abuse and Neglect Practice* (2nd ed., 1998), *Incest: A Mother's Nightmare: A Practical Legal Guide for Parents and Professionals* (1997), and *Evidence in Child Abuse and Neglect Cases* (3rd ed., 1997). He is the author of 100 articles and chapters on child abuse. He is a frequent speaker, having made more than 200 presentations in the United States, Canada, and Europe. His writing has been cited by more than 140 courts, including the U.S. Supreme Court. He is on the faculty of the National Council of Juvenile and Family Court Judges and the National Judicial College. He has received several awards, including the "Distinguished Contribution to Child Advocacy" award from the Division of Child, Youth, and Family Services of the American Psychological Association.

Lucy Berliner, MSW, is Director of the Harborview Center for Sexual Assault and Traumatic Stress in Seattle, Washington. She is Clinical Associate Professor, University of Washington School of Social Work and Department of Psychiatry and Behavioral Sciences. Her activities include clinical practice with child and adult victims of trauma and crime, research on the impact of trauma and the effectiveness of clinical and societal interventions, and participation in local and national social policy initiatives to promote the interests of trauma and crime victims. She is on the editorial boards of leading journals concerned with interpersonal violence, has authored numerous peer-reviewed articles and book chapters, and has served or serves on local and national boards of organizations, programs, and professional societies.

John Briere, PhD, is Associate Professor of Psychiatry and Psychology at the University of Southern California School of Medicine and Director of the Psychological Trauma Clinic of Los Angeles County–USC Medical Center. He is currently president of the International Society for Traumatic Stress Studies (ISTSS). A fellow of the American Psychological Association, he is recipient of the Robert S. Laufer Memorial Award for Scientific Achievement and the Outstanding Professional Award (1999) from the American Professional Society on the Abuse of Children. He is author of various articles, chapters, books, and psychological tests in the areas of child abuse and psychological trauma.

C. Terry Hendrix, MA, has been an active member of APSAC for the past decade and was named to the President's Honor Roll in 1995. He was appointed to the APSAC

Board of Directors in 1999 and is presently serving his second term as treasurer and a member of the executive committee. His academic training was in counseling psychology and organizational behavior, and he served in the U.S. Army as a clinical psychology technician. He joined Sage Publications in 1984 as an acquiring editor for both journals and books. During the past 17 years, he has been instrumental in the development of the Sage lists in interpersonal violence and criminology, as well as serving as editorial director and vice president for a 4-year term. Prior to joining Sage, he was an acquiring editor for Wadsworth Publishing Company and co-founder and editorial director of Brooks/Cole for 18 years. In his current role as Senior Editor at Sage Publications, Terry manages the acquisition, development, and maintenance of all U.S.-based journals in criminology and interpersonal violence, including *Child Maltreatment, Journal of Interpersonal Violence, Trauma, Violence & Abuse,* and *Violence Against Women.*

Carole Jenny, MD, MBA, is Professor of Pediatrics at Brown University School of Medicine. She contributes to the professional literature and is a frequent speaker at conferences. She is Director of the Child Protection Program at Hasbro Children's Hospital, Providence, Rhode Island.

Theresa A. Reid, PhD, was Executive Director of APSAC from 1988 to 1997, when she resigned to raise her daughter and finish her doctorate at the University of Chicago. She is currently revising her dissertation for publication as a book, entitled *What's Wrong With the Way We Talk About Sexual Abuse, and How to Fix It.* In the last few years, Dr. Reid has lectured internationally on organizational development and sexual abuse awareness, and has served as Associate Editor of *Child Maltreatment.* Dr. Reid has been President of the Board of Directors of the Chicago Children's Advocacy Center since 1999.

About the Contributors

Veronica D. Abney, LCSW, DCSW, is a licensed clinical social worker and diplomat in clinical social work in private practice in Santa Monica, California, specializing in the treatment of child, adolescent, and adult survivors of childhood sexual trauma. She is an adjunct lecturer in social work in the Department of Psychiatry at the UCLA School of Medicine. She is a senior candidate member of the Institute of Contemporary Psychoanalysis and is interested in the application of modern psychoanalytic theories in cross-cultural and adult survivor treatment. She is completing her doctoral dissertation on African American psychoanalysts. She is past president of the American Professional Society on the Abuse of Children and is a board member of the California Professional Society on the Abuse of Children. She is Associate Editor of *Child Maltreatment* and *Trauma, Violence, and Abuse*. Her publications include "Transference and Countertransference Issues Unique to Long-Term Group Psychotherapy of Adult Women Molested as Children: The Trials and Rewards: A Rationale for Cultural Competency, African Americans and Sexual Child Abuse," in *Sexual Abuse in Nine North American Cultures*.

Nelson J. Binggeli, MS, is a doctoral student in counseling psychology at Georgia State University. He is interested in the social significance of child abuse and neglect, the ethics of human rights, social justice, social responsibility (particularly for the helping professions), and social actions (such as public education and political advocacy). Clinically, he has worked in college counsel-

ing centers, a psychiatric hospital, and other community settings. His guiding vision is the progressive transformations of human societies through the promotion of children's basic human rights and the healing of personal and collective traumas.

Maureen Black, PhD, is Professor in the Department of Pediatrics and Director of the Growth and Nutrition Clinic at the University of Maryland School of Medicine. She is a fellow of the American Psychological Association and a past president of the Society of Pediatric Psychology and the Division of Child, Youth, and Family Services of the American Psychological Association. Her research interests include growth deficiency, micronutrient supplementation, obesity prevention, child neglect, adolescent pregnancy and parenting, and the evaluation of intervention strategies to promote healthy growth and development.

Robert W. Block, MD, is Presidential Professor and Daniel C. Plunket Chair of the Department of Pediatrics, University of Oklahoma College of Medicine, Tulsa, Oklahoma. He is the Chief Child Abuse Examiner for Oklahoma. He was a founding member of the Oklahoma Child Death Review Board, serving as its chair from 1993 to 1998. He is a member of the Committee on Child Abuse and Neglect of the American Academy of Pediatrics, and he is Medical Director for the Tulsa Children's Justice Center, Tulsa's advocacy center for child abuse investigations.

575

Barbara L. Bonner, PhD, a clinical child psychologist, is Associate Professor and Director of the Center on Child Abuse and Neglect in the Department of Pediatrics at the University of Oklahoma Health Sciences Center. Her clinical and research interests include the assessment and treatment of abused children, forensic evaluation of alleged sexually abused children, prevention of child fatalities, and treatment of children and adolescents with inappropriate or illegal sexual behavior. She currently serves on the Board of Councilors of the International Society for the Prevention of Child Abuse and Neglect and is past president of the American Professional Society on the Abuse of Children.

Marla R. Brassard, PhD, is Associate Professor of Psychology and Education at Teachers College, Columbia University. Her research focuses on the mental injuries and behavioral problems that result from parental psychological maltreatment and the contextual factors that moderate the effect of maltreatment, particularly the role of schools, teachers, and peer relationships. She also studies psychological aggression in teacher-student and peer relationships and its impact on children's functioning. Clinically, she has worked in a prison, schools, and clinics with maltreated and other troubled children and youth.

David L. Chadwick, MD, is Director, Emeritus, of the Center for Child Protection at the Children's Hospital in San Diego, having retired from that position on January 1, 1997. He is Associate Clinical Professor of Pediatrics at the University of California, San Diego School of Medicine. He is now self-employed as a consultant in the field of child protection health care. In that capacity, he provides consultation and other forms of assistance to institutions and persons who can use his extensive knowledge of this field. His recent clients include a number of children's hospitals, community hospitals, and federal, state, and county governmental agencies seeking assistance in improving child maltreatment programs that need a health component, in addition to prosecutors and other attorneys seeking expert consultation about individual cases, especially those involving physical abuse, or on issues involving child abuse reporting. He is a frequent expert witness in litigated cases in-

volving physical abuse. He is a frequent speaker on a variety of topics related to child maltreatment, and he is engaged in research on children's injuries, abuse prevention, and developmental work to improve the health and health information about dependent and foster children. Dr. Chadwick is the author of numerous articles and book chapters on child maltreatment, and he is the recipient of a number of awards for his work in that field.

Mark Chaffin, PhD, is a psychologist and Associate Professor of Pediatrics and Clinical Associate Professor of Psychiatry and Behavioral Sciences at the University of Oklahoma Health Sciences Center in Oklahoma City, Oklahoma. He currently serves as Director of Research at the OUHSC Center on Child Abuse and Neglect. He has served on the board of directors of the American Professional Society on the Abuse of Children and is currently editor-in-chief of the journal *Child Maltreatment*. He has published numerous empirical articles and book chapters on the topic of child abuse and neglect.

Deborah Daro, PhD, is a research fellow at the Chapin Hall Center for Children at the University of Chicago. Prior to joining Chapin Hall in January 1999, she served as Director of the National Center on Child Abuse Prevention Research, a program of the National Committee to Prevent Child Abuse. With more than 20 years of experience in evaluating child abuse treatment and prevention programs, she has directed some of the largest multisite program evaluations completed in the field. She has published and lectured widely and has served as president of the American Professional Society on the Abuse of Children, and she is currently on the Executive Council of the International Society for the Prevention of Child Abuse and Neglect.

Howard A. Davidson, JD, is Director of the American Bar Association Center on Children and the Law in Washington, D.C., and has been so since the founding of the center in 1978. The center works to improve court systems that serve children and to enhance legal responses to child abuse and neglect, child sexual exploitation, foster care, adoption, representation of children, parental child abduction, child and adolescent health, and other child welfare-related issues. He served as chair and vice chair of the U.S. Advisory Board on Child Abuse and Neglect and is a founding board member of the National Center for Missing and Exploited Children. His many books and published writings cover a wide range of legal issues affecting children involved in the court system, including *Legal Rights of Children, Children's Rights in America, Establishing Ombudsman Programs for Children and Youth, The Impact of Domestic Violence on Children,* and a set of legal commentaries for the American Psychiatric Press book, *Family Violence: A Clinical and Legal Guide.* His article, "Child Protection Policy and Practice at Century's End," appeared in the fall 1999 issue of the *Family Law Quarterly.*

Anne Cohn Donnelly, DPH, is Resident Fellow and Professor at the Kellogg School of Management at Northwestern University in Evanston, Illinois. In addition to teaching nonprofit governance, she is assisting the school in operating a center on nonprofit management. She served as Executive Director of the National Committee to Prevent Child Abuse from 1980 to 1997. Prior to that, in addition to serving as Congressional Science Fellow and White House Fellow in Washington, D.C., she has directed a number of research projects on child abuse and neglect treatment and prevention. She has written and lectured widely on child abuse and neglect.

Howard Dubowitz, MD, MS, is Professor of Pediatrics and Codirector of the Center for Families at the University of Maryland, Baltimore. He is chair of the Child Maltreatment Committee of the American Academy of Pediatrics, Maryland Chapter, and he is on the Maryland State Council of Child Abuse and Neglect. He recently completed two terms on the APSAC board. He edited *Neglected Children: Research, Practice and Policy* (1999) and coedited the *Handbook on Child Protection Practice* (2000). He is a clinician, researcher, and educator, and he is active in the policy arena at the state and national levels, representing APSAC on the National Child Abuse Coalition.

Byron Egeland, PhD, is the Irving B. Harris Professor of Child Development and Direc-

tor of the Mother-Child Project, a 20-year longitudinal study of high-risk children and their families. He is a coinvestigator on the national evaluation and study of the JOBS and New Chance Programs for families on welfare and is a fellow in the American Psychological Association, the American Psychological Society, and the American Association of Applied and Preventive Psychology. He is on the board of directors of a number of organizations, including Prevent Child Abuse America. He has published articles and book chapters in the areas of child maltreatment, the development of high-risk children, factors influencing development, child psychopathology, and intervention with high-risk families.

Diana M. Elliott, PhD, is Clinical Associate Professor of Psychiatry and Behavioral Sciences at the University of Southern California. She has published a number of research articles and chapters on the short-term and long-term impacts of interpersonal trauma. She lectures on various issues related to the assessment and treatment of interpersonal violence. She also maintains a private practice in Cerritos, California, where she conducts assessments and provides long-term treatment to victims of child abuse and other forms of violence.

Martha Farrell Erickson, PhD, is Director of the University of Minnesota's Children, Youth and Family Consortium. She is a developmental psychologist specializing in parent-child attachment, child abuse prevention, and community-based approaches to strengthening families. With Byron Egeland, she developed STEEP (Steps Toward Effective, Enjoyable Parenting), a program for parents and infants. She consults and trains professionals in the United States and abroad. She is coauthor of *Infants, Toddlers, and Families: A Framework for Support and Intervention* (1999). She is also author of numerous journal articles, book chapters, and the weekly syndicated column "Growing Concerns." She appears regularly on television as the child and family expert on the KARE-11 *Today Show.* She also serves on several boards, including Prevent Child Abuse America.

C. Christine Fair, MA, works at RAND, a public policy research institution. At

RAND, she has worked on a wide array of projects that address issues germane to the health and well-being of women and children. In recent projects, she has studied prenatal substance exposure, child care, the USDA's Child and Adult Care Food Program, and assisted reproductive technologies. She has also worked on several education- and compensation-related projects for the Department of Defense.

David Finkelhor, PhD, is Director of the Crimes Against Children Research Center, Codirector of the Family Research Laboratory, and Professor of Sociology at the University of New Hampshire. He has been studying the problems of child victimization, child maltreatment, and family violence since 1977. He is well known for his conceptual and empirical work on the problem of child sexual abuse, reflected in publications such as *Sourcebook on Child Sexual Abuse* (1986) and *Nursery Crimes* (1988). He has also written about child homicide, missing and abducted children, children exposed to domestic and peer violence, and other forms of family violence. In his recent work, he has tried to unify and integrate knowledge about all the diverse forms of child victimization in a field he has termed *developmental victimology*. He is editor and author of 10 books and more than 75 journal articles and book chapters. He has received grants from the National Institute of Mental Health, the National Center on Child Abuse and Neglect, the U.S. Department of Justice, and a variety of other sources. In 1994, he was given the Distinguished Child Abuse Professional Award by the American Professional Society on the Abuse of Children.

William N. Friedrich, PhD, is Professor and Consultant at the Mayo Clinic and Mayo Medical School in Rochester, Minnesota. He is a diplomate in both clinical and family psychology with the American Board of Professional Psychology; the author of five professional books, four of which focus on sexual abuse treatment and assessment; and the developer of the Child Sexual Behavior Inventory (CSBI). He has also authored more than 120 academic papers, chapters, and reviews and was the consultant to NCCAN's only two grants awarded to investigate sexually intrusive behavior in preteens.

Ann F. Garland, PhD, is Associate Professor of Psychiatry at the University of California, San Diego, and Associate Director of the Child and Adolescent Services Research Center at Children's Hospital, San Diego. She is the principal investigator of NIMH-funded research projects investigating methods for evaluating the effectiveness of community-based youth mental health services. She has also written extensively about factors that predict the need for and use of mental health services among youth in the child welfare system. In addition, she is the supervising psychologist at the Children's Hospital Out-Patient Psychiatry Clinic.

Gail S. Goodman, PhD, is Professor of Psychology at the University of California, Davis. In addition to her current appointment at the University of California, she has served on the faculties of the University of Denver (including as Director of the Dual Degree Program in Psychology and Law), the State University of New York at Buffalo, and the University of California, Riverside. Dr. Goodman has been the president of two divisions and one section of the American Psychological Association. She is the author of numerous scientific publications and the recipient of numerous federal grants.

Sandra A. Graham-Bermann, PhD, is Associate Professor in the Department of Psychology and Women's Studies Program at the University of Michigan. She studies the impact of different forms of family violence on children's social and emotional adjustment. This work spans the ages from 3 to 13 and includes children in a variety of contexts such as preschools, community settings, and shelters for battered women. Using a nested ecological framework, she is able to demonstrate which children are most affected by family violence, in what ways, and how best to intervene for children with particular adjustment profiles. She is consultant to local domestic violence programs and Head Start schools. Nationally, she is a consultant to the U.S. Department of Justice, the U.S. Department of Health and Human Services, and the National Academy of Sciences. In addition to authoring numerous research journal articles, her new book, with coeditor Jeff Edleson, is titled *Domestic Violence in the Lives of Children: The Future of Research, Intervention, and Policy* (2001).

Stuart N. Hart, PhD, is Professor Emeritus of Counseling and Educational Psychology and Founding Director of the Office for the Study of the Psychological Rights of the Child in the School of Education of Indiana University Purdue University Indianapolis (Indiana). He has worked with children with problems and special needs and those serving children in schools, hospitals, group homes, county and state detention centers, government settings, and in private practice. He has conducted research and presented and published extensively on the topics of children's rights and the psychological maltreatment of children. He is co-chair of the Psychological Maltreatment Task Force of the American Professional Society on the Abuse of Children, chair of the Children's Rights Committee of the International School Psychology Association, and past president of the Indiana Psychological Association, the National Association of School Psychologists (USA), the National Committee for the Rights of the Child (USA), and the International School Psychology Association.

Debra B. Hecht, PhD, is a clinical child psychologist and Assistant Professor of Pediatrics at the Center on Child Abuse and Neglect at the University of Oklahoma Health Sciences Center. Clinical and research interests include developing appropriate assessment and treatment programs for children who have been abused and their families. She also participates in the evaluation of services being provided to children and families.

Charles F. Johnson, MD, is Professor of Pediatrics at the Ohio State University College of Medicine and Director of the Child Abuse Program at Children's Hospital in Columbus, Ohio. He specializes in pediatrics, particularly child development. He has published more than 50 articles on hyperactivity, phenylketonuria, the hand in physical diagnosis, parenting, and various topics in child maltreatment. He has also written 10 book chapters on child abuse topics, including the chapter on child abuse in *Nelson's Textbook of Pediatrics.* He has published poetry and cartoons and has exhibited his paintings. He edits *SCAN,* the newsletter of the Section on Child Abuse and Neglect of the American Academy of Pediatrics, and serves on the Section Committee. As an active clinician and consultant, he frequently appears in court.

Susan J. Kelley, PhD, is Dean of the College of Health and Human Sciences at Georgia State University in Atlanta, Georgia. She received her PhD in Developmental Psychology from Boston College and her BS and MS in Nursing from Boston University. She has specialized in the field of child abuse since 1980 and has published more than 50 journal articles and book chapters on various aspects of child abuse. She is an editorial board member of several journals dealing with child abuse, including *Child Maltreatment, Journal of Child Sexual Abuse,* and *Trauma, Violence and Abuse: A Review Journal.* She served as the editor-in-chief of the *APSAC Advisor* from 1990 to 1996. She is the author of *Pediatric Emergency Nursing* (2nd ed.). She is a member of APSAC's advisory board and served on APSAC's board of directors for 7 years. Dr. Kelley's research focuses on the impact of abuse and neglect on children and families. Her most recent work addresses the relationship between substance abuse and child abuse and grandparents raising grandchildren. She is founder and director of Project Healthy Grandparents, a community-based program providing services to families where grandparents are raising grandchildren in parent-absent homes. Most of the grandchildren in the program have been abused, neglected, and abandoned by their birth parents. Currently, Dr. Kelley is directing a 5-year federal demonstration project funded by the Office of Child Abuse and Neglect to reduce the impact of neglect in grandchildren raised by grandparents.

David J. Kolko, PhD, is Associate Professor of Child Psychiatry, Psychology, and Pediatrics at the University of Pittsburgh School of Medicine. At Western Psychiatric Institute and Clinic, he directs the Special Services Unit, a treatment research program for youth referred by the juvenile court. He is also a consultant for the Family Intervention Center at Children's Hospital of Pittsburgh, a child abuse program specializing in forensic interviewing and medical evaluation. Dr. Kolko's federal and state grant funding has been directed toward the study and treatment of disruptive disorders, childhood firesetting, juvenile sexual offending, child physical abuse, and adolescent depression.

He currently serves as principal investigator for a study designed to evaluate a treatment program that integrates clinical services and probation for juvenile sexual abusers and for a clinical trial examining the effectiveness of multimodal, community-based treatment for young children with disruptive disorders. Dr. Kolko is serving a second term on the board of directors of the American Professional Society on the Abuse of Children and is chair of its research committee. His primary clinical research interests involve the evaluation of cognitive-behavioral and family system treatments for youth involved as victims or offenders of violent/coercive behavior.

John Landsverk, PhD, is Professor in the School of Social Work at San Diego State University and Director of the NIMH-funded Child and Adolescent Services Research Center at Children's Hospital, San Diego. He has continuing research interests in the delivery of mental health services for children and adolescents who are involved with public systems such as child welfare, probation, mental health, and education and in the impact of home visitation on the health and development of children at risk for maltreatment. He is the principal investigator of an NIMH-funded national study of mental health services across child welfare agencies; coprincipal investigator of a projected 20-year longitudinal study of foster children funded by the Agency for Children, Youth, and Families; and the coprincipal investigator for an NIMH-funded study of patterns of mental health care among youth in child welfare, probation, substance abuse services, mental health, and the SED sector of education.

Kenneth V. Lanning was a special agent with the FBI for more than 30 years. He was assigned to the Behavioral Science Unit and the National Center for the Analysis of Violent Crime at the FBI Academy in Quantico, Virginia, for 20 years. He is a founding member of the board of directors of the American Professional Society on the Abuse of Children (APSAC) and is a former member of the APSAC advisory board. He is a current member of the advisory board of the Association for the Treatment of Sexual Abusers (ATSA) and the Boy Scouts of America Youth Protection Expert Advisory Panel. He is the 1996 recipient of the Out-

standing Professional Award from APSAC for outstanding contributions to the field of child maltreatment and the 1997 recipient of the FBI Director's Annual Award for Special Achievement for his career accomplishments in connection with missing and exploited children. He has lectured before and trained thousands of police officers and criminal justice professionals.

Louanne Lawson, PhD, RN, is Assistant Professor at the University of Arkansas for Medical Sciences, where she teaches nursing theory and research utilization in the graduate program. Her forensic nursing career began in 1985, when she became the clinical nurse specialist for the child abuse identification and education team at Arkansas Children's Hospital. She is the Sexual Assault Nurse Examiner (SANE) Educational and Preceptorship Program Coordinator for Arkansas and, over the past 5 years, has created educational opportunities for more than 175 SANEs. Currently, she is investigating the process of treatment for sexual behavior problems from the perspective of youth who have molested children. Furthermore, she is actively participating in the development of a pencil-and-paper self-report instrument for use with intrafamilial child sexual abusers. Her publications are indexed in CINAHL, PsycInfo, and Medline.

Laurel K. Leslie, MD, is a research scientist at the Child and Adolescent Services Research Center; Assistant Clinical Professor of Pediatrics at the University of California, San Diego; and Adjunct Research Assistant Professor at San Diego State University School of Public Health. Her research interests focus on the developmental and mental health needs of underserved children, the impact of policy initiatives on access to care for underserved children, and collaborative models of care. Areas of special interest include the health, developmental, and mental health needs of children in foster care and the identification and treatment of children with attention deficit disorder in primary care. She also serves as a practicing pediatrician with the East County Community Health Services and as a consultant to the Healthy Child Care America initiative in San Diego County. She has been active in the American Academy of Pediatrics' efforts to define the role of the pediatrician of the future. She served for the past 3 years on the

Task Force on the Future of Pediatric Education II, a national initiative funded by the Packard Foundation Center for the Future of Children addressing the role of the pediatrician in the provision of health care in the 21st century. She is currently working on a collaborative venture between the American Academy of Pediatrics and Johnson & Johnson to develop leadership training programs for pediatricians.

Elizabeth Letourneau, PhD, is Assistant Professor at the Family Services Research Center of the Medical University of South Carolina. Her research and clinical work has focused on the assessment and treatment of sex offenders, and she has numerous publications in this area.

Thomas D. Lyon, JD, PhD, is Professor of Law at the University of Southern California. His PhD is in developmental psychology, and his research and writing concern child witnesses and child abuse. He has authored or coauthored half a dozen book chapters, and his work has appeared in *Child Development; Law and Human Behavior; Cornell Law Review; Southern California Law Review Pacific Law Journal; Harvard Women's Law Journal; Psychology, Public Policy, and Law; Contemporary Psychology; Applied Developmental Science;* and *Developmental and Behavioral Pediatrics.*

Teresa F. Parnell, PsyD, is a licensed psychologist and certified family mediator in private practice in Altamonte Springs, Florida. She serves children, adolescents, and adults with specialization in child abuse, domestic violence, divorce/custody, and Munchausen by proxy syndrome. She has taught as an adjunct faculty member at Nova Southeastern University, the University of Central Florida, and Rollins College. She has made presentations at national and regional conferences. She is the lead editor of *Munchausen by Proxy Syndrome: Misunderstood Child Abuse.*

Karen J. Saywitz, PhD, is Professor at the University of California, Los Angeles, School of Medicine, Department of Psychiatry and Biobehavioral Sciences. She is Director of Child and Adolescent Psychology at the Harbor-UCLA Medical Center. She has authored numerous articles regarding the capabilities, limitations, and needs of children involved in the legal system. In her research on interviewing children and preparing them for court, she develops and tests innovative interventions to enhance children's memory performance, communicative competence, emotional resilience, and their resistance to suggestion. She has served as the president of the American Psychological Association's Division of Child Youth and Family Services. Dr. Saywitz has won awards for her pioneering research, outstanding teaching, and distinguished clinical service. She consults to the U.S. Department of Health and Human Services, the U.S. Department of Justice, State Justice Institute, and the Office of Juvenile Justice and Delinquency. She lectures nationally and internationally for organizations such as the American Academy of Pediatrics, American Psychological Association, American Academy of Child and Adolescent Psychiatry, and the National Judicial College.

Jane F. Silovsky, PhD, is Assistant Professor at the Center on Child Abuse and Neglect in the Department of Pediatrics at the University of Oklahoma Health Sciences Center. She conducts treatment outcome research with children who have sexual behavior problems and children who have experienced traumatic events, including child maltreatment.

Paul Stern, JD, is a senior deputy prosecuting attorney for Snohomish County, Washington. He has been involved in the prosecution of child sexual and physical abuse cases since 1985. He has tried more than 120 felony jury cases, predominately involving child abuse, sexual assault, or homicide. He served on the board of directors for the American Professional Society on the Abuse of Children for 6 years. He currently sits on many professional advisory boards. He serves on Washington State's Sexual Offender Treatment Provider Advisory Committee and was appointed to the Governor's Advisory Committee on DNA. He has lectured throughout the United States and in Australia, South Africa, and the United Kingdom on issues regarding the prosecution of child abuse and neglect. He has written several articles about the prosecution of interpersonal violence, including a manual on the prosecution of sexual assault cases.

His book, *Preparing and Presenting Expert Testimony in Child Abuse Litigation,* was published in 1997.

Karen Boyd Worley, PhD, is Director of the Family Treatment Program and the Adolescent Sexual Adjustment Project in the Department of Pediatrics for the University of Arkansas Medical Sciences Center at Arkansas Children's Hospital. The Family Treatment Program provides treatment for families in which there has been sexual abuse. The Adolescent Sexual Adjustment Project provides outpatient assessment and treatment for adolescent perpetrators of sexual abuse. She is active on a number of state boards addressing child abuse issues, provides statewide training and consultation, and has several publications on child maltreatment.

Gail L. Zellman, PhD, is a social and clinical psychologists at RAND, a public policy research institution. At RAND, her work focuses on a range of youth and family policies, including child abuse, teenage pregnancy and contraceptive use, substance use and prevention, child care, and parenting and parent school involvement. She also has studied the implementation of policy innovations in such diverse organizations as public schools, the military, and health maintenance organizations. With support from NCCAN, she conducted a national study of mandated reporters that produced a number of articles and a RAND report. Her current work focuses on prenatal substance exposure, family contributions to children's cognitive and emotional outcomes, and child care. She also maintains a small therapy practice in which she specializes in work with couples and families.